BERGER-BURR'S

ULTRALIGHT and MICROLIGHT AIRCR OF THE WORLD

Alain-Yves Berger
Norman Burr

SECOND EDITION 1985/6

Foulis

Haynes
®

ALAIN-YVES BERGER

Frenchman Alain-Yves Berger has been passionately fond of the third dimension ever since he was a boy, an enthusiasm which eventually led him to start the monthly *Pilote Prive* magazine in 1973. Twelve years on, the publication is now the best seller in its field, covering all aspects of leisure aviation, and Alain-Yves is its editorial director.

One of the first Europeans to fly a hang glider, in April 1973, he gave the sport its French name of 'vol libre' (free flight), but gave up hang gliding in 1976, after a serious accident when his aircraft suffered an in-flight failure. Two years later, walking with much difficulty but seeking a way of getting airborne again, he realised that the aviation world was witnessing the start of a revolution and wrote the first article on the subject in the French press, christening this new flying 'aviation ultralegere', a phrase which rapidly became shortened to 'ULM' (ultraleger motorise). Through *Pilote Prive* he began regular coverage of this new breed of machine and in June 1982 published Europe's first yearbook for the sport in the form of a special edition of *Pilote Prive*. This grew into a regular ultralight magazine called *UlmMag*, the only French-language publication devoted exclusively to ultralights.

Forty-two year-old Alain-Yves and his much younger wife Joss fly have flown ultralights of many kinds, and as Joss is one of those rare women who not only flies but is also interested in engines, it was only natural that she should write the engines chapter.

In early 1983 the pair were flying 'three-up' in a *Quicksilver MXII* but this practice, forbidden under French regulations, ended in due course when Joss produced a new ultralight, Gael, that November (3.7 kg without engine). And to ensure that every member of the family got some airtime in, Alain-Yves began 1985 by giving his 12 year-old son Mickael his first flying lessons in his new two-seater Jokair *Maestro*.

NORMAN BURR

As far back as he can remember, 36 year-old Norman Burr has had a fascination for things mechanical, a fascination which led him at the age of 18 to take an apprenticeship with Rolls Royce Aero Engines in Bristol, combined with studies for an engineering degree at the nearby University of Bath.

But the conventional aircraft industry was not for him, and he left the company after graduation, feeling that engineering on such a grand scale, however impressive in terms of its results, was just too remote and impersonal to be inspiring. Shortly afterwards he accepted the offer of a Masters Degree research project and returned to university. Finding the writing of his thesis a pleasant task, he decided to write for a living and got a job as assistant editor of a works management magazine in London. This was to be the start of a varied and often hectic career in technical journalism, which culminated in his going freelance in 1982.

Enjoying his new-found independence, he explored various writing avenues, and, intrigued by the emergence at last of aviation on a human scale, approached the British Microlight Aircraft Association with the offer of journalistic help. Almost before he knew it, he found himself appointed editor of the association's magazine, and took over the post in March 1982.

Ably assisted by the magazine's technical editor Peter Lovegrove, and by his wife Wendy who helps with advertising and administration, he has in the intervening three years developed *Flightline* into a magazine which, although modestly presented by comparison with some of its big-budget contemporaries, is nevertheless widely respected and enjoyed at home and abroad. The link with Alain-Yves Berger, which was forged when he approached the Frenchman with the suggestion that they co-operate over the coverage of the '82 London-Paris, led to the publication of the first edition of *Berger-Burr's* and to his recognition as a world authority on this new aviation industry.

He beat Berger, incidentally, in the race to take their offspring aloft by flying to Crete with Wendy when their son Tom was minus seven months old; Alain-Yves, however, is claiming that flights in Boeings don't count...

Illustrations

Unless otherwise credited, all illustrations in this book are provided by the aircraft builders

Main front cover picture Thor Air *Thor 1A* (Canada)

Inset front cover pictures, clockwise from top Winton *Sportsman* (Australia); Binder *Mistral* (West Germany); Mignet *HM1000 Balerit* (France); Squadron *Fokker D-VII* (United States); Diehl *XTC* (United States); Cascade *Kasperwing 180-BX* (United States)

Back cover Southdown International *Puma Sprint* (Great Britain) on the Iceland Breakthrough expedition, photo by Jean Luc Cheron

Title page Air Creation *Safari GT 1+1 Quartz 18* (France)

Pages 2-7 Microflight *Spectrum* (Great Britain); background photo by Ann Welch

Production Team

Design: covers by Haynes Publishing, *remainder* by Norman Burr Media Services

Typesetting Mill Studio, Sudbury, Suffolk

Translation Stan Abbott, Steve Figures

Administration Wendy Burr

Printed in England by J H Haynes & Co Ltd

Published by Haynes Publishing Group, Sparkford, Yeovil, Somerset BA22 7JJ, England

Haynes Publications Inc, 861 Lawrence Drive, Newbury Park, California 91320, USA

British Library cataloguing in publication data

Berger, Alain-Yves
Berger-Burr's Ultralight & Microlight Aircraft of the World - 2nd ed.
1. Ultralight aircraft - handbooks, manuals, etc.
I. Title II. Burr, Norman
629.133'340426 TL685.15

ISBN 0-85429-481-3

Library of Congress catalog card number 85-80550

A Foulis aviation book
First published 1985
©Alain-Yves Berger and Norman Burr

Acknowledgements

Special thanks are due to the following contributors

Luigi Accusani
Hal Adkins
Marco Bartolozzi
Dave Becker
Joss Berger
Curt Bjornemark
Alan Blain
Michael Bradford
Joachim Fassbender
Rob Fox
Dave Garrison
Janic Geelen
Bogoljub Jeremic
Marton Ordody
Bertrand Piccard
Paul H Poberezny
Michael Schonherr
Willi Tacke
Martin Velek
Ann Welch
Victor Whitmore
The staff of L'Aquilone magazine

plus the hundreds of aircraft builders whose support has made this book possible.

This book is dedicated to the next generation of pilots: Tom, Mickael and Gael

Contents

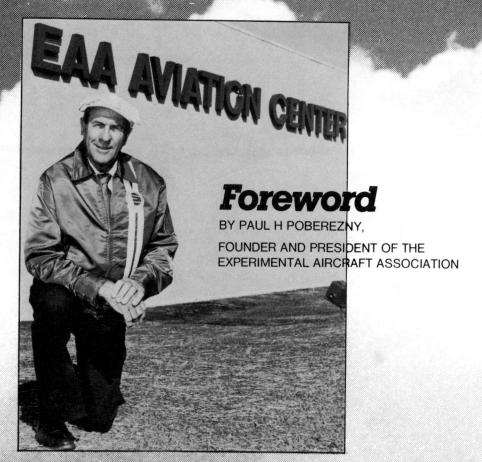

Foreword

BY PAUL H POBEREZNY,

FOUNDER AND PRESIDENT OF THE
EXPERIMENTAL AIRCRAFT ASSOCIATION

PAUL H POBEREZNY IS THE FOUNDER AND PRESIDENT OF THE EXPERIMENTAL AIRCRAFT ASSOCIATION, PRESIDENT OF THE FEDERATION AERONAUTIQUE INTERNATIONAL'S CIACA COMMITTEE, AND CHAIRMAN OF THE BOARD OF THE NON-PROFIT MAKING EAA AVIATION FOUNDATION. EAA'S ULTRALIGHT DIVISION IS THE OFFICIAL UNITED STATES REPRESENTATIVE FOR ULTRALIGHT AFFAIRS TO THE FAI.

To imitate the birds may be mankind's oldest dream. The freedom of personal flight is one of our greatest triumphs.
EAA has been involved in the ultralight and microlight movement from the very beginning. These elemental, inexpensive flying machines have opened the skies to thousands of men and women who may not have become airborne under other circumstances. We have watched and assisted as the pilots and aircraft have evolved and matured. Today, the world of very light flight is becoming an important and accepted part of the aviation community. We look forward to a bright future of even greater pilot proficiency and better, more airworthy ultralights and microlights. Whether you are a seasoned ultralight pilot or just entering this exciting sport for the first time, I think you will find this comprehensive, yet concise book both enjoyable and valuable. Welcome to the family of light aviation - I'll be looking for you in the sky.

Paul H. Poberezny

Introduction

When we decided to write a second edition of *Berger-Burr's,* it was not without some trepidation. The first edition had proved a mammoth task, and neither of us fancied a repetition of the enormous workload it had imposed. Yet we were deeply gratified by the enthusiastic response of reviewers and public alike, and anxious to build on the foundations it had laid.

So instead we approached some of the many contacts built up while writing the first edition, and appointed 'country editors' to help with writing and research in the principal ultralight-producing nations. This system not only ensures that we don't get old before our time, but also means that we have someone on the spot to sort out queries and give us the latest possible information. Our country editors' names are listed on the contents page, so we will confine ourselves here to saying a blanket 'thanks guys' to the team who made this second edition possible. However, there are others whose efforts, no less important, would go unsung if they were not recorded here. In particular, FAI president Ann Welch OBE, whose international contacts have proved invaluable, *Glider Rider* magazine, for helping us with many illustrations, Dave Garrison for helping with the history section, and of course EAA president Paul H Poberezny for writing the foreword.

This international co-operation has produced a noticeably more comprehensive book than previously, with new sections from Italy, Hungary, New Zealand, South Africa, Sweden and Yugoslavia, plus for the first time entries from Rumania, Czechoslovakia, Japan and China. There's more to come from China particularly, for Zhang Ruying, head of the Popular Aviation Committee of Nanjing Society of Aeronautics & Astronautics, has offered to act as country editor for the third edition, an offer which unfortunately came too late for this edition. The only other disappointment is Poland; despite the enthusiasm of Polish Aeroklub president Wladyslaw Hermaszewski, who distributed information to homebuilders there on our behalf, we have not had any feedback.

With two-axis and hybrid machines so much less common than before, we have used the colour section not to introduce the various control systems but simply to take the reader on a world ultralight tour, a feat which, incidentally, has yet to be achieved in real life. The other principal change is the inclusion of a history section.

Although we've altered the style to make the book easier to use and more attractive, the arrangement of information is virtually identical to before, except that we've ditched the paragraph numbers because they didn't seem to serve any useful purpose, and by popular demand added two items of information to each descripion: production status and noise level.

The result, we hope, is a book which you will find both useful and enjoyable. Safe flying.

Alain-Yves and
Joss Berger

Norman Burr

Using this Book

In deciding what to include in this book, we have applied two criteria: first, the aircraft has to be available to the public either at the time of going to press or at least during the currency of the book, and second the aircraft has to be under 331 lb (150 kg) empty weight.

We have, however, bent these guidelines on a number of occasions. With countries whose output of machines for public sale is small, we have included some home-builts, while in most countries we have included a few heavier aircraft, principally two-seaters which are likely to be useful trainers for ultralight pilots.

In a few cases companies were suffering financial problems at the time of going to press and were not trading, and in such instances we explain in the text the situation at that time. We felt this was a wiser policy than simply omitting those companies, because it is quite common for a firm in difficulties to re-emerge under a new name but with substantially similar products. The countries in this book are arranged alphabetically and the manufacturers alphabetically within each country. Within manufacturers we often break with alphabetical order in favour of a historical approach, so the descriptions read on from one machine to another, two-seaters usually being dealt with last.

Each aircraft is described according to a standard format, an example being shown on the page opposite. First comes the maker's name and address, plus those of any agents abroad, followed by a sub-heading giving the make and model of the aircraft, plus its control system in standard form. The model name is printed in italic, a style which is continued throughout the book.

Immediately under the sub-heading comes a summary, divided into sentences, as follows: **first,** basic format of aircraft; **second,** design of wing(s) and (if present) tail; **third,** control system including description of control surfaces (if present); **fourth,** wing structure; **fifth,** undercarriage format and suspension design; **sixth,** ground steering; **seventh,** braking; **eighth,** structure of fuselage or equivalent; **ninth,** engine(s) and propeller(s) arrangement. Sometimes there are one or more additional sentences, describing material specifications etc. At the end of the summary we give the production status of the aircraft. To save space we sometimes cross-refer from one summary to another; note that when we say 'summary as .... aircraft' we mean just that: the summaries are the same. This does not mean that the aircraft are identical, merely that the differences are too minor to be apparent from such a broad description.

The detailed description follows the summary and is divided into five paragraphs; it is here that the differences between similar aircraft are explained. The **General** paragraph is a descriptive text and includes prices and options where known. Next come four paragraphs whose titles are self-explanatory: **External dimensions and areas, Power plant, Weights and loadings,** and finally **Performance**. Unless otherwise stated, these last four paragraphs refer to the standard version of the machine.

Having explained the system, we must emphasise that any book like this is reliant on the honesty of the aircraft builders, since we cannot possibly verify all the data independently, and draw readers' attention to the disclaimer at the front of the book. Very few aircraft are so unusual that there is nothing their data can be compared to; in most cases readers will be able to cross check with similar machines and draw their own conclusions if, for instance, two machines of similar weight, power, wing area, and configuration shown radically different maximum speeds.

Finally, the following points are worth noting:

1 Where we have been unable to obtain an item of information, we print 'NC' (not communicated).

2 Where we know a figure is only approximate, we print it in italic.

3 Unless otherwise stated, all prices are ex-factory (ie excluding delivery charges) and do not include taxes. Normally, prices are quoted in the currency of the country where the aircraft is made.

4 Power per unit area and wing loading are calculated from the main wing area, plus where applicable the area of the canard. However, fully flying canards are regarded purely as control surfaces and are not normally included in such calculations.

5 All propellers are two-blade unless otherwise stated.

6 Landing distances are quoted without the use of any brakes which may be fitted.

7 Trike nomenclature: trikes consist of two distinct parts - trike unit and wing - and many trike units can be flown successfully with a variety of wings. Thus by juggling trike unit and wing combinations, a huge

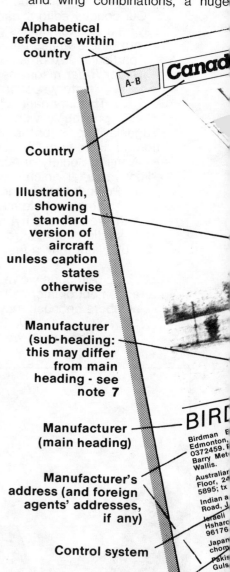

Alphabetical reference within country

Country

Illustration, showing standard version of aircraft unless caption states otherwise

Manufacturer (sub-heading: this may differ from main heading - see note 7

Manufacturer (main heading)

Manufacturer's address (and foreign agents' addresses, if any)

Control system

Summary

number of different aircraft can be created. It is impossible to list the characteristics of every one, so instead we mate each trike unit to a typical wing and detail that combination. Where the two parts come from different manufacturers, we list the aircraft under the trike unit manufacturer but give both makers' names in the sub-heading. Thus, under the Medway heading you will find a sub-heading Medway/Pegasus *Hybred 440/Typhoon XL*, indicating that the aircraft consists of a Medway *Hybred 440* trike unit and a Pegasus *Typhoon XL* wing.

Where the makers' names are doubled up but there is only one model name, the aircraft is sold complete as a joint venture between the two companies. Conversely, where there is only one maker but a double name for the model, this indicates that both trike unit and wing are from the same manufacturer but are sold separately. The simple rule with all these double names is **trike unit first, wing second.**

To find the address of a wing manufacturer, consult the index. Either the company will also make trike units, in which case it will have a listing in its own right, or its address will be in the index.

8 Unless otherwise stated, all information in this book is believed correct as at December 1984.

Rotax 277-powered form is one of Canada's most successful ultralights.
Created by Polish-born Vladimir Talanczuk, who designed and built a number of light aircraft, hang gliders and even a gyrocopter in his native country before emigrating to Canada in 1981, the *Chinook* is actually the eleventh machine to come from Vladimir's drawing board - hence its WT11 suffix.

Although the Birdman company was founded in 1972 to make hang gliders and later went on to make the *Quicksilver*-like *Atlas* range with various control systems, all links with unconventional controls were firmly broken with the *Chinook*, which sets out unashamedly to attract conventional pilots. Introduced in 1983, this tube and Dacron aircraft has gained a reputation for nimble handling and, despite its enclosed cockpit, good visibility. Former company test pilot Dennis Maland gave a graphic demonstration of the aircraft's abilities at the '83 Oshkosh, when he deliberately deployed his emergency parachute, floated down with it for a while, then detached it from the aircraft, landed the machine and dashed out into the crowd to catch the 'chute as it approached the ground!

Initially offered with a V-belt reduction on its Rotax 277 engine, the *Chinook WT-11 277* is now available with either a toothed-belt reduction or the Rotax integral gearbox. Our data gives figures for the toothed-belt 277-engined version; with a gearbox the reduction ratio becomes 2.6/1, the prop is changed to a 60x28 (1.52x0.71 m), thrust is increased to 200 lb (91 kg) and weight slightly reduced, so performance should be a little better than shown below. For pilots wanting still more thrust, the WT-11 377 is available, with Rotax 377 engine, though in that form the *Chinook* falls well outside the ultralight category in the US. Where different, data for the 377-engined version is shown in parentheses.

All versions take 15 min to rig with two people and are sold as 40-100 h kits. Prices are C$5995 and C$6150 respectively.

EXTERNAL DIMENSIONS & AREAS - Length overall 17.5 ft, 5.33 m. Height overall 5.8 ft, 1.78 m. Wing span 35.0 ft, 10.67 m. Constant chord 4.0 ft, 1.22 m. Dihedral 1.5°. Sweepback 0°. Tailplane span 8.3 ft, 2.54 m. Fin height 3.9 ft, 1.19 m. Total wing area 140 ft², 13.0 m². Total aileron area 13.2 ft², 1.24 m². Tailplane area 20.4 ft², 1.89 m². Total elevator area 11.0 ft², 1.02 m². Aspect ratio 8.8/1. Wheel track 5.2 ft, 57 m. Wheelbase 11.7 ft, 3.57 m. Tailwheel diameter overall 5 inch, 13 cm. Main wheels diameter overall 16 inch, 41 cm.

POWER PLANT - Rotax 277 (Rotax 377) engine. Max power 28(36) hp at 6000 rpm. Propeller diameter and pitch 54(60)x32(30) inch, 1.37(1.52)x0.81(0.76) m. Toothed-belt (gear) reduction, ratio 2.5(2.6)/1. Max static thrust 180 (220) lb, 81(100) kg. Power per unit area 0.20(0.26) hp/ft², 2.2(2.8) hp/m². Fuel capacity 6.0 US gal, 5.0 Imp gal, 22.7 litre.

WEIGHTS & LOADINGS - Empty weight 625(628) lb, 113(122) kg. Max take-off weight 625(628) lb, 283(285) kg. Payload 375(358) lb, 170(162) kg. Max wing loading 4.46(4.49) lb/ft², 21.8(21.9) kg/m². Max power loading 22.3(17.4) lb/hp, 10.1(7.9) kg/hp. Load factors +6.0, -3.0 recommended; +7.6, -3.5 ultimate.

PERFORMANCE* - Max level speed 60(66) mph, 97(106) kph. Never exceed speed 85 mph, 137 kph. Max cruising speed 55 mph, 88 kph. Economic cruising speed 25 mph, 40 kph. Max climb rate at sea level 700(900) ft/min, 3.6(4.6) m/s. Min sink rate at sea level 325(350) ft/min at 32(35) mph, 1.65(1.78) m/s at 51(56)

GENERAL - As can be seen from the dealer list and production figures above, the *Chinook WT-11* in its basic

kph. Best glide ratio with power off 10/1 at 45(46) mph, 72(74) kph. Take-off distance 100 ft, 30 m. Landing distance 100 ft, 30 m. Service ceiling 10,000(11,000) ft, 3050(3350) m. Range at average cruising speed 220(110) mile, 354(177) km. Noise level 55 dB at 500 ft, 150 m.
*Under the following test conditions - Airfield altitude 2400 ft, 732 m. Ground temperature 23°F, -5°C. Ground pressure 1011 mB. Ground windspeed 0 mph, 0 kph. Test payload 227 lb, 103 kg.

BIRDMAN CHINOOK WT-11 2S447 and WT-11 2S503

(Three-axis)

Summary as Chinook WT-11 277 and WT-11 377 except:
Tandem two-seater. 45%-span ailerons.
Production status: current; 50 completed (WT-11 2S447 model), 20 completed (WT-11 2S503 model).

GENERAL - Very similar to the solo machine in concept, the 2S version of the *Chinook* has a wider span and the option of two big Rotax twins - either the 447 or the 503, the aircraft's name being suffixed accordingly. Apart from larger ailerons, all the other flying surfaces are the same.
Our data below refers to the 503-engined version; where different, figures for the 447 are the same as for the single-seater and prices for 60-100 h kits are C$6800 or C$7040, depending on which engine is required.

EXTERNAL DIMENSIONS & AREAS - See *Chinook WT-11 277* and *WT-11 377* except: Wing span 37.0 ft, 11.28 m. Total wing area 148 ft², 13.7 m². Total aileron area 14.5 ft², 1.34 m². Aspect ratio 9.3/1.

POWER PLANT - Rotax 447 (Rotax 503) engine. Max power 40(47) hp at 6000 rpm. Propeller diameter and pitch 60x38(28) inch, 1.52x0.97(0.71) m. Gear (toothed-belt) reduction, ratio 2.6(2.2)/1. Max static thrust 240(270) lb, 108(122) kg. Power per unit area 0.27(0.32) hp/ft², 2.9(3.4) hp/m². Fuel capacity 5.0 US gal, 4.2 Imp gal, 18.9 litre.

WEIGHTS & LOADINGS - Empty weight 333(340) lb, 151(154) kg. Max take-off weight 761(768) lb, 345(348) kg. Payload 428 lb, 194 kg. Max wing loading 5.14(5.19) lb/ft², 25.2(25.4) kg/m². Max power loading 19.0(16.3) lb/hp, 8.6(7.4) kg/hp. Load factors +3.9, -2.0 recommended; +4.5, -2.5 ultimate.

PERFORMANCE* - Max level speed 68(72) mph, 110 (116) kph. Never exceed speed 85 mph, 137 kph. Economic cruising speed 60 mph, 97 kph. Economic cruising speed 55 mph, 88 kph. Stalling speed 38 mph, 61 kph. Max climb rate at sea level 600(700) ft/min, 3.1(3.6) m/s. Min sink rate at sea level 360 ft/min at 45 mph, 1.8 m/s at 72 kph. Best glide ratio with power off 11/1 at 52 mph, 84 kph. Take-off distance 200 ft, 61 m. Landing distance 150 ft, 46 m. Service ceiling 8000(8500) ft, 2440(2590) m. Range at average cruising speed 86 mile, 138 km. Noise level 62 dB at 500 ft, m.
*Under the following test conditions - Airfield altitude 2400 ft, 732 m. Ground temperature 23°F, -5°C. Ground pressure 1011 mB. Ground windspeed 0 mph, 0 kph. Test payload 378 lb, 171 kg.

The very manoeuvrable Chinook really showed its paces at Oshkosh '84.

BIRDMAN CHINOOK WT-11 277 and WT-11 377

(Three-axis)

Single-seat single-engined high wing monoplane with conventional three-axis control. Wing has unswept leading and trailing edges, and constant chord; conventional tail. Pitch control by elevator on tail, yaw control by fin-mounted rudder; roll control by 42%-span ailerons; control inputs through stick for pitch/roll and pedals for yaw. Wing braced from below by struts; wing profile modified UA 80/1; 85% double-surface. Undercarriage has three wheels in tail-dragger formation; bungee suspension on all wheels. Push-right go-right tailwheel steering connected to yaw control; also differential braking. Brakes on main wheels. Aluminium-alloy tube airframe, totally enclosed. Engine mounted at wing height, driving pusher propeller.
Production status: current; over 350 completed (WT-11 277 model), 80 completed (WT-11 377 model).

N

Ltd, 7939 Argyll Road, 4A9; tel (403) 468-0001; tx ohn Craig. General manager: ral sales manager: Gordon

sic Flying Machines Pty, 3rd et, Sydney 2000; tel 02-264-Contact: Jack deLissa
International, Seward, A B Nair ay; tel 628 222.
tonit Ultralight Aircraft Ltd, 5 Petach-Tikva 49353; tel (03) Navon Yekutiel and Giora Gazit.
Yasutomo & Co Ltd, No. 7-5, 2-o, Naka-ku, Yokohama 231.
Nova International, B-82, Block 5, , Karachi; tx 24174 ENCON PK.
agent: Nova International, PO Box tel 477-1214; tx 203147 BARAD

General description — Model

Data on external dimensions and areas

Data on power plant

Data on weights and loadings

Data on performance

Glossary

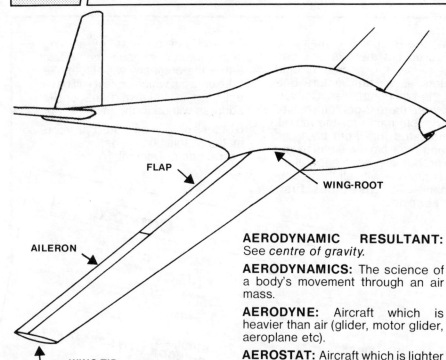

FLAP

WING-ROOT

AILERON

WING-TIP

Norman Burr

A-FRAME: The rigid tubular structure used to control a weight-shift aircraft. It is attached to the wing at the top and its horizontal lower bar is moved by the pilot: forward for up, backwards for down, leftwards for clockwise/right, rightwards for anti-clockwise/left. This *bar* is normally straight, but is sometimes shaped to extend the pilot's reach, in which case it is known as a *B-bar*.

▼

AERODYNAMIC RESULTANT: See *centre of gravity*.

AERODYNAMICS: The science of a body's movement through an air mass.

AERODYNE: Aircraft which is heavier than air (glider, motor glider, aeroplane etc).

AEROSTAT: Aircraft which is lighter than air (airship or hot-air balloon).

AILERONS: Control surfaces on trailing edges of wings which deflect differentially (eg the left aileron is lowered when the right aileron is raised) in order to roll the aircraft.

AIR BRAKES: Devices which extend from an aircraft to increase its drag, thereby slowing it down. Spoilers are often used in this way.

AIRCRAFT: Generic term for all aviation machines whether aerodyne or aerostat.

AIRFIELD: Land which is specially equipped with runways, hangars, control tower etc for aeroplanes and gliders to take-off and land. Ultra-lights and microlghts do not require prepared airfields.

AIRFRAME: The structure of an aircraft, not including the wings and tail. This term is not used to describe trike units.

AIRSCREW: See *propeller*.

AIRSPEED INDICATOR: See *anemometer*.

ALL FLYING: See *fully flying*.

ALL MOVING: See *fully flying*.

ALL-UP WEIGHT: This is calculated before each flight by adding together the weights of all the components which will take to the air, such as aircraft, pilot, fuel, clothing, instruments etc, in order to avoid exceeding the maximum recommended take-off weight.

ALTIMETER: The instrument which measures the altitude or height (see *altitude*) by making use of differences in atmospheric pressure.

ALTIPORT: A mountain airfield which may or may not have buildings and hard surfaces.

ALTITUDE: The vertical elevation above sea level. It must not be confused with height, which is the vertical elevation above the ground. If you calibrate the altimeter with the atmospheric pressure at sea level, it will register on the ground the height of the terrain upon which you are standing. In flight your altitude above sea level must always be above the heights indicated on relief route maps. If you calibrate your altimeter to the atmospheric pressure registered at your take-off point, it will indicate 0 and thereafter register your height above that ground. We refer to the atmospheric pressure above sea level as QNH, and this may be obtained by phoning the airfield or its nearest meteorological office. The QFE is the atmospheric pressure registered on the ground.

ALUMINIUM: Alloys based on ths light metal, such as Duralumin, are currently widely used in aeronautics. The metallurgical classifications vary from country to country - aviation quality Duralumin is type AU4G1 in France, 6061 in the USA, and seamless HT30 in Great Britain. The end of the classification indicates the type of heat treatment given to the metal. Note that aluminium to French class AU3G does not offer sufficient strength and is therefore prohibited for aeronautical structures.

ALUMINUM: US spelling for *aluminium*.

AMPHIBIOUS: This class of aircraft can land and take-off on land or water. Typically, the wheels retract into a portion of the fuselage which can then be sealed like a boat, and the wings carry small floats. See *seaplane*.

ANEMOMETER: Instrument which measures the relative speed of the wing. It can also indicate the speed of the aircraft through the air (but not over the ground).

ANGLE OF ATTACK: The angle between the wing profile and the relative direction of the wind. The relative wind consists of one component due to the actual wind direction and another due to the movement of the aircraft through the air.

ANGLE OF SWEEP: See *sweep*.

ANHEDRAL: Negative *dihedral*.

A.S.I.: Abbreviation for airspeed indicator. See *anemometer*.

ASPECT RATIO: The ratio between the square of the wing span and the wing's surface area. A modern glider has an aspect ratio of 20/1 while a supersonic machine could be less than 3/1. Example: the ratio for an aircraft of 11 m span and 13 m² is 121/13=9.3.

AXES: The movements of any aircraft in flight are composed of rotations about the three axes passing through its centre of gravity - pitch (up-down), roll (clockwise-anticlockwise), and yaw (left-right). Three-axis control allows the pilot to control independently the aircraft's movement in each axis, usually with a stick for pitch and roll (backwards for up, forwards for down, leftwards for anti-clockwise, rightwards for clockwise) and pedals for yaw (push left for left, push right for right). Such an arrangement is known as **conventional three-axis control**; alternative arrangements are known as **unconventional three-axis control** and sometimes use just a stick, with a mixer mechanism to apportion the left-right control movement into roll and yaw elements.

In practice roll is normally accompanied by yaw and vice versa, with the pilot co-ordinating the controls to avoid a sideslip or skid; the single-stick arrangement avoids the need for such co-ordination. Other designers avoid the need for yaw/roll co-ordination in a different way, by simply dispensing with the roll control. These aircraft are known as **two-axis** machines.

Strictly speaking, **weight-shift** aircraft are also two-axis machines, but they are generally regarded as a distinct category. They are controlled by the pilot altering the relative positions of the wing and the aircraft's centre of gravity, usually by means of an A-frame. Most weight-shift aircraft are trikes, and note that, with such machines, the 'missing' axis is not roll but yaw, the latter being available only through induced roll.

Hybrid aircraft use a combination of weight-shift and one or more control surfaces.

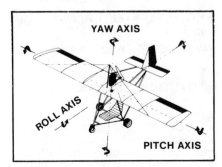

YAW AXIS
ROLL AXIS
PITCH AXIS

AXLE-FLEX: Suspension system relying on the distortion of the axle under stress. The term is usually reserved for metal axles.

B-BAR: See *A-frame.*

BANK: Angle formed between the aircraft and the horizontal when rolling.

BAR: See *A-frame.*

BATTEN: Another word for the *rib* in a Rogallo wing.

BIPLANE: This is an aircraft with two wings placed one above the other. These should be of similar weight and plan. If one is significantly superior, or if they are significantly staggered, the aircraft is not a biplane but a double monoplane or tandem monoplane.

BOWSPRIT: See *cross-tube.*

BOX-SECTION: This is a structural arrangement to increase rigidity. Without its lid, a box's sides can easily be deformed, but once the lid is in place one has a rigid structure which is difficult to deform.

BRACING: The wires or struts which increase the strength and rigidity of the wings and tail. The undercarriage may be strengthened by bracing it to the wings and the wings themselves may be braced by means of struts or wires running from the kingpost on the top of the aircraft.

BUNGEE: An elastic strap.

BUTTERFLY TAIL: Another description for V-tail - see *tail.*

CABLE; Used in two senses: either a cable to brace the structure or a method of transmitting a control input.

CAGE: Framework around the pilot.

CANARD: A design where a small supplementary lifting surface is carried ahead of the main wing. This forward wing can be movable to vary the angle of attack, or fixed with a control surface to vary the pitch.

CANOPY: A construction of one or more pieces of transparent material to shield the pilot; it is normally made from Lexan, plexiglass, or perspex.

CANTILEVER: A wing which is self-supporting, ie one which is not supported by wires and/or struts.

CASTOR: A wheel which castors is free to swivel in respose to ground forces and cannot be controlled by the pilot.

CEILING: The maximum altitude which an aircraft can attain. In truth there are two ceilings, the theoretical ceiling which we have just defined and the service ceiling, which is the maximum height at which there is still some ability to manoeuvre.

CENTRE OF GRAVITY: The point in the aircraft through which its mass appears to act. This is a downward force.

CENTRING: The position of the centre of gravity, which must remain within certain limits so as not to affect the stability or manoeuvrability of the aircraft.

CHORD: The distance betwen the leading and trailng edges of the wing. With some wings this is constant for any cross-section from the root to the tip. With other wings it reduces towards the tip, hence the term tapering chord. The mean chord is the arithmetic mean of the root chord and the tip chord; thus an aircraft with a root chord of 120 cm and a tip chord of 90 cm would have a mean chord of 105 cm. For wings with a steady rate of taper, the wing area can be calculated by multiplying the mean chord by the wing span.

C.H.T.G.: Abbreviation for cylinder head temperature gauge.

COMPOSITE: A structure using two or more different materials irrevocably bonded together - eg a wing using aluminium tube surrounded by polystyrene and covered with a glass-fibre skin.

CONTROL: See *axes.*

THE CONTROLS: They act upon the movable surfaces to change the motion of the aircraft about one or more of its axes (see *axes*).

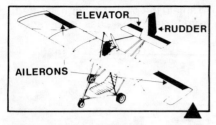

CONTROL SURFACE: Any movable area which can be used to control the aircraft in one or more axes (eg rudder, spoiler).

CONVENTIONAL TAIL: See *tail*.

CROSS-TUBE: The main tube supporting the width of a Rogallo wing. When fixed at its centre to the keel structure, it is known as a rigid cross-tube. When not so attached, it is called a floating cross-tube. Some Rogallo wings have no cross-tube, but use instead a forward-projecting tube, or bowsprit, to which are attached bracing wires from the leading edges.

CRUCIFORM TAIL: See *tail*.

CRUISE: The part of the flight between the end of the climb after take-off and the start of the descent before landing.

CRUISING SPEED: The speed of the aircraft in zero wind at the various engine settings which can be maintained without excessive engine strain. Note that the maximum speed in level flight requires the engine to be performing at peak rpm and is impossible to maintain for long periods without the performance of the engine deteriorating.

DERIGGING: See *rigging*.

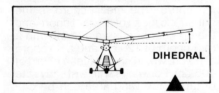

DIHEDRAL: The angle between the horizontal and the wing when the aircraft is seen face on. This plays a part in determining an aircraft's stability in flight.

DOUBLE MONOPLANE: See *bi-plane*.

DOUBLE-SURFACE: See *surface*.

DRAG: The total of all the forces upon the aircraft which resist its forward motion.

DUOPOLE: See *pole*.

E.G.T.G.: Abbreviation for exhaust gas temperature gauge.

ELEVATOR: A control which moves the aircraft about the pitch axis (see *axes*).

ELEVONS: A control surface giving combined pitch and roll control.

EMPTY WEIGHT: The weight of the aircraft alone, ie without fuel, lubricants or anything else.

END PLATE: Another word for *saumon*.

ENDURANCE: The length of time an aircraft is capable of flying. It is a function of its fuel capacity and consumption and is measured in hours and minutes. It must not be confused with range, which is a distance in miles or kilometres.

FAIRING: Any moulding or similar added to an aircraft to improve its aerodynamic characteristics. A nose fairing is called a pod.

FIN: See *stabiliser*.

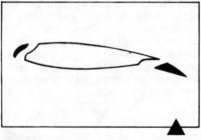

FLAPS: In order to delay the stall at low speeds, various high-lift devices are employed. Though seldom used in ultralights and microlights, leading edge flaps (slats) prevent the early breakdown of the airflow over the top surface of the wing. The most common type used are flaps attached to the trailing edge of the wing, which work by changing the wing profile to make it supply more lift. Split flaps are when the lower portion of the trailing edge is lowered. Fowler flaps actually increase the wing area before being lowered.

FLEX-WING: Any wing which relies on airflow to give it its correct profile. This term is usually reserved for describing *Rogallo wings*.

FLOATING CROSS-TUBE: See *cross-tube*.

FLYING WING: This distinct class of aircraft has no fuselage but has its tail surfaces attached directly to the rear of the aerofoil - ie, it is an aircraft without a tail.

FREE-FLIGHT: A flight made without the use of the engine, a practice often called soaring.

FULLY FLYING: When, on a two- or three-axis aircraft, there are no fixed surfaces in a particular axis, the moving surfaces are known as fully flying - eg an aircraft with a rudder but no fin has a fully flying rudder.

FUSELAGE: Where the structural components of an ultralight or microlight, excluding wings and tail, are made from a glass-fibre moulding or similar, rather than tubing, that structure is called the fuselage. This term is not used to describe trike units. (Note that in general aviation, 'fuselage' has a rather broader meaning).

GLIDE RATIO: The ratio between the distance an aircraft travels forward in a glide and the distance it descends from its starting point, in zero wind. It is given as a ratio to 1 for each speed, ie an aircraft with a glide ratio of 10/1 will move forward 10 miles for every 1 mile descent. The maximum glide ratio is only available at one particular speed.

GROUND EFFECT: An aerodynamic effect due to the cushion of air trapped between the ground and the wings.

GROUND ROLL: Strictly speaking, this is any manoeuvre on the ground. However, it is now used to express either the distance travelled from standstill to the instant of take-off, or the distance from touch-down to standstill.

GROUND RUN: See *ground roll*.

HANG-POINT: Point of attachment of a trike unit to a Rogallo wing.

HEIGHT: Not to be confused with *altitude*.

HIGH-WING: See *wing*.

HORIZONTAL STABILISER: See *tail*.

HYBRID: See *axes*.

INCLINED FIXED PLANE: See *stabiliser*.

INVERTED V-TAIL: See *tail*.

JOYSTICK: See *stick*.

KEEL: A rigid member on the underside of the fuselage or as a skid under the tail to confer greater rigidity. In a trike it is the principal structure from which the trike unit is hung, being made up of a tube or tubes which form the main load bearers and also determine the angle of attack of the wing.

KEEL POCKET: A vertical area of wing underneath the rear of the main surface of a Rogallo wing.

KINGPOST: A rigid mast above the midpoint of the wing, to which bracing is attached.

LAMINAR: A smooth (ie non-turbulent) flow of air over a surface.

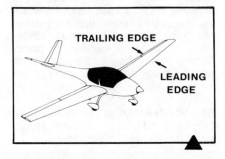

LEADING EDGE: The front edge of the wing.

LENGTH: The length of an aircraft is the distance from the frontmost to the rearmost part.

LIFT: The force generated by the movement of air round the wing and which enables an aircraft to fly.

LIFTING SURFACE: The total area of all the surfaces of an aircraft which generate lift.

LOAD FACTOR: The ratio between the real and apparent weight of an aircraft. The apparent weight is the weight which acts when not in level flight in still air, eg when banking or making a violent change of direction or in great turbulence, all of which involve a sharp rise in apparent weight.

This load is measured in g, where 1 g is the force of gravity. Obviously, excessive load factors will cause breakage of an aircraft's structure, so designers should always supply the limits within which their aircraft must be flown. This is given in postive/negative values of g. Some tend to exaggerate the structural strength of their machines, so we feel we must mention that most light aircraft can only tolerate up to +4g, -2g, except those certified as stronger and probably designed for aerobatics. The table below shows the effect of acceleration during a turn on the apparent weight of a pilot.

Bank	0°	35°	45°	60°
Load factor	1	1.15	1.4	2
Weight of pilot (kg)	80	92	112	160
Weight of aircraft (kg)	200	230	280	400
% gain	0	15	40	100

LONGERON: A stiffening member or beam in the fuselage.

LOW-WING: See *wing*.

MAXIMUM TAKE-OFF WEIGHT: The maximum weight at which an aircraft is authorised to take off. This is a function of various parameters, eg its structural strength, power, wing loading, etc.

MICROLIGHT AIRCRAFT: See *ultralight aircraft*.

MID-WING: See *wing*.

MIXER: A mechanism allowing one control to move two or more differently oriented control surfaces, or conversely, a mechanism allowing a control surface to be moved by more than one control.

MONOBLOC: Another word for *fully flying*.

MONOPLANE: A hybrid, two-or three-axis aircraft with a single wing. For double monoplane or tandem monoplane, see *biplane*.

MONOPOLE: See *pole*.

MOTOR GLIDER: Gliders (as opposed to hang-gliders) or sail-planes which have auxiliary engines to assist cross-country flight. In some cases the engines are powerful enough to permit self-launching.

NOSE ANGLE: The included angle between the leading edges of a Rogallo wing.

ONE-PLUS-ONE: An aircraft with two seats but whose payload is too small to permit two full-size adults to be carried.

PARASOL-WING: See *wing*.

PAYLOAD: The weight which an aircraft can safely lift. It should not be less than the weight of the pilot!

PITCH: See *axes*.

POD: A non-structural fairing on the front of an airframe or trike unit.

POLE: Upright structural member on a trike unit. A monopole trike unit has only one pole; duopoles have two.

POWER PACK: A group of components consisting of the engine and its accessories (starter, exhaust etc), propeller and where fitted a reduction system. Usually just referred to as the engine. (See also *propeller*).

POWER-TO-WEIGHT RATIO: The ratio between maximum take-off weight of the aircraft and its maximum engine power. Note that the higher the ratio the poorer the rate of climb.

PREFLIGHT: The check before each flight to ensure that all the components of the aircraft are in good order.

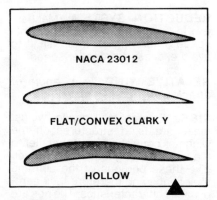

NACA 23012

FLAT/CONVEX CLARK Y

HOLLOW

PROFILE: The shape of the wing which defines its aerodynamic properties. Certain profiles give better lift and others permit faster flight.

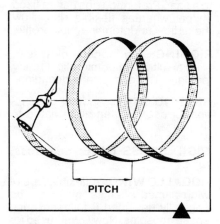

PITCH

PROPELLER: This may be tractor (pulls the aircraft through the air) or pusher. It may be two-, three-, or four-bladed and is defined by its length and pitch. Pitch here must not be confused with the pitch movement of an aircraft; it refers to the screw-thread principle, the pitch being the distance a screw travels forward in one rotation. The circle drawn by the propeller as it turns is given as its diameter.

PUSHER: See *propeller*.

QFE: The atmospheric pressure on the ground (see *altitude*).

QNH: The atmospheric pressure at sea level (see *altitude*).

RANGE: The maximum distance an aircraft can travel in still air on a single flight. This is a function of speed, fuel capacity and fuel consumption and is expressed in miles or kilometres. Do not confuse it with *endurance* which is expressed in units of time.

RATE OF CLIMB: The opposite of the rate of sink: the vertical speed of an aircraft is its climb. As with sink, it is measured with a variometer.

REDUCTION SYSTEM: Mechanism for gearing down the rotational speed of the engine output shaft to avoid excessive propeller speed.

RELATIVE WIND: See *angle of attack.*

RIBS: Except in Rogallo wings, these are fixed structures on the wings or control surfaces parallel to the aircraft's longitudinal axis, which give these portions of the airframe their shape and therefore their aerodynamic characteristics. The ribs are attached to the spars and to them are fixed the upper and lower surfaces. With Rogallo wings, the ribs do a similar job but are not rigidly attached to a spar. Preformed ribs have a fixed shape, whereas flexible ribs allow the airflow to determine their profile.

RIGGING: The process of assembling an ultralight or microlight ready for flight. The opposite is derigging.

RIGGING WIRE: Another description for *cable*. Often abbreviated to rigging.

RIGID CROSS-TUBE: See *cross-tube.*

ROGALLO WING: A flexible type of wing named after its inventor, who originally designed it for recovering space capsules. Now widely used for hang-gliding and weight-shift aircraft.

ROLL: See *axes.*

RUDDER: The vertical control surface which affects the direction of the aircraft in the yaw plane. It is normally operated by applying pressure on the rudder bar with the feet. Trikes do not have a rudder.

RUDDER BAR: A bar to which are fitted two pedals which control the rudder.

RUDDERON: Another word for *tip-rudder.*

RUDDERVATOR: In a V-tail the two movable surfaces serve the same function as the three surfaces in a conventional tail. These two surfaces

are called the ruddervators and control pitch and yaw.

SAIL WING: Aerodyne made specifically for free flying. Rogallo wings are often called sails.

SAUMONS: Vertical surfaces fixed to the wing tips, designed to stop

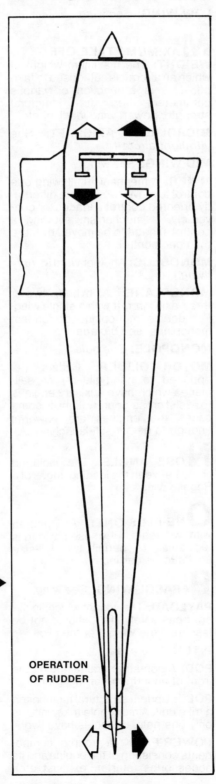

OPERATION OF RUDDER

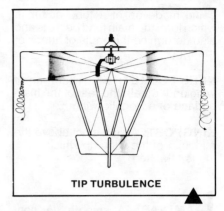

TIP TURBULENCE

seepage of air over the tips and thus reduce turbulence over the tips and improve the performance of the wing. They may be present upon any other structure, eg on a horizontal stabiliser, to serve a similar purpose. Occasionally they are movable, in which case they become control surfaces.

SEAPLANE: An aircraft which can only land and take off on water. Not to be confused with an *amphibian.*

SEAPLANE BASE: A stretch of water which may be used by seaplanes and amphibians.

SECTION: In aviation as in nautical circles, a section is a circumferential member along the longitudinal axis of the fuselage, braced by longerons parallel to that axis. The principal section is, as the name implies, the section at the widest point of the fuselage. The size of the fuselage is defined by its length, height and width at principal section. It is also worth noting that this principal section equals the area of the fuselage perpendicular to the relative wind, in level flight and still air.

SERVICE CEILING: See *ceiling.*

SINGLE-SURFACE: See *surface.*

SKIN: See *surface.*

SLATS: See *flaps.*

SOARING: See *free-flight.*

SPAR: A stiffening member or beam in the wing.

SPEED: The speed of an aircraft is made up of various elements, all of which imply their own particular speeds of air flowing over the various lifting surfaces.
Approach speed is that speed which should be maintained as an aircraft prepares to land. It if is too low the aircraft will land short or stall, too high and the ground roll will be lengthened.

Climb speed - see *rate of climb*.

Cruising speed - see *cruise*.

Take-off speed is the speed at which the wings start to carry the aircraft. Take-off is not solely due to the speed of the aircraft but also to the angle of attack between the wing and the relative wind. This relative wind is itself dependent on speed. Take-off commences when lift generated by the wing is sufficient to counteract the weight of the aircraft.

Maximum speed is the speed obtained in horizontal flight with the engine generating maximum power.

Groundspeed is an essential concept. The mechanics of flight depend on the aircraft's passage through the air and not, as in a car, its crossing the ground. So if one is flying at 60 mph in the same direction as a wind of 30 mph, the airspeed will be 60 mph but the groundspeed will be 90 mph. Conversely, if one is facing a head wind of 30 mph the airspeed indicator will still read 60 mph but one will only pass over the ground at 30 mph.

At or below **stalling speed** the wings no longer carry the aircraft. The stall is due not only to the speed but also to the angle of attack between the wing and the relative wind. This relative wind is itself dependent on speed. At the stall speed, the airflow over the wing breaks down and therefore the lift collapses.

SPIN: A fairly rapid descent in conjunction with rotation about the roll axis. It is not advisable to perform this manoeuvre in an ultralight or microlight.

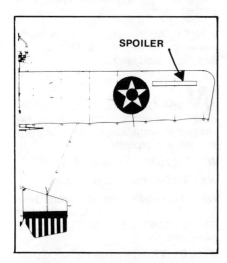

SPOILER: A spoiler is a movable surface, usually attached to the top of the wing, which disrupts the airflow

and hence reduces the lift on that wing. Thus, when a spoiler is deployed on one wing, it creates roll; when spoilers are deployed on both wings, they act as air brakes.

Note that a spoiler works in the opposite way to an aileron; a spoiler reduces lift, an aileron increases it. Some aircraft use a combination of aileron and spoiler for roll control.

Spoileron is a rather nebulous term. Usually it means a large spoiler used as the sole means of roll control (ie without ailerons), but since some spoilers are also used in this way, much confusion has arisen about the difference between the two terms.

One manufacturer's spoiler is another's spoileron and, since this book is largely compiled from information supplied by manufacturers, that inconsistency is inevitably reflected in our descriptions. If in doubt, readers should ask manufacturers for more detail.

SPOILERON: See *spoiler*.

STABILISER: A fixed surface in association with a control surface. A vertical fixed surface is known as a fin, a horizontal fixed surface is known as a tailplane (except in canard aircraft of course), and a fixed surface used with a ruddervator is called an inclined fixed plane.

STALLING SPEED: See *speed*.

STERN POST: The extreme rear of the fuselage.

STICK: The control stick of a two- or three-axis aircraft. Sometimes called joystick.

STREAMLINING: Smooth low-drag surface round any portion of an aircraft.

SURFACE: Covering material of the aircraft (Dacron, laminate, wood, linen, metal, etc) placed on the structure to form the outer surface. Where the wing structure is covered only on its upper side, the wing is known as single-surface. Where part or all of the underside is covered, the wing is known as double-surface, with a percentage to indicate how much of the underside is covered. Thus 100% double-surface means that none of the upper surface is visible from the underside. Double-surface wings offer greater performance than their single-surface equivalents, but tend to be heavier and more complex. Skin is another word for surface.

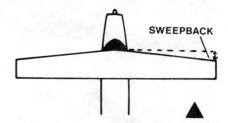

SWEEPBACK: Looking from above the aircraft, the angle between an edge of a wing and a line drawn at right angles across the aircraft. Where only one figure is shown for sweepback, it is normally the figure for the leading edge.

T-TAIL: See *tail*.

TAIL: The collection of vertical, horizontal or sloping surfaces comprising fixed and movable parts at the rear of the aircraft. Most commonly, it is a T-shape, either an upright T with the elevator above the rudder, this arrangement being known as a **T-tail**, or an inverted T with rudder above elevator, an arrangement so common that it has become termed a **conventional tail**. The vertical tail surface is made up of a fixed stabiliser and a movable rudder, while the

T-tail.

horizontal surface comprises a fixed stabiliser and movable elevator. If there is no fixed portion to these surfaces they are called *fully-flying*.

Similarly, V-tails (ie tails using ruddervators) may also come upright or inverted, and with or without stabilisers. Upright V-tails are simply called **V-tails**, while those turned through 180° are known as **inverted V-tails**. When used with V-tails, stabilisers are known as inclined fixed planes.

The **cruciform tail** has an X shape with areas of rudder above and below the horizontal surface.

Two-rudder and **two-fin** tails, as their names imply, have a rudder at

Glossary

V-tail

each tip of the horizontal surface, forming either an H or a U with the horizontal surface.

TAIL-DRAGGER: See *undercarriage.*

TAILPLANE: See *stabiliser.*

TANDEM: Two seats one behind the other.

TANDEM MONOPLANE: See *biplane.*

THREE-AXIS: See *axes.*

THRUST: In the mechanics of flight, the force created by the propeller in powered flight.

THRUST LINE: The line through the aircraft along which the power supplied by its motor(s) appears to act. In a multi-engined aircraft this is the resultant of the forces supplied by each engine. A component for drag is also included in the resultant.

TIP DRAGGERS: Another word for *tip rudders.*

TIP RUDDERS: Rudders mounted on the ouboard ends of the main wing.

TIP TURBULENCE: See *saumons.*

TORQUE: A force of rotation in the rolling plane produced by the working of the engine. It is greatest when power output is high and speed is low, such as at take-off.

TRACTOR: See *propellor.*

TRAILING EDGE: The rear edge of the wing.

TRAPEZE: See *A-frame.*

TRICYCLE: See *undercarriage.*

TRIKE: A weight-shift aircraft consisting of a trike unit and a Rogallo wing.

TRIKE UNIT: That part of a weight-shift Rogallo-winged aircraft that is suspended below the wing - ie the cage, undercarriage and power pack.

TURBULENCE: Disturbed air moving in a haphazard fashion.

TWIN-BOOM: This is an aircraft where the rear portion of the fuselage is split into two booms upon which the tail is carried.

TWO-AXIS: See *axes.*

TWO-FIN TAIL: See *tail.*

TWO-SEATER: Aircraft with two seats and with a payload sufficient to allow both seats to be occupied by full-size adults. If the seats are placed one behind the other the aircraft is referred to as a tandem two-seater. If they are placed alongside one another, the aircraft is a side-by-side two-seater.

ULTRALIGHT AIRCRAFT: This is not just a powered aircraft of very low weight but a legal definition which varies from country to country. The term ultralight is not universal; Britain uses 'microlight', France 'ULM', West Germany 'UL', and so on. As the basis of their legislation, many countries use the FAI definition of a microlight, which is as follows: 'a one or two seat aircraft whose empty weight does not exceed 150 kg and with a wing area in square metres of not less than W/10, where W is the weight in kilograms'. Increasingly, there is a move to allow a further 25 kg for two-seat training aircraft.

UNDERCARRIAGE: The structure which serves for rolling, take-off and landing, sometimes called the undercart for short when it uses wheels (it can also consist of skis or floats). Most undercarriages consist of three wheels; looking from above, if there is one wheel at the front of the aircraft and two behind, the aircraft has a tricycle undercarriage. If there are two wheels at the front and one behind, it has a tail-dragger undercarriage (sometimes called a classical or tailwheel undercarriage). On a tail-dragger undercarriage, the rear wheel can be replaced by a skid or strip of metal.

Tricycle undercarriage.

With the vast majority of tricycle undercarriages, the two rear wheels are designed to take most of the load. In the few cases where the nosewheel does most of the work, we have used the term double tail-dragger.

The undercarriage is a mono when it consists of a principal wheel (or single ski) under the fuselage, and a small wheel or tail skid situated in the same longitudinal plane. It is called mono because only one wheel tracks along the ground. Each wing of such a device has supple metal supports to prevent the wing tips touching the ground and being damaged.

Tail-dragger undercarriage.

An undercarriage may be fixed or retractable, depending on whether or not it can retract into the fuselage and wing. The holes into which the wheels retract can be fitted with covers to streamline the surface. (See also *amphibian*).

V-TAIL: See *tail.*

VARIOMETER: Instrument which measures the vertical speed of the aircraft - positive when climbing or negative when descending. Often called vario for short.

VERTICAL STABILISER: See *stabiliser.*

V.N.E: Abbreviation for velocity never to be exceeded. This limit is fixed for each aircraft.

WASHOUT: Twist built into a wing. In some aircraft this can be altered in flight to give roll control - see *wing warping.*

WEIGHT: The force of gravity.

WEIGHT-SHIFT: See *axes.*

WHEELBASE: The distance between the centre of the nosewheel or tailwheel and the centre line of the main wheels.

WHEEL TRACK: The distance between the centres of the main wheels.

WINGLET: Another word for *saumon.*

WINDSCREEN: A surface of transparent material to protect the pilot from the elements. Do not confuse this with *canopy*.

WINDSOCK: A fabric tube placed at the top of a mast to indicate wind direction.

WING: All the lifting surfaces of an aircraft, split into two or four sub-wings depending on whether the aircraft is a monoplane or biplane. Normally these sub-wings are just called wings. According to its wing position in relation to the fuselage, an aircraft may be **parasol-winged** (above and clear of the fuselage), **high-winged** (attached to the top of the fuselage), **mid-winged** (attached to the centre of the fuselage), or **low-winged** (bottom surface flush with the bottom of the fuselage).

WING-LOADING: The ratio between the mass of the aircraft and its wing's surface area. In our descriptions of the aircraft we have chosen to define the wing loading of each machine using the maximum take-off weight, as this appears to be the most representative, but unladen or empty-weight wing loadings are also often found.

WING-ROOT: The portion of the wing where it joins the fuselage.

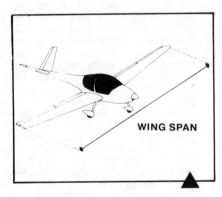

WING SPAN

WING SPAN: The length of the wing measured between its two extremities (the tips), at right angles to the longitudinal axis of the fuselage.

WING TIPS: The outermost edges of the wings.

WING WARPING: Now no longer a popular method of roll control, thanks to the advent of ailerons, this method achieves roll control by twisting the whole of one wing to reduce the lift provided, thereby causing that wing to drop relative to the other, unaltered, wing.

WIRE: When used in a description of an aircraft's structure, another word for *cable*.

Y AW: See *axes*.

CONVERSION TABLE

US/Imperial to Metric

To convert . . .	to . . .	multiply by . . .
Inches (inch)	Millimetres (mm)	25.40
Inches (inch)	Centimetres (cm)	2.540
Inches (inch)	Metres (m)	0.0254
Feet (ft)	Metres (m)	0.3048
Miles (mile)	Kilometres (km)	1.609
Nautical Miles (n mile)	Kilometres (km)	1.853
Square inches (in^2 or sq inch)	Square centimetres (cm^2 or sq cm)	6.452
Square feet (ft^2 or sq ft)	Square metres (m^2 or sq m)	0.0929
Cubic inches (in^3 or cu inch)	Cubic centimetres (cm^3 or cc)	16.39
Cubic feet (ft^3 or cu ft)	Cubic metres (m^3 or cu m)	0.0283
Cubic inches (in^3 or cu inch)	Litres (litre)	0.01639
US pints (US pint)	Litres (litre)	0.4731
Imperial pints (Imp pint)	Litres (litre)	0.5683
US gallon (US gal)	Litres (litre)	3.785
Imperial gallon (Imp gal)	Litres (litre)	4.546
Miles per hour (mile/h or mph)	Kilometres per hour (km/h or kph)	1.609
Knots (n mile/h or kt)	Kilometres per hour (km/h or kph)	1.853
Feet per minute (ft/min)	Metres per second (m/s)	0.00508
Ounces (oz)	Grams (g)	28.35
Pounds (lb)	Kilograms (kg)	0.4536
US tons (US ton)	Tonnes (t)	0.9072
Imp tons (Imp ton)	Tonnes (t)	1.016
Horsepower (hp)	Metric horsepower (hp)	1.014
Horsepower (hp)	Watts (W)	745.7
Horsepower per square foot (hp/ft^2 or hp/sq ft)	Metric horsepower per square metre (hp/m^2 or hp/sq m)	10.91
Pounds per horsepower (lb/hp)	Kilograms per metric horsepower (kg/hp)	0.4474
Ounces per square inch (oz/in^2 or oz/sq in)	Grams per square centimetre (g/cm^2 or g/sq cm)	4.394
Pounds per square foot (lb/ft^2 or lb/sq ft)	Kilograms per square metre (kg/m^2 or kg/sq m)	4.882

Metric to US/Imperial

To convert . . .	to . . .	multiply by . . .
Millimetres (mm)	Inches (inch)	0.03937
Centimetres (cm)	Inches (inch)	0.3937
Metres (m)	Inches (inch)	39.37
Kilometres (km)	Feet (ft)	3.282
Kilometres (km)	Miles (mile)	0.6215
Kilometres (km)	Nautical miles (n mile)	0.5397
Square centimetres (cm^2 or sq cm)	Square inches (in^2 or sq inch)	0.1550
Square metres (m^2 or sq m)	Square feet (ft^2 or sq ft)	10.76
Cubic centimetres (cm^3 or cc)	Cubic inches (in^3 or cu inch)	0.06102
Cubic metres (m^3 or cu m)	Cubic feet (ft^3 or cu ft)	35.31
Litres (litre)	Cubic inches (in^3 or cu inch)	61.02
Litres (litre)	US pints (US pint)	2.114
Litres (litre)	Imperial pints (Imp pint)	1.760
Litres (litre)	US gallon (US gal)	0.2642
Litres (litre)	Imperial gallon (Imp gal)	0.220
Kilometres per hour (km/h or kph)	Miles per hour (mile/h or mph)	0.6215
Kilometres per hour (km/h or kph)	Knots (n mile/h or kt)	0.5397
Metres per second (m/s)	Feet per minute (ft/min)	196.9
Grams (g)	Ounces (oz)	0.03527
Kilograms (kg)	Pounds (lb)	2.205
Tonnes (t)	US tons (US ton)	1.102
Tonnes (t)	Imperial tons (Imp ton)	0.9842
Metric horsepower (hp)	Horsepower (hp)	0.9864
Watts (W)	Horsepower (hp)	0.001341
Metric horsepower per square metre (hp/m^2 or hp/sq m)	Horsepower per square foot (hp/ft^2 or hp/sq ft)	0.09164
Kilograms per metric horsepower (kg/hp)	Pounds per horsepower (lb/hp)	2.235
Grams per square centimetre (g/cm^2 or g/sq cm)	Ounces per square inch (oz/in^2 or oz/sq in)	0.2276
Kilograms per square metre (kg/m^2 or kg/sq m)	Pounds per square foot (lb/ft^2 or lb/sq ft)	0.2048

Miscellaneous

1. 1 US gal = 0.8327 Imp gal; 1 US ton = 0.8929 Imp ton = 2000 lb.
2. To convert from °F to °C, subtract 32 and then divide by 1.8; to convert from °C to °F, multiply by 1.8 and then add 32.
3. All conversions in this table are accurate to four significant figures. They may not agree exactly with conversions in the text, because of rounding after conversion.

History

'One can fly over long distances using a very simple machine, without any abnormal effort, and this sort of free flight and motion through the air gives more pleasure than any other type of sport!' - Otto Lilienthal.

Introduction

The first edition of *Berger-Burr's* provided a snapshot of what the sport was like in 1983 and also included some obsolete but historically important machines. What it did not do, however, was to put these machines in perspective, to explain the evolution of the worldwide movement which produced them - an omission we were determined to remedy for the second edition. What was needed, we decided, was something to bring the reader up to that 1983 datum.

However, when we sat down to write what we believe is the first English-language history of the sport, we found ourselves confronted with a very fundamental problem. When did ultralighting begin?

The instinctive reaction of most pilots would be to say that it developed from hang gliding in the late '70s, but history is never that simple! In fact, ultralighting is a rebirth, a return to the love of slow-speed flight which the earliest aviators felt so keenly, but which was subsequently lost in the quest for military superiority and commercial practicality. In a very real sense, the first ultralighter was the first heavier-than-air aviator. We must turn the clock back a lot further . . .

Up to 1909

Many excellent books have been written about the exploits of the 19th century pioneers, and in a section this length it is hard to do justice to these redoubtable characters. Nevertheless we must at least acknowledge the contribution of men like General Resnier de Goue, the Frenchman who in 1806 at the age of 77 became the world's first hang glider pilot by launching himself from the ramparts of Angouleme, some 250 ft (76 m) above the River Charente. Hitherto, would-be aviators had tried to copy the birds by fitting their arms (and sometimes legs) with imitations of wings, which they proceeded to flap wildly as they plummeted to earth. But the general went far further, building a machine with a batten-stiffened flexible wing and a tail which, though solidly attached to the wing, was steerable by the pilot's legs.

His first flight rewarded him with a ducking in the Charente and his second with a broken leg, but the point had been made. Others had simply managed to fall slower with their machines than without them, but Resnier was almost able to control the course of his second flight - and it *was* a flight, not just a fall.

Not until the great German pioneer Lilienthal did matters develop further, though it was not for want of trying. The Englishman Cayley, for example, not wishing to become airborne himself at the age of 80, press-ganged his coachman to be his test pilot. But after an inconclusive attempt this brave man exclaimed, 'Sir - you engaged me to drive your horses, not to fly!' and refused to try again. Across the Channel, in 1857, Breton Jean-Marie Le Bris gained the honour of being the first to go soaring, managing to get 300 ft (90 m) above the ground. On another occasion Le Bris mounted his glider on top of a carriage, and the coachman set the horses to gallop. The glider took off rapidly, but the rope holding him in the glider caught round the seat of the carriage, ripping out the seat and the driver with it. They both alighted unharmed, having achieved the first recorded flight of a two-seater, albeit inadvertently!

Finally we come to the greatest of all the pre-Wright brothers pioneers, the German Otto Lilienthal, whose first glider and flights date from 1891. Like Resnier de Goue, he tried to forget the birds. He started badly: the engine with which he was experimenting worked on the paddle rather than the propeller principle, despite the fact that the latter had been known for a long time - indeed Da Vinci had realised its aeronautical potential centuries before.

But aerodynamically he was unquestionably on the right track. Sometimes monoplanes, sometimes biplanes, all of Lilienthal's flying machines had a similar structure of bamboo woven with rattan cane and covered with waxed cotton. Even his first two birds were built with separate wings, one either side of the pilot, and that was the end of the one-piece wing for a long time. These wings were made up of radiating ribs which allowed the fabric to form deeply concave fan shaped sections, especially at the wing-tip lobes. This, just like the eagle's tip feathers, gave increased stability. At the back, he had an empennage with a vertical fin and an adjustable elevator, a combination which today we would call hybrid control, since pitch control was by control surfaces, but yaw was by weight-shift, Otto moving his legs or entire body whilst being supported simply by resting his elbows on the 'fuselage', without any harness!

Incredibly, Otto made more than 2000 flights like this, running to take-off from the top of a 100 ft (30 m) hill and covering sometimes 1000 ft (300 m) before landing. This equates to a glide ratio of around 10/1, not far short of the performance of modern hang gliders! Otto's motto goes a long way towards explaining his success: 'To design a flying machine is nothing; building it isn't much; flight testing it is what matters.'

On 9 August 1896, five years after his first flight, Otto took off once more. No one knows for sure whether his biplane was caught by a strong gust, which combined with too much up elevator to cause a vicious stall and dive from which he could not recover, or if the top wing simply broke up in mid-air. Whichever it was, Otto's back was broken, and he died the following day.

But Lilienthal had not died in vain. He had laid the foundations of heavier than air flight, foundations which the Wright brothers were to build on so successfully just seven years later. In fact the focus of progress shifted across the Atlantic very soon after Lilienthal's death, for Frenchman Octave Chanute was resident in the US at the time, and combined the works of Mouillard and Lilienthal with some new ideas of his own, attaching to his gliders a tail with movable control surfaces (designed by Penaud, another Frenchman). These strut and wire-braced biplanes flew in 1896 at the hands of test pilots Avery and Herring, and showed the way for the Wright brothers and for Ferdinand Ferber. To Ferber should go the honour of being the first ultralight pilot, in 1908, though this was not his first successful flight, as he had three years earlier managed a 150 ft (45 m) flight with a glide ratio of 8/1 in what we would now call a motor glider. Although this machine, a biplane like all the early designs, had a 12 hp Peugeot engine driving two propellers on the same axis, it was nevertheless essentially designed to be a glider, though at the time no one was interested in such subtle distinctions. Orville & Wilbur's *Flyer* flew in 1903, and what followed is common knowledge, history with a capital H: the conquest of the sky and on out into space.

But in the headlong rush from Ferber's powered glider to the most sophisticated powered glider yet, the Space Shuttle

Francis Melvin Rogallo, liberator!

By
Alain-Yves Berger,
with additional
material from
Dave Garrison

*Independence Day 1969, and Bill Bennett celebrates
by gliding around the Statue of Liberty after a
powerboat-assisted take-off.*

Columbia, something had been lost; the birdman had taken a wrong turning.

1909 to 1939

In the First World War, aircraft were conscripted into uniform. Then between the wars there were dreams of aerial buses which had to be realised. All this drive forward tended to exclude those who wished to fly at low speed and purely for fun. Such indulgence was considered almost treasonable by some, and as a curiosity by most of the rest.

It hadn't always been so: Alberto Santos-Dumont, despite an income larger than the budget of a small country, nevertheless designed his 1909 *Demoiselle 20* with quantity production in mind. He wanted to bring aviation to the masses. Just three years later in the USA, the same G M Bellanca who was to give his name to so many light aircraft was sufficiently smitten with Santos-Dumont's offspring to create an exact forerunner, using contemporary technology, of the pioneering ultralight designs of the '70s, the Australian *Scout* and the *Kolb Flyer.*

Of course it would be wrong to say there was no pleasure flying going on before the advent of ultralights, but it was certainly not the popular pastime it is today. In Europe between the wars, though rapid progress was being made by the gliding fraternity, biplanes like de Pischof's 1921 45 hp *Aerial Scooter* and Farman's 1923 60 hp *Le Sport* were beginning a pursuit of power which eclipsed their contemporaries. Nevertheless, Henri Mignet rediscovered the joys of simple flight with his 20 hp *Pou-du-Ciel,* as did Taylor in the first of the American *Cubs,* while other notable designs included the *E-2* two-seater of 1931 with 37 hp, and the *Cycloplane* of the same year, looking like a microlight with its two-stroke 25 hp engine. There were others too, like the British 22 hp BAC *Drone* motor glider of 1933, the 36 hp Aeronca *C-3* two-seater of 1934, and the 36 hp Czech Praga *Baby* of 1935.

1940 to 1969

After the second war, Europe especially needed fresh designs to stimulate its war-shattered economy, and the Jodel *Bebe* single-seater which could be built at home and which even on 25 hp was capable of taking off from a large lawn, was almost ideal. So much so, that it gave rise to a whole new family of truly light aircraft. But despite the good intentions of its creators Edouard Joly and Jean Delemontez, the old problem resurfaced. The aeronautical equivalent of a Sunday drive simply didn't provide enough sales to survive on, and by the early '50s Jodel had turned to the two-seater market, graduating from 65 to 75 and eventually to 90 hp. The power race had begun all over again!

There was one notable exception to this preference for power and speed, the American gliding fanatic Volmer Jensen. However, we are getting ahead of ourselves. . .

Curiously, it was astronautics which re-kindled interest in low-speed flight. The principal character in this re-awakening is called Francis Melvin Rogallo, an American aeronautical engineer. In 1936, this quiet character joined Langley Research Center at Hampton, Virginia, the only government-financed aeronautical research laboratory on that side of the Atlantic. He left Langley in 1970 after 34 years of loyal service, retiring to Kitty Hawk in North Carolina. There, in the very spot where the *Wright Flyer* began powered flight, Rogallo continued work on an invention which was to revolutionise unpowered flight - the delta flexwing, or as we now know it, the Rogallo wing.

Until Frances and his wife Gertrude Sugden patented the first version of their flexwing in 1948, wings had always been designed to be essentially rigid. Early designs used a lozenge-shape; then they experimented with a triangle and finally came the classic Rogallo shape, a delta wing. The trick is in the profile; the wing forms two half-cones and, seen from behind, two half-cylinders. These are flexible fabric lobes which inflate in flight, being attached to the nose and two leading edges of the triangle, but left free at the trailing edge.

Meanwhile, Rogallo had been nominated director of the Low Speed Vehicle Branch of Langley. They were studying methods of recovering the first stage of Saturn rockets after launching, and especially the space capsules of the Gemini and Apollo programmes. Our man, naturally, thought of using his flexwings as pilotable parachutes.

The military got involved: they asked Ryan Aeronautical to design a system based on the Rogallo wing, and on 23 May 1961, NASA test pilot Lou Everett took off in the first Rogallo ever to leave the ground under power, a prototype using a Continental O-200 100 hp light aero engine and simply called *Flex-Wing.* A few months and several disappointments later, the *Flex-Wing* was tried again with a 180 hp Lycoming, as a four-seater with a 1100 lb (500 kg) empty weight. This attained the magnificent speed of 60 mph (97 kph) and only made up for it by not stalling until 24 mph (39 kph). It was followed by the *Fleep* (a contraction of *Flex-Wing* and *Jeep*), which abandoned the simple rudder of its predecessor in favour of an empennage and a keel. This was capable of carrying 990 lb (450 kg) at 64 mph (103 kph), but used 220 hp! Next came the *Flex Flyer* at the end of 1963, a side-by-side two seater with a canard. With a 595 lb (270 kg) empty weight and a useful load of 282 lb (128 kg), it was capable of 76 mph (122 kph). We must not forget the *Flex Bee,* the only microlight of the lot.

With just 28 ft² (2.6 m²) of wing area it carried 66 lb (30 kg) of TV cameras at 65 mph (105 kph) to more than 4900 ft (1500 m), all on a 9.5 hp McCulloch MC-40 engine - a machine with military potential for remote-control reconnaissance.

The 'NASA connection' also generated some false starts, as a freight carrier towed behind a helicopter, as a precision parachute, or as a folding wing mounted on ejection seats to allow American 'advisers' in Vietnam to regain the security of their own lines without having to walk. Each test was as inconclusive as the others.

One of the first people to realise the fun potential of Rogallo's creation was Californian Barry Palmer, who began building Rogallos in 1961 and by 1969 was motorising them with first one chainsaw motor, then two, and later with a 15 hp snowmobile unit. But his efforts remained a curiosity, rather than blossoming into a new sport. In fact the link between the NASA work and the mainstream evolution of hang gliding is much less direct, and arose in a quite unexpected way - through water skiing.

By the end of the '60s, the really passionate water skiers were no longer content just to jump ramps. Since 1964 French champion Bernard Danis had lifted off the water by harnessing himself to a kite behind a powerful outboard. This had made some others envious, amongst them his competitor and friend Bill Moyes.

Bill is an Australian aeronautical engineer who had worked for NASA and knew about the disappointments experienced with Rogallo's wings. On returning to Australia, he adapted one of these wings as a ski kite, and in 1968 he made it controllable by adding the triangle of tubes which was to become known as the trapeze or A-frame. The following year, at the water-skiing world championships in Copenhagen, Bill Moyes caused a sensation: in flight, he released the cable attaching him to the outboard and glided down to land on the water. Hang-gliding had been born.

Bernard Danis took Moyes' innovations back to France and that September, together with Jean-Francois Moveau and Christian Raisin, he effected the first hang-glider flights above the lake of Annecy. Meanwhile, Moyes' partner Bill Bennett went to preach the word in the US. He combined this with the national water-ski championships at Berkeley, and on 4 July, Independence Day, he started a flight around the Statue of Liberty. At first towed behind an outboard, he released the cable, glided for a long time, and landed at the feet of the statue.

The symbolism of this historic flight, captured by the picture on the first page of this section, was not lost on American enthusiasts, who realised that thanks to Rogallo they had indeed attained liberty and independence in the skies.

Ann Welch

Another hang glider which was to have a major influence on the ultralight movement was the Fledge, *from which the Pterodactyls were developed.*

1970 to 1976

The new toy quickly caught on. Someone decided to dispense with the water and the outboard. At first they used snow, so they could retain the skis, but soon they sprinted from the summit of rounded hills. This is when Richard Miller's *Bamboo Butterfly* appeared, with its bamboo frame carrying a Rogallo-style covering of polyethylene. Richard's creation broke no new ground technologically and rewarded him with multiple fractures and contusions, but it did prove one thing: that had they not been so hopelessly preoccupied with flapping their arms like birds, early aviators could have flown long before Lilienthal. After all, there's nothing new about bamboo, and the polyethylene could easily have been replaced by waxed cloth, or the large leaves from a banana tree.

Proper hang-gliders arrived in the Old World at the end of 1972, with a Californian machine which Christian Paul-Depasse brought into France and market-ed under the name *Deltaplane.* Hardly had the Deltaplane taken off, than Bernard Danis brought out his own version, the *Delta Manta* which became the best selling hang-glider of its time in Europe. Hang-gliding developed as one would expect, with a number of serious or fatal accidents, caused by mistakes or foolishness - it is not for us to judge. But we would do well to remember Otto Lilienthal's dying words: 'This is the price of progress!'

Once again, designers followed the well-trodden aviation path of modifying what is basically a glider to accept a motor. At first they called the result a powered hang-glider, and only later did the terms ultralight and its FAI equivalent microlight come into use.

But before we chart the mainstream development of the sport, we must mention three early machines which are ultralights in spirit even though they have no hang-gliding roots - Bob Hovey's *Whing Ding*, Homer Kolb's *Kolb Flyer* and Michel Colomban's *Cri Cri*. All three designers simply set out to create a light, fun aircraft, and only later found that their machines were attracting ultralight enthusiasts. The American *Whing Ding*, which first made its appearance in 1970, is still available in somewhat modified form today (see Aircraft Specialties) and was the progenitor of a whole series of Hovey designs, though Bob's predilection for biplanes has limited their influence on the mainstream of the sport. By contrast, Homer Kolb's *Kolb Flyer* was a tube-and-fabric ultralight in what was to become the classic American configuration, and its influence would have been enormous had this genial, modest man not flown it purely for his own and his neighbours' amusement for fully 10 years. Only in 1980, by which time it was no longer revolutionary, did the world realise what a gem he had produced.

The *Cri Cri* is different again. It is not listed

UlmMag

Summer '73, and a youthful Alain-Yves Berger takes-off with a Delta Manta from a little hill in a southern suburb of Paris. Thanks to a glide ratio of only 2.5/1 at 24 mph (39 mph), this particular flight ended in the netting of the tennis courts.

in this book (though there is a small photo in the glossary under 'canopy') and is not a microlight according to the FAI definition, but we detailed it in our first edition out of respect for its unique appeal, as the smallest twin in the world. Unveiled in 1973 at the French 'Oshkosh', it was an instant hit, with its 139 lb (63 kg) empty weight, Plexiglas blister canopy, a low wing as thick as a handspan and tiny 16.1 (4.90 m) span. Power came from two 8 hp Stihl chainsaw engines of only 8 hp each, but thanks to its tiny wing area it can cruise at very non-ultralight speeds, around 125 mph (200 kph) being normal for the higher powered later versions. It remains a fascinating machine, but one aimed at conventional pilots and intended for normal airfields, rather than the fore-runner of the new ultralight breed.

That same year, however, that forerunner appeared, for Bill Bennett was following in Barry Palmer's footsteps and attempting to motorise a Californian hang-glider. It was treated by the media as a huge joke. Bill had coupled a 12 hp engine to a

pusher propeller (known as the Bumchop-per) and mounted the package on his back. This was a seductive solution to the problem of powering a hang glider: there was no modification required other than a supplementary harness; the pilot still launched by running, his motorised back-pack then acting like a winch to get him to greater and more useful altitudes.

It did not, however, work particularly well, as the prop was almost completely masked by his large back, and what little efficiency remained was further reduced by the thick wire guard with which Bill was prudent enough to surround the package. So while gliding Rogallos were advancing rapidly in America and elsewhere, it was left to the Europeans to take up the challenge of finding a practical method of motorising them. The Americans had other things on their minds, for they were about to begin their love affair with hybrid and later three-axis controls, an ardour which shows no sign of cooling right to this day.

Why did American power pilots turn so

decisively to fixedwings? Part of the answer is undoubtedly Volmer Jensen, a gliding enthusiast who began his career in 1925 by building a Chanute biplane from plans published in *Popular Mechanic* magazine. He was smitten for life by the rustic pleasures of weight-shift and hybrid controls, and in 1941 completed his own design for a downhill glider called the *VJ-11,* a strut and wire braced biplane in the Chanute style but with the addition of a T-tail. Later he built a light aircraft and a slightly heavier amphibian, but. despite these sidetracks he remained throughout the bleak (for low-speed flight enthus-iasts) days of the '50s and '60s one of the few designers who never ceased to think in terms of sporting aircraft, especially those capable of being foot-launched and easily transported. But even he could not go against the current of history; his ideas were years ahead of their time and the '60s would be over before people realised the fact.

However, by 1970 the world was catching up with him. Jensen, by then no longer a

Bernard Schreier

Hang gliding came to Europe around the beginning of '73; here we see Christian Paul-Depasse with his Deltaplane *flying at Beynes, near Paris.*

practising aeronautical engineer, stumbled across hang-gliding at Santa Ana in California. He was inspired! He built a monoplane hang-glider with a cruciform empennage and a rudder and called it the *VJ-23 Swingwing*. It was particularly advanced for its time and with the technology of its day could only be constructed with difficulty, so it was followed in 1974 by the *VJ-24 Sunfun*. Like its predecessor this needed an engine (of around 10 hp) to get the best out of it, and in motorised form is still in production (see Volmer Aircraft) - a testimony to its designer's farsightedness.

Across in France, the oil crisis had arrived. Hang glider pilots were finding travel to the mountainous regions a long and expensive business, while gliding enthusiasts too were hit, as the price of towing increased dramatically. Parisian architect Jean-Marc Geiser realised that if the Rogallo could be effectively motorised, 'hang gliding' from the flatlands would become a reality, and glider pilots too would have an alternative. He sat down at

his drawing board in 1974 and chewed over the problem . . .

What emerged was to become the Motodelta: a happy marriage between a Danis *Delta-Manta* Rogallo and what we would now call a trike unit, though unlike modern trike units this one incorporated a tail boom and fin/rudder assembly. Fitted with a 12 hp flat twin, this assembly first flew in May 1975, without any major problems, and represented a major advance. Constructed from glassfibre, polystyrene, polyester and epoxy, the 'trike unit' was suspended from its wing by a single streamlined mast and did away as far as possible with the spider's web of cables. No trapeze here - instead a single top-mounted stick was attached to the wing, the conventional-control theme being continued by fitting rudder pedals in the normal fixedwing position.

The French authorities were completely disorientated by this sudden apparition, for which they had no applicable regulations and which could land and take-off almost anywhere. The bureaucratic logic

was inescapable: 'If it isn't a hang glider - and it can't be, because it has an engine - then it must be a lightplane, and if it's a lightplane the pilot must have a license and the aircraft must be certificated as a homebuilt'. On top of all this, Jean-Marc Geiser is a perfectionist to extremes. A combination of careful development, bureaucratic problems, and a few mishaps, meant that the Motodelta didn't go on sale until 1982, fully seven years later!

By that time the trike proper was well established and within a few months production ceased, but there is a happy ending to the story, for the design has re-emerged virtually unchanged in Japan (see Moto Hung, Other Countries section).

We do not know how much of the Motodelta was due to Geiser's inventiveness and how much he was inspired by others, but certainly he was not the only person thinking along such lines in the early '70s. Almost simultaneously with the Motodelta, a Daf-powered trike-like device appeared in Italy, while a glance at Dan

Poynter's *Hang Gliding* book, published in 1973, reveals an aircraft carrying the number N4411 and consisting of a Bensen gyrocopter with its blades replaced by a Rogallo but with its rudder retained.

There were two other noteworthy French pioneers. J Duvaleix flew a tubular-construction hybrid-control machine very like a modern trike but with twin fins, exposed to the wash from the pusher prop, each with its own rudder. Between the fins was a monobloc elevator. Controls were conventional stick and rudder, though there was an element of weight-shift in its control system as the pilot could alter the angle of a trellis of tubes and cables. Behind the pilot, mounted to the wing support struts, was a 1500 cc VW engine of some 45 hp. No more was heard of this unique machine.

Even odder was the unfinished prototype built by Jean-Pierre Grammare. Beneath a Danis 213 ft² (19.8 m²) Rogallo was suspended what we can only describe as a GRP sarcophagus, inside which the pilot lay flat on his stomach. This assembly was suspended from a triangular arrangement of tubes fixed to the wing and which also carried the main wheels of the undercarriage. Fortunately, Grammare never got as far as test-flying his *Chrysalide,* and in deference to his life expectancy turned instead to other homebuilding projects, which he has completed successfully.

Now for the first time since Cayley and his reluctant coachman-turned test pilot, an Englishman enters the story - Len Gabriels, founder of the Skyhook company.

Hang gliding was growing strongly in the UK, and just as elsewhere pilots were getting fed up with hauling their gear up hills before take-off. Gradually the back-pack idea was discredited, and small wing-mounted power packs were substituted. These early experiments went largely unrecorded, even in log books let alone the press, because the pioneers were uncomfortably aware that the addition of an engine made the craft liable to registration and airworthiness legislation, and the pilot liable to licensing.

Foremost amongst these clandestine experimenters was Len, who himself cannot remember whether his first keel-mounted power pack was tried in late '73 or early '74 (his logbook being curiously blank at this point!), but he does recall that the McCulloch-engined machine was not a great success, providing enough thrust to assist flight but not enough for a flat-land take-off. One way and another, it didn't seem worth the hassle, and it was not until 1977 that he pursued the idea seriously.

But across the English Channel, French-men Maurice Bruneau and Dr Peres were thinking along similar lines, and early in 1975 mounted a 4 hp Flymo motor on their *Delta Manta.* Near Paris that same year, Veliplane proprietor Roland Magallon was also hard at work, clandestinely testing various methods of powering his company's products. At first he fitted a triangular structure of tubes to his trapeze and tapered it back to support a 12 hp McCulloch engine at the end of this 'fuselage'. Later he replaced the engine with one of 15 hp, which drove its prop at a dizzy 9000 rpm, but he prudently concluded that it wasn't wise to market such a device, believing that it wasn't possible to make it safe. His interest in power remained, but it would be a few years before he would make his greatest contribution. The day of the trike was yet to come.

Meanwhile in the Antipodes, ultralighting had taken off, in every sense. The first flights of the Ron Wheeler's *Scout* (see Australian section) took place in May 1974, and the aircraft went on sale immediately, the world's first commercially available fixedwing ultralight (Bob Hovey's *Whing Ding* was only offered as plans). Santos-Dumont would have been proud of it - a light aircraft reduced to the absolute minimum, a latter-day *Demoiselle* with a conventional tail and relieved of its hotch-potch of wires.

Grammare's remarkable creation of 1975 used a Danis wing plus a 25 hp Hirth engine, and was built near Rouen in Normandy. Happily, it never flew!

Ann Welch

Though it is now known the world over as a highly successful ultralight, the Eipper Quicksilver started life as a fixedwing hang glider. Here we have two shots of it in that form, one of an early version (above) and one rather later (below).

Ann Welch

25

The Australian Department of Transport were quicker off the mark than their European counterparts, and in 1976 created the first ultralight legislation, bringing the *Scout* within the law and really opening up the market. One of the first to take advantage of this was Col Winton, who that year introduced his *Cricket,* a design as influential in its homeland as the *Quicksilver* was to be in the US.

Back in America, things were really warming up. There was still no quantity production of ultralights, but a wide variety of new designs was appearing. At the '75 Oshkosh, for example, Larry Haig showed his extraordinary 150 lb (68 kg) *American Eaglet* with 12 hp McCulloch engine, a beautiful ultralight motor glider which we featured in our first edition. However, with its completely enclosed cockpit, it appealed more to licensed pilots or sailplane enthusiasts than to hang gliders, and it thus met with only limited success. Georges Applebay's *Zia,* which we describe in this edition, was unveiled in its canard guise at the next Oshkosh, but this too remained more of a curiousity than a force in the marketplace. Well before either of these came the Birdman *TL-1A* and *TL-1B* by Emmett M Taly, an interesting design produced from 1976-82 and

likely to be revived by the British firm Tirith, as you can read under that heading. In truth, however, none of these designs really launched the movement in the US in the way the *Scout* had in Australia; that would have to wait until 1977.

Meanwhile, a Mormon from Utah called John Chotia had since 1975 been working on a two-axis ultralight which was to be a major influence on the growth of the US ultralight movement . . .

1977

By 1977 a pattern was emerging, with the movement polarised into two camps. While Europeans were playing around with powered Rogallos, power flyers in Australia were adopting the same stance as the Americans, who had spurned the creation of their native son in favour of aircraft with control surfaces, some like Jensen's creations derived from fixed-wing hang-gliders, others like the *Whing Ding* designed from the outset for power. In the US they became known as ultralights, in Britain they were microlights (since in the UK there already existed a category of very light aircraft known as ultralights), whilst in France they were

known as motorised ultralights or ULM for short.

The British were still doggedly pursuing ways of motorising Rogallos, and four men were making the running. Len Gabriels mounted two of the biggest model aircraft engines he could find on a Skyhook *Sunspot* and on 15 July '77 took off from 'a pimple of hill' in conditions of almost nil-lift. Encouraged, he fitted a McCulloch and tried again on 11 August, taking off at the *bottom* of a 300 ft (90 m) hill and landing at the top, feeling on top of the world in more senses than one.

He decided to demonstrate the machine at the big hang-gliding meeting at Mere the following month, but was crestfallen when he arrived to find that the motor wouldn't start. To make matters worse, Murray Rose and Simon Wootton from rival hang glider manufacturer Chargus had produced a similar tool based on a *Midas E,* and were merrily giving demonstrations! The fourth pioneer, Steve Hunt, was at the time working for a third Rogallo manufacturer, Hiway, and tried a different approach. Early that year he had coupled a McCulloch to a ducted fan and mounted the ensemble on a *Scorpion D* wing. It was less than successful, but he had made his entry into the microlight world,

Another French attempt at motorising a hang-glider, this one dating from 1977 and using an engine attached to the pilot's harness but connected to the keel tube.

and Britain would hear a great deal from this tireless Australian from then on.

Not to be outdone, across in France Camille Lefevre and Philippe Peauger built a twin-engined two-seater by mounting one 10 hp McCulloch on the front of a *Delta Manta* and another on the rear. And it flew very well, confounding the sceptics at that year's homebuilders gathering in Brienne-le Chateau.

Despite these developments, it was the US which was making the running now. Following Volmer Jensen's lead, a whole series of fixedwing hang gliders were being successfully motorised. The *Icarus V* flying wing appeared, with its tip rudders and swept-back wing, while Larry Mauro's *Easy Riser* biplane started to sell in large numbers, using McCulloch 12 hp or Chrysler 8 hp two-strokes. Hang gliding record holder Don Mitchell fitted his *BF-10* with a motor, though he still used the pilot's legs as undercarriage, an arrangement which persisted until his *B-10 Mitchell Wing* ultralight proper appeared. Then there was the *Manta Fledge IIB*, copied by many but immortalised by Jack McCornack, who derived from it the famous Pterodactyl series of machines and produced a great deal of favourable publicity for the movement by making a long-distance proving flight in each new model.

And last but by no means least was the famous *Quicksilver,* created in 1972 by Bob Lovejoy. Unlike many of its contemporaries, it was designed from the outset to have a tail, and so was a natural for conversion into a relatively conventional-looking ultralight. Its success in this guise was staggering, and far outstripped anything it had achieved as a hang glider. In the years to come thousands of *Quicks* would be produced, plus many more machines of the same genre from other manufacturers. The *Quicksilver's* single-surface tube and Dacron construction, tubular empennage with fully flying rudder, and straightforward undercarriage were copied all over the world, not just because they worked, but also because diligent development and effective marketing gave the product a reputation which imitators were only too ready to trade on.

Two- and three-axis ultralights became more and more numerous, outnumbering their forerunners. In Australia, there was the Kimberley *Sky Rider,* designed to the legislation which the *Scout* had prompted, while in America the MGI *Teratorn* and Bill Adaska's Rotec *Rally* made their appearance. Bill, ex-Bell and ex-Aerospatiale employee who had specialised until then in helicopters, went on to sell over 2000 *Rallys* in the next four years! The pre-history of ultralight aviation ended that year, at the first meeting of American pioneers at Brook Fields Aerodrome near Marshall, halfway between Chicago and Detroit. At that event, held from 1 to 3 July, John Moody, who had involuntarily looped three times the year before at Oshkosh, climbed to 4250 ft (1300 m) with his *Easy Riser* and a 12 hp engine. Now we were really flying!

1978

It is 1978, and in the USA ultralight aviation is sweeping all before it, as one innovative design after another leaves the drawing board and takes to the air, proving that tube and Dacron technology has finally come of age. Construction of Klaus Hill's V-tailed *Hummer,* which made its first flight in November 1977, began in earnest and gave Klaus a place amongst the cream of American pioneers, particularly when he followed it with the *Humbug,* on which the *Vector* and many other designs were modelled. Sadly, like other aviation

In 1978 French pioneer Bernard Danis mated a Soarmaster unit to this SK 2SS wing of 168 ft² (15.6 m), and climbed to 5990 ft (1825 m) in the southern Alps on 5 August.

pioneers, he gained his experience in the hardest possible way, being killed during a test flight on 10 October 1979.

Then there was the composite-construction Striplin *Flac,* which took its name from 'foot-launched air cycle', a reflection of the early American legislation requiring ultralights to be foot-launched if they were to be exempt from lightplane rules. Right from the start, Ken Striplin intended his *Flac* to incorporate an undercarriage, but he pretended it was an auxiliary one, to get round the legislation.

Different control systems and configurations abounded. Ultralite Soaring's *Wizard* suspended its pilot in a harness between the tubes of the cage, but also had an elevator. Others, like the Ultralight Flight's *Mirage,* used a cruciform tail with elevators and rudder, with spoilers on top of the wing. Still others used ruddervators on an inverted V-tail, where the ailerons improve their efficiency, as is the case with the Ultraflight Sales *Lazair* from Canada. The choice was growing almost by the hour.

This was the year, too, when John Chotia's efforts finally came good, his first two prototypes of the two-axis *Weedhopper* making their maiden flights in February 1978. Carrying the type number *JC-24,* as they were his 24th design, they led to a pre-production machine the following year and large-scale production in 1980.

Tragically, only one year later, on 27 October 1981, Chotia followed in Hill's footsteps and was killed while test flying one of his own machines. We remember him as a big good-natured man with strict morals (even when in France he wouldn't taste the wine!), but farsighted enough to see that ultralight aviation had to turn to research into small engines. Even though his own single-cylinder Chotia 460 was notoriously unreliable, he was nevertheless the first person to create an engine specifically for ultralight use. While his engineering was questionable, his grasp of history certainly wasn't: he realised that he was taking part in an aviation rebirth,

and shortly before he died confessed to having been largely inspired by Santos-Dumont's *Demoiselle.*

By comparison, Europe was pretty quiet, and undoubtedly the major event of the year was the first successful crossing of the English Channel by microlight, when on 9 May Dave Cook (later to found CFM - see British section) took a *VJ-23E* across to France. Like Chotia, he too had a sense of history, landing near the spot from where Bleriot had started his first ever crossing, 69 years earlier. He'd taken 1 h 15 min to fly from Deal in Kent to Les Baraques in northern France, much longer than Bleriot's 37 min but without the benefit of the extra 15 hp provided by the Frenchman's Anzani.

Len Gabriels soldiered on, by now using a *Safari* wing, and that summer Steve Hunt made his first successful powered flights in a *Super Scorpion* with a Soarmaster-style power pack fitted.

We say 'Soarmaster-style' because these American power packs were both imported and imitated in Europe, having become quite popular among US hang glider pilots. But only in Europe were they to develop into an ultralight proper: America in 1978 was fixedwing oriented and already ultralighting and hang gliding had gone their separate ways.

At France's Brienne-le-Chateau meeting that year there were exhibits from Mobiplane, Bernard Danis with his powered hang-gliders, and Roland Magallon. Steadily, powered hang gliders were becoming better understood and more widely used. Now you could buy power kits, using two 9 hp Stihl engines supplied by two students at Orignac in the Pyrenees.

Meanwhile at Coulommiers in Seine et Marne, Claude Chudzik had built a single-seater which was entirely his own work. One of the first, if not *the* first, applications of a motorcycle engine to an ultralight, it used a front-mounted Yamaha 347 cc engine, delivering 36 hp at 7000 rpm to a tractor propellor. A boom extended backwards to a conventional tail, with rudder

operated by a rudder bar and elevators by a stick. The wing was a rigidly attached Rogallo which could be flexed in flight to provide roll control - an original, true three-axis design.

We must also record the contribution of Helmut Wilden in West Germany, whose single seater flew for the first time that year and caused quite a stir. This three-axis aircraft used a 20 hp Limbach engine, which could be swapped for a Wankel KM 24 motor of 27 hp to allow the aircraft to be used as a two-seat side-by-side machine! But only one was built: to borrow a phrase from rugby, this try was not to be converted.

1979

In America things were really humming, and were given a further boost by the introduction in 1979 of the *Eagle.* Designed as a safe beginner's machine, Larry Newman and Bryan Allen's American Aerolights company was to sell large numbers of these canard aircraft over the coming years, bringing flying to thousands who had never known it before.

There was a lot to be done if the Europeans were to make up for lost time. Even two more Channel crossings in 1979 weren't enough. Gerry Breen and Len Gabriels, using Hiway *Scorpion* and Skyhook *Bluebird* powered Rogallos respectively, demonstrated the increasing reliability of powered hang-gliders, but they were still tricky to fly, as the wing mounting of the engine meant that the thrust line altered whenever the pitch was changed. Something better was needed if the safety of everyday pilots was to be assured - and that something was the trike.

Roland Magallon visited Jean-Marc Geiser and took a long look at the Motodelta. Plenty of people had allied pure weight-shift control to a wing-mounted engine, and here was hybrid control with a 'fuselage' - much more stable in flight, but rather complex and expensive. Why not combine the best of

After his cross-Channel flight, Dave Cook was much in demand by airshow organisers. Here his VJ-23 stands on the tarmac at Biggin Hill near London, awaiting its slot in Britain's most prestigious annual show.

Dave Cook

UlmMag

*Roland Magallon with the first prototype trike, photographed at
Guyancourt airport near Paris in 1979, before its maiden flight.*

both worlds, by replacing the Motodelta's 'fuselage' with a simple tubular framework and dispensing with the rudder? That should produce a cheap, safe, flying machine.

It did indeed. Magallon is thus credited - rightly we think - with the invention of the trike, but as it was more a logical development than a flash of genius, it is quite possible that others who have failed to reach the record books had the same idea at the same time, or perhaps even earlier. But it was Magallon who produced and marketed it, Magallon who did for the trike what Henry Ford did for the motor car.

He called the first version *Mosquito* and marketed it in October 1979, continuing with it until 1981. The prototype had flown with a McCulloch MC-101A motor of 125 cc, delivering 10 hp at 8000 rpm to a direct-drive prop with ground adjustable pitch. But soon he was offering it with a Solo 210 which produced around 12 hp at much less frantic revs.

Inevitably, it wasn't long before the idea crossed the Channel, where Gerry Breen was still busy with powered hang-gliders. That year he'd swapped his Soarmaster-powered *Olympus 160* for a powered *Super Scorpion,* which he took on a 202

mile (325 km) trip from Tredegar to Norwich, but despite this achievement he recognised the deficiencies of keel-mounted wings, and when he saw a picture of Magallon's trike in the French hang gliding magazine *Vol Libre,* he knew that the days of the Soarmasters were numbered.

He showed the picture to Frank Tarjanyi at Hiway, who promptly constructed Britain's first trike - a monopole - and it wasn't long before Hiway was churning out *Skytrikes* by the dozen. Interestingly though, these were to a different configuration, Steve Hunt having modified the

Len Gabriels skirts London on his way to France on board the Bluebird *in 1979.*

design to duopole before commencing production. For his part, Frank still preferred the monopole, and shortly afterwards left to join Graham Slater in setting up Ultra Sports, where they put the monopole into production as the *Tripacer*. At this point the cross-Channel cross-fertilisation process began again, the French soon adopting the monopole for their own designs. The configuration has since become almost standard among modern trikes.

Away from the Rogallo scene, little was happening in Europe, but a few seeds were being sewn. In October '79 Paul Baker and Dave Garrison brought two Pterodactyl *Pfledges* into Britain - the first US-style ultralights to reach the UK - and by the following February were busy importing kits and selling complete aircraft.

1980 to 1982

By 1980 the American scene had ceased to be something which can be fairly described in a short history like this. The industry was mushrooming at an astonishing pace, and at times it seemed that even the manufacturers themselves couldn't keep pace with it. Lightplane manufacturers, who were still thoroughly in the doldrums, could only look on in wonderment at this upstart sport which was achieving what they had so signally failed to do in the preceeding six decades - bring aviation to the common man.

From this point on, all the models of any significance are chronicled in our first edition, and readers will get a much better feel for the sport from that volume than from any summary which we could produce in the little space available here. But before we close, we have a few loose ends to ties up in Europe.

In the Old World the race was on to produce a viable two-seat trike, and to this day we are not certain which country won. In our first edition on p36 we credited Nick Wrigley with the honour, since he turned up at the British Microlight Aircraft Association's inaugural fly-in at Wellesbourne in June 1980 with a Sachs-engined side-by-side two-seater which flew very well. However we have since learned that the previous month Magallon had tried a tandem machine with a 340 cc Sachs which produced 30 hp at 10,000 rpm. It also produced a dreadful noise, and he soon ditched it in favour of two Solo engines, these being replaced in turn by a Hirth 438 cc unit in September 1981.

At Brienne that year, Magallon, Danis and other early French constructors timidly showed their trikes. No more control surfaces: the Motodelta was forgotten, superseded just as Geiser was feeling confident enough about it to begin serious production, and the Americans had not yet arrived.

At least, they hadn't in France. Across in England, the first *Eagles* had been brought in by Gerry Breen that January

and were finding a ready market among flyers who wanted cheap aviation but didn't fancy a trike. Gerry had opened the floodgates, and before the year was out just about every significant make of American ultralight was being imported into the UK. The invasion had begun.

The following year the Transatlantic onslaught reached France, machines like the *Weedhopper, Vector 600, Quicksilver, Rally* and *Goldwing* having an enormous impact throughout 1981. The early imports were all single-seaters, for it was not until early 1982 that the Americans thought seriously about two-

seaters; until then, US pilots needed a license before they could take up a passenger.

The appearance in Europe of viable fixed-wings broadened the appeal of the sport overnight. Pilots of lightplanes or gliders, who had been put off by what was to them the strange appearance and reversed controls of the trikes, suddenly found that there was a whole range of ultralights in which they could feel at home. To feed this new market, new manufacturers sprang up, some developing their own versions of American products (such as Eurowing, which built *Goldwings* in Scot-

Bob Calvert, later to captain the British team for the first Microlight World Championships in 1985, put British triking on the map in 1982 with a world record flight of 16,168 ft (4928 m) in this Mainair/Solar Wings Tri-Flyer 330/Typhoon.

British Microlight Aircraft Association

Only two years old but already a historic shot: the British Microlight Aircraft Association's first display team poses at the '83 Biggin Hill show, following in the footsteps of Dave Cook four years earlier. From left to right: Adrian Mol (Goldwing), Angus Fleming (Lazair), Derek Cracknell (Eagle), Fred Dawcett (Pathfinder), Gerry Breen (Pathfinder), Julian Rimmer (Puma), Steve Hunt (Pathfinder), Sally Huxtable (Tripacer/Demon), Pete Davies (Phantom), Mairi Barr, Iain Barr (Tiger Cub), and Ron Bott (BMAA secretary). Also present was Dave Kent with a Duet.

land), others creating designs of their own.

Firmly in the latter category was Steve Hunt, who by 1981 had left Hiway to form his own company Huntair. He was determined to produce a machine in which conventional pilots would feel at home, and he succeeded so well that his *Pathfinder* became a best seller on both sides of the Channel.

His creation acquitted itself brilliantly in the '82 London-Paris, a marvellous, happy occasion which was symbolic in many ways, not just because it was a race between the capitals of the two countries which spearheaded ultralighting in Europe, but also because it was dominated by the new European machinery, which in many cases was proving superior to the American aircraft which had inspired it - and cheaper, thanks to the strength of the dollar.

Admittedly, a *Vector* won the fixedwing

class, but second was a Belgian Butterfly and every other place in the top ten was occupied by a *Pathfinder,* apart from a sole *Lazair* in equal sixth. And in the flexwing class of course, there wasn't an American to be seen. The London-Paris was a turning point in European ultralighting, the occasion when the sport came of age and the media was forced to take it seriously, if only because to the newspapers' eternal disappointment no one dropped in the Channel.

Sadly, this was to be the high point of Hunt's career, for shortly afterwards he introduced the ill-fated *Pathfinder II* in an attempt to produce a machine light enough for the West German market and fast enough to beat the American *Phantom.* The two requirements were simply not compatible, and the result was a machine with very little reserve of strength once its envelope was exceeded, as Hunt himself found to his cost when

he hit severe turbulence in the 1983 French Grand Prix and was killed.

It is easy to look at the list of pioneer ultralighters who paid for their passion with their lives and to conclude, quite erroneously, that ultralighting is a dangerous sport. But the test pilot's job has never been an easy one, let alone being test pilot for a new technology in a little known realm of flight, and one can easily argue that the pioneers did extremely well to achieve as much as they did with the meagre resources at their disposal.

Let us simply be grateful that they have left us with a rapidly maturing and, for the properly trained pilot in a properly constructed machine, safe sport. Thousands of ultralighters can now benefit from their efforts, enjoying rallies, fly-ins, and local and international competitions, and will no doubt continue to laugh at the frontiers which, from on high, we have never been able to see very well.

TRAVELLING LIGHT

Until someone manages to circumnavigate the globe by ultralight, the next best thing must surely be a world tour to sample the machinery in each ultralight manufacturing country. And that's just what we're about to embark on in this colour section, starting with what must be regarded as the home of ultralight aviation, the country with more machines than the rest of the world put together – the USA.

In fact there's so much to see in the States that we're going to fly round America first before setting off overseas, starting not in California as you might expect, but in neighbouring Arizona, where this fast, slick *Sadler Vampire* is built by American Microflight

Now let's follow the Colorado River, heading for Grand Junction in the Mountain State, the home of Sport Flight Engineering, whose *Sky Pup* (main picture) offers flying at the other end of the market from the *Sadler Vampire,* simple low-cost fun for the homebuilder.

Next it's time to remember our ultralight roots, with a stop over in Texas, the home of Rotec and the *Rally Champ* (above left). Though considerably developed over the years, this is still basically the same *Rally* on which thousands of ultralighters have had their first taste of flight.

Still heading east, we have our first taste of float flying in Florida, where HighCraft Aero-Marine developed its amphibian *Buccaneer XA-280* (now built by Advanced Aviation), here shown with wheels retracted (above centre).

Now let's look north to a completely different environment, as we travel up the East Coast to New Jersey and an aircraft that has started a whole new flying sub-culture of its own – the *Paraplane* (lower right). Maybe it's not unique any more, but it's still remarkable.

Much more conventional but no less successful is Fisher's *FP-202 Koala* (above right), taking to the skies above the company's Ohio factory. We're heading west again now, but we've one more stop to make before we hit California . . .

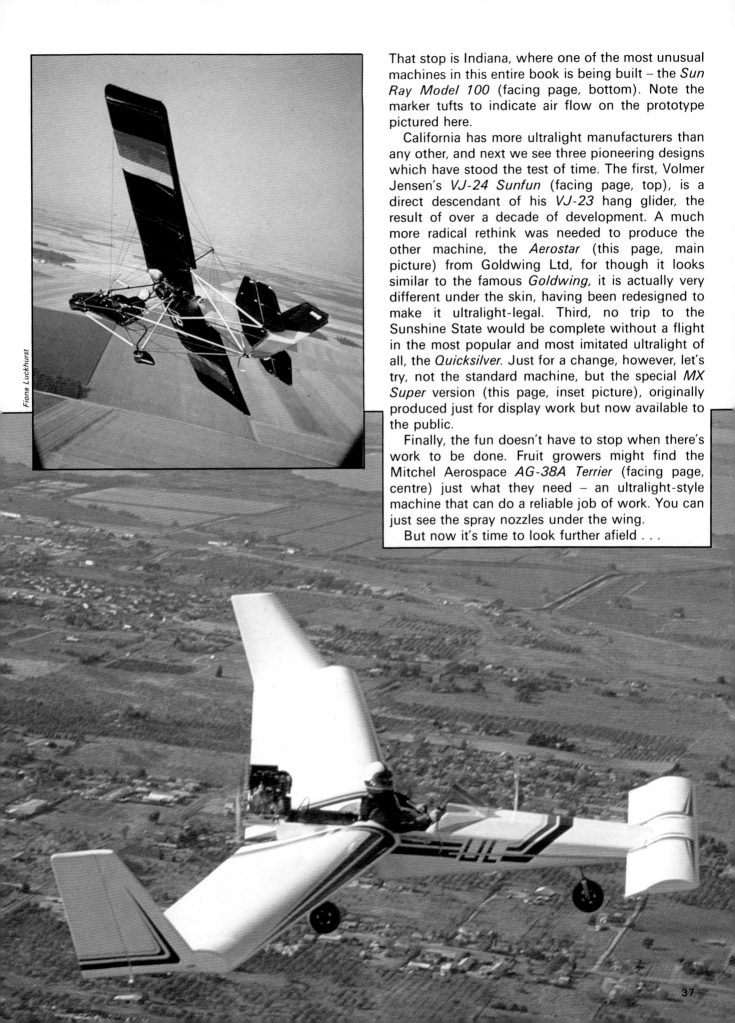

Fiona Luckhurst

That stop is Indiana, where one of the most unusual machines in this entire book is being built – the *Sun Ray Model 100* (facing page, bottom). Note the marker tufts to indicate air flow on the prototype pictured here.

California has more ultralight manufacturers than any other, and next we see three pioneering designs which have stood the test of time. The first, Volmer Jensen's *VJ-24 Sunfun* (facing page, top), is a direct descendant of his *VJ-23* hang glider, the result of over a decade of development. A much more radical rethink was needed to produce the other machine, the *Aerostar* (this page, main picture) from Goldwing Ltd, for though it looks similar to the famous *Goldwing,* it is actually very different under the skin, having been redesigned to make it ultralight-legal. Third, no trip to the Sunshine State would be complete without a flight in the most popular and most imitated ultralight of all, the *Quicksilver.* Just for a change, however, let's try, not the standard machine, but the special *MX Super* version (this page, inset picture), originally produced just for display work but now available to the public.

Finally, the fun doesn't have to stop when there's work to be done. Fruit growers might find the Mitchel Aerospace *AG-38A Terrier* (facing page, centre) just what they need – an ultralight-style machine that can do a reliable job of work. You can just see the spray nozzles under the wing.

But now it's time to look further afield . . .

New Zealand Wings

South African Aero News

Rob Fox

Let's fly right across the Pacific, to Japan. Ultralight flying is not big business in the Land of the Rising Sun, but one notable design is being produced – the Moto Hung *DW-2000 Bee Bird* (inset, top left). The name may not be familiar, but the shape will be, for this is the famous French design of the mid-70s, the Motodelta *G-11,* produced under licence long after it has ceased to be available in Europe.

Heading south to Australasia, we start with that small but very microlight-oriented country, New Zealand. By far the most important project there is the *Bantam* (inset, top right), by Micro Aviation, the first entirely Kiwi fixed-wing microlight, here shown in production form.

Across in Australia, they have one problem in common with the New Zealanders, in that their regulations are in a state of flux as we go to press. But this hasn't stopped the flow of new designs, among them the *Javelin* (main picture) from Flight 95 Australia and the *SVX1* (inset, bottom right) by SV Aircraft.

Now it's time to start the long haul to Europe, but *en route* we'll drop in to Natal in South Africa, the home of Microlight Flight Systems, whose two-seat *Shadow* was the first African microlight ever exhibited at Oshkosh (inset, bottom left). The machine is rather reminiscent of the *Quicksilver MXII,* except that it has tandem seating.

Rob Fox

Norman Burr

Our first stop in Europe is Great Britain, where microlight flying is evolving in a distinctly different direction from the rest of the Continent, following the imposition of strict airworthiness regulations which have turned out to favour trikes. This, coupled with the introduction of some excellent new Rogallos, has made the flexwing king of the skies, in sharp contrast to the trend in neighbouring France.

Here we see one of the best of the latest crop of two-seat trikes, the *Gemini Flash* (main picture) from Mainair, plus an interesting machine at the other end of the trike spectrum – the Medway/Aerial Arts/130 SX *Half Pint* (inset, bottom left), built to be under 70 kg empty weight and thus exempt from the airworthiness regulations.

Though they aren't figuring strongly in the sales charts at present, behind the scenes there is plenty of three-axis activity, especially at Tirith, whose *Firebird FB-2* (inset, top left) has grown another seat and another engine since the prototype was featured in our first edition.

Finally, we have the pretty *Pipistrelle 2C* (inset, bottom right) from Southdown Aerostructure, originally a French design but now extensively re-engineered to suit British regulations – which leads us nicely on to the French machines proper . . .

Norman Burr

France is remarkable for the variety of aircraft offered, greater perhaps even than the US, since designers there don't shun flexwings. And here we see perhaps the best weight-shift machine in France, the Cosmos *Bidulm 44* with La Mouette wing (facing page).

Most French buyers, however, are turning to fixed-wing machines, and undoubtedly among the most successful of these is the Aviasud *Sirocco* (this page, main picture), winner of numerous competitions and awards and now also manufactured in Britain by Midland Ultralights.

Our next aircraft, France Aerolights' *First Agri* (below left), is shown here flying from an airfield, but that perhaps does not do it justice, for the remarkable aspect of this machine is its very supple undercarriage, which allows it to land safely *across* a ploughed field. Finally in this brief look at French ultralights, we have an aircraft which will be instantly recognisable to anyone who remembers the pre-war flying scenes: the Mignet *HM-14* (below right), the famous *Flying Flea* which captured the ultralight spirit long before the word was invented, and which has inspired a number of aircraft in this book, including one from Henri Mignet's own family.

UltraMag

From France we cross the border to Belgium, where a small but active industry is producing, among other things, the Dynali *Chickinox* (facing page, bottom left), a single-surface tube-and-Dacron machine which has been well received not only at home but also in neighbouring France.

Moving into West Germany, we find a healthy mixture of flex-wing and fixed-wing machines, the latter category including the *Ultra* (facing page, top right) from the famous Scheibe glider factory.

Typical of West German trikes is this *Enduro* with *Focus 18* wing (facing page, top left), made by the Munich-based company Schmidtler Bern. A very different approach is evident in the NST *Minimum* (main picture), an interesting cross between the old-style powered hang-glider and a modern trike.

Continuing south into Switzerland, we find the small microlight fraternity locked in a struggle to survive against a strong environmental lobby. As a result, local products are few, but one of them is this interesting *Fun Fly* (facing page, centre right) by Dominique Loup, pictured here at the French 'Oshkosh' – Brienne-le-Chateau – in July 1984.

Willi Tacke

We cross the border to Italy now, where ultralights are much less well established than further north in Europe. However, this British-designed Polaris *Air Dinghy* (facing page) shows what can be done with a very conventional Italian Rogallo plus a little imagination.

One doesn't normally think of neighbouring Yugoslavia as microlighting country either, yet the enthusiasts there are certainly active, none more so than Durin Slobodan and Durin Milan, whose Komarac *Mosquito II* shown above left made its first flight as long ago as May 1979.

Moving north again to Hungary, we find much more activity, though unlike Yugoslavia it is exclusively weight-shift. Our picture above right shows the MMRK *Hidroden,* and shows also that the flying enthusiasts there need no lessons on how to enjoy themselves!

Next stop is Czechoslovakia, whose most modern ultralight project to date is this CVUT *SP-1* (below), pictured outside its hangar shortly after completion. But our travels aren't over yet . . .

Letectví a kosmonautica

Our last stop in Europe is Sweden, where we find this very soaring-oriented Radab *Windex 1100* (below). The next shot might also have been taken in Sweden, but appearances can be deceptive! For now we are heading back to the US, via Canada, home of this Ultravia *Super Pelican* (inset, top right), pictured on its final tests before entering production.

And to round off this colour section, another Canadian, this time with a touch of nostalgia – the Graham Lee-designed Circa *Baby Nieuport* (main picture), a World War I replica complete with highly appropriate registration.

Werner Bekker landing his Thruster Aircraft Thruster 85 Utility *with his dog Sheeba as passenger.*

The best is yet to come

by Rob Fox

When a flimsy, tubular-frame *Scout* lifted off from a football field near Sydney on arguably the first flight of an ultralight a mere 14 years ago, who could have imagined the remarkable impact that short event would have on the world of aviation?

The *Scout,* now much modified, is still in production more than a decade later. Four other distinct and popular ultralights in production today also had their genesis in another very early model, the *Cricket,* the forerunner of many second-generation ultralights in other countries.

Mercifully, Australia was never burdened with the foot-launch drama that plagued the Americans in their converted hang gliders. We were also fortunate in another important area: regulations evolved quickly, putting the country at the forefront of the ultralight movement. Even though it took the D of A five years to legalise ultralights, the *Scout* was still the world's first legal ultralight. Since then the legislation has continued to evolve, the latest, very significant, change coming in early 1985 when the Department of Aviation introduced *Air Navigation Order 95:10 (Issue Two),* which allows the use of ultralights with a heavier empty weight and permits pilots to fly cross-country.

As the ultralight fraternity has gained in confidence, so its wish for self-regulation has grown. Out of this wish was born the Australian Ultralight Federation, which the legislators have agreed shall be the body charged with regulating ultralights in Australia in much the same way as its counterparts in gliding, hang gliding and parachuting control their respective sports. The AUF - although still in a turbulent, embryonic stage - has achieved much that outsiders considered impossible in such a short time: acceptable legislation and federal funding.

The original *ANO 95:10,* which stood from November 1976, was updated with *Issue Two* to permit single-place ultralights weighing less than 115 kg empty (254 lb) and with an empty wing loading of 11 kg/m^2 maximum (2.25 lb/ft^2) to operate free of licensing and other bureaucratic constraints and to fly cross-country, but not above 500 ft AGL (152 m) or within controlled or restricted airspace. Although this marked a tremendous advance on the original

▶

▷ rules, it still did not include two-place trainers or some of the heavier single-seaters, because the authorities were concerned about the legal responsibilities involved with carrying a passenger and about the increasingly high performance of relatively heavy solo machines. These matters had been bones of contention between the D of A and the AUF for a number of years.

Finally, on 25 March 1985, the problem was solved by the introduction of *ANO 95:25,* giving Australia two classes of ultralights. This second class has the same operational constraints as *ANO 95:10* machines, but includes two-place trainers with a maximum take-off weight of 400 kg (882 lb) and single-place ultralights with a maximum take-off weight of 290 kg (639 lb). Operations manuals are being drawn up for it, because *ANO 95:25* deals with the more sophisticated types of aircraft, and thus has more constraints. These include aircraft registration, airworthiness and maintenance requirements (similar to the British *BCAR Section S*), and the need for the operator to hold an AUF pilot certificate (an AUF student certificate in the case of trainees). But there are no air navigation charges and none are envisaged because no government facilities are used.

It is still early days for the AUF, which faces a great challenge in making the airworthiness system work, but it has already secured adequate funding (A$100,000 for the first year of operations) and the 'loan' of a full-time ex-D of A airways surveyor, which augurs well.

Hopefully this will pave the way for what the D of A regards as the permanent regulation for this class of ultralight, *ANO 95:55.* This regulation will replace the temporary *ANO 95:25* and promises a degree of operational freedom hitherto thought impossible: flights up to 5000 ft AGL (1520 m), with flying time to be logged and credited against a PPL, making the introduction to the world of conventional aviation an affair within the reach of the most modest budget.

As can be seen from this section, a number of 'real little aircraft' have been built in Australia in anticipation of the new regulations and it appears their creators have been limited only by their own imaginations. Not only are these machines bringing the wonder of flight to many who have hitherto only dreamed of it, but they have provided those farmers who must cover hundreds of miles during their work with a tool as useful as a tractor. One such farmer completed the whole of his lambing season in weather you wouldn't want to ride a motorbike in, let alone attempt to fly, and yet managed to save many newborn lambs by landing his ultralight near any sheep experiencing difficulties. He even used it to transport sick animals back with him.

There are many other useful applications, but at the moment there is no possibility of either class of ultralight being put to commercial use in Australia, as they are regulated purely as sport aircraft. But the fun has just begun!

For more information on ultralights in Australia, contact: Australian Ultralight Federation Inc, PO Box 181, Abbotsford, Victoria 3067.

AIR-AM

Air-Am Aviation Industries, PO Box 149, Fyshwick, ACT 2609; tel 062 804003.

AIR-AM *HORNET*

(Three-axis)

Single-seat single-engined low-wing monoplane with conventional three-axis control. Wing has swept back leading and trailing edges, and tapering chord; no tail. Pitch/roll control by elevon; yaw control by tip rudders. Cantilever wing; wing profile NC; 100% double-surface. Composition-construction airframe, totally enclosed. Other details NC.

Production status: see text.

Artist's impression of the two-seat Hornet; the engine is in the nose with shaft drive to a ducted fan at the rear. Expected performance with a 55 hp engine is 115 mph (185 kph) cruise and 1000 ft/min (5.1 m/s) climb.

GENERAL - This book would not be complete without some mention of the fate of David Betteridge's remarkable 1977 design, the *Hornet.* Originally intended to be a rigid-wing hang-glider - David's company Free Flight was a hang-glider manufacturer at the time - construction of this tail-less composite machine began in 1978 and the first example took to the air the following year in the hands of Colin Scott.

From that the production *Hornet 130S* evolved, with direct-drive Konig SC430 engine and ducted fan, but the company went into receivership in 1984 and were purchased by Air-Am the same year. At the time of writing no aircraft are being marketed, but the intention is to produce the *Hornet* as an *ANO 95-10(2)* aircraft, and David Betteridge has been retained to redesign the wing accordingly.

The story does not end there, however, for the company also intends to develop a larger two-seat version to be fully certified and registered as a general-aviation aircraft, the first such machine to be developed from an ultralight in Australia.

In view of the early stage of these projects at the time of going to press, we are omitting our data paragraphs in this instance.

AIRBORNE WINDSPORTS

Airborne Windsports Pty Ltd, 39 Griffith St, Charlestown; tel 049 439599.

AIRBORNE WINDSPORTS
EXPLORER II SINGLE-SEAT
(Weight-shift)

Single-seat single-engined flex-wing aircraft with weight-shift control. Rogallo wing with keel pocket. Pilot suspended below wing in trike unit, using bar to control pitch and roll/yaw by altering relative positions of trike unit and wing. Wing braced from above by kingpost and cables, from below by cables; bowsprit construction with NC% double-surface; preformed ribs. Undercarriage has three wheels in tricycle formation; no suspension on any wheels. Push-right go-left nosewheel steering independent from aerodynamic controls. No brakes. Aluminium-alloy tube trike unit, with optional pod. Engine mounted below wing, driving pusher propeller.

Production status: current, number completed NC.

GENERAL - The *Explorer II* is believed to be the only weight-shift ultralight manufactured in Australia. Indeed the country has seen very few such aircraft, a reflection of the fact that Australia never suffered the foot-launch regulation imposed in the USA and thus all ultralights had wheeled undercarriages from the outset. But the rapid improvement in the performance of trikes has seen it stage a comeback in this country.
The *Explorer II* is available as a single-seater powered by a EC25PS Fuji Robin engine (detailed below) or as a tandem two-up machine when fitted with the EC44 unit (listed separately), both versions sharing the same straightforward monopole structure. The two-place has been used solo for successful aero-towing of hang gliders, with the tow rig passing along the thrust line through the propeller hub and top reduction pulley. There is no precedent for such activity in Australia and the Department of Aviation is looking at legislation to govern tow launching by ultralight.
Either model can be derigged single-handed for roof-top transportation in 20 minutes. Standard features on the *Explorer II* are the Moyes *220 Delta* wing, foot-operated throttle and recoil start for in-flight use after a session of soaring. Optional are a streamlined pod, floats, electric start, a choice of wing colours and the usual instrument packages.
Price: NC.

EXTERNAL DIMENSIONS & AREAS - NC.

POWER PLANT - Robin EC25PS engine. Max power 18 hp at NC rpm. Other data NC.

WEIGHTS & LOADINGS - Empty weight 187 lb, 85 kg. Other data NC.

PERFORMANCE* - Never exceed speed 55 mph, 88 kph. Max cruising speed 40 mph, 64 kph. Stalling speed 18 mph, 29 kph. Take-off distance 130 ft, 40 m. Other data NC.

*Under unspecified test conditions.

AIRBORNE WINDSPORTS
EXPLORER II TWO-SEAT
(Weight-shift)

See Explorer II Single-Seat *except: Tandem two-seater.*

Production status: current, number completed NC.

GENERAL - See *Explorer II Single-Seat.*
EXTERNAL DIMENSIONS & AREAS - NC.
POWER PLANT - Robin EC44 engine. Max power 50 hp at NC rpm. Other data NC.
WEIGHTS & LOADINGS - Empty weight 243 lb, 110 kg. Other data NC.
PERFORMANCE* - Never exceed speed 66 mph, 106 kph. Max cruising speed 45 mph, 72 kph. Stalling speed 22 mph, 35 kph. Take-off distance 100 ft, 30 m. Other data NC.
*Under unspecified test conditions.

EASTWOOD

Geoff Eastwood Aircraft, Aldinga Airfield, Aldinga, South Australia S173; tel 085 565404.

EASTWOOD *TYRO MKII*
(Three-axis)

Single-seat single-engined high-wing monoplane with conventional three-axis control. Wing has unswept leading and trailing edges, and constant chord; cruciform tail. Pitch control by fully flying tail; yaw control by fin-mounted rudder; roll control by half-span ailerons; control inputs through stick for pitch/roll and pedals for yaw. Wing braced from below by struts; wing profile NACA 4418; 100% double-surface. Undercarriage has three wheels in taildragger formation; leaf-spring suspension on tailwheel and bungee suspension on main wheels. Push-right go-right tailwheel steering connected to yaw control. No brakes. Aluminium-alloy tube airframe, with pod. Engine mounted at wing height, driving tractor propeller.

Production status: current, 47 completed.

GENERAL - The *Tyro* was built in 1981 after four years of research and development by Geoff Eastwood at the South Coast Air Centre in South Australia, and like several other ultralights its ancestry can be traced to the *Cricket* way back in 1976. The strut-braced high-wing design has had few changes over the years, except the addition of a new cockpit pod and a new engine - Rotax 447 with geared reduction drive.

Because the type has been sold in plan and basic kit form for so long, very few *Tyros* look the same, and individual tastes have created everything from remarkably sophisticated machines, with totally enclosed fuselage, to the basic aircraft with pod. Construction is all aluminium with the flying surfaces covered using the Stits process with heat-shrunk Dacron and a dope finish. The main spar is 6061T6 alloy tube with the ribs cut from 0.024 inch (6 mm) aluminium sheet and the leading edge from 2024T3 0.020 inch (5 mm) sheet. Plans allow for construction using simple hand tools or alternatively the company can supply a fully built and test-flown *Tyro MkII*. Lessons are offered to buyers in a two-place ultralight but it is not clear whether this is the company's own design, and if it is whether it will be offered for sale to the public.

Price of the *Tyro MkII* in kit form is A$5000 including power pack, while plans cost A$65.

EXTERNAL DIMENSIONS & AREAS - Length overall 17.5 ft, 5.36 m. Height overall 6.5 ft, 1.98 m. Wing span 29.2 ft, 8.89 m. Constant chord 3.8 ft, 1.17 m. Dihedral 2°. Sweepback 0°. Tailplane span 7.5 ft, 2.29 m. Fin height 3.8 ft, 1.17 m. Total wing area 115 ft^2, 10.7 m^2. Total aileron area 8.4 ft^2, 0.78 m^2. Fin area 3.5 ft^2, 0.33 m^2. Rudder area 6.5 ft^2, 0.60 m^2. Total elevator area 17.5 ft^2, 1.63 m^2. Aspect ratio 7.4/1. Wheel track 5.0 ft, 1.52 m. Wheelbase 11.5 ft, 3.51 m. Tailwheel diameter overall 3 inch, 8 cm. Main wheels diameter overall 12 inch, 30 cm.

POWER PLANT - Rotax 447 engine. Max power 43 hp at 6400 rpm. Propeller diameter and pitch 68x28 inch, 1.73x 0.71 m. Gear reduction, ratio 2.6/1. Max static thrust NC. Power per unit area 0.37 hp/ft^2, 4.0 hp/m^2. Fuel capacity 5.4 US gal, 4.5 Imp gal, 20.4 litre.

WEIGHTS & LOADINGS - Empty weight 250 lb, 113 kg. Max take-off weight 460 lb, 209 kg. Payload 210 lb, 95 kg. Max wing loading 4.00 lb/ft^2, 19.5 kg/m^2. Max power load-

ing 10.7 lb/hp, 4.9 kg/hp. Load factors +4.0, -2.0 recommended; +6.3, -3.2 ultimate.

PERFORMANCE* - Max level speed 75 mph, 121 kph. Never exceed speed 85 mph, 137 kph. Economic cruising speed 65 mph, 105 kph. Stalling speed 22 mph, 35 kph. Max climb rate at sea level 1000 ft/min, 5.1 m/s. Min sink rate 400 ft/min at 40 mph, 2.0 m/s at 64 kph. Best glide ratio with power off 7/1 at 40 mph, 64 kph. Take-off distance 60 ft, 18 m. Landing distance 200 ft, 61 m. Range at average cruising speed 150 mile, 241 km. Other data NC.

*Under the following test conditions - Test payload 210 lb, 95 kg. Other data NC.

ELITE

Elite Aircraft, 2 Yardley Drive, Mulgrave 3170, Victoria; tel 03560 1705. Designer/builder: Alan Clarke.

ELITE *MACRO*

(Three-axis)

Single-seat single-engined low-wing monoplane with conventional three-axis control. Wing has swept back leading and trailing edges, and constant chord; T-tail. Pitch control by fully flying tail; yaw control by fin-mounted rudder; roll control by 30%-span ailerons; control inputs through stick for pitch/roll and pedals for yaw. Cantilever wing; wing profile NC; 100% double-surface. Undercarriage has three wheels in tail-dragger formation; rubber suspension on tailwheel and axle-flex suspension on main wheels. Push-right go-right tailwheel steering connected to yaw control. No brakes. Aluminium-alloy monocoque airframe, partially enclosed. Engine mounted at wing height, driving tractor propeller.

Production status: prototype.

Rob Fox

Alan Clarke stands proudly by the first Macro.

GENERAL - The Elite Aircraft *Macro* is the result of two years of development work, the intention being to produce a fast cross-country ultralight with high strength and durability, good crash protection and minimal dimensions. After experimentation with composite materials and space-frame aluminium structures, designer/builder Alan Clarke chose an all-metal (2024T3 aluminium alloy) monocoque construction.

The lower fuselage is built from 0.025 inch (6 mm) aluminium, double laminated from firewall to cockpit. Turtledecks and flying surfaces are made of 0.016 inch (4 mm) alloy sheet. The cantilever wing spar and carry-through consist of a built up I-beam, while wing ribs are hand-beaten aluminium.

Powered by a single-cylinder 18 hp Fuji Robin, the *Macro* first flew in May 1984 after ten weeks construction. With a stall speed of approximately 44 mph and an empty weight of just 198 lb (90 kg), the *Macro* appears to be well within the new regulations governing cross-country ultralight operations in Australia.

Price: A$8500.

EXTERNAL DIMENSIONS & AREAS - Length overall 13.0 ft, 3.96 m. Height overall 3.0 ft, 0.91 m. Wing span 23.0 ft, 7.01 m. Constant chord 2.9 ft, 0.86 m. Dihedral 3°. Sweepback 5°. Tailplane span 5.3 ft, 1.63 m. Fin height 2.7 ft, 0.81 m. Total wing area 64 ft², 5.9 m². Total aileron area 5.0 ft², 0.46 m². Fin area 2.5 ft², 0.23 m². Rudder area 4.5 ft²,

0.42 m². Tailplane area 6.0 ft², 0.56 m². Total elevator area 4.5 ft², 0.56 m². Aspect ratio 8.3/1. Wheel track 3.9 ft, 1.20 m. Other data NC.

POWER PLANT - Robin EC25PS engine. Max power 18 hp at 5500 rpm. Propeller diameter and pitch 32x15 inch, 0.81x0.38 m. No reduction. Max static thrust 100 lb, 45 kg. Power per unit area 0.28 hp/ft², 3.1 hp/m². Fuel capacity 4.8 US gal, 4.0 Imp gal, 18.2 litre.

WEIGHTS & LOADINGS - Empty weight 198 lb, 90 kg. Max take-off weight 400 lb, 181 kg. Payload 202 lb, 92 kg. Max wing loading 6.25 lb/ft², 30.7 kg/m². Max power loading 22.2 lb/hp, 10.1 kg/hp. Load factors +6.0, -6.0 recommended; +10.0, -10.0 ultimate.

PERFORMANCE* - Max level speed 75 mph, 121 kph. Never exceed speed 110 mph, 177 kph. Max cruising speed 65 mph, 105 kph. Economic cruising speed 65 mph, 105 kph. Stalling speed 40 mph, 64 kph. Max climb rate at sea level 700 ft/min, 3.6 m/s. Min sink rate 500 ft/min, 2.5 m/s at NC speed. Best glide ratio with power off 12/1 at NC speed. Take-off distance 300 ft, 91 m. Landing distance 300 ft, 91 m. Service ceiling NC. Range at average cruising speed 180 mile, 290 km. Noise level NC.

*Under the following test conditions - Airfield altitude 300 ft, 91 m. Ground temperature 59°F, 15°C. Other data NC.

ELITE *MACRO II*

(Three-axis)

Side-by-side two-seat twin-engined low-wing monoplane with conventional three-axis control. Wing has swept back leading and trailing edges, and constant chord; conventional tail. Pitch control by fully flying tail; yaw control by fin-mounted rudder; roll control by 30%-span ailerons; control inputs through stick for pitch/roll and pedals for yaw. Cantilever wing; wing profile NC; 100% double-surface. Undercarriage has three wheels in tricycle formation; no suspension on nosewheel and axle-flex suspension on main wheels. Push-right go-right nosewheel steering connected to yaw control. No brakes. Aluminium-alloy monocoque airframe, partially enclosed. Engine mounted at wing height, driving tractor propeller.

Production status: prototype.

GENERAL - Construction of the *Macro II* began in July 1984 and it is essentially a larger, two-seat version of the *Macro*. Structurally it is built in a very similar manner, but there are a number of differences in configuration, notably the use of two wing-mounted engines. Also, the tail is conventional rather than having the high elevator of the solo machine, and the undercarriage is tricycle rather than tail-dragger. At the time of writing the aircraft was complete but unflown so no performance details were available. Projected price is A$14,000.

EXTERNAL DIMENSIONS & AREAS - Length overall 16.0 ft, 4.88 m. Height overall 4.0 ft, 1.22 m. Wing span 35.0 ft, 10.67 m. Constant chord 3.5 ft, 1.07 m. Dihedral 3°. Sweepback 5°. Tailplane span 7.2 ft, 2.20 m. Fin height 4.3 ft, 1.3 m. Total wing area 127 ft², 11.8 m². Aspect ratio 9.6/1. Wheel track 4.9 ft, 1.50 m. Other data NC.

POWER PLANT - Two Robin EC25PS engines. Max power 18 hp each at 5500 rpm. Propeller diameter and pitch 32x15 inch, 0.81x0.38 m. No reduction. Max static thrust 200 lb, 91 kg. Power per unit area 0.28 hp/ft², 3.1 hp/m². Fuel capacity 7.2 US gal, 6.0 Imp gal, 27.3 litre.

WEIGHTS & LOADINGS - Empty weight 415 lb, 188 kg. Max take-off weight 770 lb, 349 kg. Payload 355 lb, 161 kg. Max wing loading 6.06 lb/ft², 29.6 kg/m². Max power loading 21.4 lb/hp, 9.7 kg/hp. Load factors +5.0, -5.0 recommended; +7.0, -7.0 ultimate.

PERFORMANCE - NC.

ELITE *PROTOTYPE*

(Three-axis)

Single-seat single-engined high-wing monoplane with conventional three-axis control. Wing has unswept leading and trailing edges, and constant chord; conventional tail. Pitch control by elevator on tail; yaw control by fin-mounted rudder; roll control by full-span flaperons; control inputs through stick for pitch/roll and pedals for yaw. Wing braced from below by struts; wing profile NC; 100% double-surface. Undercarriage has three wheels in tail-dragger formation; bungee suspension on tailwheel and axle-flex suspension on main wheels. Push-right go-right tailwheel steering connected to yaw control. No brakes. Aluminium-alloy tube airframe, totally enclosed Engine mounted below wing, driving tractor propeller.

Production status: prototype.

GENERAL - Currently under construction by Elite Aircraft and as yet unnamed is a machine designed to fall within the latest proposed Australian ultralight regulations, and which should have great appeal to Piper *Cub* fanatics.
The aircraft is a *Cub* lookalike and has been designed with simplicity of construction uppermost as it is intended to be produced in kit and plan form. The wing remains much the same as in the *Macro* series and is again an all-metal construction, but on this aircraft it is strut-braced. The spaceframe fuselage is built on to a crash-resistant monocoque cockpit.
Thanks to full-span flaperons, the aircraft's speed range should be quite good, as our (calculated) figures show, but as the aircraft had not been flown at the time of writing, no other performance data is available. Projected price is A$8000.

EXTERNAL DIMENSIONS & AREAS - Length overall 15.0 ft, 4.57 m. Height overall 4.8 ft, 1.45 m. Wing span 32.0 ft, 9.75 m. Constant chord 3.3 ft, 1.00 m. Dihedral 0.75°. Sweepback 0°. Tailplane span 7.2 ft, 2.20 m. Fin height 3.9 ft, 1.20 m. Total wing area 108 ft², 10.0 m². Total aileron area 20.0 ft², 1.86 m². Aspect ratio 9.5/1. Wheel track 4.0 ft, 1.22 m. cm. Main wheels diameter overall 12 inch, 30 cm. Other data NC.

POWER PLANT - Robin EC25PS engine. Max power 18 hp at 5500 rpm. Propeller diameter and pitch 40x20 inch, 1.02x0.51 m. V-belt reduction, ratio 1.5/1. Max static thrust 140 lb, 64 kg. Power per unit area 0.17 hp/ft², 1.8 hp/m². Fuel capacity 4.8 US gal, 4.0 Imp gal, 18.2 litre.

WEIGHTS & LOADINGS - Empty weight 240 lb, 109 kg. Max take-off weight 470 lb, 213 kg. Payload 230 lb, 104 kg. Max wing loading 4.35 lb/ft², 21.3 kg/m². Max power loading 26.1 lb/hp, 11.8 kg/hp. Load factors +6.0, -6.0 recommended; +8.0, -8.0 ultimate.

PERFORMANCE* - Max level speed 69 mph, 111 kph. Stalling speed 25 mph, 40 kph. Other data NC.

*Under unspecified test conditions.

FACET

Facet Aircraft, 6/57 Allingham Street, Condell Park.

FACET *SAPPHIRE*
(Three-axis)

Single-seat single-engined high-wing monoplane with conventional three-axis control. Wing has swept back leading and trailing edges, and tapering chord; conventional tail. Pitch control by fully flying tail; yaw control by fin-mounted rudder; roll control by flaperons; control inputs through stick for pitch/roll and pedals for yaw. Wing braced from below by struts; wing profile NC; 100% double-surface. Undercarriage has two wheels plus tailskid; glass-fibre suspension on tailskid and main wheels. No ground steering. No brakes. Composite-construction airframe, partially enclosed. Engine mounted at wing height, driving pusher propeller.

Production status: current, number completed NC.

GENERAL - The *Sapphire*, developed and built by Scott Winton (son of *Cricket* designer Col Winton) is surely one of the prettiest ultralights on the market today. This high-wing strut-braced pusher with tail-dragger undercarriage has beautifully sleek sailplane lines, but has the ability to handle a wide range of airfield and weather conditions.

So often today's slick ultralights sacrifice this versatility for top-end performance, and a mile of smooth runway is needed to launch these little rockets: not so the *Sapphire*. Thanks to its unusual combination of wing design and flaps, allied to a choice of two powerful engines, the *Sapphire* can handle the short rough strips so commonly found in Australia. Despite being extensively tested over 12 months, only a few minor problems needed rectifying before the aircraft went into full production.

A composite construction of glass-fibre, foam and aluminium, the *Sapphire* is robust even in basic form and a fully aerobatic version has been built that is even stronger. This has been co-developed with *Sapphire*-owner George Markey, basically for his personal use, as the Department of Aviation has no policy at present on exemptions from the Air Navigation Order to permit aerobatics in ultralights. Markey is said to be so impressed with the performance of this special that he was attempting, at the time of writing, to get his *Sapphire SA-1* fully certified.

The wings of the *Sapphire* are made from laminated glass-fibre/foam ribs with a pre-moulded glass-fibre skin. An unusual feature of the aircraft is the position of the pilot, who is seated between the D-sections of both wings, where a gap-cover would normally be. The tail boom is an alloy tube neatly bonded to the glass-fibre forward fuselage and ending forward of the main undercarriage legs. Initial examples were powered by KFM horizontally opposed twins, but as with so many others, a switch to the Rotax 377 (optionally 447) has been effected. Our data below refers to the smaller-engined version.

A tricycle undercarriage model with a four-cylinder Konig engine has been built, but this is understood to be a one-off and for production no change from the current specification is being considered. In standard form the aircraft retails at A$9800 complete.

EXTERNAL DIMENSIONS & AREAS - Length overall 16.0 ft, 4.88 m. Height overall 4.0 ft, 1.22 m. Wing span 29.0 ft, 8.84 m. Chord at root 2.5 ft, 0.76 m. Chord at tip 1.5 ft, 0.46 m. Dihedral 0.5°. Sweepback 0.5°. Tailplane span 7.7 ft, 2.35 m. Total wing area 100 ft², 9.3 m². Total aileron area 8.0 ft², 0.74 m². Total elevator area 12.0 ft², 1.11 m². Aspect ratio 8.4/1. Wheel track 4.5 ft, 1.37 m. Wheelbase 10.1 ft,

3.08 m. Main wheels diameter overall 11 inch, 28 cm. Other data NC.

POWER PLANT - Rotax 377 engine. Max power 35 hp at 6000 rpm. Propeller diameter and pitch 52x49 inch, 1.32x 1.24 m. Gear reduction, ratio 2.6/1. Max static thrust NC. Power per unit area 0.35 hp/ft², 3.8 hp/m². Fuel capacity 5.8 US gal, 4.8 Imp gal, 22.0 litre.

WEIGHTS & LOADINGS - Empty weight 310 lb, 141 kg. Max take-off weight 550 lb, 249 kg. Payload 240 lb, 109 kg. Max wing loading 5.50 lb/ft², 26.8 kg/m². Max power loading 15.7 lb/hp, 7.1 kg/hp. Load factors +4.0, -2.0 recommended; +6.5, -4.0 ultimate.

PERFORMANCE* - Max level speed 92 mph, 148 kph. Never exceed speed 110 mph, 177 kph. Max cruising speed 80 mph, 129 kph. Economic cruising speed 80 mph, 129 kph. Stalling speed 33 mph, 53 kph. Max climb rate at sea level 1200 ft/min, 6.1 m/s. Min sink rate 450 ft/min at 43 mph, 2.3 m/s at 69 kph. Best glide ratio with power off 10/1 at NC speed. Landing distance 250-300 ft, 76-91 m. Range at average cruising speed 190 mile, 306 km. Other data NC.

*Under unspecified test conditions.

FLIGHT 95 AUSTRALIA

Flight 95 Australia Pty Ltd, 316 Pacific Highway, Lindfield, New South Wales 2070; tel 02533 1865. Designer/builder: Leigh Wakelan of Flying Ultralight Machines.

FLIGHT 95 AUSTRALIA *JAVELIN*
(Three-axis)

Single-seat single-engined high-wing monoplane with conventional three-axis control. Wing has unswept leading and trailing edges, and constant chord; cruciform tail. Pitch control by elevator on tail; yaw control by fin-mounted rudder; roll control by 30%-span ailerons; control inputs through stick for pitch/roll and pedals for yaw. Wing braced from below by struts; wing profile NC; single-surface. Undercarriage has three wheels in tail-dragger formation; axle-flex suspension on all wheels. Push-right go-right tailwheel steering connected to yaw control. Brakes NC. Aluminium-alloy tube airframe, with pod. Engine mounted below wing, driving tractor propeller.

Production status: current, number completed NC.

GENERAL - The *Javelin*, designed by Leigh Wakelan of Flying Ultralight Machines but marketed by Flight 95 Australia, first appeared on the scene in April 1984 at the Sport Aircraft Association of Australia's Mangalore convention. A direct development of its predecessor the *Mustang*, from which it differs principally in being strut- rather than cable-braced, it was originally powered by Fuji Robin single- and twin-cylinder engines with belt reduction, but the *Javelins* which appeared later that year at the Yarrawonga fly-in sported the very popular Rotax 377 with gear reduction, and it is in that form which we detail it below.
The engine is mounted below the rectangular section

Rob Fox

Rob Fox

The Javelin *from Flight 95 Australia, here shown with belt reduction (gear is now standard); for another illustration, see colour section.*

aluminium fuselage boom in tractor configuration, with a tuned exhaust passing up and over the mainplane to deflect engine noise upwards. V-strut bracing of the mainplane to the leading edge and rear spars makes rigging easier and quicker than with the *Mustang*. All flying surfaces are covered in brightly coloured single-surface Dacron matching the baked enamel finish of the airframe and the glass-fibre pod.

The pilot is seated within a hefty A-frame in the area below the mainplane, which can be left open but is normally semi-enclosed by a pod, with a screen to deflect propwash. The *Javelin* has acquired a reputation for good flight characteristics, managing to combine positive control at very low speeds with featherlight inputs at cruise.

Price is A$5670 complete.

EXTERNAL DIMENSIONS & AREAS - Length overall 16.3 ft, 4.97 m. Wing span 28.0 ft, 8.53 m. Constant chord 4.9 ft, 1.50 m. Sweepback 0°. Total wing area 138 ft², 12.8 m². Aspect ratio 5.7/1. Other data NC.

POWER PLANT - Rotax 377 engine. Max power 35 hp at NC rpm. Propeller diameter and pitch 50xNC inch, 1.27xNC m. Gear reduction, ratio 2.6/1. Max static thrust NC. Power per unit area 0.25 hp/ft², 2.7 hp/m². Fuel capacity 5.8 US gal, 4.8 Imp gal, 22.0 litre.

WEIGHTS & LOADINGS - Empty weight 240 lb, 109 kg. Other data NC.

PERFORMANCE* - Max level speed 55 mph, 88 kph. Stalling speed 19 mph, 31 kph. Max climb rate at sea level 800 ft/min, 4.1 m/s. Other data NC.

*Under unspecified test conditions.

GEONIC

Geonic Aero Industries Pty Ltd, 10 Geonic Street, Woodridge 4114; tel 209 5533; tx 43310. General manager: Norman P St John. Manufacturing manager: Peter Adams.

GEONIC *ROUSEABOUT*
(Three-axis)

Single-seat single-engined high-wing monoplane with conventional three-axis control. Wing has unswept leading and trailing edges, and constant chord; conventional tail. Pitch control by fully flying tail; yaw control by fin-mounted rudder; roll control by full-span ailerons; control inputs through stick for pitch/roll and pedals for yaw. Wing braced from below by struts; wing profile NASA GA(W)-2; 100% double-surface. Undercarriage has three wheels in tricycle formation; coil-spring suspension on nosewheel and Kevlar/carbon-fibre suspension on main wheels. Push-right go-right nosewheel steering connected to yaw control. Optional nosewheel brake. Composite-construction airframe, partially enclosed. Engine mounted above wing, driving pusher propeller.

Production status: current, 6 completed.

GENERAL - Although the *Rouseabout* is similar in appearance to the *Resurgam MKII*, beneath its beautiful lines lies a vastly different bird. Developed in 1983, it made its first flight in November of that year, although the public had to wait until the Sport Aircraft Association of Australia's

both pictures : Rob Fox

The Rouseabout, *with Don Adams at the controls.*

Mangalore convention the following April to catch its first glimpse.

Built by Don and Peter Adams with the late Gordon Bedson of Resurgam fame as design consultant, the *Rouseabout's* wing is structured around a 4 inch diameter x 0.047 inch thick (102 x 1.2 mm) aluminium tube with 0.875x0.375 inch (22x10 mm) spruce cap strips epoxied top and bottom. The leading edge is formed of glass-fibre extending back through 45% of the chord, with the remainder covered with synthetic fabric. Full-span flaperons complete the wing, which uses the extremely thin NASA GA(W)-2 aerofoil section, only 13% thick with maximum depth at 40% of chord. The trailing edge is square and only 0.5 inch (13 mm) thick, with a slight undercamber at the rear of the section.

The prototype utilised full-span flaperons with three-stage flap positioning at 10°, 25° and 40°. Adverse yaw is elimated by Don Adams' ingenious system whereby only the up-going flaperon moves when roll control is required, the control surface on the opposite wing remaining in its preset flap position.

The fuselage differs from Gordon Bedson's *Resurgam* in both shape and structure. The prototype used an aluminium sub-frame and tail boom, but production aircraft are expected to be of carbon-fibre/Kevlar composition with an integral tail boom, permitting a stronger, lighter and less labour-intensive construction.

Whereas the *Resurgam* is a true homebuilder's project for building from plans, the *Rouseabout* has been developed as a very comprehensive components kit. A fuselage shell with all control runs installed, leading-edge torsion box and spar assembly all complete, and ready-to-install metal sub-

assemblies and components, comprise the A$12,500 package.

A two-seat tandem trainer is at present being developed, possibly using two JPX engines, but at the time of writing no further details were available. The Geonic company, incidentally, is also Australian agent for the Canadian *Pelican* series of aircraft, made by Ultravia (see Canadian section).

EXTERNAL DIMENSIONS & AREAS - Length overall 18.3 ft, 5.56 m. Height overall 9.0 ft, 2.74 m. Wing span 30.0 ft, 9.14 m. Constant chord 4.0 ft, 1.22 m. Dihedral 2.5°. Sweepback 0°. Tailplane span 7.0 ft, 2.13 m. Fin height 9.0 ft, 2.74 m. Total wing area 128 ft^2, 11.9 m^2. Total elevator area 14.0 ft^2, 1.30 m^2. Aspect ratio 7.0/1. Wheel track 5.0 ft, 1.52 m. Wheelbase 6.0 ft, 1.83 m. Nosewheel diameter overall 12 inch, 30 cm. Main wheels diameter overall 12 inch, 30 cm. Other data NC.

POWER PLANT - Konig SD570 engine. Max power 30 hp at 4000 rpm. Propeller diameter and pitch 60x33 inch, 1.52x0.84 m. Toothed-belt reduction, ratio 1.7/1. Max static thrust 250 lb, 113 kg. Power per unit area 0.23 hp/ft^2, 2.5 hp/m^2. Fuel capacity 5.8 US gal, 4.8 Imp gal, 22.0 litre.

WEIGHTS & LOADINGS - Empty weight 287 lb, 130 kg. Max take-off weight 573 lb, 260 kg. Payload 287 lb, 130 kg. Max wing loading 4.48 lb/ft², 21.8 kg/m². Max power loading 19.1 lb/hp, 8.7 kg/hp. Load factors +3.8, -2.0 recommended; +6.0, -3.0 ultimate.

PERFORMANCE* - Max level speed 86 mph, 138 kph. Never exceed speed 104 mph, 167 kph. Max cruising speed 81 mph, 130 kph. Economic cruising speed 67 mph, 108 kph. Stalling speed 29 mph, 47 kph. Max climb rate at sea level 600 ft/min, 3.1 m/s. Min sink rate 100 ft/min at 35 mph, 0.5 m/s at 56 kph. Best glide ratio with power off 13/1 at 35 mph, 56 kph. Take-off distance 200 ft, 61 m. Landing distance 200 ft, 61 m. Service ceiling 10,000 ft, 3050 m. Range at average cruising speed 150 mile, 241 km. Noise level NC.

*Under the following test conditions - Airfield altitude 0 ft, 0 m. Ground temperature 59°F, 15°C. Ground pressure 1013 mB. Ground windspeed 0 mph, 0 kph. Test payload 130 lb, 59 kg.

KIMBERLEY

Gary Kimberley, 255 Woniora Road, Blakenhurst, New South Wales 2221; tel 02546 4143.

KIMBERLEY *SKY RIDER*
(Three-axis)

Single-seat single-engined high-wing monoplane with conventional three-axis control. Wing has unswept leading edge, swept forward trailing edge, and tapering chord; flaps fitted; cruciform tail. Pitch control by fully flying tail; yaw control by fully flying rudder; roll control by half-span ailerons; control inputs through stick for pitch/roll and pedals for yaw. Wing braced from above by kingpost and cables, from below by cables; wing profile NC; single-surface. Undercarriage has three wheels in tail-dragger formation; suspension NC. Ground steering by differential braking; castoring tailwheel. Brakes on main wheels. Aluminium-alloy tube airframe, completely open. Engine mounted at wing height, driving tractor propeller.

Production status: see text.

Kimberley Sky Rider *with McCulloch Mc101 engine.*

GENERAL - To 1985 eyes there is nothing remarkable about Gary Kimberley's *Sky Rider,* as it is a straightforward tube-and-Dacron high-wing machine whose most distinguishing feature is its use of flaps, unusual in such a slow-speed machine. It is easy to forget, however, that it was designed as long ago as 1978, and that it was a very sophisticated ultralight in its time - good enough, in fact, to win the 'outstanding individual achievement' award from the EAA that year. It was that award which persuaded Gary to market what had up to that point been purely a one-off, and since then plans have been sold in 14 countries.

Being a homebuilt - kits and complete aircraft have never been available - engine choice is up to the builder, a maximum of 50 hp being recommended, but we detail below three popular choices - the McCulloch Mc101, Robin EC25PS and Cuyuna 430. Our data is based on the McCulloch-engined version with figures for the others, where different, in parentheses.

Though we have not heard from Gary for some time, to the best of our knowledge the plans still cost US$35 plus US$4 for airmail postage.

EXTERNAL DIMENSIONS & AREAS - Length overall* *19.0* ft, *5.79* m. Height overall 7.8 ft, 2.38 m. Wing span 32.3 ft, 9.85 m. Chord at root 5.0 ft, 1.52 m. Chord at tip 4.0 ft, 1.22 m. Dihedral 2°. Sweepback 0°. Elevator span 10.3 ft, 3.14 m. Rudder height 5.0 ft, 1.52 m. Total wing area 144 ft², 13.4 m². Total aileron area 17.5 ft², 1.63 m². Rudder area

9.5 ft², 0.88 m². Total elevator area 20.0 ft², 1.86 m². Aspect ratio 7.1/1. Wheel track 4.5 ft, 1.37 m. Wheelbase 13.0 ft, 3.96 m. Tailwheel diameter overall 4 inch, 10 cm. Main wheels diameter overall 12 inch, 30 cm.

POWER PLANT - McCulloch Mc101 (Robin EC25PS) (Cuyuna 430) engine. Max power 12(20)(30) hp at NC rpm. Propeller diameter and pitch 54(NC)(NC)x27(NC)(NC) inch, 1.37(NC)(NC)x0.69(NC)(NC) m. Chain (belt)(NC) reduction, ratio 4.0(2.5)(NC)/1. Max static thrust NC. Power per unit area 0.08(0.14)(0.21) hp/ft², 0.9(1.5)(2.2) hp/m². Fuel capacity** 1.2 US gal, 1.0 Imp gal, 4.5 litre.

WEIGHTS & LOADINGS - Empty weight** 195(210)(220) lb, 88(95)(100) kg. Max take-off weight 400 lb, 181 kg. Payload** 205(190)(180) lb, 93(86)(82) kg. Max wing loading 2.78 lb/ft², 13.5 kg/m². Max power loading 33.3(20.0) (13.3) lb/hp, 15.1(9.1)(6.0) kg/hp. Load factors +3.0, -1.0 design limit; >+4.5, >-1.0 ultimate.

PERFORMANCE* - Max level speed 43(50)(NC) mph, 69(80)(NC) kph. Never exceed speed 65 mph, 105 kph. Cruising speed 40(45)(48) mph, 64(72)(77) kph. Stalling speed with land flaps**** 20(21)(NC) mph, 32(34)(NC) kph. Max climb rate at sea level *150(300)(400)* ft/min, *0.8(1.5) (2.0)* m/s. Min sink rate 300 ft/min at 28 mph, 1.5 m/s at 45 kph. Best glide ratio with power off 6/1 at 33 mph, 53 kph. Take-off distance 250(200)(NC) ft, 76(61)(NC) m. Landing distance 160(200)(NC) ft, 49(61)(NC) m. Service ceiling *5000(10,000)(NC)* ft, *1520(3050)(NC)* m. Range at average cruising speed** 40(30)(NC) mile, 64(48)(NC) km. Noise level NC.

*Depends on engine installation.

**With standard tank - 3.6 US gal, 3.0 Imp gal, 13.6 litre optional.

***Under unspecified test conditions.

****For McCulloch-engined version - Stalling speed with flaps up 25 mph, 40 kph. Stalling speed with ground effect 18 mph, 29 kph. Equivalent figures for other versions NC.

LABAHAN

Robert Labahan, 6 Victoria Road, Seville 3139; tel 059 644730.

LABAHAN *RANGER*

(Three-axis)

Single-seat single-engined high-wing monoplane with conventional three-axis control. Wing has unswept leading and trailing edges, and constant chord; cruciform tail. Pitch control by elevator on tail; yaw control by fin-mounted rudder; roll control by full-span ailerons; control inputs through stick for pitch/roll and pedals for yaw. Wing braced from above by kingpost and cables, from below by cables; wing profile in-house; 100% double-surface. Undercarriage has three wheels in tail-dragger formation; bungee suspension on tailwheel and torsion-bar suspension on main wheels. Push-right go-right tailwheel steering connected to yaw control. No brakes. Aluminium-alloy tube airframe, with optional pod. Engine mounted at wing height, driving tractor propeller.

Production status: see text.

Robert Labahan flying a Ranger *in 1981.*

Rob Fox

GENERAL - Robert Labahan designed the *Ranger* in June 1981 as a more practical concept than the Catto *CA15* he was flying at the time. The first flight of this, his first design, took place that August, and Labahan claims the aircraft enjoys a high degree of control combined with a high roll rate.

The *Ranger* is designed for simple construction and building time is about 80 h; the wings comprise aluminium-alloy tube for the leading edge and rear spar and preformed tube ribs. The leading-edge skin is alloy sheet covered with Dacron and dope finished, as are all the flying surfaces. Rigging time for one person is claimed at 10 min.

Although originally conceived as a one-off, three aircraft have now been built, successive machines incorporating various improvements, including a pod. Price: NC.

EXTERNAL DIMENSIONS & AREAS - Length overall 15.5 ft, 4.72 m. Height overall 7.5 ft, 2.29 m. Wing span 25.0 ft, 7.62 m. Constant chord 3.8 ft, 1.14 m. Dihedral 1.5°. Sweepback 0°. Tailplane span 6.0 ft, 1.83 m. Fin height 3.5 ft, 1.07 m. Total wing area 94 ft², 8.7 m². Total aileron area 12.0 ft², 1.11 m². Fin area 4.5 ft², 0.42 m². Rudder area 4.0 ft², 0.37 m². Tailplane area 7.0 ft², 0.65 m². Total elevator area 5.0 ft², 0.46 m². Aspect ratio 6.6/1. Wheel track 11.0 ft, 3.35 m. Wheelbase 4.0 ft, 1.22 m. Tailwheel diameter overall 4 inch, 10 cm. Main wheels diameter overall 11 inch, 28 cm.

POWER PLANT - Robin EC25PS engine. Max power 15 hp at 5000 rpm. Propeller diameter and pitch 36x12 inch, 0.91x0.30 m. No reduction. Max static thrust 95 lb, 43 kg. Power per unit area 0.16 hp/ft², 1.7 hp/m². Fuel capacity 1.8 US gal, 1.5 Imp gal, 7.0 litre.

WEIGHTS & LOADINGS - Empty weight 160 lb, 73 kg. Max take-off weight 350 lb, 159 kg. Payload 190 lb, 86 kg. Max wing loading 3.72 lb/ft², 18.3 kg/m². Max power loading 23.3 lb/hp, 10.6 kg/hp. Load factors +5.0, -2.0 recommended; +7.0, -2.0 ultimate.

PERFORMANCE* - Max level speed 50 mph, 80 kph. Never exceed speed 70 mph, 113 kph. Max cruising speed 45 mph, 72 kph. Economic cruising speed 38 mph, 61 kph. Stalling speed 24 mph, 39 kph. Max climb rate at sea level 270 ft/min, 1.4 m/s. Min sink rate 320 ft/min at 32 mph, 1.6 m/s at 51 kph. Best glide ratio with power off 9/1 at 35 mph, 56 kph. Take-off distance 250 ft, 76 m. Landing distance 300 ft, 91 m. Service ceiling 11,000 ft, 3350 m. Range at average cruising speed 40 mile, 64 km. Noise level NC.

*Under the following test conditions - Airfield altitude 320 ft, 98 m. Ground temperature 64°F, 18°C. Ground pressure NC. Ground windspeed 0 mph, 0 kph. Test payload 165 lb, 75 kg.

Robert Labahan at the controls of the Arrow.

LABAHAN *ARROW*

(Three-axis)

Single-seat single-engined high-wing monoplane with conventional three-axis control. Wing has unswept leading and trailing edges, and constant chord; cruciform tail. Pitch control by fully flying tail; yaw control by fin-mounted rudder; roll control by half-span ailerons; control inputs through stick for pitch/roll and pedals for yaw. Wing braced from below by struts; wing profile NACA 2412; 100% double-surface. Undercarriage has two wheels in tandem with additional wheels at wing tips; bungee suspension on tailwheel and no suspension on main wheel. Push-right go-right tailwheel steering connected to yaw control. Brake on main wheel. Glass-fibre/aluminium-alloy tube airframe, totally enclosed. Engine mounted below wing, driving pusher propeller.

Production status: see text.

GENERAL - The *Arrow* was designed while Robert Labahan was working for another ultralight manufacturer and is intended as an efficient tourer-cum-motorglider. The aircraft was built in four months and the successful first flight, on 22 May 1983, lasted 20 min. Labahan, who has logged many hours on the machine since, claims it is a joy to fly and, because of its good glide ratio, can also achieve an excellent endurance. A 3-4 h flight can end with a third of a tank of petrol still left and Robert has proved the point by undertaking many cross-country flights in the *Arrow*, the longest being 240 mile (386 km). Good control in rough weather is also claimed and the machine has been flown to 11,200 ft (3410 m) in still air.

The wings are built of plywood ribs over a metal spar and covered with Dacron, while the fuselage is of tube construction with a thin glass-fibre shell and a tube tail boom. The overall structure is strong and the aircraft is approved for limited aerobatics.

Like the *Ranger,* the *Arrow* is not a production aircraft in the normal sense, but is built only on request. Price: NC.

EXTERNAL DIMENSIONS & AREAS - Length overall 16.5 ft, 5.03 m. Height overall 4.0 ft, 1.22 m. Wing span 31.0 ft, 9.45 m. Constant chord 3.3 ft, 1.00 m. Dihedral 3°. Sweepback 0°. Elevator span 6.0 ft, 1.83 m. Fin height 3.5 ft, 1.07 m. Total wing area 98 ft², 9.1 m². Total aileron area 15.0 ft², 1.39 m². Fin area 7.0 ft², 0.65 m². Rudder area 4.5 ft², 0.42 m². Total elevator area 10.0 ft², 0.93 m². Aspect ratio 9.8/1. Wheelbase 11.0 ft, 3.35 m. Tailwheel diameter overall 3 inch, 8 cm. Main wheel diameter overall 10 inch, 25 cm.

POWER PLANT - Robin EC25PS engine. Max power 14 hp at 4800 rpm. Propeller diameter and pitch 30x20 inch, 0.76x0.51 m. No reduction. Max static thrust 80 lb, 36 kg. Power per unit area 0.14 hp/ft², 1.5 hp/m². Fuel capacity 5.3 US gal, 4.4 Imp gal, 20.0 litre.

WEIGHTS & LOADINGS - Empty weight 238 lb, 108 kg. Max take-off weight 420 lb, 191 kg. Payload 182 lb, 83 kg. Max wing loading 4.29 lb/ft², 21.0 kg/m². Max power loading 30.0 lb/hp, 13.6 kg/hp. Load factors +5.5, -4.0 recommended; +8., -6.0 ultimate.

PERFORMANCE* - Max level speed 82 mph, 132 kph. Never exceed speed 92 mph, 148 kph. Max cruising speed 75 mph, 121 kph. Economic cruising speed 63 mph, 101 kph. Stalling speed 33 mph, 53 kph. Max climb rate at sea level 340 ft/min, 1.7 m/s. Min sink rate 220 ft/min at 36 mph, 1.1 m/s at 58 kph. Best glide ratio with power off 19/1 at 45 mph, 72 kph. Take-off distance 500 ft, 152 m. Landing distance 500 ft, 152 m. Service ceiling 6000 ft, 1830 m. Range at average cruising speed 240 mile, 386 km. Noise level NC.

*Under the following test conditions - Airfield altitude 500 ft, 152 m. Ground temperature 59°F, 15°C. Ground pressure NC. Ground windspeed 10 mph, 16 kph. Test payload 180 lb, 82 kg.

LABAHAN *HITCHIKER*
(Three-axis)

Single-seat single-engined high-wing monoplane with conventional three-axis control. Wing has swept back leading and trailing edges, and constant chord; conventional tail. Pitch control by fully flying tail; yaw control by fin-mounted rudder; roll control by full-span flaperons; control inputs through stick for pitch/roll and pedals for yaw. Wing braced from below by struts; wing profile in-house; 100% double-surface. Undercarriage has three wheels in tail-dragger formation; bungee suspension on tailwheel and torsion-bar suspension on main wheels. Push-right go-right tailwheel steering connected to yaw control. Brakes NC. Aluminium-alloy tube/wood airframe, with optional pod. Engine mounted at wing height, driving pusher propeller.

Production status: prototype.

GENERAL - The *Hitchiker* is the third aircraft designed by Robert Labahan and, unlike his *Arrow* which sacrifices short field performance for cross-country ability, it is designed with only limited cross-country work but good short-field performance in mind. The aircraft has the 277 Rotax engine with geared drive, which although giving only 27hp, nonetheless provides good performance thanks to the rigid wooden wing and lightweight construction. Intended as a long-life machine, the design incorporates oversize tubes with sleeved holes.

Robert Labahan takes the Hitchiker *up for its first flight.*

The *Hitchiker* incorporates full span flaperons which are set positive for take-off and landing and negative for cruising, an arrangement which also allows the fuselage to fly at a better angle relative to the airflow, thereby reducing trim drag. The pilot sits reclined as in a high-performance glider, to minimise frontal area and drag, and for winter flying there is provision for a full pilot enclosure. A removable fuel tank is provided, so it can be filled away from the aircraft, a useful feature on cross-country flights.

For transport the *Hitchiker* requires a small trailer, as it breaks down into a 16 ft (4.9 m) fuselage, two 13x4 ft (4.0x1.2 m) panels and two 3x2 ft (0.9x0.6 m) elevators. Rigging time is quoted as 10 min. The *Hitchiker* is designed for quick construction at low cost and, unlike Labahan's other aircraft, is planned to go into series production after intensive testing. Price: A$5000.

EXTERNAL DIMENSIONS & AREAS - Length overall 15.8 ft, 4.80 m. Height overall 4.5 ft, 1.37 m. Wing span 26.5 ft, 8.08 m. Constant chord 3.8 ft, 1.14 m. Dihedral 3°. Sweepback 12°. Elevator span 6.5 ft, 1.98 m. Fin height 4.0 ft, 1.22 m. Total wing area 99 ft^2, 9.2 m^2. Total flaperon area 18.0 ft^2, 1.67 m^2. Fin area 5.0 ft^2, 0.46 m^2. Rudder area 5.0 ft^2, 0.46 m^2. Total elevator area 10.5 ft^2, 0.98 m^2. Aspect ratio 7.1/1. Wheel track 4.0 ft, 1.22 m. Wheelbase 11.0 ft, 3.35 m. Tailwheel diameter overall NC. Main wheels diameter overall NC.

POWER PLANT - Rotax 277 engine. Max power 27 hp at 6250 rpm. Propeller diameter and pitch 50x38 inch, 1.27x 0.97 m. Gear reduction, ratio 2.6/1. Max static thrust 175 lb, 79 kg. Power per unit area 0.27 hp/ft^2, 2.9 hp/m^2. Fuel capacity 6.6 US gal, 5.5 Imp gal, 25.0 litre.

Rob Fox

WEIGHTS & LOADINGS - Empty weight 220 lb, 100 kg. Max take-off weight 450 lb, 204 kg. Payload 230 lb, 104 kg. Max wing loading 4.55 lb/ft², 22.2 kg/m². Max power loading 16.7 lb/hp, 7.6 kg/hp. Load factors +6.0, -4.0 recommended; +9.0, -6.0 ultimate.

PERFORMANCE* - Max level speed 70 mph, 113 kph. Never exceed speed 80 mph, 129 kph. Max cruising speed 60 mph, 97 kph. Economic cruising speed 50 mph, 80 kph. Stalling speed 26 mph, 42 kph. Max climb rate at sea level 870 ft/min, 4.4 m/s. Min sink rate 380 ft/min at 35 mph, 1.9 m/s at 56 kph. Best glide ratio with power off 9/1 at 40 mph, 64 kph. Take-off distance 150 ft, 46 m. Landing distance 200 ft, 61 m. Service ceiling NC. Range at average cruising speed 180 mile, 290 km. Noise level NC.

*Under the following test conditions - Airfield altitude 320 ft, 98 m. Ground temperature 59°F, 15°C. Ground pressure NC. Ground windspeed 0 mph, 0 kph. Test payload 200 lb, 91 kg.

Three views of the Stratos, *with designer Charles Ligeti.*

LGT

LGT Aero Nautical, PO Box 362, North Balwyn, Victoria 3104; tel 03859 6600. Director: Charles K Ligeti.

LGT *STRATOS*
(Three-axis)

Single-seat single-engined double monoplane in tandem with outboard ends joined; conventional three-axis control. Forward wing has swept back leading and trailing edges, rear wing has swept back leading edge and unswept trailing edge; both wings tapering chord; flaps on rear wing; no tail. Pitch control by elevator on forward wing; yaw control by tip rudders; roll control by four 40%-span ailerons; control inputs through stick for pitch/roll and pedals for yaw. Forward wing braced by rear wing and vice-versa; wing profile Wortmann FX 67-K-170; 100% double-surface. Undercarriage has two wheels in tandem with additional wheels at wing tips; coil-spring suspension on tailwheel and coil-spring plus shock-

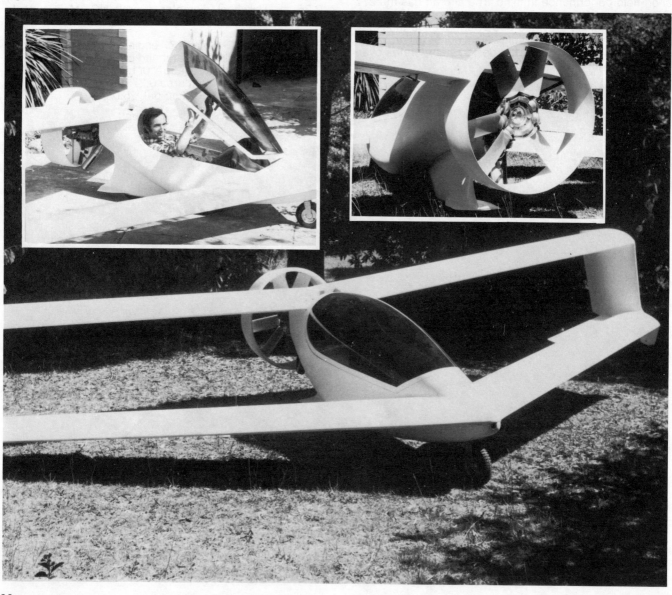

absorber suspension on main wheel. Push-right go-right main wheel steering independent from yaw control. Main wheel brake. Composite-construction airframe, totally enclosed. Engine mounted between wings, driving pusher propeller.

Production status: prototype.

GENERAL - The LGT *Stratos* is a high-performance ultralight developed and constructed by Charles Ligeti to a design that is radical both aeronautically and technologically. The holder of an MSc in chemistry, Ligeti gave himself a part-time education in aeronautical engineering and advanced composite materials with the object of producing a high-performance, very small ultralight, and the result is a most unusual machine, unlike anything else in this book with the possible exception of the American Summit *Trident T-3*.

Initial design studies began in Czechoslovakia in 1976 but legal difficulties and problems with availability of materials led to the postponement of the project, which was resumed with the construction of the prototype in Australia in May 1983, after extensive testing of quarter-scale radio-controlled and free-flying models which apparently met the design goals.

The aim of the *Stratos* is to combine the efficiency of a canard, the large wing area but small span of a tandem wing, and the structural advantages of an externally braced biplane. The swept back forward wing is joined with the high rear wing at the tips by vertical fins carrying control surfaces which act as rudders if used differentially or air brakes if deployed simultaneously. This configuration is claimed to yield increased pilot protection, greater wing stiffness, and lower weight and induced drag, which in turn give higher performance at both ends of the speed range. Both wings have ailerons, while the rear wing also has flaps.

The structure is fabricated over shaped rigid foam and laminated with Kevlar and glass-fibre, with spars of carbon fibre. This soaring-oriented machine has a glider-style undercarriage with a single main wheel incorporating a drum brake, while the fully enclosed cockpit features a forward opening Plexi-glass canopy raised by a gas strut, with a semi-supine seat incorporating the standard fuel tank and filled with expanded aluminium foil. The aircraft has an integral dual-charged ballistic recovery system designed by the manufacturer.

Charles concedes that 'construction and development were not without difficulties', particularly with the power pack. The *Stratos* was originally designed for a normal two-blade pusher propeller but the unreliability of the chosen power plants prompted a switch to a ducted fan with three-cylinder Konig radial engine.

Another interesting point is that, to the best of our knowledge, the *Stratos* is the only ultralight which can be transported rigged, simply by turning it sideways and loading it onto a trailer. The flight test programme began in January 1985, but we must point out that the performance figures below are calculations rather than test results. If they are confirmed in practice Charles will indeed have created a remarkable aircraft.

The projected price of the machine is A$15,000.

EXTERNAL DIMENSIONS & AREAS - Length overall 7.9 ft, 2.42 m. Height overall 3.1 ft, 0.93 m. Wing span 16.6 ft, 5.06 m (forward wing); 17.4 ft, 5.31 m (rear wing). Chord at root NC (forward wing); 2.5 ft, 0.75 m (rear wing). Chord at tip NC (forward wing); 2.1 ft, 0.65 m (rear wing). Dihedral NC (forward wing); 3.5° (rear wing). Sweepback 30° (forward wing); NC (rear wing). Fin height 2.2 ft, 0.66 m. Forward wing area 36.6 ft^2, 3.4 m^2. Rear wing area 39.9 ft^2, 3.7 m^2. Total wing area 76.4 ft^2, 7.1 m^2. Total aileron area 4.8 ft^2, 0.45 m^2. Fin area 8.6 ft^2, 0.80 m^2. Rudder area 2.2 ft^2, 0.20 m^2. Total elevator area 3.1 ft^2, 0.29 m^2. Aspect ratio 7.5/1 (forward wing); 7.6/1 (rear wing). Wheelbase 4.9 ft, 1.50 m. Tailwheel diameter overall 8 inch, 21 cm. Main wheel diameter overall 10 inch, 26 cm.

POWER PLANT - Konig SC430 engine. Max power 26 hp at 4200 rpm. Ducted fan diameter and pitch 24x* inch, 0.61x* m. No reduction. Max static thrust NC. Power per unit area 0.34 hp/ft^2, 3.7 hp/m^2. Fuel capacity 5.8 US gal, 4.8 Imp gal, 22.0 litre.

WEIGHTS & LOADINGS - Empty weight 172 lb, 78 kg. Max take-off weight 379 lb, 172 kg. Payload 207 lb, 94 kg. Max wing loading 4.96 lb/ft^2, 24.2 kg/m^2. Max power loading 14.6 lb/hp, 6.6 kg/hp. Load factors +6.0, -4.0 recommended; +9.0, -6.0 ultimate.

PERFORMANCE** - Max level speed 137 mph, 220 kph. Never exceed speed 168 mph, 270 kph. Max cruising speed 115 mph, 185 kph. Economic cruising speed 106 mph, 170 kph. Stalling speed (with power on) 32 mph, 52 kph. Max climb rate at sea level 830 ft/min, 4.2 m/s. Best glide ratio with power off 19/1 at NC speed. Service ceiling 14,800 ft, 4500 m. Range at average cruising speed 423 mile, 680 km. Other data NC.

*Ground adjustable for pitch.

**Under unspecified test conditions.

POUR LE MERITE

Pour le Merite Ultralights, Lot 2, Whroo Graytown Road, Adlerfeld, Via Nagambie; tel 058 561622. Designer/builder: Werner Bekker.

POUR LE MERITE *BLUE MAX SABRE IK and SABRE IR*

(Three-axis)

Single-seat single-engined high-wing monoplane with conventional three-axis control. Wing has unswept leading and trailing edges, and constant chord; cruciform tail. Pitch control by fully flying tail; yaw control by fin-mounted rudder; roll control by full-span ailerons; control inputs through stick for pitch/roll and pedals for yaw. Wing braced from below by struts; wing profile NC; 100% double-surface. Undercarriage has three wheels in tail-dragger formation; coil-spring suspension on tailwheel and axle-flex suspension on main wheels. No ground steering; castoring tailwheel. No brakes. Aluminium-alloy tube airframe, with pod. Engine mounted at wing height, driving tractor propeller.

Production status: prototype.

GENERAL - As in the USA, one design dominated the early Australian ultralight scene with various clones following. The Americans had Bob Lovejoy's *Quicksilver*, while in

Rob Fox

The first Blue Max Sabre 1K *takes shape.*

Australia in 1976 the one to copy was Col Winton's *Cricket* which later became the *Jackeroo.* Its genes can be found today in the *Bunyip, Tyro* and the *Blue Max Sabre.*

When Werner Bekker flew his twin-engined *Jackeroo* 1270 mile (2045 km) across the Nullarbor desert from Kalgoolie to Adelaide, he was so impressed with this superb little basic aircraft that when it went out of production he decided to build on the concept and include a number of new features. The idea was to create a more efficient and reliable aircraft for long cross-country flights, something which would take Werner's Kalgoolie-Adelaide flight in its stride. With a wide track undercarriage and big balloon tyres, the *Blue Max Sabre* is expected to cope easily with rough, unprepared landing fields. Other changes include the choice of engine; the four-cylinder Konig radial is used on the prototype (detailed below), but the 503 Rotax will be offered as an option, the aircraft name acquiring a *1K* or *1R* suffix depending on which is fitted. The tail feathers differ in shape and size and a large pod to take the pilot out of the elements is a standard feature. The main airframe is constructed from rectangular-section aluminium-alloy tube bolted and TIG welded. The main spar comprises double upper and lower tubes and there is a single trailing-edge tube. Ribs, leading edge and tips are of glass-fibre, with diagonal cables bracing the bones of the wings which are covered with synthetic fabric and dope finished. The tailplane is also built of aluminium tube, with glass-fibre ribs.

Test flying of the Konig-powered prototype was due to start in April 1985, projected prices being A$8750 for either version.

EXTERNAL DIMENSIONS & AREAS - Length overall 14.8 ft, 4.50 m. Height overall 6.4 ft, 1.95 m. Wing span 27.0 ft, 8.23 m. Constant chord 4.4 ft, 1.34 m. Dihedral 2.5°. Sweepback 0°. Tailplane span 7.5 ft, 2.30 m. Total wing area 122 ft^2, 11.3 m^2. Total aileron area 14.0 ft^2, 1.30 m^2. Total elevator area 12.4 ft^2, 1.15 m^2. Aspect ratio 6.0/1. Wheel track 9.8 ft, 3.00 m. Wheelbase 6.0 ft, 1.83 m. Tailwheel diameter overall 3 inch, 8 cm. Main wheels diameter overall 13 inch, 32 cm. Other data NC.

POWER PLANT - Konig SD570 engine. Max power 28 hp at 4200 rpm. Propeller diameter and pitch 51x* inch, 1.30x* m. Toothed-belt reduction, ratio 1.8/1. Max static thrust NC. Power per unit area 0.23 hp/ft^2, 2.5 hp/m^2. Fuel capacity 5.0 US gal, 4.2 Imp gal, 18.9 litre.

WEIGHTS & LOADINGS - Empty weight 254 lb, 115 kg. Max take-off weight 495 lb, 225 kg. Payload 241 lb, 109 kg. Max wing loading 4.06 lb/ft^2, 19.9 kg/m^2. Max power loading 17.7 lb/hp, 8.0 kg/hp. Load factors +4.2, -2.8 recommended; NC ultimate.

PERFORMANCE -** Max level speed 60 mph, 97 kph. Never exceed speed 80 mph, 129 kph. Max cruising speed 55 mph, 88 kph. Economic cruising speed 50 mph, 80 kph. Stalling speed 30 mph, 48 kph. Max climb rate at sea level 700 ft/min, 3.6 m/s. Min sink rate NC. Best glide ratio with power off 10/1 at 35 mph, 56 kph. Take-off distance 100 ft, 30 m. Landing distance 150 ft, 46 m. Service ceiling 15,000 ft, 4570 m. Range at average cruising speed 300 mile, 483 km. Noise level NC.

*Adjustable for pitch.

**Under unspecified test conditions.

RESURGAM

Resurgam Aviation, 59 Sierra Drive, Tamborine N 4272; tel 075 451762. Plans and kits from: Resurgam Aviation, PO Box 6, Bundarra, 2359 New South Wales; tel 2382 06712 (M). Proprietor: Celia Bedson.

RESURGAM *RESURGAM MKII*
(Three-axis)

Single-seat single-engined high-wing monoplane with conventional three-axis control. Wing has unswept leading and trailing edges, and constant chord; conventional tail. Pitch control by fully flying tail; yaw control by fin-mounted rudder; roll control by 40%-span ailerons; control inputs through stick for pitch/roll and pedals for yaw. Wing braced from below by struts; wing profile NACA 4415; 100% double-surface. Undercarriage has three wheels in tricycle formation; coil-spring suspension on nosewheel and glass-fibre suspension on main wheels. Push-right go-right nosewheel steering connected to yaw control. No brakes. Wood airframe, partially enclosed. Engine mounted at wing height, driving pusher propeller.

Production status: current, over 40 completed.

GENERAL - Improbable though it may sound, the *Resurgam* was designed by Gordon Bedson back in 1948, to be powered by a JAP engine. Propeller manufacturer Bedson resurrected his design with the advent of the ultralight and it has stood the test of time very well, though sadly Gordon is no longer around to witness the continued success of his creation, as he was killed in 1984 on the maiden flight of a two-seat prototype, the *Magra*. The company is now being run by his widow Celia.

Gordon Bedson flying the Resurgam MkII *at the 1984 Mangalore airshow.*

The *Resurgam MkII* differs from earlier versions in that the triangulated alloy tube rear fuselage has been replaced by a single tube. Ailerons are standard on the *MkII*, whereas earlier models allowed a choice of spoilers or ailerons. The wing centre section is attached to the fuselage, with the wings located by six pip-pins and supported by a single strut. An unusual feature is that derigging can be accomplished without disconnecting any control cables. The wing comprises a single spruce and ply spar to which ply/foam composite ribs are epoxied and reinforced with glass-fibre. Foam is used for the leading and trailing edges, the former being covered with glass-fibre and the latter with plywood.

The *Resurgam* was designed specifically as a homebuilt and has been constructed not only in Australia but also in four overseas countries. Builders have formed themselves into ROBA, the Resurgam Owners & Builders Association, and are brought up to date continuously by a comprehensive bi-monthly news report.

The basic *Resurgam* is designed for building from tried and tested materials - spruce and plywood - and the average homebuilder needs about 350 h to complete the task. For those who lack the time for this type of manufacture, ready-built assemblies are offered, including glass-fibre fuselage shell, leading edges, ribs, spars, control assemblies, nosewheel struts, seat and main undercarriage. The latter is built from a laminated composite of 0.125 inch (3 mm) plywood layers shaped to an aerofoil and covered with layers of Kevlar and glass-fibre. Using these components, which cost about A$3000, building time is cut to some 200 h. Plans cost A$95.

Some earlier aircraft used the 320 cc Skylark engine, but now there is a choice of three European units, the cheapest being the attractive French JPX PUL425 twin which develops 22 bhp at 4400 rpm. This engine gives 141 lb (64 kg) static thrust, weighs 37 lb (17 kg) complete, is available with electric start and costs approximately A$1250. Konig engines are also offered, either the SC430 three-cylinder 24 hp unit or the SD570 with 30 bhp, both with standard electric start and optional reduction drive. Prices range from A$1240 ex-factory for the direct-drive three-cylinder to A$1858 for the four-cylinder with reduction. All come with mountings, exhaust, ignition wiring loom, throttle and choke levers with flexible controls, but props are extra, various two and three-blade adjustable-

Rob Fox

pitch devices being available for A$235-330. Other engines have been considered but none of sufficient power have proved light enough to meet the *ANO 95-10* requirements. Our data below refers to a Resurgam MkII with SD570 engine and typical prop.

EXTERNAL DIMENSIONS & AREAS - Length overall 19.5 ft, 5.94 m. Height overall 7.5 ft, 2.29 m. Wing span 30.0 ft, 9.14 m. Constant chord 4.0 ft, 1.22 m. Dihedral 2°. Sweepback 0°. Elevator span 8.0 ft, 2.44 m. Fin height 4.0 ft, 1.22 m. Total wing area 120 ft², 11.1 m². Total aileron area 12.0 ft², 1.11 m². Fin area 4.0 ft², 0.37 m². Rudder area 0.55 ft², m². Total elevator area 10.0 ft², 0.93 m². Aspect ratio 7.5/1. Wheel track 5.3 ft, 1.63 m. Wheelbase 5.8 ft, 1.78 m. Nosewheel diameter overall 10 inch, 25 cm. Main wheels diameter overall 10 inch, 25 cm.

POWER PLANT - Konig SD570 engine. Max power 28 hp at 4200 rpm. Propeller diameter and pitch 51x32 inch, 1.30x0.81 m. Toothed-belt reduction, ratio 1.8/1. Max static thrust 180 lb, 82 kg. Power per unit area 0.23 hp/ft², 2.5 hp/m². Fuel capacity 5.0 US gal, 4.2 Imp gal, 19.0 litre.

WEIGHTS & LOADINGS - Empty weight 220 lb, 100 kg. Max take-off weight 440 lb, 200 kg. Payload 220 lb, 100 kg. Max wing loading 3.67 lb/ft², 18.0 kg/m². Max power loading 15.7 lb/hp, 7.1 kg/hp. Load factors +6.0, -NC recommended; +9.0, -NC ultimate.

PERFORMANCE* - Never exceed speed 72 mph, 116 kph. Max cruising speed 56 mph, 90 kph. Stalling speed 31 mph, 50 kph. Max climb rate at sea level 500 ft/min, 2.5 m/s. Best glide ratio with power off 14/1 at NC speed. Take-off distance 200 ft, 61 m. Landing distance 150 ft, 46 m. Range at average cruising speed 150 mile, 241 km. Other data NC.

*Under unspecified test conditions.

SKYLARK

Skylark, Lot 7, Whiteside Road, Officer, Victoria 3809; tel 707 2076. Designer/builder: Ron Lang.

SKYLARK *SKYLARK*
(Three-axis)

Single-seat single-engined high-wing monoplane with conventional three-axis control. Wing has unswept leading and trailing edges, and constant chord; cruciform tail. Pitch control by elevator on tail; yaw control by fin-mounted rudder; roll control by full-span ailerons; control inputs through stick for pitch/roll and pedals for yaw. Wing braced from above by kingpost and cables, from below by cables; wing profile NC; 100% double-surface. Undercarriage has three wheels in tail-dragger formation; axle-flex suspension on all wheels. Push-right go-right tailwheel steering connected to yaw control. No brakes. Aluminium-alloy tube airframe, completely open. Engine mounted at wing height, driving tractor propeller.

Production status: current, 3 completed.

GENERAL - Ron Lang has been manufacturing the Skylark 320 25 hp horizontally opposed two-stroke engine for eight years, and the *Skylark* ultralight is designed specifically to mate with that engine. It is built on tried and tested tube-and-Dacron lines with the emphasis on strengthening the airframe without overburdening the whole structure.

Lang felt the market was moving away from the basic ultralight concept and that the aircraft entering the market were far too sophisticated and expensive. His straightfor-

ward *Skylark* is a high-wing cable-braced three-axis machine with the Skylark engine mounted above the main fuselage boom and the large pulley of the reduction drive centred on the boom. The double-tuned exhausts pass rearward over the mainplane to deflect noise upwards. The wing has leading- and trailing-edge spars of alloy tube and compression struts of the same material. Preformed ribs of 1.2 cm (0.47 inch) diameter tube are rivetted to the spars and the wing is braced diagonally with cables, its frame being covered by stretching presewn Ripstop Dacron over it, as with the tailplane and full-span ailerons. The *Skylark* is available as a complete or part kit, but since building time is only around 30 h, complete kits have proved more popular. Price: A$3500.

EXTERNAL DIMENSIONS & AREAS - Length overall 14.1 ft, 4.30 m. Height overall 6.6 ft, 2.00 m. Wing span 27.9 ft, 8.50 m. Constant chord 3.9 ft, 1.20 m. Dihedral 5°. Sweepback 0°. Tailplane span 6.6 ft, 2.00 m. Fin height 3.3 ft, 1.00 m. Total wing area 112 ft^2, 10.4 m^2. Aspect ratio 6.9/1. Other data NC.

POWER PLANT - Skylark 320 engine. Max power 25 hp at 5000 rpm. Propeller diameter and pitch 48x27 inch, 1.21x0.68 m. V-belt reduction, ratio 2.1/1. Max static thrust NC. Power per unit area 0.22 hp/ft^2, 2.4 hp/m^2. Fuel capacity 2.6 US gal, 2.2 Imp gal, 10.0 litre.

WEIGHTS & LOADINGS - Empty weight 195 lb, 88 kg. Other data NC.

PERFORMANCE* - Max level speed 48 mph, 77 kph. Never exceed speed 55 mph, 88 kph. Max cruising speed 46 mph, 74 kph. Economic cruising speed 35 mph, 56 kph. Stalling speed 25 mph, 40 kph. Max climb rate at sea level 400 ft/min, 2.0 m/s. Take-off distance 100 ft, 30 m. Range at average cruising speed 70 mile, 113 km. Other data NC.

*Under unspecified test conditions.

SPORT AIRCRAFT

Sport Aircraft, PO Box 101, Hahndorf, South Australia 5245; tel 08388 7534. Managing director: Reg Schwartz. Designer/pilot: John Kittle.

SPORT AIRCRAFT *SUPA PUP II* (Three-axis)

Single-seat single-engined high-wing monoplane with conventional three-axis control. Wing has unswept leading and trailing edges, and constant chord; flaps fitted; conventional tail. Pitch control by elevator on tail; yaw control by fin-mounted rudder; roll control by 35%-span ailerons; control inputs through stick for pitch/roll and pedals for yaw. Wing braced from below by struts; wing profile NC; 100% double-surface. Undercarriage has three wheels in tail-dragger formation; glass-fibre suspension on tailwheel and torsion-bar suspension on main wheels. No ground steering, castoring tailwheel. Brakes NC. Steel-tube airframe, totally enclosed. Engine mounted below wing, driving tractor propeller.

Production status: current, number completed NC.

GENERAL - Reg Schwartz and John Kittle have developed a number of vastly different ultralights for display at

The Supa Pup II: *latest models have a slightly different tail from this example, with a fin and rudder change to increase their resemblance to the* Cub.

successive Sport Aircraft Association of Australia Mangalore conventions, the Australian 'Oshkosh' held each Easter. In 1981 their high-wing pusher *Sundowner* with lattice rear fuselage like an early *Resurgam* earned them top honours, and at the same time they were also busy flight testing a 22 hp 81 mph low-wing all wooden monoplane, the *Swift*.

However, both designs were shelved with the appearance the following year of their neat, chunky Piper *Cub*-styled *Supa Pup*, the first Australian ultralight with 'real aeroplane' appearance and handling. This machine converted many aviators who had hitherto been sceptical about ultralights, and a number were ordered and built before the pair returned the following Easter with the *Supa Pup II*, a sleek tailwheel machine evoking images of a baby *Citarbria Decathlon*. Powered by a four-stroke Global engine, the *Supa Pup* made many onlookers think a 'big boy' had strayed into the ultralight park.

Since then, four years' development and A$200,000 have brought the *Supa Pup II* close to being a fully certified aircraft, and test pilot Kittle has made non-stop flights in excess of 5 h to prove its capabilities and comfort. The company claims the machine should enjoy a service life of at least 25 years.

Fuselage construction accuracy is maintained with a fully rotating jig for welding the three sizes of 531-grade steel tubing. Wings are fabricated from pressed alloy ribs with a D-section leading edge, tube trailing edge and fabricated main spar, the frame being Dacron-covered and dope finished. Stainless-steel rods secure the tailplane, and there are aircraft bearings in all the bell cranks, ailerons being pushrod actuated and the rudder and elevator cable-controlled.

The machine is available ready to fly for A$12,940 or as a kit for A$10,340. Instead of the Global, customers may order a 45 hp Rotax 447 with 2.6/1 gear reduction, which reduces prices by A$640, but our data below refers to the standard version.

EXTERNAL DIMENSIONS & AREAS - Length overall 18.3 ft, 5.56 m. Height overall 5.8 ft, 1.75 m. Wing span 27.3 ft, 8.33 m. Sweepback 0°. Total wing area 105 ft^2, 9.8 m^2. Aspect ratio 7.1/1. Other data NC.

POWER PLANT - Global engine. Max power 35 hp at NC rpm. Propeller diameter and pitch 54x27 inch, 1.37x0.69 m. No reduction. Max static thrust NC. Power per unit area 0.33 hp/ft^2, 3.6 hp/m^2. Fuel capacity 9.6 US gal, 8.0 Imp gal, 36.3 litre.

WEIGHTS & LOADINGS - Empty weight 380 lb, 172 kg. Max take-off weight 630 lb, 286 kg. Payload 250 lb, 113 kg. Max wing loading 6.00 lb/ft^2, 29.2 kg/m^2. Max power loading 18.0 lb/hp, 8.2 kg/hp. Load factors +6.0, -4.0 recommended; NC ultimate.

PERFORMANCE* - Max level speed 100 mph, 161 kph. Never exceed speed 110 mph, 177 kph. Max cruising speed 90 mph, 145 kph. Stalling speed 32 mph, 51 kph. Max climb rate at sea level 800 ft/min, 4.1 m/s. Take-off distance 350 ft, 107 m. Landing distance 600 ft, 183 m. Range at average cruising speed** 300 mile, 483 km. Other data NC.

*Under unspecified test conditions.
**Without using 30 min reserve.

SV AIRCRAFT

SV Aircraft Pty Ltd, PO Box 85, Locksley Road, Nagambie; tel 057942 711. Workshop foreman: Glen Lyon.

SV AIRCRAFT *SV8 BANDIT*

(Three-axis)

Single-seat single-engined high-wing monoplane with conventional three-axis control. Wing has unswept leading and trailing edges, and constant chord; flaps fitted; V-tail. Pitch/yaw control by ruddervator; roll control by 90%-span ailerons; control inputs through stick for pitch/roll and pedals for yaw. Cantilever wing; wing profile SV419; 100% double-surface. Undercarriage has two wheels in tandem plus additional wheels on wing tips; rubber suspension on tailwheel and no suspension on main wheel. Push-right go-right main wheel steering connected to yaw control. Brake on main wheel. Composite-construction airframe, totally enclosed. Engine mounted at wing height, driving pusher propeller.

Production status: current, 6 completed.

GENERAL - Sander Veenstra was involved in the Australian ultralight scene right at the start in the late '70s and like many others he began with the *Scout*, converting it to a twin-engined machine using Victa lawnmower motors. Subsequently he built several *Mitchell Wings* and *Crickets* and early in 1980 started work on his own design,

the *Bluebird*, a high-wing, high-boom strut-braced pusher aircraft of tube and doped polyfibre construction, using a cockpit of gussetted alloy tube and a wrap-round screen. From this came the *Thermite*, a sleek machine with bullet-like fuselage and one-piece polycarbon canopy which we illustrated in our first edition on p43. This glass-fibre/aluminium tube aircraft had a high boom, alloy tube spars, welded primary structure, foam ribs laminated with glass-fibre, a preformed glass-fibre wing skin, seven-eighths span ailerons, and an Avon Sabre drop tank.

A production run of 14 was commenced, but it is not clear how many were actually built before construction ceased in early 1984, for Veenstra quickly tired of production aircraft in favour of one-off purpose-built machines.

A sailplane pilot at heart with a passion for motorgliders, he made the V-tail his trade mark, along with monowheel landing gear and direct-drive props which he carved himself. He also stuck with the Robin EC25PS engine.

Sander's next production aircraft was the *SV8 Bandit*, a high-performance clipped-wing motorglider bearing an obvious resemblance to the *Thermite,* but using an upright V-tail as opposed to an inverted one. Early examples used a welded aluminium-alloy tube structure, but this was replaced for weight and cost reasons by a Kevlar/glass-fibre fuselage, though the tubular main spar was retained. The *SV8 Bandit,* which costs A$7500 complete, was followed into production by the *SVXI Farmate*, but around a dozen other designs have been built as prototypes. These range from the twin-engine two-seat *SV10 Tardis* to the *SV7* - a 43 ft (13 m) span motorglider - and an ultra lightweight sailplane with *Bandit* lines for hang gliding.

Tragically, on 6 March 1985 Veenstra was killed making the second test flight of yet another prototype, an open frame lightweight machine with tail-dragger undercarriage and, for the first time, a reduction drive. He had always built

Rob Fox

Rob Fox

The SV8 Bandit in flight, with (inset), Sander Veenstra at the controls. The SV7 motorglider is in the background.

to the upper weight limit and this was his first major diversion from the 'strong and heavy' philosophy. He had not flown an open type for many years and it is thought this may have contributed to the accident, in which he stalled at 80 ft (24 m) after take-off.

The fate of his company was unknown at the time of writing but his widow Judy says she wants production to continue.

EXTERNAL DIMENSIONS & AREAS - Length overall 16.4 ft, 5.00 m. Height overall 3.3 ft, 1.00 m. Wing span 26.2 ft, 8.00 m. Constant chord 2.9 ft, 0.87 m. Dihedral 0°. Sweepback 0°. Tailplane span 5.7 ft, 1.75 m. Inclined fixed surface height 3.8 ft, 1.15 m. Total wing area 73 ft^2, 6.8 m^2. Total aileron area 10.2 ft^2, 0.95 m^2. Inclind fixed surface area NC. Rudder area 15.6 ft^2, 1.45 m^2. Aspect ratio 9.4/1. Wheelbase 10.2 ft, 3.10 m. Tailwheel diameter overall 3 inch, 8 cm. Main wheels diameter overall 10 inch, 25 cm.

POWER PLANT - Robin EC25PS engine. Max power 18 hp at 6000 rpm. Propeller diameter and pitch 30x18 inch, 0.76x0.46 m. No reduction. Max static thrust NC. Power per unit area 0.25 hp/ft^2, 2.6 hp/m^2. Fuel capacity 7.1 US gal, 5.9 Imp gal, 27.0 litre.

WEIGHTS & LOADINGS - Empty weight 225 lb, 102 kg. Max take-off weight 475 lb, 215 kg. Payload 250 lb, 113 kg. Max wing loading 6.51 lb/ft^2, 31.6 kg/m^2. Max power loading 26.4 lb/hp, 12.0 kg/hp. Load factors +5.0, -5.0 recommended; +7.0, -6.0 ultimate.

PERFORMANCE* - Max level speed 100 mph, 161 kph. Never exceed speed 120 mph, 193 kph. Max cruising speed 75 mph, 121 kph. Economic cruising speed 65 mph, 105 kph. Stalling speed 35 mph, 56 kph. Max climb rate at sea level 500 ft/min, 2.5 m/s. Min sink rate 250 ft/min at 45 mph, 1.3 m/s at 72 kph. Best glide ratio with power off 20/1 at 55 mph, 88 kph. Take-off distance 500 ft, 152 m. Landing distance 700 ft, 213 m. Service ceiling 8500 ft, 2590 m. Range at average cruising speed 300 mile, 483 km. Noise level NC.

*Under the following test conditions - Airfield altitude 450 ft, 137 m. Ground temperature 68°F, 20°C. Ground pressure NC. Ground windspeed 10 mph, 16 kph. Test payload 210 lb, 95 kg.

Rob Fox

SV AIRCRAFT *SVX1 FARMATE*
(Three-axis)

Summary as SV8 Bandit *except: Wing braced from below by struts. Undercarriage has three wheels in tail-dragger formation; rubber suspension on tailwheel and leaf-spring suspension on main wheels. Push-right go-right tailwheel steering connected to yaw control. Brakes on main wheels.*

Production status: current, 9 completed.

GENERAL - The *SVXI Farmate* is of essentially similar construction to the *Bandit* but caters for those who want to combine the sleek lines and performance of baby motor-gliders with the attributes of a more conventiaonal ultra-light, namely the ability to operate from short, rough fields and carry equipment and gear. The main differences are the conventional tailwheel undercarriage and the addition of strut-bracing to the wings, which are two-piece, pre-formed glass-fibre shells over laminated foam and glass-fibre ribs, with alloy tube main spars and a single strut each side. All fittings are stainless-steel.

Price ready to fly is A$7500 in standard form, as detailed below, but at extra cost customers can have a poly V-belt 1.7/1 reduction drive fitted.

EXTERNAL DIMENSIONS & AREAS - See *SV8 Bandit* except: Height overall 3.6 ft, 1.10 m. Constant chord 3.3 ft, 1.00 m. Dihedral 2°. Total wing area 84 ft², 7.8 m². Aspect

Farmates *on the production line. For another illustration, see colour section.*

ratio 8.2/1. Wheel track 3.9 ft, 1.20 m. Main wheels diameter overall 10 inch, 25 cm.

POWER PLANT - See *SV8 Bandit* except: Propeller diameter and pitch 32x18 inch, 0.81x0.46 m. Max static thrust 100 lb, 45 kg. Power per unit area 0.21 hp/ft², 2.3 hp/m².

WEIGHTS & LOADINGS - Empty weight 265 lb, 120 kg. Max take-off weight 500 lb, 227 kg. Payload 235 lb, 107 kg. Max wing loading 5.95 lb/ft², 29.1 kg/m². Max power loading 27.8 lb/hp, 12.6 kg/hp. Load factors +5.0, -4.0 recommended; +7.0, -5.5 ultimate.

PERFORMANCE* - Max level speed 85 mph, 137 kph. Never exceed speed 100 mph, 161 kph. Max cruising speed 65 mph, 105 kph. Economic cruising speed 55 mph, 88 kph. Stalling speed 35 mph, 56 kph. Max climb rate at sea level 400 ft/min, 2.0 m/s. Min sink rate 300 ft/min at 45 mph, 1.5 m/s at 72 kph. Best glide ratio with power off 10/1 at 45 mph, 72 kph. Take-off distance 500 ft, 152 m. Landing distance 400 ft, 122 m. Service ceiling 5000 ft, 1520 m. Range at average cruising speed 250 mile, 402 km. Noise level NC.

**Under the following test conditions -* Airfield altitude 450 ft, 137 m. Ground temperature 68°F, 20°C. Ground pressure NC. Ground windspeed 8 mph, 13 kph. Test payload 200 lb, 91 kg.

SV AIRCRAFT *TARDIS* (Three-axis)

Side-by-side two-seat twin-engined high-wing monoplane with conventional three-axis control. Wing has unswept leading and trailing edges, and constant chord; conventional tail. Pitch control by fully flying tail; yaw control by fin-mounted rudder; roll control by 90%-span ailerons; control inputs through stick for pitch/roll and pedals for yaw. Wing braced from below by struts; wing profile SV419; 100% double-surface. Undercarriage has three wheels in tail-dragger formation; rubber suspension on tailwheel and leaf-spring suspension on main wheels. Push-right go-right tailwheel steering connected to yaw control. No brakes. Composite-construction airframe, totally enclosed. Engines mounted below wing, driving pusher propellers.

Production status: see text.

GENERAL - The *Tardis* is essentially a larger, two-seat version of the discontinued *Thermite* (see *SV8 Bandit*) from which it differs in having twin engines and a conventional tail. The twin 244 cc Robins use belt reduction drives with pusher props mounted behind and just below the trailing edge on outriggers from the fuselage. Entry to the cockpit is from either side as the polycarbon canopy is hinged along its centre line.

The *Tardis* was built as a one-off to prove the two-seat concept and at the time of writing is mothballed pending finalisation of Department of Aviation two-seat regulations. We include it, however, because unlike the other Veenstra one-offs this machine may well be put into production during the currency of this book, projected price being around A$10,000.

EXTERNAL DIMENSIONS & AREAS - Length overall 20.3 ft, 6.20 m. Height overall 3.9 ft, 1.20 m. Wing span 36.1 ft, 11.00 m. Constant chord 3.3 ft, 1.00 m. Dihedral 2°. Sweepback 0°. Tailplane span 7.5 ft, 2.30 m. Fin height 3.6 ft, 1.10 m. Total wing area 116 ft², 10.8 m². Total aileron area 16.1 ft², 1.50 m². Fin area 6.5 ft², 0.60 m². Rudder area 3.8 ft², 0.35 m². Total elevator area 12.9 ft², 1.2 m². Aspect ratio 11.2/1. Wheel track 4.9 ft, 1.50 m. Wheelbase NC. Tailwheel diameter overall 4 inch, 10 cm. Main wheels diameter overall 13 inch, 32 cm.

POWER PLANT - Two Robin EC25PS engines. Max power 18 hp each at 6000 rpm. Propellers diameter and pitch 40x30 inch, 1.02x0.76 m. Poly V-belt reduction, ratio 1.7/1. Max static thrust 260 lb, 118 kg. Power per unit area 0.31 hp/ft², 3.3 hp/m². Fuel capacity 14.5 US gal, 12.1 Imp gal, 55.0 litre.

WEIGHTS & LOADINGS - Empty weight 485 lb, 220 kg. Max take-off weight 900 lb, 408 kg. Payload 415 lb, 188 kg. Max wing loading 7.76 lb/ft², 37.8 kg/m². Max power loading 25.0 lb/hp, 11.3 kg/hp. Load factors +4.0, -2.5 recommended; +6.5, -4.0 ultimate.

PERFORMANCE* - Max level speed 70 mph, 113 kph. Never exceed speed 100 mph, 161 kph. Max cruising speed 65 mph, 105 kph. Economic cruising speed 60 mph, 97 kph. Stalling speed 42 mph, 68 kph. Max climb rate at sea level 350 ft/min, 1.8 m/s. Best glide ratio with power off 10/1 at 50 mph, 80 kph. Take-off distance 450 ft, 137 m. Landing distance 650 ft, 198 m. Range at average cruising speed 200 mile, 322 km. Other data NC.

*Under the following test conditions - Airfield altitude 450 ft, 137 m. Ground temperature 72°F, 22°C. Ground pressure NC. Ground windspeed NC. Test payload 390 lb, 177 kg.

THRUSTER AIRCRAFT

Thruster Aircraft Australia Pty Ltd, 458 The Boulevarde, Kirrawee, New South Wales 2232; tel 02542 1990 and 02524 5914; tx AA 73953. General manager: David Belton. Designer/production: Steve Cohen.

European and Middle Eastern agent: Thruster Aircraft (UK) Ltd, Barton, Bolventor, Launceston, Cornwall PL15 7TZ, England; tel 056686 514 and 08406 517. Director: Ian Stokes.

THRUSTER AIRCRAFT *THRUSTER 85*
(Three-axis)

Single-seat single-engined high-wing monoplane with conventional three-axis control. Wing has unswept leading and trailing edges, and constant chord; cruciform tail. Pitch control by elevator on tail; yaw control by fin-mounted rudder; roll control by full-span ailerons; control inputs through stick for pitch/roll and pedals for yaw. Wing braced from below by struts; wing profile NC; 100% double-surface. Undercarriage has three wheels in tail-dragger formation; axle-flex suspension on all wheels. Push-right go-right tailwheel steering connected to yaw control. No brakes. Aluminium-alloy tube airframe, with pod. Engine mounted at wing height, driving tractor propeller.

Production status: current, see text for number completed.

GENERAL - The *Thruster* first appeared in 1983 but was not designer-builder Steve Cohen's first foray into the ultralight industry. Cohen successfully manufactured and flew hang gliders for many years before creating his *Yellow Thing*, a rigid-winged pusher aircraft which was born out of a joint venture with Hawker De Havilland but proved too complicated for mass production.

His first production ultralight was the rigid wing *Stolero* with a 98 cc kart engine in tractor configuration, Robin singles and twins being later adopted. Then came the *Condor*, of which production ceased in 1980, and in 1981 Cohen designed the *Avenger* against the strong rumour that the Air Navigation Order would change to allow a higher weight limit. Much of the *Yellow Thing* experience was employed in this aircraft, which had alloy-tube spars, glass-fibre ribs and leading edge and an open bolted alloy-tube airframe. This was further developed as the *Avenger*

Rob Fox

Designer Steve Cohen warms up a Thruster 85 *with Rotax 377.*

II in 1982 with a fully enclosed cockpit and 440 Robin, but when it became obvious that *ANO 95-22* for 'heavy' ultralights was still a long way off, the project was mothballed.

The *Thruster* was born to comply with the existing *ANO 95-10* and first flew in November 1982, 47 having been built by March '83, of which 15 were exported to New Zealand. With the company growing, David Belton joined to handle marketing and leave Steve free to develop the *Thruster*, the firm being renamed Ultralight Aviation before changing again, to its present title, in 1985. Production is now running at three aircraft per week.

All *Thrusters* feature a batten-framed aerofoil section and double-surface wings which can be racked on removal to facilitate rigging, plus a glass-fibre pod with polycarbon screen. The current version, the *Thruster 85*, is the result of three years' design updating in the course of production and differs from the original model in having a smaller span and length and in having a Rotax engine with gear reduction instead of the earlier belt system.

Instrumentation including ASI and tachometer is standard as are wing bags and clear anodising of all aluminium alloy. The aircraft is available in three ready-to-fly models depending on the choice of engine, the Rotax 277 (A$6450), 377 (A$6950) or 503 (A$7250), the latter being recommended for use with floats, which are available for an extra A$950. All three versions are dimensionally identical,

but we have no other data valid for the 277 model. Our figures below are refer to the 377-engined machine; where different, data for the 503 is shown in parentheses.

EXTERNAL DIMENSIONS & AREAS - Length overall 17.4 ft, 5.30 m. Height overall 6.2 ft, 1.90 m. Wing span 25.5 ft, 7.78 m. Constant chord 5.3 ft, 1.61 m. Sweepback 0°. Total wing area 135 ft², 12.5 m². Aspect ratio 4.8/1. Other data NC.

POWER PLANT - Rotax 377 (Roax 503) engine. Max power 40(50) hp at NC rpm. Propeller diameter and pitch NC. Gear reduction, ratio 2.6/1. Max static thrust NC. Power per unit area 0.30(0.37) hp/ft², 3.2(4.0) hp/m². Fuel capacity 6.6 US gal, 5.5 Imp gal, 25.0 litre.

WEIGHTS & LOADINGS - Empty weight 298(309) lb, 135(140) kg. Max take-off weight 595(617) lb, 270(280) kg. Payload 298(309) lb, 135(140) kg. Max wing loading 4.41(4.57) lb/ft², 21.6(22.4) kg/m². Max power loading 14.9(12.3) lb/hp, 6.8(5.6) kg/hp. Load factors +4.0, -2.0 recommended; NC ultimate.

PERFORMANCE* - Max level speed 77(81) mph, 124 (130) kph. Never exceed speed 92 mph, 148 kph. Economic cruising speed 60(63) mph, 97(101) kph. Stalling speed 31(37) mph, 50(60) kph. Max climb rate at sea level 800(1000) ft/min, 4.1(5.1) m/s. Range at average cruising speed 190(NC) mile, 306(NC) km. Other data NC.

*Under unspecified test conditions.

THRUSTER AIRCRAFT
THRUSTER UTILITY (Three-axis)

Summary as Thruster 85 *except: No pod.*

Production status: see text.

GENERAL - The *Thruster 85 Utlity*, which we detail below, and *Thruster Twoplace*, which we list separately, have both been produced in anticipation of some eagerly awaited legislation. Not wishing to be left behind when the Department of Aviation and the AUF eventually agree on the Air Navigation Order for ultralights weighing more than 115 kg (254 lb) and for two-seat trainers, the company has gained experience of high-payload machines by making a number of utility aircraft for the farmer who needs space to carry tools and equipment, or even his dog!

With an empty weight of 150 kg (331 lb), these aircraft are currently outside Australian legislation, but a lot of work on a two-seater is under way in Britain at Thruster Aircraft (UK). Although this is being done with an eye to the European market, the UK effort is also highly relevant to Australia, because Australian and British airworthiness regulations are very similar. The company may thus be able to shortcut the inevitable delays of the embryonic Australian airworthiness system by making use of the relatively well established arrangements in the UK.

The trainer costs A$8950 complete and shares the basic airframe of the *Thruster 85* but has a larger wing and side-by-side seating with dual flying and engine controls. The *Thruster Utility* is A$400 cheaper and is effectively the two-seater minus one seat and its pod, though as you can see from the picture accompanying the introduction to this section, some examples have been fitted with transparent panels around the nose. Both models use the same Rotax 503 powerplant and can be had with floats for an extra A$950.

EXTERNAL DIMENSIONS & AREAS - See *Thruster 85* except: Wing span 31.5 ft, 9.60 m. Total wing area 164 ft², 15.2 m². Aspect ratio 6.1/1.

POWER PLANT - See Rotax 503-engined version of *Thruster 85* except: Power per unit area 0.30 hp/ft², 3.3 hp/m². Fuel capacity NC.

WEIGHTS & LOADINGS - Empty weight 331 lb, 150 kg. Max take-off weight 772 lb, 350 kg. Payload 441 lb, 200 kg. Max wing loading 4.71 lb/ft², 23.0 kg/m². Max power loading 15.4 lb/hp, 7.0 kg/hp. Load factors +4.0, -2.0 recommended; NC ultimate.

PERFORMANCE* - Max level speed 69 mph, 111 kph. Never exceed speed 92 mph, 148 kph. Economic cruising speed 58 mph, 93 kph. Stalling speed 38 mph, 61 kph. Max climb rate at sea level 800 ft/min, 4.1 m/s. Other data NC.

*Under unspecified test conditions.

THRUSTER AIRCRAFT
THRUSTER TWOPLACE
(Three- axis)

Summary as Thruster 85 *except: Side-by-side two-seater.*

Production status: see Thruster Utility *text.*

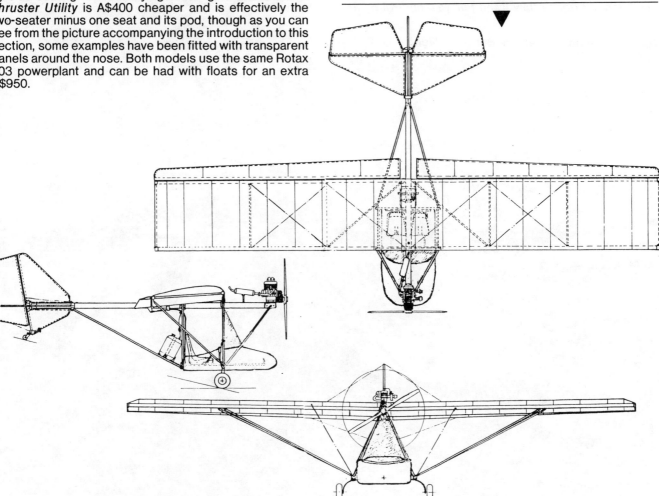

GENERAL - See *Thruster Utility* text.

EXTERNAL DIMENSIONS & AREAS - See *Thruster Utility*.

POWER PLANT - See *Thruster Utility*.

WEIGHTS & LOADINGS - Empty weight 331 lb, 150 kg. Max take-off weight 816 lb, 370 kg. Payload 485 lb, 220 kg. Max wing loading 4.97 lb/ft², 24.3 kg/m². Max power loading 16.3 lb/hp, 7.4 kg/hp. Load factors +4.0, -2.0 recommended; NC ultimate.

PERFORMANCE - See *Thruster Utility*.

UAI

Ultralight Aircraft Industries (Aust) Pty Ltd, PO Box 104, Goolwa, South Australia 5214; tel 085 552222. Managing director: Tony Peters. Secretary: Wendy Peters.

UAI *BUNYIP and WOMBAT*
(Three-axis)

Single-seat single-engined high-wing monoplane with conventional three-axis control. Wing has unswept leading and trailing edges, and constant chord; cruciform tail. Pitch control by fully flying tail; yaw control by fin-mounted rudder; roll control by full-span ailerons; control inputs through stick for pitch/roll and pedals for yaw. Wing braced from below by struts; wing profile NACA 4415; 100% double-surface. Undercarriage has three wheels in tail-dragger formation (Bunyip), in tricycle formation with additional tailwheel (Wombat); suspension NC on tailwheel (Bunyip), rubber suspension on nosewheel (Wombat); leaf-spring suspension on main wheels. Push-right go-right steering (tailwheel on Bunyip, nosewheel on Wombat) connected to yaw control. No brakes. Aluminium-alloy tube and box-section airframe, partially enclosed. Engine mounted at wing height, driving tractor propeller.

Production status: current, 16 completed.

GENERAL - The *Bunyip* is designed very much with the rural and pastoral industries in mind and most of the aircraft sold are operating in the South Australia outback. They have become invaluable for checking stock and oversee-

The Wombat *and (inset) the* Bunyip *in flight.*

Rob Fox

ing the hundreds of miles of fencing on large farms, as well as waterpoint inspection and even mustering.

Before design and development began, market reasearch into the rural sector was carried out by managing director Tony Peters. Five prototypes were built and with the aid of a federal government research and development grant, the *Bunyip* went into production at the rate of one a fortnight. In March 1984 it was joined by the *Wombat*, a tricycle undercarriage version to cater for those unfamiliar with the quirks of tailwheel aircraft.

Both aircraft are unusual in that they have all-metal wings, with an aviation grade aluminium-alloy web main spar, ribs of alloy sheet and the skins of aviation-grade Alclad. The fuselage, fin, rudder assembly and the all-flying elevator are made from 6061T6 aluminium with TIG welding of all components.

With the main area of operations being from rough, unprepared fields and paddocks, much work went into the rugged undercarriages, the main gear consisting of three-leaf springs coupled with wide aluminium-alloy hubs and pneumatic tyres.

UAI claims that full roll control is retained even at a high sink rate near the stall speed, with only a lowering of the nose needed to return the aircraft quickly to straight and level flight. The company also claims there is no violent pitch down even with the stick held right back.

An engine change was imminent at the time of writing, to a Hunting design with gear reduction, but our data below refers to the Robin-engined version, which was still available at the time of going to press and which costs A$11,000 regardless of undercarriage chosen.

A tandem two-place is due in early 1985 but it will only be available to dealers and approved ultralight flying schools, and no more details are yet available.

EXTERNAL DIMENSIONS & AREAS - Length overall 14.8 ft, 4.5 m. Height overall 6.6 ft, 2.00 m. Wing span 27.6 ft, 8.41 m. Constant chord 4.3 ft, 1.32 m. Dihedral 1°. Sweepback 0°. Tailplane span 7.2 ft, 2.20 m. Total wing area 120 ft^2, 11.1 m^2. Aspect ratio 6.3/1. Wheel track 5.5 ft, 1.68 m. Nosewheel diameter overall (*Wombat*) 10.5 inch, 27 cm. Main wheels diameter overall 12.5 inch, 32 cm. Other data NC.

POWER PLANT - Robin EC44 engine. Max power 50 hp at 6400 rpm. Propeller diameter and pitch 57x38 inch, 1.45x 0.97 m. Poly V-belt reduction, ratio 2.4/1. Max static thrust 250 lb, 113 kg. Power per unit area 0.42 hp/ft^2, 4.5 hp/m^2. Fuel capacity 6.1 US gal, 5.1 Imp gal, 23.0 litre.

WEIGHTS & LOADINGS - Empty weight 330 lb, 150 kg. Max take-off weight 660 lb, 299 kg. Payload 660 lb, 150 kg. Max wing loading 5.50 lb/ft^2, 26.9 kg/m^2. Max power loading 13.2 lb/hp, 6.0 kg/hp. Load factors +4.0, -2.0 recommended; +6.6, -3.0 ultimate.

PERFORMANCE* - Max level speed 81 mph, 130 kph. Never exceed speed 92 mph, 148 kph. Max cruising speed 75 mph, 121 kph. Economic cruising speed 50 mph, 93 kph. Stalling speed 31 mph, 50 kph. Max climb rate at sea level 800 ft/min, 4.1 m/s. Min sink rate *400* ft/min at 46 mph, *2.0* m/s at 74 kph. Best glide ratio with power off 10/1 at 46 mph, 74 kph. Take-off distance 100 ft, 30 m. Landing distance 150 ft, 46 m. Service ceiling NC. Range at average cruising speed 138 mile, 222 km. Noise level 60 dB at 300 ft, 91 m.

*Under the following test conditions - Airfield altitude 45 ft, 14 m. Ground temperature 64°F, 18°C. Ground pressure NC. Ground windspeed 0 mph, 0 kph. Test payload 330 lb, 150 kg.

WAACO

West Australia Aircraft Co, 20 Twyford Street, Box Hill, 3129 Victoria; tel 03 890 2889. Managing director: Max Kremke.

WAACO *STAGGERBIPE*

(Three-axis)

Single-seat single-engined biplane with conventional three-axis control. Wings have unswept leading and trailing edges, and constant chord; conventional tail. Pitch control by elevator on tail; yaw control by fin-mounted rudder; roll control by full-span ailerons; control inputs through stick for pitch/roll and pedals for yaw. Wings braced by struts; wing profile NACA 4112; 100% double-surface. Undercarriage has three wheels in tail-dragger formation; suspension NC on tailwheel and axle-flex suspension on main wheels. Push-right go-right tailwheel steering connected to yaw control; also differential braking. Brakes on main wheels. Aluminium-alloy tube airframe, totally or partially enclosed. Engine mounted between wings, driving tractor propeller.

Production status: prototype.

GENERAL - Under development since 1979, Max Kremke's *Staggerbipe* really got moving after a visit to Oshkosh in 1981 when Kremke reckoned his project was in keeping with the way the industry was moving. He wanted to create an enthusiast's aircraft built from easily obtainable, locally produced, off-the-shelf materials, a 'Ferrari of the skies' which would appreciate over the years.

The design and construction of the *Staggerbipe* is quite innovative and the workmanship remarkable. The fuselage comprises 6063T5 aluminium square tubing with rivetted and bonded gussets. The formers are wood, the windscreen specially moulded polycarbon. Cowls are of pre-moulded glass-fibre as are the fuel tank and seat, while the landing gear is made from chrome alloy tube.

Wings have a main spar of Australian silver quandong, which although 5-10% heavier than spruce is 50% stronger and locally a third of the price. The 42 ribs are Klegecell foam capped with profiled plywood, and the leading edge and tips are premoulded glass-fibre.

All fittings are 2024T6 alloy, with chrome alloy N-struts and main struts, a design claimed to be A$800 cheaper than flying wires and easier to set up and break-down. Vertical and horizontal stabilisers are of foam between aluminium ribs, covered in glass-fibre, as are the rudder and elevators. Pitch trim is via an anodised crank casting which changes the incidence of the horizontal stabiliser. Ailerons are full-span on the smaller, lower wing and are of the Friese type, but will become flaperons on the production model of which the airframe will be covered with HS90 1.7 oz polyfibre.

An interesting part of the project has been the stress analysis, which was done in Chile by Pat Urrutia, a long-time associate of Kremke's who recently emigrated.

The prototype is powered by a modifed VW1300 of 44 hp, but the kit will provide the owner with any desired option so long as it weighs about 45 kg (100 lb), possibilities being the four-stroke Lotus or Global units, and Rotax or Robin two-strokes.

If good looks and quality are any guide to performance, the _Staggerbipe_ should go like a dream when it becomes available in kit form after comprehensive test-flying. Kit prices will be A$5000-7000 excluding engine and instruments. Options under consideration include floats and retractable undercarriage.

EXTERNAL DIMENSIONS & AREAS - Length overall 14.4 ft, 4.40 m. Height overall 4.3 ft, 1.30 m. Wing span NC (bottom); 20.3 ft, 6.19 m (top). Constant chord NC (bottom wing); 3.0 ft, 0.91 m (top wing). Dihedral 1° (bottom wing); 1° (top wing). Sweepback 0°. Tailplane span 6.0 ft, 1.83 m. Fin height 2.7 ft, 0.81 m. Total wing area 116 ft², 10.7 m². Total aileron area 12.0 ft², 1.11 m². Fin area 1.2 ft², 0.11 m². Rudder area 2.9 ft², 0.27 m². Tailplane area NC. Total elevator area 6.5 ft², 0.60 m². Aspect ratio NC (bottom wing); 6.8/1 (top wing). Wheel track 5.0 ft, 1.52 m. Wheelbase 12.0 ft, 3.66 m. Tailwheel diameter overall NC. Main wheels diameter overall 12 inch, 30 cm.

POWER PLANT - VW 1300 engine. Max power 43 hp at 3600 rpm. Propeller diameter and pitch 54x34 inch, 1.37x 0.86 m. No reduction. Max static thrust 190 lb, 86 kg. Power per unit area 0.37 hp/ft², 4.0 hp/m². Fuel capacity 6.6 US gal, 5.5 Imp gal, 25.0 litre.

WEIGHTS & LOADINGS - Empty weight 330 lb, 150 kg. Max take-off weight 585 lb, 266 kg. Payload 255 lb, 116 kg. Max wing loading 5.04 lb/ft², 24.9 kg/m². Max power loading 13.6 lb/hp, 6.2 kg/hp. Load factors +6.6, -3.3 recommended; +10.0, -5.0 ultimate.

The Staggerbipe _prototype before covering in 1984 and (inset) an artist's impression of the finished aircraft, showing the machine in totally enclosed form (it may be flown partially enclosed by removing the doors)._

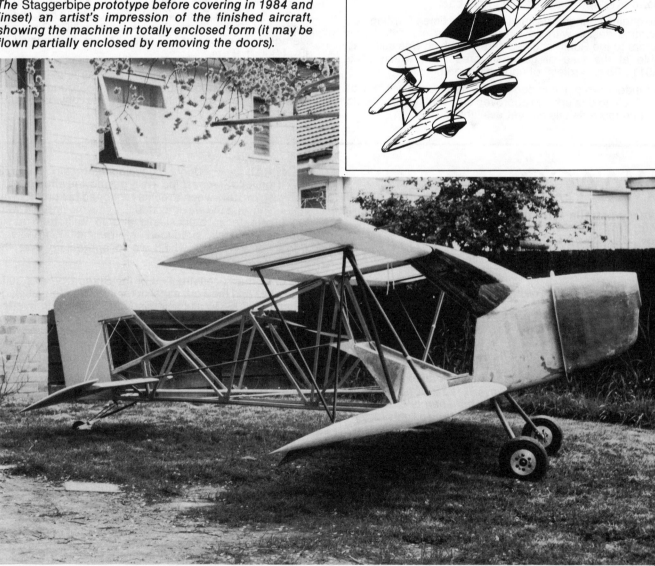

Rob Fox

PERFORMANCE* - Max level speed 90 mph, 145 kph. Never exceed speed 120 mph, 193 kph. Max cruising speed 80 mph, 129 kph. Economic cruising speed 75 mph, 121 kph. Stalling speed 35 mph, 56 kph. Max climb rate at sea level 850 ft/min, 4.3 m/s. Min sink rate 250 ft/min at 48 mph, 1.3 m/s at 77 kph. Best glide ratio with power off 9.5/1 at 50 mph, 80 kph. Take-off distance 100 ft, 30 m. Landing distance 150 ft, 46 m. Service ceiling NC. Range at average cruising speed 270 mile, 434 km. Noise level NC.

*Under the following test conditions - Test payload 231 lb, 105 kg. Other data NC.

WHEELER

Ron Wheeler Aircraft (Sales) Pty Ltd, 152 Bellevue Parade, Carlton, New South Wales 2218; tel 02546 2501.

WHEELER
SCOUT MK3-RN and MK3-RX

(Three-axis)

Single-seat single-engined high-wing monoplane with conventional three-axis control. Wing has unswept leading edge, swept forward trailing edge, and tapering chord; conventional tail. Pitch control by fully flying tail; yaw control by fully flying rudder; roll control by wing warping; control inputs through stick for pitch/roll and pedals for yaw. Wing braced from above by kingpost and cables, from below by cables; wing profile NC; 100% single-surface. Undercarriage has three wheels in tail-dragger formation; suspension NC on tailwheel and axle-flex suspension on main wheels. Push-right go-right tailwheel steering connected to yaw control. No brakes. Aluminium-alloy tube airframe, with optional pod. Engine mounted at wing height, driving tractor propeller.

Production status: current, number completed NC.

GENERAL - Ron Wheeler's *Scout* is without doubt one of the world's oldest ultralight designs, and was put into production as long ago as 1976. The ultimate in simple tube-and-Dacron designs, with its single-surface wing and rudimentary airframe, it could never be described as a cross-country machine, but it has certainly given a lot of pilots a lot of fun over the years. Along the way it has spawned derivatives in Britain (Flylite), West Germany (Mahe) and New Zealand (Canterbury Microlights), all of which we list separately.

Considering its age, the *Scout* has changed remarkably little. Originally a two-axis machine with Pixie Major engine, it gained a modified front axle and seat support to become the *Scout Mk2* and then had roll control and a Robin EC25PS added to create the *Mk3*, which at one stage was known as the *Mk3/3/R.* A *Mk4* version is believed to be imminent, incorporating changes developed by Canterbury Microlights in New Zealand, but no details have yet been released of this derivative and as recently as 1985 Ron Wheeler was still advertising the *Mk3,* which is now available in two forms - *Mk3-RN* with Robin engine (the version detailed below) or the otherwise identical *Mk3-RX* with 35 hp Rotax 377.

Prices including tax are A$3950 and A$4700 respectively, a pod being an optional extra on either at A$195.

Finally, we should just mention a couple of other *Scout* derivatives which Ron produced around 1982 but which to the best of our knowledge did not reach production. One was called the *Viva Scout,* a semi-enclosed machine with *Scout*-like wing but using a fin as well as a rudder, while the other was a biplane, using two *Scout*-like wings, a between-wings engine location, and a low-boom. This aircraft too had a vertical stabiliser.

EXTERNAL DIMENSIONS & AREAS - Length overall 17.1 ft, 5.20 m. Height overall 6.2 ft, 1.90 m. Wing span 28.8 ft, 8.77 m. Chord at root 6.5 ft, 1.98 m. Chord at tip 1.3 ft, 0.40 m. Dihedral NC°. Sweepback 0°. Elevator span 10.5 ft, 3.20 m. Rudder height 4.8 ft, 1.47 m. Total wing area 109 ft^2, 10.1 m^2. Rudder area NC. Total elevator area 12.5 ft^2, 1.16 m^2. Aspect ratio 7.6/1. Wheel track 4.5 ft, 1.37 m. Wheelbase 12.5 ft, 3.80 m. Tailwheel diameter overall 4 inch, 10 cm. Main wheels diameter overall 12 inch, 31 cm.

POWER PLANT - Robin EC25PS engine. Max power 18 hp at NC rpm. Propeller diameter and pitch 48xNC inch, 1.23xNC m. V-belt reduction, ratio 2.2/1. Max static thrust 130 lb, 59 kg. Power per unit area 0.17 hp/ft^2, 1.8 hp/m^2. Fuel capacity 1.6 US gal, 1.3 Imp gal, 6.0 litre.

WEIGHTS & LOADINGS - Empty weight 130 lb, 59 kg. Max take-off weight 310 lb, 141 kg. Payload 180 lb, 82 kg. Max wing loading 2.84 lb/ft^2, 14.0 kg/m^2. Max power loading 17.2 lb/hp, 7.8 kg/hp. Load factors NC recommended; >+3.0, >-3.0 ultimate.

PERFORMANCE* - Max level speed 53 mph, 85 kph. Never exceed speed 75 mph, 120 kph. Max cruising speed 47 mph, 75 kph. Economic cruising speed 47 mph, 75 kph. Stalling speed 20 mph, 32 kph. Max climb rate at sea level 550 ft/min, 2.8 m/s. Min sink rate 470 ft/min at 40 mph, 2.4 m/s at 64 kph. Best glide ratio with power off 7/1 at 40 mph,

The Scout Mk3-RN.

64 kph. Take-off distance 130 ft, 40 m. Landing distance 100 ft, 30 m. Service ceiling 9900 ft, 3000 m. Range at average cruising speed 56 mile, 90 km. Noise level NC.

Under unspecified test conditions.

WHEELER _SEA SCOUT_

(Three-axis)

Summary as Scout Mk3-RN and Mk3-RX *except: Undercarriage has two floats, no wheels.*

Production status: current, number completed NC.

GENERAL - The *Sea Scout* is simply a *Scout Mk3* with its tailwheel removed and its main wheels replaced by floats. As with the landplane, there is a choice of Robin or Rotax engines, prices including tax being A$4650 and A$5400 respectively; again, a pod is a A$195 extra.

EXTERNAL DIMENSIONS & AREAS - Wing-related data as *Scout Mk3-RN and Mk3-RX. Other data NC.*

POWER PLANT - See *Scout Mk3-RN and Mk3-RX.*

WEIGHTS & LOADINGS - NC.

PERFORMANCE - NC.

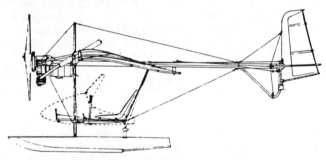

Sea Scout *with Robin EC25PS engine; the dotted line shows location of optional pod.*

WINTON

Winton Aircraft, 23 Foxwell Road, Coomera, 4210 Queensland; tel 075 532027. Designer/builder: Col Winton.

WINTON _SPORTSMAN_

(Three-axis)

Single-seat single-engined mid-wing monoplane with conventional three-axis control. Wing has unswept leading and trailing edges, and constant chord; cruciform tail. Pitch control by fully flying tail; yaw control by fin-mounted rudder; roll control by full-span ailerons; control inputs through stick for pitch/roll and pedals for yaw. Wing bracing see text; wing profile NC; 100% double-surface. Undercarriage has three wheels in tricycle formation; no suspension on nosewheel and torsion-bar suspension on main wheels. Push-right go-right nosewheel steering connected to yaw control; also differential braking. Brakes on main wheels. Aluminium-alloy tube airframe, partially enclosed or completely open (full enclosure optional). Engine mounted above wing, driving pusher propeller.

Production status: see text.

GENERAL - Well known ultralight designer Col Winton of *Grasshopper, Cricket* and *Jackeroo* fame designed and built the *Sportsman* to meet the anticipated heavyweight ANO, and it first appeared in Queensland in 1984, powered by a 1300 cc VW engine coupled to a direct-drive pusher propellor.

In 1981, Winton and 250 other Australians took a Qantas Boeing 747 with 16 Australian-designed aircraft, including two ultralights, in the cargo hold to the EAA's Oshkosh air show where the *Grasshopper* took one of the top awards. The design was sold and Winton went on to produce the *Jackeroo*, which has since ceased production.

With the failure of the heavyweight legislation to arrive, the *Sportsman* has been redesigned and re-engined to conform with the latest *ANO 95:10(2)*. Details were sketchy at the time of writing but a water-cooled two-stroke with geared reduction drive is understood to be on the new model, while external dimensions and appearance are much as the original *Sportsman*.

The sleek glass-fibre sailplane-style body can be removed to allow the pilot to fly surrounded only by the tubular aluminium-alloy airframe, an ideal arrangement for the prevailing conditions on Australia's Gold Coast. An over-the-wing, streamlined-section brace strut appeared on later models and it is not clear whether these will be incorporated on the new lightweight version. Original kits came as a complete body moulding with fully finished airframe and wings.

Projected prices for the new version are A$4500 for the basic kit, A$6000 for the kit with engine, and A$8000 ready to fly. In view of the lack of data on the latest model, we detail below the VW-powered version.

EXTERNAL DIMENSIONS & AREAS - Length overall 15.0 ft, 4.57 m. Wing span 25.0 ft, 7.62 m. Constant chord 4.6 ft, 1.40 m. Sweepback 0°. Total wing area 115 ft², 10.7 m². Aspect ratio 5.4/1. Other data NC.

POWER PLANT - VW 1400 engine. Max power 40 hp at 3200 rpm. Propeller diameter and pitch 54x28 inch, 1.37x 0.71 m. No reduction. Max static thrust 240 lb, 109 kg. Power per unit area 0.35 hp/ft², 3.7 hp/m². Fuel capacity NC.

WEIGHTS & LOADINGS - Empty weight 331 lb, 150 kg. Max take-off weight 560 lb, 254 kg. Payload 229 lb, 104 kg. Max wing loading 4.87 lb/ft², 23.7 kg/m². Max power loading 14.0 lb/hp, 6.4 kg/hp. Load factors NC.

PERFORMANCE* - Max level speed 115 mph, 185 kph. Max cruising speed 81 mph, 130 kph. Stalling speed 35 mph, 56 kph. Max climb rate at sea level 1000 ft/min, 5.1 m/s. Other data NC.

Under unspecified test conditions.

A Winton Sportsman *at the Yarrawonga fly-in. This example has the VW engine and over-wing struts. For another* Sportsman *illustration, see front cover.*

Belgium

Researched by
Alain-Yves Berger

One of Belgium's best - Dynali's Chickinox Monoplace.

Workable laws and a viable market

by Alain-Yves Berger

Since our last edition the August 1982 rules, Belgium's first attempt at microlight legislation, have been replaced by the royal decree of 21 September 1983, which defines a microlight as single- or two-seater with an empty weight not exceeding 150 kg (331 lb), a wing area of at least 10 m² (108 ft²) and with a maximum empty wing-loading of 10 kg/m² (2.05 lb/ft²). Take-off weight is not allowed to exceed 230 kg (507 lb) for single-seaters or 350 kg (772 lb) for two-seaters, the former being permitted engines of up to 25 kW (34 hp) and the latter up to 35 kW (47 hp), their respective noise levels being limited to 92 dB and 98 dB.

Belgian legislation differentiates between microlights with aerodynamic controls and trikes, which the lawmakers call 'DPMs', standing for Delta Plane Motorise or powered hang glider. This term will bring a smile to the faces of Europe's pioneering hang-glider pilots, who will recall that the *Deltaplane*, produced in 1973 by Christian Paul-Depasse in France, was simply one particular model of hang glider. Imagine what would happen if a parallel situation arose in motoring, and all traffic legislation used the description 'Model T' instead of 'car'! Still, it is at least an improvement on the French civil servant who, wishing to distinguish between weight-shift and two/three-axis microlights, christened the latter 'multi-axis'!

All Belgian microlights must withstand +5g and -3g before structural failure, and must carry at least an ASI, altimeter (the legislation limits operations to 450 m above ground level (1370 ft)).rev counter, compass and seat harness. Additionally a log must be kept, recording mechanical incidents and important maintenance, repairs, replacement of parts, and engine overhauls - an excellent initiative which would surely be welcomed in other countries since it provides a guarantee of good upkeep and a precaution against ageing and its effects, about which little is yet known. It's also a valuable document for secondhand buyers.

Modified theoretical and practical exams are now required to permit solo flying, the pilot being allowed to carry a passenger after 30 h. The microlight pilot is also obliged to keep a log of flights, including their duration and the place of take-off, a legal requirement which has yet to permeate bureaucratic thinking in neighbouring France. Microlight hours can count towards a light aircraft private pilot's licence, up to a maximum of 10 h. Other regulations govern the use of airfields exclusively by microlights, their flying rules and the authorisation of instructors.

The bilingual Federation Belge D'Aviation Micro-Legere/Belgische Micro-Luchtvaart Federatie (FBAM/BMLF) was founded in April 1981, its first president being Hugo Paridaens, who was succeeded by Alain Vercammen-Grandjean and in turn by Jacqueline Fernandes-Villela. The current president is Charles Vandermeulen. After a two-

▷ year trial period, it was recognised as a new member federation of both the national body - the Belgian Royal Aero Club - and the FAI (Federation Aeronautique Internationale).

Thanks to the country's unquestionable dynamism, Belgium has won for itself an enviable place in the microlight world, aided in part by the sport's comprehensive administration. The future now seems well assured in this country, small in area but rich in ideas. The Belgian market, wide open to imports as befits the most cosmopolitan country in Europe, is currently served by five national manufacturers, two making flexwings and the three fixedwings, a total of 11 single- and two-seat models.

Unfortunately, conflicts of interest between the two sectors have led to a state of near warfare between professionals in the Belgian microlight movement, which can only be deplored. Of course the same can also be said for a good many other countries where the differences run deep despite their being more land, more people and a bigger market to share, but it's particularly disturbing when this happens in a relatively small, close-knit industry and particulary sad to find that, having avoided the cultural divide which it is so easy to fall into in this bilingual country, the microlight community has created a divide of its own.

The saving grace is that such politics always interest the industry far more than the pilots, who simply get on with enjoying the flying...

For more information on microlights in Belgium, contact: Federation Belge D'Aviation Micro-Legere/Belgische Micro-Luchtvaart Federatie (FBAM/BMLF), 1 rue Montoyer, B1040 Brussels.

BUTTERFLY COMPANY

Butterfly Company, 2 avenue du Chateau, 1080 Bruxelles; tel (02) 428 9166. Proprietors: R Mossoux and J C Vinois.

BUTTERFLY COMPANY
BUTTERFLY (Two-axis)

Single-seat single-engined double monoplane in tandem with two-axis control. Wings have unswept leading and trailing edges, and constant chord; tail has vertical surfaces only. Pitch control by fully flying wing; yaw control by fin-mounted rudder; no separate roll control; control inputs through stick for pitch/yaw. Cantilever wings;

This Butterfly *was built in 1983 by BN.*

wing profile NC; 100% double-surface. Undercarriage has three wheels in tail-dragger formation; no suspension on tailwheel and axle-flex suspension on main wheels. Push-right go-right tailwheel steering independent from yaw control. No brakes. Aluminium-alloy/steel tube airframe, completely open. Engine mounted between wings, driving pusher propeller.

Production status: see text.

GENERAL - Mechanical and aeronautical engineer Raymond Mossoux was for 30 years responsible for repair and structural checking of the fleet of the Belgian national airline, Sabena. In 1978, in response to fans of the Mignet formula - the famous *Flying Flea* two-axis double monoplane on which the variable-incidence front wing took the place of an elevator - he began developing a foot-launched ultralight glider of that configuration. Using preformed 2024T3 sheet longerons and moulded plastic ribs covered in heat-shrunk Dacron, he built an airframe of 35 kg (77 lb) empty weight that was nonetheless able to withstand +6g, -6g, as was proved by Belgian aeronautical administration tests. The first flight, however, was not foot-launched, the

prototype being towed behind a car as a an airspeed of 28 kph (17 mph) was required. The original runners were to be replaced by a conventional undercarriage with a steerable tailwheel the following year.

The *Butterfly* was first motorised in September 1980 when a 9 hp engine driving a 50 cm (20 inch) propeller was mounted on the rear wing. The following March Raymond brought out a second prototype specifically intended for power, on which the wings were set further apart and the rear wing redesigned to give a better glide angle. It was fitted with a 10 hp Stihl chainsaw motor which proved rather feeble, so that August a young engineer called Jean-Claude Vinois who had completed his studies working for Raymond co-operated with Bosch to produce a two-cylinder Stihl with electronic ignition producing 40 kg (88 lb) thrust. Raymond began production of five kits and the following February formed the Butterfly Company.

The aircraft was presented at the homebuilders' convention at Brienne-le-Chateau in France where it proved an instant hit. Journalist Rene Thierry of Belgian national TV flew one to second place in the two/three-axis class of the '82 London-Paris.

With ten aircraft already sold in Belgium, France and Netherlands, Raymond was approached in January 1983 by the BN manufacturing company (Brugeoise et Nivelles) which was interested in producing the machine. He designed a new model geared to the firm's manufacturing methods while Jean-Claude completed a reduction drive which raised thrust to 50 kg (110 lb) and cut noise by 5 dB. This new *Butterfly*, manufactured by BN and fitted with two extra spoilers to quicken turn response and improve crosswind handling, was unveiled at the Le Bourget Salon in June 1983 and the following month was placed sixth in the French Grand Prix after fuel feed problems.

Meanwhile a new company had been formed to market the BN *Butterfly*, Ultralight Aeronautic SA, run by Mme E de Middelaer, J P van Erps, A van Joo and J P Vanophalvens. Legal proceedings were in process at the time of writing between license owner Butterfly Company, manufacturer BN, and marketing company Ultralight Aeronautic. Our data comes from the Butterfly Company and refers to the pre-BN version of the machine; specifications may change in the light of the forthcoming judgement. A Rene Thierry article on this interesting aircraft appeared in the March '84 issue of *UlmMag*.
Price: NC.

EXTERNAL DIMENSIONS & AREAS - Length overall 11.5 ft, 3.50 m. Height overall 4.5 ft, 1.36 m. Wing span 20.3 ft, 6.19 m (front); 14.3 ft, 4.36 m (rear). Constant chord 3.9 ft, 1.20 m (front wing); 3.9 ft, 1.20 m (rear wing). Dihedral* 4° (front wing); 4° (rear wing). Sweepback 0°. Fin height NC.

Total wing area 126 ft², 11.7 m². Fin area 10.8 ft², 1.00 m². Rudder area 6.5 ft², 0.60 m². Aspect ratio 5.2/1 (front wing); 3.6/1 (rear wing). Wheel track 3.3 ft, 1.0 m. Wheelbase 6.6 ft, 2.00 m. Tailwheel diameter overall 3 inch, 8 cm. Main wheels diameter overall 8 inch, 21 cm.

POWER PLANT - JCV engine. Max power 22 hp at 6800 rpm. Propeller diameter and pitch 30x18 inch, 0.77x0.45 m. No reduction. Max static thrust 108 lb, 49 kg. Power per unit area 0.17 hp/ft², 1.9 hp/m². Fuel capacity 2.6 US gal, 2.2 Imp gal, 10.0 litre.

WEIGHTS & LOADINGS - Empty weight 110 lb, 50 kg. Max take-off weight 309 lb, 140 kg. Payload 199 lb, 90 kg. Max wing loading 2.45 lb/ft², 12.0 kg/m². Max power loading 14.0 lb/hp, 6.4 kg/hp. Load factors NC recommended; +6.0, -6.0 ultimate.

PERFORMANCE** - Max level speed 68 mph, 110 kph. Never exceed speed 75 mph, 120 kph. Max cruising speed 50 mph, 80 kph. Economic cruising speed 40 mph, 65 kph. Stalling speed 22 mph, 35 kph. Max climb rate at sea level 390 ft/min, 2.0 m/s. Min sink rate 240 ft/min at 32 mph, 1.2 m/s at 52 kph. Best glide ratio with power off 12/1 at 32 mph, 52 kph. Take-off distance 100 ft, 30 m. Landing distance 65 ft, 20 m. Service ceiling 10,000 ft, 3050 m. Range at average cruising speed 103 mile, 165 km. Noise level NC.

On outboard section of wing only.

**Under unspecified test conditions.*

BN *BUTTERFLY 04*
(Two-axis)

Summary as Butterfly *except: Side-by-side two-seater.*
Production status: see text.

GENERAL - While BN was producing the *Butterfly*, the company also designed and built a side-by-side two-seater, the *Butterfly 04*, which made its first flight on 1 March 1984 and was displayed at the Brussels Salon des Vacances, where we had the chance to snatch a photograph and glean some all too brief details of it. Since then we have heard little of substance about either the solo or dual machines, neither of which was being produced at the time of writing.

EXTERNAL DIMENSIONS & AREAS - Length overall 12.4 ft, 3.78 m. Height overall 4.6 ft, 1.40 m. Wing span 26.9 ft, 8.20 m (front); NC (rear). Constant chord 3.9 ft, 1.20 m

(front wing); 3.9 ft, 1.20 m (rear wing). Dihedral* 6° (front wing); 6° (rear wing). Sweepback 0°. Fin height 3.3 ft, 1.02 m. Front wing area 101 ft², 9.3 m². Rear wing area 69 ft², 6.4 m². Total wing area 170 ft², 15.8 m². Fin area 3.7 ft², 0.34 m². Rudder area 6.5 ft², 0.60 m². Aspect ratio 7.2/1 (front wing); NC (rear wing). Wheel track 4.3 ft, 1.30 m. Wheelbase 7.5 ft, 2.30 m. Tailwheel diameter overall 4 inch, 10 cm. Main wheels diameter overall 10 inch, 26 cm.

POWER PLANT - KFM 107R engine. Max power 25 hp at 6300 rpm. Propeller diameter and pitch 45x20 inch, 1.14x 0.50 m. V-belt reduction, ratio 2.0/1. Max static thrust 154 lb, 70 kg. Power per unit area 0.15 hp/ft², 1.6 hp/m². Fuel capacity 10.6 US gal, 8.8 Imp gal, 40.0 litre.

WEIGHTS & LOADINGS - Empty weight 260 lb, 118 kg. Max take-off weight 626 lb, 284 kg. Payload 366 lb, 166 kg. Max wing loading 3.68 lb/ft², 18.0 kg/m². Max power loading 25.0 lb/hp, 11.4 kg/hp. Load factors NC recommended; +6.0, -6.0 ultimate.

PERFORMANCE - NC.

* On outboard section of wing only.

DYNALI

Dynali SA, 24 rue Delporte, 1050 Bruxelles; tel (02) 649 5505. Contact: Jacky Tonet.

Overseas sales: Ste Hariscain, Department Aeronautique, 103 rue de Croissy, 78230 Le Pecq, France; tel (3) 976 5836. Contact: Jean-Bernard and Jeanine Hariscain.

DYNALI
CHICKINOX MONOPLACE

(Two-axis)

Single-seat single-engined high-wing monoplane with two-axis° control. Wing has unswept leading and trailing edges, and constant chord; flaps fitted; cruciform tail. Pitch control by fully flying tail; yaw control by fully flying rudder; no separate roll control; control inputs through stick for pitch/yaw. Wing braced from below by struts; wing profile mono-convexe; single-surface. Undercarriage has three wheels in tricycle formation; axle-flex suspension on all wheels. Ground steering by differential braking. Brakes on main wheels. Aluminium-alloy/stainless-steel tube airframe, with pod. Engine mounted below wing, driving pusher propeller.*

Production status: current, 35 completed.

*See text.

GENERAL - Jacky Tonet from Brussels was already well known in the biking world, in which he excels, when he began an equally successful venture with 'aerial motor-bikes'. Surrounding himself with aeronautical experts, he came up with the prototype *Chickinox* single-seater, a two-axis stick-only machine using technology well proven in the high-power two-wheeled sector: a 304 stainless-steel tubular structure with high-strength argon welding. Little used because of its weight and until recently inferior quality to aviation-grade Duralumin, the stainless-steel oversized tubes used by Jacky have proved themselves as safe as the traditional 6061 and AU4G1 Duralumins. Dynali

employs two welders approved by the Belgian authorities and all welded parts undergo physical and chemical tests under the auspices of the same ministry.

A prototype flown in turn by Patrick Dupont and Patrick Thouze at the French Six Hours at Blagnac near Toulouse in June '84, which required 6 h flying in good but extremely turbulent conditions, interrupted only by refuelling stops, was placed third in the general two/three-axis class behind the Belgian *Butterfly* and the Sonaca *Falcon*, and first in the all-classes distance section with 470 km completed (292 mile). Just two weeks previously the same aircraft had demonstrated its reliability at the hands of Dupont in the Round Belgium Rally.

A photo of the take-off at Blagnac appears in our colour section, with a picture of a production machine accompanying the introduction to this section.

Production began that autumn and the first aircraft off the line was flight tested by Alain-Yves Berger in the March '85 issue of *UlmMag*, which commented on its extraordinary flying qualities. In flight safety terms, it appears to be the natural successor to the famous *Quicksilver MX,* not stalling in the practical sense but parachuting at the rate of 3-5 m/s (680-980 ft/min). It is practically impossible to spin because of its similar dihedral to the *Quick*, and indeed the wing in general appears very similar, except that it is strut-braced.

The leading edge is made of 65x5 mm (2.6x0.2 inch) tube and is connected to the 45x5mm (1.8x0.2 inch) trailing edge by three compression struts, while six ribs hold the profile.

This comparison with the *Quick* should not be taken too far, however, for the *Chickinox* has a much stronger structure - it is questionable whether Bob Lovejoy's bird would pass the rigorous Belgian airworthiness tests - and has much better performance.

UlmMag's tester held the *Chickinox* at nearly 120 kph (75 mph) indicated for 15 min with 105 kg (231 lb) on board at -5C (23F), a temperature in which he was grateful for the glass-fibre fairing and the huge windscreen of the production model, his only regret being the absence of a trim tab on the fully flying tail.

Currently under test are spoilers which will also act as air brakes and which will be available as a retro-fit for existing two-axis machines.

May '85 tax-paid price of the aircraft, including pod and detachable windscreen, is FF43,000 in kit form or FF45,000 assembled and flight-tested.

EXTERNAL DIMENSIONS & AREAS - Length overall 16.4 ft, 5.00 m. Height overall 7.2 ft, 2.20 m. Wing span 30.8 ft, 9.40 m. Constant chord 4.6 ft, 1.39 m. Dihedral 7.5°. Sweepback 0°. Elevator span 8.4 ft, 2.56 m. Rudder height NC. Total wing area 142 ft², 13.2 m². Rudder area 8.1 ft², 0.75 m². Total elevator area 23.7 ft², 2.20 m². Aspect ratio 6.7/1. Wheel track 6.0 ft, 1.83 m. Wheelbase 5.7 ft, 1.75 m. Nosewheel diameter overall 10 inch, 26 cm. Main wheels diameter overall 16 inch, 40 cm.

POWER PLANT - Rotax 377 engine. Max power 34 hp at 6750 rpm. Propeller diameter and pitch 54x35 inch, 1.38x 0.90 m. Gear reduction, ratio 2.6/1. Max static thrust 220 lb, 100 kg. Power per unit area 0.24 hp/ft², 2.6 hp/m². Fuel capacity 7.4 US gal, 6.2 Imp gal, 28.0 litre.

WEIGHTS & LOADINGS - Empty weight 289 lb, 131 kg. Max take-off weight 507 lb; 230 kg. Payload 218 lb, 99 kg. Max wing loading 3.57 lb/ft², 17.4 kg/m². Max power loading 14.9 lb/hp, 6.8 kg/hp. Load factors +6.0, -3.0 recommended; NC ultimate.

PERFORMANCE ** - Max level speed 68 mph, 110 kph.

Never exceed speed 81 mph, 130 kph. Max cruising speed 59 mph, 95 kph. Economic cruising speed 44 mph, 70 kph. Stalling speed 25 mph, 40 kph. Max climb rate at sea level 790 ft/min, 4.0 m/s. Min sink rate 300 ft/min at 40 mph, 1.5 m/s at 65 kph. Best glide ratio with power off 10/1 at 40 mph, 65 kph. Take-off distance 130 ft, 40 m. Landing distance 80 ft, 25 m. Service ceiling 13,100 ft, 4000 m. Range at average cruising speed 211 mile, 340 km. Noise level 90 dB at 33 ft, 10 m.

**Under the following test conditions - Airfield altitude 246 ft, 75 m. Ground temperature 59°F, 15°C. Ground pressure 1013 mB. Ground windspeed 4 mph, 7 kph. Test payload 225 lb, 102 kg.

DYNALI *CHICKINOX BIPLACE*
(Two-axis)

Summary as Chickinox Monoplace *except: Tandem two-seater. Pod optional.*

Production status: current, number completed NC.

GENERAL - A tandem two-seater *Chickinox,* with dual control but otherwise very similar to the solo machine, was scheduled for testing in May 1985 and is said to retain the flying qualities of the single-seater. It has a Rotax 447 engine and will be sold at FF59,000 tax-paid, assembled and test-flown. Options are a pod and detachable windscreen for FF2951 and, later, spoiler/airbrake kits as on the single-seater.

EXTERNAL DIMENSIONS & AREAS - See *Chickinox Monoplace* except: Wing span 36.1 ft, 11.00 m. Total wing area 164 ft², 15.3 m². Rudder area 8.1 ft², 0.75 m². Aspect ratio 7.9/1. Nosewheel diameter overall 16 inch, 40 cm.

POWER PLANT - Rotax 447 engine. Max power 41 hp at 6750 rpm. Propeller diameter and pitch 54x39 inch, 1.38x 1.00 m. Gear reduction, ratio 2.6/1. Max static thrust 243 lb, 110 kg. Power per unit area 0.25 hp/ft², 2.7 hp/m². Fuel capacity 7.9 US gal, 6.6 Imp gal, 30.0 litre.

WEIGHTS & LOADINGS - Empty weight 328 lb, 149 kg. Max take-off weight 772 lb, 350 kg. Payload 443 lb, 201 kg.

Jacky Tonnet takes a passenger up in the prototype Chickinox Biplace.

Max wing loading 4.71 lb/ft², 22.9 kg/m². Max power loading 18.9 lb/hp, 8.5 kg/hp. Load factors +6.0, -3.0 recommended; NC ultimate.

PERFORMANCE** - Max level speed 62 mph, 100 kph. Never exceed speed 81 mph, 130 kph. Max cruising speed 53 mph, 85 kph. Economic cruising speed 40 mph, 65 kph. Stalling speed 25 mph, 40 kph. Max climb rate at sea level 510 ft/min, 2.6 m/s. Min sink rate 300 ft/min at 37 mph, 1.5 m/s at 60 kph. Best glide ratio with power off 10/1 at 3l mph, 60 kph. Take-off distance 180 ft, 55 m. Landing distance 100 ft, 30 m. Service ceiling NC. Range at average cruising speed 103 mile, 165 km. Noise level NC.

**Under the following test conditions - Airfield altitude 246 ft, 75 m. Ground temperature 59°F, 15°C. Ground pressure 1013 mB. Ground windspeed 3 mph, 5 kph. Test payload 441 lb, 200 kg.

FUN AVIATION

Fun Aviation SA, 5 rue du Maieur, 5880 Tourinnes-Saint-Lambert; tel (010) 658134. Proprietor: Thierry Greiner.

FUN AVIATION
MICRO FUN/Suitable Rogallo
(Weight-shift)

Single-seat single-engined flex-wing aircraft with weight-shift control. Rogallo wing. Pilot suspended below wing in trike unit, using bar to control pitch and roll/yaw by altering relative positions of trike unit and wing. Wing braced from above by kingpost and cables, from below by cables. Undercarriage has three wheels in tricycle formation; no suspension on nosewheel and coil-spring suspension on main wheels. Push-right go-left nosewheel steering independent from aerodynamic controls. Optional nosewheel brake. Aluminium-alloy tube trike unit, completely open. Engine mounted below wing, driving pusher propeller. Other details NC.

Production status: see text.

GENERAL - In this and the next two listings we show three trikes marketed by Fun Aviation - a single-seater and a pair of two-seaters, one side-by-side and one tandem, both the dual machines using the same wing. The range sounds logical enough, but behind it lies a complex tale which we feel obliged to explain at some length.

Thierry Greiner set up Fun Aviation in December '83 to manufacture under licence the solo and dual trikes designed by Microbel (see separate entry), Bernard Gosselet's company with which he had just finished a long apprenticeship. Production of the two Microbel models began, the single-seater renamed *Micro Fun* and the two-seater *Big Fun*.

In May 1984, Fun Aviation opened its own microlight centre and school at Tourinnes-Saint-Lambert, and that summer acquired manufacturing rights to Fulmar's wings and trikes. Detailed in our first edition, this firm was set up in 1981 by Pierangelo Mezzapesa and offered the single-seat *Trident* and tandem two-seat *Jumbo* trikes, as well as at one time manufacturing the *Weedhopper* for the European agents of the American company. Fulmar was declared bankrupt in June 1984, but Pierangelo bought back the rights to the name, and that August Fun Aviation set up its own wing fac-

This 1984 picture of a Micro Fun *trike unit shows clearly the Microbel-style rear suspension units; there's also a Microbel sticker on the front strut.*

tory and resumed production of the *Rival* solo and the *Jumbo* dual wings as well as of two trike units, the *Trident* single-seater and the *Tyger II* two-seater, whilst also assuring a Fulmar spares service.

The two-seater *Tyger II* was developed from Pierangelo's original *Tiger* but had not reached the flying stage when Fulmar went bust. Its test programme was completed by Fun Aviation with the help of Pierangelo himself, who went on to acquire new business interests, becoming vice-president of the Belgian microlight federation and launching a French-language hang gliding and microlighting publication called *Ultralight Magazine* in spring '85.

Meanwhile Fun Aviation and Microbel were having their differences and the firms broke links at the end of 1984. Legal proceedings were in train at the time of writing and Bernard Gosselet won a court order in February 1985 granting him the rights to the name Microbel. Nevertheless, the first issue of *Ultralight Magazine* featured a buyer's guide from which Microbel products were absent and in which Fun Aviation was still credited with the production of the *Micro Fun* and the *Big Fun*, even though they were conceived to the best of our knowledge under the Microbel name by Bernard Gosselet and are still fitted with Robin engines. We must leave it to the courts to judge the rights and wrongs of this confusing situation. In the meantime we reproduce without prejudice the data below, along with prices quoted in a letter from Fun Aviation in December 1984: *Micro Fun* trike unit FB165,000, *Big Fun* trike unit FB195,000, *Tyger II* trike unit FB173,000. Recommended wings include the Pegasus *Typhoon S4* (FB80,000) for the single-seater and the Pegasus *Typhoon XL* (FB118,000) for the two-seater, plus of course the com-

pany's own *Jumbo* (FB91,000) and *Jumbo Nova* (FB87,000).

We give below data for the *Micro Fun,* and list that for the *Big Fun* and *Tyger II* separately in turn. The data below contains many approximations, because the company did not specify which wing the trike unit was mated to when the figures were taken.

EXTERNAL DIMENSIONS & AREAS - Length overall *11.5* ft, *3.50* m. Height overall *12.5* ft, *3.80* m. Wing span *32.8* ft, *10.00* m. Chord at root *8.2* ft, *2.50* m. Chord at tip *3.3* ft, *1.00* m. Dihedral 1°. Total wing area *183* ft², *17.0* m². Aspect ratio *5.9/1.* Wheel track 6.6 ft, 2.00 m. Wheelbase 4.9 ft, 1.50 m. Nosewheel diameter overall 15 inch, 37 cm. Main wheels diameter overall 15 inch, 37 cm. Other data NC.

POWER PLANT - Robin EC34PM engine. Max power 32 hp at 6500 rpm. Propeller diameter and pitch 59x30 inch, 1.50x0.75 m. Toothed-belt reduction, ratio NC. Max static thrust NC. Power per unit area *0.17* hp/ft², *1.9* hp/m². Fuel capacity 5.3 US gal, 4.4 Imp gal, 20.0 litre.

WEIGHTS & LOADINGS - Empty weight *220* lb, *100* kg. Max take-off weight *441* lb, *200* kg. Payload *220* lb, *100* kg. Max wing loading *2.41* lb/ft², *11.8* kg/m². Max power loading *13.8* lb/hp, *6.3* kg/hp. Load factors +5.0, -2.0 recommended; +6.0, -3.0 ultimate.

PERFORMANCE* - Max level speed *47* mph, *75* kph. Never exceed speed *62* mph, *100* kph. Max cruising speed *44* mph, *70* kph. Economic cruising speed *31* mph, *50* kph. Stalling speed *25* mph, *40* kph. Max climb rate at sea level *790* ft/min, *4.0* m/s. Min sink rate *300* ft/min at *31* mph, *1.5* m/s at *50* kph. Best glide ratio with power off *7/1* at *28* mph, *45* kph. Take-off distance *130* ft, *40* m. Landing distance *180* ft, *55* m. Service ceiling *11,500* ft, *3500* m. Range at average cruising speed *218* mile, *350* km. Noise level *55* dB at 490 ft, 150 m.

*Under the following test conditions - Airfield altitude 328 ft, 100 m. Ground temperature 59°F, 15°C. Ground pressure 1000 mB. Ground windspeed 9 mph, 15 kph. Test payload 198 lb, 90 kg.

FUN AVIATION
BIG FUN/JUMBO
(Weight-shift)

Side-by-side two-seat single-engined flex-wing aircraft with weight-shift control. Rogallo wing with keel pocket. Pilot suspended below wing in trike unit, using bar to control pitch and roll/yaw by altering relative positions of trike unit and wing. Wing braced from above by kingpost and cables, from below by cables; floating cross-tube construction with 85% double-surface enclosing cross-tube; preformed ribs. Undercarriage has three wheels in tricycle formation; no suspension on nosewheel and coil-spring suspension on main wheels. Push-right go-left nosewheel steering independent from aerodynamic controls. Optional nosewheel brake. Aluminium-alloy tube trike unit, completely open. Engine mounted below wing, driving pusher propeller.

Production status: see Micro Fun/Suitable Rogallo *text.*

GENERAL - See *Micro Fun/Suitable Rogallo* text.

EXTERNAL DIMENSIONS & AREAS - Length overall 13.1 ft, 4.00 m. Height overall 12.5 ft, 3.80 m. Wing span 34.4 ft, 10.50 m. Chord at root 9.2 ft, 2.80 m. Chord at tip 3.3

ft, 1.00 m. Dihedral 1°. Nose angle 130°. Total wing area 215 ft², 20.0 m². Aspect ratio 5.5/1. Wheel track 6.6 ft, 2.00 m. Wheelbase 5.2 ft, 1.60 m. Nosewheel diameter overall 16 inch, 40 cm. Main wheels diameter overall 16 inch, 40 cm. Other data NC.

POWER PLANT - Robin EC44 engine. Max power 45 hp at 6500 rpm. Propeller diameter and pitch 59x35 inch, 1.50x 0.90 m. Toothed-belt reduction, ratio 2.6/1. Max static thrust 291 lb, 132 kg. Power per unit area 0.21 hp/ft², 2.3 hp/m². Fuel capacity 5.3 US gal, 4.4 Imp gal, 20.0 litre.

WEIGHTS & LOADINGS - Empty weight 287 lb, 130 kg. Max take-off weight 772 lb, 350 kg. Payload 485 lb, 220 kg. Max wing loading 3.59 lb/ft², 17.5 kg/m². Max power loading 17.2 lb/hp, 7.8 kg/hp. Load factors +5.0, -2.0 recommended; +6.0, -3.0 ultimate.

PERFORMANCE* - Max level speed 53 mph, 85 kph. Never exceed speed 62 mph, 100 kph. Max cruising speed 50 mph, 80 kph. Economic cruising speed 37 mph, 60 kph. Stalling speed 25 mph, 40 kph. Max climb rate at sea level 690 ft/min, 3.5 m/s. Min sink rate 370 ft/min at 37 mph, 1.9 m/s at 60 kph. Best glide ratio with power off 6.5/1 at 34 mph, 55 kph. Take-off distance 165 ft, 50 m. Landing distance 230 ft, 70 m. Service ceiling 11,500 ft, 3500 m. Range at average cruising speed 137 mile, 220 km. Noise level 55 dB at 492 ft, 150 m.

*Under the following test conditions - Airfield altitude 328 ft, 100 m. Ground temperature 59°F, 15°C. Ground pressure 1000 mB. Ground windspeed 9 mph, 15 kph. Test payload 353 lb, 160 kg.

FUN AVIATION
TYGER II/JUMBO
(Weight-shift)

Summary as Big Fun/Jumbo *except: Tandem two-seater. No suspension. Nosewheel brake standard. Optional pod.*

*Production status: current; 10 completed (*Tyger II), *100 completed (*Jumbo).*

GENERAL - See *Micro Fun/Suitable Rogallo* text.

EXTERNAL DIMENSIONS & AREAS - See *Big Fun/ Jumbo* except: Wheelbase 5.9 ft, 1.80 m. Nosewheel diameter overall 12 inch, 30 cm. Main wheels diameter overall 16 inch, 40 cm. Other data NC.

POWER PLANT - Citroen 652 cc engine. Max power 36 hp at 5750 rpm. Propeller diameter and pitch 59x35 inch, 1.50x0.90 m. V-belt reduction, ratio 2.5/1. Max static thrust 254 lb, 115 kg. Power per unit area 0.17 hp/ft², 1.8 hp/m². Fuel capacity 6.6 US gal, 5.5 Imp gal, 25.0 litre.

WEIGHTS & LOADINGS - Empty weight 331 lb, 150 kg. Max take-off weight 772 lb, 350 kg. Payload 441 lb, 200 kg. Max wing loading 3.59 lb/ft², 17.5 kg/m². Max power loading 21.4 lb/hp, 9.7 kg/hp. Load factors +5.0, -2.0 recommended; +6.0, -3.0 ultimate.

PERFORMANCE* - See *Big Fun/Jumbo* except: Min sink rate 350 ft/min at 37 mph, 1.8 m/s at 60 kph. Best glide ratio with power off 8/1 at 34 mph, 55 kph. Take-off distance 130 ft, 40 m. Landing distance 165 ft, 50 m. Range at

The 1984 Big Fun/Jumbo, *using Microbel-style suspension and a Robin engine.*

The Tyger II *trike unit uses a four-stroke Citroen engine.*

average cruising speed 93 mile, 150 km. Noise level NC.

*Under the following test conditions - Airfield altitude 328 ft, 100 m. Ground temperature 64°F, 18°C. Ground pressure NC. Ground windspeed 9 mph, 15 kph. Test payload 441 lb, 200 kg.

Microbel's SC377 trike unit features the company's distinctive suspension.

MICROBEL

La Microbel, 62 avenue Bel Horizon, 1341 Ceroux-Mousty; tel 010 611703. Proprietor: Bernard Gosselet.

MICROBEL/PEGASUS
SC377/TYPHOON S4 LARGE
(Weight-shift)

Single-seat single-engined flex-wing aircraft with weight-shift control. Rogallo wing with keel pocket. Pilot suspended below wing in trike unit, using bar to control pitch and roll/yaw by altering relative positions of trike unit and wing. Wing braced from above by kingpost and cables, from below by cables; floating cross-tube construction with 55% double-surface enclosing cross-tube; preformed ribs. Undercarriage has three wheels in tricycle formation; no suspension on nosewheel and coil-spring suspension on main wheels. Push-right go-left nosewheel steering independent from aerodynamic controls. No brakes. Aluminium-alloy tube trike unit, completely open. Engine mounted below wing, driving pusher propeller.

Production status: current, number completed NC.

GENERAL - It is with some satisfaction that we include Microbel in this book, as Microbel's founder Bernard Gosselet was among the pioneers of hang gliding in Belgium and he was already flying an authentic Christian-Paul Depasse *Deltaplane* in 1975.

Bernard designed and built his first trike units in l981, fitted with a Solo 210 motor and his own reduction drive. Production was small-scale and about 15 were sold through Fulmar, a company which has since disappeared (see Fun Aviation). At the end of that year Bernard devised the celebrated Microbel suspension system, capable of 20 cm (8 inch) compression under a 2 kg (4.4 lb) shock loading, a capability scarcely matched since. It combines a telescopic shock absorber for each main wheel with a system of six articulated tubes, an extremely effective mechanism. Bernard put the single-seater into production in 1982, and in the same year introduced his side-by-side two-seater, the first the Continent had seen as earlier British designs from Hornet, Skyhook and UAS had not been seriously marketed abroad.

In 1982 and 1983 the company built about 50 of the two models, with Roland Coddens acting as distributor, but next year came the agreement with Fun Aviation. This deal allowed Fun Aviation to build and distribute both these Robin-engined machines under license, renaming them *Micro Fun* and *Big Fun* respectively, and an example of the latter was flight-tested by Jean-Luc Prignol for the November 1984 issue of *UlmMag*.

However, the deal has since ended in legal proceedings, as we explain under Fun Aviation, and Bernard has therefore recommended small-scale production of both his *SC377* and *SL477* trike units, which are little changed except for the adoption of Rotax power. Incidentally, Microbel also fits Rotax 377 engines to the Aviasud *Sirocco* on behalf of Belgian importer Roland Coddens.

Prices for the trike units only are FB139,000 for the *SC 377*, which we detail below, and FB169,000 for the *SL 447* two-seater, which we list separately. Either can be fitted with any wing of the buyer's choice, but we detail them with the most popular options, the Pegasus *Typhoon S4 Large* and Southdown International *Sprint* respectively.

EXTERNAL DIMENSIONS & AREAS - Length overall 12.8 ft, 3.90 m. Wing span 34.0 ft, 10.36 m. Chord at root 8.5 ft, 2.68 m. Dihedral 0°. Nose angle 122°. Total wing area 180 ft², 16.7 m². Aspect ratio 6.4/1. Other data NC.

POWER PLANT - Rotax 377 engine. Max power 34 hp at 6500 rpm. Propeller diameter and pitch 57x35 inch, 1.45x 0.90 m. Gear reduction, ratio 2.6/1. Max static thrust 231 lb, 105 kg. Power per unit area 0.19 hp/ft², 2.0 hp/m². Fuel capacity 5.3 US gal, 4.4 Imp gal, 20.0 litre.

WEIGHTS & LOADINGS - Empty weight 220 lb, 100 kg. Max take-off weight 507 lb, 230 kg. Payload 287 lb, 130 kg. Max wing loading 2.82 lb/ft², 13.8 kg/m². Max power loading 14.9 lb/hp, 6.8 kg/hp. Load factors +6.5, -4.5 recommended; NC ultimate.

PERFORMANCE* - Max climb rate at sea level 980 ft/min, 5.0 m/s. Other data NC.

*Under unspecified test conditions.

MICROBEL/SOUTHDOWN INTERNATIONAL SL447/SPRINT

(Weight-shift)

Side-by-side two-seat single-engined flex-wing aircraft with weight-shift control. Rogallo wing with fin. Pilot suspended below wing in trike unit, using bar to control pitch and roll/yaw by altering relative positions of trike unit and wing. Wing braced from above by kingpost and cables, from below by cables; floating cross-tube construction with 70% double-surface enclosing crosstube; preformed ribs. Undercarriage has three wheels in tricycle formation; no suspension on nosewheel and coil-spring suspension on main wheels. Push-right go-left nosewheel steering independent from aerodynamic controls. Nosewheel brake. Aluminium-alloy tube trike unit, completely open. Engine mounted below wing, driving pusher propeller.

Production status: current, number completed NC.

GENERAL - See *SC377/Typhoon S4 Large* text.

EXTERNAL DIMENSIONS & AREAS - Length overall 11.2 ft, 3.41 m. Wing span 35.0 ft, 10.67 m. Chord at root 8.7 ft, 2.65 m. Chord at tip 2.5 ft, 0.76 m. Dihedral -2°. Nose angle 130°. Fin height 3.8 ft, 1.16 m. Total wing area 180 ft², 16.7 m². Fin area 7.2 ft², 0.67 m². Aspect ratio 6.8/1. Other data NC.

POWER PLANT - Rotax 447 engine. Max power 41 hp at 6500 rpm. Propeller diameter and pitch 57x35 inch, 1.45x

0.90 m. Gear reduction, ratio 2.6/1. Max static thrust 287 lb, 130 kg. Power per unit area 0.23 hp/ft², 2.5 hp/m². Fuel capacity 5.3 US gal, 4.4 Imp gal, 20.0 litre.

WEIGHTS & LOADINGS - Empty weight 271 lb, 123 kg. Max take-off weight 717 lb, 325 kg. Payload 445 lb, 202 kg. Max wing loading 3.98 lb/ft², 19.5 kg/m². Max power loading 17.5 lb/hp, 7.9 kg/hp. Load factors +4.0, -2.0 recommended; >+6.0, >-3.0 ultimate.

PERFORMANCE* - Max climb rate at sea level 590 ft/min, 3.0 m/s. Min sink rate 430 ft/min at 37 mph, 2.2 m/s at 60 kph. Other data NC.

*Under unspecified test conditions.

MICROBEL TD447/Suitable Rogallo

(Weight-shift)

Summary similar to SL447/Sprint except: Tandem two-seater.

Production status: prototype.

GENERAL - Bernard advises us that a prototype tandem two-seater trike unit, the *TD 447*, had just made its first flight as we went to press, though he did not say which wing it was mated to. It is fitted with a 41 hp Rotax 447 and is expected to sell at FB169,000. Details are subject to change and data has not yet been released.

EXTERNAL DIMENSIONS & AREAS - NC.

POWER PLANT - See *SL447/Sprint* except: Power per unit area NC.

WEIGHTS & LOADINGS - NC.

PERFORMANCE - NC.

Jacques Callies takes off in a Sonaca Falcon from the French 'Oshkosh' at Brienne-le-Chateau in 1984.

SONACA

Sonaca SA, Marketing Falcon, Route Nationale 5, 6200 Gosselies; tel 071 342211; tx 51241.

SONACA *FALCON* (Three-axis)

Summary as American Aircraft Falcon *(USA section).*
Production status: current, 45 completed.

GENERAL - Sonaca is one of the two most important Belgian aviation firms, formed before World War II, semi-nationalised and employing some 1600 people. The company makes F16 fighters for NATO as well as parts for the European *A310* and *A320 Airbus*. The involvement of top aerospace firms like Sonaca, echoed in France by the Matra group through its Zenith subsidiary, and by Zodiac, can do nothing but good for the image of microlight aviation, still regarded in some quarters as something of an aeronautical joke.

The first contact between Sonaca and Larry Newman of American Aircraft was made in March 1984 when an arrangement was made to manufacture the *Falcon* under licence for the European, African and Asian markets. Three American-built single-seaters were delivered to Sonaca that August, followed by 10 machines in pieces for assembly in Belgium. At the end of 1984 the Belgian firm embarked on its first in-house production run, and by May 1985 some 45 had been delivered in Belgium and abroad.

Static tests under Belgian airworthiness rules showed that the main wing as produced in the USA could only support +4.5g ultimate, so Sonaca-produced machines have undergone 29 modifications to bring them into line with the norms enforced in many European countries. Structural reinforcement has been added to the main wing, canard, fuselage, undercarriage, engine mountings, seat belt and fuel tank, while other modifications involve both the design itself and the method of component manufacture. For example, the ribs at the wing root and tips are now made as a single piece rather than assembled from several pieces, the American arrangement having been shown by Sonaca's fatigue tests to be susceptible to cracking, in theory as well as practice.

UlmMag magazine took part in this research through managing director Jacques Callies and Jacques Mangenot, director of Meaux-Esbly aerodrome east of Paris, the latter flying a *Falcon* in the French championships at Millau-Larzac in the summer of 1984. Following these tests, a detailed report was given to the Belgian company, while Jacques Mangenot wrote an article on his experience in the January 1985 edition, under the evocative headline *A machine in which to wave at the Gods!* The result of all this work is a machine which is a credit to the Americans who conceived it, Larry Newman, Bryan Allen and Ben Abruzzo, though sadly we have to report that the latter has recently passed away.

The future of the single-seat *Falcon* in Belgium now seems assured, but the same cannot unfortunately be said for the two-seat version, for as we write there are still areas of disagreement between Larry Newman and Sonaca. We fervently hope that in due course these will be ironed out, allowing production of this most interesting machine to commence in Europe.

Price of the single-seat *Falcon* in the form detailed below, with Rotax 277 engine, is FB470,000, but from 9 May '85 normal fitment has been the more powerful 34 hp Rotax 377, which adds FB7500 to the price. Integral visor (with optional canopy) and internal wind-breaks to cover the nosewheel hole can be added for a further FB7500, while an American Para Flite ballistic recovery system is a FB40,000 option.

EXTERNAL DIMENSIONS & AREAS - See American Aircraft *Falcon* (USA section).

POWER PLANT - See American Aircraft *Falcon* (USA section).

WEIGHTS & LOADINGS - Empty weight 278 lb, 126 kg. Max take-off weight 525 lb, 238 kg. Payload 347 lb, 112 kg. Max wing loading 2.91 lb/ft^2, 14.2 kg/m^2. Max power loading 20.2 lb/hp, 9.2 kg/hp. Load factors +6.0, -3.0 recommended; +7.0, NC ultimate.

PERFORMANCE* - Max level speed 63 mph, 102 kph. Never exceed speed 75 mph, 120 kph. Max cruising speed 60 mph, 96 kph. Economic cruising speed 50 mph, 80 kph. Stalling speed 27 mph, 43 kph. Max climb rate at sea level 650 ft/min, 3.3 m/s. Min sink rate 250 ft/min at 35 mph, 1.3 m/s at 56 kph. Best glide ratio with power off 15/1 at 43 mph, 69 kph. Take-off distance 200 ft, 61 m. Landing distance NC. Service ceiling 15,000 ft, 4570 m. Range at average cruising speed 52 mile, 83 km. Noise level 91 dB at 30 ft, 10 m.

*Under the following test conditions - Airfield altitude 0 ft, 0 m. Ground temperature 59°F, 15°C. Ground pressure 1013 mB. Ground windspeed 0 mph, 0 kph. Test payload 210 lb, 95 kg.

Canada

Researched by Hal Adkins

Spectrum's Beaver RX-550.

Regulation without stagnation

by Victor Whitmore, President of the Ultralight Pilots Association of Canada

Canadian ultralight pilots enjoy probably the best ultralight flying anywhere in the world. Variety of terrain, variety of aircraft types available, and good regulation all play a positive role in allowing full enjoyment of the sport. The terrain varies from west coast to east coast, from the Rocky Mountains, to flat land prairies, to lake-spotted cottage country, to rolling hills. Canadians can soar over ridges and valleys, fly with floats onto thousands of lakes, or just plain have fun at a very challenging endeavour.

Ultralights flown in Canada include types from other countries in addition to several home-grown designs. The American influence plays a large part in the Canadian market, not only in the import of their designs, but also in the export of our machinery to that vastly larger market. Since the ultralight standards of the two countries are fairly similar, most current designs fit into both sets of regulations. Generally, Canadian designs are not limited by stall or top speed, as in *FAR Part 103,* but most comply with a wing-loading requirement.

Designs have changed significantly over the past couple of years as demand for a 'better mouse trap' continues. Eager designers have set up new companies to challenge early leaders such as Eipper and Ultraflight Sales, maker of the *Lazair,* and designs have shifted from single-surface wings with hybrid control to more sophisticated machines featuring double-surface strut-braced wings, enclosed or semi-enclosed cockpits, and full three-axis controls. There are even some scaled-down replicas of light aircraft. Birdman's *Chinook,* Spectrum's *Beaver,* and Ultravia's *Pelican* all subscribe to these trends and all are Canadian companies competing in the world market. Even more designs are in the prototype or pre-production stage. All these companies are competing in a tight market that was largely stagnant in 1984 but shows signs of steady growth in 1985 and beyond. The boom times are past and we are now settling into a more mature period based on new designs, whose greater safety is helping to attract new blood to the sport.

The past two years have also seen significant changes in regulation. From 1 April 1983 all ultralights had to be registered and to carry that registration number. The following July brought pilot licensing, complete with mandatory training and testing, and shortly afterwards the definition of an ultralight was slightly modified to allow more weight while retaining the wing-loading element. All these regulations are the result of a conscious effort on the part of the ultralight community - especially the Ultralight Pilots Association of Canada - and the Department of Transport, and the results are now beginning to show. The accident rate has declined, but enthusiasts are still able to enjoy the sport to the full.

With variety of terrain, loads of machines to choose from, and meaningful regulations, the sport in Canada continues unabated. And the future looks great!

For more information on ultralights in Canada, contact: UPAC, 169 Romfield Circuit, Thornhill, Ontario L3T 3H7; tel (416) 889-7261.

Hal Adkins

BIRDMAN

Birdman Enterprises Ltd, 7939 Argyll Road, Edmonton, Alberta T6C 4A9; tel (403) 468-0001; tx 0372459. President: John Craig. General manager: Barry Metcalfe. General sales manager: Gordon Wallis.

Australian agent: Basic Flying Machines Pty, 3rd Floor, 249 Pitt Street, Sydney 2000; tel 02-264-5895; tx AA25415. Contact: Jack deLissa.

Indian agent: Nova International, Sewaar, A B Nair Road, Juhu, Bombay; tel 628 222.

Israeli agent: Kanfonit Ultralight Aircraft Ltd, 5 Hsharon Street, Petach-Tikva 49353; tel (03) 961765. Contacts: Navon Yekutiel and Giora Gazit.

Japanese agent: Yasutomo & Co Ltd, No. 7-5, 2-chome, Okina-cho, Naka-ku, Yokohama 231.

Pakistani agent: Nova International, B-82, Block 5, Gulshen-E-Iqbal, Karachi; tx 24174 ENCON PK.

Saudi Arabian agent: Nova International, PO Box 1427, Riyadh; tel 477-1214; tx 203147 BARAD SJ.

The very manoeuvrable Chinook *really showed its paces at Oshkosh '84.*

BIRDMAN *CHINOOK WT-11 277 and WT-11 377*

(Three-axis)

Single-seat single-engined high-wing monoplane with conventional three-axis control. Wing has unswept leading and trailing edges, and constant chord; conventional tail. Pitch control by elevator on tail; yaw control by fin-mounted rudder; roll control by 42%-span ailerons; control inputs through stick for pitch/roll and pedals for yaw. Wing braced from below by struts; wing profile modified UA 80/1; 85% double-surface. Undercarriage has three wheels in tail-dragger formation; bungee suspension on all wheels. Push-right go-right tailwheel steering connected to yaw control; also differential braking. Brakes on main wheels. Aluminium-alloy tube airframe, totally enclosed. Engine mounted at wing height, driving pusher propeller.

Production status: current; over 350 completed (WT-11 277 model), 80 completed (WT-11 377 model).

GENERAL - As can be seen from the dealer list and production figures above, the *Chinook WT-11* in its basic

Rotax 277-powered form is one of Canada's most successful ultralights.

Created by Polish-born Vladimir Talanczuk, who designed and built a number of light aircraft, hang gliders and even a gyrocopter in his native country before emigrating to Canada in 1981, the *Chinook* is actually the eleventh machine to come from Vladimir's drawing board - hence its *WT11* suffix.

Although the Birdman company was founded in 1972 to make hang gliders and later went on to make the *Quicksilver*-like *Atlas* range with various control systems, all links with unconventional controls were firmly broken with the *Chinook,* which sets out unashamedly to attract conventional pilots. Introduced in 1983, this tube and Dacron aircraft has gained a reputation for nimble handling and, despite its enclosed cockpit, good visibility. Former company test pilot Dennis Maland gave a graphic demonstration of the aircraft's abilities at the '83 Oshkosh, when he deliberately deployed his emergency parachute, floated down with it for a while, then detached it from the aircraft, landed the machine and dashed out into the crowd to catch the 'chute as it approached the ground!

Initially offered with a V-belt reduction on its Rotax 277 engine, the *Chinook WT-11 277* is now available with either a toothed-belt reduction or the Rotax integral gearbox. Our data gives figures for the toothed-belt 277-engined version; with a gearbox the reduction ratio becomes 2.6/1, the prop is changed to a 60x28 (1.52x0.71 m), thrust is increased to 200 lb (91 kg) and weight slightly reduced, so performance should be a little better than shown below. For pilots wanting still more thrust, the *WT-11 377* is available, with Rotax 377 engine, though in that form the *Chinook* falls well outside the ultralight category in the US. Where different, data for the 377-engined version is shown in parentheses.

All versions take 15 min to rig with two people and are sold as 40-100 h kits. Prices are C$5995 and C$6150 respectively.

EXTERNAL DIMENSIONS & AREAS - Length overall 17.5 ft, 5.33 m. Height overall 5.8 ft, 1.78 m. Wing span 35.0 ft, 10.67 m. Constant chord 4.0 ft, 1.22 m. Dihedral 1.5°. Sweepback 0°. Tailplane span 8.3 ft, 2.54 m. Fin height 3.9 ft, 1.19 m. Total wing area 140 ft², 13.0 m². Total aileron area 13.4 ft², 1.24 m². Fin area 7.8 ft², 0.72 m². Rudder area 4.4 ft², 0.40 m². Tailplane area 20.4 ft², 1.89 m². Total elevator area 11.0 ft², 1.02 m². Aspect ratio 8.8/1. Wheel track 5.2 ft, 1.57 m. Wheelbase 11.7 ft, 3.57 m. Tailwheel diameter overall 5 inch, 13 cm. Main wheels diameter overall 16 inch, 41 cm.

POWER PLANT - Rotax 277 (Rotax 377) engine. Max power 28(36) hp at 6000 rpm. Propeller diameter and pitch 54(60)x32(30) inch, 1.37(1.52)x0.81(0.76) m. Toothed-belt (gear) reduction, ratio 2.5(2.6)/1. Max static thrust 180 (220) lb, 81(100) kg. Power per unit area 0.20(0.26) hp/ft², 2.2(2.8) hp/m². Fuel capacity 6.0 US gal, 5.0 Imp gal, 22.7 litre.

WEIGHTS & LOADINGS - Empty weight 250(270) lb, 113(122) kg. Max take-off weight 625(628) lb, 283(285) kg. Payload 375(358) lb, 170(162) kg. Max wing loading 4.46(4.49) lb/ft², 21.8(21.9) kg/m². Max power loading 22.3(17.4) lb/hp, 10.1(7.9) kg/hp. Load factors +6.0, -3.0 recommended; +7.0, -3.5 ultimate.

PERFORMANCE* - Max level speed 60(66) mph, 97(106) kph. Never exceed speed 85 mph, 137 kph. Max cruising speed 55 mph, 88 kph. Economic cruising speed 50(52) mph, 80(84) kph. Stalling speed 25 mph, 40 kph. Max climb rate at sea level 700(900) ft/min, 3.6(4.6) m/s. Min sink rate 325(350) ft/min at 32(35) mph, 1.65(1.78) m/s at 51(56)

kph. Best glide ratio with power off 10/1 at 45(46) mph, 72(74) kph. Take-off distance 100 ft, 30 m. Landing distance 100 ft, 30 m. Service ceiling 10,000(11,000) ft, 3050(3350) m. Range at average cruising speed 220(110) mile, 354(177) km. Noise level 55 dB at 500 ft, 150 m.

*Under the following test conditions - Airfield altitude 2400 ft, 732 m. Ground temperature 23°F, -5°C. Ground pressure 1011 mB. Ground windspeed 0 mph, 0 kph. Test payload 227 lb, 103 kg.

BIRDMAN
CHINOOK WT-11 2S447 and WT-11 2S503
(Three-axis)

Summary as Chinook WT-11 277 and WT-11 377 *except: Tandem two-seater. 45%-span ailerons.*

Production status: current; 50 completed (WT-11 2S447 model), 20 completed (WT-11 2S503 model).

GENERAL - Very similar to the solo machine in concept, the *2S* version of the *Chinook* has a wider span and an option of two big Rotax twins - either the 447 or the 503, the aircraft's name being suffixed accordingly. Apart from larger ailerons, all the other flying surfaces are the same.

Our data below refers to the 447-engined aircraft; where different, figures for the 503-engined version are given in parentheses. Rigging times are the same as for the single-seater and prices for 60-100 h kits are C$6800 or C$7040, depending on which engine is required.

EXTERNAL DIMENSIONS & AREAS - See *Chinook WT-11 277 and WT-11 377* except: Wing span 37.0 ft, 11.28 m. Total wing area 148 ft², 13.7 m². Total aileron area 14.5 ft², 1.34 m². Aspect ratio 9.3/1.

POWER PLANT - Rotax 447 (Rotax 503) engine. Max power 40(47) hp at 6000 rpm. Propeller diameter and pitch 60x38(28) inch, 1.52x0.97(0.71) m. Gear (toothed-belt) reduction, ratio 2.6(2.2)/1. Max static thrust 240(270) lb, 108(122) kg. Power per unit area 0.27(0.32) hp/ft², 2.9(3.4) hp/m². Fuel capacity 5.0 US gal, 4.2 Imp gal, 18.9 litre.

WEIGHTS & LOADINGS - Empty weight 333(340) lb, 151(154) kg. Max take-off weight 761(768) lb, 345(348) kg. Payload 428 lb, 194 kg. Max wing loading 5.14(5.19) lb/ft², 25.2(25.4) kg/m². Max power loading 19.0(16.3) lb/hp, 8.6(7.4) kg/hp. Load factors +3.9, -2.0 recommended; +4.5, -2.5 ultimate.

PERFORMANCE* - Max level speed 68(72) mph, 110 (116) kph. Never exceed speed 85 mph, 137 kph. Max cruising speed 60 mph, 97 kph. Economic cruising speed 55 mph, 88 kph. Stalling speed 38 mph, 61 kph. Max climb rate at sea level 600(700) ft/min, 3.1(3.6) m/s. Min sink rate 360 ft/min at 45 mph, 1.8 m/s at 72 kph. Best glide ratio with power off 11/1 at 52 mph, 84 kph. Take-off distance 200 ft, 61 m. Landing distance 150 ft, 46 m. Service ceiling 8000(8500) ft, 2440(2590) m. Range at average cruising speed 86 mile, 138 km. Noise level 62 dB at 500 ft, 150 m.

*Under the following test conditions - Airfield altitude 2400 ft, 732 m. Ground temperature 23°F, -5°C. Ground pressure 1011 mB. Ground windspeed 0 mph, 0 kph. Test payload 378 lb, 171 kg.

Hal Adkins

Graham Lee's Baby Nieuport *was fitted with a 430 Cuyuna when flown at Oshkosh '843 .*

CIRCA REPRODUCTIONS

G Lee Circa Reproductions, 8027 Argyll Road, Edmonton, Alberta T6C 4A9; tel (403) 474-3948. Owner/designer: Graham Lee.

CIRCA REPRODUCTIONS
BABY NIEUPORT

(Three-axis)

Single-seat single-engined biplane with conventional three-axis control. Wings have swept back leading and trailing edges, and constant chord (bottom wing), negative-tapering chord (top wing); cruciform tail. Pitch control by elevator on tail; yaw control by fully flying rudder; roll control by 20%-span ailerons; control inputs through stick for pitch/roll and pedals for yaw. Wings braced by struts and transverse X-cables; wing profile semi Clark Y 11%; 100% double-surface. Undercarriage has two wheels plus tailskid; glass-fibre suspension on tailskid and bungee suspension on main wheels. No ground steering. No brakes. Aluminium-alloy tube airframe, partially enclosed. Engine mounted between wings, driving tractor propeller.

Production status: see text.

GENERAL - Graham Lee's very attractive and realistic seven-eighths scale *Nieuport 11* replica was finished and test flown just in time to make the '84 Oshkosh, and was generally admired as one of the nicest looking World War I replicas at the show, complete with its fake Lewis machine gun and clever C-IRCA registration.

At the time of writing it is only available in plan form, at C\$95 (US\$75), so the powerplant is largely up to the builder.

Graham says any engine of 25-40 hp could be used, mated to a suitable reduction so that the prop speed comes down to 1700-2000 rpm, and our figures below may be considered typical for a machine with 25 hp. The prototype at Oshkosh, incidentally, used a 430 Cuyuna.

Wing design is unusual in that the top wing's chord is larger at tip than at root, thanks to negative-tapering ailerons. Wing design is to an extent the builder's choice, as the standard figure below may be increased to 125 ft² (11.6 m²).

Construction is basically tube and ceconite fabric, the structure being pop-rivetted together. No rib stitching is required, as the fabric is fixed to the airframe with contact cement and then shrunk on with a hot iron. Build time is estimated at 600 h, and with careful construction it may be built light enough to qualify as a US-legal ultralight. However, we've never met a homebuilder yet who didn't build in a few 'refinements' as he or she went along, so it would be safer for US buyers to construct it under experimental-category rules, to ensure that they aren't left with an illegal machine if it comes out a bit heavy. Canadian regulations are less stringent, so the problem is unlikely to arise as far as the home market is concerned.

Transportation requires a car top carrier for the wings and a trailer to hold the fuselage, and though no special tools are required, rigging takes a couple of hours.

EXTERNAL DIMENSIONS & AREAS - Length overall 16.3 ft, 4.95 m. Height overall 7.5 ft, 2.29 m. Wing span NC (bottom); 21.5 ft, 6.55 m (top). Constant chord (bottom wing) 3.5 ft, 1.07 m. Chord at root (top wing) 3.5 ft, 1.07 m. Chord at tip (top wing) 3.9 ft, 1.19 m. Dihedral 5°. Sweepback 5°. Tailplane span 8.0 ft, 2.44 m. Rudder height 2.6 ft, 0.79 m. Total wing area 114 ft², 10.6 m². Total aileron area 8.8 ft², 0.81 m². Rudder area 3.0 ft², 0.28 m². Tailplane area 14.0 ft², 1.30 m². Total elevator area 7.5 ft², 0.70 m². Aspect ratio NC (bottom wing); 6.2/1 (top wing). Wheel track 4.8 ft, 1.45 m. Wheelbase 12.0 ft, 3.66 m. Main wheels diameter overall 24 inch, 61 cm.

POWER PLANT - Output 25 hp at 5000 rpm. Propeller diameter and pitch 72x36 inch, 1.83x0.91 m. Reduction ratio 2.9/1. Power per unit area 0.22 hp/ft², 2.4 hp/m². Fuel capacity 12.6 US gal, 10.5 Imp gal, 47.7 litre. Other data NC.

WEIGHTS & LOADINGS - Empty weight NC. Max take-off weight 475* lb, 215* kg. Payload NC. Max wing loading 4.17* lb/ft^2, 20.3* kg/m^2. Max power loading 19.0 lb/hp, 8.6 kg/hp. Load factors +4.5*, -3.5* recommended; +6.0*, -5.0* ultimate.

PERFORMANCE -** Max level speed 64 mph, 103 kph. Never exceed speed 90 mph, 145 kph. Max cruising speed 63 mph, 101 kph. Economic cruising speed 48 mph, 77 kph. Stalling speed 26 mph, 42 kph. Max climb rate at sea level 500 ft/min, 2.5 m/s. Best glide ratio with power off NC/1 at 35 mph, 56 kph. Take-off distance 300 ft, 91 m. Landing distance 200 ft, 61 m. Range at average cruising speed 263 mile, 422 km. Other data NC.

*Max take-off weight quoted (and used for derived data) is practical limit; aircraft stressed for 550 lb, 249 kg.

** Under the following test conditions - Airfield altitude 2500 ft, 762 m. Ground temperature 64°F, 18°C. Ground pressure NC. Ground windspeed 3 mph, 5 kph. Test take-off weight 465 lb, 211 kg.

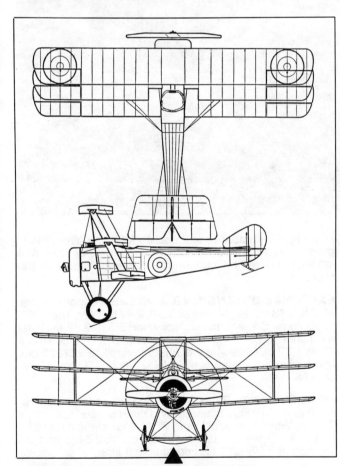

CIRCA REPRODUCTIONS
SOPWITH TRIPLANE
(Three-axis)

Single-seat single-engined triplane with conventional three-axis control. Wings have unswept leading and trailing edges, and constant chord; cruciform tail. Pitch control by elevator on tail; yaw control by fin-mounted rudder; roll control by ailerons on all three wings; control inputs through stick for pitch/roll and pedals for yaw. Wings braced by struts and transverse X-cables; wing profile NC; double-surface. Undercarriage has two

wheels plus tailskid; suspension NC. Ground steering NC. Brakes NC. Aluminium-alloy tube airframe, partially enclosed. Engine mounted between bottom and centre wings, driving tractor propeller.

Production status: prototype.

GENERAL - Due to be released in July '85 is this replica *Sopwith Triplane*. As we write, the machine is still at the design stage and little information is available. However, we presume that the construction will be on similar principles to the *Baby Nieuport*.
Price: NC.

EXTERNAL DIMENSIONS & AREAS - NC.

POWER PLANT - NC.

WEIGHTS & LOADINGS - NC.

PERFORMANCE - NC.

SKY KING

Sky King International, 419 Wellesley Street E, Toronto, Ontario M4X 1H5; tel (416) 923-9917. President: Richard Spence.

Israeli agent: APCO (see separate listing in Other Countries section).

French agent: Avulnor (see separate listing).

West German agent: Ultra-Flug (see separate listing).

SKY KING VECTOR 627SR
(Three-axis)

Single-seat single-engined high-wing monoplane with conventional or unconventional three-axis control. Wing has unswept leading edge, swept forward trailing edge, and tapering chord; V-tail. Pitch/yaw control by ruddervator; roll control by one-third span spoilerons; control inputs through stick for pitch/roll and pedals for yaw, or stick for pitch/yaw/roll*. Wing braced from above by kingpost and cables, from below by cables; wing profile NC; double-surface. Undercarriage has three wheels in tricycle formation with additional tailwheel; no suspension on nosewheel and rubber suspension on main wheels. Push-right go-right nosewheel steering connected to yaw control, or no ground steering*. No brakes. Aluminium-alloy tube airframe, completely open. Engine mounted at wing height, driving pusher propeller.*

Production status: see text.

*See text.

GENERAL - Although the Sky King company may not be familiar to ultralight enthusiasts, its product certainly is, for this Canadian firm bought in mid '84 the rights to the famous *Vector*, one of the best liked early tube and Dacron designs.
Introduced in 1980 as the *Vector 600* by the Skysports International company, which produced it jointly with Gemini International, the *Vector* was a descendent of ultralight pioneer Klaus Hill's *Humbug*. Gemini later went its own way and produced the *Hummingbird* series, which

Norman Burr

The Vector's *greatest moment of glory came when Jacques Breuvart took this 330 Robin-engined* 610 *to outright victory in the '82 London-Paris.*

not surprisingly also bore a relationship to the *Humbug*, while Skysports was absorbed by Vector Aircraft Corp. The latter was itself bought up by Aerodyne Systems at the end of '82, and it was when Aerodyne went bankrupt in 1984 that Sky King stepped in.

Through all the management changes the aircraft has steadily evolved. The two Chrysler engines were replaced for the US market with a single Zenoah G25B to create the *Vector 610,* which also had larger spoilerons, saumons, and some strengthening. In Europe, *Vector 610s* were often powered by 250 or 330 Robin engines. Next came the *Vector 627,* again very similar to its predecessors but with a stiffer tail to resist vibration and a 377 Rotax engine.

All these variants used unconventional three-axis control, with a single stick controlling pitch (fore and aft) and yaw/roll together (side to side) through a mixer. With the *Vector 627SR,* however, came conventional three-axis controls allied to a steerable nosewheel, with the added novelty that the aircraft could easily be converted back to single-stick control in the style of the standard *Vector 627.* This feature was designed to appeal to inexperienced pilots, who could get the feel of the plane before having to learn hand and foot co-ordination.

Now the only version available, the *Vector 627SR* costs US$5790 ready to fly and takes 45 min to rig. We are not certain of the present production arrangements, since Sky King initially said that its first priority was servicing existing

customers with spares and update kits. The aircraft is in production at APCO in Israel and it is possible that manufacture will be concentrated there, at least in the short term.

EXTERNAL DIMENSIONS & AREAS - Length overall 18.0 ft, 5.48 m. Height overall 8.0 ft, 2.44 m. Wing span 35.3 ft, 10.76 m. Sweepback 0°. Tail span 8.5 ft, 2.59 m. Total wing area 154 ft², 14.3 m². Aspect ratio 8.1/1. Wheel track 4.3 ft, 1.32 m. Nosewheel diameter overall 12 inch, 29 cm. Main wheels diameter overall 12 inch, 29 cm. Other data NC.

POWER PLANT - Rotax 377 engine. Max power 36 hp at 6500 rpm. Propeller diameter and pitch 54x26 inch, 1.37x 0.66 m. V-belt reduction, ratio 2.3/1. Max static thrust 260 lb, 118 kg. Power per unit area 0.23 hp/ft², 2.5 hp/m². Fuel capacity 5.0 US gal, 4.2 Imp gal, 18.9 litre.

WEIGHTS & LOADINGS - Empty weight 252 lb, 114 kg. Max take-off weight 500 lb, 227 kg. Payload 248 lb, 112 kg. Max wing loading 3.24 lb/ft², 15.8 kg/m². Max power loading 13.9 lb/hp, 6.3 kg/hp. Load factors +5.7, -2.8 design; NC ultimate.

PERFORMANCE ** -** Max level speed 55 mph, 88 kph. Never exceed speed 63 mph, 101 kph. Max cruising speed 48 mph, 77 kph. Economic cruising speed 40 mph, 64 kph. Stalling speed 27 mph, 43 kph. Max climb rate at sea level 1000 ft/min, 5.1 m/s. Best glide ratio with power off 8/1 at NC speed. Other data NC.

***Under unspecified test conditions.**

SKYSEEKER

Skyseeker Aircraft Corp, PO Box 243, 101 Brady Road, Winnipeg, Manitoba R3V 1L6; tel (204) 261-3330.

SKYSEEKER *SKYSEEKER MKII*
(Three-axis)

Side-by-side two-seat single-engined high-wing monoplane with conventional three-axis control. Wing has unswept leading and trailing edges, and constant chord; cruciform tail. Pitch control by fully flying tail; yaw control by fully flying rudder; roll control by half-span ailerons; control inputs through stick for pitch/roll and pedals for yaw. Wing braced from above by kingpost and cables, from below by cables; wing profile NC; single-surface. Undercarriage has three wheels in tail-dragger formation; bungee suspension on all wheels. Push-right go-right tailwheel steering connected to yaw control. No brakes. Aluminium-alloy tube airframe, with optional pod. Engine mounted below wing, driving pusher propeller.

Production status: current, number completed NC.

GENERAL - This company, formerly known as Skye Treck, can be traced back to 1979, making it one of the country's oldest ultralight concerns.
The *Skyseeker MkII* is derived from the company's first ultralight, the single-seat *Skyseeker MkI*, but unlike the *MkI* the aircraft uses full three-axis controls. The *MkI*, now out of production, was a hybrid control machine with weight-shift assisted by an elevator and rudder.
Though in general one could describe the tube-and-Dacron *Skyseeker MkII* as 'Quicksilver like', there are in fact various differences between the Canadian product and the venerable Eipper machine. The most obvious is that it uses tail-dragger undercarriage, but there is also a fully flying tail and ailerons, not spoilerons, for roll control.
Power comes from the biggest Rotax, the 503, the company having standardised on Rotax power after fitting various engines in its earlier aircraft, including Cuyuna 215 and Komet K-55 units.
Sold as a kit requiring 50 h to construct, the *Skyseeker MkII* costs C$7750 and has a rigging time of 1 h.

EXTERNAL DIMENSIONS & AREAS - Length overall 19.0 ft, 5.79 m. Height overall 9.8 ft, 2.97 m. Wing span 36.0 ft, 10.97 m. Constant chord 5.0 ft, 1.52 m. Dihedral 5°. Sweepback 0°. Elevator span 9.2 ft, 2.80 m. Rudder height 5.0 ft, 1.52 m. Total wing area 180 ft^2, 16.7 m^2. Total aileron area 9.0 ft^2, 0.84 m^2. Aspect ratio 7.2/1. Wheel track 4.2 ft, 1.27 m. Tailwheel diameter overall 3 inch, 8 cm. Main wheels diameter overall 20 inch, 51 cm. Other data NC.

POWER PLANT - Rotax 503 engine. Max power 50 hp at NC rpm. Propeller diameter and pitch 52x34 inch, 1.32x 0.86 m. Reduction type NC, ratio 2.5/1. Max static thrust NC. Power per unit area 0.28 hp/ft^2, 3.0 hp/m^2. Fuel capacity 5.0 US gal, 4.2 Imp gal, 18.9 litre.

WEIGHTS & LOADINGS - Empty weight 330 lb, 150 kg. Max take-off weight 760 lb, 345 kg. Payload 430 lb, 195 kg. Max wing loading 4.22 lb/ft^2, 20.7 kg/m^2. Max power loading 15.2 lb/hp, 6.9 kg/hp. Load factors NC.

PERFORMANCE* - Max level speed 50 mph, 80 kph. Cruising speed 40 mph, 64 kph. Stalling speed 21 mph, 34 kph. Max climb rate at sea level 450 ft/min, 2.3 m/s. Other data NC.

**Under unspecified test conditions.*

SKYSEEKER *SKYSEEKER MKIII*
(Three-axis)

Summary as Skyseeker MkII *except: Single-seater.*

Production status: current, number completed NC.

GENERAL - In effect the *Skyseeker MkIII* is a single-seat version of the *MkII*, sharing many of the dual machine's dimensions though with an extra 4 ft (1.22 m) added to the span. Standard power plant is the Rotax 277, as in the example detailed below, although the Rotax 377 is an option and there are also some Cuyuna 215-engined examples around.
Because this aircraft is structurally similar to the old hybrid-control *MkI*, the company offers update kits to bring the latter up to *MkIII* specification.
Sold as a 35 h kit for C$6250 with Rotax 277 (price with 377: NC), the aircraft can be had with various options, including pod, skis, floats, instruments, a 50x34 inch prop (1.27x0.86 m), and a seat cushion.

EXTERNAL DIMENSIONS & AREAS - See *Skyseeker MkII* except: Wing span 32.0 ft, 9.75 m. Total wing area 160 ft^2, 14.9 m^2. Aspect ratio 6.4/1. Main wheels diameter overall 16 inch, 41 cm.

POWER PLANT - Rotax 277 engine. Max power 28 hp at 6250 rpm. Propeller diameter and pitch 50x26 inch, 1.27x 0.66 m. V-belt reduction, ratio 2.2/1. Max static thrust 180 lb, 82 kg. Power per unit area 0.18 hp/ft^2, 1.9 hp/m^2. Fuel capacity 5.0 US gal, 4.2 Imp gal, 18.9 litre.

WEIGHTS & LOADINGS - Empty weight 252 lb, 114 kg. Max take-off weight 496 lb, 225 kg. Payload 244 lb, 111 kg. Max wing loading 3.10 lb/ft^2, 15.1 kg/m^2. Max power loading 17.7 lb/hp, 8.0 kg/hp. Load factors +4.0, -2.0 recommended; NC ultimate.

PERFORMANCE* - Max level speed 60 mph, 97 kph. Never exceed speed 75 mph, 121 kph. Max cruising speed 45 mph, 72 kph. Economic cruising speed 42 mph, 68 kph. Stalling speed 20 mph, 32 kph. Max climb rate at sea level 750 ft/min, 3.8 m/s. Min sink rate 250 ft/min at 30 mph, 1.3 m/s at 48 kph. Best glide ratio with power off 6/1 at NC speed. Take-off distance 50 ft, 15 m. Landing distance 25 ft, 8 m. Service ceiling 10,000 ft, 3050 m. Range at average cruising speed 210 mile, 338 km. Noise level NC.

**Under unspecified test conditions.*

SPECTRUM

Spectrum Aircraft Inc, No. 3, 9531 192nd Street, Surrey, British Columbia V3T 4W2; tel (604) 888-2045 or (605) 888-1747. President: Peter B L Keate. Director of R&D: Larry Croome. Director of production: Martin Dennis. Sales and marketing manager: Allan K Hunkin.

SPECTRUM *BEAVER RX-28 and RX-35*
(Three-axis)

Single-seat single-engined high-wing monoplane with conventional three-axis control. Wing has swept back

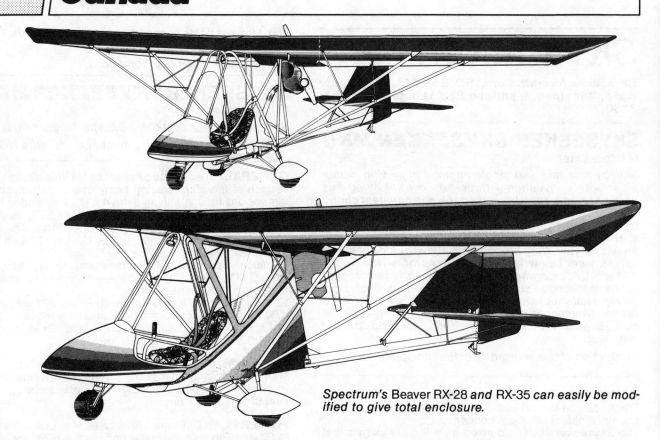

Spectrum's Beaver RX-28 *and* RX-35 *can easily be modified to give total enclosure.*

leading and trailing edges, and tapering chord; conventional tail. Pitch control by elevator on tail; yaw control by fin-mounted rudder; roll control by 75%-span ailerons; control inputs through stick for pitch/roll and pedals for yaw. Wing braced from below by struts; wing profile NC; 100% double-surface. Undercarriage has three wheels in tricycle formation with additional tailwheel; bungee suspension on nosewheel and coil-spring suspension on main wheels. Ground steering by differential braking. Brakes on main wheels. Aluminium-alloy tube airframe, with pod (total enclosure optional). Engine mounted below wing, driving pusher propeller.*

Production status: current, over 125 completed (total of all Beaver *variants).*

GENERAL - Introduced in 1983, the *Beaver* has rapidly blossomed into a range of aircraft, all of them using tube-and-Dacron construction and the same basic configuration.

Cheapest of the range is the *Beaver RX-28,* which as its title suggests has 28 hp courtesy of its Rotax 277 engine. This model is ultralight legal in the US, unlike its larger brother, the *Beaver RX-35,* which is identical except for its Rotax 377 power unit. Our data below refers to the 277-engined version; where different, figures with the 377 are given in parentheses.

Various refinements have been incorporated since we wrote about the *Beaver* in our first edition. Coil-spring suspension has been fitted to the main wheels, the belt reduction system has been changed for the Rotax gearbox, and nylon compression plugs are now fitted to all down tubes, a change which company R&D chief Larry Croome says saves weight and complication and results in a 'strong, positive attachment'. A pod became standard fitment soon after the aircraft was announced, but now pilots can go one

stage further and opt for full enclosure. A further subtle but useful change has been to reduce the tailplane span from 8.0 to 7.8 ft (2.44 to 2.36 m) to allow the aircraft to fit into a standard 8 ft trailer.

Worthy of note on all *Beavers* is the undercarriage, which although basically of tricycle configuration has an additional tailwheel, so that the aircraft can be used as a tail-dragger if required. This of course leaves the question of deciding which wheel to ground steer from, and the company's answer is, quite simply, to use neither. Instead, independently operable main-wheel brakes are fitted.

The aircraft are sold as 40-50 h kits with a rigging time of around 20 min, prices being US$5950 for the *RX-28* and US$6325 for the *RX-35*.

EXTERNAL DIMENSIONS & AREAS - Length overall 17.7 ft, 5.39 m. Height overall 5.7 ft, 1.73 m. Wing span 31.0 ft, 9.45 m. Chord at root 5.5 ft, 1.68 m. Chord at tip 4.7 ft, 1.43 m. Dihedral 1.5°. Sweepback 0°. Tailplane span 7.8 ft, 2.36 m. Fin height 3.0 ft, 0.91 m. Total wing area 148 ft², 13.7 m². Total aileron area 22.0 ft², 2.04 m². Fin area 4.5 ft², 0.42 m². Rudder area 6.6 ft², 0.61 m². Tailplane area 24.1 ft², 2.24 m². Total elevator area 10.1 ft², 0.94 m². Aspect ratio 6.5/1. Wheel track 4.5 ft, 1.37 m. Wheelbase 4.7 ft, 1.44 m. Nosewheel diameter overall 10 inch, 25 cm. Main wheels diameter overall 11 inch, 28 cm.

POWER PLANT - Rotax 277 (Rotax 377) engine. Max power 28(35) hp at 6300(6500) rpm. Propeller diameter and pitch 60(64)x28(30) inch, 1.52(1.63)x0.71(0.76) m. Gear reduction, ratio 2.6/1. Max static thrust 210(NC) lb, 95(NC) kg. Power per unit area 0.19(0.24) hp/ft², 2.0(2.6) hp/m². Fuel capacity 5.0 US gal, 4.2 Imp gal, 18.9 litre.

WEIGHTS & LOADINGS - Empty weight 253(268) lb, 115(122) kg. Max take-off weight 524(539) lb, 238(244) kg.

Payload 271 lb, 123 kg. Max wing loading 3.54(3.64) lb/ft², 17.4(17.8) kg/m². Max power loading 18.7(15.4) lb/hp, 8.5(7.0) kg/hp. Load factors +5.0(4.8), -2.0(1.9) recommended; +7.5(7.3), -3.0(2.9) ultimate.

PERFORMANCE* - Max level speed 58(64) mph, 93(103) kph. Never exceed speed 70 mph, 113 kph. Max cruising speed 48(55) mph, 77(88) kph. Economic cruising speed 40(42) mph, 64(68) kph. Stalling speed 24(25) mph, 39(40) kph. Max climb rate at sea level 800(1100) ft/min, 4.1(5.6) m/s. Min sink rate 375(385) ft/min at 38(39) mph, 1.9(2.0) m/s at 61(63) kph. Best glide ratio with power off 8/1 at 40(42) mph, 64(68) kph. Take-off distance 90(60) ft, 27(18) m. Landing distance 110(115) ft, 34(35) m. Service ceiling 12,000(13,000) ft, 3660(3960) m. Range at average cruising speed 100(90) mile, 161(145) km. Noise level 81 dB at 100 ft, 30 m.

*Under the following test conditions - Airfield altitude 75 ft, 23 m. Ground temperature 32°F, 0°C. Ground pressure NC. Ground windspeed NC. Test payload 208 lb, 94 kg.

Designed as a workhorse: Spectrum's Beaver RX-550SP. For an illustration of the RX-550, see introduction to Canadian section.

SPECTRUM
BEAVER RX-35 FLOATER

(Three-axis)

Summary as Beaver RX-28 and RX-35 *except: Floatplane; no wheels or brakes.*

Production status: current, see Beaver RX-28 and RX-35 *for number completed.*

GENERAL - This aircraft is a seaplane derivative of the solo *Beaver,* and is available only with the Rotax 377 engine. US enthusiasts will be disappointed to learn that even with the FAA's 'floatplane credit', the weight of the *Beaver RX-35 Floater* exceeds the ultralight limit, but it does make an excellent experimental-category marine machine.
Price is identical to the *Beaver RX-35.*

EXTERNAL DIMENSIONS & AREAS - See *Beaver RX-28 and RX-35* except: Undercarriage dimensions not applicable.

POWER PLANT - See *Beaver RX-35.*

WEIGHTS & LOADINGS - Empty weight 328 lb, 149 kg. Max take-off weight 582 lb, 264 kg. Payload 254 lb, 115 kg. Max wing loading 3.93 lb/ft², 19.3 kg/m². Max power loading 16.6 lb/hp, 7.5 kg/hp. Load factors +4.5, -2.0 recommended; +6.75, -3.0 ultimate.

PERFORMANCE* - Max level speed 60 mph, 97 kph. Never exceed speed 70 mph, 113 kph. Max cruising speed 51 mph, 82 kph. Economic cruising speed 42 mph, 68 kph. Stalling speed 25 mph, 40 kph. Max climb rate at sea level 950 ft/min, 4.8 m/s. Min sink rate 390 ft/min at 39 mph, 2.0 m/s at 63 kph. Best glide ratio with power off 7/1 at 41 mph, 66 kph. Take-off distance 150 ft, 46 m. Landing distance 150 ft, 46 m. Service ceiling 12,000 ft, 3660 m. Range at average cruising speed 80 mile, 129 km. Noise level 81 dB at 100 ft, 30 m.

*Under the following test conditions - Airfield altitude 75 ft, 23 m. Ground temperature 32°F, 0°C. Ground pressure NC. Ground windspeed NC. Test payload 208 lb, 94 kg.

SPECTRUM
BEAVER RX-550 and RX-550SP

(Three-axis)

Summary as Beaver RX-28 and RX-35 *except:* Beaver RX-550 *is tandem two-seater. Total enclosure not available on either machine.*

Production status: current, see Beaver RX-28 and RX-35 *for number completed.*

GENERAL - Conceived initially as a trainer, the *Beaver RX-550* shares the same control surfaces as the solo machines from which it is derived, but has a 4 ft (1.22 m) greater span and consequently greater wing area.
One notable feature which is particularly valuable for teaching is that the instructor's controls have a built-in mechanical advantage over those of the student, making it easy to over-ride any foolish moves which the novice may make. Power comes from the Rotax 447.
This is replaced by the big Rotax 503 for the heaviest-duty *Beaver* of them all, the *RX-550SP.* The letters *SP* stand for special purpose, the idea being to take a standard *RX-550,* remove the second seat to produce a cargo area, fit a more powerful engine, tougher undercarriage and a larger fuel tank, the latter integral with the seat. The result is a workhorse which has already seen service in wild-life parks and for surveying and which has obvious potential for many other duties such as crop-spraying. Rigging time on both models is around 20 min, and both are sold as 55-75 h kits. Prices are US$7250 for the *RX-550* and US$7600 for the *RX-550SP.* An option on the two-seater is the larger fuel tank from the *SP.* Our data below refers to the standard *RX-550;* where different, data for the *RX-550SP* is shown in parentheses.

EXTERNAL DIMENSIONS & AREAS - Wing span 35.0 ft, 10.67 m. Chord at root 5.6 ft, 1.70 m. Chord at tip 4.7 ft, 1.42 m. Tailplane span 7.8 ft, 2.36 m. Fin height 3.0 ft, 0.91 m. Total wing area 170 ft², 15.8 m². Total aileron area 22.0 ft², 2.04 m². Fin area 4.5 ft², 0.42 m². Rudder area 6.6 ft², 0.61 m². Tailplane area 24.1 ft², 2.24 m². Total elevator area 10.1 ft², 0.94 m². Aspect ratio 7.2/1. Wheel track 4.8 ft, 1.47 m. Wheelbase 5.5 ft, 1.68 m. Nosewheel diameter overall 11 inch, 28 cm. Main wheels diameter overall 16 inch, 41 cm.

POWER PLANT - Rotax 447 (Rotax 503) engine. Max power 42(48) hp at 6400(6200) rpm. Propeller diameter and pitch 64x30(32) inch, 1.63x0.76(0.81) m. Gear reduction, ratio 2.6/1. Max static thrust 310(NC) lb, 141(NC) kg. Power per unit area 0.25(0.28) hp/ft², 2.7(3.0) hp/m². Fuel capacity 5.0(9.0) US gal, 4.2(7.5) Imp gal, 18.9(34.1) litre.

WEIGHTS & LOADINGS - Empty weight 329(385) lb, 149(175) kg. Max take-off weight 736(905) lb, 334(411) kg. Payload 407(520) lb, 185(236) kg. Max wing loading 4.33(5.32) lb/ft², 21.1(26.0) kg/m². Max power loading 17.5(18.9) lb/hp, 8.0(8.6) kg/hp. Load factors +4.5, -2.0 recommended; +6.75, -3.0 ultimate.

PERFORMANCE* - Max level speed 60(75) mph, 97(121) kph. Never exceed speed 70(80) mph, 113(129) kph. Max cruising speed 49(60) mph, 79(97) kph. Economic cruising speed 41(48) mph, 66(77) kph. Stalling speed 27(29) mph, 43(47) kph. Max climb rate at sea level 600(800) ft/min, 3.1(4.1) m/s. Min sink rate 380(400) ft/min at 42(43) mph, 1.9(2.0) m/s at 68(69) kph. Best glide ratio with power off 7(7.5)/1 at 45(48) mph, 72(77) kph. Take-off distance 175 ft, 53 m. Landing distance 230(240) ft, 70(73) m. Service ceiling 10,500(12,000) ft, 3200(3660) m. Range at average cruising speed 80(110) mile, 129(177) km. Noise level 81(NC) dB at 100(NC) ft, 30(NC) m.

*Under the following test conditions - Airfield altitude 75 ft, 23 m. Ground temperature 32°F, 0°C. Ground pressure NC. Ground windspeed NC. Test payload 383(408) lb, 174(185) kg.

SPECTRUM
BEAVER RX-550 FLOATER
(Three-axis)

Summary as Beaver RX-28 and RX-35 except: Tandem two-seater. Floatplane; no wheels or brakes. Total enclosure not available.

Production status: current, see Beaver RX-28 and RX-35 for number completed.

GENERAL - Just as the *RX-35 Floater* bears a close relationship to the landplane *RX-35,* so the *RX-550 Floater* is directly derived from the two-seat *RX-550* - just the job for those wanting a bush plane to go lake-hopping with a passenger. Apart from the floats, the only change of any significance is the adoption of the Rotax 503 engine from the *RX-550SP.*
As with the *Beaver RX-550,* the large fuel tank is an optional extra; our data below refers to the standard version. Price is US$7600.

EXTERNAL DIMENSIONS & AREAS - See *Beaver RX-550 and RX-550SP* except: Undercarriage dimensions not applicable.

POWER PLANT - See *Beaver RX-550SP.*

WEIGHTS & LOADINGS - Empty weight 450 lb, 204 kg. Max take-off weight 905 lb, 411 kg. Payload 455 lb, 206 kg. Max wing loading 5.32 lb/ft², 26.0 kg/m². Max power loading 18.9 lb/hp, 8.6 kg/hp. Load factors +4.5, -NC recommended; +6.75, -NC ultimate.

PERFORMANCE* - Max level speed 70 mph, 113 kph. Never exceed speed 80 mph, 129 kph. Max cruising speed 54 mph, 87 kph. Economic cruising speed 46 mph, 74 kph.

Stalling speed 30 mph, 48 kph. Max climb rate at sea level 700 ft/min, 3.6 m/s. Min sink rate 400 ft/min at 43 mph, 2.0 m/s at 69 kph. Best glide ratio with power off 6.5/1 at 46 mph, 74 kph. Take-off distance 275 ft, 84 m. Landing distance 200 ft, 61 m. Service ceiling 11,000 ft, 3350 m. Range at average cruising speed 62 mile, 100 km. Noise level NC.

*Under the following test conditions - Airfield altitude 75 ft, 23 m. Ground temperature 32°F, 0°C. Ground pressure NC. Ground windspeed NC. Test payload 383 lb, 174 kg.

TESORI

Tesori Aircraft Ltd, 7219 104 Street, Edmonton, Alberta T6E 4B8; tel (403) 439-7878; tx 037-2036. President: Robert Tesori. Manager: John Cameron.

TESORI PONY
(Three-axis)

Single-seat single-engined high-wing monoplane with conventional three-axis control. Wing has unswept leading and trailing edges, and constant chord; conventional tail. Pitch control by elevator on tail; yaw control by fin-mounted rudder; roll control by half-span ailerons; control inputs through stick for pitch/roll and pedals for yaw. Wing braced from below by struts; wing profile NC; 100% double-surface. Undercarriage has three wheels in tail-dragger formation; axle-flex suspension on all wheels. Push-right go-right tailwheel steering connected to yaw control. No brakes. Aluminium-alloy monocoque airframe, totally enclosed. Engine mounted below wing, driving tractor propeller.

Production status: prototype.

GENERAL - The product of one of Canada's newest ultralight companies, the *Pony* made its first appearance at Oshkosh '84 in prototype form and at the time of writing had not reached production.
Although it wasn't ready to take to the air at Oshkosh, it created quite a lot of interest, not just because of its eye-catching colour scheme, but also because its all-alloy monocoque construction, with aluminium-alloy wings covered with ceconite, promises to be a long-life structure.
Projected price is US$9000.

EXTERNAL DIMENSIONS & AREAS - Length overall 19.0 ft, 5.79 m. Height overall 6.0 ft, 1.83 m. Wing span 30.0 ft, 9.14 m. Constant chord 5.0 ft, 1.52 m. Dihedral 5°. Sweepback 0°. Tailplane span 8.0 ft, 2.44 m. Fin height 4.0 ft, 1.22 m. Total wing area 150 ft², 13.9 m². Tailplane area 16.0 ft², 1.49 m². Total elevator area 8.0 ft², 0.74 m². Aspect ratio 6.0/1. Other data NC.

POWER PLANT - KFM 107 engine. Max power 26 hp at 6000 rpm. Propeller diameter and pitch 72xNC inch, 1.83xNC m. V-belt reduction, ratio 2.2/1. Max static thrust NC. Power per unit area 0.17 hp/ft², 1.9 hp/m². Fuel capacity 6.0 US gal, 5.0 Imp gal, 22.7 litre.

WEIGHTS & LOADINGS - Empty weight 250 lb, 113 kg. Max take-off weight 500 lb, 227 kg. Payload 250 lb, 113 kg. Max wing loading 3.33 lb/ft², 16.3 kg/m². Max power load-

Hal Adkins

A busy scene at Oshkosh, as the Pony *is prepared for display, its engine cover removed to show the monocoque structure.*

ing 19.2 lb/hp, 8.7 kg/hp. Load factors +6.0, -4.0 recommended; NC ultimate.

PERFORMANCE* - Max level speed 70 mph, 113 kph. Never exceed speed 100 mph, 161 kph. Max cruising speed 65 mph, 105 kph. Economic cruising speed 60 mph, 97 kph. Stalling speed 24 mph, 39 kph. Max climb rate at sea level 600 ft/min, 3.1 m/s. Take-off distance 200 ft, 61 m. Landing distance 150 ft, 46 m. Other data NC.

*Under unspecified test conditions.

THOR-AIR

Thor-Air Inc, 457 Fenmar Drive, Weston, Ontario M9L 2R6; tel (416) 745-4657; tx 065-27383. General manager: Guenter Weber.

US agent: Thor-Air Inc, 56 Harvester Ave, Batavia, New York 14020; tel (716) 343-2396.

THOR-AIR *THOR T-1 and T-1-A* (Three-axis)

Single-seat single-engined high-wing monoplane with conventional three-axis control. Wing has swept back leading and trailing edges, and tapering chord; conventional tail. Pitch control by elevator on tail; yaw control by fin-mounted rudder and tip rudders; roll control by yaw-induced roll from tip-rudders; control inputs through stick for pitch/roll and pedals for yaw. Wing braced from below by struts; wing profile Clark Y; 100% double-surface. Undercarriage has three wheels in tail-dragger formation; bungee suspension on all wheels. Push-right go-right tailwheel steering connected to yaw control. No brakes. Aluminium-alloy tube airframe, completely open (partially enclosed optional). Engine mounted below wing, driving tractor propeller.

Production status: current; 65 completed (T-1), 30 completed (T-1-A).

GENERAL - It would be easy to dismiss Thor-Air's *T-1* as just another tube-and-Dacron machine in the modern strut-braced idiom, were it not for the aircraft's most unusual method of roll control. The pilot's inputs are conventional enough, but what happens when the stick is moved from side to side is certainly not. Instead of ailerons or spoilers, the stick moves a tip rudder which not only induces roll through yaw but also creates drag, thus heightening the roll effect.

As you can see from our pictures - both here and on the front cover - there is also a fixed fin at each wing tip, forming a kind of saumon.

That apart, the machine looks conventional enough in ultralight terms, with the popular Rotax 277 and gearbox to lift it aloft. The company is particularly proud of its undercarriage design, which it says is robust enough to handle repeated rough-field landings.

Pilots wanting more power can opt for the Rotax 447 engine, in which form the aircraft is known as the *T-1-A*. Our data below refers to the standard *T-1;* where different, figures for the *T-1-A* are shown in parentheses.

Sold as kits requiring 30 h build time, the aircraft cost US$6280 (*T-1*) and US$6660 (*T-1-A*). Rigging time on either is 45 min and options include a rather appealing transparent semi-enclosure, cockpit heater, skis and floats.

EXTERNAL DIMENSIONS & AREAS - Length overall 13.8 ft, 4.21 m. Height overall 7.8 ft, 2.38 m. Wing span 32.2 ft, 9.81 m. Chord at root 5.5 ft, 1.68 m. Chord at tip 5.0 ft, 1.52 m. Dihedral 13°. Sweepback 34°. Tailplane span 8.0 ft, 2.44 m. Rear fin height 2.5 ft, 0.76 m. Total wing area 167 ft², 15.5 m². Rear fin area 4.0 ft², 0.37 m². Rear rudder area 4.2 ft², 0.39 m². Tailplane area 18.0 ft², 1.67 m². Total elevator area 8.0 ft², 0.74 m². Aspect ratio 6.2/1. Wheel track 4.9 ft, 1.49 m. Wheelbase 12.0 ft, 3.66 m. Tailwheel diameter overall 4 inch, 10 cm. Main wheels diameter overall 12 inch, 30 cm.

POWER PLANT - Rotax 277 (Rotax 447) engine. Max

The twin-cylinder Thor-Air T-1-A, *with optional semi-enclosure.*

power 28(42) hp at 6500 rpm. Propeller diameter and pitch 60(68)x24(28) inch, 1.52(1.73)x0.61(0.71) m. Gear reduction, ratio 2.6/1. Max static thrust NC. Power per unit area 0.17(0.25) hp/ft^2, 1.8(2.7) hp/m^2. Fuel capacity 5.0 US gal, 4.2 Imp gal, 18.9 litre.

WEIGHTS & LOADINGS - Empty weight 238(263) lb, 108(119) kg. Max take-off weight 500 lb, 227 kg. Payload 262(237) lb, 119(108) kg. Max wing loading 2.99 lb/ft^2, 14.6 kg/m^2. Max power loading 17.9(11.9) lb/hp, 8.1(5.4) kg/hp. Load factors +3.0, -2.0 recommended; NC ultimate.

PERFORMANCE* - Max level speed 60(65) mph, 97(105) kph. Never exceed speed 80 mph, 129 kph. Max cruising speed 55(60) mph, 88(97) kph. Economic cruising speed 45(55) mph, 72(88) kph. Stalling speed 28 mph, 45 kph. Max climb rate at sea level 450(800) ft/min, 2.3(4.1) m/s. Min sink rate NC. Best glide ratio with power off 9/1 at 35 mph, 56 kph. Take-off distance 100(40) ft, 30(12) m. Landing distance 200 ft, 61 m. Service ceiling 12,000 ft, 3660 m. Range at average cruising speed 135(100) mile, 217(161) km. Noise level NC.

*Under the following test conditions - Airfield altitude 600 ft, 183 m. Ground temperature 59°F, 15°C. Ground pressure 1013 mB. Ground windspeed 0 mph, 0 kph. Test payload 200 lb, 91 kg.

THOR-AIR *THOR T-1-2*
(Three-axis)

Summary as T-1 and T-1-A *except: Side-by-side two-seater.*

Production status: current, 20 completed.

GENERAL - Most two-seaters share many common parts with the solo machines from which they are derived, but the

Thor-Air's two-seater with optional semi-enclosure.

T-1-2 takes this a stage further, by using a dimensionally identical airframe, though the tubing is heavier gauge. The power pack is the same as the *T-1-A* too, so it should be a relatively easy job for the single-seat owner who wants to fly with a friend to convert his or her machine to *T-1-2* specification.
The two-seater comes with a centre throttle, two sticks and two sets of rudder pedals and sells at US$7482; options, rigging time and build time are as for the single-seater.

EXTERNAL DIMENSIONS & AREAS - See *T-1 and T-1-A.*

POWER PLANT - See *T-1-A.*

WEIGHTS & LOADINGS - Empty weight 320 lb, 145 kg. Max take-off weight 700 lb, 318 kg. Payload 380 lb, 172 kg. Max wing loading 4.19 lb/ft^2, 20.5 kg/m^2. Max power loading 16.7 lb/hp, 7.6 kg/hp. Load factors +3.0, -2.0 recommended; NC ultimate.

PERFORMANCE* - Max level speed 60 mph, 97 kph. Never exceed speed 80 mph, 129 kph. Max cruising speed 55 mph, 88 kph. Economic cruising speed 45 mph, 72 kph. Stalling speed 28 mph, 45 kph. Max climb rate at sea level 500 ft/min, 2.5 m/s. Min sink rate NC. Best glide ratio with power off 9/1 at NC speed. Take-off distance 200 ft, 61 m.

Landing distance 200 ft, 61 m. Service ceiling 12,000 ft, 3660 m. Range at average cruising speed 100 mile, 161 km. Noise level NC.

Under the following test conditions - Airfield altitude 600 ft, 183 m. Ground temperature 59°F, 15°C. Ground pressure 1013 mB. Ground windspeed 0 mph, 0 kph. Test payload 380 lb, 172 kg.

THOR-AIR *THOR T-2*
(Three-axis)

Summary as T-1 *and* T-1-A *except: Yaw control by fully flying rudder with separate fin; roll control by half-span ailerons. Partially enclosed (total enclosure optional).*

Production status: prototype.

GENERAL - As we write, the *T-2* is no more than a prototype and the manufacturer has released only limited information and no illustrations. However, it appears to be a 'conventionalised' *T-1,* dimensionally very similar but with ailerons replacing the tip rudders and tip fins. Cockpit arrangements also seem a little different.
Price: NC.

EXTERNAL DIMENSIONS & AREAS - See *T-1 and T-1-A* except: Total aileron area 16.0 ft², 1.49 m².

POWER PLANT - See *T-1.*

WEIGHTS & LOADINGS - See *T-1.*

PERFORMANCE - See *T-1* except: Never exceed speed 90 mph, 145 kph.

ULTRAFLIGHT SALES

Ultraflight Sales Ltd, PO Box 370, Port Colborne, Ontario L3K 1B7; tel (416) 735-8352; tx 061-5497. President: Dale Kramer.

British agent: AMF Microflight Ltd, Membury Airfield, Lambourn, Berkshire RG16 7TL; tel 0488 72224; tx 848507 MIFLI. Director: Angus Fleming.

ULTRAFLIGHT SALES
LAZAIR SERIES III and SERIES III EC
(Three-axis)

Single-seat twin-engined high-wing monoplane with conventional three-axis control. Wing has unswept leading edge, swept forward trailing edge, and tapering chord; inverted V-tail. Pitch/yaw control by ruddervator; roll control by 40%-span ailerons; control inputs through stick for pitch/roll and pedals for yaw. Wing braced from below by struts; wing profile NC; 100% double-surface.

Undercarriage has four wheels in tail-dragger formation; no suspension on any wheels. Ground steering by differential braking (also differential engine output). Brakes on main wheels. Aluminium-alloy tube airframe; completely open (Series III), totally enclosed (Series III EC). Engines mounted at wing height, driving tractor propellers.

Production status: current, number completed NC.

GENERAL - The *Lazair* is a remarkable aircraft in many respects, not least for the way in which it has stood the test of time. Created by Dale Kramer as long ago as 1978, progressive development has kept it competitive. Even the older aircraft don't look like first generation ultralights, and more than one observer has remarked that if the original design were introduced today, it would still look fresh and modern.

But the essence of the *Lazair* has never changed - a machine with good soaring ability, an inverted V-tail, and twin direct-drive engines mounted on a wing incorporating foam ribs, an aluminium-alloy leading edge, and transparent covering - originally Mylar but later changed to Tedlar in the interests of ultraviolet resistance.

Other changes centre around the control arrangements, engine type and undercarriage design. Early aircraft had a top-mounted stick with a mixer to apportion movement between ruddervators and ailerons; rudder pedals were an option and could easily be disconnected in flight to bring the machine back to stick-only control. By the time the *Series III* arrived, the position was reversed, pedals being standard and single-stick to special order only. The stick mounting was altered too, to the conventional bottom position. The company's latest literature makes no mention of the stick-only option and we suspect it has been dropped. Early *Lazairs* had Pioneer 100 cc engines of 5.5 hp each, but by 1982 these had been replaced by the present Rotax 185 units. These 9.5 hp engines allowed Dale to fit a wider, more stable undercarriage without ruining the performance, so for the *Series III* the *Lazair* was turned into a true tail-dragger, without the additional nosewheel of earlier machines. The twin tailwheels were made to castor rather than being fixed straight ahead, and the main wheels were fitted with spats and individual disc brakes, each operated by the tip of a rudder pedal to permit ground steering.

Options include glass-fibre reinforced polyester skis and floats and, more importantly, a very attractive cockpit enclosure made of similar material and using a polycarbonate windshield. This enclosure is removable in about 10 min and has a dramatic effect on performance, as can be seen from our figures below. They refer to the standard *Series III:* where different, data for the *Series III EC,* as the enclosed version is now known (it was introduced as the *Series IV*), is shown in parentheses.

At a time when other manufacturers' prices are going through the roof, it is pleasing to report that since our last edition the price of a ready-built *Series III* has risen by a mere C$5 to C$8195, while the kit price is exactly the same at C$6450. Equivalent prices for the *Series III EC* are C$9550 and C$7795 respectively.

EXTERNAL DIMENSIONS & AREAS - Length overall 14.0(16.0) ft, 4.27(4.88) m. Height overall 6.3 ft, 1.92 m. Wing span 36.3 ft, 11.07 m. Chord at root 4.8 ft, 1.47 m. Chord at tip 3.1 ft, 0.94 m. Dihedral 2°. Sweepback 0°. Tailplane span 6.7 ft, 2.03 m. Inclined fixed surface height NC. Total wing area 142 ft², 13.2 m². Total aileron area 4.8 ft², 0.45 m². Inclined fixed area NC. Total ruddervator area

8.6 ft², 0.80 m². Aspect ratio 9.3/1. Wheel track 3.9 ft, 1.18 m. Wheelbase 10.0 ft, 3.05 m. Tailwheels diameter overall 4 inch, 10 cm. Main wheels diameter overall 16 inch, 41 cm. Optional floats: length 10.0 ft, 3.05 m; width 25 inch, 0.65 m; height 14 inch, 0.36 m; weight of pair including mounts 60 lb, 27 kg. Optional skis: length 68 inch, 1.72 m; width 13.5 inch, 0.34 m; weight each 13 lb, 5.9 kg.

POWER PLANT - Two Rotax 185 engines. Max power 9.5 hp each at 5800 rpm. Propeller diameter and pitch 28xNC inch, 0.71xNC m. No reduction. Max static thrust 140 lb, 64 kg. Power per unit area 0.13 hp/ft², 1.4 hp/m². Fuel capacity 5.0 US gal, 4.2 Imp gal, 18.9 litre.

WEIGHTS & LOADINGS - Empty weight 220(253) lb, 100(115) kg. Max take-off weight 490 lb, 222 kg. Payload 270(237) lb, 122(108) kg. Max wing loading 3.45 lb/ft², 16.8 kg/m². Max power loading 25.8 lb/hp, 11.7 kg/hp. Load factors* +4.0, -1.3(2.0) recommended; NC ultimate.

PERFORMANCE - Max level speed 55(61) mph, 88(98) kph. Never exceed speed 55(62) mph, 88(100) kph. Cruising speed 40(50) mph, 64(80) kph. Stalling speed 20(24)

Main picture: Lazair Series III EC. Close-up inset: These biblade carbon-fibre propellers were abandoned ... (other inset) for the early Series IIIs but are now being fitted again.

mph, 32(39) kph. Max climb rate at sea level 400(375) ft/min, 2.0(1.9) m/s. Best glide ratio with power off 12(NC)/1 at NC speed. Take-off distance 120(135) ft, 37(41) m. Landing distance 75-100 ft, 23-30 m. Range at average cruising speed 167(208) mile, 269(335) km. Other data NC.

Load limits calculated with jury struts installed (included in stated price) and at all-up weights of 420 lb (191 kg) and 440 lb (200 kg) for the Series III and Series III EC respectively.

**Stalling speed, glide ratio and landing distance obtained under unspecified test conditions. Other figures obtained under the following test conditions - Airfield altitude 0 ft, 0 m. Ground temperature 59°F, 15°C. Ground pressure 1013 mB. Ground windspeed 0 mph, 0 kph. Test payload 170 lb, 77 kg.*

ULTRAFLIGHT SALES
LAZAIR ELITE and ELITE EC
(Three-axis)

Summary as Lazair Series III and Series III EC.

Production status: current, number completed NC.

GENERAL - Although the *Series III* and *Series III EC* perform well for aircraft with only 19 hp to lift them aloft, there are pilots who want more power, and for them the *Elite* and *Elite EC* models have been introduced.

These machines use JPX PUL425 engines driving conventional wooden props and apart from some strengthening are otherwise identical to their *Series III* counterparts. Prices for the *Lazair Elite* are C\$9895 ready to fly or C\$8250 in kit form, equivalent figures for the *Lazair Elite EC* being C\$11,295 and C\$9595 respectively. Rigging and build times are the same as the Rotax-engined machines - around 25 min and 150 h respectively. Options are also the same. Our data below refers to the standard *Lazair Elite;* where different, figures for the enclosed model are shown in parentheses.

EXTERNAL DIMENSIONS & AREAS - See *Lazair Series III and Series III EC.*

POWER PLANT - Two JPX PUL425 engines. Max power 20 hp each at 4400 rpm. Propeller diameter and pitch 34x20 inch, 0.86x0.51 m. No reduction. Max static thrust 190 lb, 86 kg. Power per unit area 0.28 hp/ft^2, 3.0 hp/m^2. Fuel capacity 5.0 US gal, 4.2 Imp gal, 18.9 litre.

WEIGHTS & LOADINGS - Empty weight 254(287) lb, 115(130) kg. Max take-off weight 490 lb, 222 kg. Payload 236(203) lb, 107(92) kg. Max wing loading 3.45 lb/ft^2, 16.8 kg/m^2. Max power loading 12.3 lb/hp, 5.6 kg/hp. Load factors* +6.6(6.0), -2.8(2.5) recommended; NC ultimate.

PERFORMANCE** - Max level speed 62(67) mph, 100(108) kph. Never exceed speed 70 mph, 113 kph. Cruising speed 55(60) mph, 88(97) kph. Stalling speed 22(25) mph, 35(40) kph. Max climb rate at sea level 700(650) ft/min, 3.6(3.3) m/s. Best glide ratio with power off NC(10)/1 at NC speed. Take-off distance 60(75) ft, 18(23) m. Range at average cruising speed 138(150) mile, 222(241) km. Other data NC.

*Load limits calculated at all-up weights of 464 lb (210 kg) and 494 lb (224 kg) for the Elite *and* Elite EC *respectively.*

**Stalling speed and glide ratio obtained under unspecified test conditions. Other figures obtained under the following test conditions - Airfield altitude 0 ft, 0 m. Ground temperature 59°F, 15°C. Ground pressure 1013 mB. Ground windspeed 0 mph, 0 kph. Test payload 170 lb, 77 kg.

ULTRAFLIGHT SALES
LAZAIR SS and SS EC
(Three-axis)

Summary similar to Lazair Series III and Series III EC.

Production status: current, number completed NC.

GENERAL - The letters *SS* stand for Surveillance Special, this aircraft being designed for police work rather than fun flying. As with the other solo machines, it comes in open or enclosed form, the principal difference on the *SS* being the engines used. Initially the model was announced with WAM 342 units, but it is now fitted with electric-start KFM 107E engines. Cap strips are added to the D-cells to make the wing strong enough to handle the extra power, and 90° dive brakes are fitted, along with extra instrumentation.

Our data below refers to the standard *Lazair SS;* where different, figures for the enclosed model are shown in parentheses. Prices for the *SS* are C\$9995 in kit form, or C\$11,895 ready to fly, equivalent prices for the enclosed model being C\$11,295 and C\$13,495 respectively.

EXTERNAL DIMENSIONS & AREAS - See *Lazair Series III and Series III EC* except: Total wing area (including dive brakes) 154 ftXX, 14.3 m^2.

POWER PLANT - Two KFM 107E engines. Max power 25 hp each at NC rpm. Propeller diameter and pitch 34x20 inch, 0.86x0.51 m. No reduction. Max static thrust NC. Power per unit area 0.32 hp/ft^2, 3.5 hp/m^2. Fuel capacity 5.0 US gal, 4.2 Imp gal, 18.9 litre.

WEIGHTS & LOADINGS - Empty weight 314(344) lb, 142(156) kg. Max take-off weight 650 lb, 295 kg. Payload 336(306) lb, 152(139) kg. Max wing loading 4.22 lb/ft^2, 20.6 kg/m^2. Max power loading 13.0 lb/hp, 5.9 kg/hp. Load factors +4.0, -2.0 recommended; NC ultimate.

PERFORMANCE* - Max level speed 75(80) mph, 121(129) kph. Never exceed speed 75 mph, 121 kph. Cruising speed 60(65) mph, 97(105) kph. Stalling speed 27(29) mph, 43(47) kph. Max climb rate at sea level 700(650) ft/min, 3.6(3.3) m/s. Take-off distance 85(110) ft, 26(34) m. Other data NC.

*Under the following test conditions - Airfield altitude 0 ft, 0 m. Ground temperature 59°F, 15°C. Ground pressure 1013 mB. Ground windspeed 0 mph, 0 kph. Test payload 170 lb, 77 kg.

ULTRAFLIGHT SALES
LAZAIR II and II EL
(Three-axis)

Summary as Lazair Series III and Series III EC *except: Side-by-side two-seater. Total enclosure not available.*

Production status: current, number completed NC.

GENERAL - First announced at the end of 1982 but not produced until the following year, the *Lazair II* has followed a similar evolutionary path to the solo machines, except that the earlier style undercarriage has been retained, the additional nosewheel - or in this case nosewheels - still being fitted. Like the *Lazair SS,* it was initially fitted with WAM 342 engines, but it now comes either with JPX PUL425 units (as used on the *Elite*) or KFM 107E engines (as used on the *SS*). Construction is very similar to the solo machines, but the wing has a greater span and area. Prices for the *Lazair II* are C\$9995 in kit form or C\$12,125 ready to fly; equivalent figures for the *Lazair II EL* are C\$10,995 and C\$13,245 respectively. Dimensions, weights and performance figures below refer to the *Lazair II;* where different, data for the *Lazair II EL* is shown in parentheses.

EXTERNAL DIMENSIONS & AREAS - Length overall

Two's company in the Lazair II.

14.0 ft, 4.27 m. Height overall 6.3 ft, 1.92 m. Wing span 38.0 ft, 11.58 m. Total wing area 151 ft², 14.0 m². Aspect ratio 9.6/1. Other data NC.

POWER PLANT (Lazair II) - See *Lazair Elite and Elite EC* except: Power per unit area 0.26 hp/ft², 2.9 hp/m².

POWER PLANT (Lazair II EL) - See *Lazair SS and SS EC* except: Power per unit area 0.33 hp/ft², 3.6 hp/m².

WEIGHTS & LOADINGS - Empty weight 287(330) lb, 130(150) kg. Max take-off weight 725 lb, 329 kg. Payload 438(395) lb, 199(179) kg. Max wing loading 4.80 lb/ft², 23.5 kg/m². Max power loading 18.1(14.5) lb/hp, 8.2(6.6) kg/hp. Load factors +4.0, -2.0 recommended; NC ultimate.

PERFORMANCE* - Max level speed 55(59) mph, 88(95) kph. Never exceed speed 55 mph, 88 kph. Cruising speed 40(45) mph, 64(72) kph. Stalling speed 25(28) mph, 40(45) kph. Max climb rate at sea level 360(450) ft/min, 1.8(2.3) m/s. Take-off distance 300(250) ft, 91(76) m. Other data NC.

*Under the following test conditions - Airfield altitude 0 ft, 0 m. Ground temperature 59°F, 15°C. Ground pressure 1013 mB. Ground windspeed 0 mph, 0 kph. Test payload 340 lb, 154 kg.

ULTRAVIA

Ultravia Aero Inc, 795 l'Assomption, Repentigny, Montreal, Quebec J6A 5H5; tel (514) 585-6132; tx 05-268897. Designer and president: Jean Rene Lepage. Production vice-president: Guy Charette. Marketing vice-president: Lorraine Chauvin.

Australian agent: Geonic (see separate listing).

British agent: World Wide Racing Services (see separate listing).

ULTRAVIA
LE PELICAN, SUPER PELICAN and PELICAN LONG-NOSE (Three-axis)

Single-seat single-engined high-wing monoplane with conventional three-axis control. Wing has unswept leading and trailing edges, and constant chord; cruciform tail. Pitch control by elevator on tail; yaw control by fin-mounted rudder; roll control by 45%-span ailerons; control inputs through stick for pitch/roll and pedals for yaw. Wing braced from below by struts; wing profile NC; 100%

Compare the front of this Pelican Longnose *with the* Super Pelican *shown in the colour section.*

double-surface. Undercarriage has three wheels in tail-dragger formation; axle-flex suspension on all wheels. Push-right go-right tailwheel steering connected to yaw control; also optional differential braking. Optional brakes on main wheels. Aluminium-alloy tube airframe, partially enclosed (total enclosure optional). Engine mounted below wing, driving tractor propeller.

Production status: current, number completed NC.

GENERAL - Conceived by Jean Rene Lepage as a marriage between traditional flying and modern materials, the *Pelican* is often compared with the Aeronca *C-2.* Despite its conventional - by ultralight standards - tube-and-Dacron construction, the *Pelican* in its various forms has a definite feel of nostalgia about it, especially since the spoilers used on the prototype were replaced by ailerons.

Of the three versions, the closest to the Aeronca are undoubtedly the *Le Pelican* and the *Super Pelican.* Both use flat-twin four-stroke engines - the 18 hp Briggs & Stratton for the first (though at one time the 22 hp Onan was also an option), and the Global 35 hp for the second - and both as a result have the Aeronca-like stubby nose, not just for aesthetic reasons but because the relatively heavy four-stroke engines would upset the aircraft's centre of gravity if mounted further forward. The third version, the *Pelican Longnose,* uses the popular Rotax 277 and gear reduction, a much lighter power pack, and is lengthened accordingly. Despite its engine weight, the *Le Pelican* is the lightest of the three, as it lacks the stronger undercarriage and differential ailerons of the later versions. All three aircraft are otherwise very similar and can be rigged in around 40 min.

A popular option, and one which seems to make the aircraft look 'just right', is floats, while a particularly useful option is doors to give total enclosure for winter flying. Skis are also available.

Price for the *Longnose* without options is US$4995 for a 150 h kit; other prices NC. Our data below refers to the *Le Pelican* in basic form; where different, figures for the *Super Pelican* and *Pelican Longnose* are shown in parentheses, in that order.

As we write, the *Super Pelican* is being put through the very stringent British airworthiness regulations by importer World Wide Racing Services, as you can read in the British section.

EXTERNAL DIMENSIONS & AREAS - Length overall 14.0(14.0)(15.0) ft, 4.27(4.27)(4.57) m. Height overall 6.0(6.5)(6.5) ft, 1.83(1.98)(1.98) m. Wing span 35.0 ft, 10.67 m. Constant chord 3.9 ft, 1.18 m. Dihedral 2.5°. Sweepback 0°. Tailplane span 8.0 ft, 2.44 m. Fin height 3.8 ft, 1.14 m. Total wing area 136 ft², 12.6 m². Aspect ratio 9.0/1. Wheel track 6.0(NC)(NC) ft, 1.83(NC)(NC) m. Wheelbase 11.0(NC)(NC) ft, 3.35(NC)(NC) m. Tailwheel diameter overall 4 inch, 10 cm. Main wheels diameter overall 20(NC)(NC) inch, 51(NC)(NC) cm.

POWER PLANT - Briggs & Stratton (Global) (Rotax 277) engine. Max power 18(35)(28) hp at 3600(3200)(6000) rpm. Propeller diameter and pitch 43(57)(60)xNC(NC)(28) inch, 1.09(1.45)(1.52)xNC(NC)(0.71) m. No (no) (gear) reduction, ratio 1.0(1.0)(2.6)/1. Max static thrust NC(250) (220) lb, NC(113)(100) kg. Power per unit area 0.13(0.26) (0.21) hp/ft², 1.4(2.8)(2.2) hp/m². Fuel capacity 5.0 US gal, 4.2 Imp gal, 18.9 litre.

WEIGHTS & LOADINGS - Empty weight 230(250)(240) lb, 104(113)(109) kg. Max take-off weight 525 lb, 238 kg. Payload 295(275)(285) lb, 134(125)(129) kg. Max wing loading 3.86 lb/ft², 18.9 kg/m². Max power loading 29.1 (15.0)(18.8) lb/hp, 13.2(6.8)(8.5) kg/hp. Load factors +4.0, -2.0 recommended; +6.0, -3.0 ultimate.

PERFORMANCE* - Max level speed 60(63)(63) mph, 97(101)(101) kph. Never exceed speed 90 mph, 145 kph. Max cruising speed 55(63)(60) mph, 88(101)(97) kph. Economic cruising speed 50(NC)(50) mph, 80(NC)(80) kph. Stalling speed 27(28)(26) mph, 43(45)(42) kph. Max climb rate at sea level 400(950)(900) ft/min, 2.0(4.8)(4.6) m/s. Min sink rate NC(NC)(250) ft/min at NC(NC)(30) mph, NC(NC)(1.3) m/s at NC(NC)(48) kph. Best glide ratio with power off NC(NC)(11)/1 at NC(NC)(35) mph, NC(NC)(56) kph. Take-off distance NC(50)(75) ft, NC(15)(23) m. Landing distance NC(100)(NC) ft, NC(30)(NC) m. Service ceiling NC(NC)(15,000) ft, NC(NC)(4570) m. Range at maximum cruising speed 275(262)(150) mile, 442(422)(241) km. Noise level NC.

*Data for Le Pelican *and* Super Pelican *obtained under unspecified test conditions. Data for* Pelican Longnose *obtained under the following test conditions -* Airfield altitude 0 ft, 0 m. Ground temperature 65°F, 18°C. Ground pressure NC. Ground windspeed 0 mph, 0 kph. Test payload 200 lb, 91 kg.

A modeller's idea of how the Pelican Club *will look.*

ULTRAVIA *PELICAN CLUB*
(Three-axis)

Side-by-side two-seat single-engined high-wing mono-plane with conventional three-axis control. Wing has unswept leading and trailing edges, and constant chord; conventional tail. Pitch control by elevator on tail; yaw control by fin-mounted rudder; roll control by 45%-span ailerons; control inputs through stick for pitch/roll and pedals for yaw. Wing braced from below by struts; wing profile NC; 100% double-surface. Undercarriage has three wheels in tail-dragger formation; axle-flex suspension on all wheels. Push-right go-right tailwheel steering connected to yaw control; also differential braking. Brakes on main wheels. Composite-construction airframe, totally enclosed. Engine mounted below wing, driving tractor propeller.

Production status: current, number completed NC.

GENERAL - Despite describing it as a production aircraft, Ultravia has so far released little information on its *Pelican Club*, and our picture, the only available one, is of a model.
At first sight one could describe the machine as simply a two-seat *Pelican Longnose* with a bigger engine and deeper chord, but a glance at the specifications shows that a lot of redesigning has gone on. The tube-and-Dacron fuselage has gone in favour of a composite construction (it is not clear whether this applies to the wings as well), and although the picture does not show how, the intention is to make the aircraft's tail-dragger undercarriage convertible to tricycle.
Prices are US$200 for plans, or US$3500-8200 for kits in various stages of completion.

EXTERNAL DIMENSIONS & AREAS - Length overall 19.5 ft, 5.94 m. Height overall 8.3 ft, 2.54 m. Wing span 35.0 ft, 10.67 m. Constant chord 4.5 ft, 1.37 m. Dihedral 1.5°. Sweepback 0°. Tailplane span 8.0 ft, 2.44 m. Total wing area 156 ft², 14.5 m². Aspect ratio 7.9/1. Other data NC.

POWER PLANT - Rotax 447 engine. Max power 40 hp at 6000 rpm. Propeller diameter and pitch 60xNC inch, 1.52xNC m. Gear reduction, ratio 2.6/1. Max static thrust 350 lb, 159 kg. Power per unit area 0.26 hp/ft², 2.8 hp/m². Fuel capacity 10.0 US gal, 8.3 Imp gal, 37.9 litre.

WEIGHTS & LOADINGS - Empty weight 320 lb, 145 kg. Max take-off weight 775 lb, 352 kg. Payload 455 lb, 206 kg. Max wing loading 4.97 lb/ft², 24.3 kg/m². Max power loading 19.4 lb/hp, 8.8 kg/hp. Load factors +4.0, -2/0 recommended; +6.0, -3.0 ultimate.

PERFORMANCE* - Max level speed 85 mph, 137 kph. Never exceed speed 110 mph, 177 kph. Max cruising speed 75 mph, 121 kph. Economic cruising speed 70 mph, 113 kph. Stalling speed 33 mph, 53 kph. Max climb rate at sea level 580 ft/min, 2.9 m/s. Min sink rate 350 ft/min at 38 mph, 1.8 m/s at 61 kph. Best glide ratio with power off 10/1 at 45 mph, 72 kph. Take-off distance 150 ft, 46 m. Landing distance 200 ft, 61 m. Service ceiling 13,000 ft, 3960 m. Range at average cruising speed 300 mile, 483 km. Noise level NC.

*Under the following test conditions - Airfield altitude 0 ft, 0 m. Ground temperature 65°F, 18°C. Ground pressure NC. Ground windspeed 0 mph, 0 kph. Test payload 430 lb, 195 kg.

ZENAIR

Zenair Ltd, King Road, Nobleton, Ontario LOG 1 NO; tel (416) 859-4556. Designer: Chris Heintz.

US agents in various states - contact manufacturer for list.

ZENAIR
ZIPPER and ZIPPER RX

(Three-axis)

Single-seat single-engined high-wing monoplane with conventional three-axis control. Wing has unswept leading edge, swept forward trailing edge, and tapering chord; conventional tail. Pitch control by elevator on tail; yaw control by fully flying rudder; roll control by 60%-span ailerons; control inputs through stick for pitch/roll and pedals for yaw. Wing braced from below by struts; wing profile Princeton Sailwing; 100% double-surface. Undercarriage has three wheels in tricycle formation; no suspension on nosewheel and glass-fibre suspension on main wheels. Push-right go-right nosewheel steering connected to yaw control. No brakes. Rivetted aluminium-alloy airframe, with optional pod. Engine mounted at wing height (above wing on Zipper RX*), driving tractor propeller.*

Production status: current, number completed NC.

GENERAL - Winner of the Best New Design award at Sun 'n Fun '84, the *Zipper* is an aluminium-alloy and Dacron ultralight with a difference. Instead of the round boom

Glider Rider

Hal Adkins

found on so many designs, Chris Heintz's creation uses sheet alloy rivetted to four longerons to form a box-section, which is not only a very rigid arrangement but also gives the aircraft a distinctive look.

Another obvious recognition point is the wing design derived from the sailwing principle developed at the University of Princeton. Best described as a flexwing, since it has no compression struts or ribs, it has its spar rivetted to the back of the D-section leading edge, the assembly being hinged to the airframe just above the pilot. When the wing fabric has been rolled up, the spar can simply be swung back parallel to the tail boom and the aircraft towed on its own wheels - at least for short distances up to 30 mph (48 kph). Longer hauls need a trailer. A rigging time of only 5 min must make this one of the quickest ultralights to get airborne.

Similar originality is evident with the control surfaces, which feature Junkers-type ailerons, behind and slightly below the trailing edge, and a fully flying rudder. The rivetted alloy construction is extended to the tail, an all-metal construction without the usual Dacron covering.

Unidirectional glass-fibre is used for the main gear, and although the nosewheel is not similarly suspended, it does offer good manoeuvrability - the *Zipper* will make a 360° turn in only 20 ft (6 m), not much more than its own length.

Two powerplants are offered, the standard *Zipper* coming with a JPX PUL425 engine and the otherwise identical *Zipper RX* using a Rotax 277. Both are sold complete,

At Oshkosh '83 the Zipper *turned up with JPX engine (main picture), but by Sun 'n Fun next spring the Rotax option had been added (inset).*

including ASI, tachometer and fuel gauge, prices being US$4980 and US$5180 respectively. Options include a pod, 16 inch (41 cm) main wheels, wheel pants, floats, skis, strobe, prop spinner, and modified rudder pedals for taller people. A trailer is also available.

Our data below refers to the standard *Zipper;* where different, figures for the *Zipper RX* are shown in parentheses.

EXTERNAL DIMENSIONS & AREAS - Length overall 16.0 ft, 4.88 m. Height overall 5.5(NC) ft, 1.68(NC) m. Wing span 28.0 ft, 8.53 m. Chord at root 6.0 ft, 1.83 m. Chord at tip 4.0 ft, 1.22 m. Dihedral 3°. Sweepback 0°. Tailplane span 7.5 ft, 2.29 m. Rudder height NC. Total wing area 143 ft², 13.3 m². Total aileron area 10.0 ft², 0.93 m². Rudder area 6.0 ft², 0.56 m². Tailplane area 15.0 ft², 1.39 m². Total elevator area 7.0 ft², 0.65 m². Aspect ratio 5.5/1. Wheel track 5.0 ft, 1.52 m. Wheelbase 5.0 ft, 1.52 m. Nosewheel diameter overall 10 inch, 25 cm. Main wheels diameter overall 10 inch, 25 cm.

POWER PLANT - JPX PUL425 (Rotax 277) engine. Max power 26(28) hp at 4600(6000) rpm. Propeller diameter and pitch 41(60)x16(28) inch, 1.04(1.52)x0.41(0.71) m. No (gear) reduction, ratio 1.0(2.5)/1. Max static thrust 140 (220) lb, 64(100) kg. Power per unit area 0.18(0.20) hp/ft², 2.0(2.1) hp/m². Fuel capacity 5.0 US gal, 4.2 Imp gal, 18.9 litre.

WEIGHTS & LOADINGS - Empty weight 220(240) lb, 100(109) kg. Max take-off weight 440(480) lb, 200(218) kg. Payload 220(240) lb, 100(109) kg. Max wing loading 3.08(3.36) lb/ft², 15.0(16.4) kg/m². Max power loading 16.9(17.1) lb/hp, 7.7(7.9) kg/hp. Load factors +4.0, -2.0 recommended; +6.0, -3.0 ultimate.

PERFORMANCE* - Max level speed 45(48) mph, 72(77) kph. Never exceed speed 55 mph, 88 kph. Max cruising speed 35(38) mph, 56(61) kph. Economic cruising speed 35 mph, 56 kph. Stalling speed 18(19) mph, 29(31) kph. Max climb rate at sea level 400(550) ft/min, 2.0(2.8) m/s. Min sink rate 200(205) ft/min, 1.02(1.04) m/s at NC speed. Best glide ratio with power off 8/1 at 29(30) mph, 47(48) kph. Take-off distance 100(80) ft, 30(24) m. Landing distance 80 ft, 24 m. Service ceiling >8000 ft, >2440 m. Range at average cruising speed 70 mile, 113 km. Noise level 70(72) dB at 300 ft, 91 m.

*Under the following test conditions - Airfield altitude 0 ft, 0 m. Ground temperature 59°F, 15°C. Ground pressure 1013 mB. Ground windspeed 0 mph, 0 kph. Test payload NC.

ZENAIR
ZIPPER II and ZIPPER AG
(Three-axis)

Summary as Zipper and Zipper RX *except:* Zipper II *is side-by-side two-seater.*

Production status: current, number completed NC.

GENERAL -

Although very similar to the single-seat *Zipper,* the Zipper II has a wing of greater span and area. In the power department, the single JPX engine is replaced by two of the same, somewhat derated to 22 hp and fitted with a special exhaust system to keep noise down. Dual rudder pedals and throttles are fitted, with a single central stick.

For agricultural use, Zenair offers the *Zipper AG,* which is basically a *Zipper II* without the second seat and with Micro Ag spray equipment added, which enables the machine to cover a typical field of 2000x600 ft (610x180 m) in half an hour. Without spray equipment, the *Zipper AG* may be used as a high performance solo fun machine - for instance with skis or floats - and is priced at US$6580 ready to fly in landplane form, the same price as the *Zipper II.* Spray equipment costs some US$2000 depending on specification and is available either from Zenair or from Micro Ag Systems, PO Box 391, Lake Geneva, Wisconsin 53147, USA. Options on both machines are similar to the solo aircraft, except that the larger wheels are standard on the *Zipper AG.* Our data below refers to the *Zipper II* in standard form; where different, figures for the *Zipper AG* are shown in parentheses.

EXTERNAL DIMENSIONS & AREAS - See *Zipper and Zipper RX* except: Height overall 6.0 ft, 1.83 m. Wing span 29.5 ft, 8.99 m. Total wing area 148 ft², 13.7 m². Rudder area 8.0 ft², 0.74 m². Aspect ratio 5.9/1. Nosewheel diameter overall 10(16) inch, 25(41) cm. Main wheels diameter overall 10(16) inch, 25(41) cm.

POWER PLANT - Two JPX PUL425 engines. Max power 22 hp each at 4500 rpm. Propeller diameter and pitch 41x16 inch, 1.04x0.41 m. No reduction. Total max static thrust 240 lb, 109 kg. Power per unit area 0.30 hp/ft², 3.2 hp/m². Fuel capacity 5.0 US gal, 4.2 Imp gal, 18.9 litre.

WEIGHTS & LOADINGS - Empty weight 270(260) lb, 122(118) kg. Max take-off weight 700(600) lb, 318(272) kg. Payload 430(340) lb, 195(154) kg. Max wing loading 4.73(4.05) lb/ft², 23.2(19.9) kg/m². Max power loading 15.9(13.6) lb/hp, 7.2(6.2) kg/hp. Load factors +3.0(4.0), -1.5(2.0) recommended; +5.0(6.0), -2.5(3.0) ultimate.

PERFORMANCE* - Max level speed 48(52) mph, 77(84) kph. Never exceed speed 55 mph, 88 kph. Max cruising speed 35 mph, 56 kph. Economic cruising speed 35 mph, 56 kph. Stalling speed 24(21) mph, 39(34) kph. Max climb rate at sea level 550(750) ft/min, 2.8(3.8) m/s. Min sink rate 300(200) ft/min, 1.5(1.0) m/s at NC speed. Best glide ratio with power off 6(8)/1 at 32(30) mph, 51(48) kph. Take-off distance 110(70) ft, 34(21) m. Landing distance 100(80) ft, 30(24) m. Service ceiling >8000(>10,000) ft, >2440 (>3050) m. Range at average cruising speed 42(45) mile, 68(72) km. Noise level 68 dB at 300 ft, 91 m.

*Under the following test conditions - Airfield altitude 0 ft, 0 m. Ground temperature 59°F, 15°C. Ground pressure 1013 mB. Ground windspeed 0 mph, 0 kph. Test payload NC.

France

Researched by Alain-Yves Berger,
Editorial Director of
UlmMag and Pilote Prive
magazines

One of the best of the current crop of French two-seater fixedwings, the Jokair Maestro.

This time the growth will last!

by Alain-Yves Berger

At the risk of being accused of chauvinism, one could reasonably claim that ultralights - or ULMs as they are known here - were born in France at the end of the first decade of the 20th century. Whereas Orville and Wilbur Wright's *Flyer* weighed some 605 lb (274 kg) in 1903 and its direct successors were around twice as heavy, Santos-Dumont's *Demoiselle 19* and *20* of 1907 and 1908 weighed only 254 lb (107 kg) and 315 lb (143 kg) respectively. However, it is not only by virtue of their empty weight that these aircraft can claim to be the world's first ultralights, but also through their configuration and philosophy.

With a high wing mounted on a 'tubular' bamboo framework, wire-bracing top and bottom, cruciform tail and a little two-cylinder 20 hp (later 35 hp) engine driving a twin-blade tractor prop, they call to mind many of today's fixed-wing tube-and-Dacron ultralights. Indeed John Chotia, father of the 1977 American *Weedhopper*, proudly proclaimed himself to have been largely inspired by the *Demoiselle 20*. As Santos-Dumont's machine could land or take off from a lawn of less than 330 ft (100 m), he would use it as a leisure aircraft to visit his friends living round the outskirts of Paris, just as ultralights are used today (air traffic zones permitting!).

None of this history, of course, made any difference in 1974, when the world recession hit France just like everywhere else, producing a slump in sales of aeroplanes and gliders and the disappearance of various manufacturers. Between 1974 and 1984, the number of registrations of light commercial aircraft plummeted from 323 to about 100 a year. This crisis also caused a disproportionate rise in the price of aircraft and the hourly cost of flying, which almost quadrupled in a decade. These costs combined with bureaucratic constraints caused first stagnation and then decline in French aviation.

But a new wind had already started to blow, with the arrival in 1973 of the first hang-gliders, a source of new hope as most practitioners came from outside the traditional aviation circles. Its acceptable costs, relative absence of red tape and its very dissociation from the jaded and moribund structure of most other aviation sports appeared to promise it a bright future. Unfortunately, outside the Alps, the Pyrenees and the Massif Central, France is a predominantly flat country and this fact quickly inspired the first hang-glider pilots, faced with excessive journeys to

▶

▷ sites, to seek ways of taking off from the flatlands. Foot-launching behind a winch or a car was at that time considered too dangerous and met with little success and these circumstances gave birth to the first ultralights in 1974, with the appearance of Jean-Marc Geiser's Motodelta *G10*. As in the USA, some pioneers chose to fit one or two motors to the hang-glider wing itself, while others added tailplanes or attached control surfaces, and still others fitted these wings with cages made from flexwing tubing and fitted with a two- or three-wheel undercarriage. There were, however, hardly any successful attempts like those of Volmer Jensen or Homer Kolb in the USA to impose a conventional aeroplane control system on an ultralight, despite a few attempts at motorising rigid or semi-rigid machines as early as 1973.

We had to wait until 1979 for an ultralight to make its commercial debut in France, when Roland Magallon, who ran the now-defunct Veliplane and Aeronautic companies, invented the trike. Now the sport was starting to grow, and two years later came the first three-axis imports and the first flights of the *Baroudeur,* the earliest French-built fixedwing commercially available. Ultralight aviation enjoyed a remarkable growth between summer '82 and September '83, thanks to the absence of stifling regulations, low purchase price and positive interest from the media, witness the coverage of the '82 London-Paris.

But this boom period ended abruptly with the three fatal accidents of the 1983 Grand Prix de France which, like the London-Paris, was organised by Bernard Lamy. Added to other serious and fatal accidents that year, this otherwise attractive competition had a deplorable impact on the image of the sport. New trainees deserted schools, which still lacked a serious system of instruction. Sales stopped abruptly for the majority of manufacturers who were not geared to the export market, and the onset of winter completed the rout. In the early months of 1984 even the least pessimistic in the trade agreed that ultralight aviation was destined to follow the skateboard into oblivion or at best obscurity. But little by little, a tentative recovery began, aided by an unseasonally fine autumn. It has continued steadily, until now one can fly with a high degree of safety, thanks to the efforts of bodies like the Federation Francaise des Planeurs Ultralegers Motorises (FFPLUM - the French ultralight aircraft federation), the Service de la Formation Aeronautique (SFACT - the aeronautical training service) which set up a pilot training system, and the Syndicat Francais des Constructeurs d'Aeronefs Ultralegers (SCAUL - the association of ultralight aircraft manufacturers) which established and ensured the application of airworthiness standards. At last we have a set of regulations which are neither too permissive nor too restrictive.

As the sport evolves, we are also seeing a reversal of the earlier preference for flexwings, with a marked predominance now of two- and three-axis aircraft. While it cannot match the US for sheer volume, France now indisputably produces the widest variety of ultralights in the world, and at competitive prices, from 30,000 to 120,000FF. There seems every chance too that 1985 will see the ultralight enjoying widespread use as agricultural aid. In common with other countries, military applications too are being researched here, and this could open up another new market.

For more information on ULMs in France, contact: FFPLUM, chemin de la Sacristie, 84140 Montfavet; tel (90) 325675. President: Alain Dreyer. Pilote Prive *and* UlmMag *magazines are at 50 rue de Chabrol, 75010 Paris; tel (1) 770 1287.*

AEIM

AEIM Department ULM, 11 rue de Verdun, 54014 Nancy Cedex; tel (8) 396 2417. Contact: G Boxstael and Jean-Jacques Colin.

AEIM/SYNAIRGIE *EPSILON*
(Weight-shift)

Tandem two-seat single-engined flex-wing aircraft with weight-shift control. Rogallo wing with keel pocket. Pilot suspended below wing in trike unit, using bar to control pitch and roll/yaw by altering relative positions of trike unit and wing. Wing braced from above by kingpost and cables, from below by cables; rigid cross-tube construction with single-surface; ribs NC. Undercarriage has three wheels in tricycle formation; no suspension on nosewheel and coil-spring suspension on main wheels. Push-right go-left nosewheel steering independent from aerodynamic controls. Nosewheel brake. Steel/aluminium-alloy tube trike unit, completely open. Engine mounted below wing, driving pusher propeller.

Production status: current, 4 completed.

GENERAL - Translated, AEIM stands for the Meurthe and Moselle association for maladjusted adults and children, an organisation assisted by government grants which specialises in building trikes designed by Jean-Jacques Colin.

Colin's machines were produced by the UAI company between January and July 1984, but the progressive installation of facilities at AEIM enabled the association to turn out 14 pre-production machines between August 1984 and January 1985, while since February the total production rate has been around 10 aircraft and 20 engines a month.

The sturdy construction of these duopole trike units makes them useful as trainers or for agricultural work, and in fact Jean-Jacques conceived them with crop-spraying in mind, hardly surprising as his father Jacques is a technical adviser to the ministry of agriculture. The trike options therefore include a 29.1 US gal (24.2 Imp gal, 110 litre) polyester spray tank fitted with a visual gauge, mixer, electric pump and pressure regulator. Two 16 ft (5 m) booms, each with nine spray units, can treat a 39 ft (12 m) swathe with a low-volume mix at a rate of 1.3-2.7 US gal/acre (1.1-2.2 Imp gal/acre, 12-25 litre/hectare). Alternatively, a newly developed pulverisation system can deliver 0.32-4.0 US gal/acre (0.27-3.3 Imp gal/acre, 3-15 litre/hectare), thanks to four small electric sprayjets which give a 46 ft (14 m) spread.

AEIM produces only one basic design of trike unit, but

AEIM Epsilon *with spray equipment attached.*

offers it with one or two-seats and each of these in turn with a choice of wings.

Initial production was all mated to wings from Synairgie, a new company specialising in heavy-duty wings for agricultural four-stroke trikes, float flying and similar high-payload applications. The firm was formed at the end of 1984 by a group including Rene Coulon, owner of *Vol Libre* magazine, the hang gliding and ultralight publication, and Vol Libre Diffusion, the hang gliding and ultralight accessories chain. Its director is Michel Baduel, formerly with the MB company.

The company's simplest Rogallo is the *Pelican,* a single-surface design which comes in two sizes depending on whether it has to support a solo or dual payload. When mated to the AEIM trike unit, the combination is known as the *Epsilon,* regardless of whether the aircraft is a solo or dual machine. Customers who want higher performance can opt for the double-surface *Sphinx.* This is also available in two sizes - 204 or 229 ft² (19.0 or 21.2 m²), both with the same span - and produces the *Epsilon Plus* when fitted to a one- or two-seat trike unit. All four wings have similar geometry.

Power comes from direct-drive Volkswagen four-cylinder four-stroke units converted for aircraft use by the association, five units being offered: 1600 cc (48 hp), 1800 cc (63 hp), 1900 cc (68 hp), 2100 cc (75 hp) and 2200 cc (80 hp).

To further complicate this bewildering array of options, Jean-Jacques has indicated that AEIM is likely to produce its own wings in due course. Moreover, in spring 1985 the company's trikes became available with La Mouette wings. However, we have no data on these variants, and for our listings have selected two of the more popular two-seat Synairgie-winged variants, the *Epsilon* with 1600 engine, which we detail below, and the *Epsilon Plus* with 1800 unit, which we list separately.

Prices for complete aircraft are 51,012FF and 55,649FF respectively. Wings may be bought separately from Synairgie (address in index), as follows: large *Pelican* 16,800FF, small *Sphinx* 15,400FF, large *Sphinx* 18,700FF. The small *Pelican* is available to special order only - price on request.

EXTERNAL DIMENSIONS & AREAS - Length overall 11.5 ft, 3.50 m. Height overall 12.5 ft, 3.80 m. Wing span 36.1 ft, 11.00 m. Chord at root 8.6 ft, 2.60 m. Chord at tip 3.3 ft, 1.00 m. Dihedral 3°. Nose angle 123°. Depth of keel pocket NC. Total wing area 229 ft², 21.2 m². Keel pocket area 2.7 ft², 0.25 m². Aspect ratio 5.7/1. Wheel track 5.8 ft, 1.75 m. Wheelbase 5.3 ft, 1.6 m. Nosewheel diameter overall 16 inch, 40 cm. Main wheels diameter overall 16 inch, 40 cm.

POWER PLANT - VW 1600 AEIM engine. Max power 48 hp at 2600 rpm. Propeller diameter and pitch 55xNC inch, 1.40xNC m. No reduction. Max static thrust 276 lb, 125 kg. Power per unit area 0.21 hp/ft², 2.3 hp/m². Fuel capacity 7.1 US gal, 5.9 Imp gal, 27.0 litre.

WEIGHTS & LOADINGS - Empty weight 373 lb, 169 kg. Max take-off weight 870 lb, 394 kg. Payload 497 lb, 225 kg. Max wing loading 3.80 lb/ft², 18.6 kg/m². Max power loading 18.1 lb/hp, 8.2 kg/hp. Load factors NC recommended; +6.0, -3.0 ultimate.

PERFORMANCE* - Max level speed 44 mph, 70 kph. Never exceed speed 62 mph, 100 kph. Max cruising speed 40 mph, 65 kph. Economic cruising speed 34 mph, 55 kph. Stalling speed 21 mph, 33 kph. Max climb rate at sea level 490 ft/min, 2.5 m/s. Min sink rate 370 ft/min at 31 mph, 1.9 m/s at 50 kph. Best glide ratio with power off NC. Take-off distance 165 ft, 50 m. Landing distance 130 ft, 40 m. Service ceiling 9840 ft, 3000 m. Range at average cruising speed 112 mile, 180 km. Noise level NC.

*Under unspecified test conditions.

AEIM trikes are easily recognisable by their distinctive balloon tyres and rear-axle arrangement. This one is an Epsilon Plus.

AEIM/SYNAIRGIE
EPSILON PLUS
(Weight-shift)

Summary as Epsilon *except: floating cross-tube construction with 70% double-surface enclosing cross-tube; preformed ribs.*

Production status: current, 10 completed.

GENERAL - See *Epsilon.*

EXTERNAL DIMENSIONS & AREAS - See *Epsilon* except: Nose angle 126°.

POWER PLANT - VW 1800 AEIM engine. Max power 63 hp at 2100 rpm. Propeller diameter and pitch 59x30 inch, 1.48x0.77 m. No reduction. Max static thrust 364 lb, 165 kg. Power per unit area 0.28 hp/ft^2, 3.0 hp/m^2. Fuel capacity 7.1 US gal, 5.9 Imp gal, 27.0 litre.

WEIGHTS & LOADINGS - Empty weight 382 lb, 173 kg. Max take-off weight 1044 lb, 473 kg. Payload 662 lb, 300 kg. Max wing loading 4.56 lb/ft^2, 22.3 kg/m^2. Max power loading 16.6 lb/hp, 7.5 kg/hp. Load factors NC recommended; +6.0, -3.0 ultimate.

PERFORMANCE* - Max level speed 62 mph, 100 kph. Never exceed speed 78 mph, 125 kph. Max cruising speed 50 mph, 80 kph. Economic cruising speed 37 mph, 60 kph. Stalling speed 23 mph, 38 kph. Max climb rate at sea level 1080 ft/min, 5.5 m/s. Min sink rate 310 ft/min at 34 mph, 1.6 m/s at 55 kph. Best glide ratio with power off NC. Take-off distance 130 ft, 40 m. Landing distance 130 ft, 40 m. Service ceiling 9840 ft, 3000 m. Range at average cruising speed 156 mile, 250 km. Noise level NC.

**Under unspecified test conditions.*

AEROKART

Aerokart SARL. Registered office: plateau de Louze, RN7, 38150 Roussillon; tel (74) 29 5951; tx 900793. Factory: chemin de Petiteux, 38370 Les-Roches-de-Condrieu; tel (74) 56 3046. Proprietors: Bernard Charpenel and Rene Feltrin.

AEROKART BABY 12
(Two-axis)

Single-seat single-engined high-wing monoplane with two-axis control. Wing has unswept leading and trailing edges, and constant chord; cruciform tail. Pitch control by elevator on tail; yaw control by fin-mounted rudder; no separate roll control; control inputs through stick for pitch/yaw. Wing braced from above by kingpost and cables, from below by cables; wing profile AK 8414; 28% double-surface. Undercarriage has three wheels in tricycle formation; no suspension on nosewheel and rubber suspension on main wheels. Push-right go-right nosewheel steering independent from yaw control. No brakes. Steel/aluminium-alloy tube airframe, with optional pod. Engine mounted at wing height, driving tractor propeller.

Production status: current, 3 completed.

GENERAL - Most companies begin with solo machines and then progress to two-seaters, but Aerokart is an exception. The company's first serious production effort was the two-seat *Aerokart 5320,* as we explain under that heading, and it was not until 1984 that the company began production of an economy two-axis single-seater derived from it, the *Baby 12.* This in turn has been developed into a complete *Baby* range, the other models all being two-seaters to fill the gap between the *Baby 12* and the company's flagship, the *Aerokart 5320.*

The company is thus able to offer anything from a two-axis machine with almost single-surface wing and tractor propeller to a three-axis double-surfaced aircraft with pusher prop. Airframe, control surfaces and three-axis control system are identical on all the two-seaters, even on the *Aerokart 5320;* company policy is to reduce costs by structural simplification and standardisation, which allows Aerokart's nine models to be built *a la carte* according to the taste and needs of the buyer.

Our data below refers to the *Baby 12,* which sells at 26,939FF as a kit or 29,469FF assembled and test flown; other models we list separately.

EXTERNAL DIMENSIONS & AREAS - Length overall 15.1 ft, 4.60 m. Height overall 8.2 ft, 2.50 m. Wing span 27.9 ft, 8.50 m. Constant chord 4.9 ft, 1.51 m. Dihedral 8°. Sweepback 0°. Tailplane span 9.8 ft, 3.00 m. Fin height 3.3 ft, 1.00 m. Total wing area 138 ft^2, 12.8 m^2. Fin area 4.1 ft^2, 0.38 m^2. Rudder area 6.8 ft^2, 0.63 m^2. Tailplane area 17.8 ft^2, 1.65 m^2. Total elevator area 11.4 ft^2, 1.06 m^2. Aspect ratio 5.6/1. Wheel track 4.3 ft, 1.30 m. Wheelbase 4.2 ft, 1.29 m. Nosewheel diameter overall 10 inch, 26 cm. Main wheels diameter overall 16 inch, 40 cm.

POWER PLANT - Rotax 277 engine. Max power 26 hp at 6000 rpm. Propeller diameter and pitch 60x29 inch, 1.52x0.73 m. Gear reduction, ratio 2.6/1. Max static thrust 172 lb, 78 kg. Power per unit area 0.19 hp/ft^2, 2.0 hp/m^2. Fuel capacity 5.3 US gal, 4.4 Imp gal, 20.0 litre.

WEIGHTS & LOADINGS - Empty weight 207 lb, 94 kg. Max take-off weight 463 lb, 210 kg. Payload 256 lb, 116 kg. Max wing loading 3.36 lb/ft^2, 16.4 kg/m^2. Max power loading 17.8 lb/hp, 8.1 kg/hp. Load factors +6.0, -4.0 recommended; NC ultimate.

PERFORMANCE* - Max level speed 44 mph, 70 kph. Never exceed speed 62 mph, 100 kph. Max cruising speed 37 mph, 60 kph. Economic cruising speed 28 mph, 45 kph. Stalling speed 16 mph, 25 kph. Max climb rate at sea level

500 ft/min, 2.5 m/s. Min sink rate 300 ft/min at 22 mph, 1.5 m/s at 35 kph. Best glide ratio with power off 6/1 at 28 mph, 45 kph. Take-off distance 50 ft, 15 m. Landing distance 80 ft, 25 m. Service ceiling 8200 ft, 2500 m. Range at average cruising speed 84 mile, 135 km. Noise level NC.

Under the following test conditions - Airfield altitude 718 ft, 219 m. Ground temperature 72°F, 22°C. Ground pressure NC. Ground windspeed 7 mph, 12 kph. Test payload 212 lb, 96 kg.

AEROKART *BABY 22*

(Two-axis)

Summary as Baby 12 *except: Side-by-side two-seater. Wing profile AK 8410.*

Production status: current, 4 completed.

GENERAL - The *Baby 22* is a two-seat version of the *Baby 12,* with larger engine, greater span, height and length, but an identical tail. For further details see *Baby 12.*
Prices for the *Baby 22* are 38,448FF in kit form, or 40,978FF assembled and test flown.

EXTERNAL DIMENSIONS & AREAS - Length overall 19.7 ft, 6.00 m. Height overall 8.9 ft, 2.70 m. Wing span 34.2 ft, 10.40 m. Constant chord 4.9 ft, 1.51 m. Dihedral 8°. Sweepback 0°. Tailplane span 9.8 ft, 3.00 m. Fin height 3.3 ft, 1.00 m. Total wing area 168 ft², 15.6 m². Fin area 4.1 ft², 0.38 m². Rudder area 6.8 ft², 0.63 m². Tailplane area 17.8 ft², 1.65 m². Total elevator area 11.4 ft², 1.06 m². Aspect ratio 6.9/1. Wheel track 5.6 ft, 1.70 m. Wheelbase 5.3 ft, 1.60 m. Nosewheel diameter overall 16 inch, 40 cm. Main wheels diameter overall 16 inch, 40 cm.

POWER PLANT - Rotax 447 engine. Max power 42 hp at 6500 rpm. Propeller diameter and pitch 60x26 inch, 1.52x0.67 m. Gear reduction, ratio 2.6/1. Max static thrust 287 lb, 130 kg. Power per unit area 0.25 hp/ft², 2.7 hp/m². Fuel capacity 10.6 US gal, 8.8 Imp gal, 40.0 litre.

WEIGHTS & LOADINGS - Empty weight 331 lb, 150 kg. Max take-off weight 883 lb, 400 kg. Payload 552 lb, 250 kg. Max wing loading 5.26 lb/ft², 25.6 kg/m². Max power loading 21.0 lb/hp, 9.5 kg/hp. Load factors +6.0, -4.0 recommended; NC ultimate.

PERFORMANCE* - Max level speed 56 mph, 90 kph. Never exceed speed 68 mph, 110 kph. Max cruising speed 44 mph, 70 kph. Economic cruising speed 31 mph, 50 kph. Stalling speed 22 mph, 35 kph. Max climb rate at sea level 500 ft/min, 2.5 m/s. Min sink rate 390 ft/min at 25 mph, 2.0 m/s at 40 kph. Best glide ratio with power off 6/1 at 31 mph, 50 kph. Take-off distance 100 ft, 30 m. Landing distance 80 ft, 25 m. Service ceiling 8200 ft, 2500 m. Range at average cruising speed 137 mile, 220 km. Noise level NC.

Under the following test conditions - Airfield altitude 718 ft, 219 m. Ground temperature 72°F, 22°C. Ground pressure NC. Ground windspeed 7 mph, 12 kph. Test payload 397 lb, 180 kg.

AEROKART *BABY 23, 231, 232, 233, and 234*

(Three-axis)

Side-by-side two-seat single-engined high-wing monoplane with conventional three-axis control. Wing has unswept leading and trailing edges, and constant chord; cruciform tail. Pitch control by elevator on tail; yaw control by fin-mounted rudder; roll control by 80%-span ailerons; control inputs through stick for pitch/roll and pedals for yaw. Wing braced from above by kingpost and cables, from below by cables (except Baby 234: wing braced from below by struts); wing profile AK 8410; 28% double-surface (Baby 23 and Baby 232), 100% double-surface (other variants). Undercarriage has three wheels in tricycle formation; no suspension on nosewheel and rubber suspension on main wheels. Push-right go-right nosewheel steering connected to yaw control. No brakes. Steel/aluminium-alloy tube airframe, with optional pod. Engine mounted below wing, driving tractor propeller (Baby 23 and Baby 231), driving pusher propeller (other variants).

Production status: current, 4 completed (total of all Baby 23 variants).

GENERAL - Designed as larger-engined three-axis version of the *Baby 22*, the *Baby 23* has itself spawned a range of variants. Thus the *Baby 23* has a tractor prop, kingpost-and-cable bracing and 28% double-surface, but customers may order it with 100% double-surface, in which form it is dubbed *Baby 231*. Fitting a pusher prop (with the same engine position) turns the base model into a *Baby 232*, while making both these modifications produces a *Baby 233*. Finally comes the *Baby 234*, which is a strut-braced version of the *Baby 233*.

Kit prices are as follows, with ready-to-fly equivalents in parentheses. *Baby 23* - 46,712FF (49,713FF), *Baby 231* - 49,494FF (52,698FF), *Baby 232* - 52,555FF (55,885FF), *Baby 233* - 55,337FF (58,870FF), *Baby 234* - 58,902FF (62,435FF). Our data below refers to the basic model.

EXTERNAL DIMENSIONS & AREAS - See *Baby 22* except: Dihedral 2.5°. Total wing area 194 ft², 18.0 m². Total aileron area 25.9 ft², 2.40 m². Aspect ratio 6.0/1.

POWER PLANT - Rotax 503 engine. Max power 53 hp at 7200 rpm. Propeller diameter and pitch 60x29 inch, 1.52x0.73 m. Toothed-belt reduction, ratio 2.5/1. Max static thrust 331 lb, 150 kg. Power per unit area 0.27 hp/ft², 2.9 hp/m². Fuel capacity 10.6 US gal, 8.8 Imp gal, 40.0 litre.

WEIGHTS & LOADINGS - Empty weight 340 lb, 154 kg. Max take-off weight 927 lb, 420 kg. Payload 587 lb, 266 kg. Max wing loading 4.78 lb/ft², 23.3 kg/m². Max power loading 17.5 lb/hp, 7.9 kg/hp. Load factors +5.7, -3.8 recommended; NC ultimate.

PERFORMANCE* - Max level speed 59 mph, 95 kph. Never exceed speed 68 mph, 110 kph. Max cruising speed 47 mph, 75 kph. Economic cruising speed 37 mph, 60 kph. Stalling speed 22 mph, 35 kph. Max climb rate at sea level 590 ft/min, 3.0 m/s. Min sink rate 360 ft/min at 25 mph, 1.8 m/s at 40 kph. Best glide ratio with power off 6.5/1 at 37 mph, 60 kph. Take-off distance 100 ft, 30 m. Landing distance 90 ft, 28 m. Service ceiling 9840 ft, 3000 m. Range at average cruising speed 130 mile, 210 km. Noise level NC.

*Under the following test conditions - Airfield altitude 718 ft, 219 m. Ground temperature 57°F, 14°C. Ground pressure 990 mB. Ground windspeed 3 mph, 5 kph. Test payload 397 lb. 180 kg.

AEROKART *AEROKART 5320*

(Three-axis)

Summary as Baby 234 *except: Wing has unswept leading edge, swept forward trailing edge, and tapering chord. Wing profile AK 8312.*

Production status: current, number completed NC.

GENERAL - Included in our first edition, this firm actually began its activities at the end of 1981 with the construction of the first Aerokart, a prototype tandem two-seater with a V-tail which was never put into production. In February 1982 Aerokart SARL was formed by Bernard Charpenel and Rene Feltrin who still run the company, and 3 June '82 saw the first flight of the *Aerokart 4315* side-by-side two-seater which had the hallmarks of the company's aircraft today: 100% double-surface wings, and engine mounted in front driving a pusher propellor at the trailing edge.

The company worked on this two-seater (there was also a single-seat *Aerokart 3315*, but this was not pursued) until the end of 1982 to bring it into line with French legislation which stipulated a maximum wing loading of 15 kg/m². Production began in November 1982 and was soon concentrated on the *Aerokart 4320* powered by the Hirth 2701R-03 engine. This three-axis two-seater, effectively a stronger, strut-braced *Aerokart 4315*, was featured in our first edition and flight-tested for *UlmMag* by Bernard Chansaud in September 1983. The following year the machine was fitted with a Rotax 503 engine and given a one-piece welded steel airframe, being renamed *Aerokart 5320* as a result.

Prices are 62,000FF in kit form or 66,000FF ready to fly, a nosewheel brake costing 556FF extra and a pod a further 1602FF.

EXTERNAL DIMENSIONS & AREAS - See *Baby 22* except: Height overall 8.2 ft, 2.50 m. Chord at root 6.3 ft, 1.90 m. Chord at tip 5.6 ft, 1.70 m. Dihedral 2.5°. Total wing area 203 ft², 18.7 m². Total aileron area 25.9 ft², 2.40 m². Aspect ratio 5.8/1.

POWER PLANT - See *Baby 23* except: Power per unit area 0.26 hp/ft², 2.8 hp/m².

WEIGHTS & LOADINGS - Empty weight 380 lb, 172 kg. Max take-off weight 994 lb, 450 kg. Payload 614 lb, 278 kg. Max wing loading 4.90 lb/ft², 24.1 kg/m². Max power loading 18.8 lb/hp, 8.5 kg/hp. Load factors +6.0, -3.0 recommended; NC ultimate.

PERFORMANCE* - Max level speed 71 mph, 115 kph. Never exceed speed 81 mph, 130 kph. Max cruising speed 59 mph, 95 kph. Economic cruising speed 50 mph, 80 kph. Stalling speed 28 mph, 45 kph. Max climb rate at sea level 690 ft/min, 3.5 m/s. Min sink rate 350 ft/min at 31 mph, 1.8 m/s at 50 kph. Best glide ratio with power off 7/1 at 50 mph, 80 kph. Take-off distance 100 ft, 30 m. Landing distance 100 ft, 30 m. Service ceiling 11,480 ft, 3500 m. Range at

average cruising speed 149 mile, 240 km. Noise level NC.

Under the following test conditions - Airfield altitude 718 ft, 219 m. Ground temperature 72°F, 22°C. Ground pressure NC. Ground windspeed 7 mph, 12 kph. Test payload 413 lb, 187 kg.

AEROKART *AGRIKART*

(Three-axis)

Summary similar to Aerokart 5320 *except: Single-seater.*

Production status: current, number completed NC.

GENERAL - For agricultural use the company offers a version of the *Aerokart 5320* known as the *Agrikart,* which is effectively an *Aerokart 5320* with one seat removed and spray equipment fitted by the Berthoud company.
Prices are 87,800FF in kit form or 92,000FF ready to fly; options include a nosewheel brake for 556FF and a pod for 911FF.

EXTERNAL DIMENSIONS & AREAS - Similar to *Aerokart 5320.*

POWER PLANT - See *Aerokart 5320.*

WEIGHTS & LOADINGS - NC.

PERFORMANCE - NC.

AEROKIT INDUSTRIE

Aerokit Industrie, Rustrel, 84400 Apt; tel (90) 74 5469/5695. Proprietors: Serge Pellenc and Olivier Richard.

AEROKIT INDUSTRIE
AEROKIT BIPLACE

(Two-axis)

Side-by-side two-seat single-engined high-wing monoplane with two-axis control. Wing has unswept leading and trailing edges, and constant chord; conventional tail. Pitch control by elevator on tail; yaw control by fully flying rudder; no separate roll control; control inputs through stick for pitch/yaw. Wing braced from above by kingpost and cables, from below by cables; wing profile NC; single-surface. Undercarriage has three wheels in tricycle formation; rubber suspension on nosewheel and suspension NC on main wheels. Ground steering by differential braking. Brakes on all wheels. Steel/aluminium-alloy tube airframe, completely open. Engine mounted below wing, driving pusher propeller.

Production status: current, 3 completed.

GENERAL - The prototype of this two-axis two-seater was described in our first edition. It is now workshop built to a delivery time of about four weeks and with the airframe guaranteed for a year. Designed by Olivier Richard and built in 1983 with help from Hugues Deleband and Christian Risbourg, the *Aerokit* was born directly out of experience gained on other microlights as a member of staff with one of the country's first schools, Le Centre National de Formation ULM. A private company despite its title, the school was based at Rustrel aerodrome in Vaucluse where the *Aerokit* is now built.
Quite obviously inspired by the celebrated *Quicksilver MX II* whose layout it retains, this 'a la francaise' variation of the

grand old American nonetheless differs from it considerably from a technological point of view.

The company has abandoned the *Quicksilver's* Duralumin 6061 in favour of an airframe partly of Duralumin AU4G1 and partly of welded steel. Other differences include wider track and rubber-band suspension on the nosewheel.

Initially conceived as a two-axis machine but with the option of spoilers, the *Aerokit* has remained with neither spoilers nor ailerons, control inputs being solely by means of the joystick. The generous size of the rudder and elevators nonetheless give it a reassuringly good roll rate, sufficient to make it handle well. Pilot comfort has been particularly well catered for, with the adoption of bucket seats and headrests.

Price is 59,000FF including all taxes, assembled and test flown.

EXTERNAL DIMENSIONS & AREAS - Length overall 17.8 ft, 5.43 m. Height overall 9.8 ft, 2.98 m. Wing span 32.7 ft, 9.95 m. Constant chord 5.0 ft, 1.53 m. Dihedral 5°. Sweepback 0°. Total wing area 164 ft², 15.2 m². Aspect ratio 6.5/1. Wheel track 5.1 ft, 1.54 m. Wheelbase 5.3 ft, 1.61 m. Other data NC.

POWER PLANT - Rotax 503 engine. Max power 45 hp at 6500 rpm. Propeller diameter and pitch 57x34 inch, 1.45x0.86 m. V-belt reduction, ratio 2.5/1. Max static thrust 287 lb, 130 kg. Power per unit area 0.27 hp/ft², 3.0 hp/m². Fuel capacity 2.6 US gal, 2.2 Imp gal, 10.0 litre.

WEIGHTS & LOADINGS - Empty weight 298 lb, 135 kg. Max take-off weight 784 lb, 355 kg. Payload 485 lb, 220 kg. Max wing loading 4.78 lb/ft², 23.3 kg/m². Max power loading 17.4 lb/hp, 7.9 kg/hp. Load factors +5.0, -3.0 recommended; NC ultimate.

PERFORMANCE* - Max level speed 62 mph, 100 kph. Never exceed speed 68 mph, 110 kph. Max cruising speed 56 mph, 90 kph. Economic cruising speed 47 mph, 75 kph. Stalling speed 19 mph, 30 kph. Max climb rate at sea level 590 ft/min, 3.0 m/s. Min sink rate 390 ft/min, 2.0 m/s at NC speed. Best glide ratio with power off 7/1 at 28 mph, 45 kph. Take-off distance >65 ft, >50 m. Landing distance 130 ft, 40 m. Service ceiling 9840 ft, 3000 m. Range at average cruising speed 112 mile, 180 km. Noise level NC.

*Under the following test conditions - Airfield altitude 262 ft, 110 m. Ground temperature 68°F, 20°C. Ground pressure NC. Ground windspeed NC. Test payload 199 lb, 90 kg.

Flashback to 1983, as the Agriplane team line up with two Condors *and, on the right, the prototype solo machine. Note the distinctive dog-leg at the top of the monopole, and the all-round suspension.*

Main picture: Agriplane Condor at work spraying a Van Gogh landscape. Inset: A similar machine equipped for powder spreading.

AGRIPLANE

Groupe Roland Perinet et Cie, Department Agriplane, route de Poitiers, 86110 Mirebeau; tel (49) 50 4434; tx 790334. Proprietors: Roland Perinet, Patrice Renaud, Jean-Claude Armaing.

AGRIPLANE CONDOR 1985
(Weight-shift)

Tandem two-seat/single-seat* single-engined flex-wing aircraft with weight-shift control. Rogallo wing with keel pocket. Pilot suspended below wing in trike unit, using bar to control pitch and roll/yaw by altering relative positions of trike unit and wing. Wing braced from above by kingpost and cables, from below by cables; rigid cross-tube construction with 35% double-surface not enclosing cross-tube; preformed ribs. Undercarriage has three wheels in tricycle formation; rubber suspension on all wheels. Push-right go-left nosewheel steering independent from aerodynamic controls. Nosewheel brake.

Aluminium-alloy tube trike unit, completely open. Engine mounted below wing, driving pusher propeller.

Production status: current, 25 completed.

*See text.

GENERAL - The Perinet group is one of the most important in France in the agricultural equipment sector, dealing in everything from tractors to helicopters - and ultralights. It is also one of the biggest French exporters in this field, so not surprisingly the company was one of the first to produce a trike specifically designed for spraying work, unveiling its *Condor* to the press as early as 1980, at a time when few other manufacturers had even begun to grasp the potential for this rather specialist application.

This first machine was built by a Perinet subsidiary, La Culture de l'Air 2000, and designed by Roland Perinet and Patrice Renaud, making its first flights in February 1981 - incontestably the world's first agricultural trike.

Fitted with a 40 hp Hirth motor with electric start, it was

117

shown at the Salon de l'Aeronautique et de l'Espace in June that year, but was not marketed until the following March, as the company wanted to get a full summer's spraying experience under its belt. Described in our previous edition, this 1982 model was also the subject of two articles in the August '82 *Pilot Prive*.

The same procedure was followed before the launch of a second series, and with good reason, for it had become evident that a few hours' experience would not produce a pilot trained for the tricky disciplines of very low altitude flying. The costs of spraying by ultralight might be very different from a helicopter or lightplane, but the training problem was just the same. As there was no specialist training available in France at the time, the company concentrated on exporting to countries where agriculture was based on large fields and thereby posed the least risk to pilots.

The 1982 and 1983 *Condors* incorporated a 23.8 US gal (19.9 Imp gal, 90 litre) tank for spray material in the back and base of the pilot's seat, while a kit enabled the machine to be converted into a conventional two-seater. It used a 248 ft² (23.0 m²) wing and 39 ft (12.0 m) spray booms. Two similar models also appeared in 1983, both equipped with a less powerful 29 hp engine and a smaller wing (18.0 m², 194 ft²) for agricultural use or as simple single-seaters. These were the *Calao* with 13 ft (4.0 m) booms and the *Choucas* with 20 ft (6.0 m) booms.

The 1985 *Condor* is very much in the same family as its predecessors - a conventional tandem two-seater of deliberately rustic construction and proven solidity to which the buyer can fit a system either for spreading powders (by means of a spreader with two hydraulically operated contra-rotating discs), low-volume liquids (using spray booms), or an ultra-low volume system (using rotating nozzles). The latter gives the following performance: spread 12.0 m (39 ft), rate 1 hectare/min (2.5 acre/min), spray quantity range 0.13-6.6 US gal/h (0.11-5.5 Imp gal/h, 0.5-25 litre/h).

Booms are made from carbon-fibre and other composites and the 2 hp two-stroke pump has a recoil start. Spray jets are opened by an electric switch and the chemical tank holds 25.2 US gal (20.9 Imp gal, 95 litre), products being continually mixed automatically. The system can cover 7-37 acre (3-15 hectare) per load. Set-up time is 10 min and equipment weight 66 lb (30 kg).

Prices on request.

EXTERNAL DIMENSIONS & AREAS - Length overall 13.1 ft, 4.00 m. Height overall 8.2 ft, 2.50 m. Wing span 32.8 ft, 10.00 m. Chord at root 9.8 ft, 3.00 m. Chord at tip 2.6 ft, 0.80 m. Total wing area 215 ft², 20.0 m². Aspect ratio 5.0/1. Other data NC.

POWER PLANT - Hirth engine. Max power 40 hp at NC rpm. Power per unit area 0.19 hp/ft², 2.0 hp/m². Other data NC.

WEIGHTS & LOADINGS - Empty weight 298 lb, 135 kg. Max take-off weight 739 lb, 335 kg. Payload 441 lb, 200 kg. Max wing loading 3.44 lb/ft², 16.8 kg/m². Max power loading 18.5 lb/hp, 8.4 kg/hp. Load factors +4.0, -2.0 recommended; +6.0, -3.0 ultimate.

PERFORMANCE* - Max level speed 50 mph, 80 kph. Never exceed speed 59 mph, 95 kph. Economic cruising speed 37 mph, 60 kph. Stalling speed 24 mph, 38 kph. Max climb rate at sea level 790 ft/min, 4.0 m/s. Take-off distance 100 ft, 30 m. Landing distance 165 ft, 50 m. Service ceiling 13,100 ft, 4000 m. Range at average cruising speed 75 mile, 120 km. Other data NC.

*Under the following test conditions - Airfield altitude 0 ft, 0 m. Ground temperature 59°F, 15°C. Ground pressure 1013 mB. Ground windspeed 0 mph, 0 kph. Test payload 331 lb, 150 kg.

AGRIPLANE X 13
(Weight-shift)

Summary as Condor *except: Single-seater.*

Production status: current, 65 completed.

GENERAL - Agriplane's *X 13* was brought out in 1984 and is a single-seater trike of the same power as the *Condor*

1985 and of similar construction. Designed to take the same spraying systems as the *Condor 1985*, it differs principally in its wing design, for though the principal dimensions are the same, the wing can be derigged in 5 min thanks to the use of two half cross-booms.
Prices on request.

EXTERNAL DIMENSIONS & AREAS - See *Condor 1985*.

POWER PLANT - See *Condor 1985*.

WEIGHTS & LOADINGS - Empty weight 331 lb, 150 kg. Max take-off weight 772 lb, 350 kg. Payload 441 lb, 200 kg. Max wing loading 3.59 lb/ft², 17.5 kg/m². Max power loading 19.3 lb/hp, 8.8 kg/hp. Load factors +4.0, -2.0 recommended; +6.0, -3.0 ultimate.

PERFORMANCE* - See *Condor 1985* except: Stalling speed 22 mph, 35 kph. Take-off distance 165 ft, 50 m. Range at average cruising speed NC.

Agriplane X 13 *at work with spray equipment.*

AIR CREATION

Air Creation, Zone Industrielle Lavilledieu, 07170 Villeneuve-de-Berg; tel (75) 36 2410. Proprietor: Gilles Bru.

AIR CREATION
◀ *SAFARI MONO/ALPHAPLUS 17*

(Weight-shift)

Single-seat single-engined flex-wing aircraft with weight-shift control. Rogallo wing with keel pocket. Pilot suspended below wing in trike unit, using bar to control pitch and roll/yaw by altering relative positions of trike unit and wing. Wing braced from above by kingpost and cables, from below by cables; floating cross-tube construction with 50% double-surface enclosing cross-tube; preformed ribs. Undercarriage has three wheels in tricycle formation; no suspension on any wheels. Push-right go-left nosewheel steering independent from aerodynamic controls. Nosewheel brake. Aluminium-alloy tube trike unit, with optional pod. Engine mounted below wing, driving pusher propeller.

Production status: current, number completed NC.

GENERAL - Gilles Bru is well known among hang-glider pilots, having worked for five years with Eole 2000. In December 1982 he started his own company under the title of Air Concept, but this name was already in use by a French sailmaker specialising in Dacron wings for hang gliders, so to avoid confusion, Gilles renamed his company Air Creation in 1983. Neither firm is connected with the ConceptAir accessories company set up in 1985 by Alain-Yves Berger and associates.

Universally recognised as a serious-minded but dynamic company, Air Creation remains, with the Cosmos/La mouette partnership, one of the last French firms producing complete trikes, rather than just wing or trike unit - if one excludes the small numbers of trike units produced by Eole 2000. In fact, Air Creation still works closely with the latter, and some models of Rogallo are in production at both addresses.

Air Creation's first wing was the *Alpha*, detailed in our first edition and introduced in 1983. The range was enlarged in 1984 by the introduction of the *Quartz*, which is now available in four versions. In 1985 came a replacement for the *Alpha*, the *Alphaplus*, a development of the *Alpha* with improved handling and flying characteristics; this comes in three versions. Also, at the start of 1985 the company brought out the *ADAC 23*, a single-surface sail for the crop-spraying market.

Turning now to the trike units, the *Safari* range, announced in 1983, gave rise to the *Safari GT* range the following year; both were featured in our first edition and are still in production. However, as the pod which previously distinguised the *GT* is now an option on all models, the principal difference between the two series has become the suspension, all *GTs* now being fitted with oleo-pneumatic units. For '85, *GTs* can also be fitted optionally with aerofoil-section tubes. *Safaris* come in solo or dual versions, while the *GT* can be had as a single-seater, one-plus-one, or two-seater. All models include as standard a brake, foot and hand throttles, and high-capacity fuel tank. Earlier Air Creation trike units used Robin engines, but now only the cheapest model retains the Japanese motor, all others being Rotax-powered.

The company's products were reviewed in *UlmMag* by Norbert Seyve in an article on flexwing manufacture entitled *Wing and trike: a happy marriage*. Excellent competition results in 1984 proved the quality of these machines: second, third, fifth and sixth places in the French championships; first and second in the French Grande Course. With a strong position in the home market, Air Creation is currently exporting some 30% of its production.

So as not to overwhelm the reader with a surfeit of detail from up to 40 different combinations of trike unit and wing, we list just six complete combinations, selected by Gilles himself; below is the *Safari Mono/Alphaplus 17* with Robin EC25PS, while five others are listed separately.

To permit readers to work out their own permutations, we give prices separately, as follows. Note that all figures include 18.6% VAT. Wings for single-seaters: *Alphaplus 17* (can also be used on a one-plus-one) 13,500FF, *Quartz*

16 15,000FF, *Quartz 18* 15,500FF. Wings for two-seaters: *ADAC 23* 14,500FF, *Alphaplus 18* 16,000FF, *Alphaplus 20* 16,500FF, *Quartz 18* 18,000FF, *Quartz 20* 18,500FF. Trikes/engines: *Safari Mono*/Robin EC25PS 17,000FF assembled, 14,000FF kit; *Safari Mono*/Rotax 377 21,500FF assembled, 18,000FF kit; *Safari Bi*/Rotax 447 24,500FF assembled, 20,500FF kit; *Safari GT Mono*/Rotax 377 24,500FF assembled; *Safari GT 1+1*/Rotax 377 25,000FF assembled; *Safari GT Bi*/Rotax 447 28,500FF assembled.

EXTERNAL DIMENSIONS & AREAS - Length overall 12.5 ft, 3.80 m. Height overall 11.5 ft, 3.50 m. Wing span 32.8 ft, 10.00 m. Chord at root 8.2 ft, 2.50 m. Chord at tip 2.7 ft, 0.80 m. Dihedral 4°. Nose angle 120°. Depth of keel pocket NC. Total wing area 190 ft², 17.6 m². Keel pocket area NC. Aspect ratio 5.7/1. Wheel track 5.3 ft, 1.60 m. Wheelbase 5.9 ft, 1.80 m. Nosewheel diameter overall 12 inch, 30 cm. Main wheels diameter overall 12 inch, 30 cm.

POWER PLANT - Robin EC25PS engine. Max power 18 hp at 6500 rpm. Propeller diameter and pitch 51xNC inch, 1.30xNC m. Multi V-belt reduction, ratio 2/1. Max static thrust NC. Power per unit area 0.09 hp/ft², 1.0 hp/m². Fuel capacity 6.1 US gal, 5.1 Imp gal, 23.0 litre.

WEIGHTS & LOADINGS - Empty weight 176 lb, 80 kg. Max take-off weight 441 lb, 200 kg. Payload 265 lb, 120 kg. Max wing loading 2.32 lb/ft², 11.4 kg/m². Max power loading 24.5 lb/hp, 11.1 kg/hp. Load factors NC recommended; +6.0, -3.0 ultimate.

Safari GT Mono *trike unit.*

PERFORMANCE* - Max level speed 50 mph, 80 kph. Never exceed speed 68 mph, 110 kph. Max cruising speed 44 mph, 70 kph. Economic cruising speed 25 mph, 40 kph. Stalling speed 17 mph, 28 kph. Max climb rate at sea level 490 ft/min, 2.5 m/s. Min sink rate 260 ft/min at 22 mph, 1.3 m/s at 35 kph. Best glide ratio with power off 7/1 at 24 mph, 38 kph. Take-off distance 100 ft, 30 m. Landing distance 115 ft, 35 m. Service ceiling 9840 ft, 3000 m. Range at average cruising speed 156 mile, 250 km. Noise level NC.

*Under the following test conditions - Airfield altitude 426 ft, 130 m. Ground temperature 55°F, 13°C. Ground pressure 1002 mB. Ground windspeed 3 mph, 5 kph. Test payload 165 lb, 75 kg.

AIR CREATION *SAFARI GT MONO/QUARTZ 16*
(Weight-shift)

Summary as Safari Mono/Alphaplus 17 *except: 80% double-surface. Oleo-pneumatic suspension on all wheels.*

Production status: current, number completed NC.

GENERAL - See *Safari Mono/Alphaplus 17.*

EXTERNAL DIMENSIONS & AREAS - See *Safari Mono/Alphaplus 17* except: Chord at tip 5.6 ft, 1.70 m. Dihedral 6°. Nose angle 122°. Total wing area 174 ft², 16.2 m². Aspect ratio 6.2/1.

POWER PLANT - Rotax 377 engine. Max power 36 hp at 6500 rpm. Propeller diameter and pitch 59xNC inch, 1.50xNC m. Gear reduction, ratio 2.6/1. Max static thrust 254 lb, 115 kg. Power per unit area 0.21 hp/ft², 2.2 hp/m². Fuel capacity 6.1 US gal, 5.1 Imp gal, 23.0 litre.

WEIGHTS & LOADINGS - Empty weight 243 lb, 110 kg. Max take-off weight 574 lb, 260 kg. Payload 331 lb, 150 kg. Max wing loading 3.30 lb/ft², 16.0 kg/m². Max power loading 15.9 lb/hp, 7.2 kg/hp. Load factors NC recommended; +6.0, -3.0 ultimate.

PERFORMANCE* - Max level speed 68 mph, 110 kph. Never exceed speed 68 mph, 110 kph. Max cruising speed 62 mph, 100 kph. Economic cruising speed 31 mph, 50 kph. Stalling speed 24 mph, 40 kph. Max climb rate at sea level 790 ft/min, 4.0 m/s. Min sink rate 330 ft/min at 27 mph, 1.7 m/s at 43 kph. Best glide ratio with power off 8/1 at 28 mph, 45 kph. Take-off distance 130 ft, 40 m. Landing distance 150 ft, 45 m. Service ceiling 11,500 ft, 3500 m. Range at average cruising speed 200 mile, 320 km. Noise level NC.

*Under the following test conditions - Airfield altitude 426 ft, 130 m. Ground temperature 55°F, 13°C. Ground pressure 1002 mB. Ground windspeed 2 mph, 3 kph. Test payload 165 lb, 75 kg.

AIR CREATION *SAFARI GT 1+1/ ALPHAPLUS 17* and *SAFARI GT 1+1/QUARTZ 18*

(Weight-shift)

Tandem one-plus-one seat single-engined flex-wing aircraft with weight-shift control. Rogallo wing with keel pocket. Pilot suspended below wing in trike unit, using bar to control pitch and roll/yaw by altering relative positions of trike unit and wing. Wing braced from above by kingpost and cables, from below by cables; floating cross-tube construction with 50% double-surface (Alphaplus 17 wing), 80% double-surface (Quartz 16 wing) enclosing cross-tube; preformed ribs. Undercarriage has three wheels in tricycle formation; oleopneumatic suspension on all wheels. Push-right go-left nosewheel steering independent from aerodynamic controls. Nosewheel brake. Aluminium-alloy tube trike unit, with optional pod. Engine mounted below wing, driving pusher propeller.

Production status: current, number completed NC.

GENERAL - See *Safari Mono/Alphaplus 17. Data below refers to Safari GT 1+1/Alphaplus 17; where different, figures for Safari GT 1+1/Quartz 16 are shown in parentheses.*

EXTERNAL DIMENSIONS & AREAS - Length overall 12.5 ft, 3.80 m. Height overall 11.5 ft, 3.50 m. Wing span 32.8 ft, 10.00 m. Chord at root 8.2 ft, 2.50 m. Chord at tip 2.7(5.6) ft, 0.80(1.70) m. Dihedral 4(6)°. Nose angle 120(122)°. Depth of keel pocket NC. Total wing area 190(194) ft², 17.6(18.0) m². Keel pocket area NC. Aspect ratio 5.7(5.6)/1. Wheel track 5.3 ft, 1.60 m. Wheelbase 5.9 ft, 1.80 m. Nosewheel diameter overall 12 inch, 30 cm. Main wheels diameter overall 12 inch, 30 cm.

POWER PLANT - See *Safari GT Mono/Quartz 16* except: Power per unit area 0.19 hp/ft², 2.0 hp/m².

Safari GT 1+1 *trike unit. See title page for an illustration of this unit mated to a* Quartz 18 *wing.*

WEIGHTS & LOADINGS - See *Safari GT Mono/Quartz 16* except: Max wing loading 3.02(2.96) lb/ft², 14.8(14.4) kg/m².

PERFORMANCE* - Max level speed 50(62) mph, 80(100) kph. Never exceed speed 68 mph, 110 kph. Max cruising speed 44(56) mph, 70(90) kph. Economic cruising speed 25(28) mph, 40(45) kph. Stalling speed 19(21) mph, 30(33) kph. Max climb rate at sea level 790 ft/min, 4.0 m/s. Min sink rate 270(310) ft/min at 22(23) mph, 1.4(1.6) m/s at 35(38) kph. Best glide ratio with power off 7(8)/1 at 23(24) mph, 38(40) kph. Take-off distance 80(100) ft, 25(30) m. Landing distance 115(130) ft, 35(40) m. Service ceiling 11,500 ft, 3500 m. Range at average cruising speed 174(200) mile, 280(320) km. Noise level NC.

*Under the following test conditions - Airfield altitude 426 ft, 130 m. Ground temperature 55°F, 13°C. Ground pressure 1002 mB. Ground windspeed 3 mph, 5 kph. Test payload 165 lb, 75 kg.

AIR CREATION *SAFARI GT BI/ ALPHAPLUS 20* and *SAFARI GT BI/QUARTZ 20*

(Weight-shift)

Tandem two-seat single-engined flex-wing aircraft with weight-shift control. Rogallo wing with keel pocket. Pilot suspended below wing in trike unit, using bar to control pitch and roll/yaw by altering relative positions of trike unit and wing. Wing braced from above by kingpost and cables, from below by cables; floating cross-tube construction with 40% double-surface (Alphaplus 20 wing), 70% double-surface (Quartz 20 wing) enclosing cross-tube; preformed ribs. Undercarriage has three wheels in tricycle formation; oleo-pneumatic suspension on all wheels. Push-right go-left nosewheel steering independent from aerodynamic controls. Nosewheel brake. Aluminium-alloy tube trike unit, with optional pod. Engine mounted below wing, driving pusher propeller.

Production status: current, number completed NC.

GENERAL - See *Safari Mono/Alphaplus 17. Data below refers to Safari GT Bi/Alphaplus 20; where different,*

figures for *Safari GT Bi/Quartz 20* are shown in parentheses.

EXTERNAL DIMENSIONS & AREAS - Length overall 13.1 ft, 4.00 m. Height overall 11.5 ft, 3.50 m. Wing span 32.8 ft, 10.00 m. Chord at root 9.8 ft, 3.00 m. Chord at tip 3.3 ft, 1.00 m. Dihedral 4(6)°. Nose angle 120(122)°. Depth of keel pocket NC. Total wing area 214 ft², 19.8 m². Keel pocket area NC. Aspect ratio 5.1/1. Wheel track 5.9 ft, 1.80 m. Wheelbase 5.9 ft, 1.80 m. Nosewheel diameter overall 16 inch, 40 cm. Main wheels diameter overall 16 inch, 40 cm.

POWER PLANT - Rotax 447 engine. Max power 42 hp at 6500 rpm. Propeller diameter and pitch 59xNC inch, 1.50xNC m. Gear reduction, ratio 2.6/1. Max static thrust 287 lb, 130 kg. Power per unit area 0.20 hp/ft², 2.1 hp/m². Fuel capacity 6.1 US gal, 5.1 Imp gal, 23.0 litre.

WEIGHTS & LOADINGS - Empty weight 287 lb, 130 kg. Max take-off weight 795 lb, 360 kg. Payload 508 lb, 230 kg. Max wing loading 3.71 lb/ft², 18.2 kg/m². Max power loading 18.9 lb/hp, 8.6 kg/hp. Load factors NC recommended; +6.0, -3.0 ultimate.

PERFORMANCE* - Max level speed 50(56) mph, 80(90) kph. Never exceed speed 62 mph, 100 kph. Max cruising speed 44(50) mph, 70(80) kph. Economic cruising speed 31 mph, 50 kph. Stalling speed 22(23) mph, 35(37) kph. Max climb rate at sea level 690 ft/min, 3.5 m/s. Min sink rate 410(450) ft/min at 24(26) mph, 2.1(2.3) m/s at 40(42) kph. Best glide ratio with power off 7(8)/1 at 26(28) mph, 43(45) kph. Take-off distance 100(115) ft, 30(35) m. Landing distance 130 ft, 40 m. Service ceiling 9840 ft, 3000 m. Range at average cruising speed 156 mile, 250 km. Noise level NC.

*Under the following test conditions - Airfield altitude 426 ft, 130 m. Ground temperature 68°F, 20°C. Ground pressure 1010 mB. Ground windspeed 0 mph, 0 kph. Test payload 309 lb, 140 kg.

Air Creation's Safari GT Bi *trike unit can be had with a* Quartz 20 *wing (main picture) or an* Alphaplus 20 *(inset).*

AVIASUD

Aviasud Engineering, domaine de la Suviere, route de la Bouverie, 83480 Le Puget-sur-Argens; tel (94) 40 0480. Proprietors: Francois Goethals and Bernard d'Otreppe.

British agent: Midland Ultralights (see separate listing).

South African agent: Aviation 2000 (see separate listing).

US agent: Aviasud Ultralights, PO Box 89, Beasley, Texas 77417; tel (409) 387-2226.

AVIASUD *SIROCCO*
(Three-axis)

Single-seat single-engined high-wing monoplane with conventional three-axis control. Wing has swept back leading and trailing edges, and constant chord; conventional tail. Pitch control by fully flying tail with trim antitab; yaw control by fin-mounted rudder; roll control by 40%-span spoilerons; control inputs through stick for pitch/roll and pedals for yaw. Wing braced from above by kingpost and cables, from below by cables; wing profile TK7315M; 100% double-surface. Undercarriage has three wheels in tricycle formation; glass-fibre suspension on all wheels. Push-right go-right nosewheel steering independent from yaw control. Nosewheel brake. Composite-construction airframe, partially enclosed (total enclosure optional). Engine mounted below wing, driving pusher propeller.

Production status: current, 110 completed.

GENERAL - This company was formed by Francois Goethals and Bernard d'Otreppe to manufacture and market the first model of Bernard Broc's three-axis single-seater *Libellule* (dragonfly in English). This aircraft went into limited production (three a month) at the start of November 1981 as did the *Mk III* model which was described in our first edition under Broc. (Bernard is still active in his own right with a quite different design, as you can read under Broc.)

In January 1983 the *Libellule* was superseded at Aviasud by the *Sirocco* which made its first flight on 26 July 1982. It was designed by Francois and Bernard using a computer to calculate exact loadings. Despite its similar configuration to the the original *Libellule* and its original title of *Libellule Mk II,* this was in effect a completely new aircraft. Francois is a specialist in fluid mechanics and Bernard in the study of composite materials and they therefore subjected the *Sirocco* to a very comprehensive series of tests, both static and in-flight. In particular these enabled them to optimise the use of Paul McCready's American TK7315 wing section with 14% thickness and to test the wing to destruction at +6.7g, -3.6g at full load.

The single-seat *Sirocco* quickly found its place among the ultralight nobility, emerging victorious from nearly every European competition it entered. Its prize list includes first places in the 1983 French Grand Prix, the 1984 French championships (flown by Patrick Fourticq) and the French Grande Course of the same year with Francois Goethals at the controls, while in the US it won the Most Outstanding Design Award at Oshkosh '83. An undoubted export success, about 15 countries are now flying the *Sirocco,* including most European nations, Australia, South Korea and the USA.

During 1984 the *Sirocco* swapped its JPX PUL425 engine, as detailed in our first edition, for the Rotax 377 with gear reduction. At the same time it was given a new spring system for the undercarriage and an optional integral enclosed canopy. In Britain the aircraft is built under license by Midland Ultralights to a somewhat different specification, as required by UK airworthiness regulations. The American market is supplied from France, a three-cylinder Konig engine being fitted for this application. Our data below refers to the French version with standard tank (double size is optional); where different, figures for the US version are shown in parentheses. The British version is listed separately, under Midland Ultralights.

Those wanting to read more about the *Sirocco* have plenty of choice. French-language reports have appeared in *UlmMag* in July 1983 and March 1984, while reports in English have appeared in the EAA's publication *Ultralight* (November '83) and in the BMAA's magazine *Flightline* (March-April '85), the latter report being of the British version.

With good glide angle, well co-ordinated control response, exceptional stability and manoeuvrability, the *Sirocco* can legitimately claim to be the best European-designed single-seater generally available at the price, which is 77,920FF including tax. In the US, it is priced at US$9305 ready to fly.

EXTERNAL DIMENSIONS & AREAS - Length overall 19.0 ft, 5.80 m. Height overall 8.9 ft, 2.70 m. Wing span 33.2 ft, 10.12 m. Constant chord at root 4.6 ft, 1.38 m. Dihedral 1°. Sweepback 10°. Elevator span 7.2 ft, 2.20 m. Fin height 3.3 ft, 1.10 m. Total wing area 151 ft², 14.1 m². Total spoileron area 6.9 ft², 0.64 m². Fin area 4.3 ft², 0.40 m². Rudder area 4.1 ft², 0.38 m². Total elevator area 15.6 ft², 1.45 m². Aspect ratio 7.3/1. Wheel track 5.9 ft, 1.80 m. Wheelbase 6.1 ft, 1.85 m. Nosewheel diameter overall 13 inch, 32 cm. Main wheels diameter overall 13 inch, 32 cm.

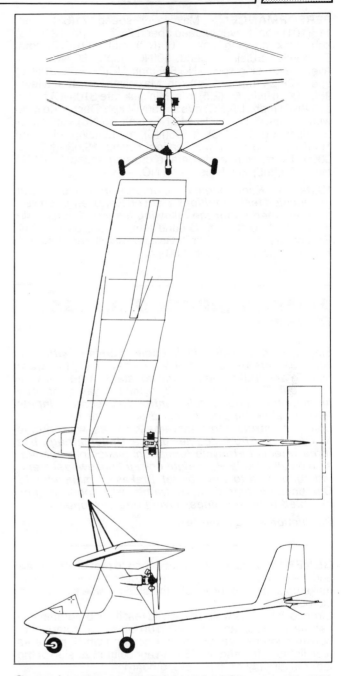

General arrangement of the original Sirocco, *with JPX PUL425 engine. For an illustration of the* Sirocco *in flight, see colour section.*

POWER PLANT - Rotax 377 (Konig SC430) engine. Max power 35(27) hp at 6600(4600) rpm. Propeller diameter and pitch 57(55)x33(24) inch, 1.45(1.40)x0.85(0.61) m. Gear (no) reduction, ratio 2.6(1.0)/1. Max static thrust 232(150) lb, 105(68) kg. Power per unit area 0.23(0.18) hp/ft², 2.5(1.9) hp/m². Fuel capacity 5.3 US gal, 4.4 Imp gal, 20.0 litre.

WEIGHTS & LOADINGS - Empty weight 287(252) lb, 130(114) kg. Max take-off weight 552(544) lb, 250(247) kg. Payload 265(292) lb, 120(132) kg. Max wing loading 3.66(3.60) lb/ft², 17.7(17.5) kg/m². Max power loading 15.8(20.1) lb/hp, 7.1(9.1) kg/hp. Load factors NC recommended; +6.7, -3.6 ultimate.

PERFORMANCE* - Max level speed 71(63) mph, 115(101) kph. Never exceed speed 75(71) mph, 121(115) kph. Max cruising speed 68(NC) mph, 110(NC) kph. Economic cruising speed 50(NC) mph, 80(NC) kph. Average cruising speed NC(60) mph, NC(97) kph. Stalling speed 28(24) mph, 45(39) kph. Max climb rate at sea level 980(500) ft/min, 5.0(2.5) m/s. Min sink rate 310(NC) ft/min at 34(NC) mph, 1.6(NC) m/s at 55(NC) kph. Best glide ratio with power off 11(12)/1 at 40(NC) mph, 65(NC) kph. Take-off distance 115(NC) ft, 35(NC) m. Landing distance 165(NC) ft, 50(NC) m. Service ceiling 19,680(NC) ft, 6000(NC) m. Range at average cruising speed 156(177) mile, 250(285) km. Noise level NC.

*Data on Konig-engined machine obtained under unspecified test conditions. Data on Rotax-engined version obtained under the following test conditions - Airfield altitude 0 ft, 0 m. Ground temperature 59°F, 15°C. Ground pressure 1013 mB. Ground windspeed 0 mph, 0 kph. Test payload 220 lb, 100 kg.

AVIASUD *SIROCCO BIPLACE*
(Three-axis)

Side-by-side two-seat single-engined biplane with conventional three-axis control. Wings have swept forward leading and trailing edges, and constant chord; conventional tail. Pitch control by fully flying tail; yaw control by fin-mounted rudder; roll control NC; control inputs through stick for pitch/roll and pedals for yaw. Wings braced by struts and transverse X-cables; wing profile NACA 2412; 100% double-surface. Undercarriage has three wheels in tricycle formation; glass-fibre suspension on all wheels. Push-right go-right nosewheel steering connected to yaw control. Brakes on main wheels. Composite-construction airframe, with pod. Engine mounted between wings, driving tractor propeller.

Production status: see text.

GENERAL - Aviasud does not intend to rest on its laurels and 1985 will see the appearance of two new models to make up a range of products: the side-by-side two-up version of the
Sirocco, a biplane which began its test flight programme in February 1985; and the *AP 100 Alize*, a composite-construction tandem two-seater flexwing which made its first flights at the end of 1984. An agricultural version of the latter is already on the drawing board.
Although still at prototype stage at the time of writing, both aircraft were due to have their public unveiling and market launch at the Salon International de l'Aeronautique et de l'Espace at Paris' Le Bourget aerodrome in June 1985. We give below the data so far released on the biplane; readers should note that the wing size and engine type may be changed before production and that the performance figures are only calculations. Details of the *AP 100 Alize* we list separately.
Prices: NC.

EXTERNAL DIMENSIONS & AREAS - Length overall 19.3 ft, 5.90 m. Height overall 7.1 ft, 2.15 m. Wing span 30.7 ft, 9.35 m (bottom); 30.7 ft, 9.35 m (top). Dihedral 3° (bottom wing); 3° (top wing). Sweepforward 5°. Elevator span 9.2 ft, 2.80 m. Total wing area *216* ft², *20* m². Aspect ratio *8.7/1* (bottom wing); *8.7/1* (top wing). Wheel track 5.6 ft, 1.70 m. Nosewheel diameter overall 13 inch, 33 cm. Main wheels diameter overall 13 inch, 33 cm. Other data NC.

POWER PLANT - *Rotax 462* engine. Max power 52 hp at 7200 rpm. Propeller diameter and pitch 66xNC inch, 1.67xNC m. Gear reduction, ratio 2.6/1. Max static thrust NC. Power per unit area *0.24* hp/ft², *2.6* hp/m². Fuel capacity 10.6 US gal, 8.8 Imp gal, 40.0 litre.

WEIGHTS & LOADINGS - Empty weight 358 lb, 162 kg. Max take-off weight 861 lb, 390 kg. Payload 503 lb, 228 kg. Max wing loading *3.99* lb/ft², *19.5* kg/m². Max power loading 16.6 lb/hp, 7.5 kg/hp. Load factors +3.8, -1.5 recommended; +5.7, -2.3 ultimate.

PERFORMANCE* - Max level speed 87 mph, 140 kph. Never exceed speed 106 mph, 170 kph. Stalling speed 31 mph, 50 kph. Max climb rate at sea level 690 ft/min, 3.5 m/s. Service ceiling 13,120 ft, 4000 m. Range at average cruising speed 248 mile, 400 km. Other data NC.

*Under unspecified test conditions.

AVIASUD *AP 100 ALIZE*
(Weight-shift)

Tandem two-seat single-engined flex-wing aircraft with weight-shift control. Rogallo wing. Pilot suspended below wing in trike unit, using bar to control pitch and roll/yaw by altering relative positions of trike unit and wing. Wing braced from above by kingpost and cables, from below by cables; 80% double-surface. Undercarriage has three wheels in tricycle formation; glass-fibre suspension on all wheels. Push-right go-left nosewheel steering independent from aerodynamic controls. Nosewheel brake. Composite-construction trike unit, with pod. Engine mounted below wing, driving pusher propeller. Other details NC.

Production status: see Sirocco Biplace *text.*

GENERAL - See *Sirocco Biplace.*

EXTERNAL DIMENSIONS & AREAS - NC.

POWER PLANT - Rotax 447 engine. Max power 42 hp at 6500 rpm. Propeller diameter and pitch 57x37 inch, 1.45x0.95 m. Gear reduction, ratio 2.6/1. Max static thrust 276 lb, 125 kg. Power per unit area NC. Fuel capacity 6.6 US gal, 5.5 Imp gal, 25.0 litre.

WEIGHTS & LOADINGS - Empty weight 287 lb, 130 kg. Max take-off weight 733 lb, 330 kg. Payload 442 lb, 200 kg. Max wing loading NC. Max power loading 17.5 lb/hp, 7.9 kg/hp. Load factors NC recommended; +6.0, -3.8 ultimate.

PERFORMANCE - NC.

AVULNOR

Avulnor SARL (Aviation Ultralegere de Normandie), aerodrome de Granville-Breville, 50290 Brehal; tel (33) 90 6513.

AVULNOR *VECTOR 627SR*
(Three-axis)

Summary as Sky King *Vector 627SR (see Canadian section).*

Production status: current, number completed NC.

GENERAL - Avulnor took over the distribution in France of the *Vector 627 SR* on behalf of the then manufacturer, the American Aerodyne firm, in 1983. Since then, the design rights have passed to Sky King International, which we list in our Canadian section.

The successor to the *Vector 600* and *610,* this machine was detailed in our first edition. The European version acquired a Rotax 377 engine in 1983 in place of the Rotax 277, which itself replaced the original Zenoah G25B1, and the Rotax twin is now standard fitment in North America too.

Based at a regional aerodrome, Avulnor is known in France not only for its aircraft but also for its well run flight training school. Its *Vector 627 SRs* have benefitted considerably from these years of experience and, as can be seen by comparing the data below with that in the Canadian section, have various differences in specification. Price: NC.

EXTERNAL DIMENSIONS & AREAS - Length overall 18.6 ft, 5.66 m. Height overall 8.3 ft, 2.54 m. Wing span 35.8 ft, 10.92 m. Sweepback 0°. Total wing area 154 ft², 14.3 m². Aspect ratio 8.3/1. Wheel track 4.3 ft, 1.31 m. Nosewheel diameter overall 12 inch, 30 cm. Main wheels diameter overall 12 inch, 30 cm. Other data NC.

POWER PLANT - Rotax 377 engine. Max power 36 hp at 6500 rpm. Propeller diameter and pitch 54x26 inch, 1.37x0.66 m. Notched V-belt reduction, ratio 2.0/1. Max static thrust 242 lb, 100 kg. Power per unit area 0.23 hp/ft², 2.5 hp/m². Fuel capacity 5.3 US gal, 4.4 Imp gal, 20.0 litre.

WEIGHTS & LOADINGS - Empty weight 252 lb, 114 kg. Max take-off weight 530 lb, 240 kg. Payload 278 lb, 126 kg. Max wing loading 3.44 lb/ft², 16.8 kg/m². Max power loading 14.7 lb/hp, 6.7 kg/hp. Load factors +5.7, -2.8 recommended; NC ultimate.

PERFORMANCE* - Max level speed 56 mph, 90 kph. Never exceed speed 71 mph, 115 kph. Max cruising speed 50 mph, 80 kph. Economic cruising speed 47 mph, 75 kph. Stalling speed 27 mph, 44 kph. Max climb rate at sea level 1000 ft/min, 5.1 m/s. Min sink rate NC ft/min at 44 mph, NC m/s at 70 kph. Best glide ratio with power off 11/1 at NC speed. Take-off distance 100 ft, 30 m. Landing distance 200 ft, 61 m. Service ceiling 10,000 ft, 3050 m. Range at average cruising speed 137 mile, 220 km. Noise level NC.

*Under the following test conditions - Airfield altitude 0 ft, 0 m. Ground temperature 64°F, 18°C. Ground pressure 1013 mB. Ground windspeed 0 mph, 0 kph. Test payload 212 lb, 96 kg.

BARDOU

Robert Bardou, Bugard, 65320 Trie-sur-Baise; tel (62) 35 5450.

BARDOU *CHOUCAS 1/Suitable Rogallo, CHOUCAS 2CC/ Suitable Rogallo, and CHOUCAS 2T/Suitable Rogallo*

(Weight-shift)

Single-seat (Choucas 1), *side-by-side two-seat* (Choucas 2CC), *tandem two-seat* (Choucas 2T), *single-engined flex-wing aircraft with weight-shift control. Rogallo wing. Pilot suspended below wing in trike unit, using bar to control pitch and roll/yaw by altering relative positions*

Four-stroke units can be accomodated in the two-seaters; this is a Choucas 2T *with Citroen Visa engine enlarged to 800 cc and developing 53 hp.*

Like all Bardou's machines, the Choucas 1 *trike unit can be tailored to the buyer's preferences.*

This Choucas 2CC *has a Rotax 377 engine.*

of trike unit and wing. Wing braced from above by kingpost and cables, from below by cables; other details depend on wing chosen. Undercarriage has three wheels in tricycle formation; glass-fibre suspension on all wheels. Push-right go-left nosewheel steering independent from aerodynamic controls. Nosewheel brake. Composite-construction trike unit, partially enclosed (total enclosure optional). Engine mounted below wing, driving pusher propeller.

Production status: current, number completed NC.

GENERAL - As described in our first edition, this crafts-man specialises in the manufacture of 'a la carte' trike units for flexwings with the customer choosing his or her own wing and engine. Robert Bardou draws on the very latest technology to manufacture his streamlined machines, using laminated glass-fibre/epoxy-resin reinforced with Kevlar, braced by tubular carbon longerons - the last word in strutural materials.

He currently produces three models, the single-seat *Choucas 1,* the side-by-side two-seater *Choucas 2CC,* and the tandem two-seat *Choucas 2T.* The single-seater can be fitted with any engine of up to 35 hp, Robert designing an appropriate metal mounting frame for each installation, while the two-seaters can take any currently available ultralight engine, including the four-stroke BMW and Citroen units, as well as the VW which has been used for the last 40 years by light aircraft homebuilders.

Common to all three models is the undercarriage, with the main legs and front forks built from unidirectional glass-fibre and carbon-fibre, spats on the main wheels, and a drum brake on the self-centring nosewheel.

The single-seater and the tandem two-seater are fitted with moulded bucket seats and the side-by-side version with a leatherette padded bench seat. The passenger seat on the *Choucas 2T* can be removed so the aircraft can be used as a single-seater for aerial work. New in 1985 for the *Choucas 1* is an integral *Falcon-* or *Sirocco-*style canopy, an interesting option which also enables its designer to offer an integral streamlined pod for single-seat three-axis machines such as the Zodiac *Ultrastar*.

Buyers can opt either for a complete machine, in which case the price is obviously dependent on the wing and engine chosen, or for a basic kit minus either of these items. Kit prices for the *Choucas 1, Choucas 2CC*, and *Choucas 2T* are 9450FF, 10,550FF, and 11,790FF respectively.

EXTERNAL DIMENSIONS & AREAS - NC.

POWER PLANT - NC.

WEIGHTS & LOADINGS - NC.

PERFORMANCE - NC.

BROC

Ets Bernard Broc, Borne, 43350 Saint-Paulien; tel (71) 00 4321.

BROC *PAPILLON*
(Three-axis)

Single-seat twin-engined high-wing monoplane with conventional three-axis control. Wing has constant chord; no tail, canard wing. Pitch control by elevators on canard; yaw control by fully flying tip rudders; roll control by ailerons with double mixer; control inputs through stick for pitch/roll and pedals for yaw. Wing braced from below by struts; wing profile NC; 100% double-surface. Undercarriage has three wheels in tricycle formation; coil-spring suspension on nosewheel and glass-fibre suspension on main wheels. Push-right go-right nosewheel steering connected to yaw control. Nosewheel brake. Composite-construction airframe, totally enclosed. Engines mounted at wing height, driving tractor propellers.

Production status: prototype.

GENERAL - Fired by his passion for aeronautical research, Bernard Broc designed and built the first *Libellule* (dragonfly in English), which made its maiden flight in May 1981. On 14 July, Bastille Day, the same year

he rallied the 435 mile (700 km) from Paris to Avignon in just under 7 h to set a duration and distance record. This *Libellule Mk I* was a single-seat two-axis machine employing a *Fledgling* sail developed in the USA by the amiable and sadly missed Klaus Hill.

The aircraft was subsequently much changed with commercial production in mind and was known first as the *Libellule Mk II* and then as the *Sirocco,* by which time it had become a three-axis machine with spoilers and a wing completely redesigned by Francois Goethals and Bernard d'Otreppe. It was put into production in January 1983 by Aviasud, and is listed separately in this section.

These models were detailed in our first edition, as was the *Libellule Mk III,* also a conventional three-axis machine but fitted with a 24 hp Konig SC430.

Next, in May 1983, came the first flights of Bernard's *Epervier* (sparrow hawk in English), a low wing cantilever monoplane with a Worthmann FX63-137 wing profile and a NACA 0012 profile for its T-tail. This interesting machine never went into production, but deserves at least a brief description here, full details being given in our first edition.

A three-axis single-seater, it was fitted with ailerons and three-position flaps, acting as high-lift generators at 2° and 15° and as air brakes at 70°. Thanks to its two Konig SC430 engines, mounted in push-pull configuration on a central pod behind the pilot, it was one of the highest performance machines of its day, with a remarkable 20/1 glide at 34 mph (55 kph), maximum level speed 81 mph (130 kph), never exceed speed 93 mph (150 kph), landing speed 22 mph (35 kph) and maximum climb of 1000 ft/min (5.1 m/s). Excellent aerodynamics enabled it to fly some 520 mile (840 km) on one engine at 40 mph (65 kph), while consuming only 1.6 US gal/h (1.3 Imp gal/h, 6.0 litre/h).

A worthy successor, as far as originality goes, is Bernard's latest creation, the *Papillon* (butterfly in English), which made its first flight in Autumn 1984. This three-axis staggered biplane is perhaps best considered as a monoplane with a novel form of canard, for its cantilever front wing acts as a large canard and carries the elevators, while the rear strut-braced wing carries fully-flying tip rudders and ailerons. The composite technology dear to Bernard is once again in evidence, not only in the wings but also in the integral glass-fibre fuselage, which is actually the front part of the *Epervier*.

The *Papillon* was still at prototype stage at the time of writing, with the designer open to manufacturing proposals, so no price had yet been set.

EXTERNAL DIMENSIONS & AREAS - Length overall 10.2 ft, 3.10 m. Height overall 4.9 ft, 1.50 m. Wing span 26.3 ft, 8.00 m. Constant chord 3.3 ft, 0.99 m. Canard chord 3.3 ft, 0.99 m. Total wing area 162 ft², 15.0 m². Main wing area 87 ft², 8.1 m². Canard area 75 ft², 6.9 m². Aspect ratio (of main wing) 7.9/1. Other data NC.

POWER PLANT - Two Konig engines, type NC. Max power 25 hp each at NC rpm. Propellers diameter and pitch 42x18 inch, 1.07x0.45 m. No reduction. Max static thrust 216 lb, 98 kg. Power per unit area 0.31 hp/ft², 3.3 hp/m². Fuel capacity NC.

WEIGHTS & LOADINGS - Empty weight 320 lb, 145 kg. Max take-off weight 651 lb, 295 kg. Payload 331 lb, 150 kg. Max wing loading 4.02 lb/ft², 19.7 kg/m². Max power loading 13.0 lb/hp, 5.9 kg/hp. Load factors +6.0, -4.0 recommended; +9.0, -6.0 ultimate.

PERFORMANCE* - Max level speed 83 mph, 150 kph. Never exceed speed 106 mph, 170 kph. Max cruising speed 75 mph, 120 kph. Economic cruising speed 62 mph, 100 kph. Stalling speed 34 mph, 55 kph. Max climb rate at sea level 980 ft/min, 5.0 m/s. Min sink rate 490 ft/min at 47 mph, 2.5 m/s at 75 kph. Other data NC.

*Under unspecified test conditions.

CENTRAIR

Centrair SA, BP 44, aerodrome, 36300 Le Blanc; tel (54) 37 0796; tx 750272 F. Proprietors: Marc and Mme Ranjon.

CENTRAIR *PARA-FAN*
(Ascending parachute)

Single-seat single-engined motorised parachute. Ram-air parachute. Pilot suspended below wing in trike unit, using pedals to tension rigging lines and thus control yaw; no other aerodynamic controls. Parachute braced by rigging lines; 100% double-surface. Undercarriage has three wheels in tricycle formation; no suspension on nosewheel and glass-fibre suspension on main wheels. Push-right go-right nosewheel steering connected to yaw control. No brakes. Aluminium-alloy tube trike unit, completely open. Engine mounted below wing, driving pusher propeller.

Production status: current, 6 completed.

GENERAL - An ex-Navy pilot of more than 7000 h, Marc Ranjon has accumulated just about every license, permit and qualification that an overactive aviation bureacracy can churn out. He set up his business with his wife in 1967 at le Blanc airfield in the centre of France, Centrair at that time consisting of four people, and 4300 ft² (400 m²) of rented accommodation. The firm's bread and butter was the import of German Schleicher sailplanes and agencies for various light aircraft, and by 1973 the the staff had risen to around 20, where it stayed until 1977 when the company entered the construction field by building the *ASW 20* racing glider under licence as the *ASW 20F.* More than 140 of these have now been built.

Marc, who is interested in just about anything that permits him to divorce himself from Planet Earth, at one time manufactured Christian Paul-Depasse's *Deltaplane* hang gliders, and followed the evolution of the ultralight movement with interest, building a few of J M Geiser's *Motodeltas* at the end of the '70s. This single-seat flexwing with hybrid controls has since disappeared in Europe, though it is still made in Japan (see Other Countries section).

But other projects beckoned. In 1981 the company launched its high-performance *Pegase* sailplane, while Marc became France's leading sailplane pilot, dealing many blows to the West German hegemony which had gone unchallenged for 25 years. Other projects followed and by the end of 1984 Centrair was worth 20M FF, employed 100 people and owned 75,000 ft² (7000 m²) of property, with Marc and his wife still at the helm.

Just when his friend Alain-Yves Berger had all but given up trying to persuade Marc to get back into ultralights, he came up with a motorised parachute, the *Para-Fan*. The idea of attaching what is in effect a trike unit onto a parachute was not stolen from the Steve Snyder's *Paraplane* (see US section), but actually predates the latter, for it was in 1980 that Marc suggested it, together with Jean Gamaury, a sailplane and lightplane pilot and a member of the *Pilote Prive* editorial team. But Jean, the holder of a parachute licence and a notorious devotee of such devices, left his picture of the machine laying around in his mental developing bath, and it was left to the Paraplane to add the developer. Finally came the fixer, when another member of the *UlmMag/Pilote Prive* team, airline pilot and ultralight expert Gerard Fletzer, made the first crossing of the English Channel by powered parachute, flying a Paraplane over the water on 13 October 1984.

Only a month later *Para-Fan* number 001 made its first flights, five in total with three propellor breakages. It was followed by 002 in January 1985 and then by 003, which ended its career in just 3 min at the hands of Jean Gamaury. Number 004 came out shortly before 005, this time Marc making the first flight, in view of Jean's all too short previous attempts. Out of this successful machine came *Para-Fan* 01 which by the time of writing had logged many successful hours and explored the whole domain between short take-off and vertical landing. The duet has become a trio with the addition of instructor Christine Moroko, and delivery of the first poduction machines was scheduled for June 1985.

Price of the complete *Para-Fan*, test-flown and including flight training and an 80pp manual, is 49,500FF.

EXTERNAL DIMENSIONS & AREAS - Length overall 8.2 ft, 2.50 m. Height overall before flight 5.6 ft, 1.70 m. Wing span 33.1 ft, 10.10 m. Constant chord 10.2 ft, 3.11 m. Sweepback 0°. Total wing area 338 ft², 31.4 m². Aspect ratio 3.2/1. Nosewheel diameter overall 10 inch, 26 cm. Main wheels diameter overall 16 inch, 40 cm.

POWER PLANT - Rotax 377 engine. Max power 34 hp at 6500 rpm. Propeller diameter and pitch 59 inch x 17°, 1.50 m x 17°. Gear reduction, ratio 2.6/1. Max static thrust NC. Power per unit area 0.10 hp/ft², 1.1 hp/m². Fuel capacity 3.2 US gal, 2.6 Imp gal, 12.0 litre.

WEIGHTS & LOADINGS - Empty weight 220 lb, 100 kg. Max take-off weight 441 lb, 200 kg. Payload 220 lb, 100 kg. Max wing loading 1.30 lb/ft², 6.4 kg/m². Max power loading 13.0 lb/hp, 5.9 kg/hp. Load factors NC.

PERFORMANCE* - Max level speed 22 mph, 36 kph. Never exceed speed NC. Cruising speed 22 mph, 36 kph. Stall at 18° wing incidence. Max climb rate at sea level 590 ft/min, 3.0 m/s. Max sink rate with power off 1180 ft/min, 6.0 m/s at 20 mph, 32 kph. Best glide ratio with power off 2.5/1 at 22 mph, 36 kph. Take-off distance 65-130 ft, 20-40

m. Landing distance 0-65 ft, 0-20 m. Service ceiling 13,120 ft, 4000 m. Range at average cruising speed 22 mile, 35 km. Noise level 58 dB at 330 ft, 100 m.

*Under the following test conditions - Airfield altitude 0 ft, 0 m. Ground temperature 59°F, 15°C. Ground pressure 1013 mB. Ground windspeed 0 mph, 0 kph. Test payload 209 lb, 95 kg.

CMV

Construction de Machines Volantes SARL (CMV), 2 bis, avenue Montesquieu, 91200 Athis-Mons; tel (6) 048 51 22; tx 231067 F. Proprietor: Antoine Modica. Test pilots: Eric Techer and Olivier Texier.

African agent: CMV Afrique (address from manufacturer). Contact: M Loubhovet.

Arabian Gulf agent: Middle East Trade Center (address from manufacturer). Contact: Khaled Akkawi.

Central and South American agent: CIRI Industries, Caracas, Venezuala. Contact: M Froidefond and M Tonneli.

Israeli agent: Kanfonit Industrie (address from manufacturer).

Spanish agent: M Abayrade (address from manufacturer).

Flashback to 20 November '81, as Marc Ranjon prepares to take the first Pegase *for its first flight.*

CMV/AIR CREATION *NINJA MONO/ALPHAPLUS 18*
(Weight - shift)

Single-seat single-engined flex-wing aircraft with weight-shift control. Rogallo wing with keel pocket. Pilot suspended below wing in trike unit, using bar to control pitch and roll/yaw by altering relative positions of trike unit and wing. Wing braced from above by kingpost and cables, from below by cables; floating cross-tube construction with 40% double-surface enclosing cross-tube; preformed ribs. Undercarriage has three wheels in tricycle formation; suspension NC on nosewheel and rubber suspension on main wheels. Push-right go-left nosewheel steering independent from aerodynamic controls. Optional nosewheel brake. Aluminium-alloy tube trike unit, completely open. Engine mounted below wing, driving pusher propeller.

Production status: current, 4 completed.

GENERAL - Launched in February 1982, the CMV company started by developing two prototypes simultaneously. The first, the *Stampa*, was a variation on the theme of Larry Mauro's *Easy Riser* biplane (see US section, UFM of Kentucky); it was still two-axis controlled but fitted with a variable-incidence canard for pitch, by Bela Nogrady who has since gone on to run his own company (see separate entry). This prototype was damaged on its first flight and as it exhibited neither the flying qualities nor the performance anticipated, and because the *Easy Riser* airframe appeared to lack rigidity, CMV abandoned it.

The second prototype was a tandem two-seater trike, the *Eclair* (lightning in English), which made its first flights quite satisfactorily in March 1982. Development was completed that summer with a 248 ft² (23.0 m²) sail which was earmarked for the production machines. These went on the market that September with Hirth 270R 438 cc 40 hp engines and toothed-belt reductions. At the end of that year came the *Eclair S,* a 'deluxe' version, while the following March both were superceded by the *Eclair V.*

This aircraft, described in our first edition, married the refinements of the *S* with an electric-start 50 hp Robin EC44 engine and an *Alpha 20* wing from Air Concept (now Air Creation - see separate listing).

CMV went on to make an agreement with the Fabrications Aeronautiques ATESMA company and early in 1984 was working on a prototype *Eclair 2000* using aviation-certified technology. This was a duopole two-seater with a sprung main undercarriage and dual controls with adjustable pedals, and could be converted into a single-seater by the removal of one seat and relocation of the hang point. While very advanced for its time, this aircraft unfortunately never reached production.

Right from the start, Antoine aimed mainly at the export market, gradually building up a network of agents, and this proved a shrewd strategy. With its rustic appearance, the *Eclair* faced considerable competition in the home market from more elaborate products and did not sell well, but in countries with more severe climates the various *Eclair* models built a solid export base for the company.

To win a share of the home market while consolidating overseas, the *Ninja* range replaced the *Eclair* range in March 1984, design of the *Ninja Mono* having started in January '84 on receipt of a military order from Portugal. *Ninja* means 'the best' in Japanese, and certainly the new models offer a number of improvements. All models boast thicker structural tubes, and extension of the two rear engine-mounting tubes to the hang point to give better support while taxying. The rear strut on the engine mounting is removable to allow the thrust line to be varied as required, the main undercarriage is silentbloc-mounted and the reduction ratio altered from 2.2 to 2.4/1, while the front wheel goes up from 12 to 16 inch (30-40 cm) in diameter and acquires an optional drum brake.

Undoubtedly the most novel feature is the floating hangpoint, which accomodates yaw movements by twisting of silentbloc bushes. Pitch movement is through pivoting about the axis of the wing/trike unit attachment bolt and roll by the rotating a nylon collar around the keel, the collar carrying the ends of the two cross-tube halves.

Standard equipment on all *Ninjas* includes hand and foot throttles, anodised tubing and stainless-steel front mudguard. Our data below refers to the *Ninja Mono* with Air Creation *Alphaplus 18* wing, a combination which costs 32,240FF assembled and test flown; the *Ninja Bi* and *Ninja Agri* are listed separately. Options include enamelled tubes to customer's colour choice for 1500FF, nosewheel brake for 500FF, and three alternative Air Creation wings: *Quartz 18, Quartz 20* and *Alphaplus 20.* Prices correct on 1 March 1985.

EXTERNAL DIMENSIONS & AREAS - Length overall 11.2 ft, 3.40 m. Height overall 11.8 ft, 3.60 m. Wing span 34.4 ft, 10.50 m. Chord at root 11.2 ft, 3.40 m. Chord at tip 1.0 ft, 0.30 m. Dihedral 4°. Nose angle 120°. Depth of keel pocket NC. Total wing area 194 ft², 18.0 m². Keel pocket area NC. Aspect ratio 6.1/1. Wheel track 5.3 ft, 1.60 m. Wheelbase 6.4 ft, 1.96 m. Nosewheel diameter overall 16 inch, 40 cm. Main wheels diameter overall 16 inch, 40 cm.

POWER PLANT - Robin EC25PS engine. Max power 18 hp at 6200 rpm. Propeller diameter and pitch 47xNC inch, 1.19xNC m. Toothed-belt reduction, ratio 2.4/1. Max static thrust 143 lb, 65 kg. Power per unit area 0.09 hp/ft², 1.0 hp/m². Fuel capacity 2.6 US gal, 2.2 Imp gal, 10.0 litre.

WEIGHTS & LOADINGS - Empty weight 199 lb, 90 kg. Max take-off weight 386 lb, 175 kg. Payload 188 lb, 85 kg. Max wing loading 1.99 lb/ft², 9.7 kg/m². Max power loading 21.4 lb/hp, 9.7 kg/hp. Load factors +6.0, -3.0 recommended; NC ultimate.

PERFORMANCE* - Max level speed 44 mph, 70 kph. Never exceed speed 53 mph, 85 kph. Max cruising speed 47 mph, 75 kph. Economic cruising speed 37 mph, 60 kph. Stalling speed 22 mph, 35 kph. Max climb rate at sea level 490 ft/min, 2.5 m/s. Min sink rate 200 ft/min at 37 mph, 1.0 m/s at 60 kph. Best glide ratio with power off 8/1 at 37 mph, 60 kph. Take-off distance 65 ft, 20 m. Landing distance 195 ft, 60 m. Service ceiling 6560 ft, 2000 m. Range at average cruising speed 75 mile, 120 km. Noise level NC.

*Under the following test conditions - Airfield altitude 423 ft, 129 m. Ground temperature 64°F, 18°C. Ground pressure 1020 mB. Ground windspeed 0 mph, 0 kph. Test payload 188 lb, 85 kg.

CMV/AIR CREATION *NINJA BI/ ALPHAPLUS 20*
(Weight-shift)

Summary as Ninja Mono/Alphaplus 18 *except: Tandem two-seater. Optional pod.*

Production status: current, 20 completed.

GENERAL - The prototype *Ninja Bi* made its first flight in September 1983 with Olivier Tessier at the controls, the

POWER PLANT - Robin EC44PM engine. Max power 50 hp at 6500 rpm. Propeller diameter and pitch 56xNC inch, 1.41xNC m. Toothed-belt reduction, ratio 2.4/1. Max static thrust 276 lb, 125 kg. Power per unit area 0.23 hp/ft², 2.5 hp/m². Fuel capacity 6.3 US gal, 5.3 Imp gal, 24.0 litre.

WEIGHTS & LOADINGS - Empty weight 338 lb, 153 kg. Max take-off weight 691 lb, 313 kg. Payload 353 lb, 160 kg. Max wing loading 3.23 lb/ft², 15.8 kg/m². Max power loading 13.8 lb/hp, 6.3 kg/hp. Load factors +6.0, -3.0 recommended; NC ultimate.

PERFORMANCE* - Max level speed 50 mph, 80 kph. Never exceed speed 59 mph, 95 kph. Max cruising speed 50 mph, 80 kph. Economic cruising speed 44 mph, 70 kph. Stalling speed 22 mph, 35 kph. Max climb rate at sea level 550 ft/min, 2.8 m/s. Min sink rate 250 ft/min at 44 mph, 1.3 m/s at 70 kph. Best glide ratio with power off 7/1 at 44 mph, 70 kph. Take-off distance 65 ft, 20 m. Landing distance 260 ft, 80 m. Service ceiling 8200 ft, 2500 m. Range at average cruising speed 87 mile, 140 km. Noise level NC.

*Under the following test conditions - Airfield altitude 423 ft, 129 m. Ground temperature 61°F, 16°C. Ground pressure 1020 mB. Ground windspeed 0 mph, 0 kph. Test payload 353 lb, 160 kg.

CMV/AIR CREATION *NINJA AGRI/GAMMA 23*
(Weight-shift)

Summary as Ninja Mono/Alphaplus 18 *except: Wing has fixed cross-tube construction with single-surface.*

Production status: current, 31 completed.

GENERAL - The aerial work *Ninja Agri* was developed as a result of an order in spring 1984 for 18 aircraft for Mexico. Built in June that year, the prototype made its first test flights the following month. When the first order was delivered at the end of August, the design was also launched simultaneously in Israel, the Ivory Coast and Venezuala.

Like most workhorse ultralights, the *Ninja Agri* can also be used as a two-seater for pleasure flying or training, the trike unit being very similar to the *Ninja Bi*. The wing, however, is quite different, for the aircraft uses a design specially manufactured for CMV by Air Creation, the fixed-crosstube, single-surface *Gamma*. Assembled, test flown and equipped for crop spraying, the aircraft costs 71,240FF. There are no optional wings, but other extras are as for *Ninja Mono*.

EXTERNAL DIMENSIONS & AREAS - Length overall 11.5 ft, 3.50 m. Height overall 11.8 ft, 3.60 m. Wing span 32.8 ft, 10.00 m. Chord at root 11.5 ft, 3.50 m. Chord at tip 1.7 ft, 0.50 m. Dihedral 4°. Nose angle 130°. Depth of keel pocket NC. Total wing area 248 ft², 23.0 m². Keel pocket area NC. Aspect ratio 4.3/1. Wheel track 5.3 ft, 1.60 m. Wheelbase 7.1 ft, 2.15 m. Nosewheel diameter overall 16 inch, 40 cm. Main wheels diameter overall 16 inch, 40 cm.

POWER PLANT - See *Ninja Bi/Alphaplus 20* except: Power per unit area 0.20 hp/ft², 2.2 hp/m². Fuel capacity 3.2 US gal, 2.7 Imp gal, 12.0 litre.

WEIGHTS & LOADINGS - Empty weight 371 lb, 168 kg. Max take-off weight 724 lb, 328 kg. Payload 353 lb, 160 kg.

first production machines emerging two months later, but it was not until January 1985 that the machine went onto the market in its present form. Connecting rods provide dual control on this model, while other features, common to all *Ninjas,* are described under *Ninja Mono*. The electric-start Robin EC44PM benefits from the same reduction-drive change as the solo machine, in this case raising thrust by 22 lb (10 kg) to 276 lb (125 kg).

The *Ninja Mono's* novel hang point is also used on this model, wing options too being the same as for the solo machine, though we detail below the *Ninja Bi* mated to an Air Concept *Alphaplus 20,* in which form it costs 42,640FF assembled and test flown. Other options are also as for the single-seater, but in addition a pod is available.

Planned for summer 1985 is a new model, the *Nimitz,* developed from the *Ninja Bi* and fitted with Pierre Fayet floats. Another 'top secret' project under test at the time of writing was an engine adaption for operation in high-altitude countries.

EXTERNAL DIMENSIONS & AREAS - Length overall 13.1 ft, 4.00 m. Height overall 11.8 ft, 3.60 m. Wing span 32.8 ft, 10.00 m. Chord at root 9.8 ft, 3.00 m. Chord at tip 3.3 ft, 1.00 m. Dihedral 4°. Nose angle 120°. Depth of keel pocket NC. Total wing area 214 ft², 19.8 m². Keel pocket area NC. Aspect ratio 5.1/1. Wheel track 5.3 ft, 1.60 m. Wheelbase 7.1 ft, 2.15 m. Nosewheel diameter overall 16 inch, 40 cm. Main wheels diameter overall 16 inch, 40 cm.

Max wing loading 2.92 lb/ft², 14.3 kg/m². Max power loading 14.5 lb/hp, 6.6 kg/hp. Load factors +6.0, -3.0 recommended; NC ultimate.

PERFORMANCE* - Max level speed 50 mph, 80 kph. Never exceed speed 56 mph, 90 kph. Max cruising speed 44 mph, 70 kph. Economic cruising speed 37 mph, 60 kph. Stalling speed 19 mph, 30 kph. Max climb rate at sea level 490 ft/min, 2.5 m/s. Min sink rate 300 ft/min at 37 mph, 1.5 m/s at 60 kph. Best glide ratio with power off 6/1 at 37 mph, 60 kph. Take-off distance 50 ft, 15 m. Landing distance 260 ft, 80 m. Service ceiling 6560 ft, 2000 m. Range at average cruising speed 44 mile, 70 km. Noise level NC.

*Under the following test conditions - Airfield altitude 423 ft, 129 m. Ground temperature 61°F, 16°C. Ground pressure 1013 mB. Ground windspeed 0 mph, 0 kph. Test payload 353 lb, 160 kg.

This agricultural version of the Eclair, the Eclair Land, was used as a flying test bed for the Ninja Agri. Note the double-surface wing on this prototype.

COSMOS

Cosmos SARL, rue du Stade, 21121 Fontaine-les-Dijon; tel (80) 57 4747. Manager: Renaud Guy.

La Mouette SARL, 1 rue de la Petite-Fin, 21121 Fontaine-les-Dijon; tel (80) 56 6647; tx MOUETTE 350053 F. Proprietors: Gerard and Jean-Marc Thevenot.

US agent: Skylines Enterprises, PO Box 4384, Salinas, California 93912; tel (408) 422-2781.

COSMOS/LA MOUETTE
DRAGSTER II 25/PROFIL 17, 34/PROFIL 17, and 34 FC/PROFIL 19 MONO
(Weight-shift)

Single-seat single-engined flex-wing aircraft with weight-shift control. Rogallo wing without keel pocket or fin. Pilot suspended below wing in trike unit, using bar to control pitch and roll/yaw by altering relative positions of trike unit and wing. Wing braced from above by kingpost and cables, from below by cables; floating cross-tube construction with 60% double-surface

Cosmos Dragster II 34 *with optional pod.*

enclosing cross-tube; preformed ribs. Undercarriage has three wheels in tricycle formation; no suspension on nosewheel, cable-stretch suspension on main wheels (Dragster II 25), bungee suspension on main wheels (other models). Push-right go-left nosewheel steering independent from aerodynamic controls. Optional nosewheel brake. Aluminium-alloy tube trike unit, with optional pod. Engine mounted below wing, driving pusher propeller.

Production status: current, 150 completed.

GENERAL - The Cosmos story started in 1975, when La Mouette was set up to manufacture and sell hang gliders designed by the Thevenot brothers, Gerard and Jean-Marc. Their first wing was actually called *La Mouette* (seagull in English) and was an ultralight glider with a cylindro-conical sail, revolutionary at a time when most Rogallos used the classic triangular plan. Gerard graduated from Strasbourg university where he specialised in fluid mechanics, and turned out to be one of world's best hang glider pilots, several times French, European and World champion, flying of course, his own wings!
La Mouette has become one of the industry's most impor-

Cosmos Dragster II 25 *with front strut (not standard on this model).*

133

tant names, especially on the export front where its efforts were rewarded by a government diploma in 1982, with production units in the USA and Japan. It entered the ultralight market in 1980 as importer of the British Ultra Sports *Tripacer* trike unit (see our first edition, p139), mating it to its own wings. But the brothers wanted to build their own trike units, and so in 1982 set up a sister company called Cosmos, to be run by Renaud Guy.

The prototype of Cosmos' first machine, the *Dragster*, flew early in 1982 and the model was marketed that August, to be replaced in 1984 by the updated *Dragster II*. For the two-seat market the company offers the *Bidulm*, and both are well proven designs enjoying an excellent reputation and faultless finish, their truly industrialised manufacture minimising performance and handling differences between individual machines. There is also an agricultural version, the *Cosmagri*.

From a design point of view, the trikes follow modern monopole practice, their most notable features being the use of gold-anodised aircraft-quality tubing and their particularly good collapsability. Folded, a *Dragster II* measures just 6.9x2.6x3.3 ft (2.1x0.8x1.0 m) which allows it to be carried on a very light trailer or in an estate car, with the wing on the roofrack.

There are three *Dragster II* versions, the *25*, the 34 and *34 FC* - the number refers to the type of Robin engine and *FC* to Fortes Charges (high loader in English) - the latter using a front strut of aerofoil section, which not only looks nice but also offers less drag than the normal round tubes. Cosmos has a reputation for excellent after-sales service, and all its models meet the rigorous West German ultralight regulations (the gutesiegel).

Early *Dragsters* used La Mouette's *Azur 17* or *19* wings, but these have been replaced by two new series with an equally good reputation: the *Atlas* and the *Profil*, both easily recognisable by their lack of either fin or keel pocket, and both available in various sizes. La Mouette wings are also sold to other trike unit manufacturers at home and abroad, which is why production of the recently introduced *Profil* had already exceeded 200 by May '85.

We detail below three typical trike unit/wing combinations, while the two-seaters and the agricultural machine are listed separately. Data below refers to a *Dragster II 25* trike unit with *Profil 17* wing, which costs 30,250FF assembled and flight-tested, though the trike unit, like most Cosmos products, can be obtained as a kit together with a 50pp manual and a handbook. Where different, figures for the *Dragster II 34/Profil 17* (37,050FF) and *Dragster II FC/Profil 19 Mono* (38,550FF) are shown in parentheses in that order. Options: nosewheel drum brake 355FF, electric start for Robin EC34 1900FF, pod 2605FF, floating hang-point for *Profil 19 Mono* wing 4860FF, extra tank to treble fuel capacity 600FF.

Wings alone (no kits available): *Atlas 18*, 9700FF, *Profil 17*, 13,900FF, *Profil 19 Mono*, 15,400FF.

There is plenty of further reading in the specialist press. French-language reports appear in *UlmMag* - a *Dragster* flight test by Jean-Pierre Mathias in July 1983 and a distance record attempt by the same author in September 1984 - while in the USA, a hang-glider towing demonstration by Pacific Windcraft's Jean-Michel Bernasconi and Gerard Thevenot of La Mouette in the summer of 1984 prompted a particularly eulogistic article in *Whole Air*.

EXTERNAL DIMENSIONS & AREAS - Length overall 16.4(16.4)(19.0) ft, 5.00(5.00)(5.80) m. Height overall 8.2 ft, 2.50 m. Wing span 34.4 ft, 10.50 m. Chord at root 8.0(8.0)(9.5) ft, 2.45(2.45)(2.90) m. Chord at tip 3.1(3.1)(3.4) ft, 0.95(0.95)(1.05) m. Dihedral 1°. Nose angle 120°. Total wing area 175(175)(205) ft², 16.3(16.3)(19.0) m². Aspect ratio 6.8(6.8)(5.8)/1. Wheel track 5.6(NC)(NC) ft, 1.70(NC)

Detail of Dragster II *nosewheel assembly when fitted with optional brake.*

(NC) m. Wheelbase NC(5.9)(NC) ft, NC(1.80)(NC) m. Nosewheel diameter overall 13(13)(NC) inch, 32(32)(NC) cm. Main wheels diameter overall 13(13)(NC) inch, 32(32) (NC) cm.

POWER PLANT - Robin EC25PS (EC34PM)(EC34PM) engine. Max power 18(32)(32) hp at 6000(6500)(6500) rpm. Propeller diameter and pitch 54(54)(59)x24(30)(27) inch, 1.37(1.37)(1.50)x0.60(0.76)(0.68) m. Notched V-belt reduction, ratio 2.4/1. Max static thrust 143(177)(209) lb, 65(80)(95) kg. Power per unit area 0.10(0.18)(0.16) hp/ft², 1.1(2.0)(1.7) hp/m². Fuel capacity 2.6 US gal, 2.2 Imp gal, 10.0 litre.

WEIGHTS & LOADINGS - Empty weight 166(199)(220) lb, 75(90)(100) kg. Max take-off weight 426(426)(464) lb, 193(193)(210) kg. Payload 260(227)(243) lb, 118(103) (110) kg. Max wing loading 2.43(2.43)(2.26) lb/ft², 11.8 (11.8)(11.1) kg/m². Max power loading 23.7(13.3)(14.5) lb/ hp, 10.7(6.0)(6.6) kg/hp. Load factors +6.0, -3.0 recommended; +9.0, -5.0(5.0)(4.0) ultimate.

PERFORMANCE* - Max level speed 50(53)(53) mph, 80(85)(85) kph. Never exceed speed 59(59)(65) mph, 95(95)(105) kph. Max cruising speed 44 mph, 70 kph. Economic cruising speed 31(34)(31) mph, 50(55)(50) kph. Stalling speed 24(26)(22) mph, 40(42)(35) kph. Max climb rate at sea level 490(690)(790) ft/min, 2.5(3.5)(4.0) m/s. Min sink rate 300(390)(300) ft/min at 28(28)(23) mph, 1.5(2.0)(1.5) m/s at 45(45)(38) kph. Best glide ratio with power off 8.8(6.6)(7.4)/1 at 30(30)(24) mph, 48(48)(40) kph. Take-off distance 100 ft, 30 m. Landing distance 80 ft, 25 m. Service ceiling 8200(13,120)(13,120) ft, 2500(4000)

(4000) m. Range at average cruising speed 93(62)(62) mile, 150(100)(100) km. Noise level 63(65)(65) dB at 490 ft, 150 m.

Under the following test conditions - Airfield altitude 262 ft, 80 m. Ground temperature 61°F, 16°C. Ground pressure 1016 mB. Ground windspeed 6 mph, 10 kph. Test payload 209 lb, 95 kg.

COSMOS/LA MOUETTE *BIDULM 34/PROFIL 19 BI, 44/PROFIL 19 BI, and 50/PROFIL 19 BI* (Weight-shift)

Summary as Dragster II 25/Profil 17 *except: Tandem two-seater. Coil spring suspension on nosewheel, no suspension on main wheels (Bidulm 34), bungee suspension on main wheels (other models).*

Production status: current, number completed NC.

GENERAL - Cosmos' offering in the two-seat market is, like the solo *Dragster II,* a monopole device of conventional construction, but using the aerofoil front strut discussed under the latter heading.

Originally fitted with the *Azur 19 Bi* wing, the *Bidulm* has since 1984 used either the *Profil -* in *17, 19 Mono* or *19 Bi* forms - or the *Atlas 22.*

Cosmos Bidulm 44, *fitted with optional extra tank, in flight with La Mouette wing. For another picture see colour section.*

Three engines are offered, Robin EC34PM, Robin EC44PM or Rotax 503, the trike units taking the titles *Bidulm 34, 44* and *50* respectively. We detail all three with the same *Profil 19 Bi* wing. Data below refers to the Robin EC34PM-engined machine which costs 42,000FF ready to fly; where different, figures for the EC44PM- and Rotax 503-engined machines (49,000FF and 44,850FF respectively) are shown in parentheses, in that order.

Options are as for the solo machines, except that the pod costs 2750FF; in addition, dual control for the front wheel can be fitted for an extra 217FF. The *Profil 19 Bi* can be purchased separately for 16,200FF, the same price as the *Atlas 22.* Load factors quoted below are correct for both these wings. Other wing prices are listed under the solo machines.

EXTERNAL DIMENSIONS & AREAS - See *Dragster II 34 FC/Profil 19 Mono* except: Wheel track 6.1 ft, 1.85 m. Wheelbase 6.1(6.4)(6.4) ft, 1.85(1.95)(1.95) m. Nosewheel diameter overall 16 inch, 40 cm. Main wheels diameter overall 16 inch, 40 cm.

POWER PLANT - Robin EC34PM (Robin EC44PM) (Rotax 503) engine. Max power 32(50)(45) hp at 6500 rpm. Propeller diameter and pitch 59(62)(62)x27(28)(28) inch, 1.50(1.57)(1.57)x0.68(0.72)(0.72) m. Notched V-belt reduction, ratio 2.4/1. Max static thrust 209(309)(309) lb, 95(140)(140) kg. Power per unit area 0.16(0.24)(0.22) hp/

ft², 1.7(2.6)(2.4) hp/m². Fuel capacity 2.6 US gal, 2.2 Imp gal, 10.0 litre.

WEIGHTS & LOADINGS - Empty weight 265(298)(287) lb, 120(135)(130) kg. Max take-off weight 618 lb, 280 kg. Payload 353(320)(331) lb, 160(145)(150) kg. Max wing loading 3.01 lb/ft², 14.7 kg/m². Max power loading 19.3 (12.4)(13.7) lb/hp, 8.8(5.6)(6.2) kg/hp. Load factors +6.0, -3.0 recommended; +9.0, -4.0 ultimate.

PERFORMANCE* - Max level speed 53 mph, 85 kph. Never exceed speed 59 mph, 95 kph. Max cruising speed 44 mph, 70 kph. Economic cruising speed 37 mph, 60 kph. Stalling speed 30 mph, 48 kph. Max climb rate at sea level 390(590)(590) ft/min, 2.0(3.0)(3.0) m/s. Min sink rate 390 ft/min at 31 mph, 2.0 m/s at 50 kph. Best glide ratio with power off 7.6/1 at 34 mph, 55 kph. Take-off distance 165(130)(130) ft, 50(40)(40) m. Landing distance 130 ft, 40 m. Service ceiling 6560(13,120)(13,120) ft, 2000(4000) (4000) m. Range at average cruising speed 87(44)(37) mile, 140(70)(60) km. Noise level 65(70)(72) dB at 490 ft, 150m.

*Under the following test conditions - Airfield altitude 262 ft, 180 m. Ground temperature 61°F, 16°C. Ground pressure 1016 mB. Ground windspeed 6 mph, 10 kph. Test payload 353 lb, 160 kg.

COSMOS/LA MOUETTE
COSMAGRI/ATLAS 22

(Weight-shift)

Single-seat single-engined flex-wing aircraft with weight-shift control. Rogallo wing without keel pocket or fin. Pilot suspended below wing in trike unit, using bar to control pitch and roll/yaw by altering relative positions of trike unit and wing. Wing braced from above by kingpost and cables, from below by cables; fixed cross-tube construction with 25% double-surface not enclosing cross-tube; preformed ribs. Undercarriage has three wheels in tricycle formation; coil-spring suspension on nosewheel and bungee suspension on main wheels. Push-right go-left nosewheel steering independent from aerodynamic controls. Optional nosewheel brake. Aluminium-alloy tube trike unit, completely open. Engine mounted below wing, driving pusher propeller.

Production status: current, number completed NC.

GENERAL - Introduced in February 1985, having made its first flights the previous November, the *Cosmagri* is an agricultural version of the *Bidulm 50,* fitted with a twin carburettor variant of the Rotax 503.

The trike unit is modified by fitting all-round suspension and by removing the dual seating (though the owner may reinstate it to go pleasure flying after a hard day's spraying), a seat-tank being substituted. In the Rogallo department, the aircraft is also obviously different, using as standard equipment the 'workhorse' *Atlas 22* wing, with 25% double-surface, a design not normally seen on the two-seaters.

Its moulded glass-fibre seat-tank carries not only the fuel but also 23.8 US gal (19.8 Imp gal, 90 litre) of chemicals, the latter being automatically mixed and delivered by an independent servo-operated centrifugal pump. The nylon filter is very accessible and spraying is controlled by a foot-operated electric valve, pressure being adjustable in flight by means of a regulator and pressure gauge. Other instruments fitted as standard include anemometer, tachometer, and chemical-level gauge. With two 30 ft (9 m) spray booms, land can be covered in 40 ft (12 m) strips. Optionally, the system can be adapted to take products in micro-granular form. All trike components are treated against corrosion.

The *Cosmagri* can be easily converted into a two-seater for pleasure flying or school use and can also be fitted with equipment for towing hang gliders.
Price with *Atlas 22* wing and agricultural equipment, assembled and test-flown: 98,100FF.

EXTERNAL DIMENSIONS & AREAS - Length overall 19.0 ft, 5.80 m. Height overall 6.6 ft, 2.00 m. Wing span 36.8 ft, 11.20 m. Chord at root 10.5 ft, 3.20 m. Chord at tip 3.9 ft, 1.20 m. Dihedral 2°. Nose angle 120°. Total wing area 237 ft^2, 22.0 m^2. Aspect ratio 5.7/1. Wheel track 6.1 ft, 1.85 m. Wheelbase 6.3 ft, 1.90 m. Nosewheel diameter overall NC. Main wheels diameter overall NC.

POWER PLANT - Rotax 503 engine. Max power 52 hp at 6500 rpm. Propeller diameter and pitch 62x27 inch, 1.57x0.69 m. Notched V-belt reduction, ratio 2.4/1. Max static thrust 331 lb, 150 kg. Power per unit area 0.22 hp/ft^2, 2.4 hp/m^2. Fuel capacity 5.3 US gal, 4.4 Imp gal, 20.0 litre.

WEIGHTS & LOADINGS - Empty weight 353 lb, 160 kg. Max take-off weight 773 lb, 350 kg. Payload 419 lb, 190 kg. Max wing loading 3.26 lb/ft^2, 15.9 kg/m^2. Max power loading 14.9 lb/hp, 6.7 kg/hp. Load factors +6.0, -3.0 recommended; +9.0, -4.0 ultimate.

PERFORMANCE* - Max level speed 44 mph, 70 kph. Never exceed speed 53 mph, 85 kph. Max cruising speed 37 mph, 60 kph. Economic cruising speed 28 mph, 45 kph. Stalling speed 22 mph, 35 kph. Max climb rate at sea level 590 ft/min, 3.0 m/s. Min sink rate 300 ft/min at 24 mph, 1.5 m/s at 40 kph. Best glide ratio with power off 7.8/1 at 28 mph, 45 kph. Take-off distance 130 ft, 40 m. Landing distance 65 ft, 20 m. Service ceiling 13,120 ft, 4000 m. Range at average cruising speed 56 mile, 90 km. Noise level 72 dB at 490 ft, 150 m.

*Under the following test conditions - Airfield altitude 262 ft, 80 m. Ground temperature 61°F, 16°C. Ground pressure 1016 mB. Ground windspeed 6 mph, 10 kph. Test payload 209 lb, 95 kg.

CROSES

SARL Croses Airplume, 63 route de Davaye, 71000 Charnay-les-Macon; tel (85) 34 1611. Proprietors: Emilien and Yves Croses.

CROSES *POUPLUME*

(Two-axis)

Single-seat single-engined double monoplane in tandem with two-axis control. Wings have unswept leading and trailing edges, and constant chord; tail has vertical surfaces only. Pitch control by fully flying wing; yaw control by fin-mounted rudder; no separate roll control; control inputs through stick for pitch/yaw. Wings braced from below by struts; wing profile NACA 23012; 100% double-surface. Undercarriage has two wheels plus tailskid; glass-fibre suspension on tailskid and main wheels. Ground steering by differential braking. Brakes on main wheels. Fuselage partially enclosed; materials see text. Engine mounted at fuselage height, driving tractor propeller.

Production status: see text.

GENERAL - Emilien Croses designed and constructed his first homebuilt as long ago as 1947, since when he has created another 11, including the famous *Criquet* (grasshopper in English). All of them are based on the Mignet *Flying flea* formula, having two wings in tandem with the high front wing acting also as an elevator. Most of these light aircraft were two-axis controlled by joystick alone, although some were fitted with ailerons, transforming them into three-axis machines with conventional stick-and-rudder controls.

The prototype of the single-seater *Pouplume* was undoubtedly one of the first ultralights in the world since, when it made its first flight in 1961, the word hadn't even been invented! Emilien designed and built it for the Bourges international competition, which he won. The task consisted of a 6 mile (10 km) closed circuit, with aircraft limited to a single-cylinder engine of maximum capacity 175 cc.

No doubt inspired by this achievement, amateurs have since then built a dozen *Pouplumes,* following bundles of plans which can be bought for 1000FF. Though the machines built so far have been of traditional wood and fabric construction, Emilien's son Yves, the founder in 1983 of Croses SARL, anticipates that laminated glass-fibre fuselages will be ready for sale by the end of 1985. Data below refers to the wood/fabric version with a JPX PUL425 engine, though in practice of course each builder makes

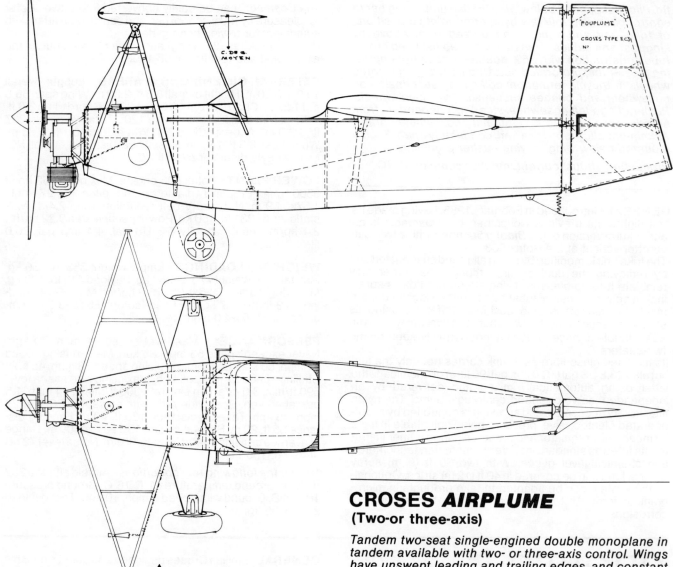

his or her own choice, the 40 hp Hirth being another possibility.

EXTERNAL DIMENSIONS & AREAS - Length overall 15.9 ft, 4.80 m. Height overall 5.9 ft, 1.80 m. Wing span 25.7 ft, 7.80 m. Sweepback 0°. Total wing area 183 ft², 17.0 m². Other data NC.

POWER PLANT - JPX PUL 425 engine. Max power 26 hp at 4600 rpm. Propeller diameter and pitch NC. No reduction. Max static thrust NC. Power per unit area 0.14 hp/ft², 1.5 hp/m². Fuel capacity 2.6 US gal, 2.2 Imp gal, 10.0 litre.

WEIGHTS & LOADINGS - Empty weight 287 lb, 130 kg. Max take-off weight 497 lb, 225 kg. Payload 210 lb, 95 kg. Max wing loading 2.71 lb/ft², 13.2 kg/m². Max power loading 19.1 lb/hp, 8.7 kg/hp. Load factors +4.5, -NC recommended; NC ultimate.

PERFORMANCE* - Max level speed 75 mph, 120 kph. Max cruising speed 62 mph, 100 kph. Economic cruising speed 44 mph, 70 kph. Stalling speed 16 mph, 25 kph. Landing distance 80 ft, 24 m. Other data NC.

*Under unspecified test conditions.

CROSES *AIRPLUME*
(Two-or three-axis)

Tandem two-seat single-engined double monoplane in tandem available with two- or three-axis control. Wings have unswept leading and trailing edges, and constant chord; tabs fitted; tail has vertical surfaces only. Pitch control by fully flying wing; yaw control by fin-mounted rudder; no separate roll control (two-axis version), roll control by 60%-span ailerons (three-axis version); control inputs through stick for pitch/yaw (two-axis version), through stick for pitch/roll and pedals for yaw (three-axis version). Wings braced from below by struts; wing profile NACA 23012; 100% double-surface. Undercarriage has three wheels in tail-dragger formation; glass-fibre suspension on all wheels. Push-right go-right tailwheel steering connected to yaw control; also differential braking. Brakes on main wheels. Steel tube/wood airframe, partially enclosed. Engine mounted at fuselage height, driving tractor propeller.

Production status: current, 24 completed.

GENERAL - Readers of our first edition may remember that we forecast the appearance of a tandem two-seater of similar configuration to the *Pouplume*, and this has now emerged, the prototype *Airplume* making its first flight on 1 April 1983. Twenty-four production models have been built since, all with Mignet-formula two-axis controls.
However, thanks as much to customer demand as to a remark by Alain-Yves Berger about the prototype's han-

level 590 ft/min, 3.0 m/s. Min sink rate 200 ft/min at 37 mph, 1.0 m/s at 60 kph. Best glide ratio with power off 10/1 at 37 mph, 60 kph. Take-off distance 130 ft, 40 m. Landing distance 130 ft, 40 m. Service ceiling 8200 ft, 2500 m. Range at average cruising speed 156 mile, 250 km. Noise level NC.

Under the following test conditions - Airfield altitude 984 ft, 300 m. Ground temperature 64°F, 18°C. Ground pressure NC. Ground windspeed 0 mph, 0 kph. Test payload 384 lb, 174 kg.

EOLE 2000

Eole 2000 SARL, ZI La Mariniere, rue Gustave-Eiffel, Bondoufle, 91000 Evry; tel (3) 078 5939. Proprietors: Patrick Biscueil, Jean-Pierre Danis.

EOLE 2000
SAFARI GTX/ALPHA 15
(Weight-shift)

Single-seat single-engined flex-wing aircraft with weight-shift control. Rogallo wing with keel pocket. Pilot suspended below wing in trike unit, using bar to control pitch and roll/yaw by altering relative positions of trike unit and wing. Wing braced from above by kingpost and cables, from below by cables; floating cross-tube construction with 60% double-surface enclosing cross-tube; preformed ribs. Undercarriage has three wheels in tricycle formation; suspension NC. Push-right go-left nosewheel steering independent from aerodynamic controls; also optional differential braking. Nosewheel brake (optional main wheel brakes). Aluminium-alloy tube trike unit, completely open. Engine mounted below wing, driving pusher propeller.

Production status: current, number completed NC.

GENERAL - Eole 2000 is one of the main French manufacturers of hang glider and trike wings and was set up in 1977 by Patrick Biscueil, who since 1974 had worked in hang glider manufacturing at Roland Magallon's now defunct Veliplane company, as well as running a hang-gliding school and having launched himself with great gusto and some success into the competition scene.

His co-founder at Eole 2000 was Jean-Pierre Mathias, now a staff writer with *UlmMag,* who in 1984 set the non-stop trike distance record. The company began as a distributor for other now defunct French manufacturers and later for Wasp (also defunct), Hiway and Flexiform. Two years later Patrick set up a factory at Salins-les-Bains in the Jura where he built the *Orion* glider and his own version of the *Skylane.* In 1980 he began the production of trike wings based on the *Orion,* these being dubbed *Centaure* when marketed by his own company and *Sabre* when sold by Bernard Danis, whose manufacturing presence has all but ceased since our first edition. The same year, the company built 100 *Condor* wings for Agriplane crop-spraying trikes.

In 1981 came the single and two-person *Alpha* hang gliding and trike wings which were, with slight modifications, known as the *Tempete* at Bernard Danis or *Samourai* at Veliplane. The same year, Patrick and Eric Bunodiere established Pro-Delta at Gemenos between Toulon and Marseille to manufacture a 60% double-surface version of

dling in turbulence and high temperatures, Yves modified the machine to three-axis stick-and-rudder controls by adding conventional ailerons. As a result, this interesting two-seater, which offers remarkable performance for a dual machine with 35 hp engine, is now available in both two- and three-axis versions.

The Macon-based manufacturer sells it in kit form. The basic kit costs 16,841FF and includes fuselage, tail fin, main undercarriage, tailskid, and fuel tank, the structure being made of glass-fibre reinforced with Kevlar and carbon strips. Kit two includes eight half-length longerons, 38 ribs, four side panels and all the other wooden components ready-machined, while number three includes wings with hinges in position and ready for covering and costs 16,080FF. A further 8700FF buys kit four, with struts, hinges, links, dual controls, axles and engine mount.

Yves Croses was on the point of linking up with an industrialist at the time of writing and led us to believe that ready-built *Airplumes* would be available at the end of 1985, while glass-fibre laminated carbon-reinforced wings were also envisaged.

EXTERNAL DIMENSIONS & AREAS - Length overall 17.1 ft, 5.20 m. Height overall 6.3 ft, 1.90 m. Wing span 25.7 ft, 7.80 m. Constant chord 3.9 ft, 1.20 m. Dihedral 5°. Sweepback 0°. Fin height 2.7 ft, 0.80 m. Total wing area 183 ft², 17.0 m². Front wing area 102 ft², 9.5 m². Rear wing area 81 ft², 7.5 m². Rudder area 8.6 ft² 0.80 m². Aspect ratio 6.5/1. Wheel track 5.7 ft, 1.70 m. Tailwheel diameter overall 5 inch, 12 cm. Main wheels diameter overall 14 inch, 35 cm.

POWER PLANT - Cuyuna ULII-02 engine. Max power 35 hp at 6500 rpm. Propeller diameter and pitch 62x24 inch, 1.60x0.60 m. Notched V-belt reduction, ratio 2.4/1. Max static thrust 221 lb, 100 kg. Power per unit area 0.19 hp/ft², 2.1 hp/m². Fuel capacity 6.4 US gal, 5.3 Imp gal, 24.0 litre.

WEIGHTS & LOADINGS - Empty weight 375 lb, 170 kg. Max take-off weight 773 lb, 350 kg. Payload 397 lb, 180 kg. Max wing loading 4.22 lb/ft², 20.6 kg/m². Max power loading 22.1 lb/hp, 10.0 kg/hp. Load factors +5.7, -3.5 recommended; NC ultimate.

PERFORMANCE* - Max level speed 78 mph, 125 kph. Never exceed speed 87 mph, 140 kph. Max cruising speed 62 mph, 100 kph. Economic cruising speed 56 mph, 90 kph. Stalling speed 19 mph, 30 kph. Max climb rate at sea

the *Alpha* and to research a single-surface wing which became the *Omega*.

Bunodiere's *Quartz* has not done well on the hang gliding market since its launch in 1983, but the success of the triking version, built by Gilles Bru at Air Creation (see separate listing) has compensated for this. Air Creation was in fact set up with help from Patrick Biscueil, and the two companies still co-operate closely.

In 1983 Eole 2000 manufactured some 865 Rogallos, but like all French manufacturers was hit by the 1984 recession and now has only one factory, on the southern outskirts of Paris. The company's most recent design, introduced in 1984, is the dual *Lambda* wing, which was built to conform to the rules of the ultralight manufacturers' syndicate, of which Roland Magallon is president. The fact that, at the time of writing, the wing had still not received the syndicate's seal of approval would appear to have more to do with personality differences among syndicate menbers than with any of the 'technical problems' quoted!

Eole 2000's position in France is somewhat analagous to that of Flexiform in the UK, in that although wing manufacture is its main business, a few trike units are also built. Currently Eole 2000 makes its own versions of the single- and two-seat trike units in production at Air Creation, calling them *Safari GTX* and *Safari GTX Bi* respectively. Principal differences between them and their Air Creation counterparts are a different design of engine mount and the option of independently operable main-wheel brakes. We detail below the solo trike unit with a typical wing, the *Alpha 15*, while a dual version with the *Lambda 21* is listed separately.

Prices, including VAT at 18.6%, are as follows. Trike units without engine: *Safari GTX*, 12,500FF; *Safari GTX Bi*, 15,000FF. Wings for single-seaters: *Alpha 15*, 13,000FF; *Alpha 17*, 13,500FF; *Omega 17*, 11,000FF; *Quartz 16*, 15,000FF; *Quartz 18*, 18,000FF. Wings for two-seaters: *Alpha 18*, 15,000FF; *Alpha 20*, 16,000FF; *Lambda 21*, 15,200FF. Note that the *Quartz 18* can also be used on two-seaters.

EXTERNAL DIMENSIONS & AREAS - Length overall 12.2 ft, 3.70 m. Height overall 11.5 ft, 3.50 m. Wing span 32.2 ft, 9.80 m. Chord at root 8.6 ft, 2.60 m. Chord at tip 3.0 ft, 0.90 m. Dihedral 5°. Nose angle 122°. Total wing area 165 ft², 15.3 m². Aspect ratio 6.3/1. Wheelbase 5.3 ft, 1.60 m. Nosewheel diameter overall 13 inch, 32 cm. Main wheels diameter overall 16 inch, 40 cm. Other data NC.

POWER PLANT - Rotax 377 engine. Max power 34 hp at 7000 rpm. Propeller diameter and pitch 59xNC inch, 1.50xNC m. Gear reduction, ratio 2.6/1. Max static thrust 220 lb, 100 kg. Power per unit area 0.21 hp/ft², 2.2 hp/m². Fuel capacity 2.6 US gal, 2.2 Imp gal, 10.0 litre.

WEIGHTS & LOADINGS - Empty weight 237 lb, 107 kg. Max take-off weight 441 lb, 200 kg. Payload 204 lb, 93 kg. Max wing loading 2.67 lb/ft², 13.1 kg/m². Max power loading 13.0 lb/hp, 5.9 kg/hp. Load factors NC.

PERFORMANCE* - Never exceed speed 56 mph, 90 kph. Max cruising speed 40 mph, 65 kph. Economic cruising speed 31 mph, 50 kph. Stalling speed 19 mph, 30 kph. Other data NC.

*Under unspecified test conditions.

◄ EOLE 2000
SAFARI GTX BI/LAMBDA 21
(Weight-shift)

Summary as Safari GTX/Alpha 15 *except: Tandem two-seater. Fixed cross-tube constrction with 30% double-surface not enclosing cross-tube. Air suspension on all wheels.*

Production status: current; number completed NC (Safari GTX), 1250 completed (Lambda 21).

GENERAL - This two-seater machine is available with either a gear-reduction Rotax 447 engine or a toothed-belt reductio Rotax 503, developing 48 hp. The former is detailed below. For further information, see *Safari GTX/ Alpha 15*.

EXTERNAL DIMENSIONS & AREAS - Length overall 12.2 ft, 3.70 m. Wing span 33.8 ft, 10.30 m. Chord at root 10.8 ft, 3.30 m. Chord at tip 4.3 ft, 1.30 m. Dihedral 4°. Nose angle 132°. Total wing area 232 ft², 21.5 m². Aspect ratio 4.9/1. Wheel track 5.9 ft, 1.80 m. Nosewheel diameter overall 13 inch, 32 cm. Main wheels diameter overall 16 inch, 40 cm. Other data NC.

POWER PLANT - Rotax 447 engine. Max power 43 hp at NC rpm. Propeller diameter and pitch 59xNC inch, 1.50xNC m. Gear reduction, ratio 2.6/1. Max static thrust 287 lb, 130 kg. Power per unit area 0.19 hp/ft², 2.0 hp/m². Fuel capacity 6.1 US gal, 5.1 Imp gal, 23.0 litre.

WEIGHTS & LOADINGS - Empty weight 287 lb, 130 kg. Max take-off weight 772 lb, 350 kg. Payload 485 lb, 220 kg. Max wing loading 3.33 lb/ft², 16.3 kg/m². Max power loading 18.0 lb/hp, 8.1 kg/hp. Load factors NC recommended; +6.0, -3.0 ultimate.

PERFORMANCE* - Never exceed speed 62 mph, 100 kph. Cruising speed 34 mph, 55 kph. Stalling speed 22 mph, 35 kph. Range at average cruising speed 112 mile, 180 km. Other data NC.

*Under unspecified test conditions.

FRANCE AEROLIGHTS

Jean-Francois Metz/France Aerolights SA, aerodrome de Libourne, Les Artigues de Lussac, 33570 Lussac; tel (57) 84 7322. President: Jean-Francois Metz. Director general: Francois Thovex. Director technical: Jean-Marc Ducournau. Chief pilot: Patrick Thouze.

FRANCE AEROLIGHTS
FIRST ONE
(Three-axis)

Single-seat single-engined high-wing monoplane with conventional three-axis control. Wing has unswept leading edge, swept forward trailing edge, and tapering chord; cruciform tail. Pitch control by elevator on tail; yaw control by fin-mounted rudder; roll control by 45%-span ailerons; control inputs through stick for pitch/roll and pedals for yaw. Wing braced from below by struts; wing profile Clark Y; 100% double-surface. Undercarriage has three wheels in tricycle formation; no sus-

pension on nosewheel and rubber suspension on main wheels. Push-right go-right nosewheel steering connected to yaw control. Brakes on main wheels. Aluminium-alloy tube airframe, with optional pod. Engine mounted wing height, driving tractor propeller.

Production status: current, number completed NC.

GENERAL - France Aerolights was set up in 1983 by two former French agents for Weedhopper, Jean-Marc Ducournau and Bruno Ziegler, and began by working on two very different series of aircraft: the *First,* which we describe here, and the *Mach,* which we list separately.
The former shared a similar configuration to the *Weedhopper* and comprised the single-seater *First One* and the side-by-side two-seater *First Two,* both of Duralumin tube and Dacron manufacture and described fully in our first edition. Control was two-axis by means of a joystick alone, although they could be converted to three-axis. The prototype *First One* made its maiden flight in January 1983 but a total of only l3 aircraft had been produced when the company ran into financial difficulties.
Fortunately, Jean-Francois Metz, an industrialist from Orleans whose own *Mach 01* had not been delivered, bought the company's assets from the receiver and relaunched it with all guns blazing at the beginning of June 1984. At the Blois ultralight meeting that September the firm was able to show new versions of the *First One* and *First Two,* revised and adapted to conventional three-axis control.
Production of the aircraft has been rationalised and properly industrialised and these two machines are consequently offered at very competitive prices, making them among the cheapest on the French market: 39,950FF for the single-seater and 52,500FF for the two-seater. Moreover, the quality of the aircraft has not suffered despite their remarkably affordable price; if anything the opposite is true. Deliveries of the aircraft started in early 1985.
Data below refers to the *First One* with Rotax 377 engine (the 447 is an option); figures for the *First Two* are given separately.

Main picture: First One *with optional pod.* Inset: First Two.

EXTERNAL DIMENSIONS & AREAS - Length overall 18.4 ft, 5.60 m. Height overall 6.6 ft, 2.00 m. Wing span 26.3 ft, 8.00 m. Chord at root 7.8 ft, 2.35 m. Chord at tip 4.4 ft, 1.35 m. Dihedral 3°. Sweepback 0°. Total wing area 159 ft^2, 14.8 m^2. Aspect ratio 4.3/1. Wheel track 3.8 ft, 1.15 m. Wheelbase 4.9 ft, 1.50 m. Nosewheel diameter overall 12 inch, 30 cm. Main wheels diameter overall 16 inch, 40 cm. Other data NC.

POWER PLANT - Rotax 377 engine. Max power 37 hp at 6250 rpm. Propeller diameter and pitch 61xNC inch, 1.55xNC m. Gear reduction, ratio 2.6/1. Max static thrust NC. Power per unit area 0.23 hp/ft^2, 2.5 hp/m^2. Fuel capacity 5.3 US gal, 4.4 Imp gal, 20.0 litre.

WEIGHTS & LOADINGS - Empty weight 265 lb, 120 kg. Max take-off weight 530 lb, 240 kg. Payload 120 lb, 265 kg. Max wing loading 3.33 lb/ft^2, 16.2 kg/m^2. Max power loading 14.3 lb/hp, 6.5 kg/hp. Load factors +3.8, -1.5 recommended; +6.0, -2.3 ultimate.

PERFORMANCE* - Max level speed 56 mph, 90 kph. Never exceed speed 68 mph, 110 kph. Max cruising speed 56 mph, 90 kph. Economic cruising speed 44 mph, 70 kph. Stalling speed 20 mph, 32 kph. Max climb rate at sea level 590 ft/min, 3.0 m/s. Min sink rate 550 ft/min at 24 mph, 2.8 m/s at 40 kph. Best glide ratio with power off 6/1 at 37 mph, 60 kph. Take-off distance 100 ft, 30 m. Landing distance 100 ft, 30 m. Service ceiling 9840 ft, 3000 m. Range at average cruising speed 137 mile, 220 km. Noise level NC.

*Under the following test conditions - Airfield altitude 164 ft, 50 m. Ground temperature 64°F, 18°C. Ground pressure 1018 mB. Ground windspeed 0 mph, 0 kph. Test payload 265 lb, 120 kg.

FRANCE AEROLIGHTS
FIRST TWO
(Three-axis)

Summary as First One *except: Side-by-side two-seater.*

Production status: see text.

GENERAL - This aircraft, whose background is described under *First One,* is a two-seat version of the latter which follows its design closely. Principal changes are the use of a larger wing, wider track and more powerful engine. The Rotax 447, optional on the single-seater, is standard fitment on the dual machine and it is in this form that we detail it below, though a Rotax 462 can be had as an option. Price is given under *First One,* but readers should note that the *First Two* was due to be phased out in summer '85 in favour of a tandem two-seater with completely different wing. At the time of writing the new machine is unnamed, but *Second Two* would seem a logical choice!.

EXTERNAL DIMENSIONS & AREAS - Length overall 18.4 ft, 5.60 m. Height overall 6.6 ft, 2.00 m. Wing span 29.7 ft, 9.04 m. Chord at root 8.2 ft, 2.50 m. Chord at tip 4.9 ft, 1.50 m. Dihedral 3°. Sweepback 0°. Total wing area 185 ft², 17.2 m². Aspect ratio 4.8/1. Wheel track 4.8 ft, 1.45 m. Wheelbase 4.9 ft, 1.50 m. Nosewheel diameter overall 12 inch, 30 cm. Main wheels diameter overall 16 inch, 40 cm. Other data NC.

POWER PLANT - Rotax 447 engine. Max power 41 hp at 6500 rpm. Propeller diameter and pitch 61xNC inch, 1.55xNC m. Gear reduction, ratio 2.6/1. Max static thrust NC. Power per unit area 0.22 hp/ft², 2.4 hp/m². Fuel capacity 5.3 US gal, 4.4 Imp gal, 20.0 litre.

WEIGHTS & LOADINGS - Empty weight 320 lb, 145 kg. Max take-off weight 806 lb, 365 kg. Payload 486 lb, 220 kg. Max wing loading 4.36 lb/ft², 21.2 kg/m². Max power loading 19.7 lb/hp, 8.9 kg/hp. Load factors +3.8, -1.5 recommended; +6.0, -2.3 ultimate.

PERFORMANCE* - Max level speed 50 mph, 80 kph. Never exceed speed 62 mph, 100 kph. Max cruising speed 50 mph, 80 kph. Economic cruising speed 40 mph, 65 kph. Stalling speed 23 mph, 38 kph. Max climb rate at sea level 590 ft/min, 3.0 m/s. Min sink rate 550 ft/min at 24 mph, 2.8 m/s at 40 kph. Best glide ratio with power off 6/1 at 37 mph, 60 kph. Take-off distance 130 ft, 40 m. Landing distance 130 ft, 40 m. Service ceiling 9840 ft, 3000 m. Range at average cruising speed 168 mile, 270 km. Noise level NC.

*Under the following test conditions - Airfield altitude 164 ft, 50 m. Ground temperature 64°F, 18°C. Ground pressure 1018 mB. Ground windspeed 0 mph, 0 kph. Test payload 486 lb, 220 kg.

FRANCE AEROLIGHTS
AGRI FIRST and ENDURO
(Three-axis)

Summary as First One *except: Enduro is side-by-side three-seater.*

Production status: current, number completed NC.

GENERAL - Apart from being an excellent pilot, having won the trike class in the '82 London-Paris on a Danis *Mercure/Sabre 23,* Francois Thovex is among the most experienced crop-spraying pilots. So not surprisingly the company's new model for 1985 is an aerial workhorse, the *Agri First,* on which the advanced static and flight tests were completed in the last few months of 1984.

Despite its name, this new machine shares only some of the basic features of the rest of the *First* range. As can be seen from its fuselage construction, raised mudguard and excellent rough-ground suspension, it is conceived solely for crop-spraying, rather than being simply an extrapolation from an existing machine, like most crop-spraying ultralights.

The aircraft has an extremely comfortable leatherette-covered bucket seat for the pilot and it can be fitted, for export, with extra seats at either side, replacing the spraying units, making it the world's first three-seat ultralight! In this form the aircraft is known as the *Enduro.* These two seats can be removed and replaced by stretchers for casualty evacuation or by other civil or military loads.

Innovation is evident in the spraying equipment too, with a completely new system based on a similar principle to the graphic designer's airbrush, in which the paint is spread at an angle by means of a controllable jet of compressed air.

Robust rear suspension of the Agri First.

The *Agri First* looks destined for a bright future in Europe and abroad as its price is very competitive, at 74,718FF for the all-terrain *Enduro* version without agricultural fittings or 110,298FF for the fully equipped *Agri First,* with spray booms and 48 US gal (40 Imp gal, 180 litre) tank for chemicals in liquid or granular form. The latter uses a 66 hp Rotax 532 engine and is the version detailed below, while the *Enduro* 'makes do' with the 52 hp Rotax 462. Both are liquid-cooled.

EXTERNAL DIMENSIONS & AREAS - See *First Two* except: Wheel track 4.9 ft, 1.50 m. Wheelbase 5.1 ft, 1.55 m. Nosewheel diameter overall 16 inch, 40 cm. Main wheels diameter overall 24 inch, 60 cm.

POWER PLANT - Rotax 532 engine. Max power 66 hp at 6500 rpm. Propeller diameter and pitch 65xNC inch,

Test flying an Agri First, *before installation of spraying equipment. Insets show nosewheel arrangement and seating permutations, with one extra seat fitted and the remaining bay left vacant for load carrying.*

1.65xNC m. Gear reduction, ratio NC. Max static thrust NC. Power per unit area 0.36 hp/ft², 3.8 hp/m². Fuel capacity 5.3 US gal, 4.4 Imp gal, 20.0 litre.

WEIGHTS & LOADINGS - Empty weight 364 lb, 165 kg. Max take-off weight 927 lb, 420 kg. Payload 563 lb, 257 kg. Max wing loading 5.01 lb/ft², 24.4 kg/m². Max power loading 14.0 lb/hp, 6.4 kg/hp. Load factors NC.

PERFORMANCE* - Max level speed 50 mph, 80 kph. Never exceed speed 68 mph, 110 kph. Max cruising speed NC. Economic cruising speed NC. Stalling speed 17 mph, 28 kph. Max climb rate at sea level 790 ft/min, 4.0 m/s. Min sink rate 550 ft/min at 24 mph, 2.8 m/s at 40 kph. Best glide ratio with power off 6/1 at 37 mph, 60 kph. Take-off distance 65 ft, 20 m. Landing distance 100 ft, 30 m. Service ceiling 7870 ft, 2400 m. Range at average cruising speed 124 mile, 200 km. Noise level NC.

*Under the following test conditions - Airfield altitude 164 ft, 50 m. Ground temperature 64°F, 18°C. Ground pressure 1018 mB. Ground windspeed 0 mph, 0 kph. Test payload 474 lb, 215 kg.

FRANCE AEROLIGHTS
MACH 01
(Three-axis)

Single-seat single-engined high-wing monoplane with conventional three-axis control. Wing has unswept leading and trailing edges, and constant chord; cruciform

P Pouleau

tail. Pitch control by elevator on tail; yaw control by fin-mounted rudder; roll control by full-span flaperons; control inputs through stick for pitch/roll and pedals for yaw. Cantilever wing; wing profile GA-PC 1; 100% double-surface. Undercarriage has three wheels in tricycle formation; no suspension on nosewheel and glass-fibre suspension on main wheels. Push-right go-right nosewheel steering connected to yaw control; also differential braking. Brakes on main wheels. Composite-construction airframe, partially enclosed (total enclosure optional). Engine mounted above wing, driving pusher propeller.

Production status: see text.

GENERAL - No less remarkable than the Agri First is the new version of the single-seater Mach 01, whose speed range with a 52 hp Rotax 462 extends from 28 to 93 mph (45 to 150 kph), thanks to what for an ultralight are revolutionary aerodyanamics. Its wing, with winglets to control the tip vortices, uses the modern self-stabilising GA-PC 1 section adapted by Jean-Marc Ducournau, a section more often found on business jets than on lightplanes, let alone ultralights. It is, moreover, fitted with flaperons, ailerons which when deployed together act as flaps at 10° 20° or as airbrakes at 30°.

With an all-Kevlar airframe, carbon-fibre wing-bracing, and honeycomb engine mountings incorporating aviation-quality Duralumin, it is one of the most futuristic ultralights around. The tail boom, for instance, comes in unidirectional carbon-fibre wrapped in a layer of filaments, technology which has only just arrived at the big wheels in the aviation industry. The tail itself consists, on the third prototype, of a honeycomb construction incorporating a metal framework to which the control surfaces are attached, which them-

Mach 01 prototype on test with canopy fitted.

selves are entirely in Kevlar, as are the winglets and wheel spats. Unidirectional glass-fibre provides the suspension. But the most remarkable feature is the wing, which weighs just 53 lb (24 kg). It uses a unidirectional carbon-fibre longeron which carries a skin made from a honeycomb and glass-fibre/epoxy resin sandwich.

At the time of writing the third prototype is flying. The first had spars and ribs from stamped and bonded Duralumin and glass-fibre winglets and made its maiden flight in October 1982, but sadly the 1984 Blois event at which the company was relaunched was marked by the total destruction of this prototype, when an ill-attempted aerobatic manoeuvre ended with the death of pilot Alain Molia. The aircraft was exonerated, but the France Aerolights team was deeply shocked by the tragedy and decided to change its marketing plans, with the result that deliveries are not now expected before 1986. A second prototype began its test flight programme in February 1985 and the third a few weeks later.

The price is yet to be fixed, but this Ferrari of the ultralight world will not be cheap, probably costing around 120,000FF. Normal engine fitment will be the Rotax 462, but for the US a KFM 107ER will be substituted, to keep the machine within the American ultralight definition. Our data below refers to the Rotax-engined version; where different, figures for the US-specification machine are shown in parentheses.

EXTERNAL DIMENSIONS & AREAS - Length overall 19.7 ft, 6.00 m. Height overall 7.3 ft, 2.20 m. Wing span 30.2 ft, 9.20 m. Constant chord 4.9 ft, 1.50 m. Dihedral 2°. Sweepback 0°. Tailplane span 8.2 ft, 2.50 m. Fin height 5.3 ft, 1.60 m. Total wing area 149 ft², 13.8 m². Total flaperon area NC. Fin area 4.8 ft², 4.50 m². Rudder area 7.0 ft², 0.65 m². Tailplane area 15.1 ft², 1.40 m². Total elevator area 10.8 ft², 1.00 m². Aspect ratio 6.1/1. Wheel track 4.9 ft, 1.50 m. Wheelbase 8.5 ft, 2.60 m. Nosewheel diameter overall 10 inch, 26 cm. Main wheels diameter overall 12 inch, 30cm.

POWER PLANT - Rotax 462 (KFM 107ER) engine. Max power 52(30) hp at NC rpm. Propeller diameter and pitch 46(NC)xNC(NC) inch, 1.16(NC)x(NC)(NC) m. Gear (V-belt) reduction, ratio 2.6(NC)/1. Max static thrust NC. Power per unit area 0.35(0.20) hp/ft², 3.8(2.2) hp/m². Fuel capacity 10.6 US gal, 8.8 Imp gal, 40.0 litre.

WEIGHTS & LOADINGS - Empty weight 291(252) lb, 132(114) kg. Max take-off weight 578 lb, 262 kg. Payload 287(326) lb, 130(148) kg. Max wing loading 3.88 lb/ft², 19.0 kg/m². Max power loading 11.1(19.3) lb/hp, 5.0(8.7) kg/hp. Load factors +3.8, -3.8 recommended; +6.0, -6.0 ultimate.

PERFORMANCE* - Max level speed 93(63) mph, 150 (101) kph. Never exceed speed 99(70) mph, 160(113) kph. Max cruising speed 81(60) mph, 130(97) kph. Economic cruising speed 69(55) mph, 111(88) kph. Stalling speed 28(26) mph, 45(42) kph. Max climb rate at sea level 980(NC) ft/min, 5.0(NC) m/s. Min sink rate 390(NC) ft/min at 37(NC) mph, 2.0(NC) m/s at 60(NC) kph. Best glide ratio with power off 12/1 at 47(NC) mph, 75(NC) kph. Take-off distance 100(NC) ft, 30(NC) m. Landing distance 115(NC) ft, 35(NC) m. Service ceiling 11,480(NC) ft, 3500(NC) m. Range at average cruising speed 156(NC) mile, 250(NC) km. Noise level 65(NC) dB at 490 ft, 150 m.

*Under the following test conditions - Airfield altitude 164 ft, 50 m. Ground temperature 64°F, 18°C. Ground pressure 1018 mB. Ground windspeed 0 mph, 0 kph. Test payload 239(278) lb, 108(126) kg.

FRANCE AEROLIGHTS
MACH 20
(Three-axis)

Summary similar to Mach 01 *except: Side-by-side two-seater.*

Production status: see text.

GENERAL - Following the completion of the *Mach 01*, a two-seat version, currently on the drawing board, will be constructed. This *Mach 20* will draw on the test experience of the solo machine and the first prototype should fly in 1985. If it lives up to its promise, it must have every chance of winning a place in the future market for ATLs (avions tres legers, very light aircraft) in Europe and ARVs (air recreational vehicles) in the USA, as much through its selling price as its likely performance. For once, an ultralight manufacturer could find himself leading trumps on his own deal...

EXTERNAL DIMENSIONS & AREAS - NC.

POWER PLANT - NC.

WEIGHTS & LOADINGS - NC.

PERFORMANCE - NC.

GARDAN

Societe de Avions Yves Gardan, 580 rue Helene-Boucher, Zone Industrielle, 78530 Buc; tel (3) 956 2882. Proprietor: Yves Gardan.

GARDAN GY-120
(Three-axis)

Tandem two-seat single-engined parasol-wing monoplane with conventional three-axis control. Wing has unswept leading and trailing edges, and constant chord; cruciform tail. Pitch control by elevator on tail; yaw control by fin-mounted rudder; roll control by half-span ailerons; control inputs through stick for pitch/roll and pedals for yaw. Wing braced from above by kingpost and cables, from below by cables; wing profile Gardan; 100% double-surface. Undercarriage has three wheels in tail-dragger formation; coil-spring suspension on tailwheel and rubber suspension on main wheels. Push-right go-right tailwheel steering connected to yaw control; also optional differential braking. Brakes on main wheels. Aluminium-alloy tube airframe, partially enclosed. Engine mounted below wing, driving tractor propeller.

Production status: prototype.

GENERAL - Yves Gardan is the celebrated aeronautical engineer who in 1947 designed the *SIPA-90*, which won the 75 hp national two-seater race and thereby attracted a state order for 100 aircraft to help aeroclubs rebuild their war-devastated fleet. Some 115 were produced and two years later his *GY-20 Minicab* took the world straight-line distance record and the under 500 kg speed record: 1135 mile (1826 km) from Paris, France to Rabat, Morocco in 10 h, an average of 109 mph (175 kph) for the 65 hp Continental-engined aircraft. Over 100 *Minicabs* were built and indeed some are still under construction by home-builders in North America, under the name *Cavalier*.

That year Yves also creatd the *SIPA-200 Minijet*, a side-by-side two-seat single-engined light jet capable of 249 mph (400 kph) in level flight with 358 lb (160 kg) thrust. In 1952 a 90 hp version of the *Minicab* with retractable undercarriage, the *Super-Cab*, appeared. In 1954 came the *SIPA-300* single-engined tandem two-seater jet and the following year saw the arrival of the *SIPA-1000 Coccinelle* 90 hp side-by-side two-seater.

Still hard at work, in 1957 he designed the *SIPA 1100* 4.5 tonne military twin, while in 1960 the famous 180 hp *GY-80 Horizon* was brought out, which in 1966 rose to fame when it took the Cannes international Grand Prix in competition with the highest-performance twins of the time. It completed the 3443 mile (5540 km) course in 23 h, an average speed of 152 mph (245 kph).

Some 270 *Horizons* were built by the company that eventually became Aerospatiale, but the aircraft's promising 1969 successor, the *GY-100,* was never put into production as aviation's economic crisis was already approaching. Indeed, since 1962 Yves has specialised in civil and military aircraft equipment and in components for hovercraft including the 450 tonne *M5OO*.

Finally, in June 1982, Yves turned his eyes to ultralights and began work on the three-axis tandem two-seat *GY-120*, building the prototype that October. Featured in our first edition, it appeared at Le Bourget show in June 1983, making its first flight on 27 April 1984 and embarking on a long and rigorous programme of static and in-flight tests based on those undergone by light commercial aircraft. Indeed the load factors to which the *GY-120* has been designed correspond to the international *FAR 23* utility category, applicable to aircraft of less than 3.7 tonnes, as an ATL (avion tres leger - very light aeroplane) version is planned.

Though at present fitted with a 40 hp Hirth 270, the *GY-120* has been designed to take any engine of from 35 to 60 hp at the choice of the buyer, which is just as well as the Hirth has been abandoned by almost every French manufacturer in favour of Robin and Rotax power. Its sale price and launch date had not been fixed at the time of going to press, but options will include a fuselage fairing, three-axis dual controls, differential braking, instrumentation and containers for agricultural or military loads. Our data below refers to the prototype.

EXTERNAL DIMENSIONS & AREAS - Length overall 19.0 ft, 5.80 m. Height overall 8.2 ft, 2.50 m. Wing span 32.8 ft, 10.00 m. Constant chord at root 5.8 ft, 1.75 m. Dihedral 2°. Sweepback 0°. Tailplane span 9.2 ft, 2.80 m. Fin height 4.3 ft, 1.30 m. Total wing area 189 ft^2, 17.5 m^2. Total aileron area 20.5 ft^2, 1.90 m^2. Fin area 7.5 ft^2, 0.70 m^2. Rudder area 7.0 ft^2, 0.65 m^2. Tailplane area 15.3 ft^2, 1.42 m^2. Total elevator area 14.0 ft^2, 1.30 m^2. Aspect ratio 5.7/1. Wheel track 5.8 ft, 1.80 m. Wheelbase 14.8 ft, 4.50 m. Nosewheel diameter overall 5 inch, 13 cm. Main wheels diameter overall 16 inch, 14 cm.

POWER PLANT - Hirth 270R-03E engine. Max power 40 hp at 7000 rpm. Propeller diameter and pitch 55xNC inch, 1.40xNC m. Toothed-belt reduction, ratio 2.7/1. Max static thrust NC. Power per unit area 0.21 hp/ft^2, 2.3 hp/m^2. Fuel capacity 7.9 US gal, 6.6 Imp gal, 30.0 litre.

WEIGHTS & LOADINGS - Empty weight 320 lb, 145 kg. Max take-off weight 751 lb, 340 kg. Payload 431 lb, 195 kg. Max wing loading 3.97 lb/ft^2, 19.4 kg/m^2. Max power loading 18.8 lb/hp, 8.5 kg/hp. Load factors +NC recommended; +6.6, -3.3 ultimate.

PERFORMANCE* - Max level speed 75 mph, 120 kph. Never exceed speed 87 mph, 140 kph. Max cruising speed 68 mph, 110 kph. Economic cruising speed 47 mph, 75 kph. Stalling speed 23 mph, 38 kph. Max climb rate at sea level 490 ft/min, 2.5 m/s. Min sink rate 350 ft/min at 40 mph, 1.8 m/s at 65 kph. Best glide ratio with power off 10/1 at 40 mph, 65 kph. Take-off distance 130 ft, 40 m. Landing distance 115 ft, 35 m. Service ceiling 8200 ft, 2500 m. Range at average cruising speed 240 mile, 400 km. Noise level NC.

*Under the following test conditions - Airfield altitude 0 ft, 0 m. Ground temperature 59°F, 15°C. Ground pressure 1013 mB. Ground windspeed 0 mph, 0 kph. Test payload 431 lb, 195 kg.

JOKAIR

Jokair SARL, Le Moulin de la Chausee, 18580 Maule; tel (3) 475 8065. Proprietors: Patrick and Laurence Lemonnier.

JOKAIR *MAESTRO*

(Three-axis)

Side-by-side two-seat single-engined high-wing monoplane with conventional three-axis control. Wing has unswept leading and trailing edges, and constant chord; cruciform tail. Pitch control by elevator on tail; yaw control by fin-mounted rudder; roll control by full-span ailerons; control inputs through stick for pitch/roll and pedals for yaw. Wing braced from above by kingpost and cables, from below by cables; wing profile NACA 4412; 100% double-surface. Undercarriage has three wheels in tricycle formation; coil-spring suspension on nosewheel and oleo-pneumatic suspension on main wheels. Push-right go-right nosewheel steering connected to yaw control. Optional nosewheel brake. Aluminium-alloy tube airframe, with pod. Engine mounted at wing height, driving tractor propeller.

Production status: current, 18 completed by May 1985.

GENERAL - Self-taught aviator Patrick Lemonnier conceived and built the prototype of his *Patrilor*, which first flew in May 1982, without so much as a plan to go on. With the third prototype of this side-by-side two-seat three-axis machine, Jean Toulorge successfully completed the London-Paris that year.

That November, Francois de Cande and Andre Gabry's Aile company put the *Patrilor 3* into production. Patrick joined the staff to develop the aircraft, along with the single-seat *PX 2000*.

Unfortunately, his work was interrupted in 1983 by the company's financial difficulties, due partly to faulty production which caused individual aircraft to vary considerably, some having a mediocre performance which quickly

Jokair Maestro *with optional skis and Rotax 462. For another illustration, see introduction to French section.*

earned the aircraft a bad reputation, despite the pleasant characteristics of the prototype sampled by Alain-Yves Berger.

Incidentally, before the failure Patrick completed another prototype called the *X3*, again a side-by-side two-seat three-axis machine but with a metal lattice-work fuselage, and though this never reached production, the sole example was sold early in 1984 and one year later had logged over 600 h.

Undaunted, Patrick unveiled a third side-by-side three-axis aircraft, the *Maestro*, to the homebuilders' meeting at Brienne-le-Chateau in July '84, one month and 250 h after its maiden flight. Reviewing it for *Pilote Prive*, Alain-Yves Berger found it had good performance, control co-ordination to match the best lightplane and handling like a top-notch single-seater, an appraisal backed by Michel Barry, an engineer and teacher at the aerodynamics laboratory of the Ville-d'Avray technology instutite, who tested the wing in a wind tunnel.

The *Maestro* quickly gained a reputation as France's best workshop-produced three-axis two-seater. Its labour-intensive construction dictates relatively high prices, but the extraordinary finish is an excellent compensation, especially as unlike the *Patrilor 3*, each example seems better than the last.

With construction from aviation-quality Duralumin tubing, mostly deliberately oversized, suspension worthy of a crop-sprayer, fine sailwork in shrink-coated Dacron painted with polyurethane, firm controls and properly machined fittings, its airframe quality is comparable to a light aircraft.

Its strength was well demonstrated when both occupants escaped unhurt after a major pilot error destroyed the prototype by colliding with a telephone pole.

Maestros are only available delivered, assembled and test-flown, with a choice of two engines: the Rotax 503, in which form we describe it below, or the 52 hp liquid-cooled Rotax 462 developing 298 lb (135 kg) thrust. Prices are 64,900FF and 67,300FF respectively. Options: electric-start for Rotax 462 2600FF; seat covers/Duralumin wheel rims/instrument pack 4900FF; nosewheel disc brake 1265FF; trailer 8500FF; Pierre Fayet steerable floats 11,500FF; Pierre Fayet skis 1500FF; basic painting 3500FF; further customisation 3000FF.

Patrick Lemonnier was working on a solo machine at the time of writing, based on similar technology and likely to appear during summer 1985. This should be something well worth waiting for.

EXTERNAL DIMENSIONS & AREAS - Length overall 19.0 ft, 5.80 m. Height overall 8.2 ft, 2.50 m. Wing span 34.4 ft, 10.50 m. Constant chord 5.4 ft, 1.62 m. Dihedral 2°. Sweepback 0°. Tailplane span 7.9 ft, 2.40 m. Fin height 4.4 ft, 1.32 m. Total wing area 183 ft², 17.0 m². Total aileron area 26.9 ft², 2.50 m². Fin area 6.6 ft², 0.61 m². Rudder area 8.0 ft², 0.75 m². Tailplane area 26.9 ft², 2.50 m². Total elevator area 9.8 ft², 0.91 m². Aspect ratio 6.5/1. Wheel track 5.2 ft, 1.58 m. Wheelbase 4.5 ft, 1.38 m. Nosewheel diameter overall 12 inch, 30 cm. Main wheels diameter overall 16 inch, 40 cm.

POWER PLANT - Rotax 503 engine. Max power 46 hp at NC rpm. Propeller diameter and pitch 65xNC inch, 1.66xNC m. Toothed-belt reduction, ratio 2.5/1. Max static thrust 260 lb, 118 kg. Power per unit area 0.25 hp/ft², 2.7 hp/m². Fuel capacity 7.4 US gal, 6.2 Imp gal, 28.0 litre.

WEIGHTS & LOADINGS - Empty weight 368 lb, 167 kg. Max take-off weight 883 lb, 400 kg. Payload 514 lb, 233 kg. Max wing loading 4.83 lb/ft², 23.5 kg/m². Max power loading 19.2 lb/hp, 8.7 kg/hp. Load factors NC recommended; +8.0, -4.0 ultimate.

PERFORMANCE* - Max level speed 68 mph, 110 kph. Never exceed speed 87 mph, 140 kph. Max cruising speed

56 mph, 90 kph. Economic cruising speed 47 mph, 75 kph. Stalling speed 24 mph, 40 kph. Max climb rate at sea level 590 ft/min, 3.0 m/s. Min sink rate 490 ft/min at 34 mph, 2.5 m/s at 55 kph. Best glide ratio with power off 11/1 at 34 mph, 55 kph. Take-off distance 130 ft, 40 m. Landing distance 165 ft, 50 m. Service ceiling 11,480 ft, 3500 m. Range at average cruising speed 81 mile, 130 km. Noise level NC.

Under the following test conditions - Airfield altitude 196 ft, 60 m. Ground temperature 61°F, 16°C. Ground pressure 1016 mB. Ground windspeed 3 mph, 5 kph. Test payload 419 lb, 190 kg.

LANOT

Lanot Aviation SARL, Zone Induspal de Lons, BP 111 LONS, avenue Gay-Lussac, 64143 Billere Cedex; tel (59) 62 5227. Proprietor: M C Lanot.

LANOT *AQUITAIN*

(Three-axis)

Side-by-side two-seat twin-engined high-wing monoplane with conventional three-axis control. Wing has unswept leading and trailing edges, and constant chord;

flaps fitted; conventional tail. Pitch control by elevator on tail; yaw control by fin-mounted rudder; roll control by 80%-span ailerons; control inputs through stick for pitch/roll and pedals for yaw. Wing braced from below by struts; wing profile Kiceniuck; 100% double-surface. Undercarriage has three wheels in tricycle formation; glass-fibre suspension on all wheels. Push-right go-right nosewheel steering connected to yaw control. Brakes on main wheels. Aluminium-alloy tube/composite-construction airframe, partially enclosed. Engines mounted at wing height, driving pusher propellers.

Production status: prototype, 2 completed.

GENERAL - An interesting newcomer to the French scene is Lanot Aviation, which was just putting the finishing touches to its *Aquitain* as we went to press. The aircraft is named after the Aquitaine province of south-west France, whose lands are watered by the Garonne and its tributaries and whose major cities are Toulouse, the aeronautical capital of France, and Bordeaux, whose wines offer armchair aviators a reliable means of getting airborne! However, we digress.

M Lanot operates very discreetly, and has sent just one very short release to the French press accompanied by an artist's impression of the *Aquitain*. However, our spies - or to be precise, our Mata Hari Joelle Nogrady, the other half of the brain behind the *Avionette* described elsewhere in

this section - recently informed us of the *Aquitain's* progress. Apparently it made its first flight at the end of April 1985, and first results were very encouraging.

Other information is rather sparse, but the aircraft is certainly unusual in that it is a side-by-side two-seater, an uncommon configuration for a composite aircraft, with only a defunct British machine, the Jordan *Duet* (see our first edition), and the American Striplin *Sky Ranger Silver Cloud* as antecedents. Like the early versions of its American counterpart, which seems a long way from attaining the sort of success it deserves, the French machine is also a twin, with its two 25 hp KFM 107ER engines mounted on the leading edge of wing's centre section, which is constructed integrally with the fuselage. But the engines in this case drive pusher props through long transmission shafts, an arrangement which directs the slipstream directly over the control surfaces.

It is too early to judge the *Aquitain's* flying qualities, but undoubtedly it is one of the most beautiful two-seaters around, and one offering remarkable visibility to boot. Certainly there is no obvious reason why the aircraft should not fly well; the problems associated with long drive shafts seem to have been satisfactorily resolved, albeit thanks only to the Taylor system improved by the late Jean Grinvalds, sadly killed in April 1985 in a crash involving his four-seat *Orion* lightplane. Also, the flexing problems associated with single-boom fuselages carrying a conventional tailplane have also been mastered.

So, now that our curiosity has been well and truly aroused, we'll just have to wait and see...

EXTERNAL DIMENSIONS & AREAS - Length overall 18.0 ft, 5.50 m. Height overall 9.8 ft, 3.00 m. Wing span 38.9 ft, 11.85 m. Chord at root 4.9 ft, 1.50 m. Chord at tip 4.9 ft, 1.50 m. Dihedral 3°. Sweepback 0°. Tailplane span 9.8 ft, 3.00 m. Fin height 4.9 ft, 1.50 m. Total wing area 215 ft^2, 20.0 m^2. Total aileron area 32.3 ft^2, 3.00 m^2. Fin area 6.5 ft^2, 0.60 m^2. Rudder area 9.7 ft^2, 0.90 m^2. Tailplane area 16.1 ft^2, 1.50 m^2. Total elevator area 16.1 ft^2, 1.50 m^2. Aspect ratio 7.9/1. Wheel track 6.2 ft, 1.90 m. Wheelbase 4.9 ft, 1.50 m. Nosewheel diameter overall 12 inch, 30 cm. Main wheels diameter overall 12 inch, 30 cm.

POWER PLANT - Two KFM 107ER engines. Max power 25 hp each at 6500 rpm. Propellers diameter and pitch 47x16° inch, 1.20x16° m. Notched V-belt reduction, ratio 2.0/1. Max static thrust 176 lb, 80 kg. Power per unit area 0.23 hp/ft^2, 2.5 hp/m^2. Fuel capacity 11.4 US gal, 9.5 Imp gal, 43.0 litre.

WEIGHTS & LOADINGS - Empty weight 386 lb, 175 kg. Max take-off weight 882 lb, 400 kg. Payload 496 lb, 225 kg. Max wing loading 4.10 lb/ft^2, 20.0 kg/m^2. Max power loading 17.6 lb/hp, 8.0 kg/hp. Load factors +6.0, -4.0 recommended; +10.0, -6.0 ultimate.

PERFORMANCE* - Max level speed 68 mph, 110 kph. Never exceed speed 78 mph, 125 kph. Max cruising speed 53 mph, 85 kph. Economic cruising speed 40 mph, 65 kph. Stalling speed 25 mph, 40 kph. Max climb rate at sea level 780 ft/min, 4.0 m/s. Min sink rate 200 ft/min at 31 mph, 1.0 m/s at 50 kph. Best glide ratio with power off 10/1 at 44 mph, 70 kph. Take-off distance 260 ft, 80 m. Landing distance 195 ft, 60 m. Service ceiling 8200 ft, 2500 m. Range at average cruising speed 174 mile, 280 km. Noise level 72 dB at 330 ft, 100 m.

**Under the following test conditions* - Airfield altitude 984 ft, 300 m. Ground temperature 72°F, 22°C. Ground pressure 1015 mB. Ground windspeed 5 mph, 8 kph. Test payload 456 lb, 207 kg.

LATECOERE

Societe Industrielle d'Aviation Latecoere (SILAT). Office: 79 avenue Marceau, 75116 Paris; tel (1) 720 0105; tx 613712 F. Factory: 135 rue du Periole, 31079 Toulouse Cedex; tel (61) 48 1110; tx 531714 F. President: Pierre-Jean Latecoere. I/c ultralight programme: Messrs Legrand (father and son).

LATECOERE *LATE 225*
(Three-axis)

Single-seat single-engined high-wing monoplane with conventional three-axis control. Wing has swept back leading and trailing edges, and constant chord; no tail, canard wing. Pitch control by elevator on canard; yaw control by rudder at rear of fuselage; roll control by tip surfaces; control inputs through stick for pitch/roll and pedals for yaw. Wing braced from below by struts; wing profile NC; 100% double-surface. Undercarriage has three wheels in tricycle formation plus water rudder; suspension NC. Push-right go-right nosewheel and water-rudder steering connected to yaw control. Brakes on main wheels. Composite-construction airframe, totally enclosed. Engine mounted at wing height, driving pusher propeller.

Production status: prototype.

GENERAL - Pierre-Georges Latecoere is one of the greatest names in French aeronautics. He founded SILAT in 1917 and manufactured Breguet aeroplanes for World War I, but he was already looking ahead to civilian applications, and in 1918 turned his mind to establishing a France-South America air link.

It was a revolutionary idea for its time but 12 years later he had achieved the seemingly impossible. Starting from Toulouse, where he based his firm, the first of many aerospace companies in the city, in 1918 passengers could reach only Barcolona but later the route map was extended with Rabat and Casablanca in Morocco, and Dacar in Senegal. Toulouse to Dakar non-stop was achieved in October 1927 and later Rio-Buenos Aires. Then came his crowning achievement, the first crossing of the South Atlantic, by Jean Mermoz in Late 283 in May 1930.

The firm completed 83 design studies, built 39 prototypes and 11 production series, a total of 776 aircraft. Among them were the Late 280 two-engined airliner of 1928, the Late 300 *Croix du Sud* (Southern Cross) at the controls of which Mermoz disappeared over the South Atlantic, the *Late 521 Lieutenant de Vaisseau Paris* freight and passenger flying boat of 1935, and the *Late 531* six-engined flying boat in 1943.

Subsequently Aeropostale concentrated on production of aerospace components, for civil programmes like *Caravelle, Concorde, Airbus*, the *Falcon 10, 20* and *50*, and Aerospatial helicopters, as well as military projects such as the *Mystere IV, Mirage III, Etandard IVM, Mirage V, Alpha Jet, Jaguar* etc, and the *Ariane* rocket. To that can be added various special engines, experimental materials and numerous electronic systems.

This policy of diversification has been maintained under Jean-Pierre Latecoere, son of the founder, but Alain-Yves Berger was to say the least surprised when at the 1983 le Bourget show two SILAT representatives confided in him that this diversification had reached the ultralight end of the

Latecoere's Late 225; the inset shows a radio-controlled model built before the prototype was constructed.

aviation spectrum. They were working on a prototype called the *Late 225,* shown at the '84 Hanover and Cannes shows and looking like something out of Burt Rutan's hangar. The machine first flew that autumn with a JPX PUL425 24 hp engine, in which form we detail it below, though that motor has since been replaced by a 30 hp KFM.

Designed and built to the lightplane *FAR 23* category N regulations, this amphibian has most unusual control surfaces for a canard machine, allied to a short fuselage which ends in a seaplane hull. The main wheels can be raised and the nosewheel is retractable, with a door to cover its compartment. An ingenious trick is that the aircraft can be rigged or derigged by one person in just 5 min by means of three pins: one for each wing at the junction with the strut and one for the canard. Regrettably we have no further details of this interesting machine, as its test programme began without any data being released, other than that below.

EXTERNAL DIMENSIONS & AREAS - Length overall 16.2 ft, 4.95 m. Height overall 7.1 ft, 2.15 m. Wing span 26.3 ft, 8.03 m. Constant chord 4.8 ft, 1.45 m. Sweepback 13°. Canard span 9.5 ft, 2.90 m. Canard chord 2.1 ft, 0.64 m. Total wing area 147 ft², 13.7 m². Main wing area 127 ft², 11.85 m². Canard area 20 ft², 1.85 m². Aspect ratio (of main wing) 5.4/1. Wheel track 5.4 ft, 1.65 m. Other data NC.

POWER PLANT - JPX PUL425 engine. Max power 24 hp at 4500 rpm. Propeller diameter and pitch NC. No reduction. Max static thrust NC. Power per unit area 0.16 hp/ft², 1.8 hp/m². Fuel capacity 6.1 US gal, 5.1 Imp gal, 23.0 litre.

WEIGHTS & LOADINGS - Empty weight 280 lb, 127 kg. Max take-off weight 569 lb, 258 kg. Payload 289 lb, 131 kg. Max wing loading 3.87 lb/ft², 18.8 kg/m². Max power loading 23.7 lb/hp, 10.8 kg/hp. Load factors NC.

PERFORMANCE* - Max level speed 75 mph, 120 kph. Max cruising speed 62 mph, 100 kph. Economic cruising speed 53 mph, 85 kph. Stalling speed 28 mph, 45 kph. Max climb rate at sea level 530 ft/min, 2.7 m/s. Take-off distance (ground) 245 ft, 75 m. Take-off distance (water) 720 ft, 220 m. Service ceiling 11,150 ft, 3400 m. Other data NC.

*Under the following test conditions - Airfield altitude 0 ft, 0 m. Ground temperature 59°F, 15°C. Ground pressure 1013 mB. Ground windspeed 0 mph, 0 kph. Test payload 176 lb, 80 kg.

MIGNET

Society d'Exploitation des Aeronefs Henri Mignet, Logis des Pierrieres, Saint-Romain-de-Benet, 17600 Saujon; tel (46) 02 2600. Proprietors: Pierre and Alain Mignet.

MIGNET *HM 1000 BALERIT*

(Two- axis)

Side-by-side two-seat single-engined double monoplane in tandem with two-axis control. Wings have unswept leading and trailing edges, and constant chord; tail has vertical surfaces only. Pitch control by fully flying wing; yaw control by fully flying rudder with separate fin; no separate roll control; control inputs through stick for pitch/yaw. Wings braced from below by struts; wing profile Mignet 3.60.12 P; 100% double-surface. Undercarriage has three wheels in tricycle formation; rubber suspension on all wheels. Push-right go-right nosewheel steering independent from yaw control; also differential braking. Brakes on main wheels. Aluminium-alloy tube/wood airframe, with optional pod. Engine mounted below wing, driving pusher propeller.

Production status: prototype.

GENERAL - We doubt if any of our readers need reminding of the name of Henry Mignet, father of the famous *Pou-du-Ciel* (flying flea), with its two-axis controls by wheel or stick according to builder's preference. More than any other single machine, it unleashed the fearsome enthusiasm of homebuilders and helped the movement spread throughout the aviation world before World War II. What is much less commonly realised, however, is that Mignet is also in a sense a father of the microlight movement.
It is now over 50 years since the first flight of the Mignet *HM 14,* on 11 September 1984, and as we write the Reseau du Sport de l'Air, the French homebuilders' group, has recen-

The prototype HM 1000 Balerit *on trial; for another illustration, see front cover. The* HM 14 *which inspired it is illustrated in the colour section.*

tly celebrated that anniversary at Brienne-le-Chateau near Troyes. It is worth recalling the characteristics and performance figures of the *HM 14,* as these show it was certainly a microlight according to the FAI definition. The span of the front wing was 19.7 ft (6.00 m) and of the rear 13.1 ft (4.00 m), both with a constant 4.6 ft (1.40 m) chord, giving a total wing area of 129 ft^2 (12.0 m^2) and an empty weight of 287 lb (130 kg). The 20 hp air-cooled Aubier-Dunne two-stroke twin allowed a take-off run of 330 ft (100 m) in nil wind, a landing speed of 19 mph (30 kph) and a cruise of 50-62 mph (80-100 kph).
Fifty years on, not many microlights can achieve such performance figures with an engine as small as that. However Henri Mignet was a prisoner of his own time, for while both mass-produced and metal-built aircraft had appeared in most industrialised countries by the '30s, the great majority of two-seaters were still wood and fabric. Moreover wood was more accessible to both the budget and the abilities of homebuilders. Aiming, with the help of Georges Houard and his monthly *Les Ailes,* to popularise light aircraft, Mignet could hardly have chosen anything other than wood from which to build his *Pou-du-Ciel.*
Half a century later his son Pierre and nephew Alain, wanting to perpetuate the family tradition with a two-seater microlight, have turned to more up-to-date technology. The fuselage of their *HM 1000* is made from 2017A Duralumin tubes, while the wing longerons are made from wood on the prototype with Duralumin and Klegecell ribs and Dacron covering, although the pair inform us that the wood will almost certainly be replaced by Duralumin on production models.
The *HM 1000* has been christened *Balerit,* meaning hawk in the dialect of Saintonge province, or more particularly a small falcon called the crecerelle.
Construction of the prototype began in July 1983 and was finished the following February, Pierre Mignet making the first flight on 8 April. The dual-control *Balerit* has the useful feature of folding wings, the front reducing from 29.5 to 13.1 ft (9.00 to 4.00 m) and the rear from 23.0 to 8.0 ft (7.00 to 2.45 m). In addition the front wing can be pivoted to

reduce its width to 6.6 ft (2.00 m) for ease of transport. The wings are retained in their flying position by means of four bayonet bolts.

Anticipated price for the *HM 1000 Balerit* is about 63,500FF when fitted with the Rotax 503 engine, replacing the Hirth 493 of the prototype detailed below.

As we write, in spring '85, the test programme is continuing and preparations for production are under way.

EXTERNAL DIMENSIONS & AREAS - Length overall 16.4 ft, 5.00 m. Height overall 6.1 ft, 1.85 m. Wing span 29.5 ft, 9.00 m (front); 23.0 ft, 7.00 m (rear). Constant chord 4.9 ft, 1.50 m (front wing); 3.9 ft, 1.20 m (rear wing). Dihedral 3° (front wing); 3° (rear wing). Sweepback 0°. Fin height NC. Total wing area 215 ft², 20.0 m². Front wing area 140 ft², 13.0 m². Rear wing area 75 ft², 7.0 m². Fin area 3.2 ft², 0.30 m². Rudder area 9.7 ft², 0.90 m². Aspect ratio 6.2/1 (front wing); 7.0/1 (rear wing). Wheel track 5.9 ft, 1.80 m. Wheelbase 6.3 ft, 1.90 m. Nosewheel diameter overall 16 inch, 40 cm. Main wheels diameter overall 16 inch, 40cm.

POWER PLANT - Hirth 493 engine. Max power 42 hp at 6750 rpm. Propeller diameter and pitch 56x29 inch, 1.42x0.73 m. Toothed-belt reduction, ratio 2.5/1. Max static thrust 276 lb, 125 kg. Power per unit area 0.20 hp/ft², 2.1 hp/m². Fuel capacity 5.3 US gal, 4.4 Imp gal, 20.0 litre.

WEIGHTS & LOADINGS - Empty weight 386 lb, 175 kg. Max take-off weight 828 lb, 375 kg. Payload 441 lb, 200 kg. Max wing loading 3.85 lb/ft², 18.8 kg/m². Max power loading 19.7 lb/hp, 8.9 kg/hp. Load factors +3.5, -1.5 recommended; +7.0, -3.0 ultimate.

PERFORMANCE* - Max level speed 62 mph, 100 kph. Never exceed speed 75 mph, 120 kph. Max cruising speed 50 mph, 80 kph. Economic cruising speed 37 mph, 60 kph. Stalling speed 24 mph, 40 kph. Max climb rate at sea level 490 ft/min, 2.5 m/s. Min sink rate 390 ft/min at 34 mph, 2.0 m/s at 55 kph. Take-off distance 115 ft, 35 m. Landing distance 80 ft, 25 m. Range at average cruising speed 124 mile, 200 km. Other data NC.

*Under the following test conditions - Airfield altitude 49 ft, 15 m. Ground temperature 68°F, 20°C. Ground pressure NC. Ground windspeed 0 mph, 0 kph. Test payload 320 lb, 145 kg.

NOGRADY

Avions Nogrady, 7 rue Jean-Mermoz, 40000 Mont-de-Massan. Proprietors: Bela and Joelle Nogrady.

NOGRADY
AN2/15 AVIONETTE
(Three-axis)

Side-by-side two-seat single-engined mid-wing monoplane with conventional three-axis control. Wing has unswept leading edge, trailing edge unswept inboard and swept forward outboard, chord constant inboard, tapering outboard; air brakes fitted; cruciform tail. Pitch

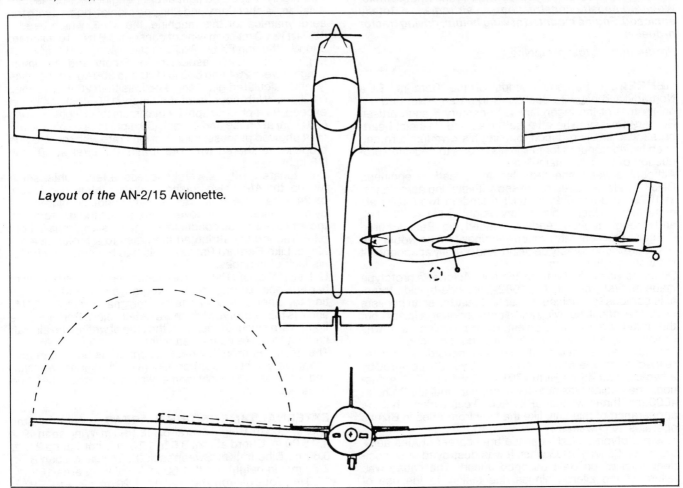

Layout of the AN-2/15 Avionette.

Bela Nogrady's second prototype featured a V-tail.

control by elevator on tail; yaw control by fin-mounted rudder; roll control by 40%-span ailerons; control inputs through stick for pitch/roll and pedals for yaw. Cantilever wing; wing profile Worthmann FX 66-S-171; 100% double-surface. Undercarriage has two wheels in tandem plus underwing skids; bungee/glass-fibre suspension on both wheels. Push-right go-right tailwheel steering connected to yaw control. Main wheel brake. Wood/composite-construction airframe, totally enclosed. Engine mounted at wing height, driving tractor propeller.

Production status: prototype.

GENERAL - Personal friends of the Bergers, Bela Nogrady and his wife Joelle are living an adventure not unlike that of the legendary 17th century French artisan Bernard Palissy, who after setbacks and financial heartbreak was finally reduced to using his own furniture and even his floorboards for fuel in his efforts to begin the production of the first enamelware!

Although a well respected telecommunications engineer, Bela has always been obsessed with making aeroplanes. In 1976 he designed and built a tandem two-seater all-metal motor glider with an empty weight of 441 kg (200 kg), and though it was ready for test-flying Bela ignored Berger's passionately argued warnings that he would one day regret such a hasty decision, and brutally abandoned it in favour of microlights.

Described in our first edition, the AN 2 *Avionette* prototype made its first flights in July 1982. This side-by-side three-axis composite machine at first had quarter-span spoilers on its low, cantilever wing and a conventional tailplane, but the latter proved a problem during taxiing and was replaced by a V-tail with fully flying ruddervators.

This tail was re-used on the second, considerably more refined, prototype which first flew in May 1983, powered by a two-cylinder 43 hp Hirth 2701 R-33 with a 2.2/1 reduction. The engine was actually a stopgap until the 30 hp at 4000 rpm three-cylinder JPX PAL640 came along, but the appearance of this unit, like the lady from Arles in Bizet's opera, is still awaited!

This prototype ended its all too brief career at Ales aerodrome on 20 May 1983 when it was destroyed in an accident from which Bela escaped unhurt. The cause was failure of the aileron hinges due mainly to the use of automotive-grade ball bearings. But, spurred on by a wave of support from readers and staff at *Pilote Prive/UlmMag*, Bela began work on a third prototype which reverted to a conventional tailplane but was otherwise similar to its predecessor.

Two highly respected light aircraft engineers from Issoire Aviation, Michel Barry and Philippe Moniot, helped with the aerodynamics for this machine, the *AN-3*, which used a 42.7 ft (13.00 m) span wing of constant 3.3 ft (1.10 m) chord and Worthmann FX 66-S-171 profile, giving a 152 ft^2 (14.1 m^2) area and 12/1 aspect ratio. Empty and maximum weights were 264 and 660 lb (120 and 300 kg) respectively, and calculated glide angle no less than 26.4 at 45 mph (72 kph). With speeds of 112 mph (180 kph) for never exceed, 94 mph (150 kph) for maximum level flight, 81 mph (130 kph) at cruise and 24 mph (39 mph) at take-off, the aircraft showed promise; minimum sink rate with three-blade propeller feathered was 140 ft/min (0.7 m/s) at 30 mph (48 kph).

Unfortunately, after several successful test flights, some two up, the *AN 3* also crashed and was totally destroyed, on 24 June 1984. Bela was left very seriously injured, but by some miracle he recovered from what the doctors had thought a hopeless condition, spending six months in hospital. The inquiry attributed the crash to a broken aileron hinge. Like Bernard Palissy, Bela had become a victim of his lack of finances.

But, still following Palissy's example and with the benefit of hard-gained experience, the Nogradys are gradually putting together a new *Avionette*, designated the *AN 2/15*, and it is this prototype which we detail below. Performance figures are calculations, for at the time of writing the aircraft had yet to make its maiden flight.

The design is probably best described as an ATL motor-glider (very light aircraft) or ARV (air recreational vehicle), and as it is obviously some way from production, no price is quoted.

EXTERNAL DIMENSIONS & AREAS - Length overall 23.2 ft, 7.05 m. Height overall 6.1 ft, 1.85 m. Wing span 49.2 ft, 15.00 m. Chord at root 3.6 ft, 1.10 m. Chord at tip 2.0 ft, 0.60 m. Dihedral 3°. Sweepback 0°. Tailplane span 8. ft, 2.70 m. Fin height 5.3 ft, 1.60 m. Total wing area 162 ft^2, 15.0 m^2. Total aileron area 12.9 ft^2, 1.20 m^2. Fin area 7.6 ft^2,

0.71 m². Rudder area 5.3 ft², 0.49 m². Tailplane area 11.9 ft², 1.10 m². Total elevator area 9.3 ft², 0.86 m². Aspect ratio 15/1. Wheelbase 14.8 ft, 4.5 m. Nosewheel diameter overall 5 inch, 12 cm. Main wheels diameter overall 14 inch, 36 cm.

POWER PLANT - VW 1700 engine. Max power 65 hp at 3900 rpm. Propeller diameter and pitch 51x47 inch, 1.30x1.20 m. No reduction. Max static thrust NC. Power per unit area 0.40 hp/ft², 4.3 hp/m². Fuel capacity 15.9 US gal, 13.3 Imp gal, 60.0 litre.

WEIGHTS & LOADINGS - Empty weight 530 lb, 240 kg. Max take-off weight 1060 lb, 480 kg. Payload 530 lb, 240 kg. Max wing loading 6.54 lb/ft², 35.3 kg/m². Max power loading 16.3 lb/hp, 7.4 kg/hp. Load factors +5.3, -2.6 recommended; +8.0, -4.0 ultimate.

PERFORMANCE* - Max level speed 112 mph, 180 kph. Never exceed speed 125 mph, 202 kph. Max cruising speed 112 mph, 180 kph. Economic cruising speed 87 mph, 140 kph. Stalling speed 37 mph, 60 kph. Max climb rate at sea level 980 ft/min, 5.0 m/s. Min sink rate 120 ft/min at 40 mph, 0.6 m/s at 65 kph. Best glide ratio with power off 28/1 at 47 mph, 75 kph. Take-off distance 330 ft, 100 m. Landing distance 330 ft, 100 m. Service ceiling 26,240 ft, 8000 m. Range at average cruising speed 497 mile, 800 km. Noise level NC.

*Under the following test conditions - Airfield altitude 0 ft, 0 m. Ground temperature 15°F, 59°C. Ground pressure 1013 mB. Ground windspeed 0 mph, 0 kph. Test payload 530 lb, 240 kg.

PIEL

Plans: Mme C Piel, Le Mas, 19300 Dannetz-Eygletons; tel (55) 93 0979. Kits: M R Francois, 99 rue des Heraults, 37170 St Avertin; tel (47) 27 4529 between 8 and 9 pm.

PIEL *CP-150 ONYX*

(Three-axis)

Single-seat single-engined double monoplane in tandem with conventional three-axis control. Front wing has unswept leading and trailing edges, and constant chord; rear wing has swept back leading edge, unswept trailing edge, and tapering chord; no tail. Pitch control by fully flying wing; yaw control by tip rudders; roll control by 30%-span ailerons on rear wing; control inputs through stick for pitch/roll and pedals for yaw. Cantilevered wings; wing profiles NACA 23012 and 23015; 100% double-surface. Undercarriage has three wheels in tricycle formation; glass-fibre suspension on all wheels. Push-right go-right nosewheel steering connected to yaw control. Brakes to builder's preference. Wood airframe (plans-built version), composite-construction airframe (kit-built version), partially enclosed. Engine mounted between wings, driving pusher propeller.

Production status: see text.

GENERAL - Claude Piel died in August 1982 after a long and painful illness, but his memory lives in any pilot who has ever flown one of the excellent light aircraft he created. A highly accomplished aeronautical engineer, he built a Mignet *Pou-du-Ciel* as an amateur in 1948 and then in the early '50s, in addition to his professional aeronautical activities, designed a whole family of light and sporting aircraft, some factory produced and others made by homebuilders the world over.

After his 'early works', the *CP-20 Pinocchio* and the *CP-40 Donald*, came the fabulous *CP-30 Emeraude*, one of the finest machines of its time. From it came the *CP-60 Diamand* and the tandem two-seater *CP-70 Beryl*, while the *CP-100 Super Emeraude* was the basis for the *CAP-10* aerobatic two-seater which is still successfully produced by Avions Mudry at Bernay. Believing that variety is the spice of life, he also designed a racer, the *CP-80,* and the push-pull twin *CP-500* for homebuilders.

Finally at the end of 1981, when he was already terminally ill, he completed the plans for his single-seater *CP-150 Onyx* microlight. Sadly, he never saw it fly; construction of first machine was delayed by his death and the *Onyx* did not make its first flight until spring '83.

Intended as a trailer-transportable machine for low power engines of 16-26 hp - Claude designed it around a 12 hp Solo - the *Onyx* is a tandem wing double monoplane with variable pitch front wing, so that it acts as an elevator as on the Mignet machines. The front wing has a smaller span than the rear and is stabilised by an anti-servo tab. Both are cantilevered, the front one being hinged on two aerofoiled struts, incidence being varied by means of push rods. The rear wing is fitted with ailerons and has two large fins at either tip, each with a rudder which, when activated simultaneously, can also act as air brakes.

Several machines were under construction in France at the time of writing and four were expected to fly before the end of 1985. One *CP-150* builder in Tourraine, M R Francois, has designed and built moulds for the fuselage (with less rectangular lines than the original wooden construction), and also for the undercarriage, both of which are made of glass-fibre, Kevlar and carbon. The wings and wingtip fins and rudders were still to be built along traditional wood and fabric lines with Klegecell ribs. For 13,000FF he can supply a Kevlar/carbon reinforced glass-fibre fuselage complete with integral chassis, floor, seat-tank of 7.9 US gal capacity (6.6 Imp gal, 30.0 litre), structural reinforcements for wing mountings, access panels, undercarriage and front wing struts.

The Francois version weighs empty some 22 lb (10 kg) more than the original detailed below. For those preferring the latter, average build time is likely to be about 900 h, using the plans which Claude's widow can still supply. Like all Claude's plans, these are extremely detailed and perfectly comprehensible, a splendid example of draughtsmanship. Price for the complete book is 500FF in France (carriage abroad extra).

EXTERNAL DIMENSIONS & AREAS - Length overall 11.4 ft, 3.45 m. Height overall 5.3 ft, 1.61 m. Wing span 14.5 ft, 4.46 m (front); 23.8 ft, 7.30 m (rear). Constant chord (front wing) 2.8 ft, 0.84 m. Chord at root (rear wing) 5.3 ft, 1.60 m. Chord at tip (rear wing) 3.3 ft, 1.00 m. Dihedral 0° (front wing); 0° (rear wing). Sweepback 0°. Fin height 3.4 ft, 1.05 m. Total wing area 138 ft², 12.8 m². Front wing area 40 ft², 3.7 m². Rear wing area 98 ft², 9.1 m². Total aileron area 6.8 ft², 0.60 m². Fin area 8.9 ft², 0.83 m². Rudder area 6.8 ft², 0.63 m². Aspect ratio 5.4/1 (front wing); 5.9/1 (rear wing). Wheel track 4.9 ft, 1.50 m. Wheelbase 5.5 ft, 1.68 m. Tailwheel diameter overall 8 inch, 20 cm. Main wheels diameter overall 10 inch, 25 cm.

POWER PLANT - Solo engine. Max power 12 hp at NC rpm. Power per unit area 0.09 hp/ft², 0.9 hp/m². Fuel capacity 7.9 US gal, 6.6 Imp gal, 30.0 litre. Other data NC.

This first composite-construction fuselage for the CP-150 Onyx was presented at the Tours show in 1983. Its lines are noticeably more rounded than the wood-built version in our other picture.

TISSERAND

Claude Tisserand, Fior di Linu. Pietranera, 20200 Bastia; tel (95) 31 6767.

TISSERAND *PUCE-DU-CIEL/ Suitable Rogallo*
(Weight-shift)

Single-seat single-engined flex-wing aircraft with weight-shift control. Rogallo wing. Pilot suspended below wing in trike unit, using bar to control pitch and roll/yaw by altering relative positions of trike unit and wing. Wing braced from above by kingpost and cables, from below by cables. Undercarriage has three wheels in tricycle formation; coil-spring suspension on nosewheel and glass-fibre/wood suspension on main wheels. Push-right go-left nosewheel steering independent from aerodynamic controls. Brakes NC. Wood trike unit, completely open. Engine mounted below wing, driving pusher propeller.

Production status: plans-built, number completed NC.

WEIGHTS & LOADINGS - Empty weight 243 lb, 110 kg. Load factors NC recommended; +4.0, -2.0 ultimate. Other data NC.

PERFORMANCE* - Max level speed 62 mph, 100 kph. Max cruising speed 50 mph, 80 kph. Economic cruising speed 37 mph, 60 kph. Stalling speed 22 mph, 35 kph. Max climb rate at sea level 350 ft/min, 1.8 m/s. Take-off distance 165 ft, 50 m. Landing distance 165 ft, 50 m. Other data NC.

*Under unspecified test conditions.

Puce-du-Ciel *trike unit.*

GENERAL - The combination of a heart dedicated to do-it-yourself and a passion for microlights led Claude Tisserand to build his own trike unit in 1981, designing it to fit a variety of solo wings then available. Called the *Puce-du-Ciel* out of respect for Henri Mignet (see separate listing) and his famous *Pou-du-Ciel* ('puce' actually translates as a rather more pleasant type of flea than a 'pou'!), this streamlined trike unit is built to take the 26 hp JPX PUL425 but can be adapted to any other engine of similar power.

The aircraft was the subject of an article in *UlmMag* by Claude Tisserand in March 1984 and the magazine subsequently followed the experience of a homebuilder constructing one, starting with Claude's plans which he sells for 170FF plus postage. This particular builder went on to buy a JPX 18 hp engine for 7531FF (the 26 hp would have cost 8776FF), a prop for 1000FF, wheels 600FF, materials and sundries 3,500FF, and a secondhand wing at 8000FF, a total of 20,801FF with the smaller engine.

The trike unit is unusual in that it uses wood, with aviation-quality 2 mm (0.078 inch) panelling attached to eight 15 mm square-section (0.59 inch) pine stringers. Timber is also in evidence in the main undercarriage, where glass-fibre and epoxy-resin struts have a 3-4 mm (0.12-0.16 inch) balsa core which acts as a spring. Up front there are stainless-steel forks which turn in a nylon bearing sleeved in 40 mm Duralumin (1.57 inch), with a coil spring to take the shocks. Three aviation-quality 40x1.25 mm (1.57x0.05 inch) Duralumin tubes support the hang point and can be folded to allow trailer transport.

The designer estimates an average build time of about 200 h.

EXTERNAL DIMENSIONS & AREAS - NC.

POWER PLANT - NC.

WEIGHTS & LOADINGS - NC.

PERFORMANCE - NC.

TISSERAND *HYDROPLUM*

(Three-axis)

Single-seat single-engined high-wing monoplane with conventional three-axis control. Wing has unswept leading and trailing edges, and constant chord; conventional tail. Pitch control by elevator on tail; yaw control by fin-mounted rudder; roll control by 40%-span spoilers; control inputs through stick for pitch/roll and pedals for yaw. Wing braced from below by struts; wing profile NACA 2415; 100% double-surface. Undercarriage has three retractable wheels in tail-dragger formation plus two under-wing floats; suspension NC on tailwheel and coil-

▼

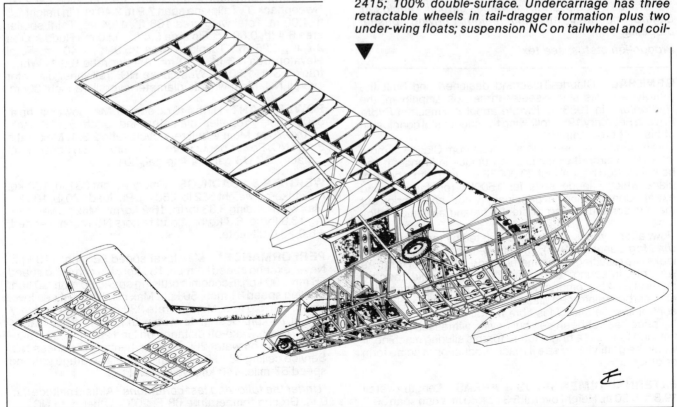

spring suspension on main wheels. Ground steering NC. No brakes. Wood/fabric airframe, partially enclosed. Engine mounted at wing height, driving pusher propeller.

Production status: see text.

GENERAL - Claude Tisserand designed and built the prototype of his single-seater three-axis amphibian, the *Hydroplum,* in 1983 and wrote about it himself in *Pilote Prive* in February 1984 following the successful conclusion of his test programme.

This is another homebuilders' project from Claude, a most interesting aircraft which is so far unique in France: it can be built in 800 h for about 30,000FF starting with a book of plans which Claude sells for 1500FF (postage abroad extra). Construction is principally wood and fabric, but there is some use also of steel tube and aluminium-alloy tube.

Now, after a year's experience (related by the designer in *UlmMag* January 1985), the success of the *Hydroplum* looks like resulting in commercial production, in kit form. As we write, in spring 1985, a first 'mini-kit' should soon be made available, comprising longerons and composite wing ribs, carbon reinforced glass-fibre undercarriage, elevator control linkage and glass-fibre floats.

No price has yet been set, but having witnessed its evolution and forecast a bright future for this alluring machine, it would be gratifying to see it reach production in some form or other.

EXTERNAL DIMENSIONS & AREAS - Length overall 19.3 ft, 5.90 m. Height overall 5.3 ft, 1.60 m. Wing span 30.3 ft, 9.25 m. Constant chord 4.6 ft, 1.40 m. Dihedral 2.8°. Sweepback 0°. Tailplane span 7.9 ft, 2.40 m. Fin height 3.3 ft, 1.00 m. Total wing area 166 ft², 15.4 m². Total spoiler area 6.4 ft², 0.60 m². Fin area 5.4 ft², 0.50 m². Rudder area 2.7 ft², 0.25 m². Tailplane area 25.9 ft², 2.40 m². Total elevator area 4.3 ft², 0.40 m². Aspect ratio 6.6/1. Wheel track 5.3 ft, 1.60 m. Wheelbase NC. Tailwheel diameter overall NC. Main wheels diameter overall 12 inch, 30cm.

POWER PLANT - Hirth 440 cc engine. Max power 40 hp at 6500 rpm. Propeller diameter and pitch 55x28 inch, 1.40x0.70 m. Multi V-belt reduction, ratio 2.3/1. Max static thrust NC. Power per unit area 0.24 hp/ft², 2.6 hp/m². Fuel capacity 5.3 US gal, 4.4 Imp gal, 20.0 litre.

WEIGHTS & LOADINGS - Empty weight 331 lb, 150 kg. Max take-off weight 552 lb, 250 kg. Payload 220 lb, 100 kg. Max wing loading 3.33 lb/ft², 16.2 kg/m². Max power loading 13.8 lb/hp, 6.3 kg/hp. Load factors NC recommended; +6.0, -3.0 ultimate.

PERFORMANCE* - Max level speed 68 mph, 110 kph. Never exceed speed 81 mph, 130 kph. Max cruising speed 56 mph, 90 kph. Economic cruising speed 50 mph, 80 kph. Stalling speed 31 mph, 50 kph. Max climb rate at sea level 980 ft/min, 5.0 m/s. Min sink rate 330 ft/min at 44 mph, 1.7 m/s at 70 kph. Best glide ratio with power off 13/1 at 44 mph, 70 kph. Take-off distance on land 200 ft, 60 m. Take-off distance on water 260 ft, 80 m. Landing distances NC. Service ceiling 9840 ft, 3000 m. Range at average cruising speed 87 mile, 140 km. Noise level NC.

*Under the following test conditions - Airfield altitude 0 ft, 0 m. Ground temperature 68°F, 20°C. Other data NC.

ULAC

ULAC Aviation SARL, aerodrome, 78210 Saint-Cyr-l'Ecole; tel (3) 045 0940 and (3) 955 3699. Proprietor: Georges Borgeaud.

ULAC *X-100*

(Three-axis)

Tandem two-seat single-engined high-wing monoplane with conventional three-axis control. Wing has unswept leading and trailing edges, and constant chord; conventional tail. Pitch control by elevator on tail; yaw control by fin-mounted rudder; roll control by half-span ailerons; control inputs through stick for pitch/roll and pedals for yaw. Wing braced from below by struts; wing profile NC; 100% double-surface. Undercarriage has three wheels in tricycle formation; coil-spring suspension on nosewheel and glass-fibre suspension on main wheels. Push-right go-right nosewheel steering connected to yaw control. Brakes on main wheels. Aluminium-alloy tube airframe, with pod. Engine mounted at wing height, driving pusher propeller.

Production status: current, number completed NC.

GENERAL - Georges Borgeaud acquired the European and African rights to the Maxair Sports' *Hummer* (see US section) in August 1981. This was a single-seater three-axis machine with unconventional controls in that the stick operated spoilers, and was developed from the original two-axis stick-only configuration on which the stick operated ruddervators.

The aircraft was the brainchild of the late Klaus Hill who died test flying his *Voyager* ultralight glider in October 1979. Also the creator of the famous *Fledge* wing, Klaus had completed the prototype *Hummer* two years pre-

viously. From it he developed the *Humbug* and the *Vector 600* (see Sky King International, Canadian section).

Meanwhile Swiss-born Georges Borgeaud had founded ULAC and set up its first factory at Monthey in the Valais canton of that country, where he developed his tandem two-seat conventional three-axis machine, the *X-99* from the *Hummer*. Featured in the Swiss section of our first edition, the main changes made by Georges were to heighten and reinforce the wing, fit larger main wheels, adapt the tailwheel to push-right go-right configuration, add spoilers and fit a 40 hp 438 cc Hirth 272R engine.

This aircraft first flew in California in early 1982 and in 1983 Georges began work on a new version of it, the *X-100*, with a twin-carburettor Rotax 503 and a conventional tail like Maxair's *Drifter,* itself developed from the *Hummer* at the instigation of Roy Pinner, a Maxair agent in the USA.

The *X-100* made its first flights early in 1984, during which year Georges decided to leave Switzerland and set up a factory at Saint-Cyr aerodrome near Paris.

Assembled and test flown, the aircraft costs 79,900FF.

EXTERNAL DIMENSIONS & AREAS - Length overall 20.3 ft, 6.20 m. Height overall 8.6 ft, 2.60 m. Wing span 34.4 ft, 10.50 m. Constant chord 4.3 ft, 1.32 m. Dihedral 2.5°. Sweepback 0°. Tailplane span 10.7 ft, 3.25 m. Fin height 5.5 ft, 1.67 m. Total wing area (including ailerons) 163 ft^2, 15.1 m^2. Total aileron area 13.5 ft^2, 1.25 m^2. Fin area 11.1 ft^2, 1.03 m^2. Rudder area 8.8 ft^2, 0.82 m^2. Tailplane area 21.0 ft^2, 1.95 m^2. Total elevator area 14.5 ft^2, 1.35 m^2. Aspect ratio 8.0/1. Wheel track 6.9 ft, 2.10 m. Wheelbase 8.4 ft, 2.55 m. Nosewheel diameter overall 16 inch, 40 cm. Main wheels diameter overall 16 inch, 40 cm.

POWER PLANT - Rotax 503 engine. Max power 53 hp at 6500 rpm. Propeller diameter and pitch 54x40 inch, 1.37x1.02 m. Notched V-belt reduction, ratio 2.2/1. Max static thrust 329 lb, 149 kg. Power per unit area 0.33 hp/ft^2, 3.5 hp/m^2. Fuel capacity 5.8 US gal, 4.8 Imp gal, 22.0 litre.

WEIGHTS & LOADINGS - Empty weight 384 lb, 174 kg. Max take-off weight 795 lb, 360 kg. Payload 411 lb, 186 kg.

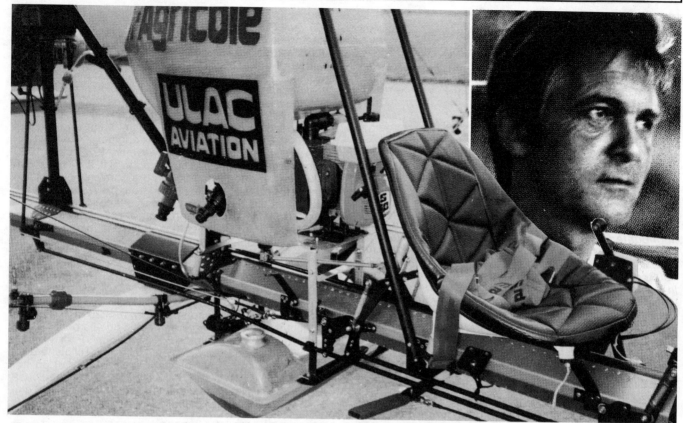

The X-Agricole *can carry either a second seat or spraying equipment. Inset: ULAC proprietor Georges Borgeaud.*

Max wing loading 4.87 lb/ft², 23.8 kg/m². Max power loading 15.0 lb/hp, 6.8 kg/hp. Load factors +4.0, -2.0 recommended; NC ultimate.

PERFORMANCE* - Max level speed 75 mph, 120 kph. Never exceed speed 81 mph, 130 kph. Max cruising speed 62 mph, 100 kph. Economic cruising speed 56 mph, 90 kph. Stalling speed 32 mph, 52 kph. Max climb rate at sea level 390 ft/min, 2.0 m/s. Min sink rate 590 ft/min at 34 mph, 3.0 m/s at 55 kph. Best glide ratio with power off 8/1 at 36 mph, 58 kph. Take-off distance 230 ft, 70 m. Landing distance 165 ft, 50 m. Service ceiling 13,120 ft, 4000 m. Range at average cruising speed 124 mile, 200 km. Noise level 65 dB at 490 ft, 150 m.

*Under the following test conditions - Airfield altitude 492 ft, 150 m. Ground temperature 50°F, 10°C. Ground pressure NC. Ground windspeed 0 mph, 0 kph. Test payload 388 lb, 176 kg.

ULAC *X-AGRICOLE*
(Three-axis)

Summary as X-100 *except: Single- or two-seat*. Wing braced from above by kingpost and cables, from below by cables.*

Production status: current, number completed NC.

*See text.

GENERAL - Georges has developed an agricultural version of the *X-100*, called the *X-Agricole*, of which the first production models were distributed early in 1985. The fully equipped, ready-to-fly *X-Agricole* costs 120,000FF and differs from the *X-100* in that it uses kingpost-and-cable bracing, which ensures that there are no struts to interfere with the spray booms.

The aircraft can also be used simply as a tandem two-seater; for agricultural work, the rear seat is replaced by a glass-fibre chemical tank, with a capacity of 26 US gal (22 Imp gal, 100 litre), beneath which are positioned the pump and pressure regulator. The spray booms under each wing, giving a spread of 33 ft (10 m), can each be replaced by two atomisers, spraying equipment being Swiss-manufactured by the specialist Fischer company.

Studies by Ciba-Geigy attribute the *X Agricole* with the ability to spray 99 acre/h (40 hectares/h) with insecticides or pesticides, or half this area with herbicides or fungicides. It should be remembered that despite its primary purpose as an agricultural workhorse, the *X Agricole* retains the excellent finish of the *X-99* and *X-100* and like them can be fitted with wheel spats, cockpit fairing and windscreen, all new options for 1985.

EXTERNAL DIMENSIONS & AREAS - See *X-100.*

POWER PLANT - See *X-100.*

WEIGHTS & LOADINGS - See *X-100* except: Empty weight and payload dependent on equipment fitted.

PERFORMANCE** - Max level speed 62 mph, 100 kph. Never exceed speed 68 mph, 110 kph. Working speed 40 mph, 65 kph. Stalling speed 34 mph, 55 kph. Max climb rate at sea level 300 ft/min, 1.5 m/s. Min sink rate 680 ft/min at 37 mph, 3.5 m/s at 60 kph. Best glide ratio with power off 6/1 at 37 mph, 60 kph. Take-off distance 230 ft, 70 m. Landing distance 165 ft, 50 m. Service ceiling NC. Range at average cruising speed 93 mile, 150 km. Noise level 65 dB at 490 ft, 150 m.

**Under the following test conditions - Airfield altitude 492 ft, 150 m. Ground temperature 50°F, 10°C. Ground pressure NC. Ground windspeed 0 mph, 0 kph. Test payload 773 lb, 350 kg.

This prototype Djins 385 *used the old tube-and-Dacron wing and a twin-carburettor Rotax 503. Inset gives a close-up of the dual controls.*

ULM TECHNIC AM

ULM Technic Aero-Marine, 65 route de Blois, 41400 Pontlevoy; tel (54) 32 6066. Proprietor: Tony Minguet.

ULM TECHNIC AM *DJINS 385* (Three-axis)

Side-by-side two-seat single-engined high-wing monoplane with conventional three-axis control. Wing has unswept leading and trailing edges, and constant chord; cruciform tail. Pitch control by elevator on tail; yaw control by fully flying rudder; roll control by full-span flaperons; control inputs through stick for pitch/roll and pedals for yaw. Wing braced from below by struts; wing profile NACA 4412; 100% double-surface. Undercarriage has three wheels in tricycle formation; bungee suspension on nosewheel and no suspension on main wheels. Push-right go-right nosewheel steering connected to yaw control. Nosewheel brake. Composite wing, aluminium-alloy tube airframe, with pod. Engine mounted at wing height, driving tractor propeller.

Production status: current, 10 completed.

GENERAL - This company was formed as ULM Aerotechnic when Alain Bernet's first prototype, the *Alto 822*, went into production in 1982, Alain having come into microlights from hang gliding in 1979 when he fitted two 9 hp Stihl kart motors to a *Quicksilver* hang-glider.

The following year he built a high-wing single-seater with a tubular airframe in the shape of a double trihedron and powered by two 9 hp Solos. After the addition of a canard, this was displayed at Le Bourget airshow, but despite substantial investment by Air Ceffelec this *Ceffelec 811* was not commercially produced due to a disagreement with Alain.

Instead, he developed it into a side-by-side two-seater two-axis machine with a cruciform tail and rectangular plan single-surface wing, and showed it at the '82 homebuilders' meet at Brienne-le-Chateau. Alain formed ULM Aerotechnic with Tony Minguet and converted the aircraft into a conventional three-axis machine by adding ailerons, calling the result the *Alto 822*.

After the company name change to the present title in '83, and other upheavals, Tony rechristened the unfinished prototype aircraft the *Djins 300* and entrusted its development to well known aeronautical engineer Marc Faure. Working free of charge, he did a full set of design calculations, completely redesigning the tail and adding full-span flaperons, to act as ailerons when applied differentially or as flaps when applied simultaneously, through up to 30°.

At the end of 1983 the aircraft was given a new trapezoid-plan double-surface wing, battened to maintain a Clark Y profile. Tony assiduously swapped the Hirth engines for a twin-carburettor 53 hp Rotax 503, fitted with a governor modified by Tony to ensure that neither cylinder-head temperature exceeded 210°C, even though Rotax's own maximum is much higher, at 260°C. With a 2.5/1 toothed-belt reduction, this aircraft was flight tested for *UlmMag's* May '84 issue.

Though the test went well enough, the company was not satisfied and in 1985 replaced the model with the *Djins 385,* which sports a composite-construction wing, with 2x0.08 inch (50x2 mm) Duralumin leading edge encased in Klegecell, the profile coming from a glass-fibre/polyester resin former. The trailing edge spar comprises two 7.8x0.08 inch (20x2 mm) Duralumin tubes joined by Klegecell, while in each wing two compression struts, two X-cables and 13 Klegecell ribs ensure rigidity.

Between the root and the first rib of each wing is a 6.6 US gal (5.5 Imp gal, 25.0 litre) glass-fibre tank including a 0.8 US gal (0.7 Imp gal, 3.0 litre) reserve. This new wing raises the never exceed speed from 81 to 99 mph (130 to 160 kph).

The flaperons are of polyurethane foam with a glass-fibre and Kevlar/epoxy coating and have a self-stopping notch-free control, while the fixed tail surfaces are of honeycomb with a heat-pressed glass-fibre coating.

All in all Tony Minguet, who limits his output and markets his products little, being motivated it seems more by enthusiasm than money, has good reason to be proud of his latest creation.

All aircraft are sold delivered and flight tested, prices depending on the power unit fitted. In standard trim the *Djins 385* uses a Rotax 447 and cost 65,000FF, in which form we detail it below, but buyers may choose instead the single-carb 503 (46 hp, 66,750FF), twin-carb 503 (53 hp, 67,333FF), 462 (51 hp, 68,171FF), or 532 (64 hp, 70,700FF), all these options except the gear-reduction 462 having toothed-belt reductions.

EXTERNAL DIMENSIONS & AREAS - Length overall 19.2 ft, 5.85 m. Height overall 5.6 ft, 1.70 m. Wing span 33.1 ft, 10.10 m. Constant chord 6.1 ft, 1.85 m. Dihedral 2°. Sweepback 0°. Tailplane span 9.8 ft, 3.00 m. Rudder height 4.9 ft, 1.50 m. Total wing area 215 ft^2, 20.0 m^2. Total aileron area 32.3 ft^2, 3.00 m^2. Rudder area 16.1 ft^2, 1.50 m^2. Tailplane area 14.4 ft^2, 1.34 m^2. Total elevator area 16.4 ft^2, 1.52 m^2. Aspect ratio 5.7/1. Wheel track 4.3 ft, 1.30 m. Wheelbase 4.6 ft, 1.40 m. Nosewheel diameter overall 12 inch, 30 cm. Main wheels diameter overall 16 inch, 40cm.

POWER PLANT - Rotax 447 engine. Max power 40 hp at 6500 rpm. Propeller diameter and pitch 61x30 inch, 1.55x0.75 m. Gear reduction, ratio 2.6/1. Max static thrust 276 lb, 125 kg. Power per unit area 0.19 hp/ft^2, 2.0 hp/m^2. Fuel capacity 13.2 US gal, 11.0 Imp gal, 50.0 litre.

WEIGHTS & LOADINGS - Empty weight 377 lb, 171 kg. Max take-off weight 838 lb, 380 kg. Payload 461 lb, 209 kg. Max wing loading 3.90 lb/ft^2, 19.0 kg/m^2. Max power loading 21.0 lb/hp, 9.5 kg/hp. Load factors +5.0, -2.0 recommended; +5.5, -2.5 ultimate.

PERFORMANCE - NC.

ULM TECHNIC AM
DJINS 385 TWIN

(Three-axis)

Summary as Djins 385 *except: Twin-engined.*
Production status: prototype.

GENERAL - Tony Minguet's latest idea is to transform the *Djins 385* into a twin-engine aircraft with two single-cylinder Rotax 277 units, one on the front of each half-wing. Their output, usually 27 hp, can be upped to 30 hp maximum with the use of Rotax-approved exhaust pipes.

This machine had not yet completed its test flight programme at the time of going to press, although readings already taken indicate that the machine will maintain 62-65 mph (100-105 kph) level speed at 6200 rpm, well below full-power revs of 7000 rpm. A 4500 rpm cruise produces 50 mph (80 kph) and the minimum flying speed is about 31 mph (50 kph). With a 440 lb (200 kg) load the climb rate was some 790 ft/min (4.0 m/s) even using only 6000 rpm, and - most important for any light or ultralight twin - the *Djins 385 Twin* has demonstrated its ability to maintain level flight on one engine.

Price with engines boosted to 30 hp each will be 70,470FF, assembled and test flown.

EXTERNAL DIMENSIONS & AREAS - See *Djins 385.*

POWER PLANT - Two Rotax 277 engines. Max power 30 hp each at 7000 rpm. Propeller diameter and pitch NC. Gear reduction, ratio 2.6/1. Max static thrust NC. Power per unit area 0.28 hp/ft^2, 3.0 hp/m^2. Fuel capacity 13.2 US gal, 11.0 Imp gal, 50.0 litre.

Test flying the Djins 385 Twin *prototype, using the old tube-and-Dacron wing from the* Djins 300.

WEIGHTS & LOADINGS - See *Djins 385* except: Empty weight NC. Payload NC.

PERFORMANCE* - Max level speed 68 mph, 110 kph. Never exceed speed 99 mph, 160 kph. Max cruising speed 59 mph, 95 kph. Economic cruising speed 50 mph, 80 kph. Stalling speed 28 mph, 45 kph. Max climb rate at sea level 980 ft/min, 5.0 m/s. Min sink rate 450 ft/min at 37 mph, 2.3 m/s at 60 kph. Best glide ratio with power off 7/1 at 40 mph, 65 kph. Take-off distance 165 ft, 50 m. Landing distance 165 ft, 50 m. Service ceiling 6560 ft, 2000 m. Range at average cruising speed 155 mile, 250 km. Noise level 66 dB at 490 ft, 150 m.

*Under the following test conditions - Airfield altitude 230 ft, 70 m. Ground temperature 59°F, 15°C. Ground pressure 1013 mB. Ground windspeed 9 mph, 15 kph. Test payload 463 lb, 210 kg.

Ultralair's JC 24D *uses a Rotax 277 engine.*

ULTRALAIR

Ultralair SA, ZI, no. 2, Batterie 200, rue Jean-Marie Frouin, 59309 Valenciennes Cedex; tel (27) 31 0031; tx 810604 ULTRALAIR F. Proprietor: Marc Mathot.

ULTRALAIR *JC 24D and JC 24D SPORT*

(Two-axis)

Single-seat single-engined high-wing monoplane with two-axis control. Wing has swept back leading edge, unswept trailing edge, and tapering chord; conventional tail. Pitch control by elevator on tail; yaw control by fin-mounted rudder; no separate roll control; control inputs through stick for pitch/yaw. Wing braced from below by struts; wing profile NC; 60% double-surface. Undercarriage has three wheels in tricycle formation; no suspension on any wheels. Push-right go-right nosewheel steering independent from aerodynamic controls. Nosewheel brake. Aluminium-alloy tube airframe, with optional pod. Engine mounted above wing, driving tractor propeller.

Production status: current; numbers completed 34 (JC 24D), 8 (JC 24D Sport), 1250 (JC24 C, including some US production), 1830 (JC 24B, all US production), NC (other solo US versions).

GENERAL - Ultralair's *JC 24D* and *JC 24D Sport* are the latest in a line which began in the US in 1977, where Weedhopper of Utah was founded by former NASA engineer John Chotia. His first *Weedhopper*, the *JC 24,* and evolved from 1978 to 1980 through a series of prototypes and production machines, including the *24B, 24C,*

24BL, 24P Penguin (a 'clipped wing' non-flying basic trainer), the *24C* and the *31A.* The *24BL* was dubbed *Weedhopper Two,* despite being only a solo machine, but later that title was transferred to the *31A,* which was a genuine two-seater but only enjoyed a limited distribution, largely among the company's dealers.

On 27 October 1981, John was killed test-flying the prototype of his new *Rocket* and Weedhopper was declared insolvent although John's widow Susan Boman continued running it to some extent, as we explained in our first edition. Subsequently, a company called Nova Air started promoting the design in the US, but Nova went out of business shortly before this edition went to press.

Though the *Weedhopper* never regained its US market, it did have a European agent in Brussels and dealers in Belgium and France. Ultralair was set up in April 1983 and took over the manufacturing licence for Europe, Africa and the Middle East. Belgian-born founder Marc Mathot clearly meant business from the outset, setting up a true production line rather than the semi-workshop arrangements previously at Brussels, and making useful improvements before his spring '83 relaunch of the solo and dual machines as *JC 24C* and *JC 31C* respectively, the initial emphasis being on the two-seater.

Much the most important change was a switch to Rotax power. The *Weedhopper* had acquired a dubious reputation, thanks largely to the unreliability of Chotia's own single-cylinder two-stroke, which was supposed to generate 28 hp at 4100 rpm. In reality, the Chotia-powered *Weedhopper* was one of the best microlights of its time for teaching students how to cope with breakdowns on cross-countries!

Mark fits the latest solo *Weeds* with a 277 (for the *JC 24D*) or a 377 (*JC24 D Sport*). These 1985 D-series models retain the configuration of their single-surface predecessors but have 60% double-surface and many detail improvements. Apart from its larger engine, the *Sport* differs from the basic model in having a reinforced structure and twice the number of battens.

An Ultralair JC 31C takes off during the 1984 Grand Prix de Paris; inset shows the JC 31D fitted with spraying equipment.

Construction is from unwelded 6061T6 Duralumin with cast fittings. Both models have anodised tubing with an additional polyester enamel finish, and come with compass, altimeter, ASI, rev counter, chtg, flying hours counter, key-operated ignition and engine-kill button.

Sharply priced considering their quality, the aircraft are available ready to fly or as a well presented 8-10 h kit complete with instruction book. Ready-to-fly prices (all including 18.6% VAT): *JC 24D* 37,500FF, *JC24 D Sport* 42,500FF. Options: three-blade prop 2372FF; special colours 854FF; aircraft cover 1067FF; engine cover 200FF; prop cover 100FF; skis and mountings 3200FF, Lexan windscreen (standard on *Sport*) 300FF, electric start (*Sport* only) 2600FF, Paul Fayet floats (*Sport* only) 9800FF.

Our data below refers to the *JC 24D;* where different, figures for the *JC 24D Sport* are shown in parentheses.

EXTERNAL DIMENSIONS & AREAS - Length overall 17.0 ft, 5.18 m. Height overall 5.8 ft, 1.75 m. Wing span 27.6 ft, 8.40 m. Chord at root 7.8 ft, 2.39 m. Chord at tip 4.1 ft, 1.25 m. Dihedral 7°. Sweepback 3°. Tailplane span NC. Fin height 1.8 ft, 0.55 m. Total wing area 168 ft², 15.6 m². Fin area 6.4 ft², 0.59 m². Rudder area 8.4 ft², 0.78 m². Tailplane area 14.8 ft², 1.37 m². Total elevator area 9.4 ft², 0.87 m². Aspect ratio 4.5/1. Wheel track 4.3 ft, 1.32 m. Wheelbase 3.3 ft, 1.01 m. Nosewheel diameter overall 13 inch, 33 cm. Main wheels diameter overall 16 inch, 40 cm.

POWER PLANT - Rotax 277 (Rotax 377) engine. Max power 24(35) hp at 5950(6950) rpm. Propeller diameter and pitch 57 inch x 13°, 1.45 m x13°. Gear reduction, ratio 2.6/1. Max static thrust 166(NC) lb, 75(NC) kg. Power per unit area 0.14(0.21) hp/ft², 1.5(2.2) hp/m². Fuel capacity 5.3 US gal, 4.4 Imp gal, 20.0 litre.

WEIGHTS & LOADINGS - Empty weight 247(260) lb, 112(118) kg. Max take-off weight 497(525) lb, 225(238) kg. Payload 249(265) lb, 113(120) kg. Max wing loading 2.96(3.13) lb/ft², 14.4(15.3) kg/m². Max power loading 20.7(15.0) lb/hp, 9.4(6.8) kg/hp. Load factors +5.0(6.0), -2.0(3.0) recommended; +6.0(8.0), -3.0(4.0) ultimate.

PERFORMANCE* - Max level speed 56(62) mph, 90(100) kph. Never exceed speed 68(84) mph, 110(135) kph. Max cruising speed 45(53) mph, 75(85) kph. Economic cruising speed 40(39) mph, 65(64) kph. Stalling speed 20(21) mph, 32(34) kph. Max climb rate at sea level 490(980) ft/min, 2.5(5.0) m/s. Min sink rate 390 ft/min at 35 mph, 2.0 m/s at 56 mph. Best glide ratio with power off 8.7(8.9)/1 at 36(37) mph, 58(60) kph. Take-off distance 130(65) ft, 40(20) m. Landing distance 130 ft, 40 m. Service ceiling 9840 ft, 3000 m. Range at average cruising speed 99(78) mile, 160(125) km. Noise level 62(63) dB at 490 ft, 150 m.

**Under the following test conditions* - Airfield altitude 279 ft, 85 m. Ground temperature 57°F, 14°C. Ground pressure 1015 mB. Ground windspeed 9 mph, 15 kph. Test payload 210 lb, 95 kg.

ULTRALAIR *JC 31D*
(Two-axis)

Summary as JC 24D and JC 24D Sport except: Side-by-side two-seater.

Production status: current; numbers completed 250 (total of JC 31C and JC 31D, includes 68 US-built JC 31C), 28 (JC 31B, all US production), NC (other dual US versions).

GENERAL - Ultralair has developed the two-seater *Weedhopper* along parallel lines to the solo machine, substituting a liquid-cooled Rotax 462 for the fickle Chotiah 460 to create the *JC 31C,* and retaining it for the latest

1985 model, the *JC 31D*, which differs from the single-surface *JC 31C* by having 60% double-surface, a reinforced structure, and superior finish.

Price (all figures include 18.6% VAT) is 55,000FF complete, including instrumentation and transport cover; a 16 h kit is also available, using identical parts but adding an integral windscreen. Options are as for the *JC 24D*, plus: 64 hp Rotax 532 4500FF, reserve fuel tank 1220FF, floats and fixings 11,500FF, retractable tricycle undercarriage (for use with floats to create an amphibian) 8500FF.

Agricultural equipment is also available, a complete set of spraying gear costing 40,612FF, including a 15.9 US gal (13.2 Imp gal, 60 litre) chemical tank, which can be replaced by a 29.1 US gal tank (24.2 Imp gal, 110 litre) for 1400FF. The spray system and its pump can spray 0.5-5.3 US gal/acre (0.4-4.4 Imp gal/acre, 5-50 litre/hectare).

EXTERNAL DIMENSIONS & AREAS - See *JC 24D* and *JC 24D Sport* except: Length overall 17.4 ft, 5.30 m. Height overall 6.3 ft, 1.90 m. Wing span 30.5 ft, 9.30 m. Sweepback 2.7°. Tailplane span 8.0 ft, 2.44 m. Fin height 1.9 ft, 0.57 m. Total wing area 185 ft^2, 17.2 m^2. Rudder area 8.9 ft^2, 8.3 m^2. Aspect ratio 5.0/1. Wheel track 4.6 ft, 1.40 m. Wheelbase 4.4 ft, 1.34 m.

POWER PLANT - Rotax 462 engine. Max power 52 hp at 6700 rpm. Propeller diameter and pitch 59 inch x 15°, 1.50 m x 15°. Gear reduction, ratio 2.6/1. Max static thrust NC. Power per unit area 0.28 hp/ft^2, 3.0 hp/m^2. Fuel capacity 5.3 US gal, 4.4 Imp gal, 20.0 litre.

WEIGHTS & LOADINGS - Empty weight 362 lb, 164 kg. Max take-off weight 905 lb, 410 kg. Payload 543 lb, 246 kg. Max wing loading 4.89 lb/ft^2, 23.8 kg/m^2. Max power loading 17.4 lb/hp, 7.9 kg/hp. Load factors +5.0, -2.0 recommended; +6.0, -3.0 ultimate.

PERFORMANCE* - Max level speed 59 mph, 95 kph. Never exceed speed 75 mph, 120 kph. Max cruising speed 50 mph, 80 kph. Economic cruising speed 40 mph, 65 kph. Stalling speed 24 mph, 39 kph. Max climb rate at sea level 590 ft/min, 3.0 m/s. Min sink rate 690 ft/min at 37 mph, 3.5 m/s at 60 kph. Best glide ratio with power off 6.5/1 at 36 mph, 58 kph. Take-off distance 130 ft, 40 m. Landing distance 130 ft, 40 m. Service ceiling 9840 ft, 3000 m. Range at average cruising speed 68 mile, 110 km. Noise level 65 dB at 490 ft, 150 m.

*Under the following test conditions - Airfield altitude 279 ft, 85 m. Ground temperature 57°F, 14°C. Ground pressure 1015 mB. Ground windspeed 9 mph, 15 kph. Test payload 386 lb, 175 kg.

WONDER MUDRY

Mudry Aviation, aerodrome, 27300 Bernay. Prop rietor: Auguste Mudry. Wonder, 77 rue des Rosiers, 93403 Saint-Oouen; tel (1) 257 1150; tx 280340 F. Proprietor: M Grimalds.

WONDER MUDRY *LE TROPIQUE*

(Three-axis)

Side-by-side two-seat single-engined biplane with conventional three-axis control. Wings have unswept leading and trailing edges, and constant chord; two-fin tail. Pitch control by elevator on tail; yaw control by fin-mounted rudder; roll control by half-span ailerons; control inputs through stick for pitch/roll and pedals for yaw. Cantilever wings; wing profile NACA Series 23 modified; 100% double-surface. Undercarriage has four wheels in tail-dragger formation; suspension NC on tailwheels and glass-fibre suspension on main wheels. Push-right go-right tailwheel steering connected to yaw control. Brakes on main wheels. Glass-fibre/carbon-fibre/Kevlar airframe, totally enclosed. Engine mounted between wings, driving pusher propeller. Honeycomb composite construction.

Production status: see text.

GENERAL - The association between the multinational Wonder company and Auguste Mudry, the well-known builder of the *CAP-10, 20* and *21* aerobatic planes, appears to have come to an early end. Readers of our first edition will recall that this co-operation led to the construction of a three-axis side-by-side two-seater microlight prototype which was destined to take the three-cylinder radial JPX PAL1300.

At the time of writing, this engine, which develops 52 hp at 3200 rpm, had yet to become available, while for its part the *Tropique* prototype was destroyed during one of its first flights after a severe flutter appeared in the tailplane. Fortunately for the test pilot the problem surfaced during take-off and he escaped unhurt.

This interesting project appears to have been taken no further and we have received no information since the accident; under the circumstances we are omitting our data paragraphs in this instance.

ZENITH

Zenith Aviation SA, Groupe Matra, 19 rue Lavoisier, 92000 Nanterre; tel (1) 725 9022; tx 610166 F. Factory: boulevard Sagnat, BP3, 42230 Roche-la-Moliere; tel (77) 90 0611; tx 330139 F. Director general: Stanislas Durand. Export manager: R Granger.

Italian agent: Nanni (see Italian section).

US agent: Joseph Fleming, 50 Coconut Row, Suite 212, Palm Beach, Florida 33480.

Other countries: OFEMA, 58 avenue Marceau, 75008 Paris; tel (1) 720 7117.

Military enquiries: H de Beaufort, 5 Villa Mozart, 75016 Paris, tel (1) 524 0533.

ZENITH
BAROUDEUR LOISIRS and BAROUDEUR AGRICOLE

(Three-axis)

Side-by-side two-seat single-engined high-wing monoplane with conventional three-axis control. Wing has unswept leading and trailing edges, and constant chord; cruciform tail. Pitch control by elevator on tail; yaw control by fin-mounted rudder; roll control by 66%-span ailerons; control inputs through stick for pitch/roll and pedals for yaw. Wing braced from above by kingpost and

cables, from below by cables; wing profile NC; 100% double-surface. Undercarriage has three wheels in tri-cycle formation; rubber suspension on nosewheel and rubber/axle-flex suspension on main wheels. Push-right go-right nosewheel steering connected to yaw control. No brakes. Aluminium-alloy tube airframe, partially enclosed. Engine mounted at wing height, driving tractor propeller.

Production status: current, over 100 completed.

A Baroudeur Loisirs *aloft over the flatlands of northern Italy, where it is imported by the Nanni company. Inset shows* Baroudeur Agricole *at work.*

GENERAL - Roland Magallon was one of the first hang gliders in France and through his Veliplane company became one of Europe's biggest manufacturers. But the company, ceased production early in 1985 and Roland quit as president of the ultralight manufacturers' association, of whose formation he had been a prime mover. Best known for his popularisation of the trike - his machines were the first to go into serious production - construction of the *Baroudeur* meant that Roland became the first manufac-turer in the world to offer hang gliders, weight-shift ultralights and one- and two-seat three-axis machines, albeit under two different banners as Veliplane handled the hang gliders and trikes, while a separate company, Aeronautic 2000, was formed by Magallon and Hubert de Beaufort in 1981 to distribute the *Baroudeur*.
Roland is currently concentrating on training and aerial work at Veliplane Club on Meaux/Esbly and Persan-Beaumont airfields, so this fiery character is still, we are happy to say, involved with the sport.
Designed by Roland and Philippe Tisserand (see separate listing), the aircraft was initially made in both solo and two-seat form, but production of the single-seater - flight-tested

in June 1982 *Pilote Prive* - ceased in summer '83. Since September 1983, Zenith has made the two-seater under licence from Aeronautic 2000 and enjoys worldwide marketing rights. A subsidiary of Solex, itself a part of the Matra group, Zenith employs 250 and specialises in high-technology aerospace work, especially light alloy forgings. Zenith has genuinely 'productionised' the *Baroudeur,* so that every one off the line is the same as the last. Drawing on its general and military aviation experience, Zenith offers a well stocked spares service, backed by service bulletins, and in March '84 started work on the airworthi-ness calculations necessary for the *Baroudeur's* approval under the French ultralight manufacturers' association scheme, successfully completing stringent static and fly-ing tests the following month.
An indication of its abilities came in the '84 Tour de Paris, when three machines were among just seven out of 22 starters to finish, one winning its category, as reported in *UlmMag* November '84. The contest covered a 620 mile (1000 km) triangle with pilots allowed only refuelling stops.

Intermediate landings, ground support or radio contact were prohibited, quite a challenge in the very poor weather of that May.

Many readers will regret the emergence of the ultralight as a military machine, but our book would be less than complete if we did not record the fact. Following successful 'live' rocket-launching tests at 30-1000 ft (10-300 m) with targets 2600 ft (800 m) away, a military version of the *Baroudeur* has gone on sale, using 89 mm ground-to-air missiles capable of piercing 2.4 ft (70 mm) armour or of showering 1600 steel pellets through a 130 ft (40 m) arc - and it costs 1200 times less than a conventional fighter. There is an agricultural version too, with 41 ft (12.5 m) spray booms equipped with 20 nozzles and fed by a 19.8 US gal tank (16.6 Imp gal, 75 litre).

The aircraft occupies only 5.2x6.6 ft (1.6x2.0 m), while the wing folds down to a 10 inch x 19.8 ft (25 cm x 6 m) cylinder for roof rack transport. New for the '85 *Baroudeurs* is the gear-reduction liquid-cooled Rotax 462, more powerful than the 50 hp Robin EC44PM, which along with other Rotax units is still an option. Our data below refers to the standard machine, the *Baroudeur Loisirs,* which costs 57,000FF ready to fly or 50,000FF as a kit; the crop-spraying *Baroudeur Agricole* comes fully equipped for 95,000FF. Military prices on demand.

Options: *Flotabilite* version with Fayet floats, mountings and steering 11,800FF; fabric/polyester pod and windscreen 5000FF; two supplementary fuel tanks inside wings 1900FF; mudguards for main wheels 500FF; instruments as required.

EXTERNAL DIMENSIONS & AREAS - Length overall 19.7 ft, 6.00 m. Height overall 8.2 ft, 2.5 m. Wing span 36.1 ft, 11.0 m. Constant chord 5.1 ft, 1.55 m. Dihedral 2°. Sweepback 0°. Tailplane span 8.0 ft, 2.45 m. Fin height 3.0 ft, 0.90 m. Total wing area 183 ft², 17.0 m². Total aileron area 16.1 ft², 1.50 m². Fin area 4.3 ft², 0.40 m². Rudder area 9.7 ft², 0.90 m². Tailplane area 15.6 ft², 1.45 m². Total elevator area 9.1 ft², 0.85 m². Aspect ratio 7.5/1. Wheel track 5.2 ft, 1.60 m. Wheelbase NC. Nosewheel diameter overall 11 inch, 28 cm. Main wheels diameter overall 14 inch, 35 cm.

POWER PLANT - Rotax 462 engine. Max power 52 hp at NC rpm. Propeller diameter and pitch 39x20 inch, 1.00x0.5 m. Gear reduction, ratio 2.6/1. Max static thrust 331 lb, 150 kg. Power per unit area 0.28 hp/ft², 3.1 hp/m². Fuel capacity 5.3 US gal, 4.4 Imp gal, 20.0 litre.

WEIGHTS & LOADINGS - Empty weight 364 lb, 165 kg. Max take-off weight 762 lb, 345 kg. Payload 397 lb, 180 kg. Max wing loading 4.16 lb/ft², 20.3 kg/m². Max power loading 14.7 lb/hp, 6.6 kg/hp. Load factors +6.0, -2.5 recommended; NC ultimate.

PERFORMANCE* - Max level speed 62 mph,100 kph. Never exceed speed 75 mph, 120 kph. Max cruising speed 56 mph, 90 kph. Economic cruising speed 37 mph, 60 kph. Stalling speed 29 mph, 46 kph. Max climb rate at sea level 590 ft/min, 3.0 m/s. Min sink rate 350 ft/min at 44 mph, 1.8 m/s at 70 kph. Best glide ratio with power off 7/1 at 44 mph, 70 kph. Take-off distance 130 ft, 40 m. Landing distance 130 ft, 40 m. Service ceiling 14,760 ft, 4500 m. Range at average cruising speed 93 mile, 150 km. Noise level NC.

*Under the following test conditions - Airfield altitude 0 ft, 0 m. Ground temperature 59°F, 15°C. Ground pressure 1013 mB. Ground windspeed 0 mph, 0 kph. Test payload 397 lb, 180 kg.

ZODIAC

Zodiac Micro-Aviation, 58 boulevard Galliene, 92130 Issy-les-Moulineaux; tel (1) 554 9280; tx 270569 F. President: Jean-Francois Perard.

ZODIAC *ULTRASTAR*

(Three-axis)

Summary as Kolb UltraStar (see US section) except: rubber suspension on tailwheel and suspension NC on main wheels. Optional brakes on main wheels. Optional pod.

Production status: current, 130 completed.

GENERAL - Best known perhaps for its famous inflatable canoes, the Zodiac group comprises a number of subsidiaries in the leisure and survival equipment fields. As well as being France's major manufacturer of civilian and military parachutes, Zodiac also makes runway over-run and aircraft carrier arrester nets, dirigibles and parts for ejector seats. Group companies include Zodiac Espace, Astral Marine, Aerazur-EFA, Parachutes de France and Sevylor International, plus subsidiaries in North America, Argentina and major European countries.

In fact Zodiac can fairly claim to be the oldest ultralight firm still in business, for in 1909 it was already building aeroplanes whose characteristics and performance would classify them today as ultralights. So in a sense they were turning the clock back when in April 1983 Zodiac startled the ultralight world with the announcement that it was licensed to build and market Homer Kolb's three-axis *UltraStar* (see US section) throughout the whole world, barring North America.

Since then this aircraft has been built in France on a proper production line and with consistent quality, and has done much to restore the image of the sport after the disastrous '83 French Grand Prix and subsequent slump. Zodiac has a name to maintain, and took on the project with great seriousness; the appearance of firms of unquestionable reputation has combined with sound training methods and higher manufacturing standards to make the media and public reconsider their view that microlighting was a high risk game of minority interest.

Much of the credit for this dynamic but responsible approach must go to Zodiac's Jean-Francois Perard; thanks to him and to his counterparts at Zenith and other top-notch companies, the public can enjoy the beneficial aspects of general aviation without being burdened with the sort of constraint that would be difficult to accept in a leisure activity. Impeccable after-sales service and proper service bulletins are two results of this commitment; another is Jean-Francois' policy of only enlisting dealers who already have a proven track record in general aviation.

Zodiac did a lot of research on the *UltraStar* in the process of production engineering its manufacture (after discovering that the US version required no less than 350 qualified man-hours to complete!), and then subjected the result to an exacting series of flying and static tests even though the original has a proven record. Aided by a switch from Cuyuna ULII-02 to Rotax 377 power, this approach has made the latest version of the French-built *UltraStar* one of the best three-axis machines around, very pleasant to fly and with control co-ordination comparable with the best lightplanes.

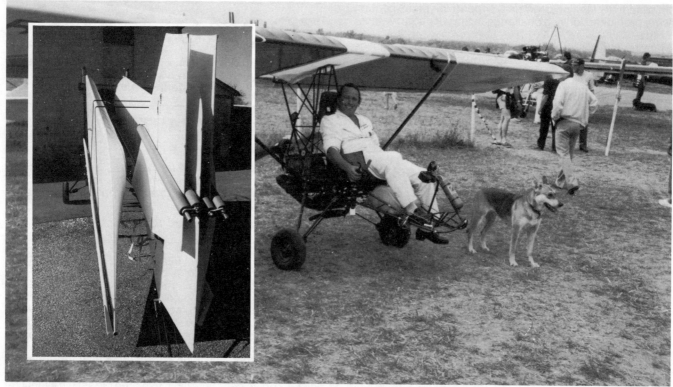

Flashback to summer '84, as the then company test pilot, Bernard Denambride, demonstrates the Ultrastar; dog is optional. Inset shows aircraft ready for transport.

Zodiac president Jean-Francois Perard (right) and M Prignol try the company's latest creation, the Twinstar.

Moreover, it remains one of the easiest ultralights to rig, requiring only about 10 min for one person, and being portable on a specially designed trailer.

Because the aircraft's chrome-molybdenum steel structure requires argon- welding, which the company does not consider within the capabilities of the average homebuilder, no kits are available. Price ready to fly is 58,850FF. Options: glass-fibre pod with tilting windscreen for ease of access, 2350FF; floats with mountings, steering etc, 11,800FF; special trailer, 5000FF; brakes, NC.

EXTERNAL DIMENSIONS & AREAS - Length overall 19.8 ft, 6.05 m. Height overall 5.4 ft, 1.64 m. Wing span 27.7 ft, 8.44 m. Constant chord 5.5 ft, 1.68 m. Dihedral 1°. Sweepback 0°. Tailplane span 7.6 ft, 2.32 m. Fin height 4.6 ft, 1.39 m. Total wing area 145 ft², 13.5 m². Total aileron area 32.3 ft², 0.30 m². Fin area 5.3 ft², 0.49 m². Rudder area 6.4 ft², 0.59 m². Tailplane area 9.2 ft², 0.85 m². Total elevator area 9.7 ft², 0.90 m². Aspect ratio 5.3/1. Wheel track 4.9 ft, 1.50 m. Wheelbase 16.5 ft, 5.04 m. Tailwheel diameter overall 6 inch, 15 cm. Main wheels diameter overall 16 inch, 40 cm.

POWER PLANT - Rotax 377 engine. Max power 35 hp at 6500 rpm. Propeller diameter and pitch 50x31 inch, 1.27x0.80 m. Multi V-belt reduction, ratio 2.0/1. Max static thrust NC. Power per unit area 0.24 hp/ft², 2.6 hp/m². Fuel capacity 5.3 US gal, 4.4 Imp gal, 20.0 litre.

WEIGHTS & LOADINGS - Empty weight 276 lb, 125 kg. Max take-off weight 551 lb, 250 kg. Payload 276 lb, 125 kg. Max wing loading 3.80 lb/ft², 18.5 kg/m². Max power loading 15.7 lb/hp, 7.1 kg/hp. Load factors +4.0, -2.0 recommended; +6.5, -3.0 ultimate.

PERFORMANCE* - Max level speed 75 mph, 120 kph. Never exceed speed 81 mph, 130 kph. Max cruising speed 75 mph, 120 kph. Economic cruising speed 50 mph, 80 kph. Stalling speed 25 mph, 40 kph. Max climb rate at sea level 980 ft/min, 5.0 m/s. Min sink rate 300 ft/min at 37 mph, 1.5 m/s at 60 kph. Best glide ratio with power off 13/1 at 40 mph, 65 kph. Take-off distance 130 ft, 40 m. Landing distance 165 ft, 50 m. Service ceiling 9840 ft, 3000 m. Range at average cruising speed 155 mile, 250 km. Noise level 59** dB at 490 ft, 150 m.

*Under the following test conditions - Airfield altitude 0 ft, 0 m. Ground temperature 59°F, 15°C. Ground pressure 1013 mB. Ground windspeed 0 mph, 0 kph. Test payload 551 lb, 250 kg.

**With three-blade propeller.

ZODIAC *TWINSTAR*

(Three-axis)

Summary as Kolb UltraStar (see US section) except: Side-by-side two-seater. Rubber suspension on tailwheel and suspension NC main wheels. Optional brakes on main wheels. Pod fitted.

Production status: see text.

GENERAL - Zodiac's side-by-side two-seat version of the *UltraStar,* the *TwinStar,* had just appeared on the market

at the time of writing, though it is not a new design, as we explain under Kolb *TwinStar* (see US section).

Built in France to the same standards as its single-seat counterpart, the aircraft also shares its technology, with undercarriage of chrome molybdenum steel tubes, and wings of rivetted Duralumin covered with heat-shrunk Dacron. The main fuselage boom, engine mounts and seats use 5 inch (127 mm) 6061T6 aluminium-alloy.

The aircraft was due to have its French launch at Le Bourget air show in June 1985.

Price, assembled and test-flown and complete with pod, is 80,000FF.

EXTERNAL DIMENSIONS & AREAS - See Zodiac *UltraStar* except: Length overall 20.3 ft, 6.05 m. Height overall 5.9 ft, 1.80 m. Wing span 30.2 ft, 9.20 m. Dihedral 2°. Total wing area 161 ft^2, 15.0 m^2. Aspect ratio 5.6/1. Wheelbase NC. Tailwheel diameter overall NC.

POWER PLANT - Rotax 447 engine. Max power 40 hp at 7000 rpm. Propeller diameter and pitch 66xNC inch, 1.68xNC m. Gear reduction, ratio 2.6/1. Max static thrust NC. Power per unit area 0.25 hp/ft^2, 2.7 hp/m^2. Fuel capacity 5.3 US gal, 4.4 Imp gal, 20.0 litre.

WEIGHTS & LOADINGS - Empty weight 320 lb, 145 kg. Max take-off weight 871 lb, 395 kg. Payload 551 lb, 250 kg. Max wing loading 5.41 lb/ft^2, 26.3 kg/m^2. Max power loading 21.8 lb/hp, 9.9 kg/hp. Load factors +4.0, -2.0 recommended; +6.5, -3.0 ultimate.

PERFORMANCE* - Max level speed 81 mph, 130 kph. Never exceed speed 93 mph, 150 kph. Max cruising speed 75 mph, 120 kph. Economic cruising speed 50 mph, 80 kph. Stalling speed 31 mph, 50 kph. Other data NC.

*Under the following test conditions - Airfield altitude 0 ft, 0 m. Ground temperature 59°F, 15°C. Ground pressure 1013 mB. Ground windspeed 0 mph, 0 kph. Test payload NC.

Great Britain

Researched by Norman Burr, Editor of Flightline, magazine of the British Microlight Aircraft Association

Eastern Airsports HG&MC

A busy scene at the start of the 1984 Norfolk Air Race, with Dick Clegg's Mainair Tri-Flyer/Southdown *Sprint in the foreground and a Skyhook* Pixie *behind.*

Suddenly, we're respectable!

by Norman Burr

Although microlight aircraft are evolving along different lines in different countries, there seems to be a remarkably consistent pattern to the evolution of the sport itself. First comes the pioneering period, when brave souls take to the air in untried machinery, usually out of the public eye. Second comes a time of explosive growth, when veteran and novice alike sample this new form of flight, often without suitable training, and sooner or later a rash of accidents results. The third phase - being pilloried by the media - follows promptly, and usually creates sufficient public pressure to precipitate phase four, a flood of often ill-conceived regulations. If you are lucky, there is a phase five, recovery into a safe and well organised sport.

Britain can't claim to be a pioneering ultralight country as far as machinery is concerned - our early trikes were inspired by the French and most of the rest were American imports - but we have set the pace as far as evolution is concerned, having the unhappy distinction of reaching phase two - the rash of accidents - earlier than anyone else, thanks to crashes of the ill-fated *Scorpion* in 1982. France had its crisis year in '83, with the public outcry over the deaths in the French Grand Prix, and the US in '84, following the infamous *Twenty-Twenty* television programme.

Now, two years after the *Scorpion* nearly killed our sport, we are entering phase five - and it feels good. The schools are busy, the number of license holders is growing, and the choice of models is steadily increasing as one by one the microlights filter through the sieve of airworthiness regulations. Things are still far from perfect, but if we haven't yet hit that strong thermal we are at least clear of the sink.

The problems that remain centre around one word: airworthiness. Ever since March '83 when the Civil Aviation Authority (CAA) published its first draft of *BCAR Section S,* the microlight airworthiness regulations, there have been two separate problems - how to deal with new machines, and how to deal with existing ones, the cut-off date between the two having been fixed at 1 January 1984. Anything manufactured after that date must carry a permit to

▷ fly before it can legally take-off. This doesn't mean that the CAA inspects each individual aircraft; instead, a type approval system is operated, where the manufacturer must demonstrate that one sample machine complies with *Section S* to the satisfaction of the CAA. Once the sample machine has complied, the manufacturer itself must have its premises and production methods inspected by the authority, to prove that it is capable of producing aircraft which consistently match the quality and characteristics of the sample machine. Then and only then may the manufacturer produce and sell replicas of the sample machine; each example must be the subject of an individual application for a permit to fly, but this is normally only a formality once the type has been approved.

The system sounds unwieldy, and it is, but it does work provided the manufacturer has enough time and money to undertake the rigorous testing and even more rigorous paperwork required. And there lay the rub for several British manufacturers; at the very time when they needed a good cash flow to fund the airworthiness programme on their machines, the public held back even from placing deposits, waiting to see which aircraft made the grade. Starting from scratch, it can take typically 12-18 months and £30,000 to get type approval, and if you have neither the cash nor a roaring export trade to rely on in the meantime, you go broke. MBA, manufacturers of the *Tiger Cub,* are absent from this edition for just that reason, and they are not the only example.

However, trike manufacturers have withstood the pressures much better than fixed-wing builders, firstly because their hang-gliding activities often give them a relatively secure financial base, and secondly because the simplicity of a trike means that the stress analysis and testing work is far easier and cheaper. They have also been greatly helped by the absence of suitable three-axis trainers, whose designers are finding it extremely difficult to satisfy the airworthiness requirements while remaining under the 150 kg limit. This conflict of legislation has produced pressure for a French-style 175 kg limit for two-seaters, but until that battle is won most budding pilots will continue to be trained on flexwings and will naturally opt for a trike when they go looking for a machine of their own.

So what happens to the pre-1984 machines? Theoretically, they too have to conform, but since there isn't the faintest hope of proving, by calculation or demonstration, that for example a Chrysler *Eagle* will take +6g and -4g, concessions have had to be made. Each type is being examined on its own merits and eventually will get a permit to fly with strings, the number of strings depending on how far the aircraft deviates from *Section S.* And all aircraft, pre- or post-1984, must have an annual inspection.

Against this background, the £30,000 grant given by the CAA to the BMAA to set up the airworthiness scheme on its behalf seems positively niggardly, and it's not surprising that the cash ran out long before the task was completed. But the system is rolling now, with the inspector network set up and the paperwork churning out, and despite the cash problem there is every prospect that by the end of 1986 the vast majority of UK microlights will have the coveted permit to fly, still issued by the CAA but with the BMAA taking an ever greater self-regulatory role as time goes on.

It's all a far cry from the pioneering days, and the challenge now is not to build an aircraft and fly it, but to build and fly to the highest international standards. There is no better test of this than the first Microlight World Championships, scheduled for France in August 1985, where the British team will be up against the best that the rest of the world can offer. It should prove a fascinating challenge.

For more information on microlights in Great Britain, contact: British Microlight Aircraft Association, New Street, Deddington, Oxford OX5 4SP; tel 0869 38888.

AERO-TECH

Aero-Tech International, Unit 2, Boundary Road, Buckingham Road Industrial Estate, Brackley, Northants NN13 5ES; tel 0280 700290. Directors: Malcolm McBride, Chris Taylor.

South African agent: Aero-Tech International (see separate listing).

Design company: Microknight Aviation Ltd, Fox Chase, 56 Eastfield Road, Westbury on Trym, Bristol BS9 4AG; tel 0272 622852. Directors: Norman Shearer, George Haffey. Designer: Mike Whittaker.

AERO-TECH *MW5 SORCERER*
(Three-axis)

Single-seat single-engined high-wing monoplane with conventional three-axis control. Wing has unswept leading and trailing edges, and constant chord; conventional tail. Pitch control by fully flying tail; yaw control by fully flying rudder; roll control by 43%-span ailerons; control inputs through stick for pitch/roll and pedals for yaw.

Wing braced from below by struts; wing profile NACA 4412; 100% double-surface. Undercarriage has three wheels in tricycle formation; no suspension on any wheels. Push-right go-right nosewheel steering connected to yaw control. No brakes. Aluminium-alloy tube/wood airframe, with pod. Engine mounted at wing height, driving tractor propeller.

Production status: see text.

GENERAL - Though Aero-Tech is a new name to the industry, the people behind it are all well known characters in the microlight business. Malcolm McBride was one of two pilots who attempted a Lands End-John O'Groats marathon flight in one day in 1983 using a Skyriders *Phantom* (see our first edition), getting as far as Inverness before fog stopped further progress. His enthusiasm for the industry thoroughly whetted, he later joined Chris Taylor at British Robin importer Nicklow, and together they formed Aero-Tech to take over Nicklow's engine business and develop it into a fully fledged microlight dealership and school.

In fact the company has become rather more than a dealership, as Aero-Tech has taken over the marketing of the *MW5 Sorcerer,* designed by Mike Whittaker.

Featured in our first edition as the Whittaker *MW5,* this neat, simple machine was originally aimed at home-

Norman Burr

Edwin A Shackleton

Cutaway of the MW5 Sorcerer; insets show (with pod) the prototype as it appeared at Woburn '84 and sporting a Hunting engine, and (without pod) the MW4, whose unusual one-piece tail attracted great interest but was cumbersome to transport.

builders. Together with several colleagues from British Aerospace at Bristol, Mike first turned his attention to the microlight world in 1981. With three designs for heavier aircraft under his belt, Mike created the *MW4*, a one-off which flew well but was plagued with engine trouble from its twin-cylinder Solo.

This machine used a novel one-piece cruciform tail attached to the tail boom by a universal joint, an arrangement not unlike that of Santos-Dumont's 1910 *Demoiselle!* Though it worked well enough, this design proved difficult to break down for transport, and a conventional tail was therefore substituted to create the *MW5*, which made its first public appearance at the BMAA's Woburn Rally in 1984, fitted with a Hunting HS260A engine.

At the time the intention was to produce kits for homebuilders, and the group set up a company, Microknight, to do this, but the advent of airworthiness legislation made the attraction of working through an established organisation like Aero-Tech irresistable.

At the time of writing three *MW5 Sorcerers* are under construction by homebuilders in addition to the prototype already flying. These will be used as 'guinea pigs' to sort out the machine's type approval, whereupon Aero-Tech will probably market complete kits, using a 330 Robin engine and incorporating flying surfaces produced under subcontract by Microknight.

Price is not fixed at the time of writing but is expected to be under £5000 for a complete kit.

EXTERNAL DIMENSIONS & AREAS - Length overall 16.5 ft, 5.03 m. Height overall 8.3 ft, 2.51 m. Wing span 28.0 ft, 8.54 m. Constant chord 5.0 ft, 1.52 m. Dihedral 2°. Sweepback 0°. Tailplane span 8.5 ft, 2.59 m. Rudder height 3.8 ft, 1.16 m. Total wing area 140 ft², 13.0 m². Total aileron area 11.0 ft², 1.02 m². Rudder area 11.4 ft², 1.06 m². Total elevator area 20.0 ft², 1.86 m². Aspect ratio 5.6/1. Wheel track 4.5 ft, 1.37 m. Wheelbase 3.8 ft, 1.16 m. Nosewheel diameter overall 10 inch, 25 cm. Main wheels diameter overall 13 inch, 33 cm.

POWER PLANT - Robin EC34PM engine. Max power 35 hp at 7000 rpm. Propeller diameter and pitch 54x27 inch, 1.37x0.69 m. Toothed-belt reduction, ratio 2.3/1. Max static thrust 200 lb, 91 kg. Power per unit area 0.25 hp/ft², 2.7 hp/m². Fuel capacity 3.6 US gal, 3.0 Imp gal, 13.6 litre.

WEIGHTS & LOADINGS - Empty weight 285 lb, 129 kg. Max take-off weight 530 lb, 240 kg. Payload 245 lb, 111 kg. Max wing loading 3.79 lb/ft², 18.5 kg/m². Max power loading 15.1 lb/hp, 6.9 kg/hp. Load factors +4.0, -2.0 recommended; +6.0, -3.0 ultimate.

PERFORMANCE* - Max level speed 60 mph, 97 kph. Never exceed speed 85 mph, 137 kph. Max cruising speed 55 mph, 88 kph. Economic cruising speed 50 mph, 80 kph.

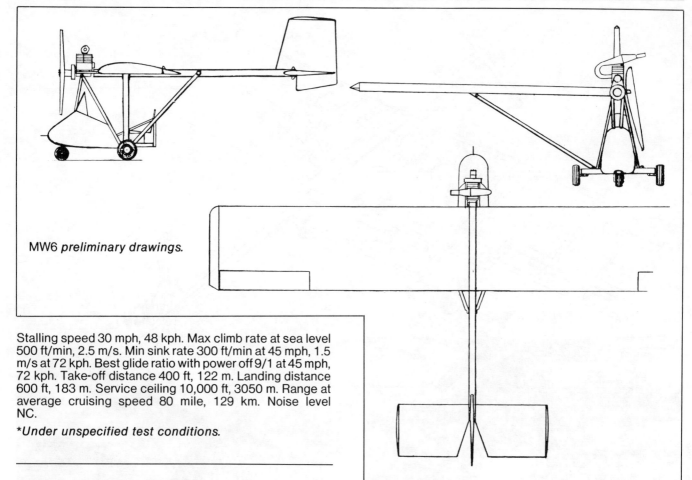

MW6 *preliminary drawings.*

Stalling speed 30 mph, 48 kph. Max climb rate at sea level 500 ft/min, 2.5 m/s. Min sink rate 300 ft/min at 45 mph, 1.5 m/s at 72 kph. Best glide ratio with power off 9/1 at 45 mph, 72 kph. Take-off distance 400 ft, 122 m. Landing distance 600 ft, 183 m. Service ceiling 10,000 ft, 3050 m. Range at average cruising speed 80 mile, 129 km. Noise level NC.

*Under unspecified test conditions.

AERO-TECH *MW6*

(Three-axis)

Summary as MW5 Sorcerer except: Tandem two-seater. 37%-span ailerons. Rubber suspension on main wheels.

Production status: see text.

GENERAL - A logical progression from the *MW5 Sorcerer* and of similar configuration, the *MW6* is Mike Whittaker's two-seater. The *MW6* is larger than the solo aircraft in almost every dimension, but shares a common chord. Power comes from the Robin EC44PM.

In parallel with the *MW5* type-approval programme, three of these dual machines are under construction by home-builders, and in due course kits are likely to be offered by Aero-Tech, though at the time of writing it is too early to say what the price will be. First flights are not expected before October '85, so our performance data below is based on calculations.

Like its single-seat stablemate, the *MW6* will probably acquire a suitably Arthurian name before being marketed, maintaining a tradition started with one of Mike's early designs, the *Excalibur,* and continued with the *Sorcerer* and the Microknight name itself. King Arthur (an early English monarch who came from the Bristol area, for the benefit of non-British readers!) was according to legend a gallant character who performed deeds of great bravery and chivalry, aided by the powerful magic of his sorcerer Merlin. Now Mike and his friends are hoping that the *MW6* will bring a little magic into student pilots' lives...

EXTERNAL DIMENSIONS & AREAS - Length overall 17.5 ft, 5.33 m. Height overall 8.5 ft, 2.59 m. Wing span 32.0 ft, 9.75 m. Constant chord 5.0 ft, 1.52 m. Dihedral 2°. Sweepback 0°. Tailplane span 9.0 ft, 2.74 m. Rudder height 4.5 ft, 1.37 m. Total wing area 160 ft^2, 14.9 m^2. Total aileron area NC. Rudder area 14.0 ft^2, 1.30 m^2. Total elevator area 24.5 ft^2, 2.28 m^2. Aspect ratio 6.4/1. Wheel track 5.0 ft, 1.52 m. Wheelbase 4.0 ft, 1.22 m. Nosewheel diameter overall 10 inch, 25 cm. Main wheels diameter overall 13 inch, 33 cm.

POWER PLANT - Robin EC44PM engine. Max power 50 hp at 7000 rpm. Propeller diameter and pitch 66x27 inch, 1.68x0.69 m. Toothed-belt reduction, ratio 2.6/1. Max static thrust NC. Power per unit area 0.31 hp/ft^2, 3.4 hp/m^2. Fuel capacity NC.

WEIGHTS & LOADINGS - Empty weight 300 lb, 136 kg. Max take-off weight 750 lb, 340 kg. Payload 450 lb, 204 kg. Max wing loading 4.69 lb/ft^2, 22.8 kg/m^2. Max power loading 15.0 lb/hp, 6.8 kg/hp. Load factors +4.0, -2.0 recommended; +6.0, -3.0 ultimate.

PERFORMANCE* - Max level speed *60* mph, *97* kph. Never exceed speed 85 mph, 137 kph. Max cruising speed *55* mph, *88* kph. Economic cruising speed *50* mph, *80* kph. Stalling speed *35* mph, *56* kph. Other data NC.

*Under unspecified test conditions.

AIR PROGRESS INTERNATIONAL

Air Progress International Ltd, Wycombe Air Park, Booker, nr Marlow, Bucks; tel 0494 29432/449810. Chairman and managing director: Phil Read. Other board members: Christopher J Garville (Garville Corp), William McDermitt (Squadron Aviation), S J Horner (Midland Bank), Tony Bianchi.

AIR PROGRESS INTERNATIONAL
SPAD XIII, SE5a and FOKKER D-VII
(Three-axis)

Summary as Squadron Aviation SPAD XIII (see US section).

Production status: see text.

GENERAL - Air Progress International is a company set up by ex-motorcycle racing champion Phil Read to manufacture Squadron Aviation's World War I replicas in Europe.

At the time of writing these American aircraft were being submitted to the British type-approval system and their final specifications were therefore not settled. We understand that British-built machines will be very similar to the US originals, so we are cross-referring our data below to the US section, but readers should note that the versions eventually put on sale in the UK may differ in some details.

The company expects to complete the airworthiness procedures during 1985, but as we write no prices are available.

EXTERNAL DIMENSIONS & AREAS - See appropriate entry under Squadron Aviation (US section).

POWER PLANT - See appropriate entry under Squadron Aviation (US section).

WEIGHTS & LOADINGS - See appropriate entry under Squadron Aviation (US section).

PERFORMANCE - See appropriate entry under Squadron Aviation (US section).

For illustrations of Squadron machines, see front cover and US section.

AMF

AMF Microflight Ltd, Membury Airfield, Lambourn, Berkshire RG16 7TL; tel 0488 72224; tx 848507 MIFLI. Director: Angus Fleming.

AMF *CHEVRON*
(Three-axis)

Side-by-side two-seat single-engined mid-wing mono-plane with conventional three-axis control. Wing has swept forward leading and trailing edges, and tapering chord; conventional tail. Pitch control by elevator on tail;

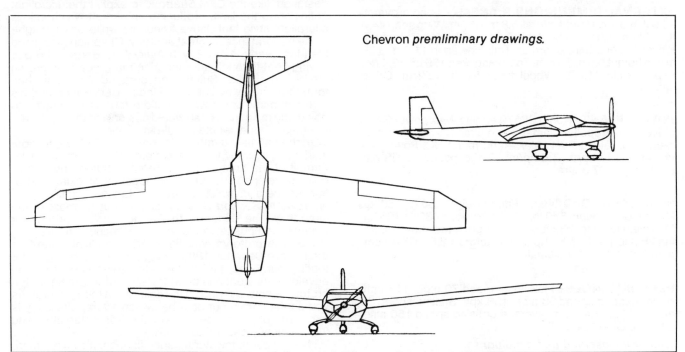

Chevron *premliminary drawings.*

yaw control by fin-mounted rudder; roll control by 39%-span ailerons; control inputs through stick for pitch/roll and pedals for yaw. Cantilever wing; wing profile 16% laminar flow; 100% double-surface. Undercarriage has three wheels in tricycle formation; no suspension on nosewheel and glass-fibre suspension on main wheels. Push-right go-right nosewheel steering connected to yaw control. Nosewheel brake. Composite-construction airframe, totally enclosed. Engine mounted at wing height, driving tractor propeller.

Production status: see text.

GENERAL - The microlight business is full of people who produce promises first and results much later, if at all, so it is refreshing to find a company whose approach is just the opposite. To most microlighters, Angus Fleming is known simply as the British agent for Canadian Lazair, though a few more knowledgeable souls will also be aware that his company is heavily involved with gliding, as its bread and butter is the manufacturer of glider trailers. What is not generally realised is that the company has very quietly spent the last two years developing its own composite-construction two-seater.

At the time of writing - July '85 - only the prototype is flying, but Angus was expecting to satisfy the UK airworthiness requirements within a couple of months, so there is a sporting chance that the aircraft will be a marketing reality by the time you read this. As is to be expected, the Chevron is gliding-oriented, with an aspect ratio of 11/1. It has a distinctive, angular shape and an equally distinctive swept-forward wing, derigging being by wing removal - as on a glider.

Power comes from a four-cylinder electric-start Konig which Angus describes as exceptionally quiet. Flight characteristics are said to be forgiving, as befits a machine intended for training. Little other information is available on this promising newcomer, except that the price will be around £10,000.

EXTERNAL DIMENSIONS & AREAS - Length overall 22.9 ft, 6.99 m. Height overall 5.8 ft, 1.75 m. Wing span 44.0 ft, 13.41 m. Chord at tip 2.0 ft, 0.61 m. Dihedral 5°. Sweep-forward at one-third chord 5°. Tailplane span 11.0 ft, 3.35 m. Fin height 5.8 ft, 1.75 m. Total wing area 176 ft^2, 16.4 m^2. Aspect ratio 11.0/1. Wheel track 5.0 ft, 1.52 m. Other data NC.

POWER PLANT - Konig SD570 engine. Max power 30 hp at NC rpm. Propeller diameter and pitch NC. Toothed-belt reduction, ratio 1.75/1. Max static thrust NC. Power per unit area 0.17 hp/ft^2, 1.8 hp/m^2. Fuel capacity 7.2 US gal, 6.0 Imp gal, 27.3 litre.

WEIGHTS & LOADINGS - Empty weight 330 lb, 150 kg. Max take-off weight 760 lb, 345 kg. Payload 430 lb, 195 kg. Max wing loading 4.32 lb/ft^2, 21.0 kg/m^2. Max power loading 25.3 lb/hp, 11.5 kg/hp. Load factors +2.0, -1.5 recommended; +4.0, -4.0 ultimate.

PERFORMANCE* - Max level speed 70 mph, 113 kph. Never exceed speed 98 mph, 158 kph. Stalling speed 35 mph, 56 kph. Range at average cruising speed 150 mile, 241 km. Other data NC.

*Under unspecified test conditions.

AVIATION COMPOSITES

Aviation Composites, Pound Lane, Thatcham, Newbury, Berkshire RG13 4TQ; tel 0635 69002/69027. Managing director: Malcolm Lawrence.

South African agent: Aviation 2000 (see separate listing).

AVIATION COMPOSITES MERCURY

(Three-axis)

Side-by-side two-seat single-engined mid-wing monoplane with conventional three-axis control. Wing has swept back leading and trailing edges, and tapering chord; no tail, canard wing. Pitch control by elevator on canard; yaw control by tip rudders; roll control by three-quarter span ailerons; control inputs through stick for pitch/roll and pedals for yaw. Cantilever wing; wing profile NC; 100% double-surface. Undercarriage has three wheels in tricycle formation; no suspension on nosewheel and glass-fibre suspension on main wheels. Ground steering by differential braking. Brakes on main wheels. Composite-construction airframe, totally enclosed. Engine mounted above wing, driving pusher propeller.

Production status: prototype.

GENERAL - The greatly missed Colin Chapman, founder of Lotus Cars, left behind many automotive testimonies to his engineering skills, but only one aeronautical legacy - the Mercury.

Conceived by Chapman as long ago as late 1981, it is designed, like the CFM Shadow, to exploit the microlight definition to the limit, producing an aircraft which enjoys microlight-style leglislative freedoms while offering light-plane performance. In great secrecy, Chapman discussed his ideas early in 1982 with Alain-Yves Berger, the pair having kept in touch after meeting many years before on the racing circuits. Suitably encouraged, Chapman then formed a three-way link with Eipper, Bert Rutan, and his own company; Lotus would build a four-stroke engine to power the machine, Rutan would design and test fly the aircraft, and Eipper would handle marketing.

With the untimely death of Chapman in 1983, a question-mark hung over the future of the project, but it survived the turmoil of the post-Chapman reorganisation and is now being developed by Aviation Composites, an existing aviation concern in which Lotus has taken a stake. Type-approval to Section S is envisaged, but as most of the aircraft will be exported this is not such a priority for Aviation Composites as for other UK manufacturers.

The original prototype was flown in the hands of Rutan over the Mojave Desert in 1983, using a two-stroke engine for testing purposes, and in the intervening two years the development work has been transferred to Britain, with a prototype now carrying a UK registration (see picture). As you can see from our data below, structural efficiency is excellent, performance nothing short of remarkable, and fuel efficiency second to none.

With such a mouthwatering specification, it's all the more

Chapman's legacy on display: the prototype Mercury; *inset is of a model, showing general layout.*

frustrating that the aircraft has yet to go on sale. In mid 1984 Lotus engineer Patrick Peal told Norman Burr that it would be available by the end of that year, but at the time of writing (July '85) production was still not under way. There is no doubt that development problems with the engine, which is still very much a Lotus responsibility, are a major cause of the delay, but we are equally confident that the aircraft will eventually reach the market. So much time and prestige has gone into the project that we would be surprised if our third edition still listed the *Mercury* as a prototype.
Price: NC.

EXTERNAL DIMENSIONS & AREAS - Length overall 18.0 ft, 5.49 m. Height overall 5.8 ft, 1.77 m. Wing span 32.5 ft, 9.91 m. Chord at root 4.0 ft, 1.22 m. Chord at tip 2.5 ft, 0.76 m. Dihedral 20°. Sweepback NC. Canard span 13.0 ft, 3.96 m. Canard chord 2.5 ft, 0.76 m. Fin height 3.8 ft, 1.14 m. Total wing area 136.5 ft², 12.7 m². Main wing area 104 ft², 9.7 m². Canard area 32.5 ft², 3.0 m². Total aileron area NC. Total fin area 5.2 ft², 0.48 m². Total rudder area 2.7 ft², 0.25 m². Total elevator area 25.5 ft², 2.34 m². Aspect ratio (of main wing) 10.2/1. Wheel track 6.6 ft, 2.01 m. Wheelbase 5.6 ft, 1.71 m. Nosewheel diameter overall 10 inch, 25 cm. Main wheels diameter overall 15 inch, 38 cm.

POWER PLANT - Lotus Magnum 4.50 engine. Max power 50 hp at 2500 rpm. Propeller diameter and pitch NC. Integral reduction (camshaft drive), ratio 2/1. Max static thrust NC. Power per unit area 0.37 hp/ft², 3.9 hp/m². Fuel capacity 6.0 US gal, 5.0 Imp gal, 22.7 litre.

WEIGHTS & LOADINGS - Empty weight 325 lb, 147 kg. Max take-off weight 800 lb, 363 kg. Payload 475 lb, 215 kg. Max wing loading 5.86 lb/ft², 28.6 kg/m². Max power load-ing 16.0 lb/hp, 7.3 kg/hp. Load factors +4.0, -2.0 recommended; +6.0, -4.0 ultimate.

PERFORMANCE* - Max cruising speed 115 mph, 185 kph. Economic cruising speed 92 mph, 148 kph. Stalling speed 32 mph, 51 kph. Max climb rate at sea level 650 ft/min, 3.3 m/s. Min sink rate 250 ft/min at 52 mph, 1.3 m/s at 84 kph. Best glide ratio with power off 12/1 at 58 mph, 93 kph. Take-off distance 210 ft, 64 m. Landing distance 250 ft, 76 m. Service ceiling 10,000 ft, 3050 m. Range at average cruising speed 300 mile, 483 km. Other data NC.

*Under unspecified test conditions.

AVIATION COMPOSITES *ROVER* (Three-axis)

Side-by-side two-seat single-engined high-wing monoplane with conventional three-axis control. Wing has swept back leading edge, unswept trailing edge, and tapering chord; conventional tail. Pitch control by elevator on tail; yaw control by fin-mounted rudder; roll control by 55%-span ailerons; control inputs through stick for pitch/roll and pedals for yaw. Wing braced from below by struts; wing profile NACA 4415 (root), NACA 4412 (tip); 100% double-surface. Undercarriage has three wheels in tricycle formation; no suspension on nosewheel and glass-fibre suspension on main wheels. Push-right go-right nosewheel steering connected to yaw control; also differential braking. Brakes on main

Outwardly similar to this AES Sky Ranger, the Rover will use a Lotus engine in place of the Hunting unit pictured here.

wheels. Composite-construction fuselage, partially enclosed (total enclosure optional). Engine mounted above wing, driving tractor propeller.

Production status: prototype.

GENERAL - This aircraft bears no relationship whatever to its Chapman-inspired stablemate, and is in fact a derivative of the Striplin *Sky Ranger* (see US section).

In 1981 David Wilson ran a company called Aero & Engineering Services (AES) and acquired the sole European rights to the Striplin *Lone Ranger* and *Sky Ranger* machines, making a number of modifications before putting his own version into production. By increasing the wing section and mounting it more squarely, he improved controllability in adverse weather conditions, and for same reason he increased the size of all the control surfaces, constructing them of wood and fabric rather than with a foam core.

Various engines were offered, including Chryslers, a Zenoah, and a Hunting HS525A, before David decided to design a 'productionised' version and seek proper finance to get the machines into quantity production. Concentrating on the two-seater, he produced a prototype outwardly very similar to the AES *Sky Ranger* but simpler and quicker to build and with provision for the Lotus four-cylinder four-stroke engine. He called it the *Rover* and set up Rover Aviation to build it, closing AES after some 12 aircraft had been built. But the new company never got off the ground due to a series of financial problems, and David went to work instead for Aviation Composites. However, he refused to let the project die, and persuaded his new employer to take it under its wing.

At the time of writing only the prototype exists, and that had yet to fly with a Lotus engine, so production is clearly some way off.

Price: NC.

EXTERNAL DIMENSIONS & AREAS - Length overall 17.0 ft, 5.18 m. Height overall 8.0 ft, 2.44 m. Wing span 36.0 ft, 10.97 m. Chord at root 5.0 ft, 1.52 m. Chord at tip 4.0 ft, 1.22 m. Dihedral 5°. Sweepback 1.5°. Tailplane span 9.0 ft, 2.74 m. Fin height 3.5 ft, 1.07 m. Total wing area 162 ft^2, 15.1 m^2. Total aileron area 16.6 ft^2, 1.54 m^2. Fin area 6.2 ft^2, 0.58 m^2. Rudder area 4.4 ft^2, 0.41 m^2. Tailplane area 10.0 ft^2, 0.93 m^2. Total elevator area 9.1 ft^2, 0.85 m^2. Aspect ratio 8.0/1. Wheel track 5.0 ft, 1.52 m. Wheelbase 4.8 ft, 1.46 m. Nosewheel diameter overall 11 inch, 28cm. Main wheels diameter overall 14 inch, 36 cm.

POWER PLANT - Lotus Magnum 4.50 engine. Max power 50 hp at 2500 rpm. Propeller diameter and pitch 58x42 inch, 1.47x1.07 m. Integral reduction (camshaft drive), ratio 2/1. Max static thrust NC. Power per unit area 0.31 hp/ft^2, 3.3 hp/m^2. Fuel capacity 9.6 US gal, 8.0 Imp gal, 36.3 litre.

WEIGHTS & LOADINGS - Empty weight 330 lb, 150 kg. Max take-off weight 760 lb, 345 kg. Payload 430 lb, 195 kg. Max wing loading 4.69 lb/ft^2, 22.8 kg/m^2. Max power loading 15.2 lb/hp, 6.9 kg/hp. Load factors +4.0, -2.0 recommended; +6.0, -3.0 ultimate.

PERFORMANCE* - Max level speed 85 mph, 137 kph. Never exceed speed 100 mph, 161 kph. Max cruising speed 78 mph, 126 kph. Economic cruising speed 65 mph, 105 kph. Stalling speed 28 mph, 45 kph. Max climb rate at sea level 550 ft/min, 2.8 m/s. Min sink rate 260 ft/min, 1.3 m/s at NC speed. Best glide ratio with power off 15/1 at 39 mph, 63 kph. Take-off distance 210 ft, 64 m. Landing distance 350 ft, 107 m. Service ceiling 10,000 ft, 3050 m. Range at average cruising speed 250 mile, 402 km. Noise level NC.

*Under unspecified test conditions.

CFM

Metal-Fax Ltd t/a Cook Flying Machines, Unit 2D, Eastlands Industrial Estate, Leiston, Suffolk IP16 4LL; tel 0728 832353; tx 987703 METAL-FAX CHACOM G. Managing director: Dave Cook. Sales/marketing manager: T M Plewman. Technical manager: C S Buck.

CFM *SHADOW*

(Three-axis)

Tandem two-seat single-engined high-wing monoplane with conventional three-axis control. Wing has swept back leading edge, swept forward trailing edge, and tapering chord; flaps fitted; two-fin tail. Pitch control by elevator on tail; yaw control by fully flying ventral rudder; roll control by half-span ailerons; control inputs through stick for pitch/roll and pedals for yaw. Wing braced from below by struts; wing profile CFM; 100% double-surface. Undercarriage has three wheels in tricycle formation with additional tailskid; bungee suspension on nose-wheel and glass-fibre suspension on main wheels. Ground steering by differential braking; castoring nose-wheel. Brakes on main wheels. Honeycomb laminate fuselage, totally enclosed. Engine mounted below wing, driving pusher propeller.

Production status: current, 9 completed.

GENERAL - It is very rare for a designer to get an aircraft 'right first time', and even rarer when that machine is a complex high-performance product, but Dave Cook's *Shadow* falls into that category.

Featured in our first edition as a prototype, this remarkable aircraft's chief change during the past two years has been its power plant. Originally flown with a Robin 440 engine, it

later underwent trials with a Rotax 503 and in 1984 entered production with a gear-reduction Rotax 447. Along the way it has collected two official world records - for distance in a straight line (339 miles, 545 km) on 3 April '84 and speed over 3 km (79 mph, 126 kph) on 4 August '83 - and also set an unofficial endurance record of 5 h 40 min.

The *Shadow* is a complex machine, designed to exploit fully the 150 kg microlight weight limit, to offer a performance bridge between tube-and-Dacron microlights and light aircraft. To achieve this, it makes extensive use of modern materials, with honeycomb laminates for the fuselage. Wings use an in-house profile with plywood I-section spars stiffened at the flanges by the addition of a fabricated aluminium-alloy box-section. Foam ribs support plywood leading and glass-fibre trailing edges, the whole wing being covered with Dacron and sealed with dope. Ground steering uses hydraulic disc brakes and a castoring nosewheel.

Originally conceived as a one-plus-one, the aircraft is now sold as a full two-seater, not because the design has changed significantly, but because UK airworthiness regulations - which the aircraft passed in full in May '85 - dictate that any aircraft with two seats must carry a full two-seat payload. When Dave Cook and his team loaded up the *Shadow* accordingly, they were delighted to find that their aircraft was stronger than they thought. The *Shadow* subsequently gained full British type-approval.

One thing the *Shadow* is not is a microlight trainer, for even with flaps the landing and take-off speeds are considerably above the microlight norm. To use a motoring analogy, it is the Ferrari of the air, though unlike the latter it may have practical applications too, as CFM is at the time of writing developing a crop-spraying package for the aircraft. Other options include floats, long-range tank, parachute, and additional instruments.

At £9000 ready to fly, the *Shadow* is far from cheap, but a kit version is promised at £4900 including power pack.

EXTERNAL DIMENSIONS & AREAS - Length overall 21.0 ft, 6.40 m. Height overall 5.7 ft, 1.73 m. Wing span 32.9

Test flying the Shadow *prototype; production aircraft use a gear reduction rather than the belt-drive shown here. Note the disc brakes on the main wheels.*

ft, 10.03 m. Chord at root 5.8 ft, 1.77 m. Chord at tip 4.0 ft, 1.22 m. Dihedral 0°. Sweepback NC. Tailplane span 8.0 ft, 2.44 m. Fin height 2.0 ft, 0.61 m. Total wing area 162 ft², 15.0 m². Total aileron area 16.0 ft², 1.49 m². Fin area 3.0 ft², 0.28 m². Rudder area 8.0 ft², 0.74 m². Tailplane area 11.5 ft², 1.07 m². Total elevator area 8.0 ft², 0.74 m². Aspect ratio 6.7/1. Wheel track 5.0 ft, 1.52 m. Wheelbase 6.0 ft, 1.83 m. Nosewheel diameter overall 10 inch, 25 cm. Main wheels diameter overall 13 inch, 33 cm.

POWER PLANT - Rotax 447 engine. Max power 40 hp at 6500 rpm. Propeller diameter and pitch 51x38 inch, 1.30x0.97 m. Gear reduction, ratio 2.6/1. Max static thrust 240 lb, 109 kg. Power per unit area 0.25 hp/ft², 2.7 hp/m². Fuel capacity 6.0 US gal, 5.0 Imp gal, 22.7 litre.

WEIGHTS & LOADINGS - Empty weight 331 lb, 150 kg. Max take-off weight 732 lb, 332 kg. Payload 401 lb, 182 kg. Max wing loading 4.52 lb/ft², 22.1 kg/m². Max power loading 18.3 lb/hp, 8.3 kg/hp. Load factors +4.0, -2.0 recommended; +6.0, -3.0 ultimate.

PERFORMANCE* - Max level speed 95 mph, 153 kph. Never exceed speed 108 mph, 174 kph. Max cruising speed 75 mph, 121 kph. Economic cruising speed 65 mph, 105 kph. Stalling speed 28 mph, 45 kph. Max climb rate at sea level 800 ft/min, 4.1 m/s. Min sink rate 250 ft/min at 45 mph, 1.3 m/s at 72 kph. Best glide ratio with power off 18/1 at 45 mph, 72 kph. Take-off distance 225 ft, 69 m. Landing distance 200 ft, 60 m. Service ceiling 16,000 ft, 4880 m. Range at average cruising speed 150 mile, 240 km. Noise level 81 dB at 500 ft, 150 m.

*Under the following test conditions - Airfield altitude 105 ft, 32 m. Ground temperature 59°F, 15°C. Ground pressure 1013 mB. Ground windspeed 12 mph, 19 kph. Test payload 371 lb, 168 kg.

FLIGHT RESEARCH

Flight Research, Rochester House, Ashfield Crescent, Ross-on-Wye, Herefordshire HR9 5PH; tel 0989 67678. Designer/test pilot: Rupert Sweet-Escott. Production manager: Mike Evans. Storeman: Eric Caulfield. Secretary: Louise McCarthy.

Asian agent: Ray Wijerwardene, AG Aero Reseach Ltd, 133 Dharmapala, Mawatha, Colombo 7, Sri Lanka.

Spanish agent: James Machin (address from manufacturer).

Swedish agent: Flight Production, Frojavan IOC, 83200 Froson. Contact: Robert Krockmar.

FLIGHT RESEARCH/PEGASUS
NOMAD 425F/TYPHOON S4 MEDIUM
(Weight-shift)

Single-seat single-engined flex-wing aircraft with weight-shift control. Rogallo wing with keel pocket. Pilot suspended below wing in trike unit, using bar to control pitch and roll/yaw by altering relative positions of trike unit and wing. Wing braced from above by kingpost and cables, from below by cables; floating cross-tube construction with 55% double-surface enclosing cross-tube; preformed ribs. Undercarriage has three wheels in tricycle formation; no suspension on any wheels. Push-right go-right nosewheel steering independent from aerodynamic controls. Nosewheel brake. Aluminium-alloy tube trike unit, completely open. Engine mounted below wing, driving pusher propeller.

Production status: current, 9 completed (total of all Nomad single-seat variants).

GENERAL - Though only 23, Rupert Sweet-Escott has packed a great deal of flying experience into his life, first taking to the air at the age of 13 and later working for Breen Hang Gliders, Birdman Sports and Solar Wings, with a period at college inbetween.

He left Solar Wings in November '81 to build his own trike units, which he mates to the Pegasus *Typhoon S4 Medium* wing - an understandable choice, as this is the power version of the free-flight Solar Wings *Typhoon S4 Medium* with which he is so familiar.

Rupert's trikes are probably the most individual machines on the market, and are aimed less at power pilots than at those who regard an engine as a necessary evil, for instance hang gliders who have the misfortune to live in flat country. The pilot flies in the prone position, to minimise drag, and has an in-flight restart to allow peaceful soaring. The first *Nomads* were the most unusual of all: a Solo-engined triple-pole machine with tail-dragger undercarriage, the tailwheel being steered by the pilot's feet, followed by the first production model, the *Nomad 425F*, which replaced the Solo with a JPX PUL425 but was otherwise similar. Rupert finds the JPX produces enough thrust

Rupert poses proudly with his Solo-engined prototype.

even at tickover to maintain level flight, which gives the machine exceptional range, a point he is planning to prove during 1985 with a long-distance attempt starting from northern Scotland.

Although at the time of writing the *Nomad 425* is still available, it is being phased out in favour of the *Nomad 425F* (to which our data below refers), a much neater monopole design with conventional tricycle undercarriage (though still with push-right go-right steering operated by the feet), revised engine mountings and an integral prone harness. This aircraft is offered at the same price as the tail-dragger version (£1294 without wing but otherwise ready to fly), with kits and plans available later.

Crash survivability in the *Nomad 425F* is said to be very good, thanks to an integral harness which hinges to provide easy access and is said to minimise the risk of spinal injuries. Although the aircraft is under the 70 kg limit at which UK airworthiness regulations become applicable, the company intends to take it through the type-approval system anyway, and similarly intends to apply for CAA-approval as a microlight manufacturer. These moves reflect Rupert's desire to dispel any impression that his *Nomads* are simply latter-day powered hang-gliders, with all the pitch stability problems which these early machines experienced. In fact he tells us they are actually more pitch stable power-on than off.

Other company plans include research into carbon-fibre structures and the development of its own novel Rogallo with internal bracing, for free- or power-flight.

EXTERNAL DIMENSIONS & AREAS - Length overall 11.0 ft, 3.35 m. Wing span 32.5 ft, 9.91 m. Chord at root 8.0 ft, 2.44 m. Chord at tip 3.3 ft, 1.01 m. Dihedral 0°. Nose angle 122°. Total wing area 166 ft^2, 15.4 m^2. Aspect ratio 6.4/1. Wheel track 5.2 ft, 1.60 m. Wheelbase 5.9 ft, 1.80 m. Nosewheel diameter overall 13 inch, 32 cm. Main wheels diameter overall 13 inch, 32 cm. Other data NC.

POWER PLANT - JPX PUL425 engine. Max power 26 hp at 4600 rpm. Propeller diameter and pitch 39x30 inch, 1.00x0.76 m. No reduction. Max static thrust 166 lb, 75 kg.

Power per unit area 0.16 hp/ft^2, 1.69 hp/m^2. Fuel capacity 2.4 US gal, 2.0 Imp gal, 9.1 litre.

WEIGHTS & LOADINGS - Empty weight 137 lb, 62 kg. Max take-off weight 358 lb, 162 kg. Payload 221 lb, 100 kg. Max wing loading 2.16 lb/ft^2, 10.5 kg/m^2. Max power loading 13.8 lb/hp, 6.2 kg/hp. Load factors +4.0, -2.0 recommended; +6.5, -3.0 ultimate.

PERFORMANCE* - Max level speed 51 mph, 82 kph. Never exceed speed 69 mph, 111 kph. Max cruising speed 45 mph, 72 kph. Economic cruising speed 28 mph, 45 kph. Stalling speed 18 mph, 29 kph. Max climb rate at sea level >800 ft/min, >4.1 m/s. Min sink rate 200 ft/min at 22 mph, 1.0 m/s at 35 kph. Best glide ratio with power off 10.5/1 at 28 mph, 45 kph. Take-off distance 45 ft, 14 m. Landing distance 25 ft, 8 m. Service ceiling NC. Range at average cruising speed 140 mile, 225 km. Noise level NC.

*Under the following test conditions - Airfield altitude 0 ft, 0 m. Ground temperature 78°F, 26°C. Ground pressure NC. Ground windspeed 0 mph, 0 kph. Test payload 160 lb, 73 kg.

FLIGHT RESEARCH/PEGASUS
NOMAD TRIBE/TYPHOON S4 LARGE

(Weight-shift)

Summary as Nomad 425F *except: Two-seater. Coil-spring suspension on nosewheel.*

Production status: prototype.

GENERAL - The *Nomad Tribe* is Flight Research's first two-seater, and at the time of writing is only a prototype, with both tandem and side-by-side seating arrangements being tried. It follows the design of the solo machine quite closely, though the undercarriage has been made more forgiving and the engine may be changed for a JPX PAL640 by the time the aircraft reaches production. To cope with the higher payload, the largest version of the *Typhoon S4* is being used.

Prices have not yet been fixed, but options are likely to be as for the *Nomad 425F:* a trailer for £195, self-pivoting aerofoils for the lateral struts at £15 per set including nylon bushes, extra pilot covering, camera brackets and ski attachments.

EXTERNAL DIMENSIONS & AREAS - Length overall 12.8 ft, 3.90 m. Wing span 34.0 ft, 10.36 m. Chord at root 8.5 ft, 2.68 m. Dihedral 0°. Nose angle 122°. Total wing area 180 ft^2, 16.7 m^2. Aspect ratio 6.4/1. Wheel track 5.2 ft, 1.60 m. Wheelbase 5.9 ft, 1.80 m. Nosewheel diameter overall 14 inch, 36 cm. Main wheels diameter overall 14 inch, 36 cm. Other data NC.

POWER PLANT - See *Nomad 425F* except: Power per unit area 0.14 hp/ft^2, 1.6 hp/m^2.

WEIGHTS & LOADINGS - NC.

PERFORMANCE* - Max level speed *62* mph, *100* kph. Never exceed speed *65* mph, *105* kph. Max cruising speed *45* mph, *72* kph. Economic cruising speed *35* mph, *56* kph. Stalling speed 24 mph, 39 kph. Max climb rate at sea level 300 ft/min, 1.5 m/s. Min sink rate 300 ft/min, 1.5 m/s at NC

speed. Best glide ratio with power off *9/1* at *34* mph, *55* kph. Take-off distance 120 ft, 37 m. Landing distance 40 ft, 12 m. Other data NC.

*Under the following test conditions - Airfield altitude 120 ft, 37 m. Ground temperature 45°F, 7°C. Ground pressure NC. Ground windspeed 0 mph, 0 kph. Test payload 340 lb, 154 kg.

FLEXIFORM

Lite Air Industries Ltd t/a Flexiform Sky Sails, Brown Street Mill, Macclesfield SK11 6SA; tel 0625 33382. Director: Mike Hurtley.

FLEXIFORM *DUAL STRIKER TRIKE*

(Weight-shift)

Tandem two-seat single-engined flex-wing aircraft with weight-shift control. Rogallo wing with keel pocket. Pilot suspended below wing in trike unit, using bar to control pitch and roll/yaw by altering relative positions of trike unit and wing. Wing braced from above by kingpost and cables, from below by cables; bowsprit construction with 60% double-surface; preformed ribs. Undercarriage has three wheels in tricycle formation; no suspension on any wheels. Push-right go-left nosewheel steering independent from aerodynamic controls. Optional brakes on main wheels. Aluminium-alloy tube trike unit, with optional pod. Engine mounted below wing, driving pusher propeller.

Production status: see text.

This is the Dual Striker Trike *sold on the UK market until the start of '84. Since then the machine has been for export only, with a later-style wing of smaller area.*

GENERAL - Though one of the best known companies in the British microlight industry, Flexiform has actually produced very few complete aircraft, as by far the majority of its output is *Strikerlight, Striker,* and *Dual Striker* wings for other trike unit manufacturers. However, a small number - approximately 20 - of complete two-seat trikes have been built since 1981, when the *Dual Striker Trike* was first put into production. The aircraft was actually the first tandem two-seat trike generally available in the UK, and used a 440 Robin power pack supplied by Mainair and identical to that used on the Rochdale company's own machines. This was fitted to a robust duopole trike unit mated to a *Dual Striker* wing.

With sales of wings far outstripping those of complete aircraft, the company has decided to get the wing through the airworthiness regulations first, with the result that the complete *Dual Striker Trike* is no longer available on the home market. However, it is still offered for export at an unspecified price.

A long list of changes have been made to the wing for *Section S* purposes, including triple-tube leading edges and uprights, an extended bowsprit reinforced with a nylon swivel, extra top side rigging, back rigging bolted to the keel sides, a new sail shape with reduced area, higher aspect ratio and more washout, a larger keel pocket and 'tail', more double-surface area (now a genuine 60%), a fully enclosed wing-tip compressive strut, a higher lift profile, 'never-kinks' at all rigging attachment points, and velcro fasteners that are easy to replace.

EXTERNAL DIMENSIONS & AREAS - Length overall 16.2 ft, 4.94 m. Height overall *14.0* ft, *4.27* m. Wing span 37.3 ft, 11.36 m. Nose angle 149°. Total wing area 214 ft²,

Geoff Hayden

19.9 m². Aspect ratio 6.5/1. Wheel track 5.8 ft, 1.77 m. Wheelbase 6.6 ft, 2.01 m. Nosewheel diameter overall 15 inch, 38 cm. Main wheels diameter overall 16 inch, 41 cm. Other data NC.

POWER PLANT - Robin EC44 engine. Max power 50 hp at 6800 rpm. Propeller diameter and pitch 62x27 inch, 1.58x0.70 m. Toothed-belt reduction, ratio 2.3/1. Max static thrust 275 lb, 125 kg. Power per unit area 0.23 hp/ft², 2.5 hp/m². Fuel capacity 4.8 US gal, 4.0 Imp gal, 18.2 litre.

WEIGHTS & LOADINGS - Empty weight 263 lb, 119 kg. Max take-off weight 624 lb, 283 kg. Payload 361 lb, 164 kg. Max wing loading 2.92 lb/ft², 14.2 kg/m². Max power loading 12.5 lb/hp, 5.7 kg/hp. Load factors NC recommended; +6.0, -3.0 ultimate.

PERFORMANCE* - Max level speed 55 mph, 88 kph. Never exceed speed 65 mph, 105 kph. Max cruising speed 50 mph, 80 kph. Economic cruising speed 45 mph, 72 kph. Stalling speed 28 mph, 45 kph. Max climb rate at sea level 850 ft/min, 4.3 m/s. Min sink rate 500 ft/min at 30 mph, 2.5 m/s at 48 kph. Best glide ratio with power off 5/1 at 30 mph, 48 kph. Take-off distance 100 ft, 30 m. Landing distance 120 ft, 35 m. Service ceiling 11,000 ft, 3350 m. Range at average cruising speed 70 mile, 113 km. Noise level NC.

*Under the following test conditions - Test payload 336 lb, 152 kg.

FLYLITE (EAST ANGLIA)

Flylite (East Anglia), Mattishall Road, East Dereham, Norfolk NR20 3BU; tel 0362 4907. Proprietor: Bob Adams.

FLYLITE (EAST ANGLIA)
SUPER SCOUT
(Three-axis)

Single-seat single-engined high-wing monoplane with conventional three-axis control. Wing has unswept leading edge, swept forward trailing edge, and tapering chord; conventional tail. Pitch control by fully flying tail; yaw control by fully flying rudder; roll control by wing warping; control inputs through stick for pitch/roll and pedals for yaw. Wing braced from above by kingpost and cables, from below by cables; wing profile NC; single-surface. Undercarriage has three wheels in tail-dragger formation; NC suspension on tailwheel and axle-flex suspension on main wheels. Push-right go-right tailwheel steering connected to yaw control. No brakes. Aluminium-alloy tube airframe, with pod. Engine mounted at wing height, driving tractor propeller.

Production status: current, number completed NC.

GENERAL - Though there is no connection between Bob Adams' *Super Scout* and the New Zealand machine of the same name built by Canterbury Microlights, the philosophy behind each is the same - to refine the venerable Ron Wheeler *Scout Mk3* into something more versatile.

The Flylite machine has one feature lacking in its antipodean counterpart, however, in that its roll control system has been redesigned. Wing warping is still used, but now there are cable-operating control rods linking the top of both wings, running from the leading edge to aft of the existing roll control point. The idea is to improve control of the trailing edge, and it certainly works, according to *Flightline's* tester Eric Woods, who put the machine through its paces in the May-June '84 edition. He commented: 'The magic ingredient that Bob has added is adequate lateral control. The controls are well balanced and certainly as effective as most other three-axis machines I have flown'.

The other refinements are relatively routine - a pod, better wheels and a foot-protector plate - and take the aircraft to within a whisker of the 70 kg empty weight limit above which it would have to have UK airworthiness type approval.

Despite these changes, the aircraft remains a machine for lightish pilots and lightish winds, rather than something for a cross-country sprint, but in *Super Scout* guise it is certainly more practical than the original and remains competitively priced at £2500.

EXTERNAL DIMENSIONS & AREAS - Length overall 17.6 ft, 5.35 m. Height overall 6.4 ft, 1.94 m. Wing span 28.8 ft, 8.77 m. Chord at root 6.5 ft, 1.98 m. Chord at tip 1.3 ft, 0.40 m. Dihedral NC°. Sweepback 0°. Elevator span 10.5 ft, 3.20 m. Rudder height 4.8 ft, 1.47 m. Total wing area 109 ft², 10.1 m². Rudder area NC. Total elevator area 12.5 ft², 1.16 m². Aspect ratio 7.6/1. Wheel track 4.5 ft, 1.37 m. Wheelbase 12.5 ft, 3.80 m. Tailwheel diameter overall 4 inch, 10 cm. Main wheels diameter overall 12 inch, 31 cm.

POWER PLANT - Robin EC25PS engine. Max power 21 hp at 6500 rpm. Propeller diameter and pitch 48xNC inch, 1.23xNC m. V-belt reduction, ratio 2.2/1. Max static thrust 130 lb, 59 kg. Power per unit area 0.19 hp/ft², 2.1 hp/m². Fuel capacity 1.6 US gal, 1.3 Imp gal, 6.0 litre.

WEIGHTS & LOADINGS - Empty weight 152 lb, 69 kg. Max take-off weight 357 lb, 162 kg. Payload 205 lb, 93 kg. Max wing loading 3.28 lb/ft², 16.2 kg/m². Max power loading 17.0 lb/hp, 7.7 kg/hp. Load factors +NC recommended; >+3.0, >-3.0 ultimate.

PERFORMANCE* - Max level speed *45* mph, *72* kph. Never exceed speed 75 mph, 121 kph. Max cruising speed *40* mph, *64* kph. Economic cruising speed *40* mph, *64* kph. Stalling speed 22 mph, 35 kph. Max climb rate at sea level *250* ft/min, *1.3* m/s. Min sink rate 470 ft/min at 40 mph, 2.4 m/s at 64 kph. Best glide ratio with power off 8/1 at 40 mph, 64 kph. Take-off distance *200* ft, *61* m. Landing distance *100* ft, *30* m. Service ceiling NC. Range at average cruising speed 62 mile, 100 km. Noise level NC.

*Under the following test conditions - Airfield altitude 100 ft, 30 m. Ground temperature 46°F, 8°C. Ground pressure NC. Ground windspeed 10-15 mph, 16-24 kph. Test payload *155* lb, *70* kg.

GARDNER

Dega-Applied Technology, 114 Wymondley Road, Hitchin, Herts SG4 9PX; tel 0462 57474; tx 827547 CG BUS G. REF DEGA. Proprietor: Derek Gardner.

GARDNER *T-M SCOUT*

(Three-axis)

Single-seat single-engined biplane with conventional three-axis control. Wings have unswept leading and trailing edges, and constant chord; conventional tail. Pitch control by elevator on tail; yaw control by fin-mounted rudder; roll control by wing-warping; control inputs through stick for pitch/roll and pedals for yaw. Wings braced by struts and transverse X-cables; wing profile NC; approximately 50% double-surface. Undercarriage has two wheels plus tailskid; suspension NC on tailskid and bungee suspension on main wheels. Ground steering NC. No brakes. Airframe materials see text, partially enclosed cockpit. Engine mounted between wings, driving tractor propeller.

Production status: see text.

GENERAL - There is no better indicator of the short-term health of an industry than the start-up rate of new companies, and no better indicator of its long-term prospects than the calibre of people behind those companies. In both respects, Gardner is a welcome newcomer to the British microlight scene. After a long and distinguished career in automotive engineering - as a transmission designer at Ferguson, as a designer of racing cars, and as engineering and marketing vice president at Borg Warner's transmission component group - lifelong aviation enthusiast Derek Gardner finally decided to combine business and pleasure by starting up his own microlight enterprise. His product is Britain's first home-grown World War I replica, a two-thirds version of the Thomas-Morse S4. Designed as a pursuit-pilot trainer by Englishman B Douglas Thomas and built in the US by the Thomas-Morse Aircraft Corp, the original machine is perhaps best remembered now for its role in the film *The Great Waldo Pepper*.

Four years in design and construction, the prototype *T-M Scout* was due to be unveiled just as we went to press, and looks to be beautifully finished. A mixture of materials is used, the fuselage being a one-piece moulding of glass laminate bonded with polyester resin, with attachment points reinforced by plywood. Wings have a wooden two-spar construction with alloy ribs and Aerolene covering, a similar material being used for the tail surfaces. Undercarriage is tubular steel with a light wooden fairing of aerofoil-section.

Power comes from a Konig SC430 with electric start but no on-board battery, the prototype having direct drive, though a reduction will be added for production. Polished aluminium heat shields protect the fuselage moulding from engine heat, the whole engine compartment being shrouded by a flame-resistant GRP cowling. Derek tells us that particular attention has been paid to noise reduction on the already quiet Konig engine, with a special reverse-flow silencer fitted.

Clearly a lot of thought has gone into the design, and the race is now on between Derek's company and Air Progress International to see who can produce the first UK-legal replica. Derek's contestant is planned to retail at £5150 for

a 150-200 h kit. Readers should note that our performance figures below are based on calculations.

EXTERNAL DIMENSIONS & AREAS - Length overall 14.2 ft, 4.32 m. Height overall 5.9 ft, 1.80 m. Wing span 16.9 ft, 5.16 m (bottom); 18.8 ft, 5.74 m (top). Constant chord 3.0 ft, 0.91 m (bottom wing); 3.6 ft, 1.09 m (top wing). Sweepback 0°. Total wing area* 108 ft², 10.0 m². Aspect ratio NC. Main wheels diameter overall 20 inch, 51 cm. Other data NC.

POWER PLANT - Konig SC430 engine. Max power 24 hp at 4200 rpm. Propeller diameter and pitch NC. No reduction. Max static thrust NC. Power per unit area 0.22 hp/ft², 2.4 hp/m². Fuel capacity 2.4 US gal, 2.0 Imp gal, 9.0 litre.

WEIGHTS & LOADINGS - Empty weight 154 lb, 70 kg. Max take-off weight 390 lb, 177 kg. Payload 236 lb, 107 kg. Max wing loading 3.61 lb/ft², 17.7 kg/m². Max power loading 16.3 lb/hp, 7.4 kg/hp. Load factors +4.0, -2.0 recommended; +6.0, -3.0 ultimate.

PERFORMANCE -** Max level speed 62 mph, 100 kph. Max cruising speed 52 mph, 84 kph. Economic cruising speed 48 mph, 77 kph. Stalling speed 33 mph, 53 kph. Max climb rate at sea level 400 ft/min, 2.0 m/s. Range at average cruising speed 54 mile, 87 km. Other data NC.

Including undercarriage fairing.

***Under the following test conditions -** Airfield altitude 0 ft, 0 m. Ground temperature 59°F, 10°C. Ground pressure 1013 mB. Ground windspeed 0 mph, 0 kph. Test payload 236 lb, 107 kg.

GO-PLANE

Go-Plane Aviation Ltd, Sandhills, Porchfield, Isle of Wight PO30 4IH; tel 0983 524713.

GO-PLANE *MICROMET*

(Three-axis)

Single-seat single-engined low-wing monoplane with conventional three-axis control. Wing has unswept leading and trailing edges, and constant chord; conventional tail. Pitch control by elevator on tail; yaw control by fin-mounted rudder; roll control by 60%-span ailerons; control inputs through stick for pitch/roll and pedals for yaw. Cantilever wing; wing profile NACA 4415; 100% double-surface. Undercarriage has three wheels in tail-dragger formation; axle-flex suspension on all wheels. Push-right go-right tailwheel steering connected to yaw control. No brakes. Aluminium-alloy sheet monocoque airframe, totally enclosed. Engine mounted above wing, driving tractor propeller.

Production status: prototype.

GENERAL - The Levi family, designers of the *Air Dinghy* which we feature in our Italian section, are also developing this very different machine - an all-alloy 'mini lightplane', under the microlight weight limit but with a small wing area and built very much along conventional aviation principles. Its monocoque structure consists of pop-rivetted aluminium-alloy sheet, controls are conventional three-axis, and a KFM 107ER is used for the power plant, a logical choice since the Levis are familiar with the engine from experience with the *Air Dinghy*.

As we write, the first prototype is still under construction, so data is rather sparse. Price has yet to be decided.

EXTERNAL DIMENSIONS & AREAS - Length overall 16.4 ft, 5.00 m. Height overall 6.0 ft, 1.83 m. Wing span 25.1 ft, 7.66 m. Constant chord 3.6 ft, 1.10 m. Dihedral 10°. Sweepback 0°. Tailplane span 7.0 ft, 2.14 m. Fin height 2.6 ft, 0.80 m. Total wing area 91 ft^2, 8.4 m^2. Tailplane area 11.5 ft^2, 1.07 m^2. Aspect ratio 7.0/1. Other data NC.

POWER PLANT - KFM 107ER engine. Max power 25 hp at 6500 rpm. Propeller diameter and pitch NCx30 inch, NCx30 m. V-belt reduction, ratio 2.1/1. Max static thrust 132 lb, 60 kg. Power per unit area 0.27 hp/ft^2, 3.0 hp/m^2. Fuel capacity 3.5 US gal, 2.9 Imp gal, 13.2 litre.

WEIGHTS & LOADINGS - NC.

PERFORMANCE - NC.

Micromet *preliminary drawings.*

HORIZON

Horizon Aerosails, Truleigh Sands, Truleigh Manor Farm, Edburton, nr Henfield, West Sussex BN4 9LL; tel 079156 236. Director: Tony Leaney.

HORIZON *SUNRISE*
(Three-axis)

Tandem two-seat single-engined high-wing monoplane with conventional three-axis control. Wing has unswept leading edge, swept forward trailing edge, and tapering chord; cruciform tail. Pitch control by elevator on tail; yaw control by fin-mounted rudder; roll control by ailerons; control inputs through stick for pitch/roll and pedals for yaw. Wing braced from above by kingpost and cables, from below by cables; wing profile NACA 6412; 100% double-surface. Undercarriage has three wheels in tricycle formation; suspension on all wheels, type NC. Push-right go-right nosewheel steering connected to yaw control. Brakes NC. Aluminium-alloy tube airframe, totally enclosed. Engine mounted below wing, driving pusher propeller.

Production status: prototype.

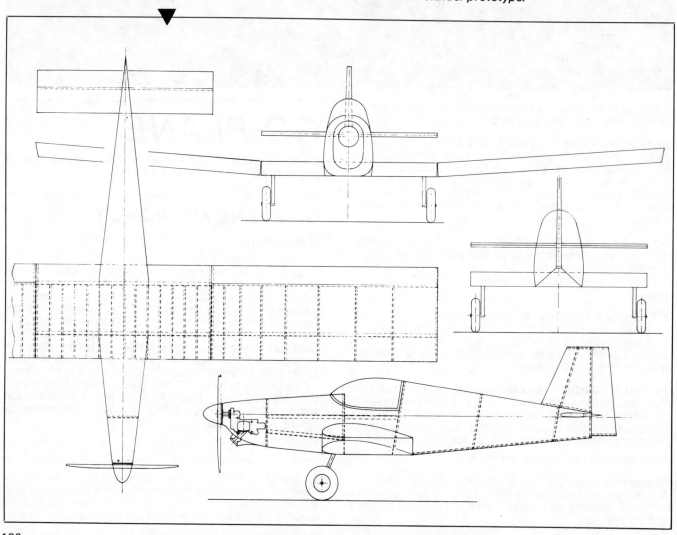

POWER PLANT - Rotax 447 engine. Max power 40 hp at NC rpm. Propeller diameter and pitch 60xNC inch, 1.52xNC m. Gear reduction, ratio 2.6/1. Max static thrust 250 lb, 113 kg. Power per unit area 0.24 hp/ft², 2.6 hp/m². Fuel capacity 6.0 US gal, 5.0 Imp gal, 22.7 litre.

WEIGHTS & LOADINGS - Empty weight 331 lb, 150 kg. Max take-off weight 763 lb, 346 kg. Payload 432 lb, 196 kg. Max wing loading 4.57 lb/ft², 22.3 kg/m². Max power loading 19.1 lb/hp, 8.7 kg/hp. Load factors NC recommended; +6.0, -4.5 ultimate.

PERFORMANCE* - Max level speed 72 mph, 116 kph. Max cruising speed 65 mph, 105 kph. Stalling speed 34 mph, 55 kph. Max climb rate at sea level 680 ft/min, 3.5 m/s. Other data NC.

*Under unspecified test conditions except: Climb rate refers to solo flying.

HORNET

Templeward Ltd t/a Hornet Microlights, Bankfoot Mills, Wibsey Bank, Bankfoot, Bradford, W Yorkshire BD6 3JU; tel 0274 308642/603645. Managing director/test pilot: Richard Wolfenden. Secretary: Ron Wolfenden. Chief inspector: Roger Patrick. Chief engineer/prop man: Ernest Robinson.

HORNET/SOUTHDOWN INTERNATIONAL *DUAL TRAINER/RAVEN* (Hybrid)

Side-by-side two-seat single-engined flex-wing aircraft with hybrid control. Rogallo wing with fin and saumons; spoilers fitted for air braking. Pilot suspended below wing in trike unit, using bar to control pitch and roll/yaw by altering relative positions of trike unit and wing; slider on control bar actuates spoilers. Wing braced from above by kingpost and cables, from below by cables; floating cross-tube construction with 100% double-surface enclosing cross-tube; preformed ribs. Undercarriage has three wheels in tricycle formation; no suspension on any wheels. Push-right go-left nosewheel steering independent from aerodynamic controls. Nosewheel brake. Aluminium-alloy tube trike unit, with optional pod. Engine mounted below wing, driving pusher propeller.

Production status: current, 45 completed (total of all Dual Trainer trike units and earlier equivalents, fitted with various wings).

GENERAL - The advent of airworthiness legislation has posed real problems for the smaller British manufacturers, who have only a small turnover to generate the funds to get their aircraft type-approved. Some, like SMD, have temporarily at least given up, but Hornet's response has been to rely on a combination of training income, export orders and component sales. The latter was a natural outlet for the firm as Hornet has always produced an unusually high proportion of its trike units in-house, making its own pods, props, and reduction drives (the company bought the rights to the Sharp reduction drives featured in our first edition).

But now that the airworthiness scheme is working

GENERAL - Even though the Horizon name is new to this book, seasoned microlight enthusiasts may notice something familiar about the above address, for Truleigh Sands was the location of two pioneering British microlight companies - Ultra Sports, since absorbed into the Pegasus concern, and Huntair, which closed about a year after founder Steve Hunt's death.

That closure prompted some hard thinking at Horizon, since at the time of the closure Horizon's stock in trade was wing manufacture, especially for Huntair, and the result of the rethink was a decision to take the plunge and become a fully fledged aircraft manufacturer.

Next door at Huntair two dual machines had been designed - Steve Hunt's *Two-Four Project,* which was never built, and the company's swansong, the Hewland-engined *Wayfarer* prototype, designed by Fred Dorsett and Tom Knight after Steve's death and resembling a two-seat *Phantom* - but Horizon decided to start afresh. Ken Jones, who had worked with Billy Brooks on the *Dragon,* was brought in to create a straightforward tube-and-Dacron two-seat trainer/tourer with non-structural glass-fibre enclosure.

Aided by young Belgian engineer Peter de Maeyer, and of course Tony Leaney, who describes himself as the factory's 'general dogsbody', Ken created the *Sunrise,* powered by a Rotax 447 with gear reduction and using a NACA 6412 section. As we write, in May '85, the aircraft has yet to make its maiden flight (our picture is of a working model and our performance figures calculations), and various items are not finalised. The kingpost-and-cable bracing may be replaced by struts if the weight limit permits, and brakes may be added. Similarly, suspension design is still undecided. Clearly, it would be over-optimistic to expect type approval much before the end of the year, but with UK schools crying out for a practical three-axis aircraft at a practical price, there should be a ready market for the machine once the legalities are complete, especially if the projected cost of £6000 ready to fly becomes a reality.

EXTERNAL DIMENSIONS & AREAS - Length overall 21.4 ft, 6.53 m. Height overall 8.2 ft, 2.50 m. Wing span 30.5 ft, 9.30 m. Chord at root 5.6 ft, 1.72 m. Chord at tip 5.3 ft, 1.63 m. Dihedral 2°. Sweepback 0°. Tailplane span 9.8 ft, 3.00 m. Fin height 4.9 ft, 1.50 m. Total wing area 167 ft², 15.5 m². Total aileron area 20.7 ft², 1.92 m². Fin area 10.1 ft², 0.94 m². Rudder area 7.3 ft², 0.68 m². Tailplane area 16.8 ft², 1.56 m². Total elevator area 12.6 ft², 1.17 m². Aspect ratio 5.6/1. Wheel track 4.9 ft, 1.50 m. Wheelbase 5.9 ft, 1.80 m. Nosewheel diameter overall 13 inch, 33 cm. Main wheels diameter overall 13 inch, 33 cm.

Great Britain

relatively smoothly, Richard Wolfenden has decided to take the plunge and produce two UK-legal trike units, the *Dual Trainer* which we describe here and the *Invader* which we list separately. The entire range of single-seaters has been dropped, the company having decided that its principal asset is the side-by-side seating position of its dual machines, an arrangement which has many advantages for training but which has been abandoned by every other British manufacturer in the quest for less drag and more speed. Only Pegasus, with its still experimental *Forger*, is showing any interest in competing for a share in this market.

Sensibly, Richard has decided on a thorough update of each machine before submitting it for airworthiness approval. Though the *Dual Trainer* is based on the *Supreme 440* listed in our last edition, it has been re-engined with a Rotax 447 in place of the Robin EC44 and now boasts a much more sophisticated wing, Southdown International's *Raven*, though Skyhook's *Cutlass CD* is still available for export to countries where ruggedness and simplicity are more important than speed. Gone too are the twin tanks which were a feature of the Robin-engined machine.

At the time of writing the *Dual Trainer/Raven* is still under development, so no performance figures are available. For the same reason the price must be regarded as provisional, at £4345 ready to fly and including instrumentation.

EXTERNAL DIMENSIONS & AREAS - Length overall 10.5 ft, 3.20 m. Height overall NC. Wing span 36.0 ft, 10.97 m. Chord at root 10.0 ft, 3.05 m. Chord at tip 1.3 ft, 0.41 m. Dihedral -3°. Nose angle 130°. Fin height 3.3 ft, 1.02 m. Total wing area 160 ft², 14.9 m². Fin area 12.0 ft², 1.11 m². Aspect ratio 8.1/1. Wheel track 4.4 ft, 1.33 m. Wheelbase

The Dual Trainer/Cutlass CD *will be similar to this* Supreme 440/Cutlass CD *pictured at the '84 Woburn Rally, but with single tank and its Robin engine replaced by a Rotax.*

4.9 ft, 1.50 m. Nosewheel diameter overall 15.5 inch, 39 cm. Main wheels diameter overall 15.5 inch, 39 cm.

POWER PLANT - Rotax 447 engine. Max power 40 hp at NC rpm. Propeller diameter and pitch 60x34 inch, 1.52x0.86 m. Gear reduction, ratio 2.6/1. Max static thrust 310 lb, 141 kg. Power per unit area 0.25 hp/ft², 2.7 hp/m². Fuel capacity 6.6 US gal, 5.5 Imp gal, 25.0 litre.

WEIGHTS & LOADINGS - Empty weight 302 lb, 137 kg. Max take-off weight 741 lb, 336 kg. Payload 439 lb, 199 kg. Max wing loading 4.63 lb/ft², 22.6 kg/m². Max power loading 18.5 lb/hp, 8.4 kg/hp. Load factors +4.0, -2.0 recommended; +6.0, -3.0 ultimate.

PERFORMANCE - NC.

HORNET/SKYHOOK SAILWINGS
DUAL TRAINER/CUTLASS CD
(Weight-shift)

Summary as Dual Trainer/Raven *except: Weight-shift control. Rogallo wing with keel pocket, no saumons or spoilers. Rigid cross-tube construction with 30% double-surface not enclosing cross-tube.*

Production status: see Dual Trainer/Raven.

GENERAL - This aircraft, described in more detail under *Dual Trainer/Raven*, is part of a new range which is still under development, so no performance figures are available. We quote below performance figures from the earlier *Supreme 440/Cutlass CD*, which was very similar apart from its use of a Robin EC44 instead of a Rotax 447. Other manufacturers with experience of both engines have concluded that substitution of one for the other makes little difference to performance (Southdown International, for

Norman Burr

instance, quotes the same figures regardless of engine fitment), so the data below should also be representative for the *Dual Trainer/Cutlass CD.*

EXTERNAL DIMENSIONS & AREAS - Length overall 12.7 ft, 3.87 m. Height overall 12.5 ft, 3.80 m. Wing span *36.0* ft, *10.97* m. Total wing area 198 ft², 18.4 m². Aspect ratio *6.5/1.* Wheel track 4.4 ft, 1.33 m. Wheelbase 4.9 ft, 1.50 m. Nosewheel diameter overall 15.5 inch, 39 cm. Main wheels diameter overall 15.5 inch, 39 cm. Other data NC.

POWER PLANT - See *Dual Trainer/Raven* except: Power per unit area 0.20 hp/ft², 2.2 hp/m².

WEIGHTS & LOADINGS - Empty weight 293 lb, 133 kg. Max take-off weight 685 lb, 311 kg. Payload 392 lb, 178 kg. Max wing loading 3.46 lb/ft², 16.9 kg/m². Max power loading 17.1 lb/hp, 7.8 kg/hp. Load factors NC recommended; >+3.75, -NC ultimate.

PERFORMANCE* - Max level speed 60 mph, 97 kph. Never exceed speed 68 mph, 110 kph. Max cruising speed 45 mph, 72 kph. Economic cruising speed 40 mph, 64 kph. Stalling speed 26 mph, 42 kph. Max climb rate at sea level 850 ft/min, 4.3 m/s. Take-off distance 45 ft, 14 m. Landing distance 110 ft, 35 m. Other data NC.

*Under the following test conditions - Airfield altitude 950 ft, 290 m. Ground temperature 68°F, 20°C. Ground pressure NC. Ground windspeed 10 mph, 16 kph. Test payload 203 lb, 92 kg.

HORNET/SOUTHDOWN INTERNATIONAL *INVADER/RAVEN* (Hybrid)

Side-by-side two-seat single-engined flex-wing aircraft with hybrid control. Rogallo wing with fin and saumons; spoilers fitted for air braking. Pilot suspended below wing in trike unit, using bar to control pitch and roll/yaw by altering relative positions of trike unit and wing; slider on control bar actuates spoilers. Wing braced from above by kingpost and cables, from below by cables; floating cross-tube construction with 100% double-surface enclosing cross-tube; preformed ribs. Undercarriage has three wheels in tricycle formation; coil-spring suspension on nosewheel and rubber suspension on main wheels. Push-right go-left nosewheel steering independent from aerodynamic controls. Nosewheel brake. Aluminium-alloy tube/glass-fibre trike unit, partially enclosed. Engine mounted below wing, driving pusher propeller.

Production status: current, 12 completed (total of all Invader trike units, fitted with various wings).

GENERAL - The unique appearance of Hornet's *Invader* has made it a controversial machine right from its inception in 1983. Offering better weather protection than any other

British trike, plus extremely easy rigging, the design has much to commend it. Unencumbered by either a front strut or a front wire - the only British trike thus constructed - the occupants have an excellent forward view from the comfy cockpit, and can also get airborne more quickly than all their clubmates, as the aircraft's rigging is confined to the wing. Thanks to the use of taper-roller bearings on stainless-steel axles, the trike unit can be towed complete on its own wheels using a standard caravan-type ball hitch on the nose. Moreover, the design incorporates suspension on all three wheels and self-stabilising steering, so that the aircraft runs true even if the pilot makes a less than perfect landing.

Unlike Hornet's other machines, the _Invader_ is a monopole, of aerofoil-section tube, the complete trike unit having been tested in a wind tunnel.

However, early examples of the _Invader_ did not live up to the company's performance expectations; straight line speed was quite good, but climb rate unimpressive, a factor which some observers attributed to the masking effect of the 'fuselage' on the prop airflow. Matters were improved by the substitution of a higher-lift wing, the _Sprint,_ for the _Dual Striker_ originally used, and can be expected to take another turn for the better now that the _Raven_ has in turn replaced the _Sprint._ At the same time, the aircraft has been re-engined, a Rotax 447 replacing the Robin EC34PM and

EC44 2P1 units previously offered. Other alterations include a Kevlar 'fuselage' to replace the rather weighty glass-fibre affair, and the fitment of a nosewheel brake in place of the rather complicated main-wheel brakes on earlier models.

Richard tells us that with Rotax engine, _Raven_ wing and the latest prop, the climb is excellent, so perhaps this interesting design will now have a chance to reach its full potential. However, as the aircraft is still under development with the aim of satisfying UK airworthiness legislation, no performance figures are available.

Provisional price is £4750, ready to fly and including instruments.

EXTERNAL DIMENSIONS & AREAS - See _Dual Trainer/Raven_ except: Wheel track 4.3 ft, 1.32 m. Wheelbase 4.6 ft, 1.40 m. Nosewheel diameter overall 11.5 inch, 29 cm.

POWER PLANT - See _Dual Trainer/Raven_ except: Fuel capacity 5.4 US gal, 4.5 Imp gal, 20.0 litre.

WEIGHTS & LOADINGS - See _Dual Trainer/Raven_ except: Empty weight 310 lb, 141 kg. Payload 431 lb, 195 kg.

PERFORMANCE - NC.

LANCASHIRE MICROLIGHT

Alphacraft Ltd t/a Lancashire Microlight, Red Rose Court, Unit 2B, Sunnyhurst Road, Blackburn, Lancashire; tel 0254 691300. Director: Nigel Heap.

LANCASHIRE MICROLIGHTS/ FLEXIFORM _MICRO-TRIKE 330/MEDIUM STRIKER_
(Weight-shift)

Single-seat single-engined flex-wing aircraft with weight-shift control. Rogallo wing with keel pocket. Pilot suspended below wing in trike unit, using bar to control pitch and roll/yaw by altering relative positions of trike unit and wing. Wing braced from above by kingpost and cables; from below by cables; bowsprit construction with >70% double-surface; preformed ribs. Undercarriage has three wheels in tricycle formation; suspension NC. Push-right go-left nosewheel steering independent from aerodynamic controls. No brakes. Aluminium-alloy tube trike unit, with optional pod. Engine mounted below wing, driving pusher propeller.

Production status: see text.

GENERAL - Many British readers will be surprised to see this company in our second edition, since its products have been absent from the British market since early 1984, when Nigel Heap and his co-directors decided that the cost of proving compliance with the airworthiness regulations could not be borne by a company with only a small annual production.

However, the parent company to Lancashire Microlight,

Norman Burr

Alphacraft, is still active in non-microlight work and, Nigel tells us, is still able to handle export orders. We are therefore repeating the data carried in our first edition for the _Micro-Trike 330/Medium Striker_ (below) and the _Micro-Trike 440/Dual Striker_ (see next listing), though readers should note that latest _Dual Strikers_ have a smaller area and are likely to be slightly faster as a result (see Flexiform).

The company also made a _Micro-Trike 250/Medium Striker,_ but as the demand for single-seaters with the Robin EC25PS engine is now virtually non-existant, this model must be regarded as discontinued for practical purposes.

The products themselves are thoroughly conventional monopole trike units, usually mated to Flexiform wings (as in our data), and were notable more for their competitive pricing than anything else. Prices are now NC. Future plans for the company are much more adventurous and include work on an advanced composite-construction trike unit with two seats and a four-stroke engine, possibly the Lotus motor. Production, however, will not start until late '85 at the earliest.

EXTERNAL DIMENSIONS & AREAS - Length overall 13.8 ft, 4.19 m. Height overall 9. ft, 3.00 m. Wing span 33.0 ft, 10.06 m. Dihedral 0.5°. Nose angle 150°. Depth of keel pocket 1.2 ft, 0.37 m. Total wing area 200 ft², 18.6 m². Keel pocket area 3.5 ft², 0.33 m². Aspect ratio 5.4/1. Wheel track NC. Wheelbase NC. Nosewheel diameter overall 14 inch, 36 cm. Main wheels diameter overall 14 inch, 36 cm.

POWER PLANT - Robin EC34PM engine. Max power 32 hp at 6500 rpm. Propeller diameter and pitch 54x30 inch, 1.37x0.76 m. Toothed-belt reduction, ratio 2.5/1. Max static thrust 210 lb, 95 kg. Power per unit area 0.16 hp/ft², 1.7 hp/m². Fuel capacity 4.8 US gal, 4.0 Imp gal, 18.2 litre.

WEIGHTS & LOADINGS - Empty weight 195 lb, 88 kg. Max take-off weight 437 lb, 198 kg. Payload 242 lb, 110 kg. Max wing loading 2.19 lb/ft², 10.6 kg/m². Max power loading 13.7 lb/hp, 6.2 kg/hp. Load factors +4.5, -2.0 recommended; NC ultimate.

PERFORMANCE* - Max level speed 45 mph, 72 kph. Never exceed speed 55 mph, 88 kph. Max cruising speed 45 mph, 72 kph. Economic cruising speed 45 mph, 72 kph. Stalling speed 25 mph, 40 kph. Max climb rate at sea level 1000 ft/min, 5.1 m/s. Min sink rate 350 ft/min at 27 mph, 1.8 m/s at 43 kph. Best glide ratio with power off 8/1 at 27 mph, 43 kph. Take-off distance 70 ft, 21 m. Landing distance 120 ft, 37 m. Service ceiling NC. Range at average cruising speed 108 mile, 174 km. Noise level NC.

*Under the following test conditions - Airfield altitude 0 ft, 0 m. Ground temperature 50°F, 10°C. Ground pressure NC. Ground windspeed 0 mph, 0 kph. Test payload 168 lb, 76 kg.

LANCASHIRE MICROLIGHTS/ FLEXIFORM *MICRO-TRIKE 440/DUAL STRIKER*

(Weight-shift)

Summary as Micro-Trike/Medium Striker except: Tandem two-seater. Wing 65% double surface. Nosewheel brake.

Production status: see Micro-Trike 330/Medium Striker text.

GENERAL - See *Micro-Trike 330/Medium Striker.*

EXTERNAL DIMENSIONS & AREAS - Length overall 14.0 ft, 4.27 m. Height overall 10.1 ft, 3.08 m. Wing span 38.0 ft, 11.58 m. Chord at root 9.0 ft, 2.74 m. Chord at tip 3.5 ft, 1.07 m. Dihedral 2°. Nose angle 150°. Depth of keel pocket 1.2 ft, 0.37 m. Total wing area 250 ft², 23.2 m². Keel pocket area 3.5 ft², 0.33 m². Aspect ratio 6.0/1. Wheel track NC. Wheelbase NC. Nosewheel diameter overall 16 inch, 40 cm. Main wheels diameter overall 16 inch, 40 cm.

POWER PLANT - Robin EC44 2PM engine. Max power 50 hp at 7000 rpm. Propeller diameter and pitch 62x27 inch, 1.57x0.69 m. Toothed-belt reduction, ratio 2.5/1. Max static thrust 300 lb, 136 kg. Power per unit area 0.20 hp/ft², 0.22 hp/m². Fuel capacity 4.8 US gal, 4.0 Imp gal, 18.2 litre.

Norman Burr

Micro-Trike 440 with optional pod. This particular example achieved second place in the 1983 Norfolk Air Race, piloted by Paul Kavanagh/Colin Lloyd and fitted with a Sprint wing.

WEIGHTS & LOADINGS - Empty weight 243 lb, 110 kg. Max take-off weight 639 lb, 290 kg. Payload 396 lb, 180 kg. Max wing loading 2.56 lb/ft², 12.5 kg/m². Max power loading 12.8 lb/hp, 5.6 kg/hp. Load factors +4.5, -2.0 recommended; NC ultimate.

PERFORMANCE* - Max level speed 45 mph, 72 kph. Never exceed speed 55 mph, 88 kph. Max cruising speed 45 mph, 72 kph. Economic cruising speed 40 mph, 64 kph. Stalling speed 25 mph, 40 kph. Max climb rate at sea level 650 ft/min, 3.3 m/s. Min sink rate 350 ft/min at 27 mph, 1.8 m/s at 43 kph. Best glide ratio with power off 8/1 at 27 mph, 43 kph. Take-off distance 130 ft, 40 m. Landing distance 200 ft, 61 m. Service ceiling NC. Range at average cruising speed 90 mile, 145 km. Noise level NC.

*Under the following test conditions - Airfield altitude 0 ft, 0 m. Ground temperature 50°F, 10°C. Ground pressure NC. Ground windspeed 0 mph, 0 kph. Test payload 336 lb, 152 kg.

MAINAIR

Mainair Sports Ltd, Shawclough Road, Rochdale, Lancs OL12 6LN; tel 0706 55131; tx 635091. Managing director: John Hudson. Sales manager: Paul Frain. Power manager: Geoff Ball. Wing production manager: Hughie McGovern.

MAINAIR/PEGASUS *TRI-FLYER 330/TYPHOON S4 MEDIUM and MERLIN/TYPHOON S4 MEDIUM*

(Weight-shift)

Single-seat single-engined flex-wing aircraft with weight-shift control. Rogallo wing with keel pocket. Pilot suspended below wing in trike unit, using bar to control pitch and roll/yaw by altering relative positions of trike unit and wing. Wing braced from above by kingpost and cables, from below by cables; floating cross-tube con-

Main picture: Geoff Ball test flying a Merlin/Typhoon S4. Inset: close up of the engine on the same machine. Since these pictures were taken, the trike unit has changed little, except that the tank has been increased in size and moved behind the pilot, and a toothed-belt reduction fitted. The very latest machines also have rubber suspension.

struction with 55% double-surface enclosing cross-tube; preformed ribs. Undercarriage has three wheels in tricycle formation; rubber suspension on all wheels. Push-right go-left nosewheel steering independent from aerodynamic controls. Nosewheel brake. Aluminium-alloy tube trike unit, completely open (Tri-Flyer 330) with pod (Merlin). Engine mounted below wing, driving pusher propeller.

Production status: current, approximately 150 completed (total Mainair production of Robin 330-engined trike units).

GENERAL - One of the biggest and most vigorous companies in UK microlighting, Mainair's position in the British industry is somewhat analagous to that of Maxair in the US, in that it not only builds aircraft but also supplies other companies with hardware and the public with a wide range of aviation goodies.

However, with the UK market now heavily oriented towards two-seaters, the company has undertaken only detail development work on its full-size solo machines since our last edition, the main improvement for '85 being the adoption of rubber suspension all round from the now defunct one-plus-one Rapier model. They remain straightforward monopole trike units which can be mated with a variety of wings, our data below referring to a Tri-Flyer 330 with Pegasus Typhoon S4 Medium, one of the most popular choices. Other suitable Rogallos include the Striker and Lightning Phase II.

The Merlin was originally conceived as a complete aircraft in conjunction with Airwave, but demand for Airwave hang-gliders was such that wing production never got under way, and as a result the Merlin has become simply a deluxe version of the Tri-Flyer 330, sold with whatever wing the customer requires. The only difference between the two trike units is the pod and fabric side panels, which not only keep the pilot warm but make the aircraft a little quicker than its cheaper stablemate detailed below.

At the time of writing the single-seaters have no UK type approval and are being manufactured only for export, a situation which will probably prevail until Mainair develops its own solo wing. Both models will then will be phased out in favour of the Scorcher, which we describe separately. Prices (trike units only) are £1600.00 for the Tri-Flyer 330 and £1939.14 for the Merlin, a wide range of options being available for both machines.

EXTERNAL DIMENSIONS & AREAS - Length overall 11.0 ft, 3.35 m. Wing span 32.5 ft, 9.91 m. Chord at root 8.0 ft, 2.44 m. Chord at tip 3.3 ft, 1.01 m. Dihedral 0°. Nose angle 122°. Total wing area 166 ft², 15.4 m². Aspect ratio 6.4/1. Wheel track 4.6 ft, 1.40 m. Wheelbase 5.8 ft, 1.76 m. Nosewheel diameter overall 13 inch, 32 cm. Main wheels diameter overall 13 inch, 32 cm. Other data NC.

POWER PLANT - Robin EC34PM engine. Max power 35 hp at 7000 rpm. Propeller diameter and pitch 54x30 inch, 1.37x0.76 m. Toothed-belt reduction, ratio 2.3/1. Max static thrust 198 lb, 90 kg. Power per unit area 0.21 hp/ft², 2.3 hp/m². Fuel capacity 5.7 US gal, 4.8 Imp gal, 21.6 litre.

WEIGHTS & LOADINGS - Empty weight 216 lb, 98 kg. Max take-off weight 463 lb, 210 kg. Payload 247 lb, 112 kg. Max wing loading 2.79 lb/ft², 13.6 kg/m². Max power loading 13.2 lb/hp, 6.0 kg/hp. Load factors +4.0, -2.0 recommended; +6.5, -3.0 ultimate.

PERFORMANCE* - Max level speed 45 mph, 72 kph. Never exceed speed 53 mph, 85 kph. Max cruising speed 35 mph, 56 kph. Economic cruising speed 30 mph, 48 kph. Stalling speed 22 mph, 35 kph. Max climb rate at sea level 600 ft/min, 3.1 m/s. Take-off distance 80-100 ft, 24-30 m. Landing distance 120-170 ft, 37-52 m. Range at average cruising speed 90 mile, 145 km. Other data NC.

*Under unspecified test conditions.

MAINAIR/SOUTHDOWN INTERNATIONAL
TRI-FLYER 440 SPRINT and GEMINI SPRINT

(Weight-shift)

Tandem two-seat single-engined flex-wing aircraft with weight-shift control. Rogallo wing with fin. Pilot suspended below wing in trike unit, using bar to control pitch and roll/yaw by altering relative positions of trike unit and wing. Wing braced from above by kingpost and cables, from below by cables; floating cross-tube construction with >70% double-surface enclosing cross-tube; preformed and composite ribs. Undercarriage has three wheels in tricycle formation; optional rubber suspension on nosewheel and standard rubber suspension on main wheels. Push-right go-left nose-wheel steering independent from aerodynamic controls. Nosewheel brake. Aluminium-alloy tube trike unit, completely open (Tri-Flyer 440) with pod (Gemini).

Production status: current, approximately 90 completed (total of both types).

GENERAL - Mainair's original Tri-Flyer Two-Seater was introduced in 1982 and most of the early machines were mated to Flexiform wings. However, later that year the same trike unit was also supplied with Southdown's Lightning DS, the combination being known as Puma MS, the MS standing for Mainair Sports to distinguish the machine from the original Puma which used an Ultra Sports trike unit.

In 1983, when Southdown introduced the Sprint wing, Mainair again married the Tri-Flyer Two-Seater to the Southdown product to produce a combination initially known as Puma Sprint MS. However, by this time the complications over the Puma name were becoming incomprehensible even to the manufacturers (see our first edition, p137!), so the machine has since been known simply by the names of its component parts. Along the way, the trike unit has been re-named Tri-Flyer 440.

Through all these complications the trike unit itself has remained basically the same, the principal change being the addition of suspension, first as rubber inserts in the telescopic rear struts and now optionally for the nosewheel as well. Most machines use the familiar upside down mounting for the 440 Robin, but some were made with 'right way up' mountings and an underslung tank, before Mainair, like Ultra Sports, reverted to the original arrangement for reliability reasons.

Latterly the Tri-Flyer 440 Sprint has been easily outsold by the Gemini Sprint, which is the same machine with a pod and fabric side panels - items which can be purchased separately to upgrade the open machine to Gemini Sprint specification. These two aircraft tied with their all-Southdown rival, the Puma Sprint, for the honour of being the first ever machine to receive type approval under the UK airworthiness scheme.

Rigging the Tri-Flyer 440 Sprint *(foreground) and* Gemini Sprint *(background). Both these examples have the standard Robin engine, the one nearest the camera using the 'right way up' engine mounting and underslung tank.*

A comparision test of three Robin-engined machines - *Gemini Sprint, Puma Sprint* and what is now Pegasus' *Panther XL* - appeared in the July-August '84 issue of *Flightline.* Our *Gemini Sprint* data below is largely taken from that test; the *Tri-Flyer 440* is some 11 lb (5 kg) lighter and a little slower. For 1985 a 447 Rotax with gear reduction is an option on either variant, and though no performance figures were available at the time of going to press, the Rotax version is claimed to be some 20 lb (9 kg) lighter, use around 30% less fuel and be slightly quieter. Other options include main-wheel spats, nosewheel enclosure, nosewheel suspension, rear seat steering, instruments and parachute system.

In basic form the *Tri-Flyer 440 Sprint* costs £3926.96 ready to fly, while the *Gemini Sprint* costs a further £217.40.

EXTERNAL DIMENSIONS & AREAS - Length overall 11.2 ft, 3.41 m. Height overall NC. Wing span 35.0 ft, 10.67 m. Chord at root 8.7 ft, 2.65 m. Chord at tip 2.5 ft, 0.76 m. Dihedral -2°. Nose angle 130°. Fin height 3.8 ft, 1.16 m. Total wing area 180 ft², 16.7 m². Fin area 7.2 ft², 0.67 m². Aspect ratio 6.8/1. Wheel track 5.0 ft, 1.52 m. Wheelbase 6.2 ft, 1.88 m. Nosewheel diameter overall 16 inch, 40 cm. Main wheels diameter overall 16 inch, 40 cm.

POWER PLANT - Robin EC44PM engine. Max power 50 hp at 6800 rpm. Propeller diameter and pitch 62x30 inch, 1.57x0.76 m. Toothed-belt reduction, ratio 2.7/1. Max static thrust 275 lb, 125 kg. Power per unit area 0.28 hp/ft², 3.1 hp/m². Fuel capacity 5.7 US gal, 4.8 Imp gal, 21.6 litre.

WEIGHTS & LOADINGS - Empty weight 309 lb, 140 kg. Max take-off weight 745 lb, 338 kg. Payload 431 lb, 195 kg. Max wing loading 4.14 lb/ft², 20.2 kg/m². Max power loading 14.9 lb/hp, 6.8 kg/hp. Load factors +4.0, -2.0 recommended; >+6.0, >-3.0 ultimate.

PERFORMANCE* - Max level speed 65 mph, 105 kph. Never exceed speed 70 mph, 113 kph. Cruising speed 40 mph, 64 kph. Stalling speed 30 mph, 48 kph. Max climb rate at sea level 440 ft/min, 2.2 m/s. Min sink rate 400 ft/min, 2.0 m/s at NC speed. Best glide ratio with power off 6/1 at 35 mph, 56 kph. Take-off distance 560 ft, 170 m, to clear obstacle of 50 ft, 15 m. Landing distance 490 ft, 150 m to clear obstacle of 50 ft, 15 m. Service ceiling 10,000 ft, 3050 m. Range at average cruising speed 75 mile, 121 km. Noise level 82 dB at 500 ft, 150 m.

*Under the following test conditions - Airfield altitude 200 ft, 61 m. Ground temperature 59°F, 15°C. Ground pressure 1013 mB. Ground windspeed 0 mph, 0 kph. Test payload 397 lb, 180 kg.

MAINAIR
TRI-FLYER 440 FLASH and GEMINI FLASH

(Weight-shift)

Summary as Tri-Flyer 440 Sprint and Gemini Sprint *except: Rogallo wing with fin and keel pocket. 75% double-surface.*

Production status: current, 38 completed (total of both types).

GENERAL - The *Gemini Flash* is the flagship of the Mainair range, and a source of great pride to the company as it is the first complete aircraft it has ever produced.
Its *Gemini* trike unit is identical to that used on the *Gemini Sprint,* but is mated to the company's own *Flash* wing, a design which lives up to its name, being the fastest dual wing in UK production at the time of writing. Although the design draws on the company's experience with the *Sprint,* the *Flash* has a number of features of its own, of which the most obvious is the unusally small vertical area - just a small fin above the wing and a tiny keel pocket beneath. Less obvious but equally interesting are the 'riblets', upper surface battens inserted from the under-

Mainair's Flash *wing is easily recognisable by its distinctive shaped vertical surfaces. See colour section for a picture of the* Gemini Flash.

Norman Burr

side, the object being to produce a taut, low-drag profile.
Though designed as a high-performance machine rather than a trainer - its stall is sharper and its landing speed higher than a *Typhoon XL* for example - the *Flash* is nevertheless now in service with a number of British schools.
The aircraft may be supplied minus pod as the *Tri-Flyer 440 Flash;* both versions have full UK type-approval. Engine and other options are as for the *Sprint*-winged machines, and prices in basic form are £4073.93 for the open machine and £4291.32 for the podded version, both ready to fly. Our data below refers to a *Gemini Flash* with Robin engine.

EXTERNAL DIMENSIONS & AREAS - Length overall 11.2 ft, 3.40 m. Height overall 12.5 ft, 3.80 m. Wing span 34.6 ft, 10.55 m. Mean chord 4.8 ft, 1.48 m. Dihedral -2°. Nose angle 130°. Fin height 1.0 ft, 0.30 m. Depth of keel pocket 0.5 ft, 0.15 m. Total wing area 168 ft², 15.6 m². Total vertical area 5.7 ft², 0.53 m². Aspect ratio 7.1/1. Wheel track 5.0 ft, 1.52 m. Wheelbase 6.2 ft, 1.88 m. Nosewheel diameter overall 16 inch, 40 cm. Main wheels diameter overall 16 inch, 40 cm.

POWER PLANT - See *Tri-Flyer 440 Sprint and Gemini Sprint* except: Power per unit area 0.30 hp/ft², 3.2 hp/m².

WEIGHTS & LOADINGS - Empty weight 322 lb, 146 kg. Max take-off weight 758 lb, 344 kg. Payload 437 lb, 198 kg. Max wing loading 4.51 lb/ft², 22.1 kg/m². Max power loading 15.2 lb/hp, 6.9 kg/hp. Load factors +4.0, -2.0 recommended; +6.0, -3.0 ultimate.

PERFORMANCE* - Max level speed 69 mph, 111 kph. Never exceed speed 89 mph, 143 kph. Max cruising speed 60 mph, 97 kph. Economic cruising speed 48 mph, 77 kph. Stalling speed 29 mph, 47 kph. Max climb rate at sea level 490 ft/min, 2.5 m/s. Min sink rate 350 ft/min, 1.8 m/s at NC speed. Best glide ratio with power off 8.5/1 at 38 mph, 61 kph. Take-off distance 590 ft, 180 m to clear obstacle of 50 ft, 15 m. Landing distance 520 ft, 160 m to clear obstacle of 50 ft, 15 m. Service ceiling 10,000 ft, 3050 m. Range at average cruising speed 75 mile, 121 km. Noise level 82 dB at 500 ft, 150 m.

*Under the following test conditions - Airfield altitude 200 ft, 61 m. Ground temperature 50°F, 10°C. Ground pressure 1013 mB. Ground windspeed 10 mph, 16 kph. Test payload 437 lb, 198 kg.

MAINAIR *MIRAC*

(Weight-shift)

Summary as Gemini Sprint *except: Rogallo wing with fin and keel pocket. 75% double-surface. Nosewheel suspension standard.*

Production status: current, 2 completed.

GENERAL - The *Mirac* is Mainair's military version of the *Gemini Flash,* the principal modification being the removal of the passenger seat to provide a cargo space. A strap-on passenger seat is an option, enabling the *Mirac* to be used as a rescue vehicle.
As with the civilian machines, Robin 440 or Rotax 447 engines are available (our data below refers to the former), and in addition a wide range of other equipment can be fitted according to customer specification. Skis, radios,

Steve Figures

The trike unit from the Mirac (the name stands for Microlight Reconnaissance Aircraft) at Popham Trade Fair in March '84, with 'right way up' engine mounting, since altered.

Kevlar armour, parachute, fire extinguisher and a range of instruments are all available, while the frame comes in a choice of two colours - olive drab or khaki.
Price: £4900.03.

EXTERNAL DIMENSIONS & AREAS - See *Gemini Flash.*

POWER PLANT - See *Gemini Flash* except: Fuel capacity 9.6 US gal, 8.0 Imp gal, 36.3 litre.

WEIGHTS & LOADINGS - See *Gemini Flash.*

PERFORMANCE - See *Gemini Flash* except: Range at average cruising speed 120 mile, 193 km.

MAINAIR
MICROTUG/Suitable Rogallo
(Weight-shift)

Summary similar to Gemini Sprint.
Production status: current, 3 trike units completed.

GENERAL - Together with Pegasus, Mainair has been in the forefront of the development of hang glider towing systems, and the *Microtug* trike unit has been engineered specifically for the job. It consists of a *Gemini* trike unit with the addition of a tow-line release system and mirrors for the pilot. The release mechanism is located at the rear of the propeller and is operated by a foot release in the pod; it also releases automatically if the glider flies too high above the tug, to prevent the tug being tipped nose-down into a dangerous situation.

However, as we write the *Microtug* is not being marketed seriously because Mainair had yet to find a suitable wing for it. The three which have been built have been flown with *Typhoon XL* wings, but John Hudson tells us that better control at very low speeds is needed; his problem is that the development of most modern Rogallos is taking them in precisely the opposite direction, with higher stall and top speeds. John says that Airwave is working on a special towing wing using *Flash* hardware, while another obvious possibility is Pegasus' *Typhoon XLT.*
Price: NC.

EXTERNAL DIMENSIONS & AREAS - Wing data NC. Other data see *Gemini Flash.*

POWER PLANT - See *Gemini Flash* except: Power per unit area NC.

WEIGHTS & LOADINGS - NC.

PERFORMANCE - NC.

Mainair test pilot Geoff Ball at the controls of the Skybike, bringing a new meaning to the term 'off-road bike'.

MAINAIR *SKYBIKE*

(Weight-shift)

Single-seat single-engined* flex-wing aircraft with weight-shift control. Rogallo wing with fin and keel pocket. Pilot suspended below wing in 'trike unit', using bar to control pitch and roll/yaw by altering relative positions of trike unit and wing. Wing braced from above by kingpost and cables, from below by cables; floating cross-tube construction with 75% double-surface enclosing cross-tube; preformed ribs. Undercarriage has four wheels in T-formation; motorcycle suspension on front pair, suspension NC on rear pair. Push-right go-left nosewheel steering independent from aerodynamic controls. Motorcycle brakes. Aluminium-alloy tube trike unit, completely open, incorporating motorcycle. Engine* mounted below wing, driving pusher propeller.

Production status: prototype.

*Second engine not used for flight.

GENERAL - Unique is a rather overworked word, but there is certainly no other machine in *Berger-Burr's* like the *Skybike*. It is easier to understand this strange device from a picture than from words, but basically it consists of a *Gemini Flash* with the front of the trike unit lopped off and a small single-seat off-road motorcycle, the Yamaha YZ80, bolted on instead. The front wheel of the bike takes the place of the trike nosewheel and is steered in the normal trike manner, which means that the pilot's feet are on the handlebars while the aircraft is flying or manoeuvring, but once the aircraft has come to a stop the bike may be detached in some 2 min and ridden away just like any other motorcycle. In the air, the little Yamaha's engine is switched off, the aircraft and bike powerplants being entirely separate.

Conceived as a military vehicle following interest from the British Army in the *Mirac,* the *Skybike* has obvious commercial potential too, and the company has taken out patents not only on the machine shown in our picture but also on a second prototype, which uses a single engine and gearbox with a control enabling the craft to be switched from wheel drive to propeller drive. Our data below refers to the first machine.

Price: NC.

EXTERNAL DIMENSIONS & AREAS - See *Gemini Flash* except: Height overall NC. Wheelbase NC. Nosewheel diameter overall not applicable. Motorcycle wheels diameter overall NC.

POWER PLANT - Rotax 447 engine. Max power 40 hp at NC rpm. Gear reduction, ratio 2.6/1. Power per unit area 0.24 hp/ft², 2.6 hp/m². Other data NC.

WEIGHTS & LOADINGS - Empty weight** 386 lb, 175 kg. Max take-off weight** 761 lb, 345 kg. Payload 375 lb, 170 kg. Max wing loading 4.53 lb/ft², 22.1 kg/m². Max power loading 19.0 lb/hp, 8.6 kg/hp. Load factors NC.

PERFORMANCE* - Never exceed speed 80 mph, 129 kph. Max climb rate at sea level 900 ft/min, 4.6 m/s. Take-off distance 165 ft, 50 m. Landing distance 130 ft, 40 m. Service ceiling 10,000 ft, 3050 m. Range at average cruising speed 60 mile, 97 km. Other data NC.

*Under the unspecified test conditions.

**Including motorcycle.

MAINAIR/FLEXIFORM
ASTRA/STRIKERLIGHT
(Weight-shift)

Single-seat single-engined flex-wing aircraft with weight-shift control. Rogallo wing with keel pocket. Pilot suspended below wing in trike unit, using bar to control pitch and roll/yaw by altering relative positions of trike unit and wing. Wing braced from above by kingpost and cables, from below by cables; bowsprit construction with 25% double-surface; preformed ribs. Undercarriage has three wheels in tricycle formation; no suspension on any wheels. Push-right go-left nosewheel steering independent from aerodynamic controls. No brakes. Aluminium-alloy tube trike unit, completely open. Engine mounted below wing, driving pusher propeller.

Production status: prototype.

GENERAL - Mainair's contestant in the sub-70 kg stakes had yet to make its maiden flight as we went to press, and indeed only received its name on the day this was written! However, we know that the *Astra* is a conventional monopole trike unit, built to a simple specification to ensure that even with wing it gets under the 70 kg limit at which UK airworthiness regulations become mandatory. Power will be by Rotax, either a 185 or 277 depending on how the weight arithmetic works out, and the wing will be the customer's choice, the company having no plans to develop one of its own for this category. Possible wings include the Skyhook *Zeus C* or *Gipsy*, and the Aerial Arts *130 SX,* but we list it here with what is likely to be its first flying partner, Flexiform's lightweight wing developed specifically for sub-70 trikes, the *Strikerlight*.
This new wing is a development of earlier Flexiform designs, and shares their bowsprit configuration and 150° nose angle. The most obvious difference is the sailcut, for the cloth is laid spanwise to save weight, and the result of this and other weight-reducing measures is a wing weighing only 52 lb (24 kg). An even lighter version, using lighter cloth to save a further 4 lb (2 kg), is also planned.
Trike unit prices are NC, but the wing costs £1165.22 (standard version) or £1204.35 (lightweight version).

EXTERNAL DIMENSIONS & AREAS - Length overall 16.0 ft, 4.88 m. Wing span 34.1 ft, 10.4 m. Chord at root 12.0 ft, 3.66 m. Chord at tip 2.5 ft, 0.76 m. Dihedral 0°. Nose angle 150°. Depth of keel pocket 1.3 ft, 0.38 m. Total wing area 194 ft², 18.0 m². Keel pocket area 4.5 ft², 0.41 m². Aspect ratio 6.0/1. Other data NC.

POWER PLANT - Rotax single-cylinder engine. Other data NC.

WEIGHTS & LOADINGS - NC.

PERFORMANCE - NC.

MAINAIR *SCORCHER*
(Weight-shift)

Summary similar to Merlin/Typhoon S4 Medium *except: Rogallo wing with fin and keel pocket. 85% double-surface.*

Production status: see text.

GENERAL - After the enthusiastic reception given to the *Gemini Flash,* Mainair has turned its attention back to the solo market, which has been relatively neglected in the UK since the advent of airworthiness legislation. Manufacturers concentrated first on legalising their dual designs, with the result that at the time of writing (June '85), the only legally saleable single-seat flexwings were the sub-70 kg machines which are exempt from airworthiness legislation; not one standard-weight solo trike had received type-approval.
Mainair's *Scorcher* is intended to remedy this situation. Like the *Gemini Flash,* the *Scorcher* will be an all-Mainair aircraft, in contrast to earlier Mainair solos which have all used other manufacturers' wings. Few details have yet been released on the *Scorcher's* wing, but it would be odd if the new Rogallo did not bear a family resemblance to its bigger brother. Of unusually small area - among British wings only the *130 SX* is smaller - it will be mated to an updated version of the *Merlin* trike unit, on which the principal change will be the adoption of Rotax power. The combination of a small, tight wing and a twin-cylinder Rotax - the 377 and 447 are likely options - should certainly produce a fast, nimble machine. Our data below refers to the 377-engined version; where different, figures for the 447 are shown in parentheses.
Price: NC.

EXTERNAL DIMENSIONS & AREAS - Total wing area 136 ft², 12.6 m². Wheel track 4.6 ft, 1.40 m. Wheelbase 5.8 ft, 1.76 m. Nosewheel diameter overall 13 inch, 32 cm. Main wheels diameter overall 13 inch, 32 cm. Other data NC.

POWER PLANT - Rotax 377 (Rotax 447) engine. Max power 35(40) hp at NC rpm. Propeller diameter and pitch NC. Gear reduction, ratio 2.6/1. Max static thrust NC. Power per unit area 0.26(0.29) hp/ft², 2.8(3.2) hp/m². Fuel capacity 5.7 US gal, 4.8 Imp gal, 21.6 litre.

WEIGHTS & LOADINGS - NC.

PERFORMANCE - NC.

MEDWAY

Medway Microlights, 6 Beatty Cottages, Allhallows, Rochester, Kent ME3 9PE; tel 0634 270780/ 270868. Chief executive: Chris Draper.

MEDWAY/AERIAL ARTS
HALF PINT/130 SX
(Weight-shift)

Single-seat single-engined flex-wing aircraft with weight-shift control. Rogallo wing with keel pocket. Pilot suspended below wing in trike unit, using bar to control pitch and roll/yaw by altering relative positions of trike unit and wing. Wing braced from above by kingpost and cables, from below by cables; floating cross-tube construction with 65% double-surface enclosing cross-tube; preformed ribs. Undercarriage has three wheels in tricycle formation; no suspension on any wheels. Push-right go-left nosewheel steering independent from aerodynamic controls. No brakes. Aluminium-alloy tube trike unit, completely open. Engine mounted below wing, driving pusher propeller.

Production status: current, number completed NC.

GENERAL - Medway Microlights started from very small beginnings in 1982 - so small in fact that it has the rare distinction of escaping the *Berger-Burr* net when our first edition was prepared - but since then the firm has gone

Norman Burr

Ian Grayland, designer of the 130 SX *wing, demonstrates the* Half Pint *at the aircraft's debut in March '85. For another illustration, see colour section.*

from strength to strength, and was one of the first to get company approval under the British airworthiness scheme. Medway makes only trike units, and its latest design, the *Half Pint,* attracted great interest on its debut at the Popham Trade Show in March '85. When mated to the Aerial Arts *130 SX* wing which it is designed to complement, it makes perhaps the neatest of all the sub-70 kg aircraft on the British market. Two things give the machine its visual appeal: firstly, the wing is unusually small in both span and area for a triking Rogallo, and secondly the use of the JPX PUL425 engine without reduction drive gives the trike unit a tidy, uncluttered appearance.

Much more important, of course, is how it flies. Aerial Arts has hitherto concentrated on making free-flight wings, and the *130 SX* is in fact a development of its *Clubman CFX* hang glider, but it has been re-engineered specifically for the sub-70 kg class, with sail elasticity and leading-edge flex calculated to get the best out of the very limited thrust of such machines. And the exercise seems to have worked: with such a small wing, one would expect a respectable level speed, but the surprise is that the aircraft also glides remarkably well, according to Keith Vinning of *Flightline* magazine, who tested the machine in the July-

August '85 issue. Both topside and underside are battened, and there are transparent inspection panels built into the wing at wear points - a nice touch.

Price is £2400 complete, and options include a B-bar, mylar-coated leading edges and a larger tank, the latter a no-cost option which holds 5.0 Imp gal (6.0 US gal, 22.7 litre).

EXTERNAL DIMENSIONS & AREAS - Wing span 29.0 ft, 8.84 m. Total wing area 128 ft^2, 11.9 m^2. Aspect ratio 6.6/1. Wheel track 5.2 ft, 1.57 m. Wheelbase 5.2 ft, 1.57 m. Nosewheel diameter overall 10 inch, 25 cm. Main wheels diameter overall 10 inch, 25 cm. Other data NC.

POWER PLANT - JPX PUL425 engine. Max power 26 hp at 4600 rpm. Propeller diameter and pitch 39x30 inch, 1.00x0.76 m. No reduction. Max static thrust 166 lb, 75 kg. Power per unit area 0.20 hp/ft^2, 2.2 hp/m^2. Fuel capacity 2.4 US gal, 2.0 Imp gal, 9.1 litre.

WEIGHTS & LOADINGS - Empty weight 143 lb, 65 kg. Max take-off weight 362 lb, 164 kg. Payload 219 lb, 99 kg. Max wing loading 2.83 lb/ft^2, 13.8 kg/m^2. Max power loading 13.9 lb/hp, 6.3 kg/hp. Load factors NC recommended; +5.7, -NC ultimate.

PERFORMANCE* - Max level speed 45 mph, 72 kph. Never exceed speed 70 mph, 113 kph. Cruising speed 35 mph, 56 kph. Stalling speed 20 mph, 32 kph. Max climb rate at sea level 350 ft/min, 1.8 m/s. Min sink rate 200 ft/min at 28 mph, 1.0 m/s at 45 kph. Best glide ratio with power off NC. Take-off distance 50 ft, 15 m. Landing distance 50 ft, 15 m. Service ceiling 7000 ft, 2130 m. Range at average cruising speed 120 mile, 193 km. Noise level NC.

Under the following test conditions - Airfield altitude 400 ft, 122 m. Ground temperature 59°F, 15°C. Ground pressure NC. Ground windspeed 8-12 mph, 13-19 kph. Test payload 155 lb, 70 kg.

MEDWAY/PEGASUS
HYBRED 440/TYPHOON XL
(Weight-shift)

Tandem two-seat single-engined flex-wing aircraft with weight-shift control. Rogallo wing with keel pocket. Pilot suspended below wing in trike unit, using bar to control pitch and roll/yaw by altering relative positions of trike unit and wing. Wing braced from above by kingpost and cables, from below by cables; floating cross-tube construction with 55% double-surface enclosing cross-tube; preformed ribs. Undercarriage has three wheels in tricycle formation; no suspension on any wheels. Push-right go-left nosewheel steering independent from aerodynamic controls. No brakes. Aluminium-alloy tube trike unit, with optional pod. Engine mounted below wing, driving pusher propeller.

Production status: current, number completed NC.

GENERAL - Medway's *HyBred 440* is the latest version of a series of trike units which the company has built in small numbers over the past two years. Most have been two-seaters with 440 Robin engines and the company has now standardised on this design, but a few have had a 330 fitted and an even smaller number have been produced with a single-seat, though the structure is otherwise identical. This latest machine, which was on the verge of full type-approval as we went to press, is basically a conventional tandem trike, but it is easily recognisable by its novel 'double monopole' - two vertical struts where a monopole would normally be situated. At the base these are bolted either side of the rectangular-section horizontal tube, while at the top they are sleeved together just below the hang point.

Type-approved aircraft will use the latest version of Pegasus' *Typhoon XL* wing, as detailed under Pegasus *Panther XL* and *Pegasus XL*. Our data below was measured with an aircraft equipped with the slightly larger older version, but is valid for both types except that the latest wing is a shade faster. Engine used in the aircraft detailed below is the Robin EC44 2PM, the standard unit, but a Rotax 447 has been tried and is likely to be an option by the time this book is published. The company co-operates closely with Pegasus, building for the latter under subcontract the distinctive semi-cylindrical section tank used for the Rotax-engined *Pegasus XL*, and it is highly likely that the complete Rotax power pack (tank included of course!) will find its way back to Medway and onto the *Hybred 440*.
Price ready to fly: £3900.

EXTERNAL DIMENSIONS & AREAS - Length overall 10.0 ft, 3.05 m. Wing span 34.0 ft, 10.36 m. Chord at root 10.0 ft, 3.05 m. Chord at tip 3.5 ft, 1.07 m. Dihedral 0°. Nose angle 122°. Total wing area 195 ft^2, 18.1 m^2. Aspect ratio 5.9/1. Wheel track 5.3 ft, 1.63 m. Wheelbase 6.0 ft, 1.83 m.

Nosewheel diameter overall 12 inch, 30 cm. Main wheels diameter overall 12 inch, 30 cm. Other data NC.

POWER PLANT - Robin EC44 2PM engine. Max power 50 hp at 6500 rpm. Propeller diameter and pitch 58x33 inch, 1.47x0.84 m. Toothed-belt reduction, ratio 3.0/1. Max static thrust 300 lb, 136 kg. Power per unit area 0.26 hp/ft^2, 2.8 hp/m^2. Fuel capacity 5.4 US gal, 4.5 Imp gal, 20.4 litre.

WEIGHTS & LOADINGS - Empty weight 326 lb, 148 kg. Max take-off weight 780 lb, 354 kg. Payload 454 lb, 206 kg. Max wing loading 4.00 lb/ft^2, 19.6 kg/m^2. Max power loading 15.6 lb/hp, 7.1 kg/hp. Load factors NC.

PERFORMANCE* - Max level speed 60 mph, 97 kph. Never exceed speed 70 mph, 113 kph. Max cruising speed 50 mph, 80 kph. Economic cruising speed 45 mph, 72 kph. Stalling speed 24 mph, 40 kph. Max climb rate at sea level 400 ft/min, 2.0 m/s. Best glide ratio with power off 6/1 at 35 mph, 56 kph. Take-off distance 150 ft, 46 m. Landing distance 180 ft, 55 m. Noise level 84 dB at 500 ft, 152 m.

Under the following test conditions - Test payload 352 lb, 160 kg.

MICROFLIGHT

Microflight Aircraft Ltd, Shobdon Airfield, Hereford HR6 9NR; tel 056881 723/8864/606. Managing director: John Hollings. Design director: Mike Campbell-Jones. Financial director: D Corbett. Marketing director: D Taylor.

MICROFLIGHT
SPECTRUM
(Three-axis)

Single-seat single-engined high-wing monoplane with conventional three-axis control. Wing has swept back leading edge, unswept trailing edge, and tapering chord; cruciform tail. Pitch control by elevator on tail; yaw control by fin-mounted rudder; roll control by ailerons; control inputs through stick for pitch/roll and pedals for yaw. Wing braced from below by struts; wing profile NC; 100% double-surface. Undercarriage has three wheels in tricycle formation; coil-spring suspension on nosewheel and spring-disc suspension on main wheels. Push-right go-right nosewheel steering connected to yaw control. Optional nosewheel brake. Aluminium-alloy tube airframe, partially enclosed. Engine mounted above wing, driving tractor propeller.

Production status: prototype.

GENERAL - Even by the tortuous standards of the British microlight industry, whose development times are increased enormously by the country's airworthiness legislation, the *Spectrum* has had a frustratingly slow birth. Originally conceived by Mike Campbell-Jones in 1982 as the *Ladybird* (see our first edition), it at that time looked set to be put into production by trike manufacturer Hiway. However, Hiway went broke before the deal could be signed, and when the firm re-emerged it turned its back on power, leaving Mike with a design but no way of getting it to the public.

So later that year he joined forces with John Hollings to start Microflight, rename the aircraft *Spectrum* (there is no

Norman Burr

Spectrum *evolution: inset is a flashback to '82 and the original Hiro-engined* Ladybird, *while the main picture shows Mike Campbell-Jones at the controls of the* Spectrum *prototype with floats, fabric-covered wing and Robin 330 engine; further shots of the* Spectrum *at this stage in its development appear at the front of the book, pp2-7.*

connection with the Canadian machines of the same name) and begin a long search for finance which was not successfully concluded until 1984. Meanwhile, Mike was constantly updating the prototype, ditching the Hiro engine in favour of a 330 Robin and then a 377 Rotax, replacing the novel wing-warping system with ailerons, and then, after briefly reinstating the wing-warping, returning to ailerons and at the same time designing a totally new composite-construction wing.

The essence of the machine, however, has remained the same throughout. The *Spectrum* is designed to appeal to gliding enthusiasts, and just to reinforce the point is billed as a 'microlight motor glider' by Microflight. A lot of work has gone into drag reduction, such as adding a fairing to compensate for the drag of the twin-cylinder engine, and substituting aerofoil-section struts for the original round tubes.

At the time of writing, spring 1985, the first composite wing was just being taken out of the moulds. Data below refers to the tube-and-Dacron winged prototype, but John Hollings tells us that he expects the figures for the new version to be virtually identical, with the possible exception of the glide angle, which he hopes will rise as high as 18/1.

Price: £3800 as landplane, £5000 with floats.

EXTERNAL DIMENSIONS & AREAS - Length overall 16.4 ft, 5.00 m. Height overall 6.9 ft, 2.10 m. Wing span 37.5 ft, 11.43 m. Dihedral 2°. Sweepback 6°. Total wing area 146 ft², 13.6 m². Aspect ratio 9.6/1. Other data NC.

POWER PLANT - Rotax 377 engine. Max power 35 hp at NC rpm. Propeller diameter and pitch 62x27 inch, 1.57x0.69 m. Gear reduction, ratio 2.6/1. Max static thrust 220 lb, 100 kg. Power per unit area 0.24 hp/ft², 2.6 hp/m². Fuel capacity 6.0 US gal, 5.0 Imp gal, 22.7 litre.

WEIGHTS & LOADINGS - Empty weight 276 lb, 125 kg. Max take-off weight 556 lb, 252 kg. Payload 280 lb, 127 kg. Max wing loading 3.81 lb/ft², 18.5 kg/m². Max power loading 15.9 lb/hp, 7.2 kg/hp. Load factors +4.0, -2.7 recommended; +6.0, -4.0 ultimate.

PERFORMANCE* - Max level speed 65 mph, 105 kph. Never exceed speed 75 mph, 121 kph. Max cruising speed 50 mph, 80 kph. Economic cruising speed 43 mph, 69 kph. Stalling speed 30 mph, 48 kph. Max climb rate at sea level 800 ft/min, 4.1 m/s. Min sink rate 270 ft/min at 35 mph, 1.4 m/s at 56 kph. Best glide ratio with power off 14/1 at 43 mph, 69 kph. Take-off distance ft, 75 m. Landing distance 215 ft, 65 m. Service ceiling 12,000 ft, 3660 m. Range at average cruising speed 143 mile, 230 km. Noise level NC.

*Under the following test conditions - Airfield altitude 320 ft, 98 m. Ground temperature 56°F, 13°C. Ground pressure 1010 mB. Ground windspeed 5 mph, 8 kph. Test payload 223 lb, 101 kg.

Eastern Airsports

MIDLAND ULTRALIGHTS LTD.

MIDLAND ULTRALIGHTS

Midland Ultralights Ltd, Kilworth Marina, North Kilworth, Lutterworth, Leics LE17 6JB; tel 0858 880484; tx TANGO G 342251. Chief executive: Derek Hucker. Director and test pilot: Iain Barr.

MIDLAND ULTRALIGHTS *SIROCCO 377GB*

(Three-axis)

Summary as Aviasud Sirocco (see French section).

Production status: current, 6 completed.

GENERAL - Midland Ultralights builds the Aviasud *Sirocco* under license and at first sight the British machine could easily be mistaken for its French cousin. However, many subtle alterations have had to be made to satisfy UK airworthiness regulations, which have resulted in a more robust but slightly heavier machine, appropriately retitled *Sirocco 377GB*.

Principal changes to the airframe are a different nosewheel mounting (the original is designed to sheer in a very heavy

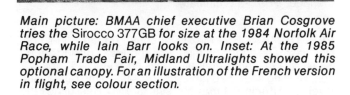

Norman Burr

Main picture: BMAA chief executive Brian Cosgrove tries the Sirocco 377GB for size at the 1984 Norfolk Air Race, while Iain Barr looks on. Inset: At the 1985 Popham Trade Fair, Midland Ultralights showed this optional canopy. For an illustration of the French version in flight, see colour section.

landing, but the UK authorities took a dim view of this idea), stops on the controls, different pedals, thicker control and trim-operating cables, a piano hinge on the trim tab, and thicker leading-edge cables, up from 2 mm to 5 mm diameter. The power pack has received attention too, with an extra silencer added, fuel drains and taps, and a sight gauge protected by a sleeve.

Price: £5600 ready to fly.

EXTERNAL DIMENSIONS & AREAS - See Aviasud *Sirocco* (French section).

Snowbird *evolution: main picture shows cutaway of latest version; insets show same machine flying and a model of the original open-cockpit design.*

POWER PLANT - Rotax 377 engine. Max power 35 hp at 6750 rpm. Propeller diameter and pitch 52x32 inch, 1.32x0.81 m. Gear reduction, ratio 2.6/1. Max static thrust 220 lb, 100 kg. Power per unit area 0.23 hp/ft^2, 2.5 hp/m^2. Fuel capacity 5.3 US gal, 4.4 Imp gal, 20.0 litre.

WEIGHTS & LOADINGS - Empty weight 300 lb, 136 kg. Max take-off weight 529 lb, 240 kg. Payload 229 lb, 104 kg. Max wing loading 3.50 lb/ft^2, 17.1 kg/m^2. Max power loading 15.1 lb/hp, 6.9 kg/hp. Load factors +4.0, -2.0 recommended; +6.7, -3.6 ultimate.

PERFORMANCE* - Max level speed 69 mph, 111 kph. Never exceed speed 86 mph, 138 kph. Max cruising speed 69 mph, 111 kph. Economic cruising speed 45 mph, 72 kph. Stalling speed 28 mph, 45 kph. Max climb rate at sea level 1200 ft/min, 6.1 m/s. Min sink rate NC. Best glide ratio with power off 12/1 at 45 mph, 72 kph. Take-off distance 500 ft, 152 m to clear obstacle of 50 ft, 15 m. Take-off roll 70 ft, 21 m. Landing distance 500 ft, 152 m to clear obstacle of 50 ft, 15 m. Landing roll 165 ft, 50 m. Service ceiling 10,500 ft, 3200 m. Range at average cruising speed 186 mile, 299 km. Noise level NC.

*Under the following test conditions - Airfield altitude 0 ft, 0 m. Ground temperature 59°F, 15°C. Ground pressure 1013 mB. Ground windspeed 0 mph, 0 kph. Test payload 229 lb, 104 kg.

NOBLE HARDMAN

Noble Hardman Aviation Ltd, Penbidwal House, Pandy, Gwent NP7 8EA; tel 087382 367; tx 437269. Managing director: David Hardman. Designer: Dr David Noble. Engineering director: Philip Noble.

French agent: GH Aviation, 1713 Notre Dame, 06220 Golfe-Juan; tel (93) 63 6351; tx 470776. Contact: G H Humpheries.

NOBLE HARDMAN *SNOWBIRD* (Three-axis)

Side-by-side two-seat single-engined high-wing mono-plane with conventional three-axis control. Wing has unswept leading and trailing edges, and constant chord; flaps fitted; cruciform tail. Pitch control by elevator on tail; yaw control by fin-mounted rudder; roll control by half-span ailerons; control inputs through stick for pitch/roll and pedals for yaw. Wing braced from below by struts; wing profile NACA 4412; 100% double-surface. Undercarriage has three wheels in tricycle formation; coil-spring suspension on nosewheel and bungee suspension on main wheels. Push-right go-right nosewheel steering connected to yaw control. Brakes on main wheels. Aluminium-alloy tube airframe, totally enclosed. Engine mounted below wing, driving tractor propeller.

Production status: prototype.

GENERAL - With the demise of the *Dragon,* there is a pressing need for a tough three-axis trainer for the British market - not an easy machine to design, because it must on the one hand satisfy the UK airworthiness regulations and on the other weigh no more than 150 kg, unlike some Continental countries where an extra 25 kg is allowed for training machines.

Noble Hardman's *Snowbird* is one such entrant for that market, though at the time of writing it is only in prototype form. Nevertheless, it has put in a lot of hours since we featured it in our first edition, and any passing resemblence which that earlier version may have had to its distant relative the *Ladybird* (see Microflight) has now well and truly disappeared.

Along the way it has become a very un-microlight looking machine with a totally enclosed cockpit, though it is still tube-and-Dacron built, and has acquired half-span flaps on the inboard halves of its trailing edges. The flaps have three positions - clean aerofoil, take-off, and steep descent.

Intended for sale at the very competitive price of £6500, the *Snowbird* was intended to have the four-cylinder Lotus engine, though the data below refers to the prototype, which is using an Arrow GT500.

EXTERNAL DIMENSIONS & AREAS - Length overall 22.3 ft, 6.80 m. Height overall 7.87 ft, 2.40 m. Wing span 31.8 ft, 9.70 m. Constant chord 5.2 ft, 1.60 m. Dihedral 2°. Sweepback 0°. Tailplane span 7.87 ft, 2.40 m. Fin height 4.3 ft, 1.31 m. Total wing area 163 ft², 15.1 m². Total aileron area 3.2 ft², 0.30 m². Fin area 4.5 ft², 0.42 m². Rudder area 6.6 ft², 0.61 m². Tailplane area 15.0 ft², 1.39 m². Total elevator area 8.8 ft², 0.82 m². Aspect ratio 6.2/1. Wheel track 5.6 ft, 1.70 m. Wheelbase 4.6 ft, 1.40 m. Nosewheel diameter overall 12 inch, 30 cm. Main wheels diameter overall 12 inch, 30 cm.

POWER PLANT - Arrow GT500 engine. Max power 60 hp at NC rpm. Propeller diameter and pitch NC. No reduction. Max static thrust 331 lb, 150 kg. Power per unit area 0.37 hp/ft², 4.0 hp/m². Fuel capacity 7.1 US gal, 5.9 Imp gal, 27.0 litre.

WEIGHTS & LOADINGS - Empty weight 331 lb, 150 kg. Max take-off weight 772 lb, 350 kg. Payload 441 lb, 200 kg. Max wing loading 4.74 lb/ft², 23.2 kg/m². Max power loading 12.9 lb/hp, 5.8 kg/hp. Load factors +4.0, -2.5 recommended; +6.0, -3.75 ultimate.

PERFORMANCE* - Max level speed 65 mph, 105 kph. Never exceed speed 90 mph, 145 kph. Max cruising speed 60 mph, 97 kph. Economic cruising speed 45 mph, 72 kph. Stalling speed 34 mph, 55 kph. Max climb rate at sea level 1200 ft/min, 6.1 m/s. Take-off distance 245 ft, 75 m. Landing distance 330 ft, 100 m. Range at average cruising speed 174 mile, 280 km. Other data NC.

*Under the following test conditions - Airfield altitude NC. Ground temperature 68°F, 20°C. Ground pressure 1013 mB. Ground windspeed 0 mph, 0 kph. Test payload 441 lb, 200 kg.

PEGASUS

Pegasus Transport Systems Ltd, PO Box 29, Marlborough, Wiltshire SN8 1PF; tel 0672 53504. Factory: George Lane, Marlborough, Wiltshire SN8 4DA; tel 0672 54414; tx 449703 TELSER G. Managing director: Rick Hogarth. Other directors include: Murray Rose, Graham Slater, Mark Southall.

PEGASUS *PANTHER XL and* PEGASUS *XL*
(Weight-shift)

Tandem two-seat single-engined flex-wing aircraft with weight-shift control. Rogallo wing with keel pocket. Pilot suspended below wing in trike unit, using bar to control pitch and roll/yaw by altering relative positions of trike unit and wing. Wing braced from above by kingpost and cables, from below by cables; floating cross-tube construction with 55% double-surface enclosing cross-tube; preformed ribs. Undercarriage has three wheels in tricycle formation; coil-spring suspension on nosewheel and no suspension on main wheels. Push-right go-left nosewheel steering independent from aerodynamic controls. Optional nosewheel brake. Aluminium-alloy tube trike unit, with pod. Engine mounted below wing, driving pusher propeller.

Production status: current, see text for number completed.

GENERAL - Though the name Pegasus is new to the microlight world, the company has been in existence in the military field since 1973, and in 1981 formed a liaison with Murray Rose's Chargus company to pursue commercial and military applications of the Chargus *Titan 38* side-by-side two-seat trike. Little came of the arrangement at the time, as Chargus stopped trading the following year, but in 1984 the Pegasus name hit the microlight headlines with the news that it had acquired Rogallo manufacturer Solar Wings, along with the rights to the Ultra Sports trike units normally sold with them. With the names came many of their personnel, especially Mark Southall of Solar Wings and Graham Slater of Ultra Sports, and by persuading Murray Rose and ex-Chargus employee Robin Goodwin to also join the new group, Pegasus amassed one of the biggest teams of design talent in Europe.

With the Chargus designs being rather outdated, it's not surprising that Pegasus' first offerings are basically Ultra Sports/Solar Wings products. The Pegasus *Panther XL* is virtually identical to the Ultra Sports/Solar Wings *Panther Dual 440* which we featured in our last edition, the main changes being that the *Typhoon XL* wing now has a slightly smaller area and the upside-down engine mounting of the Robin 440 has been reinstated, the 'right-way-up' system having proved unreliable. The Robin 330 option has been dropped and two previously optional features - nosewheel brake and pod - are now standard; wheel spats are now also a standard fitment.

Though not as fast as some of its rivals, the *Panther XL* has earned a good reputation with schools, who appreciate its very gentle stall, light roll control and relatively high bar force in pitch, a combination of features which makes it the most idiot-proof dual wing on the British market.

For the same price as the *Panther XL* - £4100 ready to fly - the company also offers the *Pegasus XL,* an identical machine except that it has a Rotax 447 engine with gear reduction. Our data below refers to the Robin-engined machine; where different, figures for the Rotax version are shown in parentheses.

Total production of this two-seater, including all engine variants and all the examples manufactured under the Ultra Sports/Solar Wings banner, is now well over 100.

Norman Burr

Easy recognition point for those not adept at identifying engines is the tank position: below engine on Pegasus XL *(main picture shows prototype, right inset shows production arrangement)* above on Panther XL *(left inset).* The latter is shown without its standard fitment spats. The third inset shows the front suspension (the mudguard is non-standard).

EXTERNAL DIMENSIONS & AREAS - Length overall 13.0 ft, 3.96 m. Height overall 11.0 ft, 3.35 m. Wing span 34.0 ft, 10.36 m. Nose angle 122°. Total wing area 188 ft², 17.5 m². Aspect ratio 6.1/1. Wheel track 5.0 ft, 1.52 m. Wheelbase 5.9 ft, 1.80 m. Nosewheel diameter overall 13 inch, 33 cm. Main wheels diameter overall 13 inch, 33 cm. Other data NC.

POWER PLANT - Robin EC44 2PM (Rotax 447) engine. Max power 40 hp at NC rpm. Propeller diameter and pitch 60x29(NC) inch, 1.52x0.74(NC) m. Toothed-belt (gear) reduction, ratio 2.6/1. Max static thrust 275(NC) lb, 125(NC) kg. Power per unit area 0.21 hp/ft², 2.3 hp/m². Fuel capacity 5.8 US gal, 4.8 Imp gal, 22.0 litre.

WEIGHTS & LOADINGS - Empty weight 328(320) lb, 149(145) kg. Max take-off weight 772 lb, 350 kg. Payload 444(452) lb, 201(205) kg. Max wing loading 4.11 lb/ft², 20.0 kg/m². Max power loading 19.3 lb/hp, 8.8 kg/hp. Load factors +4.0, -2.0 recommended; +6.0, -4.0 ultimate.

PERFORMANCE* - Max level speed *60* mph, *97* kph. Never exceed speed 67 mph, 107 kph. Cruising speed 52 mph, 83 kph. Stalling speed 28 mph, 45 kph. Max climb rate at sea level 385(400) ft/min, 1.95(2.03) m/s. Range at average cruising speed 121(127) mile, 195(204) km. Other data NC.

*Under unspecified test conditions except - Test payload for stalling speed measurement 444(452) lb, 201(205) kg.

PEGASUS
PEGASUS TUG XL and TUG XLT
(Weight-shift)

Summary as Panther XL and Pegasus XL.

Production status: prototype, production late 1985.

GENERAL - The *Pegasus Tug* is the company's workhorse trike unit, very similar to that used with the *Panther XL* and *Pegasus XL* except that the biggest Rotax is fitted, the 503. For use as a tourer/trainer, it can be supplied with a *Typhoon XL* wing, the complete aircraft being dubbed *Pegasus Tug XL,* but for banner or hang-glider towing the larger *Typhoon XLT* is used, creating the *Pegasus Tug XLT.*
A lot of effort has gone into the development of safe hang-glider towing equipment, and the *Pegasus Tug XLT*

All pictures: Norman Burr

The Pegasus Tug XLT prototype, pictured at Popham Trade Fair in March '85. The glider release mechanism can be seen just under the tank. Inserts show the release mechanism close up and the rubber-mounted prop boss through which the tow line passes.

features a through-the-prop towing line, with release mechanisms at the glider end and the trike end. The latter is situated just above the engine and is controlled by a foot pedal in the pod.

Our data below refers to the larger-winged machine, which costs £4500. Price of smaller version: NC.

EXTERNAL DIMENSIONS & AREAS - See *Panther XL and Pegasus XL* except: Length overall NC. Height overall NC. Wing span 37.0 ft, 11.28 m. Total wing area 204 ft², 19.0 m². Aspect ratio 6.7/1.

POWER PLANT - Rotax 503 engine. Max power 46 hp at NC rpm. Propeller diameter and pitch 60xNC inch, 1.52xNC m. Toothed-belt reduction, ratio 2.6/1. Max static thrust NC. Power per unit area 0.23 hp/ft², 2.4 hp/m². Fuel capacity 5.8 US gal, 4.8 Imp gal, 22.0 litre.

WEIGHTS & LOADINGS - Empty weight 331 lb, 150 kg. Max take-off weight 772 lb, 350 kg. Payload 441 lb, 200 kg. Max wing loading 3.78 lb/ft², 18.4 kg/m². Max power loading 16.8 lb/hp, 7.6 kg/hp. Load factors +4.0, -2.0 recommended; +6.0, -4.0 ultimate.

PERFORMANCE* - Never exceed speed 57 mph, 92 kph. Cruising speed 52 mph, 83 kph. Stalling speed 24 mph, 39 kph. Max climb rate at sea level when towing** 500 ft/min, 2.5 m/s. Other data NC.

Under unspecified test conditions except - Test payload for stalling speed measurement 441 lb, 200 kg.

**Drag from towed object NC.*

PEGASUS *FORGER T.503*

(Weight-shift)

Summary similar to Panther XL and Pegasus XL *except: Side-by-side two-seater.*

Production status: prototype.

GENERAL - The *Forger T.440* prototype is effectively an updated version of the old Chargus *Titan 38,* and was originally developed for military use. As we went to press, the aircraft was about to be re-engined with an identical power unit to the *Pegasus Tug XLT,* and re-named *Forger T.503* accordingly. It will probably also share the same wing as the towing machine, though probably with composite leading edges, a feature which may in due course be extended to other Pegasus wings. The company believes there is also a market for a civilian version, and is likely to introduce a trainer based on the *Forger T.503,* though no release date has been fixed. Price: NC.

EXTERNAL DIMENSIONS & AREAS - For wing data see *Pegasus Tug XLT.* Other data NC.

POWER PLANT - See *Pegasus Tug XLT.*

WEIGHTS & LOADINGS - NC.

PERFORMANCE - NC.

PEGASUS/MAINAIR
SOLAR FLASH
(Weight-shift)

Summary as Pegasus XL *except: Rogallo wing with fin and keel pocket. 75% double-surface.*

Production status: see text.

GENERAL - This aircraft, which was still secret as we went to press, is Pegasus' response to the need for a fast two-seater.

While its *Typhoon XL* and *XLT* wings are very well liked as training and workhorse Rogallos, neither can match the speed of the *Flash,* so with commendable pragmatism Pegasus director Rick Hogarth decided to buy complete wings from Mainair to mount on his own trike units.

The result will be called the *Solar Flash* and will be marketed as the top of the line Pegasus model, possibly with a specially luxurious pod as standard. Basically, however, the trike unit will be identical with that of the *Pegasus XL.* Performance will obviously be similar to the Rotax-engined version of Mainair's *Gemini Flash,* though Rick hopes to better the latter by using a special prop and is aiming at a maximum level speed of over 70 mph (113 kph).

Likely options include a specially quiet engine/prop combination, which could be a winner in countries with strict noise regulations, like West Germany and the Netherlands. Price: NC.

EXTERNAL DIMENSIONS & AREAS - Length overall 11.2 ft, 3.40 m. Height overall NC. Wing span 34.6 ft, 10.55 m. Mean chord 4.8 ft, 1.48 m. Dihedral -2°. Nose angle 130°. Fin height 1.0 ft, 0.30 m. Depth of keel pocket 0.5 ft, 0.15 m. Total wing area 168 ft², 15.6 m². Total vertical area 5.7 ft², 0.53 m². Aspect ratio 7.1/1. Wheel track 5.0 ft, 1.52 m. Wheelbase 5.9 ft, 1.80 m. Nosewheel diameter overall 13 inch, 33 cm. Main wheels diameter overall 13 inch, 33 cm.

POWER PLANT - See *Pegasus XL* except: Power per unit area 0.24 hp/ft², 2.6 hp/m².

WEIGHTS & LOADINGS - Empty weight 331 lb, 150 kg. Other data NC.

PERFORMANCE - NC.

PEGASUS *SOLO*
(Weight-shift)

Summary similar to Panther XL and Pegasus XL *except: Single-seat. Rubber suspension on nosewheel and coil-spring suspension on main wheels.*

Production status: prototype.

GENERAL - Though there is no doubt about which wing will be on top of Pegasus' first standard-weight single-seat trike (provisionally called the *Solo*), the *Typhoon S4 Large* being the obvious choice, the company has no less than three trike units it can draw on - Chargus' *T250,* Ultra Sports' *Tripacer,* and a prototype developed by Robin Goodwin.

Shapes of the Solo to come? Since our main picture was taken at the Norfolk Air Race in July '84, Sally Huxtable's much modified Tripacer has had its 330 Robin replaced with a Rotax, though she fitted the 377 rather than the 277 as the aircraft is frequently used for display and competition work. Underslung tank is also non-standard. Insets show the GMD 330 and a close-up of its front suspension.

Norman Burr

Of the three, the prototype is perhaps the most interesting, and dates from the period when Robin ran his own company, in between leaving Chargus and joining Pegasus. Prop manufacture was his stock in trade, but he did turn up at the Weston Park fly-in in July '83 with a very neat 330 Robin-engined trike unit called the *GMD 330* which he later mated to a Southdown *Lightning Phase II* wing to produce the *Lynx*. This very promising machine never got into production, but some of its features, particularly its suspension system, are likely to be incorporated into the *Solo,* which we understand will otherwise draw heavily on the *Tripacer*. It seems unlikely that the new machine will bear much relationship to the *T250,* which is not surprising as the latter is an old design and was in any case far outsold by the very popular *Tripacer*.

No price or release date has been fixed, but what is certain is that the *Solo* will use a 277 Rotax engine.

Just to add a final twist to the saga, we understand that the one and only *GMD 330* is being used as a flying test bed to evaluate composite materials for future Pegasus designs...

EXTERNAL DIMENSIONS & AREAS - Length overall 12.8 ft, 3.90 m. Wing span 34.0 ft, 10.36 m. Chord at root 8.5 ft, 2.68 m. Dihedral 0°. Nose angle 122°. Total wing area 180 ft², 16.7 m². Aspect ratio 6.4/1. Other data NC.

POWER PLANT - Rotax 277 engine. Max power 28 hp at NC rpm. Power per unit area 0.16 hp/ft², 1.7 hp/m². Other data NC.

WEIGHTS & LOADINGS - NC.

PERFORMANCE - NC.

PHOENIX

Phoenix Aircraft Co, c/o 2 Watford Road, Crick, Northants; tel 0788 822416. Principal: Chris Harrison. Stress/design: K Wadolkowski.

PHOENIX *FALCON*
(Three-axis)

Single-seat single-engined high-wing monoplane with conventional three-axis control. Wing has unswept leading and trailing edges, and constant chord; cruciform tail. Pitch control by elevator on tail; yaw control by fin-mounted rudder; roll control by 40%-span spoilers; control inputs through stick for pitch/roll and pedals for yaw. Wing braced from above by kingpost and cables, from below by cables; wing profile NC; 100% double-surface. Undercarriage has three wheels in tricycle formation; bungee suspension on all wheels. Push-right go-right nosewheel steering connected to yaw control. No brakes. Aluminium-alloy tube airframe, with pod. Engine mounted at wing height, driving tractor propeller.

Production status: prototype.

GENERAL - With the British market heavily biased towards trikes and the three-axis manufacturers trying to establish a foothold by offering more sophistication than the average flexwing, the straightforward US-style tube-and-Dacron microlight has been rather left out in the cold.

So while Chris Harrison's *Falcon* appears thoroughly unremarkable in concept - in fact it looks very much like a

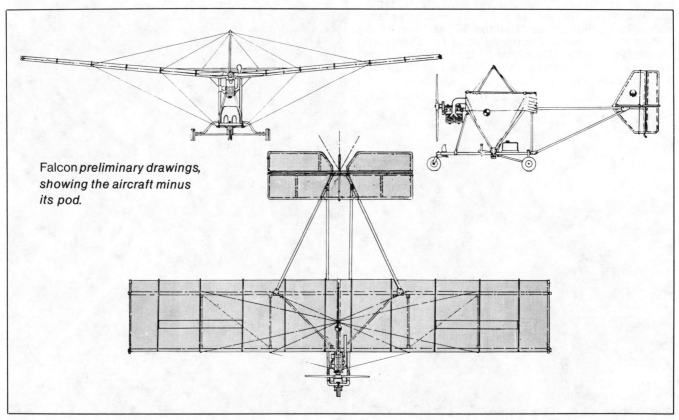

Falcon preliminary drawings, showing the aircraft minus its pod.

Mirage - it will nevertheless be the only machine of its kind on the British market, with the exception of imported *Quicksilvers.* In practice the venerable American is likely to have the market to itself for a while longer at least, for the aircraft's type-approval process still had some way to go at the time of going to press (July '85). But if Phoenix's projected price of under £4000 can be turned into a reality, the *Falcon* could well find a following among those desiring a simple, unpretentious machine.

EXTERNAL DIMENSIONS & AREAS - Length overall 16.5 ft, 5.03 m. Height overall 7.5 ft, 2.29 m. Wing span 30.0 ft, 9.14 m. Constant chord 5.0 ft, 1.52 m. Dihedral 5°. Sweepback 0°. Tailplane span 10.0 ft, 3.05 m. Fin height 4.5 ft, 1.37 m. Total wing area 150 ft^2, 13.9 m^2. Total spoiler area 9.0 ft^2, 0.84 m^2. Fin area NC. Rudder area NC. Tailplane area 15.0 ft^2, 1.39 m^2. Total elevator area 13.0 ft^2, 1.21 m^2. Aspect ratio 6.0/1. Wheel track 5.0 ft, 1.52 m. Wheelbase 6.8 ft, 2.06 m. Nosewheel diameter overall 16 inch, 40 cm. Main wheels diameter overall 16 inch, 40 cm.

POWER PLANT - Robin EC34PM engine. Max power 35 hp at 6000 rpm. Propeller diameter and pitch 54x27 inch, 1.37x0.69 m. Notched V-belt reduction, ratio 2.8/1. Max static thrust NC. Power per unit area 0.23 hp/ft^2, 2.5 hp/m^2. Fuel capacity 6.0 US gal, 5.0 Imp gal, 22.7 litre.

WEIGHTS & LOADINGS - Empty weight 140 lb, 309 kg. Max take-off weight 560 lb, 254 kg. Payload 251 lb, 114 kg. Max wing loading 3.73 lb/ft^2, 18.3 kg/m^2. Max power loading 16.0 lb/hp, 7.3 kg/hp. Load factors +4.0, -2.0 recommended; +6.0, -3.0 ultimate.

PERFORMANCE - NC.

The pre-production Wren *as it looked on 24 June 1985; normally, the tank will be an aluminium unit behind the seat.*

QUESTAIR

Questair Ltd, Charlton Marshall, Blandford, Dorset DT11 9NE; tel 0258 55664. Directors: Mike Coghlan, David Dreux, S G Dreux, G Newby.

QUESTAIR/AERIAL ARTS
WREN/130 SX
(Weight-shift)

Single-seat single-engined flex-wing aircraft with weight-shift control. Rogallo wing with keel pocket. Pilot suspended below wing in trike unit, using bar to control pitch and roll/yaw by altering relative positions of trike unit and wing. Wing braced from above by kingpost and cables, from below by cables; floating cross-tube construction with 65% double-surface enclosing cross-tube; preformed ribs. Undercarriage has three wheels in tricycle formation; optional rubber suspension on all wheels. Push-right go-left nosewheel steering independent from aerodynamic controls. No brakes. Aluminium-alloy tube trike unit, with optional pod. Engine mounted below wing, driving pusher propeller.

Production status: see text.

GENERAL - After several years as an instructor and dealer, Questair's Mike Coghlan decided in 1985 to branch out into manufacture, a logical decision as both the makes with which he was principally associated - SMD and Huntair - had ceased production. Huntair never really recovered from the death of its founder Steve Hunt, while SMD though still in business is not building aircraft at present, as we explain under the company's own entry.

Questair's offering is a trike unit to compete in the rapidly growing sub-70 kg sector. Known as the *Wren,* the machine was still under development as we went to press, which is why our performance figures are approximate. We show it with JPX PUL425 engine and Aerial Arts *130 SX* wing, the most likely production combination, but a KFM 107ER is also a possibility. Much of the test flying has in fact been done with a Robin EC25PS, one prototype and one pre-production aircraft having been built.

Like the SMD trike units with which the company is so familiar, the *Wren* is a duopole, which makes it the only sub-70 duopole on the British market. It is also unusual in offering an optional pod and suspension, refinements not normally found on machines this light for fear of breaking the all-important 70 kg barrier. Mike tells us that the torsional rubber suspension units will absorb over 3g before bottoming, the axle being built in three sections for easy repair and portability - by removing two bolts, it reduces to just 24 inch (61 cm) wide.

Another feature is a hang point which may be interchanged with the steering mount, both being made from stainless steel as are all other important fittings. All bolt holes in tubes are bushed.

Price in basic form, with *130 SX* wing, is £1975. Apart from the pod and suspension, options include a long-range tank, main wheel spats, and electronic instruments, the latter a Questair speciality.

Incidentally, *Pathfinder II* owners may also be interested in another Questair speciality, strengthening kits for the wing and empennage.

EXTERNAL DIMENSIONS & AREAS - Height 11.4 ft, 3.47 m. Wing span 29.0 ft, 8.84 m. Total wing area 128 ft², 11.9 m². Aspect ratio 6.6/1. Wheel track 4.6 ft, 1.40 m. Wheelbase 5.1 ft, 1.55 m. Nosewheel diameter overall 8.5 inch, 22 cm. Main wheels diameter overall 8.5 inch, 22 cm. Other data NC.

POWER PLANT - JPX PUL425 engine. Max power 26 hp at 4600 rpm. Propeller diameter and pitch NC. No reduction. Max static thrust NC. Power per unit area 0.20 hp/ft², 2.2 hp/m². Fuel capacity 2.4 US gal, 2.0 Imp gal, 9.1 litre.

WEIGHTS & LOADINGS - Empty weight 150 lb, 68 kg. Max take-off weight 374 lb, 170 kg. Payload 225 lb, 102 kg. Max wing loading 2.92 lb/ft², 14.3 kg/m². Max power loading 14.4 lb/hp, 6.5 kg/hp. Load factors +4.0, -2.5 recommended; +6.0, -4.0 ultimate.

PERFORMANCE* - Max level speed *54* mph, *87* kph. Never exceed speed 70 mph, 113 kph. Max cruising speed *47* mph, *76* kph. Economic cruising speed *39* mph, *63* kph. Stalling speed *23* mph, *37* kph. Max climb rate at sea level *400* ft/min, *2.0* m/s. Min sink rate *250* ft/min at *28* mph, *1.0* m/s at *45* kph. Range at average cruising speed *77* mile, *124* km. Other data NC.

**Under the following test conditions* - Airfield altitude 80 ft, 24 m. Ground temperature 59°F, 14°C. Ground pressure 998 mB. Ground windspeed 6 mph, 10 kph. Test payload 175 lb, 79 kg.

SHEFFIELD MICROLIGHT

Big Boys Toys Ltd t/a Sheffield Microlight Aircraft, 52 Crescent Road, Nether Edge, Sheffield S7 1HN; tel 0742 585644. Director: Peter Jackson.

SHEFFIELD MICROLIGHT
AEROSPACE 70/Suitable Rogallo
(Weight-shift)

Single-seat single-engined flex-wing aircraft with weight-shift control. Rogallo wing. Pilot suspended below wing in trike unit, using stick to control pitch and roll/yaw by altering relative positions of trike unit and wing. Wing braced from above by kingpost and cables, from below by cables. Undercarriage has three wheels in

Sheffield Microlights' Aerospace 70 *as it looked in early '85, with extra control bar, WAM 342 engine and a small experimental fuel tank of 1.3 Imp gal capacity (1.6 US gal, 5.9 litre). The top lever is an in-flight restart.*

tricycle formation; rubber suspension on all wheels. Push-right go-left nosewheel steering independent from aerodynamic controls. Nosewheel brake. Aluminium-alloy tube trike unit, completely open. Engine mounted below wing, driving pusher propeller.

Production status: prototype.

GENERAL - This company was founded to make the *Trident* trike unit, a conventional monopole device which was supplied with various engines and produced in small quantities until early 1983. Since then, however, Sheffield Microlight has been developing a much more radical machine, called the *Aerospace 70,* the number indicating that its all-up weight with wing is under the 70 kg limit at which UK airworthiness regulations apply.

Progress has been slow, since the company has been undertaking non-microlight work as well, but a very interesting aircraft has resulted, offering a novel solution to the problem of reducing pilot-induced drag on an ultra-light machine. Rather than adopt a fully prone position as on the Flight Research machines, Peter Jackson places the pilot in a semi-supine position close to the wing. The normal geometry of the wing wires is retained, resulting in a bar running under the base tube of the trike unit and necessitating a separate control bar further up the A-frame. Since our picture was taken this extra bar has been replaced by a top-mounted stick.

Drag is further cut by providing retractable main wheels, which can be moved inwards and forwards by levers either side of the base tube. The wheels are kingpin-mounted on their axles and constrained to face forwards regardless of their fore-and-aft position, which allows the pilot to land safely, albeit bicycle-style, even if they refuse to lock out.

The power unit is unconventional too, the prototype originally using a direct-drive WAM 342 engine with a

ducted fan. However, when these engines were withdrawn by the manufacturer for modifications, Peter substituted a Solo single with reduction drive, a move which puts the weight over 70 kg when the *Typhoon S4 Large* is used. So at the time of going to press the hunt was on for a lighter wing, the most likely candidate being Flexiform's *Strikerlight*.

A price of £1250 is quoted for the trike unit ready built, but in view of the development work still going on this should be regarded as provisional.

EXTERNAL DIMENSIONS & AREAS - NC.

POWER PLANT - Modified Solo engine. Max power 20 hp at 6000 rpm. Ducted fan diameter and pitch 25xNC inch, 0.64xNC m (3-blade). Toothed-belt reduction, ratio 2.0/1. Max static thrust NC. Power per unit area NC. Fuel capacity 2.4 US gal, 2.0 Imp gal, 9.1 litre.

WEIGHTS & LOADINGS - NC.

PERFORMANCE - NC.

SIGH WING

Sigh Wing Ltd, 81 Roodegate, Basildon, Essex; tel 0268 26999. Proprietor: Bill Morris.

French agent: John Byrne, 107 avenue Felix Faure, 75015 Paris.

SIGH WING/HARLEY
PARA-TRIKE/288

(Ascending parachute)

Single-seat single-engined motorised parachute. Ram-air parachute with 9 cells. Pilot suspended below wing in trike unit, using sticks to tension rigging lines and thus control yaw; no other aerodynamic controls. Parachute braced by rigging lines, number NC; 100% double-surface. Undercarriage has three wheels in tricycle for-mation; no suspension on any wheels. Push-right go-left nosewheel steering independent from aerodynamic controls. No brakes. Aluminium-alloy tube trike unit, completely open. Engine mounted below wing, driving pusher propeller. Canopy made from ripstop nylon. Bracing lines made from Kevlar.

Production status: current, 2 completed.

GENERAL - Britain's first and so far only home-grown ascending parachute, Sigh Wing's creation consists of the company's *Para-Trike* 'trike unit' mated to a Harley *288* 'chute. It is unusally generously powered for a machine of its type, with a 377 Rotax as standard - the version to which our data refers - and the even more powerful 447 as an option.

Partly because of this, the machine is heavier than most of its competitors, and comes above the 70 kg limit at which UK airworthiness type-approval becomes mandatory. We imagine this has caused a certain amount of head-scratching at the CAA, as the staff there try to decide how *Section S* should be applied to this most unusual machine, and as a result the aircraft is being aimed largely at the export market at the time of writing. Only a prototype has been retained in the UK.

One possible route to UK sales would be to build a sub-70 kg version, and Bill tells us this is very much on the cards, though no decision has yet been made.
Price: £3680 complete, instruments extra.

EXTERNAL DIMENSIONS & AREAS - Length overall* 5.0 ft, 1.52 m. Height overall before flight 5.0 ft, 1.52 m. Height overall during flight NC. Wing span 28.0 ft, 8.53 m. Constant chord 11.0 ft, 3.35 m. Sweepback 0°. Total wing area 288 ft^2, 26.7 m^2. Aspect ratio 2.7/1. Wheel track 5.0 ft, 1.52 m. Wheelbase NC. Nosewheel diameter overall 10 inch, 25 cm. Main wheels diameter overall 10 inch, 25cm.

POWER PLANT - Rotax 377 engine. Max power 37 hp at 6200 rpm. Propeller diameter and pitch 62x36 inch, 1.57x0.91 m. Gear reduction, ratio 2.6/1. Max static thrust 260 lb, 118 kg. Power per unit area 0.13 hp/ft^2, 1.4 hp/m^2. Fuel capacity 2.4 US gal, 2.0 Imp gal, 9.1 litre.

WEIGHTS & LOADINGS - Empty weight 204 lb, 93 kg. Max take-off weight 510 lb, 231 kg. Payload 306 lb, 139 kg. Max wing loading 1.77 lb/ft^2, 8.7 kg/m^2. Max power loading 13.8 lb/hp, 6.2 kg/hp. Load factors +6.0, -NC recommended, +7.0, -NC ultimate.

PERFORMANCE** - Max level speed 40 mph, 64 kph. Never exceed speed 65 mph, 105 kph. Max cruising speed 40 mph, 64 kph. Economic cruising speed 30 mph, 48 kph. Max climb rate at sea level 600 ft/min, 3.1 m/s. Take-off distance 40 ft, 12 m. Landing distance 30 ft, 9 m. Service ceiling 15,000 ft, 4570 m. Other data NC.

Trike unit only.

***Under the following test conditions* - Ground windspeed 8 mph, 13 kph. Test payload 512 lb, 232 kg.

Prototype two-seater from Sigh Wing.

SIGH WING/HARLEY
PARA-TRIKE TWO-SEAT/450
(Ascending parachute)

Summary similar to Para-Trike/288 except: Tandem two-seater.

Production status: prototype.

GENERAL - In the works at Sigh Wing is a two-seat version of the *Para-Trike* using a very similar trike unit to the solo machine but with tandem seating. A much larger canopy is used, but we have no further details of this still experimental machine, which has the honour of being the only two-seat motorised parachute in this book.

EXTERNAL DIMENSIONS & AREAS - Total wing area 450 ft^2, 41.8 m^2. Other data NC.

POWER PLANT - NC.

WEIGHTS & LOADINGS - NC.

PERFORMANCE - NC.

SKYHOOK

Skyhook Sailwings Ltd, Vale Mill, Chamber Road, Hollinwood, Oldham, Greater Manchester OL8 4PG; tel 061-624 9231; tx 667849. Managing director: Len Gabriels.

SKYHOOK *PIXIE*

(Weight-shift)

Single-seat single-engined flex-wing aircraft with weight-shift control. Rogallo wing with keel pocket. Pilot suspended below wing in trike unit, using bar to control pitch and roll/yaw by altering relative positions of trike unit and wing. Wing braced from above by kingpost and cables, from below by cables; floating cross-tube construction with 55% double-surface enclosing cross-tube; preformed ribs. Undercarriage has three wheels in tricycle formation; no suspension on any wheels. Push-right go-left nosewheel steering independent from aerodynamic controls. No brakes. Aluminium-alloy tube trike unit, completely open. Engine mounted below wing, driving pusher propeller.

Production status: current, number completed NC.

GENERAL - Len Gabriels' Skyhook company is one of the oldest in the British hang glider and microlight industry, and has survived since 1972 not least because Len is willing to innovate around a problem, instead of following others. Though not all his ideas have reached production - his *Experimental* three-axis trike and the remarkable *Orion*, a canard hang-glider/microlight, never got past the prototype stage - this amiable maverick has given the market plenty to think about over the years. In 1981, for instance, when the hunt was on for a reliable two-stroke powerful enough for a two-seat trainer, Len circumnavigated the problem by building a power pack with two single-cylinder Solo engines, each with its own reduction drive, powering contra-rotating props.

The Pixie *trike unit folds into a remarkably small package.*

Two years later, when the British industry was gloomily awaiting the impending airworthiness legislation and the customers were holding back to see which aircraft satisfied the regulations, he again produced a novel solution in the form of the *Pixie,* a trike of under 70 kg empty weight and hence exempt from the airworthiness regs. There was nothing particularly new about the idea - some of the earliest British trikes, like the Hiway *Skytrike Mk1/Super Scorpion C,* fell into the same category - but unlike the latter the *Pixie* has a respectable performance, rather than just being a marginal machine for light pilots in fine weather.

Len first showed the aircraft at the BMAA's 1983 AGM, and without doubt it was the star of the show, a back to basics machine which was the complete antithesis of the 'more power, more weight' route being followed by the rest of the industry. Since then the concept has been echoed by other manufacturers - notably Medway, Mainair, Sheffield Microlight and, on a slightly different tack, Flight Research - and a whole new sub-culture of British triking has appeared.

Although the *Pixie* normally comes complete with Skyhook's own *Zeus C* wing, it can also be supplied with the company's *Gipsy* or *Apollo* Rogallos, the latter incidentally having no connection with the Hungarian products of the same name.

To confuse the issue further, the trike unit may soon be sold separately to other Rogallo manufacturers, as Skyhook is heavily involved in sub-contract sail work for Mainair and can therefore make trike units faster than wings. Flexiform is seeking a trike unit to fit its new *Strikerlight,* while Gold Marque is starting trials with its *Javelin* wing. This represents a radical departure for the latter firm; the Nikite trike units planned for its wings in 1983 never got into quantity production, so this will be Gold Marque's first serious involvement with power flying.

Clearly, by the time our next edition is prepared there could be a whole list of *Pixie* derivatives to describe, but below we detail just the standard version with *Zeus C* wing, which sells at £1960. Substitution of the *Gipsy* wing reduces the price by £200.

EXTERNAL DIMENSIONS & AREAS - Length overall 12.3 ft, 3.76 m. Wing span 34.0 ft, 10.36 m. Dihedral 0°. Nose angle 120°. Total wing area 195 ft², 18.1 m². Aspect ratio 5.9/1. Wheel track 4.4 ft, 1.35 m. Wheelbase 5.3 ft, 1.63 m. Nosewheel diameter overall 12 inch, 30 cm. Main wheels diameter overall 12 inch, 30 cm. Other data NC.

POWER PLANT - Solo engine. Max power 14 hp at 5500 rpm. Propeller diameter and pitch 50x30 inch, 1.27x0.76 m. V-belt reduction, ratio 2.3/1. Max static thrust 110 lb, 50 kg. Power per unit area 0.07 hp/ft², 0.8 hp/m². Fuel capacity 1.3 US gal, 1.1 Imp gal, 5.0 litre.

WEIGHTS & LOADINGS - Empty weight 148 lb, 67 kg. Max take-off weight 380 lb, 172 kg. Payload 232 lb, 105 kg. Max wing loading 1.95 lb/ft², 9.5 kg/m². Max power loading 27.1 lb/hp, 12.3 kg/hp. Load factors +4.0, -NC recommended; +6.0, -NC ultimate.

PERFORMANCE* - Max level speed 45 mph, 72 kph. Economic cruising speed 35 mph, 56 kph. Stalling speed 25 mph, 40 kph. Max climb rate at sea level 300 ft/min, 1.5 m/s. Min sink rate 240 ft/min, 1.2 m/s at NC speed. Best glide ratio with power off 9/1 at 28 mph, 45 kph. Take-off distance 105 ft, 32 m. Landing distance 100 ft, 30 m. Range at average cruising speed 44 mile, 71 km. Noise level 64 dB at 500 ft, 150 m.

Under the following test conditions - Airfield altitude 1000 ft, 305 m. Ground temperature NC. Ground pressure NC. Ground windspeed 15 mph, 24 kph. Test payload 185 lb, 84 kg.

SMD

Southern Microlight Developments, 55 Carters Avenue, Hamworthy, Poole; tel 0202 672266. Proprietor: Chris Scoble.

SMD *VIPER/Suitable Rogallo*
(Weight-shift)

Single-seat single-engined flex-wing aircraft with weight-shift control. Rogallo wing. Pilot suspended below wing in trike unit, using bar to control pitch and roll/yaw by altering relative positions of trike unit and wing. Undercarriage has three wheels in tricycle formation. Trike unit partially enclosed. Engine mounted below wing, driving pusher propeller. Other details NC.

Production status: prototype.

GENERAL - Although he shuns publicity, south coast constructor Chris Scoble has earned himself a good reputation as a trike builder during the five years he has been involved with the sport, initially making homebuilts for his own amusement and then branching out into small-scale production of the *Gazelle* trike unit and its two-seat derivative.

However, like many small manufacturers, he has been forced to radically rethink his approach following the introduction of airworthiness testing, due to the costs involved, and is not manufacturing at the time of writing. Instead he has concentrated on engine testing - he did much development work on the Hewland twin - and constructing an advanced prototype called the *Viper*. At present the machine is best described as a latter-day Motodelta *G-11* without the rudder (see Other Countries section, Moto-Hung), naturally with a Hewland engine.

As we write the aircraft has yet to make its maiden flight and it is not clear in what form it will be offered to the public. If Chris decides to take the plunge and become a fully fledged manufacturer, he is likely to engineer the design for superplastic aluminium rather than glass-fibre, with the prototype being used as a buck for the moulds.

Wing has yet to be decided.

EXTERNAL DIMENSIONS & AREAS - NC.

POWER PLANT - Hewland twin-cylinder engine. Other data NC.

WEIGHTS & LOADINGS - NC.

PERFORMANCE - NC.

SNIPE

SNIPE Aircraft Developments Ltd, 622-640 Woodborough Road, Nottingham NG3 5FS; tel 0602 624131; tx 342351 TRANSCO G L. Directors: J M Chapman, Arthur Luff.

SNIPE *DIAMOND*
(Three-axis)

Single-seat single-engined double monoplane in tandem with outboard ends joined; conventional three-axis control. Forward wing has swept back leading and trailing edges, rear wing has swept forward leading and trailing edges; both wings constant chord; no tail. Pitch control by elevators on rear wing; yaw control by tip fin/ rudder assemblies; roll control by ailerons at outboard end of wings; control inputs through stick for pitch/roll and pedals for yaw. Forward wing braced by rear wing and vice-versa; wing profile NC; 100% double-surface. Undercarriage has three wheels in tricycle formation; suspension NC. Push-right go-right nosewheel steering connected to yaw control. No brakes. Sheet aluminium airframe, totally enclosed. Engine mounted between wings, driving pusher propeller.

Production status: prototype.

GENERAL - This company was formed in 1982 to develop, manufacture and market a series of designs by Arthur Luff, a former Rolls Royce engineer, RAF VR pilot and gliding instructor.

The range of designs stems from a single basic configuration and covers four machines. First is an unpowered, self-landing low-cost sailplane, as submitted to the British Gliding Association's homebuilt design competition in 1981, and then come a single-seat lightplane and a two-seat lightplane trainer for low-cost flying training and towing. Fourth is the machine of interest to us here - the *Diamond*.

Arthur has aimed at simplicity of construction with all these machines, not just for low cost but also for ease of repair. The *Diamond*, for instance, uses folded sheet alloy for its fuselage, the panels being two-dimensional so that replacements are easy to produce. A similar system is used for the wing structure, the covering being aluminium-alloy sheet for the leading edge and polyester fabric elsewhere.

The 'joined wing' arrangement is very unusual and appears in only two other aircraft in this book - the Australian *Stratos* and the American *Trident T-3*, with, arguably, Bernard Broc's *Papillon* (see French section) as a third example. As a way of retaining the clean airflow of a cantilever wing, without its associated structural problems, it has obvious advantages, and has enabled the *Diamond* to slot into the sub-70 kg category in the UK, thus exempting it from airworthiness legislation.

At the time of writing the aircraft had not long made its maiden flight and development was still proceeding, so no performance figures have been released. For the same reason the price is not yet fixed, though the target figure is £3500 complete.

EXTERNAL DIMENSIONS & AREAS - Length overall 13.4 ft, 4.08 m. Height overall 6.1 ft, 1.86 m. Wing span 24.0 ft, 7.32 m. Constant chord 3.0 ft, 0.91 m (rear wing); 3.0 ft,

0.91 m (forward wing). Dihedral 3° (forward wing); 8° (rear wing). Sweepback 20° (forward wing); -20° (rear wing). Total wing area 132 ft², 12.3 m². Wheel track 4.0 ft, 1.22 m. Wheelbase 5.0 ft, 1.52 m. Nosewheel diameter overall 10 inch, 25 cm. Main wheel diameter overall 10 inch, 25 cm.

POWER PLANT - JPX PUL425 engine. Max power 22 hp at 4600 rpm. Propeller diameter and pitch 39xNC inch, 1.00xNC m. No reduction. Max static thrust NC. Power per unit area 0.17 hp/ft², 1.8 hp/m². Fuel capacity NC.

WEIGHTS & LOADINGS - Empty weight 150 lb, 68 kg. Max take-off weight 370 lb, 168 kg. Payload 220 lb, 100 kg. Max wing loading 2.80 lb/ft², 13.7 kg/m². Max power loading 16.8 lb/hp, 7.6 kg/hp. Load factors +5.0, -3.0 design; NC ultimate.

PERFORMANCE - NC.

SOUTHDOWN AEROSTRUCTURE

Southdown Aerostructure Ltd, Lasham Airfield, Alton, Hants GU34 5SR; tel 025623 359. Directors: Sir Charles Dorman, Ken Fripp, M K Fripp, F G Irving, Robert Jacquet, P Kelsey.

SOUTHDOWN AEROSTRUCTURE PIPISTRELLE 2C

(Three-axis)

Single-seat single-engined high-wing monoplane with conventional three-axis control. Wing has unswept lead- *ing and trailing edges, and constant chord; V-tail. Pitch/ yaw control ruddervators; roll control by 34%-span ailerons assisted by 18%-span spoilers; control inputs through stick for pitch/roll and pedals for yaw. Wing braced from below by struts; wing profile Worthmann FX63-137; 100% double-surface. Undercarriage has three wheels in tail-dragger formation; no suspension on tailwheel and glass-fibre suspension on main wheels. Push-right go-right tailwheel steering connected to yaw control. No brakes. Composite-construction airframe, partially enclosed. Engine mounted below wing, driving pusher propeller.*

Production status: see text.

GENERAL - The pretty *Pipistrelle* first came to the attention of the British microlighting fraternity at Biggin Hill aerodrome in September '82, when Alain Pochet took off on the London-Paris in a JPX-engined example.

That aircraft, like the rest of the first 20, was built in France by the Aerostructure company, featured in our first edition but no longer active as a microlight constructor. At the time we predicted that construction would soon be transferred to the UK, and so it has proved, with Southdown Aerostructure being set up specifically for that purpose, *Pipistrelle* designer Robert Jacquet being one of the directors. However, the intervening two years have seen only two aircraft built, both prototypes of a new version, the *Pipistrelle 2C*, designed to satisfy UK airworthiness regulations. For the record, the first *Pipistrelle* of all flew in 1981 and was designated *P2A*, production models coming the following March and being dubbed *P2B*.

The design makes extensive use of GRP, only the two wing struts being aluminium alloy. The fuselage is made of two half shells bonded together, while derigging is very easy, since the wings and tail surfaces are fixed to the fuselage glider-style, perhaps not surprisingly as Robert Jacquet had previously designed the *JP-15/34* and *15/36* sailplanes. Another gliding carry-over is the use of a combination of ailerons and spoilers for roll control, the other axes being looked after by differential ruddervators.

Considerable redesigning has been necessary to satisfy the UK authorities, but the aircraft is making steady progress in the hands of Ken Fripp and his team and should receive its type-approval during 1985. Ken is an experienced aircraft man, with years in the business to his credit at Southdown Aerostructure's sister company Southdown Aero Services, which specialises in glider work. While on the subject of names, incidentally, we had better point out that neither company has any connection with Southdown International.

No price had been fixed at the time of writing.

EXTERNAL DIMENSIONS & AREAS - Length overall 16.4 ft, 5.00 m. Height overall 5.3 ft, 1.63 m. Wing span 36.7 ft, 11.20 m. Constant chord 3.9 ft, 1.20 m. Dihedral 0°. Sweepback 0°. Tailplane span 8.9 ft, 2.72 m. Tailplane height NC. Total wing area 143 ft^2, 13.2 m^2. Total aileron area 12.2 ft^2, 1.13 m^2. Total spoiler area 1.8 ft^2, 0.17 m^2. Inclined fixed area 19.1 ft^2, 1.77 m^2. Ruddervator area 11.4 ft^2, 1.06 m^2. Aspect ratio 9.5/1. Wheel track 3.5 ft, 1.08 m. Wheelbase 8.5 ft, 2.60 m. Tailwheel diameter overall 8 inch, 20 cm. Main wheels diameter overall 16 inch, 40cm.

POWER PLANT - JPX PUL425 engine. Max power 26 hp at 4600 rpm. Propeller diameter and pitch 35x20 inch, 0.90x0.52 m. No reduction. Max static thrust 141 lb, 64 kg. Power per unit area 0.18 hp/ft^2, 2.0 hp/m^2. Fuel capacity 6.0 US gal, 5.0 Imp gal, 22.7 litre.

WEIGHTS & LOADINGS - Empty weight 287 lb, 130 kg. Max take-off weight 551 lb, 250 kg. Payload 265 lb, 120 kg. Max wing loading 3.85 lb/ft^2, 18.9 kg/m^2. Max power loading 21.2 lb/hp, 9.6 kg/hp. Load factors +4.0, -2.0 recommended; +6.0, -3.0 ultimate.

PERFORMANCE* - Max level speed 62 mph, 100 kph. Never exceed speed 75 mph, 120 kph. Max cruising speed 56 mph, 90 kph. Stalling speed 27 mph, 44 kph. Best glide ratio with power off 12/1 at 31 mph, 50 kph. Take-off distance 115 ft, 35 m. Landing distance 230 ft, 70 m. Range at average cruising speed 112 mile, 180 km. Noise level 79 dB at 490 ft, 150 m.

*Under the following test conditions - Airfield altitude 490 ft, 150 m. Ground temperature 50°F, 10°C. Ground pressure 998 mB. Ground windspeed 0 mph, 0 kph. Test payload 243 lb, 110 kg.

Pipistrelle 2C, *now built in Britain. For another illustration, see colour section.*

SOUTHDOWN INTERNATIONAL

Southdown International Ltd, 6a Carlton Terrace, Portslade, E Sussex BN4 1XF; tel 0273 422013. Directors: Roy Venton-Walters and Keith Reynolds.

Overseas sales: Agents in most Western European countries; contact manufacturer for list.

South African agent: Aero-Tech (see separate listing).

SOUTHDOWN INTERNATIONAL *PUMA SPRINT*

(Weight-shift)

Tandem two-seat single-engined flex-wing aircraft with weight-shift control. Rogallo wing with fin. Pilot suspended below wing in trike unit, using bar to control pitch and roll/yaw by altering relative positions of trike unit and wing. Wing braced from above by kingpost and cables, from below by cables; floating cross-tube construction with >70% double-surface enclosing cross-tube; preformed ribs. Undercarriage has three wheels in tricycle formation; optional rubber suspension on all wheels. Push-right go-left nosewheel steering independent from aerodynamic controls. Optional brakes on main wheels. Aluminium-alloy tube trike unit, with optional pod. Engine mounted below wing, driving pusher propeller.

Production status: current, number completed NC.

GENERAL - In terms of wing design, Southdown International is undoubtedly the most innovative company in the British industry. In 1981 it was Southdown Sailwings, as the company was then known, which introduced the first concealed floating cross-boom two-seat triking wing, the *Lightning DS,* thus opening up the two-seat trike market not only in Britain but all over Europe. Designed by Ian Grayland (who went on to form Aerial Arts) and Roy Venton-Walters, this wing was mated with an Ultra Sports trike unit to form the famous *Puma,* a tandem two-seat trainer which appealed not only because of its flying characteristics but also because it could be purchased 'off the shelf' as an entity, under one easily remembered name.

The success of the *Puma* spawned numerous derivatives using the same wing but different trike units, producing a situation so complicated that in our last edition we felt obliged to offer some explanatory notes on the origins of all the variants. Fortunately, the intervening two years have clarified things, as there is now only one aircraft bearing the *Puma* name, the *Puma Sprint.* This machine, unlike the original *Puma,* is an all-Southdown product and uses a monopole trike unit more notable for its excellent finish than any peculiarity of design. It is mated to the *Sprint* wing, a smaller, cleaner derivative of the *Lightning DS.*

Though much faster than the old *DS* thanks in no small measure to the use of very high sail tension, the *Puma Sprint* has proved extremely popular not only as a tourer but also as a trainer, and has sold well throughout Western Europe. Together with the related *Gemini Sprint* (see Mainair), it also has the honour of being the first aircraft to pass the stringent British airworthiness requirements.

There have been other notable achievements too, of which the most famous was the aircraft's use by Gerry Breen and Simon Baker on the Iceland Breakthrough expedition (see back cover), during which a previously unnavigable river was successfully travelled by a team of canoeists, backed by two microlights for supply and reconnaisance duties. Gerry later used a similar aircraft for an unofficial record attempt, taking a *Puma Sprint,* his then fiancee Manuela Thormann, and a considerable number of extra fuel tanks on a 550 mile (342 km) non-stop flight from northern Scotland to southern England in May 1984.

The design has altered during its two and half years' production, the principal changes being to the power pack. The original Robin EC44PM unit can now be replaced as an option by a Rotax 447, our data below referring to the Robin-engined machine; where different, figures for the Rotax version are shown in parentheses. For countries where noise regulations are especially stringent, a Hirth engine can be substituted.

In basic form the *Puma Sprint* costs £4134, to which can be added a long-range tank, skis, main wheel spats, main wheel brakes, all-wheel suspension, a pod, and a base-tube deflexor wire to reduce the chance of base-tube breakages under repeated heavy landings. Floats are also available, to turn the aircraft into an amphibian, but for regular marine use, Southdown recommends the seaplane *Seasprint,* which we list separately.

This Christmas message, which our politicians would do well to remember for the rest of the year, was Sally Denman's novel way of making a card for the folks back home in America, courtesy of pilot/photographer David Young and his Puma Sprint. In the background is Blenheim Palace.

EXTERNAL DIMENSIONS & AREAS - Length overall 11.2 ft, 3.41 m. Height overall 12.5 ft, 3.81 m. Wing span 35.0 ft, 10.67 m. Chord at root 8.7 ft, 2.65 m. Chord at tip 2.5 ft, 0.76 m. Dihedral -2°. Nose angle 130°. Fin height 3.8 ft, 1.16 m. Total wing area 180 ft², 16.7 m². Fin area 7.2 ft², 0.67 m². Aspect ratio 6.8/1. Wheel track 5.3 ft, 1.62 m. Wheelbase 6.2 ft, 1.89 m. Nosewheel diameter overall 13 inch, 33 cm. Main wheels diameter overall 13 inch, 33cm.

POWER PLANT - Robin EC44PM (Rotax 447) engine. Max power 45 hp at 6800(NC) rpm. Propeller diameter and pitch 62(NC)x27(NC) inch, 1.58(NC)x0.70(NC) m. Toothed-belt (gear) reduction, ratio 2.7(2.6)/1. Max static thrust 280(NC) lb, 127(NC) kg. Power per unit area 0.25 hp/ft², 2.7 hp/m². Fuel capacity 2.4 US gal, 2.0 Imp gal, 9.1 litre.

WEIGHTS & LOADINGS - Empty weight 304(298) lb, 138(135) kg. Max take-off weight 725 lb, 329 kg. Payload 421(427) lb, 191(194) kg. Max wing loading 4.03 lb/ft², 19.7 kg/m². Max power loading 16.1 lb/hp, 7.3 kg/hp. Load factors +4.0, -2.0 recommended; >+6.0, >-3.0 ultimate.

PERFORMANCE* - Max level speed 62 mph, 100 kph. Never exceed speed 70 mph, 113 kph. Cruising speed 40 mph, 64 kph. Stalling speed 30 mph, 48 kph. Max climb rate at sea level 355 ft/min, 1.8 m/s. Min sink rate 390 ft/min at 37 mph, 1.9 m/s at 60 kph. Best glide ratio with power off NC. Take-off distance 712 ft, 217 m to clear obstacle of 500 ft, 152 m. Landing distance 620 ft, 189 m. Service ceiling NC. Range at average cruising speed 34(NC) mile, 55(NC) km. Noise level NC.

*_Under the following test conditions_ - Airfield altitude 550 ft, 168 m. Ground temperature 57°F, 14°C. Ground pressure NC. Ground windspeed 0-6 mph, 0-10 kph. Test payload 421 lb, 191 kg.

SOUTHDOWN INTERNATIONAL _SEASPRINT_

(Weight-shift)

Summary as Puma Sprint _except: Undercarriage has two floats, no wheels. No brakes._

Production status: current, number completed NC.

GENERAL - The _Seasprint_ is the marine version of the _Puma Sprint,_ and apart from its undercarriage is the same aircraft, though extra attention is given to corrosion resistance. The Hirth engine is not an option on this variant, but otherwise any relevant option from the _Puma Sprint_ list can be specified.
Price on application.

EXTERNAL DIMENSIONS & AREAS - See _Puma Sprint_ for wing data. Other data NC.

POWER PLANT - See _Puma Sprint._

WEIGHTS & LOADINGS - NC.

PERFORMANCE - NC.

SOUTHDOWN INTERNATIONAL _AGRASPRINT_

(Weight-shift)

Summary as Puma Sprint _except: Single-seater._

Production status: current, number completed NC.

GENERAL - Conceived as an agricultural version of the _Puma Sprint,_ the _Agrasprint_ is aimed largely at Third World countries and is marketed in co-operation with the company's South African agent.
The normal tandem seating is replaced by a single seat/tank unit, of capacity 22.4 US gal (18.7 Imp gal, 85 litre), though the fuel capacity stays as before. The spray booms are equipped with Micronair applicators which can be adjusted to give any droplet size between 80 and 1000 microns, the latter corresponding to an application rate of 5.4 US gal/acre (4.5 Imp gal/acre, 51 litre/hectare). Coverage rate is 2.5 acre/min (1.0 hectare/min) with a swathe width of 45 ft (13 m).
Like most agricultural trikes, the _Agrasprint_ can easily be converted back to standard two-seat specification. Rigging time from trailer to spraying is 30 min. Price on application; options are as for the _Puma Sprint._

EXTERNAL DIMENSIONS & AREAS - See _Puma Sprint._

POWER PLANT - See _Puma Sprint._

WEIGHTS & LOADINGS - See _Puma Sprint_ except: Empty weight NC. Payload NC.

PERFORMANCE - NC.

SOUTHDOWN INTERNATIONAL _RAVEN_

(Hybrid)

Summary as Puma Sprint _except: Hybrid control. Rogallo wing with fin and saumons. Spoilers added for air braking, actuated by slider on control bar. 100% double-surface._

Production status: current, number completed NC.

GENERAL - The _Raven_ Southdown's third generation triking wing, and represents a radical departure from normal flexwing design in that it is not purely a fully flying wing, but also has control surfaces, in the form of spoilers.

These are provided not for roll control but to lower the approach speed, and their inclusion amounts to a recognition by the company that as wings get faster and faster, they become harder for the novice to land and need bigger fields. The _Raven_ is Southdown's attempt to have the best of both worlds - a wing faster than a _Sprint_, but easier to handle.

There are other novel features too. Saumons are provided to increase the effective aspect ratio of the wing - already high for a flexwing at 8.1/1 - and to delay onset of the stall. Roy tells us that some remarkable results have been achieved in testing, with the aircraft remaining controllable even when fully stalled. Wing area is right down at the legal minimum for a UK-legal two-seater, and the whole area is double surfaced, using an L48 profile. Besides its aerodynamic advantages, the double-surfacing means there are two layers of fabric to share the trailing edge loads, allowing greater sail tension and thus lower washout.

The full double-surfacing is made possible by what Southdown calls its Isoflex trailing-edge system, a semi free-floating underside attachment of the outboard wing sections which is claimed to virtually eliminate torsional resistance of the fabric 'box-section' formed by the double-surface and hence allow free flexure in washout.

Seen for the first time at the BMAA's annual general meeting in November '84, the _Raven_ is at the time of writing still undergoing type-approval, so although a few have been sold for export it is too early to judge whether it represents the great leap forward claimed for it. But if the company's past record is anything to go by, it will certainly give its competitors something to think about.

Price is £4343 when mated to an identical trike unit to that of the _Puma Sprint,_ or £1575 separately. Options are as for the _Puma Sprint._

EXTERNAL DIMENSIONS & AREAS - Length overall 10.5 ft, 3.20 m. Height overall 12.5 ft, 3.81 m. Wing span 36.0 ft, 10.97 m. Chord at root 10.0 ft, 3.05 m. Chord at tip

Norman Burr

1.3 ft, 0.41 m. Dihedral -3°. Nose angle 130°. Fin height 3.3 ft, 1.02 m. Total wing area 160 ft², 14.9 m². Fin area 12.0 ft², 1.11 m². Aspect ratio 8.1/1. Wheel track 5.3 ft, 1.62 m. Wheelbase 6.2 ft, 1.89 m. Nosewheel diameter overall 13 inch, 33 cm. Main wheels diameter overall 13 inch, 33cm.

POWER PLANT - See *Puma Sprint* except: Power per unit area 0.28 hp/ft², 3.0 hp/m².

WEIGHTS & LOADINGS - Empty weight 304(298) lb, 138(135) kg. Max take-off weight 741 lb, 336 kg. Payload 437(443) lb, 198(201) kg. Max wing loading 4.63 lb/ft², 22.6 kg/m². Max power loading 16.5 lb/hp, 7.5 kg/hp. Load factors +4.0, -2.0 recommended; +6.0, -3.0 ultimate.

PERFORMANCE* - Max level speed 83 mph, 134 kph. Never exceed speed 108 mph, 174 kph. Max cruising speed 75 mph, 121 kph. Economic cruising speed 56 mph, 90 kph. Stalling speed 25 mph, 40 kph. Max climb rate at sea level 1200 ft/min, 6.1 m/s. Min sink rate 340 ft/min at 28 mph, 1.7 m/s at 45 kph. Best glide ratio with power off 9.2/1 at 54 mph, 87 kph. Take-off distance 120 ft, 37 m. Landing distance 180 ft, 55 m. Service ceiling 18,000 ft, 5500 m. Range at average cruising speed 112(NC) mile, 180(NC) km. Noise level 73 dB at 500 ft, 152 m.

*Under the following test conditions - Airfield altitude 200 ft, 61 m. Ground temperature 50°F, 10°C. Ground pressure NC. Ground windspeed 5 mph, 8 kph. Test payload 80 lb, 176 kg.

This prototype Raven flew at the '85 Popham Trade Fair, though without its saumons. Photographed just as the Southdown team was derigging, some of the battens have been removed so the profile is not as normal, but the spoilers can be seen clearly marked.

TIGER CUB DEVELOPMENTS

Tiger Cub Developments, Larkfield, Retford Road, Mattersey, Doncaster, S Yorks DN10 5HG; tel 0777 817975. Proprietor: Russ Light.

TIGER CUB DEVELOPMENTS
TIGER CUB SERIES II
(Three-axis)

Single-seat single-engined biplane with conventional three-axis control. Wings have unswept leading and trailing edges, and constant chord; conventional tail. Pitch control by fully flying tail; yaw control by fin-

mounted rudder; roll control by ailerons on lower wing; control inputs through stick for pitch/roll and pedals for yaw. Wings braced by struts and transverse X-cables; wing profile NC; 100% double-surface. Undercarriage has three wheels in tail-dragger formation; coil-spring suspension on tailwheel and axle-flex suspension on main wheels. Push-right go-right tailwheel steering connected to yaw control. No brakes. Aluminium-alloy tube/ foam airframe, partially enclosed. Engine mounted between wings, driving tractor propeller.

Production status: prototype.

GENERAL - The *Tiger Cub* story began at the BMAA's 1981 annual general meeting, when Tom Wright and Russ Light of MBA showed their *Microbipe,* a Robin EC25PS-engined prototype which attracted so much attention that the company was virtually catapulted into manufacture.

Long delays ensued as the company frantically tried to develop the prototype into something which it felt confident enough to sell the public, by which time the aircraft had evolved into a very different machine, with larger engine, greater span, greater weight and a boxed-in tailboom of foam and tubing, in place of the original purely tubular structure. Known by the rather long-winded title of *Super Tiger Cub 440,* universally abbreviated to *Tiger Cub,* kits for this aircraft finally started leaving the factory early in 1983, the first completed aircraft appearing that summer. That year was a tough one for the sport in Britain, and the success of the little biplane, with over 150 kits sold, was one of the few bright spots of the year.

However, as enthusiastic owners leapt into their aircraft for their maiden flights, stories began to spread that all was not well, that the aircraft was tricky to handle in inexperienced hands. A number of accidents ensued, mostly minor fortunately, but the word was out. Sales plummeted as buyers waited to see what reaction the CAA's test pilots would have to the machine when they took it aloft on its *Section S* type-approval flights.

MBA struggled manfully on, but with the financial demands of type-approval coinciding with a drop in sales it was a hopeless task, and in 1984 the company folded, leaving a lot of very worried *Tiger Cub* owners.

Happily, MBA director Russ Light bought the rights to the aircraft and set up Tiger Cub Developments to carry on where MBA left off, the intention being to develop a UK-legal *Tiger Cub,* then sell update kits for earlier machines and finally start production of the properly developed machine. At the time of writing (July '85) Russ was just completing a new prototype designed from the outset to be UK-legal, and which we have christened *Tiger Cub Series II* in the absence of a better title. Though the design was not finalised - the aircraft had yet to make its maiden flight - principal changes will include replacement of the fully flying rudder by a fin and rudder arrangement, addition of trim system to the fully flying tail, revised main undercarriage for greater stability, and considerable attention to drag reduction, including a more rounded fuselage shape with partially enclosed cockpit. Also, the iron-on adhesive-backed fabric covering for the foam has been abandoned in favour of a new heat-shrink process. The result, Russ believes, will be a prettier, cleaner, faster, more comfortable and better handling machine.

Our summary above is as accurate as we can make it at the time of going to press, but the data below refers to the *Super Tiger Cub 440,* as no figures for the new machine

Norman Burr

Tiger Cubs *gather at the '84 Woburn Rally; the aircraft nearest the camera was constructed by then MBA dealer Flylite, which also sells the* Super Scout *(see separate listing).*

have been released. As explained above, the rudder area will almost certainly change, but otherwise we understand that no major changes are envisaged for the principal dimensions, weights, or power pack.
Price: NC.

EXTERNAL DIMENSIONS & AREAS - Length overall 13.3 ft, 4.05 m. Height overall 5.5 ft, 1.68 m. Wing span 21.0 ft, 6.40 m (bottom); 21.0 ft, 6.40 m (top). Constant chord 3.0 ft, 0.91 m (bottom wing); 3.5 ft, 1.07 m (top wing). Dihedral 5° (bottom wing); 0° (top wing). Sweepback 0°. Tailplane span 7.0 ft, 2.13 m. Rudder height 2.9 ft, 0.88 m. Total wing area 136 ft^2, 12.6 m^2. Total aileron area 13.8 ft^2, 1.28 m^2. Rudder area 6.3 ft^2, 0.59 m^2. Total elevator area 14.6 ft^2, 1.36 m^2. Aspect ratio 6.4/1. Wheel track 4.2 ft, 1.28 m. Wheelbase NC ft, m. Tailwheel diameter overall 4 inch, 10 cm. Main wheels diameter overall 13 inch, 33 cm.

POWER PLANT - Robin EC44 engine. Max power 50 hp at 7000 rpm. Propeller diameter and pitch 54x33 inch, b 37x0.84 m. Toothed-belt reduction, ratio 2.4/1. Max static thrust 220 lb, 100 kg. Power per unit area 2.72 hp/ft^2, 29.7 hp/m^2. Fuel capacity 6.0 US gal, 5.0 Imp gal, 22.7 litre.

WEIGHTS & LOADINGS - Empty weight 265 lb, 120 kg. Max take-off weight 500 lb, 227 kg. Payload 235 lb, 107 kg. Max wing loading 3.68 lb/ft^2, 18.0 kg/m^2. Max power loading 10.0 lb/hp, 4.5 kg/hp. Load factors +6.0, -4.0 recommended; +9.0, -7.0 ultimate.

PERFORMANCE* - Max level speed 80 mph, 129 kph. Never exceed speed 85 mph, 137 kph. Max cruising speed 70 mph, 113 kph. Economic cruising speed 60 mph, 97 kph. Stalling speed 30 mph, 48 kph. Max climb rate at sea level 900 ft/min, 4.6 m/s. Min sink rate 500 ft/min at 36 mph, 2.5 m/s at 58 kph. Best glide ratio with power off 7/1 at 35 mph, 56 kph. Take-off distance on short grass 60 ft, 18 m. Landing distance on short grass 80 ft, 24 m. Service ceiling 10,000 ft, 3050 m. Range at average cruising speed 115 mile, 185 km. Noise level NC.

*Under the following test conditions - Airfield altitude 0 ft, 0 m. Ground temperature 50°F, 10°C. Ground pressure NC. Ground windspeed 0 mph, 0 kph. Test payload 185 lb, 84kg.

TIRITH

Tirith Microplane Ltd, 77 Alston Drive, Bradwell Abbey, Milton Keynes MK13 9HG; tel 0908 311544; tx 826813 AQUATC G. Managing director: Brian Hogan. Commercial director: Mike Wright. Chief engineer: M Ward.

West German agent: Wirth Brennstoffe, Dusseldorfer Strasse 5, 4053 Juchen 3, Otzenrath. Contact: Thomas Wirth.

TIRITH *FIREBIRD FB-1*

(Three-axis)

Single-seat twin-engined high-wing monoplane with conventional three-axis control. Wing has unswept leading and trailing edges, and constant chord; conventional tail. Pitch control by elevator on tail; yaw control by fin-mounted rudder; roll control by 40%-span ailerons; control inputs through stick for pitch/roll and pedals for yaw. Wing braced from below by struts; wing profile Goetingen 797; 100% double-surface. Undercarriage has three wheels in tricycle formation; no suspension on nosewheel and glass-fibre suspension on main wheels. Push-right go-right nosewheel steering connected to yaw control. Nosewheel brake. Composite-construction airframe, partially enclosed. Engines mounted below wing, driving pusher propellers.

Production status: prototype.

GENERAL - Included in our first edition at a very early stage in its evolution, when it was known simply as the *Firebird,* the *Firebird FB-1* has changed a great deal since we last went to press. At that time this interesting partially enclosed design had a single WAM WAE342 engine, 60% span flaps and a Worthmann FS67-170-17 profile, but since then a lot of development hours have been flown. The design team, led by J Webb and Prof D Howe of Cranfield College of Aeronautics, decided that more power was necessary and solved the problem by the simple expedient of adding a second engine. Also, the flaps were removed and a different wing profile substituted.

Aimed very much at the experienced pilot who wants to fly a conventional-feeling aircraft but at microlight costs, the *Firebird* is a composite-construction machine of foam and glass-reinforced epoxy, supplemented with a tubular aluminium-alloy frame where appropriate. It splits into six major components for transport, and may be reassembled without tools or the need for any pre-flight adjustments.

One reason for the aircraft's long gestation period has undoubtedly been the development work found necessary on the engines. The 30 hp WAE342 was originally conceived as a target drone engine, and though it offered exceptional power for its weight, the manufacturers found that in its original form it was not sufficiently reliable for microlight use, and withdrew it from the market not long after its introduction. Despite this setback, the Tirith team remained loyal to the unit, and in effect allowed their prototype to be used as a flying test bed for a radically redesigned version of the engine. Unlike most microlight engines, the WAM unit will be certified, under *JAR22 sub-part H* of the British regulations, and this should more than dispel any remaining doubts about the WAE342's reliability, especially as the engines are derated to give only 20 hp each in this application. This reduced output comes much lower in the rev band, at 4500 instead of 7000, which suits the direct-drive/ducted fan arrangement of the *FB-1* admirably.

The aircraft itself, of course, has to pass the *BCAR Section S* microlight standards, and at the time of writing the type-approval process was well advanced, though its big sister, the two-seat *Firebird FB-2,* will probably be given greater priority as the British market is currently screaming for a UK-legal fixedwing trainer.

Projected price for the single-seater is £6740 complete.

EXTERNAL DIMENSIONS & AREAS - Length overall 18.4 ft, 5.61 m. Height overall 9.0 ft, 2.74 m. Wing span 29.6 ft, 9.03 m. Constant chord 5.2 ft, 1.60 m. Dihedral 0°. Sweepback 0°. Tailplane span 11.3 ft, 3.45 m. Fin height 3.5 ft, 1.07 m. Total wing area 156 ft^2, 14.5 m^2. Total aileron area 9.9 ft^2, 0.92 m^2. Fin area 7.6 ft^2, 0.71 m^2. Rudder area 4.7 ft^2, 0.44 m^2. Tailplane area 19.9 ft^2, 1.85 m^2. Total elevator area 14.9 ft^2, 1.38 m^2. Aspect ratio 5.6/1. Wheel track 5.7 ft, 1.76 m. Wheelbase 5.8 ft, 1.78 m. Nosewheel diameter overall 11 inch, 28 cm. Main wheels diameter overall 11 inch, 28 cm.

POWER PLANT - Two WAM WAE342 engines. Max power 20 hp each at 4500 rpm. Ducted fans diameter and pitch 33x24 inch, 0.84x0.61 m. No reduction. Max static thrust 212 lb, 96 kg. Power per unit area 0.26 hp/ft^2, 2.8 hp/m^2. Fuel capacity 9.2 US gal, 7.7 Imp gal, 35.0 litre.

WEIGHTS & LOADINGS - Empty weight 313 lb, 142 kg. Max take-off weight 573 lb, 260 kg. Payload 260 lb, 118 kg. Max wing loading 3.67 lb/ft^2, 17.9 kg/m^2. Max power loading 14.3 lb/hp, 6.5 kg/hp. Load factors +4.0, -2.0 recommended; +6.0, -3.0 ultimate.

PERFORMANCE* - Max level speed 65 mph, 105 kph. Never exceed speed 84 mph, 135 kph. Max cruising speed 60 mph, 97 kph. Economic cruising speed 55 mph, 88 kph. Stalling speed 26 mph, 42 kph. Max climb rate at sea level 650 ft/min, 3.3 m/s. Min sink rate 350 ft/min at 40 mph, 1.8 m/s at 64 kph. Best glide ratio with power off 7/1 at 40 mph, 64 kph. Take-off distance 300 ft, 91 m. Landing distance 300 ft, 91 m. Service ceiling NC. Range at average cruising speed 120 mile, 193 km. Noise level 65 dB at 500 ft, 152 m.

*Under the following test conditions - Airfield altitude 200 ft, 61 m. Ground temperature 68°F, 20°C. Ground pressure 1000 mB. Ground windspeed 0 mph, 0 kph. Test payload 231 lb, 105 kg.

TIRITH *FIREBIRD FB-2*

(Three-axis)

Summary as Firebird FB-1 *except: Side-by-side two-seater.*

Production status: prototype.

GENERAL - Derived from the *Firebird FB-1,* this two-seater uses an identical power plant and is very similar dimensionally, principal changes being a greater wing span and more fixed horizontal area in the tailplane.

The two ducted-fan power plants give the *Firebirds* an unmistakable appearance and a distinctive crisp though

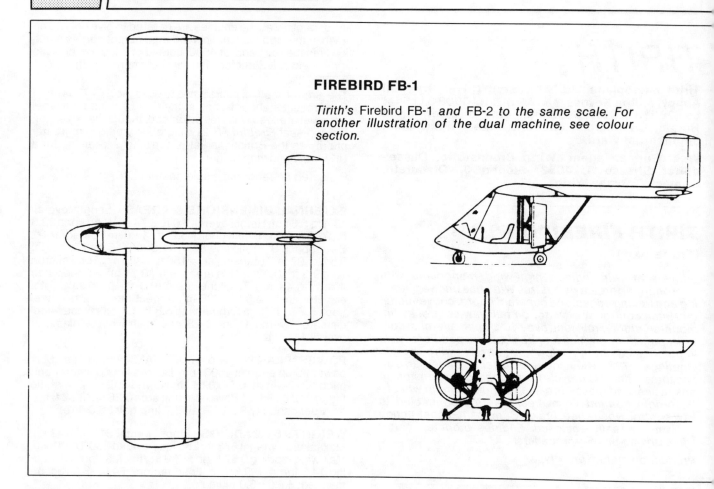

FIREBIRD FB-1

Tirith's Firebird FB-1 *and* FB-2 *to the same scale. For another illustration of the dual machine, see colour section.*

not unpleasant engine note. This becomes all the more distinctive if one of the engines is revving at a slightly different speed to the other, producing the beats phenomenon which generations of high-school physics masters have amused themselves demonstrating with tuning forks!

Though the aircraft is currently only a prototype, it is unlikely to change significantly before production, as the type-approval process was well advanced at the time of going to press. The company's manufacturing facilities had already been approved by the CAA, one of the first to be so endorsed, in 1984. This is good news for the fixedwing schools in Britain, who are in dire need of a reliable UK-legal trainer. Tirith's two-seater, with side-by-side seating and the added reassurance of two engines, could be just what the schools have been waiting for.

Projected price is £7610.

EXTERNAL DIMENSIONS & AREAS - See *Firebird FB-1* except: Length overall 19.0 ft, 5.78 m. Wing span 31.2 ft, 9.50 m. Total wing area 164 ft², 15.2 m². Tailplane area 26.2 ft², 2.43 m². Aspect ratio 5.9/1.

POWER PLANT - See *Firebird FB-1* except: Power per unit area 0.24 hp/ft², 2.6 hp/m².

WEIGHTS & LOADINGS - Empty weight 362 lb, 148 kg. Max take-off weight 794 lb, 360 kg. Payload 467 lb, 212 kg. Max wing loading 4.84 lb/ft², 23.7 kg/m². Max power loading 19.9 lb/hp, 9.0 kg/hp. Load factors +4.0, -2.0 recommended; +6.0, -3.0 ultimate.

PERFORMANCE* - See *Firebird FB-1* except: Stalling speed 30 mph, 48 kph. Max climb rate at sea level 400 ft/min, 2.0 m/s.

**Under the following test conditions* - See *Firebird FB-1* except: Test payload 231 lb, 105 kg.

TIRITH *ULTRA 1*
(Two-axis)

Single-seat single-engined low-wing monoplane with two-axis control. Wing has unswept leading and trailing edges, and constant chord; V-tail. Pitch control by 'ruddervator'; yaw/roll control by three spoilers on each wing (two upper, one lower); control inputs through stick for pitch/yaw/roll. Cantilever wing; wing profile NC; 100% double-surface. Undercarriage has two wheels plus tailskid; no suspension on tailskid and bungee suspension on main wheels. No ground steering. No brakes. Composite construction fuselage, completely open. Engine mounted above wing, driving pusher propeller.

Production status: prototype.

GENERAL - Readers of our first edition may remember a pretty but rather delicate-looking aircraft called the Birdman *TL-1B*, which featured an unusual control system with sequentially operated spoilers to provide yaw/roll control. It was produced by a Florida company unconnected with the Canadian firm of the same name, and since the manufacturer was defunct even then - the company never fully recovered from the death of the aircraft's creator, Emmett M Tally, in the prototype in 1976 - we did not expect to see the *TL-1B* in these pages again, especially as it had acquired a reputation for being underpowered and laborious to build!

However, on the very day we went to press, Brian Hogan told us that Tirith was busy building a prototype of a greatly improved but visually similar model, having bought the

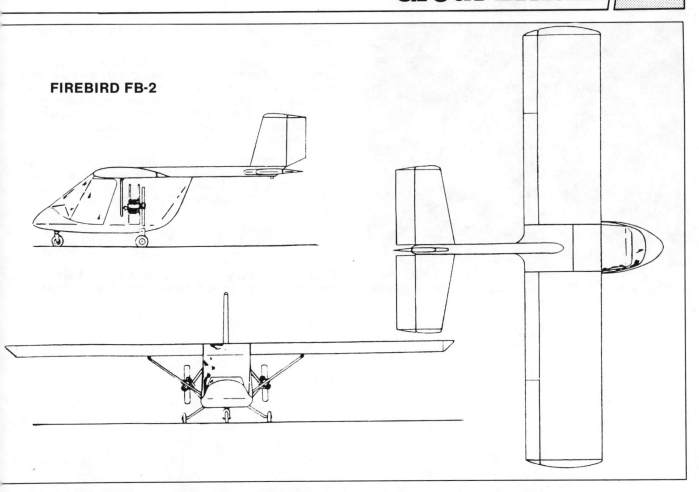

FIREBIRD FB-2

design rights in 1984. Composites are now used instead of timber - Brian reckoned that up to 1000 h could be expended on making a decent job of building the original design - and the airframe's stressing has been thoroughly overhauled.

Brian expects the new version to weigh around 143 lb (65 kg) empty, nicely under the 70 kg limit at which UK type-approval becomes mandatory, but nevertheless it will be designed to *Section S* requirements, even though the principal market for the aircraft is seen as North America. In fact Tirith has a transatlantic partner in the project, the Canadian firm Elco Aviation. Power unit has yet to be decided: a McCulloch engine is being considered but will probably be rejected in favour of something more powerful. No price has been quoted, but the intention is to produce kits which can genuinely be completed by two people in one week. In view of the relatively early stage of the project, we are omitting our data paragraphs in this instance.

Tirith's Ultra 1 *will be based on this Birdman* TL-1B.

WORLD WIDE RACING SERVICES

Embermere Ltd t/a World Wide Racing Services, 281 Hithermoor Road, Stanwell Moor, Staines, Middlesex TW19 6AZ; tel 0753 682019; tx 849234. Director: Charles Pinion.

WORLD WIDE RACING SERVICES
SUPER PELICAN
(Three-axis)

Summary as Ultravia Super Pelican *(see Canadian section).*

Production status: prototype.

GENERAL - World Wide Racing Services is the UK agent for the Canadian Ultravia company, and at the time of writing was well advanced in its attempts to get one of the

company's products, the *Super Pelican,* through the UK airworthiness regulations.

As the UK version of the machine was still in prototype form at the time of writing, it is too early to say how it will differ from the original, though we know that drag struts have been added to the wings and the wing roots redesigned. Also the ailerons and engine mounts have been the subject of major changes. It seems likely that the undercarriage will be strengthened too.

In view of the provisional nature of the information, we are omitting our data in this instance; readers may safely assume that the UK version will be very similar to its Canadian counterpart, but will be a little heavier.
Price:NC.

Flashback to early '84, as the first British-built Super Pelican *takes shape in Charles Pinion's workshops.*

Researched by Dr Marton Ordody, of the hang-gliding executive of the Hungarian NAEC.

Hungary

Predating the recent British interest in aerotowing by some three years, the MAV Tornado 1250/Denever made its first successful hang-glider tow on 10 October 1981, this picture being taken some 14 months later. The towing lines can be clearly seen at the rear.

Triking, Eastern European style by Norman Burr

With the Hungarians being active in international hang-gliding competitions, it is perhaps inevitable that the trike should be the dominant form of microlight there, so much so that this short section on Hungarian machines contains nothing else. What is particularly gratifying is that in Hungary there are definitely aircraft for sale, rather than just the one-offs which one finds in most other parts of the Eastern Bloc. We have a hunch that the first World Microlight Championships, due to be held in France in August 1985, will attract much interest in Hungary and that it will not be too long before the country's microlighters follow the footsteps of their hang-gliding colleagues and enter international competition. Here's hoping...

For more information on microlights in Hungary, contact: Dr Marton Odody, c/o Hungarian NAEC hang gliding executive, 1093 Bp, Szamuely u. 44; tel 170351.

APOLLO

Apollo Hang Gliders Manufacturer, H-3300 Eger, Olasz U31; tel 3636 13196. Director: Zolton Molnar.

APOLLO
CX and CX TANDEM
(Weight-shift)

Single-seat (CX) or side-by-side two-seat (CX Tandem) single-engined flex-wing aircraft with weight-shift control. Rogallo wing with keel pocket. Pilot suspended below wing in trike unit, using bar to control pitch and roll/yaw by altering relative positions of trike unit and wing. Wing braced from above by kingpost and cables, from below by cables; floating cross-tube construction with 60% double-surface enclosing cross-tube; preformed ribs. Undercarriage has three wheels in tricycle formation; no suspension on nosewheel and axle-flex suspension on main wheels. Push-right go-left nosewheel steering independent from aerodynamic controls. No brakes. Aluminium-alloy tube trike unit, with optional pod. Engine mounted below wing, driving pusher propeller.

Production status: current; 50 completed (CX), 20 completed (CX Tandem).

GENERAL - The wing of Apollo's *CX* is a typical modern Rogallo with enclosed floating cross-tube and 60% double-surface, but it is rather large for solo flight by current Western European standards, at 202 ft² (18.8 m²).

Main picture: the Apollo CX *with spray bar attached.*
Inset: Apollo CX Tandem *in flight.*

However, there is logic in this arrangement, for the *CX* is not solely a fun machine: with the wing slightly strengthened, it can also be used for crop-spraying or converted into the two-seat *CX Tandem,* when the high payload of the large wing comes into its own.

In fact this machine reminds us of the early Skyhook trikes from Britain, which like the Apollo machines were duopoles, a configuration which lends itself to this modular approach much better than monopoles. Skyhook's *TR1* trike unit with *Cutlass* wing could be converted into a *TR2* two-seater simply by fitting a dual seat and a pokier power pack, and a similar approach is evident at Apollo, which fits the 26 hp engine from the East German Trabant car in the solo aircraft, but substitutes a tuned version developing 40 hp for the *CX Tandem,* which despite its name has side-by-side seating. The quoted noise output of these units, incidentally, is described by Apollo as *just* inside the legal limit!

Price of the Apollo *CX* is Ft60,000, the *CX Tandem* costing Ft5000 more. Options in both cases are a pod for Ft5000 and a harness for Ft4000. Our data below refers to the *CX;* where different, figures for the *CX Tandem* are shown in parentheses.

EXTERNAL DIMENSIONS & AREAS - Length overall 12.5 ft, 3.80 m. Height overall 11.2 ft, 3.40 m. Wing span 34.8 ft, 10.60 m. Chord at root 9.4 ft, 2.85 m. Chord at tip 3.3 ft, 1.00 m. Dihedral 2°. Nose angle 123°. Depth of keel pocket 0.9 ft, 0.27 m. Total wing area 202 ft², 18.8 m². Keel pocket area 2.9 ft², 0.27 m². Aspect ratio 6.0/1. Wheel track 3.9 ft, 1.20 m. Wheelbase NC. Nosewheel diameter overall 13 inch, 32 cm. Main wheels diameter overall 13 inch, 32 cm.

POWER PLANT - Trabant engine. Max power 26(40) hp at 4200 rpm. Propeller diameter and pitch 55x28(35) inch, 1.40x0.70(0.90) m. V-belt reduction, ratio 1.7/1. Max static thrust 187(243) lb, 85(110) kg. Power per unit area 0.13(0.20) hp/ft², 1.4(2.1) hp/m². Fuel capacity 2.6 US gal, 2.2 Imp gal, 10.0 litre.

WEIGHTS & LOADINGS - Empty weight 243(253) lb, 110(115) kg. Max take-off weight 463(650) lb, 210(295) kg. Payload 220(397) lb, 100(180) kg. Max wing loading 2.29(3.22) lb/ft², 11.2(15.7) kg/m². Max power loading 17.8(16.3) lb/hp, 8.1(7.4) kg/hp. Load factors +3.0, -1.0 recommended; +6.0, -4.0 ultimate.

PERFORMANCE* - Max level speed 50(56) mph, 80(90) kph. Never exceed speed 62 mph, 100 kph. Max cruising speed 44(47) mph, 70(75) kph. Economic cruising speed 37(40) mph, 60(65) kph. Stalling speed 22(30) mph, 35(48) kph. Max climb rate at sea level 490(300) ft/min, 2.5(1.5) m/s. Min sink rate 300(390) ft/min at 28(34) mph, 1.5(2.0) m/s at 45(55) kph. Best glide ratio with power off 8(6)/1 at 30(37) mph, 48(60) kph. Take-off distance 65(165) ft, 20(50) m. Landing distance 130(260) ft, 40(80) m. Service ceiling 9800(6600) ft, 3000(2000) m. Range at average cruising speed 75(50) mile, 120(80) km. Noise level 55(60) dB at 330 ft, 100 m.

*Under the following test conditions - Airfield altitude 390 ft, 120 m. Ground temperature 77°F, 25°C. Ground pressure 1020 mB. Ground windspeed 6 mph, 10 kph. Test payload 209(419) lb, 95(190) kg.

HODGEP

Hodgep Maschinenfabrik, H-6801 Hodmezovasarhely, Pf 19; tel 64 12911; tx 84232.

Export sales: Technika, H-1475 Budapest, Pf 125; tel 339-992 or 338-305; tx 225765.

HODGEP
DRAGON S, T and A
(Weight-shift)

Single-seat (except: Dragon T is tandem two-seat) single-engined flex-wing aircraft with weight-shift control. Rogallo wing with keel pocket. Pilot suspended below wing in trike unit, using bar to control pitch and roll/yaw by altering relative positions of trike unit and wing. Wing braced from above by kingpost and cables, from below by cables; floating cross-tube construction with 60% double-surface enclosing cross-tube; flexible ribs. Undercarriage has three wheels in tricycle formation; no suspension on any wheels. Push-right go-left nosewheel steering independent from aerodynamic controls. No brakes. Aluminium-alloy tube trike unit, completely open. Engine mounted below wing, driving pusher propeller.

Production status: prototype.

GENERAL - The *Dragon* is a very important aircraft for the Hungarians, as it is the country's first attempt to build a machine which will be competitive in export markets.

▼

The Hlamot II power pack used the club's own gear reduction...

...while the Hlamot III boasts triple carbs and three cylinders.

The trike unit is a modern monopole design with a snoot to allow plenty of forward bar movement, the overall appearance being not unlike the *Puma Sprint* from Britain, apart from the *Dragon's* distinctive vertical tank. Little information is available on the design of the *Strucc-2* wing, but we know that unlike most modern Rogallos it uses flexible battens.

Although the two-seater prototype we illustrate uses a Trabant engine, it is intended to offer two alternative units, the Konig SD570 (28 hp at 4000 rpm) or the Rotax 503 (51 hp at 6670 rpm), in order to appeal to the West German market, at which the aircraft is principally targetted. There will be three airframe options too, all with the same Rogallo: the *Dragon A*, a solo machine, the *Dragon T*, a two-seater for training, and the *Dragon A*, a single-seater for agricultural work.

Unfortunately, the company does not explain which engine goes with which variant, but we believe our data below will be representative of a *Dragon T* with Trabant engine. Prices have yet to be announced, but will probably start at under Ft100,000.

EXTERNAL DIMENSIONS & AREAS - Length overall 14.8 ft, 4.50 m. Height overall 11.5 ft, 3.50 m. Wing span 34.8 ft, 10.60 m. Chord at root 8.5 ft, 2.60 m. Chord at tip 3.3 ft, 1.00 m. Dihedral 0°. Nose angle 125°. Depth of keel pocket 0.7 ft, 0.20 m. Total wing area 184 ft^2, 17.1 m^2. Keel pocket area 3.2 ft^2, 0.30 m^2. Aspect ratio 6.6/1. Wheel track 5.6 ft, 1.70 m. Wheelbase 3.3 ft, 1.00 m. Nosewheel diameter overall 10 inch, 25 cm. Main wheels diameter overall 14 inch, cm.

POWER PLANT - Trabant engine. Max power 42 hp at 6000 rpm. Propeller diameter and pitch 55x28 inch, 1.40x 0.70 m. V-belt reduction, ratio 2.0/1. Max static thrust 243 lb, 110 kg. Power per unit area 0.23 hp/ft^2, 2.5 hp/m^2. Fuel capacity 3.2 US gal, 2.6 Imp gal, 12.0 litre.

WEIGHTS & LOADINGS - Empty weight 240 lb, 109 kg. Max take-off weight 683 lb, 310 kg. Payload 443 lb, 201 kg. Max wing loading 3.71 lb/ft^2, 18.1 kg/m^2. Max power loading 16.7 lb/hp, 7.6 kg/hp. Load factors +3.0, -1.0 recommended; +6.0, -3.0 ultimate.

PERFORMANCE* - Max level speed 45 mph, 72 kph. Never exceed speed 56 mph, 90 kph. Max cruising speed 40 mph, 65 kph. Economic cruising speed 37 mph, 60 kph. Stalling speed 26 mph, 42 kph. Max climb rate at sea level 390 ft/min, 2.0 m/s. Min sink rate 350 ft/min at 34 mph, 1.8 m/s at 55 kph. Best glide ratio with power off 7/1 at 37 mph, 60 kph. Take-off distance 165 ft, 50 m. Landing distance 330 ft, 100 m. Service ceiling 8200 ft, 2500 m. Range at average cruising speed 93 mile, 150 km. Noise level NC.

*Under unspecified test conditions.

MAV

MAV Aeroclub, H-1146 Budapest, Thokoly ut 41; tel 361 634468. Leader of club hang-gliding section: Fereno Hlacs.

◄ MAV *TORNADO 1250/ DENEVER*

(Weight-shift)

Single-seat or side-by-side two-seat* single-engined flex-wing aircraft with weight-shift control. Rogallo wing with keel pocket. Pilot suspended below wing in trike

By flying with single seat but retaining the 46 hp engine, the Tornado 1250/Denever *can double the climb rate quoted in our data.*

unit, using bar to control pitch and roll/yaw by altering relative positions of trike unit and wing. Wing braced from above by kingpost and cables, from below by cables; floating cross-tube construction with 55% double-surface enclosing cross-tube; preformed ribs. Undercarriage has three wheels in tricycle formation; no suspension on any wheels. Push-right go-left nosewheel steering independent from aerodynamic controls. No brakes. Aluminium-alloy tube trike unit, completely open. Engine mounted below wing, driving pusher propeller.

Production status: one-off.

*See text.

GENERAL - Although the MAV trike is only a one-off, its inclusion is more than justified by the obviously resourceful and inventive nature of its designers. Not only must the MAV club rank among the world pioneers in hang-glider towing by trike (see the picture accompanying the section introduction), but also it has put a lot of work into turning the East German Trabant car engine, which seems to be the standard motor for Hungarian trikes, into a specialised microlight power pack.

In its basic form the Trabant is an in-line two-stroke twin of 594 cc capacity giving 26 hp DIN, but as early as 1980 MAV was tuning the engine and mating it to an integral gearbox to form the Hlamot II power pack, well before Rotax produced its now famous reduction of similar design. And when the club decided that even in tuned form the engine was just not powerful enough, it set out to engineer the Hlamot III three-cylinder version with a full 46 hp and triple carburettors. As this was fitted to the trike in 1982, the *Tornado 1250/Denever* must surely rate as the world's first in-line three-cylinder microlight.

With so much development work surrounding the aircraft, and with the machine having been flown solo and as a side-by-side two-seater, it is rather hard to come up with typical data! However, we describe it below in what is probably its most interesting form, as a three-cylinder two-seater.

EXTERNAL DIMENSIONS & AREAS - Length overall 14.8 ft, 4.50 m. Height overall 11.2 ft, 3.40 m. Wing span 32.8 ft, 10.00 m. Chord at root NC. Chord at tip 2.6 ft, 0.80 m. Dihedral 0°. Nose angle 122-125°. Depth of keel pocket 0.8 ft, 0.25 m. Total wing area 175 ft², 16.3 m². Keel pocket area 8.6 ft², 0.80 m². Aspect ratio 6.2/1. Wheel track 6.6 ft, 2.0 m. Wheelbase NC. Nosewheel diameter overall 8 inch, 20 cm. Main wheels diameter overall 8 inch, 20 cm.

POWER PLANT - MAV-modified Trabant engine. Max power 46 hp at 9000 rpm. Propeller diameter and pitch 56x35 inch, 1.43x0.90 m. Gear reduction, ratio 3.2/1. Max static thrust 276 lb, 125 kg. Power per unit area 0.26 hp/ft²,

2.8 hp/m². Fuel capacity 2.6 US gal, 2.2 Imp gal, 10.0 litre.

WEIGHTS & LOADINGS - Empty weight 243 lb, 110 kg. Max take-off weight 639 lb, 290 kg. Payload 397 lb, 180 kg. Max wing loading 3.65 lb/ft², 17.8 kg/m². Max power loading 13.9 lb/hp, 6.3 kg/hp. Load factors +2.5, -1.0 recommended; +6.0, -2.0 ultimate.

PERFORMANCE** - Max level speed 44 mph, 70 kph. Never exceed speed 56 mph, 90 kph. Max cruising speed 40 mph, 65 kph. Economic cruising speed 34 mph, 55 kph. Stalling speed 25 mph, 40 kph. Max climb rate at sea level 490 ft/min, 2.5 m/s. Min sink rate 350 ft/min at 31 mph, 1.8 m/s at 50 kph. Best glide ratio with power off 6/1 at 34 mph, 55 kph. Take-off distance 165 ft, 50 m. Landing distance 330 ft, 100 m. Service ceiling 13,100 ft, 4000 m. Range at average cruising speed 50 mile, 80 km. Noise level NC.

**Under unspecified test conditions.

MMRK

MMRK Aeroclub, Pf 184, H-1368 Budapest, V Sem melweisu 9.II.4; tel 00361 180303. Secretary: Feren Kiss.

MMRK *HIDRODEN*

(Weight-shift)

Single-seat single-engined flex-wing aircraft with weight-shift control. Rogallo wing with keel pocket. Pilot suspended below wing in trike unit, using bar to control pitch and roll/yaw by altering relative positions of trike unit and wing. Wing braced from above by kingpost and cables, from below by cables; floating cross-tube construction with 55% double-surface enclosing cross-tube; preformed ribs. Undercarriage has two floats, no wheels. Water steering by rudder aft of port float, independent from aerodynamic controls. No brakes. Aluminium-alloy tube trike unit, completely open. Engine mounted below wing, driving pusher propeller.

Production status: one-off.

GENERAL - The MMRK Aeroclub is the flyer's club of the agricultural and technical university in Budapest, and the *Hidroden* is as far as we know the club's first microlight design.

It uses a similar *Denever* wing to the MAV trike - we say similar because although the span and area are the same, some of the other dimensions are not - mated to a trike unit of the club's own design, using what appear to be glassfibre floats. Water steering is controlled by pedals connected to a single rudder on the rear of the port float, as can be seen on the picture in our colour section, while in the air the controls are the same as a normal trike.

Once again the Trabant engine is used, this time with V-belt reduction rather than the gear unit developed by MAV. To the best of our knowledge there are no plans for production.

▲

EXTERNAL DIMENSIONS & AREAS - Length overall 10.5 ft, 3.20 m. Height overall 11.2 ft, 3.40 m. Wing span 32.8 ft, 10.00 m. Chord at root 10.5 ft, 3.20 m. Chord at tip 2.6 ft, 0.80 m. Dihedral 2°. Nose angle 122°. Depth of keel pocket 1.3 ft, 0.38 m. Total wing area 175 ft², 16.3 m². Keel pocket area 3.2 ft², 0.30 m². Aspect ratio 6.2/1. Beam 5.2 ft, 1.6 m.

POWER PLANT - Trabant engine. Max power 25 hp at 3800 rpm. Propeller diameter and pitch 59x34 inch, 1.50x 0.86 m. V-belt reduction, ratio 2.0/1. Max static thrust 243 lb, 110 kg. Power per unit area 0.14 hp/ft², 1.5 hp/m². Fuel capacity 2.6 US gal, 2.2 Imp gal, 10.0 litre.

WEIGHTS & LOADINGS - Empty weight 220 lb, 100 kg. Max take-off weight 408 lb, 185 kg. Payload 187 lb, 85 kg. Max wing loading 2.33 lb/ft², 11.4 kg/m². Max power loading 16.3 lb/hp, 7.4 kg/hp. Load factors +2.0, -1.0 recommended; +6.0, -3.0 ultimate.

PERFORMANCE* - Max level speed NC. Never exceed speed 52 mph, 83 kph. Max cruising speed 50 mph, 80 kph. Economic cruising speed 31 mph, 50 kph. Stalling speed 21 mph, 35 kph. Max climb rate at sea level 590 ft/min, 3.0 m/s. Min sink rate 410 ft/min at 28 mph, 2.1 m/s at 45 kph. Best glide ratio with power off 5/1 at 30 mph, 48 kph. Take-off distance 490 ft, 150 m. Landing distance 100 ft, 30 m. Service ceiling 6600 ft, 2000 m. Range at average cruising speed 31 mile, 50 km. Noise level NC.

*Under unspecified test conditions.

Italy

Catching up fast

by Marco Bartolozzi, President of the Associazione Italiana Piloti di Ultraleggero

At present, ultralights here are governed by a simple law dated 14 March 1985, which exempts them from all the complications of general aviation. Unfortunately, there is also a technical enclosure which determines weights and dimensions for the ultralight category, and since the original law was presented over five years ago, these figures reflect yesterday's state of the art: 30 kg empty weight for hang-gliders and 40 kg for ultralights with engines not exceeding 5 hp.

Obviously this definition was drafted for hang-gliders and powered hang-gliders only, and was never modified to bring it into line with practical modern machines. However, it is much easier to change a technical enclosure than a law proper, since the former can be done by the National Aviation Authority, whereas the latter must go through parliament, so the legal limbo which the modern ultralight finds itself in should soon be over. From what we know at present, we are likely to get US-style regulations along the lines of *FAR Part 103,* with two-seaters being allowed for training purposes. This autumn the regulations for schools, forbidden flying areas, exams etc should also be published, allowing the sport to get established on a formal basis at last.

Instruction will be given under the supervision of the Aero Club of Italy and will we hope rely on established ultralight schools rather than just on local aero clubs. There are already over 40 ultralight schools working, whereas the aero clubs are all in tough financial straits and may not be able to tackle the job in the right way.

Even with these difficulties, ultralighting has caught on well in Italy. There are now some 700 pilots here, mostly in the north of the country, about 500 of them trikers. Most of the rest fly *Eagles,* imported since 1979 by Giesse Team of Torino, and now made here by an associated company, Ultrasport. Apart from this company and the others listed in this section, there are various imports: Rotecs can be had through Eximco in Milano, Aviasud products from Spin in Torino, and *Weedhoppers* from Gava-Light in Pavia. The last-named have sold well, especially the two-seater, largely because of their attractive price. A purely Italian fixedwing has yet to emerge, because the small market does not justify the investment involved, but it is now possible to create an all-Italian trike, by mating a wing from one of our three hang-glider manufacturers - Moyes Italia, Polaris, and Cama - with a Nanni, FIU or CSAM trike unit.

Finally, I must mention the Italian ultralight pilots association, the AIPU. Though not officially formed until 24 February 1984, the need for a pilots' association had become evident about a year earlier, and in February '83 I asked the specialist press for help in gathering information about how many ultralighters Italy had, and what their experience was. About 500 replies were received, some confusing, some false, but out of them came a figure of around 350 'real' pilots. Of these over 150 met at the inaugural meeting, and from then on the organisation has grown continuously, with over 200 by the end of '84 and over 300 by the following March. Total membership by the end of '85 is estimated at around 500. Present officials include myself as president, Erio Atti and Dino Panzacchi from Bologna, Luigi Aprile from Milano, and Rodolfo Bianchorosso from Rome.

For more information on ultralights in Italy, contact: AIPU, Str Madonna di Fatima, 3-10025 Pino Torinese (TO). L'Aquilone magazine is at Via del Lavoro, 17 Bologna.

Close up of the Hawk B *cockpit, showing how the doors unzip for summer flying. Instruments are optional.*

CERTANO

Pietro Certano & C SRL, Via Torino 72/A, 10040 Druento To; tel (011) 9846503/9846728; tx 211094 CERTAO I. President: Giancarlo Gianello.

CERTANO *HAWK B*
(Three-axis)

Summary as CGS Hawk B *(USA section).*
Production status: current, 35 completed.

GENERAL - The Certano company builds the lighter version of the American CGS *Hawk,* the *Hawk B,* under

license but fits a larger engine, a Rotax 377 instead of the single-cylinder 277. We understand from Certano president Giancarlo Gianello that the aircraft are identical in all other respects, though interestingly the empty weight of the Italian-made machine is only 6 lb (2.7 kg) up on that of its American counterpart, despite a difference of around 22 lb (10 kg) in engine weights.
Price: NC.

EXTERNAL DIMENSIONS & AREAS - See CGS *Hawk B* (USA section).

POWER PLANT - Rotax 377 engine. Max power 35 hp at 6250 rpm. Propeller diameter and pitch 60x30 inch, 1.52x0.76 m. Gear reduction, ratio 2.4/1. Max static thrust NC. Power per unit area 0.26 hp/ft², 2.8 hp/m². Fuel capacity 5.0 US gal, 4.2 Imp gal, 18.9 litre.

WEIGHTS & LOADINGS - Empty weight 251 lb, 114 kg. Max take-off weight 530 lb, 240 kg. Payload 279 lb, 127 kg. Max wing loading 3.93 lb/ft², 19.0 kg/m². Max power loading 15.1 lb/hp, 6.9 kg/hp. Load factors +4.0, -2.0 recommended; +6.0, -4.0 ultimate.

PERFORMANCE* - Max level speed NC. Never exceed speed 80 mph, 129 kph. Max cruising speed 70 mph, 113 kph. Economic cruising speed 55 mph, 88 kph. Stalling speed 26 mph, 42 kph. Max climb rate at sea level *700* ft/min, *3.6* m/s. Min sink rate 250 ft/min at 30 mph, 1.3 m/s at 48 kph. Best glide ratio with power off NC. Take-off distance 150 ft, 45 m. Landing distance 95 ft, 29 m. Service ceiling NC. Range at average cruising speed 100 mile, 161 km. Noise level NC.

**Under the following test conditions -* Airfield altitude 0 ft, 0 m. Ground temperature NC. Ground pressure NC mB. Ground windspeed 0 mph, 0 kph. Test payload 211 lb, 96 kg.

CERTANO *HAWK B II*
(Three-axis)

Summary as CGS Hawk II *(USA section).*
Production status: current, 10 completed.

GENERAL - Certano's version of the American two-seat *Hawk II,* called the *Hawk B II,* is identical in all respects to the US machine except that the Rotax 503 engine is fitted as standard instead of the 447.
Price: NC.

EXTERNAL DIMENSIONS & AREAS - See CGS *Hawk II* (USA section).

POWER PLANT - See CGS *Hawk II* (USA section) except: Rotax 503 engine. Max power 50 hp at NC rpm. Max static thrust NC. Power per unit area 0.37 hp/ft², 4.0 hp/m².

WEIGHTS & LOADINGS - See CGS *Hawk II* (USA section) except: Max power loading 16.0 lb/hp, 7.3 kg/hp.

PERFORMANCE* - Never exceed speed 85 mph, 137 kph. Max cruising speed 70 mph, 113 kph. Economic cruising speed 55 mph, 88 kph. Stalling speed 29 mph, 47 kph. Other data NC.

*Under unspecified test conditions.

CONERO

Conero Air Sport, Contrada Marignano 10, 62018 Porto Potenza (Macerata); tel (0733) 672202.

CONERO *VOYAGER*
(Three-axis)

Single-seat version has summary similar to Freedom Flyers Ascender II+; side-by-side two-seat version has summary similar to Ascender II+2 (see US section).

Production status: current, number completed NC.

GENERAL - Although we have not heard from this company directly, our sources in Italy tell us that it produces a local version of the *Ascender,* as latest versions of Jack McCornack's famous *Pterodactyl* are known. Apparently the machines come with one or two seats, are well finished and sharply priced, but unfortunately we have no further details.

EXTERNAL DIMENSIONS & AREAS - NC.

POWER PLANT - NC.

WEIGHTS & LOADINGS - NC.

PERFORMANCE - NC.

CSAM

CSAM srl, Via Boscovich, 17-20124 Milano; tel (02) 6554742.

CSAM *SIRIO*

(Three-axis)

Summary similar to Aviasud Sirocco (see French section) except: Roll control by ailerons. Wing braced from below by struts.

Production status: current, number completed NC.

GENERAL - Information from this company is very sparse, but we know that the *Sirio* is a copy of the French Aviasud *Sirocco,* but with modified wing, incorporating ailerons for roll control instead of spoilers, and using strut bracing instead of kingpost-and-cable. We understand that a two-seat version is on the drawing board. CSAM also produces a complete line of trike units, but unfortunately we have no further details.

EXTERNAL DIMENSIONS & AREAS - NC.

POWER PLANT - NC.

WEIGHTS & LOADINGS - NC.

PERFORMANCE - NC.

FIU

Fabbrica Italiana Ultraleggeri; address NC. All enquiries through French agent: Virginia Winds, La Maree, Chapelle Voland, 39140 Bletterans; tel (84) 48 6577.

FIU *SIGMA*
(Three-axis)

Single-seat single-engined high-wing monoplane with conventional three-axis control. Wing has unswept leading and trailing edges, and constant chord; cruciform tail. Pitch control by elevator on tail; yaw control by fin-mounted rudder; roll control by full-span ailerons; control inputs through stick for pitch/roll and pedals for yaw. Wing braced from below by struts; wing profile NC; NC% double-surface. Undercarriage has three wheels in tail-dragger formation; suspension NC. Ground steering NC. Brakes NC. Aluminium-alloy tube airframe, completely open. Engine mounted below wing, driving pusher propeller.

Production status: current, number completed NC.

GENERAL - Though it looks very like a Kolb *Ultrastar* (see US section), the FIU *Sigma* is actually quite different structurally, relying on aluminium-alloy tubing rather than welded steel. Another difference is the availability of a four-stroke engine, the Citroen Avion unit, which may be ordered in place of the KFM 107 Maxi usually fitted. Our data below refers to the two-stroke version; where different, figures for the four-stroke machine are shown in parentheses.
FIU is unusual in that it produces both fixedwing and flexwing machines (the latter admittedly using other manufacturers' wings), and to reduce production costs the company has standardised as much as possible, so that many undercarriage and power pack components are the same throughout the range.
A 10 min rigging time is claimed for the *Sigma;* no price is quoted.

EXTERNAL DIMENSIONS & AREAS - Wing span 27.6 ft, 8.40 m. Constant chord 5.3 ft, 1.61 m. Sweepback 0°. Total wing area 145 ft², 13.5 m². Aspect ratio 5.2/1. Other data NC.

POWER PLANT - KFM 107 Maxi (Citroen Avion) engine. Max power 30(34) hp at NC rpm. Propeller diameter and pitch NC. Reduction type and ratio NC. Max static thrust 243(220) lb, 110(100) kg. Power per unit area 0.21(0.23) hp/ft², 2.2(2.5) hp/m². Fuel capacity 3.4 US gal, 2.9 Imp gal, 13.0 litre.

WEIGHTS & LOADINGS - Empty weight *236* lb, *107* kg. Load factors NC recommended; +4.0, -3.0 ultimate. Other data NC.

PERFORMANCE - NC.

FIU *ZG/Suitable Rogallo*
(Weight-shift)

Single- or two-seat* single-engined flex-wing aircraft with weight-shift control. Rogallo wing. Pilot suspended below wing in trike unit, using bar to control pitch and roll/yaw by altering relative positions of trike unit and wing. Wing braced from above by kingpost and cables, from below by cables. Undercarriage has three wheels in tricycle formation; suspension NC. Push-right go-left nosewheel steering independent from aerodynamic controls. Brakes NC. Aluminium-alloy tube trike unit, completely open. Engine mounted below wing, driving pusher propeller.

Production status: current, number completed NC.

*See text.

GENERAL - With the *ZG* trike unit being made to order

with one or two seats and a wide variety of engines, it is virtually impossible to describe a standard machine and we are therefore omitting our data paragraphs in this case. The basic structure weighs 51 lb (23 kg) and will accept most engines from 49 to 104 lb weight (22-47 kg), including Rotax 277, 377 and 503, and the KFM 107 in both 25 hp and 30 hp versions. As on the *Sigma*, the four-stroke Citroen Avion unit is also available.

Rigging time is 15 min for the solo version and 20 min for the dual, when mated to a typical Rogallo. No prices are available.

The bare bones of the Fox Mono *trike unit, minus power pack...*

NANNI

Nanni Delta, Via Ruffini 6/c, 40133 Bologna; tel 051-370811/2; tx NAGIBO 511607. Sales manager: Giancarlo Nanni. Production director: Andrea Nanni. Test pilots: Stefano Nanni and Ilio Bergamini.

NANNI/PEGASUS *FOX MONO*
(Weight-shift)

Single-seat single-engined flex-wing aircraft with weight-shift control. Rogallo wing with keel pocket. Pilot suspended below wing in trike unit, using bar to control pitch and roll/yaw by altering relative positions of trike

...and with Jonathan Export engine being installed.

unit and wing. Wing braced from above by kingpost and cables, from below by cables; floating cross-tube construction with 55% double-surface enclosing cross-tube; preformed ribs. Undercarriage has three wheels in tricycle formation; no suspension on any wheels. Push-right go-left nosewheel steering independent from aerodynamic controls. Nosewheel brake. Aluminium-alloy tube trike unit, with optional pod. Engine mounted below wing, driving pusher propeller.

Production status: current, 20 completed (total of all Nanni models).

GENERAL - The Nanni company makes trike units which are used with a variety of wings, but which are engineered around the *Typhoon* range from British manufacturer Pegasus.

This smallest trike, the *Fox Mono*, consists of Nanni's *Fox*

22CV trike unit mated to a *Typhoon S4 Large* to give the machine described below, the trike unit being a thoroughly conventional lightweight machine in the modern idiom, with monopole construction.

Power comes not from the ubiquitous Robin or Rotax units but from the Jonathan single-cylinder engine, which is available in two forms - the Elite, with horizontal cylinder, and the Export, with vertical cylinder. Outputs are the same but the Export has a different reduction (2.5/1) giving rather less thrust (142 lb, 60 kg).

Price (trike unit only) is L2,033,000, with an instrument pod costing an extra L127,000 and a pilot's pod L212,000.

EXTERNAL DIMENSIONS & AREAS - Length overall 12.8 ft, 3.90 m. Height overall 11.0 ft, 3.35 m. Wing span 34.0 ft, 10.36 m. Chord at root 8.5 ft, 2.68m. Dihedral 0°. Nose angle 122°. Total wing area 180 ft², 16.7 m². Aspect ratio 6.4/1. Wheel track 5.2 ft, 1.60 m. Wheelbase 5.9 ft, 1.80 m. Other data NC.

POWER PLANT - Jonathan Elite engine. Max power 22 hp at 7800 rpm. Propeller diameter and pitch 55xNC inch, 1.40xNC m. Toothed-belt reduction, ratio 3.3/1. Max static thrust 154 lb, 70 kg. Power per unit area 0.12 hp/ft², 1.3 hp/m². Fuel capacity 2.6 US gal, 2.2 Imp gal, 10.0 litre.

WEIGHTS & LOADINGS - Empty weight 176 lb, 80 kg. Max take-off weight 485 lb, 220 kg. Payload 309 lb, 140 kg. Max wing loading 2.69 lb/ft², 13.2 kg/m². Max power loading 22.0 lb/hp, 10.0 kg/hp. Load factors +6.5, -4.5 recommended; NC ultimate.

PERFORMANCE* - Max level speed 56 mph, 90 kph. Never exceed speed 62 mph, 100 kph. Max cruising speed 47 mph, 75 kph. Economic cruising speed 40 mph, 64 kph. Stalling speed 32 mph, 20 kph. Min sink rate 280 ft/min at 29 mph, 1.4 m/s at 47 kph. Best glide ratio with power off 5/1 at NC speed. Other data NC.

*Under the following test conditions - Test payload 187 lb, 85 kg. Other data NC.

NANNI/PEGASUS *FOX BI*

(Weight-shift)

Summary as Fox Mono *except: Tandem two-seater. No suspension on nosewheel and rubber suspension on main wheels.*

Production status: current, see Fox Mono *for number completed.*

GENERAL - The *Fox Bi* is a completely separate design from the single-seat *Fox Mono,* rather than just a strengthened version of it, and uses duopole construction rather than the lightweight low-drag monopole arrangement on the solo machine.

Two versions of the *Fox Bi* are available, both using a Pegasus *Typhoon XL* wing, but mated to either a *Fox 42CV* trike unit or a *Fox 50CV* trike unit. The only difference between the two is the power pack, either a Rotax 447 or a Robin EC44.

Interestingly, the performance figures for the two do not differ greatly, confirming what we have long suspected, that Rotax power output figures tend to be rather conservative compared with those of their rivals. Our data below refers to the Rotax-engined version; where different, figures for the Robin-engined machine are shown in parentheses. The manufacturer's test figures below were taken with a 195 ft² (18.1 m²) *Typhoon XL,* but readers should note that

latest versions of the wing are slightly smaller (see Pegasus, British section). The *Fox Bi* would probably be a little faster if thus equipped.

Prices are L3,815,000 with Rotax power and L4,660,000 with the Robin, options being as for the solo machine.

EXTERNAL DIMENSIONS & AREAS - Length overall 13.1 ft, 3.98 m. Height overall 11.0 ft, 3.35 m. Wing span 34.0 ft, 10.36 m. Chord at root 10.0 ft, 3.05 m. Chord at tip 3.5 ft, 1.07 m. Dihedral 0°. Nose angle 122°. Total wing area 195 ft², 18.1 m². Aspect ratio 5.9/1. Other data NC.

POWER PLANT - Rotax 447 (Robin EC44) engine. Max power 42(50) hp at 6500 rpm. Propeller diameter and pitch 59(61)xNC inch, 1.50(1.55)xNC m. Gear (toothed-belt) reduction, ratio 2.4/1. Max static thrust 278(320) lb, 126(145) kg. Power per unit area 0.22(0.26) hp/ft², 2.3(2.8) hp/m². Fuel capacity 5.3 US gal, 4.4 Imp gal, 20.0 litre.

WEIGHTS & LOADINGS - Empty weight 287(304) lb, 130(138) kg. Max take-off weight 750 lb, 340 kg. Payload 463(445) lb, 210(202) kg. Max wing loading 3.85 lb/ft², 18.8 kg/m². Max power loading 17.9(15.0) lb/hp, 8.1(6.8) kg/hp. Load factors +6.0, -3.5 recommended; +6.5, -4.5 ultimate.

PERFORMANCE* - Max level speed 53 mph, 85 kph. Never exceed speed 68 mph, 110 kph. Max cruising speed 44(45) mph, 70(72) kph. Economic cruising speed 39 mph, 62 kph. Stalling speed 24 mph, 38 kph. Max climb rate at sea level 980(1220) ft/min, 5.0(6.2) m/s. Other data NC.

*Under the following test conditions - Test payload 209 lb, 95 kg.

Nanni Fox 50CV *trike unit.*

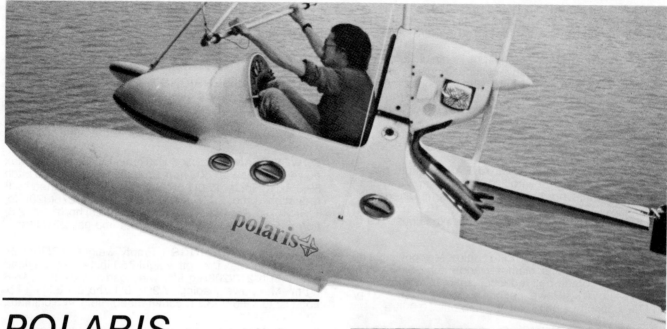

POLARIS

Polaris SRL, Via Flaminia 208, 06021 Costacciaro (PG); tel 075-9170186.

POLARIS *AIR DINGHY*
(Weight-shift)

Single-seat single-engined flex-wing aircraft with weight-shift control. Rogallo wing with keel pocket. Pilot suspended below wing in 'trike unit', using bar to control pitch and roll/yaw by altering relative positions of 'trike unit' and wing. Wing braced from above by kingpost and cables, from below by cables; floating cross-tube construction with single-surface; preformed ribs. Undercarriage has two floats, no wheels. Push-right go-right water rudders independent from aerodynamic controls. No brakes. Composite-construction 'trike unit', partially enclosed. Engine mounted below wing, driving pusher propeller.

Production status: current, approximately 10 completed.

GENERAL - From the hang point upwards this aircraft is a normal trike, using the well known Polaris *Delta* wing, a simple single-surface design.

However, the rest of the machine bears no relationship to a normal trike unit at all. Designed by British water sports enthusiast Sonny Levi, who is particularly well known on the powerboat scene, it is built by Polaris under license from his Go Plane company (see British section). The bottom half of the machine consists of a monocoque fuselage with two integral floats, constructed in grp/Kevlar. A KFM engine is mounted in the normal trike position behind the pilot's head, and there is one small water rudder on the end of each float, controlled by pedals. The pedals are not connected to the wing, so in the air the machine behaves exactly like a normal trike.

Strictly a seaplane, not an amphibian, the *Air Dinghy* has a similar weight and performance to a conventional solo trike, with take-off at around 20 mph (32 kph). Because the lower part is transported complete - either on a boat or a trailer - rigging time is very short, only 10 min being

A British design, made in Italy - the Air Dinghy. *For another illustration, see colour section.*

claimed. Alternatively, if the owner can't be bothered to rig at all, the bottom half of the machine can be used as a hydroplane, the low draught allowing it to be used even in shallow lagoons.

This very original machine sells at £5000 sterling, including a few hours free training if desired.

EXTERNAL DIMENSIONS & AREAS - Length overall 12.9 ft, 3.93 m. Height overall 8.0 ft, 2.44 m. Wing span 34.1 ft, 10.40 m. Nose angle 120°. Total wing area 200 ft², 18.6 m². Aspect ratio 5.8/1. Beam 6.7 ft, 2.04 m. Other data NC.

POWER PLANT - KFM 107ER engine. Max power 25 hp at 6500 rpm. Propeller diameter and pitch 50x32 inch, 1.27x0.81 m. V-belt reduction, ratio 2.1/1. Max static thrust 132 lb, 60 kg. Power per unit area 0.13 hp/ft², 1.3 hp/m². Fuel capacity 3.5 US gal, 2.9 Imp gal, 13.2 litre.

WEIGHTS & LOADINGS - Empty weight 230 lb, 104 kg. Max take-off weight 550 lb, 249 kg. Payload 320 lb, 145 kg. Max wing loading 2.75 lb/ft², 13.4 kg/m². Max power loading 22.0 lb/hp, 10.0 kg/hp. Load factors NC.

PERFORMANCE* - Max level speed 50 mph, 80 kph. Never exceed speed 60 mph, 97 kph. Max cruising speed 45 mph, 72 kph. Economic cruising speed 40 mph, 64 kph. Stalling speed 20 mph, 32 kph. Other data NC.

*Under unspecified test conditions.

ULTRASPORT

Ultrasport SRL, Frazione Montebruno, 10060 Garzigliana, Torino; tel (0121) 531484/5; tx 210310 PPTO I. Sales and administration manager: Marco Bartolozzi. Production manager: Luigi Accusani.

Northern European agent: Continental Aerolights (see separate listing, Other Countries section).

Far Eastern agent: Devcon Enterprise, Pemimpin Industrial Building, Singapore.

ULTRASPORT *EAGLE XL*
(Three-axis)

Single-seat single-engined high-wing monoplane with conventional three-axis control. Wing has swept back leading and trailing edges, and tapering chord; no tail, canard wing. Pitch control by elevator on canard; yaw control by tip rudders; roll control by 15%-span spoilers; control inputs through stick for pitch/roll and pedals for yaw. Wing braced from above by kingpost and cables, from below by cables; wing profile NC; 50% double-surface. Undercarriage has three wheels in tricycle formation; no suspension on nosewheel and axle-flex suspension on main wheels. Push-right go-right nosewheel steering connected to yaw control. Nosewheel brake. Aluminium-alloy tube airframe, completely open. Engine mounted below wing, driving pusher propeller.

Production status: current, approximately 4000 completed (total US and Italian production of all solo Eagle variants).

GENERAL - One of the most famous ultralights of all and certainly one of the most popular, the *Eagle* was undoubtedly the easiest to fly of all the early machines and was produced in large quantities in the US by American Aerolights.

This tube-and-Dacron aircraft quickly gained a reputation for being well-nigh idiot-proof, thanks to the spin- and stall-resistant canard design, and thus appealed greatly to the inexperienced pilot who, in the days before dual training, was of necessity largely self-taught.

Various control arrangements have been used over the years. The original design, and probably still the most numerous worldwide, had hybrid controls, with a swing seat linked to the elevator to control pitch and a tiller to control tip rudders; there was no separate roll control. In November '81 came the *Eagle SL,* a two-axis variant which was identical to the original except for having a fixed seat, the tiller controlling pitch as well as yaw. Thirdly came the *Eagle XL* in 1982, with spoilers added to give full conventional three-axis control.

In fact the *XL* was more than just an *SL* with spoilers, as the wing had more double-surface and a higher aspect ratio, while the tip rudders were redesigned and enlarged. As pilots grew more experienced, they grew frustrated at the original design's limitations in gusty weather and its tendency to weathercock; the *XL* was an attempt to provide them with a higher-performance machine.

These airframe changes have been paralleled by many engine changes, early models using twin Chrysler engines, followed by the Zenoah G25B (often replaced in Europe by the Robin EC25PS), the Cuyuna 215RR and the Cuyuna 430RR, the latter·two being offered concurrently, as the 430 engine was intended only for heavier pilots and came

By substituting floats for the main wheels, the Eagle XL *can be quickly turned into a seaplane.*

with a strengthened airframe. It was, however, fitted as standard in the *XL.*

Following a long legal battle over royalties, between designers Horst Honacker/Romauld Drlik and American Aerolights, the latter stopped production of the *Eagle* and later reformed the company as American Aircraft to concentrate on its unrelated *Falcon* design. Production rights for the *Eagle* were then transferred to Ultrasport, which has decided to build only the three-axis version and its two-seat equivalent. Italian-built *Eagle XLs* are very similar to their US counterparts, the most obvious difference being that the Cuyuna 430RR has been dropped in favour of a Rotax 377. Prices are L7,900,000 in kit form or L9,900,000 ready-to-fly, wheel spats being optional in either case.

EXTERNAL DIMENSIONS & AREAS - Length overall 13.0 ft, 3.96 m. Height overall 8.0 ft, 2.44 m. Wing span 34.0 ft, 10.36 m. Chord at root 7.0 ft, 2.13 m. Chord at tip 2.0 ft, 0.61 m. Dihedral 5°. Sweepback 22.5°. Canard span 10.0 ft, 3.05 m. Canard chord 2.0 ft, 0.61 m. Rudder height NC. Total wing area 175 ft^2, 16.3 m^2. Main wing area 155 ft^2, 14.4 m^2. Canard area 20 ft^2, 0.65 m^2. Total spoiler area 5.0 ft^2, 0.46 m^2. Total rudder area 8.0 ft^2, 0.74 m^2. Total elevator area NC. Aspect ratio (of main wing) 7.5/1. Wheel track 7.0 ft, 2.13 m. Wheelbase 5.0 ft, 1.52 m. Nosewheel diameter overall 10 inch, 25 cm. Main wheels diameter overall 10 inch, 25 cm.

POWER PLANT - Rotax 377 engine. Max power 34 hp at 6500 rpm. Propeller diameter and pitch 54x34 inch, 1.37x0.86 m. V-belt reduction, ratio 2.2/1. Max static thrust 230 lb, 104 kg. Power per unit area 0.19 hp/ft^2, 2.1 hp/m^2. Fuel capacity 4.0 US gal, 3.3 Imp gal, 15.1 litre.

WEIGHTS & LOADINGS - Empty weight 230 lb, 104 kg. Max take-off weight 500 lb, 227 kg. Payload 270 lb, 122 kg. Max wing loading 2.86 lb/ft^2, 13.9 kg/m^2. Max power loading 14.7 lb/hp, 6.7 kg/hp. Load factors +4.0, -1.5 recommended; +6.5, -2.5 ultimate.

PERFORMANCE* - Max level speed 50 mph, 80 kph. Never exceed speed 63 mph, 101 kph. Max cruising speed 50 mph, 80 kph. Economic cruising speed 38 mph, 61 kph. Stalling speed 22 mph, 35 kph. Max climb rate at sea level 1000 ft/min, 5.1 m/s. Min sink rate 400 ft/min at 26 mph, 2.0 m/s at 42 kph. Best glide ratio with power off 6/1 at 38 mph, 61 kph. Take-off distance 100 ft, 30 m. Landing distance 100 ft, 30 m. Service ceiling 13,000 ft, 3960 m. Range at average cruising speed 80 mile, 129 km. Noise level 65 dB at 500 ft, 150 m.

Under the following test conditions - Airfield altitude 0 ft, 0 m. Ground temperature 59°F, 15°C. Ground pressure 1013 mB. Ground windspeed 0 mph, 0 kph. Test payload 185 lb, 84 kg.

ULTRASPORT *EAGLE XL* 2-PLACE
(Three-axis)

Summary as Eagle XL *except: Side-by-side two-seater.*

Production status: current, approximately 250 completed (total US and Italian production of all dual Eagle *variants).*

GENERAL - Like the solo machine, the two-seater *Eagle* first appeared with a swing seat, but unlike the solo model this control arrangement never went into production, all aircraft sold to the public being three-axis machines - effectively two-seat *Eagle XLs*. With the move to Italy, they have become that in name as well as fact, adopting the *XL* suffix and sharing many components with the solo aircraft, as is evident from our data below.
Power comes from a Rotax 503, which replaced the Cuyuna 430RR used on the prototype and has been fitted to all two-seat *Eagles*, American or Italian, ever since.
Price is L9,900,000 in kit form or L11,800,000 complete, wheel spats being optional in either case.

EXTERNAL DIMENSIONS & AREAS - See *Eagle XL* except: Height overall 9.0 ft, 2.74 m. Canard span 11.0 ft, 3.35 m. Total wing area 180 ft², 16.7 m². Canard area 25 ft², 2.3 m². Nosewheel diameter overall 15 inch, 38 cm. Main wheels diameter overall 15 inch, 38 cm.

POWER PLANT - Rotax 503 engine. Max power 44 hp at 6300 rpm. Propeller diameter and pitch 56x34 inch, 1.42x0.86 m. V-belt reduction, ratio 2.0/1. Max static thrust 280 lb, 127 kg. Power per unit area 0.24 hp/ft², 2.6 hp/m². Fuel capacity 4.0 US gal, 3.3 Imp gal, 15.1 litre.

WEIGHTS & LOADINGS - Empty weight 275 lb, 125 kg. Max take-off weight 675 lb, 306 kg. Payload 400 lb, 181 kg.

Max wing loading 3.75 lb/ft², 18.3 kg/m². Max power loading 15.3 lb/hp, 7.0 kg/hp. Load factors +3.0, -1.5 recommended; +5.0, -2.0 ultimate.

PERFORMANCE* - Max level speed 55 mph, 88 kph. Never exceed speed 63 mph, 101 kph. Max cruising speed 55 mph, 88 kph. Economic cruising speed 43 mph, 69 kph. Stalling speed 28 mph, 45 kph. Max climb rate at sea level 500 ft/min, 2.5 m/s. Min sink rate 600 ft/min, 3.1 m/s at NC speed. Best glide ratio with power off 5/1 at 43 mph, 69 kph. Take-off distance 300 ft, 91 m. Landing distance 200 ft, 61 m. Service ceiling 6500 ft, 1980 m. Range at average cruising speed 45 mile, 72 km. Noise level 75 dB at 500 ft, 152 m.

Under the following test conditions - Airfield altitude 0 ft, 0 m. Ground temperature 59°F, 15°C. Ground pressure 1013 mB. Ground windspeed 0 mph, 0 kph. Test payload 353 lb, 160 kg.

ULTRASPORT *FOXCAT*
(Three-axis)

Summary similar to American Aircraft Falcon (*see US section*).

Production status: current, number completed NC.

GENERAL - The *Foxcat* is Ultrasport's version of American Aircraft's *Falcon*, and like its counterpart in Belgium (see Sonaca) has been greatly strengthened compared to the original design. Fuselage and wings are now entirely made from Kevlar and carbon-fibre.
Price: NC.

EXTERNAL DIMENSIONS & AREAS - NC.

POWER PLANT - NC.

WEIGHTS & LOADINGS - NC.

PERFORMANCE - NC.

ULTRASPORT *FOXCAT TWO-PLACE*
(Three-axis)

Summary similar to American Aircraft Falcon (*see US section*) *except: Two-seater.*

Production status: prototype.

GENERAL - Ultrasport is now working on a two-seat version of its *Foxcat* using the new Arrow GT500 engine. As we go to press, no information is available other than that below.

EXTERNAL DIMENSIONS & AREAS - NC.

POWER PLANT - Arrow GT500 engine. Max power 60 hp at NC rpm. Other data NC.

WEIGHTS & LOADINGS - Empty weight 375 lb, 170 kg. Max take-off weight 882 lb, 400 kg. Payload 507 lb, 230 kg. Max wing loading NC. Max power loading 14.7 lb/hp, 6.7 kg/hp. Load factors NC.

PERFORMANCE* - Cruising speed 93 mph, 150 kph. Other data NC.

Under unspecified test conditions.

New Zealand

Researched by Janic Geelen, Associate Editor of New Zealand Wings magazine

Proudly owned by Derek Krippner, this Ultra Flight Systems Trike uses a 215 cc engine and is mated to a Vampyr 162 wing.

The Kiwis' key to the skies

by Janic Geelen

More than 300 microlights are currently flying in New Zealand, and that, for a country with only 3 million people, must make New Zealand the nation with the most microlights per head of population in the world. Microlight flying had a quiet, almost secret beginning back in 1979, when an enterprising chap in Stratford imported a *Scout Mk1* powered by the tiny Pixie engine. This microlight was never registered and was kept out of Ministry of Transport sight. It still exists in a museum at Queenstown.

The first truly public appearance of a microlight came in November 1980 at Hamilton, where a privately imported *Quicksilver* was on display. The public didn't see it fly - that was reserved for 'those in the know' - but this secrecy didn't last very long. All credit for this change must go to a group of hang-glider pilots who founded the Microlight Association of New Zealand in 1981. The founders were all very familiar with the special niche hang-gliding had in New Zealand aviation, whereby, with the full approval of the Ministry of Transport's Civil Aviation Division, the Hang Gliding Association had set up the rules, controlled safety, and approved both modifications and new designs for the sport. They were thus were able to draft a similar system for microlights, again with Ministry approval, making the rules restrictive enough to satisfy the Ministry that all would be well, while leaving the system sufficiently free from bureaucracy to satisfy most of those who already had microlights.

The minimum requirements were simple. A microlight pilot had to be over 16 years old and have a medical - then he could obtain a student pilot's license from the Ministry. No previous flying experience was required, although it was recommended that the pilot should have 2-3 h dual instruction on a light aircraft. Ownership of a microlight required membership of MAANZ and an aircraft registration from the Ministry, while the machine itself had to be fitted with an ASI, altimeter, and compass. MAANZ controlled all type-approvals and individually approved owners so they could maintain their own machines under a permit-to-fly system. Flying was forbidden over built-up areas and near controlled airports, except under special circumstances, such as airshows.

Until the advent of two-place microlights this system worked extremely well, with 280 official MAANZ registrations by September 1984. There were, however, over 50 unregistered machines (including two-seaters) in the country, whose owners were 'rugged

New Zealand Wings

▷ individualists' and were not members of MAANZ. Some were hang-glider pilots who only fitted their trike units every now and then, while others were farmers whose microlights never ventured beyond the confines of their own properties.

However, the advent of the two-seater invoked further Ministry interest, for there was now the possibility of passengers being killed. Moreover, the higher payload of the two-seater meant that commercial work, in particular aerial spraying, became practical. Believe it or not, one enterprising microlight pilot actually shot deer from his machine, which he fitted with an extra seat for the shooter!

So during 1983 a set of new rules for microlights was proposed by the Ministry, creating two classes based on empty weight. As a result, confusion reigned and still does. Some microlights have been registered under MAANZ rules, while identical machines have been registered under regular light aircraft permit-to-fly regulations, while an unknown number have simply not been registered at all! Type approval is another area of concern, with approvals being issued either by MAANZ or by the Ministry; some types have never been approved because their importers have never supplied any information, yet they continue to fly as though approval had been granted.

Thus the 1985 microlight scene in New Zealand is one of consolidation. New types are imported from time to time and production of local machines is steady, but most microlight pilots are sitting on the sidelines waiting for the rules to change yet again, waiting for a sensible pattern of control to emerge for this, the fastest growing sector of aviation in New Zealand today.

For more information on microlights in New Zealand, contact: MAANZ, PO Box 14520, Panmure, Auckland. New Zealand Wings *magazine is at PO Box 305, Feilding; tel 36-240.*

CANTERBURY MICROLIGHTS

Canterbury Microlights, 118 Rockinghorse Road, Christchurch 7; tel 884.765. Proprietor: Merv Thompson.

CANTERBURY MICROLIGHTS
SUPER SCOUT
(Three-axis)

Single-seat single-engined high-wing monoplane with conventional three-axis control. Wing has unswept leading edge, swept forward trailing edge, and tapering chord; conventional tail. Pitch control by fully flying tail; yaw control by fully flying rudder; roll control by wing warping; control inputs through stick for pitch/roll and pedals for yaw. Wing braced from above by kingpost and cables, from below by cables; wing profile has lifting section, reflex trailng edge; single-surface. Undercarriage has three wheels in tail-dragger formation; axle-flex suspension on all wheels. Push-right go-right tailwheel steering connected to yaw control. No brakes. Aluminium-alloy tube airframe, completely open. Engine mounted at wing height, driving tractor propeller.

Production status: see text.

GENERAL - Since 1981 sales of the Skycraft *Scout Mk3* have outstripped all other microlights in New Zealand, over 50 having been supplied. The agent, L M Wright & Co of Dunedin, has done much more than just sell *Scouts* - the company has kept in touch with owners and relayed suggestions for improvements to the Australian manufacturer, and as a result significant changes have been incorporated into the *Mk4* which was due to reach the New Zealand market in early 1985.

Meanwhile Merv Thompson, a *Scout* owner from Christchurch, has incorporated his own range of improvements in the *Mk3,* and has dubbed the modified aircraft *Super Scout.* Because Merv makes airframe spares for the *Scout* (as well as for other microlights), the only Australian-built

New Zealand Wings

components of the *Super Scout* are the fuselage and wing spars - everything else is made at Christchurch.

The extensive modifications include a KFM electric start engine, instrument console (NZ$50), heavy-duty undercarriage (NZ$148 main wheels, NZ$85 tailwheel), long-range tank (NZ$120), large upholstered seat (NZ$38), and a bracing and flying wires safety attachment kit (NZ$66), prices in parentheses being the costs of the individual items to owners of existing *Scouts* who want to upgrade their machines to *Super Scout* specification.

The *Super Scout* first flew in April 1984 and the KFM motor has proved very smooth and reliable, giving improved performance and payload compared with the standard power unit. An unspecified number of production examples have now been built, a complete new *Super Scout* costing NZ$7200; instruments are optional.

To avoid confusion, we must point out that Merv's aircraft has no connection with the British machine of the same name, produced by Flylite.

EXTERNAL DIMENSIONS 6 AREAS - Length overall 16.0 ft, 4.88 m. Height overall 7.0 ft, 2.13 m. Wing span 28.5 ft, 8.69 m. Chord at root 6.5 ft, 1.98 m. Chord at tip 3.5 ft, 1.07 m. Dihedral 4°. Sweepback 0°. Tailplane span 10.0 ft, 3.05 m. Fin height 4.0 ft, 1.22 m. Total wing area 126 ft^2, 11.7 m^2. Tailplane area 22.0 ft^2, 2.0 m^2. Aspect ratio 6.4/1. Tailwheel diameter overall 4 inch, 10 cm. Main wheels diameter overall 12 inch, 30 cm. Other data NC.

POWER PLANT - KFM 107ER engine. Max power 25 hp at 6300 rpm. Propeller diameter and pitch 54x24 inch, 1.37x0.61 m. Notched V-belt reduction, ratio 2.0/1. Max static thrust 176 lb, 80 kg. Power per unit area 0.20 hp/ft^2, 2.1 hp/m^2. Fuel capacity 3.8 US gal, 3.2 Imp gal, 14.5 litre.

WEIGHTS 6 LOADINGS - Empty weight 142 lb, 64 kg. Max take-off weight 367 lb, 166 kg. Payload 225 lb, 102 kg. Max wing loading 2.91 lb/ft², 14.2 kg/m². Max power loading 14.7 lb/hp, 6.6 kg/hp. Load factors +6.0, -2.0 recommended; +8.0, -2.5 ultimate.

PERFORMANCE* - Max level speed 65 mph, 105 kph. Never exceed speed 75 mph, 121 kph. Max cruising speed 55 mph, 88 kph. Economic cruising speed 45 mph, 72 kph. Stalling speed 20 mph, 32 kph. Max climb rate at sea level 800 ft/min, 4.1 m/s. Min sink rate 200 ft/min at 27 mph, 1.0 m/s at 43 kph. Best glide ratio with power off 7/1 at 30 mph, 48 kph. Take-off distance 90 ft, 25 m. Landing distance 120 ft, 35 m. Service ceiling 12,500 ft, 3800 m. Range at average cruising speed 140 mile, 225 km. Noise level 85 dB at 50 ft, 15 m.

*Under the following test conditions - Airfield altitude 300 ft, 90 m. Ground temperature 59°F, 15°C. Ground pressure 1016 mB. Ground windspeed 5 mph, 8 kph. Test payload 171 lb, 78 kg.

DELORE

Delore, 62 Sparks Road, Christchurch 2; tel 381.889. Manager: Terry Delore.

DELORE
SKY-TRIKE/Suitable Rogallo
(Weight-shift)

Single-seat single-engined flex-wing aircraft with weight-shift control. Rogallo wing. Pilot suspended below wing in trike unit, using bar to control pitch and roll/yaw by altering relative positions of trike unit and wing. Undercarriage has three wheels in tricycle formation; torsion-bar suspension on all wheels. Push-right go-left nosewheel steering independent from aerodynamic controls. No brakes. Aluminium-alloy tube trike unit, completely open. Engine mounted below wing, driving pusher propeller.

Production status: see text.

GENERAL - Terry Delore is a hang-glider from Christchurch, who has also turned his skills to standard class gliding, where he has attained some success at New Zealand Championship level.

It is his hang-gliding activities, however, which have led him into aircraft building, as he started building powered hang-gliders, then moved to making improvements to imported trikes, and finally to complete local manufacture of trike units.

His *Sky-Trike* is a duopole design based on one of the earliest English trikes, the Hiway *Skytrike*, but has been modified in a number of ways, principally with a sprung undercarriage and a stronger framework, which unlike the original Hiway machine incorporates a front strut. Some 20 examples have been built in three years, making it the most common trike unit in the country, though at the time of writing Terry was in Italy furthering his gliding experience, so no aircraft were being produced; it is not known if production will recommence on his return.

Sky-Trikes are generally sold to pilots who already own a Rogallo, so the trike unit is flown with a wide variety of wings, including Ultra Light Systems *Chevron A* and *B*,

Terry Delore's first prototype Skytrike *takes off on a trial flight, on this occasion using a* Chevron B *wing.*

Wedgetail III and *Swift*; Pacific Kites *Lancer 4* and *Vampyr* (all sizes); and Moyes *Mega II*, *Mega III* and *Meteron*.

Two engine sizes are offered - the 250 Robin single and the 330 twin - and customers can choose either the standard tank (in which form we detail it below) or a tank one-third as large.

Much of the data is obviously dependent on the wing and engine used, but Terry says that a 450 ft/min (2.3 m/s) climb and a cruise of 40 mph (64 kph) are typical. Prices start at NZ$2500 for the trike unit.

Note: in the following data, where a figure is dependent on the engine fitted, figures for the Robin EC25PS are given first, followed in parentheses by those for the EC34PM.

EXTERNAL DIMENSIONS & AREAS - Wheel track 5.0 ft, 1.52 m. Wheelbase 4.5 ft, 1.37 m. Nosewheel diameter overall 10 inch, 25 cm. Main wheels diameter overall 10 inch, 25 cm. Other data NC.

POWER PLANT - Robin EC25PS (EC34PM) engine. Max power 22 (30) hp at NC rpm. Propeller diameter and pitch 54x27 inch, 1.37x0.69 m. V-belt reduction, ratio 2.5/1. Max static thrust NC. Power per unit area NC. Fuel capacity 4.0 US gal, 3.3 Imp gal, 15.0 litre.

WEIGHTS & LOADINGS - NC.

PERFORMANCE - NC.

This photo, taken in June 1984, shows the Bantam *prototype; compare it to the shot in the colour section, taken just five months later, of the production B-10 version.*

MICRO AVIATION

Micro Aviation NZ Ltd, c/o Post Office, Te Kowhai. Co-designers and managers: John Smith and Max Clear.

MICRO AVIATION
B-10 BANTAM
(Three-axis)

Single-seat single-engined high-wing monoplane with conventional three-axis control. Wing has unswept leading and trailing edges, and constant chord; cruciform tail. Pitch control by elevator on tail; yaw control by fin-mounted rudder; roll control by full-span ailerons; control inputs through stick for pitch/roll and pedals for yaw. Wing braced from above by kingpost and cables, from below by cables; wing profile NC; 100% double-surface. Undercarriage has three wheels in tricycle formation; no suspension on nosewheel and glass-fibre suspension on main wheels. Push-right go-right nosewheel steering connected to yaw control. No brakes. Aluminium-alloy tube airframe, with pod. Engine mounted at wing height, driving tractor propeller.

Production status: current, 12 completed.

New Zealand Wings

GENERAL - The *Bantam* is New Zealand's first microlight to receive full Ministry type approval, and was designed at Te Kowhai by John Smith and Max Clear. It first flew in early 1983 and quickly showed its superiority over the imported microlights then available.

Max is a well known figure in the homebuilding fraternity, and already had a Turbulent and a Pitts Special under his belt when microlights appeared on the scene. He let hang-gliding enthusiasts use his airstrip to test fly their micro-lights back in 1980, and was soon hooked himself, purchasing a *Mirage*. When the *Phantom* was announced in 1982 it gave him the final inspiration for the *Bantam*, and others who saw the design were so quick to support the scheme that 10 *Bantams* had been ordered before the first metal had been cut.

The *Bantam* uses similar construction materials to the *Phantom* and looks superficially similar, but there the connection ends. Its design is entirely new and everthing except the engine is New Zealand-sourced.

Constructed like the rest of the machine to aircraft standards, the wing is a solid affair with preformed metal ribs of similar cross-section to a Jodel *D.11* wing. This section was chosen because the Jodel has a proven good short airstrip performance, and the *Bantam* has inherited all the Jodel's good flying features as a result. A recent flight test by *Aviation News*' Murray Kirkus mentioned that it was well built, adequately powered, comfortable and easy to fly, with the handling characteristics expected of an conventional aircraft, light well balanced controls, and a most effective rudder and full-span ailerons.

The future of the *Bantam* seems assured, with a healthy order book and every possibility of exports in 1985. Price including NZ sales tax is NZ$9900.

EXTERNAL DIMENSIONS & AREAS - Length overall 17.0 ft, 5.18 m. Height overall 8.0 ft, 2.44 m. Wing span 28.5 ft, 8.69 m. Chord 4.3 ft, 1.30 m. Dihedral 2.5°. Sweepback 0°. Tailplane span 8.0 ft, 2.44 m. Fin height 4.7 ft, 1.42 m. Total wing area 121 ft², 11.2 m². Total aileron area 21.0 ft², 1.95 m². Fin area NC. Rudder area 10.0 ft², 0.93 m². Tailplane area 12.6 ft², 1.17 m². Total elevator area 12.6 ft², 1.17 m². Aspect ratio 6.7/1. Wheel track 5.2 ft, 1.57 m. Wheelbase 4.6 ft, 1.40 m. Nosewheel diameter overall 11 inch, 28 cm. Main wheels diameter overall 11 inch, 28cm.

POWER PLANT - Rotax 503 engine. Max power 51 hp at 6600 rpm. Propeller diameter and pitch 58x27 inch, 1.47x0.69 m. Notched V-belt reduction, ratio 2.0/1. Max static thrust NC. Power per unit area 0.42 hp/ft², 4.6 hp/m². Fuel capacity 9.8 US gal, 8.1 Imp gal, 37.0 litre.

WEIGHTS & LOADINGS - Empty weight 280 lb, 127 kg. Max take-off weight 551 lb, 250 kg. Payload 271 lb, 123 kg. Max wing loading 4.55 lb/ft², 22.3 kg/m². Max power loading 10.8 lb/hp, 4.9 kg/hp. Load factors NC recommended; +9.0, -6.0 ultimate.

PERFORMANCE* - Max level speed 62 mph, 100 kph. Never exceed speed 81 mph, 130 kph. Max cruising speed 58 mph, 93 kph. Economic cruising speed 46 mph, 74 kph. Stalling speed 24 mph, 39 kph. Max climb rate at sea level 550 ft/min, 2.8 m/s. Min sink rate 600 ft/min, 3.0 m/s at NC speed. Take-off distance 150 ft, 45 m. Service ceiling 12,000 ft, 3660 m. Range at average cruising speed 230 mile, 371 km. Other data NC.

*Under the following test conditions - Airfield altitude 110 ft, 35 m. Ground temperature 54°F, 12°C. Ground pressure NC. Ground windspeed NC. Test payload 192 lb, 87 kg.

ULTRA FLIGHT SYSTEMS

Ultra Flight Systems, 40 Pukete Road, PO Box 10052, Te Rapa, Hamilton; tel 492.303. Manager: Steve Edridge.

ULTRA FLIGHT
TRIKE/VAMPYR
(Weight-shift)

Single-seat single-engined flex-wing aircraft with weight-shift control. Rogallo wing with keel pocket. Pilot suspended below wing in trike unit, using bar to control pitch and roll/yaw by altering relative positions of trike unit and wing. Wing braced from above by kingpost and cables, from below by cables; floating cross-tube construction with 75% double-surface enclosing cross-tube; preformed ribs. Undercarriage has three wheels in tricycle formation; no suspension on nosewheel and axle-flex suspension on main wheels. Push-right go-left nosewheel steering independent from aerodynamic controls. No brakes. Aluminium-alloy tube trike unit, completely open. Engine mounted below wing, driving pusher propeller.

Production status: current, 12 completed.

GENERAL - Steve Edridge of Hamilton was a keen and experienced hang-glider pilot when he first tried power flying, building his first trike unit towards the end of 1981. Since then he has produced some five similar machines for sale each year.
Steve adopts a different solution from Terry Delore to the problem of achieving good controllability on rough terrain, preferring a monopole construction, which allows the rear axles to be set at a shallow angle and braced with cables to provide a degree of flexure - a common enough arrangement internationally but unique in New Zealand, and one which has given the *Trike* a reputation for good ground handling.
Local production of hang-gliders has all but ceased, and at no time have complete trikes been available from a New Zealand factory. So Steve sells his trike units to existing hang-glider pilots who either wish to 'go power' or who wish to have the option of both - a limited market, as Steve explains: 'There are only about 400 hang-gliders in New Zealand and many of these are unsuitable for conversion; knowing many of the owners, I think it unlikely that many of the suitable ones will ever become available for conversion.'
While the *Trike* may be flown with a wide variety of wings, it is best suited to the *Shark*, *Vampyr 162*, *Vampyr 175*, *Vampyr 185* and *Lancer 4* double-surface Rogallos. The data below is for the *Trike* mated to a *Vampyr 175*. For an illustration of an Ultra Flight Systems machine, see the introductory page of this section.
Price of the trike unit only is NZ$2800.

EXTERNAL DIMENSIONS & AREAS - Wing span 34.0 ft, 10.4 m. Chord at root 6.0 ft, 1.83 m. Chord at tip 1.0 ft, 0.30 m. Dihedral 1.5°. Depth of keel pocket 0.8 ft, 0.23 m.

Total wing area 175 ft², 16.3 m². Keel pocket area 3.0 ft², 0.28 m². Aspect ratio 6.6/1. Wheel track 6.6 ft, 2.0 m. Wheelbase 6.6 ft, 2.0 m. Nosewheel diameter overall 12 inch, 30 cm. Main wheels diameter overall 12 inch, 30 cm. Other data NC.

POWER PLANT - Rotax engine. Max power 28 hp at 5500 rpm. Propeller diameter and pitch 52x28 inch, 1.32x0.71 m. Gear reduction, ratio 2.25/1. Max static thrust 185 lb, 84 kg. Power per unit area 0.16 hp/ft², 1.7 hp/m². Fuel capacity NC.

WEIGHTS & LOADINGS - Empty weight 195 lb, 88 kg. Max take-off weight 490 lb, 222 kg. Payload 295 lb, 134 kg. Max wing loading 2.80 lb/ft², 13.6 kg/m². Max power loading 17.5 lb/hp, 7.9 kg/hp. Load factors +4.0, -2.0 recommended; +6.0, -4.0 ultimate.

PERFORMANCE* - Max level speed 45 mph, 72 kph. Never exceed speed 55 mph, 88 kph. Max cruising speed 40 mph, 64 kph. Economic cruising speed 40 mph, 64 kph. Stalling speed 22 mph, 35 kph. Max climb rate at sea level 650 ft/min, 3.3 m/s. Min sink rate 210 ft/min at 25 mph, 1.1 m/s at 40 kph. Best glide ratio with power off 5/1 at 30 mph, 48 kph. Take-off distance 120 ft, 35 m. Landing distance 300 ft, 90 m. Service ceiling 9000 ft, 2740 m. Range at average cruising speed 150 mile, 241 km. Noise level NC.

*Under the following test conditions - Airfield altitude 200 ft, 60 m. Ground temperature 57°F, 14°C. Ground pressure NC. Ground windspeed 8 mph, 13 kph. Test payload 180 lb, 82 kg.

South Africa

Researched by Dave Becker of South African Aeronews

Of American origin but now very much a South African product, the Thunderbird *is attracting great interest. This is the first South African-built example.*

Building a sport - and an industry by Dave Becker

Although the sport here is nowhere near as large as in some countries, microlighting has grown tremendously in South Africa since the first Rotec *Rally* was registered in June 1980. As in most countries, the first machines were made by fitting small motors to hang gliders, and in 1979-80 a few hybrid-control *Quicksilvers, Rallys, Eagles, Easy Risers,* and *Mitchell Wings* were imported. Many were never registered, so it is difficult today to know how many early imports there were, but compulsory registration was soon introduced - much earlier than elsewhere - making the historian's job much easier!

A lot has happened since then. The April '85 register shows 434 entries, and in addition there are many unregistered machines here - the author knows of at least 100, so a conservative estimate of the current total would be around 550. Present regulations demand that all aircraft conform to *LS1,* a type-approval document which sets out the basic requirements for microlight aircraft, and be checked by one of 25 approved persons for a nominal fee. On the licensing front, the original requirement for microlighters to have a student pilot's license has given way to the MPL (microlight pilot's license), which needs 20 h flying, including 15 h solo, with an approved instructor. At present many aircraft and pilots do not meet these standards and the aviation authority here, the DCA, plans to start getting tough with those not conforming to these basic requirements: of the seven fatalities since the sport started, most were to unlicensed pilots in unregistered aircraft.

Most microlight activities are controlled by MISASA - the Microlight Section of the Aero Club of South Africa - and the two biggest events of the year are undoubtedly the airshow, held at Springs this year on 4 May, and the race to Durban which followed on 6-11 May. Both are usually well supported. An annual microlight competition and rally is also planned, though there have already been many events at club level.

Our first locally produced microlight was the *M Fledge,* a *Fledgling* derivative built by George Killen and powered by a tiny Sachs motor. George flew one of these from Durban to Cape Town, quite a feat for its time. Since then the industry has had its ups and downs, with mergers, take-overs and, not surprisingly in view of South Africa's economic crisis, some company failures. Micro Aircraft of Durban has emerged as a clear leader, its *CDL* being by far the most numerous microlight here. Other strong contenders are Microlight Flight Systems, also of Durban, and

▷ Aeroventure of Pretoria, but in Cape Town production has been suspended of the promising *Phoenix*.
Of the imports, the *Quicksilver* is still the most popular, but there has been a swing to European machinery of late, especially trikes which have only recently become popular. The exchange rate, however, means that imports are expensive.
Despite the recession, the industry seems set to flourish in the next year. Hopefully the export trade, begun in 1984, will continue to increase and this in turn should keep local prices down.

For more information on microlights in South Africa, contact: MISASA, c/o South African Aeronews (official journal of the Aero Club of South Africa), PO Box 10467, Vorna Valley 1686; tel 011-805 2220.

AERO-TECH

Aero-Tech International, PO Box 8086, Edenglen, Edenvale 1610; tel 609-3063/4.

AERO-TECH *PUMA SPRINT, SEASPRINT and AGRASPRINT*
(Weight-shift)

Summary as appropriate Southdown International model (see Great Britain section).

Production status: current, number completed NC.

GENERAL - Aero-Tech International in South Africa is an offshoot of the British company of the same name. Although the latter is best known for its marketing of the Whittaker fixedwing designs, its South African subsidiary is more involved with flexwings, and sells Southdown International products under its own name.
Most of the aircraft are imported, but some local component manufacture has started, and it is possible that Pegasus wings will be used on future machines, producing a trike unit/wing combination which is uniquely South African. However, at the time of writing the aircraft are all-Southdown with specifications identical to the British machines, so we are omitting our data paragraphs in this instance.
Prices: *Puma Sprint* R9450, other models NC.

AEROTECHNICS

Aerotechnics (Pty) Ltd, 19-21 Hewett Avenue, Epping, Cape Town; tel 216093. Proprietor: J A Botha, 11 Jameson Road, Door de Kraal, Bellville 7530.

AEROTECHNICS *VALKYRIE*
(Three-axis)

Single-seat single-engined high-wing monoplane with conventional three-axis control. Wing has unswept leading and trailing edges, and constant chord; cruciform tail. Pitch control by elevator on tail; yaw control by fin-mounted rudder; roll control by half-span ailerons; control inputs through stick for pitch/roll and pedals for yaw. Wing braced from below by struts; wing profile NC; 100% double-surface. Undercarriage has three wheels in tri-

South African Aeronews

cycle formation; suspension NC. Ground steering NC. Brakes NC. Aluminium-alloy tube airframe, completely open. Engine mounted at wing height, driving pusher propeller.

Production status: one-off.

GENERAL - This straightforward tube-and-Dacron machine was produced in 1981 and demonstrated at the Aviation Africa airshow that year; for its time it was unusual in having strut bracing instead of kingpost-and-cable. Production was planned and considerable interest shown, but no further examples have ever been produced and it seems now that the *Valkyrie* will remain a one-off, though the sole example is still registered.

EXTERNAL DIMENSIONS & AREAS - Wing span 32.8 ft, 10.00 m. Constant chord 4.6 ft, 1.40 m. Dihedral 0°. Sweepback 0°. Total wing area 140 ft², 13.0 m². Aspect ratio 7.7/1. Other data NC.

POWER PLANT - Cuyuna 430R engine. Max power 30 hp at NC rpm. Reduction type NC, ratio 2.0/1. Power per unit area 0.21 hp/ft², 2.3 hp/m². Other data NC.

WEIGHTS & LOADINGS - Empty weight 260 lb, 118 kg. Other data NC.

PERFORMANCE - NC.

AEROVENTURE

Aeroventure (Pty) Ltd, PO Box 1392, Silverton 0127. Managing director: Doug Davey.

MEDIA AIRCRAFT *BUSH PATROL*
(Three-axis)

Single-seat single-engined high-wing monoplane with conventional three-axis control. Wing has unswept lead-

ing and trailing edges, and constant chord; cruciform tail. Pitch control by elevator on tail; yaw control by fully flying rudder; roll control by spoilers; control inputs through stick for pitch/roll and pedals for yaw. Wing braced from above by kingpost and cables, from below by cables; wing profile NC; single-surface. Undercarriage has three wheels in tail-dragger formation; suspension NC on tailwheel and bungee suspension on main wheels. Ground steering NC. Brakes NC. Aluminium-alloy tube airframe, completely open. Engine mounted above wing, driving pusher propeller.

Production status: obselete, 4 completed.

GENERAL - Though no longer in production, we include the *Bush Patrol* because it was one of South Africa's first home-grown microlights.

Intended as a rugged no-frills machine, the design owes a lot to the Rotec *Rally,* right down to the 'crash bars' in front of the pilot. Though we list it here with spoilers, we have seen pictures of a *Bush Patrol* with ailerons mounted on the trailing edge of the wing, just as on the early *Rallys.* Later *Rallys* had spoilers instead, and it seems that the African product evolved along parallel lines.

Only four *Bush Patrols* were built, all by Media Aircraft, predecessor of Aeroventure.

EXTERNAL DIMENSIONS & AREAS - Wing span 32.0 ft, 9.75 m. Constant chord 4.8 ft, 1.48 m. Total wing area 155 ft², 14.4 m². Aspect ratio 6.6/1. Other data NC.

POWER PLANT - Cuyuna 430 engine. Max power 43 hp at NC rpm. Toothed-belt reduction, ratio 2.4/1. Power per unit area 0.28 hp/ft², 3.0 hp/m². Other data NC.

WEIGHTS & LOADINGS - NC.

PERFORMANCE* - Max level speed 45 mph, 72 kph. Max cruising speed 35 mph, 56 kph. Stalling speed with power off 18 mph, 29 kph. Stalling speed with power on 16 mph, 26 kph. Max climb rate at sea level 600 ft/min, 3.0 m/s. Best glide ratio with power off 7/1 at NC speed. Take-off distance 90 ft, 27 m. Landing distance 60 ft, 18 m. Service ceiling 10,000 ft, 3050 m. Other data NC.

*Under unspecified test conditions.

In flight with a Dual Patrol.

AEROVENTURE *DOLPHIN*
(Three- axis)

Summary as Bush Patrol *except: Side-by-side two-seater. Push-right go-right tailwheel steering connected to yaw control.*

Production status: current, over 14 completed (total of Media Aircraft Dual Patrol *and Aeroventure* Dolphin *production).*

GENERAL - Introduced under the Media Aircraft banner as the *Dual Patrol,* this aircraft was renamed *Dolphin* by the Aeroventure company. Just as the solo machine was similar in concept to a Rotec *Rally 2,* so the dual aircraft resembled the *Rally 3,* though it differed in many details. As with the *Rally 3,* a Rotax 503 provides the power.
The first *Dual Patrol* was registered in December 1982 and unlike the single-seater the model is still available, though only to special order as it is being phased out in favour of an unnamed new aircraft believed to be similar to an Eipper *GT,* but with two seats.
Quite apart from this project, by the time you read this Aeroventure's output may have expanded again, as reports just as we were going to press suggested that the company would be building the *Thunderbird* on behalf of Sport Aviation. However, as these reports are unconfirmed at the time of writing, we list the latter under the Sport Aviation heading.
Price for *Dolphin*: NC.

EXTERNAL DIMENSIONS & AREAS - Wing span 40.0 ft, 12.19 m. Constant chord 5.0 ft, 1.52 m. Total wing area 200 ft², 18.6 m². Aspect ratio 8.0/1. Other data NC.

POWER PLANT - Rotax 503 engine. Other data NC.

WEIGHTS & LOADINGS - NC.

PERFORMANCE - See *Bush Patrol* except: Stalling speed with power off 20 mph, 32 kph. Stalling speed with power on 22 mph, 35 kph. Max climb rate at sea level 330 ft/min, 1.7 m/s. Take-off distance 115 ft, 35 m.

AIRMAN

Aircraft Manufacturers, 16 Perth Street, Pietermaritzburg 3201. Proprietors: Neville and Peter Reid-Robertson.

AIRMAN *SPURWING*

(Two-axis)

Single-seat single-engined high-wing monoplane with two-axis control. Wing has swept back leading and trailing edges, and constant chord; no tail, canard wing. Pitch control by fully flying canard; yaw control by tip rudders; no separate roll control; control inputs through stick for pitch/yaw. Wing braced from above by kingpost and cables, from below by cables; wing profile NC; 100% double-surface. Undercarriage has three wheels in tricycle formation; suspension NC. No ground steering. Brakes NC. Wooden wing, aluminium-alloy tube airframe, completely open. Engine mounted below wing, driving pusher propeller.

Production status: one-off.

GENERAL - This being the first edition of *Berger-Burr's* to include a South African section, we are listing a few of the more significant historical machines, and in that category undoubtedly belongs the *Spurwing.*
Constructed in early 1979 by the Reid-Robertson brothers, it was based on an *Icarus V* hang glider, with its painstakingly built-up wooden wing and tip rudders. Pitch control was by fully flying canard, supported not by two parallel tubes either side of the pilot, Pterodactyl-style, but by a single large-diameter strut from the centre of the leading edge, aided by lesser struts from the nosewheel area.
The engine position was also noticeably higher than on a 'Dactyl. In fact the power pack was an Airman speciality, a 100 cc Yamaha unit with notched V-belt reduction and a very respectable thrust. These units were marketed separately for use on *Mitchell Wings,* for which the company was South African agent.
Unlike its power pack, the *Spurwing* itself remained unique. To the best of its constructors' knowledge, no others were ever built, and unfortunately the whereabouts of the one and only example is now unknown, as it was never registered.

EXTERNAL DIMENSIONS & AREAS - NC.

POWER PLANT - Yamaha KT100S engine. Notched V-belt reduction, ratio NC. Max static thrust 105 lb, 48 kg. Other data NC.

WEIGHTS & LOADINGS - NC.

PERFORMANCE - NC.

ASCHENBORN

Richard Aschenborn, PO Box 698, Groblersdal 0470.

ASCHENBORN *HARTEBEES*
(Three-axis)

Summary as Aircraft Specialties Delta Bird *(see US section) except: Undercarriage has two wheels plus tailskid; bungee suspension on main wheels. No ground steering. Brakes NC.*

Production status: prototype.

GENERAL - Richard Aschenborn's *Hartebees* is basically a *Delta Bird* built under license, but there are a few differences between his machine and the Bob Hovey version. The Dacron wing covering has been changed for ceconite, a larger fuel tank is fitted, the tailwheel deleted, and, on the prototype at least, a less powerful version of the 430 Cuyuna is used. The American machine is fitted with a Cuyuna ULII-02, but Richard has stayed with the older 430R model and a smaller prop.
The net result of all these changes is a machine about 10 lb (4.5 kg) lighter and with a similar cruise speed, though the climb rate is down. A roll rate of 45° in 1.5 s can be achieved.
The prototype *Hartebees* was registered in December 1983 but at the time of writing (April '85) no production models had been built. This is possibly the result of pressure of work from Richard's other projects, as we understand that he is working on a two-seater version of the *Hartebees,* which will be offered with a crop-spraying

kit as an option. Construction of the two-seater started in 1984 but no details have been released.
Prices: NC.

EXTERNAL DIMENSIONS & AREAS - See Aircraft Specialties *Delta Bird* (US section).

POWER PLANT - Cuyuna 430R engine. Max power 30 hp at 5500 rpm. Propeller diameter and pitch 54x27 inch, 1.37x0.69 m. V-belt reduction, ratio 2.0/1. Max static thrust NC. Power per unit area 0.20 hp/ft^2, 2.1 hp/m^2. Fuel capacity 4.8 US gal, 4.0 Imp gal, 18.0 litre.

WEIGHTS & LOADINGS - See Aircraft Specialties *Delta Bird* (US section) except: Empty weight 220 lb, 100 kg. Payload 207 lb, 94 kg. Load factors +3.0, -4.5 recommended; NC ultimate.

PERFORMANCE* - Never exceed speed 60 mph, 97 kph. Max cruising speed 45 mph, 72 kph. Stalling speed 22 mph, 35 kph. Max climb rate at sea level 400 ft/min, 2.0 m/s. Other data NC.

*Under unspecified test conditions.

AVIATION 2000

Aviation 2000, PO Box 70710, The Willows, Pretoria 0041. Also: Shop 21, Willows Shopping Centre, Pretoria; tel 012 871186/7. Proprietors: Fanie van Rensburg, Bernard Schutte.

AVIATION 2000 *BASIC 2000*
(Three-axis)

Summary as Eipper Quicksilver MX *(see US section).*
Production status: current, number completed NC.

GENERAL - Aviation 2000 is the South African agent for several notable foreign manufacturers, including Aviasud (see French section), Aviation Composites (see GB section), and Eipper.
Through Aviation 2000 the last-named has supplied a large

number of the evergreen *Quicksilver MX* to the African market and, encouraged by the success of this American favourite, Aviation 2000 in spring '85 announced that it was to build its own version of the machine under license.
The *Basic 2000,* as it is known, is aimed very much at the novice pilot with little cash to spend. Specification is right down to the minimum required under the *LS1* airworthiness regulations, and though the price had not been fixed at the time of going to press, it is expected to be around R5000.
The company quotes identical specifications for the *Basic 2000* as the figures we present in the US section for the *MX* - indeed some of Aviation 2000's publicity material for the *Basic 2000* actually uses pictures of the American machine - so readers should refer to Eipper *Quicksilver MX* for data.

DWYNN

Willie Dwynn; tel 3317811/2/3 work, 659 1464 home.

DWYNN *DWYNN TRIKE/ Suitable Rogallo*

(Weight-shift)

Single-seat single-engined flex-wing aircraft with weight-shift control. Rogallo wing. Pilot suspended below wing in trike unit, using bar to control pitch and roll/yaw by altering relative positions of trike unit and wing. Wing braced from above by kingpost and cables, from below by cables. Undercarriage has three wheels in tricycle formation; no suspension on any wheels. Push-right go-left nosewheel steering independent from aerodynamic controls. No brakes. Aluminium-alloy tube trike unit, completely open. Engine mounted below wing, driving pusher propeller.

Production status: trike unit one-off.

GENERAL - Willie Dwynn's *Dwynn Trike* was one of South Africa's first trike units and was fitted to various hang

South African Aeronews

gliders. Powered by a direct-drive Sachs 150 engine, the machine was never put into production; in fact it could be said to have been ahead of its time, not in terms of its technology, but because trikes are only now beginning to catch on in South Africa.

The only example built was damaged in a ground accident in October '84 when the throttle jammed open.

EXTERNAL DIMENSIONS & AREAS - NC.

POWER PLANT - Sachs 150 engine. No reduction. Other data NC.

WEIGHTS & LOADINGS - NC.

PERFORMANCE - NC.

FG AVIATION

FG Aviation, PO Box 16087, Atlasville 1460; tel 894 5770.

FG AVIATION *FG AVION 1*
(Three-axis)

Single-seat single-engined high-wing monoplane with conventional three-axis control. Wing has unswept leading and trailing edges, and constant chord; flaps fitted; conventional tail. Pitch control by elevator on tail; yaw control by fin-mounted rudder; roll control by two-thirds

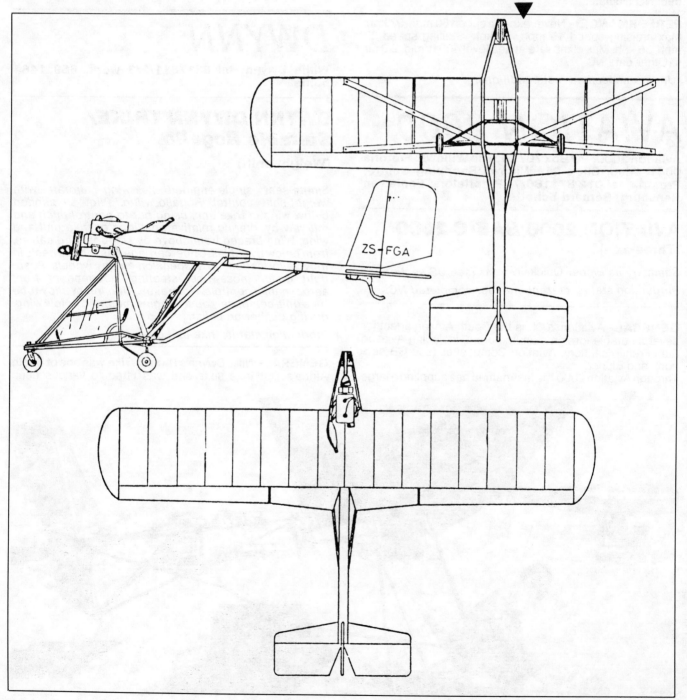

ZS-FGA

span ailerons; control inputs through stick for pitch/roll and pedals for yaw. Wing braced from below by struts; wing profile NC; NC% double-surface. Undercarriage has three wheels in tricycle formation with additional tailskid; suspension NC. Ground steering NC. Brakes NC. Tubular airframe, completely open. Engine mounted at wing height, driving tractor propeller.

Production status: prototype.

GENERAL - Announced just as we were going to press, FG Aviation's *FG Avion 1* is another example of how South Africa's microlight industry is 'growing up', producing its own designs rather than just importing foreign ones.

The machine was exhibited in incomplete form at the Springs show in May '85, having not yet flown, so little information is available. However, it appears to be a conventional high-wing tube-and-Dacron machine, whose main point of interest is the provision of Fowler flaps inboard of the differential ailerons. Workmanship on the prototype was very good, and it was obvious that the builders are well versed in standard aircraft-building techniques.

One of the options looks most intriguing - electronically operated trim tabs - though no details are given. The extras list also includes a 720 channel radio, intercom, helmet, navigation lights, strobes, trailer and parachute. No instruments appear on the options list, as a full set of gauges is to be fitted as standard, including ASI, vario, altimeter, compass, egtg and tachometer.

FG AVIATION *FG AVION 2*
(Three-axis)

Summary as FG Avion 1 *except: Two-seater.*

Production status: prototype.

GENERAL - Parallel with the development of the *FG Avion 1* solo machine, the company is also working on a two-seater, appropriately called the *FG Avion 2*. The two aircraft are of similar configuration, and use the same Zenoah G50D power unit. Despite having a larger wing, the two-seater is claimed to have almost the same empty weight. Options and instrumentation are as for the single-seater. Again, no prices are yet available, and readers should note that the data below is based on calculations.

EXTERNAL DIMENSIONS & AREAS - Wing span 32.0 ft, 9.75 m. Constant chord 5.1 ft, 1.56 m. Sweepback 0°. Total wing area 163 ft², 15.2 m². Aspect ratio 6.3/1. Other data NC.

POWER PLANT - See *FG Avion 1* except: Power per unit area 0.32 hp/ft². 3.4 hp/m².

WEIGHTS & LOADINGS - Empty weight 269 lb, 122 kg. Max take-off weight 816 lb, 370 kg. Payload 547 lb, 248 kg. Max wing loading 5.01 lb/ft², 24.3 kg/m². Max power loading 15.7 lb/hp, 7.1 kg/hp. Load factors NC.

PERFORMANCE* - Max level speed 60 mph, 97 kph. Never exceed speed 75 mph, 120 kph. Cruising speed 55 mph, 88 kph. kph. Stalling speed 37 mph, 59 kph. Max climb rate at sea level 240 ft/min, 1.2 m/s. Take-off distance 490 ft, 150 m, to clear obstacle of 52 ft, 16 m. Landing distance 260 ft, 80 m, to clear obstacle of 52 ft, 16 m. Take-off roll 195 ft, 60 m. Landing roll 165 ft, 50 m. Service ceiling 10,000 ft, 3050 m. Other data NC.

*Under the following test conditions - Airfield altitude 0 ft, 0 m. Ground temperature 59°F, 15°C. Ground pressure 1013 mB. Ground windspeed 0 mph, 0 kph. Pilot weight 194 lb, 88 kg, passenger weight 194 lb, 88 kg.

No prices are yet available, and readers should note that the data below is based on calculations.

EXTERNAL DIMENSIONS & AREAS - Wing span 30.0 ft, 9.14 m. Constant chord 5.0 ft, 1.52 m. Sweepback 0°. Total wing area 151 ft², 14.0 m². Aspect ratio 6.0/1. Other data NC.

POWER PLANT - Zenoah G50D engine. Max power 52 hp at 5800 rpm. Power per unit area 0.34 hp/ft², 3.7 hp/m². Fuel capacity 10.6 US gal, 8.8 Imp gal, 40.0 litre. Other data NC.

WEIGHTS & LOADINGS - Empty weight 265 lb, 120 kg. Max take-off weight 595 lb, 270 kg. Payload 330 lb, 150 kg. Max wing loading 3.94 lb/ft², 19.3 kg/m². Max power loading 11.4 lb/hp, 5.2 kg/hp. Load factors NC.

PERFORMANCE* - Max level speed 60 mph, 97 kph. Never exceed speed 75 mph, 120 kph. Cruising speed 55 mph, 88 kph. kph. Stalling speed 33 mph, 53 kph. Max climb rate at sea level 300 ft/min, 1.5 m/s. Take-off distance 330 ft, 100 m, to clear obstacle of 52 ft, 16 m. Landing distance 195 ft, 60 m, to clear obstacle of 52 ft, 16 m. Take-off roll 130 ft, 40 m. Landing roll 100 ft, 30 m. Service ceiling 10,000 ft, 3050 m. Other data NC.

*Under the following test conditions - Airfield altitude 0 ft, 0 m. Ground temperature 59°F, 15°C. Ground pressure 1013 mB. Ground windspeed 0 mph, 0 kph. Pilot weight 194 lb, 88 kg.

FISHER

Fisher Flying Products Manufacturing Pty Ltd, Box 1512, Empangeni, Natal 3880; tel 0351-2668142. Managing director: E T D Phelps.

FISHER *FP-202 KOALA*
(Three-axis)

Summary as Fisher FP-202 Koala (see US section) *except: Flaps fitted, 41%-span ailerons.*

Production status: current, number completed NC.

GENERAL - Fisher Flying Products was started in 1984 to manufacture the *FP-202 Koala* under contract from the American parent company of the same name. By the end of October 1984 the factory had almost completed a prototype and production was already under way, with a staff of 30 people.

Most of the aircraft will be exported back to the US, 10 having been shipped by the time of going to press, but the prototype was registered in South Africa with the letters ZS-VII on 11 December 1984, for test flying. South African-built machines are sold in the US in ready-to-fly form complete with instruments, while those produced in America are sold as kits. Specifications for the two versions differ slightly, as the kit-built machines have larger ailerons but no flaps. Despite this, weight is slightly lower on the Natal-built version.

Price in USA: US$5750 complete.

EXTERNAL DIMENSIONS & AREAS - See Fisher *FP-202 Koala* (US section) except: Total aileron area 12.0 ft², 1.11 m². Flap area NC.

POWER PLANT - See Fisher *FP-101* (US section) except: Power per unit area 0.21 hp/ft², 2.3 hp/m².

South African Aeronews

South Africa's first FP-202 Koala; inset shows production of wing ribs.

WEIGHTS & LOADINGS - See Fisher *FP-202 Koala* (US section) except: Empty weight 245 lb, 111 kg. Payload 255 lb, 116 kg.

PERFORMANCE - See Fisher *FP-202 Koala* (US section) except: Stalling speed 24 mph, 39 kph. Max climb rate at sea level 750 ft/min, 3.8 m/s. Min sink rate 250 ft/min at 40 mph, 1.3 m/s at 64 kph. Best glide ratio with power off 9/1 at 40 mph, 64 kph. Take-off distance 130 ft, 40 m. Landing distance 125 ft, 38 m.

KILLEY

George Killey (EL Props), PO Box 7754, Petit 1512; tel 011 964 1410.

KILLEY
M FLEDGE FLYING WING
(Hybrid)

Single-seat single-engined high-wing monoplane with hybrid control. Wing has swept back leading and trailing edges, and tapering chord; no tail. Pitch control by weight-shift; yaw control by tip rudders; no separate roll control; control inputs through weight-shift for pitch and stick for yaw. Wing braced from above by kingpost and

cables, from below by cables; wing profile NC; NC% double-surface. Undercarriage has three wheels in tricycle formation; suspension NC. Ground steering NC. Brakes NC. Aluminium-alloy tube airframe, completely open. Engine mounted below wing, driving pusher propeller.

Production status: see text.

GENERAL - George Killey may not be an internationally known microlight pioneer, but as far as South Africans are concerned he ranks with the Gerry Breens and Jack McCornacks of this world, for it was George who flew his *M Fledge*, South Africa's first home-produced microlight, some 1300 miles (2090 km) from Durban to Cape Town in the days when pilots felt they'd done well if 10 h came up without some mechanical problem intervening.

George's prototype was registered on 1 August 1980 as ZS-UMF, but had actually been flying for some time before this, using a direct-drive Sachs motor. Originally George built his own cage and attached it to a standard Manta *Fledge* wing complete with tip rudders, producing an aircraft not unlike the Pterodactyl *Pfledgling 430D* featured in our first edition. Later aircraft used stronger wings but

254

Main picture: A typical Killey M Fledge, (if there is such a thing!), with Cuyuna motor and canard. Insets show ZS-UMF, the first African-built Fledge, and a two-seater with canard and Rotax 503. Note that the dual machine has tandem seating, unlike its American cousin, Freedom Fliers' Ascender II+2.

were of similar configuration - flying wing with swing seat for pitch control, plus tip rudders for yaw.

At this point, however, the story gets complicated, as some of these machines were modified in just the way that Jack McCornack altered the *Pfledge* to create the *Ptraveler,* by fixing the seat and adding a canard. Others were built this way from new, some with a second seat, and all these variants could be had with a choice of engine. In addition to the original Sachs, over the years fitments have included the 430 Cuyuna, Rotax 503, Yamaha KT100S and Yamaha 350.

Though only 10 *M Fledges* are registered, at least 20 are known to exist, and of these it is unlikely that there are two the same. We thus admit defeat in our attempts to provide meaningful data, and can only refer readers to George Killey, who we understand will still build the machine to order at a price depending on specification, with or without canard, second seat, instrument panel, etc etc...

The best we can do is to summarise the two basic configurations, one above and the other under a separate heading.

KILLEY
M FLEDGE CANARD

(Two- axis)

See M Fledge Flying Wing except: Single- or two-seat, two-axis control. No tail, canard wing. Pitch control by fully flying canard; control inputs through stick for pitch/ yaw.

Production status: see M Fledge Flying Wing text.

GENERAL - See *M Fledge Flying Wing* text.

South African Aeronews

MICRO AIRCRAFT CO

Micro Aircraft Co, 26 Brunning Place, Jacobs 4052; tel 473436. Managing director: Colin Liddle.

Sales enquiries: Microlight Marketing, PO Box 39, Gillitts 3603; tel 031 743743. Contacts: Victor Hugo, Piet Van Rensburg.

MICRO AIRCRAFT CO
GRASSHOPPER

(Two-axis)

Single-seat single-engined high-wing monoplane with two-axis control. Wing has unswept leading edge, swept forward trailing edge, and tapering chord; cruciform tail. Pitch control by fully flying tail; yaw control by fully flying rudder; no separate roll control; control inputs through stick for pitch/yaw. Wing braced from above by kingpost and cables, from below by cables; wing profile NC; single-surface. Undercarriage has three wheels in tail-dragger formation; no suspension on tailwheel and axle-flex suspension on main wheels. Push-right go-right tailwheel steering connected to yaw control. No brakes. Aluminium-alloy tube airframe, completely open. Engine mounted at wing height, driving tractor propeller.

Production status: obsolete, 32 completed.

GENERAL - Though this aircraft is obsolete, this section would not be complete without a mention of the *Grass-hopper,* the machine on which the Liddle brothers, Colin and Douglas, cut their manufacturing teeth back in 1980

before going on to become South Africa's most successful microlight constructors.

Very similar to the early versions of the Australian *Scout,* the first *Grasshopper* was registered ZS-UNB on 11 December 1980 and the machine was subsequently produced in what was for the time large quantities. It differed from its Australian cousin principally in its choice of power plant, the Yamaha KT100S being used.

EXTERNAL DIMENSIONS & AREAS - Length overall 16.0 ft, 4.88 m. Height overall 8.0 ft, 2.44 m. Wing span 28.0 ft, 8.53 m. Chord at root 6.0 ft, 1.83 m. Chord at tip 2.0 ft, 0.61 m. Dihedral 6°. Sweepback 0°. Tailplane span 8.0 ft, 2.44 m. Rudder height NC. Total wing area 120 ft², 11.1 m². Rudder area 10.0 ft², 0.93 m². Total elevator area 16.0 ft², 1.49 m². Aspect ratio 6.5/1. Wheel track 5.3 ft, 1.63 m. Wheelbase 13.0 ft, 3.96 m. Tailwheel diameter overall 6 inch, 15 cm. Main wheels diameter overall 10 inch, 25cm.

POWER PLANT - Yamaha KT100S engine. Max power 15 hp at 10,000 rpm. Propeller diameter and pitch 48x27 inch, 1.22x0.69 m. V-belt reduction, ratio 4.0/1. Max static thrust 110 lb, 50 kg. Power per unit area 0.13 hp/ft², 1.4 hp/m². Fuel capacity 1.3 US gal, 1.1 Imp gal, 5.0 litre.

WEIGHTS & LOADINGS - Empty weight 130 lb, 59 kg. Max take-off weight 351 lb, 159 kg. Payload 220 lb, 100 kg. Max wing loading 2.93 lb/ft², 14.3 kg/m². Max power loading 23.4 lb/hp, 10.6 kg/hp. Load factors +2.5, -2.0 recommended; +4.0, -3.0 ultimate.

PERFORMANCE* - Max level speed 50 mph, 80 kph. Never exceed speed 59 mph, 95 kph. Max cruising speed 37 mph, 60 kph. Economic cruising speed 31 mph, 50 kph. Stalling speed 17 mph, 28 kph. Max climb rate at sea level 400 ft/min, 2.0 m/s. Min sink rate NC. Best glide ratio with power off 6/1 at 25 mph, 40 kph. Take-off distance 165 ft, 50 m. Landing distance 80 ft, 25 m. Service ceiling 3000 ft, 910 m. Range at average cruising speed 50 mile, 80 km. Noise level NC.

*Under the following test conditions - Test payload 220 lb, 100 kg. Other data NC.

MICRO AIRCRAFT CO
GRASSHOPPER MKII
(Three-axis)

Summary as Grasshopper *except: Conventional three-axis control. Wing has unswept leading and trailing edges, and constant chord. Roll control by quarter-span spoilerons; control inputs through stick for pitch/roll and pedals for yaw.*

Production status: obsolete, 12 completed.

GENERAL - Like the *Scout,* the *Grasshopper* soon evolved into a three-axis machine, the Liddle brothers calling this, their first aircraft with full conventional controls, the *Grasshopper MkII.* However, the pair chose a very different route from Ron Wheeler in Australia, putting their own stamp on the machine by designing a new wing for it, a square-section constant-chord sail with spoilers. Ron, on the other hand, simply added wing warping to the existing design.
The other major change was a more powerful engine, the 430 Cuyuna being adopted.

EXTERNAL DIMENSIONS & AREAS - Wing span 28.0 ft, 8.53 m. Constant chord 5.5 ft, 1.68 m. Sweepback 0°. Tailplane span 8.0 ft, 2.44 m. Rudder height NC. Total wing area 154 ft^2, 14.3 m^2. Rudder area 12.0 ft^2, 1.11 m^2. Total elevator area 20.0 ft^2, 1.86 m^2. Aspect ratio 5.1/1. Wheel track 5.3 ft, 1.63 m. Wheelbase 13.0 ft, 3.96 m. Tailwheel diameter overall 6 inch, 15 cm. Main wheels diameter overall 10 inch, 25 cm. Other data NC.

POWER PLANT - Cuyuna 430 engine. Max power 36 hp at 5800 rpm. Propeller diameter and pitch 36x16 inch, 0.91x0.41 m. No reduction. Max static thrust 165 lb, 75 kg. Power per unit area 0.23 hp/ft^2, 2.5 hp/m^2. Fuel capacity 2.6 US gal, 2.2 Imp gal, 10.0 litre.

WEIGHTS & LOADINGS - Empty weight 176 lb, 80 kg. Max take-off weight 397 lb, 180 kg. Payload 220 lb, 100 kg. Max wing loading 2.58 lb/ft^2, 12.6 kg/m^2. Max power loading 11.0 lb/hp, 5.0 kg/hp. Load factors +2.6, -2.0 recommended; +6.0, -4.0 ultimate.

PERFORMANCE* - Max level speed 50 mph, 80 kph. Never exceed speed 65 mph, 105 kph. Max cruising speed 40 mph, 64 kph. Economic cruising speed 35 mph, 56 kph. Stalling speed 22 mph, 35 kph. Max climb rate at sea level 600 ft/min, 3.1 m/s. Min sink rate 250 ft/min, 1.3 m/s at NC speed. Best glide ratio with power off 7/1 at 30 mph, 48 kph. Take-off distance 65 ft, 20 m. Landing distance 65 ft, 20 m. Service ceiling 8000 ft, 2440 m. Range at average cruising speed 50 mile, 80 km. Noise level NC.

*Under the following test conditions - Test payload 220 lb, 100 kg. Other data NC.

MICRO AIRCRAFT CO CDL SINGLE-SEAT
(Three-axis)

Single-seat single-engined high-wing monoplane with conventional three-axis control. Wing has unswept leading and trailing edges, and constant chord; cruciform tail. Pitch control by elevator on tail; yaw control by fully flying rudder; roll control by quarter-span spoilerons; control inputs through stick for pitch/roll and pedals for yaw. Wing braced from above by kingpost and cables,

South African Aeronews

Beginning of a highly successful line - the first production prototype of the CDL Single-Seat takes to the air.

from below by cables; wing profile NC; single-surface. Undercarriage has three wheels in tricycle formation; no suspension on nosewheel and axle-flex suspension on main wheels. Push-right go-right nosewheel steering connected to yaw control. No brakes. Aluminium-alloy tube airframe, completely open. Engine mounted below wing, driving pusher propeller.

Production status: obsolete, approximately 10 completed.

GENERAL - Having gained some experience of *Quicksilver*-style wings and *Quicksilver*-style power packs with the *Grasshopper MkII,* Colin and David Liddle next decided to go the whole hog and produce a complete aircraft of similar configuration to the famous Eipper machine. The first example was registered ZS-UTJ on 9 June 1982, and the brothers were sufficiently proud of it to call the machine after their initials - *CDL.*
Though the American inspiration was evident, the *CDL Single-Seat* was rather more than just a *Quicksilver MX* clone, boasting such improvements as nosewheel steering, an A-frame kingpost, and an aerofoil-section leading-edge tube. In single-seat form the *CDL* is a rare bird, for it was followed almost immediately by the two-seater which we describe separately, and which proved so successful that the solo machine was dropped after only a few had been sold. It was, however, the first genuinely South African design to get into series production, as opposed to a series of one-offs, and marked the emergence of MAC as the country's leading microlight producer.

EXTERNAL DIMENSIONS & AREAS - Wing span 28.0 ft, 8.53 m. Other data NC.

POWER PLANT - Cuyuna 430 engine. Max power 30 hp at NC rpm. V-belt reduction, ratio NC/1. Fuel capacity 5.3 US gal, 4.4 Imp gal, 20.0 litre.

South African Aeronews

WEIGHTS & LOADINGS - Empty weight 231 lb, 105 kg. Max take-off weight 463 lb, 210 kg. Payload 231 lb, 105 kg. Max wing loading NC. Max power loading 15.4 lb/hp, 7.0 kg/hp. Load factors NC.

PERFORMANCE* - Max level speed 42 mph, 68 kph. Cruising speed 32 mph, 51 kph. Stalling speed 20 mph, 32 kph. Max climb rate at sea level 600 ft/min, 3.1 m/s. Take-off distance 100 ft, 30 m. Landing distance 80 ft, 25 m. Other data NC.

*Under unspecified test conditions.

MICRO AIRCRAFT CO CDL
(Three-axis)

Summary as CDL Single-Seat *except: Tandem two-seater. Optional pod.*

Production status: current; 110 completed (Cuyuna-engined version), 45 completed (Rotax-engined version).

GENERAL - With the introduction of a two-seat version of the *CDL,* the Liddle brothers' business really took off. Introduced in 1982, this machine was South Africa's first locally manufactured two-seater and soon supplanted its single-seat parent to become the company's bread and butter, selling over 100 units over the next three years. At first, sales were handled by Placo, the local Piper agent,

but later on Microlight Marketing took over, leaving the Liddle brothers to get on with production and development. This arrangement took the *CDL* to the position of market leader in 1983/4.

Thanks partly to the use of the tuned version of the Cuyuna twin, developing 43 hp, the *CDL* has good performance for a machine of its type, better than Eipper's *Quicksilver MXII,* which is handicapped by the extra drag of its side-by-side seating arrangement. Better performance still became available in early 1984, when a Rotax option was introduced, using the twin-carburetter 53 hp variant of the engine. Our data below refers to the Cuyuna-engined machine; where different, figures for the Rotax-engined version are shown in parentheses.

Though sales have dropped off during '85, at the time of writing (May) both versions of this well liked workhorse are still available. Local prices compare very favourably with those of US imports, which are heavily handicapped by the dollar exchange rate, the Cuyuna model selling at R6400. No price is quoted for the Rotax version. Options on either include instruments and a pod.

EXTERNAL DIMENSIONS & AREAS - Length overall 17.0 ft, 5.18 m. Height overall 9.0 ft, 2.74 m. Wing span 34.5 ft, 10.52 m. Constant chord 5.0 ft, 1.52 m. Dihedral 5°. Sweepback 0°. Tailplane span 9.0 ft, 2.74 m. Rudder height NC. Total wing area 173 ft², 16.0 m². Total spoileron area NC. Rudder area 12.5 ft², 1.16 m². Tailplane area 21.6 ft², 2.01 m². Total elevator area 18.5 ft², 1.72 m². Aspect ratio 6.1/1. Wheel track 5.4 ft, 1.65 m. Wheelbase 6.4 ft, 1.95 m. Nosewheel diameter overall 12 inch, 30 cm. Main wheels diameter overall 12 inch, 30 cm.

POWER PLANT - Cuyuna 430 (Rotax 503) engine. Max power 43(53) hp at 6800 rpm. Propeller diameter and pitch 54x24(30) inch, 1.37x0.61(0.76) m. V-belt reduction, ratio 2.0/1. Max static thrust NC(276) lb, NC(125) kg. Power per unit area 0.25(0.31) hp/ft², 2.7(3.3) hp/m². Fuel capacity NC(5.3) US gal, NC(4.4) Imp gal, NC(20.0) litre.

WEIGHTS & LOADINGS - Empty weight 309 lb, 140 kg. Max take-off weight 750 lb, 340 kg. Payload 441 lb, 200 kg. Max wing loading 4.34 lb/ft², 21.3 kg/m². Max power loading 17.4(14.2) lb/hp, 7.9(6.4) kg/hp. Load factors +2.6, -2.0 recommended; +6.0, -4.0 ultimate.

PERFORMANCE* - Max level speed 50(55) mph, 80(88) kph. Never exceed speed 65 mph, 105 kph. Max cruising speed 40 mph, 64 kph. Economic cruising speed 35 mph, 56 kph. Stalling speed 22(26) mph, 35(42) kph. Max climb rate at sea level 600(700) ft/min, 3.1(3.6) m/s. Min sink rate 350 ft/min, 1.8 m/s at NC speed. Best glide ratio with power off 7/1 at 30(27) mph, 48(43) kph. Take-off distance NC(100) ft, NC(30) m. Landing distance NC(100) ft, NC(30) m. Service ceiling NC(10,000) ft, NC(3050) m. Range at average cruising speed NC(80) mile, NC(129) km. Noise level NC.

*Under the following test conditions - Test payload 441 lb, 200 kg. Other data NC.

MICRO AIRCRAFT CO *CL2*

(Three-axis)

Side-by-side two-seat single-engined high-wing mono-plane with conventional three-axis control. Wing has unswept leading and trailing edges, and constant chord; conventional tail. Pitch control by elevator on tail; yaw control by fully flying rudder with separate fin; roll control by full-span ailerons; control inputs through stick for pitch/roll and pedals for yaw. Wing braced from below by struts; wing profile semi-symmetrical; 100% double-surface. Undercarriage has three wheels in tricycle formation; coil-spring/oleo suspension on nosewheel and axle-flex suspension on main wheels. Push-right go-right nosewheel steering connected to yaw control. Brakes on main wheels. Aluminium-alloy tube airframe, totally enclosed. Engine mounted below wing, driving pusher propeller.

Production status: prototype.

GENERAL - Micro Aircraft's *CL2* is the company's entrant into the upmarket three-axis sector, where buyers want something more sophisticated than a single-surface wing.

At the time of writing (May '85) it is only a prototype, but it is already clear that the *CL2* is Colin and Doug's most complex machine to date, with fully double-surfaced wing, full-span ailerons, strut bracing, brakes, fully enclosed cockpit and suspension all round. The power pack is borrowed from the Rotax 503-engined version of the *CDL*. Conceived as a two-seater, the addition of a third seat is under consideration.

With the poor economic climate in South Africa, no production date for the aircraft has been fixed, and therefore no price.

EXTERNAL DIMENSIONS & AREAS - Length overall 18.0 ft, 5.49 m. Height overall 8.0 ft, 2.44 m. Wing span 32.0 ft, 9.76 m. Constant chord 4.2 ft, 1.27 m. Dihedral 2°.

Sweepback 0°. Tailplane span 9.4 ft, 2.87 m. Fin height 4.4 ft, 1.34 m. Total wing area 134 ft², 12.4 m². Total aileron area 38.0 ft², 3.53 m². Fin area 7.8 ft², 0.72 m². Rudder area 9.0 ft², 0.84 m². Tailplane area 7.8 ft², 0.72 m². Total elevator area 7.8 ft², 0.72 m². Aspect ratio 7.6/1. Wheel track 5.0 ft, 1.52 m. Wheelbase 6.0 ft, 1.83 m. Nosewheel diameter overall 12 inch, 30 cm. Main wheels diameter overall 12 inch, 30 cm.

POWER PLANT - See Rotax-engined version of *CDL* except: Power per unit area 0.40 hp/ft², 4.3 hp/m².

WEIGHTS & LOADINGS - Empty weight *320* lb, *145* kg. Max take-off weight *761* lb, *340* kg. Payload *441* lb, *200* kg. Max wing loading *5.68* lb/ft², *27.4* kg/m². Max power loading *14.4* lb/hp, *6.4* kg/hp. Load factors +4.0, -1.5 recommended; +6.0, -3.0 ultimate.

PERFORMANCE* - Max level speed 85 mph, 137 kph. Never exceed speed 100 mph, 161 kph. Max cruising speed 70 mph, 113 kph. Economic cruising speed 65 mph, 105 kph. Stalling speed 30 mph, 48 kph. Max climb rate at sea level 800 ft/min, 4.1 m/s. Min sink rate NC. Best glide ratio with power off 8/1 at 40 mph, 64 kph. Take-off distance 100 ft, 30 m. Landing distance 65 ft, 20 m. Service ceiling 12,000 ft, 3660 m. Range at average cruising speed 150 mile, 241 km. Noise level NC.

*Under unspecified test conditions.

MICROLIGHT FLIGHT SYSTEMS

Microlight Flight Systems (Pty) Ltd, 53 Old Main Road, Hillcrest 3600, Natal; tel 031 753920. Managing director: John Young.

US agent: Freedom Fliers (see separate listing).

MICROLIGHT FLIGHT SYSTEMS *XCR*

(Hybrid)

Single-seat single-engined high-wing monoplane with hybrid control. Wing has swept back leading and trailing edges, and constant chord; no tail, canard wing. Pitch control by elevator on canard; yaw control by tip rudders; no separate roll control; control inputs through weight-shift for pitch and tiller for yaw. Wing braced from above by kingpost and cables, from below by cables; wing profile NC; approximately 50% double-surface. Undercarriage has three wheels in tricycle formation; no suspension on nosewheel and steel-spring suspension on main wheels. Push-right go-left nosewheel steering connected to yaw control. No brakes. Aluminium-alloy tube airframe, with optional pod. Engine mounted below wing, driving pusher propeller.

Production status: see text.

GENERAL - Based on the famous *Eagle*, now produced by Ultrasport in Italy but originally an American design, the

South African Aeronews

XCR was flown at the first of the annual Pretoria (and later Springs) to Durban air races. In fact the name reflects this competition history, the initials standing for 'cross-country racer'. Since this is not an activity that the standard *Eagle* exactly excels at, we will not quibble with the manufacturer's claim to have many improvements to the original design! We don't have many details of the changes, but certainly the rear undercarriage, always a weak point on early *Eagles,* was radically redesigned.

Although at the time of writing one *XCR* is still being built, bringing the total to 21, this looks like being the last of the line as the company's emphasis has now firmly shifted to the three-axis sector, with the *Shadow,* which we describe separately.

Power for the *XCR* came from the 430 Cuyuna, as was used for the heavier-payload versions in the States before the advent of Rotax power. Two states of tune were offered, 35 or 43 hp; our figures below refer to the less powerful version. Some aircraft also had larger tanks fitted, up to 5.3 US gal (4.4 Imp gal, 20.0 litre), while a fairing was another option.

EXTERNAL DIMENSIONS & AREAS - Wing span 36.0 ft, 10.97 m. Total wing area 190 ft², 17.7 m². Other data NC.

POWER PLANT - Cuyuna 430RR engine. Max power 35 hp at NC rpm. Propeller diameter and pitch 60x24 inch, 1.52x0.61 m. Toothed-belt reduction, ratio 2.0/1. Max static thrust NC. Power per unit area 0.18 hp/ft², 2.0 hp/m². Fuel capacity 3.2 US gal, 2.6 Imp gal, 12.0 litre.

WEIGHTS & LOADINGS - Empty weight 220 lb, 100 kg. Max take-off weight 573 lb, 260 kg. Payload 353 lb, 160 kg. Max wing loading 3.02 lb/ft², 14.7 kg/m². Max power loading 16.4 lb/hp, 7.4 kg/hp. Load factors NC.

PERFORMANCE* - Max level speed 55 mph, 88 kph. Economic cruising speed 37 mph, 60 kph. Stalling speed

An XCR *with optional fairing.*

23 mph, 37 kph. Max climb rate at sea level 850 ft/min, 4.3 m/s. Service ceiling 17,500 ft, 5330 m. Other data NC.

*Under unspecified test conditions.

MICROLIGHT FLIGHT SYSTEMS *SHADOW and SHADOW TRAINER*
(Three-axis)

Tandem two-seat single-engined high-wing monoplane with conventional three-axis control. Wing has unswept leading and trailing edges, and constant chord; cruciform tail. Pitch control by elevator on tail; yaw control by fully flying rudder; roll control by spoilers, % span NC; control inputs through stick for pitch/roll and pedals for yaw. Wing braced from above by kingpost and cables, from below by cables; wing profile NC; single-surface. Undercarriage has three wheels in tricycle formation; suspension NC on nosewheel and steel-spring suspension on main wheels. Push-right go-right nosewheel steering connected to yaw control. Brakes NC. Aluminium-alloy tube airframe, completely open. Engine mounted below wing, driving pusher propeller.

Production status: current, 16 completed.

GENERAL - Although the output of the MFS company under John Young has yet to approach that of its obvious rival MAC, John's firm is very much the rising star of the South African industry, especially now that its distribution problems are sorted out. Building on the good reputation of his hybrid-control *XCR,* he introduced his first three-axis machine, the *Shadow,* and unlike MAC decided to go straight for the two-seat market, rather than develop a solo machine first.

South African Aeronews

First production prototype of the Shadow. *For another* Shadow *illustration, see colour section.*

MFS in 1984 became the first and so far only South African company to exhibit at the EAA's Oshkosh convention in Wisconsin, and the machine was extremely well received there, not because of any revolutionary technology but because it is very well finished and, thanks to the strength of the dollar, competitively priced - US$5000 for a 25 h kit in late '84, though this may well change in view of the vagaries of international exchange rates. As we write, in April '85, two *Shadows,* known in the US as *Shadow Trainers* to emphasise what John Young sees as their main market there, have been sold to American buyers.

This success, though tiny by American standards, has been a big shot in the arm for the South African microlight community, pleased at last to see some aircraft going the other way across the Atlantic. It's strange what currency fluctuations can make possible - two years ago we would have rated the chances of anyone trying to sell *Quicksilver*-type machines to Americans about as high as those of a Japanese whisky salesman in Scotland or an English wine importer in France!

Comparisons with the rival MAC *CDL* are inevitable, especially as the price is similar, at R6500. In fact, the most obvious recognition point between the two is the kingpost arrangement, the *Shadow* retaining the Eipper-style single post and its rival opting for a double arrangement in the form of an inverted V.

Although we have heard reports from US sources of a single-seat *Shadow* being developed, we have no definite news at the time of going to press. Similarly, we can add nothing to reports that the company intends to build under license a 30 hp KFM-engined machine, called the *Leone T7* and designed by Aviazone Ultraleggera Italiana.

Data below refers to the standard tandem two-seater with 53 hp engine (some have been built with the 48 hp Rotax 503).

EXTERNAL DIMENSIONS & AREAS - Length overall 18.7 ft, 5.69 m. Height overall 10.1 ft, 3.08 m. Wing span 32.0 ft, 9.75 m. Constant chord 5.0 ft, 1.52 m. Sweepback 0°. Total wing area 160 ft², 14.9 m². Aspect ratio 6.4/1. Other data NC.

POWER PLANT - Rotax 503 engine. Max power 53 hp at 6800 rpm. Propeller diameter and pitch 53x27 inch, 1.35x0.69 m. Reduction type and ratio NC. Max static thrust NC. Power per unit area 0.33 hp/ft², 3.6 hp/m². Fuel capacity 5.3 US gal, 4.4 Imp gal, 20.0 litre.

WEIGHTS & LOADINGS - Empty weight 321 lb, 146 kg. Max take-off weight 700 lb, 318 kg. Payload 379 lb, 172 kg. Max wing loading 4.38 lb/ft², 21.3 kg/m². Max power loading 13.2 lb/hp, 6.0 kg/hp. Load factors NC.

PERFORMANCE* - Never exceed speed 60 mph, 97 kph. Max cruising speed 45 mph, 72 kph. Stalling speed 26 mph, 42 kph. Max climb rate at sea level 650 ft/min, 3.3 m/s. Take-off distance 300 ft, 91 m to clear obstacle of 50 ft, 15 m. Take-off roll 100 ft, 30 m. Landing roll 80 ft, 24 m. Service ceiling 12,000 ft, 3660 m. Other data NC.

*Under the following test conditions - Airfield altitude 7500 ft, 2290 m. Test payload 379 lb, 172 kg.

South African Aeronews

SOCHEN

Edwin Sochen, PO Box 42, Wendywood, Sandton 2144; tel 011 802 3545.

Factory: Court Helicopters, PO Box 2546, Cape Town 8000; tel 021 931 2288.

SOCHEN *ES-1 PHOENIX*
(Three-axis)

Single-seat single-engined high-wing monoplane with conventional three-axis control. Wing has unswept leading edge, swept forward trailing edge, and tapering chord; cruciform tail. Pitch control by elevator on tail; yaw control by fully flying rudder; roll control by full-span ailerons; control inputs through stick for pitch/roll and pedals for yaw. Wing braced from below by struts; wing profile NC; 100% double-surface. Undercarriage has three wheels in tricycle formation; suspension NC. Push-right go-right nosewheel steering connected to yaw control; also differential braking. Brakes on main wheels. Aluminium-alloy tube airframe, completely open. Engine mounted below wing, driving pusher propeller.

Production status: one-off.

GENERAL - Edwin Sochen was the proud owner of a *Quicksilver MX* until it got destroyed in a storm. He set out to rebuild it, but in the process created a completely new aircraft, of much more sophisticated design.
The *ES-1 Phoenix* which resulted boasted a strut-braced double-surfaced wing with ailerons, a steerable nose-wheel, and independently operable brakes. Edwin, however, was not satisfied and reckoned that a two-seater would be more appropriate. Consequently the *ES-1 Phoenix* remained a one-off and the *Phoenix CII* was created, a side-by-side two-seater of very similar configuration.
Two prototypes were built and production then handed over to Court Helicopters; for a while it looked as though the future of Edwin's creation was assured. However, production was suspended after only 11 had been built and the project has since been abandoned, partly because of the harsh economic climate in South Africa at present.
Whether the *Phoenix CII* will re-emerge only time will tell; the matter seems to be out of Edwin's hands as he has relinquished all rights to Court Helicopters. However, he is working on a new design of his own and hopes to have it fly-

ing during 1985, so hopefully we have not heard the last of his creations.
We have no data for Edwin's single-seat *ES-1 Phoenix*, other than that it used a 430 Cuyuna engine. Data for the *Phoenix CII* we list separately.

SOCHEN *PHOENIX CII*
(Three-axis)

Summary as ES-1 Phoenix *except: Side-by-side two-seater. Leaf-spring suspension on main wheels.*

Production status: see ES-1 Phoenix *text.*

GENERAL - See *ES-1 Phoenix.*

EXTERNAL DIMENSIONS & AREAS - Wing span 32.0 ft, 9.75 m. Other data NC.

POWER PLANT - Rotax 503 engine. Max power 52 hp at NC rpm. Propeller diameter and pitch 58xNC inch, 1.47xNC m. Other data NC.

WEIGHTS & LOADINGS - Empty weight 315 lb, 143 kg. Other data NC.

PERFORMANCE* - Max level speed 65 mph, 105 kph. Max cruising speed 50 mph, 80 kph. Stalling speed 28 mph, 45 kph. Max climb rate at sea level 350 ft/min, 1.8 m/s. Take-off distance 230 ft, 70 m. Landing distance 100 ft, 30 m. Range at average cruising speed *100* mile, *161* km. Other data NC.

*Under the following test conditions - Airfield altitude 5500 ft, 1680 m. Ground temperature 59°F, 15°C. Ground pressure NC. Ground windspeed NC. Total pilot and passenger weight 313 lb, 142 kg.

SOLAR WINGS

Solar Wings, PO Box 214, Gillitts 3603; tel 031 742929. Managing director: Aidan De Gersigny.

SOLAR WINGS *WINDLASS TRIKE*
(Weight-shift)

Single-seat single-engined flex-wing aircraft with weight-shift control. Rogallo wing with keel pocket. Pilot suspended below wing in trike unit, using bar to control pitch and roll/yaw by altering relative positions of trike unit and wing. Wing braced from above by kingpost and cables, from below by cables; floating cross-tube construction with 60% double-surface enclosing cross-tube; preformed ribs. Undercarriage has three wheels in tricycle formation; suspension NC. Push-right go-left nosewheel steering independent from aerodynamic controls. Brakes NC. Aluminium-alloy tube trike unit, completely open. Engine mounted below wing, driving pusher propeller.

Production status: current, 4 completed.

GENERAL - On seeing the name of this company, many readers will have assumed that it is a South African offshoot of the British firm Pegasus, which used to market its wings under the Solar Wings banner. However, this is

South African Aeronews

emphatically not so, and Rick Hogarth of Pegasus has assured us that his company has no connection with Solar Wings in South Africa.

South African Aeronews

In fact the company is well established and independent, Aidan de Gersigny having been building hang gliders since 1976 and various one-off microlights since around 1980. He has now produced over 300 Rogallos, apparently quite independently of any European manufacturers, and has also constructed wings for the Microlight Flight Systems *XCR* under subcontract. Undoubtedly, however, he draws on European designs when creating his products, and admits that the wing for the *Windlass Trike* is based on Airwave's highly successful *Magic* hang glider wing, produced in Britain. Confusingly, the quoted wing area for the *Windlass Trike* is identical to that of Pegasus' *Typhoon S4 Medium,* though the span and percentage double-surface area are different. Unfortunately, deadlines do not permit us to clarify the matter further.

Origins apart, Aidan's creation is a simple conventional trike, and was displayed at the Springs meeting in May '85. It is of monopole construction and uses the popular Rotax 277 power pack, rigging time being quoted as 20 min. At the time of writing (May '85) the aircraft had yet to receive its airworthiness approval, so the specifications below must be regarded as provisional.
Price: R4700.

EXTERNAL DIMENSIONS & AREAS - Wing span 34.0 ft, 10.36 m. Total wing area 166 ft², 15.4 m². Aspect ratio 7.0/1. Other data NC.

POWER PLANT - Rotax 277 engine. Max power 28 hp at NC rpm. Propeller diameter and pitch 60x28 inch, 1.52x0.71 m. Gear reduction, ratio 2.6/1. Max static thrust NC. Power per unit area 0.17 hp/ft², 1.8 hp/m². Fuel capacity 2.6 US gal, 2.2 Imp gal, 10.0 litre.

WEIGHTS & LOADINGS - Empty weight 192 lb, 87 kg. Other data NC.

PERFORMANCE* - Never exceed speed 55 mph, 88 kph. Max cruising speed 40 mph, 64 kph. Stalling speed 20 mph, 32 kph. Max climb rate at sea level 800 ft/min, 4.1 m/s. Min sink rate 350 ft/min, 1.8 m/s at NC speed. Take-off distance 100 ft, 30 m. Other data NC.

*Under unspecified test conditions.

SPORT AVIATION

Sport Aviation SA, 97 9th Street, Linden 2195; tel 012 835 040 work, 011 782 4049 home. Managing director: Louis Meyer.

SPORT AVIATION *THUNDERBIRD*
(Three-axis)

Side-by-side two-seat single-engined high-wing monoplane with conventional three-axis control. Wing has swept back leading edge, swept forward trailing edge, and tapering chord; flaps fitted; cruciform tail. Pitch control by elevator on tail; yaw control by fin-mounted rudder; roll control by 60%-span ailerons; control inputs through stick for pitch/roll and pedals for yaw. Wing braced from below by struts; wing profile NC; 100% double-surface. Undercarriage has three wheels in tricycle formation; suspension NC. Nosewheel steering. No brakes. Aluminium-alloy tube airframe, with pod. Engine mounted above wing, driving tractor propeller.

Production status: prototype.

GENERAL - Louis Meyer's *Thunderbird* is developed from a *Spitfire II* which was imported in 1984 and registered ZS-VJF on 8 January the following year. At the time of importing, the *Spitfire II* was being produced by the American company Worldwide Ultralight Industries, and Louis negotiated a license agreement with the firm so that he could construct his own version in South Africa.
However, around the time the imported *Spitfire II* was registered, the WUI company folded. Former WUI employee Fred Bell has since restarted production of the model, as you can read under Bell in the US section, but we are not sure where this leaves Louis. Better legal brains than ours must decide whether he has thus become Bell's licensee, or is now independent from the Americans.
Anyway, licensee or independent, Louis has been getting on with the job, and on 12 April '85 registered his own prototype with the letters ZS-VKE, retitling the aircraft *Thunderbird.* It is this machine which we illustrate with the introduction to this section. Just to confuse the situation further, we ought to record that the same name was used by WUI, but for a different model!
A comparision of the data supplied by the two manufac-

turers reveals a few differences between the African *Thunderbird* and the American *Spitfire II.* Louis' machine has a small sweepback on the leading edge and ailerons of 60% span, whereas Fred Bell describes his as unswept and lists the ailerons as only one-third span. Power plants are the same but the Sport Aviation machine is slightly heavier. Construction is still tube and Dacron, except for the tail, where Louis has decided to use doped, painted ceconite instead.
At the time of writing (April '85), Louis is still setting up for production so only the prototype exists. However, it has been well received, including a favourable flying report by John Pocock in the April '85 edition of *South African Aeronews,* and appears to have a promising future as a strong high-performance microlight.
Projected price is under R14,000 for the standard version detailed below, with a twin-carb Rotax 503 or a liquid-cooled Rotax available on option.

EXTERNAL DIMENSIONS & AREAS - Wing span 30.0 ft, 9.14 m. Total wing area 154 ft², 14.3 m². Aspect ratio 5.8/1. Other data NC.

POWER PLANT - Rotax 503 engine. Max power 48 hp at NC rpm. Power per unit area 0.31 hp/ft², 3.4 hp/m². Other data NC.

WEIGHTS & LOADINGS - Empty weight 360 lb, 163 kg. Max take-off weight 750 lb, 340 kg. Payload 390 lb, 177 kg. Max wing loading 4.87 lb/ft², 23.8 kg/m². Max power loading 15.6 lb/hp, 7.1 kg/hp. Load factors NC.

PERFORMANCE* - Never exceed speed 90 mph, 145 kph. Max cruising speed 70 mph, 113 kph. Stalling speed** 38 mph, 61 kph. Other data NC.

*Under unspecified test conditions, except for stall speeds (see below).

**With pilot and passenger and without use of flaps; with pilot only and full flaps, stalling speed is 20 mph, 32 kph for a 212 lb, 96 kg pilot.

ULTRALITE AIRCRAFT

Ultralite Aircraft Co (Pty) Ltd, PO Box 128, Bergvlei 2012; tel 011 802 3614/2007. Managing director: Roy Jude.

ULTRALITE AIRCRAFT *STRIKER*
(Three-axis)

Single-seat single-engined high-wing monoplane with conventional three-axis control. Wing has unswept leading and trailing edges, and constant chord; conventional tail. Pitch control by fully flying tail; yaw control by fully flying rudder; roll control by 40%-span ailerons; control inputs through stick for pitch/roll and pedals for yaw. Wing braced from below by struts; wing profile NC; 100% double-surface. Undercarriage has three wheels in tricycle formation; coil-spring suspension on all wheels. Push-right go-right nosewheel steering connected to yaw control. Nosewheel brake. Aluminium-alloy tube airframe, with optional pod. Engine mounted below wing, driving pusher propeller.

Production status: current, 8 completed.

GENERAL - The *Striker* was intended to be a South Africa-produced version of the American Teman *Mono-Fly*, and the project started with the import of one such machine, which was registered ZS-UWR on 11 May 1983 and simultaneously dubbed *Striker*. Subsequently Roy Jude modified it to a two-seater and renamed it *Striker II.*

To the best of our knowledge, there are no other *Mono-Fly*-type machines in South Africa - imports, renamed imports, or local products - and certainly no others had appeared on the official register by the time of going to press. This is in sharp contrast to the manufacturer's quoted production figures of 8 for the solo machine and 4 for the two-seater. Another oddity is that the manufacturer's data, which we reproduce below for the *Striker* and under a separate heading for the *Striker II,* differs markedly from that of the *Mono-Fly.* Deeper inspection of the figures reveals that the two-seater is claimed to be identical in dimensions, weight, and power pack to its solo stablemate, and to offer an identical climb rate, even when a passenger is carried! We can only quote the figures in good faith, printing them exactly as supplied apart from the correction of a couple of obvious errors, and leave it to the reader to judge their accuracy, bearing in mind that the DCA, the government department which regulates aviation in South Africa, has cancelled the aircraft's provisional flight authority. Roy Jude quotes a price of R8000 for the single-seater and R9200 for the dual machine, options being a four-point harness, ASI and altimeter in either case.

EXTERNAL DIMENSIONS & AREAS - Length overall 18.0 ft, 5.49 m. Height overall 6.0 ft, 1.83 m. Wing span 32.0 ft, 9.75 m. Constant chord 4.0 ft, 1.22 m. Dihedral 3°. Sweepback 0°. Elevator span 5.0 ft, 1.52 m. Rudder height 5.0 ft, 1.52 m. Total wing area 148 ft², 13.7 m². Total aileron area 12.0 ft², 1.11 m². Rudder area 8.0 ft², 0.74 m². Elevator area 12.0 ft², 1.11 m². Aspect ratio 6.9/1. Wheel track 5.0 ft, 1.52 m. Wheelbase 5.0 ft, 1.52 m. Nosewheel diameter overall 8 inch, 20 cm. Main wheels diameter overall 8 inch, 20 cm.

POWER PLANT - Rotax 503 engine. Max power 50 hp at 6500 rpm. Propeller diameter and pitch 54x34 inch, 1.37x0.86 m. Belt reduction, ratio 2.2/1. Max static thrust

NC. Power per unit area 0.34 hp/ft², 3.6 hp/m². Fuel capacity 5.8 US gal, 4.8 Imp gal, 22.0 litre.

WEIGHTS & LOADINGS - Empty weight 350 lb, 159 kg. Max take-off weight 750 lb, 340 kg. Payload 400 lb, 181 kg. Max wing loading 5.07 lb/ft², 24.8 kg/m². Max power loading 15.0 lb/hp, 6.8 kg/hp. Load factors +4.0, -3.0 recommended; +9.0, -9.0 ultimate.

PERFORMANCE* - Max level speed 95 mph, 153 kph. Never exceed speed 110 mph, 177 kph. Max cruising speed 80 mph, 129 kph. Economic cruising speed 75 mph, 121 kph. Stalling speed 32 mph, 51 kph. Max climb rate at sea level 1200 ft/min, 6.1 m/s. Min sink rate NC. Best glide ratio with power off 8/1 at 40 mph, 64 kph. Take-off distance 150 ft, 46 m. Landing distance 150 ft, 46 m. Service ceiling 12,000 ft, 3660 m. Range at average cruising speed 300 mile, 483 km. Noise level 60 dB at NC height.

*Under the following test conditions - Airfield altitude 5500 ft, 1680 m. Ground temperature 28°F, -2°C. Ground pressure 1031 mB. Ground windspeed 5 mph, 8 kph. Test payload 250 lb, 113 kg.

South African Aeronews

▲

ULTRALITE AIRCRAFT
STRIKER II
(Three-axis)

Summary as Striker *except: Tandem two-seater.*

Production status: current, 4 completed.

GENERAL - See *Striker.*

EXTERNAL DIMENSIONS & AREAS - See *Striker.*

POWER PLANT - See *Striker.*

WEIGHTS & LOADINGS - See *Striker.*

PERFORMANCE* - See *Striker* except: Stalling speed 42 mph, 68 kph. Take-off distance 300 ft, 91 m. Landing distance 300 ft, 91 m.

*Under the following test conditions - Airfield altitude 5500 ft, 1680 m. Ground temperature 28°F, -2°C. Ground pressure 1031 mB. Ground windspeed 5 mph, 8 kph. Test payload 380 lb, 172 kg.

▼

South African Aeronews

Soviet Union

Researched by Martin Velek of Kosmonautika magazine.

Young talent will out!

by Norman Burr

In our first edition we expressed the hope that the next version of *Berger-Burr's* would be better informed about the Soviet scene, and we are happy to report that this time we have managed to obtain both more aircraft data and more illustrations of the work of Soviet enthusiasts.

Credit for this must go to the Martin Velek of the excellent Czechoslovakian magazine *Kosmonautika*, who has been monitoring Soviet publications on our behalf and to whom we are greatly indebted. However, we must also say thank you to Yu Postnikov of the USSR Federation of Aeronautic Sports, who has undertaken to distribute information about Berger-Burr's direct to Soviet constructors, an arrangement which bodes well for future editions. He tells us that the only microlights - or mikrosamolyot as they are called in Russian - currently in the USSR are homebuilts, but it is clear from the descripions below that there is no shortage of enthusiasm, especially among young engineers. Moreover, as you can read below, some of the designs may yet reach production. Let's hope so...

For more information on mikrosamolyots in the Soviet Union, contact the USSR Federation of Aeronautic Sports, BP 395, Moscow 123362; tel 491-86-61. Kosmonautika magazine is at Jungmannova 24, 113 66 Praha 1, Czechoslovakia; tel 2606 51-9, 2615 51-8.

BABAKHOV

C/o Kharkov Aviation Institute.

BABAKHOV *KhAI-33M*

(Three-axis)

Single-seat single-engined high-wing monoplane with three-axis control. Two-fin T-tail. Yaw control by fin-mounted rudders; roll control by full-span ailerons. Wing braced from below by struts; 100% double-surface. Undercarriage has one float integral with fuselage; no wheels. Ground steering by yaw control only. Engine mounted below wing, driving pusher propeller. Other details NC.

Production status: see text.

GENERAL - Two students at the aircraft construction faculty of Kharkov Aviation Institute, A and M Babakhov, undertook as their final-year project to design this interesting ultralight seaplane, which they dubbed the *KhAI-33M*, after the initials of the college.

Not content with this, the pair on graduating turned their plans into reality, producing the machine pictured here. The pilot sits on a large punt-type float which is integral with the fuselage and which appears to divide in two at the rear, to form two booms to support the two-fin tail.

We understand that the aircraft is being considered for such work as primary training in the aeroclubs of the DOSAAF, patrolling of water reserves and meteorological

sampling, so although to the best of our knowledge only one *KhAI-33M* has been produced to date, the designers may yet have the pleasure of seeing their creation produced in quantity.

EXTERNAL DIMENSIONS & AREAS - NC.

POWER PLANT - Engine type NC. Max power 40 hp. Other data NC.

WEIGHTS & LOADINGS - Max take-off weight 662 lb, 300 kg. Max power loading 16.6 lb/hp, 7.5 kg/hp. Other data NC.

PERFORMANCE* - Cruising speed 53 mph, 85 kph. Other data NC.

*Under unspecified test conditions.

BYELYI

Address NC.

BYELYI *A-6*
(three-axis)

Single-seat single-engined high-wing monoplane with three-axis control. Conventional tail. Pitch control by elevator on tail; yaw control by fin-mounted rudder; roll control by full-span ailerons. Wing braced from below by struts; profile NC; 100% double-surface. Undercarriage has three wheels in tricycle formation; suspension see text. Composite-construction airframe, completely open. Engine mounted above wing, driving pusher propeller. Other details NC.

Production status: see text.

GENERAL - Flown at the second All-union Amateur-built Aircraft Rally, this composite-construction machine by Byelyi looks superficially like the Soviet Union's answer to the Aviasud Sirocco, apart from the strange nose fairing, which we presume is an instrument housing.

Described in the report of the rally as a 'sport lightplane', the A-6's general layout is very reminiscent of the French machine, especially the tapering tail boom and the main-wheel undercarriage, which appears to use glass-fibre as the suspension medium.

There the resemblence ends, however. The nosewheel arrangement is quite different, the engine is mounted higher, just above the wing, full-span ailerons are fitted and, most important of all, the wing span and area are much smaller. Indeed, a glance at the technical data reveals that the A-6 is not a microlight according to the FAI definition, as the wing loading is too high.

The rally report gives no details of the A-6's availability, but as far as we know it is purely a one-off.

EXTERNAL DIMENSIONS & AREAS - Length overall 14.8 ft, 4.50 m. Wing span 22.6 ft, 6.90 m. Mean chord 2.6 ft, 0.8 m. Total wing area 59 ft², 5.5 m². Aspect ratio 8.6/1. Other data NC.

POWER PLANT - Engine type NC. Max power 25 hp. Power per unit area 0.42 hp/ft², 4.5 hp/m². Other data NC.

WEIGHTS & LOADINGS - Empty weight 238 lb, 108 kg. Max take-off weight 437 lb, 198 kg. Payload 199 lb, 90 kg. Max wing loading 7.41 lb/ft², 35.9 kg/m². Max power loading 17.5 lb/hp, 7.9 kg/hp. Load factors NC.

PERFORMANCE - NC.

KHARKOV

Address NC.

KHARHOV *EKRANOLET*

Side-by-side two-seat single-engined mid-wing monoplane. T-tail. Yaw control by fin-mounted rudder. Cantilever wing; wing profile NC; 100% double-surface. Undercarriage see text. Fuselage partially enclosed. Engine mounted above wing, driving tractor propeller. Other details NC.

Production status: see text.

GENERAL - This radical design from a group of young engineers at Kharkov had reached the stage of being a flying aerodynamic mockup at the time of going to press. In

Letectvi Kosmonautika

fact, according to one of the designers, V Matyushin, two models have been built - the one pictured here and a second, improved, version.

Power for the mockup in our photo comes from an uprated Raduga 7 model engine, and it has a span of 4.9 ft (1.50 m) with the same overall length.

The *Ekranolet's* most striking feature is its wing design, which uses pronounced anhedral for the inboard part and pronounced dihedral outboard, an arrangement which brings the wing virtally down to ground level at mid-span and allows a wheel or skid to mounted on the underside.

It is clearly too early to have any idea of whether the *Ekranolet* will ever be more than a one-off, but in our next edition we hope at least to have some information on how it flies...

EXTERNAL DIMENSIONS & AREAS - NC.

POWER PLANT - NC.

WEIGHTS & LOADINGS - NC.

PERFORMANCE - NC.

KHIRGIZIA

Address NC.

KHIRGIZIA *NLO-01*

Single-seat single-engined mid-wing monoplane. Tapering chord; conventional tail. Wing braced from below by struts. Tubular airframe (material NC) totally enclosed. Engine mounted above wing, driving pusher propeller. Other details NC.

Production status: prototype.

GENERAL - This 'mikrosamolyot' with its tiny wing area would probably not qualify as a microlight in the eyes of the FAI, because its wing loading would be too high, but it is none the less interesting for that. The product of some 30 young enthusiasts, students in the transport division of the technicians college in the Soviet republic of Khirgizia, it was due to make its maiden flight shortly after we went to press. Unfortunately, no further data is available.

EXTERNAL DIMENSIONS & AREAS - NC.

POWER PLANT - NC.

WEIGHTS & LOADINGS - NC.

PERFORMANCE - NC.

KRONSTADT

Address NC.

KRONSTADT *DELFIN*

Side-by-side two-seat single-engined low-wing monoplane. Conventional tail. Yaw control by fin-mounted rudder. Cantilever wing; 100% double-surface. Undercarriage has three wheels in tricycle formation. Steering see text. Brakes see text. Fuselage (material NC) totally enclosed. Engine mounted above wing, driving tractor propeller. Other details NC.

Production status: see text.

GENERAL - This practical looking machine is the product of young constructors at the Public Design Bureau at Kronstadt. Powered by a four-cylinder 50 hp engine, the aircraft is described as having 'twin steering', possibly a reference to steering being available by differential braking as well as from the nosewheel.

Little other information is available, other than the name of one of the designers - P Lyavin. Maximum weight is quoted as 1146 lb (520 kg), and in the data below we have assumed that that figure refers to maximum take-off weight.

No information is given about the production prospects of the *Delfin*, but if the reception given to the machine by

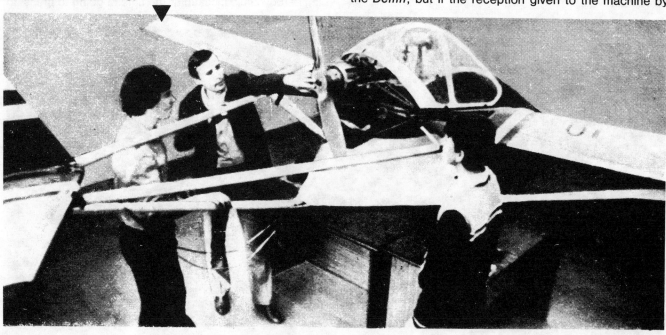

Letectvi Kosmonautika

Soviet aeronautical engineers is anything to go by, then this Kronstadt design has a promising future.

EXTERNAL DIMENSIONS & AREAS - NC.

POWER PLANT - Engine type NC. Max power 50 hp. Other data NC.

WEIGHTS & LOADINGS - Max take-off weight 1146 lb, 520 kg. Max power loading 22.9 lb/hp, 10.4 kg/hp. Other data NC.

PERFORMANCE* - Max level speed 84 mph, 135 kph. Other data NC.

*Under unspecified test conditions.

KRONSTADT *OSA*

Side-by-side two-seat* single-engined high-wing monoplane. Conventional tail. Pitch control by elevator on tail; *yaw control by fin-mounted rudder. Wing braced from below by struts. Undercarriage has three wheels in tricycle formation. Fuselage (material NC) partially enclosed. Engine mounted below wing, driving tractor propeller. Other details NC.*

Production status: see text.

*see note in text.

GENERAL - Another product of Kronstadt students, the *Osa* (wasp in Russian) is much more of a fun aircraft than the *Delfin*, but like the *Delfin* is said to have been highly acclaimed by Soviet engineers.

Information on the machine is sparse, and it is not even clear whether the aircraft has one seat or two, but the generous maximum take-off weight suggests that the *Osa* is stressed for two. Power comes from an aircooled motorcycle engine of large (for a microlight) capacity - 750 cc. No power output is quoted.

Letectvi Kosmonautika

To the best of our knowledge, the *Osa* is a one-off and not intended for production.

EXTERNAL DIMENSIONS & AREAS - NC.

POWER PLANT - Cross 750 engine. Other data NC.

WEIGHTS & LOADINGS - Max take-off weight 705 lb, 320 kg. Other data NC.

PERFORMANCE ** - Max level speed 62 mph, 100 kph. Other data NC.

***Under unspecified test conditions.*

KUIBYCHEV

Address NC.

KUIBYCHEV *A-11M*

(Three-axis)

Single-seat single-engined low-wing monoplane. Wing has swept back leading and trailing edges; conventional tail. Yaw control by fin-mounted rudder. Cantilever wing; 100% double-surface. Undercarriage has three wheels in tricycle formation. Fuselage (material NC) totally enclosed. Engine mounted above wing, driving tractor propeller. Other details NC.

Production status: see text.

GENERAL - Though not intended for full-blooded aerobatics, this is an unashamedly sporting machine, and one which its designers openly admit was inspired by Western developments, particularly the trend towards lighter materials. 'Advanced constructional principles' are used in the aircraft, from which we can safely assume that modern composite technology has been used in its construction.

As with the Byelyi *A-6*, our information on this machine is gleaned from a report of the All-union Amateur-built Aircraft Rally, which does not tell us anything about the designers, other than that they are a group of students from Kuibychev - presumably from the aeronautical institute in the town. Readers of our first edition will remember that the *Strekoza* was produced by the same college.

The report describes the design as progressive and says that, given time, there is a 'strong possibility' that the design group will be able to develop a sport aircraft 'well suited to today's needs', the implication being that the *A-11M*, or a derivative of it, may be put into production.

EXTERNAL DIMENSIONS & AREAS - Length overall 14.4 ft, 4.40 m. Wing span 17.4 ft, 5.30 m. Mean chord 2.2 ft, 0.67 m. Total wing area 38 ft², 3.6 m². Aspect ratio 7.9/1. Other data NC.

POWER PLANT - Engine type NC. Max power 40 hp. Power per unit area 1.04 hp/ft², 11.2 hp/m². Other data NC.

WEIGHTS & LOADINGS - Empty weight 273 lb, 124 kg. Max take-off weight 472 lb, 214 kg. Payload 199 lb, 90 kg. Max wing loading 12.3 lb/ft², 60.1 kg/m². Max power loading 11.8 lb/hp, 5.4 kg/hp. Load factors NC.

PERFORMANCE - NC.

Sweden

Researched by Curt Bjornemark

Where practicality comes first

by Norman Burr

In Sweden the chief impetus behind the microlight movement comes not from hang gliders wanting to power fly but from flying clubs who see the microlight as a route to cheaper airtime. It is no accident, therefore, to find that all the aircraft in this section are three-axis machines - in sharp contrast to neighbouring Norway, where imported British trikes are well liked.

Sweden has relatively liberal laws as far as weight limits are concerned, 175 kg (386 lb) unladen being permitted for two-seaters. Moreover, once the aircraft has demonstrated its ability to fly under that weight, extras may be added up to a maximum wing loading of 25 kg/m² (5.12 lb/ft²), the intention being to encourage practical aircraft rather than machines which in local weather conditions would only be flyable a few days each year. In keeping with the 'mini aeroplane' approach, all aircraft must be noise tested and type approved for airworthiness, while pilots require a license.

In general, the Swedes seem to look askance at machines without a conventional configuration and conventional three-axis controls. The Swedish airforce's chief designer is on record as saying that canards are the wrong approach for microlights, while weight-shift control has come in for criticism too. In fact, in a review of microlight flying over the period 1981-4, prepared by Ingvar Arnbacke and Olle Lofgren, the authors went so far as to recommend that only machines with conventional stick-and-rudder controls be permitted. To be fair to the authors though, they did also comment that a separate microlight association would be a healthy development, and we suspect that if one were formed it might be able to soften some of these rather rigid views.

For more information on microlights in Sweden, contact: Kungl Svenska Aeroklubben Skeppsbron (Royal Swedish Aero Club), Box 1212, S-11182 Stockholm; tel 08/232365.

JONSSON

Sven Jonsson, Radjursvagen 3, 65468 Karlstad.

Plans available from: Heiner Neumann & Dieter Reich, Fichtenstrasse 7, D-8077 Reichertshofen 2, West Germany; tel 08453 467. Alternatively: Anechostrasse 16, 8000 Munchen 82, West Germany.

JONSSON *ULF-1*

(Three-axis)

Single-seat single-engined high-wing monoplane with conventional three-axis control. Wing has unswept leading edge, swept forward trailing edge, and tapering chord; conventional tail. Pitch control by elevator on tail; yaw control by fin-mounted rudder; roll control by 30%-span ailerons; control inputs through stick for pitch/roll and pedals for yaw. Cantilever wing; wing profile Wortmann 63-137; 100% double-surface. Undercarriage has two skids in tandem; glass-fibre suspension on tailskid and rubber suspension on main skid. No ground steering; castoring tailskid. No brakes. Wood airframe, partially enclosed. Engine mounted above wing, driving pusher propeller.

Production status: plans built, number completed NC.

GENERAL - We do not claim to include an exhaustive selection of motor gliders in this book, but Sven Jonsson's *ULF-1* was an example we couldn't resist. It started life as a *ULF-1* foot-launched glider as designed by Heiner Neumann and Dieter Reich in West Germany, but Sven's addition of an 8 hp Jonsereds engine has made it eligible for our book.

The aircraft is a simple structure, around 95% of it being wood, with the pilot straddling the front skid during foot launch, hauling him or herself back onto the seat once airborne. If you can find a hillside of 15°, says Sven, then 15-18 steps are all you need even on a windless day, just 8 being sufficient if there's a wind of of 9 mph or so (14 kph). With a flat field and a windless day, however, sometimes an extra horsepower is needed, as our picture shows!

With the *ULF-1*, the accent is on low build cost - around £1000 sterling in materials, and anything up to 3000 h in time. One novel cost-saving device is the front suspension, which we rather flatteringly describe as 'rubber' in our summary above, but which actually consists of several tennis balls secured between skid and fuselage.

Drawings are available from the West German designers for DM385. The plans package contains about 30 A1 size drawings; kits are not available.

EXTERNAL DIMENSIONS & AREAS - Length overall 18.2 ft, 5.55 m. Height overall 8.4 ft, 2.55 m. Wing span 34.1 ft, 10.40 m. Chord at root 5.2 ft, 1.60 m. Chord at tip 3.8 ft, 1.15 m. Dihedral 2°. Sweepback 0°. Tailplane span NC. Fin height NC. Total wing area 144 ft², 13.4 m². Total aileron area 14.6 ft², 1.36 m². Fin area 9.3 ft², 0.86 m². Rudder area 6.0 ft², 0.56 m². Tailplane area 9.7 ft², 0.9 m². Total elevator area 27.4 ft², 2.55 m². Aspect ratio 8.1/1.

Lars Douren

POWER PLANT - Jonsereds engine. Max power 8 hp at 7000 rpm. Propeller diameter and pitch 26x7.5 inch, 0.66x 0.19 m. No reduction. Max static thrust NC. Power per unit area 0.06 hp/ft², 0.6 hp/m². Fuel capacity 1.0 US gal, 0.8 Imp gal, 3.79 litre.

WEIGHTS & LOADINGS - Empty weight 99 lb, 45 kg. Max take-off weight 302 lb, 137 kg. Payload 203 lb, 92 kg. Max wing loading 2.10 lb/ft², 10.2 kg/m². Max power loading 37.8 lb/hp, 17.1 kg/hp. Load factors +4.0, -2.0 recommended; NC ultimate.

PERFORMANCE* - Max level speed 44 mph, 70 kph. Never exceed speed 44 mph, 70 kph. Max cruising speed 34 mph, 55 kph. Economic cruising speed 34 mph, 55 kph. Stalling speed 16 mph, 25 kph. Max climb rate at sea level 200 ft/min, 1.0 m/s. Min sink rate 160 ft/min at 28 mph, 0.8

(inset left) full of anticipation on a crisp winter's morning...(inset right) Posing for the cameraman before the off...(main picture) And with a little help, Sven Jonsson takes the ULF-1 aloft.

m/s at 45 kph. Best glide ratio with power off 15/1 at 34 mph, 55 kph. Take-off distance** 16 ft, 5 m. Landing distance 20 ft, 6 m. Service ceiling NC. Range at average cruising speed 47 mile, 75 km. Noise level 65 dB at 13 ft, 4 m.

*Under the following test conditions - Airfield altitude 144 ft, 44 m. Ground temperature 10°F, -12°C. Ground pressure 1040 mB. Ground windspeed NC. Test payload 176 lb, 80 kg.

** Horse assisted.

KGK

KGK Aircraft AB, Box 213, 19123 Sollentuna; tel 8-923213/4 or 8-923000; tx 19504 KGKS.

British agent: Scandesign Ltd, 30 Bilton Road, Greenford, Middlesex UB6 7DS; tel 01-997 4530.

KGK *TIERRA 2*
(Three-axis)

Summary as Teratorn Tierra 2 (*see US section*).
Production status: current, 25 completed.

GENERAL - KGK is the European agent for the American Teratorn company, but in practice has concentrated its marketing effort on just one model, Teratorn's two-seater *Tierra 2*, which it has modified subtly to suit European needs and regulations.

Although the rules still vary from country to country, the 150 kg microlight definition is steadily giving way to 175 kg as far as two-seat trainers are concerned, and it is no accident that KGK's version of the Tierra 2 weighs in at 384 lb (174 kg), making it microlight-legal in Sweden, Finland, Norway, France and Spain. The US aircraft tips the scales at a full 400 lb (181 kg), the difference being due to the use of a smaller fuel tank and very careful weight control during manufacture, which is now partially carried out in Sweden. The power unit is exactly the same apart from a small change in prop pitch.

However, legality is one thing, marketing is another. Swedish regulations insist that the aircraft is flyable under 175 kg, but once that has been demonstrated, extras may be added up to a maximum wing loading of 25.0 kg/m² (5.12 lb/ft²). So in view of the Swedish weather, KGK fits as standard the full enclosure and some instrumentation, and offers as an option the US-size fuel tank, double the capacity of the one detailed below. Hydraulic brakes are standard, just as on the US machine, but the aircraft may be supplied without if required, saving Kr2224 and a few kg weight on the figures quoted below.

KGK's *Tierra 2* costs Kr82,598, with options as follows: skis Kr3827, floats Kr20,472, Tierra-Kote anticorrosion treatment Kr346, sea prop (with polyurethane edge) Kr769.

EXTERNAL DIMENSIONS & AREAS - See Teratorn *Tierra 2* (US section).

POWER PLANT - See Teratorn *Tierra 2* (US section) except: Propeller diameter and pitch 72x47 inch, 1.83x 1.19 m. Fuel capacity 6.0 US gal, 5.0 Imp gal, 22.7 litre.

WEIGHTS & LOADINGS - See Teratorn *Tierra 2* (US section) except: Empty weight 384 lb, 174 kg. Max take-off weight 900 lb, 408 kg. Payload 516 lb, 234 kg.

PERFORMANCE* - Max level speed 75 mph, 121 kph. Never exceed speed 85 mph, 137 kph. Max cruising speed 68 mph, 109 kph. Economic cruising speed 63 mph, 101 kph. Stalling speed 34 mph, 55 kph. Max climb rate at sea level 850 ft/min, 4.3 m/s. Min sink rate 400 ft/min at 45 mph, 2.0 m/s at 72 kph. Best glide ratio with power off 7/1 at NC speed. Take-off distance 140 ft, 43 m. Landing distance 200 ft, 60 m. Service ceiling NC. Range at average cruising speed 93 mile, 150 km. Noise level 64 dB at 1000 ft, 300 m.

*Under the following test conditions - Airfield altitude 0 ft, 0 m. Ground temperature 59°F, 15°C. Ground pressure 1009 mB. Ground windspeed 2 mph, 3 kph. Test payload 441 lb, 200 kg.

MFI

Malmo Research & Development Co (MFI), Smedstorpsgatan, 21228 Malmoe; tel 4640-180705 or 4640 290435. President: Rud Abelin. Technical manager: Bjorn Andreasson.

MFI *BA-12 SLANDAN*

(Three-axis)

Single-seat single-engined high-wing monoplane with conventional three-axis control. Wing has unswept leading and trailing edges, and constant chord; V-tail. Pitch/yaw control by ruddervator; roll control by 30%-span ailerons; control inputs through stick for pitch/roll and pedals for yaw. Wing braced from below by struts; wing profile 15% laminar; 100% double-surface. Undercarriage has three wheels in tricycle formation with additional tailskid; axle-flex suspension on all wheels. Push-right go-right nosewheel steering connected to yaw control. Brakes on main wheels. Composite construction airframe, partially enclosed (totally enclosed optional). Engine mounted at wing height, driving tractor propeller.

Production status: current, 5 under construction in Feb '85.

GENERAL - The *BA-12 Slandan* (Slandan is Swedish for Dragonfly) is a vitally important aircraft to the Swedish flying fraternity, as it is the country's first home-grown general purpose microlight, the other machines being either imported or having the accent on gliding.

Designer Bjorn Andreasson is an respected aeronautical engineer with a wealth of experience and has produced a machine which when tested by the Royal Swedish Aero Club and the Swedish civil aviation board was found to be completely viceless, even in winds of 35-40 mph (56-65 kph) or crosswinds of up to 23 mph (37 kph). In fact the RSAC was so impressed that it decided to build the aircraft in its own workshops for flying clubs, once the first batch of five have been completed by MFI to prove the tooling. Because of its flying characteristics, the authorities will accept *Slandan* time as normal lightplane time for pilot licensing purposes - another big boost for the project.

This composite-construction machine has its cabin made in six pieces bonded together to form what is claimed to be a very strong structure, while the wings use two spars pressed in a simple tool. Ribs are 0.375 inch (10 mm) foam clad with glass-fibre, while a glass-fibre/Kevlar/glass-fibre sandwich is used for the skin. The tail boom is made in two halves bonded together and carries part of the fuel load. Landing gear legs are of high-tensile steel, machined to save weight, and all controls are pushrods.

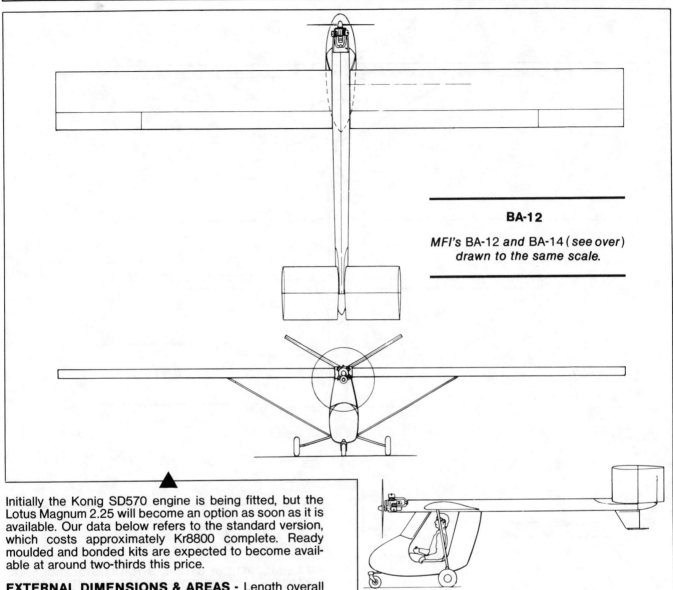

BA-12

*MFI's BA-12 and BA-14 (see over)
drawn to the same scale.*

Initially the Konig SD570 engine is being fitted, but the Lotus Magnum 2.25 will become an option as soon as it is available. Our data below refers to the standard version, which costs approximately Kr8800 complete. Ready moulded and bonded kits are expected to become available at around two-thirds this price.

EXTERNAL DIMENSIONS & AREAS - Length overall 17.1 ft, 5.20 m. Height overall 6.6 ft, 2.00 m. Wing span 32.8 ft, 10.00 m. Constant chord 3.3 ft, 1.00 m. Dihedral 1.5°. Sweepback 0°. Total wing area 108 ft^2, 10.0 m^2. Aspect ratio 10.0/1. Other data NC.

POWER PLANT - Konig SD570 engine. Max power 28 hp at 4200 rpm. Propeller diameter and pitch 51xNC inch, 1.30xNC m (3-blade). Toothed-belt reduction, ratio 1.7/1. Max static thrust 192 lb, 87 kg. Power per unit area 0.26 hp/ft^2, 2.8 hp/m^2. Fuel capacity 5.3 US gal, 4.4 Imp gal, 20.0 litre.

WEIGHTS & LOADINGS - Empty weight 298 lb, 135 kg. Max take-off weight 551 lb, 250 kg. Payload 254 lb, 115 kg. Max wing loading 5.10 lb/ft^2, 25.0 kg/m^2. Max power loading 19.7 lb/hp, 8.9 kg/hp. Load factors £4.4, -2.2 recommended; £6.6, -3.3 ultimate.

PERFORMANCE* - Max level speed 68 mph, 110 kph. Never exceed speed 118 mph, 190 kph. Max cruising speed 62 mph, 100 kph. Stalling speed 25 mph, 40 kph. Max climb rate at sea level 800 ft/min, 4.1 m/s. Take-off distance 165 ft, 50 m. Landing distance 165 ft, 50 m. Service ceiling 4000 ft, 1220 m. Other data NC.

*Under unspecified test conditions.

MFI *BA-14 TWO-SEAT*

(Three-axis)

Summary as BA-12 Slandan *except: Side-by-side two-seater. Flaps fitted. 25%-span ailerons. Totally enclosed.*

Production status: prototype.

GENERAL - Inspired by the reception given to the single-seater, Bjorn Andreasson is now working on a two-seater of similar design, the intention being to power it with a 65 hp Rotax similar to that used by KGK on its *Tierra 2*. Other notable differences from the solo machine include the use of flaps and slightly more rounded wing shapes, while doors are likely to be a standard fitment rather than an option. At the time of writing the first aircraft was still under construction, so our data below must be regarded as provisional. Projected price is approximately Kr13,200 complete.

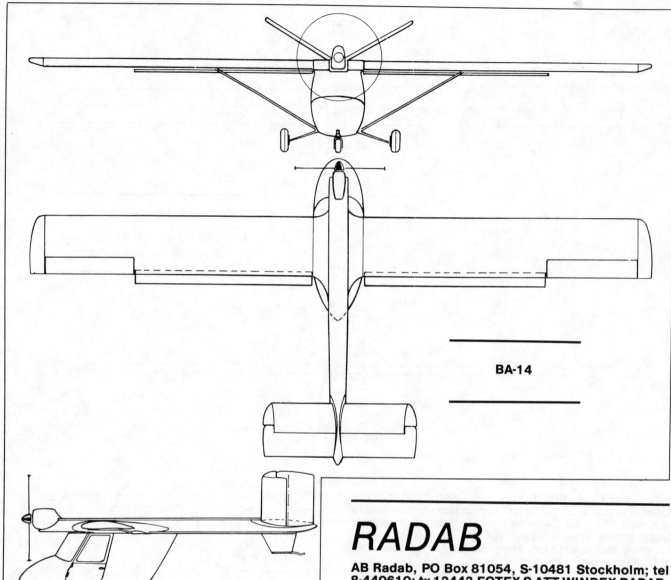

BA-14

EXTERNAL DIMENSIONS & AREAS - Length overall *17.4* ft, *5.30* m. Height overall *6.9* ft, *2.10* m. Wing span *36.1* ft, *11.00* m. Constant chord *3.3* ft, *1.00* m. Dihedral *1.5°*. Sweepback *0°*. Total wing area *138* ft², *12.8* m². Aspect ratio *11.0/1.* Wheel track *6.6* ft, *2.00* m. Wheelbase *5.2* ft, *1.60* m. Other data NC.

POWER PLANT - *Rotax 532* engine. Max power *65* hp at *6500* rpm. Propeller diameter and pitch NC. Gear reduction, ratio NC. Max static thrust NC. Power per unit area *0.47* hp/ft², *5.1* hp/m². Fuel capacity *5.3* US gal, *4.4* Imp gal, *20.0* litre.

WEIGHTS & LOADINGS - Load factors *+4.4, -2.2* recommended; *+6.6, -3.3* ultimate. Other data NC.

PERFORMANCE* - Max level speed *93* mph, *150* kph. Stalling speed *25* mph, *40* kph. Take-off distance *195* ft, *60* m. Other data NC.

*Under unspecified test conditions.

RADAB

AB Radab, PO Box 81054, S-10481 Stockholm; tel 8-440610; tx 12443 FOTEX S ATT WINDEX RADAB. Managing director: Harald Unden. Technical director: S O Ridder.

RADAB *WINDEX 1100*

(Three-axis)

Single-seat single-engined mid-wing monoplane with conventional three-axis control. Wing has unswept leading edge, swept forward trailing edge, and chord with double taper; 22.5% trailing-edge flaps; cruciform tail. Pitch control by elevator on tail; yaw control by fin-mounted rudder; roll control by 36%-span ailerons; control inputs through stick for pitch/roll and pedals for yaw. Cantilever wing; wing profile see text; 100% double-surface. Undercarriage has one wheel with skids at wing tips and tail; no suspension. No ground steering. Brake on wheel. Composite-construction airframe, totally enclosed. Engine mounted above wing, driving tractor propeller.

Production status: prototype.

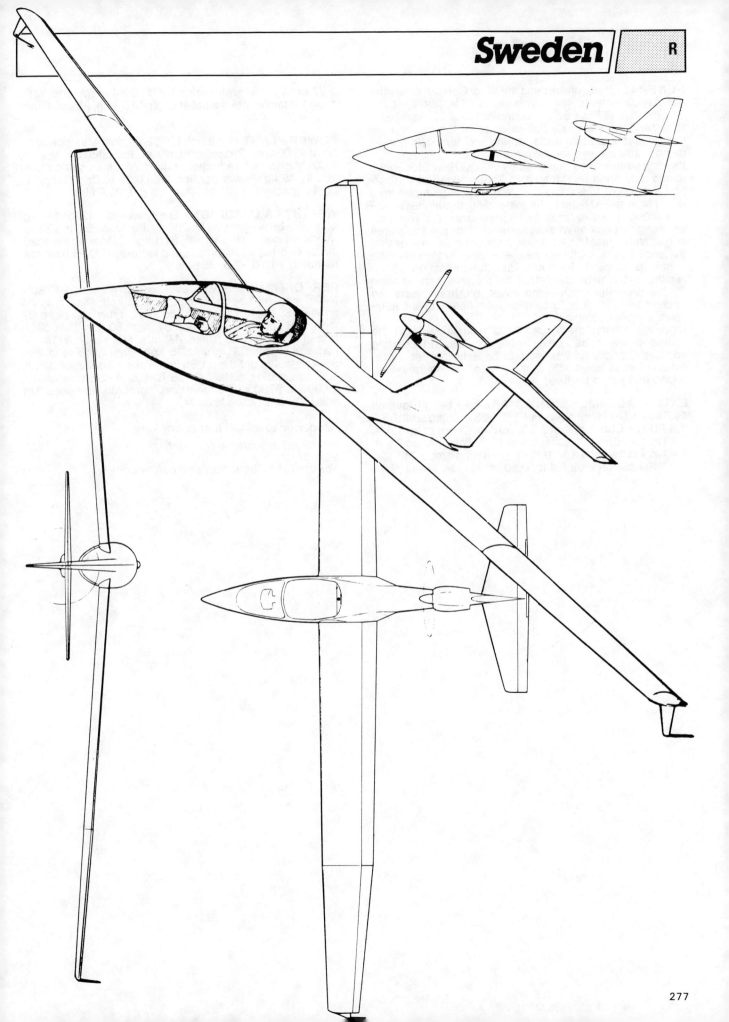

Sweden

GENERAL - Designed around the West German airworthiness requirements for sailplanes, *LFSM (1975) LTK-Gruppe A,* and their British equivalent *JAR 22 Aerobatic Category,* the *Windex 1100* is aimed at the motorglider market and is built for good soaring and aerobatic performance rather than short take-off.

Its wing section was designed by RIT (KTH) in Stockholm and is described by Radab as a 'forward-loaded laminar-flow section of 17% thickness', while the flaps move from -5° for high speed flight to 70° for landing, this highest position acting as a dive brake for glide path control. The rearward engine position was chosen so that the prop operates in relatively undisturbed air, and should also ensure that the pilot has a relatively peaceful time even when the engine is running. To counteract the deflection of the slipstream by the horizontal tail, the propeller shaft is tilted 8°, the propeller pitch being adjustable from inside the cockpit, which makes for easy in-flight restarting and maximum cruise efficiency.

Since we featured the *Windex 1100* in our first edition, the company has made considerable progress with testing and certification, and expects to be able to offer a pre-moulded kit in late 1985. At the time of writing, however, prices had yet to be fixed.

EXTERNAL DIMENSIONS & AREAS - Length overall 14.8 ft, 4.50 m. Height overall 4.1 ft, 1.25 m. Wing span 36.1 ft, 11.00 m. Chord at root 2.5 ft, 0.75 m. Chord at tip 1.4 ft, 0.43 m. Dihedral 3.5°. Sweepback 0°. Tailplane span 7.9 ft, 2.40 m. Fin height 4.1 ft, 1.25 m. Total wing area 80 ft², 7.4 m². Total aileron area 5.4 ft², 0.50 m². Rudder area 2.9 ft², 0.27 m². Total elevator area 3.7 ft², 0.34 m². Aspect ratio 16.4/1. Main wheel diameter overall 10 inch, 25 cm. Other data NC.

POWER PLANT - Limbach L275E engine. Max power 22 hp at 7200 rpm. Propeller diameter and pitch 39x** inch, 1.00x** m. V-belt reduction, ratio 1.6/1. Max static thrust 100 lb, 45 kg. Power per unit area 0.28 hp/ft², 3.0 hp/m². Fuel capacity 5.3 US gal, 4.4 Imp gal, 20.0 litre.

WEIGHTS & LOADINGS - Empty weight 242 lb, 110 kg. Max take-off weight 506 lb, 230 kg. Payload 264 lb, 120 kg. Max wing loading 6.33 lb/ft², 31.1 kg/m². Max power loading 23.0 lb/hp, 10.5 kg/hp. Load factors +7.0, -5.0 recommended; +10.5, -7.5 ultimate.

PERFORMANCE* - Max level speed 149 mph, 240 kph. Never exceed speed 179 mph, 287 kph. Max cruising speed 133 mph, 214 kph. Economic cruising speed 97 mph, 156 kph. Stalling speed 37 mph, 60 kph. Max climb rate at sea level 790 ft/min, 4.0 m/s. Min sink rate 140 ft/min at 47 mph, 0.7 m/s at 75 kph. Best glide ratio with power off 30/1 at 53 mph, 85 kph. Take-off distance 325 ft, 100 m. Landing distance 325 ft, 100 m. Service ceiling 19,000 ft, 5790 m. Range at average cruising speed 311 mile, 500 km. Noise level NC.

*Under unspecified test conditions.

**In-flight adjustable for pitch.

For another illustration see colour section.

Switzerland

Flashback to happier times: the beginnings of ultralighting in Switzerland, with the gathering in summer '81 of four Fledge-winged homebuilts, constructed by members of the Delta Club of Lausanne. From left to right: the creations of Jacques Rollet, Felix Faessler, Pierre Teuscher and Bertrand Piccard.

Grounded by a mountain of prejudice
by Bernard Piccard, Secretary General of the Swiss Ultralight Aircraft Association (SULV/ASUL).

Talking about ultralight aviation in Switzerland is like discussing pornography in a convent! Banned in the 'land of freedom' by federal order since 4 July 1984, ultralight flight has been blamed for every sin since the creation by so-called ecological groups which seem more preoccupied with politics than Mother Nature. However did we arrive a such a state of affairs?

Following initial pressure from ultralight pilots, supported by the Swiss hang gliding federation and represented from 1983 by Swiss Ultralight Aviation Association (SULV/ASUL), the Swiss authorities approved two trial periods, with the aim of gaining experience of these new aircraft so that adequate regulations could be drafted. The draconian noise requirements (60 dB at 100m) and the safety measures imposed turned the ultralight into the safest and most environmentally acceptable motorised aircraft flying. Some pilots even succeeded in reducing the noise level of their aircraft still further, to 53 dB measured at 150 m with their foot on the gas!

The controls brought in by the federal aviation office were even breached on a number of occasions by the bells of a herd of cows or a churchbell in a neighbouring village. Who would have imagined bells could be louder than an ultralight at take-off! The battle seemed won, the dream was becoming reality: aviation, ecology and democracy living in harmony.

But we were forgetting about the 'eco-militants', for years deprived of political victories and abandoned by their supporters who had tired of so many defeats. Microlight aviation, the passion of a mere minority, furnished the ideal charger on which to ride into battle; it would be the perfect whipping boy. The Swiss authorities saw in this situation an excellent opportunity to prove their concern for the environment without broaching delicate issues like industrial pollution, nuclear power and so on. Thus, despite the federal aviation office's favourable report and in violation of International Civil Aviation Organisation rules, Switzerland became in 1984 the only country to exercise a total ban on ultralight aviation, apart from East Germany. The Government declared itself 'anxious to preserve the environment from any attack, albeit a minimal one'.

But this aberration has much more far-reaching consequences. The banning order actually affects all aircraft with a wing-loading of less than 20 kg/m^2, in other words the whole gamut of modern light, slow, low-powered aeroplanes which create the least pollution! So if you want to fly in Switzerland it is now, thanks to the federal order of July 4, 1984, mandatory to choose a heavy and therefore powerfully engined machine which is consequently louder than a good ultralight.

Despite all this, ultralight aviation is not dead. The SULV/ASUL, backed by Swiss aeronautical interests, is leading a publicity campaign which aims to present the true face of this new and promising form of aviation, including its 'ecological' applications in agriculture, photography, survey work and pilot training, and has decided also to use legal channels to seek the annulment of the discriminatory legislation against ultralights.

The struggle is pitched towards the future. But it should be understood by ultralight bodies in neighbouring countries that just as long as pilots fail to understand that ultralight aviation must be practised with respect for nature and for those on the ground, and that self-imposed noise limitations represent our sole means of survival, then jealous people the world over will continue to conspire against us. And we will have succeeded only in scuttling our own ship.

This message comes from a country where ultralight aviation is completely forbidden and is directed towards the 'free world'. Let us act together to ensure the survival of our passion through our own self-discipline so the Swiss example is not followed by others.

For more information on ultralights in Switzerland, contact: SULV/ASUL, avenue de l'Avenir 19, CH-1012 Lausanne; tel 021 28 8083.

FUN FLY

Fun Fly, 1 Comte-Geraud, CH-1213 Geneve. Proprietors: Dominique Loup and Francis Riat.

FUN FLY *FUN FLY*
(Three-axis)

Side-by-side two-seat single-engined mid-wing monoplane with conventional three-axis control. Wing has unswept leading and trailing edges, and constant chord; conventional tail. Pitch control by elevator on tail; yaw control by fin-mounted rudder; roll control by 55%-span ailerons; control inputs through stick for pitch/roll and pedals for yaw. Cantilever wing; wing profile NACA 23015; 100% double-surface. Undercarriage has three wheels in tricycle formation; coil-spring suspension on nosewheel and no suspension on main wheels. Push-right go-right nosewheel steering connected to yaw control. Nosewheel brake, plus emergency stop system for main wheels. Wood wing, aluminium-alloy tube airframe, completely open. Engine mounted at wing height, driving pusher propeller.

Production status: current, 1 completed.

GENERAL - Hang-glider pilot Dominique Loup was one of the first Europeans to import a motorised Catto *CA15* from the USA. After a few years' use this aircraft was destroyed on the ground by a gale and Dominique began reconstructing it, giving it elevons like a *Mitchell Wing* and converting it to two-axis control. But then he received his baptism in aerobatics as a passenger in a Mudry *CAP-10* at Annemasse airfield just across Lake Geneva in France, and came home contaminated by that dangerous virus, *aerobaticus-virulens*. There were two possible cures: get a private pilot's licence and work up to an aerobatics rating, or build a two-seat aerobatic three-axis ultralight.

Now not every Swiss is either rich or a banker, so Dominique chose the latter cure. He told the story in September 1984 *UlmMag*, writing: 'I began by defining the load requirements of the aircraft: it would be a two-seater robust enough for rough field operation as well as two-up aerobatics but still capable of being flown solo; quick to rig and derig; a high performance wing and powerful engine; car-toppable and able to carry luggage. I then considered possible layouts: to maximise the sensation of flying I wanted maximum visibility, so the wing had to be either above or behind the crew. Above would be no good for aerobatics, so it went behind. The engine would have to go

Brienne-le-Chateau fly-in 1984, and Dominque Loup briefs Francis Riat before his first flight in the Fun Fly. *A further picture appears in the colour section.*

behind too; up front it would be too noisy and anyway I wanted to see the countryside.

'Four months passed from the time we first put pen to paper in mid May until its first flight on 15 September '83 at Motier in Switzerland. I'm a teacher and I spent my summer holiday in the workshop, the actual construction taking about two-and-a-half months. I had help calculating the centre of gravity, and we knew the correct angle of incidence from sketches of the low Reynolds number NACA 23015 profile. But imagine the anguish of taking off in an aircraft which you have designed yourself from A to Z. Will it fly? If so, how well? How will it react?'

With power pack built by Max Brugger, an aeronautics professional and a keen homebuilder in the best traditions of the Swiss watch industry, the aircraft made its first flights. Dominique admitted to just one error: the front wheel was too high, giving the wing too much incidence on the ground. 'It was impossible to land correctly,' he described. 'As soon as this wheel touched the ground it bounced back up, increasing the angle of attack.' The result was a series of kangaroo hops, the wheel finally breaking just as Dominique realised what was happening. He corrected the fault and fitted suspension for good measure.

After about 70 h, including more than 40 h two-up, the only other modification has been to enlarge the tail as this was not big enough for engine-off gliding. Dominique also introduced dual controls and adjustable seats for trimming purposes. Future developments include a pod and plans for an amphibian.

At the end of July 1984 Dominique showed off his *Fun Fly* at the homebuilders' meet at Brienne-le-Chateau in France, to which he flew non-stop from Switzerland, about 220 miles (350 km). The aircraft proved a big hit, but on the advice of his friends at *UlmMag*, he strengthened the tail assembly, which was mounted on two single beams and might be liable to twisting. At the end of '84 Dominique offered plans to homebuilders, hoping to follow that with 150 h kits for 5000-6000SF. With Swiss ultralight legislation having taken the worst possible turn, Dominique has teamed up with Francis Riat and the pair are now thinking of basing their manufacturing in France. The *Fun Fly* is a very pleasant machine to pilot and many will wish them well despite their limited means.

EXTERNAL DIMENSIONS & AREAS - Length overall 18.0 ft, 5.50 m. Height overall 7.2 ft, 2.20 m. Wing span 36.4 ft, 11.10 m. Constant chord 4.9 ft, 1.50 m. Dihedral 1°. Sweepback 0°. Tailplane span 9.8 ft, 3.00 m. Fin height 4.9 ft, 1.50 m. Total wing area 188 ft², 17.5 m². Total aileron area 19.4 ft², 1.80 m². Fin area 4.3 ft², 0.40 m². Rudder area 6.5 ft², 0.60 m². Tailplane area 19.4 ft², 1.80 m². Total elevator area 11.8 ft², 1.10 m². Aspect ratio 7.0/1. Wheel track 4.9 ft, 1.50 m. Wheelbase 4.9 ft, 1.50 m. Nosewheel diameter overall 12 inch, 30 cm. Main wheels diameter overall 16 inch, 40 cm.

POWER PLANT - Rotax 503 engine. Max power 51 hp at 6900 rpm. Propeller diameter and pitch 63x31 inch, 1.60x0.80 m. Gear reduction, ratio 3.1/1. Max static thrust 331 lb, 150 kg. Power per unit area 0.27 hp/ft², 2.9 hp/m². Fuel capacity 12.7 US gal, 10.6 Imp gal, 48.0 litre.

WEIGHTS & LOADINGS - Empty weight 384 lb, 174 kg. Max take-off weight 828 lb, 375 kg. Payload 444 lb, 201 kg. Max wing loading 4.40 lb/ft², 21.4 kg/m². Max power loading 16.2 lb/hp, 7.4 kg/hp. Load factors NC recommended; +10.0, -10.0 ultimate.

PERFORMANCE* - Max level speed 75 mph, 120 kph. Never exceed speed 99 mph, 160 kph. Max cruising speed 65 mph, 105 kph. Economic cruising speed 53 mph, 85 kph. Stalling speed 28 mph, 45 kph. Max climb rate at sea level 980 ft/min, 5.0 m/s. Min sink rate 300 ft/min at 47 mph, 1.5 m/s at 75 kph. Best glide ratio with power off 15/1 at 50 mph, 80 kph. Take-off distance 165 ft, 50 m. Landing distance 165 ft, 50 m. Service ceiling 16,400 ft, 5000 m. Range at average cruising speed 280 mile, 450 km. Noise level NC.

*Under the following test conditions - Airfield altitude 0 ft, 0 m. Ground temperature 59°F, 15°C. Ground pressure 1013 mB. Ground windspeed 0 mph, 0 kph. Test payload 444 lb, 201 kg.

GIGAX

Hans Gigax, Merkurstrasse 10, CH-4142 Munchenstein; tel (061) 46 0703.

GIGAX *FOX-D and SHERPA*

See Ikarus (West German section).

NEUKOM

Segelflugzeugbau Albert Neukom, Flugplatz, CH-8213, Neunkirch; tel (053) 61553.

NEUKOM *AN-20B*

(Three-axis)

Single-seat single-engined high-wing monoplane with conventional three-axis control. Wing has unswept leading and trailing edges, and constant chord; T-tail. Pitch control by elevator on tail; yaw control by fin-mounted rudder; roll control by one-third span ailerons; control inputs through stick for pitch/roll and pedals for yaw. Wing braced from below by struts; wing profile Worthmann FX 63-137; 100% double-surface. Undercarriage has three wheels in tricycle formation with additional tailskid; no suspension on nosewheel and glass-fibre suspension on main wheels. Push-right go-right nosewheel steering connected to yaw control. Brakes on main wheels. Glass-fibre fuselage, partially enclosed. Engine mounted at wing height, driving pusher propeller. Wing and T-tail have wood spars, ribs in styrofoam and covered with epoxied glass-fibre.

Production status: see text.

GENERAL - Our previous edition featured the various prototypes designed and built by Albert Neukom, who was sadly killed at the controls of one of his own machines just as our first French-language edition was coming out, in September 1983. Various Neukom machines are still made by homebuilders and two of his models, the *AN-22* and *AN-20,* are scheduled for production in West Germany (see Albatros and LTB-Borowski respectively). So while his designs may live on, the Neukom name will be sadly absent from the list of manufacturers in future editions of *Berger-Burr's,* making this an appropriate opportunity to show our respect for this gifted designer by briefly retelling the story of his inspired aeronautical career.

Albert Neukom's name is respected as much in the world of conventional gliding (thanks to the *Elfe 15* and *Elfe 17*) as among homebuilders, for whom he created his single-seat *AN-100.* His first microlight, the *AN-20,* made its first flights in 1978 and had a T-tail mounted on a round-section Kevlar

Switzerland

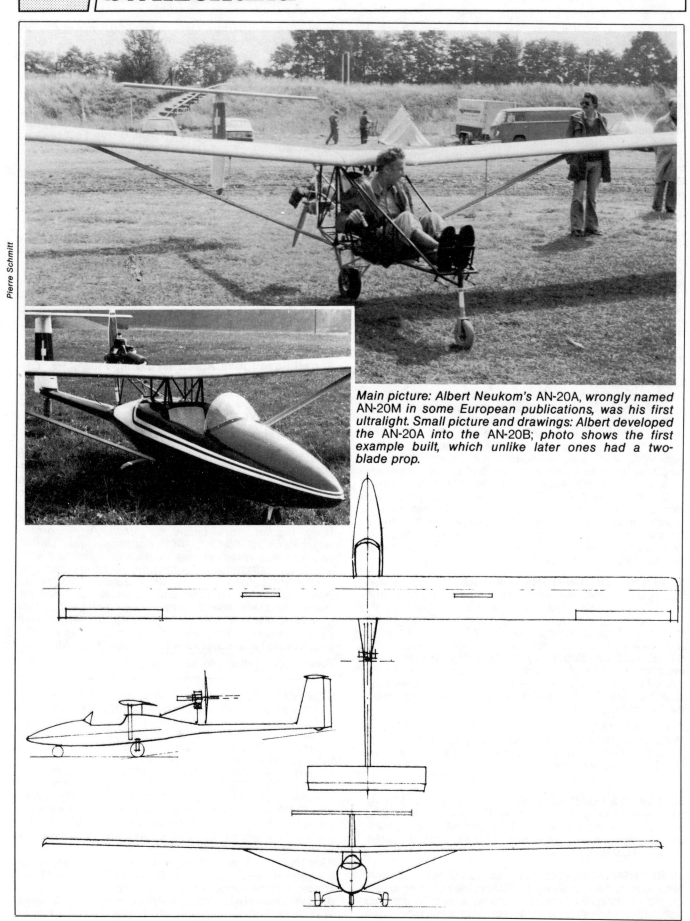

Pierre Schmitt

Main picture: Albert Neukom's AN-20A, wrongly named AN-20M in some European publications, was his first ultralight. Small picture and drawings: Albert developed the AN-20A into the AN-20B; photo shows the first example built, which unlike later ones had a two-blade prop.

boom connected to the fuselage at wing height. The tubular fuselage sat on what was essentially a monowheel undercarriage directly below the centre of the wing, though there was also a nosewheel steered from the rudder bar as well as a tailwheel, mounted on the bottom of the fin in line with the other two.

This machine was featured in various publications under the designation *AN-20M*, a great surprise to Albert who told us he had never called this first model by any name other than *AN-20*, although it eventually became the *AN-20A* to distinguish it from the later *AN-20B*. The prototype was shown at the 1982 homebuilders' meet at Brienne-le-Chateau.

The *AN-20B* was evolved directly from its predecessor, retaining the recangular plan wings, each braced by a single aerofoil-section strut. A significant change was the addition of air brakes as well as a glass-fibre fairing and windscreen, enclosing the fuselage right back to the trailing edge of the wing, where it merged into the tail boom. As this boom was no longer at wing height, the tailplane had to be redesigned so that it no longer extended below the boom. Similarly the engine, previously fitted below the tail boom, was remounted on a tubular structure above it, level with the wing. Production models were fitted with the three-cylinder Konig SC430 driving a three-blade pusher prop. A tricycle undercarriage with drum brakes on the main wheels replaced the earlier configuration.

EXTERNAL DIMENSIONS & AREAS - Length overall 17.7 ft, 5.40 m. Height overall 3.9 ft, 1.20 m. Wing span 41.3 ft, 12.60 m. Constant chord 2.6 ft, 0.80 m. Dihedral 2°. Sweepback 0°. Tailplane span 8.0 ft, 2.45 m. Fin height 3.2 ft, 0.95 m. Total wing area 109 ft², 10.1 m². Total aileron area 8.5 ft², 0.79 m². Fin area 6.6 ft², 0.61 m². Rudder area NC. Tailplane area 8.4 ft², 0.78 m². Total elevator area 4.2 ft², 0.39 m². Aspect ratio 15.8/1. Wheel track 4.7 ft, 1.43 m. Wheelbase NC. Nosewheel diameter overall 8 inch, 21 cm. Main wheels diameter overall 8.5 inch, 22 cm.

POWER PLANT - Konig SC430 engine. Max power 24 hp at 4200 rpm. Propeller diameter and pitch 42xNC inch, 1.06xNC m (3-blade). Belt reduction, ratio 1.8/1. Max static thrust 121 lb, 55 kg. Power per unit area 0.22 hp/ft², 2.4 hp/m². Fuel capacity 5.3 US gal, 4.4 Imp gal, 20.0 litre.

WEIGHTS & LOADINGS - Empty weight 287 lb, 130 kg. Max take-off weight 508 lb, 230 kg. Payload 221 lb, 100 kg. Max wing loading 4.68 lb/ft², 22.8 kg/m². Max power loading 21.2 lb/hp, 9.6 kg/hp. Load factors NC recommended; +5.3, -2.6 ultimate.

PERFORMANCE* - Max level speed 93 mph, 150 kph. Never exceed speed 99 mph, 160 kph. Max cruising speed 68 mph, 110 kph. Economic cruising speed 59 mph, 95 kph. Stalling speed 31 mph, 50 kph. Max climb rate at sea level 500 ft/min, 2.5 m/s. Min sink rate 160 ft/min at 37 mph,

Brienne-le-Chateau 1982, and the AN-21R, *shortly before its London-Paris adventure.*

0.8 m/s at 60 kph. Best glide ratio with power off 18/1 at 37 mph, 60 kph. Take-off distance 360 ft, 110 m. Landing distance 330 ft, 100 m. Service ceiling 11,500 ft, 3500 m. Range at average cruising speed 186 mile, 300 km. Noise level NC.

*Under unspecified test conditions.

NEUKOM *AN-21R*

(Three-axis)

Single-seat single-engined high-wing monoplane with conventional three-axis control. Wing has swept back leading and trailing edges, and tapering chord; no tail, canard wing. Pitch control by elevator on canard; yaw control by tip rudders; roll control by one-third span ailerons; control inputs through stick for pitch/roll and pedals for yaw. Wing braced from below by struts; wing profile Worthmann FX 63-137; 100% double-surface. Undercarriage has three wheels in tricycle formation; no suspension on nosewheel and glass-fibre suspension on main wheels. Push-right go-right nosewheel steering connected to yaw control. Nosewheel brake. Aluminium-alloy tube/fabric fuselage, totally enclosed. Engine mounted at wing height, driving pusher propeller.

Production status: one-off.

GENERAL - The *AN-21R* was a prototype designed and built for Albert Neukom's own amusement. As he confirmed to us, the machine was never intended for production. In fact, he told us: 'I wanted to design a single-seat canard aircraft, as much to try out this formula as for my own pleasure.'

Of hybrid technology (duralumin tubular structure with composite materials for the wing, canard and rudders), the prototype made its first flights in 1980 and remains unique, with no direct descendants. It was originally called the *AN-21* but it was later sold to a German, Klaus-Jurgen Richter, who flew it in the London to Paris race in September 1982, where many enthusiasts admired its exquisite detailing. It became known as the *AN-21R*, this last letter referring to Mr Richter himself.

EXTERNAL DIMENSIONS & AREAS - Length overall 16.1 ft, 4.90 m. Height overall 7.9 ft, 2.40 m. Wing span 41.3 ft, 12.60 m. Mean chord 2.8 ft, 0.85 m. Canard span 9.8 ft, 3.00 m. Canard chord 1.7 ft, 0.53 m. Total wing area 132 ft², 12.3 m². Main wing area 115 ft², 10.7 m². Canard area 17 ft², 1.6 m². Aspect ratio (of main wing) 14.8/1. Other data NC.

POWER PLANT - Konig SC430 engine. Max power 25 hp at 4200 rpm. Power per unit area 0.19 hp/ft^2, 2.0 hp/m^2. Other data NC.

WEIGHTS & LOADINGS - NC.

PERFORMANCE* - Max level speed 81 mph, 130 kph. Stalling speed 26 mph, 42 kph. Max climb rate at sea level 500 ft/min, 2.5 m/s. Other data NC.

*Under unspecified test conditions.

NEUKOM *AN-22*

(Three-axis)

Summary as Albatros AN22 (see West German section).

Production status: see text.

GENERAL - This single-seat, three-axis, conventional-control aircraft designed by Albert Neukom made its first flights in March 1983. Production versions are factory built and sold by Albatros in West Germany, and as we give further information under that heading, the data paragraphs have been omitted in this case. Albert also worked on a two-seat version of the aircraft, the *AN-22 Twin*, at his Neunkirch works in 1983.

An early example of an AN-22, *photographed at Brienne-le-Chateau in '83. A recent model is illustrated under Albatros in our West German section.*

PICCARD

Piccard Aviation, 19 avenue de l'Avenir, CH-1012 Lausanne; tel (021) 28 8083 (Piccard) and (021) 28 1895 (de Kalbermatten). Proprietors: Bertrand Piccard and Laurent de Kalbermatten.

PICCARD *EUREKA*

(Three-axis)

Single-seat single-engined low-wing monoplane with conventional three-axis control. Wing has unswept leading edge, swept forward trailing edge, and tapering chord; cruciform tail. Pitch control by elevator on tail; yaw control by fin-mounted rudder; roll control by wing warping; control inputs through stick for pitch/roll and pedals for yaw. Wing braced from above and below by cables; wing profile NACA 23015 modified; 100% double-surface. Undercarriage has three wheels in tail-dragger formation; suspension NC on tailwheel and rubber suspension on main wheels. Push-right go-right tailwheel steering connected to yaw control. No brakes. Aluminium-alloy tube airframe, partially enclosed. Engine mounted at wing height, driving tractor propeller.

Production status: prototype.

GENERAL - Piccard Aviation was formed at the end of 1982 by Bertrand Piccard, son of underwater research

Main picture: Test flying Piccard's Eureka. *Insets: The* Eureka *features a novel semi-elliptical plan wing and simple stowage arrangements.*

vessel builder Dr Jacques Piccard and grandson of Prof Auguste Piccard, who set a world altitude record of 52,500 ft (16,000 m) with a stratospheric balloon in 1931 and dived his bathyscope to 35,800 ft (10,916 m) in 1960.

Clearly, pioneering runs in the family, and Bertrand was a founder member of both the Swiss hang gliding and ultralight federations. Part of the *UlmMag* editorial team and co-editor of the Swiss chapter in our first edition, he took up hang gliding in 1974 and acquired some international fame with his aerobatics on hang gliders modified by himself from 1976. He is a hang gliding instructor in Switzerland which remains one of the best

locations for the sport in Europe. Alain-Yves Berger recalls that in 1976 he and Bertrand achieved what must have been one of the first 'IFR' hang-glider flights when they flew two gliders down through a bank of cloud 1000-1300 ft thick (300-400 m) which filled a Swiss valley.

Bertrand came into ultralights in 1981, first with flexwings and then with fixedwings. He finished the 1983 French Grand Prix sixth on a two-seater and has taken part in more than 120 displays at which he was often the only representative of ultralight aviation. His partner Laurent de Kalbermatten was also one of Europe's hang gliding pioneers and was the first Swiss champion in 1974. A light aircraft pilot, he has always been obsessed by aviation and was soon seduced by the possibilities opened up by ultralights. Long before the public had heard of 'les ULM', he had already built about five original machines, both three-axis and hybrid-control. In 1980 he became president of the Swiss ecological aviation committee, which later became the Swiss ultralight association.

The *Eureka* stems from a project he had been working on for several years, to build an easily portable single-seat three-axis ultralight. He took on the running of the technical department and, being an economist by training, was due to play a part in marketing the new product.

Unfortunately this firm's apparently promising future was thrown into doubt when the outright ban on ultralight aviation was enacted in 1984. Bernard himself expresses succinctly in the introduction to this section the near universal view of the sport's followers in Switzerland. A direct repercussion of the decision is unfortunately a virtual halt on work on the *Eureka*, just at the crucial moment when the prototype was undergoing its proving flights and having reportedly minor faults correc-

ted. It is therefore impossible at present to make presumptions about the future of this aircraft, but we publish below the data relevant to the prototype, and wish them and their fellow ultralighters a brighter future.

EXTERNAL DIMENSIONS & AREAS - Wing span 24.0 ft, 7.30 m. Chord at root 6.7 ft, 2.05 m. Chord at tip 0 ft, 0 m. Dihedral 3°. Sweepback 0°. Tailplane span 8.2 ft, 2.50 m. Total wing area 115 ft², 10.7 m². Fin area 12.9 ft², 1.2 m². Aspect ratio 5.0/1. Wheel track 4.8 ft, 1.45 m. Tailwheel diameter overall 2.5 inch, 10 cm. Main wheels diameter overall 12 inch, 30 cm. Other data NC.

POWER PLANT - Rotax 277 engine. Max power 27 hp at 6200 rpm. Propeller diameter and pitch 55xNC inch, 1.4xNC m. Gear reduction, ratio 2.6/1. Max static thrust 198 lb, 90 kg. Power per unit area 0.23 hp/ft², 2.5 hp/m². Fuel capacity 2.6 US gal, 2.2 Imp gal, 10.0 litre.

WEIGHTS & LOADINGS - Empty weight 216 lb, 98 kg. Max take-off weight 481 lb, 218 kg. Payload 265 lb, 120 kg. Max wing loading 4.18 lb/ft², 20.4 kg/m². Max power loading 17.8 lb/hp, 8.1 kg/hp. Load factors +6.0, -4.0 recommended; +9.5, -6.0 ultimate.

PERFORMANCE* - Max level speed 68 mph, 110 kph. Max cruising speed 62 mph, 100 kph. Economic cruising speed 50 mph, 80 kph. Stalling speed 31 mph, 50 kph. Max climb rate at test site 590 ft/min, 3.0 m/s. Best glide ratio with power off 6/1 at 44 mph, 70 kph. Take-off distance 100 ft, 30 m. Landing distance 165 ft, 50 m. Range at average cruising speed 99 mile, 160 km. Other data NC.

*Under the following test conditions - Airfield altitude 2790 ft, 850 m. Ground temperature 50°F, 10°C. Ground pressure 1005 mB. Ground windspeed 3 mph, 5 kph. Test payload 198 lb, 90 kg.

United States

Researched by Hal Adkins, Contributing Editor to Ultralight Flying magazine, author and photographer

The Rotec Sea Panther *was developed largely because of demand from offshore pilots in Florida.*

Ultralights - Growing and changing by Hal Adkins

Only a few short years ago the presence of a three-axis ultralight at a major US fly-in such as Oshkosh or Sun 'n Fun would have caused quite a stir. This situation has now been utterly reversed, so much so that three-axis machines are the norm, two-axis the exception and hybrids practically non-existant. Changes come quickly to the US ultralight scene.

The ultralight industry and the sport have both matured, as have the machines themselves. Although aluminium-alloy tube and Dacron are still prevalent, composites and welded materials are becoming more apparent. Enclosed or semi-enclosed cockpits are being built into new designs, and almost all of the 'bugs in the teeth' type ultralights now offer some kind of optional pod. Clearly, the public wants airplane-like ultralights, especially those pilots who can no longer fly general-aviation aircraft for financial or medical reasons, and the manufacturers are giving them what they want.

One particularly popular avenue is replicas, the venerable *J-3 Cub* being a favourite for replication, and we have gone from aircraft which 'fly like a Cub' - a common advertising hook in recent years - to planes that actually *look* like Cubs. Some of the more faithful imitations will actually deceive you at a distance into thinking that they're the real McCoy, the more so when painted the familiar Cub yellow. Also in the same vein and growing in popularity are the Heath *Parasol* lookalikes, often using a repli-Cub airframe. Another fun approach is to build a World War I fighter replica, an idea pioneered by the bright yellow *Jenny* biplane ultralight that caused such a stir a couple of years back. They're all structurally similar, but change a tail here, add a cowling there, paint it the appropriate colours and you're all ready for a mock dogfight with your friends, with realism aided by dummy machine guns, some with flashing strobe lights in the barrels.

Rising in popularity are the more off-beat aircraft that US ultralight regulations embrace. Relatively small solo balloons have caught the imagination of would-be balloonists hitherto put off by the often high price of conventional propane burners, who find they can carry the whole device in the back of a car - adventure on a budget. Gyrocopters, statistically one of the safest aircraft to fly but at one time overbuilt and powered by rare and expensive engines, have benefitted from the latest generation of reliable two-strokes developed for winged ultralights, and are now much lighter, using more aluminium and glass-fibre. Powered or ascending parachutes, probably the easiest aircraft of all to fly, have been very well received by people looking for their first flight experience.

Ultralight sales have slowed in the last year, due partly to some very biased media coverage, and many companies attending trade shows did so under an umbrella of doom, fearful of finding small crowds with their wallets firmly in their pockets. But generally the response is still good, with pilots proving much more knowledgeable and demanding than in the past - no doubt educated by the mamy publications they have access to - but still willing to spend.

With recent government and public hearings on the future course of ultralight aviation has come the realisation that the government will almost certainly be implenting new regulations covering both the aircraft and their pilots, bringing to an end the two-year period of self-regulation which the sport has enjoyed. Behind these changes is the fact that self-regulation has not worked as well as had been hoped; the general consensus among ultralight producers is that government-imposed standards will increase public confidence and thus stimulate sales. However, there is no such consensus amongst the pilots, many of whom are opposed to any form of federal intervention and want self-regulation - such as it is - to continue. They feel that once the government starts making and enforcing rules on ultralight operation, the fun flying days will be gone. Only time will tell who is right.

As we write, in early 1985, ultralights in the US are still operating under *FAR Part 103*, which defines an ultralight aircraft as a single-place machine with an empty weight of 254 lb or less, a straight and level speed not exceeding 63 mph and a stall speed of not more than 27 mph. Such an aircraft may be flown without any form of license or aircraft registration. Two-place ultralights are allowed for training purposes only, no solo flights being permitted except for maintenance, or travel to and from the lesson site. Use the same machine for any other purpose, and you'll need a pilot's license to take a passenger, while the aircraft will have to be registered as a homebuilt experimental machine, with an N-number displayed. How long these rules will remain in force is not clear, but no changes are likely before 1986 at the earliest.

Whatever happens, ultralight aviation in the US will remain at heart what it has always been - a way for the ordinary man or woman to enjoy and afford the freedom of flight. Thanks to the headlong evolution from the powered hang-gliders of yesterday to the mini-aircraft of today, an evolution which at one time saw companies introducing improved models every few months, the American public has the world's largest selection of ultralights to choose from, and lo, don't we love it!

For more information on ultralights in the US, contact the EAA Ultralight Association, Wittman Airfield, Oshkosh, Wisconsin 54903-2591; tel (414) 426-4800. Ultralight Flying magazine (formerly Glider Rider) *is at PO Box 6009, Chattanooga, Tennessee 37401; tel (615) 629-5375.*

ADVANCED AVIATION

Advanced Aviation, PO Box 16716, 323 N Ivey Lane, Orlando, Florida 32861; tel (305) 298-2920. President: Wayne Richter. Marketing director: Angel Matos.

ADVANCED AVIATION *COBRA*
(Three-axis)

Single-seat single-engined high-wing monoplane with conventional three-axis control. Wing has unswept leading and trailing edges, and constant chord except for triangular wing tips; cruciform tail. Pitch control by elevator on tail; yaw control by fully flying rudder; roll control by half-span spoilerons; control inputs through stick for pitch/roll and pedals for yaw. Wing braced from above by kingpost and cables, from below by cables; wing profile NC; 90% double-surface. Undercarriage has three wheels in tricycle formation; torsion-bar suspension on all wheels. Push-right go-right nosewheel steering connected to yaw control. Optional nosewheel brake. Aluminium-alloy tube airframe, completely open. Engine mounted below wing, driving pusher propeller.

Production status: current, number completed NC.

GENERAL - This company can be traced back to the dawn of ultralighting, being founded in 1978 as Lafayette Aviation Inc and taking its present name in 1982. As with many US ultralight constructors, the early products were hybrid control machines - the *Hi-Nuski* (later called *Hi-Nuski Huski* and finally just *Huski*), *Huski II* and *Coyote* -but by 1983 production was concentrated on a three-axis machine, the *Cobra,* first shown to the public at the '82 Oshkosh.

Glider Rider

Though still using tube and Dacron construction, the *Cobra* has little else in common with these earlier designs, and features a double-surface wing, torsion-bar suspension and spoilerons. The design has changed little since our first edition, except that the steerable nosewheel has become a standard fitment.

Sold as a 30-40 h kit for US$5454, the *Cobra* has a rigging time of 25 min. Options include floats and wheel spats.

EXTERNAL DIMENSIONS & AREAS - Length overall 17.5 ft, 5.33 m. Height overall 9.3 ft, 2.82 m. Wing span 35.0 ft, 10.67 m. Sweepback 0°. Total wing area 155 ft^2, 14.4 m^2. Aspect ratio 7.9/1. Other data NC.

POWER PLANT - Cuyuna ULII-02 engine. Max power 35 hp at 6200 rpm. Propeller diameter and pitch 54x29 inch, 1.37x0.74 m. Planetary gear reduction, ratio 2.1/1. Max static thrust 225 lb, 102 kg. Power per unit area 0.23 hp/ft^2, 2.4 hp/m^2. Fuel capacity 4.8 US gal, 18.2 Imp gal, 18.2 litre.

WEIGHTS & LOADINGS - Empty weight 245 lb, 111 kg. Max take-off weight 525 lb, 238 kg. Payload 280 lb, 127 kg. Max wing loading 3.39 lb/ft^2, 16.5 kg/m^2. Max power loading 15.0 lb/hp, 6.8 kg/hp. Load factors +5.0, -3.0 design; NC ultimate.

PERFORMANCE* - Max level speed 63 mph, 101 kph. Never exceed speed 70 mph, 113 kph. Max cruising speed

Glider Rider

55 mph, 88 kph. Economic cruising speed 50 mph, 80 kph. Stalling speed 26 mph, 42 kph. Max climb rate at sea level 800 ft/min, 4.1 m/s. Best glide ratio with power off 9/1 at NC speed. Take-off distance 80 ft, 24 m. Landing distance 100 ft, 30 m. Other data NC.

*Under unspecified test conditions.

ADVANCED AVIATION *KING COBRA, COBRA ENFORCER, COBRA VIP and AG COBRA* (Three-axis)

Summary as Cobra *except: Side-by-side two-seater* (King Cobra), *single-seater (other models). Brakes on main wheels.*

Production status: current, number completed NC.

GENERAL - A logical development from the *Cobra,* the *King Cobra* is the company's entrant in the dual stakes, and follows closely the configuration of the solo machine. Wing span is marginally increased, though the distinctive scalloped trailing edge remains, and the most powerful Cuyuna available is bolted in - the 430RR with 43 hp. Disc brakes for the main wheels complete the re-engineering process.

Sold with full dual controls as standard equipment, the *King Cobra* costs US$6666 for a 40 h kit with a 30 min set up time. Options include floats and wheel spats.

Advanced Aviation has also produced three solo derivaties of the *King Cobra's* two-seat airframe. The *Cobra Enforcer* comes with siren and blue light and is intended for police use, while the *Cobra VIP* comes with an extra wide seat and single controls in place of the dual arrangements, leaving sufficient room and payload for even the most gargantuan of pilots. Third is the *AG Cobra,* a crop-dusting version. Figures for all three are very similar to those of the *King Cobra* given below, except that a 1000 ft/min climb

Easy to recognise because of the distinctive trailing-edge shape common to all Cobras, *the* King Cobra *(main picture) and* Cobra Enforcer *(inset) are both based on the same airframe.*

(5.1 m/s) is claimed for the police version, which weighs around 25 lb (11 kg) less than the dual machine. Prices: NC.

EXTERNAL DIMENSIONS & AREAS - Length overall 19.7 ft, 5.99 m. Height overall 9.3 ft, 2.84 m. Wing span 35.3 ft, 10.76 m. Sweepback 0°. Total wing area 162 ft², 15.1 m². Aspect ratio 7.7/1. Other data NC.

POWER PLANT - Cuyuna 430RR engine. Max power 43 hp at 7000 rpm. Propeller diameter and pitch 72x32 inch, 1.83x0.81 m. Planetary gear reduction, ratio 3.0/1. Max static thrust NC. Power per unit area 0.27 hp/ft², 2.8 hp/m². Fuel capacity 4.8 US gal, 4.0 Imp gal, 18.2 litre.

WEIGHTS & LOADINGS - Empty weight 325 lb, 147 kg. Max take-off weight 775 lb, 352 kg. Payload 450 lb, 204 kg. Max wing loading 4.78 lb/ft², 23.3 kg/m². Max power loading 18.0 lb/hp, 8.2 kg/hp. Load factors NC.

PERFORMANCE - See *Cobra* except: Max climb rate at sea level 450 ft/min, 2.3 m/s. Best glide ratio with power off 7/1 at NC speed. Take-off distance 275 ft, 84 m. Landing distance 250 ft, 76 m.

ADVANCED AVIATION
HIGHCRAFT BUCCANEER

(Three-axis)

See HighCraft Aero-Marine.

ADVANCED AVIATION
SEAWOLF

(Three-axis)

Single-engined biplane with conventional three-axis control. Bottom wing has unswept leading edge, swept forward trailing edge, and tapering chord; top wing has unswept leading and trailing edges, and constant chord; cruciform tail. Pitch control by elevator on tail; yaw control by fin-mounted rudder; roll control NC; control inputs NC. Wings braced by struts and transverse X-cables; wing profile NC; NC% double-surface. Under-carriage has three retractable wheels in tricycle formation plus under-wing floats; suspension NC. Ground steering NC. Brakes NC. Aluminium-alloy tube airframe, totally enclosed. Engine mounted above wings, driving pusher propeller.

Production status: prototype.

GENERAL - Announced just as we went to press, the *Seawolf* is quite unconnected with earlier Advanced Aviation designs apart from retaining tube and Dacron construction, and is described by the company as a cabin-class amphibian lightplane. The configuration is unusual, with staggered wings, retractable landing gear and pusher prop, but few other details are available at the time of writing. We have no hard news even of the seating configuration, though as pilot weights of up to 420 lb (191 kg) are envisaged the machine will almost certainly be a two-

seater. A variety of engines from 35 to 65 hp are under consideration.
Price: NC.

EXTERNAL DIMENSIONS & AREAS - Length overall 21.3 ft, 6.49 m. Wing span 23.5 ft, 7.16 m (bottom); 23.5 ft, 7.16 m (top). Sweepback 0°. Total wing area 165 ft², 15.3 m². Aspect ratio 6.9/1. Other data NC.

POWER PLANT - NC.

WEIGHTS & LOADINGS - NC.

PERFORMANCE - NC.

ADVANCED COMPOSITE TECHNOLOGY

Advanced Composite Technology, 5053 Merriam, Shawnee Mission, Kansas 66203; tel (913) 384-1813. Alternatively: 6315 S Hydraulic, Wichita, Kansas 67216. President: Mark Calder.

ADVANCED COMPOSITE TECHNOLOGY *WREN*
(Three-axis)

Single-seat single-engined high-wing monoplane with conventional three-axis control. Wing has swept back leading edge, swept forward trailing edge, and tapering chord; conventional tail. Pitch control by elevator on tail;

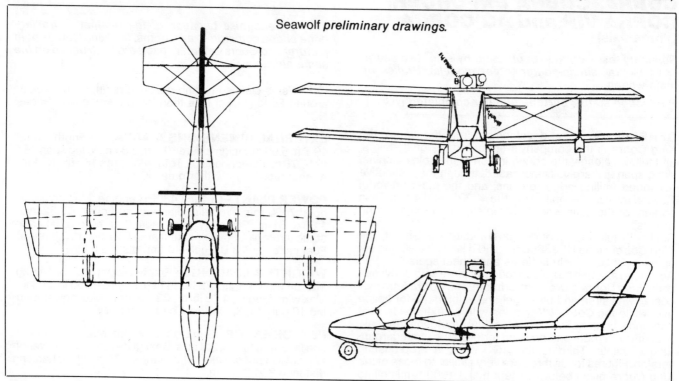

Seawolf *preliminary drawings.*

yaw control by fin-mounted rudder; roll control by half-span ailerons; control inputs through stick for pitch/roll and pedals for yaw. Wing braced from below by struts; 100% double-surface. Undercarriage has two wheels plus tailskid. Composite-construction airframe, totally enclosed. Engine mounted below wing, driving tractor propeller. Other details NC.

Production status: see text.

An early picture of the prototype Wren; *the machine has changed little in appearance since.*

GENERAL - Featured in our first edition under Wren Aviation, the Mark Calder-designed *Wren* was first conceived in 1981, with the intention of reaching the market in 1983. The present company was presumably set up to facilitate that, but we have no news of production arrangements, though firm prices are quoted, of US$5295 for a 250-500 h kit and US$100 for plans.

How practical it would be to build from plans we are not sure, since the construction is quite complex. The woodwork - incorporating fir, birch, plywood, pine and redwood - should be no problem, but the wings use glass-fibre/Kevlar/carbon-fibre in an epoxy matrix over foam cores, a rather daunting structure for the average homebuilder.

Initially listed with Zenoah and Kawasaki engines, the *Wren* now uses a Rotax 277 power plant. Rigging time is 15-25 min.

EXTERNAL DIMENSIONS & AREAS - Wing span 36.0 ft, 10.97 m. Sweepback 0°. Total wing area 160 ft², 14.9 m². Aspect ratio 8.1/1. Other data NC.

POWER PLANT - Rotax 277 engine. Max power 28 hp at NC rpm. Propeller diameter and pitch 58x27 inch, 1.47x0.69 m. Reduction type NC, ratio 2.25/1. Max static thrust NC. Power per unit area 0.18 hp/ft², 1.9 hp/m². Fuel capacity 4.5 US gal, 3.8 Imp gal, 17.0 litre.

WEIGHTS & LOADINGS - Empty weight 233 lb, 106 kg. Max take-off weight 500 lb, 227 kg. Payload 267 lb, 121 kg. Max wing loading 3.13 lb/ft², 15.2 kg/m². Max power loading 17.9 lb/hp, 8.1 kg/hp. Load factors NC recommended; +8.5, -5.0 ultimate.

PERFORMANCE* - Max level speed 60 mph, 97 kph. Never exceed speed 95 mph, 153 kph. Cruising speed 55 mph, 88 kph. Stalling speed 23 mph, 37 kph. Max climb rate at sea level 1200 ft/min, 6.1 m/s. Range at average cruising speed 155 mile, 249 km. Other data NC.

*Under unspecified test conditions.

double-surface. Undercarriage has three wheels in tail-dragger formation. Totally enclosed. Engine mounted below wing, driving tractor propeller.

Production status: prototype.

GENERAL - This very *Cub*-like machine appeared as a prototype at Oshkosh '84 and since then the company has been setting up for production. The last we heard of the aircraft was a short report in *Light Plane World* in January '85, at which time the production engineering process was still incomplete. The intention was to use a sandwich structure wing and a doped fabric finish, but no other structural information was given. Since then, however, the aircraft has been listed at US$7995 complete, with a rigging time of 12-20 min.

EXTERNAL DIMENSIONS & AREAS - Wing span 30.0 ft, 9.14 m. Constant chord 3.9 ft, 1.18 m. Sweepback 0°. Total wing area 116 ft², 10.8 m². Aspect ratio 7.8/1. Other data NC.

POWER PLANT - KFM 107ER engine. Max power 25 hp at NC rpm. Propeller diameter and pitch 54x19 inch, 1.37x0.48 m. Reduction type NC, ratio 2.1/1. Max static thrust NC. Power per unit area 0.22 hp/ft², 2.3 hp/m². Fuel capacity 5.0 US gal, 4.2 Imp gal, 18.9 litre.

WEIGHTS & LOADINGS - Empty weight 250 lb, 113 kg. Max take-off weight 503 lb, 228 kg. Payload 253 lb, 115 kg. Max wing loading 4.34 lb/ft², 21.1 kg/m². Max power loading 20.1 lb/hp, 9.1 kg/hp. Load factors NC.

PERFORMANCE* - Max level speed 63 mph, 101 kph. Never exceed speed 70 mph, 113 kph. Cruising speed 55 mph, 88 kph. Stalling speed 25 mph, 40 kph. Max climb rate at sea level 500 ft/min, 2.5 m/s. Range at average cruising speed 172 mile, 277 km. Other data NC.

*Under unspecified test conditions.

AERO INNOVATIONS

Aero Innovations, Rt 1, Box 1175, Pipe Creek, Texas 78063; tel (512) 535-4412. General manager: Norris Warner.

AERO INNOVATIONS *FIESTA*
(Three-axis)

Single-seat single-engined high-wing monoplane with conventional three-axis control. Wing has unswept leading and trailing edges, and constant chord; flaps fitted; cruciform tail. Pitch control by elevator on tail; yaw control by fin-mounted rudder; roll control by half-span ailerons; control inputs through stick for pitch/roll and pedals for yaw. Wing braced from below by struts; 100%

AEROTECH DYNAMICS

Aerotech Dynamics Corp, Route 1, Box 125, Lawtey, Florida 32058; tel (904) 964-6741. Offices: 660 Madison Ave, Suite 404, New York, New York 10021.

AEROTECH DYNAMICS *WIND RIDER*
(Three-axis)

Single-seat single-engined high-wing monoplane with conventional three-axis control. Wing has unswept lead-

ing and trailing edges, and constant chord; cruciform tail. Pitch control by elevator on tail; yaw control by fully flying rudder; roll control by half-span ailerons; control inputs through stick for pitch/roll and pedals for yaw. Wing braced from above by kingpost and cables, from below by cables; single-surface. Undercarriage has three wheels in tricycle formation. Aluminium-alloy tube airframe, completely open. Engine mounted below wing, driving pusher propeller. Other details NC.

Production status: see text.

AEROTECH DYNAMICS
WIND RIDER II
(Three-axis)

Summary as Wind Rider except: two-seater.

Production status: see Wind Rider text.

GENERAL - See *Wind Rider*.

EXTERNAL DIMENSIONS & AREAS - Wing span 39.0 ft, 11.89 m. Constant chord 5.0 ft, 1.52 m. Sweepback 0°. Total wing area 195 ft², 18.1 m². Aspect ratio 7.8/1. Other data NC.

POWER PLANT - Rotax 503 engine. Max power 48 hp at NC rpm. Propeller diameter and pitch 60x30 inch, 1.52x0.76 m. Reduction type NC, ratio 2.0/1. Max static thrust NC. Power per unit area 0.25 hp/ft², 2.7 hp/m². Fuel capacity 10.0 US gal, 8.3 Imp gal, 37.9 litre.

WEIGHTS & LOADINGS - Empty weight 300 lb, 136 kg. Max take-off weight 700 lb, 318 kg. Payload 400 lb, 181 kg. Max wing loading 3.59 lb/ft², 17.6 kg/m². Max power loading 14.6 lb/hp, 6.6 kg/hp. Load factors NC.

PERFORMANCE* - Max level speed 45 mph, 72 kph. Never exceed speed 60 mph, 97 kph. Cruising speed 40 mph, 64 kph. Stalling speed 22 mph, 35 kph. Max climb rate at sea level 600 ft/min, 3.1 m/s. Other data NC.

Under unspecified test conditions.

AEROTIQUE

Aerotique Aviation, Jonesburg Airport, Route 1, Box 146, Jonesburg, Missouri 63351; tel (314) 488 3108. President: Bob Cowan.

AEROTIQUE *PARASOL*
(Three-axis)

Single-seat single-engined parasol-wing monoplane with conventional three-axis control. Wing has unswept leading and trailing edges, and constant chord; conventional tail. Pitch control by elevator on tail; yaw control by fin-mounted rudder; roll control by half-span ailerons; control inputs through stick for pitch/roll and pedals for yaw. Wing braced from below by struts; wing profile NC; 100% double-surface. Undercarriage has two wheels plus tailskid; no suspension on tailskid and bungee suspension on main wheels. No ground steering. No brakes. Wood wing, aluminium-alloy tube airframe, partially enclosed. Engine mounted below wing, driving tractor propeller.

Production status: see text.

GENERAL - Little information is available about this company or its products, but we know that the Wind Rider is based on the obscure but quite conventional tube and Dacron *Aerostat 340,* which we featured in our first edition under Aerolight Flight Development. Aerotech Dynamics bought the rights to this machine and renamed it *Wind Rider,* though it is not clear what changes were made in the process nor whether the Kawasaki TA440 was retained. We suspect, however, that the main emphasis is now on a two-seat version using a Rotax 503, whose data we list separately; no data is available for the solo machine.

Glider Rider

Flashback to Oshkosh '83, where the Parasol *appeared in prototype form with a Cuyuna engine.*

GENERAL - First shown at the '83 Oshkosh, the *Parasol* was subsequently put into production on the strength of the reception received. The design is a replica of the Heath *Parasol* of the '20s, and uses a mixture of traditional and modern construction. Wings are wood and fabric, but under the fuselage skin lurks an airframe of rectangular-section alloy tubing.

The machine has received a lot of interest from the American press, including a flight test in the December '84 *Ultralight Flying,* and this helped to swell the order book to the point where a production rethink was needed. Even by October '84 around 50 were on order, yet only three had been delivered. At that time the company said it was gearing up to 20 per month, but early in 1985 the situation was confused by the announcement of a company reorganisation, in which current president Bob Cowan bought out his former partner Rich Kohm.

At the time of writing (July '85), it is not clear whether the *Parasol* is in production or whether it has been abandoned in favour of two other designs which Bob is known to be interested in developing: replicas of the Pietenpol *Air Camper* and *Scout,* dual and solo machines respectively which he hopes to sell in both the ultralight and home-built markets.

Last published prices for the *Parasol* were US$6500 and US$7995 for 350-400 h kits and fly-away machines respectively.

EXTERNAL DIMENSIONS & AREAS - Length overall 17.5 ft, 5.33 m. Height overall 6.2 ft, 1.89 m. Wing span 32.0 ft, 9.75 m. Constant chord 4.5 ft, 1.37 m. Sweepback 0°. Total wing area 144 ft², 13.4 m². Aspect ratio 7.1/1. Other data NC.

POWER PLANT - Rotax 277 engine. Max power 27 hp at 6200 rpm. Propeller diameter and pitch 68x24 inch, 1.73x0.61 m. Gear reduction, ratio 2.6/1. Max static thrust NC. Power per unit area 0.19 hp/ft², 2.0 hp/m². Fuel capacity 5.0 US gal, 4.2 Imp gal, 18.9 litre.

WEIGHTS & LOADINGS - Empty weight 250 lb, 113 kg. Max take-off weight 520 lb, 236 kg. Payload 270 lb, 122 kg. Max wing loading 3.61 lb/ft², 17.6 kg/m². Max power loading 19.3 lb/hp, 8.7 kg/hp. Load factors +6.0, -2.5 design; NC ultimate.

PERFORMANCE* - Max level speed 60 mph, 97 kph. Never exceed speed 78 mph, 126 kph. Cruising speed 55 mph, 88 kph. Stalling speed 22 mph, 35 kph. Max climb rate at sea level 700 ft/min, 3.6 m/s. Best glide ratio with power off 12/1 at NC speed. Other data NC.

*Under unspecified test conditions.

AIRBORNE

Airborne Balloons & Airships USA Inc, 2967 Coors Court, Unit E, Santa Rosa, California 95407; tel (707) 546-7124. President: Richard H Pingrey. Vice-president: Jimmy G Marshall.

AIRBORNE BALLOONS *AX3-21*
(Hot-air balloon)

Single-seat hot-air balloon. 12 gores. Height control by temperature of contained air, rotation control by directional vents; control inputs through burner valve for height increase, vent/parachute deflation rope for height decrease, directional vent ropes for rotation. Envelope braced by horizontal and vertical nylon load tapes, with double overlap seams. No undercarriage. No ground steering. No brakes. Stainless-steel tube chair. No engine. Envelope made from nylon ripstop fabric.

Production status: current, number completed NC.

GENERAL - Airborne Balloons & Airships has designed its *AX3-21* and *AX4-31* ultralight balloons to carry just one person, as required by the FAA regulations for ultralight aircraft, the principal difference between the two models being the size of the envelope.

As with all balloons, the lifting capability is determined by the volume of the envelope, the weight of the balloon including pilot and fuel, the temperature inside the envelope compared to that outside, and the particular atmospheric conditions at the time of the flight. To fly higher or to carry more weight, either the envelope volume must be increased or the temperature differential must be raised. However, too high an internal temperature will damage the fabric of the bag, so there is a practical limit in terms of altitude and weight lift for any hot-air balloon.

Thus the company has designed two balloons, to meet the needs of different weight pilots and different conditions. For normal conditions, where the pilot weighs under 200 lb (91 kg) and the craft is to be operated at or below altitudes of 4000 ft (1220 m) AMSL, the *AX3-21* with its 21,000 ft³ (181 m³) envelope is recommended. For heavier pilots or greater altitudes, the 31,000 ft³ (268 m³) *AX4-31* would be the better choice.

Both use 12 gore envelopes and come with left and right rotation vents, so the pilot can rotate the craft in any direction he or she pleases.

Standard equipment with each envelope includes a chair-type car (rather than the traditional basket) with seat cushions and carrying bag, a basic burner complete with all fuel lines etc, a padded aluminium propane cylinder with both liquid and vapour pilot light valve and regulator system, an altimeter and temperature indicator flags. The car carries an overhead burner frame with lexan support rods and includes a storage locker.

Optional burner equipment includes a liquid burner back-up, a dual blast valve system and an electronic blast valve with its control buttom mounted next to the instruments. A further option is to replace the standard tank (detailed below) with either a double size or an 11.5 US gal (9.6 Imp gal, 43.5 litre) tank.

Depending on options, prices are US$4995-7500 for the AX3-21 and US$5665-8570 for the AX4-31.

EXTERNAL DIMENSIONS, AREAS & VOLUMES - Height overall 40.0 ft, 12.19 m. Diameter overall 35.0 ft, 10.67 m. Volume fully inflated 21,000 ft³, 181 m³. Other data NC.

POWER PLANT - Propane burner, max output 9.0M BTU/h, 9.5M kJ/h. Specific output 1.0M BTU/h per 15 lb/in², 1.1M kJ/h per 100 kN/m². Fuel capacity 10.0 US gal, 8.3 Imp gal, 38.0 litre.

WEIGHTS & LOADINGS - NC.

PERFORMANCE* - Max climb rate at sea level 800 ft/min, 4.1 m/s. Max sink rate 900 ft/min, 4.6 m/s. Service ceiling 20,000 ft, 6100 m. Endurance 1.0 h.

*In still air, other test conditions unspecified.

AIRBORNE BALLOONS *AX4-31*
(Hot-air balloon)

Summary as AX3-21.

GENERAL - See *AX3-21*.

EXTERNAL DIMENSIONS, AREAS & VOLUMES - Height overall 45.0 ft, 13.71 m. Diameter overall 40.0 ft, 12.19 m. Volume fully inflated 31,000 ft³, 878 m³. Other data NC.

POWER PLANT - See *AX3-21*.

WEIGHTS & LOADINGS - Empty weight 155 lb, 70 kg.

Max take-off weight 600 lb, 272 kg. Payload 445 lb, 202 kg.

PERFORMANCE - See *AX3-21*.

AIRBORNE WING DESIGN

Airborne Wing Design, 7572 Telfer Way, Sacramento, California 95823; tel (916) 395-3374.

AIRBORNE WING DESIGN
AVENGER
(Three-axis)

Single-seat single-engined high-wing monoplane with conventional three-axis control. Wing has unswept leading and trailing edges, and constant chord; conventional tail. Pitch control by elevator; yaw control by rudder; roll control by half-span ailerons; control inputs through stick for pitch/roll and pedals for yaw. Wing braced from below by struts. Undercarriage has three wheels in tricycle formation. Tubular airframe, completely open. Engine mounted below wing, driving pusher propeller. Other details NC.

Production status: see text.

GENERAL - Though listed as recently as January 1985 at a price of US$5500 for a 60-70 h kit, with ready to fly machines available for an extra US$1000, we have heard nothing of this Rotax-engined machine since its announce-

ment with a 430 Cuyuna back in mid '83, and are unsure of its availability.

Data is similarly sparse, but the aircraft appears to be conventional tube-and-Dacron device with strut bracing, whose only distinguishing feature is a higher than usual ground clearance.

EXTERNAL DIMENSIONS & AREAS - Length overall 17.0 ft, 5.18 m. Wing span 31.0 ft, 9.45 m. Constant chord 4.4 ft, 1.33 m. Sweepback 0°. Total wing area 135 ft², 12.5 m². Aspect ratio 7.1/1. Other data NC.

POWER PLANT - Rotax 277 engine. Max power 28 hp at NC rpm. Propeller diameter and pitch 54x32 inch, 1.37x0.81 m. Reduction type NC, ratio 2.0/1. Max static thrust NC. Power per unit area 0.21 hp/ft², 2.2 hp/m². Fuel capacity 5.0 US gal, 4.2 Imp gal, 18.9 litre.

WEIGHTS & LOADINGS - Empty weight 242 lb, 110 kg. Max take-off weight 542 lb, 246 kg. Payload 300 lb, 136 kg. Max wing loading 4.01 lb/ft², 19.7 kg/m². Max power loading 19.4 lb/hp, 8.8 kg/hp. Load factors NC.

PERFORMANCE* - Max level speed 60 mph, 97 kph. Never exceed speed 70 mph, 113 kph. Cruising speed 45 mph, 72 kph. Stalling speed 18 mph, 29 kph. Max climb rate at sea level 600 ft/min, 3.1 m/s. Range at average cruising speed 173 mile, 278 km. Other data NC.

*Under unspecified test conditions.

AIR COMMAND

Air Command, 106 Sycamore, Excelsior Springs, Missouri 64024; tel (816) 637-3784. Designer: Dennis Fetters.

AIR COMMAND
447 COMMANDER
(Gyroplane)

Single-seat single-engined gyroplane with three-axis control. Rotor has constant chord; conventional tail. Pitch/roll control by angling rotor, yaw control by fin-mounted rudder; control inputs through stick for pitch/roll and pedals for yaw. Two-blade rotor with laminar-section blades. Undercarriage has three wheels in tricycle formation; suspension NC. Push-right go-right nosewheel steering connected to yaw control. Brakes on main wheels. Aluminium-alloy tube airframe, completely open. Engine mounted below rotor, driving pusher propeller.

Production status: current, number completed NC.

GENERAL - Interest in ultralight-legal gyroplanes is growing fast in the US, and the *447 Commander* is designed to satisfy this market. Straight and level top speed comes out right on the ultralight limit at 63 mph (101 kph), and weight is comfortably within bounds, even with a Rotax 447 doing the pushing.

The heart of any gyroplane, of course, is the rotor blades, and the *447 Commander* uses units built by McCutchen Sky Wheels in Denver. Air Command Designer Dennis Fetters reckons these are exceptionally tough, and was quoted in the March '85 edition of *Ultralight Flying* as saying that 'we can actually throw lawn chairs up at them at full rpm - it chews the lawn chairs up, but only scratches the rotors'. Nevertheless, we would prefer not be offered the first flight after such a test!

Yaw control is provided by a conventional fin/rudder

Glider Rider

forward speed is needed before the blades are turning fast enough to lift the craft. As an option, therefore, this machine offers a pre-rotate system, which temporarily connects the engine to the rotors to get them moving before the take-off roll begins. Other options are a rotor tachometer and a rotor brake.

In standard form the craft costs US$4200 for a kit claimed to take only a couple of hours to assemble. Rigging time is similarly short, only 10 min.

EXTERNAL DIMENSIONS & AREAS - Length overall 10.7 ft, 3.25 m. Height overall 7.0 ft, 2.13 m. Rotor diameter 23.0 ft, 7.01 m. Other data NC.

POWER PLANT - Rotax 447 engine. Max power 40 hp at 6000 rpm. Propeller diameter and pitch NC (4-blade). Gear reduction, ratio 2.6/1. Max static thrust NC. Fuel capacity 5.0 US gal, 4.2 Imp gal, 18.9 litre.

WEIGHTS & LOADINGS - Empty weight 225 lb, 102 kg. Max take-off weight 550 lb, 249 kg. Payload 325 lb, 147 kg. Max power loading 13.8 lb/hp, 6.2 kg/hp. Load factors NC.

PERFORMANCE* - Max level speed 63 mph, 101 kph. Never exceed speed 150 mph, 241 kph. Cruising speed 45 mph, 72 kph. Max climb rate at sea level 1000 ft/min, 5.1 m/s. Range at average cruising speed 225 mile, 362 km. Other data NC.

*Under unspecified test conditions.

assembly, operated by pedals and made of glass-fibre, while the other two axes are controlled by the stick. Hydraulic disc brakes for the main wheels are a standard fitment. Our data below does not quote a stall speed, because Dennis insists that his machine is impossible to stall. Indeed, in the same article he remarked that 'it'll fly backwards without losing altitude'. This attribute allows gyroplanes to make literally pinpoint landings, but the same cannot usually be said of take-offs, because plenty of

AIRCORE

Aircore Industries Inc, 4700 188th NE, Arlington, Washington 98223; tel (206) 435-3737. President: James Scott.

Sales: Eastside Ultralight Inc at the same address.

AIRCORE *CADET*

(Three-axis)

Single-seat single-engined high-wing monoplane with conventional three-axis control. Wing has unswept leading and trailing edges, and constant chord; conventional tail. Pitch control by elevator on tail; yaw control by fin-mounted rudder; roll control by 66%-span ailerons; control inputs through yoke for pitch/roll and pedals for yaw. Wing braced from below by struts; wing profile NC; 60% double-surface. Under carriage has three wheels in tricycle formation; no suspension on nosewheel and leaf-spring suspension on main wheels. Push-right go-right nosewheel steering connected to yaw control. No brakes. Aluminium-alloy tube airframe, completely open. Engine mounted at wing height, driving tractor propeller.

Production status: current, 39 complete.

GENERAL - Aircore Industries is basically a father and son operation, which originated when Jim Scott and Jim Scott Jnr started modifying Weedhoppers and eventually decided to produce their own machine. With the *Cadet*, the emphasis is very much on a low-cost no-frills flying machine. Construction is straightforward tube and Dacron with strut bracing and a tractor prop, and there's a conventional tail supported on a single large-diameter tube, strut braced from underneath. Perhaps the only

unusual feature is the use of a control yoke instead of a stick.

Tester James Campbell, writing in the March '85 edition of *Ultralight Aircraft* magazine, commented that the finish was not as good as on some more expensive machines, though he found nothing to make him doubt the airworthiness of the *Cadet*. He rated the aircraft as reasonably easy to fly, with surprisingly effective ailerons.

Aircore claims a respectable performance from this single-cylinder machine, the stall speed being commendably low, while the price is a highly competitive US$3995 for a kit taking an estimated 10-20 h to build. Rigging time is quoted as 20-40 min.

We understand that two additional versions of the *Cadet*, a fully double-surfaced single-seater and a two-seater, are being designed and that the latter is likely to fly during 1985.

EXTERNAL DIMENSIONS & AREAS - Length overall 17.0 ft, 5.18 m. Height overall 8.0 ft, 2.44 m. Wing span 30.0 ft, 9.14 m. Chord 5.5 ft, 1.67 m. Dihedral 3°. Sweepback 0°. Tailplane span 7.8 ft, 2.39 m. Fin height 8.0 ft, 2.44 m. Total wing area 164 ft², 15.2 m². Total aileron area 14.0 ft², 1.30 m². Fin area 5.0 ft², 0.46 m². Rudder area 5.0 ft², 0.46 m². Tailplane area NC. Total elevator area 20.0 ft², 1.86 m². Aspect ratio 5.5/1. Wheel track 5.3 ft, 1.63 m. Wheelbase 5.5 ft, 1.68 m. Nosewheel diameter overall 10 inch, 25 cm. Main wheels diameter overall 10 inch, 25 cm.

POWER PLANT - Rotax 277 engine. Max power 28 hp at 6000 rpm. Propeller diameter and pitch 60x28 inch, 1.52x0.71 m. Quadruple V-belt reduction, ratio 2.6/1. Max static thrust 190 lb, 86 kg. Power per unit area 0.17 hp/ft², 1.8 hp/m². Fuel capacity 5.0 US gal, 4.2 Imp gal, 18.9 litre.

WEIGHTS & LOADINGS - Empty weight 247 lb, 112 kg. Max take-off weight 550 lb, 249 kg. Payload 303 lb,

137 kg. Max wing loading 3.35 lb/ft², 16.4 kg/m². Max power loading 19.6 lb/hp, 8.9 kg/hp. Load factors +4.0, -2.0 recommended; +6.0, -4.0 ultimate.

PERFORMANCE* - Max level speed 52 mph, 84 kph. Never exceed speed 65 mph, 105 kph. Max cruising speed 47 mph, 76 kph. Economic cruising speed 37 mph, 60 kph. Stalling speed 18 mph, 29 kph. Max climb rate at sea level 600 ft/min, 3.1 m/s. Min sink rate 320 ft/min at 35 mph, 1.6 m/s at 56 kph. Best glide ratio with power off 8/1 at 26 mph, 42 kph. Take-off distance 100 ft, 30 m. Landing distance 100 ft, 30 m. Service ceiling 10,000 ft, 3050 m. Range at average cruising speed 100 mile, 161 km. Noise level 62 dB at 250 ft, 75 m.

*Under the following test conditions - Airfield altitude 140 ft, 45 m. Ground temperature 58°F, 14°C. Ground pressure 1013 mB. Ground windspeed 7 mph, 11 kph. Test payload 210 lb, 95 kg.

AIRCRAFT DESIGNS

Aircraft Designs Inc, 11082 Bel Aire Court, Cuper tino, California 95014; tel (408) 255-2194. Presi dent: Martin Hollmann. Vice president: Doug Kendrick.

AIRCRAFT DESIGNS
BUMBLE BEE

(Gyroplane)

Single-seat single-engined gyroplane with three-axis control. Rotor has constant chord; conventional tail. Pitch/roll control by angling rotor, yaw control by fin-mounted rudder; control inputs through stick for pitch/roll and pedals for yaw. Two-blade rotor with laminar-section blades. Undercarriage has three wheels in tricycle formation; no suspension on nosewheel and bungee suspension on main wheels. Push-right go-right nosewheel steering connected to yaw control. Nosewheel brake. Aluminium-alloy tube airframe, with pod. Engine mounted below rotor, driving pusher propeller. Blades made from glass-fibre.

Production status: prototype.

GENERAL - Although the *Bumble Bee* is hardly what the word 'ultralight' normally conjours up, this gyroplane is undoubtedly an ultralight from the legal point of view. It meets all the current FAA ultralight requirements regarding speeds, weight and fuel capacity, and in one respect is superior to any winged machine - not only does it fall comfortably within the FAA's 27 mph (43 kph) minimum stall speed, but it is said to remain controllable right down to 5 mph (8kph) airspeed.

Moreover, like most gyroplanes, it can fly in winds that would have most ultralights firmly grounded. Aircraft Designs reckons the *Bumble Bee* is spin proof and has a control response similar to a normal three-axis ultralight. A Rotax 447 provides the power, though a Kawasaki TA440 engine has also been used.

Features include a field assembly time of only 15 min, easy folding for transport and storage, and a small pod containing a large instrument panel and fitted with a windscreen. The *Bumble Bee* is supplied as a kit with all welding and machining done, and all glass-fibre parts finished. Building time is estimated at 200-400 h. Price: US$5500.

EXTERNAL DIMENSIONS & AREAS - Length overall 12.0 ft, 3.66 m. Height overall 8.0 ft, 2.44 m. Rotor diameter 23.0 ft, 7.01 m. Chord 7.0 inch, 17 cm. Tailplane span 4.0 ft, 1.22 m. Fin height 3.0 ft, 0.91 m. Area swept by rotor 415 ft², 38.6 m². Solidity ratio 31/1. Wheel track 7.5 ft, 2.29 m. Wheelbase 5.0 ft, 1.52 m. Nosewheel diameter overall 11 inch, 28 cm. Main wheels diameter overall 16 inch, 41 cm. Other data NC.

POWER PLANT - Rotax 447 engine. Max power 40 hp at 6200 rpm. Propeller diameter and pitch 60x38 inch, 1.52x0.96 m. Gear reduction, ratio 2.9/1. Max static thrust 270 lb, 122 kg. Fuel capacity 5.0 US gal, 4.2 Imp gal, 18.9 litre.

WEIGHTS & LOADINGS - Empty weight 220 lb, 100 kg. Max take-off weight 500 lb, 227 kg. Payload 280 lb, 127 kg. Max power loading 12.5 lb/hp, 5.7 kg/hp. Load factors +3.5, -1.0 recommended; +5.3, -1.5 ultimate.

PERFORMANCE* - Max level speed 63 mph, 101 kph. Never exceed speed 80 mph, 129 kph. Max cruising speed 63 mph, 101 kph. Economic cruising speed 45 mph, 72 kph. Minimum controllable speed 5 mph, 8 kph. Max climb rate at sea level 1200 ft/min, 6.1 m/s. Min sink rate with power off 600 ft/min, 3.0 m/s at NC speed. Take-off distance 100 ft, 30 m. Landing distance 0 ft, 0 m. Service ceiling 16,000 ft, 4880 m. Range at average cruising speed 63 mile, 101 km. Noise level 90 dB at 5 ft, 1.5 m.

*Under unspecified test conditions.

AIRCRAFT DEVELOPMENT

Aircraft Development, 1326 N Westlink Boulevard, Wichita, Kansas 67212; tel (316) 722 7736. Proprietor: Richard Jimenez.

Overseas agents: none; enquiries invited.

AIRCRAFT DEVELOPMENT
EZ-1
(Three-axis)

Single-seat single-engined low-wing monoplane with conventional three-axis control. Wing has unswept leading and trailing edges, and constant chord; con-ventional tail. Pitch control by fully flying tail; yaw control by fully flying rudder; roll control by ailerons; control inputs through stick for pitch/roll and pedals for yaw. Cantilever wing; wing profile see text; 100% double-surface. Undercarriage has three wheels in tricycle formation; no suspension on nosewheel and glass-fibre suspension on main wheels. Ground steering by differential braking; castering nosewheel. Brakes on main wheels. Composite construction airframe, completely open. Engine mounted above wing, driving pusher propeller.

Production status: current, 1 built.

GENERAL - Since we wrote about the *EZ-1* in our first edition, the aircraft has progressed from design to reality, with the first example now flying.

On the *EZ-1* Richard Jimenez has pioneered a construction technique that has many people in the industry interested. Basically, portions of the machine are held together with a type of Scotch tape developed by 3M Corporation, the aluminium skin of the flying surfaces being bonded to the airframe by an extremely tough double-sided tape. Richard is very willing to send out samples of this tape, along with pieces of aluminium to try it with; in fact every one of his comprehensive information packs (US$10) contains these items to try for yourself.

3M Corporation also had a hand in the undercarriage design, supplying a special unidirectional glass-fibre material for the main-wheel suspension struts. This material tends to turn the kinetic energy from a rough landing into heat, rather than simply storing it momentarily and then rebounding the aircraft back into the air.

The *EZ-1* has a very thick wing which is designed to give plenty of lift and prevent the aircraft exceeding the

EZ-1 development: the sketch shows Richard's original concept of the machine; note how, on the finished aircraft in the photo, a tubular structure has been added behind the pilot's head.

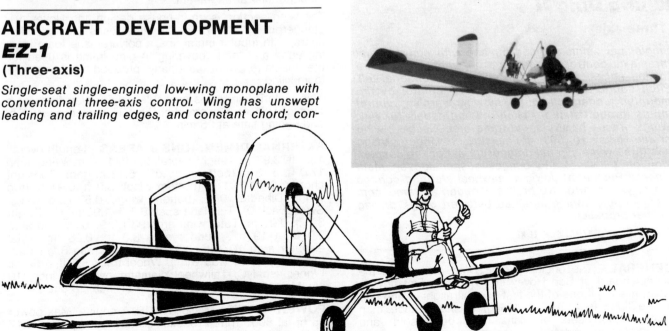

63 mph (101 kph) maximum speed limit for ultralights in the US. Large control surfaces are designed to give good control authority and are interchangeable for ease of building and maintenance. Engine was initially a 20 hp Zenoah, but larger units were being evaluated at the time of going to press.

Richard admits that building an *EZ-1* from scratch would take around 1000 h (though he will sell plans for US$100), and that on the other hand the cost would be prohibitive if the purchaser wanted all the parts and assemblies prefabricated, though this route would bring the construction time down to some 40 h. He recommends that buyers strike a happy medium between the time and money, so various degrees of assembly are offered to suit the purchaser's preference, at prices from US$3500 to US$8500. A rigging time of 10 min is claimed.

Later, Richard plans to market more sophisticated versions of he *EZ-1* dubbed the *EZ-2* and *EZ-3*.

EXTERNAL DIMENSIONS & AREAS - Length overall 17.5 ft, 5.33 m. Height overall 6.5 ft, 2.0 m. Wing span 31.0 ft, 9.45 m. Chord 4.3 ft, 1.30 m. Dihedral 5°. Sweepback 0°. Tailplane span 9.5 ft, 2.90 m. Fin height 4.3 ft, 1.30 m. Total wing area 129 ft², 12.0 m². Total aileron area 15.6 ft², 1.44 m². Rudder area 11.0 ft², 1.02 m². Total elevator area 22.0 ft², 2.04 m². Aspect ratio 7.4/1. Wheel track 3.8 ft, 1.14 m. Wheelbase 4.3 ft, 1.32 m. Nosewheel diameter overall 11 inch, 28 cm. Main wheels diameter overall 11 inch, 28 cm.

POWER PLANT - Zenoah G25B engine. Max power 20 hp at 6500 rpm. Propeller diameter and pitch 50x20 inch, 1.27x0.51 m. V-belt reduction, ratio 2.0/1. Max static thrust 130 lb, 59 kg. Power per unit area 0.16 hp/ft², 1.7 hp/m². Fuel capacity 4.3 US gal, 3.6 Imp gal, 16.3 litre.

WEIGHTS & LOADINGS - Empty weight 234 lb, 106 kg. Max take-off weight 505 lb, 229 kg. Payload 271 lb, 123 kg. Max wing loading 3.91 lb/ft², 19.1 kg/m². Max power loading 25.3 lb/hp, 11.5 kg/hp. Load factors +6.0, -3.0 recommended; +9.0, -4.5 ultimate.

PERFORMANCE* - Max level speed 50 mph, 80 kph. Never exceed speed 70 mph, 113 kph. Max cruising speed 45 mph, 72 kph. Economic cruising speed 40 mph, 64 kph. Stalling speed 25 mph, 40 kph. Max climb rate at sea level 340 ft/min, 1.7 m/s. Min sink rate NC. Best glide ratio with power off 8/1 at NC speed. Take-off distance 300 ft, 90 m. Landing distance 200 ft, 60 m. Service ceiling 9500 ft, 2900 m. Range at average cruising speed 77 mile, 124 km. Noise level NC.

*Under unspecified test conditions.

AIRCRAFT SPECIALTIES

Aircraft Specialties Co, PO Box 1074, Canyon Country, California 91351; tel (805) 252-4054. Proprietor: R W Hovey.

AIRCRAFT SPECIALTIES
Whing Ding II

(Three-axis)

Single-seat single-engined biplane with conventional three-axis control. Wings have unswept leading and trailing edges, and constant chord; conventional tail. Pitch control by fully flying tail; yaw control by fin-mounted rudder; roll control by wing warping; control inputs through stick for pitch/roll and pedals for yaw. Wings braced by struts and transverse X-cables; wing profile Hovey 10; 60% double-surface. Undercarriage has three wheels in tail-dragger formation; no suspension on tailwheel and bungee suspension on main wheels. Push-right go-right tailwheel steering connected to yaw control. No brakes. Wooden airframe, completely open. Engine mounted between wings, driving pusher propeller.

Production status: see text.

GENERAL - The original *Whing Ding* came from the design board of Bob Hovey in 1970, and first flew in 1971, making it one of the first ever ultralights - and one of the lightest, at 122 lb (55kg) finished. Since then some 14,000 sets of plans have been sold, and remarkably, an updated version of this wood, foam and fabric machine, known as the *Whing Ding II* or *WD-II* for short, is still available.

However the years have shown up its limitations, for this pioneering ultralight was designed as an off-airport fun machine, and was not intended for even limited cross-country flight, the first example having only enough fuel for half an hour or so. In practice, fuel capacity varies from builder to builder, but the figure shown below is typical.

Engines vary too - we know of one *Whing Ding* in France with a JPX PUL425 unit - but the McCulloch 101A kart engine with 3.8/1 reduction is probably the most popular arrangement.

The wing section is an in-house design, the Hovey 10, staggered by 4°. Their structure uses two wooden spars, with tubular metal ribs, a polyurethane foam leading edge and fabric covering. A pine frame is used for the fuselage, with mahogany plywood cladding and foam filling.

This historic aircraft is available only in plan form, at a cost of US$30. Construction time is quoted as 400 h, and rigging time at 25 min.

EXTERNAL DIMENSIONS & AREAS - Length overall 13.0 ft, 3.96 m. Height overall 5.3 ft, 1.63 m. Wing span 17.0 ft, 5.18 m (bottom); 17.0 ft, 5.18 m (top). Constant chord 3.0 ft, 0.91 m (bottom wing); 3.0 ft, 0.91 m (top wing). Dihedral 0.5° (bottom wing); 0.5° (top wing). Sweepback 0°. Tailplane span 6.3 ft, 1.93 m. Fin height 3.0 ft, 0.91 m. Total wing area 98 ft², 9.10 m². Fin area 2.0 ft², 0.19 m². Rudder area 3.0 ft², 0.28 m². Total elevator area 10.0 ft², 0.93 m². Aspect ratio 6.1/1 (bottom wing); 5.7/1 (top wing). Wheel track 5.0 ft, 1.52 m. Wheelbase NC. Tailwheel diameter overall 4 inch, 10 cm. Main wheels diameter overall 11 inch, 28 cm.

POWER PLANT - McCulloch 101A engine. Max power 15 hp at 8000 rpm. Propeller diameter and pitch 48x17 inch, 1.22x0.43 m. V-belt reduction, ratio 3.8/1. Max

R F Morton

This Whing Ding II *was built in France by British engineer Robin Morton, while working there for Airbus Industrie. Constructed with the UK airworthiness regulations in mind, it is rather longer (14.5 ft, 4.42 m) and heavier (194 lb, 88 kg) than most examples, and therefore will probably have the Wheeler Pixie engine shown here replaced by a more powerful unit to cope with the extra weight.*

static thrust NC. Power per unit area 0.15 hp/ft², 1.6 hp/m². Fuel capacity 0.5 US gal, 0.4 Imp gal, 2.0 litre.

WEIGHTS & LOADINGS - Empty weight 122 lb, 55 kg. Max take-off weight 310 lb, 140 kg. Payload 188 lb, 85 kg. Max wing loading 3.16 lb/ft², 15.4 kg/m². Max power loading 20.7 lb/hp, 9.3 kg/hp. Load factors +3.0, 3.0- recommended; +4.5, -4.5 ultimate.

PERFORMANCE* - Max level speed 50 mph, 80 kph. Never exceed speed 80 mph, 129 kph. Max cruising speed 40 mph, 64 kph. Economic cruising speed 35 mph, 56 kph. Stalling speed 25 mph, 40 kph. Max climb rate at sea level 300 ft/min, 1.5 m/s. Min sink rate 600 ft/min at 35 mph, 3.1 m/s at 56 kph. Best glide ratio with power off 5/1 at 35 mph, 56 kph. Take-off distance 125 ft, 40 m. Landing distance 175 ft, 55 m. Service ceiling NC. Range at average cruising speed 50 mile, 80 km. Noise level NC.

*Under unspecified test conditions.

AIRCRAFT SPECIALTIES
BETA BIRD

(Three-axis)

Single-seat single-engined high-wing monoplane with conventional three-axis control. Wing has unswept leading and trailing edges, and constant chord; conventional tail. Pitch control by elevator on tail; yaw control by fin-mounted rudder; roll control by full-span ailerons; control inputs through stick for pitch/roll and pedals for yaw. Wing braced from below by struts; wing profile Hovey BB-14; 100% double-surface. Undercarriage has three wheels in tail-dragger formation; no suspension on tailwheel and bungee suspension on main wheels. Push-right go-right tailwheel steering connected to yaw control, plus differential braking. Brakes on main wheels. Wooden airframe, completely open. Engine mounted below wing, driving pusher propeller.

Production status: see text.

GENERAL - We are bending our own rules slightly by including the *Beta Bird*, as this aircraft is too heavy to be a microlight, let alone an ultralight. However, the machine is very much in the ultralight spirit, with the pilot sitting out front in the 'bugs in the teeth' position, and moreover is directly derived from an ultralight, the

Whing Ding II. Like an ultralight, it has good short-field capabilities.

The *Beta Bird* is basically a strengthened and enlarged *Whing Ding II* with the bottom wing removed and a more powerful engine substituted. Roll control is different though, with full-span ailerons instead of wing-warping. For easy transport and storage, the wings fold. Unlike its biplane stablemate, the *Beta Bird* is not only available as plans. Bob does not supply complete kits, but material kits and some prefabricated parts can be purchased. No special tools or skills are said to be needed to build the aircraft, even from plans, which cost US$60.

EXTERNAL DIMENSIONS & AREAS - Length overall 16.0 ft, 4.88 m. Height overall 6.5 ft, 1.98 m. Wing span 25.5 ft, 7.77 m. Chord 3.5 ft, 1.07 m. Dihedral 0.5°. Sweepback 0°. Total wing area 88 ft², 8.2 m². Total aileron area 28.0 ft², 2.60 m². Fin area 3.0 ft², 0.28 m². Rudder area 6.0 ft², 0.56 m². Tailplane area 18.0 ft², 1.67 m². Total elevator area 9.0 ft², 0.84 m². Aspect ratio 7.4/1. Wheel track 5.5 ft, 1.68 m. Tailwheel diameter overall 5 inch, 13 cm. Main wheels diameter overall 16 inch, 41 cm.

POWER PLANT - Volkswagen 1600 engine. Max power 50 hp at 3000 rpm. Propeller diameter and pitch 54x24 inch, 1.37x0.61 m. No reduction. Max static thrust NC. Power per unit area 0.57 hp/ft², 6.1 hp/m². Fuel capacity 7.5 US gal, 6.3 Imp gal, 28.4 litre.

WEIGHTS & LOADINGS - Empty weight 405 lb, 184 kg. Max take-off weight 630 lb, 286 kg. Payload 225 lb, 102 kg. Max wing loading 7.16 lb/ft², 34.9 kg/m². Max power loading 12.6 lb/hp, 5.7 kg/hp. Load factors *+4.0, -1.5* recommended; +6.0, -2.3 ultimate.

PERFORMANCE* - Max level speed 85 mph, 137 kph. Never exceed speed 100 mph, 161 kph. Max cruising speed 80 mph, 129 kph. Economic cruising speed 65 mph, 105 kph. Stalling speed 45 mph, 72 kph. Max climb rate at sea level 700 ft/min, 3.6 m/s. Min sink rate 630 ft/min at 50 mph, 3.2 m/s at 80 kph. Best glide ratio with power off 7/1 at 50 mph, 80 kph. Take-off distance 250 ft, 75 m. Landing distance 250 ft, 75 m. Service ceiling NC. Range at average cruising speed 120 mile, 193 km. Noise level NC.

*Under unspecified test conditions.

AIRCRAFT SPECIALTIES
DELTA BIRD
(Three-axis)

Single-seat single-engined biplane with conventional three-axis control. Wings have unswept leading and trailing edges, and constant chord; conventional tail. Pitch control by elevator on tail; yaw control by fin-mounted rudder; roll control by full-span ailerons on top wing; control inputs through stick for pitch/roll and pedals for yaw. Wings braced by struts and transverse X-cables; wing profile NC; 100% double-surface. Undercarriage has three wheels in tail-dragger formation; axle-flex suspension on tailwheel and bungee suspension on main wheels. Push-right go-right tailwheel steering connected to yaw control. No brakes. Aluminium-alloy tube airframe, completely open. Engine mounted between wings, driving tractor propeller.

Production status: current, 100 completed.

GENERAL - First unveiled at the 1982 Oshkosh, the *Delta Bird* is Bob Hovey's entrant in the modern ultralight stakes. Gone is the traditional wood airframe of his earlier designs, and in its place comes tube and Dacron construction.

Gone too is the pusher prop, and instead the engine is mounted in tractor position on a triangular framework just ahead of the main airframe, with the exhaust tucked out of harm's way between the undercarriage legs. But the full-span ailerons of the *Beta Bird* are retained, and form the entire trailing edge of the upper wing.

Engine is the latest version of the Cuyuna twin, the ULII-02, developing 35 hp in this installation and driving through a 2.3/1 reduction.

The adoption of modern materials means that the *Delta Bird* is offered in kit as well as plan form. A kit costs US$4600, while plans can be had for US$40. Customers wanting a *Delta Bird* in kit form may obtain one from Ken Knowles Sport Aircraft or from Aircraft Spruce & Specialty Co - see separate listings for addresses.

Bob Hovey says building time from plans is 350 h, while Ken Knowles quotes 150-250 h for completion of his kit. Rigging time of a completed aircraft is 35 min.

EXTERNAL DIMENSIONS & AREAS - Length overall 15.0 ft, 4.57 m. Height overall 6.0 ft, 1.83 m. Wing span 20.2 ft, 6.16 m (bottom); 24.0 ft, 7.32 m (top). Constant

Glider Rider

chord 3.5 ft, 1.07 m (bottom wing); 3.5 ft, 1.07 m (top wing). Dihedral 0.5° (bottom wing); 0.5° (top wing). Sweepback 0°. Tailplane span 8.0 ft, 2.44 m. Fin height 3.0 ft, 0.91 m. Total wing area 152 ft^2, 14.1 m^2. Total aileron area 22.0 ft^2, 2.04 m^2. Fin area 5.0 ft^2, 0.46 m^2. Rudder area 5.0 ft^2, 0.46 m^2. Tailplane area 10.0 ft^2, 0.93 m^2. Total elevator area 10.0 ft^2, 0.93 m^2. Aspect ratio 6.0/1 (bottom wing); 6.9/1 (top wing). Wheel track 6.0 ft, 1.83 m. Wheelbase NC. Tailwheel diameter overall 4 inch, 10 cm. Main wheels diameter overall 11 inch, 28 cm.

POWER PLANT - Cuyuna ULII-02 engine. Max power 35 hp at 6000 rpm. Propeller diameter and pitch 60x27 inch, 1.52x0.69 m. V-belt reduction, ratio 2.3/1. Max static thrust NC. Power per unit area 0.23 hp/ft^2, 2.5 hp/m^2. Fuel capacity 3.5 US gal, 2.9 Imp gal, 13.2 litre.

WEIGHTS & LOADINGS - Empty weight 230 lb, 104 kg. Max take-off weight 427 lb, 194 kg. Payload 197 lb, 90 kg. Max wing loading 2.81 lb/ft^2, 13.8 kg/m^2. Max power loading 12.2 lb/hp, 5.5 kg/hp. Load factors +4.0, -4.0 recommended; +6.0, -6.0 ultimate.

PERFORMANCE* - Max level speed 48 mph, 77 kph. Never exceed speed 80 mph, 129 kph. Max cruising speed 45 mph, 72 kph. Economic cruising speed 40 mph, 64 kph. Stalling speed 26 mph, 42 kph. Max climb rate at sea level 600 ft/min, 3.1 m/s. Min sink rate 600 ft/min at 35 mph, 3.1 m/s at 56 kph. Best glide ratio with power off 5/1 at 35 mph, 56 kph. Take-off distance 125 ft, 40 m. Landing distance 175 ft, 55 m. Service ceiling NC. Range at average cruising speed 60 mile, 97 km. Noise level NC.

*Under unspecified test conditions.

AIRCRAFT SPECIALTIES
DELTA HAWK
(Three-axis)

Summary as for Delta Bird *except: Undercarriage has two wheels plus tailskid; axle-flex suspension on tailskid and bungee suspension on main wheels. Push-right go-right tailskid steering connected to yaw control; also differential braking. Brakes on main wheels. Aluminium-alloy airframe, partially enclosed.*

Production status: current, 136 completed.

GENERAL - Closely related to the *Delta Bird*, the *Delta Hawk* is Bob Hovey's answer to those who like a little more by way of creature comforts. The cockpit is partially enclosed, and to further enhance the 'real airplane' look, the fabric fueslage is taken right back to the tail, replacing the simple single-tube boom on the *Delta Bird*.

Brakes are fitted to the main wheels, capable of independent operation to augment the tailskid and rudder when manoeuvring.

The other major change is the use of the Kawasaki TA440 engine in place of the Cuyuna, the small increase in power offsetting the greater weight of the airframe. Indeed the *Delta Hawk* has markedly superior performance to the *Delta Bird*, as can be seen from the performance figures, a phenomenon probably attributable to its generally cleaner shape.

Plans for the *Delta Hawk* can be bought from Bob for US$80, for which price the buyer gets the plans for the *Delta Bird* too; build time is estimated at 450 h. As with the *Delta Bird*, those wanting a *Delta Hawk* in kit form

should contact either Ken Knowles Sport Aircraft (kit price US$5500, build time 200-300 h) or Aircraft Spruce & Specialty Co. Ready-to-fly machines can also be supplied, by arrangement with Bob Hovey.
Rigging time for the *Delta Hawk* is 35 min.

EXTERNAL DIMENSIONS & AREAS - See *Delta Bird* except: Length overall 15.6 ft, 4.75 m. Dihedral 0.25° (bottom wing); 0.25° (top wing). Wheel track 6.6 ft, 2.01 m. Wheelbase 6.3 ft, 1.91 m.

POWER PLANT - Kawasaki TA440 engine. Max power 38 hp at 6200 rpm. Propeller diameter and pitch 60x27 inch, 1.52x0.69 m. V-belt reduction, ratio 2.6/1. Max static thrust 220 lb, 100 kg. Power per unit area 0.25 hp/ft^2, 2.7 hp/m^2. Fuel capacity 3.5 US gal, 2.9 Imp gal, 13.2 litre.

WEIGHTS & LOADINGS - Empty weight 248 lb, 112 kg. Max take-off weight 453 lb, 205 kg. Payload 205 lb, 93 kg. Max wing loading 2.98 lb/ft^2, 14.5 kg/m^2. Max power loading 11.9 lb/hp, 5.4 kg/hp. Load factors +4.0, -4.0 recommended; +6.0, -6.0 ultimate.

PERFORMANCE* - Max level speed 55 mph, 88 kph. Never exceed speed 80 mph, 129 kph. Max cruising speed 50 mph, 80 kph. Economic cruising speed 45 mph, 72 kph. Stalling speed 26 mph, 42 kph. Max climb rate at sea level 700 ft/min, 3.6 m/s. Min sink rate 600 ft/min at 40 mph, 3.1 m/s at 64 kph. Best glide ratio with power off 6/1 at 40 mph, 64 kph. Take-off distance 150 ft, 45 m. Landing distance 150 ft, 45 m. Service ceiling NC. Range at average cruising speed 60 mile, 97 km. Noise level NC.

*Under unspecified test conditions.

AIRCRAFT SPECIALTIES
SUPER HAWK
(Three-axis)

Summary as Delta Bird except: Wing profile Hovey 14. Push-right go-right tailwheel steering connected to yaw control; also differential braking. Brakes on main wheels. Aluminium-alloy tube airframe, partially enclosed.

Production status: current, number completed NC.

GENERAL - Another variation on the *Delta Bird* theme is the *Super Hawk*, which unlike its stablemates has a fully aluminium-skinned airframe. This gives a superior aerodynamic performance to the *Delta Bird* and *Delta Hawk*, allowing slightly faster level flight and cruise speeds, and slower sink.
These improvements are achieved despite the substitution of a single-cylinder engine for the twins of the other aircraft, the Rotax 277 being the chosen power unit.
This top of the range machine sells through Ken Knowles Sport Aircraft at US$5619 in kit form, no assembly time being quoted. For details of plans availabilty, contact Bob Hovey.

EXTERNAL DIMENSIONS & AREAS - See *Delta Bird*.

POWER PLANT - Rotax 277 engine. Max power 28 hp at 6000 rpm. Propeller diameter and pitch 60x27 inch, 1.52x0.69 m. Gear reduction, ratio 2.25/1. Max static thrust NC. Power per unit area 0.18 hp/ft^2, 2.0 hp/m^2. Fuel capacity 3.5 US gal, 2.9 Imp gal, 13.2 litre.

WEIGHTS & LOADINGS - Empty weight 245 lb, 111 kg. Max take-off weight 485 lb, 220 kg. Payload 240 lb, 109 kg. Max wing loading 3.19 lb/ft², 15.6 kg/m². Max power loading 17.3 lb/hp, 7.9 kg/hp. Load factors +4.0, -4.0 recommended; +6.0, -6.0 ultimate.

PERFORMANCE* - Max level speed 58 mph, 93 kph. Never exceed speed 80 mph, 129 kph. Max cruising speed 55 mph, 88 kph. Economic cruising speed 45 mph, 72 kph. Stalling speed 26 mph, 42 kph. Max climb rate at sea level 700 ft/min, 3.6 m/s. Min sink rate 500 ft/min at 35 mph, 2.5 m/s at 56 kph. Best glide ratio with power off 6/1 at 35 mph, 56 kph. Take-off distance 125 ft, 40 m. Landing distance 175 ft, 55 m. Service ceiling NC. Range at average cruising speed 70 mile, 113 km. Noise level NC.

*Under unspecified test conditions.

AIRCRAFT SPRUCE & SPECIALTY

Aircraft Spruce & Specialty Co, PO Box 424, Fullerton, California 92632; tel (714) 870-7551.

AIRCRAFT SPECIALTIES
DELTA BIRD

See Aircraft Specialties.

AIRCRAFT SPECIALTIES
DELTA HAWK

See Aircraft Specialties.

CATTO *GOLDWING ST*

See Catto.

LIGHT MINIATURE AIRCRAFT
LM-1

See Light Miniature Aircraft.

SPORT FLIGHT ENGINEERING
SKY PUP

See Sport Flight Engineering.

THE AIRPLANE FACTORY

The Airplane Factory, 7111 Brandvista Avenue, PO Box 24035, Dayton, Ohio 45424; tel (513) 849-6533.

THE AIRPLANE FACTORY
EINDECKER
(Three-axis)

Single-seat single-engined mid-wing monoplane with conventional three-axis control. Wing has unswept leading and trailing edges, and constant chord; cruciform tail. Pitch control by elevator on tail; yaw control by fin-mounted rudder; roll control by one-third span spoilers; control inputs through stick for pitch/roll and pedals for yaw. Wing braced from above by kingpost and cables, from below by cables; 100% double-surface. Undercarriage has three wheels in tail-dragger formation. Push-right go-right tailwheel steering connected to yaw control. Steel-tube airframe, partially enclosed. Engine mounted at wing height, driving tractor propeller. Other details NC.

Production status: current, number completed NC.

GENERAL - Of all the replicas available on the US ultralight market, the *Eindecker* is perhaps the most faithful reproduction of all, not least because it is nearly the same size as the original - fifteen sixteenths of the size, to be exact. All the cables and bracing are arranged just as on the original, and of course the decals and colours are faithfully copied.
Sometimes called *Das Ultralighterfighter,* it is modelled on the Fokker *Eindecker* of World War I fame, but under the skin the structure is modern enough, with a chrome-moly steel tubular airframe and aluminium-alloy tubing for the wings' leading and trailing edges. The designers, Walter and Doug Hoy, already had 10 years' experience of home-built supplies manufacturing when they turned constructor themselves, and perhaps because of this they have paid particular attention to ease of assembly. For instance, the Dacron wing covering is supplied pre-sewn, so that it slides on like a sock, contributing to what is claimed to be genuine 40 h construction time.
When exhibited at Oshkosh in 1983 the machine drew quite a few stares, but the public had to wait until the following year's Sun 'n Fun to see it fly. Since then it has undergone one or two changes - acquiring a steerable tailwheel instead of a skid for instance - but has retained every bit of its nostalgic appeal.
Price: US$5500 in kit form; options are a fake machine gun and hub caps in the original style.

EXTERNAL DIMENSIONS & AREAS - Length overall 20.5 ft, 6.25 m. Height overall 8.0 ft, 2.44 m. Wing span 36.0 ft, 10.97 m. Constant chord 4.3 ft, 1.30 m. Sweepback 0°. Total wing area 154 ft², 14.3 m². Aspect ratio 8.4/1. Other data NC.

POWER PLANT - Rotax 277 engine. Max power 28 hp at 6200 rpm. Propeller diameter and pitch 72x33 inch,

Glider Rider

Glider Rider

Eindecker *at Oshkosh '83 and (inset) in the air, fitted with optional hub caps.*

1.83x0.84 m. Gear reduction, ratio 2.6/1. Max static thrust 275 lb, 125 kg. Power per unit area 0.18 hp/ft^2, 2.0 hp/m^2. Fuel capacity 4.4 US gal, 3.7 Imp gal, 16.7 litre.

WEIGHTS & LOADINGS - Empty weight 251 lb, 114 kg. Max take-off weight 500 lb, 227 kg. Payload 249 lb, 113 kg. Max wing loading 3.25 lb/ft^2, 15.9 kg/m^2. Max power loading 17.9 lb/hp, 8.1 kg/hp. Load factors +4.0, -2.0 recommended; +6.0, -3.0 ultimate.

PERFORMANCE* - Max level speed 63 mph, 101 kph. Never exceed speed 70 mph, 113 kph. Cruising speed 50 mph, 80 kph. Stalling speed 23 mph, 37 kph. Max climb rate at sea level 500 ft/min, 2.5 m/s. Best glide ratio with power off 7.8/1 at NC speed. Take-off distance 50 ft, 15 m. Landing distance 75 ft, 23 m. Other data NC.

*Under unspecified test conditions.

AIR TECH

Air Tech Inc, Rt 4 Box 48, Vacherie, Louisiana 70090; tel (504) 265-3075.

AIR TECH *SS/Z*

(Three-axis)

Single-seat single-engined high-wing monoplane with unconventional three-axis control. Wing has unswept leading and trailing edges, and constant chord; cruciform tail. Pitch control by elevator on tail; yaw control by fully flying rudder; roll control by spoilerons; control inputs through stick for pitch/yaw and pedals for roll. Wing braced from below by struts;

wing profile NC; single-surface. Undercarriage has three wheels in tail-dragger formation; suspension NC on tailwheel and bungee suspension on main wheels. Ground steering by differential braking; castoring tailwheel. Brakes on main wheels. Aluminium-alloy tube airframe, completely open. Engine mounted at wing height, driving pusher propeller.

Production status: current, 10 completed.

GENERAL - While obviously borrowing many ideas from the famous *Quicksilver MX,* not least its unconventional three-axis control with pedals controlling spoilerons, this straightforward tube-and-Dacron ultralight is rather more than just another *Quicksilver* clone.
True, the wing design, tail design and engine location clearly show the Eipper heritage, but three things in particular distinguish the *SS/Z* from straightforward imitations. Firstly, the designer has dispensed with the kingpost and cable bracing in favour of struts, to the benefit of both portability and aerodynamics. Secondly, it is a taildragger, and thirdly it sports curved tubes in front of the pilot - rather in the style of a Rotec *Rally* - to protect his or her feet in the event of a mishap.
Unconventional three-axis control is still a subject of controversy among microlight pilots. Some maintain that the controls should be standardised in the conventional fashion to prevent possible confusion, while others point out that using the pedals for roll control allows both spoilerons to be operated simultaneously as air brakes, which can be useful if the pilot is trying to drop quickly into a tight field.
The *SS/Z* is sold ready to fly (US$5495) or as a 30 h kit (US$4995), fitted with either a Cuyuna ULII-02 or a

Rotax 377, the latter version being detailed below. Prices include brakes and wheel spats. Rigging time is 30 min single-handed, or 15 min with an assistant.
Air Tech, incidentally, is closely connected with the Ultra Classics company which we list separately.

EXTERNAL DIMENSIONS & AREAS - Length overall 18.0 ft, 5.49 m. Height overall 6.5 ft, 1.98 m. Wing span 30.0 ft, 9.14 m. Constant chord 5.0 ft, 1.52 m. Dihedral 5°. Sweepback 0°. Tailplane span 9.0 ft, 2.74 m. Rudder height NC. Total wing area 150 ft^2, 13.9 m^2. Total spoileron area NC. Rudder area 15.0 ft^2, 1.39 m^2. Tailplane area 18.0 ft^2, 1.67 m^2. Total elevator area 14.0 ft^2, 1.30 m^2. Aspect ratio 6.0/1. Wheel track 12.0 ft, 3.66 m. Wheelbase 5.0 ft, 1.52 m. Tailwheel diameter overall 5 inch, 13 cm. Main wheels diameter overall 12 inch, 30 cm.

POWER PLANT - Rotax 377 engine. Max power 38 hp at 6200 rpm. Propeller diameter and pitch 56x30 inch, 1.42x0.76 m. V-belt reduction, ratio 2.0/1. Max static thrust 209 lb, 95 kg. Power per unit area 0.25 hp/ft^2, 2.7 hp/m^2. Fuel capacity 4.5 US gal, 3.8 Imp gal, 17.0 litre.

WEIGHTS & LOADINGS - Empty weight 251 lb, 114 kg. Max take-off weight 500 lb, 227 kg. Payload 249 lb, 113 kg. Max wing loading 3.33 lb/ft^2, 16.3 kg/m^2. Max power loading 13.2 lb/hp, 6.0 kg/hp. Load factors +6.0, -4.0 recommended; +8.0, -6.0 ultimate.

PERFORMANCE* - Max level speed 60 mph, 97 kph. Never exceed speed 78 mph, 126 kph. Max cruising speed 50 mph, 80 kph. Economic cruising speed 43 mph, 69 kph. Stalling speed 22 mph, 35 kph. Max climb rate at sea level 680 ft/min, 3.5 m/s. Min sink rate NC. Best glide ratio with power off 8/1 at 24 mph, 39 kph. Take-off distance 50 ft, 15 m. Landing distance 70 ft, 20 m. Service ceiling 12,000 ft, 3650 m. Range at average cruising speed 120 mile, 193 km. Noise level NC.

*Under the following test conditions - Test payload 205 lb, 93 kg. Other data NC.

AMERICAN AIRCRAFT

American Aircraft Inc, 4310 Rankin Lane NE, Albuquerque, New Mexico 87107; tel (505) 822-1419.

European, African and Asian agent: Sonaca (see Belgian section).

AMERICAN AIRCRAFT *FALCON*
(Three-axis)

Single-seat single-engined high-wing monoplane with conventional three-axis control. Wing has swept back leading and trailing edges, and tapering chord; no tail, canard wing. Pitch control by elevator on canard; yaw control by tip rudders; roll control by 66%-span ailerons; control inputs through stick for pitch/roll and pedals for yaw. Wing braced from below by struts; wing profile NACA; 100% double-surface. Under carriage has three wheels in tricycle formation with retractable front wheel; no suspension on nosewheel and torsion-bar suspension on main wheels. Push-right go-right nosewheel steering connected to yaw control. Nosewheel brake. Composite-construction airframe, partially enclosed (total enclosure optional). Engine mounted below wing, driving pusher propeller.

Production status: current, number completed NC.

GENERAL - In an industry where all too often a product is rushed into production before significant air experience has been gained, the *Falcon* is remarkable for the length of its gestation period. Although we are

Despite the logo on the wing, this is actually an American Falcon *rather than the Belgian version, being one of the machines exported to Sonaca for initial evaluation.*

uncertain about the date that Larry Newman and his colleagues first put pencil to drawing board, the aircraft was certainly undergoing test flights as long ago as 1982, with a promise of production the following year.

At that time the design was the property of American Aerolights, manufacturers of the famous *Eagle* range, and was envisaged as the the company's entrant in the high-tech high-performance end of the market, complementing the slow, simple, *Eagle.* However, following legal battles over the design rights to the latter, American Aerolights stopped trading and Larry set up a new company, American Aircraft, to concentrate on the *Falcon*, production of the *Eagle* shifting to the Italian firm Ultrasport.

All these changes have certainly not helped the *Falcon's* development programme, but it is now in series production at last and available for US$7995 ready to fly. It is an interesting design, using a fuselage constructed of a Kevlar/glass-fibre sandwich, with carbon-fibre reinforcement at stress points. Stringers are styrofoam in an epoxy matrix, while the wings have a 2024T3 aluminium-alloy D-tube with internal ribs, the ribs proper being of styrofoam with alloy capstrips. Tedlar covers all the flying surfaces.

A recent modification is the addition of a protective plate around the aperture of the retractable nosewheel, to minimise damage if the pilot forgets to lower the nosewheel on landing.

For the European, African and Asian markets, the *Falcon* is manufactured to a somewhat different specification by Sonaca (see Belgian section). The Belgian version is dimensionally and mechanically the same (though the very latest versions use a larger engine), but has a number of structural modifications in line with European airworthiness standards. The load factors we quote below are as released by American Aircraft, but we must point out that they do not appear to agree with the results of tests at Sonaca, as described in our Belgian section.

In the works at American Aircraft is a two-seat version of this machine, but no details have been released; a two-seater derivative is also being built at Ultrasport (see Italian section).

EXTERNAL DIMENSIONS & AREAS - Length overall 14.2 ft, 4.34 m. Height overall 5.5 ft, 1.67 m. Wing span 36.0 ft, 10.97 m. Chord at root 5.4 ft, 1.65 m. Chord at tip 2.5 ft, 0.76 m. Dihedral 1.5°. Sweepback 15°. Canard span 12.0 ft, 3.66 m. Canard chord 1.5 ft, 0.45 m. Rudder height NC. Total wing area 180.3 ft², 16.76 m². Main wing area 157.8 ft², 14.67 m². Canard area 22.5 ft², 2.09 m². Total aileron area 11.0 ft², 1.02 m². Total rudder area 8.2 ft², 0.76 m². Total elevator area 11.0 ft², 1.02 m². Aspect ratio (of main wing) 8.2/1. Wheel track 5.0 ft, 1.52 m. Wheelbase 6.2 ft, 1.90 m. Nosewheel diameter overall 9 inch, 22 cm. Main wheels diameter overall 10 inch, 27 cm.

POWER PLANT - Rotax 277 engine. Max power 26 hp at 6500 rpm. Propeller diameter and pitch 54x34 inch, 1.38x0.86 m (3-blade). Gear reduction, ratio 2.6/1. Max static thrust 150 lb, 68 kg. Power per unit area 0.14 hp/ft², 1.6 hp/m². Fuel capacity 5.0 US gal, 4.2 Imp gal, 19.0 litre.

WEIGHTS & LOADINGS - Empty weight 265 lb, 120 kg. Max take-off weight 530 lb, 240 kg. Payload 265 lb, 120 kg. Max wing loading 2.94 lb/ft², 14.3 kg/m². Max power loading 20.4 lb/hp, 9.2 kg/hp. Load factors +5.8, -2.9 design; NC ultimate.

PERFORMANCE* - Max level speed 63 mph, 101 kph. Never exceed speed 75 mph, 121 kph. Max cruising speed 55 mph, 88 kph. Economic cruising speed 45 mph, 72 kph. Stalling speed 27 mph, 43 kph. Max climb rate at sea level 650 ft/min, 3.3 m/s. Min sink rate 250 ft/min at 35 mph, 1.3 m/s at 56 kph. Best glide ratio with power off 15/1 at 45 mph, 72 kph. Take-off distance 200 ft, 61 m. Landing distance 250 ft, 76 m. Service ceiling 15,000 ft, 4570 m. Range at average cruising speed** 121 mile, 195 km. Noise level NC.

*Under the following test conditions - Airfield altitude 0 ft, 0 m. Ground temperature 59°F, 15°C. Ground pressure 1013 mB. Ground windspeed 0 mph, 0 kph. Test payload 200 lb, 91 kg.

**With 15 min reserve remaining.

AMERICAN AIR TECHNOLOGY

American Air Technology, 1290 Bodega Avenue, Petaluma, California 94952; tel (707) 762-1800; tx 287316 HOM. President: William Mittendorf. Vice presidents: Sam W Lloyd and Craig Catto. General manager: Sam Replin.

AMERICAN AIR TECHNOLOGY *SOLO*

(Three-axis)

Single-seat single-engined high-wing monoplane with conventional three-axis control. Wing has unswept leading edge and unswept/swept forward trailing edge (see text); constant/tapering chord (see text); conventional tail. Pitch control by elevator on tail; yaw control by fin-mounted rudder; roll control by half-span ailerons; control inputs through yoke for pitch/roll and pedals for yaw. Wing braced from below by struts; wing profile Liebeck; 100% double-surface. Undercarriage has three wheels in tricycle formation; axle-flex suspension on

nosewheel and glass-fibre suspension on main wheels. Push-right go-right nosewheel steering connected to yaw control. Nosewheel brake. Composite-construction airframe, totally enclosed, with door. Engine mounted below wing, driving tractor propeller.

Production status: prototype.

GENERAL - Craig Catto, designer of the all composite *Goldwing,* has continued in the foam and fibre tradition with this very Cessna-looking *Solo* ultralight. In fact it is so Cessna-looking that at the 1984 EAA convention at Oshkosh, Wisconsin, one of the air traffic controllers in the tower kept trying to raise the *Solo* and give it landing instructions, not realising that it was a non-radio aircraft just flying around with the rest of the ultralight crowd! Construction of the *Solo* incorporates various foam cores with Kevlar and epoxy coverings. The wing is unusual for an ultralight in that its inboard part is of constant chord, while the outboard tapers, thanks to a sweep forward by the trailing edge. Conventional three-axis controls are used, the twist being that instead of a joystick a yoke is used for elevator and ailerons. The *Solo* is clearly and unashamedly out to get the general aviation pilots into its seat.

With an empty weight nudging right on the ultralight limit, the *Solo* appears to be a sturdy craft and should be able to handle winds that would keep other ultralights on the ground. Power comes from the popular Rotax 277 with gear reduction.

Some of Craig Catto's earlier designs have been available as kits, but not so the *Solo,* which is sold in fully built-up form only, at a price of US$10,950.

EXTERNAL DIMENSIONS & AREAS - Length overall 19.5 ft, 5.94 m. Height overall 7.9 ft, 2.41 m. Wing span 30.0 ft, 9.14 m. Chord at root 4.6 ft, 1.40 m. Chord at tip 3.0 ft, 0.91 m. Dihedral 2°. Sweepback 0°. Tailplane span 7.9 ft, 2.41 m. Fin height 7.9 ft, 2.41 m. Total wing area 128 ft², 11.9 m². Total aileron area 12.0 ft², 1.11 m². Fin area 10.0 ft², 0.93 m². Rudder area 9.0 ft², 0.84 m². Tailplane area 14.0 ft², 1.30 m². Total elevator area 12.0 ft², 1.11 m². Aspect ratio 7.0/1. Wheel track 6.6 ft, 2.01 m. Wheelbase 7.0 ft, 2.13 m. Nosewheel diameter overall 12 inch, 30 cm. Main wheels diameter overall 12 inch, 30 cm.

POWER PLANT - Rotax 277 engine. Max power 27 hp at 6250 rpm. Propeller diameter and pitch 60x30 inch, 1.52x0.76 m. Gear reduction, ratio 2.6/1. Max static thrust 190 lb, 86 kg. Power per unit area 0.21 hp/ft², 2.3 hp/m². Fuel capacity 5.0 US gal, 4.2 Imp gal, 18.9 litre.

WEIGHTS & LOADINGS - Empty weight 253 lb, 115 kg. Max take-off weight 500 lb, 227 kg. Payload 247 lb, 112 kg. Max wing loading 3.91 lb/ft², 19.1 kg/m². Max power loading 18.5 lb/hp, 8.4 kg/hp. Load factors +3.0, -1.0 recommended; +8.0, -3.5 ultimate.

PERFORMANCE* - Max level speed 62 mph, 100 kph. Never exceed speed 85 mph, 137 kph. Max cruising speed 55 mph, 88 kph. Economic cruising speed 50 mph, 80 kph. Stalling speed 27 mph, 43 kph. Max climb rate at sea level 640 ft/min, 3.3 m/s. Min sink rate 270 ft/min at 34 mph, 1.4 m/s at 55 kph. Best glide ratio with power off 12/1 at 40 mph, 64 kph. Take-off distance 90 ft, 27 m. Landing distance 80 ft, 24 m. Service ceiling NC (depends on carburettor jetting). Range at average cruising speed 125 mile, 201 km. Noise level NC.

*Under the following test conditions - Airfield altitude 0 ft, 0 m. Ground temperature 59°F, 15°C. Ground pressure 1013 mB. Ground windspeed 0 mph, 0 kph. Test payload 247 lb, 112 kg.

AMERICAN AIR TECHNOLOGY
DUAL A
(Three-axis)

Side-by-side two-seat single-engined high-wing monoplane with conventional three-axis control. Wing has swept back leading and swept forward trailing edges, and tapering chord; flaps fitted; conventional tail. Pitch control by elevator on tail; yaw control by fin-mounted rudder; roll control by half-span ailerons; control inputs through stick for pitch/roll and pedals for yaw. Wing braced from below by struts; wing profile NC; 100% double-surface. Undercarriage has three wheels in tricycle formation; coil-spring suspension on nosewheel and glass-fibre suspension on main wheels. Push-right go-right nosewheel steering connected to yaw control; also differential braking. Brakes on main wheels. Composite-construction airframe, totally enclosed, with doors. Engine mounted below wing, driving tractor propeller.

Production status: prototype.

GENERAL - The *Dual A* and *Dual B* are basically two-seat derivatives of the *Solo,* but their design has been more than a scaling up operation. The wing shape is quite different, for example, while the aircraft are noticeably better equipped in the suspension and braking departments. Also, the control yoke of the *Solo* is abandoned in favour of a joystick.

The difference between the two is confined to the engine, a Rotax 532 for the *Dual A* and a Continental 0-200 for the *Dual B.* At the time of going to press, the aircraft are both in prototype form and we have little data on the Rotax-powered machine. In fact both these aircraft are strictly speaking too heavy for this book, and would not have been included were it not for their close relationship with the ultralight *Solo.* The Continental-powered machine is well above the microlight let alone the ultralight weight limit, and although Craig Catto has not released a weight for the Rotax version, it too can hardly fail to exceed the magic 331 lb (150 kg).

Like the *Solo,* the two-seaters are sold only in fully built-up form. Prices depend on specification, but range from US$15,000-17,000 for the *Dual A,* and from US$13,500-20,000 for the *Dual B.*

EXTERNAL DIMENSIONS & AREAS - Length overall NC. Height overall 8.3 ft, 2.53 m. Wing span 35.5 ft, 10.82 m. Chord at root 5.0 ft, 1.52 m. Chord at tip 3.5 ft, 1.07 m. Dihedral 2°. Sweepback 1°. Tailplane span 8.0 ft, 2.44 m. Fin height 4.0 ft, 1.22 m. Total wing area 140 ft², 13.0 m². Total aileron area 13.0 ft², 1.21 m². Fin area 12.0 ft², 3.66 m². Rudder area 5.0 ft², 0.46 m². Tailplane area 12.0 ft², 3.66 m². Total elevator area 7.0 ft², 0.65 m². Aspect ratio 9.0/1. Wheel track 7.4 ft, 2.26 m. Wheelbase 6.5 ft, 1.98 m. Nosewheel diameter overall 16 inch, 41 cm. Main wheels diameter overall 16 inch, 41 cm.

POWER PLANT - Rotax 532 engine. Other data NC.

WEIGHTS & LOADINGS - NC.

PERFORMANCE - NC.

AMERICAN AIR TECHNOLOGY
DUAL B
(Three-axis)

Summary as Dual A.

Production status: prototype.

GENERAL - See *Dual A.*

EXTERNAL DIMENSIONS & AREAS - See *Dual A* except: Length overall 23.3 ft, 7.10 m.

POWER PLANT - Continental 0-200 engine. Max power 100 hp at 2700 rpm. Propeller diameter and pitch 68xNC inch, 1.73xNC m. No reduction. Max static thrust NC. Power per unit area 0.71 hp/ft^2, 7.7 hp/m^2. Fuel capacity 30.0 US gal, 25.0 Imp gal, 113.6 litre.

WEIGHTS & LOADINGS - Empty weight 650 lb, 295 kg. Max take-off weight 1250 lb, 567 kg. Payload 600 lb, 272 kg. Max wing loading 8.93 lb/ft^2, 43.6 kg/m^2. Max power loading 12.5 lb/hp, 5.67 kg/hp. Load factors +6.8, -3.4 recommended; +10.2, -5.2 ultimate.

PERFORMANCE* - Max level speed 147 mph, 237 kph. Never exceed speed 182 mph, 293 kph. Max cruising speed 140 mph, 225 kph. Economic cruising speed 130 mph, 209 kph. Stalling speed 43 mph, 69 kph. Max climb rate at sea level 800 ft/min, 4.1 m/s. Min sink rate 500 ft/min at 56 mph, 2.5 m/s at 90 kph. Best glide ratio with power off 12/1 at 60 mph, 97 kph. Take-off distance 200 ft, 60 m. Landing distance 200 ft, 60 m. Service ceiling 14,500 ft, 4400 m. Range at average cruising speed 840 mile, 1352 km. Noise level NC.

*Under the following test conditions - Airfield altitude 0 ft, 0 m. Ground temperature 59°F, 15°C. Ground Pressure 1013 mB. Ground windspeed 0 mph, 0 kph. Test payload 600 lb, 272 kg.

AMERICAN BALLOON CO

American Balloon Co, 8220 Cooper Street, Alexandria, Virginia 22309; tel (703) 780 5572.

AMERICAN BALLOON CO
YANKEE DOODLE
(Hot-air balloon)

Single-seat hot-air balloon. Height control by temperature of contained air, other controls NC. Envelope bracing NC. No undercarriage. No ground steering. No brakes. Aluminium-alloy tube chair. No engine. Envelope made from nylon ripstop fabric.

Production status: current, number completed NC.

GENERAL - Announced in early 1984, the *Yankee Doodle* is the first venture into ultralight-legal ballooning by the American Balloon Co, which already produces a much bigger model, the *Americana.* The ultralight is of similar design, featuring a Para-Rip deflation vent, and can take a 225 lb (102 kg) pilot aloft while not exceeding an envelope temperature of 200°F, even on an 80°F day (93°C, 27°C).

The basket is of aluminium-alloy, without welds, and provides a rigid support for the burner plus a shock-insulated mount for the fuel tank. Price: NC.

EXTERNAL DIMENSIONS, AREAS & VOLUMES - Volume fully inflated 30,000 ft^3, 259 m^3. Other data NC.

POWER PLANT - Propane burner, max output 10.0M BTU/h, 10.6M kJ/h. Specific output NC. Fuel capacity 10.0 US gal, 8.3 Imp gal, 38.0 litre.

WEIGHTS & LOADINGS - Max pilot weight 225 lb, 102 kg. Other data NC.

PERFORMANCE - NC.

AMERICAN MICROFLIGHT

American Microflight Inc, 7654 E Acoma, Scottsdale, Arizona 85260; tel (602) 951-9772. President: William G Sadler.

AMERICAN MICROFLIGHT
SADLER VAMPIRE
(Three-axis)

Single-seat single-engined mid-wing monoplane with conventional three-axis control. Wing has unswept leading and trailing edges, and constant chord; flaps fitted; two-fin tail. Pitch control by elevator on tail; yaw control by fin-mounted rudders; roll control by 30% span ailerons; control inputs through stick for pitch/roll and pedals for yaw. Cantilever wing; wing profile NACA 63$_3$-218A; 100% double-surface. Undercarriage has three wheels in tricycle formation; rubber suspension on all wheels. Push-right go-right nosewheel steering connected to yaw control. Nosewheel brake. Aluminium-alloy tube airframe, partially enclosed (total enclosure optional). Engine mounted at wing height, driving pusher propeller.6061-T6 aluminium tubes, 2024 alclad skin, glass-fibre nose.

Production status: current, 25 completed.

GENERAL - In the mid '50s, Bill Sadler built and sold customised racing cars, and this racing heritage can still be seen in his *Sadler Vampire* ultralight, the lines of which remind one of the British De Havilland *Vampire* jet fighter of the same era.

One of the very few all-metal ultralights, the *Vampire* uses conventional aircraft aluminium materials and construction processes, the result being a solid machine that is stressed for more than 6g. A glass-fibre nose is the only non-metal part, and streamlines the airframe nicely, along with the Lexan canopy which is normally fitted.

The aluminium skin of the flying surfaces is bonded in place, with strategically placed rivets added to guard against peeling. This is not a constructional technique that lends itself to simple homebuilding, so not surprisingly the aircraft is only available ready to fly. Every *Sadler Vampire* comes with a serialised manual of its manufacturing history, complete with dates, builders' names, and a check-off list.

If you're a beginner or a non-pilot, Bill Sadler won't sell you one, as the *Sadler Vampire* is definitely not an

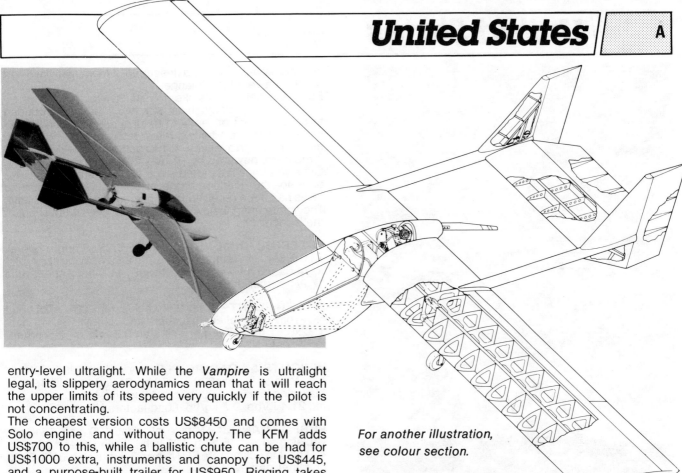

Hal Adkins

entry-level ultralight. While the *Vampire* is ultralight legal, its slippery aerodynamics mean that it will reach the upper limits of its speed very quickly if the pilot is not concentrating.

The cheapest version costs US$8450 and comes with Solo engine and without canopy. The KFM adds US$700 to this, while a ballistic chute can be had for US$1000 extra, instruments and canopy for US$445, and a purpose-built trailer for US$950. Rigging takes only 10 min.

In enclosed KFM-engined form particularly, the aircraft has very good performance, but nevertheless Bill Sadler is working on a thicker-skinned, bigger-engined version with full-span ailerons, said to be capable of over 125 mph (201 kph) while retaining landing and take-off speeds in the 30-40 mph range (48-64 kph). Take-off and landing distances should be 200-300 ft (60-90 m) and fuel economy is said to be excellent. This version will be fully aerobatic, with recommended load factors of +9g, -9g, and ultimate figures of +12g, -12g.

Data below refers to the Solo-engined machine; where different, figures for the KFM version are shown in parentheses.

EXTERNAL DIMENSIONS & AREAS - Length overall 17.5 ft, 5.33 m. Height overall 4.5 ft, 1.37 m. Wing span 28.0 ft, 8.53 m. Constant chord 4.2 ft, 1.27 m. Dihedral 0.78°. Sweepback 0°. Tailplane span 5.0 ft, 1.52 m. Total wing area 116 ft^2, 10.8 m^2. Aspect ratio 6.8/1. Other data NC.

POWER PLANT - Solo 210 cc (KFM 107ER) engine. Max power 20 (22) hp at 7000 (6000) rpm. Propeller diameter and pitch 50x24 (50x27) inch, 1.27x0.61 (1.27x0.69) m. V-belt reduction, ratio 2.4/1 (2.1/1). Max static thrust 130 (150) lb, 59 (68) kg. Power per unit area 0.17 (0.19) hp/ft^2, 1.9 (2.0) hp/m^2. Fuel capacity 4.5 US gal, 3.8 Imp gal, 17.0 litre.

WEIGHTS & LOADINGS - Empty weight 245 (253) lb, 111 (115) kg. Max take-off weight 495 (503) lb, 224 (228) kg. Payload 250 lb, 113 kg. Max wing loading 4.27 (4.34) lb/ft^2, 20.7 (21.1) kg/m^2. Max power loading 24.8 (22.9) lb/hp, 11.2 (10.4) kg/hp. Load factors +6.0, -6.0 recommended; +8.0, -8.0 ultimate.

PERFORMANCE* - Max level speed 63 mph, 101 kph. Never exceed speed 100 mph, 161 kph. Max cruising

For another illustration, see colour section.

speed 60 mph, 97 kph. Economic cruising speed 55 mph, 88 kph. Stalling speed 27 mph, 43 kph. Max climb rate at sea level 400 (600) ft/min, 2.0 (3.1) m/s. Min sink rate 200 ft/min at 40 mph, 1.0 m/s at 64 kph. Best glide ratio with power off 14/1 at 45 mph, 72 kph. Take-off distance 300 ft, 90 m. Landing distance 300 ft, 90 m. Service ceiling 12,000 ft, 3660 m. Range at average cruising speed 200 mile, 322 km. Noise level NC.

AMERICAN MICROFLIGHT
SADLER VAMPIRE TRAINER
(Three-axis)

Summary similar to Sadler Vampire *except: Side-by-side two-seater.*

Production status: prototype.

GENERAL - First shown at the Los Angeles Recreational Aircraft Expo '84, this two-seater version of the *Sadler Vampire* was still in prototype form as we went to press and little information was available. The all metal wing construction of the solo machine is retained, and to cope with the higher payload a Zenoah G50 engine is installed. No price has yet been quoted.

EXTERNAL DIMENSIONS & AREAS - NC.

POWER PLANT - Zenoah G50 engine. Other data NC.

WEIGHTS & LOADINGS - NC.

PERFORMANCE - NC.

Glider Rider

APPLEBAY

Zia-Applebay, 2111 Commercial Street NE, Albuquerque, New Mexico 87102. Proprietor: George Applebay.

APPLEBAY *ZIA*
(Three-axis)

Single-seat single-engined high-wing monoplane with conventional three-axis control. Wing has swept back leading edge, swept forward trailing edge, and tapering chord; two-fin tail. Pitch control by elevator on tail; yaw control by fin-mounted rudders; roll control NC; control inputs through stick for pitch/roll and pedals for yaw. Cantilever wing; wing profile NC; 100% double-surface. Undercarriage has three wheels in tricycle formation. Composite-construction airframe, totally enclosed. Engine mounted at wing height, driving pusher propeller. Other details NC.

Production status: see text.

GENERAL - George Applebay gave us a nasty fright when he redesigned his *Zia* motorglider. Originally conceived as a canard machine with tip rudders and no tail, we featured it thus in our first edition, only to read reports after we had gone to press of a *Zia* that bore no resemblance what-

soever to the one we had described. It looked as if we had dropped a very large clanger.

But there was no mistake. In mid '83 George showed a totally redesigned machine, with two-fin tail and intended to be sold in kit or ready to fly form as an experimental-category aircraft. After two years' development and various different design avenues, he had settled for the design pictured here, powered by a Rotax 277.

Quite what has happened since then we are not sure. No price for the machine has ever been announced, an no news has been received from the company for some time. The information below is that which was published at the launch.

EXTERNAL DIMENSIONS & AREAS - Length overall 18.0 ft, 5.49 m. Height overall 5.7 ft, 2.59 m. Wing span 46.0 ft, 14.02 m. Total wing area 118 ft², 11.0 m². Aspect ratio 17.9/1. Other data NC.

POWER PLANT - Rotax 277 engine. Max power 28 hp at NC rpm. Propeller diameter and pitch 52x24 inch, 1.32x0.61 m. Power per unit area 0.24 hp/ft², 2.5 hp/m². Other data NC.

WEIGHTS & LOADINGS - Empty weight 195 lb, 88 kg. Max take-off weight 600 lb, 272 kg. Payload 405 lb, 184 kg. Max wing loading 5.08 lb/ft², 24.7 kg/m². Max power loading 21.4 lb/hp, 9.7 kg/hp. Load factors NC.

PERFORMANCE* - Max level speed 100 mph, 161 kph. Cruising speed 75 mph, 121 kph. Stalling speed 26 mph, 42 kph. Max climb rate 650 ft/min, 3.3 m/s at 7000 ft, 2130 m. Other data NC.

*Under unspecified test conditions.

ATLANTIS

Atlantis Aviation Inc, 4230 Hoff Road, Bellingham, Washington 98225; tel (206) 733-4986.

ATLANTIS
BABY CHICKEN HAWK 250
(Three-axis)

Single-seat single-engined high-wing monoplane with conventional three-axis control. Wing has unswept leading and trailing edges, and constant chord; conventional tail. Pitch control by elevator on tail; yaw control by fin-mounted rudder; roll control by 70% span ailerons; control inputs through stick for pitch/ roll and pedals for yaw. Wing braced from above by kingpost and cables, from below by cables; wing profile NC; 100% double-surface. Undercarriage has three wheels in tricycle formation; no suspension. Push-right go-right nosewheel steering connected to yaw control. No brakes. Aluminium-alloy tube airframe, completely open. Engine mounted at wing height, driving pusher propeller.

Production status: current, see text for number completed.

GENERAL - Not widely advertised or visible to the public, the *Chicken Hawk* range of ultralights offers simple but competitive machines at reasonable prices - due, the company says, to not having to carry a large advertising budget. Atlantis is one of the USA's smaller manufacturers, with only 11 aircraft produced to date, and no indication available about how this is distributed among the company's range of models.

The *Baby Chicken Hawk 250* is the simplest of the three, a straightforward tube-and-Dacron machine using a direct drive Zenoah engine of 250 cc. Originally advertised as a two-axis machine with ailerons as an option, three-axis control has been standard since mid-1984. Wing design follows normal ultralight practice, with two rigging bays, the only unusual feature being the near vertical strut in front of the pilot, which meets the wing keel tube at approximately right angles to provide a forward attachment point for the rigging wires.

Aircraft-standard hardware is used throughout, with 0.5 inch (13 mm) material for the wing drag tubes and stainless steel for the rudder and elevator controls. Dacron weight is 3.9 oz throughout.

The cheapest way to buy a *Baby Chicken Hawk 250* is as a kit, which costs US$3595 including a 4 inch (10 cm) military-type safety belt, nylon wheels with sealed bearings, and three instruments - chtg, tachometer, and ASI/compass. All the sails come factory sewed and virtually all parts are cut to size, with some predrilled. With the help of the instructions and colour photos supplied, construction time is said to be 40-55 h.

Alternatively the aircraft may be bought factory assembled and test flown for an additional US$600, while for a further US$60 the customer can have it painted too.

Equipment options include wheel spats, coil-spring suspension on all wheels, and main-wheel brakes, the latter independently operable to help ground manoeuvring.

EXTERNAL DIMENSIONS & AREAS - Length overall 15.2 ft, 4.63 m. Height overall 7.0 ft, 2.13 m. Wing span 30.0 ft, 9.1 m. Constant chord 4.3 ft, 1.32 m. Dihedral 12°. Sweepback 0°. Total wing area* 150 ft², 13.9 m². Total aileron area 20.0 ft², 1.86 m². Aspect ratio 6.0/1. Other data NC.

POWER PLANT - Zenoah G25B1 engine. Max power 22 hp at 6500 rpm. Propeller diameter and pitch 36x16 inch, 0.91x0.41 m. No reduction. Max static thrust NC. Power per unit area 0.15 hp/ft², 1.6 hp/m². Fuel capacity 3.0 US gal, 2.5 Imp gal, 11.4 litre.

WEIGHTS & LOADINGS - Empty weight 185 lb, 84 kg. Max take-off weight 375 lb, 170 kg. Payload 190 lb, 86 kg. Max wing loading 2.50 lb/ft², 12.2 kg/m². Max power loading 17.0 lb/hp, 7.7 kg/hp. Load factors NC.

PERFORMANCE -** Never exceed speed 64 mph, 103 kph. Max cruising speed 40 mph, 64 kph. Economic cruising speed 30 mph, 48 kph. Stalling speed 22 mph, 35 kph. Max climb rate at sea level >400 ft/min, >2.0 m/s. Take-off distance 150 ft, 45 m. Landing distance *90* ft, *27* m. Other data NC.

Including ailerons.

Under the following test conditions - Test payload 188 lb, 85 kg. Other data NC.

ATLANTIS
BABY CHICKEN HAWK 277
(Three-axis)

Summary as Baby Chicken Hawk 250.

Production status: current, see Baby Chicken Hawk 250 *text for number completed.*

GENERAL - This aircraft is identical to the *Baby Chicken Hawk 250* except that a Rotax 277 engine with gear reduction is substituted for the direct-drive Zenoah. This gives a considerable increase in performance, plus, we suspect, a noticeable decrease in noise.

Naturally the buyer pays more for this sophistication, the *Baby Chicken Hawk 277* costing US$3999 as a kit. The kit comes in just the same form as for the Zenoah-engined machine, and claimed assembly time is the same. Options too are identical, including the facility for factory build and paint.

EXTERNAL DIMENSIONS & AREAS - See *Baby Chicken Hawk 250.*

POWER PLANT - Rotax 277 engine. Max power 26.5 hp at 6000 rpm. Propeller diameter and pitch 54x34 inch, 1.37x0.86 m. Gear reduction, ratio 2.6/1. Max static thrust NC. Power per unit area 0.18 hp/ft², 1.9 hp/m². Fuel capacity 3.0 US gal, 2.5 Imp gal, 11.4 litre.

WEIGHTS & LOADINGS - Empty weight 203 lb, 92 kg. Max take-off weight 475 lb, 215 kg. Payload 272 lb, 123 kg. Max wing loading 3.16 lb/ft², 15.5 kg/m². Max power loading 17.9 lb/hp, 8.1 kg/hp. Load factors NC.

PERFORMANCE* - Never exceed speed 64 mph, 103 kph. Max cruising speed 55 mph, 88 kph. Economic cruising speed 30 mph, 48 kph. Stalling speed 23 mph, 37 kph. Max climb rate at sea level 700 ft/min, 3.6 m/s. Take-off distance 100 ft, 30 m. Landing distance *90* ft, 27 m. Other data NC.

*Under the following test conditions - Test payload 188 lb, 85 kg. Other data NC.

ATLANTIS
BABY CHICKEN HAWK BIPE 277
(Three-axis)

Single-seat single-engined biplane with conventional three-axis control. Wings have unswept leading and trailing edges, and constant chord; conventional tail. Pitch control by elevator on tail; yaw control by fin-mounted rudder; roll control by 70% span ailerons on upper wing; control inputs through stick for pitch/roll and pedals for yaw. Wings braced by struts and transverse X-cables; wing profile NC; 100% double-surface. Undercarriage has three wheels in tricycle formation; no suspension. Push-right go-right nosewheel steering connected to yaw control. No brakes. Aluminium-alloy tube airframe, completely open. Engine mounted at upper wing height, driving pusher propeller.

Production status: current, see Baby Chicken Hawk 250 *text for number completed.*

GENERAL - Atlantis' offering to the biplane market is simply a *Baby Chicken Hawk 277* with an additional wing of smaller span added beneath the existing one. Controls and power plant remain exactly the same, and it is interesting to compare the effect which the second wing has on performance. Climb and never exceed speed are unchanged, but maximum cruise is down a little, as one would expect in view of the extra drag. The most dramatic effect, however, is on the stall, which comes a full 3 mph (5 kph) slower. Take-off and landing characteristics are changed too, with the take-off and landing rolls reduced.
There are three ways to obtain Atlantis' biplane. Firstly it can be bought as a kit, in similar form to the *Baby Chicken Hawk 250,* for US$4695, secondly it can be bought factory built and test flown for an additional US$700, or thirdly it can be produced by converting a *Baby Chicken Hawk 277* to biplane specification, using a conversion kit costing US$795.

Options are as for the *Baby Chicken Hawk 250,* except that paint costs US$70.

EXTERNAL DIMENSIONS & AREAS - Length overall 15.2 ft, 4.63 m. Height overall 7.0 ft, 2.13 m. Wing span 24.0 ft, 7.31 m (bottom); 30.0 ft, 9.14 m (top). Constant chord NC (bottom wing); 4.3 ft, 1.32 m (top wing). Dihedral NC (bottom wing); 12° (top wing). Sweepback 0°. Total wing area* 230 ft², 21.4 m². Total aileron area 20.0 ft², 1.86 m². Aspect ratio 7.2/1 (bottom wing); 6.0/1 (top wing). Other data NC.

POWER PLANT - See *Baby Chicken Hawk 277* except: Power per unit area 0.12 hp/ft², 1.2 hp/m².

WEIGHTS & LOADINGS - Empty weight 250 lb, 113 kg. Max take-off weight 500 lb, 226 kg. Payload 250 lb, 113 kg. Max wing loading 2.17 lb/ft², 10.6 kg/m². Max power loading 18.9 lb/hp, 8.5 kg/hp. Load factors NC.

PERFORMANCE** - Never exceed speed 64 mph, 103 kph. Max cruising speed 50 mph, 80 kph. Economic cruising speed 30 mph, 48 kph. Stalling speed 20 mph, 32 kph. Max climb rate at sea level 700 ft/min, 3.6 m/s. Take-off distance 80 ft, 24 m. Landing distance 65 ft, 20 m. Other data NC.

*Including ailerons.

**Under the following test conditions - Test payload 188 lb, 85 kg. Other data NC.

ATLANTIS
SUPER CHICKEN HAWK
(Three-axis)

Single-seat single-engined high-wing monoplane with conventional three-axis control. Wing has unswept leading and trailing edges, and constant chord; flaps fitted; cruciform tail. Pitch control by elevator on tail; yaw control by fin-mounted rudder; roll control by ailerons; control inputs through stick for pitch/roll and pedals for yaw. Wing braced from above by kingpost and cables, from below by cables; wing profile NC; 100% double-surface. Undercarriage has three wheels in tricycle formation; coil-spring suspension on all wheels. Push-right go-right nosewheel steering connected to yaw control; also differential braking. Brakes on main wheels. Aluminium-alloy tube airframe, completely open. Engine mounted at wing height, driving pusher propeller.

Production status: current, see Baby Chicken Hawk 250 *text for number completed.*

GENERAL - First advertised in mid-1984, the *Super Chicken Hawk* shows a superficial resemblence to the *Baby Chicken Hawk 250* but in fact differs from it in many ways, with an electric-start Kawasaki engine fitted instead of the Zenoah, and a considerably different airframe with a cruciform tail plus greater overall length and height. Though still of constant chord, the wing is different too, with a slightly larger span, less dihedral and the addition of three-position flaps. This top of the range machine includes many items optional on the lower models, such as the suspension, brakes and wheel spats. An ASI is added to the instrumentation, and the complete package retails at US$5195 for a kit said to take 12-16 h to build. Buyers willing to do more construction can get more basic kits for less money, the price depending on the amount of work needed for completion.

EXTERNAL DIMENSIONS & AREAS - Length overall 16.6 ft, 5.05 m. Height overall 7.9 ft, 2.41 m. Wing span 31.0 ft, 9.45 m. Sweepback 0°. Total wing area 152 ft², 14.1 m². Aspect ratio 6.3/1. Other data NC.

POWER PLANT - Kawasaki 440A engine. Max power 40 hp at NC rpm. Propeller diameter and pitch 48x32 inch, 1.22x0.81 m (3-blade). Quadruple V-belt reduction, ratio 2.2/1. Max static thrust NC. Power per unit area 0.26 hp/ft², 2.8 hp/m². Fuel capacity 5.0 US gal, 4.2 Imp gal, 18.9 litre.

WEIGHTS & LOADINGS - Empty weight 252 lb, 114 kg. Max take-off weight 502 lb, 228 kg. Payload 250 lb, 114 kg. Max wing loading 3.30 lb/ft², 16.2 kg/m². Max power loading 12.6 lb/hp, 5.7 kg/hp. Load factors NC.

PERFORMANCE* - Never exceed speed 64 mph, 103 kph. Max cruising speed 55 mph, 88 kph. Economic cruising speed 35 mph, 56 kph. Stalling speed 24 mph, 39 kph. Max climb rate at sea level >700 ft/min, >3.6 m/s. Other data NC.

*Under unspecified test conditions.

AVIAN

Avian Balloon Co, South 3722 Ridgeview Drive, Spokane, Washington 99206; tel (509) 928-6847.

AVIAN *32 CALIBRE*

(Hot-air balloon)

Single-seat hot-air balloon. Height control by temperature of contained air; control inputs through burner valve for height increase, NC inputs for height decrease and rotation. Other details NC.

Production status: current, number completed NC.

GENERAL - Avian Balloon Co makes a whole range of balloons, of which the ultralight legal *32 Calibre* of 32,000 ft³ (910 m³) is the smallest. Larger models, which are not detailed here because they are outside the ultralight definition, come in 42,000, 60,000, 80,000 and 140,000 ft³ capacities (1190, 1700, 2270 and 3970 m³).
Standard equipment on the baby of the range includes a pilot's chair with harness, a 10 US gal (8.3 Imp gal, 37.9 litre) propane tank and a propane burner. The company has released little other information, apart from the price, which is US$5250.

EXTERNAL DIMENSIONS, AREAS & VOLUMES - Height overall 47.0 ft, 14.33 m. Diameter overall 40.0 ft, 12.19 m. Volume fully inflated 32,000 ft³, 910 m³. Other data NC.

POWER PLANT - Propane burner, max output NC. Specific output NC. Fuel capacity 10.0 US gal, 8.3 Imp gal, 37.9 litre.

WEIGHTS & LOADINGS - Empty weight 147 lb, 67 kg. Other data NC.

PERFORMANCE - NC.

BEALER

Bealer Enterprises Inc, PO Box 84, 1205 First Avenue SE, Clarion, Iowa 50525; tel (515) 532-6569. President: Clair O Meyer.

BEALER *BEACHY BREEZER*

(Three-axis)

Single-seat single-engined high-wing monoplane with conventional three-axis control. Wing has swept back leading and trailing edges, and constant chord (disregarding ailerons); conventional tail. Pitch control by elevator on tail; yaw control by fin-mounted rudder; roll control by threequarter-span ailerons; control inputs through stick for pitch/roll and pedals for yaw. Wing braced from below by struts; wing profile NC; 100% double-surface. Undercarriage has three wheels in tail-dragger formation; coil-spring suspension on nosewheel and bungee suspension on main wheels. Push-right go-right tailwheel steering connected to yaw control. No brakes. Aluminium-alloy tube airframe, partially enclosed. Engine mounted below wing, driving pusher propeller.

Production status: current, number completed NC.

GENERAL - Clair O Meyer is no stranger to the US home-built fraternity, having been constructing his own machines for over 20 years, so it is perhaps not surprising that his *Beachy Breezer* ultralight gives the impression of being well thought out. Whether this relatively new design - it was introduced in summer '84 - lives up to its designer's claim to be the 'most efficient ultralight on the market today' remains to be seen, but certainly its combination of respectable fuel consumption and decent sized fuel tank should make it a genuine cross-country machine. Good crosswind landing capability is claimed, with 23 mph (37 kph) winds managable at an angle of 45°.

The *Beachy Breezer* should be comfortable over distances too, as it has a spacious cockpit which features adjustable seating, able to accommodate any pilot from 5 ft 5 inch and 145 lb to 6 ft 6 inch and 235 lb (1.65-1.98 m, 66-107 kg) without disturbing the centre of gravity - an unusual feature for an ultralight but none the less welcome for that. A lexan windshield protects the pilot from the elements and there is an external sight gauge to indicate fuel level.

Otherwise the construction of the aircraft is conventional enough, with aircraft-quality materials being used throughout. A single boom tube supports the tail, while the wing is braced by struts and jury struts. The manufacturer is particularly proud of the design of the hinges for the control surfaces, which it is claimed need no lubrication, will not corrode and are virtually indestructible.

▲

The Cuyuna 215 cc engine is mated to a Nova Power Products gear reduction and a Sterba laminated wood propeller. Price in kit form (assembly time 20-40 h) is US$5925 and rigging time is quoted as 10-20 min.

EXTERNAL DIMENSIONS & AREAS - Length overall 16.0 ft, 4.88 m. Height overall 5.0 ft, 1.52 m. Wing span 30.0 ft, 9.14 m. Chord at root 4.2 ft, 1.27 m. Chord at tip (including aileron) 5.0 ft, 1.51 m. Dihedral 0.5°. Sweepback 0.25°. Tailplane span 8.0 ft, 2.44 m. Fin height 3.8 ft, 1.14 m. Total wing area 147 ft^2, 13.6 m^2. Total aileron area 18.4 ft^2, 1.71 m^2. Fin area 7.5 ft^2, 0.70 m^2. Rudder area 3.9 ft^2, 0.36 m^2. Tailplane area NC. Total elevator area 10.3 ft^2, 0.96 m^2. Aspect ratio 6.1/1. Wheel track 5.0 ft, 1.52 m. Wheelbase 12.8 ft, 3.89 m. Tailwheel diameter overall 3 inch, 8 cm. Main wheels diameter overall 16 inch, 41 cm.

POWER PLANT - Cuyuna 215RR engine. Max power 20 hp at 6500 rpm. Propeller diameter and pitch 52x27 inch, 1.32x0.69 m. Gear reduction, ratio 2.3/1. Max static thrust 157 lb, 71 kg. Power per unit area 0.14 hp/ft^2, 1.5 hp/m^2. Fuel capacity 4.2 US gal, 3.5 Imp gal, 15.9 litre.

WEIGHTS & LOADINGS - Empty weight 245 lb, 111 kg. Max take-off weight 510 lb, 231 kg. Payload 265 lb, 120 kg. Max wing loading 3.47 lb/ft^2, 17.0 kg/m^2. Max power loading 25.5 lb/hp, 11.6 kg/hp. Load factors + 4.0, -3.0 recommended; NC ultimate.

PERFORMANCE* - Max level speed 62 mph, 100 kph. Never exceed speed 75 mph, 121 kph. Max cruising speed 55 mph, 88 kph. Economic cruising speed 48 mph, 77 kph. Stalling speed 20 mph, 32 kph. Max climb rate at sea level 800 ft/min, 4.1 m/s. Min sink rate NC. Best glide ratio with power off 10.5/1 at 35 mph, 56 kph. Take-off distance 100 ft, 30 m. Landing distance 75 ft, 23 m. Service ceiling NC. Range at average cruising speed 120 mile, 193 km. Noise level NC.

*Under the following test conditions - Airfield altitude 1162 ft, 354 m. Ground temperature 75°F, 24°C. Ground pressure NC. Ground windspeed 0-5 mph, 0-8 kph. Test payload 194 lb, 88 kg.

BEAUJON

Beaujon Aircraft Co, PO Box 2121, Ardmore, Oklahoma 73402. Proprietor: H Beaujon.

BEAUJON *MACH.07*
(Three-axis)

Single-seat single-engined high-wing monoplane with conventional three-axis control. Wing has unswept leading and trailing edges, and constant chord; cruciform tail. Pitch control by elevator on tail; yaw control by fully flying rudder with additional fin; roll control by spoilers; control inputs through stick for pitch/roll and pedals for yaw. Wing braced from below by struts; wing profile NC; single-surface. Undercarriage has three wheels in tail-dragger formation; no suspension on tailwheel and bungee suspension on main wheels. No ground steering. No brakes. Aluminium-alloy tube airframe, completely open. Engine mounted at wing height, driving tractor propeller.

Production status: see text.

GENERAL - H Beaujon was one of the first designers to offer ultralight plans to homebuilders, with his *Easy Flyer* in 1977, and was also one of the first to advise on using two-stroke engines for aeronautical purposes.

Today he offers a range of six very simple designs with the accent on low build cost, claiming that any of the six can be built from as little as US$1200 complete. Certainly he does his bit towards keeping costs down, for all six sets of plans plus a build manual were offered in August '84 for only US$9.95, and to the best of our knowledge that price still stands.

Few details of any of the aircraft are available and we have yet to see a completed example of any of the six, but as they all seem to be derived from three basic designs, we list the *Mach.07* here and the other two configurations separately.

EXTERNAL DIMENSIONS & AREAS - Length overall 18.5 ft, 5.61 m. Wing span 33.0 ft, 10.06 m. Constant chord 5.0 ft, 1.52 m. Sweepback 0°. Total wing area 165 ft², 15.3 m². Aspect ratio 6.6/1. Other data NC.

POWER PLANT - Cuyuna 430 engine. Max power 30 hp at NC rpm. Power per unit area 0.18 hp/ft², 2.0 hp/m². Fuel capacity 2.5 US gal, 2.1 Imp gal, 9.5 litre. Other data NC.

WEIGHTS & LOADINGS - Empty weight 230 lb, 104 kg. Max take-off weight 450 lb, 204 kg. Payload 220 lb, 100 kg. Max wing loading 2.73 lb/ft², 13.3 kg/m². Max power loading 15.0 lb/hp, 6.8 kg/hp. Load factors NC.

PERFORMANCE* - Cruising speed 43 mph, 69 kph. Stalling speed 20 mph, 32 kph. Max climb rate at sea level 600 ft/min, 3.1 m/s. Take-off distance 80 ft, 24 m. Landing distance 60 ft, 18 m. Other data NC.

*Under unspecified test conditions.

BEAUJON
BJ.2, MINIMAC and HARDNOSE
(Three-axis)

Single-seat single-engined high-wing monoplane with conventional three-axis control. Wing has unswept leading and trailing edges, and constant chord; cruciform tail. Pitch control by fully flying tail; yaw control by fully flying rudder; roll control by ailerons; control inputs through stick for pitch/roll and pedals for yaw. Wing braced from below by struts. Undercarriage has three wheels in tricycle formation. Aluminium-alloy tube airframe, completely open. Engine mounted below wing (BJ.2 and Hardnose), at wing height (Minimac), driving pusher propeller (BJ.2), tractor propeller (Minimac and Hardnose). Other details NC.

Production status: see Mach.07 *text.*

GENERAL - See *Mach.07.* Data below refers to the *BJ.2;* where different, figures for the *Minimac* and *Hardnose* are shown in parentheses in that order.

EXTERNAL DIMENSIONS & AREAS - Wing span 30.0(28.0)(30.0) ft, 9.14(8.53)(9.14) m. Constant chord 4.8(4.3)(4.8) ft, 1.46(1.31)(1.46) m. Sweepback 0°. Total wing area 144(120)(144) ft², 13.4(11.1)(13.4) m². Aspect ratio 6.3(6.5)(6.3)/1. Other data NC.

POWER PLANT - See *Mach.07* except: Power per unit area 0.21(0.25)(0.21) hp/ft², 2.2(2.7)(2.2) hp/m². Fuel capacity NC.

WEIGHTS & LOADINGS - Empty weight 240(235)(245) lb, 109(107)(111) kg. Max take-off weight 470(450)(470) lb, 213(204)(213) kg. Payload 230(215)(225) lb, 104(98)(102) kg. Max wing loading 3.26(3.75)(3.26) lb/ft², 15.9(18.4) (15.9) kg/m². Max power loading 15.7(15.0)(15.7) lb/hp, 7.1(6.8)(7.1) kg/hp. Load factors NC.

PERFORMANCE* - Cruising speed 48(50)(45) mph, 77(80)(72) kph. Stalling speed 23(25)(23) mph, 37(40)(37) kph. Max climb rate at sea level 600(600)(650) ft/min, 3.1(3.1)(3.3) m/s. Take-off distance 90(100)(90) ft, 27(30) (27) m. Landing distance 60(80)(60) ft, 18(24)(18) m. Other data NC.

*Under unspecified test conditions.

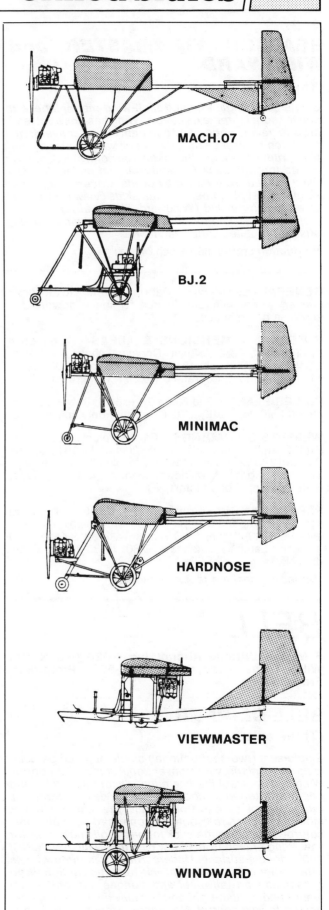

MACH.07

BJ.2

MINIMAC

HARDNOSE

VIEWMASTER

WINDWARD

BEAUJON *VIEWMASTER* and *WINDWARD*

(Three-axis)

Single-seat single-engined high-wing monoplane with conventional three-axis control. Wing has unswept leading and trailing edges, and constant chord; conventional tail. Pitch control by fully flying tail; yaw control by fully flying rudder with additional fin; roll control NC; control inputs through stick for pitch/roll and pedals for yaw. Wing braced from below by struts. Undercarriage has single wheel plus nose and tail skids (Viewmaster), two wheels plus tailskid (Windward). Wood airframe, completely open. Engine mounted below wing, driving pusher propeller. Other details NC.

Production status: see Mach.07 *text.*

GENERAL - See *Mach.07.* Data below refers to the *Viewmaster;* where different, figures for the *Windward* are shown in parentheses.

EXTERNAL DIMENSIONS & AREAS - Wing span 27.0(28.0) ft, 8.22(8.53) m. Constant chord 4.4(4.5) ft, 1.34(1.37) m. Sweepback 0°. Total wing area 120(126) ft^2, 11.1(11.7) m^2. Aspect ratio 6.1(6.2)/1. Other data NC.

POWER PLANT - See *Mach.07* except: Power per unit area 0.25(0.24) hp/ft^2, 2.7(2.6) hp/m^2. Fuel capacity NC.

WEIGHTS & LOADINGS - Empty weight 200(220) lb, 91(100) kg. Max take-off weight 420(440) lb, 191(200) kg. Payload 220 lb, 100 kg. Max wing loading 3.50(3.49) lb/ft^2, 17.2(17.1) kg/m^2. Max power loading 14.0(14.7) lb/hp, 6.4(6.7) kg/hp. Load factors NC.

PERFORMANCE* - Cruising speed 60(55) mph, 97(88) kph. Stalling speed 24 mph, 39 kph. Max climb rate at sea level 900(700) ft/min, 4.6(3.6) m/s. Take-off distance 100 ft, 30 m. Landing distance 100(80) ft, 30(24) m. Other data NC.

*Under unspecified test conditions.

BELL

F M Bell Ultralite Aircraft Inc, 1020 I-45 North, Willis, Texas 77378; tel (409) 856-5518. Proprietor: Fred Bell.

BELL *CLIPPER*

(Three-axis)

Single-seat (two-seat optional) single-engined parasol-wing monoplane with conventional three-axis control. Wing has unswept leading edge, swept forward trailing edge, and tapering chord; flaps fitted; cruciform tail. Pitch control by elevator on tail; yaw control by fin-mounted rudder; roll control by one-third span ailerons; control inputs through stick for pitch/roll and pedals for yaw. Wing braced from below by struts; wing profile NC; 100% double-surface. Undercarriage has three wheels in tail-dragger formation (tricycle formation optional); no suspension on tailwheel and bungee suspension on main wheels. Push-right go-right tailwheel steering connected to yaw control. No brakes. Steel tube airframe,

partially enclosed. Engine mounted below wing, driving tractor propeller.

Production status: current, 25 completed.

GENERAL - Fred Bell has been in the ultralight industry for a number of years, though it was only at the start of 1985 that his own company got under way. He worked at Ultralight Flight while the *Phantom* was being designed, and that aircraft obviously impressed him as much as it did the flying public, for he subsequently joined International Ultralight, where he was involved with the company's *Sidewinder,* a *Phantom* lookalike which we featured in our last edition. Later he worked as part of the Worldwide Ultralite Industries team, designing the *Spitfire,* which again owes a lot to the *Phantom.* Finally, when WUI ceased trading, Fred set up on his own, taking with him the *Spitfire,* which we describe separately, but not apparently several other WUI designs - the *Thunderbird* and *Model T,* the *Quicksilver MX* and *MXII* lookalikes (*Skyraider, Skyraider SS* and *Skyraider SST*), and the *Water Mocassin* flying boat.

The *Clipper* stands apart from all the above aircraft in that it is a fresh design, bearing no obvious resemblance to any other machine. It is not a replica, yet is unashamedly nostalgic, evoking memories of open-cockpit flying in parasol-winged aircraft. Like the *Spitfire,* it was introduced under the WUI banner, receiving its public debut at the '84 Oshkosh, but is now being produced by the Bell company at a substantially lower price. It is really several aircraft in one, as buyers can choose one or two seats, tricycle or tail-dragger undercarriage, and 28 hp or 40 hp Rotax engines. Our data below refers to a single-seat taildragger with 28 hp engine, which costs US$6395 for a 35-40 h kit, the bigger engine adding another US$200. All versions use a welded chrome-moly tubular fuselage, with wings built up out of aluminium, and Dacron covering throughout. Four-position flaps are built into the wings.

EXTERNAL DIMENSIONS & AREAS - Length overall 16.5 ft, 5.03 m. Height overall 7.5 ft, 2.29 m. Wing span 30.0 ft, 9.14 m. Chord at root 5.0 ft, 1.52 m. Chord at tip 4.5 ft, 1.37 m. Dihedral 2°. Sweepback 0°. Tailplane span 8.0 ft, 2.44 m. Fin height 3.5 ft, 1.07 m. Total wing area 152 ft^2, 14.1 m^2. Aspect ratio 5.9/1. Wheelbase 5.0 ft, 1.52 m. Tailwheel diameter overall 5 inch, 13 cm. Main wheels diameter overall 10 inch, 25 cm. Other data NC.

POWER PLANT - Rotax 277 engine. Max power 28 hp at 6400 rpm. Propeller diameter and pitch 68x28 inch, 1.73x0.71 m. Gear reduction, ratio NC. Max static thrust NC. Power per unit area 0.18 hp/ft^2, 2.0 hp/m^2. Fuel capacity 5.0 US gal, 4.2 Imp gal, 18.9 litre.

WEIGHTS & LOADINGS - Empty weight 254 lb, 115 kg. Max take-off weight 600 lb, 272 kg. Payload 346 lb, 157 kg. Max wing loading 3.9 lb/ft^2, 19.3 kg/m^2. Max power loading 21.4 lb/hp, 9.7 kg/hp. Load factors +6.0, -4.0 recommended; +9.0, -6.0 ultimate.

PERFORMANCE* - Max level speed 63 mph, 101 kph. Never exceed speed 85 mph, 137 kph. Max cruising speed 55 mph, 88 kph. Economic cruising speed 50 mph, 80 kph. Stalling speed 19 mph, 31 kph. Max climb rate at sea level 800 ft/min, 4.1 m/s. Min sink rate 450 ft/min, 2.3 m/s at NC speed. Best glide ratio with power off 6/1 at 40 mph, 64 kph. Take-off distance 150 ft, 45 m. Landing distance 200 ft, 60 m. Service ceiling 14,000 ft, 6350 m. Range at average cruising speed 100 mile, 161 km. Noise level 65 dB at 100 ft, 30 m.

*Under unspecified test conditions.

Hal Adkins

BELL
SPITFIRE and SONIC SPITFIRE
(Three-axis)

Single-seat single-engined high-wing monoplane with conventional three-axis control. Wing has unswept leading edge, swept forward trailing edge and tapering chord; flaps fitted (Spitfire only); cruciform tail. Pitch control by elevator on tail; yaw control by fin-mounted rudder; roll control by one-third span ailerons (Spitfire), full-span ailerons (Sonic Spitfire); control inputs through stick for pitch/roll and pedals for yaw. Wing braced from below by struts; wing profile NC; 100% double-surface. Undercarriage has three wheels in tricycle formation; no suspension on nosewheel and axle-flex suspension on main wheels. Push-right go-right nosewheel steering connected to yaw control. No brakes. Aluminium-alloy tube airframe, with pod. Engine mounted above wing, driving tractor propeller.

Production status: current, 300 completed.

Hal Adkins

Many early Spitfires *use a belt-reduction Kawasaki engine.*

GENERAL - As we explained in our oX2Clipper description, the ancestry of the *Spitfire* can be directly traced back to the *Phantom,* and the two certainly look alike apart from the use of strut bracing instead of kingpost and cables. However, the standard *Spitfire* also differs from the *Phantom* in having flaps, and much smaller ailerons in consequence - only one-third span instead of full-span. For full-span ailerons, one must opt for the aerobatic *Sonic Spitfire,* with its clipped wings, double-sleeved spars, diagonals, cage rails and uprights. Extra struts are also fitted, along with double hinge points and dual rudder cables, producing a strong and responsive machine.

Both versions make liberal use of aircraft-quality materials, with AN and MS hardware, and rugged chrome moly landing gear. A glass-fibre pod and windscreen are standard, as is a padded seat with integral belt and shoulder harness, and an ASI. Standard engine is now a 377 Rotax, though there are some 277 Rotax versions around and many early machines had Kawasaki TA440 units.

Price of the *Spitfire* is US$6595 for a 40 h kit, rigging time being around 15 min. The *Sonic Spitfire* costs an extra US$600. Our data below refers to the standard *Spitfire*.

EXTERNAL DIMENSIONS & AREAS - Length overall 17.8 ft, 5.44 m. Wing span 30.0 ft, 9.14 m. Chord at root 5.0 ft, 1.52 m. Chord at tip 4.5 ft, 1.37 m. Dihedral 2°. Sweep-back 0°. Tailplane span 8.0 ft, 2.44 m. Fin height 3.5 ft, 1.07 m. Total wing area 152 ft², 14.1 m². Aspect ratio 5.9/1. Nosewheel diameter overall 10 inch, 25 cm. Main wheels diameter overall 10 inch, 25 cm. Other data NC.

POWER PLANT - Rotax 377 engine. Max power 36 hp at 6400 rpm. Propeller diameter and pitch 68x28 inch, 1.73x-0.71 m. Gear reduction, ratio 2.6/1. Max static thrust 230 lb, 104 kg. Power per unit area 0.24 hp/ft², 2.6 hp/m². Fuel capacity 5.0 US gal, 4.2 Imp gal, 18.9 litre.

WEIGHTS & LOADINGS - Empty weight 254 lb, 115 kg. Max take-off weight 600 lb, 272 kg. Payload 346 lb, 157 kg. Max wing loading 3.94 lb/ft², 19.2 kg/m². Max power loading 16.7 lb/hp, 7.6 kg/hp. Load factors +6.0, -4.0 recommended; +9.0, -6.0 ultimate.

PERFORMANCE* - Max level speed 63 mph, 101 kph. Never exceed speed 85 mph, 137 kph. Max cruising speed 55 mph, 88 kph. Economic cruising speed 50 mph, 80 kph. Stalling speed 19 mph, 31 kph. Max climb rate at sea level 650 ft/min, 3.3 m/s. Min sink rate 450 ft/min, 2.3 m/s at NC speed. Best glide ratio with power off 6/1 at 40 mph, 64 kph. Take-off distance 150 ft, 45 m. Landing distance 200 ft, 60 m. Service ceiling 14,000 ft, 4270 m. Range at average cruising speed 100 mile, 161 km. Noise level 65 dB at 100 ft, 30 m.

*Under unspecified test conditions.

BELL SPITFIRE II
(Three-axis)

Summary as Spitfire *except: Side-by-side two-seater.*

Production status: current, 100 produced.

GENERAL - This machine is very similar to the standard *Spitfire,* sharing the same overall dimensions and using the same wing. As befits a two-seater, a larger engine is fitted, the Rotax 503 being standard.

A wide range of options is available, including crop spraying equipment, floats, skis, and an 80 hp engine. When the aircraft was manufactured by Worldwide Ultralite Industries, a version called the *Ambulance* was also offered, fitted with oxygen equipment, but it is not clear whether this model is still available.

Our data below refers to the standard machine, which costs US$7995 for a 30 h kit. Rigging time is much as the single-seater, around 15 min.

EXTERNAL DIMENSIONS & AREAS - See *Spitfire.*

POWER PLANT - Rotax 503 engine. Max power 48 hp at 6400 rpm. Propeller diameter and pitch 68x28 inch, 1.73x 0.71 m. Gear reduction, ratio 2.5/1. Max static thrust 350 lb, 159 kg. Power per unit area 0.32 hp/ft^2, 3.4 hp/m^2. Fuel capacity 5.0 US gal, 4.2 Imp gal, 18.9 litre.

WEIGHTS & LOADINGS - Empty weight 350 lb, 159 kg. Max take-off weight 850 lb, 386 kg. Payload 500 lb, 227 kg. Max wing loading 5.59 lb/ft^2, 27.4 kg/m^2. Max power loading 17.7 lb/hp, 8.0 kg/hp. Load factors +6.0, -4.0 recommended; +9.0, -6.0 ultimate.

PERFORMANCE* - Max level speed 80 mph, 129 kph. Never exceed speed 100 mph, 161 kph. Max cruising speed 70 mph, 113 kph. Economic cruising speed 60 mph, 97 kph. Stalling speed 30 mph, 48 kph. Max climb rate at sea level 800 ft/min, 4.1 m/s. Min sink rate 550 ft/min, 2.8 m/s at NC speed. Best glide ratio with power off 6/1 at 40 mph, 64 kph. Take-off distance 200 ft, 60 m. Landing distance 300 ft, 90 m. Service ceiling 14,000 ft, 4270 m. Range at average cruising speed NC. Noise level 65 dB at 100 ft, 30 m.

*Under unspecified test conditions.

BLISS

Bliss Aircraft Corp, 4630 Section 3B, Pacific Highway E, Fife, Washington 98424; tel (206) 922-3838. Proprietor: George Bliss.

BLISS COMMANDO
(Three-axis)

Single-seat single-engined biplane with conventional three-axis control. Wings have unswept leading and trailing edges, and constant chord; two-fin tail. Pitch control by elevator; yaw control by fin-mounted rudders; roll control by four full-span flaperons; control inputs through stick for pitch/roll and pedals for yaw. Wings braced by struts and transverse X-cables; wing profile NC; 100% double-surface. Undercarriage has three wheels in tricycle formation; bungee suspension on all wheels. Push-right go-right nosewheel steering connected to yaw control. Brakes on main wheels. Aluminium-

alloy tube and sheet airframe, totally enclosed. Engine mounted between wings, driving pusher propeller.

Production status: see text.

GENERAL - Conceived as a workhorse able to cope with rough field landings, the *Commando* is a rugged machine which at 410 lb (186 kg) is definitely not an ultralight, though it would be on the verge of microlight status in some European countries if a second seat were added and the wing enlarged - something the payload would easily permit.

The company showed the prototype to the press in mid '84 and our impression is that a lot of thought had gone into this unusual aircraft. Not only does the detailing appear to be carefully done, but there are novel features, like sight glasses incorporated into the inboard section of the upper wing, so that the pilot can see fuel level in the wing tanks at a glance. The cockpit is set in front of the wings, giving good visibility, while the engine sits behind driving a pusher prop located between the two high tail booms. Hydraulic disc brakes are fitted.

First flights were made in the prototype in November '83, and production was scheduled for mid '85 at a price of approximately US$20,000, the main targets being export markets and agricultural applications.

EXTERNAL DIMENSIONS & AREAS - Length overall 16.8 ft, 5.13 m. Height overall 5.7 ft, 1.73 m. Wing span 20.0 ft, 6.10 m (bottom); 20.0 ft, 6.10 m (top). Sweepback 0°. Total wing area 120 ft^2, 11.1 m^2. Aspect ratio 6.7/1 (bottom wing); 6.7/1 (top wing). Other data NC.

POWER PLANT - Rotax 532 engine. Max power 65 hp at 6200 rpm. Propeller diameter and pitch 66xNC inch, 1.68xNC m. Gear reduction, ratio 2.6/1. Max static thrust NC. Power per unit area 0.54 hp/ft^2, 5.9 hp/m^2. Fuel capacity 8.6 US gal, 7.2 Imp gal, 32.6 litre.

WEIGHTS & LOADINGS - Empty weight 410 lb, 186 kg. Max take-off weight 800 lb, 363 kg. Payload 390 lb, 177 kg. Max wing loading 6.67 lb/ft^2, 32.7 kg/m^2. Max power loading 12.3 lb/hp, 5.6 kg/hp. Load factors NC recommended; +9.0, -9.0 ultimate.

PERFORMANCE* - Max level speed 103 mph, 166 kph. Cruising speed 86 mph, 138 kph. Stalling speed 36 mph, 58 kph. Max climb rate at sea level 1080 ft/min, 5.5 m/s. Other data NC.

*Under unspecified test conditions.

BROCK

Ken Brock Manufacturing, 11852 Western Avenue, Stanton, California 90680; tel (714) 898-4366.

BROCK AVION
(Three-axis)

Single-seat single-engined high-wing monoplane with conventional three-axis control. Wing has unswept leading and trailing edges, and constant chord; conventional tail. Pitch control by fully flying tail; yaw control by fully flying rudder; roll control by 90%-span ailerons; control inputs through stick for pitch/roll and pedals for yaw. Wing braced from below by struts;

Hal Adkins

wing profile NC; 100% double-surface. Undercarriage has three wheels in tricycle formation; no suspension on nosewheel and spring-tube suspension on main wheels. Push-right go-right nosewheel steering con nected to yaw control. Nosewheel brake. Aluminium-alloy tube airframe, completely open. Engine mounted below wing, driving pusher propeller.

Production status: prototype.

GENERAL - The *Avion* is undoubtedly one of the more interesting recent American designs, simply because in an industry where costs and sophistication are constantly increasing, it represents an attempt to return to the basics of ultralight flying. The project started when Bob Lovejoy, who designed the *Quicksilver* in the early '70s, attended an ultralight meet some ten years later and was amazed to find how much the machinery cost, and how few machines had progressed beyond being imitations of his by then venerable *Quicksilver*. He decided that there must be room for improvement and set out to design a simple low-cost but practical three-axis ultralight. The *Avion* was the result.

Sadly, the project claimed his life, Bob being fatally injured in a test flight in 1982, not through any design defect but simply due to an oversight on his preflight inspection. Fortunately for the ultralight world, that was not the end of the *Avion,* as he had already made arrangements to market the aircraft through gyroplane manufacturer Ken Brock, and Ken spent the following two years developing the design, incorporating refine ments like a combined seat and tank, an idea he popularised on his gyroplanes. By the end of 1984 he had a prototype flying and kits became available during 1985 at US$3995, with all tubes bent and all holes drilled, allowing a building time of 25 h. Rigging time is around 30 min. One likely change from the prototype detailed below is that the Rotax 277 will probably have its V-belt reduction replaced by gears.

W.....g in the February '85 edition of *Ultralight Planes,*

Dave Martin reported that the *Avion* had delightfully light controls, and though he was concerned about the prototype's tendency to pitch down when flown hands off, he was generally very enthusiastic about this Californian newcomer.

EXTERNAL DIMENSIONS & AREAS - Length overall 15.5 ft, 4.72 m. Height overall 6.8 ft, 2.08 m. Wing span 28.0 ft, 8.5 m. Constant chord 5.0 ft, 1.52 m. Dihedral 1°. Sweepback 0°. Elevator span NC. Rudder height NC. Total wing area 140 ft^2, 13.0 m^2. Total aileron area 24.0 ft^2, 2.23 m^2. Rudder area 7.0 ft^2, 0.65 m^2. Total elevator area 18.0 ft^2, 1.67 m^2. Aspect ratio 5.6/1. Wheel track 4.4 ft, 1.35 m. Wheelbase 5.0 ft, 1.52 m. Nosewheel diameter overall 10 inch, 25 cm. Main wheels diameter overall 10 inch, 25 cm.

POWER PLANT - Rotax 277 engine. Max power 28 hp at 2800 rpm. Propeller diameter and pitch 48x28 inch, 1.22x0.71 m. V-belt reduction, ratio 2.1/1. Max static thrust 170 lb, 77 kg. Power per unit area 0.20 hp/ft^2, 2.2 hp/m^2. Fuel capacity 5.0 US gal, 4.2 Imp gal, 18.9 litre.

WEIGHTS & LOADINGS - Empty weight 250 lb, 113 kg. Max take-off weight 530 lb, 240 kg. Payload 280 lb, 127 kg. Max wing loading 3.79 lb/ft^2, 18.5 kg/m^2. Max power loading 18.9 lb/hp, 8.6 kg/hp. Load factors p/6.0, -4.0 recommended; NC ultimate.

PERFORMANCE* - Max level speed 63 mph, 101 kph. Never exceed speed 80 mph, 129 kph. Max cruising speed NC. Economic cruising speed 48 mph, 77 kph. Stalling speed 27 mph, 43 kph. Max climb rate at sea level 700 ft/min, 3.6 m/s. Min sink rate 500 ft/min at 40 mph, 2.5 m/s at 64 kph. Best glide ratio with power off 7/1 at 45 mph, 72 kph. Take-off distance 180 ft, 55 m. Landing distance 150 ft, 45 m. Service ceiling 10,000 ft, 3050 m. Range at average cruising speed 140 mile, 225 km. Noise level NC.

*Under unspecified test conditions.

diameter 22.0 ft, 6.71 m. Chord 6.0 inch, 15.2 cm. Solidity ratio 35/1. Wheel track 5.7 ft, 1.73 m. Wheelbase 3.4 ft, 1.02 m. Nosewheel diameter overall 10 inch, 25 cm. Main wheels diameter overall 12 inch, 30 cm.

POWER PLANT - McCulloch 4318 engine. Max power 90 hp at 4000 rpm. Propeller diameter and pitch 44x20 inch, 1.12x0.51 m. No reduction. Max static thrust NC. Fuel capacity 8.9 US gal, 7.4 Imp gal, 33.7 litre.

WEIGHTS & LOADINGS - Empty weight 235 lb, 107 kg. Max take-off weight 650 lb, 295 kg. Payload 415 lb, 188 kg. Max power loading 7.22 lb/hp, 3.3 kg/hp. Load factors NC.

PERFORMANCE* - Max level speed 90 mph, 145 kph. Never exceed speed 95 mph, 153 kph. Max cruising speed 70 mph, 113 kph. Economic cruising speed 50 mph, 80 kph. Minimum controllable speed NC. Max climb rate at sea level 1200 ft/min, 6.1 m/s. Min sink rate with power off 800 ft/min at 45 mph, 4.1 m/s at 72 kph. Take-off distance *250* ft, *75* m. Landing distance *10* ft, *3* m. Service ceiling 10,000 ft, 3050 m. Range at average cruising speed 125 mile, 201 km. Noise level NC.

Under unspecified test conditions.

BROCK *KB-2*
(Gyroplane)

Single-seat single-engined gyroplane with three-axis control. Rotor has constant chord; conventional tail. Pitch/roll control by angling rotor, yaw control by fin-mounted rudder; control inputs through stick for pitch/roll and pedals for yaw. Two-blade rotor with Clark Y-section blades. Undercarriage has three wheels in tricycle formation; no suspension on any wheels. Push-right go-right nosewheel steering independent from yaw control. Nosewheel brake. Aluminium-alloy tube airframe, completely open. Engine mounted below rotor, driving pusher propeller.

Production status: current, number completed NC.

GENERAL - Ken Brock's *KB-2*, although a little too fast at cruise speed and with too large a fuel capacity to be ultralight legal, is still very much in the ultralight spirit. The machine is licensed in the experimental amateur-built category and is entitled to the usual general-aviation facilities. Ken has been building gyros for a number of years, and his *KB-2* gyrocopter can be had in the form of eight part kits, so that the pilot can join the rotor fraternity without laying out all his money at once. Indeed, Ken says it's a good idea to build the gyro unpowered first, so that the pilot can accumulate time and experience in rotor control by being towed aloft by a car. The powerplant can added once the builder has gained confidence. Alternatively, the machine may be had as a complete kit.
Either way, the *KB-2* comes with detailed plans, construction drawings and step-by-step building instructions. The only tools needed are spanners, screwdriver, drill and hacksaw.
A feature of the *KB-2* is its combined seat and fuel tank, which has become so much of a Brock trademark that he now sells them separately for around US$200. The complete *KB-2* costs US$7000 and comes with a McCulloch 4318 engine as detailed below, though various alternatives are also in use.

EXTERNAL DIMENSIONS & AREAS - Length overall 12.0 ft, 3.66 m. Height overall 6.5 ft, 1.98 m. Rotor

CASCADE

Cascade Ultralites Inc, 4700 188th Street NE, Suite C, Arlington, Washington 98223; tel (206) 435-8614. Proprietor: Steve Grossruck.

Australian agent: Mobius Flying Systems, PO Box 212, Belconnen, ACT 2616; tel (062) 540499. Proprietor: Dan Fitzsimmons.

Canadian agent: various, contact manufacturer for list.

New Zealand agent: Cascade Microlites, RD1 Morrinsville; tel Tauwhare 897. Proprietor: Ken Hoult.

CASCADE *KASPERWING 180-B* and *180-BX*
(Hybrid)

Single-seat single-engined high-wing monoplane with hybrid control. Wing has unswept leading and trailing edges, and constant chord; no tail. Pitch control by weight-shift; yaw control by tip rudders; no separate roll control; control inputs through weight-shift for pitch and pedals for yaw. Wing braced from above by kingpost and cables, from below by cables; wing profile by W Kasper; single-surface. Undercarriage has three wheels in tricycle formation; no suspension on any wheels. Push-right go-left nosewheel steering independent from yaw control. No brakes. Aluminium-alloy tube airframe, with optional pod. Engine mounted below wing, driving pusher propeller.

Production status: current, 322 completed.

GENERAL - Unique is an overworked word, but it's the only one appropriate to describe the *Kasperwing's* aerodynamics. Named after Witold Kasper who collaborated

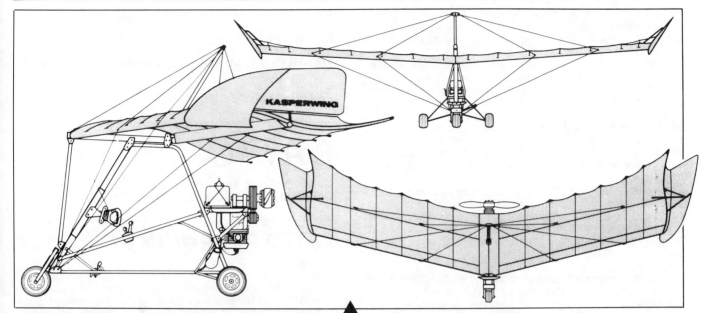

with Steve Grossruck on the aircraft's design, this hybrid machine is the only ultralight using the Kasper system, in which tip-rudders are used as wing-tip vortice controls and air brakes. This enables the aircraft to remain controllable after the stall and to fly *literally* like a bird. In fact it is possible to put the *Kasperwing* into a vertical mush.

With its low weight and excellent slow flight capabilities, this aircraft is a natural for soaring, though the turbulence associated with thermals often needs some hard work by the pilot, who has only weight-shift at his disposal for pitch control. Early *Kasperwings* used a variety of engines, but the current *180-B* model has a Zenoah unit and differs from the original *180* in having sturdier landing gear. Retrofit kits

are available for early models to bring them up to the latest specification. A smart pilot enclosure with sliding air vent and quick-remove canopy is optional, in which form the machine is dubbed *180-BX* and illustrated on our front cover. These refinements too are retrofittable.

Construction is of aircraft-quality tubing and Dacron, with stainless-steel fasteners. Rigging takes half an hour by one person, and the machine can be easily carried without a trailer, as the wing folds into a bag 21 ft long by 1 ft in diameter (6.4x0.3 m) and the rest of the aircraft will fit into the back of an estate car.

Price of the *180-B* is US$4800 in kit form or US$5300 ready to fly, while corresponding prices for the *180-BX* are US$5495 and 5795 respectively. Options on either model include wheel spats, parachute, Sea Hawk floats, and the heavy duty undercarriage developed for the *Kasperwing 180-C*. Data below refers to the 180-B; where different, figures for the 180-BX are shown in parentheses.

EXTERNAL DIMENSIONS & AREAS - Length overall 12.7(NC) ft, 3.86(NC) m. Height overall 11.0 ft, 3.34 m. Wing span 35.0 ft, 10.67 m. Total wing area 180 ft², 16.7 m². Aspect ratio 6.8/1. Wheel track 7.2 ft, 2.18 m. Wheelbase 5.2 ft, 1.57 m. Nosewheel diameter overall 11 inch, 27 cm. Main wheels diameter overall 11 inch, 27 cm. Other data NC.

POWER PLANT - Zenoah G25B engine. Max power 23 hp at NC rpm. Propeller diameter and pitch 54x27(30) inch, 1.37x0.69(0.76) m. V-belt reduction, ratio 2.5/1. Max static thrust 170 lb, 77 kg. Power per unit area 0.13 hp/ft², 1.4 hp/m². Fuel capacity 2.5(5.0) US gal, 2.1(4.2) Imp gal, 9.5(18.9) litre.

WEIGHTS & LOADINGS - Empty weight 175(220) lb, 79(100) kg. Max take-off weight 410(470) lb, 186(213) kg. Payload 235(250) lb, 107(113) kg. Max wing loading 2.28(2.61) lb/ft², 11.1(12.8) kg/m². Max power loading 17.8(20.4) lb/hp, 8.1(9.3) kg/hp. Load factors NC recommended; +7.0, -4.0 ultimate.

PERFORMANCE* - Max level speed 55 mph, 88 kph. Never exceed speed 60 mph, 97 kph. Max cruising speed 45 mph, 72 kph. Economic cruising speed 35 mph, 56 kph. Stalling speed *20(24)* mph, *32(39)* kph. Max climb rate at sea level 700(600) ft/min, 3.6(3.1) m/s. Min sink rate 200 ft/min at 23(22) mph, 1.0 m/s at 37(35) kph. Best glide ratio with power off 10(12)/1 at 23(25) mph, 37(40) kph. Take-off distance *75* ft, *23* m. Landing distance *50* ft, *15* m. Service ceiling 15,000 ft, 4570 m. Range at average cruising speed 85(175) mile, 137(282) km. Noise level NC.

*Under the following test conditions - Test payload 170 lb, 77 kg. Other data NC.

CASCADE
KASPERWING 180-C
and *180-CR*
(Three-axis)

Single-seat single-engined high-wing monoplane with conventional three-axis control. Wing has unswept leading and trailing edges, and constant chord; no tail. Pitch control by operation of both elevons; yaw control by tip rudders; roll control by spoilerons; control inputs through stick for pitch/roll and pedals for yaw. Wing braced from above by kingpost and cables, from below by cables; wing profile by W Kasper; single-surface. Undercarriage has three wheels in tricycle formation; bungee suspension on all wheels. Ground steering by differential braking; castoring nosewheel. Brakes on main wheels. Aluminium-alloy tube airframe, with optional pod. Engine mounted below wing, driving pusher propeller.

Production status: current, 6 completed.

GENERAL - To attract pilots used to conventional controls, the *Kasperwing* is also available in three-axis form, in which guise it is known as the *Kasperwing 180-C* or *180-CR* depending on whether it is fitted with a Rotax 277 or Rotax 503. The latter version is an experimental-aircraft category machine, too heavy for an ultralight, and is not detailed here.

The single-surface wing of the earlier versions is retained, but is fitted with what we have called elevons for lack of a better word, though they are used for pitch control only. Spoilerons look after roll control, both sets of surfaces being operated by a stick which may be left or right mounted to customer preference. The rudder control cables and rear-wheel drum brakes are connected to the rudder pedals and can be operated differentially or together, while the nosewheel is free to castor but is restrained by bungees.

Telescopic landing gear is bungee controlled and adjustable for different terrains, giving 3 inch travel on the front and 10 inch at the rear (8 and 25 cm). Trim adjustment is provided by fore and aft seat movement. Portability is just as good as with the earlier models, though kit construction and rigging take rather longer - 60 h and 45 min respectively.

In standard form the *Kasperwing 180-C* costs US$5895 as a kit and US$6395 ready to fly, options being as for the hybrid models, including the pod. No price is quoted for the *Kasperwing 180-CR*.

EXTERNAL DIMENSIONS & AREAS - See *Kasperwing 180-B* and *180-BX* except: Height overall NC.

POWER PLANT - Rotax 277 engine. Max power 28 hp at 6200 rpm. Propeller diameter and pitch 60x30 inch, 1.52x-0.76 m. Gear reduction, ratio 2.5/1. Max static thrust NC. Power per unit area 0.16 hp/ft^2, 1.7 hp/m^2. Fuel capacity 5.0 US gal, 4.2 Imp gal, 18.9 litre.

WEIGHTS & LOADINGS - Empty weight 245 lb, 111 kg. Max take-off weight 525 lb, 238 kg. Payload 280 lb, 127 kg. Max wing loading 2.92 lb/ft^2, 14.3 kg/m^2. Max power loading 18.8 lb/hp, 8.5 kg/hp. Load factors NC recommended; +9.0, -6.0 ultimate.

PERFORMANCE* - Max level speed 60 mph, 97 kph. Never exceed speed 85 mph, 137 kph. Max cruising speed 55 mph, 88 kph. Economic cruising speed 45 mph, 72 kph. Stalling speed 22 mph, 35 kph. Max climb rate at sea level 800 ft/min, 4.1 m/s. Min sink rate 300 ft/min, 1.5 m/s at NC speed. Best glide ratio with power off 9/1** at NC speed. Take-off distance 90 ft, 27 m. Landing distance 50 ft, 15 m. Service ceiling 15,000 ft, 4570 m. Range at average cruising speed 150 mile, 241 km. Noise level NC.

*Under unspecified test conditions.

**11/1 with pod.

CASCADE
KASPERWING TWO-SEAT

(Three-axis)

Summary similar to Kasperwing 180-C and CR *except: Tandem two-seater.*

Production status: prototype.

GENERAL - Steve Grossruck had released little information on this prototype at the time of going to press, but we understand that it is intended not only for ultralight training but also as a fun machine. It is based closely on the three-axis solo machines and may well be a derivative of the Rotax 503 engined *180-CR*, since the Rotax 503 is comfortably powerful enough for a two-seat payload. Price: NC.

EXTERNAL DIMENSIONS & AREAS - NC.

POWER PLANT - NC.

WEIGHTS & LOADINGS - Empty weight 320 lb, 145 kg. Other data NC.

PERFORMANCE - NC.

CATTO

Catto Aircraft Inc, PO Box 1104, San Andreas, California 95249; tel (209) 754-1949.

CATTO *GOLDWING ST*

(Three-axis)

Single-seat single-engined mid-wing monoplane with conventional three-axis control. Wing has swept back leading and trailing edges, and tapering chord; no tail, canard wing. Pitch control by elevator on canard; yaw control by tip rudders; roll control by half-span up-only ailerons and spoilers; control inputs through stick for pitch/roll and pedals for yaw. Cantilever wing; main-wing profile modified Liebeck; canard profile GU25; both 100% double-surface. Undercarriage has three wheels in tricycle formation; no suspension on nosewheel and steel-spring suspension on main wheels. Push-right go-right nosewheel steering connected to yaw control. Optional brakes on main wheels. Aluminium-alloy tube/glass-fibre fuselage, partially enclosed. Engine mounted above wing, driving pusher propeller. Composite-construction wing of foam and aluminium covered with glass-fibre skin.

Production status: current, approximately 1000 completed (including machines supplied by Goldwing Ltd, Aircraft Spruce & Specialty Co, and Wicks Aircraft Supply).

GENERAL - One of the most distinctive shapes in the sky and a classic amongst ultralights, the Craig Catto-designed *Goldwing* has a long history, being first seen at the 1979 Sun 'n Fun event in Florida. British-born Craig, who also designed the *Forty Niner* hang glider and the *CA14*, *CA15* and *CA16* ultralights, has since gone on to work on more conventional machines at American Air Technology, but his *Goldwing* has endured, still offering pleasant flight characteristics and a good safety record. It soars excellently, though the other side of the coin is that it needs a longer take-off roll than the average tube-and-Dacron machine.

With the advent of *FAR Part 103*, the original *Goldwing ST* version of the design ceased to be a legal ultralight, and as a result is no longer offered by Goldwing Ltd, but it is still available from elsewhere, either as plans or a kit. Craig Catto himself sells plans, while kits can be had through Aircraft Spruce & Specialty Co or Wicks Aircraft Supply (for addresses see separate entries). The Wicks kit costs US$2044.

With so many aircraft built over such a long time span, and with the most recent *Goldwing STs* being experimental-category homebuilts, it is impossible to describe a 'standard' machine. However, many have been built with direct-drive Cuyuna 430D engines, so it is in this form we detail it below.

EXTERNAL DIMENSIONS & AREAS - Length overall 12.0 ft, 3.66 m. Height overall 5.0 ft, 1.52 m. Wing span 30.0 ft, 9.14 m. Mean chord 4.0 ft, 1.22 m. Canard chord 2.0 ft, 0.61 m. Total wing area 128 ft², 11.9 m². Main wing area 115.5 ft², 10.74 m². Canard area 12.5 ft², 1.16 m². Total fin area 7.3 ft², 0.68 m². Total rudder area 6.8 ft², 0.63 m². Total elevator area 5.0 ft², 0.46 m². Aspect ratio (of main wing) 7.8/1. Nosewheel diameter overall 20 inch, 51 cm. Main wheels diameter overall 20 inch, 51 cm. Other data NC.

POWER PLANT - Cuyuna 430D engine. Max power 30 hp at 5500 rpm. Propeller diameter and pitch 36x16 inch, 0.91x0.40 m. No reduction. Max static thrust NC. Power per unit area 0.23 hp/ft², 2.5 hp/m². Fuel capacity 6.0 US gal, 5.0 Imp gal, 22.7 litre.

WEIGHTS & LOADINGS - Empty weight 220 lb, 100 kg. Max take-off weight 480 lb, 218 kg. Payload 260 lb, 118 kg. Max wing loading 3.75 lb/ft², 18.3 kg/m². Max power loading 16.0 lb/hp, 7.3 kg/hp. Load factors NC recommended; +6.0, -3.0 ultimate.

PERFORMANCE* - Max level speed 70 mph, 113 kph. Never exceed speed 85 mph, 137 kph. Max cruising speed 60 mph, 97 kph. Economic cruising speed 45 mph, 72 kph. Stalling speed 24 mph, 38 kph. Max climb rate at sea level 600 ft/min, 3.1 m/s. Min sink rate 250 ft/min at 38 mph, 1.3 m/s at 61 kph. Best glide ratio with power off 16/1 at 43 mph, 69 kph. Take-off distance 150 ft, 45 m. Landing distance 200 ft, 60 m. Service ceiling 10,000 ft, 3050 m. Range at average cruising speed 360 mile, 579 km. Noise level NC.

*Under unspecified test conditions.

Norman Burr

This Goldwing, owned by British enthusiast Norman Beadle, entered the '83 London-Paris and also has the distinction of being the first built by Eurowing, a now defunct company which was Goldwing Ltd's UK agent. Later Eurowing machines differed considerably from the US versions, but this example is virtually identical to the American apart from its Robin 330 engine and engine fairing.

CATTO *GOLDWING SP*

(Three-axis)

Summary as Goldwing ST *except: glass-fibre suspension on all wheels, brakes on main wheels, fuselage totally enclosed.*

Production status: see text.

GENERAL - Craig Catto designed the *Goldwing SP* as a high-performance version of the original *ST,* but unlike the earlier design, it was never taken up by Goldwing Ltd. One *SP* was built by Goldwing Ltd's UK agent Eurowing before the company folded, and Craig himself built one, but other than that the only *SPs* are those built from plans, which Craig still sells.

Although the aircraft looks like an *ST* with an enclosed cockpit, in reality it is rather more than that, with a different fuselage construction, using no alloy except in the bulkhead. The canard span is increased, and more attention is given to the suspension and braking departments.

Being plans built, it is hard to define a standard *SP,* but the Eurowing example, using a Konig SC430 engine, was well documented and it is that which we detail below.

EXTERNAL DIMENSIONS & AREAS - Length overall 12.0 ft, 3.66 m. Height overall 7.5 ft, 2.29 m. Wing span 30.0 ft, 9.14 m. Chord at root 4.5 ft, 1.37 m. Chord at tip 3.0 ft, 0.91 m. Canard span 12.0 ft, 3.66 m. Canard chord 1.5 ft, 0.46 m. Fin height 3.0 ft, 0.91 m. Total wing area 148 ft², 13.7 m². Main wing area 130 ft², 12.1 m². Canard area 18 ft², 1.7 m². Aspect ratio (of main wing) 6.9/1. Wheel track 5.0 ft, 1.52 m. Wheelbase 7.3 ft, 2.21 m. Nosewheel diameter overall 14 inch, 36 cm. Main wheels diameter overall 16 inch, 41 cm. Other data NC.

POWER PLANT - Konig SC430 engine. Max power 28 hp at NC rpm. Propeller diameter and pitch NC. Toothed-belt reduction, ratio NC. Max static thrust 165 lb, 75 kg. Power per unit area 0.19 hp/ft², 2.0 hp/m². Fuel capacity 6.0 US gal, 5.0 Imp gal, 22.7 litre.

WEIGHTS & LOADINGS - Empty weight 290 lb, 132 kg. Max take-off weight 540 lb, 245 kg. Payload 250 lb, 113 kg. Max wing loading 3.65 lb/ft², 17.9 kg/m². Max power loading 19.3 lb/hp, 8.8 kg/hp. Load factors NC recommended; +6.5, -3.0 ultimate.

PERFORMANCE* - Max level speed 85 mph, 137 kph. Never exceed speed 90 mph, 145 kph. Max cruising speed 70 mph, 113 kph. Economic cruising speed 50 mph, 80 kph. Stalling speed 28 mph, 45 kph. Max climb rate at sea level 700 ft/min, 3.6 m/s. Min sink rate 180 ft/min at 35 mph, 0.9 m/s at 56 kph. Best glide ratio with power off 16/1 at 45 mph, 72 kph. Take-off distance 220 ft, 67 m. Landing distance 160 ft, 48 m. Service ceiling NC. Range at average cruising speed 220 mile, 354 km. Noise level NC.

*Under the following test conditions - Airfield altitude 600 ft, 180 m. Ground temperature 48°F, 9°C. Ground pressure NC. Ground windspeed 5 mph, 8 kph. Test payload 170 lb, 77 kg.

CGS

CGS Aviation Inc, 1305 Lloyd Road, Wickliffe, Ohio 44092; tel (216) 943-3064. Owner and designer: Chuck Slusarczyk.

Canadian agent: Micronautics Inc, 236 Wood Street, Prescott, Ontario; tel (613) 925-2800.

Italian agent: Certano (see separate listing).

Japanese agent: MIE Corporation, 112-3 Chome Sasagawa, Yokka Ichi City, MIE T-510. Malaysian agent: Main Air Service, 433-1 Jalen Ampane, Kuala Lumpur; tel 478559 or 478378.

CGS *HAWK A*
(Three-axis)

Single-seat single-engined high-wing monoplane with conventional three-axis control. Wing has unswept leading and trailing edges, and constant chord; conventional tail. Pitch control by elevator on tail; yaw control by fin-mounted rudder; roll control by half-span ailerons; control inputs through stick for pitch/roll and pedals for yaw. Wing braced from below by struts; wing profile Ul-1720; 100% double-surface. Undercarriage has three wheels in tricycle formation (tail-dragger optional); axle-flex suspension on all wheels. Push-right go-right nosewheel (optional tailwheel) steering connected to yaw control. Optional main-wheel brakes. Aluminium-alloy tube airframe, totally enclosed. Engine mounted at wing height, driving pusher propeller.

Production status: current, 423 completed (total of Hawk A *and* B *production).*

GENERAL - Chuck Slusarczyk started CGS (Chuck's Glider Supplies) in 1972 and sold some 2000 hang-gliders in five years. Subsequently he made a name for himself in the powered scene by creating and distributing the Powerhawk 152 reduction unit, one of the first specifically designed for ultralights and a unit which changed the standards of the industry, not to mention the performance of its products.

When he turned his attention to designing a complete plane, the result met with almost instant success, winning the best design award at the '82 Sun 'n Fun fly-in at Lakeland, Florida, and then winning the Aircraft Recreatioal Vehicle competition at Oshkosh the following year. Although looking nothing like a *Cub,* the *Hawk* was the forerunner of all the 'Cub like' ultralights, for its handling is very similar, as many an aviation writer has observed.

Two versions of the single-seat *Hawk* are offered, the *Hawk A* for homebuilders, which is too heavy for the ultralight category though it *just* qualifies as an FAI-definition microlight, and an ultralight-legal version, the *Hawk B.* Originally the *Hawk A* used a Cuyuna ULII-02 engine and the *Hawk B* either the same unit or a Kawasaki TA440, but latterly the company has standardised on Rotax power, normal fitment being a 277 for the ultralight and a 377 for the homebuilt, though some of the latter have found their way into the sky with a 40 hp 447 on board. All variants feature an enclosed cockpit with removable side doors and use tricycle undercarriages as standard, though a tail-dragger arrangement is optional. Also common to all are four position flaps operating at 8°, 15°, 30°, and 40°. The aircraft come in kit form, the *Hawk A* taking 60 h to build and the *Hawk B* 150 h, and take 20 minutes to rig.

With the prices of the 377-engined machine and its 277-engined stablemate being identical at US$6695 plus US$150 for the optional brakes, there's a straight trade-off between the speed and cross-country ability of the homebuilt-category machine and the legislative freedom and rapid construction of the ultralight. No price is quoted for the *Hawk A* with Rotax 447.

Note: in the following data, where figures for the two Hawk A *versions differ, data for the Rotax 377-engined machine is given first, followed in parentheses by that for the 447-engined aircraft.*

EXTERNAL DIMENSIONS & AREAS - Length overall 20.7 ft, 6.30 m. Height overall 6.8 ft, 2.08 m. Wing span 28.8 ft, 8.78 m. Constant chord 4.6 ft, 1.41 m. Dihedral 3°. Sweepback 0°. Tailplane span 9.0 ft, 2.74 m. Fin height 3.6 ft, 1.09 m. Total wing area 135 ft², 12.6 m². Total aileron area 12.5 ft², 1.16 m². Fin area 7.4 ft², 0.68 m². Rudder area 5.7 ft², 0.53 m². Tailplane area 17.5 ft², 1.62 m². Total elevator area 11.4 ft², 1.06 m². Aspect ratio 6.1/1. Wheel track NC. Wheelbase 6.0 ft, 1.83 m. Nosewheel diameter overall 12 inch, 30 cm. Main wheels diameter overall 15 inch, 38 cm.

POWER PLANT - Rotax 377(447) engine. Max power 35(40) hp at 6250 rpm. Propeller diameter and pitch 60x30 inch, 1.52x0.76 m. Gear reduction, ratio 2.4/1. Max static thrust NC(340) lb, NC(154) kg. Power per unit area 0.26(0.30) hp/ft², 2.8(3.2) hp/m². Fuel capacity 5.0 US gal, 4.2 Imp gal, 18.9 litre.

WEIGHTS & LOADINGS - Empty weight 267(271) lb, 121(123) kg. Max take-off weight 547(551) lb, 248(250) kg. Payload 280 lb, 127 kg. Max wing loading 4.05(4.08) lb/ft², 19.7(19.8) kg/m². Max power loading 15.6(13.8) lb/hp, 7.1(6.3) kg/hp. Load factors +4.0, -2.0 recommended; +6.0, -4.0 ultimate.

PERFORMANCE* - Max level speed 70(80) mph, 113(129) kph. Never exceed speed 85 mph, 137 kph. Max cruising speed 65(70) mph, 105(113) kph. Economic cruising speed 60(65) mph, 97(105) kph. Stalling speed 26 mph, 42 kph. Max climb rate at sea level 800(1000) ft/min, 4.1(5.1) m/s. Min sink rate 300 ft/min at 40 mph, 1.5 m/s at 64 kph. Best glide ratio with power off 9/1 at 50 mph, 80 kph. Take-off distance *130*(100) ft, *40*(30) m. Landing distance *130*(100) ft, *40*(30) m. Service ceiling 18,000 ft, 5490 m. Range at average cruising speed 100 mile, 161 km. Noise level at full power 86 dB at 50 ft, 15 m.

*Under the following test conditions - Airfield altitude 7088 ft, 2160 m. Ground temperature 82°F, 28°C. Ground pressure NC. Ground windspeed 5 mph, 8 kph. Test payload 225 lb, 102 kg.

CGS *HAWK B*
(Three-axis)

Summary as Hawk A.

Production status: see Hawk A.

GENERAL - See *Hawk A.*

EXTERNAL DIMENSIONS & AREAS - See *Hawk A.*

POWER PLANT - See *Hawk A* except: Rotax 277 engine. Max power 28 hp at 6250 rpm. Max static thrust 220 lb, 100 kg. Power per unit area 0.21 hp/ft², 2.2 hp/m².

WEIGHTS & LOADINGS - Empty weight 245 lb, 111 kg.

Glider Rider

Max take-off weight 525 lb, 238 kg. Payload 280 lb, 127 kg. Max wing loading 3.89 lb/ft², 18.9 kg/m². Max power loading 18.8 lb/hp, 8.5 kg/hp. Load factors+4.0, -2.0 recommended;+6.0, -4.0 ultimate.

PERFORMANCE* - Max level speed 60 mph, 97 kph. Never exceed speed 85 mph, 137 kph. Max cruising speed 60 mph, 97 kph. Economic cruising speed 55 mph, 88 kph. Stalling speed 26 mph, 42 kph. Max climb rate at sea level 600 ft/min, 3.1 m/s. Min sink rate 300 ft/min at 40 mph, 1.5 m/s at 64 kph. Best glide ratio with power off 9/1 at 50 mph, 80 kph. Take-off distance 150 ft, 45 m. Landing distance 150 ft, 45 m. Service ceiling 18,000 ft, 5490 m. Range at average cruising speed 100 mile, 161 km. Noise level 86 dB at 50 ft, 15 m.

*Under the following test conditions - Airfield altitude 7088 ft, 2160 m. Ground temperature 82°F, 28 °C. Ground pressure NC. Ground windspeed 5 mph, 8 kph. Test payload 225 lb, 102 kg.

CGS *AG HAWK*
(Three-axis)

Summary as Hawk A *except: Main wheel brakes fitted as standard.*

Production status: current, 10 completed.

GENERAL - This specially rigged *Hawk* is designed for crop spraying duties, and when first announced was fitted with a Rotax 503 engine. CGS tell us that standard equipment is now the Rotax 447 engine, but even with the smaller engine the payload is generous; the data below refers to the latter version. Chemicals are contained in a 20

The Hawk A. *For a picture of the* Hawk B, *see* Certano (Italian section).

US gal tank (16.7 Imp gal, 75.7 litre), and booms and nozzles are fitted along the span of the wings to give a spray swath of nearly 30 ft (9.1 m).
Prices are US$7695 for the aircraft, plus US$2500 for the spray unit.

EXTERNAL DIMENSIONS & AREAS - See *Hawk A.*

POWER PLANT - See Rotax 447 version of *Hawk A.*

WEIGHTS & LOADINGS - Empty weight 275 lb, 125 kg. Max take-off weight 650 lb, 295 kg. Payload 375 lb, 170 kg. Max wing loading 4.8 lb/ft², 23.4 kg/m². Max power loading 16.3 lb/hp, 7.4 kg/hp. Load factors+4.0, -2.0 recommended; +4.0, -6.0 ultimate.

PERFORMANCE* - Max level speed 80 mph, 129 kph. Never exceed speed 85 mph, 137 kph. Max cruising speed 65 mph, 105 kph. Economic cruising speed 62 mph, 100 kph. Stalling speed 29 mph, 47 kph. Max climb rate at sea level 800 ft/min, 4.1 m/s. Min sink rate 300 ft/min at 40 mph, 1.5 m/s at 64 kph. Best glide ratio with power off 9/1 at 50 mph, 80 kph. Take-off distance *130* ft, *40* m. Landing distance *130* ft, *40* m. Service ceiling 18,000 ft, 5490 m. Range at average cruising speed 100 mile, 161 km. Noise level at full power 86 dB at 50 ft, 15 m.

*Under the following test conditions - Airfield altitude 7088 ft, 2160 m. Ground temperature 82°F, 28°C. Ground pressure NC. Ground windspeed 5 mph, 8 kph. Test payload 251 lb, 114 kg.

CGS *HAWK II*
(Three-axis)

Summary as Hawk A except: Tandem two-seater. Main wheel brakes fitted as standard.

Production status: current, 4 completed.

GENERAL - The two-seat version of the *Hawk* is remarkable for the commonality of parts with the single-seat version, some 65% being interchangeable. During development a slightly larger span was tried, just 2 inch (5 cm) greater than the solo machine, but the company quotes the production aircraft as having identical span and area. Chuck and his team found they needed steel tail struts and landing gear legs instead of the solo machine's aluminium, but the resulting aircraft is still instantly recognisable as a *Hawk*. As with the single-seater, doors can be removed for summer flying.

Although we have heard of two-seat *Hawks* with Rotax 503 engines, CGS tell us that standard equipment is the 447 Rotax, which itself permits a hefty 470 lb payload (213 kg), enough to take two large jovial ultralight enthusiasts aloft. It is the 447 version which we detail below, though the 503 version is in production at CGS' Italian licensee, Certano, and is detailed in the Italian section.

The US -produced machine is priced at US$8195 for a kit taking 80-125 h to build. The price excludes options, among them transparent nose and wing panels to improve visibility. Rigging time is stated as approximately 25 min. We hear also that CGS is working on an amphibious version of this aircraft, with the wheels retracting into the floats. The aircraft will be aimed at the homebuilt market, rather than as a trainer, but at the time of going to press no further details were available.

EXTERNAL DIMENSIONS & AREAS - See *Hawk A* except: *Length overall 20.7 ft, 6.30 m. Height overall 7.5 ft, 2.29 m.*

POWER PLANT - See Rotax 447-engined version of *Hawk A.*

WEIGHTS & LOADINGS - Empty weight 330 lb, 150 kg. Max take-off weight 800 lb, 363 kg. Payload 470 lb, 213 kg. Max wing loading 5.93 lb/ft^2, 28.8 kg/m^2. Max power loading 20.0 lb/hp, 9.1 kg/hp. Load factors +4.0, -2.0 recommended; +6.0, -4.0 ultimate.

PERFORMANCE* - Max level speed 80 mph, 129 kph. Never exceed speed 90 mph, 145 kph. Max cruising speed 70 mph, 113 kph. Economic cruising speed 65 mph, 105 kph. Stalling speed 30 mph, 48 kph. Max climb rate at sea level 700 ft/min, 3.6 m/s. Min sink rate 400 ft/min at 45 mph, 2.0 m/s at 72 kph. Best glide ratio with power off 9/1 at 55 mph, 88 kph. Take-off distance *175* ft, *53* m. Landing distance *175* ft, *53* m. Service ceiling 18,000 ft, 5490 m. Range at average cruising speed 100 mile, 161 km. Noise level at full power 86 dB at 50 ft, 15 m.

*Under the following test conditions - Airfield altitude 7088 ft, 2160 m. Ground temperature 82°F, 28°C. Ground pressure NC. Ground windspeed 5 mph, 8 kph. Test payload 380 lb, 172 kg.

CHANDELLE

Chandelle Aircraft, 4230 South 36th Place, Phoenix, Arizona 85040; tel (602) 437-2828.

CHANDELLE
MARK IV SERIES
(Three-axis)

Single-seat single-engined high-wing monoplane with conventional three-axis control. Wing has swept back leading edge, swept forward trailing edge, and tapering chord; cruciform tail. Pitch control by elevator on tail; yaw control by fin-mounted rudder; roll control by full-span ailerons; control inputs through stick for pitch/roll and pedals for yaw. Wing braced from below by struts; wing profile NC; single-surface. Undercarriage has three wheels in tricycle formation; no suspension on nosewheel and suspension (type NC) on main wheels. Push-right go-right nosewheel steering connected to yaw control. Brakes fitted. Aluminium-alloy tube airframe, with optional pod. Engine mounted below wing, driving pusher propeller.

Production status: current, number completed NC.

GENERAL - Chandelle is a new name to the US ultralight industry, and the company is becoming known not for any revolutionary technology - a tube-and-Dacron design with single-surface wing could hardly be that - but for very keen pricing.

The *Mark IV* which we detail here is the basis of the company's range and costs US$5395 for a 16-40 h kit, but there is also a super-cheap two-axis version, at US$2995 with single-cylinder engine or US$3295 with a twin. This economy version appears to use the same airframe as the three-axis machine, but has its differential ailerons removed, leaving the wing as constant chord with a swept forward trailing edge. An agricultural version with 45 hp engine and 20 US gal (16.7 Imp gal, 75 litre) crop spray tank is also offered, called the *Mark IV AG* and priced at US$8758.

Finally, for those who already have a power pack, the company sells the *Mark IV* without engine, in which form it costs US$3995 and is dubbed *Mark IV LE.*

EXTERNAL DIMENSIONS & AREAS - Wing span 30.3 ft, 9.25 m. Total wing area 176 ft^2, 16.4 m^2. Aspect ratio 5.2/1. Nosewheel diameter overall 16 inch, 41 cm. Main wheels diameter overall 16 inch, 41 cm. Other data NC.

POWER PLANT - Cuyuna ULII-02 engine. Max power 35 hp at NC rpm. Propeller diameter and pitch 59 inch x 13°, 1.50 inch x 13° (3-blade). Reduction type NC, ratio 2.4/1. Max static thrust NC. Power per unit area 0.20 hp/ft^2, 2.1 hp/m^2. Fuel capacity 5.0 US gal, 4.2 Imp gal, 18.9 litre.

WEIGHTS & LOADINGS - Empty weight 243 lb, 110 kg. Max take-off weight 500 lb, 227 kg. Payload 257 lb, 117 kg. Max wing loading 2.84 lb/ft^2, 13.8 kg/m^2. Max power loading 14.3 lb/hp, 6.5 kg/hp. Load factors NC.

PERFORMANCE* - Max level speed 60 mph, 97 kph. Never exceed speed 75 mph, 121 kph. Max cruising speed 50 mph, 80 kph. Economic cruising speed 40 mph, 64 kph. Stalling speed 22 mph, 35 kph. Max climb rate at sea level 650 ft/min, 3.3 m/s. Range at average cruising speed 187 mile, 302 km. Other data NC.

*Under unspecified test conditions.

CHANDELLE *MARK TWO*
(Three-axis)

Summary as Mark IV except: Two-seater.

Production status: current, number completed NC.

GENERAL - This aircraft is basically a two-seat version of the *Mark IV,* but with larger span. Price is US$6495 including full dual controls, but no other details are available.

EXTERNAL DIMENSIONS & AREAS - Wing span 33.3 ft, 10.16 m. Nosewheel diameter overall 16 inch, 41 cm. Main wheels diameter overall 16 inch, 41 cm. Other data NC.

POWER PLANT - NC.

WEIGHTS & LOADINGS - NC.

PERFORMANCE - NC.

CLOUD DANCER

Cloud Dancer Aeroplane Works, Hangar 21, Delaware Municipal Airport, Delaware, Ohio 43015; tel (614) 363-5009. (No longer trading).

CLOUD DANCER *JENNY*
(Three-axis)

Single-seat single-engined biplane with conventional three-axis control. Wings have unswept leading and trailing edges, and constant chord; conventional tail. Pitch control by elevator on tail; yaw control by fin-mounted rudder; roll control by quarter-span spoilers; control inputs through stick for pitch/roll and pedals for yaw. Wings braced by struts and transverse X-cables; wing profile NC; 100% double-surface. Undercarriage has two wheels plus tail-skid; no suspension on tailskid and bungee suspension on main wheels. No ground steering. No brakes. Aluminium-alloy tube airframe, partially enclosed. Engine mounted between wings, driving tractor propeller.

Production status: see text.

GENERAL - One of the first replica machines to hit the US ultralight market, the *Jenny* is modelled on the Curtiss *JN4-D Jenny* and was designed by Lew Parsons, who later went on to create a series of three replicas for Squadron Aviation. In fact the *Jenny* is structurally very similar to the Squadron machines, relying on aluminium and Dacron despite its traditional appearance.
For lovers of nostalgia, it's just as well that the Squadron machines are still very much alive, for at the time of writing the *Jenny* was not. The company folded in early 1985 even though according to one report the order book was healthy, and at the time of writing it is not clear whether the design will ever reappear.

EXTERNAL DIMENSIONS & AREAS - Length overall 17.0 ft, 5.18 m. Height overall 7.5 ft, 2.29 m. Wing span NC (bottom); 28.3 ft, 8.63 m (top). Sweepback 0°. Total wing area 186 ft², 17.3 m². Other data NC.

POWER PLANT - Cuyuna ULII-02 engine. Max power 35 hp at 5500 rpm. Propeller diameter and pitch 72x33 inch,

Glider Rider

1.83x0.84 m. Planetary gear reduction, ratio 3.0/1. Max static thrust 296 lb, 134 kg. Power per unit area 0.19 hp/ft², 2.0 hp/m². Fuel capacity 5.0 US gal, 4.2 Imp gal, 18.9 litre.

WEIGHTS & LOADINGS - Empty weight 248 lb, 112 kg. Max take-off weight 500 lb, 227 kg. Payload 252 lb, 114 kg. Max wing loading 2.69 lb/ft², 13.1 kg/m². Max power loading 14.3 lb/hp, 6.5 kg/hp. Load factors +4.0, -2.0 recommended; NC ultimate.

PERFORMANCE* - Max level speed 62 mph, 100 kph. Never exceed speed 69 mph, 111 kph. Max cruising speed 58 mph, 93 kph. Economic cruising speed 46 mph, 74 kph. Stalling speed 21 mph, 34 kph. Max climb rate at sea level 1000 ft/min, 5.1 m/s. Best glide ratio with power off 5.5/1 at NC speed. Range at average cruising speed 144 mile, 231 km. Other data NC.

*Under unspecified test conditions.

DELTA TECHNOLOGY

Delta Technology, 12953 E Garvey Blvd, Baldwin Park, California 91706; tel (818) 814-1467. President: Walter S Robinson.

DELTA TECHNOLOGY *HONCHO II*
(Three-axis)

Single-seat single-engined high-wing monoplane with conventional three-axis control. Wing has unswept leading and trailing edges, and constant chord; cruciform tail. Pitch control by elevator on tail; yaw control by fin-mounted rudder; roll control by half-span ailerons; control inputs through stick for pitch/roll and pedals for yaw. Wing braced from below by struts; wing profile NACA 4415; 100% double-surface. Undercarriage has three wheels in tricycle formation with additional tailwheel; no suspension on nosewheel and coil-spring suspension on main wheels. Push-right go-right nosewheel steering connected to yaw control. Optional brake. Steel/aluminium-alloy tube airframe, completely open. Engine mounted below wing, driving pusher propeller.

Production status: current, number completed NC.

GENERAL - When glider and hang-glider manufacturer Delta Sailplane Corporation folded in 1982, it seemed like the end for the ultralights it had created - the tandem under-carriage *Nomad,* tricycle *Honcho* and its more powerful brother the *Super Honcho.* Against all the odds, however, the designs have survived and are now back in serious pro-duction in the hands of Walter Robinson. His team has made various changes and now concentrates its market-ing effort on the *Honcho II,* as the latest version of the *Honcho* is known.

Improvements include a stronger undercarriage with coil-springs for the main wheels, and a revised tail design with fin-mounted rudder replacing the previous fully flying device, which had only a separate under-boom fin to do the job of vertical stabiliser. Wing covering is ceconite 7600. The variety of engines previously offered have all been abandoned in favour of Rotax power, which is now stan-dard throughout the range.

One notable feature which has not been altered is the sturdy cage around the pilot, which should give the pilot every chance in the event of an accident, though at the price of rather difficult access to the seat. A *Honcho II* was tested by Bill Cox in the 1985 edition of *Ultralight Aircraft Annual.*

Sold as a 100-150 h kit, the aircraft costs US$4980, with ready to fly machines available for an extra US$1500. Rigging time is 20 min.

EXTERNAL DIMENSIONS & AREAS - Length overall 17.5 ft, 5.35 m. Height overall 9.4 ft, 2.87 m. Wing span 32.2 ft, 9.80 m. Constant chord 4.1 ft, 1.24 m. Sweepback 0°. Total wing area 131 ft², 12.2 m². Aspect ratio 7.9/1. Other data NC.

POWER PLANT - Rotax 277 engine. Max power 27 hp at NC rpm. Propeller diameter and pitch 48x32 inch, 1.22x0.81 m. Flat-belt reduction, ratio 2.1/1. Max static thrust NC. Power per unit area 0.21 hp/ft², 2.2 hp/m². Fuel capacity 5.0 US gal, 4.2 Imp gal, 18.9 litre.

WEIGHTS & LOADINGS - Empty weight 239 lb, 108 kg. Max take-off weight 420 lb, 191 kg. Payload 181 lb, 82 kg. Max wing loading 3.21 lb/ft², 15.7 kg/m². Max power load-ing 15.6 lb/hp, 7.1 kg/hp. Load factors NC recommended; +6.7, -2.5 ultimate.

PERFORMANCE* - Max level speed 58 mph, 93 kph. Never exceed speed 70 mph, 113 kph. Cruising speed 50 mph, 80 kph. Stalling speed 25 mph, 40 kph. Max climb rate

at sea level 700 ft/min, 3.6 m/s. Min sink rate 200 ft/min, 1.0 m/s at NC speed. Best glide ratio with power off 12.7/1 at NC speed. Take-off distance 95 ft, 29 m. Landing distance NC. Service ceiling 12,500 ft, 3810 m. Range at average cruising speed 160 mile, 257 km. Noise level NC.

*Under the following test conditions - Test payload 181 lb, 82 kg. Other data NC.

DELTA TECHNOLOGY
SUPER HONCHO
(Three-axis)

Summary as Honcho II.

Production status: current, number completed NC.

GENERAL - The *Super Honcho* has benefitted from just the same development as the *Honcho II,* which it resem-bles closely. The major change is the use of a much more powerful engine, the Rotax 503, which boosts the price to US$5980 in kit form.

EXTERNAL DIMENSIONS & AREAS - See *Honcho II* except: Length overall 17.9 ft, 5.46 m. Height overall 9.9 ft, 3.02 m.

POWER PLANT - Rotax 503 engine. Max power 50 hp at NC rpm. Propeller diameter and pitch 54x32 inch, 1.37x0.81 m. Reduction type NC, ratio 2.4/1. Max static thrust NC. Power per unit area 0.38 hp/ft², 4.1 hp/m². Fuel capacity 5.0 US gal, 4.2 Imp gal, 18.9 litre.

WEIGHTS & LOADINGS - Empty weight 276 lb, 125 kg. Max take-off weight 525 lb, 238 kg. Payload 249 lb, 113 kg. Max wing loading 4.01 lb/ft², 19.5 kg/m². Max power load-ing 10.5 lb/hp, 4.8 kg/hp. Load factors NC recommended; +6.7, -3.5 ultimate.

PERFORMANCE* - Max level speed 63 mph, 101 kph. Never exceed speed 80 mph, 129 kph. Cruising speed 58 mph, 93 kph. Stalling speed 27 mph, 43 kph. Max climb rate at sea level 1580 ft/min, 8.0 m/s. Min sink rate 230 ft/min, 1.2 m/s at NC speed. Best glide ratio with power off 11.4/1 at NC speed. Take-off distance 60 ft, 18 m. Landing distance NC. Service ceiling 17,500 ft, 5330 m. Range at average cruising speed 140 mile, 225 km. Noise level NC.

*Under the following test conditions - Test payload 249 lb, 113 kg. Other data NC.

DELTA TECHNOLOGY
NOMAD II
(Three-axis)

Summary as Honcho II *except: Undercarriage has two wheels in tandem with under-wing skids; suspension NC. Ground steering NC. Brakes NC.*

Production status: current, number completed NC.

GENERAL - The *Nomad* is Delta's soaring-oriented ultralight and has a glider-style undercarriage using a single main wheel and skids under the wings. Wing span is increased to improve the glide angle, and the airframe is slightly longer.

Price: US$5380 for a 100-150 h kit.

Flashback to Oshkosh '82, and the original Honcho, *now modified as described in the text and back in production.*

EXTERNAL DIMENSIONS & AREAS - Length overall 18.9 ft, 5.75 m. Height overall 9.4 ft, 2.87 m. Wing span 36.1 ft, 11.00 m. Constant chord 4.1 ft, 1.24 m. Sweepback 0°. Total wing area 147 ft², 13.7 m². Aspect ratio 8.8/1. Other data NC.

POWER PLANT - See *Honcho II* except: Power per unit area 0.18 hp/ft², 2.0 hp/m².

WEIGHTS & LOADINGS - Empty weight 248 lb, 112 kg. Max take-off weight 442 lb, 200 kg. Payload 194 lb, 88 kg. Max wing loading 3.01 lb/ft², 14.6 kg/m². Max power loading 16.4 lb/hp, 7.4 kg/hp. Load factors NC recommended; +6.7, -2.5 ultimate.

PERFORMANCE* - Max level speed 56 mph, 90 kph. Never exceed speed 65 mph, 105 kph. Cruising speed 48 mph, 77 kph. Stalling speed 23 mph, 37 kph. Max climb rate at sea level 660 ft/min, 3.4 m/s. Min sink rate 180 ft/min, 0.9 m/s at NC speed. Best glide ratio with power off 15.8/1 at NC speed. Take-off distance 100 ft, 30 m. Landing distance NC. Service ceiling 15,000 ft, 4570 m. Range at average cruising speed 160 mile, 257 km. Noise level NC.

Under the following test conditions -* Test payload 194 lb, 88 kg. Other data NC.

DENNEY

Denney Aerocraft Company, 6140 Morris Hill Lane, Boise, Idaho 83704; tel (208) 322-1716. President: Dan Denney.

DENNEY *KITFOX*
(Three-axis)

Side-by-side two-seat single-engined high-wing monoplane with conventional three-axis control. Wing has unswept leading and trailing edges, and constant chord; cruciform tail. Pitch control by elevator on tail; yaw control by fin-mounted rudder; roll control by full-span flaperons; control inputs through stick for pitch/roll and pedals for yaw. Wing braced from below by struts; wing profile NC; 100% double-surface. Undercarriage has three wheels in tail-dragger formation; leaf-spring suspension on tailwheel and bungee suspension on main wheels. Push-right go-right tailwheel steering connected to yaw control; also differential braking. Brakes on main wheels. Steel-tube airframe, totally enclosed. Engine mounted below wing, driving tractor propeller.

Production status: current, 6 completed.

GENERAL - Dan Denney was one of the co-designers of the popular *Avid Flyer,* (see Light Aero) and has set up his own company to sell what he believes is an improved version. Called the *Kitfox,* it incorporates a number of subtle changes, of which the most important is more cockpit room, a major deficiency of the *Avid Flyer.*

The *Kitfox* is well out of the ultralight category, though it would qualify as a microlight in some countries, and is sold in the US as a homebuilt experimental aircraft. It comes as a complete kit that includes a 52 hp Rotax 503 engine, all-welded fuselage and other 4130-grade aircraft steel components, die-formed flaperons, routed and glued ribs, formed glass-fibre components, and all other necessary items except colour dope, upholstery and instruments. Some 250 h are needed to turn this collection of goodies into a flying machine.

The accent is very much on practicality, with wings that fold back parallel with the fuselage, allowing very quick rigging (5 min is claimed). A pin holds the wings folded and a towbar can then be attached so that it straddles the tailwheel assembly, obviating the need for a trailer. Dan set out to create a machine with good short-field capability, and this, combined with a rugged undercarriage, excellent visibility and dual controls, should make the *Kitfox* a good training tool.

Price is US$8200 and options include upholstery for US$225, hydraulic disc brakes for US$265 and a towbar for US$75.

EXTERNAL DIMENSIONS & AREAS - Length overall 16.9 ft, 5.14 m. Height overall 5.6 ft, 1.70 m. Wing span 31.4 ft, 9.55 m. Constant chord 4.3 ft, 1.30 m. Dihedral 2.5°. Sweepback 0°. Tailplane span 7.8 ft, 2.39 m. Fin height 4.8 ft, 1.45 m. Total wing area 128 ft^2, 11.9 m^2. Total flaperon area 16.0 ft^2, 1.49 m^2. Fin area 12.3 ft^2, 1.14 m^2. Rudder area 4.3 ft^2, 0.40 m^2. Tailplane area 16.2 ft^2, 1.51 m^2. Total elevator area 6.8 ft^2, 0.63 m^2. Aspect ratio 7.7/1. Wheel track 4.8 ft, 1.45 m. Wheelbase 12.4 ft, 3.78 m. Tailwheel diameter overall 6 inch, 15 cm. Main wheels diameter overall 20 inch, 51 cm.

POWER PLANT - Rotax 503 engine. Max power 52 hp at 6300 rpm. Propeller diameter and pitch 68x30 inch, 1.73x0.76 m. Toothed-belt reduction, ratio 2.3/1. Max static thrust 340 lb, 154 kg. Power per unit area 0.41 hp/ft^2, 4.4 hp/m^2. Fuel capacity 9.7 US gal, 8.1 Imp gal, 36.7 litre.

WEIGHTS & LOADINGS - Empty weight 380 lb, 172 kg. Max take-off weight 800 lb, 363 kg. Payload 420 lb, 191 kg. Max wing loading 6.25 lb/ft^2, 30.5 kg/m^2. Max power loading 15.4 lb/hp, 7.0 kg/hp. Load factors +3.8, -1.5 recommended; +5.7, -3.0 ultimate.

PERFORMANCE* - Max level speed 85 mph, 137 kph. Never exceed speed 95 mph, 153 kph. Max cruising speed 75 mph, 121 kph. Economic cruising speed 65 mph, 15 kph. Stalling speed 27 mph, 43 kph. Max climb rate at sea level 1480 ft/min, 7.5 m/s. Take-off distance 100** ft, 30** m. Landing distance 200 ft, 60 m. Service ceiling *20,000* ft, *6100* m. Range at average cruising speed 275 mile, 442 km. Other data NC.

*Under the following test conditions - Airfield altitude 20 ft, 6 m. Ground temperature 59°F, 15°C. Ground pressure 1013 mB. Ground windspeed 0 mph, 0 kph. Test payload 210 lb, 95 kg.

**Approximately double when used dual.

DIEHL AERO-NAUTICAL

Diehl Aero-Nautical, 1855 North Elm, Jenks, Oklahoma 74037; tel (918) 299-4445. President: Dan Diehl. Vice-president: Tom Diehl.

DIEHL AERO-NAUTICAL
XTC-UL and XTC-EXP

(Three-axis)

Single-seat single-engined mid-wing monoplane with conventional three-axis control. Wing has swept back leading edge, swept forward trailing edge, and tapering chord; no tail, canard wing. Pitch control by elevator on canard; yaw control by rudders at quarter span; roll control by quarter-span spoilers; control inputs through stick for pitch/roll and pedals for yaw. Cantilever wing; wing profile NC; 100% double-surface. Undercarriage has three retractable wheels in tricycle formation; coil-spring suspension on nosewheel and glass-fibre suspension on main wheels. Push-right go-right nosewheel steering connected to yaw control; also differential braking. Brakes on main wheels. Composite-construction airframe, partially enclosed (full enclosure optional). Engine mounted above wing, driving pusher propeller.

Production status: current, 65 completed (total of both versions).

GENERAL - Introduced at Oshkosh '82 in prototype form, the unique shape of the world's first amphibious ultralight caused quite a stir at the annual EAA fly-in and has fascinated enthusiasts ever since. At that time called the *XTC Hydrolight*, in production form this composite-construction machine with retractable undercarriage is powered by a KFM engine and is offered in two versions - the ultralight *XTC-UL*, which weighs in at 292 lb (132 kg) and the experimental-category *XTC-EXP*, weighing 330 lb (150 kg). Both use foam/glass-fibre construction, with wing spars in carbon fibre, and gain their buoyancy from the fuselage itself, which forms a hull. For float flying the nosewheel retracts forwards and the main wheels retract sideways and outwards.

Some readers may be mystified to see an aircraft weighing 292 lb classified as an ultralight, but there's no mistake: although current US legislation stipulates a 254 lb (115 kg) weight limit, a further 50 lb (23 kg) is allowed for ultralights using the fuselage to provide buoyancy, and Diehl makes full use of this concession.

Buyers have a choice of traditional Stits wing covering or transparent Tedlar, and a wide range of other options, including a bubble canopy, saltwater corrosion proofing, instrumentation, electric start, headrest, special trim, plus for the homebuilt model an extra fuel tank. There's even a video tape to help with construction, which takes 200-400 h for the ultralight, all glass-fibre parts being premoulded. Rigging time is around 20 min, the wings being removable outboard of the rudders.

Prices are US$7400 for the *XTC-UL* and US$7100 for the *XTC-EXP*, with part kits available to spread the financial load. Plans cost US$100.

Data below refers to the *XTC-UL;* where different, figures for the *XTC-EXP* are shown in parentheses.

EXTERNAL DIMENSIONS & AREAS - Length overall 14.6 ft, 4.45 m. Height overall 4.8 ft, 1.47 m. Wing span 32.0 ft, 9.75 m. Chord at root 5.0 ft, 1.52 m. Chord at tip 3.0 ft, 0.91 m. Dihedral 3°. Sweepback NC°. Canard span 8.8 ft, 2.69 m. Canard chord 1.8 ft, 0.56 m. Fin height 2.8 ft, 0.86 m. Total wing area 145 ft^2, 13.5 m^2. Main wing area 128 ft^2, 11.9 m^2. Canard area 17 ft^2, 1.6 m^2. Total spoileron area 3.0 ft^2, 0.3 m^2. Fin area 10.0 ft^2, 0.9 m^2. Total rudder area 7.0 ft^2, 0.7 m^2. Total elevator area 6.0 ft^2, 0.6 m^2. Aspect ratio (of main wing) 8.0/1. Wheel track 6.1 ft, 1.85 m. Wheelbase 9.0 ft, 1.85 m. Nosewheel diameter overall 10 inch, 25 cm. Main wheels diameter overall 10 inch, 25 cm.

POWER PLANT - KFM 107 engine. Max power 25 hp at 6100 rpm. Propeller diameter and pitch 53x22 inch, 1.35x0.56 m. V-belt reduction, ratio 2.1/1. Max static thrust 140 lb, 64 kg. Power per unit area 0.17 hp/ft^2, 1.9 hp/m^2. Fuel capacity 5.0 US gal, 4.2 Imp gal, 18.9 litre.

WEIGHTS & LOADINGS - Empty weight 292(330) lb,

Perhaps the prettiest version of all, this XTC is fitted with Tedlar wing covering and the optional bubble canopy. For another illustration, see front cover.

132(150) kg. Max take-off weight 522(560) lb, 236(254) kg. Payload 230 lb, 104 kg. Max wing loading 3.6(3.9) lb/ft², 17.5(18.8) kg/m². Max power loading 20.9(22.4) lb/hp, 9.4(10.2) kg/hp. Load factors +4.2, -NC recommended; +6.3, -NC ultimate.

PERFORMANCE* - Max level speed 62 mph, 100 kph. Never exceed speed 80 mph, 129 kph. Max cruising speed 50(60) mph, 80(97) kph. Economic cruising speed 50 mph, 80 kph. Stalling speed 27(32) mph, 43(51) kph. Max climb rate at sea level 600 ft/min, 3.1 m/s. Min sink rate 250 ft/min, 1.3 m/s at NC speed. Best glide ratio with power off 14/1 at 42 mph, 68 kph. Take-off distance 200** ft, 60** m. Landing distance 100*** ft, 30*** m. Service ceiling 10,000 ft, 3050 m. Range at average cruising speed 150 mile, 241 km. Noise level NC.

*Under the following test conditions - Airfield altitude 623 ft, 190 m. Ground temperature 85°F, 29°C. Ground pressure NC. Ground windspeed 6 mph, 10 kph. Test payload 185 lb, 84 kg.

**Land figure - twice as much on water.

***On land or water.

EASTERN ULTRALIGHTS

Eastern Ultralights, 102 Fort Meyers Drive, PO Box 21, Indian Lake Estates, Florida 33855; tel (813) 692-1526. President: Raymond Abel.

EASTERN ULTRALIGHTS *SNOOP*

(Three-axis)

Single-seat single-engined high-wing monoplane with conventional three-axis control. Wing has unswept leading and trailing edges, and constant chord; cruciform tail. Pitch control by elevator on tail; yaw control by fully flying rudder; roll control by one-third span spoilers; control inputs through stick for pitch/roll and pedals for yaw. Wing braced from above by kingpost and cables, from below by cables; wing profile NC; single-surface. Undercarriage has three wheels in tricycle formation with additional tailskid; torsion-bar suspension on all wheels. No ground steering. No brakes. Aluminium-alloy tube

airframe, with optional pod. Engine mounted below wing, driving pusher propeller.

Production status: current, see text for number completed.

GENERAL - Formerly based in New Jersey under Robert Abel, this company moved in 1985 to Florida and is now run by his brother Raymond, leaving Robert free to develop his own firm, US Aircraft, which we list separately.

The *Snoop* which Raymond is now in charge of is a straightforward tube-and-Dacron ultralight in the classic *Quicksilver MX* mould, the most obvious recognition point being the use of two angled kingposts rather than the single vertical device favoured by Eipper. The prototype *Snoop* was shown at Sun 'n Fun as long ago as '81, at which time it was a two-axis machine, but production versions all have roll control. Around 200 have been built in total, including a number of two-seat *Snoop IIs* and just four of a double-surfaced version called the *Snoop +*. The latter has a smaller span wing with ailerons and flaps, but has yet to be developed to the company's satisfaction and is not offered for sale at present.

Detailed below is the standard *Snoop*, which costs US$4790 for a 30 h kit - the same price, incidentally, as we quoted in our last edition two years ago.

EXTERNAL DIMENSIONS & AREAS - Length overall 16.1 ft, 4.90 m. Height overall 8.5 ft, 2.59 m. Wing span 33.0 ft, 10.05 m. Constant chord 5.0 ft, 1.52 m. Dihedral 7°. Sweepback 0°. Total wing area 165 ft², 15.3 m². Total spoiler area 3.0 ft², 0.28 m². Rudder area 6.0 ft², 0.56 m².

Total elevator area 6.0 ft², 0.56 m². Aspect ratio 6.6/1. Wheelbase 5.5 ft, 1.67 m. Nosewheel diameter overall 12 inch, 30 cm. Main wheels diameter overall 14 inch, 35 cm. Other data NC.

POWER PLANT - Cuyuna ULII-02 engine. Max power 35 hp at 6200 rpm. Propeller diameter and pitch 54x27 inch, 1.37x0.69 m. V-belt reduction, ratio 2.0/1. Max static thrust 200 lb, 91 kg. Power per unit area 0.21 hp/ft², 2.3 hp/m². Fuel capacity 5.0 US gal, 4.2 Imp gal, 18.9 litre.

WEIGHTS & LOADINGS - Empty weight 238 lb, 108 kg. Max take-off weight 518 lb, 235 kg. Payload 280 lb, 127 kg. Max wing loading 3.2 lb/ft², 15.3 kg/m². Max power loading 14.8 lb/hp, 6.7 kg/hp. Load factors +5.5, -3.5 recommended; +6.0, -4.0 ultimate.

PERFORMANCE* - Max level speed 50 mph, 80 kph. Never exceed speed 55 mph, 88 kph. Max cruising speed 45 mph, 72 kph. Economic cruising speed 40 mph, 64 kph. Stalling speed 18 mph, 29 kph. Max climb rate at sea level 600 ft/min, 3.1 m/s. Take-off distance 75 ft, 23 m. Landing distance 100 ft, 30 m. Service ceiling 10,000 ft, 3050 m. Range at average cruising speed 125 mile, 201 km. Other data NC.

*Under the following test conditions - Airfield altitude 60 ft, 18 m. Ground temperature 70°F, 21°C. Ground pressure NC. Ground windspeed 5 mph, 8 kph. Pilot weight 180 lb, 82 kg.

EASTERN ULTRALIGHTS
SNOOP II
(Three-axis)

Summary as Snoop *except: Side-by-side two-seater. Push-right go-right nosewheel steering connected to yaw control. Pod not available.*

Production status: current, see Snoop *text for number completed.*

GENERAL - Similar in concept to the *Snoop* but beefed up and with a larger wing, this two-seater comes with dual rudder pedals and side-mounted sticks, with a single central throttle control. Engine is a tuned version of the Cuyuna ULII-02 used for the solo machine.
Price: US$5790 for a 40-50 h kit.

EXTERNAL DIMENSIONS & AREAS - See *Snoop* except: Length overall 17.1 ft, 5.21 m. Wing span 39.0 ft, 11.88 m. Total wing area 195 ft², 18.1 m². Aspect ratio 7.8/1. Wheelbase 6.7 ft, 2.04 m.

POWER PLANT - See *Snoop* except: Max power 45 hp at 6200 rpm. Belt reduction, ratio 2.0/1. Max static thrust NC. Power per unit area 0.23 hp/ft², 2.5 hp/m².

WEIGHTS & LOADINGS - Empty weight 268 lb, 122 kg. Max take-off weight 688 lb, 312 kg. Payload 420 lb, 190 kg. Max wing loading 3.52 lb/ft², 17.2 kg/m². Max power loading 15.3 lb/hp, 6.9 kg/hp. Load factors +5.5, -3.5 design; +6.0, -4.0 ultimate.

PERFORMANCE* - See *Snoop* except: Stalling speed 17 mph, 27 kph. Take-off distance 100 ft, 30 m. Landing distance 125 ft, 38 m. Range at average cruising speed 100 mile, 161 km.

*Test conditions as Snoop *except:* Total pilot and passenger weight 360 lb, 164 kg. Engine used for test: 40 hp Cuyuna 430R.

A peaceful scene on Lake Windermere, in the heart of England's picturesque Lake District, as two local enthusiasts take a break from float-flying their Quick silver MX.

EIPPER

Eipper Industries, PO Box 1572, Temecula, California 92390; tel (714) 676-3228. President: Lyle Byrum.

British agent: The Aerolite Aviation Co Ltd, Long Marston Aviation Centre, Long Marston, Stratford-upon-Avon, Warks CV37 8RT; tel (0789) 299229. Directors: Barry and Sue Gordon.

French agent: AD'air, ZI, 17 rue des Rochettes, 91150 Morigny-Champigny; tel (6) 494 4636.

South African agent: Aviation 2000 (see separate listing).

EIPPER QUICKSILVER MX
(Three-axis)

Single-seat single-engined high-wing monoplane with unconventional three-axis control (conventional three-axis optional). Wing has unswept leading and trailing edges, and constant chord; cruciform tail. Pitch control by elevator on tail; yaw control by fully flying rudder; roll control by one-third span spoilers; control inputs through stick for pitch/yaw (pitch/roll optional) and pedals for roll (yaw optional). Wing braced from above by kingpost and cables, from below by cables; wing profile NC; 100% single-surface. Undercarriage has three wheels in tricycle formation with additional tailskid; torsion-bar suspension on all wheels. No ground steering. Nosewheel brake. Aluminium-alloy tube airframe, completely open (pod or full enclosure optional). Engine mounted below wing, driving pusher propeller.

Production status: see text; over 8000 completed.

GENERAL - No book on ultralights would be complete without a description of the *Quicksilver*, the most popular and most imitated design in the world. Conceived by Bob Lovejoy in the early '70s as a hybrid-control hang-glider, it was a natural for motorisation and was marketed as a hybrid ultralight by Dick Eipper's Eipper-formance company, later renamed Eipper Aircraft. A three-axis version followed, dubbed the *Quicksilver MX*, and so great was the success of this variant that literally dozens of firms making *Quicksilver* lookalikes sprang up right across the US.

With thousands of *Quicks*, as they are colloquially known, in service the world over, pilots were worried by reports in early 1985 that Eipper Aircraft had filed for bankruptcy, but in June '85 it was confirmed that Eipper had been reorganised and was now back in business as Eipper Industries.

Since the last of the hybrid machines, the *Quicksilver E*, was dropped from the range, the *Quicksilver MX* has been the base model. We detail it below in its most recent form, with Rotax 377 engine (earlier models used Cuyunas) and a retail price of US$4590 for a 40 h kit, though this price should be regarded as provisional because we understand that the reorganised Eipper will put the older, single-surface machines on a special-order-only basis.

A wide range of accessories is offered, including floats, a side-mounted stick, a rudder pedal conversion kit to give conventional three-axis control, and a pod or full enclosure. The latter was developed to fit the flagship of the Eipper range, the *Quicksilver GT*, but can be adapted to fit all the company's solo machines.

EXTERNAL DIMENSIONS & AREAS - Length overall 18.1 ft, 5.51 m. Height overall 9.7 ft, 2.95 m. Wing span 32.0 ft, 9.75 m. Constant chord 5.0 ft, 1.52 m. Dihedral 15°. Sweepback 0°. Tailplane span 9.1 ft, 2.77 m. Rudder height NC. Total wing area 160 ft², 14.9 m². Total spoiler area 1.5 ft², 0.14 m². Rudder area 11.3 ft², 1.05 m². Tailplane area 19.5 ft², 1.82 m². Total elevator area 11.8 ft², 1.10 m². Aspect ratio 6.4/1. Wheel track 5.8 ft, 1.75 m. Wheelbase 5.5 ft, 1.65 m. Nosewheel diameter overall 12 inch, 30 cm. Main wheels diameter overall 12 inch, 30 cm.

POWER PLANT - Rotax 377 engine. Max power 33.5 hp at 6500 rpm. Propeller diameter and pitch 52x32 inch, 1.32x0.81 m. V-belt reduction, ratio 2.0/1. Max static thrust 235 lb, 107 kg. Power per unit area 0.21 hp/ft², 2.27 hp/m². Fuel capacity 5.0 US gal, 4.2 Imp gal, 18.9 litre.

WEIGHTS & LOADINGS - Empty weight 239 lb, 108 kg. Max take-off weight 525 lb, 238 kg. Payload 286 lb, 130 kg. Max wing loading 3.28 lb/ft², 16.0 kg/m². Max power loading 15.7 lb/hp, 7.0 kg/hp. Load factors NC recommended; +6.0, -3.8 ultimate.

PERFORMANCE* - Max level speed 52 mph, 84 kph. Never exceed speed 63 mph, 101 kph. Max cruising speed 46 mph, 74 kph. Economic cruising speed 38 mph, 61 kph. Stalling speed 24 mph, 38 kph. Max climb rate at sea level 800 ft/min, 4.1 m/s. Min sink rate NC. Best glide ratio with power off 6.5/1 at 28 mph, 45 kph. Take-off distance 69 ft, 21 m. Landing distance 60 ft, 18 m. Service ceiling 10,000 ft, 3050 m. Range at average cruising speed 95 mile, 153 km. Noise level NC.

°*Under unspecified test conditions.*

EIPPER *QUICKSILVER MX SUPER*

(Three-axis)

Summary as Quicksilver MX *except: Conventional three-axis control. Roll control by full-span ailerons. Control inputs through stick for pitch/roll and pedals for yaw. 50% double-surface wing. Pod standard.*

Production status: see Quicksilver MX *text.*

GENERAL - Eipper president Lyle Byrum flew the *MX Super* at airshows in America and Europe for some two years before eventually making it publicly available. Essentially an aerobatic *MX*, it is extensively modified over the standard product and fitted with a twin carburettor version of the Rotax 503, giving it power enough to undertake limited aerobatics, such as rolls, loops, tail slides, stalls and inverted flight. Full-span ailerons replace the *MX's* spoilers and the wing is double surfaced as well as being of shorter span, though the area is unchanged. Lyle has demonstrated its potential not only at airshows but also in stunt work for television shows like *Remington Steele* and *Fantasy Island*.

A pod, inverted fuel system, four point safety harness and extra large fuel tank are all standard equipment on the *MX Super*, which is sold as an experimental category aircraft, as it is too heavy to be an ultralight. Price: NC.

EXTERNAL DIMENSIONS & AREAS - Length overall 18.6 ft, 3.20 m. Height overall 8.6 ft, 2.62 m. Wing span 28.5 ft, 8.69 m. Constant chord 5.6 ft, 1.71 m. Sweep back 0°. Total wing area 160 ft², 14.9 m². Aspect ratio 5.1/1. Other data NC.

POWER PLANT - Rotax 503 engine. Max power 52 hp at 6300 rpm. Propeller diameter and pitch 52x34 inch, 1.32x0.81 m. Reduction type NC, ratio NC. Max static thrust NC. Power per unit area 0.32 hp/ft², 3.5 hp/m². Fuel capacity 11.0 US gal, 9.2 Imp gal, 41.6 litre.

WEIGHTS & LOADINGS - Empty weight 345 lb, 156 kg. Max take-off weight 631 lb, 286 kg. Payload 286 lb, 130 kg. Max wing loading 3.94 lb/ft², 19.2 kg/m². Max power loading 12.1 lb/hp, 5.5 kg/hp. Load factors NC.

PERFORMANCE* - Max level speed 73 mph, 117 kph. Never exceed speed 85 mph, 137 kph. Max cruising speed 56 mph, 90 kph. Economic cruising speed 51 mph, 82 kph. Stalling speed 32 mph, 51 kph. Max climb rate at sea level 1000 ft/min, 5.1 m/s. Range at average cruising speed 200 mile, 322 km. Other data NC.

**Under unspecified test conditions.*

For an illustration of the MX Super, *see colour section.*

EIPPER *POLICE INTERCEPTOR*

(Three-axis)

Summary similar to Quicksilver MX.

Production status: see Quicksilver MX *text.*

GENERAL - Introduced in mid 1983 following the successful use of a modified *Quicksilver MX* by the Police Department of Downey, California, the *Police Interceptor* is basically a strengthened *MX* with the power pack from an *MXII*, a larger fuel tank and a more spacious cockpit.

Available only to police forces, the aircraft can be had with a number of options; items being developed by Eipper at the time of the launch include siren, searchlight, PA system and two-way police and aviation radios. Price: NC.

EXTERNAL DIMENSIONS & AREAS - See *Quicksilver MX*.

POWER PLANT - See *Quicksilver MXII* except: Fuel capacity 6.0 US gal, 5.0 Imp gal, 22.7 litre.

WEIGHTS & LOADINGS - Empty weight 300 lb, 136 kg. Max take-off weight 700 lb, 318 kg. Payload 400 lb, 181 kg. Max wing loading 4.38 lb/ft², 21.3 kg/m². Max power loading 15.2 lb/hp, 6.9 kg/hp. Load factors NC.

PERFORMANCE* - Max level speed 55 mph, 88 kph. Never exceed speed 63 mph, 101 kph. Cruising speed 41 mph, 66 kph. Stalling speed 28 mph, 45 kph. Max climb rate at sea level 500 ft/min, 2.5 m/s. Other data NC.

*Under unspecified test conditions.

EIPPER *QUICKSILVER MXII*
(Three-axis)

Summary as Quicksilver MX *except: Side-by-side two-seater. Brakes on main wheels. Pod or full enclosure not available.*

Production status: see Quicksilver MX *text.*

GENERAL - One of the first American two-seaters to be produced, the *Quicksilver MXII* has proved to be an invaluable training tool and is used by schools in large numbers, not only in the US but also in Europe. It's unconventional three-axis control permits the student to gain air experience without having to co-ordinate hand and foot, as the *MXII* turns quite happily by induced roll and the novice pilot can thus leave the pedals alone. Moreover, both pedals can be operated simultaneously as air brakes, a facility which is lost if the aircraft is converted to conventional controls, which as on the single-seater is available as an option, as is a second set of pedals.
Initially powered by the Cuyuna 430R engine, since early 1983 the Rotax 503 has been standard equipment. In Cuyuna form the aircraft was tested by Alain-Yves Berger and Alain Bliez in the July '82 edition of *Pilote Prive* magazine.
Price: US$6495 in kit form.

EXTERNAL DIMENSIONS & AREAS - See *Quicksilver MX.*

POWER PLANT - Rotax 503 engine. Max power 46 hp at 6500 rpm. Propeller diameter and pitch 52x34 inch, 1.32x0.81 m. V-belt reduction, ratio 2.0/1. Max static thrust NC. Power per unit area 0.28 hp/ft², 3.1 hp/m². Fuel capacity 5.0 US gal, 4.2 Imp gal, 18.9 litre.

WEIGHTS & LOADINGS - Empty weight 300 lb, 136 kg. Max take-off weight 700 lb, 317 kg. Payload 400 lb, 181 kg. Max wing loading 4.37 lb/ft², 21.3 kg/m². Max power loading 15.2 lb/hp, 6.9 kg/hp. Load factors NC recommended; +6.5, -3.5 ultimate.

PERFORMANCE* - Max level speed 45 mph, 72 kph. Never exceed speed 73 mph, 117 kph. Max cruising speed 41 mph, 66 kph. Economic cruising speed 36 mph, 58 kph. Stalling speed 24 mph, 39 kph. Max climb rate at sea level 390 ft/min, 2.0 m/s. Min sink rate 390 ft/min, 2.0 m/s at NC speed. Best glide ratio with power off 6/1 at 28 mph, 45 kph. Take-off distance 100 ft, 30 m. Landing distance 100 ft, 30 m. Service ceiling 10,000 ft, 3050 m. Range at average cruising speed 49 mile, 79 km. Noise level NC.

*Under the following test conditions - Airfield altitude 0 ft, 0 m. Ground temperature 59°F, 15°C. Ground pressure NC. Ground windspeed 0 mph, 0 kph. Test payload 350 lb, 159 kg.

Norman Burr

Quicksilver MXII *all ready to be flown solo in the '83 London-Paris, with extra fuel taking the place of the passenger.*

EIPPER *QUICKSILVER MXL*
(Three-axis)

Summary as Quicksilver MX *except: Conventional three-axis control. Control inputs through stick for pitch/roll and pedals for yaw. 100% double-surface wing, profile NC.*

Production status: current, number completed NC.

GENERAL - This aircraft is effectively a thorough modernisation of the original *Quicksilver MX* concept. Shown for the first time in 1982 as a prototype with a Cuyuna 430R engine, it uses a fully double-surface wing of reduced span and dihedral compared to the *MX,* plus a considerably reinforced structure with redesigned tail surfaces. Gone are the pedal-operated spoilers of the *MX,* in favour of conventional three-axis controls. Production models use a 377 Rotax, the power pack in fact being identical to the *MX.*
Flight tested in the February 1983 edition of *Glider Rider* by James Lawrence, the *MXL* costs US$5995 in the form of a kit taking around 40 h to assemble, with options available as on the *MX.* Rigging time is much the same as for its single-surface antecedent, at 45 min.

EXTERNAL DIMENSIONS & AREAS - Length overall 17.1 ft, 5.21 m. Height overall 9.7 ft, 2.95 m. Wing span 30.0 ft, 9.14 m. Constant chord 5.0 ft, 1.52 m. Dihedral 7.5°. Sweepback 0°. Tailplane span 9.1 ft, 2.77 m. Rudder height NC. Total wing area 150 ft², 13.9 m². Total spoiler area 1.5 ft², 0.14 m². Rudder area 11.3 ft², 1.05 m². Tailplane area 16.1 ft², 1.50 m². Total elevator area 11.8 ft², 1.10 m². Aspect ratio 6.8/1. Wheel track 5.8 ft, 1.75 m. Wheelbase 5.5 ft, 1.65 m. Nosewheel diameter overall 12 inch, 30 cm. Main wheels diameter overall 12 inch, 30 cm.

POWER PLANT - See *Quicksilver MX* except: Power per unit area 0.22 hp/ft², 2.4 hp/m².

WEIGHTS & LOADINGS - Empty weight 252 lb, 114 kg. Max take-off weight 550 lb, 249 kg. Payload 298 lb, 135 kg. Max wing loading 3.66 lb/ft², 17.8 kg/m². Max power loading 16.4 lb/hp, 7.3 kg/hp. Load factors NC recommended; +5.8, -2.9 ultimate.

PERFORMANCE* - Max level speed 61 mph, 98 kph.

Never exceed speed 74 mph, 119 kph. Max cruising speed 54 mph, 87 kph. Economic cruising speed 45 mph, 72 kph. Stalling speed 24 mph, 38 kph. Max climb rate at sea level 850 ft/min, 4.3 m/s. Min sink rate NC. Best glide ratio with power off 6/1 at NC speed. Take-off distance 75 ft, 23 m. Landing distance 75 ft, 23 m. Service ceiling 10,000 ft, 3050 m. Range at average cruising speed 113 mile, 181 km. Noise level NC.

Under the following test conditions - Airfield altitude 0 ft, 0 m. Ground temperature 59°F, 15°C. Ground pressure NC. Ground windspeed 0 mph, 0 kph. Test payload 175 lb, 79 kg.

EIPPER *QUICKSILVER MXLII*
(Three-axis)

Summary as Quicksilver MX *except: Side-by-side two-seater with conventional three-axis control. Control inputs through stick for pitch/roll and pedals for yaw. Double-surface wing. Brakes on main wheels. Pod or full enclosure not available.*

Production status: current, number completed NC.

GENERAL - Just as the *Quicksilver MXII* is directly descended from the *MX*, so the *MXLII* is a derivative of the *MXL*, sharing the same external dimensions. Power pack is the 46 hp Rotax 503, just as used in the *MXII*.
The aircraft's main claim to fame is the historic cross-Mediterranean flight made by Andre Fournel and Pierre Barret on 12 August 1984. Laden with special tanks and no less than 42 US gal (35 Imp gal, 158 litre) of fuel, 'the climb rate broke no records', as Fiona Luckhurst recorded when she described the trip in the January-February '85 edition of *Flightline*,

but an inversion helped the pair on their way. Even this fuel load was not enough for a 516 mile (830 km) flight, so the aircraft was refuelled in mid-air from a helicopter - a tricky manoeuvre, as ultralights and helicopter prop wash don't mix, but one which was accomplished successfully. In fact the only problem happened right at the end, when the chosen landing site, a jetty at Monaco, proved too much for the tired aircraft and pilots. Fortunately the aircraft was retrieved almost undamaged next day. Apart from the extra tanks, a pod, instruments and a parachute, the machine was an unmodified pre-production *MXL*. American readers, incidentally, can find an account of the trip in the November '84 edition of *Ultralight*.
Price: US$6995.

EXTERNAL DIMENSIONS & AREAS - See *Quicksilver MXL*.

POWER PLANT - See *Quicksilver MXII* except: Power per unit area 0.31 hp/ft^2, 3.3 hp/m^2.

WEIGHTS & LOADINGS - Empty weight 313 lb, 142 kg. Max take-off weight 713 lb, 323 kg. Payload 400 lb, 181 kg. Max wing loading 4.75 lb/ft^2, 23.2 kg/m^2. Max power loading 15.5 lb/hp, 7.0 kg/hp. Load factors NC.

PERFORMANCE* - Max level speed 70 mph, 113 kph. Never exceed speed 75 mph, 121 kph. Cruising speed 65 mph, 105 kph. Stalling speed 32 mph, 51 kph. Max climb rate at sea level 440 ft/min, 2.2 m/s. Other data NC.

*Under unspecified test conditions.

Making history: Michel Anglade in the Ecureuil helicopter links up with the MXLII for mid-air refuelling over the Mediterranean.

EIPPER *QUICKSILVER GT 280C and GT 400C*

(Three-axis)

Single-seat single-engined high-wing monoplane with conventional three-axis control. Wing has swept back leading edge, swept forward trailing edge, and tapering chord; flaps fitted; cruciform tail. Pitch control by elevator on tail; yaw control by fin-mounted rudder; roll control by half-span ailerons; control inputs through yoke for pitch/roll and pedals for yaw. Wing braced from above by kingpost and cables, from below by cables; wing profile NC; 100% double-surface. Undercarriage has three wheels in tricycle formation with additional tailwheel; no suspension on nosewheel and axle-flex suspension on main wheels. Push-right go-right nosewheel steering connected to yaw control. Nosewheel brake. Aluminium-alloy tube airframe, with pod (full enclosure optional). Engine mounted above wing, driving pusher propeller.

Production status: current; 50 completed by October '84 (total of all GT variants).

GENERAL - Despite retaining the *Quicksilver* name, this aircraft has no connection with earlier Eipper models, and is the fresh start on which much of the company's future prosperity depends. The prototypes, initially called *X-2* and then *Esprit,* were flying for a tantalisingly long time before the *GT* was finally put into production in the middle of '84, but by all accounts the lengthy gestation period has not been wasted, as all the published test reports comment on the careful development and high standard of finish which are evident.

Buyers can choose from cable or strut bracing (the former is detailed below, the latter listed separately) and either of two Rotax engines, giving a total of four models. The bracing is designated by the *C* or *S* suffix, while the engines are a 277 for the *280* models and a 447 for the *400* models. Some *GT 350C* and *GT 350S* models were produced using a Rotax 377, but this engine is no longer offered. The biggest-engined version is too heavy for the ultralight category, and is sold as an experimental homebuilt.

The thinking behind the *GT* is to achieve aircraft standards while retaining ultralight fun, and to heighten its appeal to conventional pilots a control yoke is fitted rather than a stick, though the stick remains an option. Four-postion flaps enhance the 'real airplane' feel. Eipper expects the struts to appeal more to the lightplane enthusiasts, though in truth strutted versions have no advantages, being heavier, less aerodynamic and less strong than their cable-braced stablemates.

Price is US$7195 for a Rotax 277-engined version, regardless of the type of wing bracing chosen. The latest price we have for the more powerful variants is US$7395, but we suspect that will have risen a little by the time you read this. Both prices refer to kits taking 35-40 h to construct. Rigging time is 20 min for the cable-braced versions, 30 min for the strutted.

In October '84, Lyle Byrum announced that the company had a tandem two-seat version, the *GT 500,* under development and that it would sell for around US$10, 000, but we have no further details of this machine.

Note: in the following data, where a figure is dependent on engine fitted, data for the 277 engined version is printed first, followed in parentheses by that

for the 447. Weight figures refer to the basic aircraft; for the US market, a throw-parachute weighing 9 lb (4 kg) is compulsory and is included in the price. Performance figures refer to aircraft thus equipped.

EXTERNAL DIMENSIONS & AREAS - Length overall 20.3 ft, 6.20 m. Height overall 7.8 ft, 2.39 m. Wing span 30.0 ft, 9.14 m. Total wing area 146 ft², 13.6 m². Chord at root 5.6 ft, 1.70 m. Chord at tip 4.3 ft, 1.32 m. Tailplane span 9.4 ft, 2.87 m. Fin height 6.8 ft, 2.06 m. Aspect ratio 6.2/1. Other data NC.

POWER PLANT - Rotax 277(447) engine. Max power 28(40) hp at 6700(7000) rpm. Propeller diameter and pitch 60x28(32) inch, 1.52x0.71(0.81) m. V-belt(gear) reduction, ratio 2.0(NC)/1. Max static thrust 220(NC) lb, 100(NC) kg. Power per unit area 0.19(0.27) hp/ft², 2.1(2.9) hp/m². Fuel capacity 5.0 US gal, 4.2 Imp gal, 18.9 litre.

WEIGHTS & LOADINGS - Empty weight 261(277) lb, 118(126) kg. Max take-off weight 520 lb, 236 kg. Payload 259(243) lb, 117(110) kg. Max wing loading 3.56 lb/ft², 17.4 kg/m². Max power loading 18.6 lb/hp, 5.9 kg/hp. Load factors   +4.0, -2.0 recommended; +6.0, -3.0 ultimate.

PERFORMANCE* - Max level speed 58(63) mph, 93(101) kph. Never exceed speed 74 mph, 119 kph. Max cruising speed 54(59) mph, 87(95) kph. Economic cruising speed 45(52) mph, 72(84) kph. Stalling speed 27** mph, 43** kph. Max climb rate at sea level 600(1000) ft/min, 3.1(5.1) m/s. Min sink rate 450 ft/min, 2.3 m at NC speed. Best glide ratio with power off 7/1 at NC speed. Take-off distance 100(75) ft, 30(23) m. Landing distance 100 ft, 30 m. Service ceiling NC. Range at average cruising speed 78(80). Noise level NC.

*Under the following test conditions - Airfield altitude 0 ft, 0 m. Ground temperature 59°F, 15°C. Ground pressure 1013 mB. Ground windspeed 0 mph, 0 kph. Test payload excluding fuel 175 lb, 79 kg.

**With flaps down.

EIPPER *QUICKSILVER GT 280S and GT 400S*

(Three-axis)

Summary as Quicksilver GT 280C and GT 400C *except: Wing braced from below by struts.*

Production status: current, see Quicksilver GT 280C and GT 400C *for number completed.*

GENERAL - See *Quicksilver GT 280C and GT 400C.*

Note: in the following data, where a figure is dependent on engine fitted, data for the 277 engined version is printed first, followed in parentheses by that for the 447. Weight figures refer to the basic aircraft; for the US market, a throw-parachute weighing 9 lb (4 kg) is compulsory and is included in the price.

EXTERNAL DIMENSIONS & AREAS - See *Quick silver GT 280C and GT 400C.*

POWER PLANT - See *Quicksilver GT 280C and GT 400C.*

Glider Rider

Main picture: Cable-braced GT with pod. One inset shows the outline of the same aircraft, the other a strut-braced GT with full enclosure.

WEIGHTS & LOADINGS - See *Quicksilver GT 280C and GT 400C* except: Empty weight 265(281) lb, 120(127) kg. Payload 255(239) lb, 116(108) kg.

PERFORMANCE* - See *Quicksilver GT 280C and GT 400C* except: Max level speed 56(61) mph, 90(98) kph. Max cruising speed 53(58) mph, 85(93) kph. Economic cruising speed 44(51) mph, 71(82) kph. Range at average cruising speed 50(55) mile, 80(88) km.

°*Under the following test conditions* - Airfield altitude 0 ft, 0 m. Ground temperature 59°F, 15°C. Ground pressure 1013 mB. Ground windspeed 0 mph, 0 kph. Test payload excluding fuel 175 lb, 79 kg.

EXPERIMENTAL AEROPLANE WORKS

Experimental Aeroplane Works, PO Box 457, Byron, California 94514; tel (209) 465-0945. Proprietor: Robert Kuklo.

EXPERMENTAL AEROPLANE WORKS *RK-1*
(Three-axis)

Single-seat single-engined high-wing monoplane with conventional three-axis control. Wing has unswept leading and trailing edges, and constant chord; cruciform tail. Pitch control by elevator on tail; yaw control by fin-mounted rudder; roll control by full-span ailerons; control inputs through stick for pitch/roll and pedals for yaw. Wing braced from below by struts; wing profile NC; 100% double-surface. Undercarriage has three wheels in taildragger formation; suspension NC on tailwheel and bungee suspension on main wheels. Push-right go-right tailwheel steering connected to yaw control. No brakes. Steel-tube airframe, completely open. Engine mounted below wing, driving pusher propeller.

Production status: see text.

GENERAL - Shown at the '83 Oshkosh, Robert Kuklo's *RK-1* bears an obvious resemblence to the Kolb *UltraStar,* though the wing bracing arrangements are more reminiscent of the earlier *Kolb Flyer.*
At the time Robert planned to have kits available by November of that year, but we have no knowledge of whether he actually got the design into production. Price: NC.

EXTERNAL DIMENSIONS & AREAS - Length overall 16.8 ft, 5.08 m. Wing span 26.5 ft, 8.08 m. Constant chord 5.7 ft, 1.74 m. Sweepback 0°. Total wing area 151 ft^2, 14.0 m^2. Aspect ratio 4.7/1. Other data NC.

POWER PLANT - Cuyuna 430R engine. Max power 30 hp at NC rpm. Propeller diameter and pitch 50x30 inch, 1.27x0.76 m. Reduction type and ratio NC. Max static thrust NC. Power per unit area 0.20 hp/ft^2, 2.1 hp/m^2. Fuel capacity 5.0 US gal, 4.2 Imp gal, 18.9 litre.

WEIGHTS & LOADINGS - Empty weight 240 lb, 109 kg. Max take-off weight 475 lb, 215 kg. Payload 235 lb, 107 kg. Max wing loading 3.15 lb/ft^2, 15.4 kg/m^2. Max power loading 15.8 lb/hp, 7.2 kg/hp. Load factors NC.

PERFORMANCE* - Max level speed 63 mph, 101 kph.

Wheeling the RK-1 *out at Oshkosh.*

Never exceed speed 100 mph, 161 kph. Cruising speed 55 mph, 88 kph. Stalling speed 25 mph, 40 kph. Max climb rate at sea level 800 ft/min, 4.1 m/s. Take-off distance 180 ft, 55 m. Landing distance 180 ft, 55 m. Other data NC.

**Under unspecified test conditions.*

FIRST CLASS

EverGreen Ultralite Inc, 14215 NE 193rd Pl, Woodinville, Washington 98072; tel (206) 487-0230. President: Bob Davis. (No longer trading).

Alternatively: First Class Aircraft Inc, PO Box 25528, Lake City, Washington 98125; tel (206) 881-9767.

EVERGREEN *SHADOW*
(Three-axis)

Single-seat single-engined high-wing monoplane with conventional three-axis control. Wing has unswept leading and trailing edges, and constant chord; cruciform tail. Pitch control by elevator on tail; yaw control by flying rudder; roll control by spoilers; control inputs through stick for pitch/roll and pedals for yaw. Wing braced from above by kingpost and cables, from below by cables; wing profile NC; 40% double-surface. Undercarriage has three wheels in tricycle formation with additional tailskid; suspension NC. No ground steering. Brakes NC. Aluminium-alloy tube airframe, completely open. Engine mounted below wing, driving pusher propeller.

Production status: see text, over 100 completed.

GENERAL - The EverGreen *Shadow* is a simple ultralight in the classic mould of the *Quicksilver,* and at first glance could easily be mistaken for the Eipper machine. Wing span, area and power unit are all the same as the *Quicksilver MX,* but the *Shadow* has saumons. Nevertheles the most notable difference between the two is the price, for at US$4495 for a 16-30 h kit, the EverGreen product comfortably undercuts the original.
However, just as we went to press we received news that EverGreen had ceased trading, so it is not clear whether the *Shadow* will remain available. The company is part of First Class Aircraft Inc, which to the best of our knowledge is still in business - a fact which will please the many enthusiasts who have been eagerly awaiting deliveries of the remarkable Pong Dragon six-cylinder twin-row radial four-stroke engine. Scheduled to reach production during 1985, this exquisitely engineered power unit will be sold separately for US$2495,

This Shadow *has been fitted with a Pong Dragon engine for test purposes.*

and at one time was also to be offered on a US$5500 version of the *Shadow,* which incidentally has no connection with the British or South African machines of the same name.

Our data below refers to the standard Rotax-engined version.

EXTERNAL DIMENSIONS & AREAS - Wing span 32.0 ft, 9.75 m. Constant chord 5.0 ft, 1.52 m. Sweep back 0°. Total wing area 160 ft², 14.9 m². Aspect ratio 6.4/1. Other data NC.

POWER PLANT - Rotax 377 engine. Max power 36 hp at NC rpm. Propeller diameter and pitch 59x12 inch, 1.50x0.30 m (3-blade). Reduction type NC, ratio 2.4/1. Max static thrust NC. Power per unit area 0.23 hp/ft², 2.4 hp/m². Fuel capacity 4.3 US gal, 3.5 Imp gal, 16.1 litre.

WEIGHTS & LOADINGS - Empty weight 251 lb, 114 kg. Max take-off weight 576 lb, 261 kg. Payload 325 lb, 147 kg. Max wing loading 3.60 lb/ft², 17.5 kg/m². Max power loading 16.0 lb/hp, 7.3 kg/hp. Load factors NC.

PERFORMANCE* - Max level speed 60 mph, 97 kph. Never exceed speed 65 mph, 105 kph. Cruising speed 45 mph, 72 kph. Stalling speed 20 mph, 32 kph. Max climb rate at sea level 900 ft/min, 4.6 m/s. Other data NC.

*Under unspecified test conditions.

EVERGREEN *SHADOW II*
(Three-axis)

See Shadow *except: Side-by-side two-seater. Optional pod.*

Production status: see Shadow *text, number completed NC.*

GENERAL - Designed principally as a trainer, the *Shadow II* is basically a strengthened *Shadow* with a Rotax 503 engine fitted in place of the 377. As with the

solo machine, a three-blade composite propellor provides the push, though on this aircraft it is driven through a Hegar toothed-belt reduction and a Flexidyne clutch. As befits a trainer, full dual controls are fitted: two sticks, two sets of rudder pedals and a single centre-mounted throttle control.

Modifications to the flying surfaces are restricted to the tail, which is double surfaced to cut drag.

Price is US$6000 for a kit taking 35-50 h to construct, but availability is in doubt (see *Shadow* text).

EXTERNAL DIMENSIONS & AREAS - See *Shadow* except: Length overall 16.0 ft, 4.88 m. Height overall 9.8 ft, 3.00 m.

POWER PLANT - Rotax 503 engine. Max power 46 hp at 5600 rpm. Propeller diameter and pitch 59x12 inch, 1.50x0.30 m (3 blade). Toothed-belt reduction, ratio 2.4/1. Max static thrust NC. Power per unit area 0.29 hp/ft², 3.1 hp/m². Fuel capacity 4.2 US gal, 3.5 Imp gal, 16.1 litre.

WEIGHTS & LOADINGS - Empty weight 310 lb, 141 kg. Max take-off weight 750 lb, 340 kg. Payload 440 lb, 200 kg. Max wing loading 4.69 lb/ft², 22.8 kg/m². Max power loading 16.3 lb/hp, 7.4 kg/hp. Load factors NC.

PERFORMANCE* - Max level speed 60 mph, 97 kph. Never exceed speed 65 mph, 105 kph. Cruising speed 50 mph, 80 kph. Stalling speed 26 mph, 42 kph. Max climb rate at sea level 450 ft/min, 2.3 m/s. Other data NC.

*Under unspecified test conditions.

FIRST STRIKE

First Strike Aviation Inc, 4 Wade Avenue, Piggott, Arkansas 72454; tel (501) 598-5126. President: Bobby Baker. Vice-president: Bruce Janes. Secretary/treasurer: Kay Baker.

FIRST STRIKE *BOBCAT*
(Three-axis)

Single-seat single-engined low-wing monoplane with conventional three-axis control. Wing has unswept leading and trailing edges, and constant chord; conventional tail. Pitch control by elevator on tail; yaw control by fin-mounted rudder; roll control by full-span ailerons; control inputs through stick for pitch/roll and pedals for yaw. Cantilever wing; wing profile see text; 100% double-surface. Undercarriage has two wheels plus tailskid; glass-fibre suspension on tailskid and no suspension on main wheels. Push-right go-right tailskid steering connected to yaw control; also optional differential braking. Optional brakes on main wheels. Wood airframe, partially enclosed. Engine mounted above wing, driving tractor propeller.

Production status: current, number completed NC.

GENERAL - The *Bobcat* is not Bobby Baker's first design, since he also created the very popular and award-winning *Mohawk,* which we featured in our last edition. However, the *Bobcat* is a totally different design, intended to be a utilitarian type ultralight able to withstand many years' operation and able to be con-

Hal Adkins

structed by the average homebuilder with the minimum of tools. Wood is used for the primary structure because of its easy working characteristics, cost and longevity, while the Stits HS90X certified covering will last indefinitely if kept painted. In the same vein, much thought was given to serviceability, with access holes where necessary and major parts easily replaceable.

No complicated jigging is needed for the fuselage construction, which Bobby says can be framed up in one day, and which uses spruce longerons and plywood bulkheads. Wings have an in-house undercambered section and are of D-tube type, with plywood-covered leading edge and spruce-capped foam ribs, each wing panel being manoeuvrable by one person using a removable handle on its upper surface. The two stabiliser halves fold upwards for easy storage.

It's no accident that the *Bobcat* looks like a small-scale version of a typical agricultural spray plane; the design allows for hardpoints to be built into the structure for the installation of crop-dusting equipment, and the machine may well find a niche in the growing field of micro-spray application.

When shown at the '84 Oshkosh, the prototype just made it under the 254 lb (115 kg) ultralight weight limit by removing the brakes, and it is in that form that we detail it here. However, in practice most *Bobcats* will be a little heavier and are likely to be registered in the experimental category.

Plans for the *Bobcat* cost US$100, or buyers can purchase the aircraft in kit form for US$3995. Part-kits can be had, with items such as pre-welded landing gear assemblies, glass-fibre cowlings and pre-cut fuselage bulkheads all available from First Strike. In addition Bobby tells us he plans to sell raw material kits through

A crowd-puller at '84 Oshkosh, this Bobcat *is fitted with the optional brakes.*

Wicks Aircraft Supply (for address see separate listing). Ready to fly machines are not offered.

EXTERNAL DIMENSIONS & AREAS - Length overall 15.3 ft, 4.65 m. Height overall 6.0 ft, 1.83 m. Wing span 27.7 ft, 8.43 m. Constant chord 4.5 ft, 1.37 m. Dihedral 3°. Sweepback 0°. Tailplane span 6.8 ft, 2.08 m. Fin height 4.0 ft, 1.22 m. Total wing area 120 ft², 11.1 m². Aspect ratio 6.4/1. Other data NC.

POWER PLANT - Rotax 277 engine. Max power 28 hp at 6000 rpm. Propeller diameter and pitch 60x30 inch, 1.52x0.76 m. Gear reduction, ratio NC. Max static thrust 220 lb, 100 kg. Power per unit area 0.23 hp/ft², 2.5 hp/m². Fuel capacity 5.0 US gal, 4.2 Imp gal, 18.9 litre.

WEIGHTS & LOADINGS - Empty weight 251 lb, 114 kg. Max take-off weight 500 lb, 227 kg. Payload 249 lb, 113 kg. Max wing loading 4.17 lb/ft², 20.5 kg/m². Max power loading 17.9 lb/hp, 8.1 kg/hp. Load factors +4.0, -3.0 recommended; +6.0, -4.0 ultimate.

PERFORMANCE* - Max level speed 63 mph, 101 kph. Never exceed speed 80 mph, 129 kph. Max cruising speed 50 mph, 80 kph. Economic cruising speed 45 mph, 72 kph. Stalling speed 27 mph, 43 kph. Max climb rate at sea level 600 ft/min, 3.1 m/s. Take-off distance 200 ft, 60 m. Landing distance 200 ft, 60 m. Other data NC.

*Under unspecified test conditions.

FISHER

Fisher Flying Products Inc, Rt 2, Box 282, South Webster, Ohio 45682; tel (614) 778-3185. Proprietor: Mike Fisher.

South African agent: Fisher Flying Products Manufacturing Pty Ltd (see separate listing).

Swedish agent: Ultralights in Sweden, Lukas Gata 9, Box 4014, S-25004 Helsingborg; tel 46 42-290677.

West German agent: Flugtechnik-Damme, Flugplatz, Postfach 1133, 2845 Damme; tel 05491 1404.

FISHER *FP-101*

(Three-axis)

Single-seat single-engined high-wing monoplane with conventional three-axis control. Wing has unswept leading and trailing edges, and constant chord; conventional tail. Pitch control by elevator on tail; yaw control by fin-mounted rudder; roll control by 55% span ailerons; control inputs through stick for pitch/roll and pedals for yaw. Wing braced from below by struts; wing profile modified Goettingen; 100% double-surface. Undercarriage has three wheels in tail-dragger formation; torsion-bar suspension on tailwheel and bungee suspension on main wheels. Push-right go-right tailwheel steering connected to yaw control; also optional differential braking. Optional brakes on main wheels. Wood airframe, partially enclosed. Engine mounted below wing, driving tractor propeller.

Production status: current, 420 completed.

Dave Stroble

GENERAL - The *FP-101* was first shown to the public at the 1982 Oshkosh fly-in, where it was parked with the ultralights but registered as an N-numbered experimental aircraft. At that time the government had yet to decide the legal definition of an ultralight, but the hoped for maximum weight was 220 lb (100 kg). A lot of people were pleasantly surprised, as was *FP-101* designer Mike Fisher, when the 254 lb (113 kg) limit was announced. This decision put the *FP-101* squarely in the ultralight class, and that's how it has been marketed, though it is interesting to note that the current *FP-101* would not qualify as a microlight under the FAI definition, on account of its relatively high wing loading, deliberately arranged to enhance stability in gusty conditions. Some earlier aircraft, which were built with a choice of Zenoah G25B or Kawasaki TA440A engines and an optional larger wing (span 34.8 ft, 10.62 m, area 140 ft², 13.0 m²) could have qualified, but we understand these variants have since been dropped.

Like all Mike's kits, it uses geodetic wood construction, giving a strong, light frame, able to absorb torsional stress without fatigue or stress cracking. Combined with modern epoxy adhesives, wood preservatives and covering materials, this gives a durable airframe which can be constructed without special tools, complex fixtures or welding. The *FP-101* is sold in kit form, with all pieces pre-cut, shaped and numbered and a full-scale set of plans; in fact, building one of Mike's creations has been likened to constructing a giant model-airplane kit. Between 150 and 200 h of work is needed.

As with all Fisher machines, power for the aircraft comes from a Rotax with tuned exhaust system and Rotax's own geared reduction drive, with helical gears in a oil bath and a built-in shock dampening system - a set-up which has become an industry standard over the past couple of years.

Price is US$4050 in kit form; plans and ready-to-fly aircraft are not available.

EXTERNAL DIMENSIONS & AREAS - Length overall 16.5 ft, 5.03 m. Height overall 5.6.ft, 1.70 m. Wing span 28.8 ft, 8.79 m. Constant chord 4.0 ft, 1.22 m. Dihedral 3°. Sweepback 0°. Tailplane span 7.5 ft, 2.29 m. Fin height 4.8 ft, 1.45 m. Total wing area 116 ft², 10.8 m². Total aileron area 16.0 ft², 1.49 m². Fin area 4.9 ft², 0.46 m². Rudder area 5.3 ft², 0.49 m². Tailplane area 13.8 ft², 1.28 m². Total elevator area 8.8 ft², 0.81 m². Aspect ratio 7.2/1. Wheel track 4.2 ft, 1.27 m. Wheelbase 13.2 ft, 4.01 m. Tailwheel diameter overall 4 inch, 10 cm. Main wheels diameter overall 13 inch, 33 cm.

POWER PLANT - Rotax 277 engine. Max power 25 hp at 6000 rpm. Propeller diameter and pitch 60x28 inch, 1.52x0.71 m. Gear reduction, ratio 2.6/1. Max static thrust 185 lb, 84 kg. Power per unit area 0.22 hp/ft², 2.3 hp/m². Fuel capacity 5.0 US gal, 4.2 Imp gal, 18.9 litre.

WEIGHTS & LOADINGS - Empty weight 240 lb, 109 kg. Max take-off weight 500 lb, 227 kg. Payload 260 lb, 118 kg. Max wing loading 4.31 lb/ft², 21.0 kg/m². Max power loading 20.0 lb/hp, 9.1 kg/hp. Load factors +4.6, -2.3 recommended; NC ultimate.

PERFORMANCE* - Max level speed 55 mph, 88 kph. Never exceed speed 75 mph, 121 kph. Max cruising speed 50 mph, 80 kph. Economic cruising speed 45 mph, 72 kph. Stalling speed 26 mph, 42 kph. Max climb rate at sea level 650 ft/min, 3.3 m/s. Min sink rate 250 ft/min at 40 mph, 1.3 m/s at 64 kph. Best glide ratio with power off 9/1 at 40 mph, 64 kph. Take-off distance 150 ft, 45 m. Landing distance 150 ft, 45 m. Service ceiling 13,000 ft, 3960 m. Range at average cruising speed 150 mile, 241 km. Noise level NC.

*Under the following test conditions - Airfield altitude 0 ft, 0 m. Ground temperature 59°F, 15°C. Ground pressure 1013 mB. Ground windspeed 0 mph, 0 kph. Test payload 200 lb, 91 kg.

FISHER *FP-202 KOALA*

(Three-axis)

Summary as FP-101 *except: 54%-span ailerons. Totally enclosed.*

Production status: current, 233 completed.

GENERAL - Mike Fisher's *FP-202 Koala* is similar in concept to the *FP-101,* but is rather larger in length, span, and weight. Despite this greater weight, the same Rotax 277 as the *FP-101* gives higher speeds in all modes except stall, so clearly the aircraft is aero-dynamically superior to its little sister. There are also some Kawasaki TA440A-engined *FP-202s* around, but the company has now standardised on the Rotax engine.

Visually the most obvious difference is the fully enclosed cockpit, but on a summer's day when the pilot has removed the side windows, observers will be reduced to comparing the tailplane shapes to decide which of Mike's creations they are looking at, as the tail on the *FP-202* is a little more rounded. Storage is effected by removing the wings, rigging taking around 15 min - as with the *FP-101.* Construction, however, takes longer - between 200 and 250 h.

The exact specifications of the *FP-202* depend on whether the aircraft is bought as a kit or ready to fly. The kit-built machine, to which this listing refers, is illustrated in our colour section and has larger ailerons but no flaps. Despite this it is slightly heavier than the factory-assembled version, which we detail in our South African section since it is manufactured by Fisher's associated company there and exported back to the US. In both cases the listings refer to Rotax-engined machines. Prices of the two variants are US$4350 and US$5750 respectively.

For those who cannot afford either the time for a kit or the cash for a ready-to-fly machine, Mike Fisher offers a quick-build kit, using a chrome-moly welded steel fuselage in place of the wood construction. This costs US$5498.

EXTERNAL DIMENSIONS & AREAS - Length overall 17.8 ft, 5.41 m. Height overall 5.6 ft, 1.71 m. Wing span 29.8 ft, 9.09 m. Constant chord 4.0 ft, 1.22 m. Dihedral 3°. Sweepback 0°. Tailplane span 7.0 ft, 2.13 m. Fin height 4.4 ft, 1.34 m. Total wing area 120 ft², 11.1 m². Total aileron area 16.0 ft², 1.49 m². Fin area 3.5 ft², 0.33 m². Rudder area 5.5 ft², 0.51 m². Tailplane area 11.5 ft², 1.07 m². Total elevator area 7.3 ft², 0.68 m². Aspect ratio 7.4/1. Wheel track 4.2 ft, 1.28 m. Wheelbase 14.5 ft, 4.42 m. Tailwheel diameter overall 4 inch, 10 cm. Main wheels diameter overall 13 inch, 33 cm.

POWER PLANT - See *FP-101* except: Power per unit area 0.21 hp/ft², 2.3 hp/m².

WEIGHTS & LOADINGS - Empty weight 250 lb, 113 kg. Max take-off weight 500 lb, 227 kg. Payload 250 lb, 113 kg. Max wing loading 4.17 lb/ft², 20.4 kg/m². Max power loading 20.0 lb/hp, 9.1 kg/hp. Load factors +4.6, -2.3 recommended; NC ultimate.

PERFORMANCE* - Max level speed 62 mph, 100 kph. Never exceed speed 75 mph, 121 kph. Max cruising speed 60 mph, 97 kph. Economic cruising speed 55 mph, 88 kph. Stalling speed 26 mph, 42 kph. Max climb rate at sea level 750 ft/min, 3.8 m/s. Min sink rate 250 ft/min at 40 mph, 1.3 m/s at 64 kph. Best glide ratio with power off 9/1 at 40 mph, 64 kph. Take-off distance 150 ft, 46 m. Landing distance 150 ft, 46 m. Service ceiling 13,000 ft, 3960 m. Range at average cruising speed 165 mile, 265 km. Noise level NC.

*Under the following test conditions - Airfield altitude 0 ft, 0 m. Ground temperature 59°F, 15°C. Ground pressure 1013 mB. Ground windspeed 0 mph, 0 kph. Test payload 200 lb, 91 kg.

FISHER *FP-303*

(Three-axis)

Single-seat single-engined low-wing monoplane with conventional three-axis control. Wing has unswept leading and trailing edges, and constant chord; flaps fitted; conventional tail. Pitch control by elevator on tail; yaw control by fin-mounted rudder; roll control by 43%-span ailerons; control inputs through stick for pitch/roll and pedals for yaw. Wing braced from below by struts; wing profile modified Goettingen; 100% double-surface. Undercarriage has three wheels in tail-dragger formation; torsion-bar suspension on tailwheel and no suspension on main wheels. Push-right go-right tailwheel steering connected to yaw control; also optional differential braking. Optional brakes on main wheels. Wood airframe, partially enclosed. Engine mounted above wing, driving tractor propeller.

Production status: current; 69 completed.

GENERAL - Although the *FP-303* shares the geodetic construction of the other Fisher aircraft, it is a totally separate design, aimed at the bottom end of the market and first shown at the 1984 Sun 'n Fun. Mike Fisher deliberately kept the machine as simple as possible, to keep construction time low (150-200 h) and price keen (US$2898), and the result is an endearing low-wing machine somewhat resembling a homebuilt Volksplane. Despite the height of its wings, it is strut-braced, the supports running from the unsprung axle of the main wheels - a novel solution to the problem of how to avoid the stresses of cantilevering on a low-wing machine.

Certainly those who think that feeling the wind in your face is a vital part of ultralight flying will have no quibble with the *FP-303,* for the pilot sits right up in the breeze, with only a tiny windscreen to keep the propwash off his or her face. Generating that propwash is the same Rotax 277 used in the other single-seaters.

A particularly low rigging time is claimed, of only 5 min.

EXTERNAL DIMENSIONS & AREAS - Length overall 16.5 ft, 5.03 m. Height overall 5.2 ft, 1.57 m. Wing span 27.7 ft, 8.44 m. Constant chord 4.0 ft, 1.22 m. Dihedral 6°. Sweepback 0°. Tailplane span 7.0 ft, 2.13 m. Fin height 5.2 ft, 1.57 m. Total wing area 111 ft², 10.3 m². Total aileron area 12.0 ft², 1.11 m². Fin area 4.5 ft², 0.42 m². Rudder area 4.4 ft², 0.41 m². Tailplane area 11.7 ft², 1.09 m². Total elevator area 8.8 ft², 0.82 m². Aspect ratio 6.9/1. Wheel track 4.2 ft, 1.27 m. Wheelbase 12.5 ft, 3.81 m. Tailwheel diameter overall 4 inch, 10 cm. Main wheels diameter overall 13 inch, 33 cm.

POWER PLANT - See *FP-101* except: Power per unit area 0.23 hp/ft², 2.4 hp/m². Fuel capacity 2.5 US gal, 2.1 Imp gal, 9.5 litre.

WEIGHTS & LOADINGS - Empty weight 235 lb, 107 kg. Max take-off weight 450 lb, 204 kg. Payload 215 lb, 98 kg. Max wing loading 4.05 lb/ft², 19.8 kg/m². Max power loading 18.0 lb/hp, 8.2 kg/hp. Load factors +4.6, -2.3 recommended; NC ultimate.

PERFORMANCE* - Max level speed 60 mph, 97 kph. Never exceed speed 70 mph, 113 kph. Max cruising speed 58 mph, 93 kph. Economic cruising speed 55 mph, 88 kph. Stalling speed 25** mph, 40** kph. Max climb rate at sea level 750 ft/min, 3.8 m/s. Min sink rate 300 ft/min at 40 mph, 1.5 m/s at 64 kph. Best glide ratio with power off 9/1 at 40 mph, 64 kph. Take-off distance 125 ft, 38 m. Landing distance 130 ft, 40 m. Service ceiling 11,000 ft, 3350 m. Range at average cruising speed 165 mile, 265 km. Noise level NC.

*Under the following test conditions - Airfield altitude 0 ft, 0 m. Ground temperature 59°F, 15°C. Ground pressure 1013 mB. Ground windspeed 0 mph, 0 kph. Test payload 185 lb, 84 kg.

**With flaps down.

FISHER *SUPER KOALA*

(Three-axis)

See FP-101 except: Side-by-side two-seater. Flaps fitted. 52%-span ailerons. Totally enclosed.

Production status: current, 6 completed.

GENERAL - In kit form the *Super Koala* costs only US$48 more than the ready-to-fly *FP-202 Koala,* so buyers have an almost straight trade-off between instant flying and the ability to explore the skies with a friend. Basically an enlarged version of the *FP-202*, the two-seat *Super Koala* uses the same tail but has a larger

wing, wider track and marginally greater overall length. The length change is due not to a longer wheelbase but to the fitting of a twin-cylinder engine, the Rotax 503 of 48 hp.

Construction time is estimated at 300-400 h from a kit costing US$5798 and rigging takes around 20 min.

EXTERNAL DIMENSIONS & AREAS - See *FP-202 Koala* except: Length overall 18.1 ft, 5.51 m. Wing span 31.0 ft, 9.45 m. Constant chord 4.5 ft, 1.37 m. Total wing area 140 ft², 13.0 m². Total aileron area 16.0 ft², 1.49 m². Aspect ratio 6.9/1. Wheel track 5.3 ft, 1.63 m.

POWER PLANT - Rotax 503 engine. Max power 48 hp at 6200 rpm. Propeller diameter and pitch 72x33 inch, 1.83x0.84 m. Gear reduction, ratio 2.6/1. Max static thrust NC. Power per unit area 0.34 hp/ft², 3.7 hp/m². Fuel capacity 5.0 US gal, 4.2 Imp gal, 18.9 litre.

WEIGHTS & LOADINGS - Empty weight 335 lb, 152 kg. Max take-off weight 725 lb, 329 kg. Payload 390 lb, 177 kg. Max wing loading 5.18 lb/ft², 25.3 kg/m². Max power loading 15.1 lb/hp, 6.9 kg/hp. Load factors +4.6, -2.3 recommended; NC ultimate.

PERFORMANCE* - Max level speed 80 mph, 129 kph. Never exceed speed 90 mph, 145 kph. Max cruising speed 75 mph, 121 kph. Economic cruising speed 70 mph, 113 kph. Stalling speed 32 mph, 51 kph. Max climb rate at sea level 500 ft/min, 2.5 m/s. Min sink rate 300 ft/min at 45 mph, 1.5 m/s at 72 kph. Best glide ratio with power off 9/1 at 45 mph, 72 kph. Take-off distance 225 ft, 69 m. Landing distance 200 ft, 60 m. Service ceiling NC. Range at average cruising speed 140 mile, 225 km. Noise level NC.

*Under the following test conditions - Airfield altitude 0 ft, 0 m. Ground temperature 59°F, 15°C. Ground pressure 1013 mB. Ground windspeed 0 mph, 0 kph. Test payload 370 lb, 168 kg.

Norman Burr

There probably aren't two 'Dactyls alike anywhere, but this one, seen at the British Microlight Aircraft Association's annual Woburn Abbey Rally, is typical of the breed. Like many British examples, it has been re-engined with a Robin twin.

FREEDOM FLIERS

Freedom Fliers Inc, PO Box 479, Rowlett, Texas 75088; tel (214) 475-8870; tx 203 941 ACTDUR. President: Gary C Vick. Marketing director: Scott M Regian. Chief pilot and R&D: Steward Cavanagh. Operations manager (production): Bob 'Mitch' Mitchell.

FREEDOM FLIERS
PTERODACTYL ASCENDER II+
(Two-axis)

Single-seat single-engine high-wing monoplane with two-axis control. Wing has swept back leading and trailing edges, and tapering chord; no tail, canard wing. Pitch control by fully flying canard; yaw control by tip rudders; no separate roll control; control inputs through stick for pitch/yaw. Wing braced from above by kingpost and cables, from below by cables; wing profile Klaus Hill Fledgling; 100% double-surface. Undercarriage has three wheels in tricycle formation; bungee suspension on nosewheel and glass-fibre suspension on main wheels. No ground steering. No brakes. Aluminium-alloy tube airframe, completely open. Engine mounted below wing, driving pusher propeller.

Production status: current, 1410 completed.

GENERAL - When Jack McCornack, creator of the legendary *Pterodactyl* in all its many forms, decided to sell the production rights to Freedom Fliers and take a break from the ultralight industry, we wondered if we were witnessing the end of an era. The industry had lost, hopefully on a temporary basis, one of its most charismatic personalities, a man with an endearing ability to deflate a hundred words of hype with a single earthy remark, and we wondered how his creation would fare without him.

Happily, the *Pterodactyl* seems to be alive and well in its new Texas home, judging by the way Freedom Fliers completed our standard pre-printed form which we sent to all manufacturers. When asked what kind of tail the aircraft had, the company replied 'None - we don't need no stinkin' tails', a touch of irreverence of which Jack would certainly approve.

There have been some changes though, for the *Pterodactyl* range has been much simplified recently, from the plethora of variants we listed in our last edition, down to just two - the *Pterodactyl Ascender II+*, which

Rear suspension of the Ascender II+.

we detail below, and the *Pterodactyl Ascender II+2*, which we list separately. One of the industry's oldest surviving designs and one of the few two-axis aircraft still in production, the *'Dactyl*, as it is colloquially known, can be traced back to Klaus Hill's *Fledgling* hang-glider, which Jack first motorised in 1978.

Various Cuyuna power units have been tried over the years and in its current form the *Ascender II+* has a Cuyuna ULII-02 engine of 35 hp. This may have found its way onto some earlier machines too, for *Pterodactyl* owners are famous/infamous for their devotion to the marque and their desire to constantly modify and improve their machines.

Introduced in 1982, the *Ascender II+* is sold for US$5536 as a kit requiring some 75 h to put together. Rigging time is around 45 min, and options include a double size fuel tank, which incidentally takes the air craft out of the ultralight category.

EXTERNAL DIMENSIONS & AREAS - Length overall 16.8 ft, 5.08 m. Height overall 9.1 ft, 2.77 m. Wing span 33.0 ft, 10.06 m. Chord at root 6.5 ft, 1.98 m. Chord at tip 4.5 ft, 1.34 m. Canard span 8.0 ft, 2.44 m. Canard chord 1.34 ft, 0.41 m. Rudder height NC. Total wing area 173 ft^2, 16.1 m^2. Main wing area 162 ft^2, 15.1 m^2. Canard area 11 ft^2, 1.0 m^2. Total rudder area NC. Aspect ratio (of main wing) 6.7/1. Wheel track 5.0 ft, 1.52 m. Wheelbase 5.0 ft, 1.52 m. Nosewheel diameter overall 16 inch, 41 cm. Main wheels diameter overall 20 inch, 51 cm.

POWER PLANT - Cuyuna ULII-02 engine. Max power 35 hp at 6200 rpm. Propeller diameter and pitch 54x27

The Freedom Fliers range - from left to right, Buckeye *(note 'chute rolled up behind trike unit),* Pterodactyl Ascender II+ *(with canard removed), and a* Shadow Trainer, *a South African-built machine from Microlight Flight Systems, for which the company is US agent (see separate listing).*

inch, 1.37x0.69 m. V-belt or notched V-belt reduction, ratio 2.0/1. Max static thrust 225 lb, 102 kg. Power per unit area 0.22 hp/ft^2, 2.3 hp/m^2. Fuel capacity 5.0 US gal, 4.2 Imp gal, 18.9 litre.

WEIGHTS & LOADINGS - Empty weight 235 lb, 107 kg. Max take-off weight 535 lb, 243 kg. Payload 300 lb, 136 kg. Max wing loading 3.30 lb/ft^2, 16.1 kg/m^2. Max power loading 15.3 lb/hp, 6.9 kg/hp. Load factors NC.

PERFORMANCE* - Max level speed 60 mph, 97 kph. Never exceed speed 63 mph, 101 kph. Max cruising speed 50 mph, 80 kph. Economic cruising speed 40 mph, 64 kph. Stalling speed 27 mph, 43 kph. Max climb rate at sea level 900 ft/min, 4.6 m/s. Min sink rate 475 ft/min at 30 mph, 2.4 m/s at 48 kph. Best glide ratio with power off 8/1 at NC speed. Take-off distance 90 ft, 27 m. Landing distance 100 ft, 30 m. Service ceiling 20,000 ft, 6100 m. Range at average cruising speed 100 mile, 161 km. Noise level NC.

*Under the following test conditions - Airfield altitude 0 ft, 0 m. Ground temperature 59°F, 15°C. Ground pressure NC. Ground windspeed 0 mph, 0 kph. Test payload 240 lb, 109 kg.

Glider Rider

FREEDOM FLIERS
PTERODACTYL ASCENDER II+2
(Three-axis)

Summary as Pterodactyl Ascender II+ *except: Side-by-side two-seater.*

Production status: see text.

GENERAL - With the single-seat *Pterodactyl Ascender II+* having a beefier frame than earlier *Pterodactyls*, it is a simple matter to turn it into a two-seater, in which form it is known as the *Pterodactyl Ascender II+2.* All that is needed is to fit a double seat (six bolts), reposition the throttle centrally and, if required, fit the double capacity tank.

When introduced in October 1982, this machine was the subject of one of Jack McCornack's by-then traditional long-distance proving flights, taking him and Robyn Solair on a 1025 mile (1649 km) trip to Mexico and back.

Last priced at US$5878 for a 60-85 h kit, this machine is no longer listed by Freedom Fliers, but so close is it to the solo aircraft that anyone wanting an *Ascender II+2* could easily create one. Jack used to sell kits to convert the solo machine to a two-seater, and we have a hunch that Freedom Fliers would not need much persuasion to do the same...

EXTERNAL DIMENSIONS & AREAS - See *Pterodactyl Ascender II+.*

POWER PLANT - See *Pterodactyl Ascender II+.*

WEIGHTS & LOADINGS - Empty weight 250 lb, 113 kg. Max take-off weight 700 lb, 318 kg. Payload 450 lb, 204 kg. Max wing loading 4.32 lb/ft², 21.0 kg/m². Max power loading 20.0 lb/hp, 9.1 kg/hp. Load factors NC.

PERFORMANCE* - Max level speed 60 mph, 97 kph. Max cruising speed 50 mph, 80 kph. Economic cruising speed 40 mph, 64 kph. Stalling speed 32 mph, 51 kph. Max climb rate at sea level 400 ft/min, 2.0 m/s. Take-off distance 200 ft, 60 m. Service ceiling 12,000 ft, 3660 m. Range at average cruising speed 82** mile, 132** km. Other data NC.

*Under unspecified test conditions.

**On standard tank.

FREEDOM FLIERS *BUCKEYE*
(Ascending parachute)

Single-seat single-engined motorised parachute. Ram-air parachute with 11 cells and square plan. Pilot suspended below wing in trike unit, using sticks to tension rigging lines and thus control yaw; no other aerodynamic controls. Parachute braced by 48 rigging lines; 100% double-surface. Undercarriage has three wheels in tricycle formation; no suspension on nosewheel and glass-fibre suspension on main wheels. Push-right go-left nosewheel steering independent from aerodynamic controls. No brakes. Aluminium-alloy tube trike unit, completely open. Engine mounted below wing, driving pusher propeller. Canopy made from 1.1 oz zero-porosity ripstop nylon. Bracing lines made from Dacron.

Production status: current, over 150 completed

GENERAL - The *Buckeye*, which Jack McCornack helped design, is the second of a new generation of air craft, the flying - or as they have come to be called - ascending parachutes, the first being Steve Snyder's *Paraplane*. The pilot sits in a motorised cage very like a trike unit, and above and behind is a ram-air parachute. A combination of propwash and ram-air effect inflates the parachute and carries the craft aloft - a delightfully simple concept which makes these machines the easiest aircraft of all to fly. There's no pitch or roll control, and no variation of airspeed; the *Buckeye* flies at a constant 26 mph (42 kph), and altering the throttle merely causes the machine to ascend or descend. Throttle forward, the craft goes up, throttle back, and it starts down. Two hand levers control yaw: pull back on the right lever to go right, pull back on the left to go left, pull back on both to flare and reduce airspeed.
The Buckeye trike unit comes in the form of a kit, requiring 6 -8 h to complete, and together with the 'chute costs US$3995 when fitted with a 35 hp Cuyuna ULII-02 engine driving through a 2/1 V-belt reduction. Alter natively, customers may pay an extra US$100 for a 37 hp Rotax 377 with gear reduction, the version detailed below. Rigging time is 15 minutes and it is claimed that a raw novice can safely solo in only 4 h.

EXTERNAL DIMENSIONS & AREAS - Length overall 8.5 ft, 2.59 m. Height overall before flight 6.0 ft, 1.83 m. Height overall during flight 22.0 ft, 6.71 m. Wing span 33.5 ft, 10.21 m. Constant chord 12.0 ft, 3.66 m. Sweep back 0°. Total wing area 400 ft², 37.2 m². Aspect ratio 2.8/1. Wheel track 6.2 ft, 1.89 m. Wheelbase 6.5 ft, 1.98 m. Nosewheel diameter overall 8 inch, 20 cm. Main wheels diameter overall 15 inch, 38 cm.

POWER PLANT - Rotax 377 engine. Max power 37 hp at 6200 rpm. Propeller diameter and pitch 54x28 inch, 1.37x0.71 m. Gear reduction, ratio 2.6/1. Max static thrust 225 lb, 102 kg. Power per unit area 0.09 hp/ft², 1.0 hp/m². Fuel capacity 2.5 US gal, 2.1 Imp gal, 9.5 litre.

WEIGHTS & LOADINGS - Empty weight 179 lb, 81 kg. Max take-off weight 379 lb, 172 kg. Payload 200 lb, 91 kg. Max wing loading 0.95 lb/ft², 4.6 kg/m². Max power loading 10.24 lb/hp, 4.6 kg/hp. Load factors NC.

PERFORMANCE* - Max level speed 26 mph, 42 kph. Never exceed speed NC. Cruising speed 26 mph, 42 kph. Stalling speed NC. Max climb rate at sea level 375 ft/min, 1.9 m/s. Sink rate with power off 960 ft/min at NC speed. Best glide ratio with power off 2.5/1 at 26 mph, 42 kph. Take-off distance 150 ft, 45 m. Landing distance 75 ft, 23 m. Service ceiling >7000 ft, >2130 m. Range at average cruising speed 30 mile, 48 km. Noise level 65 dB at 500 ft, 150 m.

*Under the following test conditions - Airfield altitude 50 ft, 15 m. Ground temperature 59°F, 15°C. Ground pressure 1013 mB. Ground windspeed 0 mph, 0 kph. Test payload 175 lb, 79 kg.

GOLDEN AGE

Golden Age Aircraft Inc, 350 East Louisiana, McKinney, Texas 75069; tel (214) 542-5632.

GOLDEN AGE
RYAN STA
(Three-axis)

Single-seat single-engined low-wing monoplane with conventional three-axis control. Wing has unswept leading and trailing edges, and constant chord; conventional tail. Pitch control by elevator on tail; yaw control by fin-mounted rudder; roll control by ailerons; control inputs through stick for pitch/roll and pedals for yaw. Wing braced from above by cables to fuselage, from below by cables to undercarriage; wing profile NC; 100% double-surface. Undercarriage has three wheels in tail-dragger formation; no suspension on any wheels. Push-right go-right tailwheel steering connected to yaw control; also differential braking. Brakes on main wheels. Steel tube airframe, partially enclosed. Engine mounted above wing, driving tractor propeller.

Production status: prototype.

GENERAL - This company is unashamedly in the nostalgia business, making replicas of the simple fun-flying machines of yesteryear. The firm first made its name with the *Waco II* replica biplane, introduced in 1983, but as we write this machine is out of production, while research is done on an improved version.
Very much in production, however, is the *Ryan STA*, earlier called the *280 Super Sport*. Resembling a *Waco II* minus its top wing, it is in fact built along similar lines with the same welded-steel construction. This very appealing tail-dragger comes with a combined seat and tank, a 12V electrical system, seat belts, shoulder harness, and three instruments - ASI, tachometer and egtg. Power comes from the ubiquitous Rotax 277 (the version detailed below), Rotax's 377 with gear drive being an option.
Other options include extra instruments, a BRS parachute system, radios, spinner, wheel spats and hydraulic brakes. In standard form the *Ryan STA* costs US$6995 as a kit or US$8995 ready-to-fly.
Golden Age Aircraft has released very little technical information about this aircraft, but claims that it satisfies *FAR Part 103*.

EXTERNAL DIMENSIONS & AREAS - Length overall 18.5 ft, 5.64 m. Wing span 30.0 ft, 9.14 m. Sweepback 0°. Wheel track 6.0 ft, 1.83 m. Other data NC.

POWER PLANT - Rotax 277 engine. Max power 28 hp at NC rpm. Propeller diameter and pitch 68x34 inch, 1.73x0.86 m. Gear reduction, ratio NC. Fuel capacity 5.0 US gal, 4.2 Imp gal, 18.9 litre. Other data NC.

WEIGHTS & LOADINGS - NC.

PERFORMANCE* - Max level speed 63 mph, 101 kph. Never exceed speed 120 mph, 193 kph. Max cruising speed 63 mph, 101 kph. Economic cruising speed 56 mph, 90 kph. Stalling speed 23 mph, 37 kph. Max climb rate at sea level 850 ft/min, 4.3 m/s. Take-off distance 75 ft, 23 m. Range at average cruising speed 250 mile, 402 km. Other data NC.

*Under unspecified test conditions.

GOLDEN AGE
RYAN STA TWO-PLACE
(Three-axis)

See Ryan STA *except: Tandem two-seater. Suspension NC.*

Production status: prototype.

GENERAL - As with the single-seater, little information is available on this aircraft, though the *Ryan STA Two-Place* is clearly directly derived from the solo machine, sharing the same wing span and overall length. The maker claims that in two-seat form it is a full-scale replica of the original *Ryan STA.*

Standard engine is the 447 Rotax (the version detailed below), but a 503 Rotax is optional. Features and options are as for the single-seater, prices being US$9995 in kit form or US$12,990 ready to fly.

EXTERNAL DIMENSIONS & AREAS - See *Ryan STA.*

POWER PLANT - Rotax 447 engine. Max power 47 hp at NC rpm. Propeller diameter and pitch 72x28 inch, 1.83x0.71 m. Gear reduction, ratio NC. Fuel capacity 5.0 US gal, 4.2 Imp gal, 18.9 litre.

WEIGHTS & LOADINGS - NC.

PERFORMANCE* - Max level speed 63 mph, 101 kph. Never exceed speed 120 mph, 193 kph. Max cruising speed 63 mph, 101 kph. Economic cruising speed 60 mph, 97 kph. Stalling speed 27 mph, 43 kph. Max climb rate at sea level 700 ft/min, 3.6 m/s. Take-off distance 175 ft, 53 m.

*Under unspecified test conditions except: Take-off distance measured when flying two-up.

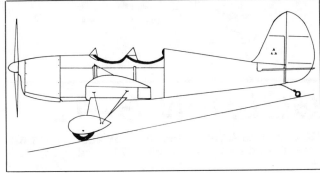

GOLDEN AGE
MONARCH
(Three-axis)

Single-seat single-engined high-wing monoplane with conventional three-axis control. Wing has unswept leading and trailing edges, and constant chord; conventional tail. Pitch control by elevator on tail; yaw control by fin-mounted rudder; roll control by ailerons; control inputs through stick for pitch/roll and pedals for yaw. Wing braced from above by kingpost and cables, from below by cables; wing profile NC; 100% double-surface. Undercarriage has three wheels in tail-dragger formation; suspension NC. Push-right go-right tailwheel steering connected to yaw control; also differential braking. Brakes on main wheels. Steel tube airframe, totally enclosed. Engine mounted below wing, driving tractor propeller.

Production status: prototype.

GENERAL - Despite being a high-wing machine, the *Monarch* is again clearly one of the *Ryan STA* family, sharing the same steel tube construction and as the other

Golden Age aircraft. The appeal, however, is rather different, for the *Monarch* is an antique-looking cabin monoplane whose most obvious rival is the Fisher *FP-202 Koala*.

Standard equipment and options are the same as for the other models in the range, and prices are the same as for the *Ryan STA*. Again, little technical data is available, but we understand that production versions will satisfy *FAR Part 103*.

EXTERNAL DIMENSIONS & AREAS - See *Ryan STA*.

POWER PLANT - See *Ryan STA* except: Propeller diameter and pitch 60x28 inch, 1.52x0.71 m.

WEIGHTS & LOADINGS - NC.

PERFORMANCE* - See *Ryan STA* except: Economic cruising speed 50 mph, 80 kph. Stalling speed 24 mph, 39 kph. Take-off distance 100 ft, 30 m.

*Under unspecified test conditions.

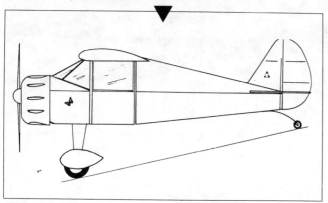

GOLDEN GATE

Golden Gate Aviation Inc, PO Box 2098, 1508 6th Street, Berkeley, California 94710; tel (415) 525-5548.

GOLDEN GATE
MOSQUITO
(Three-axis)

Single-seat single-engined high-wing monoplane with conventional three-axis control. Wing has unswept leading and trailing edges, and constant chord; cruciform tail. Pitch control by elevator on tail; yaw control by fin-mounted rudder; roll control by full-span ailerons; control inputs through stick for pitch/roll and pedals for yaw. Wing braced from above by kingpost and cables, from below by cables (strut bracing from below optional); wing profile NC; 100% double-surface. Undercarriage has three wheels in tricycle formation; no suspension on nosewheel and torsion-bar suspension on main wheels. Push-right go-right nosewheel steering connected to yaw control. Nosewheel brake. Aluminium-alloy tube airframe, with pod. Engine mounted at wing height, driving tractor propeller.

Production status: current, 8 completed.

GENERAL - It's impossible to look at the *Mosquito* without thinking of the Ultralight Flight *Phantom* and the

Bell *Spitfire*, so much does it resemble these machines. However, Hungarian-born designer Mihaly Kun, who worked for Mitchell and Manta before deciding to set up on his own, is convinced that his creation is stronger than either of them - quite a claim in view of the fact that the *Phantom* and *Spitfire* are themselves among the strongest ultralights. Available in either strut- or wire-braced forms (the latter is standard and is the version detailed below), the *Mosquito* comes very well equipped as standard, including front brake, steerable nosewheel, pod and windshield (which can be converted to full enclosure), ASI, egtg, and tachometer. For pilots wanting to do aerobatics, the wire-braced version is recommended.

Power comes from the Kawasaki TA440A engine developing 32 hp, and the price is US$4995 for a kit taking 25-60 h to assemble, or an extra US$1000 for a ready-to-fly machine. Set-up time is 20-40 min.

EXTERNAL DIMENSIONS & AREAS - Length overall 18.0 ft, 5.49 m. Height overall 8.3 ft, 2.54 m. Wing span 28.0 ft, 8.53 m. Constant chord 5.0 ft, 1.52 m. Dihedral 3°. Sweepback 0°. Tailplane span 8.0 ft, 2.44 m. Fin height 5.0 ft, 1.52 m. Total wing area 142 ft², 13.2 m². Total aileron area 20.0 ft², 1.86 m². Fin area 7.5 ft², 0.70 m². Rudder area 8.8 ft², 0.81 m². Tailplane area 12.0 ft², 1.11 m². Total elevator area 8.0 ft², 0.74 m². Aspect ratio 5.5/1. Wheel track 5.0 ft, 1.52 m. Wheelbase 4.3 ft, 1.30 m. Nosewheel diameter overall 12 inch, 30 cm. Main wheels diameter overall 11 inch, 28 cm.

POWER PLANT - Kawasaki TA440A engine. Max power 32 hp at 6000 rpm. Propeller diameter and pitch 58x30 inch, 1.47x0.76 m. Notched V-belt reduction, ratio 2.3/1. Max static thrust 200 lb, 91 kg. Power per unit area 0.23 hp/ft², 2.4 hp/m². Fuel capacity 5.0 US gal, 4.2 Imp gal, 18.9 litre.

WEIGHTS & LOADINGS - Empty weight 260 lb, 118 kg. Max take-off weight 560 lb, 254 kg. Payload 300 lb, 136 kg. Max wing loading 3.94 lb/ft², 19.2 kg/m². Max power loading 17.5 lb/hp, 7.9 kg/hp. Load factors +6.5, -9.0 recommended; +10.1, -6.6 ultimate.

PERFORMANCE* - Max level speed 63 mph, 101 kph. Never exceed speed 100 mph, 161 kph. Max cruising speed 60 mph, 97 kph. Economic cruising speed 50 mph, 80 kph. Stalling speed 26 mph, 42 kph. Max climb rate at sea level 800 ft/min, 4.1 m/s. Min sink rate 500 ft/min at 32 mph, 2.5 m/s at 51 kph. Best glide ratio with power off 8/1 at 37 mph, 60 kph. Take-off distance 150 ft, 45 m. Landing distance 150 ft, 45 m. Service ceiling 12,000 ft, 3660 m. Range at average cruising speed 100 mile, 161 km. Noise level NC.

*Under the following test conditions - Airfield altitude 62 ft, 19 m. Ground temperature 70°F, 21°C. Ground pressure NC. Ground windspeed NC. Test payload 460 lb, 209 kg.

One of the patterns from which the moulds for the Aerostar wings were made. Note the high standard of finish. For a picture of the completed aircraft, see colour section.

GOLDWING

Goldwing Ltd, Amador County Airport Building 3, PO Box 1123, Jackson, California, 95642; tel (209) 223-0384. President: Brian Glenn. General manager: Reklai Salazar.

GOLDWING LTD
AEROSTAR

(Three-axis)

Single-seat single-engined mid-wing monoplane with conventional three-axis control. Wing has swept back leading and trailing edges, and tapering chord; no tail, canard wing. Pitch control by elevator on canard; yaw control by tip rudders; roll control by half-span up-only ailerons and spoilers; control inputs through stick for pitch/roll and pedals for yaw. Cantilever wing; main-wing profile modified Liebeck; canard profile GU25; both 100% double-surface. Undercarriage has three wheels in tricycle formation; suspension NC. Push-right go-right nosewheel steering connected to yaw control. No brakes. Composite-construction fuselage, partially enclosed. Engine mounted above wing, driving pusher propeller. Composite-construction wing of foam, Kevlar and carbon fibre, with glass-fibre skin.

Production status: current, number completed NC.

GENERAL - Craig Catto's classic canard design for the *Goldwing* has spawned a number of variants since it was first shown in 1979, of which the *Aerostar* is the latest and possibly the most sophisticated. Certainly it is the best engineered from a production point of view; the original *Goldwing*, later dubbed *Goldwing ST*, had its wings built 'inside out', in that their glass-fibre skin was not laid in a mould but wrapped around the foam/aluminium-alloy core after the latter had been sanded to shape. This approach avoided expensive tooling, but demanded laborious hand finishing of the skin to give a good finish. With the *Aerostar*, the manufacturer has taken the plunge and invested in moulds so that the aircraft can be produced in quantity and with a consistently high finish.

However, it is not just the production method which has changed. To make the *Goldwing* concept light enough for *FAR Part 103*, a lot of redesigning has had to be done, and the result is an aircraft which looks similar to the original (though in fact its fuselage is slimmer and squarer in section), but is very different under the skin. Carbon-fibre and Kevlar help keep down the weight, and after flirtations with Kawasaki and Zenoah replacements for the twin-cylinder Cuyuna, the latter has finally been ditched in favour of a 277 Rotax with gear reduction, giving another useful weight saving.

Some idea of the time and investment needed can be gleaned from the fact that the *Aerostar* was originally announced in 1983, under the name *Goldwing UL*, yet only in spring 1985 reached serious production. Along the way, the company has dropped the original *Goldwing ST* (though it is still available from other sources - see Catto), and its crop-sraying derivative the *Gold Duster*. Also no longer listed is the two-seat *Goldwing II*, a decision which means that there is now no two-seat version of the *Goldwing* available anywhere, since the version developed by Goldwing's former UK agent Eurowing, the *Zephyr II*, never got past the prototype stage and the only example was destroyed when the company folded. Also shelved, possibly for good, is the *Nexus* two-seater first shown at Oshkosh '82, a very un-Goldwing looking machine (it has a tail!) which never reached production. Clearly, the company has nailed its colours firmly to the *Aerostar*.

The *Aerostar* is provisionally priced at US$7995, fully built. Kits and plans are not available.

EXTERNAL DIMENSIONS & AREAS - Length overall 13.5 ft, 4.11 m. Height overall 5.5 ft, 1.68 m. Wing span 30.5 ft, 9.30 m. Total wing area 148 ft², 13.7 m². Other data NC.

POWER PLANT - Rotax 277 engine. Max power 28 hp at 6200 rpm. Propeller diameter and pitch 50x27 inch, 1.27x0.69 m. Gear reduction, ratio 2.0/1. Max static thrust NC. Power per unit area 0.19 hp/ft², 2.0 hp/m². Fuel capacity 5.0 US gal, 4.2 Imp gal, 18.9 litre.

WEIGHTS & LOADINGS - Empty weight 254 lb, 115 kg. Max take-off weight 540 lb, 245 kg. Payload 286 lb, 130 kg. Max wing loading 3.65 lb/ft², 17.9 kg/m². Max power loading 19.3 lb/hp, 9.1 kg/hp. Load factors NC recommended; £6.0, -4.5 ultimate.

PERFORMANCE* - Max level speed 63 mph, 101 kph. Never exceed speed 70 mph, 113 kph. Cruising speed 62 mph, 100 kph. Stalling speed 26 mph, 42 kph. Max climb rate at sea level 600 ft/min, 3.1 m/s. Min sink rate 350 ft/min, 1.8 m/s at NC speed. Best glide ratio with power off 16/1 at NC speed. Range at average cruising speed 200 mile, 322 km. Other data NC.

*Under unspecified test conditions.

GREENWOOD

Greenwood Aircraft Inc, PO Box 401, Alexandria, Minnesota 56308; tel (612) 762-2020. President: George Roth. Chief test pilot: George Roth Jnr.

GREENWOOD *WITCH*
(Three-axis)

Single-seat single-engined high-wing monoplane with conventional three-axis control. Wing has unswept leading and trailing edges, and constant chord; T-tail. Pitch control by fully flying tail; yaw control by fin-mounted rudder; roll control by half-span ailerons; control inputs through stick for pitch/roll and pedals for yaw. Wing braced from below by struts; wing profile NACA 6212; 100% double-surface. Undercarriage has three wheels in tricycle formation with additional tailwheel; suspen-sion NC on nosewheel and axle-flex suspension on main wheels. Push-right go-right nosewheel steering connec-

A wing-folding demonstration on a Greenwood Witch; this is a pre-production prototype without the addit-ional tailwheel.

ted to yaw control. Nosewheel brake. Tubular airframe (materials see text), with pod. Engine mounted below wing, driving pusher propeller.

Production status: current, number completed NC.

GENERAL - If Eipper's *Quicksilver GT* had a T-tail, one might be forgiven for mistaking it for Greenwood's *Witch* - that is, until the time came to derig. Then the *Witch's* unique wing folding system would come into its own, whereby the outboard halves of the wing fold flat onto the top of the inboard halves, the whole assembly then being rotated through 90° so that the aircraft can be towed on its own wheels.

Naturally, this arrangement arouses great interest wherever the machine is flown, and this tends to over-shadow the rest of the aircraft, which is unfortunate as the *Witch* is interesting in other departments too. For instance, although the large-diameter tail boom is aluminium alloy, as are the leading edge D-cell and stamped ribs, the rest of the airframe is welded steel tube. Dacron is used to cover the wings, but the tail surfaces are all metal and incorporate a full-span trim tab for the all flying elevator.

The *Witch* has had a long gestation period, making its first flights in 1982 using an elegant but expensive cantilever wing with foam ribs and mahogany plywood capstrips. The present design was substituted for cost reasons, and plans to offer the cantilever arrangement as an option seem to have been dropped.

An interesting article on the machine by James Lawrence appeared in the 1985 edition of *Ultralight Aircraft Annual*, in which James seemed to conclude that the aircraft was very thoughtfully constructed, with the attention more on engineering than marketing. In some areas the specification is rather lacking in showroom appeal - the seat cushion for instance is an extra, the standard arrangement being simply a frame with Dacron webbing - but nevertheless it is gratifying to see this novel machine in serious if small scale production at last, especially as we understand that it may soon be joined by a two-seat version. With the price now down from US$7200 to a more realistic US$6500 complete (kits are not available), the machine deserves to find a market.

EXTERNAL DIMENSIONS & AREAS - Length overall 18.2 ft, 5.55 m. Height overall 7.0 ft, 2.13 m. Wing span 30.0 ft, 9.14 m. Constant chord 5.0 ft, 1.52 m. Dihedral 1.5°. Sweepback 0°. Total wing area 150 ft^2, 13.9 m^2. Aspect ratio 6.0/1. Other data NC.

POWER PLANT - Zenoah G25B1 engine. Max power 22 hp at 6500 rpm. Propeller diameter and pitch 54x27 inch, 1.37x0.69 m. V-belt reduction, ratio 2.5/1. Max static thrust 160 lb, 73 kg. Power per unit area 0.15 hp/ft^2, 1.6 hp/m^2. Fuel capacity 5.0 US gal, 4.2 Imp gal, 18.9 litre.

WEIGHTS & LOADINGS - Empty weight 248 lb, 113 kg. Max take-off weight 494 lb, 224 kg. Payload 246 lb, 111 kg. Max wing loading 3.29 lb/ft^2, 16.1 kg/m^2. Max power loading 22.5 lb/hp, 10.2 kg/hp. Load factors +3.8, -2.0 recommended; +5.7, -NC ultimate.

PERFORMANCE* - Max level speed 63 mph, 101 kph. Never exceed speed 90 mph, 145 kph. Max cruising speed 50 mph, 80 kph. Economic cruising speed 45 mph, 72 kph. Stalling speed 26 mph, 42 kph. Max climb rate at sea level 500 ft/min, 2.5 m/s. Best glide ratio with power off 7.6/1 at NC speed. Range at average cruising speed 225 mile, 362 km. Other data NC.

*Under unspecified test conditions.

GROVER

Grover Aircraft Corporation, PO Box 647, Hendersonville, North Carolina 28793; tel (704) 697-7958. President: Charles Harry III. General manager: George F Worton. Design engineer: Jesse D Anglin. Marketing manager: Greg Kilpatrick.

Canadian agent: Modern Aviation Canada, PO Box 5, Levis, Quebec G6V 7E2; tel (418) 835-1427. Contact: Maureen Kennedy.

French agent: Filcoa Co, Usine du Poet, Le Poet 05300; tel 9265 7208; tx 403434. Contact: Pierre Bourgeois.

GROVER *J-3 KITTEN*
(Three-axis)

Single-seat single-engined high-wing monoplane with conventional three-axis control. Wing has unswept leading and trailing edges, and constant chord; conventional tail. Pitch control by elevator on tail; yaw control by fin-mounted rudder; roll control by 40%-span ailerons; control inputs through stick for pitch/roll and pedals for yaw. Wing braced from below by struts; wing profile NASA 64; 100% double-surface. Undercarriage has three wheels in tail-dragger formation; leaf-spring suspension on tailwheel and coil-spring suspension on main wheels. Push-right go-right tailwheel steering connected to yaw control; also differential braking. Brakes on main wheels. Steel-tube airframe, totally enclosed (doors removable). Engine mounted below wing, driving tractor propeller.

Production status: current, 50 completed.

GENERAL - The *J-3 Kitten* made its first public appearance at the Lakeland, Florida Sun 'n Fun fly-in during March '84, when it won the Best New Design award. Ironically, what set the *Kitten* apart was how unlike an ultralight it was in construction, for it was the first real 'Cub-like' ultralight to come on the scene, built like a 'real aircraft', with lots of welded steel components and fabric covering. True to the 'little airplane' philosophy, when shown at Lakeland it used a four-stroke Global engine, and the thump of this turned quite a few heads sharply upward, as those more used to the snarl of two-strokes looked up to see the pretty yellow ultralight motoring through the sky.

Subsequently, Jesse Anglin, under whose name the aircraft was originally marketed, fell out with the manufacturers of the Global engine (who incidentally went on to found Nostalgair), and substituted the ubiquitous Rotax 277 for the four-stroke twin.

Kittens come in plan, kit or ready-to-fly form. Plans, professionally drawn and many of them full scale, measure 18x24 inch (45x60 cm) and cost US$75, while kits sell for US$6300 with part kits (fuselage, wing, engine) also available to spread the cost. The kits are nothing if not complete, with all instruments, wheels, tyres, nuts, bolts, washers, turnbuckles, cable, nicos, micarta ball-bearing pulleys, covering material and glue included. The Rotax engine comes complete with prop, all welding is already complete, and all brackets and fittings are made and in place. Wing ribs and spars, cowlings and fuel tank are all finished, and metal parts are primed. A construction

manual is supplied and just about the only additional item needed is paint.

Building a *Kitten* takes 100-150 h, and the completed aircraft takes 15 min to rig. Ready-to-fly machines cost US$7900.

EXTERNAL DIMENSIONS & AREAS - Length overall 16.3 ft, 4.95 m. Height overall 5.2 ft, 1.57 m. Wing span 30.0 ft, 9.14 m. Constant chord 4.0 ft, 1.22 m. Dihedral 2°. Sweepback 0°. Tailplane span 7.5 ft, 2.29 m. Fin height 3.7 ft, 1.12 m. Total wing area 120 ft², 11.1 m². Total aileron area 13.3 ft², 1.24 m². Fin area 3.0 ft², 0.28 m². Rudder area 5.0 ft², 0.47 m². Tailplane area 6.0 ft², 0.56 m². Total elevator area 5.6 ft², 0.52 m². Aspect ratio 7.5/1. Wheel track 5.0 ft, 1.52 m. Wheelbase 12.2 ft, 3.71 m. Tailwheel diameter overall 4 inch, 10 cm. Main wheels diameter overall 12 inch, 30 cm.

POWER PLANT - Rotax 277 engine. Max power 28 hp at 6250 rpm. Propeller diameter and pitch 60x28 inch, 1.62x0.71 m. Gear reduction, ratio 2.6/1. Max static thrust 210 lb, 95 kg. Power per unit area 0.23 hp/ft², 2.5 hp/m². Fuel capacity 5.0 US gal, 4.2 Imp gal, 18.9 litre.

WEIGHTS & LOADINGS - Empty weight 248 lb, 112 kg. Max take-off weight 450 lb, 204 kg. Payload 202 lb, 92 kg. Max wing loading 3.75 lb/ft², 18.4 kg/m². Max power loading 16.1 lb/hp, 7.3 kg/hp. Load factors +6.0, -4.0 recommended; NC ultimate.

PERFORMANCE* - Max level speed 62 mph, 100 kph. Never exceed speed 100 mph, 161 kph. Max cruising speed 58 mph, 93 kph. Economic cruising speed 50 mph, 80 kph. Stalling speed 24 mph, 39 kph. Max climb rate at sea level 700 ft/min, 3.6 m/s. Min sink rate 400 ft/min at 45 mph, 2.0 m/s at 72 kph. Best glide ratio with power off 11/1 at NC speed. Take-off distance *90* ft, *27* m. Landing distance *350* ft, *107* m. Service ceiling *11,000* ft, *3350* m. Range at economic cruising speed 139 mile, 223 km. Noise level NC.

*Under the following test conditions - Airfield altitude 0 ft, 0 m. Ground temperature 59°F, 15°C. Ground pressure 1013 mB. Ground windspeed 0 mph, 0 kph. Test payload 170 lb, 77 kg.

GROVER
SUPER KITTEN
(Three-axis)

Summary as J-3 Kitten.

Production status: current, number completed NC.

GENERAL - Identical in every respect to the *J-3 Kitten* except for its engine, the *Super Kitten* is too heavy for the ultralight category, and is sold as an experimental homebuilt. Power comes from the twin-cylinder Rotax 447. Though normally sold in kit form only, it is available as a finished aircraft to law enforcement agencies. Price: NC.

EXTERNAL DIMENSIONS & AREAS - See *J-3 Kitten.*

POWER PLANT - Rotax 447 engine. Max power 40 hp at NC rpm. Propeller diameter and pitch 64x32 inch, 1.63x0.81 m. Reduction type and ratio NC. Max static thrust NC. Power per unit area 0.33 hp/ft², 3.6 hp/m². Fuel capacity 5.0 US gal, 4.2 Imp gal, 18.9 litre.

WEIGHTS & LOADINGS - Max take-off weight 525 lb, 238 kg. Max wing loading 4.38 lb/ft², 21.4 kg/m². Max power loading 13.1 lb/hp, 6.0 kg/hp. Other data NC.

PERFORMANCE - NC.

GROVER
J-4 SPORTSTER
(Three-axis)

Summary as J-3 Kitten except: Parasol wing. Wing profile NC. Partially enclosed.

Production status: current, number completed NC.

GENERAL - Not content with their *J-3 Kitten* taking top honours at Sun 'n Fun, Jesse Anglin and friends turned up at Oshkosh just a few months later with what is effectively a parasol-winged version of the same machine, and proceeded to win the Grand Champion award. Called the *J-4 Sportster,* the new machine earned high praise for its standard of finish, and will appeal to those who want fresh air flying and yet prefer to have a substantial fuselage around them. Prices, purchase arrangements, build and rigging time are all the same as for the *J-3 Kitten,* the main constructional difference between the two being that on the *J-4 Sportster* the wings don't fold. Also, only the enclosed machine comes with a luggage bay cover.

This is clearly not the end of Jesse Anglin's creative efforts, for we understand that the company is working on a two-seater, and on another four-stroke design. There is also a possibility that the firm may market an ultralight-category helicopter designed by Tamarind International of Olla, Louisiana.

EXTERNAL DIMENSIONS & AREAS - See *J-3 Kitten.*

POWER PLANT - See *J-3 Kitten.*

WEIGHTS & LOADINGS - See *J-3 Kitten* except: Empty weight 240 lb, 109 kg. Payload 210 lb, 95 kg. Load factors +6.0, -3.5 recommended; NC ultimate.

PERFORMANCE* - Max level speed 62 mph, 101 kph. Never exceed speed 100 mph, 16 kph. Max cruising speed 58 mph, 93 kph. Economic cruising speed 50 mph, 80 kph. Stalling speed 24 mph, 39 kph. Max climb rate at sea level 700 ft/min, 3.6 m/s. Best glide ratio with power off 10.5/1 at NC speed. Other data NC.

*Under unspecified test conditions.

HAIMERL

Haimerl Aircraft Co, PO Box 3502, Grand Junction, Colorado 81502.

HAIMERL *FOLK-ER*
(Three-axis)

Single-seat single-engined biplane with conventional three-axis control. Aluminium-alloy tube airframe, completely open. Other details NC.

Production status: plans-built, number completed NC.

GENERAL - All we know about this obscure homebuilt biplane is the little we have gleaned from advertisements in American aviation magazines, from which we gather that it is of tubular aluminium-alloy construction, bolted rather than welded together. In view of the lack of information, we are omitting our data paragraphs in this case.

Plans cost US$40, information US$5; add US$6 for overseas.

HELICRAFT

Helicraft Inc, PO Box 16488, Baltimore, Maryland 21217.

HELICRAFT
BW-20 GYROKOPTER
(Gyroplane)

Single-seat single-engined gyroplane with three-axis control. Rotor has constant chord; tail has vertical surfaces only. Pitch/roll control by angling rotor, yaw control by fin-mounted rudder; control inputs through stick for pitch/roll and pedals for yaw. Two-blade rotor. Undercarriage has three wheels in tricycle formation. Tubular

airframe, completely open. Engine mounted below rotor, driving pusher propeller.

Production status: plans built, number completed NC.

GENERAL - Little information is available on this home-built gyroplane, which is a development of the company's unpowered design, the *BW-19*. Indeed, one way of easing the build costs is to construct the latter first and later add an engine to create a *BW-20*. Build time is estimated at 100 h.

Price of the plans is US$33, plus US$3 for airmail overseas. The same company also offers a jet-powered gyroplane, the *Helicraft Jet*, but we have no further details.

EXTERNAL DIMENSIONS & AREAS - Rotor diameter 21.0 ft, 6.40 m. Other data NC.

POWER PLANT - McCulloch 4381 engine. Max power 72 hp at NC rpm. Fuel capacity 5.0 US gal, 4.2 Imp gal, 18.9 litre. Other data NC.

WEIGHTS & LOADINGS - Empty weight 240 lb, 109 kg. Max take-off weight 550 lb, 249 kg. Payload 310 lb, 141 kg. Max power loading 7.6 lb/hp, 3.5 kg/hp. Load factors NC.

PERFORMANCE* - Max level speed 80 mph, 129 kph. Cruising speed 55 mph, 88 kph. Max climb rate at sea level 900 ft/min, 4.6 m/s. Range at average cruising speed 92 mile, 147 km. Other data NC.

*Under unspecified test conditions.

HIGHCRAFT AERO-MARINE

HighCraft Aero-Marine Inc, PO Box 1771, 110 Mingo Trail, Longwood, Florida 32750; tel (305) 339-5744. President: W Bruce Pemberton. Vice-president: John J Gruener. Head of r&d: Bobby Bailey. Secretary: Jim Walsh.

Sales and production through: Advanced Aviation (see separate listing).

Australian agent: Moyes Delta Gliders, Sydney; tel 387-2160. Proprietor: Bill Moyes.

West Indian agent: David Gillmor, St Lucia 22500; tel (809) 452-2377.

HIGHCRAFT AERO-MARINE
BUCCANEER XL/280 and XA/280
(Three-axis)

Single-seat single-engined high-wing monoplane with conventional three-axis control. Wing has unswept leading and trailing edges, and constant chord; conventional tail. Pitch control by elevator on tail; yaw control by fin-mounted rudder; roll control by 60%-span ailerons; control inputs through stick for pitch/roll and pedals for yaw. Wing braced from above by kingpost and cables, from below by cables; wing profile NC; 100% double-surface. Undercarriage has three wheels in tail-dragger formation (XL/280), plus sponsons and glass-fibre reinforced

hull (XA/280); torsion-bar suspension on tailwheel and axle-flex suspension on main wheels. Push-right go-right tailwheel steering connected to yaw control; also optional differential braking on XL/280. Optional brakes on main wheels (XL/280); no brakes (XA/280). Aluminium-alloy tube airframe; completely open (XL/280), partially enclosed (XA/280). Engine mounted above wing, driving pusher propeller.

Production status: current, number completed NC.

GENERAL - Take one look at the basic version of the *Buccaneer*, the *XL/280*, and you could be forgiven for thinking that it is a fairly straightforward cable-braced ultralight with no remarkable features. But there is a twist: it can also be very readily made into an amphibious aircraft.

The *Buccaneer XL/280* is produced and sold on behalf of HighCraft by Advanced Aviation. Kit can be had for US$5995, with the amphibian *Buccaneer XA/280* costing US7995, and for the difference between the two prices the customer can buy a kit to convert one version to the other. The conversion kit contains everything required to turn the land plane into a true ultralight-legal amphibian, for the FAA rules allow an extra 50 lb (23 kg) for aircraft using the fuselage as a flotation device, enough to keep the *XA/280* within the *FAR Part 103* rules.

A unique aspect of the amphibian's design is the foolproof system of retracting the wheels. There are no complicated mechanisms to go wrong: the pilot simply reaches over the side to lock the main wheels into their mounting points for a wheeled landing, or unlocks them and pulls them up into their holders for a marine landing. Rigging time obviously varies a bit depending on which mode the aircraft is to be operated in, but is around 20 min with two people.

There are a few sacrifices to be made for this versatility - the climb and sink are not as good on the amphibious version and the optional brakes cannot be fitted - but most of the company's customers seem to choose the *XA/280* nevertheless, attracted by its go-anywhere ability and the slightly higher speeds which the drag-reducing hull allows. And while it may not matter in Florida, its weather protection is better too...

Note: In the data below, where figures for the two versions differ, those for the XL/280 are shown first, followed in parentheses by those for the XA/280.

EXTERNAL DIMENSIONS & AREAS - Length overall 17.5(19.1) ft, 5.33(5.82) m. Height overall 7.4 ft, 2.26 m. Wing span 33.5 ft, 10.21 m. Constant chord 4.4 ft, 1.34 m. Dihedral 5°. Sweepback 0°. Tailplane span 8.3 ft, 2.53 m. Fin height 4.2 ft, 1.28 m. Total wing area 146 ft², 13.6 m². Total aileron area 18.1 ft², 1.68 m². Fin area 5.5 ft², 0.51 m². Rudder area 8.7 ft², 0.81 m². Tailplane area 8.0 ft², 0.74 m². Total elevator area 10.4 ft², 0.97 m². Aspect ratio 7.7/1. Wheel track 4.8 ft, 1.46 m. Wheelbase 12.1 ft, 3.69 m. Tailwheel diameter overall 4 inch, 10 cm. Main wheels diameter overall 10 inch, 25 cm.

POWER PLANT - Rotax 277 engine. Max power 28 hp at 6300 rpm. Propeller diameter and pitch 60x28 inch, 1.52x-0.71 m. Gear reduction, ratio 2.6/1. Max static thrust NC. Power per unit area 0.19 hp/ft², 2.1 hp/m². Fuel capacity 4.5 US gal, 3.8 Imp gal, 17.0 litre.

WEIGHTS & LOADINGS - Empty weight 228(298) lb, 103(135) kg. Max take-off weight 500(550)) lb, 227(249) kg. Payload 272(252) lb, 123(114) kg. Max wing loading 3.42(3.77) lb/ft², 16.6(18.3) kg/m². Max power loading 17.9(19.6) lb/hp, 8.1(8.9) kg/hp. Load factors +3.5(3.0), -2.5(2.0) recommended; +5.5(5.0), -4.0(3.5) ultimate.

PERFORMANCE* - Max level speed 52(55) mph, 84(88)

kph. Never exceed speed 70 mph, 113 kph. Max cruising speed 45(47) mph, 72(76) kph. Economic cruising speed 40 mph, 64 kph. Stalling speed 21(23) mph, 34(37) kph. Max climb rate at sea level 600(450) ft/min, 3.1(2.3) m/s. Min sink rate 220(280) ft/min at 26(28) mph, 1.1(1.4) m/s at 42(45) kph. Best glide ratio with power off 11(10)/1 at 32(34) mph, 51(55) kph. Take-off distance 125(175) ft, 38(53) m. Landing distance 100(150) ft, 30(46) m. Service ceiling 12,000 ft, 3660 m. Range at average cruising speed 120 mile, 193 km. Noise level NC.

Under the following test conditions - Airfield altitude 0 ft, 0 m. Ground temperature 60°F, 16°C. Ground pressure NC. Ground windspeed 0 mph, 0 kph. Test payload 197(202) lb, 89(92) kg.

For an illustration of the Buccaneer, *see colour section.*

HOUSTON

Houston Ultralights Corp, 25314 Zube Road, Hockley, Texas 77447; tel (713) 373-3095.

HOUSTON
MUSTANG I

Single-seat single-engined high-wing monoplane. Wing has unswept leading and trailing edges, and constant chord; cruciform tail. Pitch control by elevator on tail; yaw control by fin-mounted rudder; roll control see text; Wing bracing and double-surfacing see text. Undercarriage has three wheels in tricycle formation. Nosewheel steering. Aluminium-alloy tube airframe, partially enclosed. Engine mounted below wing, driving tractor propeller. Other details NC.

Production status: see text.

GENERAL - Announced just as we went to press and claimed to be especially suitable for the novice pilot, the *Mustang I* at first sight has a vaguely *Cub*-like appearance, with engine in the nose, tractor prop and fully covered airframe. However, the wing is very much in the *Quicksilver MX* vein, with kingpost and cable bracing, single surfacing and pronounced dihedral, though a strut-braced double-surface wing is offered on the same airframe for the more experienced pilot.

Construction is tube and heat-shrunk Dacron, but other than that little information is available, not even whether the controls are two- or three-axis. No data or prices have been released, nor do we know the production status of the machine.

INDUSTRIAL ELECTRIC

Industrial Electric, Box 74, Osceola, Indiana 46561; tel 219) 674-5764.

INDUSTRIAL ELECTRIC
INDIANA FLYER

Single- or two-seat (see text) single-engined mid-wing monoplane. Two-fin tail. Wing braced from below by struts. Undercarriage has three wheels in tricycle forma-

tion. Wood airframe, partially enclosed. Engine mounted below wing, driving pusher propeller.

Production status: plans-built, number completed NC.

GENERAL - This obscure machine is designed for the homebuilder who fancies a twin-boom pusher aircraft and yet has little money to spend. An odd looking design, with a fuselage shaped more like an assault craft than an aircraft, it can be built as a solo or dual machine.
The manufacturer offers a complete kit, including twin-cylinder engine of unspecified make, for US$1995, or plans for US$35. Information costs US$1.

EXTERNAL DIMENSIONS & AREAS - Wing span 32.0 ft, 9.75 m. Other data NC.

POWER PLANT - NC.

WEIGHTS & LOADINGS - NC.

PERFORMANCE - NC.

INTERNATIONAL AIRCRAFT CORP

International Aircraft Corporation, N34 W28341 Taylors Woods Road, Pewaukee, Wisconsin 53072; tel (414) 691-4452; tx 559664. President: Chip Erwin. Vice-president: Larry Whiting.

Canadian agent: Zenair (see separate listing).

INTERNATIONAL
AIRCRAFT CORP
AG-7
(Three-axis)

Single-seat twin-engined high-wing monoplane with conventional three-axis control. Wing has swept back leading edge, swept forward trailing edge, and tapering chord; flaps fitted; cruciform tail. Pitch control by elevator on tail; yaw control by fully flying rudder, roll control by half-span ailerons; control inputs through stick for pitch/roll and pedals for yaw. Wing braced from below by struts; wing profile Princeton Sailwing; 100% double-surface. Undercarriage has three wheels in tricycle formation; no suspension on nosewheel and glass-fibre suspension on main wheels. Push-right go-right nosewheel steering connected to yaw control. No brakes. Aluminium-alloy tube airframe, with optional

357

pod. Engines mounted at wing height, driving tractor propellers.

Production status: current, 150 completed (total of AG-7 and TR-7 production).

GENERAL - Chip Erwin will be familiar to many readers as the man behind the Midwest Microlites company which took over the marketing of the Waspair *Tomcat* models. But now Robin Haynes' novel canard design is out of production, as incidentally are the *Pintail* and *Pintail Trainer* derivatives which Robin designed for the defunct Little Air plane Co, featuring strut bracing and three-axis controls with ailerons.

So Chip has wiped the slate clean, setting up a new company to make a new aircraft, a workhorse machine which unlike most utilitarian ultralights is not derived from a basically recreational design. Together with Larry Whiting he has started from scratch to create the *AG-7*, deliberately restricting top speed in the interest of a low stall, and fitting flaps to further aid low-speed manoeuvring. Twin engines were adopted for reliability reasons, the choice being that well proven French twin, the JPX PUL425. The latter is unusual in that it has a large capacity for its power output - 425 cc for 22 hp - and thus revs much slower than the average ultralight engine, slow enough to dispense with a reduction drive.

Most *AG-7s* are used for crop-dusting, and the company offers as a US$2500 option its Micro-Ag spray system, with spray nozzles mounted on booms slung under the wings. Further versatility is provided by another option, floats, which cost an extra US$1220. The aircraft is available only in ready-to-fly form, at a price of US$8500.

EXTERNAL DIMENSIONS & AREAS - Length overall 15.0 ft, 4.57 m. Height overall 6.0 ft, 1.83 m. Wing span 29.0 ft, 8.84 m. Chord at root 7.0 ft, 2.13 m. Chord at tip 4.0 ft, 1.22 m. Total wing area 148 ft^2, 13.7 m^2. Aspect ratio 5.7/1. Other data NC.

POWER PLANT - Two JPX PUL425 engines. Max power 22 hp each at 4200 rpm. Propeller diameter and pitch NC. No reduction. Max static thrust NC. Power per unit area 0.30 hp/ft^2, 3.2 hp/m^2. Fuel capacity 5.0 US gal, 4.2 Imp gal, 18.9 litre.

WEIGHTS & LOADINGS - Empty weight 260 lb, 118 kg. Max take-off weight 600 lb, 272 kg. Payload 340 lb, 154 kg. Max wing loading 4.05 lb/ft^2, 19.8 kg/m^2. Max power loading 13.6 lb/hp, 6.2 kg/hp. Load factors +6.0, -3.0 recommended; NC ultimate.

PERFORMANCE* - Max level speed 55 mph, 88 kph. Never exceed speed 60 mph, 97 kph. Max cruising speed 40 mph, 64 kph. Economic cruising speed 35 mph, 56 kph. Stalling speed 19 mph, 31 kph. Max climb rate at sea level 540 ft/min, 2.7 m/s. Min sink rate NC. Best glide ratio with power off 8/1 at 30 mph, 48 kph. Take-off distance 70 ft, 21 m. Landing distance 100 ft, 30 m. Service ceiling 12,000 ft, 3660 m. Range at average cruising speed 75 mile, 121 km. Noise level 50 dB at 300 ft, 91 m.

*Under the following test conditions - Airfield altitude 0 ft, 0 m. Ground temperature 60°F, 16°C. Ground pressure NC. Ground windspeed 0 mph, 0 kph. Test payload 340 lb, 154 kg.

INTERNATIONAL AIRCRAFT CORP *TR-7*
(Three-axis)

Summary as AG-7 except: Side-by-side two-seater.

Production status: current, see AG-7 for number completed.

GENERAL - The *TR-7* is designed as a training machine for pilots intending to fly the *AG-7*, and resembles the solo machine in every respect except for its seating arrangements.
Price is US$8600.

EXTERNAL DIMENSIONS & AREAS - See *AG-7*.

POWER PLANT - See *AG-7*.

WEIGHTS & LOADINGS - Empty weight 270 lb, 122 kg. Max take-off weight 700 lb, 318 kg. Payload 430 lb, 195 kg. Max wing loading 4.73 lb/ft^2, 23.2 kg/m^2. Max power loading 15.9 lb/hp, 7.2 kg/hp. Load factors NC.

PERFORMANCE* - Max level speed 48 mph, 77 kph. Never exceed speed 55 mph, 88 kph. Cruising speed 35 mph, 56 kph. Max climb rate at sea level 460 ft/min, 2.3 m/s. Other data NC.

*Under unspecified test conditions.

KNOWLES

Ken Knowles Sport Aircraft Inc, 5398 Trail Street, Norco, California 91760; tel (714) 734-1468.

AIRCRAFT SPECIALTIES *DELTA BIRD*

See Aircraft Specialties.

AIRCRAFT SPECIALTIES *DELTA HAWK*

See Aircraft Specialties.

AIRCRAFT SPECIALTIES *SUPER HAWK*

See Aircraft Specialties.

UltraStar *in flight and (inset) folded ready for towing.*

KOLB COMPANY

Kolb Company, RD 3, Box 38, Phoenixville, Pennsylvania 19460; tel (215) 948-4136. Proprietor: Homer Kolb.

French agent: Zodiac (see separate listing).

KOLB COMPANY *ULTRASTAR*
(Three-axis)

Single-seat single-engined high-wing monoplane with conventional three-axis control. Wing has unswept leading and trailing edges, and constant chord; cruciform tail. Pitch control by elevator on tail; yaw control by fin-mounted rudder; roll control by full-span ailerons; control inputs through stick for pitch/roll and pedals for yaw. Semi-cantilevered wing braced from below by single strut; wing profile NC; 100% double-surface. Under carriage has three wheels in tail-dragger formation; torsion-bar suspension on tailwheel and no suspension on main wheels. Push-right go-right tailwheel steering connected to yaw control. No brakes. Steel-tube air frame, completely open. Engine mounted below wing, driving pusher propeller. Wings and tail surfaces have aluminium-alloy structure.

Production status: current, number completed NC.

GENERAL - In 1970 what was probably the first true ultralight aircraft was built and flown in Pennsylvania by Homer Kolb. It was of steel tube and fabric construction, had three-axis controls, was powered by twin chainsaw-type engines, and weighed less than 200 lb (91 kg). Homer

had a lot of fun with this aircraft and amazed his neighbours by proving that such a lightweight machine could actually carry a man about.

Eventually the plane was retired to a corner of a barn and all but forgotten, but as the ultralight movement gained momentum several years later, friends of Homer persuaded him to market his creation, which they naturally enough dubbed the *Kolb Flyer*. Plans were drawn up and sold to consumers, and eventually a raw materials kit became available, the design proving to be one of the most popular and successful ultralights around, with several versions flying.

Not long after the marketing of the *Kolb Flyer* got underway, Homer designed the *UltraStar,* and this too has sold widely since its introduction at the '82 Sun 'n Fun in Lakeland, Florida. Although seemingly a *Kolb Flyer* with one engine instead of two, it was actually designed on a fresh sheet of paper and has since supplanted the earlier design in the marketplace. Its features include quick-folding wings and tail surfaces that make the aircraft easy to transport and store, rigging time being around 10 min. Testing the aircraft in the October '84 edition of *Glider Rider,* Jan W Steenblik reported that the large full-span ailerons provided a very impressive roll rate, while the steerable tailwheel helped give the machine surprisingly good controllability on rough fields. In practice though, the small prop clearance and lack of suspension (apart from big soft tyres) restrict operation to reasonably good surfaces.

Just as with the *Flyer,* controls are standard three-axis, with a side-mounted stick, while power comes from a Cuyuna ULII-02 with Kolb's own reduction unit. Construction is based on standard aircraft practice, avoiding eccentric loading of fittings or bolts in bending, and using welded aircraft steel for the airframe and many important components.

As a kit requiring around 300 h to build, the *UltraStar* costs US$3695, but buyers can cut this down to 75 h by paying an extra US$800 for a ready-welded cage.

EXTERNAL DIMENSIONS & AREAS - Length overall 20.0 ft, 6.09 m. Height overall 6.0 ft, 1.83 m. Wing span 27.5 ft, 8.38 m. Constant chord 5.5 ft, 1.65 m. Dihedral 1°. Sweepback 0°. Tailplane span 7.8 ft, 2.33 m. Fin height 5.4 ft, 1.65 m. Total wing area 147 ft^2, 13.6 m^2. Total aileron area 27.0 ft^2, 2.51 m^2. Aspect ratio 5.2/1. Wheel track 4.6 ft, 1.40 m. Wheelbase 14.5 ft, 4.42 m. Tailwheel diameter overall 5 inch, 13 cm. Main wheels diameter overall 15 inch, 38 cm. Other data NC.

POWER PLANT - Cuyuna ULII-02 engine. Max power 35 hp at 6200 rpm. Propeller diameter and pitch 50x30 inch, 1.27x0.76 m. Notched flat-belt reduction, ratio 2.0/1. Max static thrust NC. Power per unit area 0.24 hp/ft^2, 2.6 hp/m^2. Fuel capacity 3.8 US gal, 3.1 Imp gal, 14.2 litre.

WEIGHTS & LOADINGS - Empty weight 245 lb, 111 kg. Max take-off weight 525 lb, 238 kg. Payload 280 lb, 127 kg. Max wing loading 3.58 lb/ft^2, 17.5 kg/m^2. Max power load ing 15.0 lb/hp, 6.8 kg/hp. Load factors +4.0, -2.0 recom mended; +6.0, -3.0 ultimate.

PERFORMANCE* - Max level speed 63 mph, 101 kph. Never exceed speed 80 mph, 129 kph. Max cruising speed 60 mph, 97 kph. Economic cruising speed 45 mph, 72 kph. Stalling speed 25 mph, 40 kph. Max climb rate at sea level >800 ft/min, >4.1 m/s. Take-off distance 100 ft, 30 m. Landing distance 100 ft, 30 m. Range at average cruising speed 98 mile, 158 km. Other data NC.

*Under unspecified test conditions.

KOLB COMPANY
ULTRASTAR KX-430
(Three-axis)

Summary as UltraStar except: Axle-flex suspension on main wheels. Optional pod.

Production status: see text.

GENERAL - Designed principally as a simpler version of the *UltraStar*, the *UltraStar KX-430* uses the same wings, tail and power pack as the *UltraStar*, but has a simplified tubular structure rather reminiscent of the Brock *Avion*. The two undercarriage legs are reduced to one to give axle-flex suspension, and the revised nose tubing allows a pod to be fitted.

Shown in prototype form at the '84 Oshkosh, the aircraft was intended to be sold only as a pre-welded kit, but at the time of writing the marketing arrangements are not clear, and no price is available.

EXTERNAL DIMENSIONS & AREAS - See *UltraStar* except: Length overall NC. Height overall NC.

POWER PLANT - See *UltraStar*.

WEIGHTS & LOADINGS - NC.

PERFORMANCE - NC.

KOLB COMPANY *FIRESTAR*
(Three-axis)

Summary similar to UltraStar except: Suspension NC. Brakes NC. Partially enclosed (total enclosure optional).

Production status: current, number completed NC.

GENERAL - Announced just as we went to press, Homer Kolb's new *FireStar* is easily recognisable from his other designs by having its engine above the tail boom rather than below it. It is also the first Kolb design to have a partially enclosed cockpit as standard, and in keeping with this change the stick has been moved from the side to the centre.

Although we do not have full details, we understand its structure is similar to earlier Kolb designs in its use of materials. Wing design is a development of the *Twin-Star*, though of smaller span, while in the power depart ment Homer has taken a leaf out of his French agent's book (see Zodiac) and opted for a Rotax 377 with gear reduction. Range should be much better than on the *UltraStar*, thanks to a larger tank.

Eager pilots anxious to get aloft will find the *FireStar* much less frustrating than earlier Kolb creations, as it is supplied completely pre-welded and with some holes drilled; moreover, aircraft in ready-to-cover form are scheduled for late summer '85.

Options include a parachute, shoulder harness, large balloon tyres, instruments, additional enclosure and pre-built wing ribs. Price: US$4995.

EXTERNAL DIMENSIONS & AREAS - Length overall 20.3 ft, 6.17 m. Height overall 5.7 ft, 1.73 m. Wing span 27.4 ft, 8.36 m. Constant chord 5.5 ft, 1.65 m. Sweep back 0°. Total wing area 148 ft^2, 13.7 m^2. Aspect ratio 5.1/1. Other data NC.

POWER PLANT - Rotax 377 engine. Max power 35 hp at 6200 rpm. Propeller diameter and pitch NC. Gear reduction, ratio 2.6/1. Max static thrust NC. Power per unit area 0.24 hp/ft^2, 2.6 hp/m^2. Fuel capacity 5.0 US gal, 4.2 Imp gal, 18.9 litre.

WEIGHTS & LOADINGS - Empty weight 254 lb, 115 kg. Max take-off weight 549 lb, 249 kg. Payload 295 lb, 134 kg. Max wing loading 3.71 lb/ft^2, 18.2 kg/m^2. Max power loading 15.7 lb/hp, 7.1 kg/hp. Load factors NC.

PERFORMANCE* - Max level speed 63 mph, 101 kph. Never exceed speed 80 mph, 129 kph. Cruising speed 50 mph, 80 kph. Stalling speed 25 mph, 40 kph. Max climb rate at sea level 1200 ft/min, 6.1 m/s. Other data NC.

*Under unspecified test conditions.

KOLB COMPANY *TWINSTAR*
(Three-axis)

Summary as UltraStar except: Side-by-side two-seater. Glass-fibre suspension on tailwheel and axle-flex sus-pension on main wheels. Push-right go-right tailwheel steering connected to yaw control; also differential braking. Brakes on main wheels. Optional pod.

Production status: current, number completed NC.

GENERAL - Designed in 1981, the *TwinStar* prototype first flew during 1982 and was presented at Oshkosh in

greater span wing with more ribs and reinforced struts, less dihedral, and a more powerful engine - a Rotax 447. The machine is remarkable for its low weight of only 285 lb (129 kg), exceptional for a three-axis two-seater with a large payload.
Price: NC.

EXTERNAL DIMENSIONS & AREAS - Length overall 20.9 ft, 6.37 m. Height overall 5.7 ft, 1.72 m. Wing span 30.0 ft, 9.14 m. Constant chord 5.5 ft, 1.65 m. Dihedral 1.5°. Sweepback 0°. Total wing area 162 ft², 15.1 m². Aspect ratio 5.6/1. Tailwheel diameter overall 5 inch, 13 cm. Main wheels diameter overall 16 inch, 41 cm. Other data NC.

POWER PLANT - Rotax 447 engine. Max power 41 hp at 6400 rpm. Propeller diameter and pitch 66xNC inch, 1.68xNC m. Gear reduction, ratio 2.6/1. Max static thrust NC. Power per unit area 0.25 hp/ft², 2.7 hp/m². Fuel capacity 5.0 US gal, 4.2 Imp gal, 18.9 litre.

WEIGHTS & LOADINGS - Empty weight 285 lb, 129 kg. Max take-off weight 625 lb, 283 kg. Payload 340 lb, 154 kg. Max wing loading 3.86 lb/ft², 18.7 kg/m². Max power loading 15.2 lb/hp, 6.9 kg/hp. Load factors +4.0, -2.0 recommended; NC ultimate.

PERFORMANCE* - Max level speed 70 mph, 113 kph. Never exceed speed 85 mph, 137 kph. Max cruising speed 65 mph, 105 kph. Economic cruising speed 55 mph, 88 kph. Stalling speed 28 mph, 45 kph. Max climb rate at sea level 750 ft/min, 3.8 m/s. Other data NC.

*Under unspecified test conditions.

August the next year. Comments on the aircraft were generally positive, except that observers regarded the change of engine position, from behind the wing to in front of it, powering a tractor instead of a pusher prop, as a retrograde step. After a number of tests the original pusher formula was reinstated, using a Rotax 447 with gear reduction, and the machine appeared in this guise at Oshkosh 1984.

In its production form, the *TwinStar* shares many features with the *KX-430* version of the *UltraStar,* and essentially is a two-seater version of that aircraft. Apart from the seating, principal differences are a slightly

LAUGHING GULL

Laughing Gull Aircraft Co, PO Box 60232, Bakersfield, California 93386; tel (805) 366-3841/ 8103. President/design engineer: Mark H Beierle. Vice-president: Danny R Romo. Treasurer: Dora I Romo. Advertising manager: Julie A Lincks.

Sales enquiries: Earthstar Aircraft Inc, Star Route, Box 313, Santa Margarita, California 93453; tel (805) 438-5235.

LAUGHING GULL
LAUGHING GULL 1277

(Three-axis)

Single-seat single-engined high-wing monoplane with conventional three-axis control. Wing has unswept leading and trailing edges, and constant chord; conventional tail. Pitch control by elevator on tail; yaw control by fin-mounted rudder; roll control by full-span ailerons; control inputs through stick for pitch/roll and pedals for yaw. Wing braced from below by struts; wing profile Gottingen 27; 100% double-surface. Undercarriage has three wheels in tricycle formation; glass-fibre suspension on all wheels. Push-right go-right nosewheel steering connected to yaw control; also differential braking. Brakes on main wheels. Steel-tube airframe, with aluminium-alloy tubing for

wing and tail structure; partially enclosed (total enclosure optional). Engine mounted below wing, driving pusher propeller. Steel tubing is welded chrome-moly 4130; aluminium-alloy to 6061-T6 or 2024-T3 specification.

Production status: current, number completed NC.

GENERAL - Though theirs is not a well known firm, the folk at Laughing Gull Aircraft Company have been around ultralights for a long time, and the *Laughing Gull 1277* is descended from the original *Laughing Gull* ultralight which has been under development since 1976. In that time five prototypes have been built with a total flight time, the company says, of over 800 h.

The result of this effort is an aircraft which at first sight looks rather like the French Aviasud *Sirocco,* and which is perhaps most notable for the apparent ruggedness of its undercarriage, all three wheels being sprung on legs made from extruded glass-fibre rod. Glass-fibre is also used for the nose-section. Wings are strut-braced for rapid rigging - 15 min is claimed - and aircraft-quality materials are used throughout.

The aircraft is available in plan, kit, or ready-to-fly form, at prices of US$95, 6395 and 6995 respectively. Kits take 180-300 h to construct. A variety of options are available, notably windows to fully enclose the cockpit; a permanent or removable left window costs US$65, and a piano-hinge and removable right window US$95.

EXTERNAL DIMENSIONS & AREAS - Length overall 18.0 ft, 5.49 m. Height overall 6.0 ft, 1.83 m. Wing span 30.0 ft, 9.14 m. Constant chord 5.0 ft, 1.52 m. Dihedral 2°. Sweepback 0°. Tailplane span 7.8 ft, 2.36 m. Fin

height 6.0 ft, 1.83 m. Total wing area 150 ft², 13.9 m². Total aileron area 22.5 ft², 2.09 m². Fin area 7.0 ft², 0.65 m². Rudder area 5.0 ft², 0.46 m². Tailplane area 10.0 ft², 0.93 m². Total elevator area 14.0 ft², 1.30 m². Aspect ratio 6.0/1. Wheel track 4.5 ft, 1.37 m. Wheelbase 6.0 ft, 1.83 m. Nosewheel diameter overall 12 inch, 29 cm. Main wheels diameter overall 12 inch, 29 cm.

POWER PLANT - Rotax 277 engine. Max power 28 hp at 6000 rpm. Propeller diameter and pitch 60x27 inch, 1.52x0.69 m. Gear reduction, ratio 2.5/1. Max static thrust 190 lb, 86 kg. Power per unit area 0.19 hp/ft², 2.0 hp/m². Fuel capacity 5.0 US gal, 4.2 Imp gal, 18.9 litre.

WEIGHTS & LOADINGS - Empty weight 250 lb, 113 kg. Max take-off weight 500 lb, 227 kg. Payload 250 lb, 113 kg. Max wing loading 3.33 lb/ft², 16.3 kg/m². Max power loading 17.9 lb/hp, 8.1 kg/hp. Load factors +6.0, -4.0 recommended; +7.5, -5.25 ultimate.

PERFORMANCE* - Max level speed 63 mph, 101 kph. Never exceed speed 80 mph, 129 kph. Max cruising speed 55 mph, 88 kph. Economic cruising speed 50 mph, 80 kph. Stalling speed 23 mph, 37 kph. Max climb rate at sea level 700 ft/min, 3.6 m/s. Min sink rate 250 ft/min at 33 mph, 1.3 m/s at 53 kph. Best glide ratio with power off 12/1 at 48 mph, 77 kph. Take-off distance 80 ft, 24 m. Landing distance 120 ft, 37 m. Service ceiling 15,000 ft, 4570 m. Range at average cruising speed 150 mile, 241 km. Noise level NC.

*Under the following test conditions - Airfield altitude 300 ft, 91 m. Ground temperature 72°F, 22°C. Ground pressure 1013 mB. Ground windspeed 0 mph, 0 kph. Test payload 200 lb, 91 kg.

LAUGHING GULL
TOUCAN-2503
(Three-axis)

Summary as Laughing Gull 1277 *except: Tandem two-seater. Wing profile NACA 23012.*

Production status: current, number completed NC.

GENERAL - Our summary above suggests that apart from its use of a different wing profile, the *Toucan-2503* is very similar to the *Laughing Gull 1277.* In fact only the concepts are similar: the two-seater is bigger in almost every dimension and a full 100 lb (45 kg) heavier. Much of the extra weight comes from the big Rotax 503 engine, which allows the aircraft to lift a generous payload.

Like the solo machine, this aircraft can be had as plans (US$110), a kit taking 220-400 h to complete (US$7995), or ready-to-fly (US$9500). Options are as for the single-seater.

EXTERNAL DIMENSIONS & AREAS - Length overall 19.8 ft, 6.02 m. Height overall 7.0 ft, 2.13 m. Wing span 32.0 ft, 9.75 m. Constant chord 5.0 ft, 1.52 m. Dihedral 2°. Sweepback 0°. Tailplane span 10.0 ft, 3.05 m. Fin height 7.0 ft, 2.13 m. Total wing area 160 ft², 14.9 m². Total aileron area 22.5 ft², 2.09 m². Fin area 10.0 ft², 0.93 m². Rudder area 7.0 ft², 0.65 m². Tailplane area 14.0 ft², 1.30 m². Total elevator area 18.0 ft², 1.67 m². Aspect ratio 6.4/1. Wheel track 5.4 ft, 1.65 m. Wheelbase 7.5 ft, 2.29 m. Nosewheel diameter overall

13 inch, 32 cm. Main wheels diameter overall 13 inch, 32 cm.

POWER PLANT - Rotax 503 engine. Max power 47 hp at 6200 rpm. Propeller diameter and pitch 60x38 inch, 1.52x0.97 m. V-belt reduction, ratio 2.5/1. Max static thrust 320 lb, 145 kg. Power per unit area 0.29 hp/ft^2, 3.2 hp/m^2. Fuel capacity 5.0 US gal, 4.2 Imp gal, 18.9 litre.

WEIGHTS & LOADINGS - Empty weight 350 lb, 159 kg. Max take-off weight 800 lb, 363 kg. Payload 450 lb, 204 kg. Max wing loading 5.00 lb/ft^2, 24.4 kg/m^2. Max power loading 17.0 lb/hp, 7.7 kg/hp. Load factors +5.0, -3.5 recommended; +6.0, -4.25 ultimate.

PERFORMANCE* - Max level speed 63 mph, 101 kph. Never exceed speed 80 mph, 129 kph. Max cruising speed 60 mph, 97 kph. Economic cruising speed 55 mph, 88 kph. Stalling speed 30 mph, 48 kph. Max climb rate at sea level 1000 ft/min, 5.1 m/s. Min sink rate NC. Best glide ratio with power off 13/1 at 55 mph, 88 kph. Take-off distance 250 ft, 76 m. Landing distance 200 ft, 61 m. Service ceiling 15,000 ft, 4570 m. Range at average cruising speed 180 mile, 290 km. Noise level NC.

*Under the following test conditions - Airfield altitude 300 ft, 91 m. Ground temperature 72°F, 22°C. Ground pressure 1013 mB. Ground windspeed 0 mph, 0 kph. Test payload 360 lb, 163 kg.

LAUGHING GULL

MINI-ULTRA GULL M118

(Two-axis)

Single-seat single-engined double monoplane in tandem with two-axis control. Wings have unswept leading and trailing edges, and constant chord; flaps fitted; no tail. Pitch control by elevons; yaw control by tip rudders on rear wing; no separate roll control; control inputs through stick for pitch/yaw. Wing bracing see text; wing profile NACA 23012; 100% double-surface. Undercarriage has three wheels in tricycle formation; glass-fibre suspension on all wheels. Push-right go-left nosewheel steering independent from yaw control. No brakes. Aluminium-alloy tube air frame, with optional pod. Engine mounted between wings, driving pusher propeller.

Production status: prototype.

GENERAL - This must be one of the most unusual air craft in this book and cannot really be likened to any other ultralight. It uses the double monoplane in tandem wing design made famous by the *Flying Flea* in the '30s, but unlike that remarkable French machine, it has no tail. Instead, the outboard ends of the two wings are joined by a broad angled strut which flares out at the back to form a rudder and fin. The front wing is further braced by a single strut on each side, both wings being of the same shape and area.
Aluminium-alloy tube is used for the airframe and wing, with a foam-backed aluminium skin for the flying surfaces, and the whole aircraft is engineered to be exceptionally light - only 160 lb (73 kg). This strict weight discipline is helped not only by choosing a light power unit, the single-cylinder Solo engine, but also by opting for two-axis control. We describe the pitch control as

'elevons' for lack of a better word, but in fact these full-span surfaces on the upper wing have no aileron function - they can only be moved simultaneously, left-right movement of the stick operating the rudders. This leaves the feet free to operate just the ground steering, resulting in another weight saving, as the simple trike arrangement of push-right go-left can then be adopted. At the time of writing the aircraft was in prototype form, but the company's intention is to sell plans for US$95 or a ready-to-fly aircraft for US$4995. Various options will be available.

EXTERNAL DIMENSIONS & AREAS - Length overall 8.0 ft, 2.44 m. Height overall 4.0 ft, 1.22 m. Wing span 16.0 ft, 4.88 m. Constant chord 2.0 ft, 0.61 m. Dihedral 0°. Sweepback 0°. Fin height 4.0 ft, 1.22 m. Total wing area 64 ft^2, 5.9 m^2. Fin area 10.0 ft^2, 0.93 m^2. Rudder area 8.0 ft^2, 0.74 m^2. Total elevon area 26.0 ft^2, 2.42 m^2. Aspect ratio of each wing 8.0/1. Wheel track 3.8 ft, 1.17 m. Wheelbase 4.0 ft, 1.22 m. Nosewheel diameter overall 12 inch, 29 cm. Main wheels diameter overall 12 inch, 29 cm.

POWER PLANT - Solo engine. Max power 18 hp at 6000 rpm. Propeller diameter and pitch 48x20 inch, 1.22x0.51 m. V-belt reduction, ratio 2.2/1. Max static thrust 140 lb, 64 kg. Power per unit area 0.28 hp/ft^2, 3.0 hp/m^2. Fuel capacity 5.0 US gal, 4.2 Imp gal, 18.9 litre.

WEIGHTS & LOADINGS - Empty weight 160 lb, 73 kg. Max take-off weight 410 lb, 186 kg. Payload 250 lb, 113 kg. Max wing loading 6.40 lb/ft^2, 31.3 kg/m^2. Max power loading 22.8 lb/hp, 10.3 kg/hp. Load factors +6.0, -4.0 recommended; +7.0, -5.0 ultimate.

PERFORMANCE* - Max level speed 60 mph, 97 kph. Never exceed speed 85 mph, 137 kph. Max cruising speed 50 mph, 80 kph. Economic cruising speed 45 mph, 72 kph. Stalling speed 26 mph, 42 kph. Max climb rate at sea level 500 ft/min, 2.5 m/s. Min sink rate 320 ft/min at 49 mph, 1.6 m/s at 79 kph. Best glide ratio with power off 11/1 at 56 mph, 90 kph. Take-off distance 160 ft, 49 m. Landing distance 140 ft, 43 m. Service ceiling 12,000 ft, 3660 m. Range at average cruising speed 200 mile, 322 km. Noise level NC.

*Under the following test conditions - Airfield altitude 300 ft, 91 m. Ground temperature 72°F, 22°C. Ground pressure 1013 mB. Ground windspeed 0 mph, 0 kph. Test payload 200 lb, 91 kg.

LAUGHING GULL

ULTRA GULL DELUXE U277

(Three-axis)

Single-seat single-engined double monoplane in tandem with conventional three-axis control. Wings have unswept leading and trailing edges, and constant chord; flaps fitted; no tail. Pitch control by elevons on forward wing; yaw control by tip-rudders on rear wing; roll control by full-span ailerons on rear wing; control inputs through stick for pitch/roll and pedals for yaw. Wing bracing see text of Mini-Ultra Gull M118; wing profile NACA 23012; 100% double-surface. Under carriage has three wheels in tricycle formation; glass-fibre suspension on all wheels. Push-right go-right nosewheel steering connected to yaw control; also differential braking. Brakes on main wheels. Steel-tube airframe, with aluminium-alloy tubing for wing and tail structure; partially enclosed. Engine mounted

between wings, driving pusher propeller. Steel tubing is welded chrome-moly 4130; aluminium-alloy to 6061-T6 or 2024-T3 specification.

Production status: prototype.

GENERAL - This aircraft is best described as a cross between the *Mini-Ultra Gull M118* and the *Laughing Gull 1277,* as it is visually similar to the former and has a similar wing structure but uses the fuselage materials and power pack of the latter - welded steel cage and glass-fibre nose. Controls are three-axis, the third dimension being added by fitting ailerons to the rear wing so that as with the two-axis machine the 'elevons' only operate as a pitch control.

Plans for the *Ultra Gull Deluxe U277* can be had for US$95, a kit for US$5795 or a completed machine for US$7500, with various options available.

EXTERNAL DIMENSIONS & AREAS - See *Mini-Ultra Gull M118* except: Total aileron area 14.0 ft², 1.30 m².

POWER PLANT - See *Laughing Gull 1277* except: Power per unit area 0.44 hp/ft², 4.7 hp/m².

WEIGHTS & LOADINGS - Empty weight 225 lb, 102 kg. Max take-off weight 500 lb, 227 kg. Payload 275 lb, 125 kg. Max wing loading 7.81 lb/ft², 38.2 kg/m². Max power loading 17.9 lb/hp, 8.1 kg/hp. Load factors +6.0, -5.0 recommended; +7.0, -6.0 ultimate.

PERFORMANCE* - Max level speed 63 mph, 101 kph. Never exceed speed 85 mph, 137 kph. Max cruising speed 60 mph, 97 kph. Economic cruising speed 55 mph, 88 kph. Stalling speed 27 mph, 43 kph. Max climb rate at sea level 900 ft/min, 4.6 m/s. Min sink rate 350 ft/min, 1.8 m/s at NC speed. Best glide ratio with power off 13/1 at 58 mph, 93 kph. Take-off distance 100 ft, 30 m. Landing distance 145 ft, 44 m. Service ceiling 20,000 ft, 6100 m. Range at average cruising speed 250 mile, 402 km. Noise level NC.

*Under the following test conditions - Airfield altitude 300 ft, 91 m. Ground temperature 72°F, 22°C. Ground pressure 1047 mB. Ground windspeed 3 mph, 5 kph. Test payload 180 lb, 82 kg

LAUGHING GULL
ULTRA GULL TWO U2503
(Three-axis)

Summary as Ultra Gull Deluxe U277 *except: Tandem two-seater, totally enclosed.*

Production status: prototype.

GENERAL - This machine is basically a two-seater version of the *Ultra Gull Deluxe U277,* though it shares few of its dimensions. A Rotax 503 engine is fitted, as in the company's more conventional two-seater, but in this case the engine is in a higher state of tune and is mated to a three-blade prop, presumably to avoid clearance problems.

Priced at US$7500 in kit form, the aircraft may also be bought as plans for US$95.

EXTERNAL DIMENSIONS & AREAS - Length overall 10.3 ft, 3.15 m. Height overall 5.0 ft, 1.52 m. Wing span 18.0 ft, 5.49 m. Constant chord 2.0 ft, 0.61 m. Dihedral 0°. Sweepback 0°. Fin height 5.0 ft, 1.52 m. Total wing area 72 ft², 6.7 m². Total aileron area 16.0 ft², 1.49 m². Fin area 12.0 ft², 1.11 m². Rudder area 10.0 ft², 0.93 m². Total elevon area 32.0 ft², 2.97 m². Aspect ratio of each wing 9.0/1. Wheel track 4.0 ft, 1.22 m. Wheelbase 5.5 ft, 1.68 m. Nosewheel diameter overall 13 inch, 32 cm. Main wheels diameter overall 13 inch, 32 cm.

POWER PLANT - Rotax 503 engine. Max power 52 hp at 6250 rpm. Propeller diameter and pitch 60x40 inch, 1.52x1.02 m (3-blade). Toothed-belt reduction, ratio 2.5/1. Max static thrust 305 lb, 138 kg. Power per unit area 0.72 hp/ft², 7.8 hp/m². Fuel capacity 12.0 US gal, 10.0 Imp gal, 45.4 litre.

WEIGHTS & LOADINGS - Empty weight 305 lb, 138 kg. Max take-off weight 800 lb, 363 kg. Payload 495 lb, 225 kg. Max wing loading 11.11 lb/ft², 54.3 kg/m². Max power loading 15.4 lb/hp, 7.0 kg/hp. Load factors +6.0, -4.0 recommended; +7.0, -5.0 ultimate.

PERFORMANCE* - Max level speed 133 mph, 214 kph. Never exceed speed 150 mph, 241 kph. Max cruising speed 105 mph, 169 kph. Economic cruising speed 45 mph, 72 kph. Stalling speed 36 mph, 58 kph. Max climb rate at sea level 850 ft/min, 4.3 m/s. Landing distance 300 ft, 91 m. Service ceiling 14,000 ft, 4270 m. Range at average cruising speed 420 mile, 676 km. Other data NC.

*Under the following test conditions - Airfield altitude 550 ft, 168 m. Ground temperature 60°F, 16°C. Ground pressure 1019 mB. Ground windspeed 7 mph, 11 kph. Test payload 290 lb, 132 kg.

LEACH

Leach Aircraft Inc, 1973 Friendship Drive, Suite F, El Cajon, California 92020; tel (619) 562-8900. (No longer trading).

LEACH *CALYPSO*
(Three-axis)

Single-seat single-engined high-wing monoplane with conventional three-axis control. Wing has unswept leading edge, swept forward trailing edge, and tapering chord; cruciform tail. Pitch control by elevator on tail; yaw control by fully flying rudder; roll control by full-span ailerons; control inputs through stick for pitch/roll and pedals for yaw. Wing braced from below by struts; wing profile NC; 100% double-surface. Undercarriage has three wheels in tricycle formation with additional tailskid; suspension NC. Push-right go-right nosewheel steering connected to yaw control. Optional brakes. Tubular airframe (material NC), with pod. Engine mounted above wing, driving pusher propeller.

Production status: see text.

GENERAL - Announced in late 1984, the Leach *Calypso* is a modern tube and Dacron design with full-span differential ailerons. A Second Chantz ballistic parachute was standard equipment, the 'parachute allowance' helping to make this otherwise overweight aircraft ultralight legal.
It looked like a welcome newcomer to the ultralight scene, but came onto the market at a time of depression in the US ultralight industry. Possibly because of this, the company ceased trading shortly after the *Calypso* was announced, and it is not clear whether the machine ever got into serious production. Standard engine was a Cuyuna, with a 377 Rotax as an option. Data below refers to the standard version.

EXTERNAL DIMENSIONS & AREAS - Length overall 19.0 ft, 5.79 m. Height overall 6.6 ft, 2.01 m. Wing span 33.0 ft, 10.06 m. Sweepback 0°. Total wing area 160 ft², 14.9 m². Aspect ratio 6.8/1. Other data NC.

POWER PLANT - Cuyuna ULII-02 engine. Max power 35 hp at 6000 rpm. Propeller diameter and pitch 54x27 inch, 1.37x0.69 m. Belt reduction, ratio 2.0/1. Max static thrust 225 lb, 102 kg. Power per unit area 0.22 hp/ft², 2.3 hp/m². Fuel capacity 5.0 US gal, 4.2 Imp gal, 18.9 litre.

WEIGHTS & LOADINGS - Empty weight 278 lb, 126 kg. Max take-off weight 500 lb, 227 kg. Payload 222 lb, 101 kg. Max wing loading 3.13 lb/ft², 15.2 kg/m². Max power loading 14.3 lb/hp, 6.5 kg/hp. Load factors +6.0, -4.0 design, NC ultimate.

PERFORMANCE* - Max level speed 63 mph, 101 kph. Never exceed speed 88 mph, 142 kph. Cruising speed 50 mph, 80 kph. Stalling speed 27 mph, 43 kph. Max climb rate at sea level 800 ft/min, 4.1 m/s. Best glide ratio with power off 9/1 at NC speed. Other data NC.

*Under unspecified test conditions.

LEADER'S INTERNATIONAL

Leader's International Inc, 212 N Mecklenburg Avenue, South Hill, Virginia 23970; tel (804) 447-4919.

LEADER'S INTERNATIONAL *JB-1000*
(Three-axis)

Single-seat single-engined high-wing monoplane with conventional three-axis control. Wing has unswept leading and trailing edges, and constant chord; conventional tail. Pitch control by fully flying elevator; yaw control by fin-mounted rudder; roll control by half-span ailerons; control inputs through stick for pitch/roll and pedals for yaw. Wing braced from below by struts; wing profile 4415; 100% double-surface. Undercarriage has two wheels plus tailskid; glass-fibre suspension on main wheels. Ground steering by differential braking; castoring tailskid. Brakes on main wheels. Aluminium-alloy tube airframe, partially enclosed. Engine mounted at wing height, driving pusher propeller.

Production status: prototype.

GENERAL - Two things stand out about the *JB-1000*. First, it is one of the very few ultralights which has its propeller spinning concentrically around its tail boom, an idea used by Swiss designer Albert Neukom but not seen on the US ultralight scene since the *Firebird Flyer* of Competition Aircraft, which we understand is now out of production. *JB-1000* designer Rolf Brand is quoted in the October '84 edition of *Glider Rider* as saying that the design ensures the controls function even if the main wing is stalled, because the airstream is parallel to the fuselage. Whether or not the aircraft actually behaves in this way is open to debate at present, because it is still at prototype stage, but the idea is certainly intriguing.
The second item of note is the aircraft's Kevlar pilot enclosure, which is a rather more substantial affair than the average pod. It is not removeable, but is part of the aircraft's structure and incorporates the pilot's seat, the idea being to build something strong around the pilot for safety reasons. The same cautious philosophy has placed an angled strut in front of the pilot to protect him or her from trees or wires in the event of a crash. Rolf inadvertently tested his design when he crashed one of the prototypes into a tree, and proved his point by living to tell the tale. By October '84 the aircraft had notched up over 200 h of airtime and it should be in full production by the time you read this, priced at US$5875 ready-to-fly; kits and plans are not available. Rigging time is 30-60 min.

EXTERNAL DIMENSIONS & AREAS - Length overall 20.3 ft, 6.20 m. Height overall 5.8 ft, 1.78 m. Wing span 30.0 ft, 9.14 m. Constant chord 5.0 ft, 1.52 m. Dihedral 2°. Sweepback 0°. Elevator span 8.5 ft, 2.60 m. Fin height 5.8

ft, 1.78 m. Total wing area 150 ft², 13.9 m². Total aileron area NC. Total fin and rudder area 15.0 ft², 1.39 m². Total elevator area 17.0 ft², 1.58 m². Aspect ratio 6.0/1. Wheel track 5.0 ft, 1.52 m. Wheelbase NC. Main wheels diameter overall 10 inch, 25 cm.

POWER PLANT - Rotax 277 engine. Max power 27 hp at 6000 rpm. Propeller diameter and pitch 60x12 inch, 1.52x0.30 m (3-blade). V-belt reduction, ratio 2.5/1. Max static thrust 170 lb, 77 kg. Power per unit area 0.18 hp/ft², 1.9 hp/m². Fuel capacity 5.0 US gal, 4.2 Imp gal, 18.9 litre.

WEIGHTS & LOADINGS - Empty weight 252 lb, 114 kg. Max take-off weight 500 lb, 227 kg. Payload 248 lb, 113 kg. Max wing loading 3.33 lb/ft², 16.3 kg/m². Max power load-ing 18.5 lb/hp, 8.4 kg/hp. Load factors +4.0, -NC recommended; +6.5, -NC ultimate.

PERFORMANCE* - Max level speed 59 mph, 95 kph. Never exceed speed 75 mph, 121 kph. Max cruising speed 50 mph, 80 kph. Economic cruising speed 45 mph, 72 kph. Stalling speed 27 mph, 43 kph. Max climb rate at sea level 420 ft/min, 2.1 m/s. Min sink rate NC. Best glide ratio with power off 7/1 at NC speed. Take-off distance 75 ft, 23 m. Landing distance 75 ft, 23 m. Service ceiling 10,000 ft, 3050 m. Range at average cruising speed 150 mile, 241 km. Noise level NC.

*Under the following test conditions - Airfield altitude 408 ft, 124 m. Ground temperature 80°F, 27°C. Ground pressure NC. Ground windspeed 4 mph, 6 kph. Test payload 210 lb, 95 kg.

LEADING EDGE AIR FOIL

Leading Edge Air Foils Inc, 331 South 14th Street, Colorado Springs, Colorado 80904; tel (303) 632-4959 or (800) 621-8386 x590.

LEADING EDGE AIR FOILS
LEAF TRIKE/Suitable Rogallo
(Weight-shift)

Single-seat single-engined flex-wing aircraft with weight-shift control. Rogallo wing. Pilot suspended below wing in trike unit, using bar to control pitch and roll/yaw by altering relative positions of trike unit and wing. Wing braced from above by kingpost and cables, from below by cables. Undercarriage has three wheels in tricycle formation; suspension NC on nosewheel and glass-fibre suspension on main wheels. Push-right go-left nosewheel steering independent from aerodynamic controls. No brakes. Aluminium-alloy tube trike unit, completely open. Engine mounted below wing, driving pusher propeller. Other details NC.

Production status: see text.

GENERAL - One of the great mysteries of ultralight aviation is why the trike has failed so utterly to make any impact on the American market. US pilots, if they know of it at all, think of the trike more as a curiosity than as a real aircraft, despite its enormous popularity in Europe and many other parts of the world.

In our last edition we included a handful of US trike manufacturers struggling to get the flexwing message across, and all but Leading Edge and Wolfe have now given up, leaving the market - such as it is - open to imported Behlen and Cosmos aircraft from West Germany and France respectively.

Because of the massive fixedwing bias of the sport in the US, Leading Edge no longer offers ready-built trike units, but as the company is one of America's leading ultralight component and accessory suppliers, it will gladly sell plans and supply parts. We quote below figures for one of the company's earlier factory-built units when mated to a typical wing.

EXTERNAL DIMENSIONS & AREAS - Length overall* 7.4 ft, 2.26 m. Height overall* 8.3 ft, 2.51 m. Width* 5.6 ft, 1.70 m. Wheelbase 5.1 ft, 1.55 m. Nosewheel diameter overall 16 inch, 41 cm. Main wheels diameter overall 20 inch, 51 cm. Other data NC.

POWER PLANT - Cuyuna ULII-02 engine. Max power 35 hp at NC rpm. Propeller diameter and pitch 54x27 inch, 1.37x0.69 m. Reduction type NC, ratio 2.0/1. Max static thrust 165 lb, 75 kg. Power per unit area NC. Fuel capacity 5.0 US gal, 4.2 Imp gal, 18.9 litre.

WEIGHTS & LOADINGS - Empty weight 149 lb, 67 kg. Payload 250 lb, 113 kg. Other data NC.

PERFORMANCE - Max level speed 45 mph, 72 kph. Max cruising speed 32 mph, 51 kph. Stalling speed 24 mph, 39 kph. Other data NC.

*Trike unit only.

**Under unspecified test conditions.

LIGHT AERO

Light Aero Inc, PO Box 45177 Dept 61, Boise, Idaho 83711; tel (208) 939-0221.

LIGHT AERO *AVID FLYER*

(Three-axis)

Summary similar to Denney Kitfox *except: Tricycle undercarriage optional.*

Production status: see text.

GENERAL - This aircraft was co-designed by Dan Denney, and provided the inspiration for the rather larger *Kitfox* which we list separately as he now sells it under his own name. To the best of our knowledge, however, the *Avid Flyer* is still available; certainly Light Aero Inc was advertising it as recently as early 1985.

This two-seat machine is aimed at the licensed pilot rather than the ultralighter and comes with dual controls. Its wing-folding system is similar to the *Kitfox*. Airframe is welded steel, again similar to the *Kitfox*, and good short-field capability is claimed. Tail-dragger undercarriage is normal, but the tricycle arrangement is optional, as are floats and skis.

Avid Flyers come as complete kits for US$8495, floats with a retractable water rudder costing an extra US$2495. A useful report on the machine appeared in the May-June 1984 *Ultralight Pilot*.

EXTERNAL DIMENSIONS & AREAS - Length overall 17.0 ft, 5.18 m. Height overall 5.4 ft, 1.65 m. Wing span 29.9 ft, 9.11 m. Constant chord 3.9 ft, 1.19 m. Sweepback 0°. Total wing area 117 ft², 10.9 m². Aspect ratio 7.6/1. Other data NC.

POWER PLANT - Cuyuna 430RR engine. Max power 43 hp at NC rpm. Propeller diameter and pitch 72xNC inch, 1.83xNC m. Planetary gear reduction, ratio 3.0/1. Max static thrust NC. Power per unit area 0.37 hp/ft², 3.9 hp/m². Fuel capacity 9.0 US gal, 7.5 Imp gal, 34.1 litre.

WEIGHTS & LOADINGS - Empty weight 360 lb, 163 kg. Max take-off weight 764 lb, 347 kg. Payload 404 lb, 183 kg. Max wing loading 6.53 lb/ft², 31.8 kg/m². Max power loading 17.8 lb/hp, 8.1 kg/hp. Load factors £3.8, -2.3 recommended; £5.7, -3.4 ultimate.

PERFORMANCE* - Never exceed speed 90 mph, 145 kph. Cruising speed 80 mph, 129 kph. Stalling speed 25 mph, 40 kph. Max climb rate at sea level** 1400 ft/min, 7.1 m/s. Min sink rate 410 ft/min at 40 mph, 2.1 m/s at 64 kph. Best glide ratio with power off 8.5/1 at NC speed. Take-off distance*** 75 ft, 23 m. Service ceiling 19,000 ft, 5790 m. Range at average cruising speed 288 mile, 463 km. Other data NC.

*Under the following test conditions - Airfield altitude 0 ft, 0 m. Ground temperature 59°F, 15°C. Ground pressure 1013 mB. Ground windspeed 0 mph, 0 kph. Test payload 165 lb, 75 kg.

**On floats - 1290 ft/min, 6.6 m/s.

***On floats - 176 ft, 54 m.

LIGHT MINIATURE AIRCRAFT

Light Miniature Aircraft Inc, 13815 NW 19th Avenue, Opa-Locka, Florida 33054; tel (305) 681-4068. President: Fred F McCallum. Senior vice-president: Fred Latulip.

LIGHT MINIATURE AIRCRAFT *LM-1*

(Three-axis)

Single-seat single-engined high-wing monoplane with conventional three-axis control. Wing has unswept leading and trailing edges, and constant chord; conventional tail. Pitch control by elevator on tail; yaw control by fin-mounted rudder; roll control by ailerons; control inputs through stick for pitch/roll and pedals for yaw. Wing braced from below by struts; wing profile Clark Y type; 100% double-surface. Undercarriage has three wheels in tail-dragger formation; no suspension on any wheels. Push-right go-right tailwheel steering connected to yaw control; also differential braking. Brakes on main wheels. Wood airframe, totally enclosed. Engine mounted below wing, driving tractor propeller.

Production status: prototype.

GENERAL - The *LM-1* prototype made one of its first public appearances at the Air Recreational Vehicle Competition, held during the 1983 Oshkosh, and to many eyes it was the best-looking aircraft in the competition, as exemplified by the constant crowds around it. The machine is basically a three-quarters scale version of the venerable *J-3 Cub* and it uses all-wood construction. Covering is of zero-porosity Dacron requiring no doping or sealing, but other covering materials can be substituted as the builder desires. The *LM-1* features removeable and foldable wings, allowing set-up to be reduced to some 10 min.

The aircraft is available in plan (US$95) or kit (US$4500) form, the latter from Wicks Aircraft Supply or Aircraft Spruce & Specialty Co (see separate listings). Kit construction takes around 480 h, while building from scratch takes around 600 h, using a step-by-step manual with 30 construction photos and 40 pages of drawings. A newsletter is put out for builders and other interested parties, to keep constructors up to date on developments of the design and give details of builders' progress. Designers Fred McCallum and Fred Latulip are thoroughly committed to their creation and offer very

good personal assistance to anyone building one of their machines.

Although too heavy for the US ultralight category, the *LM-1* is only just over the microlight weight limit, and could be made legal in some European countries with a little effort.

EXTERNAL DIMENSIONS & AREAS - Length overall 17.5 ft, 5.33 m. Height overall 5.6 ft, 1.70 m. Wing span 27.0 ft, 8.23 m. Constant chord 4.5 ft, 1.37 m. Dihedral 2°. Sweepback 0°. Tailplane span 7.4 ft, 2.26 m. Fin height 2.0 ft, 0.61 m. Total wing area 120 ft², 11.1 m². Fin area 3.5 ft², 0.33 m². Aspect ratio 6.1/1. Wheel track 4.5 ft, 1.37 m. Main wheels diameter overall 13 inch, 32 cm. Other data NC.

POWER PLANT - Cuyuna 430 engine. Max power 30 hp at 6200 rpm. Propeller diameter and pitch 54x27 inch, 1.37x0.69 m. V-belt reduction, ratio 2.1/1. Max static thrust NC. Power per unit area 0.25 hp/ft², 2.7 hp/m². Fuel capacity 5.5 US gal, 4.6 Imp gal, 20.8 litre.

WEIGHTS & LOADINGS - Empty weight 340 lb, 154 kg. Max take-off weight 600 lb, 272 kg. Payload 260 lb, 118 kg. Max wing loading 5.00 lb/ft², 24.5 kg/m². Max power loading 20.0 lb/hp, 9.1 kg/hp. Load factors +5.0, -4.5 recommended; +8.0, -6.0 ultimate.

PERFORMANCE* - Max level speed 70 mph, 113 kph. Never exceed speed 75 mph, 121 kph. Max cruising speed 65 mph, 105 kph. Economic cruising speed 55 mph, 88 kph. Stalling speed 24 mph, 39 kph. Max climb rate at sea level 350 ft/min, 1.8 m/s. Best glide ratio with power off 10/1 at 40 mph, 64 kph. Take-off distance 250 ft, 76 m. Landing distance 300 ft, 91 m. Range at average cruising speed 175 mile, 282 km. Other data NC.

*Under unspecified test conditions.

LIGHT MINIATURE AIRCRAFT
LM-1U

(Three-axis)

Summary similar to LM-1 except: Aluminium-alloy tube airframe.

Production status: see text.

GENERAL - In June '85 the two Freds announced that they were putting their plans for an ultralight version of the LM-1 into action, having earlier shelved them due to the poor state of the American ultralight market. Dubbed the LM-1U, the new version looks very similar to the experimental-category machine but is quite different structurally, using square-section alloy tube and ceconite construction in order to cut build time.
Distribution arrangments had yet to be finalised at the time of going to press, and no prices were available, but a Fisher-style system of foreign-built complete aircraft and US-manufactured kits is on the cards.

EXTERNAL DIMENSIONS & AREAS - Length overall 17.6 ft, 5.36 m. Height overall 6.5 ft, 1.98 m. Wing span 30.0 ft, 9.14 m. Constant chord 4.0 ft, 1.22 m. Sweep back 0°. Total wing area 120 ft², 11.1 m². Aspect ratio 7.5/1. Other data NC.

POWER PLANT - Rotax 277 engine. Max power 28 hp at 6800 rpm. Power per unit area 0.23 hp/ft², 2.5 hp/m². Fuel capacity 5.0 US gal, 4.2 Imp gal, 18.9 litre. Other data NC.

WEIGHTS & LOADINGS - Empty weight 250 lb, 113 kg. Max take-off weight 510 lb, 231 kg. Payload 260 lb, 118 kg. Max wing loading 4.25 lb/ft², 20.8 kg/m². Max power loading 18.2 lb/hp, 8.3 kg/hp. Load factors NC.

PERFORMANCE* - Max level speed 62 mph, 100 kph. Never exceed speed 65 mph, 105 kph. Cruising speed 55 mph, 88 kph. Stalling speed 25 mph, 40 kph. Max climb rate at sea level 500 ft/min, 2.5 m/s. Other data NC.

Under unspecified test conditions.

LIGHT MINIATURE AIRCRAFT
LM-2

(Three-axis)

Summary as LM-1 except: Wing profile NC. Suspension on main wheels NC.

Production status: see text.

GENERAL - At the time of writing the first prototype of this two-seater was still uncompleted, but work was proceeding apace. In concept it follows the LM-1 closely, using traditional wood construction and a fully enclosed cockpit, and in appearance it will resemble a three-quarter scale Taylorcraft. Undoubtedly the most novel feature is its use of a Wankel rotary engine, though unfortunately the make has not been disclosed.
Sales arrangements have not been finalised, but the target price is US$6000 in kit form.

EXTERNAL DIMENSIONS & AREAS - NC.

POWER PLANT - Wankel engine, make NC. Max power 35 hp. Fuel capacity 6.0 US gal, 5.0 Imp gal, 22.7 litre. Other data NC.

WEIGHTS & LOADINGS - Empty weight 350 lb, 159 kg. Max take-off weight 650 lb, 295 kg. Payload 300 lb, 136 kg. Max wing loading NC. Max power loading 18.6 lb/hp, 8.4 kg/hp. Load factors NC.

PERFORMANCE* - Max level speed 75 mph, 121 kph. Never exceed speed 85 mph, 137 kph. Max cruising speed 70 mph, 113 kph. Economic cruising speed 60 mph, 97 kph. Stalling speed 26 mph, 42 kph. Max climb rate at sea level 450 ft/min, 2.3 m/s. Best glide ratio with power off 10/1 at 40 mph, 64 kph. Take-off distance 250 ft, 76 m. Landing distance 300 ft, 91 m. Range at average cruising speed 175 mile, 282 km.

Under unspecified test conditions.

LOEHLE AVIATION

Loehle Enterprises Inc, Shipman's Creek Road, Wartrace, Tennessee 37183; tel (615) 857-3419. President: Mike Loehle. Marketing communications manager: Sandy Burgess.

LOEHLE AVIATION
THE FUN MACHINE

(Three-axis)

Single-seat single-engined biplane with conventional three-axis control. Wings have swept back leading and trailing edges, and constant chord; conventional tail. Pitch control by elevator on tail; yaw control by fully flying rudder; roll control by four quarter-span spoilerons; control inputs through stick for pitch/roll and pedals for yaw. Wings braced by struts and transverse X-cables; wing profile by Loehle; 100% double-surface. Undercarriage has three wheels in tricycle formation; no suspension on nosewheel and glass-fibre suspension on main wheels. Push-right go-right nosewheel steering connected to yaw control. Optional nosewheel brake. Aluminium-alloy tube airframe, with optional pod. Engine mounted between wings, driving pusher propeller. Tubing is bright dip anodised.

Production status: current, 2 completed.

GENERAL - Although production of Mike Loehle's The Fun Machine was just getting under way as we went to press, there was still little information available about the aircraft. Mike actually has four companies operating under the Loehle Enterprises banner - Loehle Aviation, UFM of Kentucky, Ritz Aircraft, and Ritz Propeller - of which the first three are aircraft producers and are listed in this book, and it is clear that The Fun Machine, the first product of Loehle Aviation, is closely related to Mike's earlier Aeroplane XP design, produced by UFM of Kentucky. The most obvious difference between the two is that The Fun Machine's wings are of equal span, whereas on the earlier aircraft the top wing is noticeably longer. Suspension arrangements are also different.
The new aircraft is a bolt-together biplane of aluminium

with a special Mylar-coated Dacron covering. It is sold in kit form for US$4995 and said to take 40 h to construct. Numerous options are available, including floats (US$1000), skis (US$390), disc brakes (US$250), ballistic parachute (US$1000), outdoor covers (US$400) and various instruments.

EXTERNAL DIMENSIONS & AREAS - Length overall 11.5 ft, 3.51 m. Height overall 6.5 ft, 1.98 m. Wing span 28.0 ft, 8.53 m (bottom); 28.0 ft, 8.53 m (top). Total wing area 174 ft², 16.2 m². Nosewheel diameter overall 16 inch, 41 cm. Main wheels diameter overall 20 inch, 51 cm. Other data NC.

POWER PLANT - Cuyuna ULII-02 engine. Max power 35 hp at 6250 rpm. Propeller diameter and pitch 54x27 inch, 1.37x0.69 m. V-belt reduction, ratio 1.9/1. Max static thrust NC. Power per unit area 0.20 hp/ft², 2.16 hp/m². Fuel capacity 5.0 US gal, 4.2 Imp gal, 18.9 litre.

WEIGHTS & LOADINGS - Empty weight 244 lb, 111 kg. Max take-off weight 500 lb, 227 kg. Payload 256 lb, 116 kg. Max wing loading 2.87 lb/ft², 14.0 kg/m². Max power loading 14.3 lb/hp, 6.49 kg/hp. Load factors NC recommended; +9.0, -5.0 ultimate.

PERFORMANCE* - Max level speed 63 mph, 101 kph. Never exceed speed 75 mph, 121 kph. Max cruising speed 60 mph, 97 kph. Economic cruising speed 25-60 mph, 40-97 kph. Stalling speed 19 mph, 31 kph. Max climb rate at sea level 1000 ft/min, 5.1 m/s. Min sink rate 290 ft/min, 1.5 m/s at NC speed. Best glide ratio with power off 8/1 at 38 mph, 61 kph. Take-off distance 100 ft, 30 m. Landing distance 100 ft, 30 m. Service ceiling NC. Range at average cruising speed 135 mile, 217 km. Noise level NC.

*Under unspecified test conditions.

LOEHLE *THE FUN MACHINE II*
(Three-axis)

Summary as The Fun Machine *except: Side-by-side two-seater.*

Production status: prototype.

GENERAL - This aircraft is a two-place homebuilt version of *The Fun Machine*. Just as the latter is a development of the *Aeroplane XP,* so this two-seater is derived from the *Aeroplane XP-2,* which we list under UFM of Kentucky. It is notably light for a two-seater, at only 250 lb (113 kg), though we print this and much of the other data as approximations (in italic), as the aircraft was being tried with two different engines at the time of going to press.
Price is US$6495 and options are as for the solo machine.

EXTERNAL DIMENSIONS & AREAS - Length overall 11.5 ft, 3.51 m. Height overall 7.0 ft, 2.13 m. Wing span 32.0 ft, 9.76 m (bottom); 32.0 ft, 9.76 m (top). Constant chord 3.0 ft, 0.91 m (bottom wing); 3.0 ft, 0.91 m (top wing). Total wing area 196.5 ft², 18.3 m². Nosewheel diameter overall 16 inch, 41 cm. Main wheels diameter overall 20 inch, 51 cm. Other data NC.

POWER PLANT - Cuyuna or Rotax engine. Max power 43 hp (Cuyuna) or 47 hp (Rotax) at NC rpm. Propeller diameter and pitch NC. V-belt reduction, ratio NC. Max static thrust NC. Power per unit area 0.22 hp/ft² (Cuyuna) or 0.24 hp/ft² (Rotax), 2.4 hp/m² (Cuyuna) or 2.6 hp/m² (Rotax). Fuel capacity 10.0 US gal, 8.3 Imp gal, 37.9 litre.

WEIGHTS & LOADINGS - Empty weight *250* lb, *113* kg. Max take-off weight *700* lb, *318* kg. Payload *450* lb, *204* kg. Max wing loading *3.56* lb/ft², *17.4* kg/m². Max power loading *16.3* lb/hp (Cuyuna) or *14.9* lb/hp (Rotax), *7.4* kg/hp (Cuyuna) or *6.8* kg/hp (Rotax). Load factors NC recommended; +9.0, -5.0 ultimate.

PERFORMANCE* - Max level speed *63* mph, *101* kph. Never exceed speed *75* mph, *121* kph. Max cruising speed *63* mph, *101* kph. Economic cruising speed *55* mph, *88* kph. Stalling speed *26* mph, *42* kph. Max climb rate at sea level *600* ft/min, *3.1* m/s. Best glide ratio with power off *8/1* at NC speed. Take-off distance *100* ft, *30* m. Landing distance *100* ft, *30* m. Range at average cruising speed *140* mile, *225* km. Other data NC.

*Under unspecified test conditions.

MATHEWS

Lyle Mathews Aircraft, 2141 Shannon Way, Mesa, Arizona 85205; tel (602) 981-2263. Designer and builder: Lyle Mathews. Builders: Mike Neutzman and Wink Turner.

MATHEWS *BREEZY*

(Three-axis)

Single- or tandem two-seat single-engined high-wing monoplane with conventional three-axis control. Wing has unswept leading and trailing edges, and constant chord; conventional tail. Pitch control by elevator on tail; yaw control by fin-mounted rudder; roll control by 75%-span ailerons; control inputs through stick for pitch/roll and pedals for yaw. Wing braced from below by struts; wing profile NC; 100% double-surface. Undercarriage has three wheels in tricycle formation; suspension NC on nosewheel and bungee suspension on main wheels. Push-right go-right nosewheel steering connected to yaw control; also differential braking. Brakes on main wheels. Aluminium-alloy tube airframe, completely open. Engine mounted below wing, driving pusher propeller.

Production status: prototype.

GENERAL - Lyle Mathews is a retired engineer from Lockheed and has worked as a stunt flyer in some 30 films. But as well as flying aircraft, he also designs them, his earliest ultralights being the *CCC* and *PUP* models which we featured in our first edition.

Lyle doesn't do all the design work himself, as not only his

Two Mathews products: (left) the Turnerkraft Biplane *and (right) the* Breezy, *which at the time this picture was taken had already notched up over 125 h of airtime.*

creations but also those of other local enthusiasts are marketed under his name. An example of this is the *Breezy,* earlier sold both under the Petit and Kindell banners, but now available through Lyle in plan form for US$20 inland, US$25 overseas. Simplicity of construction has a high priority with this design, which uses no glass-fibre or foam and opts for strut rather than cable bracing. The fuselage boom is a square-section tube, and wing covering is doped fabric.

The *Breezy* can be built in either solo or dual form, the second seat and fuel tank being located, Lyle says, directly below the centre of gravity and thus not affecting balance. Depending on the payload envisaged, either a Rotax 277 or 503 is recommended, the data below referring to a solo machine with 277 engine.

Lyle and friends spent 165 h building the prototype, and reckon the average builder will take 200-300 h.

EXTERNAL DIMENSIONS & AREAS - Length overall *17.0* ft, *5.18* m. Height overall *5.3* ft, *1.60* m. Wing span *30.0* ft, *9.14* m. Constant chord *4.6* ft, *1.40* m. Dihedral *3°*. Sweepback *0°*. Tailplane span *8.0* ft, *2.44* m. Fin height *3.3* ft, *1.02* m. Total wing area *132* ft², *12.3* m². Total aileron area *8.0* ft², *0.74* m². Fin area *6.0* ft², *0.56* m². Rudder area *8.0* ft², *0.74* m². Aspect ratio *6.8/1*. Wheel track *5.0* ft, *1.52* m. Other data NC.

POWER PLANT - Rotax 277 engine. Max power 28 hp at NC rpm. Propeller diameter and pitch 54x33 inch, 1.37x0.84 m. Gear reduction, ratio NC. Max static thrust 190 lb, 86 kg. Power per unit area 0.21 hp/ft², 2.3 hp/m². Fuel capacity 5.0 US gal, 4.2 Imp gal, 18.9 litre.

WEIGHTS & LOADINGS - Empty weight 247 lb, 112 kg. Max take-off weight 536 lb, 243 kg. Payload 289 lb, 131 kg. Max wing loading 4.06 lb/ft², 19.8 kg/m². Max power loading 19.1 lb/hp, 8.7 kg/hp. Load factors +3.5, -NC recommended; +4.0, -NC ultimate.

PERFORMANCE* - Max level speed 65 mph, 105 kph. Never exceed speed 75 mph, 121 kph. Max cruising speed 50 mph, 80 kph. Economic cruising speed 45 mph, 72 kph. Stalling speed 25 mph, 40 kph. Max climb rate at sea level 390 ft/min, 2.0 m/s. Take-off distance 210 ft, 64 m. Landing distance 160 ft, 49 m. Range at average cruising speed 300 mile, 483 km. Other data NC.

*Under the following test conditions - Airfield altitude 1375 ft, 419 m. Ground temperature 100°F, 38°C. Ground pressure NC. Ground windspeed 0 mph, 0 kph. Test payload 275 lb, 125 kg.

MATHEWS
PARASOL JUNIOR
and *J-3 JUNIOR*
(Three-axis)

Single-seat single-engined parasol-wing (high-wing for J-3 Junior) monoplane with conventional three-axis control. Wing has unswept leading and trailing edges, and constant chord; conventional tail. Pitch control by elevator on tail; yaw control by fin-mounted rudder; roll control by ailerons; control inputs through stick for pitch/roll and pedals for yaw. Wing braced from below by struts; wing profile NC; 100% double-surface. Undercarriage has three wheels in tail-dragger formation; suspension NC on tailwheel and bungee suspension on main wheels. Push-right go-right tailwheel steering connected to yaw control; also differential braking. Brakes on main wheels. Steel-tube airframe, partially enclosed. Engine mounted below wing, driving tractor propeller.

Production status: prototype.

GENERAL - The *J-3 Junior* is the fourteenth aircraft designed by the prolific Lyle Mathews, and like his company's other products is sold only as plans. This Cub-like machine can be made to look like a *Champ, Vagabond, Taylorcraft,* or of course a *Cub* by the builder making small alterations to the shape of the tail surfaces, and other similar changes. For those who want a machine looking rather like a *Baby Ace,* Lyle offers a variation on the *J-3 Junior* theme called the *Parasol Junior,* which apart from its parasol wing is a very similar machine, using the same construction principles of welded steel tube and fabric covering.

Choice of powerplant is up to the builder; our data below is accurate for a *Parasol Junior* with Rotax 277 engine, and approximately correct for a similarly engined *J-3 Junior.* Plans for the aircraft cost the same as for the *Breezy;* construction and rigging times are also similar.

EXTERNAL DIMENSIONS & AREAS - Length overall 17.0 ft, 5.18 m. Height overall 5.2 ft, 1.57 m. Wing span 30.0 ft, 9.14 m. Constant chord 4.0 ft, 1.22 m. Dihedral 2°. Sweepback 0°. Tailplane span 8.0 ft, 2.44 m. Fin height 4.0 ft, 1.22 m. Total wing area 120 ft², 11.1 m². Total aileron area 8.0 ft², 0.74 m². Fin area 3.0 ft², 0.28 m². Rudder area 8.0 ft², 0.74 m². Total elevator area 16.0 ft², 1.49 m². Aspect ratio 7.5/1. Wheel track 4.5 ft, 1.37 m. Other data NC.

POWER PLANT - Rotax 277 engine. Max power 28 hp at NC rpm. Propeller diameter and pitch 72x26 inch,

Now all we need is the wing! The prototype J-3 Junior takes shape.

1.83x0.66 m. Gear reduction, ratio 2.1/1. Max static thrust 170 lb, 77 kg. Power per unit area 0.23 hp/ft², 2.5 hp/m². Fuel capacity 5.0 US gal, 4.2 Imp gal, 18.9 litre.

WEIGHTS & LOADINGS - Empty weight 249 lb, 113 kg. Max take-off weight 498 lb, 226 kg. Payload 249 lb, 113 kg. Max wing loading 4.15 lb/ft², 20.4 kg/m². Max power loading 17.8 lb/hp, 8.1 kg/hp. Load factors NC.

PERFORMANCE* - Max level speed 85 mph, 137 kph. Never exceed speed 105 mph, 169 kph. Max cruising speed 62 mph, 100 kph. Economic cruising speed 58 mph, 93 kph. Stalling speed 24 mph, 39 kph. Max climb rate at sea level 520 ft/min, 2.6 m/s. Best glide ratio with power off 10/1 at NC speed. Take-off distance 200 ft, 61 m. Landing distance 180 ft, 55 m. Range at average cruising speed 300 mile, 483 km. Other data NC.

*Under the following test conditions - Airfield altitude 1375 ft, 419 m. Ground temperature 100°F, 38°C. Ground pressure NC. Ground windspeed 5 mph, 8 kph. Test payload 246 lb, 112 kg.

MATHEWS
SIMPLE SIMON
(Three-axis)

Summary similar to Parasol Junior.

Production status: prototype.

GENERAL - Little information is available about the *Simple Simon,* but it appears to be yet another variation on the *J-3 Junior* theme, this time with the accent on exceptional simplicity of construction. The Mathews-Neutzman-Turner team built the prototype in only 12 working days, using a similar Rotax engine to the *J-3 Junior,* and now offer plans for the same price as the *Breezy.*

EXTERNAL DIMENSIONS & AREAS - NC.

POWER PLANT - Rotax 277 engine. Other data NC.

WEIGHTS & LOADINGS - NC.

PERFORMANCE - NC.

MATHEWS
TURNERKRAFT BIPLANE
(Three-axis)

Single-seat single-engined biplane with conventional three-axis control. Wings have unswept leading and trailing edges, and constant chord; conventional tail.

Pitch control by elevator on tail; yaw control by fin-mounted rudder; roll control by full-span ailerons on upper wing; control inputs through stick for pitch/roll and pedals for yaw. Wings braced by struts and transverse X-cables; wing profile NC; 100% double-surface. Undercarriage has three wheels in tail-dragger formation (tricycle optional); suspension NC. Push-right go-right tailwheel (nosewheel optional) steering connected to yaw control. No brakes. Aluminium-alloy tube airframe, completely open. Engine mounted at upper-wing height, driving pusher propeller.

Production status: see text.

GENERAL - Designed by Wink Turner, the *Turnerkraft Biplane* is a simple machine constructed from aluminium-alloy tubing and making extensive use of pop rivetting. Ailerons are operated by push-pull tubes and the Dacron wing covering on the prototype is taped tautly in place and then protected with Latex (exterior) house paint, a method which Lyle claims gives excellent durability. Lyle describes the aircraft as rugged, but warns that it is not designed for aerobatics.

Although in March '84 the company announced that this aircraft and the *Breezy* would be available in kit form, the company now list them as 'plans only', the price for the biplane drawings being the same as for the *Breezy*.

Being a homebuilt, specifications vary considerably and builders can incorporate tail-dragger or tricycle undercarriage; our example below uses a Kawasaki engine and is valid for either type of landing gear. Construction time is 200-300 h and rigging takes 15 min.

EXTERNAL DIMENSIONS & AREAS - Length overall 17.8 ft, 5.44 m. Wing span 24.0 ft, 7.32 m (bottom); 24.0 ft, 7.32 m (top). Constant chord 3.4 ft, 1.02 m (bottom wing); 3.4 ft, 1.02 m (top wing). Sweepback 0°. Total wing area 161 ft², 15.0 m². Aspect ratio 7.2/1 (bottom wing); 7.2/1 (top wing). Other data NC.

POWER PLANT - Kawasaki TA440A engine. Max power 40 hp at NC rpm. Propeller diameter and pitch 54x28 inch, 1.37x0.71 m. Reduction type and ratio NC. Max static thrust NC. Power per unit area 0.25 hp/ft², 2.7 hp/m². Fuel capacity 5.0 US gal, 4.2 Imp gal, 18.9 litre.

WEIGHTS & LOADINGS - Empty weight 251 lb, 114 kg. Max take-off weight 490 lb, 222 kg. Payload 239 lb, 108 kg. Max wing loading 3.04 lb/ft², 14.8 kg/m². Max power loading 12.3 lb/hp, 5.6 kg/hp. Load factors NC.

PERFORMANCE* - Cruising speed 40 mph, 64 kph. Stalling speed 25 mph, 40 kph. Other data NC.

*Under unspecified test conditions.

MAVERICK

Maverick Manufacturing Inc, 12139 Glenwood Road SW, Port Orchard, Washington 98366; tel (206) 876-9175. (No longer trading).

MAVERICK *MAVERICK 500R*
(Two-axis)

Summary similar to Ultralair JC24 D (see French section).

Production status: see text.

GENERAL - We are not sure whether the Maverick company really deserves to be in this book, as we

understood from reliable sources that it had ceased trading. However its product, a *Weedhopper*-style machine, was listed in a US buyers' guide as recently as January '85, so we present here a few details. Price at that time was US$4750 for a 16 h kit.

Now that Nova Air, which took over the *Weedhopper* proper, and Custom Aircraft Conversions, which produced an imitation called the *Raven II*, are both apparently inactive, the *Maverick's* closest relative is the French Ultralair *JC24 D*.

EXTERNAL DIMENSIONS & AREAS - Length overall 17.8 ft, 5.41 m. Height overall 5.8 ft, 1.78 m. Wing span 28.0 ft, 8.53 m. Total wing area 168 ft², 15.6 m². Aspect ratio 4.7/1. Other data NC.

POWER PLANT - Rotax 277 engine. Max power 28 hp at 6500 rpm. Propeller diameter and pitch 60x28 inch, 1.52x0.71 m. Belt reduction, ratio 2.0/1. Max static thrust 180 lb, 82 kg. Power per unit area 0.17 hp/ft², 1.8 hp/m². Fuel capacity 5.0 US gal, 4.2 Imp gal, 18.9 litre.

WEIGHTS & LOADINGS - Empty weight 195 lb, 88 kg. Max take-off weight 450 lb, 204 kg. Payload 255 lb, 116 kg. Max wing loading 2.68 lb/ft², 13.1 kg/m². Max power loading 16.1 lb/hp, 7.3 kg/hp. Load factors NC recommended; +8.0, -3.0 ultimate.

PERFORMANCE* - Max level speed 55 mph, 88 kph. Never exceed speed 60 mph, 97 kph. Max cruising speed 40 mph, 64 kph. Economic cruising speed 35 mph, 56 kph. Stalling speed 25 mph, 40 kph. Max climb rate at sea level 600 ft/min, 3.1 m/s. Best glide ratio with power off 8/1 at NC speed. Range at average cruising speed 117 mile, 188 km. Other data NC.

*Under unspecified test conditions.

MAXAIR SPORTS

Maxair Sports Inc, 32 Water St, Glen Rock, Pennsylvania 17327; tel (717) 235-5512/5985/2107; tx MAXAIR 4996511.

Australian agent: Austflight, Ballina Airpark, Pacific Hwy, Ballina 2478, NSW; tel (066) 865633; tx ULAUST AA 66237.

Japanese agent: IM Products Inc, 11-4 Chuo, 1-Chome, Yashio-Shi, Saitama 340; tel 0489 972361; tx 242-8203.

Italian agent: Digirama SRL, Via Toscana 1, 00187 Roma; tel 06/4757486; tx 621040.

Central American agent: Juan Del Carmen, 20 Calle 3-50, Zona 10, Guatemala City, Guatemala; tel 681567.

MAXAIR SPORTS *HUMMER*
(Three- axis)

Single-seat single-engined high-wing monoplane with unconventional three-axis control. Wing has unswept leading and trailing edges, and constant chord; V-tail. Pitch/yaw control by ruddervator; roll control by spoilers; control inputs through stick for pitch/yaw and pedals for roll. Wing braced from above by kingpost and cables, from below by cables; wing profile NC; 100% double-surface. Undercarriage has three wheels in tail-dragger formation; leaf-spring suspension on tailwheel

Norman Burr

and no suspension on main wheels. Stick-right go-right tailwheel steering connected to yaw control. Optional brakes on main wheels. Aluminium-alloy tube airframe, with optional pod. Engine mounted below wing, driving pusher propeller.

Production status: see text.

GENERAL - Designed by ultralighting pioneer Klaus Hill, the *Hummer* dates back to 1977, when the late Klaus star ted design studies for the machine. The first production models flew the following spring, and for several years now the design has been marketed by Maxair Sports, who have continued to refine and develop it.

The most significant change has been the addition of pedal-operated spoilers to provide unconventional three-axis control, an arrangement which makes it easy for a two-axis *Hummer* to be upgraded. Incidentally, the now defunct British importer Hummer Sales did produce a series of five machines with conventional three-axis control, called the *Hummer TX*, but the idea was never taken up by Maxair.

A further development, so major that it is really a new plane, was to ditch the V-tail in favour of a conventional one. This move, allied to various other changes, produced the *Drifter* range which we describe separately and on which the company's marketing effort is now concentrated. Judging by its listings in ultralight magazines in early 1985, the *Hummer* is still available but we suspect that the two-axis variant has been dropped. Various engines have been fitted over the years, including the Robin 250 and 330 in Europe, but our data refers to two versions common in the US: the Zenoah and Rotax 277 engined three-axis machines.

The *Hummer* is sold as a 50 h kit for US$5200, with plans and part kits also available. Rigging time is 10 min.

Note: in the data below, where figures for the two versions differ, those for the Zenoah-engined aircraft are shown first, followed in parentheses by those for the Rotax version.

EXTERNAL DIMENSIONS & AREAS - Length overall 18.0 ft, 5.48 m. Height overall 8.3 ft, 2.54 m. Wing span 34.0 ft, 10.36 m. Constant chord 4.4 ft, 1.32 m. Sweepback 0°. Tail span 8.2 ft, 2.50 m. Total wing area 138 ft², 12.8 m². Aspect ratio 8.4/1. Wheel track 3.6 ft, 1.08 m. Tailwheel diameter overall 6 inch, 15 cm. Main wheels diameter overall 10 inch, 25 cm.

POWER PLANT - Zenoah G25B (Rotax 277) engine. Max power 22(28) hp at 6000(6200) rpm. Propeller diameter and pitch 52(56)x32(28) inch, 1.32(1.42)x0.81(0.71) m. V-belt reduction, ratio 2.25/1. Max static thrust 160(220) lb,

73(100) kg. Power per unit area 0.16(0.20) hp/ft², 1.7(2.2) hp/m². Fuel capacity 5.0 US gal, 4.2 Imp gal, 18.9 litre.

WEIGHTS & LOADINGS - Empty weight 185 lb, 84 kg. Max take-off weight 440 lb, 199 kg. Payload 255 lb, 116 kg. Max wing loading 3.18 lb/ft², 15.5 kg/m². Max power load ing 20.0(15.7) lb/hp, 9.0(7.1) kg/hp. Load factors +5.0, -3.0 recommended; NC ultimate.

PERFORMANCE* - Max level speed 50(60) mph, 80(97) kph. Never exceed speed 63 mph, 101 kph. Max cruising speed 45 mph, 72 kph. Economic cruising speed 30 mph, 48 kph. Stalling speed 23(24) mph, 37(39) kph. Max climb rate at sea level 400(600) ft/min, 2.0(3.1) m/s. Min sink rate 300(NC) ft/min, 1.5(NC) m/s at NC speed. Best glide ratio with power off 9/1 at 28 mph, 45 kph. Take-off distance 60(NC) ft, 18(NC) m. Landing distance 100(NC) ft, 30(NC) m. Service ceiling 10,000(NC) ft, 3050(NC) m. Range at average cruising speed 100(NC) mile, 161(NC) km. Noise level NC.

*Under unspecified test conditions.

MAXAIR SPORTS
DRIFTER DR277 and DK440

(Three-axis)

Single-seat single-engined high-wing monoplane with conventional three-axis control. Wing has unswept leading and trailing edges, and constant chord; flaps fitted; conventional tail. Pitch control by elevator on tail; yaw control by fin-mounted rudder; roll control by full-span ailerons; control inputs through stick for pitch/roll and pedals for yaw. Wing braced from above by kingpost and cables, from below by cables; wing profile NC; 100% double-surface. Undercarriage has three wheels in tail-dragger formation; axle-flex suspension on all wheels. Push-right go-right tailwheel steering connected to yaw control; also differential braking. Brakes on main wheels. Aluminium-alloy tube airframe, with optional pod. Engine mounted at wing height, driving pusher propeller.

Production status: current, 100 completed (total of all single-seat Drifter variants).

Maxair's Drifter, here shown with optional pod, offers the pilot an unparalleled view.

GENERAL - As we explain under *Hummer,* the *Drifter* can be traced back to that venerable Klaus Hill design but is in reality much more than just a re-tailed *Hummer.* The wing is stubbier and has full-span ailerons, while the undercarriage is redesigned with wider track and more rugged suspension legs, giving an aircraft which Maxair says is particularly good on rough terrain.

Originally introduced at Oshkosh '82 with Kawasaki TA440A engine and simply called *Drifter,* this model has now been retitled *Drifter DK440* to differentiate it from the more recent *Drifter DR277,* which uses a Rotax 277 and is the only variant which is ultralight legal in the US.

The aircraft are otherwise identical and both have the advantage over many rivals in that they are built by a firm which not only constructs aircraft but also supplies some 200 different parts to other ultralight and hang-glider companies. There is thus every reason to think that the fittings and detailing will be of good quality; writing in the November '84 issue of *Glider Rider,* Michael Bradford had high praise for the aircraft's finish, durability, and vice-free flying characteristics.

Both models are sold in kit form, around 45 h being needed to build the single-cylinder machine (price US$6495 including instruments) and 80 h for the twin (price NC). Ready to fly versions cost US$400 more. Rigging time is 10 min in either case. Note that in the data below, where figures for the two versions differ, those for the Rotax-engined version are shown first, followed in parentheses by those for the Kawasaki version.

EXTERNAL DIMENSIONS & AREAS - Length overall 19.0 ft, 5.79 m. Height overall 9.0 ft, 2.74 m. Wing span 30.0 ft, 9.14 m. Constant chord 5.1 ft, 1.55 m. Dihedral 2.25°. Sweepback 0°. Tailplane span 9.5 ft, 2.90 m. Fin height 4.5 ft, 1.37 m. Total wing area 152 ft², 14.1 m².

Total aileron area 20.5 ft², 1.90 m². Fin area 13.0 ft², 1.21 m². Rudder area 6.4 ft², 0.60 m². Tailplane area 27.0 ft², 2.51 m². Total elevator area 27.0 ft², 2.51 m². Aspect ratio 5.9/1. Wheel track 6.0 ft, 1.83 m. Wheelbase 15.6 ft, 4.72 m. Tailwheel diameter overall 4 inch, 10 cm. Main wheels diameter overall 12 inch, 30 cm.

POWER PLANT - Rotax 277 (Kawasaki TA440A) engine. Max power 28(38) hp at 6200(6000) rpm. Propeller diameter and pitch 60x26(NC) inch, 1.52x0.66(NC) m. V-belt reduction, ratio 2.25/1. Max static thrust 210(NC) lb, 95(NC) kg. Power per unit area 0.18(0.25) hp/ft², 2.0(2.7) hp/m². Fuel capacity 5.0 US gal, 4.2 Imp gal, 18.9 litre.

WEIGHTS & LOADINGS - Empty weight 250(270) lb, 113(122) kg. Max take-off weight 500(575) lb, 227(261) kg. Payload 250(305) lb, 113(138) kg. Max wing loading 3.29(3.78) lb/ft², 16.1(18.5) kg/m². Max power loading 17.9(15.1) lb/hp, 8.1(6.9) kg/hp. Load factors +4.5(NC), -2.0(NC) recommended; +6.0(NC), -3.3(NC) ultimate.

PERFORMANCE* - Max level speed 63(70) mph, 101(113) kph. Never exceed speed 75 mph, 121 kph. Max cruising speed 60(63) mph, 97(101) kph. Economic cruising speed 40(45) mph, 64(72) kph. Stalling speed 26(29) mph, 42(47) kph. Max climb rate at sea level 600(900) ft/min, 3.1(4.6) m/s. Min sink rate 280(300) ft/min at 33(40) mph, 1.4(1.5) m/s at 53(64) kph. Best glide ratio with power off 8.2(8.0)/1 at 40(41) mph, 64(66) kph. Take-off distance 210(150) ft, 65(46) m. Landing distance 225(235) ft, 69(72) m. Service ceiling 10,000(NC) ft, 3050(NC) m. Range at average cruising speed 118(113) mile, 190(182) km. Noise level NC.

*Under unspecified test conditions.

MAXAIR SPORTS
DRIFTER DR503

(Three-axis)

Summary similar to Drifter DR277 and DK440.

Production status: current, number completed NC.

GENERAL - Maxair's *Drifter DR503* is not an ultralight, but is aimed at lightplane pilots who want a high-performance machine with an ultralight feel. It is basically a strengthened *Drifter DR277* with a much reduced wing span and its Rotax 277 replaced by the Rotax 503, as used in the two-seater.

The result was tested in the June '85 edition of *Ultralight Flying* by Michael Bradford, who concluded that it was not for the inexperienced but was nevertheless enormous fun to fly. Sold in kit form, it costs US$7295.

EXTERNAL DIMENSIONS & AREAS - Wing span 22.0 ft, 6.71 m. Constant chord 5.1 ft, 1.55 m. Sweepback 0°. Total wing area 114 ft², 10.6 m². Aspect ratio 4.2/1. Other data NC.

POWER PLANT - Rotax 503 engine. Max power 48 hp at NC rpm. Propeller diameter and pitch 60xNC inch, 1.52xNC m. Belt reduction, ratio 2.25/1. Max static

Glider Rider

thrust NC. Power per unit area 0.42 hp/ft², 4.5 hp/m². Fuel capacity 5.0 US gal, 4.2 Imp gal, 18.9 litre.

WEIGHTS & LOADINGS - Empty weight 305 lb, 138 kg. Max take-off weight 550 lb, 249 kg. Payload 245 lb, 111 kg. Max wing loading 4.82 lb/ft², 23.5 kg/m². Max power loading 11.5 lb/hp, 5.2 kg/hp. Load factors +6.0, -4.5 design; +9.0, -6.0 ultimate.

PERFORMANCE* - Never exceed speed 95 mph, 153 kph. Cruising speed 70 mph, 113 kph. Stalling speed 35 mph, 56 kph. Max climb rate at sea level 1000 ft/min, 5.1 m/s. Other data NC.

*Under unspecified test conditions.

Two-place version of the Drifter *with optional pod.*

MAXAIR SPORTS
DRIFTER XP503 and MU503
(Three-axis)

Summary as Drifter DR277 and DK440 *except: Tandem two-seater (Drifter XP503), three-seater (Drifter MU503).*

Production status: current, number completed NC (Drifter XP503); prototype (Drifter MU503).

GENERAL - Maxair's *Drifter XP503* was conceived as a trainer for pilots wanting a solo *Drifter,* and is basically a beefed-up single-seater with an extra seat added under the wing. To cope with the extra payload, the big Rotax 503 is fitted, but the wing and overall dimensions remain the same.

Price is US$7495 for an 80 h kit including instruments.

Just as we went to press we learned that Maxair had developed a three-seat version of the *XP503* for military use, named the *MU503.* Payload is increased to 550 lb (249 kg) but we have no other details. Data below is accurate for the two-seater only.

EXTERNAL DIMENSIONS & AREAS - See *Drifter DR277 and DK440.*

POWER PLANT - See *Drifter DR503* except: Power per unit area 0.32 hp/ft², 3.4 hp/m².

WEIGHTS & LOADINGS - Empty weight 345 lb, 156 kg. Max take-off weight 790 lb, 358 kg. Payload 445 lb, 202 kg. Max wing loading 5.20 lb/ft², 25.4 kg/m². Max power loading 16.5 lb/hp, 7.5 kg/hp. Load factors NC.

PERFORMANCE* - Max level speed 63 mph, 101 kph. Max cruising speed 60 mph, 97 kph. Economic cruising speed 45 mph, 72 kph. Stalling speed 31 mph, 50 kph. Max climb rate at sea level 600 ft/min, 3.1 m/s. Best glide ratio with power off 8/1 at 46 mph, 74 kph. Take-off distance 300 ft, 91 m. Landing distance 300 ft, 91 m. Range at average cruising speed 102 mile, 165 km. Other data NC.

*Under unspecified test conditions.

MIRAGE AIRCRAFT

Mirage Aircraft Inc, 31 Pearson Way, West Springfield, Maryland 01089; tel (413) 732-5067.

MIRAGE AIRCRAFT
MIRAGE II
(Three-axis)

Single-seat single-engined high-wing monoplane with conventional three-axis control. Wing has unswept leading edge and unswept trailing edge (swept forward trailing edge optional), and constant chord (tapering chord optional); cruciform tail. Pitch control by elevator on tail; yaw control by fin-mounted rudder; roll control by 15%-span spoilerons (double spoilerons optional); control inputs through stick for pitch/roll and pedals for yaw. Wing braced from above by kingpost and cables, from below by cables; wing profile Clark Y; 90% double-surface. Undercarriage has three wheels in tricycle formation with additional tailskid; no suspension on nosewheel and bungee suspension on main wheels. Push-right go-right nosewheel steering connected to yaw control. No brakes. Aluminium-alloy tube airframe, with pod. Engine mounted above wing, driving tractor propeller.

Production status: current, number completed NC.

GENERAL - A development of the Klaus Hill-designed *Humbug,* the *Mirage* enjoyed instant success following its award-winning introduction at Sun 'n Fun '81. Originally fitted with two 15 hp Yamaha engines driving a single prop, it later acquired a 430 Cuyuna and then the Kawasaki TA440A, the latter version being known as the *Mirage MkII* because it also incorporated various other improvements. Manufactured for several years by Ultralight Flight, the *Mirage MkII* was overshadowed by the success of the *Phantom* and eventually dropped from the company's range. Mirage Aircraft was set up by a group which still believed in the design, the result of this commitment being the *Mirage II* (not to be confused with the *Mirage MkII!*).

This latest version differs from its predecessors in having as standard a higher lift aerofoil, nosewheel steering, detachable fuel tank, low-speed ASI, and a pod and windshield. Perhaps more important are the options: double spoilers to sharpen the roll rate, a tapering-chord wing, and any of five engines. Standard is a Rotax 277 with air restart or a Kawasaki 340, but at extra cost the buyer can have a Rotax 377, Rotax 447 or Kawasaki 440, choices which when allied with the wing options produce a bewildering number of permutations. The tapering wing has the same span and root chord but a 4.0 ft (1.22 m) tip chord, which reduces area to 141 ft^2 (13.1 m^2), derived quantities being altered accordingly. Where fitted, the second spoiler is of identical area to the first.

Our data below refers to a constant-chord single-spoiler wing and covers three engines: Rotax 277 first, followed where different by figures in parentheses for the Kawasaki 340 and 440 variants.

Price of standard aircraft is US$4795 for a 30 h kit, with a US$500 surcharge for factory build. A tapered wing costs US$50 extra, double spoilers US$150, a Rotax 377 US$200, and a Rotax 447 US$300; no price is quoted for the Kawasaki 440. Other options include floats and extra instruments. Rigging time is 30 min.

EXTERNAL DIMENSIONS & AREAS - Length overall 18.0 ft, 5.49 m. Height overall 8.5 ft, 2.59 m. Wing span 32.5 ft, 9.91 m. Constant chord 4.5 ft, 1.37 m. Dihedral 6°. Sweepback 0°. Tailplane span 8.0 ft, 2.44 m. Fin height 4.7 ft, 1.43 m. Total wing area 145.5 ft^2, 13.5 m^2. Total spoileron area 2.5 ft^2, 0.23 m^2. Fin area 3.6 ft^2, 0.34 m^2. Rudder area 9.6 ft^2, 0.89 m^2. Tailplane area 11.8 ft^2, 1.09 m^2. Total elevator area 10.3 ft^2, 0.96 m^2. Aspect ratio 7.3/1. Wheel track 4.0 ft, 1.22 m. Wheelbase 5.6 ft, 1.70 m. Nosewheel diameter overall 10 inch, 25 cm. Main wheels diameter overall 10 inch, 25 cm.

POWER PLANT - Rotax 277 (Kawasaki 340) (Kawasaki 440) engine. Max power 28(32)(37) hp at 6200(5000)(NC) rpm. Propeller diameter and pitch 58x27 inch, 1.47x0.69 m. Gear (toothed-belt) (toothed-belt) reduction, ratio NC(2.0)(2.0)/1. Max static thrust NC(195)(215) lb, NC(88)(95) kg. Power per unit area 0.19(0.22)(0.25) hp/ft^2, 2.1(2.4)(2.7) hp/m^2. Fuel capacity 5.0 US gal, 4.2 Imp gal, 18.9 litre.

WEIGHTS & LOADINGS - Empty weight 230(236)(246) lb, 104(107)(112) kg. Max take-off weight 500 lb, 227 kg. Payload 270(264)(254) lb, 122(120)(115) kg. Max wing loading 3.44 lb/ft^2, 16.8 kg/m^2. Max power loading 17.9 (15.6)(13.5) lb/hp, 8.1(7.1)(6.1) kg/hp. Load factors +4.2, -3.3 recommended; +6.3, -4.9 ultimate.

PERFORMANCE* - Max level speed NC(58)(61) mph, NC(93)(98) kph. Never exceed speed 70 mph, 113 kph. Max cruising speed 50(50)(55) mph, 80(80)(88) kph. Economic cruising speed 40 mph, 64 kph. Stalling speed 26 mph, 42 kph. Max climb rate at sea level 700(800)(1000) ft/min, 3.6(4.1)(5.1) m/s. Min sink rate 400 ft/min at 30 mph, 2.0 m/s at 48 kph. Best glide ratio with power off 7.5/1 at 32 mph, 51 kph. Take-off distance 120(NC)(75) ft, 36(NC)(23) m. Landing distance 120 ft, 36 m. Service ceiling >10,000 ft, >3050 m. Range at average cruising speed 150(111) (100) mile, 241(179)(161) km. Noise level 70(NC)(NC) dB at 150 ft, 46 m.

*Under the following test conditions - Airfield altitude 200 ft, 61 m. Ground temperature 60°F, 16°C. Ground pressure 1013 mB. Ground windspeed 0 mph, 0 kph. Test payload 200 lb, 91 kg.

MITCHELL AEROSPACE

Mitchell Aerospace, 1900 S Newcomb, Porterville, California 93257; tel (209) 781-8100; tx 682402 ARRWFAL TOBL.

MITCHELL AEROSPACE
B-10 MITCHELL WING
(Three-axis)

Single-seat single-engined high-wing monoplane with conventional three-axis control. Wing has swept back leading and trailing edges, and tapering chord; no tail. Pitch/roll control by elevons; yaw control by fully flying tip rudders; control inputs through stick for pitch/roll and pedals for yaw. Cantilever wing; wing profile NACA 23015; 100% double-surface. Undercarriage has three wheels in tricycle formation; no suspension on nose-wheel and axle-flex/glass-fibre suspension on main wheels. Push-right go-right nosewheel steering connected to yaw control. Nosewheel brake. Aluminium-alloy tube/wood airframe, with optional pod. Engine mounted below wing, driving pusher propeller.

Production status: current, over 2000 plans and kits sold.

GENERAL - Don Mitchell is an almost legendary figure in the US aviation scene, and worked on the famous Northrop flying wing project in the 1940s. He brought this experience with him to the hang-gliding world in the form of a rigid-wing glider called the *B-10,* which was one of the best performing hang-gliders of its time.
It was not long before an engine was added to help the *B-*

There probably aren't two B-10 Mitchell Wings *alike anywhere; this one has non-standard main wheels and a pod.*

10 climb to soaring heights, although the design remained foot-launchable. A cage and landing gear with steerable nosewheel followed rapidly, creating the *B-10 Mitchell Wing* as we know it today, an aircraft which has proved one of the world's most popular ultralights. Inevitably, most homebuilders make their own modifications as they go along, but common changes are adding a glass-fibre pod (either the factory option or one of their own) and fitting a floor-mounted stick in place of the overhead design.

Although the control arrangements are conventional enough, the general consensus amongst flight testers is that the machine is not for the inexperienced. Its flying surfaces consist of elevons acting simultaneously for pitch control and differentially for roll control, with tip rudders which can be slewed round together to act as air brakes and steepen the descent angle.

Constructing the *B-10* needs time and patience; most builders take at least 400 h to complete the machine, much of that on the plywood wing, which has a D-section spar, foam ribs and Dacron or ceconite covering. Although there have been some factory-built *B-10s,* it is now offered only as plans (US$125) or a raw materials kit (US$1295). To complete their aircraft, buyers can purchase a Zenoah engine pack for US$1595.

EXTERNAL DIMENSIONS & AREAS - Length overall 8.0 ft, 2.44 m. Height overall 4.5 ft, 1.37 m. Wing span 34.0 ft, 10.36 m. Chord at root 5.0 ft, 1.52 m. Chord at tip 2.0 ft, 0.61 m. *Dihedral 6°. Sweepback 12°. Total wing area 136 ft², 12.6 m². Aspect ratio 8.5/1. Nosewheel diameter overall 10 inch, 25 cm. Main wheels diameter overall 10 inch, 25 cm. Other data NC.

POWER PLANT - Zenoah G25B engine. Max power 22 hp at 6500 rpm. Propeller diameter and pitch 50x27 inch,

1.27x0.69 m. Toothed-belt reduction, ratio 2.25/1. Max static thrust 180 lb, 82 kg. Power per unit area 0.16 hp/ft², 1.7 hp/m². Fuel capacity 5.0 US gal, 4.2 Imp gal, 18.9 litre.

WEIGHTS & LOADINGS - Empty weight 220 lb, 100 kg. Max take-off weight 440 lb, 200 kg. Payload 220 lb, 100 kg. Max wing loading 3.24 lb/ft², 15.9 kg/m². Max power loading 20.0 lb/hp, 9.1 kg/hp. Load factors +3.0, -3.0 recommended; +6.0, -6.0 ultimate.

PERFORMANCE** - Max level speed 63 mph, 101 kph. Never exceed speed 63 mph, 101 kph. Max cruising speed 55 mph, 88 kph. Economic cruising speed 45 mph, 72 kph. Stalling speed 27 mph, 43 kph. Max climb rate at sea level 400 ft/min, 2.0 m/s. Min sink rate 180 ft/min at 45 mph, 0.9 m/s at 72 kph. Best glide ratio with power off 16/1 at 36 mph, 58 kph. Take-off distance 200 ft, 61 m. Landing distance 200 ft, 61 m. Service ceiling 10,000 ft, 3050 m. Range at average cruising speed 300 mile, 483 km. Noise level NC.

*On outboard part of wing.

**Under the following test conditions - Airfield altitude 420 ft, 128 m. Ground temperature 70°F, 21°C. Ground pressure NC. Ground windspeed 0 mph, 0 kph. Test payload 180 lb, 82 kg.

Main picture shows U-2 Super Wing *and inset, the aircraft with wings folded ready for transportation. Rigging time is 5-10 min.*

MITCHELL AEROSPACE
U-2 SUPER WING
(Three-axis)

Single-seat single-engined mid-wing monoplane with conventional three-axis control. Wing has swept back leading and trailing edges, and tapering chord; no tail. Pitch/roll control by elevon; yaw control by tip rudders; control inputs through stick for pitch/roll and pedals for yaw. Cantilever wing; wing profile modified Wortmann; 100% double-surface. Undercarriage has three wheels in tricycle formation; no suspension on any wheels. Push-right go-right nosewheel steering connected to yaw control. Nosewheel brake. Steel-tube airframe, totally enclosed. Engine mounted above wing, driving pusher propeller.

Production status: current, over 1500 plans and kits sold.

GENERAL - Like the *B-10*, the *U-2 Super Wing* is a flying wing, but with a more complex structure designed for higher performance. Certainly the aircraft performs well, as a glance at our cruise speeds below will show, and

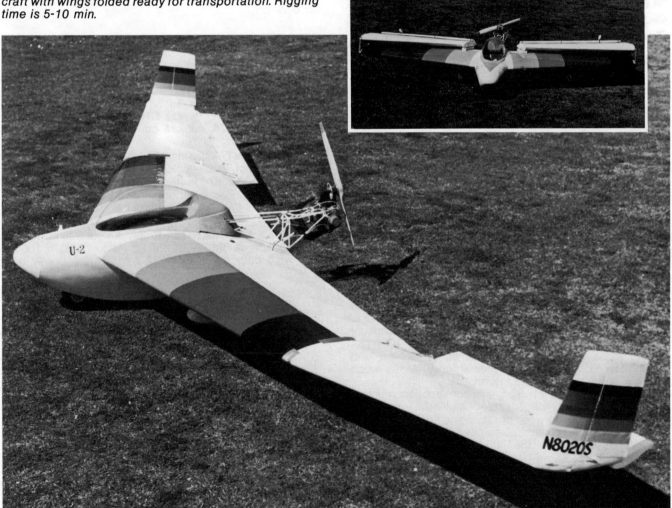

American Dick Rowley proved in the most dramatic way possible how much can be extracted from the machine when he flew his 35 hp Cuyuna ULII-02 engined example to 25,940 ft (7907 m) on 17 September 1983, a world record for class c1 a/o (landplanes under 300 kg take-off weight).

Many *U-2s* come out a little too heavy for the ultralight category, but can be made microlight legal without too much difficulty. Build time is around 250 h for the basic structure, plus some 100 h for finishing off. Standard engine is a Zenoah G25B, but there are some Cuyuna-engined examples around (like Rowley's) and we detail both below, with Zenoah data first, followed where different by figures for the Cuyuna.

The *U-2* is sold in just the same manner as the *B-10*, and for the same prices, except that the raw materials kit costs US$1995.

EXTERNAL DIMENSIONS & AREAS - See *B-10 Mitchell Wing* except: Length overall 9.0 ft, 2.74 m. Height overall 4.5 ft, 1.37 m. Wheelbase 8.0 ft, 2.44 m.

POWER PLANT - Zenoah G25B (Cuyuna 430R) engine. Max power 22(30) hp at 6500(NC) rpm. Propeller diameter and pitch 50(NC)x30(NC) inch, 1.27(NC)x0.76(NC) m. Toothed-belt reduction, ratio 2.25(NC)/1. Max static thrust 180(NC) lb, 82(NC) kg. Power per unit area 0.16(0.22) hp/ft², 1.7(2.4) hp/m². Fuel capacity 5.0 US gal, 4.2 Imp gal, 18.9 litre.

WEIGHTS & LOADINGS - Empty weight 240(300) lb, 109(136) kg. Max take-off weight 580 lb, 263 kg. Payload 340(280) lb, 154(127) kg. Max wing loading 4.26 lb/ft², 20.9 kg/m². Max power loading 26.4(19.3) lb/hp, 12.0(8.8) kg/hp. Load factors +3.0, -3.0 recommended; +6.0, -6.0 ultimate.

PERFORMANCE* - Max level speed 82(NC) mph, 132(NC) kph. Never exceed speed 90 mph, 145 kph. Max cruising speed 65(70) mph, 105(113) kph. Economic cruising speed 55(NC) mph, 88(NC) kph. Stalling speed 28(37) mph, 45(60) kph. Max climb rate at sea level 450(750) ft/min, 2.3(3.8) m/s. Min sink rate 180 ft/min at 45 mph, 0.9 m/s at 72 kph. Best glide ratio with power off 20(23)/1 at 45(49) mph, 72(79) kph. Take-off distance 200(210) ft, 61(64) m. Landing distance 200(250) ft, 61(76) m. Service ceiling 13,000(12,000) ft, 3960(3660) m. Range at average cruising speed 300(133) mile, 483(215) km. Noise level NC.

*Under these test conditions: as below for the Zenoah-engined machine, unspecified for the Cuyuna-engined version - Airfield altitude 420 ft, 128 m. Ground temperature 70°F, 21°C. Ground pressure NC. Ground windspeed 0 mph, 0 kph. Test payload NC.

MITCHELL AEROSPACE
P-38 LIGHTNING
(Three-axis)

Single-seat single-engined mid-wing monoplane with conventional three-axis control. Wing has swept forward leading and trailing edges, and constant chord; two-fin tail. Pitch control by fully flying tail; yaw control by fin-mounted rudders; roll control by full-span ailerons also useable as flaps; control inputs through stick for pitch/roll and pedals for yaw. Wing braced from above by struts; wing profile NACA 23015; 100% double-surface. Undercarriage has three wheels in tricycle formation with additional tailskids; no suspension on nosewheel and glass-fibre suspension on main wheels. Push-right go-right nosewheel steering connected to yaw control. Nosewheel brake. Aluminium-alloy/steel tube airframe, with optional pod. Engine mounted above wing, driving pusher propeller.

Production status: current, 500 plans and kits sold.

GENERAL - It's hard to imagine an aircraft more different from the *B-10* than the *P-38 Lightning*, which Don Mitchell named after the famous twin-boom fighter of World War II. With its unusual two-fin tail and its even more unusual swept forward wing incorporating 'flaperons' (ailerons usable as flaps), the *P-38* is a distinctive machine, and though too heavy for the ultralight category, is very much an ultralight in terms of its performance.

A variety of materials are used in its construction, much of the airframe being welded steel, while the spars are duralumin, epoxied to wood ribs. Leading edges are foam, with birch plywood covering. Designed for easy assembly, the aircraft is sold for US$4395 as a prefabricated and partly assembled kit with less than 200 pieces, which it is claimed needs 80 h to complete. A power pack is extra: various engines have been used since the aircraft went into production in the second quarter of 1981, but the standard unit now is the Cuyuna 430 with 32 hp, which costs US$1895 complete with ancillaries. Plans are available for US$125.

EXTERNAL DIMENSIONS & AREAS - Length overall 19.0 ft, 5.79 m. Height overall 6.5 ft, 1.98 m. Wing span 28.0 ft, 8.53 m. Constant chord 4.0 ft, 1.22 m. Dihedral 6°. Sweepforward 5°. Tailplane span 4.0 ft, 1.22 m. Fin height 3.0 ft, 0.91 m. Total wing area 112 ft², 10.4 m². Aspect ratio 7.0/1. Wheel track 4.0 ft, 1.22 m. Wheelbase 4.0 ft, 1.22 m. Nosewheel diameter overall 10 inch, 25 cm. Main wheels diameter overall *14* inch, *36* cm. Other data NC.

POWER PLANT - Cuyuna 430RR engine. Max power 32 hp at 6800 rpm. Propeller diameter and pitch 52x30 inch, 1.32x0.76 m. V-belt reduction, ratio 2.0/1. Max static thrust 220 lb, 100 kg. Power per unit area 0.29 hp/ft², 3.1 hp/m². Fuel capacity 5.0 US gal, 4.2 Imp gal, 18.9 litre.

WEIGHTS & LOADINGS - Empty weight 300 lb, 136 kg. Max take-off weight 520 lb, 236 kg. Payload 220 lb, 100 kg. Max wing loading 4.64 lb/ft², 22.7 kg/m². Max power load-

ing 16.3 lb/hp, 7.4 kg/hp. Load factors +3.0, -3.0 recommended; +6.0, -6.0 ultimate.

PERFORMANCE* - Max level speed 60 mph, 97 kph. Never exceed speed 70 mph, 113 kph. Max cruising speed 55 mph, 88 kph. Economic cruising speed 50 mph, 80 kph. Stalling speed 30 mph, 48 kph. Max climb rate at sea level 400 ft/min, 2.0 m/s. Best glide ratio with power off 7/1 at 45 mph, 72 kph. Landing distance 150 ft, 46 m. Service ceiling 10,000 ft, 3050 m. Range at average cruising speed 150 mile, 241 km. Other data NC.

*Under the following test conditions - Airfield altitude 420 ft, 128 m. Ground temperature 70°F, 21°C. Ground pressure NC. Ground windspeed 0 mph, 0 kph. Test payload NC.

MITCHELL AEROSPACE
AG-38A TERRIER
(Three-axis)

Summary as P-38 Lightning *except: Wing has unswept leading and trailing edges.*

Production status: current, number completed NC.

GENERAL - This aircraft is intended for agricultural work, and though the *AG-38* is derived from the *P-38,* in its latest *AG-38A Terrier* form it is a considerably different machine. The wing's span and area are much larger, the wing is mounted without sweep, and a Rotax 447 engine is fitted to allow an exceptionally big payload.
Depending on setting, the spray equipment can deal with 35-500 acre (14-202 ha) per flight, thanks to a 40 US gal hopper (33 Imp gal, 151 litre) mounted under the wing between the landing gear legs. An electric pump delivers the chemicals through 19 fan nozzles attached to spray bars covering the entire width of the aircraft, giving a spray swath equal to the span.
Sold as a pre-cut, pre-welded kit without engine for US$7495, it is also available in plan form for US$125. The Rotax 447 power pack costs an extra US$1995.

EXTERNAL DIMENSIONS & AREAS - Length 19.0 ft, 5.79 m. Height overall 6.9 ft, 2.10 m. Wing span 34.0 ft, 10.36 m. Constant chord 4.2 ft, 1.28 m. Dihedral 5°. Sweepback 0°. Total wing area 160 ft², 14.9 m². Aspect ratio 7.2/1. Wheelbase 4.0 ft, 1.22 m. Nosewheel diameter overall 10 inch, 25 cm. Main wheels diameter overall *14* inch, *36* cm. Other data NC.

POWER PLANT - Rotax 447 engine. Max power 42 hp at 7000 rpm. Propeller diameter and pitch 58x33 inch, 1.47x0.84 m. Gear reduction, ratio 2.25/1. Max static thrust 250 lb, 113 kg. Power per unit area 0.26 hp/ft², 2.8 hp/m². Fuel capacity 5.0 US gal, 4.2 Imp gal, 18.9 litre.

WEIGHTS & LOADINGS - Empty weight 370 lb, 168 kg. Max take-off weight 1050 lb, 476 kg. Payload 680 lb, 308 kg. Max wing loading 6.56 lb/ft², 31.9 kg/m². Max power loading 25.0 lb/hp, 11.3 kg/hp. Load factors +3.0, -2.0 recommended; +5.0, -3.0 ultimate.

PERFORMANCE* - Max level speed 70 mph, 113 kph. Never exceed speed 75 mph, 121 kph. Max cruising speed 60 mph, 97 kph. Economic cruising speed 55 mph, 88 kph. Stalling speed 30 mph, 48 kph. Max climb rate at sea level >500 ft/min, >2.5 m/s. Min sink rate 220 ft/min at 45 mph, 1.1 m/s at 72 kph. Best glide ratio with power off 8/1 at 45

mph, 72 kph. Take-off distance 250 ft, 76 m. Landing distance 200 ft, 61 m. Service ceiling >10,000 ft, >3050 m. Range at average cruising speed 200 mile, 322 km. Noise level NC.

*Under the following test conditions - Airfield altitude 420 ft, 128 m. Ground temperature 70°F, 21°C. Ground pressure NC. Ground windspeed 0 mph, 0 kph. Test payload NC.

MITCHELL WING INC

Mitchell Wing Inc, 11616 West 59th St, South Sand Springs, Oklahoma 74063; tel (918) 245-2571. (No longer trading).

MITCHELL WING INC
A-10 SILVER EAGLE
(Three-axis)

Summary as Mitchell Aerospace B-10 Mitchell Wing *except: Yaw control by tip rudders. Wing profile NC. Suspension NC. Aluminium-alloy airframe, with pod.*

Production status: see text, number completed NC.

GENERAL - As our summary shows, the *A-10 Silver Eagle* is a derivative of the famous *B-10 Mitchell Wing,* and was first shown in December '82. A bottom-mounted stick is incorporated, but by far the most significant change is to the wing, whose shape remains much the same but whose materials are totally different. The time-consuming wooden structure is abandoned in favour of a metal spar, a NASA-developed boron-containing foam, and an aluminium alloy skin, a design which unlike the *B-10* can be factory built at a sensible price.
The aluminium-skinned wing gives the aircraft a dramatic appearance, and boosted demand to the point where Don Mitchell helped set up Mitchell Wing Inc to manufacture ready to fly *A-10s* in quantity, quite apart from his kit and plan business at Mitchell Aerospace. However, we under-

stand that Mitchell Wing Inc has since closed, leaving the design in limbo, but we present details here in case Don makes other arrangements for its manufacture.

EXTERNAL DIMENSIONS & AREAS - Length overall 8.5 ft, 2.59 m. Height overall 6.2 ft, 1.88 m. Wing span 34.3 ft, 10.46 m. Chord at root 6.0 ft, 1.83 m. Chord at tip 2.0 ft, 0.61 m. *Dihedral 6°. Sweepback 12°. Total wing area 134 ft², 12.4 m². Aspect ratio 8.8/1. Nosewheel diameter overall 10 inch, 25 cm. Main wheels diameter overall 10 inch, 25 cm. Other data NC.

POWER PLANT - Zenoah G25B-1 engine. Max power 23 hp at NC rpm. Propeller diameter and pitch 54x24 inch, 1.37x0.61 m. Toothed-belt reduction, ratio 2.25/1. Max static thrust 165 lb, 75 kg. Power per unit area 0.17 hp/ft², 1.9 hp/m². Fuel capacity 3.0 US gal, 2.5 Imp gal, 11.4 litre.

WEIGHTS & LOADINGS - Empty weight 250 lb, 1 13 kg. Max take-off weight 553 lb, 251 kg. Payload 303 lb, 138 kg. Max wing loading 4.13 lb/ft², 20.2 kg/m². Max power loading 24.0 lb/hp, 10.9 kg/hp. Load factors NC recommended; +5.5, -5.5 ultimate.

PERFORMANCE ** - Max level speed 63 mph, 101 kph. Never exceed speed 80 mph, 129 kph. Max cruising speed 58 mph, 93 kph. Stalling speed 27 mph, 43 kph. Max climb rate at sea level 640 ft/min, 3.3 m/s. Best glide ratio with power off 15/1 at NC speed. Take-off distance 200 ft, 61 m. Landing distance 200 ft, 61 m. Range at average cruising speed 120 mile, 193 km. Other data NC.

*On outboard part of wing.

**Under unspecified test conditions.

MITCHELL WING INC
TU-10 DOUBLE EAGLE
(Three-axis)

Summary as Mitchell Aerospace B-10 Mitchell Wing except: Side-by-side two-seater. Yaw control by tip rudders. Wing profile NC. Suspension NC. Aluminium-alloy airframe, with pod.

Production status: see A-10 Silver Eagle text, number completed NC.

GENERAL - This aircraft is intended as a trainer for those wishing to fly the single-seat *A-10 Silver Eagle* or other Mitchell flying wings, and is very similar to the *A-10* in design, though the structure is beefed up and the wing is larger. A Rotax 447 is fitted to cope with the extra weight, and there are full dual controls.
As with the single-seater, the aircraft's future is uncertain at the time of going to press.

EXTERNAL DIMENSIONS & AREAS - Wing span 37.3 ft, 11.4 m. Total wing area 170 ft², 15.8 m². Aspect ratio 8.2/1. Other data NC.

POWER PLANT - engine. Max power 42 hp at 6000 rpm. Propeller diameter and pitch 52x30 inch, 1.32x0.76 m. Belt reduction, ratio 2.0/1. Max static thrust NC. Power per unit area 0.25 hp/ft², 2.7 hp/m². Fuel capacity 5.0 US gal, 4.2 Imp gal, 18.9 litre.

WEIGHTS & LOADINGS - Empty weight 350 lb, 159 kg. Max take-off weight 750 lb, 340 kg. Payload 400 lb, 181 kg.

Max wing loading 4.41 lb/ft², 21.5 kg/m². Max power loading 17.9 lb/hp, 8.1 kg/hp. Load factors NC.

PERFORMANCE * - Never exceed speed 80 mph, 129 kph. Max cruising speed 63 mph, 101 kph. Stalling speed 29 mph, 47 kph. Max climb rate at sea level 650 ft/min, 3.3 m/s. Range at average cruising speed 120 mile, 193 km. Other data NC.

*Under unspecified test conditions.

MONNETT

Monnett Experimental Aircraft Inc, 895 West 20th Avenue, PO Box 2984, Oshkosh, Wisconsin 54903; tel (414) 426-1212. President: John T Monnett.

MONNETT MONERAI P
(Three-axis)

Single-seat single-engined mid-wing monoplane with conventional three-axis control. Wing has unswept leading and trailing edges, and constant chord; flaps fitted; V-tail. Pitch/yaw control by ruddervator; roll control by full-span ailerons; control inputs through stick for pitch/roll and pedals for yaw. Cantilever wing; wing profile NC; 100% double-surface. Undercarriage has two wheels in tandem; no suspension on either wheel. No ground steering. Brake on main wheel. Aluminium-alloy tube/glass-fibre airframe, totally enclosed. Engine mounted above wing, driving pusher propeller.

Production status: current, number completed NC.

GENERAL - John Monnett founded his company to sell plans and some components for his *Sonerai* Formula V racer, which was voted best single-seat VW-engined aircraft at the '71 Oshkosh. Subsequently his attention turned to gliding and he produced the *Monerai*, a kit-built solo glider of average performance - 28/1 glide angle at 60 mph (97 kph), and sink of 160 ft/min (0.8 m/s). Before long he produced a powered version called appropriately enough the *Monerai P*, the sailplane becoming *Monerai S* to avoid confusion.
Too fast for a US-style ultralight and with too high a wing loading for the FAI microlight category, the aircraft appeals to soaring enthusiasts rather than tube-and-Dacron reared ultralighters - hence its provision for oxygen and radio. Full-span flaps are fitted, arranged to permit negative (up) settings for high-speed flight, positive (down) settings for thermalling, and 90° down for landing. Also notable is the

Moni *with tricycle undercarriage.*

single-pin tail surface attachment. The side-mounted stick has a bungee trim system, while the flap handle incorporates the brake.
Monerai Ps come with either a Zenoah G25B engine (the version described below) or a KFM 107 giving 25 hp at 7300 rpm, though we have also heard of one using a three-cylinder Konig.
Price: NC.

EXTERNAL DIMENSIONS & AREAS - Length overall 19.7 ft, 5.96 m. Height overall 4.3 ft, 1.32 m. Wing span 36.0 ft, 10.97 m. Constant chord 2.2 ft, 0.66 m. Sweepback 0°. Total wing area 78 ft², 7.2 m². Aspect ratio 16.6/1. Other data NC.

POWER PLANT - Zenoah G25B engine. Max power 20 hp at 6500 rpm. Propeller diameter and pitch NC. Belt reduction, ratio NC. Max static thrust NC. Power per unit area 0.26 hp/ft², 2.8 hp/m². Fuel capacity 1.0 US gal, 0.8 Imp gal, 3.8 litre.

WEIGHTS & LOADINGS - Empty weight 270 lb, 122 kg. Max take-off weight 500 lb, 227 kg. Payload 230 lb, 104 kg. Max wing loading 6.41 lb/ft², 31.2 kg/m². Max power loading 25.0 lb/hp, 11.3 kg/hp. Load factors NC recommended; +5.2, -5.2 ultimate.

PERFORMANCE* - Max level speed 90 mph, 145 kph. Never exceed speed 120 mph, 193 kph. Max cruising speed 60 mph, 97 kph. Stalling speed 40 mph, 64 kph. Max climb rate at sea level 300 ft/min, 1.5 m/s. Min sink rate 160 ft/min at 55 mph, 0.8 m/s at 88 kph. Best glide ratio with power off 22/1 at 60 mph, 97 kph. Take-off distance 500 ft, 152 m. Other data NC.

*Under unspecified test conditions.

MONNETT *MONI*
(Three-axis)

Single-seat single-engined low-wing monoplane with conventional three-axis control. Wing has unswept leading and trailing edges, and constant chord; V-tail. Pitch/yaw control by ruddervator; roll control by full-span ailerons; control inputs through stick for pitch/roll and pedals for yaw. Cantilever wing; wing profile NC; 100% double-surface. Undercarriage has two wheels in tandem with wing tip wheels (three wheels in tricycle formation optional); no suspension on either wheel (no suspension on nosewheel and axle-flex suspension on main wheels with tricycle undercarriage). Push-right go-right tailwheel steering (nosewheel with tricycle undercarriage), connected to yaw control. Air brake on main wheel (air brake under fuselage with tricycle undercarriage) plus air brakes on wings. Aluminium-alloy tube airframe, totally enclosed. Engine mounted at wing height, driving tractor propeller.

Production status: current, number completed NC.

GENERAL - A little overweight and too fast for the ultralight category, the *Moni* is nevertheless one of the top lightweight sport planes available, and was first shown by John Monnett at the '81 Oshkosh. It draws on his experience with the *Sonerai* and, particularly, the *Monex,* a high-performance one-off which John built in 1980 and which is of similar configuration.
Offered as a complete kit for US$6000 with sailplane-style undercarriage (single main wheel plus tailwheel), or for US$6400 with conventional tricycle gear, the *Moni* is a slick performer either way. Although there is a performance price to be paid for the drag of three wheels, it's one which many lightplane pilots are willing to pay, even though the handling of the monowheel arrangement is said to be excellent.

The wing uses an I-section extruded aluminium-alloy spar plus a false spar on which are mounted the 'flaperons', which hinge upwards by 8° to reduce drag in cruise. Skinning consists of a single sheet rolled round the leading edge, bonded to the ribs and rivetted to the false spar, each wing weighing only 50 lb (23 kg) and being removable for transportation. This construction method is time consuming, 500-600 h being a common build time, but the job is not difficult and the kit is very complete.

Early models used a very noisy direct-drive KFM 107 engine, but a prop change had reduced the noise by the time the *Moni* was tested in the July '84 edition of *Glider Rider*. Further improvements since then include spoilers to act as air brakes and reduce landing distance, a prop spinner and a carburettor airfilter. There's also an option of the 30 hp KFM, incorporating like the smaller engine an electric start, and a 6.0 US gal tank (5.0 Imp gal, 22.7 litre). Our data refers to the KFM 107-engined machine with standard tank and monowheel undercarriage; where different, figures for the tricycle version are shown in parentheses.

EXTERNAL DIMENSIONS & AREAS - Length overall 15.0 ft, 4.57 m. Height overall 3.3 ft, 0.99 m. Wing span 27.5 ft, 8.38 m. Constant chord 2.9 ft, 0.88 m. Sweepback 0°. Total wing area 75 ft², 7.0 m². Aspect ratio 10.1/1. Other data NC.

POWER PLANT - KFM 107 engine. Max power 22 hp at 6300 rpm. Propeller diameter and pitch 33x18 inch, 0.84x0.46 m. No reduction. Max static thrust NC. Power per unit area 0.29 hp/ft², 3.2 hp/m². Fuel capacity 4.0 US gal, 3.3 Imp gal, 15.1 litre.

WEIGHTS & LOADINGS - Empty weight 260(280) lb, 118(127) kg. Max take-off weight 560 lb, 254 kg. Payload 300(280) lb, 136(127) kg. Max wing loading 7.47 lb/ft², 36.3 kg/m². Max power loading 25.5 lb/hp, 11.5 kg/hp. Load factors +6.0, -4.0 design; NC ultimate.

PERFORMANCE* - Max level speed 120(NC) mph, 193(NC) kph. Never exceed speed 150 mph, 241 kph. Max cruising speed 110(105) mph, 177(169) kph. Economic cruising speed 80 mph, 129 kph. Stalling speed 38 mph, 61 kph. Max climb rate at sea level 500 ft/min, 2.5 m/s. Best glide ratio with power off 20(18)/1 at 50 mph, 80 kph. Take-off distance 400 ft, 122 m. Range at average cruising speed 320(300) mile, 515(483) km. Other data NC.

*Under unspecified test conditions.

NOSTALGAIR

Nostalgair Inc, PO Box 2049, Hendersonville, N Carolina 28739; tel (704) 692-8566. President: Jimm Gill. Vice-president engineering: Ken Allen. Vice-president production: Bob Counts.

NOSTALGAIR *N-3 PUP*
(Three-axis)

Single-seat single-engined high-wing monoplane with conventional three-axis control. Wing has unswept leading and trailing edges, and constant chord; conventional tail. Pitch control by elevator on tail; yaw control by fin-mounted rudder; roll control by 60%-span ailerons; control inputs through stick for pitch/roll and pedals for yaw. Wing braced from below by struts; wing profile Gotinge 847; 100% double-surface. Undercarriage has three wheels in tail-dragger formation; torsion-bar suspension on tailwheel and bungee suspension on main wheels. Push-right go-right tailwheel steering connected to yaw control; also optional differential braking. Optional brakes on main wheels. Steel-tube airframe, partially enclosed (totally enclosed optional). Engine mounted below wing, driving tractor propeller.

Production status: current, 26 completed by 9 November '84.

GENERAL - Of all the Piper *J-3 Cub* replicas, the *N-3 Pup* is probably the most faithful copy of all, using a four-stroke

engine allied to materials and construction techniques that have been around almost as long as there have been aircraft - welded steel airframe and fabric covering - to give it real old-time appeal. Nevertheless it is fully ultralight legal and mildly aerobatic.

Nostaigair was started when Jimm Gill parted company with Jesse Anglin's company (now called Grover) and set up independently to build his own *Cub* replica and to continue developing the four-stroke Global engine originally intended for Anglin's *J-3 Kitten*. This 37 hp Global flat-twin engine is a low-revving unit that needs no reduction drive. With exhaust, carburettion, air and oil filters, it weighs 76 lb (34 kg) and is claimed to consume 1.5-1.8 US gal/h (1.3-1.5 Imp gal/h, 5.7-6.8 litre/h), a figure which sounds perfectly realistic but does not agree with the N-3's quoted range, printed below.

The aircraft is supplied as a complete 75 h kit, with engine mount, fuselage, tail feathers and landing gear ready welded from 4130 chrome-moly steel, sandblasted, primered and epoxy painted. All the struts come cut to length and ready to rig, while the spars - front, rear, and aileron - are pre-drilled and treated, ready for mounting to the stamped aluminium ribs. Stits Dacron cloth comes complete with adhesive, edge tape, sealant, ultraviolet-resistant paint and, to finish the job off, some *Pup* decals. Wheels, tyres, six instruments, all hardware and fittings are supplied.

Options include carburettor heat, in-flight mixture control, door/window package, brakes, a ballistic 'chute, shoulder harness and bungee covers for the landing gear. Floats and skis can also be fitted. Rigging time is 20 min. The *N-3 Pup* costs US$6595 as a kit or US$8095 ready to fly.

Also available from Nostalgair is the heavier *Questor,* a homebuilt which is well out of the ultralight class, having a 120 mph cruise and 47 mph stall (193 and 76 kph). It costs US$7500.

EXTERNAL DIMENSIONS & AREAS - Length overall 16.5 ft, 5.03 m. Height overall 5.0 ft, 1.52 m. Wing span 30.0 ft, 9.14 m. Constant chord 4.0 ft, 1.22 m. Dihedral 5°. Sweepback 0°. Tailplane span 7.3 ft, 2.24 m. Fin height 3.5 ft, 1.07 m. Total wing area 123 ft^2, 11.4 m^2. Total aileron area 15.4 ft^2, 1.43 m^2. Fin area 6.6 ft^2, 0.61 m^2. Rudder area 4.4 ft^2, 0.41 m^2. Tailplane area 7.6 ft^2, 0.71 m^2. Total elevator area 7.6 ft^2, 0.71 m^2. Aspect ratio 7.3/1. Wheel track 7.4 ft, 2.26 m. Wheelbase 12.9 ft, 3.93 m. Nosewheel diameter overall 4 inch, 10 cm. Main wheels diameter overall 13 inch, 33 cm.

POWER PLANT - Global engine. Max power 35 hp at 3250 rpm. Propeller diameter and pitch 54x22 inch, 1.37x0.56 m. No reduction. Max static thrust 220 lb, 100 kg. Power per unit area 0.28 hp/ft^2, 3.07 hp/m^2. Fuel capacity 4.7 US gal, 3.9 Imp gal, 17.8 litre.

WEIGHTS & LOADINGS - Empty weight 250 lb, 113 kg. Max take-off weight 535 lb, 243 kg. Payload 285 lb, 129 kg. Max wing loading 4.35 lb/ft^2, 21.3 kg/m^2. Max power loading 15.3 lb/hp, 6.9 kg/hp. Load factors £6.0, -3.0 recommended; NC ultimate.

PERFORMANCE* - Max level speed 60 mph, 97 kph. Never exceed speed 90 mph, 145 kph. Max cruising speed 60 mph, 97 kph. Economic cruising speed 50 mph, 80 kph. Stalling speed 26 mph, 42 kph. Max climb rate at sea level 700 ft/min, 3.6 m/s. Min sink rate NC. Best glide ratio with power off 11/1 at NC speed. Take-off distance 100 ft, 30 m. Landing distance 200 ft, 61 m. Service ceiling 8000 ft, 2440 m. Range at average cruising speed 258 mile, 415 km. Noise level NC.

*Under unspecified test conditions.

NOSTALGAIR *N-2 MOUSE*
(Three-axis)

Summary similar to N-3 Pup.

Production status: current, number completed NC.

GENERAL - Announced by Nostalgair as we went to press was the *N-2 Mouse,* a structurally similar machine to the *N-3 Pup* but styled like an Aeronca C-2. The latter never won any prizes for elegance, and Jimm Gill readily admits that the *Mouse* is similarly ugly, though in an endearing way. Purchase arrangements, prices and options are all similar to the *Pup,* but the 35 hp Global engine is only an option, standard fitment being a similar 25 hp unit. Our data below refers to the more powerful version.

EXTERNAL DIMENSIONS & AREAS - Length overall 17.0 ft, 5.18 m. Height overall 5.0 ft, 1.52 m. Wing span 29.0 ft, 8.84 m. m. Total wing area 134 ft^2, 12.4 m^2. Aspect ratio 6.3/1. Other data NC.

POWER PLANT - See *N-3 Pup* except: Power per unit area 0.26 hp/ft^2, 2.8 hp/m^2.

WEIGHTS & LOADINGS - Empty weight 250 lb, 113 kg. Max take-off weight 525 lb, 238 kg. Payload 275 lb, 125 kg. Max wing loading 3.92 lb/ft^2, 19.2 kg/m^2. Max power loading 15.0 lb/hp, 6.8 kg/hp. Load factors NC.

PERFORMANCE* - Max level speed 63 mph, 101 kph. Never exceed speed 85 mph, 137 kph. Max cruising speed 60 mph, 97 kph. Economic cruising speed 58 mph, 93 kph. Stalling speed 27 mph, 43 kph. Max climb rate at sea level 650 ft/min, 3.3 m/s. Other data NC.

*Under unspecified test conditions.

PARAPLANE CORPORATION

Paraplane Corporation, 5801 Magnolia Avenue, Pennsauken, New Jersey 08109; tel (609) 663-2234; tx 710-8920105. Proprietor: Steve Snyder.

PARAPLANE CORPORATION
PARAPLANE PM1 and PM1-SS
(Ascending parachute)

Single-seat twin-engined motorised parachute. Ram-air parachute with 14 cells and constant chord. Pilot suspended below wing in trike unit, using pedals to tension rigging lines and thus control yaw; no other aerodynamic controls. Parachute braced by rigging lines, number NC; 100% double-surface. Undercarriage has three wheels in tricycle formation; rubber suspension on nosewheel and axle-flex suspension on main wheels. Push-right go-right nosewheel steering connected to aerodynamic controls; castoring main wheels. No brakes. Aluminium-alloy tube trike unit, completely open. Engine mounted below wing, driving pusher propeller. Trike unit made from extruded square-section

7129-T5 and 6061-T6 tube. Wing made from ripstop nylon.

Production status: current, 575 completed.

GENERAL - To Steve Snyder must go the credit for developing a completely new form of flying, and one which has proved itself to be the easiest and fastest way to obtain powered flight.

The concept is simple - a sport-type ram-air parachute with a trike unit rather than a parachutist underneath, the 'chute inflated by a combination of propwash and ram air - but the result is a strange-looking machine that caused a sensation when it appeared at the '83 Sun 'n Fun in Lakeland, Florida. Since then the aircraft has become an accepted part of the ultralight scene - accepted enough, in fact, to be imitated, by the Freedom Fliers *Buckeye*. The principal difference between the two is that the *Paraplane* is twin-engined with contra-rotating props, to ensure there is no torque reaction problem, but the controls are also a little different, in that with the *Paraplane* yaw is controlled by foot pedals not sticks.

Otherwise the principle is much the same: there are no pitch or roll controls, altitude being throttle-dependent. Airspeed is constant, regardless of throttle opening (apart from when throttled right back), and yaw control is achieved by tensioning the appropriate rigging lines. Paraplane Corporation does not quote a stall speed, but it seems that the minimum airspeed at which the pilot has any yaw control is around 9 mph (14 kph).

Two Solo engines provide the power, and the main wheels castor to allow for straight ahead landing rolls even if you come down a bit out of shape. Getting aloft can be done in two ways: if you're flying alone, you lay the 'chute on the ground behind the trike unit and then rely on forward motion of the latter to pull the 'chute out of its bag. If you have a helper, he or she holds the canopy up behind the trike unit and allows it to be pulled free as the aircraft sets off, and this method gives the shortest take-off run, typically 200-250 ft (60-75 m). Rigging time is approximately 15 min, and the whole aircraft will fit in the boot of a standard size American car.

Two versions are offered: the normal *Paraplane PM1* for

US$3995 or the *PM1-SS* with 'super standard' power system for US$4250. Options include altimeter, custom colours, and tuned exhausts.

EXTERNAL DIMENSIONS & AREAS - Length overall 5.7* ft, 1.73* m. Height overall before flight 5.6 ft, 1.71 m. Wing span 30.5 ft, 9.30 m. Constant chord 13.0 ft, 3.96 m. Sweepback 0°. Total wing area 400 ft^2, 37.2 m^2. Aspect ratio 2.3/1. Other data NC.

POWER PLANT - Two Solo engines. Max power 15 hp each at 7000 rpm. Propeller diameter and pitch 51x28 inch, 1.30x0.71 m. V-belt reduction, ratio 2.5/1. Max static thrust 200 lb, 91 kg. Power per unit area 0.08 hp/ft^2, 0.8 hp/m^2. Fuel capacity 4.5 US gal, 3.8 Imp gal, 17.0 litre.

WEIGHTS & LOADINGS - Empty weight 160 lb, 73 kg. Max take-off weight 350 lb, 159 kg. Payload 190 lb, 86 kg. Max wing loading 0.88 lb/ft^2, 4.3 kg/m^2. Max power loading 11.67 lb/hp, 5.3 kg/hp. Load factors +9.0, -NC recommended; +9.0, -NC ultimate.

PERFORMANCE -** Max level speed 26 mph, 42 kph. Max cruising speed 26 mph, 42 kph. Economic cruising speed 26 mph, 42 kph. Stalling speed see text. Max climb rate at sea level 250 ft/min, 1.3 m/s. Best glide ratio with power off 3/1*** at 21*** mph, 34*** kph. Take-off distance see text. Landing distance *30* ft, *10* m. Range at average cruising speed 30 mile, 48 km. Other data NC.

*Without wing.

**Under the following test conditions - Airfield altitude 0 ft, 0 m. Ground temperature 59°F, 15°C. Ground pressure NC. Ground windspeed 0 mph, 0 kph. Test payload 170 lb, 77 kg.

***With only one engine off - 12/1 at 26 mph, 42 kph.

PHANTOM

Phantom Aircraft Inc, 1450 NE 39th Street, Ocala, Florida 32670; tel (904) 629-5849.

PHANTOM *CLOUDANCER*

(Three-axis)

Single-seat single-engined high-wing monoplane with conventional three-axis control. Wing has unswept leading and trailing edges, and constant chord; conventional tail. Pitch control by elevator on tail; yaw control by fin-mounted rudder; roll control by full-span ailerons; control inputs through stick for pitch/roll and pedals for yaw. Wing braced from above by kingpost and cables, from below by cables. Undercarriage has three wheels in tail-dragger formation. Tubular airframe, completely open. Engine mounted at wing height, driving tractor propeller. Other details NC.

Production status: current, number completed NC.

GENERAL - If ever there was a confusingly named aircraft, this is it, so we had better start by making it clear that the Phantom company has nothing to do with the famous *Phantom* made by Ultralight Flight, nor with the *Cloud Dancer* of Ultra Sail, nor with the Cloud Dancer Aeroplane Works which manufactured the *Jenny*.

In our last edition we mentioned that Phantom was

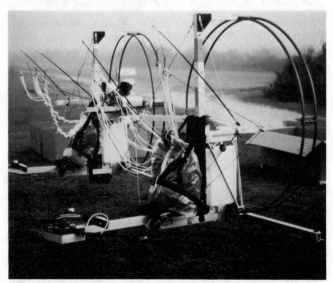

Two Paraplane *trike units freshly unpacked from their boxes. For an illustration of the aircraft in flight, see colour section.*

developing a prototype aimed at homebuilders and called the *Firecracker,* and the *Cloudancer* seems to be a simplified version of that prototype, retaining the same Zenoah power unit and high-wing tractor prop configuration, but substituting kingpost and cable bracing for the *Firecracker's* struts and deleting the cockpit, engine cover and wheel spats which gave the original its elegance. The *Cloudancer* costs US$2950, 4290 or 4950 depending on whether it is bought as a materials kit, an assembly kit, or ready to fly. Homebuilders' supplies are the company's bread and butter, and Phantom also offers kits for various other manufacturers' designs - see subsequent listings.

EXTERNAL DIMENSIONS & AREAS - Wing span 33.0 ft, 10.06 m. Constant chord 4.6 ft, 1.41 m. Sweepback 0°. Total wing area 153 ft², 14.2 m². Aspect ratio 7.1/1. Other data NC.

POWER PLANT - Zenoah G25B1 engine. Max power 23 hp at NC rpm. Propeller diameter and pitch 58x22 inch, 1.47x0.56 m. Reduction type NC, ratio 2.3/1. Max static thrust NC. Power per unit area 0.15 hp/ft², 1.6 hp/m². Fuel capacity 3.1 US gal, 2.6 Imp gal, 11.7 litre.

WEIGHTS & LOADINGS - Empty weight 242 lb, 110 kg. Max take-off weight 474 lb, 215 kg. Payload 232 lb, 105 kg. Max wing loading 3.10 lb/ft², 15.1 kg/m². Max power loading 20.6 lb/hp, 9.3 kg/hp. Load factors NC.

PERFORMANCE* - Max level speed 48 mph, 77 kph. Never exceed speed 63 mph, 101 kph. Cruising speed 43 mph, 69 kph. Stalling speed 27 mph, 43 kph. Max climb rate at sea level 500 ft/min, 2.5 m/s. Range at average cruising speed 76 mile, 122 km. Other data NC.

*Under unspecified test conditions.

BEAUJON *MACH.07*

See Beaujon.

MATHEWS *BREEZY*

See Mathews.

WICKS *BARNSTORMER*

See Wicks.

PHOENIX

Phoenix Development Inc, PO Box 271, Westmorland, Tennessee 37186; tel (615) 644-3324. President: John W Tucker.

PHOENIX *SUNBIRD*
(Three-axis)

Single-seat single-engined high-wing monoplane with conventional three-axis control. Wing has unswept leading and trailing edges, and constant chord; cruciform tail. Pitch control by elevator on tail; yaw control by fin-mounted rudder; roll control by 35%-span spoilers; control inputs through stick for pitch/roll and pedals for yaw.

Phoenix's Sunbird *with optional pod.*

Wing braced from above by kingpost and cables, from below by cables; wing profile 7%; single-surface. Undercarriage has three wheels in tail-dragger formation; bungee suspension on all wheels. Push-right go-right tailwheel steering connected to yaw control. No brakes. Aluminium-alloy tube airframe, with optional pod. Engine mounted below wing, driving tractor propeller.

Production status: current, number completed NC.

GENERAL - The easiest way to describe the Phoenix *Sunbird* is to say it is a Rotec *Rally* with a tractor prop. No doubt the manufacturer would consider that a much too sweeping generalisation, but there is no doubt that their configurations are similar, as are their wing spans and areas. The *Sunbird* is unashamedly a simple machine of modest performance, and was created by John Tucker initially for his own benefit, John finding himself priced out of the market by ever more complex and expensive ultralights.

Straightforward tube-and-Dacron construction and a single-surface wing allow the machine to be offered at the very competitive price of US$3995 in kit form. No build time is quoted for the kit, but it should not be unreasonable as all the assemblies come pre-drilled and all the cables (vinyl-coated stainless-steel) are pre-swaged. Features include an undercarriage claimed to be more rugged than most, a safety roll cage built into the structure, an in-flight restart facility and a glass-fibre fuel tank with sight gauge.

Options include a pod (US$150), ballistic parachute (US$795), floats, instrument panel and instruments, and storage covers.

EXTERNAL DIMENSIONS & AREAS - Length overall 16.2 ft, 4.94 m. Height overall 8.0 ft, 2.44 m. Wing span 30.0 ft, 9.14 m. Constant chord 5.0 ft, 1.52 m. Dihedral 4°. Sweepback 0°. Tailplane span 7.0 ft, 2.13 m. Fin height 2.6 ft, 0.79 m. Total wing area 150 ft², 13.9 m². Total spoiler area 3.0 ft², 0.28 m². Fin area 3.0 ft², 0.28 m². Rudder area 9.0 ft², 0.84 m². Tailplane area 15.0 ft², 1.39 m². Total elevator area 10.0 ft², 0.93 m². Aspect ratio 6.0/1. Wheel track 5.0 ft, 1.52 m. Wheelbase 11.0 ft, 3.35 m. Nosewheel diameter overall 4 inch, 10 cm. Main wheels diameter overall 20 inch, 51 cm.

POWER PLANT - Cuyuna ULII-02 engine. Max power 35 hp at 6250 rpm. Propeller diameter and pitch 54x27 inch, 1.37x0.69 m. Notched V-belt reduction, ratio 2.4/1. Max static thrust 200 lb, 91 kg. Power per unit area 0.23 hp/ft², 2.5 hp/m². Fuel capacity 5.0 US gal, 4.2 Imp gal, 18.9 litre.

Hal Adkins

WEIGHTS & LOADINGS - Empty weight 250 lb, 113 kg. Max take-off weight 525 lb, 238 kg. Payload 275 lb, 125 kg. Max wing loading 3.50 lb/ft², 17.1 kg/m². Max power loading 15.0 lb/hp, 6.8 kg/hp. Load factors +3.0, -3.0 recommended; +4.0, -3.0 ultimate.

PERFORMANCE* - Max level speed 50 mph, 80 kph. Never exceed speed 62 mph, 100 kph. Max cruising speed 45 mph, 72 kph. Economic cruising speed 40 mph, 64 kph. Stalling speed 20 mph, 32 kph. Max climb rate at sea level 550 ft/min, 2.8 m/s. Min sink rate 200 ft/min, 1.0 m/s at NC speed. Best glide ratio with power off 7/1 at 28 mph, 45 kph. Take-off distance 70 ft, 21 m. Landing distance 150 ft, 46 m. Service ceiling 10,000 ft, 3050 m. Range at average cruising speed 110 mile, 177 km. Noise level NC.

*Under the following test conditions - Airfield altitude 1000 ft, 305 m. Ground temperature 70°F, 21°C. Ground pressure NC. Ground windspeed 10 mph, 16 kph. Test payload 200 lb, 91 kg.

PINAIRE

Pinaire Engineering Inc, 1313 Newton Avenue, Evansville, Indiana 47715; tel (812) 477-9818. President: Lon Pinaire.

PINAIRE *ULTRA-AIRE*

(Three-axis)

Single-seat single-engined high-wing monoplane with conventional three-axis control. Wing has swept back leading and trailing edges, and constant chord; no tail, canard wing. Pitch control by elevator on canard; yaw control by tip rudders; roll control by half-span spoilerons; control inputs through stick for pitch/roll and pedals for yaw. Wing braced from above by kingpost and cables, from below by cables; wing profile modified NACA 67; single-surface. Undercarriage has three wheels in tricycle formation; glass-fibre suspension on

all wheels. Push-right go-right nosewheel steering connected to yaw control; also optional differential braking. Optional brakes on main wheels. Aluminium-alloy tube airframe, completely open. Engine mounted below wing, driving pusher propeller.

Production status: prototype.

GENERAL - Those who regret the departure from the US market of the simple, idiot-proof *Eagle* will be most interested in the *Ultra-Aire,* which in many ways is the *Eagle XL* brought up to date. A canard configuration was chosen because of its resistance to stalling, the idea being to produce an easy-to-fly fun aircraft, with good slow-flight controllability and needing minimum attention to piloting. Both wing and canard use modified NACA airfoils, designed to give improved lift at low speeds.

But although the configurations and construction materials are similar, the *Ultra-Aire* could in no way be called an *Eagle* clone; one look at the constant chord wing with its novel tip rudders and fins, shaped to act as saumons so that they block vortex generation over the wing tips, proves that Lon Pinaire has put original thought into the design. Also in marked contrast to the *Eagle,* the undercarriage has suspension on all wheels. Ground manoeuvrability is said to be particularly good, with the *Ultra-Aire* able to turn in the width of 'a city street'.

Lon, who we understand is a professional engineer, places great emphasis on the machine's strength, saying it has been stress-analysed completely, and articles on the aircraft's load testing have appeared in *Ultralight & The Light Plane* (November '84) and *Glider Rider* (October '84). Construction is of 6061-T6 aluminium, with some components using 4130 heat-treated steel. All pinned joints are in double shear, and aircraft hardware is used throughout. Production was just getting under way as we went to press, with aircraft available as a complete 40 h kit (US$6195), or in three part kits to spread the financial load, or ready to fly (US$6995). Options include brakes, wheel spats, a windshield, floats and skis. In addition the aircraft may be used with wing removed and with an optional propeller shield as a recreational vehicle, either on land, snow (with the flight skis), or water (with special hydrofoil floats).

EXTERNAL DIMENSIONS & AREAS - Length overall 14.0 ft, 4.27 m. Height overall 7.0 ft, 2.13 m. Wing span 26 ft, 7.92 m. Constant chord 5.0 ft, 1.52 m. Dihedral 5°. Sweepback 8°. Canard span 10.0 ft, 3.05 m. Canard chord 2.0 ft, 0.61 m. Fin height 2.0 ft, 0.61 m. Total wing area 150 ft², 13.94 m². Main wing area 130 ft², 12.07 m². Canard area 20 ft², 1.86 m². Total spoileron area 5.0 ft², 0.46 m². Total fin area 16.0 ft², 1.49 m². Total rudder area 6.0 ft², 0.56 m². Total elevator area 5.0 ft², 0.46 m². Aspect ratio (of main wing) 5.2/1. Wheel track 5.0 ft, 1.52 m. Wheelbase 5.8 ft, 1.78 m. Nosewheel diameter overall 11 inch, 28 cm. Main wheels diameter overall 11 inch, 28 cm.

POWER PLANT - Cuyuna ULII-02 engine. Max power 35 hp at 6250 rpm. Propeller diameter and pitch 54x27 inch, 1.37x0.69 m. V-belt reduction, ratio 2.0/1. Max static thrust 220 lb, 100 kg. Power per unit area 0.23 hp/ft², 2.5 hp/m². Fuel capacity 5.0 US gal, 4.2 Imp gal, 18.9 litre.

WEIGHTS & LOADINGS - Empty weight 250 lb, 113 kg. Max take-off weight 550 lb, 249 kg. Payload 300 lb, 136 kg. Max wing loading 3.67 lb/ft², 17.9 kg/m². Max power loading 15.7 lb/hp, 7.1 kg/hp. Load factors +6.0, -4.0 recommended; >+6.0, >-4.0 ultimate.

PERFORMANCE* - Max level speed 63 mph, 101 kph. Never exceed speed 75 mph, 121 kph. Max cruising speed 40 mph, 64 kph. Economic cruising speed 35 mph, 56 kph. Stalling speed 22 mph, 35 kph. Max climb rate at sea level 600 ft/min, 3.1 m/s. Best glide ratio with power off 8/1 at 30 mph, 48 kph. Take-off distance 110 ft, 34 m. Landing distance 200 ft, 61 m. Range at average cruising speed 115 mile, 185 km. Other data NC.

*Under the following test conditions - Airfield altitude 400 ft, 122 m. Ground temperature 85°F, 29°C. Ground pressure NC. Ground windspeed 0-5 mph, 0-8 kph. Test payload 210 lb, 95 kg.

PINAIRE *ULTRA-AIRE II*

(Three-axis)

Summary as Ultra-Aire *except: Side-by-side two-seater, 55%-span spoilerons.*

Production status: one-off.

GENERAL - Pinaire's *Ultra-Aire II* is the company's two-seater, and is based closely on the solo machine, except that it has a Rotax 447 engine and a larger main wing and canard. Dual controls are provided, with two sets of rudder pedals, two sticks and a single throttle between the seats.

Lon describes it as a one-off at the time of writing (early 1985) but expects to get it into production at a price of US$7750 in kit form, or US$8750 ready to fly.

EXTERNAL DIMENSIONS & AREAS - See *Ultra-Aire* except: Length overall 15.0 ft, 4.57 m. Wing span 32.0 ft, 9.75 m. Canard span 12.0 ft, 3.66 m. Total wing area 184 ft², 17.09 m². Main wing area 160 ft², 14.86 m². Canard area 24.0 ft², 2.23 m². Total spoileron area 6.0 ft², 0.56 m². Aspect ratio (of main wing) 6.4/1.

POWER PLANT - Rotax 447 engine. Max power 40 hp at 6500 rpm. Propeller diameter and pitch 68x28 inch, 1.73x0.71 m. Gear reduction, ratio 2.5/1. Max static thrust 320 lb, 145 kg. Power per unit area 0.22 hp/ft², 2.3 hp/m². Fuel capacity 5.0 US gal, 4.2 Imp gal, 18.9 litre.

WEIGHTS & LOADINGS - Empty weight 300 lb, 136 kg.

Max take-off weight 750 lb, 340 kg. Payload 450 lb, 204 kg. Max wing loading 4.08 lb/ft², 19.9 kg/m². Max power loading 18.8 lb/hp, 8.5 kg/hp. Load factors +5.0, -3.0 recommended; +6.0, -4.0 ultimate.

PERFORMANCE* - Max level speed 60 mph, 97 kph. Never exceed speed 70 mph, 113 kph. Max cruising speed 40 mph, 64 kph. Economic cruising speed 35 mph, 56 kph. Take-off distance 100 ft, 30 m. Landing distance 200 ft, 61 m. Range at average cruising speed 60 mile, 97 km. Other data NC.

*Under the following test conditions - Airfield altitude 400 ft, 122 m. Ground temperature 65°F, 18°C. Ground pressure NC. Ground windspeed 0-5 mph, 0-8 kph. Test payload 320 lb, 145 kg.

PIONEER

Pioneer International Aircraft Inc, PO Box 631, Manchester, Connecticut 06040; tel (203) 644-1581; tx 710-427-2994.

European agent: Mess und Fordertechnik, PO Box 800609, D-2050 Hamburg, West Germany; tel 040-725 50183; tx 217931.

PIONEER *FLIGHTSTAR*

(Three-axis)

Single-seat single-engined high-wing monoplane with conventional three-axis control. Wing has unswept leading edge, swept forward trailing edge, and tapering chord; conventional tail. Pitch control by elevator on tail; yaw control by fin-mounted rudder; roll control by full-span ailerons; control inputs through stick for pitch/roll and pedals for yaw. Wing braced from below by struts; wing profile NC; 100% double-surface. Undercarriage has three wheels in tricycle formation with additional tailskid; bungee suspension on all wheels. Push-right go-right nosewheel steering connected to yaw control. Brakes NC. Aluminium-alloy tube airframe, with optional pod. Engine mounted below wing, driving tractor propeller.

Production status: see text.

GENERAL - Pioneer International is a large corporation embracing a number of aerospace companies, and when in 1983 it announced the setting up of a company to make and produce the *FlightStar,* it seemed that a major new force was entering the US ultralight industry, a force with an established aerospace background as impeccable as Sonaca in Belgium or Zenith in France.

For a while, that's how it worked out. The product certainly did the company no disservice, being a modern tube-and-Dacron design with full-span ailerons and double-surface wing - an obvious competitor for the *Phantom,* a comparison which in itself is a compliment. Certainly the example that showed up at the '83 London-Paris, complete with optional pod as we show in our picture, attracted many admiring glances.

However, being part of a large group has its drawbacks as well as its advantages, and shortly before we went to press Pioneer announced that production of the *FlightStar* had been suspended because of worries over product liability insurance and the implications that any claims might have

Norman Burr

on the group's other activities. The latest information we have is from the June '85 edition of *Ultralight Flying,* which says that spares will continue to be available, and implies that production may be resumed in due course, but for export only.

Under the circumstances there is no point in listing prices, options etc, so we content ourselves with repeating the data published in our last edition, the aircraft having changed very little in the interim.

EXTERNAL DIMENSIONS & AREAS - Length overall 16.5 ft, 5.03 m. Height overall 7.5 ft, 2.29 m. Wing span 30.0 ft, 9.14 m. Chord at root 4.8 ft, 1.46 m. Chord at tip 4.5 ft, 1.37 m. Dihedral 2.5°. Sweepback 0°. Tailplane span 8.2 ft, 2.50 m. Fin height 4.0 ft, 1.22 m. Total wing area 144 ft², 13.4 m². Total aileron area 26.0 ft², 2.41 m². Fin area 5.0 ft², 0.46 m². Rudder area 7.0 ft², 0.65 m². Tailplane area 10.0 ft², 0.93 m². Total elevator area 11.0 ft², 1.02 m². Aspect ratio 6.3/1. Wheel track 5.1 ft, 1.55 m. Wheelbase 6.0 ft, 1.83 m. Nosewheel diameter overall 10 inch, 25 cm. Main wheels diameter overall 10 inch, 25 cm.

POWER PLANT - Kawasaki TA440A engine. Max power 38.5 hp at 6000 rpm. Propeller diameter and pitch 58x27 inch, 1.47x0.68 m. Belt reduction, ratio 2.0/1. Max static thrust 270 lb, 122 kg. Power per unit area 0.25 hp/ft², 2.9 hp/m². Fuel capacity 5.0 US gal, 4.2 Imp gal, 18.9 litre.

WEIGHTS & LOADINGS - Empty weight 247 lb, 112 kg. Max take-off weight 500 lb, 227 kg. Payload 253 lb, 115 kg. Max wing loading 3.47 lb/ft², 16.9 kg/m². Max power loading 13.0 lb/hp, 5.9 kg/hp. Load factors +6.0, -4.0 recommended; +7.8, -NC ultimate.

PERFORMANCE* - Max level speed 64 mph, 103 kph. Never exceed speed 75 mph, 121 kph. Max cruising speed 55 mph, 88 kph. Economic cruising speed 50 mph, 80 kph.

Stalling speed 25 mph, 40 kph. Max climb rate at sea level 850 ft/min, 4.3 m/s. Min sink rate 350 ft/min at 30 mph, 1.8 m/s at 48 kph. Best glide ratio with power off 7.1/1 at 35 mph, 56 kph. Take-off distance 100 ft, 30 m. Landing distance 100 ft, 30 m. Service ceiling 10,000 ft, 3050 m. Range at average cruising speed 50 mile, 80 km. Noise level NC.

*Under the following test conditions - Airfield altitude 0 ft, 0 m. Ground temperature 58°F, 14°C. Ground pressure NC. Ground windspeed 0 mph, 0 kph. Pilot weight 170 lb, 77 kg.

PIONEER *FLIGHTSTAR MC, DUALSTAR and DUALSTAR K* (Three-axis)

Summary similar to FlightStar *except:* DualStar *models are side-by-side two-seaters.* DualStar K *has brakes.*

Production status: see text.

GENERAL - These three aircraft are all derivatives of the *FlightStar* and all have the same questionmark hanging over their futures. However, if only for the record, we should explain that the *FlightStar MC* is a beefed-up export model for agricultural and military purposes, while a similarly strengthened airframe is used for the other two, which are both dual models. The *DualStar K* is the best equipped of the two, coming with brakes, instruments, and a ballistic 'chute as standard.

Our data below refers to the *FlightStar MC;* where different, figures for the *DualStar* and *DualStar K* are shown in parentheses.

EXTERNAL DIMENSIONS & AREAS - Wing span 30.0

ft, 9.14 m. Chord at root 4.8 ft, 1.46 m. Chord at tip 4.5 ft, 1.37 m. Sweepback 0°. Total wing area 144 ft², 13.4 m². Aspect ratio 6.3/1. Other data NC.

POWER PLANT - Rotax 447 (Rotax 447) (Kawasaki 440B) engine. Max power 42((42)(50) hp at NC rpm. Propeller diameter and pitch 68(68)(72)x28(28)(32) inch, 1.73(1.73) (1.83)x0.71(0.71)(0.81) m. Gear (gear) (belt) reduction, ratio 2.5(2.5)(3.0)/1. Max static thrust NC. Power per unit area 0.29(0.29)(0.35) hp/ft², 3.1(3.1)(3.7) hp/m². Fuel capacity 6.0(6.0)(5.0) US gal, (5.0)(5.0)(4.2) Imp gal, 22.7(22.7)(18.9) litre.

WEIGHTS & LOADINGS - Empty weight 345(345)(350) lb, 156(156)(159) kg. Max take-off weight 760 lb, 345 kg. Payload 415(415)(410)lb, 188(188)(186) kg. Max wing loading 5.28 lb/ft², 25.7 kg/m². Max power loading 18.1 (18.1)(15.2) lb/hp, 8.2(8.2)(6.9) kg/hp. Load factors NC.

PERFORMANCE* - Max level speed 85(60)(60) mph, 137(97)(97) kph. Never exceed speed 90(75)(75) mph, 145(121)(121) kph. Cruising speed 65(50)(50) mph, 105 (80)(80) kph. Stalling speed 27(30)(30) mph, 43(48)(48) kph. Max climb rate at sea level 1400(800)(800) ft/min, 7.1(4.1)(4.1) m/s. Range at average cruising speed 130 (NC)(83) mile, 209(NC)(134) km. Other data NC.

*Under unspecified test conditions.

QUAD CITY

Quad City Ultralight Corp, 3610 Coaltown Road, Moline, Illinois 61265; tel (309) 764-3515; tx 468556 ATTN: CHALLENGER. President: Chuck Hamilton. Vice president and designer: Dave Goulet.

QUAD CITY *CHALLENGER and CHALLENGER RX*

(Three-axis)

Single-seat single-engined high-wing monoplane with conventional three-axis control. Wing has unswept leading and trailing edges, and constant chord; conventional tail. Pitch control by elevator on tail; yaw control by fin-mounted rudder; roll control by full-span ailerons (full-span flaperons optional); control inputs through stick for pitch/roll and pedals for yaw. Wing braced from below by struts; flat-bottom wing profile with 14% camber; 100% double-surface. Undercarriage has three wheels in tricycle formation with additional tailwheel (tail-dragger optional); no suspension on nosewheel (tail-dragger undercarriage - tailwheel suspension NC) and axle-flex suspension on main wheels. Push-right go-right nosewheel steering (tail-dragger undercarriage - tailwheel steering) connected to yaw control; also optional differential braking. Optional brakes on main wheels. Aluminium-alloy tube airframe, partially enclosed (total enclosure optional). Engine mounted at wing height, driving pusher propeller.

Production status: current, 80 completed (total of all single-seat variants).

GENERAL - Quad City's *Challenger* made its debut at the 1983 Sun 'n Fun in Lakeland, Florida. Its appeal was immediate and it has been selling steadily ever since.
Part of its attraction is the way the buyer can tailor the machine to his or her own requirements. The ailerons can be converted to flaperons (US$119.95 extra) to lower the stall speed and reduce the ground runs, tricycle or tail-dragger undercarriage can be fitted (most customers prefer tricycle apparently), and side curtains can be added ((US$179.95) to make winter flying more comfy. Very much a 'little airplane', the *Challenger* was the subject of favourable flight tests in *Ultralight & Light Plane* (August '84), *Ultralight Planes* (Jan-Feb '85) and *Glider Rider* (August '84), the latter including an interesting build report by Hal Adkins.

Underneath the fabric covering lies a sturdy aluminium-alloy tube structure, the fuselage structure coming to the customer very nearly finished. To assemble the kit requires a genuine 40-70 h, rigging time being some 20 min. Early aircraft were fitted with either a 25 hp KFM 107ER or a Kawasaki, but now the *Challenger* comes with either a Rotax 277 at US$5995 or a KFM 107 Maxi at US$6295. Since the two versions are identical in performance, the extra really buys only the convenience of an electric start and the smoothness of a twin. To get more performance,

the pilot must choose the *Challenger RX,* which is identical to its stablemates except that it has a Rotax 377 or 447. The 377 increases the weight to 249 lb (113 kg) and drives a 52x32 inch prop (1.32x0.81 m) through a 2.1/1 reduction. Options on all versions are as above, plus wheel spats (US$140), brakes (US$185), and instruments (US$495).

Note: Data below refers to a tricycle-undercarriage aircraft without options and with a Rotax 277 engine. Where different, data for the KFM 107 Maxi-engined version is given in parentheses.

EXTERNAL DIMENSIONS & AREAS - Length overall 18.5 ft, 5.64 m. Height overall 6.0 ft, 1.83 m. Wing span 31.5 ft, 9.60 m. Constant chord 4.5 ft, 1.37 m. Dihedral 3°. Sweepback 0°. Tailplane span 8.0 ft, 2.44 m. Fin height 3.0 ft, 0.91 m. Total wing area 143 ft², 13.3 m². Total aileron area 15.5 ft², 1.44 m². Fin area 5.0 ft², 0.46 m². Rudder area 5.0 ft², 0.46 m². Tailplane area 16.0 ft², 1.49 m². Total elevator area 15.0 ft², 1.39 m². Aspect ratio 6.9/1. Wheel track 5.0 ft, 1.52 m. Wheelbase 5.0 ft, 1.52 m. Nosewheel diameter overall 12 inch, 30 cm. Main wheels diameter overall 12 inch, 30 cm.

POWER PLANT - Rotax 277 (KFM 107 Maxi) engine. Max power 28(30) hp at 6300(6300) rpm. Propeller diameter and pitch 52(54)x26(25) inch, 1.32(1.37)x0.66(0.64) m. V-belt reduction, ratio 2.1/1. Max static thrust 200(200) lb, 91(91) kg. Power per unit area 0.20(0.21) hp/ft², 2.1(2.3) hp/m². Fuel capacity 5.0 US gal, 4.2 Imp gal, 18.9 litre.

WEIGHTS & LOADINGS - Empty weight 235(242) lb, 107(110) kg. Max take-off weight 500 lb, 227 kg. Payload 265(258) lb, 120(117) kg. Max wing loading 3.50 lb/ft², 17.1 kg/m². Max power loading 17.9(16.7) lb/hp, 8.1(7.6) kg/hp. Load factors +4.0, -3.0 recommended; +6.0, -4.0 ultimate.

PERFORMANCE* - Max level speed 63 mph, 101 kph. Never exceed speed 80 mph, 129 kph. Max cruising speed 60 mph, 97 kph. Economic cruising speed 55 mph, 88 kph. Stalling speed 27 mph, 43 kph. Max climb rate at sea level 700 ft/min, 3.6 m/s. Min sink rate 350 ft/min at 40 mph, 1.8 m/s at 64 kph. Best glide ratio with power off 10/1 at 40 mph, 64 kph. Take-off distance 150 ft, 46 m. Landing distance 150 ft, 46 m. Service ceiling 12,500 ft, 3810 m. Range at average cruising speed 150 mile, 241 km. Noise level 90 dB at 50 ft, 15 m.

*Under the following test conditions - Airfield altitude 550 ft, m. Ground temperature 70°F, 21°C. Ground pressure NC. Ground windspeed 0 mph, 0 kph. Test payload 200 lb, 91 kg.

QUAD CITY *CHALLENGER II*
(Three-axis)

Summary as Challenger and Challenger RX *except: Tandem two-seater.*

Production status: current, 35 completed.

GENERAL - As so many ultralight manufacturers have done (and wisely), Quad City has designed a two-seater

based on its solo machine. It is very similar to the single-seater, but has more wing area thanks to a deeper chord, a longer wheelbase and of course a second seat. Power comes from the Rotax 447, and there is a trim adjustment to take care of the weight difference between solo and dual flying.

Since its introduction in 1984, the *Challenger II* has proved one of the company's fastest-selling models, and is offered at US$7195, with options as for the solo machines. Ready-to-fly aircraft are available for a surcharge.

EXTERNAL DIMENSIONS & AREAS - See *Challenger and Challenger RX* except: Length overall 19.5 ft, 5.94 m. Constant chord 5.5 ft, 1.68 m. Total wing area 175 ft^2, 16.3 m^2. Aspect ratio 5.7/1. Wheelbase 5.5 ft, 1.68 m.

POWER PLANT - Rotax 447 engine. Max power 40 hp at 6500 rpm. Propeller diameter and pitch 52x34 inch, 1.32x0.86 m. V-belt reduction, ratio 2.1/1. Max static thrust 250 lb, 113 kg. Power per unit area 0.23 hp/ft^2, 2.5 hp/m^2. Fuel capacity 5.0 US gal, 4.2 Imp gal, 18.9 litre.

WEIGHTS & LOADINGS - Empty weight 300 lb, 136 kg. Max take-off weight 800 lb, 363 kg. Payload 500 lb, 227 kg. Max wing loading 4.57 lb/ft^2, 22.3 kg/m^2. Max power loading 20.0 lb/hp, 9.1 kg/hp. Load factors +4.0, -3.0 recommended; +6.0, -4.0 ultimate.

PERFORMANCE* - Max level speed 70 mph, 113 kph. Never exceed speed 90 mph, 145 kph. Max cruising speed 60 mph, 97 kph. Economic cruising speed 55 mph, 88 kph. Stalling speed 30 mph, 48 kph. Max climb rate at sea level 500 ft/min, 2.5 m/s. Min sink rate 400 ft/min at 40 mph, 2.0 m/s at 64 kph. Best glide ratio with power off 9/1 at 40 mph, 64 kph. Take-off distance 300 ft, 91 m. Landing distance 300 ft, 91 m. Service ceiling 12,500 ft, 3810 m. Range at average cruising speed 120 mile, 193 km. Noise level 90 dB at 50 ft, 15 m.

*Under the following test conditions - Airfield altitude 550 ft, 168 m. Ground temperature 70°F, 21°C. Ground pressure NC. Ground windspeed 0 mph, 0 kph. Test payload 370 lb, 168 kg.

RANS

Rans Inc, 1104 East Highway 40 Bypass, Hays, Kansas 67601; tel (913) 625-6346.

RANS *COYOTE*

(Three-axis)

Single-seat single-engined high-wing monoplane with conventional three-axis control. Wing has unswept leading and trailing edges, and constant chord; conventional tail. Pitch control by elevator on tail; yaw control by fin-mounted rudder; roll control by 40%-span ailerons; control inputs through stick for pitch/roll and pedals for yaw. Wing braced from above by kingpost and cables, from below by cables; wing profile NC; 100% double-surface. Undercarriage has three wheels in tail-dragger formation; leaf-spring suspension on tailwheel and bungee suspension on main wheels. Push-right go-right tailwheel steering connected to yaw control; also optional

differential braking. Optional brakes on main wheels. Aluminium-alloy tube/steel tube airframe, partially enclosed (total enclosure optional). Engine mounted below wing, driving tractor propeller.

Production status: current, 33 completed.

GENERAL - Just as we were putting the first edition of *Berger-Burr's* to press, we heard some very brief details of the *Coyote* produced by the Aero-Max company (later renamed Rans) and managed to incorporate them.

Although we didn't know it at the time, the *Coyote* had already been one year in the making, and in the years since then designer Randy Schlitter has been developing and refining the aircraft, replacing, for instance, the original cable-braced suspension with the present more robust arrangement. By 1984 the machine was in serious, if small-scale, production and earning itself a reputation for being easy to fly, yet with light and responsive handling - as Randy puts it, 'a cross between a hang-glider and a *J-3 Cub*'.

The *Coyote* is a conventional enough design, with normal three-axis controls and a centre stick, but those who have seen one in the flesh reckon that its workmanship is above average. Rigging consists solely of assembling the wings, as the rest of the aircraft stays intact, and with two people takes 15 min from trailer to runway. With aluminium spars and fabric covering, the wings fold into a bag 16.0x0.5x0.25 ft (4.9x0.15x0.76m).

A Rotax 277 provides the power in the standard version, which we detail below, though more powerful engines of 36 hp and 42 hp are available. Price in December '84 was US$5995 for the kit and US$6995 ready to fly, with options as follows: doors US$250, disc brakes US$175, bush tyres US$25, 36 hp engine US$300, and 42 hp engine US$500.

A flaps option was under development as we went to press.

EXTERNAL DIMENSIONS & AREAS - Length overall 17.0 ft, 5.18 m. Height overall 5.5 ft, 1.68 m. Wing span 32.0 ft, 9.75 m. Constant chord 4.1 ft, 1.24 m. Dihedral 2°. Sweepback 0°. Tailplane span 7.8 ft, 2.36 m. Fin height 4.0 ft, 1.22 m. Total wing area 133 ft^2, 12.4 m^2. Total aileron area NC. Fin area 12.0 ft^2, 1.11 m^2. Rudder area NC. Tailplane area 12.0 ft^2, 1.11 m^2. Total elevator area 12.0 ft^2, 11.1 m^2. Aspect ratio 7.7/1. Wheel track 6.0 ft, 1.83 m. Wheelbase 13.0 ft, 3.96 m. Tailwheel diameter overall 8 inch, 20 cm. Main wheels diameter overall 13 inch, 33cm.

POWER PLANT - Rotax 277 engine. Max power 28 hp at 6250 rpm. Propeller diameter and pitch 60x28 inch, 1.52x0.71 m. Gear reduction, ratio 2.6/1. Max static thrust NC. Power per unit area 0.21 hp/ft^2, 2.3 hp/m^2. Fuel capacity 5.0 US gal, 4.2 Imp gal, 18.9 litre.

WEIGHTS & LOADINGS - Empty weight 249 lb, 113 kg. Max take-off weight 535 lb, 243 kg. Payload 286 lb, 130 kg. Max wing loading 4.02 lb/ft^2, 19.6 kg/m^2. Max power loading 19.1 lb/hp, 8.7 kg/hp. Load factors +3.5, -1.5 recommended; +6.0, -3.0 ultimate.

PERFORMANCE* - Max level speed 60 mph, 97 kph. Never exceed speed 75 mph, 121 kph. Max cruising speed 50 mph, 80 kph. Economic cruising speed 40 mph, 64 kph.

Hal Adkins

Stalling speed 25 mph, 40 kph. Max climb rate at sea level 800 ft/min, 4.1 m/s. Min sink rate 350 ft/min at 30 mph, 1.8 m/s at 48 kph. Best glide ratio with power off 10/1 at 30 mph, 48 kph. Take-off distance 60 ft, 18 m. Landing distance 75 ft, 23 m. Service ceiling 14,000 ft, 4270 m. Range at average cruising speed 150 mile, 241 km. Noise level 65 dB at 100 ft, 30 m.

Under the following test conditions - Airfield altitude 0 ft, 0 m. Ground temperature 59°F, 15°C. Ground pressure 1013 mB. Ground windspeed 0 mph, 0 kph. Test payload 286 lb, 130 kg.

RD AIRCRAFT

RD Aircraft, Box 211, Mayville, New York 14757; tel (716) 753-2111/2112. President: Robert Dart. Engineer: Emerson Stevens.

RD AIRCRAFT *SKYCYCLE*

(Three-axis)

Single-seat single-engined parasol-wing monoplane with conventional three-axis control. Wing has unswept leading and trailing edges, and constant chord; cruciform tail. Pitch control by elevator on tail; yaw control by fin-mounted rudder; roll control by 36%-span ailerons; control inputs through stick for pitch/roll and pedals for yaw. Wing braced from above by kingpost and cables, from below by cables; wing profile modified RAF-6;

100% double-surface. Undercarriage has three wheels in tail-dragger formation; axle-flex suspension on all wheels. Push-right go-right tailwheel steering connected to yaw control. No brakes. Steel-tube airframe (wood/styrofoam wing), partially enclosed. Engine mounted below wing, driving tractor propeller.

Production status: pre-production, 3 prototypes completed.

GENERAL - This simple aircraft using traditional construction methods is primarily for the homebuilder who wants a low-cost flying machine, for almost any engine of 20+ hp and around 250 cc can be used in the *Skycycle*, when allied to a suitable reduction drive. The wood and styrofoam wing, covered with fabric, should hold no surprises for the constructor, while the fuselage and tail structure are of 4130 aircraft-grade steel tube.

Although advertised in spring '84 in plan and kit form, the company will now supply finished machines too, at a price of US$7700. Plans cost US$50, the company reckoning it is possible to build the machine for as little as US$1400. The basic kit comes minus engine and costs US$2300, but factory-built aircraft are fitted with a Zenoah power unit, so it is this version we specify below. Other possible engines are 22 hp Yamaha 246, 28 hp Rotax 277, and 25 hp KFM.

In the works at RD Aircraft is a two-seater called the *Skycycle II*, but we have no details of this derivative.

EXTERNAL DIMENSIONS & AREAS - Length overall 19.7 ft, 5.99 m. Height overall 6.5 ft, 1.98 m. Wing span 31.7 ft, 9.65 m. Constant chord 5.0 ft, 1.52 m. Dihedral 2°.

Sweepback 0°. Tailplane span 7.8 ft, 2.38 m. Fin height 4.2 ft, 1.27 m. Total wing area 153 ft², 14.2 m². Total aileron area 16.3 ft², 1.51 m². Fin area 8.0 ft², 0.74 m². Rudder area 6.1 ft², 0.57 m². Tailplane area 14.0 ft², 1.30 m². Total elevator area 11.8 ft², 1.09 m². Aspect ratio 6.6/1. Wheel track 4.3 ft, 1.32 m. Wheelbase 14.2 ft, 4.32 m. Tailwheel diameter overall 2.5 inch, 6.4 cm. Main wheels diameter overall 10.5 inch, 26.7 cm.

POWER PLANT - Zenoah engine. Max power 20 hp at 5625 rpm. Propeller diameter and pitch 54x22 inch, 1.37x0.56 m. V-belt reduction, ratio 2.25/1. Max static thrust 190 lb, 86 kg. Power per unit area 0.13 hp/ft², 1.4 hp/m². Fuel capacity 5.0 US gal, 4.2 Imp gal, 18.9 litre.

WEIGHTS & LOADINGS - Empty weight 254 lb, 115 kg. Max take-off weight 454 lb, 206 kg. Payload 200 lb, 91 kg. Max wing loading 2.97 lb/ft², 14.5 kg/m². Max power loading 22.7 lb/hp, 10.3 kg/hp. Load factors +3.5, -2.0 recommended; +5.25, -3.0 ultimate.

PERFORMANCE* - Max level speed 56 mph, 90 kph. Never exceed speed 65 mph, 105 kph. Max cruising speed 50 mph, 80 kph. Economic cruising speed 40 mph, 64 kph. Stalling speed 27 mph, 43 kph. Max climb rate at sea level 500 ft/min, 2.5 m/s. Best glide ratio with power off 10/1 at 35 mph, 56 kph. Take-off distance *80* ft, *24* m. Landing distance *80* ft, *24* m. Range at average cruising speed 200 mile, 322 km. Other data NC.

*Under the following test conditions - Airfield altitude 1340 ft, 408 m. Ground temperature 75°F, 24°C. Ground pressure 1013 mB. Ground windspeed 0 mph, 0 kph. Test payload 200 lb, 91 kg.

RD AIRCRAFT
SKYCYCLE GYPSY
(Three-axis)

Summary as Skycycle *except: No suspension on main wheels.*

Production status: pre-production, 2 prototypes completed.

GENERAL - Very similar to the *Skycycle,* the *Skycycle Gypsy* has a cutaway cockpit to give the pilot more of an open-air feeling, plus a windshield to keep the propwash off his face. The undercarriage lacks the main-wheel suspension of the *Skycycle* but has a slightly wider track, while the tail surfaces are a little different in shape. Wings are identical.
Prices are as for the *Skycycle.*

EXTERNAL DIMENSIONS & AREAS - See *Skycycle* except: Length overall 20.3 ft, 6.20 m. Height overall 6.8 ft, 2.08 m. Fin area 6.9 ft², 0.65 m². Rudder area 5.6 ft², 0.52 m². Wheel track 4.5 ft, 1.37 m. Wheelbase 14.5 ft, 4.42 m. Main wheels diameter overall 15 inch, 38 cm.

POWER PLANT - See *Skycycle.*

WEIGHTS & LOADINGS - See *Skycycle.*

PERFORMANCE - See *Skycycle.*

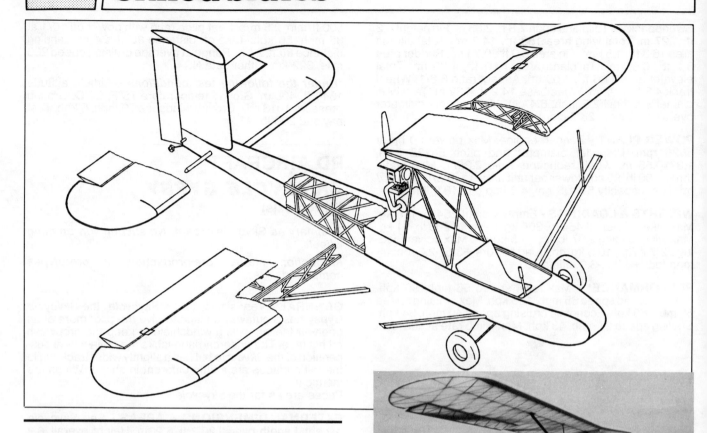

RITZ AIRCRAFT

Addresses etc: See Loehle Aviation.

RITZ *STANDARD A*
(Three-axis)

Single-seat single-engined high-wing monoplane with conventional three-axis control. Wing has unswept leading and trailing edges, and constant chord; conventional tail. Pitch control by elevator on tail; yaw control by fully flying rudder; roll control by half-span ailerons; control inputs through stick for pitch/roll and pedals for yaw. Wing braced from below by struts; wing profile Ritz; 100% double-surface. Undercarriage has three wheels in tail-dragger formation; coil-spring suspension on tailwheel and wooden-axle-flex/rubber suspension on main wheels. Push-right go-right tailwheel steering connected to yaw control. No brakes. Wood airframe, partially enclosed. Engine mounted at wing height, driving pusher propeller.

Production status: current, 75 completed.

GENERAL - Designed by the late Gerry Ritz, the *Standard A* uses a wooden geodetic structure to make a simple, light and inexpensive aircraft, which glides well but is not at its best in gusty conditions, as Michael Bradford observed when flight testing one for *Glider Rider* in May '84. Most of the wood used is machined ponderosa pine, while the curved items like rib caps, wing and stabiliser tip bows, and fuselage nose are laminated of multi-ply poplar or aspen veneer. The cantilever landing gear is laminated of hard maple veneer and is pre-moulded and sanded, ready to be bolted onto the fuselage and wheels.
Traditionally, wooden aircraft are tedious to build, but the

'structure in a slot' method used for the *Standard A* allows this machine to go together relatively quickly - the 32 wing ribs can be assembled in one evening and the whole aircraft in 200 h, it is claimed.
All metal fittings come machined and welded, ready to be bolted or epoxied in place, most fittings being aluminium alloy, with 4130 chrome-moly steel substituted on high-stress items.
The *Standard A* must be one of the cheapest ultralights on the market, at US$2495 for a complete kit. Alternatively, part kits may be purchased to spread the cost: a complete kit less engine is US$1995, wood airframe kit US$1295, power unit kit US$995, and a metal parts kit US$495. Plans cost US$40, plus another US$20 if you want the construction manual, and there are various options available, including a seat belt kit, windshield kit, parachute, decals and instruments. Since taking over the design, Mike Loehle has made various improvements, notably to the ailerons and the wing spars and struts, and now sells update kits for earlier machines.

EXTERNAL DIMENSIONS & AREAS - Length overall 17.0 ft, 5.18 m. Height overall 5.5 ft, 1.68 m. Wing span 36.0 ft, 11.0 m. Constant chord 4.0 ft, 1.22 m. Sweepback 0°. Total wing area 140 ft², 13.0 m². Aspect ratio 9.3/1. Wheel track 4.6 ft, 1.40 m. Tailwheel diameter overall 4 inch, 10 cm. Main wheels diameter overall 14 inch, 36 cm. Other data NC.

POWER PLANT - Zenoah 250 engine. Max power 22 hp at 6500 rpm. Propeller diameter and pitch 54x27 inch, 1.37x

0.69 m. V-belt reduction, ratio 2.4/1. Max static thrust NC. Power per unit area 0.16 hp/ft², 1.7 hp/m². Fuel capacity 5.0 US gal, 4.2 Imp gal, 18.9 litre.

WEIGHTS & LOADINGS - Empty weight 200 lb, 91 kg. Max take-off weight 475 lb, 215 kg. Payload 275 lb, 125 kg. Max wing loading 3.39 lb/ft², 16.5 kg/m². Max power loading 21.6 lb/hp, 9.8 kg/hp. Load factors NC recommended; +4.5, -3.0 ultimate.

PERFORMANCE* - Max level speed 55 mph, 88 kph. Never exceed speed 65 mph, 105 kph. Max cruising speed 50 mph, 80 kph. Economic cruising speed 30 mph, 48 kph. Stalling speed 15 mph, 24 kph. Max climb rate at sea level 400 ft/min, 2.0 m/s. Best glide ratio with power off 15/1 at 30 mph, 48 kph. Take-off distance 120 ft, 36 m. Landing distance 120 ft, 36 m. Range at average cruising speed 250 mile, 402 km. Other data NC.

*Under unspecified test conditions.

RITZ *CABIN MODEL*

(Three-axis)

Summary as Standard A *except: 95%-span ailerons.*

Production status: prototype.

GENERAL - Although we list both this machine and the *Standard A* from which it is derived as 'partially enclosed', the *Cabin Model* as its name suggests offers the pilot considerably more weather protection. The other significant change is to the ailerons, which are made nearly full span to increase their effectiveness.

The aircraft was still at the prototype stage as we went to press, so data is sparse, and it is not even certain whether the Zenoah engine will be retained for production. Price: NC.

EXTERNAL DIMENSIONS & AREAS - See *Standard A* except: Length overall 18.0 ft, 5.49 m. Wheel track 4.8 ft, 1.47 m.

POWER PLANT - Zenoah 250 engine. Max power 22 hp at 6500 rpm. V-belt reduction. Power per unit area 0.16 hp/ft², 1.7 hp/m². Other data NC.

WEIGHTS & LOADINGS - Empty weight 270 lb, 122 kg. Other data NC.

PERFORMANCE - NC.

ROBERTS

Roberts Sport Aircraft Inc, PO Box 9217, Yakima, Washington 98909; tel (509) 457-4377. Proprietor: Larry Roberts.

ROBERTS *SCEPTRE*

(Three-axis)

Single-seat single-engined low-wing monoplane with conventional three-axis control. Wing has swept back leading edge, swept forward trailing edge, and tapering chord; full-span flaps fitted; two-fin T-tail. Pitch control by elevator on tail; yaw control by fin-mounted rudders; roll control by half-span spoilers; control inputs through stick for pitch/roll and pedals for yaw. Cantilever wing; wing profile NACA-63 1412; 100% double-surface. Undercarriage has three wheels in tricycle formation; suspension NC. Push-right go-right nose-wheel steering connected to yaw control. Brakes on main wheels. Composite-construction airframe, totally enclosed (partially enclosure optional). Engine mounted above wing, driving pusher propeller.

Production status: see text.

GENERAL - This intriguing machine was launched in mid '84 with the publication in the EAA's *Ultralight* magazine of an interesting article by its constructor Larry Roberts. Larry explained how a project to build a one-off for a competition at the '83 Oshkosh caught the imagination of him and his sons to the extent that they decided to engineer it for production. A lot of homebuilders claim to be manufacturers of course, but Larry seems to have put his money where his mouth is, moving to a large new factory, hiring extra staff, and withdrawing from the design competition because he preferred not to attract publicity for the aircraft before it was ready for production. Certainly the EAA was

impressed enough to put a full colour picture of the *Sceptre* on the back of the same issue.

Since then there has been no further news of the project, but in view of the construction technique chosen for the production model, with components being heat-cured in large female moulds to produce a sandwich of epoxy/glass-fibre 'bread' and nomex honeycomb 'filling', this is not wholly surprising, as tooling up for such processes is

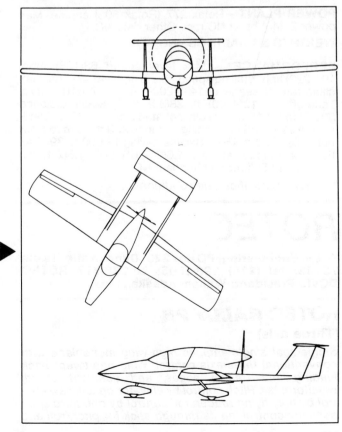

Rotec's Rally Sport *with pod and wheel spats.*

Float flying with the Rally 2B.

an expensive and lengthy task. The intention is to produce the aircraft in two forms, an ultralight with Rotax 277 and a much faster but otherwise similar machine with a Rotax 503; our data below refers to the ultralight version; where different, figures for the twin-cylinder machine are shown in parentheses.

Looking even further ahead, the company has plans for a kit version and a two-seater.

EXTERNAL DIMENSIONS & AREAS - NC.

POWER PLANT - Rotax 277 (Rotax 503) engine. Max power 22(48) hp at NC rpm. Other data NC.

WEIGHTS & LOADINGS - NC.

PERFORMANCE* - Max level speed 63(138) mph, 101(222) kph. Stalling speed 28(29) mph, 45(47) kph. Max climb rate at sea level 1400(2000) ft/min, 7.1(10.2) m/s. Take-off roll 125(100) ft, 38(30) m. Take-off distance 300(250) ft, 91(76) m to clear obstacle of 50 ft, 15 m. Landing roll 125 ft, 38 m. Landing distance 250 ft, 76 m to clear obstacle of 50 ft, 15 m. Service ceiling 13,000 ft, 3960 m. Fuel consumption at cruise 1.6(2.5) US gal/h, 1.3(2.1) Imp gal/h, 6.1(9.5) litre/h. Other data NC.

*Under unspecified test conditions.

ROTEC

Rotec Engineering, PO Box 220, Duncanville, Texas 75138; tel (214) 298-2505; tx 288-777 ROTEC DCVL. President: William Adaska.

ROTEC *RALLY 2B*
(Three-axis)

Single-seat single-engined high-wing monoplane with conventional three-axis control. Wing has swept back leading and trailing edges, and constant chord; cruciform tail. Pitch control by elevator on tail; yaw control by fully flying rudder; roll control by one-third span spoilers; control inputs through stick for pitch/roll and pedals for yaw. Wing braced from above by kingpost and cables, from below by cables; wing profile NC; single-surface. Undercarriage has three wheels in tail-dragger formation; bungee suspension on all wheels. No ground steering; castoring tailwheel. No brakes. Aluminium-alloy tube airframe, with optional pod. Engine mounted below wing, driving pusher propeller.

Production status: current, over 2000 completed.

GENERAL - One of the oldest and most famous of all ultralights, the *Rally* was designed in 1977 by Bill Adaska, who used to work as an aeronautical engineer for Bell helicopters and for the helicopter division of the French Aerospatiale company. The original aircraft were hybrid controlled and used a McCulloch engine, but were followed in 1979 by the *Rally 2,* with 17 hp Solo engine and two-axis controls. A year later came the *Rally 2B,* the first three-axis Rotec, initially retaining the Solo motor but later with a variety of units, such as 2.7/1 reduction-drive 20 hp Solo, 30 hp Chaparral twin, 28 hp Kohler, 40 hp Kawasaki or 35 hp Cuyuna. By 1983 the Rotax 377 was an option, and the company later standardised on this unit, also adopting Rotax power for all the other models in its range. Another piece of history worth noting is that the 1981 *Rally 2B* used ailerons attached to the trailing edge; these have since been replaced by spoilers.

With its simple structure and single-surface wing, the *Rally 2B* is inevitably a low-performance machine, at its best in a light wind on a warm summer's evening. The plus side of the machine's character is its spectacularly short ground rolls, which allow it to be placed in the smallest fields, and many people who were at the 1983 Popham Spring Trade Fair in England will remember watching with great amusement as Rotec owner Jack Bishop landed perfectly safely *across* the long but very narrow strip in a way that few other ultralighters could even contemplate.

To many people, these kind of attributes are what ultralight flying is all about, and one look at the production figures proves that not every pilot wants to go places fast.

Sold as a kit taking around 40 h to complete, the *Rally 2B* costs US$3500 until 31 July '85 and has a rigging time of around 30 min.

EXTERNAL DIMENSIONS & AREAS - Length overall 16.8 ft, 5.13 m. Height overall 10.3 ft, 3.15 m. Wing span 31.0 ft, 9.44 m. Constant chord 5.0 ft, 1.52 m. Total wing area 155 ft², 14.4 m². Rudder area 12.3 ft², 1.14 m². Total elevator area 7.6 ft², 0.70 m². Aspect ratio 6.2/1. Tailwheel diameter overall 5 inch, 13 cm. Main wheels diameter overall 20 inch, 51 cm. Other data NC.

POWER PLANT - Rotax 377 engine. Max power 38 hp at 6600 rpm. Propeller diameter and pitch 54x34 inch, 1.37x-0.86 m. Toothed-belt reduction, ratio 2.3/1. Max static thrust 280 lb, 127 kg. Power per unit area 0.25 hp/ft², 2.6 hp/m². Fuel capacity 3.5 US gal, 2.9 Imp gal, 13.2 litre.

WEIGHTS & LOADINGS - Empty weight 238 lb, 108 kg. Max take-off weight 480 lb, 218 kg. Payload 242 lb, 110 kg. Max wing loading 3.10 lb/ft², 15.1 kg/m². Max power loading 12.6 lb/hp, 5.7 kg/hp. Load factors +3.5, -2.0 recommended; £5.25, -3.0 ultimate.

PERFORMANCE* - Max level speed 45 mph, 72 kph. Never exceed speed 50 mph, 80 kph. Max cruising speed 45 mph, 72 kph. Economic cruising speed 40 mph, 64 kph. Stalling speed 21 mph, 34 kph. Max climb rate at sea level 680 ft/min, 3.5 m/s. Min sink rate NC. Best glide ratio with power off 7/1 at NC. Take-off distance 75 ft, 23 m. Landing distance 30 ft, 15 m. Service ceiling 10,000 ft, 3050 m. Range at average cruising speed 78 mile, 126 km. Noise level 58 dB at 500 ft, 150 m.

Under the following test conditions - Airfield altitude 0 ft, 0 m. Ground temperature 59°F, 15°C. Ground pressure NC. Ground windspeed 0 mph, 0 kph. Test payload 197 lb, 89 kg.

ROTEC *RALLY CHAMP*

(Three-axis)

Summary as Rally 2B.

Production status: current, over 100 completed.

GENERAL - Conceived as a low-cost machine to attract the pilot buying his or her first ultralight the *Rally Champ* was introduced in 1984 and is basically a bare-bones *Rally 2B* with the Rotax 277 substituted for the Rotax 377.

Weight is saved not only by the smaller engine but also by the gear reduction, and by using a lighter rudder assembly. The single-cylinder engine means that performance suffers of course (except that the glide is a little better), but the changes help the aircraft sell at a very competitive US$3200 until 31 July '85 in kit form, making it the cheapest model in the Rotec range. The kit takes around 30 h to assemble, ready-to-fly machines being available for an extra US$680. Rigging time is around 30 min.

EXTERNAL DIMENSIONS & AREAS - See *Rally 2B.*

POWER PLANT - Rotax 277 engine. Max power 28 hp at 6200 rpm. Propeller diameter and pitch 54x27 inch, 1.37x0.69 m. Gear reduction, ratio 2.6/1. Max static thrust 200 lb, 91 kg. Power per unit area 0.18 hp/ft², 1.9 hp/m². Fuel capacity 3.5 US gal, 2.9 Imp gal, 13.2 litre.

WEIGHTS & LOADINGS - Empty weight 202 lb, 92 kg. Max take-off weight 424 lb, 192 kg. Payload 222 lb, 101 kg. Max wing loading 2.74 lb/ft², 13.3 kg/m². Max power loading 15.1 lb/hp, 6.9 kg/hp. Load factors +3.5, -2.0 recommended; +5.25, -3.0 ultimate.

PERFORMANCE* - Max level speed 40 mph, 64 kph. Never exceed speed 50 mph, 80 kph. Max cruising speed 40 mph, 64 kph. Economic cruising speed 35 mph, 56 kph. Stalling speed 20 mph, 32 kph. Max climb rate at sea level 450 ft/min, 2.3 m/s. Min sink rate NC. Best glide ratio with power off 7.5/1 at NC speed. Take-off distance 100 ft, 30 m. Landing distance 50 ft, 15 m. Service ceiling 10,000 ft, 3050 m. Range at average cruising speed 85 mile, 137 km. Noise level 58 dB at 500 ft, 150 m.

Under the following test conditions - Airfield altitude 0 ft, 0 m. Ground temperature 59°F, 15°C. Ground pressure NC. Ground windspeed 0 mph, 0 kph. Test payload 207 lb, 94 kg.

For a picture of the Rally Champ, see colour section.

ROTEC *RALLY SPORT*

(Three-axis)

Summary as Rally 2B except: 75% span spoilers.

Production status: current, over 700 completed.

GENERAL - This single-seater is one of the few ultralights actually advertised as being capable of aerobatics, and has performed these manoeuvres in many airshow routines, often flown by Rotec president Bill Adaska.

The *Rally Sport* has a shorter span than the *Rally 2B* and is fitted with saumons, while in addition aero-dynamically balanced elevators are fitted around the horizontal stabiliser, to give the effect of servo tabs. The airframe is of course built stronger to handle the very heavy loads of aerobatics, while the engine is the big Rotax 503 with centrifugal clutch, allowing an excellent climb rate. To complete the package, the spoilers are increased to three-quarter span, to provide a roll rate of 150°/s.

Price is US$3960 for a 40 h kit.

EXTERNAL DIMENSIONS & AREAS - Length overall 16.6 ft, 5.05 m. Height overall 10.3 ft, 3.15 m. Wing span 27.0 ft, 8.23 m. Total wing area 135 ft², 12.5 m². Aspect ratio 5.4/1. Tailwheel diameter overall 5 inch, 13 cm. Main wheels diameter overall 20 inch, 51 cm. Other data NC.

POWER PLANT - Rotax 503 engine. Max power 48 hp at 6250 rpm. Propeller diameter and pitch 60x28 inch, 1.52x0.71 m. Toothed-belt reduction, ratio 2.3/1. Max static thrust 338 lb, 153 kg. Power per unit area 0.36 hp/ft², 3.8 hp/m². Fuel capacity 3.5 US gal, 2.9 Imp gal, 13.2 litre.

WEIGHTS & LOADINGS - Empty weight 252 lb, 114 kg. Max take-off weight 494 lb, 224 kg. Payload 242 lb, 110 kg. Max wing loading 3.66 lb/ft², 17.9 kg/m². Max power loading 10.3 lb/hp, 4.7 kg/hp. Load factors +6.0, -3.0 recommended; +9.0, -4.5 ultimate.

PERFORMANCE* - Max level speed 55 mph, 88 kph. Never exceed speed 60 mph, 97 kph. Max cruising speed 50 mph, 80 kph. Economic cruising speed 48 mph, 77 kph. Stalling speed 23 mph, 37 kph. Max climb rate at sea level 1000 ft/min, 5.1 m/s. Min sink rate 450 ft/min at 28 mph, 2.3 m/s at 45 kph. Best glide ratio

with power off 6.8/1 at NC speed. Take-off distance 70 ft, 21 m. Landing distance 75 ft, 23 m. Service ceiling 10,000 ft, 3050 m. Range at average cruising speed 83 mile, 134 km. Noise level NC.

Under the following test conditions - Airfield altitude 0 ft, 0 m. Ground temperature 59°F, 15°C. Ground pressure NC. Ground windspeed 0 mph, 0 kph. Test payload 197 lb, 89 kg.

ROTEC *RALLY 3*

(Three-axis)

Summary as Rally 2B *except: Side-by-side two-seater. Roll control by spoilers (span NC). Optional main wheel brakes.*

Production status: current, over 1500 completed.

GENERAL - One of the earliest production three-axis two-seaters, the *Rally 3* was first seen in 1981 and put on sale the following year. Sometimes known as the *Big Lifter,* the machine has since 1982 been available with a 'jump option', which includes a trapeze-type bar for the parachutist to latch onto after he or she has slid the passenger seat back out of the way and is preparing to jump. The second set of pedals is deleted from the specification to give a clear exit path. Other options include saumons, brakes, a pod, floats and skis. The sliding seat is in fact standard on all *Rally 3s* for both pilot and passenger, allowing the centre of gravity to be adjusted to suit the payload.

This military version of the Rally 3 *has been evaluated by the US Army.*

Very similar to the single-seater in concept but longer and with greater wing area, the *Rally 3* uses the same 'servo tab' arrangement as the *Rally Sport,* and is still a popular ultralight trainer, always in demand at American airshows, giving rides to anyone and everyone. It is easily recognisable from the solo aircraft by the addition of a third curved bar up front. Though a Rotax 503 is now standard, earlier machines used a Cuyuna 430R, while some aircraft imported into France were fitted with Hirth 276 engines and dubbed *Rally 4B2S.*
Price: US$4200 until 31 July '85 for a 45 h kit with 45 min rigging time.

EXTERNAL DIMENSIONS & AREAS - Length overall 17.3 ft, 5.28 m. Height overall 10.7 ft, 3.25 m. Wing span 38.0 ft, 11.58 m. Constant chord 5.0 ft, 1.52 m. Total wing area 190 ft², 17.7 m². Aspect ratio 7.6/1. Tailwheel diameter overall 5 inch, 13 cm. Main wheels diameter overall 16 inch, 41 cm. Other data NC.

POWER PLANT - See *Rally Sport* except: Power per unit area 0.25 hp/ft², 2.7 hp/m². Fuel capacity 5.0 US gal, 4.2 Imp gal, 18.9 litre.

WEIGHTS & LOADINGS - Empty weight 285 lb, 129 kg. Max take-off weight 747 lb, 339 kg. Payload 462 lb, 210 kg. Max wing loading 3.93 lb/ft², 19.2 kg/m². Max power loading 15.6 lb/hp, 7.1 kg/hp. Load factors +3.5, -2.0 recommended; +5.25, -3.0 ultimate.

PERFORMANCE* - Max level speed 45 mph, 72 kph. Never exceed speed 50 mph, 80 kph. Max cruising speed 40 mph, 64 kph. Economic cruising speed 35 mph, 56 kph. Stalling speed 22 mph, 35 kph. Max climb rate at sea level 450 ft/min, 2.3 m/s. Min sink rate NC. Best glide ratio with power off 7.1/1 at NC speed. Take-off distance 100 ft, 30 m. Landing distance 80 ft, 24 m. Service ceiling 10,000 ft, 3050 m. Range at average cruising speed 100 mile, 161 km. Noise level NC.

Under the following test conditions - Airfield altitude 0 ft, 0 m. Ground temperature 59°F, 15°C. Ground pressure NC. Ground windspeed 0 mph, 0 kph. Test payload 385 lb, 175 kg.

ROTEC *PANTHER*

(Three-axis)

Single-seat single-engined high-wing monoplane with conventional three-axis control. Wing has swept back leading and trailing edges, and constant chord; conventional tail. Pitch control by elevator on tail; yaw control by fin-mounted rudder; roll control by spoilers; control inputs through stick for pitch/roll and pedals for yaw. Wing braced from below by struts; wing profile NC; 83% double-surface. Undercarriage has three wheels in tail-dragger formation; coil-spring suspension on tailwheel and air shocks on main wheels. Push-right go-right tailwheel steering connected to yaw control. Optional brakes on main wheels. Aluminium-alloy tube airframe, totally enclosed. Engine mounted below wing, driving pusher propeller.

Production status: current, 64 completed.

GENERAL - For all its enduring popularity, the *Rally* is a design firmly linked with the dawn of ultralight aviation. The *Panther* is Rotec's entrant into the modern ultralight stakes, and is everything the *Rally* is not - double-surfaced, totally enclosed, strut-braced, and quick. And just to reinforce the point that this is a totally new design, there's a floor-mounted stick and boom-type fuselage.

Two features stand out as particularly novel. First, the *Panther* has a baggage compartment and offers as an option a cabin heater, hardly oddities in aviation generally but virtually unknown on an ultralight. Second, the company has developed an air-shock suspension system for the main gear, and has lodged a patent application for it. Rotec says the shocks allow the air craft can be dropped from a height of 5 ft (1.5 m) without damage and are adjustable for pilot weight. Though no figure for the track is given, it is quite wide, and this, combined with the air shocks and optional brakes, should give the machine good rough field capability.

Just about the only connection with the *Rally* series is the power pack, the Rotax 277 unit being very similar to that used for the *Rally Champ,* which was introduced at the same time, the two making their first appearance at Sun 'n Fun '84. On the *Panther,* however, there's an in-flight restart facility.

Sold either ready to fly for US$6760 or as a kit requiring 40 h assembly for US$5800, the *Panther* takes only about 15 min to rig, much less than the *Rally* with its plethora of cables.

EXTERNAL DIMENSIONS & AREAS - Length overall 16.8 ft, 5.13 m. Height overall 6.3 ft, 1.91 m. Wing span 34.0 ft, 10.36 m. Constant chord 4.4 ft, 1.33 m. Total wing area 148 ft², 13.7 m². Aspect ratio 7.8/1. Tailwheel

diameter overall 5 inch, 13 cm. Main wheels diameter overall 16 inch, 41 cm. Other data NC.

POWER PLANT - See *Rally Champ* except: Power per unit area 0.19 hp/ft², 2.0 hp/m². Fuel capacity 5.0 US gal, 4.2 Imp gal, 18.9 litre.

WEIGHTS & LOADINGS - Empty weight 250 lb, 113 kg. Max take-off weight 480 lb, 218 kg. Payload 230 lb, 104 kg. Max wing loading 3.24 lb/ft², 15.9 kg/m². Max power loading 17.1 lb/hp, 7.8 kg/hp. Load factors +4.0, -1.9 recommended; +6.0, -2.85 ultimate.

PERFORMANCE* - Max level speed 58 mph, 93 kph. Never exceed speed 62 mph, 100 kph. Max cruising speed 58 mph, 93 kph. Economic cruising speed 54 mph, 87 kph. Stalling speed 24 mph, 39 kph. Max climb rate at sea level 400 ft/min, 2.0 m/s. Min sink rate 400 ft/min at 29 mph, 2.0 m/s at 47 kph. Best glide ratio with power off 9/1 at NC speed. Take-off distance 120 ft, 37 m. Landing distance 75 ft, 23 m. Service ceiling 10,000 ft, 3050 m. Range at average cruising speed 172 mile, 277 km. Noise level 58 dB at 500 ft, 150 m.

Under the following test conditions - Airfield altitude 0 ft, 0 m. Ground temperature 59°F, 15°C. Ground pressure NC. Ground windspeed 0 mph, 0 kph. Test payload 207 lb, 94 kg.

ROTEC *PANTHER PLUS* and *SEA PANTHER*

(Three-axis)

Summary as Panther *except: Engine mounted above wing driving pusher propeller.*

Production status: current, 14 completed.

GENERAL - Very similar to the *Panther,* the *Panther Plus* is Rotec's first single-seater for the experimental category, as it is too heavy and too fast for the ultralight designation.

Aimed both at the ultralight pilot moving upmarket and the lightplane pilot moving down, the *Panther Plus* has a useful cross-country ability. In fact, it seems to be just the thing for a weekend away from it all: it has a useful range, thanks to a 70 mph (113 kph) cruise and an endurance of some 2.5 h at that speed, camping or fishing gear will fit nicely into the 12 ft³ luggage compartment (0.34 m³), and if your chosen landing site is less than ideal the air-shock landing gear should be able to cope.

It is based closely on the *Panther,* the principal difference being the adoption of the Rotax 447 engine, whose extra size necessitates it being mounted above the wing. The machine is FAA-approved as a homebuilt under the 51% rule, and is sold in two versions - the *Panther Plus,* which is a landplane, and the *Sea Panther,* which is the same aircraft fitted with a pair of Lightning floats instead of main wheels. Take-off distance on floats is said to be around 120 ft (36 m). Our figures below refer to the landplane.

Price for a 40 h kit is US$6800 and rigging time is as for the *Panther.*

EXTERNAL DIMENSIONS & AREAS - See *Panther* except: Height overall 6.8 ft, 2.06 m.

POWER PLANT - Rotax 447 engine. Max power 42 hp

at NC rpm. Propeller diameter and pitch 60xNC inch, 1.52xNC m. Gear reduction, ratio 2.6/1. Max static thrust NC. Power per unit area 0.28 hp/ft², 3.07 hp/m². Fuel capacity 5.0 US gal, 4.2 Imp gal, 18.9 litre.

WEIGHTS & LOADINGS - Empty weight 295 lb, 134 kg. Max take-off weight 630 lb, 286 kg. Payload 335 lb, 152 kg. Max wing loading 4.26 lb/ft², 20.9 kg/m². Max power loading 15.0 lb/hp, 6.8 kg/hp. Load factors +3.5, -1.5 recommended; +5.25, -2.25 ultimate.

PERFORMANCE* - Max level speed 70 mph, 113 kph. Never exceed speed 80 mph, 129 kph. Max cruising speed 70 mph, 113 kph. Economic cruising speed 60 mph, 97 kph. Stalling speed 26 mph, 42 kph. Max climb rate at sea level 800 ft/min, 4.1 m/s. Min sink rate 400 ft/min at 31 mph, 2.0 m/s at 50 kph. Best glide ratio with power off 9.5/1 at NC speed. Take-off distance 90 ft, 27 m. Landing distance 75 ft, 23 m. Service ceiling 10,000 ft, 3050 m. Range at average cruising speed 175 mile, 282 km. Noise level 59 dB at 500 ft, 150 m.

*Under the following test conditions - Airfield altitude 0 ft, 0 m. Ground temperature 59°F, 15°C. Ground pressure NC. Ground windspeed 0 mph, 0 kph. Test payload 207 lb, 94 kg.

For an illustration of the Sea Panther, *see introduction to US section.*

SCHMITTLE

Schmittle Aircraft Corp, PO Box 790, Severn, Maryland 21144; tel (301) 760-1706 or (301) 766-5264. Proprietor: Hugh Schmittle.

SCHMITTLE *FREEBIRD*

(Two-axis)

Single-seat single-engined flex-wing aircraft with two-axis control. Free-floating Rogallo wing with keel pocket, pitch control by fully flying tail with separate fixed surface, yaw control by tip rudders, no separate roll control. Pilot suspended below wing in trike unit; control inputs through stick for pitch and pedals for yaw. Wing braced from above by kingpost and cables, from below by cables. Undercarriage has three wheels in tricycle formation. Aluminium-alloy tube trike unit, completely open. Engine mounted below wing, driving pusher propeller. Other details NC.

Production status: prototype.

GENERAL - The history of the ultralight movement shows plenty of instances where old, almost forgotten ideas have been looked at afresh, and Hugh Schmittle's *Freebird* is another example.

It is based on the hinged-wing idea conceived by Octave Chanute before the Wright brothers turned flying from a dream into a reality and consigned Chanute's concept to obscurity. The *Freebird* has a Rogallo wing with a Pterodactyl-style trike unit hung beneath. Unlike a trike, however, the pilot has no control over the wing in pitch, which is thus free to take up whatever angle of incidence the airflow dictates. Pitch control comes from a fully-flying horizontal surface attached to the rear of the wing's keel

ROTEC *PANTHER 2 PLUS*
(Three-axis)

Summary similar to Panther *except: Two-seater.*

Production status: current, number completed NC.

GENERAL - Announced shortly before we went to press, the *Panther 2 Plus* is a two-seat version of the *Panther* and is intended both for training and for pleasure flying. Few details are available at the time of writing, other than those below.
Price until 31 July '85: US $600 for a 70 h kit.

EXTERNAL DIMENSIONS & AREAS - NC.

POWER PLANT - NC.

WEIGHTS & LOADINGS - Payload 500 lb, 227 kg. Other data NC.

PERFORMANCE* - Cruising speed 75 mph, 121 kph. Max climb rate at sea level 860 ft/min, 4.4 m/s. Range at average cruising speed 200 mile, 322 km. Other data NC.

*Under unspecified test conditions.

tube, while a separate fixed horizontal surface is mounted behind the trike unit. Tip rudders look after yaw control. The theory, Hugh Schmittle says, is that the wing's constant angle of attack makes it stall proof and ensures that the wing automatically dumps three-quarters of its positive loads and two-thirds of the negative ones.
However, it must be said that those who have seen the machine fly - it turned up at the Circle X side-show to the '84 Sun 'n Fun - have been less than convinced. At that stage the aircraft had only achieved short hops, and on hearing the theory and examining the machine, British visitor Dave Garrison concluded that it might be wise to keep it that way!
But Dave, himself one of the sport's pioneers, has learned the value of caution in such matters and was quick to qualify his remarks, pointing out in the July-August '84 *Flightline* that 'if it weren't for those pursuing ideas everyone else considers insane, we'd all still be on the ground'. Hugh Schmittle has asked Sport Flight Engineering (see separate listing) to engineer the machine for production and also to produce a two-seat version, and it will be fascinating to see if the Colorado company can prove all the doubters wrong.

EXTERNAL DIMENSIONS & AREAS - Length overall 12.5 ft, 3.81 m. Height overall 11.0 ft, 3.35 m. Wing span 32.0 ft, 9.75 m. Total wing area 180 ft², 16.7 m². Aspect ratio 5.7/1. Other data NC.

POWER PLANT - Cuyuna ULII-02 engine. Max power 35 hp at NC rpm. Propeller diameter and pitch 54x34 inch, 1.37x0.86 m. Reduction type and ratio NC. Max static thrust NC. Power per unit area 0.19 hp/ft², 2.1 hp/m². Fuel capacity 5.0 US gal, 4.2 Imp gal, 18.9 litre.

WEIGHTS & LOADINGS - Empty weight 242 lb, 110 kg. Max take-off weight 457 lb, 207 kg. Payload 215 lb, 98 kg. Max wing loading 2.54 lb/ft², 12.4 kg/m². Max power loading 13.1 lb/hp, 5.9 kg/hp. Load factors NC.

PERFORMANCE* - Max level speed 45 mph, 72 kph.

Never exceed speed 60 mph, 97 kph. Cruising speed 40 mph, 64 kph. Max climb rate at sea level 700 ft/min, 3.6 m/s. Other data NC.

*Under unspecified test conditions.

SIMPSON

Simpson Midwest Ultralights, Route 1, Box 114, Fisk, Missouri 63940; tel (314) 686-3578.

SIMPSON *LITTLE BI*

(Three-axis)

Single-seat single-engined biplane with conventional three-axis control. Wings have unswept leading and trailing edges, and constant chord; cruciform tail. Pitch control by fully flying tail; yaw control by fully flying rudder with additional fin; roll control NC; control inputs through stick for pitch/roll and pedals for yaw. Wings braced by struts and transverse X-cables; wing profile NC; 100% double-surface. Undercarriage has three wheels in tricycle formation; glass-fibre suspension on nosewheel and suspension NC on main wheels. Push-right go-right nosewheel steering. Brakes NC. Aluminium-alloy tube airframe, completely open. Engine mounted at top wing height, driving tractor propeller.

Production status: see text.

GENERAL - Since we described the Simpson *Little Bi* in our first edition as a simple lightweight biplane with no pretensions to high performance, the machine has changed little apart from the substitution of the ubiquitous Rotax 277 for the variety of units previously recommended, including Yamaha KT100S, Cuyuna 215R and Zenoah G25B. Weight has risen slightly compared with the Yamaha-engined version we described then, from 190 to 205 lb (86-93 kg), but construction remains the same, with an aluminium-alloy airframe, bolted and pop-rivetted together. Wing ribs are made of styrofoam capped with glass-fibre tape and covered with Dacron, while the nosewheel is cushioned with glass-fibre suspension.

Aimed primarily at homebuilders, some 20 of whom had bought US$55 sets of plans by November '83, the latest sales figure we have, the aircraft can also be had in the form of a basic kit. This comes without engine but with tubing cut and ribs made for US$2900 - only US$55 up on the '83 price. In this way build time can be cut to 60 h, a scratch-build operation taking up to twice as long but costing only around US$1800, the company reckons. Frankly, both times sound rather optimistic to us.

Part kits are also available to help the builder spread the

▼

financial burden. Finally, we should also mention that the company offers two other designs, the *Panda Cub* (US$5595 ready to fly) and the *Sky Bird* (US$2995 as a 75-100 h kit or US$4495 ready to fly). Both are Rotax 277-engined monoplanes with a 32.0 ft span (9.75 m) and 133 ft² area (12.4 m²), but unfortunately, we have no further information on them.

EXTERNAL DIMENSIONS & AREAS - Length overall 15.0 ft, 4.57 m. Height overall 4.0 ft, 1.22 m. Wing span 20.0 ft, 6.10 m (bottom); 24.0 ft, 7.32 m (top). Sweepback 0°. Total wing area 178 ft², 16.5 m². Other data NC.

POWER PLANT - Rotax 277 engine. Max power 28 hp at NC rpm. Propeller diameter and pitch 50x28 inch, 1.27x0.71 m. Reduction type NC, ratio 2.0/1. Max static thrust NC. Power per unit area 0.16 hp/ft², 1.7 hp/m². Fuel capacity 4.5 US gal, 3.8 Imp gal, 17.0 litre.

WEIGHTS & LOADINGS - Empty weight 205 lb, 93 kg. Max take-off weight 450 lb, 204 kg. Payload 245 lb, 111 kg. Max wing loading 2.53 lb/ft², 12.4 kg/m². Max power loading 16.1 lb/hp, 7.3 kg/hp. Load factors NC recommended; +5.0, -3.0 ultimate.

PERFORMANCE* - Max level speed 62 mph, 100 kph. Never exceed speed 70 mph, 113 kph. Max cruising speed 50 mph, 80 kph. Economic cruising speed 45 mph, 72 kph. Stalling speed 19 mph, 31 kph. Max climb rate at sea level 600 ft/min, 3.1 m/s. Range at average cruising speed 113 mile, 182 km. Other data NC.

*Under unspecified test conditions.

SKYHIGH

Skyhigh Ultralights Inc, PO Box 64, Langhorne, Pennsylvania 19047.

SKYHIGH *SKYBABY*

(Three-axis)

Single-seat single-engined high-wing monoplane with conventional three-axis control. Wing has unswept leading and trailing edges, and constant chord; conventional tail. Pitch control by elevator on tail; yaw control by fin-mounted rudder; roll control by one-third span ailerons; control inputs through stick for pitch/roll and pedals for yaw. Wing braced from above by kingpost and cables, from below by cables; wing profile NC; NC% double-surface. Undercarriage has three wheels in tail-dragger formation; suspension NC on tailwheel and bungee suspension on main wheels. Push-right go-right tailwheel steering connected to yaw control. No brakes. Wood/aluminium-alloy tube airframe, partially enclosed. Engine mounted below wing, driving pusher propeller.

Production status: plans-built, over 250 sets sold and 10 aircraft completed by November '83 (latest production figure available).

GENERAL - Intended as a low-cost route to the skies for homebuilders, the *Skybaby* incorporates a mixture of materials in its construction. Dougles fir is used for the spars, while the ribs are also made of wood, all flying surfaces being covered in heat-shrunk doped Dacron. The fuselage is a plywood structure of 0.125 inch material (3 mm), with foam to stiffen the sides, while a 3 inch (76 mm) 6061T6 aluminium-alloy tube forms the tail boom.

Glider Rider

Power unit is the choice of the builder, but a variety of engines in the 12-20 hp range will fit, McCulloch Mc-101 and Yamaha KT100S units being popular choices. Our data below refers to the former. Build cost from plans is claimed to be around US$1700 including engine, the job taking some 200 h. Though no complete kits are available, this time can be cut by buying pre-assembled components from the manufacturer. Landing gear, controls, reduction drive and seat are all available in this way. Plans consist of 11 sheets and a build manual and in 1984 cost US$55, the most recent price we have available.

EXTERNAL DIMENSIONS & AREAS - Length overall 17.0 ft, 5.18 m. Height overall 6.0 ft, 1.83 m. Wing span 32.0 ft, 9.75 m. Constant chord 4.0 ft, 1.22 m. Sweepback 0°. Total wing area 128 ft², 11.9 m². Aspect ratio 8.0/1. Other data NC.

POWER PLANT - McCulloch Mc-101 engine. Max power 12.5 hp at 9000 rpm. Power per unit area 0.09 hp/ft², 1.1 hp/m². Fuel capacity 3.0 US gal, 2.5 Imp gal, 11.4 litre. Other data NC.

WEIGHTS & LOADINGS - Empty weight 155 lb, 70 kg. Max take-off weight 360 lb, 163 kg. Payload 205 lb, 93 kg. Max wing loading 2.81 lb/ft², 13.7 kg/m². Max power loading 28.8 lb/hp, 13.0 kg/hp. Load factors NC recommended; +5.0, -3.0 ultimate.

PERFORMANCE* - Max level speed 40 mph, 64 kph. Never exceed speed 50 mph, 80 kph. Max cruising speed 35 mph, 56 kph. Stalling speed 24 mph, 39 kph. Max climb rate at sea level 225 ft/min, 1.1 m/s. Best glide ratio with power off 9/1 at NC speed. Take-off distance 200 ft, 61 m. Landing distance 100 ft, 30 m. Other data NC.

*Under the following test conditions - Pilot weight 180 lb, 82 kg. Other data NC.

SORRELL

Sorrell Aircraft Co Ltd, 16525 Tilley Road South, Tenino, Washington 98589; tel (206) 264-2866; tx 856389. President: Mark Sorrell. Vice president: Tim Sorrell. Secretary/treasurer: Lisa Sorrell. General manager: Dennis Nichols.

Australian agent: Austflight, PO Box 489, Ballina, NSW; tel 066 865633; tx AA66237.

Japanese agent: Yasutomo & Co Ltd, No. 7-5, 2-chome, Okino-Cho, Naka-Ku, Yokohama 231; tel 045-641-7801-3; tx J47759.

South African agent: Condor Aviation, 15 Pike Road, Hazelmere, 3201 Pietermariteburg; tel 0331 62938; tx 6-433535SA.

Spanish agent: Luis Rollan, Juan Bravo 25, Madrid 6; tel 1-261-3236.

SORRELL *HIPERLIGHT*

(Three-axis)

Single-seat single-engined biplane with conventional three-axis control. Wings have unswept leading and trailing edges, and constant chord; cruciform tail. Pitch control by fully flying tail; yaw control by fin-mounted rudder; roll control by full-span flaperons; control inputs through stick for pitch/roll and pedals for yaw. Wings braced by struts and transverse X-cables; wing profile NC; 100% double-surface. Undercarriage has three wheels in tail-dragger formation; axle-flex suspension on all wheels. Push-right go-right tailwheel steering connected to yaw control. No brakes. Aluminium-alloy tube/

Hal Adkins

steel tube airframe, totally enclosed. Engine mounted between wings, driving tractor propeller.

Production status: current, number completed NC.

GENERAL - The late Hobie Sorrell owned and operated a sawmill in Washington state and designed a number of lightweight sport aircraft, mostly of wood. Probably the most famous of these is the *Hiperbipe,* a negative-stagger biplane that was both comfortable and possessed of excellent performance characteristics, including aerobatic capability. An offshoot of this is the *Guppy,* also of wood and basically a scaled down version of the *Hiperbipe* that weighed in around 300 lb (136 kg).

When Hobie's sons Mark and Tim decided to enter the ultralight market, they designed a new aircraft rather than lighten the ultralight-ish *Guppy,* and the result was a machine using a welded steel fuselage structure and built-up aluminium wings. But the new machine still *looked* like a *Guppy,* for tradition dies hard in the Sorrell family. With Hobie having produced a whole series of machines carrying the *SNS* prefix (Sorrell Negative Stagger), it was perhaps inevitable that his sons' machine would retain the configuration. In fact, in the works the *Hiperlight* is known as the *SNS-8,* being the family's eighth design.

Although modestly powered, by a Rotax 277, the *Hiperlight* will comfortably exceed the FAA's 63 mph (101 kph) maximum permitted speed for an ultralight, but the brothers have won a concession allowing it to be sold as an ultralight nevertheless. To help lower the stall speed into the ultralight-legal realm, the ailerons droop simultaneously when the elevator is moved to full up, and are thus best described as flaperons. Another interesting feature is that the wings do not fold for transport - the tail does instead, an arrangement that allows a set-up time of only 10 min.

Buyers can acquire a *Hiperlight* either in pre-fabricated

form, with all surfaces Dacron-covered and just a couple of days' assembly to do, or as a kit requiring 100-150 h of work. In the latter version, the wings come as pre-sewn socks; heat-sensitive tape is applied to the wing surfaces, the sock slipped over, and then a warm iron applied to tauten the fabric and activate the tape, bonding the sock to the wing and making rib stitching unneccessary. The two versions cost US$8950 and US$7350 respectively.

Two projects under way at the time of going to press were a float version of the *Hiperlight,* said to take off in 250-300 ft (76-91 m), and an experimental-category version called the *Hiperlight EXP.* As we write, no hard data is available on either, but the latter is very similar to the ultralight except for the use of either a Rotax 377 or a 447, the extra nose weight being offset by using Stits/polydope covering throughout, which adds weight to the tail.

EXTERNAL DIMENSIONS & AREAS - Length overall 15.5 ft, 4.72 m. Height overall 5.3 ft, 1.60 m. Wing span 22.0 ft, 6.71 m (bottom); 22.0 ft, 6.71 m (top). Constant chord 3.2 ft, 0.97 m (bottom wing); 3.2 ft, 0.97 m (top wing). Dihedral 3° (bottom wing); 3° (top wing). Sweepback 0°. Total wing area 140 ft², 13.0 m². Aspect ratio 6.9/1 (bottom wing); 6.9/1 (top wing). Other data NC.

POWER PLANT - Rotax 277 engine. Max power 28 hp at 6250 rpm. Propeller diameter and pitch 60x28 inch, 1.52x0.71 m. V-belt reduction, ratio 2.5/1. Max static thrust NC. Power per unit area 0.20 hp/ft², 2.2 hp/m². Fuel capacity 5.0 US gal, 4.2 Imp gal, 18.9 litre.

WEIGHTS & LOADINGS - Empty weight 247 lb, 112 kg. Max take-off weight 500 lb, 227 kg. Payload 253 lb, 115 kg. Max wing loading 3.57 lb/ft², 17.5 kg/m². Max power loading 17.9 lb/hp, 8.1 kg/hp. Load factors +6.0, -3.0 recommended; +9.0, -6.0 ultimate.

PERFORMANCE* - Max level speed >63 mph, >101 kph. Never exceed speed 95 mph, 153 kph. Max cruising speed 63 mph, 101 kph. Economic cruising speed 55 mph, 88 kph. Stalling speed 27 mph, 43 kph. Max climb rate at sea level 700 ft/min, 3.6 m/s. Min sink rate 250 ft/min at 40 mph, 1.3 m/s at 64 kph. Best glide ratio with power off 12/1 at 40 mph, 64 kph. Take-off distance 150 ft, 46 m. Landing distance NC. Service ceiling >10,000 ft, >3050 m. Range at average cruising speed 180 mile, 290 km. Noise level NC.

*Under the following test conditions - Ground windspeed 0 mph, 0 kph. Test payload 170 lb, 77 kg. Other data NC.

SPORT FLIGHT

Sport Flight Engineering Inc, PO Box 2164, 1328 Winters, Grand Junction, Colorado 81501; tel (303) 245-3899.

SPORT FLIGHT *SKY PUP*
(Two-axis)

Single-seat single-engined high-wing monoplane with two-axis control. Wing has unswept leading and trailing edges, and constant chord; conventional tail. Pitch control by elevator on tail; yaw control by fin-mounted rudder; no separate roll control; control inputs through stick for pitch and pedals for yaw. Cantilever wing; wing profile NACA 43018; 100% double-surface. Undercarriage has two wheels plus tailskid; no suspension on tailskid and axle-flex suspension on main wheels. Push-right go-right tailskid steering connected to yaw control. No brakes. Wood/foam airframe, partially enclosed. Engine mounted below wing, driving tractor propeller.

Production status: current, number completed NC.

GENERAL - Illustrated in our colour section and developed from Steven Wood's one-off ultralight called the *Blue Light Special,* the *Sky Pup* is designed for simplicity and low cost and was announced in 1983.

The design principle is to use foam to carry shear loads and wood to carry bending loads. Ribs and fuselage panels are cut from foam and then bonded to wood capstrips and gussets, with plywood covering for the leading edge and dope and fabric covering for the rest of the flying surfaces. The use of wood extends even to the main undercarriage legs, which are designed to flex.

One of the few two-axis ultralights still available, its centre stick moves fore-and-aft only, while pedals control the rudder in the usual way. The simplicity theme continues with one of the most basic engine mountings ever seen on an ultralight, the motor being simply bolted onto a plate on the front of the fuselage. Needless to say, there are no brakes, but it is possible to use the feet, as there is a round hole in the bottom of the fuselage for this purpose.

Power comes from either a Cuyuna 215 or, latterly, a Rotax 277. We quote below the figures for the Cuyuna-engined aircraft, followed where different by those for the Rotax version.

Sold as plans (US$50) or as a basic kit without engine (US$1100), the aircraft is said to be quite simple to construct, a popular modification being to add a windscreen. Plans-built machines can be completed for US$1200-1500, while kit builders can reckon on being airborne for double the kit price. Construction time is said to be around 400 h, but most builders manage to get aloft in much less time.

EXTERNAL DIMENSIONS & AREAS - Length overall 15.9 ft, 4.85 m. Height overall 4.3 ft, 1.32 m. Wing span 31.0 ft, 9.45 m. Chord at root 4.2 ft, 1.27 m. Chord at tip 4.0 ft, 1.22 m. Dihedral 6°. Sweepback 0°. Tailplane span 6.2 ft, 1.88 m. Fin height 4.0 ft, 1.22 m. Total wing area 130 ft^2, 12.1 m^2. Fin area 4.0 ft^2, 0.37 m^2. Rudder area 5.6 ft^2, 0.52 m^2. Tailplane area 7.0 ft^2, 0.65 m^2. Total elevator area 5.0 ft^2, 0.46 m^2. Aspect ratio 7.4/1. Wheel track 5.0 ft, 1.52 m. Wheelbase 10.7 ft, 3.25 m. Main wheels diameter overall 20 inch, 51 cm.

POWER PLANT - Cuyuna 215 (Rotax 277) engine. Max power 20(28) hp at 6500 rpm. Propeller diameter and pitch 58(60)x22(29) inch, 1.47(1.52)x0.56(0.74) m. V-belt (Gear) reduction, ratio 2.3(2.6)/1. Max static thrust 120(175) lb, 54(79) kg. Power per unit area 0.15(0.22) hp/ft^2, 1.7(2.3) hp/m^2. Fuel capacity 2.5 US gal, 2.1 Imp gal, 9.5 litre.

WEIGHTS & LOADINGS - Empty weight 200 lb, 91 kg. Max take-off weight 400 lb, 181 kg. Payload 200 lb, 91 kg. Max wing loading 3.08 lb/ft^2, 15.0 kg/m^2. Max power loading 20.0(14.3) lb/hp, 9.1(6.5) kg/hp. Load factors +3.8, -1.9 limit; +5.7, -2.8 ultimate.

PERFORMANCE* - Max level speed NC(61) mph, NC(98) kph. Never exceed speed 69 mph, 111 kph. Max cruising speed 54 mph, 87 kph. Economic cruising speed NC(45) mph, NC(72) kph. Stalling speed 26 mph, 42 kph. Max climb rate at sea level 450(1050) ft/min, 2.3(5.3) m/s. Min sink rate NC(260) ft/min at NC speed. Best glide ratio with power off 12(10)/1 at NC(34) mph, NC(55) kph. Take-off distance NC(105) ft, NC(32) m. Landing distance NC(300) ft, NC(91) m. Service ceiling NC(16,000) ft, NC(4880) m. Range at average cruising speed NC(120) mile, NC(193) km. Noise level NC.

*Under unspecified test conditions for the Cuyuna-engined version; under the following test conditions for the Rotax machine - Airfield altitude 0 ft, 0 m. Ground temperature 59°F, 15°C. Ground pressure NC. Ground windspeed 0 mph, 0 kph. Test payload 200 lb, 91 kg.

SQUADRON AVIATION

Squadron Aviation Inc, PO Box 23276, Columbus, Ohio 43223; tel (614) 497-1123; tx 00233 775229-SUPPLY. President: W G McDermitt. Vice-president: Lew Parsley. Chief operating officer: Charles Kibble. Secretary/treasurer: Michael Moushey.

British agent: Air Progress International (see separate listing).

SQUADRON AVIATION
SPAD XIII
(Three-axis)

Single-seat single-engined biplane with conventional three-axis control. Wings have unswept leading and trailing edges, and constant chord; cruciform tail. Pitch control by elevator on tail; yaw control by fin-mounted rudder; roll control by spoilerons; control inputs through stick for pitch/roll and pedals for yaw. Wings braced by struts and transverse X-cables; wing profile NC; 100% double-surface. Undercarriage has two wheels plus

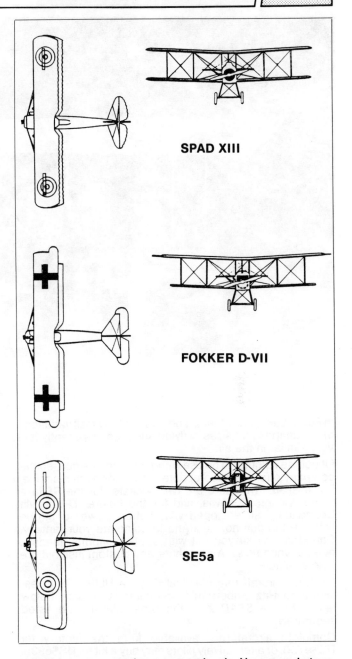

SPAD XIII

FOKKER D-VII

SE5a

tailskid; no suspension on any wheels. No ground steering; castoring tailskid. No brakes. Aluminium-alloy tube airframe, partially enclosed. Engine mounted between wings, driving tractor propeller.

Production status: current, number completed NC.

GENERAL - Even the name Squadron conjours up an image of military nostalgia, and that's just what Squadron Aviation's products are about. The company makes a range of three replica World War I fighters - the *SPAD XIII* from France, the *SE5a* from Britain and the *Fokker D-VII* from Germany - all of them scaled down to be ultralight legal and all of them sharing many common parts. Yet despite this commonality, each has its own unmistakable identity, not only because cowlings, wing spans and tail shapes vary, but also because the original colour schemes are faithfully reproduced.

These excellent copies are proving very popular, the *SPAD XIII* winning the Outstanding Replica Award at the '84 Sun

'n Fun in Lakeland, Florida, and despite the small variations in the shapes and sizes of flying surfaces, apparently feel very similar in the air.

Of course a fighter is no use without a machine gun, so the company offers the appropriate replica for each machine. For a *SPAD XIII* there are twin Vickers, for the *SE5a* a single Vickers & Lewis, and for the *Fokker D-VII* twin Spandaus - all equipped with battery-powered strobe lights in the gun nozzles! And to complete your fantasy, Squadron will kit you out with boots, uniforms, medals, even a white scarf. A parachute and custom insignia are also available.

All three aircraft use identical Cuyuna ULII-02 engines, mated to Ritz Superthrust propellers. Our data below refers to the *SPAD XIII;* the other aircraft are listed separately.

Complete aircraft are available from the factory for US$9750, or alternatively pilots may buy a kit for US$6995. Build time for the kit is 160-200 h, and rigging time is 1 h with two people.

EXTERNAL DIMENSIONS & AREAS - Length overall 16.0 ft, 4.88 m. Height overall 6.4 ft, 1.94 m. Wing span 24.0 ft, 7.32 m (bottom); 24.0 ft, 7.32 m (top). Constant chord 3.5 ft, 1.07 m (bottom wing); 3.5 ft, 1.07 m (top wing). Dihedral 3.5° (bottom wing); 3.5° (top wing). Sweepback 0°. Total wing area 168 ft², 15.6 m². Aspect ratio 6.85/1. Wheel track 3.9 ft, 1.17 m. Other data NC.

POWER PLANT - Cuyuna ULII-02 engine. Max power 35 hp at 6200 rpm. Propeller diameter and pitch 72x33 inch, 1.83x0.84 m. Gear reduction, ratio 3.0/1. Max static thrust >300 lb, >136 kg. Power per unit area 0.21 hp/ft², 2.24 hp/m². Fuel capacity 5.0 US gal, 4.2 Imp gal, 18.9 litre.

WEIGHTS & LOADINGS - Empty weight 250 lb, 113 kg. Max take-off weight 505 lb, 229 kg. Payload 255 lb, 116 kg. Max wing loading 3.01 lb/ft², 14.7 kg/m². Max power load-

ing 14.4 lb/hp, 6.5 kg/hp. Load factors +4.0, -3.0 design; NC ultimate.

PERFORMANCE* - Max level speed 63 mph, 101 kph. Never exceed speed 75 mph, 121 kph. Max cruising speed 52 mph, 84 kph. Stalling speed 22 mph, 35 kph. Max climb rate at sea level 1000 ft/min, 5.1 m/s. Best glide ratio with power off 6.5/1 at NC speed. Take-off distance 80 ft, 24 m. Landing distance 100 ft, 30 m. Range at average cruising speed 173 mile, 278 km. Other data NC.

*Under unspecified test conditions.

SQUADRON AVIATION *SE5a*
(Three-axis)

Summary as SPAD XIII.

Production status: current, number completed NC.

GENERAL - See *SPAD XIII.*

EXTERNAL DIMENSIONS & AREAS - See *SPAD XIII* except: Length overall 15.5 ft, 4.72 m. Height overall 6.7 ft, 2.03 m. Wing span 24.5 ft, 7.47 m (bottom); 24.5 ft, 7.47 m (top). Total wing area 171.5 ft², 15.9 m². Aspect ratio 7.0/1.

POWER PLANT - See *SPAD XIII* except: Power per unit area 0.20 hp/ft², 2.20 hp/m².

WEIGHTS & LOADINGS - Empty weight 251 lb, 114 kg. Max take-off weight 506 lb, 230 kg. Payload 255 lb, 116 kg. Max wing loading 2.95 lb/ft², 14.5 kg/m². Max power loading 14.5 lb/hp, 6.6 kg/hp.

PERFORMANCE - See *SPAD XIII.*

SQUADRON AVIATION
FOKKER D-VII
(Three-axis)

Summary as SPAD XIII.

Production status: current, number completed NC.

GENERAL - See *SPAD XIII.*

EXTERNAL DIMENSIONS & AREAS - See *SPAD XIII* except: Length overall 17.3 ft, 5.28 m. Height overall 7.3 ft, 2.24 m. Wing span 21.4 ft, 6.53 m (bottom); 25.0 ft, 7.62 m (top). Total wing area 162.5 ft², 15.1 m². Aspect ratio 7.1/1.

POWER PLANT - See *SPAD XIII* except: Power per unit area 0.22 hp/ft², 2.32 hp/m².

WEIGHTS & LOADINGS - Empty weight 248 lb, 112 kg. Max take-off weight 503 lb, 228 kg. Payload 255 lb, 116 kg. Max wing loading 3.10 lb/ft², 15.1 kg/m². Max power loading 14.4 lb/hp, 6.5 kg/hp.

PERFORMANCE - See *SPAD XIII.*

For an illustration of the Fokker D-VII, *see front cover.*

STARFLIGHT

StarFlight Aircraft, Liberty Landing Airport, Route 3, Box 197, Liberty, Missouri 64068; tel (816) 781-2250. President: Dick Turner.

STARFLIGHT
XC-280, XC-280HP, XC-320 and XC-320HP
(Three-axis)

Single-seat single-engined high-wing monoplane with conventional three-axis control. Wing has unswept leading and trailing edges, and constant chord; cruciform tail. Pitch control by elevator on tail; yaw control by fully flying rudder; roll control by spoilerons; control inputs through stick for pitch/roll and pedals for yaw. Wing braced from above by kingpost and cables, from below by cables; wing profile NC; single-surface. Undercarriage has three wheels in tricycle formation; no suspension on nosewheel and glass-fibre suspension on main wheels. Push-right go-right nosewheel steering connected to yaw control. Brakes NC. Aluminium-alloy tube airframe, with optional pod. Engine mounted below wing, driving pusher propeller.

Production status: current, number completed NC.

GENERAL - Like many US ultralight manufacturers, Dick Turner's StarFlight company started with a hybrid-control machine. The *Starfire*, as it was known, was developed into the three-axis *Tristar* in 1982 and by the following year production of the original machine had ended, it being clear that the market was moving towards conventional controls. At the '83 Sun 'n Fun the company introduced its third design, a strengthened and re-engined *Tristar* (the latter's Cuyuna 430RR had given way to a Rotax 377) called the *TX-1000*. These three machines were featured in our first edition, but a further derivative, the two-seater *DBL*, appeared after that book went to press.

Collectively these four are known as the *TX* series, to distinguish them from the structurally similar but updated *XC* series which replaced them in 1984. The *XC* series can be had in solo or dual form, the two-seater being known as *XC-2000* (see separate listing). Solo machines come with a choice of two wing spans and two engines: 28.5 ft (8.69 m) for the *XC-280* and 32.5 ft (9.91 m) for the *XC-320*, each with the same chord and each taking the suffix *HP* if a Rotax 377 is substituted for the usual 277. We detail below the cheapest of the four, the small-span small-engine *XC-280*, which costs US$5195 for a 35 h kit. As with all StarFlight designs, plans are also available.

Finally, just to confuse the situation, we must mention an aircraft announced just as we went to press and billed by the company as 'our inflation fighting model', at US$4750 in kit form. It revives the old *Starfire* name and, from the minimal information available to us at the time of writing, seems indistinguishable from the *XC-320*.

EXTERNAL DIMENSIONS & AREAS - Length overall 16.0 ft, 4.88 m. Height overall 8.0 ft, 2.44 m. Wing span 28.5 ft, 8.69 m. Constant chord 4.9 ft, 1.50 m. Sweepback 0°. Total wing area 140 ft², 13.0 m². Aspect ratio 5.8/1. Other data NC.

Glider Rider

StarFlight's XC-280 with optional pod and wheel spats.

POWER PLANT - Rotax 277 engine. Max power 28 hp at 6200 rpm. Propeller diameter and pitch 60x28 inch, 1.52x0.71 m. Gear reduction, ratio 2.6/1. Max static thrust 205 lb, 93 kg. Power per unit area 0.20 hp/ft², 2.2 hp/m². Fuel capacity 5.0 US gal, 4.2 Imp gal, 18.9 litre.

WEIGHTS & LOADINGS - Empty weight 232 lb, 105 kg. Max take-off weight 487 lb, 221 kg. Payload 255 lb, 116 kg. Max wing loading 3.48 lb/ft², 17.0 kg/m². Max power loading 17.4 lb/hp, 7.9 kg/hp. Load factors +6.0, -3.0 design; NC ultimate.

PERFORMANCE* - Max level speed 60 mph, 97 kph. Never exceed speed 65 mph, 105 kph. Cruising speed 45 mph, 72 kph. Stalling speed 21 mph, 34 kph. Max climb rate at sea level 600 ft/min, 3.1 m/s. Best glide ratio with power off 6/1 at NC speed. Other data NC.

*Under unspecified test conditions.

STARFLIGHT *STILETTO XC*
(Three-axis)

Summary as XC models except: Roll control by full-span ailerons. 100% double-surface. Pod standard.

Production status: current, number completed NC.

GENERAL - Often called simply *Stiletto*, this derivative of the *XC* series is StarFlight's high-performance single-seater, and although its airframe is much the same as the humbler models it has a very different wing, with full-span ailerons instead of spoilerons for roll control and full double-surfacing. In keeping with the top of the range image, a pod is standard equipment.
Michael Bradford, editor of *Ultralight Flying* magazine, tested a *Stiletto* in the January '85 edition, concluding that it was a well finished ultralight with no unique virtues but no serious faults either - a good all-rounder.
With the standard Rotax 377 engine, the price is US$5995

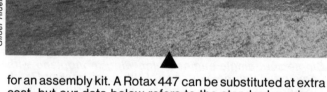

Glider Rider

for an assembly kit. A Rotax 447 can be substituted at extra cost, but our data below refers to the standard version.

EXTERNAL DIMENSIONS & AREAS - Length overall 17.0 ft, 5.18 m. Height overall 7.8 ft, 2.39 m. Wing span 29.0 ft, 8.84 m. Constant chord 5.5 ft, 1.68 m. Sweepback 0°. Total wing area 160 ft², 14.9 m². Aspect ratio 5.3/1. Other data NC.

POWER PLANT - Rotax 377 engine. Max power 32 hp at 5800 rpm. Propeller diameter and pitch 60x30 inch, 1.52x0.76 m. Gear reduction, ratio 2.6/1. Max static thrust 285 lb, 129 kg. Power per unit area 0.20 hp/ft², 2.1 hp/m². Fuel capacity 5.0 US gal, 4.2 Imp gal, 18.9 litre.

WEIGHTS & LOADINGS - Empty weight 251 lb, 114 kg. Max take-off weight 502 lb, 228 kg. Payload 251 lb, 114 kg. Max wing loading 3.14 lb/ft², 15.3 kg/m². Max power loading 15.7 lb/hp, 7.1 kg/hp. Load factors +6.0, -3.0 design; NC ultimate.

PERFORMANCE* - Max level speed 63 mph, 101 kph. Never exceed speed 75 mph, 121 kph. Cruising speed 55 mph, 88 kph. Stalling speed 25 mph, 40 kph. Max climb rate at sea level 600 ft/min, 3.1 m/s. Best glide ratio with power off 8/1 at NC speed. Other data NC.

*Under unspecified test conditions.

STARFLIGHT *XC-2000*
(Three-axis)

Summary similar to XC models except: Tandem two-seater.

Production status: current, number completed NC.

GENERAL - Very similar in construction to the solo models, the *XC-2000* is StarFlight's two-seater, and uses the larger of the company's two single-surface wings. It comes as standard with full dual controls for US$6250, but can be had with just a single set for rather less money. Another version is available, called the *Ag-Light,* and though we don't have any details, we believe that the latter is a single-seat version of the two-seat airframe, engineered for crop-spraying and similar duties. Our data below refers to the standard aircraft.

EXTERNAL DIMENSIONS & AREAS - Wing span 32.5 ft, 9.91 m. Constant chord 4.9 ft, 1.50 m. Sweepback 0°. Total wing area 160 ft², 14.9 m². Aspect ratio 6.6/1. Other data NC.

POWER PLANT - Rotax 447 engine. Max power 40 hp at NC rpm. Propeller diameter and pitch NC. Gear reduction, ratio 2.6/1. Max static thrust NC. Power per unit area 0.25 hp/ft², 2.7 hp/m². Fuel capacity 5.0 US gal, 4.2 Imp gal, 18.9 litre.

WEIGHTS & LOADINGS - Empty weight 295 lb, 134 kg. Max take-off weight 750 lb, 340 kg. Payload 455 lb, 206 kg. Max wing loading 4.69 lb/ft², 22.8 kg/m². Max power loading 18.8 lb/hp, 8.5 kg/hp. Load factors NC.

PERFORMANCE - NC.

STAR-LITE

Star-Lite Aircraft, 2219 Orange Blossom, San Antonio, Texas 78247. Designer: Mark D Brown.

STAR-LITE AIRCRAFT *STAR-LITE*
(Three-axis)

Single-seat single-engined low-wing monoplane with conventional three-axis control. Wing has swept back leading edge, swept forward trailing edge, and tapering chord; conventional tail. Pitch control by full flying tail; yaw control by fin-mounted rudder; roll control NC; control inputs through stick for pitch/roll and pedals for yaw. Cantilever wing; wing profile NC; 100% double-surface. Undercarriage has three wheels in tail-dragger formation. Composite-construction airframe, totally enclosed. Engine mounted above wing, driving tractor propeller. Other details NC.

Production status: current, number produced NC.

GENERAL - Along with many others, we have admired the sleek lines of Robert Brown's award-winning *Star-Lite,* which took first place in the ARV design competition at the '83 Oshkosh. We did not, however, expect to include it in this book, because only at the last minute did we learn that the aircraft had reached production. As is evident from our summary above and data below, information is very sparse

at the time of going to press and we do not even know in what form the aircraft is to be sold, though as the company's publicity material speaks of a 'premoulded advanced composite structure' it sounds as though kits are contemplated.

Much too fast for the US ultralight category and with what looks like too small a wing area for FAI-definition microlight status, the machine may nevertheless be eligible for ultralight/microlight status in some other countries - Australia for example. Our weight figure, incidentally, refers to the prototype which appeared at Oshkosh. Prices: NC.

EXTERNAL DIMENSIONS & AREAS - NC.

POWER PLANT - Max power 25 hp. Other data NC.

WEIGHTS & LOADINGS - Empty weight 193 lb, 87 kg. Other data NC.

PERFORMANCE* - Max level speed 110 mph, 177 kph. Cruising speed 100 mph, 161 kph. Other data NC.

*Under unspecified test conditions.

STERNER ULTRACRAFT

Sterner Ultracraft, PO Box 811, Sterling Heights, Michigan 48078; tel (313) 268-1882. (No longer trading).

STERNER ULTRACRAFT *SKY WALKER*
(Three-axis)

Single-seat single-engined high-wing monoplane with conventional three-axis control. Wing has unswept leading and trailing edges, and constant chord; flaps fitted; cruciform tail. Pitch control by elevator on tail; yaw control by fin-mounted rudder; roll control by ailerons; control inputs through stick for pitch/roll and pedals for yaw. Wing braced from below by struts. Undercarriage has three wheels in tricycle formation. Push-right go-right nosewheel steering connected to yaw control. Aluminium-alloy tube airframe, completely open. Engine mounted below wing, driving pusher propeller.

Production status: see text.

GENERAL - Readers of our first edition will recall the Airmass company and its inverted V-tailed *Sunburst* ultralight and *Sunburst II* two-seater, and may also recall that the firm subsequently disappeared, more or less simultaneously with a spate of flying wire failures which killed several *Sunburst* pilots.

Some relatively simple redesigning cured the problem, and the design was taken from Airmass' Stilwell, Kansas factory to be relaunched as the *Sunrise V* by a company called Personal Planes Inc of Norwalk, Ohio. Only a couple of months later, however, in autumn 1983, the design was on the move once more, this time to Texas, where Double Star Engineering & Manufacturing Inc renamed it yet again, as the *Lone Star,* and introduced a two-seater *Double Star* for good measure. Then in spring '84 came another twist to the saga, when Double Star announced a merger with Bob

Glider Rider

Aloft in the earlier wide-span version of the Sky Walker.

Sterner's company in Michigan, the intention being to offer the two Double Star models, plus a third called *Star Fire,* plus Bob's own *Sky Walker* design.

Finally, in early 1985 we learned that Sterner Ultracraft had ceased trading, bringing to an end what must surely be one of the unhappiest sagas in American ultralight history, John Massey's ill-fated *Sunburst* having killed four pilots and, on the face of it at least, the same number of ultralight companies. It probably travelled more miles as a set of manufacturing drawings than it ever did as an aircraft, its only moment of glory coming when Massey piloted one across the English Channel in the '82 London-Paris.

Unfortunately Bob Sterner's own *Sky Walker,* a quite unrelated and uncontroversial tube and Dacron design unusual only in that it has flaps, seems to have died along with this unlamented machine. However, despite the *Sky Walker's* obsolescence, in the interests of historical accuracy we print here a few details of the last examples built, as these have a much smaller span than the 32.0 ft (9.75 m) machine detailed in our first edition.

EXTERNAL DIMENSIONS & AREAS - Wing span 26.0 ft, 7.92 m. Constant chord 5.3 ft, 1.62 m. Sweepback 0°. Total wing area 138 ft², 12.8 m². Aspect ratio 4.9/1. Other data NC.

POWER PLANT - Cuyuna 430 engine. Max power 30 hp at NC rpm. Propeller diameter and pitch 52xNC inch, 1.32xNC m. Reduction type NC, ratio 2.1/1. Max static thrust NC. Power per unit area 0.22 hp/ft², 2.3 hp/m². Fuel capacity 5.0 US gal, 4.2 Imp gal, 18.9 litre.

WEIGHTS & LOADINGS - Empty weight 247 lb, 112 kg. Max take-off weight 467 lb, 212 kg. Payload 220 lb, 100 kg. Max wing loading 3.38 lb/ft², 16.6 kg/m². Max power loading 15.6 lb/hp, 7.1 kg/hp. Load factors NC.

PERFORMANCE* - Max level speed 62 mph, 100 kph. Never exceed speed 80 mph, 129 kph. Cruising speed 50 mph, 80 kph. Stalling speed 24 mph, 39 kph. Max climb rate at sea level 600 ft/min, 3.1 m/s. m. Range at average cruising speed 147 mile, 237 km. Other data NC.

*Under unspecified test conditions.

STRIKER

Striker Aircraft Manufacturing, 2530 N Brighton, Burbank, California 91504; tel (818) 846-8741. Alternatively: Steve Mahrle, 511 Foote Street, McKinney, Texas 75069.

STRIKER *L.Y.N.X.*

(Three-axis)

Single-seat single-engined low-wing monoplane with conventional three-axis control. Wing has constant chord; cruciform tail. Pitch control by elevator on tail; yaw control by fin-mounted rudder; roll control by ailerons; control inputs through stick for pitch/roll and pedals for yaw. Wing braced from above by struts; 100% double-surface. Undercarriage has three wheels in tail-dragger formation. Partially enclosed fuselage. Engine mounted above wing, driving tractor propeller. Other details NC.

Production status: see text.

GENERAL - Although we have never met the *L.Y.N.X's* designer, Steve Mahrle, we feel a certain kinship with him because he was a close friend of the late and greatly missed Glenn Brinks, the Californian ultralight pilot and writer who helped us greatly with our first edition but was tragically killed before it was published.

Indeed, it was the loss of Glenn, allied to the death of his father, that spurred Steve into turning the *L.Y.N.X* into a reality. To take his mind off his grief, he set about constructing the first prototype of this low-wing tractor machine, and wrote briefly about the first flights in the July '84 edition of *Ultralight* magazine. He gave few constructional details of this angular but not unattractive partially enclosed tail-dragger, which has removable wings and a 15 min rigging time, beyond stating that it was intended to be a rugged utilitarian machine with a strong cage around the pilot.

However, we were pleased to note that it was listed in the *Ultralight Planes* buyers' guide of January-February '85, implying that the aircraft is now past the prototype stage. No price was given though, so readers are advised to contact the addresses above for further information.

EXTERNAL DIMENSIONS & AREAS - Length overall 19.0 ft, 5.79 m. Wing span 33.0 ft, 10.06 m. Total wing area 145 ft², 13.5 m². Aspect ratio 7.5/1. Other data NC.

POWER PLANT - Rotax 277 engine. Max power 28 hp at NC rpm. Propeller diameter and pitch 60x28 inch, 1.52x0.71 m. Reduction type and ratio NC. Max static thrust NC. Power per unit area 0.19 hp/ft², 2.1 hp/m². Fuel capacity 5.0 US gal, 4.2 Imp gal, 18.9 litre.

WEIGHTS & LOADINGS - Empty weight 262 lb, 119 kg. Max take-off weight 525 lb, 238 kg. Payload 263 lb, 119 kg. Max wing loading 3.62 lb/ft², 17.6 kg/m². Max power loading 18.8 lb/hp, 8.5 kg/hp. Load factors NC.

PERFORMANCE* - Max level speed 55 mph, 88 kph. Never exceed speed 90 mph, 145 kph. Cruising speed 50 mph, 80 kph. Stalling speed 23 mph, 37 kph. Max climb rate at sea level 450 ft/min, 2.3 m/s. Range at average cruising speed 143 mile, 230 km. Other data NC.

*Under unspecified test conditions.

Now very much at home in conventional lightplane company - Striplin's Sky Ranger Silver Cloud *(foreground) and* Lone Ranger Silver Cloud *(behind).*

STRIPLIN

Striplin Aircraft, PO Box 2001, Lancaster, California 93539; tel (805) 945-2522. President: Ken Striplin.

STRIPLIN *LONE RANGER SILVER CLOUD*

(Three-axis)

Single-seat single-engined high-wing monoplane with conventional three-axis control. Wing has swept back leading and trailing edges, and tapering chord; conventional tail. Pitch control by fully flying tail; yaw control by fin-mounted rudder; roll control by full-span flaperons; control inputs through stick for pitch/roll and pedals for yaw. Cantilever wing; wing profile NC; 100% double-surface. Undercarriage has three wheels in tricycle formation; suspension NC on nosewheel and glass-fibre suspension on main wheels. Push-right go-right nosewheel steering connected to yaw control. Nosewheel brake. Composite-construction airframe, totally enclosed. Engine mounted below wing, driving tractor propeller.

Production status: current, number completed NC.

GENERAL - Although it looks like a thoroughly conventional composite-construction 'mini-aeroplane', the *Lone Ranger Silver Cloud* is in fact derived from a very unconventional machine indeed, the *Flac.* This tailless machine used control surfaces not unlike those of Mitchell's *B-10* and had remarkably high performance for a low-powered machine, making its first flight in 1978 fitted with two 9 hp Chrysler Westbend engines. Despite being foot-launchable (the name stands for Foot Launch Air Cycle) it had an enclosed cockpit and an undercarriage, the nosewheel being manually retractable.

This latter feature was ditched on the next variant, the *Super-Flac,* to give the pilot's legs more room, but the aircraft was otherwise similar apart from using Soarmaster rather than Chrysler engines.

The first *Lone Ranger* flew in 1980 and was basically a single-engined *Super Flac* with a triangular-section spar supporting a conventional tail. Various engines were tried, and by 1982 buyers could choose from Yamaha KT100S (15 hp), Zenoah G25B (20 hp) or Cuyuna 215R (20 hp) units. A somewhat different version was built by British agent AES, which constructed some 12 Striplin-based single- and two-seat machines (featured in our first edition) before succumbing to financial difficulties.

Meanwhile in the US development continued, with the two struts per side being reduced to one and then, in a major redesign effort announced at Sun 'n Fun 1983, eliminated altogether, an arrangement which had been purely optional hitherto. The wing had a new high-lift profile and integral full-span flaperons, and the trailing edge was different too, being swept back rather than unswept. Finally the fully flying tail was remounted lower down and the engine moved from the top of the wing to the nose.

The new version was dubbed *Silver Cloud*, at that time the intention being to retain the 'Ranger' part of the name only in the company title, which was henceforth to be Ranger Aviation. By the time production got under way in November '83, however, it had been decided to retain the Striplin name, the aircraft becoming *Lone Ranger Silver Cloud*. Although the rigging time is claimed to be only 15 min, many buyers are likely to keep the machine rigged, as the company proudly points out that the enclosed cockpit and composite construction of glass-fibre/carbon fibre/Kevlar, foam and epoxy gives the machine excellent weather resistance. Sold as a 150 h kit for US$6950 or ready built for US$8950, the aircraft is currently fitted with a Rotax 277 engine, though some may have Cuyuna 215R or Zenoah motors.

EXTERNAL DIMENSIONS & AREAS - Length overall 15.5 ft, 4.72 m. Height overall 7.0 ft, 2.13 m. Wing span 35.0 ft, 10.67 m. Chord at root 4.5 ft, 1.37 m. Chord at tip 3.5 ft, 1.07 m. Dihedral 2°. Sweepback 2°. Tailplane span 8.0 ft, 2.44 m. Fin height 3.5 ft, 1.07 m. Total wing area 136 ft², 12.6 m². Total aileron area 24.0 ft², 2.23 m². Fin area 2.0 ft², 0.19 m². Rudder area 2.5 ft², 0.23 m². Total elevator area 11.0 ft², 1.02 m². Aspect ratio 9.0/1. Wheel track 5.0 ft, 1.52 m. Wheelbase 4.5 ft, 1.37 m. Nosewheel diameter overall 12 inch, 30 cm. Main wheels diameter overall 14 inch, 36 cm.

POWER PLANT - Rotax 277 engine. Max power 28 hp at 6200 rpm. Propeller diameter and pitch 60x28 inch, 1.52x0.71 m. Toothed-belt reduction, ratio 2.6/1. Max static thrust 180 lb, 82 kg. Power per unit area 0.21 hp/ft², 2.22 hp/m². Fuel capacity 5.0 US gal, 4.2 Imp gal, 18.9 litre.

WEIGHTS & LOADINGS - Empty weight 253 lb, 115 kg. Max take-off weight 500 lb, 227 kg. Payload 247 lb, 112 kg. Max wing loading 3.68 lb/ft², 18.0 kg/m². Max power loading 17.9 lb/hp, 8.1 kg/hp. Load factors +4.6, -3.0 recommended; +6.0, -4.0 ultimate.

PERFORMANCE* - Max level speed 62 mph, 100 kph. Never exceed speed 80 mph, 129 kph. Max cruising speed 60 mph, 97 kph. Economic cruising speed 55 mph, 88 kph. Stalling speed 26 mph, 42 kph. Max climb rate at sea level 600 ft/min, 3.1 m/s. Min sink rate 300 ft/min, 1.5 m/s at NC speed. Best glide ratio with power off 12/1 at 44 mph, 71 kph. Take-off distance 150 ft, 46 m. Landing distance 200 ft, 61 m. Service ceiling 12,000 ft, 3660 m. Range at average cruising speed 250 mile, 402 km. Noise level NC.

*Under the following test conditions - Airfield altitude 2300 ft, 701 m. Ground temperature 75°F, 24°C. Ground pressure NC. Ground windspeed 0 mph, 0 kph. Test payload 180 lb, 82 kg.

STRIPLIN
SKY RANGER SILVER CLOUD
(Three-axis)

Summary similar to Lone Ranger Silver Cloud *except: Side-by-side two-seater.*

Production status: current, number completed NC.

GENERAL - The *Sky Ranger* is basically a two-seat derivative of the *Lone Ranger*, and its history has para-

lleled that of the solo machine. First shown at Oshkosh '81 with Fowler flaps, a T-tail, and a single engine mounted above the cockpit driving two props - one on each leading edge - the aircraft had changed greatly by the time it reached production *Silver Cloud* form in 1984, with more ground clearance, a single prop driven from a nose-mounted engine, wing changes paralling those on the solo aircraft, and wing-tip fuel tanks. As with the *Lone Ranger Silver Cloud,* the doors can be removed for summer flying.

Two engines are offered - the Rotax 503 with 45 hp (the version detailed below) or a Volkswagen unit with 65 hp, a prototype of the latter version being shown at Oshkosh '84. VW-derived engines, such as the Hapi or Revmaster, will also fit.

Sold as a kit for US$8950, the aircraft is also available ready built at a price depending on specification.

EXTERNAL DIMENSIONS & AREAS - Wing span 35.0 ft, 10.67 m. Total wing area 136 ft², 12.6 m². Aspect ratio 9.0/1. Other data NC.

POWER PLANT - Rotax 503 engine. Max power 46 hp at 6500 rpm. Propeller diameter and pitch 60x36 inch, 1.52x0.91 m. Power per unit area 0.34 hp/ft², 3.7 hp/m². Fuel capacity 10.0 US gal, 8.3 Imp gal, 37.9 litre. Other data NC.

WEIGHTS & LOADINGS - Empty weight 350 lb, 159 kg. Max take-off weight 1000 lb, 453 kg. Payload 650 lb, 295 kg. Max wing loading 7.35 lb/ft², 40.0 kg/m². Max power loading 21.7 lb/hp, 38.6 kg/hp. Load factors NC.

PERFORMANCE* - Max level speed 88 mph, 142 kph. Never exceed speed 100 mph, 161 kph. Cruising speed 78 mph, 126 kph. Stalling speed 32 mph, 51 kph. Max climb rate at sea level 600 ft/min, 3.1 m/s. Other data NC.

*Under unspecified test conditions.

SUMMIT

Summit Aircraft Corp, PO Box 884, Denton, Texas 76201; tel (817) 566-0060. Chairman: Charlie H Townson. President: Roland Schmitt III. Vice-president engineering: Rick Ward. Vice-president administration: Neta Watkins.

SUMMIT *TRIDENT T-3*
(Three-axis)

Single-seat single-engined double monoplane in tandem with outboard ends joined; conventional three-axis control. Forward wing has swept back leading and trailing edges, rear wing has swept forward leading and trailing edges; both wings tapering chord; no tail. Pitch control by elevator on forward wing; yaw control by tip rudders; roll control by one-third span ailerons just inboard of tip rudders; control inputs through stick for pitch/roll and pedals for yaw. Forward wing braced by rear wing and vice versa; wing profile in-house; 100% double-surface Undercarriage has three wheels in tricycle formation; no suspension on nosewheel and glass-fibre suspension on main wheels. Push-right go-right nosewheel steering connected to yaw control. Nosewheel brake. Composite-construction airframe, with optional pod. Engine mounted between wings, driving pusher propeller.

Production status: prototype.

GENERAL - The *Trident T-3* has perhaps the most remarkable configuration of any aircraft in this book, using two staggered flying wings joined at the tips and arranged to form a diamond shape both in plan and front view. The pilot sits up front on the heavily swept back front wing.

As it is only a prototype at the time of writing, it is too early to reach any conclusions about the aircraft's flying characteristics, but a lot of research seems to have gone into the design, which was invented and patented by Dr Julian Wolkovitch, the president of ACA Industries Inc, of Rancho Palos Verdes, California. The company says the 'joined wing' concept has received hundreds of hours testing in wind tunnels by experts in universties, the aircraft industry and the military, and has demonstrated inherent direct lift and sideforce capabilities. Compared with a conventional wing, advantages claimed are lower weight - the structure is said to be stronger than steel and lighter than aluminium - plus higher stiffness, less induced drag, lower wave drag and higher trimmed maximum lift coefficient.

At Oshkosh '84 great interest was shown in the prototype, though *Glider Rider* irreverently described it as 'looking like Luke Skywalker's first starship with a chair stuck on it'. It used a KFM 107ER engine with electric start.

Rigging time is not quoted but with such a clean structure it should be short. The company's intention is to sell complete pre-moulded kits, needing only hand tools to assemble, for 'in the upper US$8000 range', with a ballistic parachute offered as an option.

Readers should note that our figures below are correct for the prototype but will not necessarily be accurate for production aircraft.

EXTERNAL DIMENSIONS & AREAS - Length overall 16.7 ft, 5.08 m. Height overall 6.3 ft, 1.91 m. Wing span (tip to tip) 33.0 ft, 10.06 m. Chord at root 4.0 ft, 1.22 m. Chord at tip 3.0 ft, 0.91 m. Dihedral 7°. Sweepback 36°. Total wing area 158 ft², 14.7 m². Total aileron area 8.0 ft², 0.74 m². Total rudder area 10.0 ft², 0.93 m². Total elevator area 12.0 ft², 1.11 m². Aspect ratio 6.9/1. Wheel track 5.0 ft, 1.52 m. Wheelbase 8.3 ft, 2.51 m. Nosewheel diameter overall 10 inch, 25 cm. Main wheels diameter overall 12 inch, 30 cm. Other data NC.

Artist's impression of the Trident T-3.

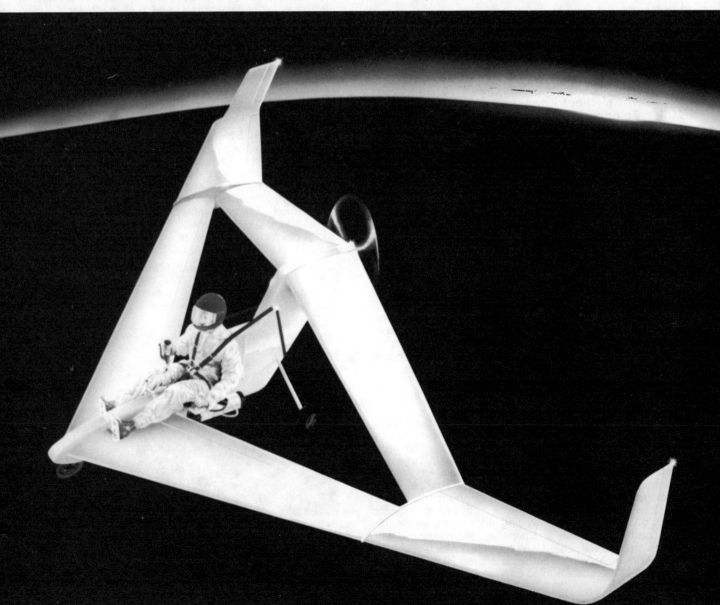

POWER PLANT - KFM 107ER engine. Max power 28 hp at 6300 rpm. Propeller diameter and pitch 54x27 inch, 1.37x0.69 m. V-belt reduction, ratio 2.1/1. Max static thrust NC. Power per unit area 0.18 hp/ft^2, 1.9 hp/m^2. Fuel capacity 5.0 US gal, 4.2 Imp gal, 18.9 litre.

WEIGHTS & LOADINGS - Empty weight 260 lb, 118 kg. Max take-off weight 510 lb, 231 kg. Payload 250 lb, 113 kg. Max wing loading 3.23 lb/ft^2, 15.7 kg/m^2. Max power loading 18.2 lb/hp, 8.3 kg/hp. Load factors +4.7, -2.3 recommended; +7.0, -3.5 ultimate.

PERFORMANCE* - Max level speed 63 mph, 101 kph. Never exceed speed 82 mph, 132 kph. Max cruising speed 55 mph, 88 kph. Economic cruising speed 45 mph, 72 kph. Stalling speed 24 mph, 39 kph. Max climb rate at sea level 500 ft/min, 2.5 m/s. Min sink rate 190 ft/min at 32 mph, 1.0 m/s at 51 kph. Best glide ratio with power off 14/1 at 39 mph, 63 kph. Take-off distance 100 ft, 30 m. Landing distance 60 ft, 18 m. Service ceiling 11,000 ft, 3350 m. Range at average cruising speed 135 mile, 217 km. Noise level NC.

**Under the following test conditions -* Airfield altitude 0 ft, 0 m. Ground temperature NC. Ground pressure NC. Ground windspeed 0 mph, 0 kph. Test payload 250 lb, 113 kg.

SUMO

Sumo Development Corporation, 8000 S Highway 99, Redding, California 96001; tel (916) 244-2676. President: Michael Koonce. Vice-president: Dave Miller. Engineering director: Paul Miller. Chairman: Howard Lesher.

SUMO *SUNSEEKER*

(Three-axis)

Single-seat single-engined high-wing monoplane with conventional three-axis control. Wing has unswept leading edge, swept forward trailing edge, and tapering chord; flaps fitted; conventional tail. Pitch control by fully flying tail; yaw control by fin-mounted rudder; roll control by ailerons; control inputs through stick for pitch/roll and pedals for yaw. Wing braced from below by struts; wing profile Goettingen 387; 100% double-surface. Undercarriage has three wheels in tricycle formation; no suspension on nosewheel and axle-flex suspension on main wheels. Push-right go-right nosewheel steering connected to yaw control. Brakes on main wheels. Steel-tube airframe, with pod. Engine mounted at wing height, driving pusher propeller.

Production status: current, 25 completed.

GENERAL - Though unremarkable in configuration, this relative newcomer to the ultralight scene definitely has a touch of class. No tube-and-Dacron construction here: instead, the airframe is a welded steel construction with aluminium-alloy sheet for the tail covering, while the wing is a composite structure incorporating flaps. A strut-supported D-cell of Nomex honeycomb is bonded by glass-fibre and attached to foam ribs which each have anti-drag struts bonded internally. Trailing edge is of aluminium-alloy, and the ailerons and flaps are alloy-skinned, with Stits covering elsewhere on the wing, which folds for transportation, rigging time being around 20 min.
Exhibited at the Los Angeles Expo in late '84, it attracted

considerable attention, with Jim Campbell commenting in the spring '85 edition of *Sport Pilot & Ultralight* that 'the construction detail appears to be exceptional'. Subsequently James Lawrence flight tested it for *Ultralight Flying* magazine and wrote one of the most glowing reports we have ever read in that publication, describing it as 'one of the finest ultralights I have ever flown' and concluding that there was no better ultralight on the market at any price.
Standard equipment includes a pod in polished aluminium-alloy to match the tail, while power comes from a Rotax 277. The machine is only available in ready-to-fly form, at a price of US$8499 including ballistic parachute.

EXTERNAL DIMENSIONS & AREAS - Length overall 18.5 ft, 5.64 m. Height overall 7.7 ft, 2.34 m. Wing span 31.5 ft, 9.60 m. Chord at root 4.8 ft, 1.47 m. Chord at tip 2.9 ft, 0.89 m. Dihedral 3°. Sweepback 0°. Total wing area 126 ft^2, 11.7 m^2. Total aileron area 16.0 ft^2, 1.49 m^2. Fin area 11.0 ft^2, 1.02 m^2. Rudder area 12.0 ft^2, 1.11 m^2. Total elevator area 16.0 ft^2, 1.49 m^2. Flap area 24.0 ft^2, 2.23 m^2. Aspect ratio 8.0/1. Wheel track NC. Wheelbase 4.3 ft, 1.30 m. Nosewheel diameter overall 10 inch, 25 cm. Main wheels diameter overall 16 inch, 41 cm.

POWER PLANT - Rotax 277 engine. Max power 28 hp at 6200 rpm. Propeller diameter and pitch 60x28 inch, 1.52x-0.71 m. Gear reduction, ratio 2.1/1. Max static thrust NC. Power per unit area 0.22 hp/ft^2, 2.4 hp/m^2. Fuel capacity 4.4 US gal, 3.7 Imp gal, 16.7 litre.

WEIGHTS & LOADINGS - Empty weight** 269 lb, 122 kg. Max take-off weight 550 lb, 249 kg. Payload 281 lb, 127 kg. Max wing loading 4.37 lb/ft^2, 21.3 kg/m^2. Max power loading 19.6 lb/hp, 8.9 kg/hp. Load factors £6.0, -6.0 recommended; £9.0, -9.0 ultimate.

PERFORMANCE* - Max level speed 63 mph, 101 kph. Never exceed speed 75 mph, 121 kph. Max cruising speed 63 mph, 101 kph. Economic cruising speed 60 mph, 97 kph. Stalling speed 25 mph, 40 kph. Max climb rate at sea level 700 ft/min, 3.6 m/s. Min sink rate 200 ft/min at 40 mph, 1.0 m/s at 64 kph. Best glide ratio with power off 14/1 at 40 mph, 64 kph. Take-off distance 150 ft, 46 m. Landing distance 100 ft, 30 m. Service ceiling 15,000 ft, 4570 m. Range at average cruising speed 250 mile, 402 km. Ground noise level 90 dB at 3.0 ft, 0.91 m.

**Under the following test conditions -* Airfield altitude 0 ft, 0 m. Ground temperature 75°F, 24°C. Ground pressure 1014 mB. Ground windspeed 0 mph, 0 kph. Test payload 200 lb, 91 kg.

***Includes parachute.*

SUN AEROSPACE

Sun Aerospace Corp, PO Box 317, Nappanee, Indiana 46550; tel (219) 773-3220. President: Russell A McDonald. Vice-president: Lee Holcomb. Treasurer: Dan Milten. Secretary: Jean Menky.

Overseas sales: World Enterprises USA, 8900 Mazanita Drive, Alta Loma, California 91701; tx 140481-WE-USA (VIA TRT). Proprietor: Dr Robert Ingram Powell.

SUN AEROSPACE
SUN RAY MODEL 100

(Three-axis)

Single-seat single-engined mid-wing monoplane with conventional three-axis control. Wing has unswept leading edge, swept forward trailing edge, and tapering chord; no tail, canard wing. Pitch control by elevator on canard; yaw control by fin-mounted rudders on inboard ends of wing; roll control by ailerons; control inputs through stick for pitch/roll and pedals for yaw. Wing structure see text; wing profile NC; 100% double-surface. Undercarriage has three wheels in tricycle formation; no suspension on nosewheel and coil-spring suspension on main wheels. Ground steering by differential braking; limited castoring nosewheel optional. Brakes on main wheels. Composite-construction fuselage, partially enclosed (totally enclosed optional). Engine mounted below raised centre portion of wing, driving pusher propeller.

Production status: prototype.

GENERAL - The dramatic shape of the *Sun Ray* caused intense interest when announced in early 1983, not just because of its unusual appearance but also because of its advanced materials, including extensive use of Kevlar.

The other side of high-technology, however, is that it takes a long time to get into serious production, and as recently as early '85 the company was still tooling up for the single-seater, now known as *Sun Ray Model 100*, while the two-seat *Model 200* seemed as far away as ever. One thing which has emerged, however, is that the aircraft cannot be safely made light enough to be an ultralight, and will now be sold as an experimental-category machine.

Nevertheless, this unusual craft should be well worth waiting for, not least for its optional hull-float and spon son package which makes it one of the most natural-looking planes on the water. Apart from these detachable items, the structure itself provides some buoyancy, thanks to the twin parallel booms bracing the canard to the rudder assemblies. Outboard of these are two half-wings with laminar profile and large dihedral, while inboard there is an inverted V-wing forming the engine housing and carrying the pusher propeller.

The *Sun Ray Model 100* is priced at US$9950, with the amphibian option costing US$1200 extra. Readers should note that our performance figures below are calculations based on improvements being built into the prototype at the time of going to press.

EXTERNAL DIMENSIONS & AREAS - Length overall 13.3 ft, 4.06 m. Height overall 6.0 ft, 1.83 m. Wing span 32.0 ft, 9.75 m. Chord at root 6.0 ft, 1.83 m. Chord at tip 2.0 ft, 0.61 m. Dihedral 6°. Sweepback 0°. Canard span 16.0 ft, 4.88 m. Canard chord 1.5 ft, 0.46 m. Total wing area 157 ft^2, 14.6 m^2. Main wing area 130 ft^2, 12.1 m^2. Canard area 27 ft^2, 2.5 m^2. Aspect ratio (of main wing) 7.9/1. Other data NC.

POWER PLANT - Kawasaki engine. Max power 52 hp at 7500 rpm. Propeller diameter and pitch 54x27 inch, 1.37x0.69 m. V-belt reduction, ratio 2.0/1. Max static thrust 245 lb, 111 kg. Power per unit area 0.33 hp/ft^2, 3.6 hp/m^2. Fuel capacity 5.0 US gal, 4.2 Imp gal, 18.9 litre.

WEIGHTS & LOADINGS - Empty weight 350 lb, 159 kg. Max take-off weight 800 lb, 363 kg. Payload 450 lb, 204 kg. Max wing loading 5.10 lb/ft^2, 24.9 kg/m^2. Max power loading 15.4 lb/hp, 7.0 kg/hp. Load factors +6.0, -6.0 recommended; +9.0, -9.0 ultimate.

PERFORMANCE* - Max level speed 90 mph, 145 kph. Never exceed speed 130 mph, 209 kph. Max cruising speed 80 mph, 129 kph. Economic cruising speed 65 mph, 105 kph. Stalling speed 40 mph, 64 kph. Max climb rate at sea level 600 ft/min, 3.1 m/s. Take-off distance 300 ft, 91 m. Landing distance 150 ft, 46 m. Service ceiling 13,000 ft, 3960 m. Range at average cruising speed 225 mile, 362 km. Other data NC.

Under the following test conditions - Airfield altitude 800 ft, 244 m. Ground temperature 72°F, 22°C. Ground pressure NC. Ground windspeed 5 mph, 8 kph. Test payload 185 lb, 84 kg.

For an illustration of the Sun Ray Model 100. *see colour section.*

TEMAN

Teman Aircraft Inc, PO Box 1489, Hawaiian Gardens, California 90716; tel (213) 402-6059. Proprietor: Bob Teman.

TEMAN
MONO-FLY and
SUPER MONO-FLY

(Three-axis)

Single-seat single-engined high-wing monoplane with conventional three-axis control. Wing has unswept leading and trailing edges, and constant chord; conventional tail. Pitch control by fully flying tail; yaw control by fully flying rudder; roll control by one-third span ailerons; control inputs through yoke for pitch/roll and pedals for yaw. Wing braced from below by struts; wing profile modified Clark Y (incidence: 6° at root, 3° at tip); 100% double-surface. Undercarriage has three wheels in tricycle formation with additional tailskid; steel-spring suspension on nosewheel and bungee suspension on main wheels. Push-right go-right nosewheel steering connected to yaw control. Nosewheel brake. Aluminium-alloy tube airframe, completely open. Engine mounted below wing, driving pusher propeller.

Production status: see text.

GENERAL - A popular choice with homebuilders because of its combination of strong airframe and simple construction, Bob Teman's *Mono-Fly* is the result of five years' development by this structural engineer, who has worked on the space shuttle and cruise missile programmes among others. Starting in 1976, he tried three different wings, four types of suspension, two tails, and several engines before settling on the *Mono-Fly* design as we know it.

Originally sold just as plans, it later became available as a kit, acquiring its present power unit, the Rotax 503, in spring '83. We described it in this form in our first edition, only to learn after publication that Bob had dubbed this version *Super Mono-Fly* on account of its superior performance to earlier aircraft, which can be found with 22 hp four-stroke Onans or 38.5 hp Kawasaki TA440s.

In practice, of course, many other power units have been fitted by homebuilders. One British enthusiast, Brian Hope, has a 377 Rotax fitted to his example, which is also non-standard in two other respects: it uses all-alloy ailerons rather than the normal foam-cored glass-fibre skinned design, and has a pod. The latter is a luxury US builders cannot afford, as the aircraft is only just under the American ultralight weight limit in its basic form and indeed was sold originally as an experimental-category machine. Writing on the project in the May-June edition of *Flightline,* Brian was full of praise for the clear and comprehensive instructions, describing them as excellent value for money at US$40.

Although to the best of our knowledge Bob is still in business, we have not heard from him for some time and our latest prices and production figures are from autumn '83, by which time 800 sets of plans had been sold and over 50 aircraft were flying. Prices then were US$3900 for an 80 h kit, or US$2515 for the same kit minus engine. Our data below refers to the *Super Mono-Fly.*

EXTERNAL DIMENSIONS & AREAS - Length overall 17.2 ft, 5.23m. Height overall 6.6 ft, 2.01 m. Wing span 30.8 ft, 9.37 m. Constant chord 4.0 ft, 1.22 m. Dihedral 3°. Sweepback 0°. Total wing area 124 ft², 11.5 m². Total aileron area 8.0 ft², 0.74 m². Rudder area 10.0 ft², 0.93 m². Total elevator area 14.0 ft², 1.30 m². Aspect ratio 7.6/1. Other data NC.

POWER PLANT - Rotax 503 engine. Max power 46 hp at 6500 rpm. Propeller diameter and pitch 52x34 inch, 1.32x0.86 m. Reduction type NC, ratio 2.0/1. Max static thrust 300 lb, 136 kg. Power per unit area 0.37 hp/ft², 4.0 hp/m². Fuel capacity* 5.0 US gal, 4.2 Imp gal, 18.9 litre.

WEIGHTS & LOADINGS - Empty weight 250 lb, 113 kg. Max take-off weight 550 lb, 249 kg. Payload 300 lb, 136 kg. Max wing loading 4.43 lb/ft², 21.6 kg/m². Max power loading 12.0 lb/hp, 5.4 kg/hp. Load factors NC recommended; +10.0, -10.0 ultimate.

PERFORMANCE - Max level speed 63 mph, 101 kph. Max cruising speed 45 mph, 72 kph. Stalling speed 20 mph, 32 kph. Max climb rate at sea level *1000* ft/min, *5.1* m/s. Take-off distance 100 ft, 30 m. Other data NC.

*Optional - 6.0 US gal, 5.0 Imp gal, 22.7 litre.

**Under unspecified test conditions.

TERATORN

Teratorn Aircraft Inc, 1604 S Shore Drive, Clear Lake, Iowa 50428; tel (515) 357-7161. President and owner: Dale Kjellsen.

Australian agent: Gary Dickinson, Suite 5003, Westfield Tower, Doncaster 3108, Melbourne, Victoria; tel 03618-482754; tx AA36444 answerback BRTFLD.

European agent: KGK (see Swedish section).

TERATORN *TIERRA UL*
(Three-axis)

Single-seat single-engined high-wing monoplane with conventional three-axis control. Wing has unswept leading and trailing edges, and constant chord; cruciform tail. Pitch control by elevator on tail; yaw control by fin-mounted rudder; roll control by 90%-span ailerons; control inputs through stick for pitch/roll and pedals for yaw. Wing braced from below by struts; wing profile thick airfoil; 100% double-surface. Undercarriage has three wheels in tail-dragger formation; bungee suspension on tailwheel and axle-flex suspension on main wheels. Push-right go-right tailwheel steering connected to yaw control. No brakes. Aluminium-alloy tube airframe, with optional pod or full enclosure. Engine mounted below wing, driving pusher propeller.

Production status: current, 400 completed.

GENERAL - This company started life as Motorized Gliders of Iowa, making the simple *Teratorn,* a tube and Dacron hybrid-control machine not unlike the early *Quick-silvers* apart from its use of tail-dragger undercarriage. Later came the *Teratorn TA,* a three-axis version of the same machine, and it was the success of these two models that encouraged Dale Kjellsen to change the company name to Teratorn Aircraft.

Both these venerable designs have now been dropped in favour of the *Tierra,* a much more sophisticated machine featuring a lot of triangulation in its tubular airframe, which gives it a distinctive 'birdcage' look. When introduced at the '83 Sun 'n Fun in Lakeland, Florida, the aircraft was claimed to be under the 254 lb (115 kg) ultralight weight

Hal Adkins

A 'naked' Tierra displays its sturdy construction.

limit, but was subsequently proved to be rather too heavy. Since then the company has managed to pare the weight down to a genuine 251 lb (114 kg), partly by substituting a 277 Rotax with gear reduction for the 377 and toothed-belt used before. Thus modified, the aircraft has been christened Tierra UL, and is selling well.

Tierra UL buyers can choose how much fresh air they want; the basic model is completely open apart from a transparent shield above the feet, but a more substantial nose fairing can be added to keep the feet warm, or alternatively the front half of the birdcage can be fully covered in to give total enclosure. The basic model costs US$4595 for a 20-30 h kit; rigging time is 20-30 min.

EXTERNAL DIMENSIONS & AREAS - Length overall 18.7 ft, 5.69 m. Height overall 5.5 ft, 1.68 m. Wing span 31.5 ft, 9.60 m. Constant chord 5.0 ft, 1.52 m. Dihedral 3°. Sweepback 0°. Tailplane span 8.9 ft, 2.72 m. Fin height 5.0 ft, 1.52 m. Total wing area 155 ft², 14.4 m². Total aileron area 15.0 ft², 1.39 m². Fin area 2.7 ft², 0.25 m². Rudder area 7.5 ft², 0.70 m². Tailplane area NC. Total elevator area 12.4 ft², 1.15 m². Aspect ratio 6.4/1. Wheel track 4.0 ft, 1.22 m. Wheelbase 12.3 ft, 3.76 m. Tailwheel diameter overall 3 inch, 8 cm. Main wheels diameter overall 6 inch, 15 cm.

POWER PLANT - Rotax 277 engine. Max power 28 hp at 6500 rpm. Propeller diameter and pitch 59x** inch, 1.50x** m (3-blade). Gear reduction, ratio 2.6/1. Max static thrust 175 lb, 79 kg. Power per unit area 0.18 hp/ft², 1.9 hp/m². Fuel capacity 5.0 US gal, 4.2 Imp gal, 18.9 litre.

WEIGHTS & LOADINGS - Empty weight 251 lb, 114 kg. Max take-off weight 500 lb, 227 kg. Payload 249 lb, 113 kg. Max wing loading 3.23 lb/ft², 15.8 kg/m². Max power loading 17.9 lb/hp, 8.1 kg/hp. Load factors +6.0, -3.0 recommended; NC ultimate.

PERFORMANCE* - Max level speed 61 mph, 98 kph. Never exceed speed 85 mph, 137 kph. Max cruising speed 50 mph, 80 kph. Economic cruising speed 45 mph, 72 kph. Stalling speed 24 mph, 39 kph. Max climb rate at sea level 650 ft/min, 3.3 m/s. Min sink rate 275 ft/min at 32 mph, 1.4 m/s at 51 kph. Best glide ratio with power off 10/1 at 32 mph, 51 kph. Take-off distance 75 ft, 23 m. Landing distance 100 ft, 30 m. Service ceiling 10,000 ft, 3050 m. Range at average cruising speed 125 mile, 201 km. Noise level NC.

*Under unspecified test conditions.

**Ground adjustable for pitch.

TERATORN *TIERRA 2*

(Three-axis)

Summary as Tierra UL *except: Side-by-side two-seater. Flaps fitted. Axle-flex suspension on all wheels. Push-right go-right tailwheel steering connected to yaw control; also differential braking. Brakes on main wheels. Partially enclosed (total enclosure optional).*

Production status: current, 600 produced.

GENERAL - With the *Tierra 2* we have a rare instance of a two-seater comfortably outselling the solo machine from which it is derived, sales running in the ratio of around 1.5/1. The aircraft has been well received in Europe too, particularly in Sweden where the European importer is based, but as it sells there with a slightly different specification we list it separately, in the Swedish section.

The *Tierra 2* is no lightweight. It shares quite a few of the *Tierra UL's* dimensions, but its wing is much larger and consequently more 'draggier', so to give the machine a good performance, Teratorn has fitted not the Rotax 503 so often found on two-seaters, but the liquid-cooled Rotax 532 with 65 hp.

The two-seater comes as standard with some weather protection, full enclosure being optional. Price is US$6895.

EXTERNAL DIMENSIONS & AREAS - Length overall 18.7 ft, 5.69 m. Height overall 6.1 ft, 1.85 m. Wing span 36.8 ft, 11.20 m. Constant chord 5.2 ft, 1.58 m. Dihedral 3°. Sweepback 0°. Tailplane span 8.9 ft, 2.72 m. Fin height 5.0 ft, 1.52 m. Total wing area 190 ft², 17.7 m². Total aileron area 20.9 ft², *1.94 m²*. Fin area 2.7 ft², 0.25 m². Rudder area 7.5 ft², 0.70 m². Tailplane area NC. Total elevator area 12.4 ft², 1.15 m². Aspect ratio 7.1/1. Wheel track 5.3 ft, 1.60 m. Wheelbase 12.3 ft, 3.76 m. Tailwheel diameter overall 5 inch, 13 cm. Main wheels diameter overall 12 inch, 30 cm.

POWER PLANT - Rotax 532 engine. Max power 65 hp at 6500 rpm. Propeller diameter and pitch 72x44 inch, 1.83x1.12 m. Gear reduction, ratio 2.6/1. Max static thrust 425 lb, 192 kg. Power per unit area 0.33 hp/ft², 3.6 hp/m². Fuel capacity 12.0 US gal, 10.0 Imp gal, 45.4 litre.

WEIGHTS & LOADINGS - Empty weight 400 lb, 181 kg. Max take-off weight 900 lb, 408 kg. Payload 500 lb, 227 kg.

Power pack of the Tierra 2; *the complete aircraft (European version) is illustrated in the Swedish section.*

Max wing loading 4.62 lb/ft², 22.5 kg/m². Max power loading 13.8 lb/hp, 6.3 kg/hp. Load factors +6.0, -3.0 recommended; NC ultimate.

PERFORMANCE* - Max level speed 80 mph, 129 kph. Never exceed speed 85 mph, 137 kph. Max cruising speed 65 mph, 15 kph. Economic cruising speed 55 mph, 88 kph. Stalling speed 31 mph, 50 kph. Max climb rate at sea level 900 ft/min, 4.6 m/s. Min sink rate 300 ft/min at 35 mph, 1.5 m/s at 56 kph. Best glide ratio with power off 10/1 at 38 mph, 61 kph. Take-off distance 125 ft, 38 m. Landing distance 150 ft, 46 m. Service ceiling 14,000 ft, 4270 m. Range at average cruising speed 200 mile, 322 km. Noise level NC.

*Under unspecified test conditions.

THOSE FLYING MACHINES

Those Flying Machines, 705 E Gardena Blvd, Gardena, California 90248; tel (213) 532-2030.

THOSE FLYING MACHINES
PEGASUS II

(Hybrid)

Single-seat single-engined high-wing monoplane with hybrid control. Wing has swept back leading and trailing edges, and tapering chord; no tail, canard wing. Pitch control by elevator on canard; yaw control by tip rudders; no separate roll control; control inputs through weight-shift for pitch/roll and tiller for yaw. Wing braced from above by kingpost and cables, from below by cables; wing profile NC; approx 30% double-surface. Undercarriage has three wheels in tricycle formation; no suspension on nosewheel and glass-fibre suspension on main wheels. Push-right go-right nosewheel steering independent from yaw control. No brakes. Aluminium-alloy tube airframe, completely open. Engine mounted below wing, driving pusher propeller.

Production status: current, number completed NC.

GENERAL - The *Eagle* may be dead (in America at least) but the *Pegasus II* lives on, and since it is very difficult to

Similar in every respect except engine to the Pegasus II, *this* Pegasus I *model is now out of production.*

Glider Rider

tell the two apart, devotees of the *Eagle* concept are unlikely to be disappointed by the Californian imitation. Although the TFM company's main thrust is now on the quite unrelated *Titan,* which we list separately, the *Pegasus II* was in early 1985 still available at the 1983 price of US$4695 ready to fly, the earlier *Pegasus I* with its single-cylinder Cuyuna 215 cc motor having been dropped.

EXTERNAL DIMENSIONS & AREAS - Length overall 15.4 ft, 4.70 m. Height overall 9.8 ft, 3.00 m. Wing span 35.2 ft, 10.72 m. Total wing area 182 ft², 16.9 m². Other data NC.

POWER PLANT - Cuyuna 430 engine. Max power 35 hp at 5800 rpm. Propeller diameter and pitch 54x36 inch, 1.37x0.91 m. V-belt reduction, ratio 2.2/1. Max static thrust 238 lb, 108 kg. Power per unit area 0.19 hp/ft², 2.1 hp/m². Fuel capacity 4.2 US gal, 3.5 Imp gal, 15.9 litre.

WEIGHTS & LOADINGS - Empty weight 203 lb, 92 kg. Max take-off weight 503 lb, 228 kg. Payload 300 lb, 136 kg. Max wing loading 2.76 lb/ft², 13.5 kg/m². Max power loading 14.4 lb/hp, 6.5 kg/hp. Load factors +6.0, -2.0 design; NC ultimate.

PERFORMANCE* - Max level speed 63 mph, 101 kph. Never exceed speed 63 mph, 101 kph. Cruising speed 45 mph, 72 kph. Stalling speed 25 mph, 40 kph. Max climb rate at sea level 850 ft/min, 4.3 m/s. Best glide ratio with power off 7/1 at NC speed. Range at average cruising speed 126 mile, 203 km. Other data NC.

*Under unspecified test conditions.

THOSE FLYING MACHINES
PEGASUS SUPRA

(Three-axis)

Summary as Pegasus II *except: Conventional three-axis control. Roll control by spoilerons; control inputs through stick for pitch/roll and pedals for yaw.*

Production status: current, number completed NC.

GENERAL - The *Pegasus Supra* is TFM's equivalent of the *Eagle XL,* with a fixed seat and conventional three-axis controls. Otherwise it is very similar to its hybrid-control stablemate, apart from a different prop and reduction ratio.
Although we list the controls as conventionally arranged, TFM has sold spoileron add-on kits for *Eagles* with the control system arranged so that both spoilerons can be operated simultaneously as air brakes, presumably via pedals as on the *Quicksilver MX.* In view of this, it is possible that some of the company's own machines are similarly equipped.
Price: US$4995 ready to fly.

EXTERNAL DIMENSIONS & AREAS - See *Pegasus II.*

POWER PLANT - See *Pegasus II* except: Propeller diameter and pitch 58x27 inch, 1.47x0.69 m. Reduction ratio 2.4/1.

WEIGHTS & LOADINGS - See *Pegasus II* except: Empty weight 224 lb, 102 kg. Payload 279 lb, 127 kg.

PERFORMANCE - See *Pegasus II* except: Stalling speed 26 mph, 42 kph. Max climb rate at sea level 800 ft/min, 4.1 m/s.

THOSE FLYING MACHINES
TITAN

(Three-axis)

Single-seat single-engined high-wing monoplane with conventional three-axis control. Wing has unswept leading and trailing edges, and constant chord; flaps fitted; tail see text. Pitch and yaw control see text; roll control by half-span ailerons; control inputs see text. Wing braced from below by struts. Undercarriage has three wheels in tricycle formation. Composite-construction airframe, partially enclosed. Engine mounted below wing, driving pusher propeller. Other details NC.

Production status: current, number completed NC.

GENERAL - Little information is available about this latest TFM machine, which is the company's first original design, bearing no relationship to the *Pegasus* models.
It uses foam-core ribs and a composite-construction pilot enclosure, but undoubtedly its most distinctive feature is the tail treatment, which one commentator described as 'Y-tail' - presumably a combination of ruddervators and a fin/rudder assembly. However, at the time of going to press we are unable to confirm this, nor are we certain of the control arrangements, though we would be surprised if conventional three-axis controls were not fitted.
The machine has flown with Zenoah, Hirth and Kawasaki 340 engines, but we only have data on Kawasaki version. Price: US$4600 ready to fly.

EXTERNAL DIMENSIONS & AREAS - Wing span 32.0 ft, 9.75 m. Constant chord 4.0 ft, 1.22 m. Sweepback 0°. Total wing area 128 ft², 11.9 m². Aspect ratio 8.0/1. Other data NC.

POWER PLANT - Kawasaki 340 engine. Max power 28 hp at NC rpm. Propeller diameter and pitch 50x26 inch, 1.27x0.66 m. Reduction type NC, ratio 2.2/1. Max static thrust NC. Power per unit area 0.22 hp/ft², 2.4 hp/m². Fuel capacity 5.0 US gal, 4.2 Imp gal, 18.9 litre.

WEIGHTS & LOADINGS - Empty weight 196 lb, 89 kg. Max take-off weight 496 lb, 225 kg. Payload 300 lb, 136 kg. Max wing loading 3.88 lb/ft², 18.9 kg/m². Max power loading 17.7 lb/hp, 8.0 kg/hp. Load factors NC.

PERFORMANCE* - Max level speed 63 mph, 120 kph. Never exceed speed 120 mph, 193 kph. Cruising speed 38 mph, 61 kph. Stalling speed 23 mph, 37 kph. Max climb rate at sea level 600 ft/min, 3.1 m/s. Range at average cruising speed 127 mile, 204 km. Other data NC.

*Under unspecified test conditions.

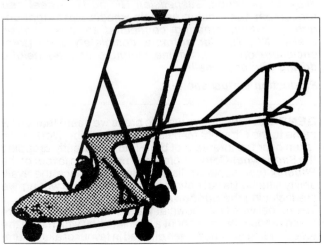

TOPA

Topa Aircraft Company, 1401 Offshore, Oxnard, California 93033. Proprietor: Chris Spangenberg.

TOPA *SCOUT*

(Three-axis)

Single-seat single-engined high-wing monoplane with conventional three-axis control. Wing has unswept leading and trailing edges, and constant chord; cruciform tail. Pitch control by elevator on tail; yaw control by fin-mounted rudder; roll control by approx 80%-span ailerons; control inputs through stick for pitch/roll and pedals for yaw. Wing braced from below by struts; wing profile NC; 100% double-surface. Undercarriage has three wheels in tail-dragger formation; suspension NC. Push-right go-right tailwheel steering connected to yaw control; also differential braking. Brakes on main wheels. Aluminium-alloy airframe, completely open. Engine mounted at wing height, driving pusher propeller.

Production status: see text.

GENERAL - Designed to give conventional pilots an ultralight feel without taking them out of reach of controlled airspace and other lightplane delights, the Topa *Scout* is not intended to be an ultralight and is overweight even for a microlight. Of pop-rivetted all-aluminium construction, it is aimed at the homebuilder who wants a docile aircraft and has only simple tools at his or her disposal. Stits Polyfiber is used for the wing covering and the recommended engine is a Rotax 503.

Though tested briefly in the September '83 issue of *Glider Rider* and advertised in the January '84 issue of the same publication, the *Scout* has received very little publicity since, and we are not sure of its present availability. The machine is basically a plans-built aircraft, though there was talk at one time of Ken Brock supplying part kits (for address see Brock).

Prices: NC.

EXTERNAL DIMENSIONS & AREAS - NC.

POWER PLANT - Rotax 503 engine. Max power 48 hp at NC rpm. Propeller diameter and pitch 60xNC inch, 1.52xNC m. Belt reduction, ratio 2.3/1. Other data NC.

WEIGHTS & LOADINGS - Empty weight 431 lb, 195 kg. Load factors NC recommended; +8.5, -NC ultimate. Other data NC.

PERFORMANCE* - Max cruising speed 50 mph, 80 kph. Economic cruising speed 40 mph, 64 kph. Stalling speed 33 mph, 53 kph. Other data NC.

*Under unspecified test conditions.

TUBE WORKS

Tube Works, 6320 Highland Road, Pontiac, Michigan 48054; tel (313) 666-1388.

ULTRA-FAB *SUNDOWNER CONVERTIBLE*

(Three-axis)

Single-seat single-engined high-wing monoplane with conventional three-axis control. Wing has unswept leading and trailing edges, and constant chord; cruciform tail. Pitch control by elevator on tail; yaw control by fully flying rudder; roll control by full-span ailerons; control inputs through stick for pitch/roll and pedals for yaw. Wing braced from below by struts; wing profile NC; 100% double-surface. Undercarriage has three wheels in tail-dragger formation; suspension NC on tail wheel and torsion-bar suspension on main wheels. Push-right go-right tailwheel steering connected to yaw control. Brakes NC. Tubular airframe, completely open (total enclosure optional). Engine mounted at wing height, driving tractor propeller.

Production status: see text.

GENERAL - Just as we went to press we heard that a new name to the ultralight manufacturers list, Tube Works, had taken over the interests of Ultra-Fab, apparently dropping the *Sundowner Convertible* in the process, in favour of the *Phoenix* (see separate listing). However, since the availability situation is not entirely clear at the time of writing, we are including the *Sundowner Convertible* anyway.

The model was first shown at the '83 Oshkosh but did not reach production until about a year later, by which time the steel landing gear had been ditched in favour of aluminium-alloy - probably for weight reasons, as the original *Sundowner* was reportedly overweight. The aircraft's most obvious attribute is its zip-on fabric cover that provides total enclosure within minutes - hence the 'convertible' name. Last quoted prices (Jan '85) were US$6495 for a 10 h kit, or US$6995 ready to fly. The standard Rotax 277 could be replaced by a 447 at extra cost, but figures below refer to the basic model.

EXTERNAL DIMENSIONS & AREAS - Length overall 17.0 ft, 5.18 m. Height overall 7.0 ft, 2.13 m. Wing span 30.5 ft, 9.30 m. Constant chord 4.8 ft, 1.46 m. Sweepback 0°. Total wing area 146 ft², 13.6 m². Aspect ratio 6.4/1. Other data NC.

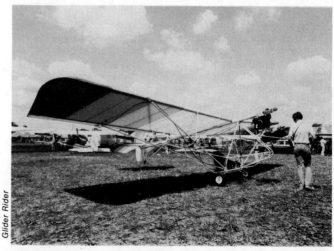

Flashback to Oshkosh '83, and the introduction of the Sundowner Convertible. **Note the cage around the pilot on which the enclosure can be mounted.**

POWER PLANT - Rotax 277 engine. Max power 28 hp a'. 6200 rpm. Propeller diameter and pitch 60x28 inch, 1.52x0.71 m. Gear reduction, ratio 2.6/1. Max static thrust 230 lb, 104 kg. Power per unit area 0.19 hp/ft², 2.1 hp/m². Fuel capacity 4.5 US gal, 3.8 Imp gal, 15.9 litre.

WEIGHTS & LOADINGS - Empty weight 248 lb, 112 kg. Max take-off weight 500 lb, 227 kg. Payload 252 lb, 114 kg. Max wing loading 3.42 lb/ft², 16.7 kg/m². Max power loading 17.9 lb/hp, 8.1 kg/hp. Load factors +6.0, -4.0 design; NC.

PERFORMANCE* - Max level speed 62 mph, 100 kph. Never exceed speed 75 mph, 121 kph. Max cruising speed 55 mph, 88 kph. Economic cruising speed 50 mph, 80 kph. Stalling speed 25 mph, 40 kph. Max climb rate at sea level 800 ft/min, 4.1 m/s. Best glide ratio with power off 7.5/1 at NC speed. Range at average cruising speed 158 mile, 253 km. Other data NC.

*Under unspecified test conditions.

TUBE WORKS *PHOENIX*
(Three-axis)

Single-seat single-engined high-wing monoplane with three-axis control. Wing has unswept leading and trailing edges, and constant chord; cruciform tail. Pitch control by elevator on tail; yaw control by fully flying rudder; roll control by spoilerons; control inputs see text. Wing braced from above by kingpost and cables, from below by cables; wing profile NC; single-surface. Undercarriage has three wheels in tricycle formation; suspension NC. No ground steering. Brakes NC. Aluminium-alloy tube airframe, completely open. Engine mounted below wing, driving pusher propeller.

Production status: current, number completed NC.

GENERAL - Announced just as we were going to press, the *Phoenix* is so new that we have been unable to get a picture of it. However, we know that it is very similar to the venerable *Quicksilver MX* in appearance, though it uses a Rotax 277 rather than the twin-cylinder unit of the Eipper product. It is not clear whether the similarity extends to the control system, in which case the *Phoenix* will have its spoilerons operated by pedals, or whether Tube Works has opted to fit as standard the conventional three-axis controls which are only optional on the *MX*.
Price: US$3995 in kit form.

EXTERNAL DIMENSIONS & AREAS - Wing span 32.0 ft, 9.75 m. Constant chord 5.0 ft, 1.52 m. Sweepback 0°. Total wing area 160 ft², 14.9 m². Aspect ratio 6.4/1. Other data NC.

POWER PLANT - Rotax 277 engine. Max power 28 hp at NC rpm. Power per unit area 0.18 hp/ft², 1.9 hp/m². Other data NC.

WEIGHTS & LOADINGS - Empty weight 234 lb, 106 kg. Max take-off weight 514 lb, 233 kg. Payload 280 lb, 127 kg. Max wing loading 3.21 lb/ft², 15.6 kg/m². Max power loading 18.4 lb/hp, 8.3 kg/hp. Load factors NC.

PERFORMANCE - Never exceed speed 64 mph, 103 kph. Other data NC.

TURNER

Turner Aircraft, 5803 Waterview Drive, Arlington, Texas 76016; tel (817) 457-5081. President and chief engineer: E L Gene Turner. Vice-president western region sales: Jerry E Turner. Vice president marketing: Jeannine E Turner. General manager: Jean M Turner.

TURNER *100 MARIAH*
(Three-axis)

Single-seat single-engined high-wing monoplane with conventional three-axis control. Wing has unswept leading and trailing edges, and constant chord; two-fin tail. Pitch control by fully flying tail; yaw control by fin-mounted rudders; roll control by ailerons; control inputs through stick for pitch/roll and pedals for yaw. Cantilever wing; wing profile NACA 63215; 100% double-surface. Undercarriage has three wheels in tricycle formation; air-spring suspension on nosewheel and spring suspension on main wheels. Push-right go-right nosewheel steering connected to yaw control. Nosewheel brake. Wood airframe (steel-tube optional), partially enclosed ((total enclosure optional). Engine mounted wing height, driving pusher propeller.

Production status: prototype.

GENERAL - Gene Turner may be a newcomer to the ultralight scene, but he's no stranger to aircraft design, having been creating and building award-winning aircraft since 1961. Among his best known machines are the popular *T-40* and *Super T-40A* homebuilts. Gene Turner, incidentally, has no connection with the *Turnerkraft*, which is available through the Mathews company.
Shown in our picture with an open cockpit, this two-fin high-wing design can be totally enclosed for winter flying. The company is particularly proud of the aircraft's safety features, which include an engine mount capable of withstanding 12g, and a 3g rollover capacity.
At the time of writing the *100 Mariah* is a prototype constructed of wood, but Gene has an alternative set of plans which would allow a steel-tube fuselage to be used instead. A variety of engines around the 20 hp mark will fit, but we believe that the figures below, supplied by Gene, were achieved with a Cuyuna 215.
Plans for the *100 Mariah* cost US$100, and materials kits are due to become available during 1985.

EXTERNAL DIMENSIONS & AREAS - Length overall 19.0 ft, 5.79 m. Height overall 6.0 ft, 1.83 m. Wing span 34.0 ft, 10.36 m. Constant chord 4.5 ft, 1.37 m. Dihedral 4°. Sweepback 0°. Tailplane span 5.8 ft, 1.77 m. Fin height 3.7 ft, 1.12 m. Total wing area 146 ft², 13.6 m². Total aileron area 12.4 ft², 1.15 m². Fin area 3.5 ft², 0.33 m². Rudder area 3.5 ft², 0.33 m². Total elevator area 14.5 ft², 1.35 m². Aspect

ratio 7.9/1. Wheel track 6.0 ft, 1.83 m. Wheelbase 7.3 ft, 2.21 m. Nosewheel diameter overall 12 inch, 30 cm. Main wheels diameter overall 12 inch, 30 cm.

POWER PLANT - Cuyuna 215 engine. Max power 20 hp at 6000 rpm. Propeller diameter and pitch 52x22 inch, 1.32x0.56 m. V-belt reduction, ratio 2.0/1. Max static thrust 125 lb, 57 kg. Power per unit area 0.14 hp/ft^2, 1.5 hp/m^2. Fuel capacity 5.0 US gal, 4.2 Imp gal, 18.9 litre.

WEIGHTS & LOADINGS - Empty weight 230 lb, 104 kg. Max take-off weight 504 lb, 229 kg. Payload 274 lb, 124 kg. Max wing loading 3.45 lb/ft^2, 16.8 kg/m^2. Max power loading 25.2 lb/hp, 11.4 kg/hp. Load factors +3.0, -1.9 recommended; +5.7, -2.9 ultimate.

PERFORMANCE* - Max level speed 60 mph, 97 kph. Never exceed speed 90 mph, 145 kph. Max cruising speed 55 mph, 88 kph. Economic cruising speed 45 mph, 72 kph. Stalling speed 28 mph, 45 kph. Max climb rate at sea level 450 ft/min, 2.3 m/s. Min sink rate 300 ft/min, 1.5 m/s at NC speed. Take-off distance 175 ft, 53 m. Landing distance 300 ft, 91 m. Other data NC.

*Under the following test conditions - Airfield altitude 720 ft, 219 m. Ground temperature NC. Ground pressure NC. Ground windspeed 5 mph, 8 kph. Test payload 270 lb, 122 kg.

UFM OF KENTUCKY

Addresses etc: See Loehle Aviation.

UFM OF KENTUCKY
AEROPLANE XP
(Three-axis)

Single-seat single-engined biplane with conventional three-axis control. Wings have swept back leading and trailing edges, and constant chord; conventional tail. Pitch control by elevator on tail; yaw control by fin-mounted rudder; roll control by spoilerons on upper wing; control inputs through stick for pitch/roll and pedals for yaw. Wings braced by struts and transverse X-cables; wing profile NC; 100% double-surface. Undercarriage has three wheels in tricycle formation; bungee suspension on all wheels. Push-right go-right nosewheel steering connected to yaw control. Nosewheel brake. Aluminium-alloy tube airframe, with optional pod. Engine mounted between wings, driving pusher propeller.

Production status: see text.

GENERAL - Mike Loehle's *Aeroplane XP* design has a distinguished ancestry which goes back to the dawn of ultralight aviation, for it is a direct descendent of the famous *Icarus II* biplane hang-glider designed by Larry Mauro. Motorised in 1975 by John Moody, it became the *Easy Riser* hybrid-control ultralight, with over 900 examples flying by 1981, built either from plans or from kits sold by dealers such as UFM of Kentucky.

This particular dealer, however, went on to develop the design in its own right, Mike producing first a two-axis design called the *Aeroplane,* with twin rudders hinged on the rear interplane struts at the wing tips and conventional

horizontal tail surfaces. Supplementing and later supplanting this came a three-axis variant, the *Aeroplane XP,* with a full conventional tail. Spoilers are used for roll control and, unusually for a machine with stick-actuated spoilers, they can both be deployed simultaneously to act as air brakes.

In 1984 Mike announced a new machine which is clearly a further development of the *Aeroplane XP* concept. Called *The Fun Machine,* it is produced by another of Mike's companies, Loehle Aviation, and listed under that name. Series production was just getting under way as we went to press, and it is not clear at the time of writing where this leaves the *Aeroplane XP.* However, Mike was still advertising it as late as February 1985, at a price of US$4955 for a 30 h kit. Rigging time is 50 min for one person and the machine folds into a package measuring some 2x4x16 ft (0.6x1.2x4.9 m), allowing car top or trailer transport.

EXTERNAL DIMENSIONS & AREAS - Length overall 11.0 ft, 3.35 m. Height overall 8.0 ft, 2.44 m. Wing span *21.7* ft, *6.61* m (bottom); 28.0 ft, 8.53 m (top). Constant chord 3.4 ft, 1.04 m (bottom wing); 3.4 ft, 1.04 m (top wing). Dihedral 15° (bottom wing); 15° (top wing). Sweepback 15°. Tailplane span 8.5 ft, 2.59 m. Fin height 3.5 ft, 1.07 m. Total wing area 170 ft^2, 15.8 m^2. Upper wing area 102.5 ft^2, 9.52 m^2. Lower wing area 67.5 ft^2, 6.27 m^2. Aspect ratio *7.0/1* (bottom wing); 7.6/1 (top wing). Wheel track 4.5 ft, 1.37 m. Wheelbase 4.5 ft, 1.37 m. Nosewheel diameter overall 20 inch, 51 cm. Other data NC.

POWER PLANT - Cuyuna ULII-02 engine. Max power 35 hp at 6200 rpm. Propeller diameter and pitch 54x30 inch, 1.37x0.76 m. V-belt reduction, ratio 2.0/1. Max static thrust 235 lb, 107 kg. Power per unit area 0.21 hp/ft^2, 2.2 hp/m^2. Fuel capacity 5.0 US gal, 4.2 Imp gal, 18.9 litre.

WEIGHTS & LOADINGS - Empty weight 245 lb, 111 kg. Max take-off weight 500 lb, 227 kg. Payload 255 lb, 116 kg. Max wing loading 2.94 lb/ft^2, 14.4 kg/m^2. Max power loading 14.3 lb/hp, 6.5 kg/hp. Load factors +6.0, -4.0 recommended; +9.0, -5.0 ultimate.

PERFORMANCE* - Max level speed 60 mph, 97 kph. Never exceed speed 70 mph, 113 kph. Max cruising speed 55 mph, 88 kph. Economic cruising speed 50 mph, 80 kph. Stalling speed 22 mph, 35 kph. Max climb rate at sea level 1000 ft/min, 5.1 m/s. Min sink rate 290 ft/min at 30 mph, 1.5 m/s at 48 kph. Best glide ratio with power off 8/1 at 28 mph, 45 kph. Take-off distance 75 ft, 23 m. Landing distance 100 ft, 30 m. Service ceiling 18,000 ft, 5490 m. Range at average cruising speed 125 mile, 201 km. Noise level NC.

*Under unspecified test conditions.

UFM OF KENTUCKY
AEROPLANE XP-2
(Three-axis)

Summary similar to Aeroplane XP *except: Side-by-side two-seater.*

Production status: see text.

GENERAL - The *Aeroplane XP-2* is a side-by-side version of the single-seat *Aeroplane XP,* but just as the solo machine may be superseded by Loehle Aviation's *The Fun Machine,* so we suspect that the introduction of *The Fun Machine II* may spell the end of the *Aeroplane XP-2.*

It was, however, listed as recently as January '85 at an

unspecified price for a 25-30 h kit. Rigging time is quoted at 35-45 min.

EXTERNAL DIMENSIONS & AREAS - Wing span 30.0 ft, 9.14 m (top). Total wing area 199 ft², 18.5 m². Other data NC.

POWER PLANT - Cuyuna ULII-02 engine. Max power 43 hp at NC rpm. Propeller diameter and pitch 72x33 inch, 1.83x0.84 m. Reduction type NC, ratio 3.0/1. Max static thrust NC. Power per unit area 0.22 hp/ft², 2.3 hp/m². Fuel capacity 10.0 US gal, 8.3 Imp gal, 37.9 litre.

WEIGHTS & LOADINGS - Empty weight 283 lb, 128 kg. Max take-off weight 750 lb, 340 kg. Payload 467 lb, 212 kg. Max wing loading 3.77 lb/ft², 18.4 kg/m². Max power loading 17.4 lb/hp, 7.9 kg/hp. Load factors NC.

PERFORMANCE* - Max level speed 63 mph, 101 kph. Never exceed speed 75 mph, 121 kph. Cruising speed 50 mph, 80 kph. Stalling speed 30 mph, 48 kph. Max climb rate at sea level 700 ft/min, 3.6 m/s. Range at average cruising speed 100 mile, 161 km. Other data NC.

Under unspecified test conditions.

ULTRA CLASSICS

Ultra Classics, Route 4, Box 48-A, Vacherie, Louisiana 70090; tel (504) 265-3077.

ULTRA CLASSICS *BEARCAT*
(Three-axis)

Single-seat single-engined high-wing monoplane with conventional three-axis control. Wing has unswept leading and trailing edges, and constant chord; cruciform tail. Pitch control by elevator on tail; yaw control by fin-mounted rudder; roll control by full-span flaperons; con-trol inputs through stick for pitch/roll and pedals for yaw. Wing braced from below by struts; wing profile NC; 100% double-surface. Undercarriage has three wheels in tail-dragger formation; axle-flex suspension on tailwheel and bungee suspension on main wheels. Push-right go-right tailwheel steering connected to yaw control; also differential braking. Brakes on main wheels. Steel-tube airframe, partially enclosed. Engine mounted below wing, driving pusher propeller.

Production status: current, 25 completed.

GENERAL - Although we list it separately, this company is closely associated with Air Tech, manufacturer of the *SS/Z*. However, the *Bearcat* is aimed at a totally different market, for it will appeal to those who want to blend a little nostalgia with their ultralight flying.

A Jack Hutchison design - the man who created the *Buccaneer* amphibian and the earliest version of the fixed-seat *Quicksilver* - the aircraft isn't intended to be a replica of any particular vintage classic, and is best described as a cross between a *J-3 Cub* and a parasol-type machine. Introduced at the '84 Sun 'n Fun in Lakeland, Florida, the *Bearcat* is now in production and is offered at US$7995 for a 40 h kit.

EXTERNAL DIMENSIONS & AREAS - Length overall 18.0 ft, 5.49 m. Height overall 6.0 ft, 1.83 m. Wing span 30.0 ft, 9.14 m. Constant chord 5.0 ft, 1.52 m. Dihedral 1°. Sweepback 0°. Tailplane span 8.0 ft, 2.44 m. Fin height 3.0 ft, 0.91 m. Total wing area 150 ft², 13.9 m². Total flaperon area NC. Fin area 4.5 ft², 0.42 m². Rudder area 8.0 ft², 0.74 m². Tailplane area NC. Total elevator area 10.0 ft², 0.93 m². Aspect ratio 6.0/1. Wheel track 6.0 ft, 1.83 m. Wheelbase 13.0 ft, 3.96 m. Tailwheel diameter overall 5 inch, 13 cm. Main wheels diameter overall 12 inch, 30 cm.

POWER PLANT - Rotax 447 engine. Max power 40 hp at 6250 rpm. Propeller diameter and pitch 68x28 inch, 1.73x0.71 m. Gear reduction, ratio 2.5/1. Max static thrust 260 lb, 118 kg. Power per unit area 0.27 hp/ft², 2.9 hp/m². Fuel capacity 5.0 US gal, 4.2 Imp gal, 18.9 litre.

WEIGHTS & LOADINGS - Empty weight 270 lb, 122 kg. Max take-off weight 650 lb, 295 kg. Payload 380 lb, 172 kg.

Max wing loading 4.33 lb/ft², 21.2 kg/m². Max power loading 16.3 lb/hp, 7.4 kg/hp. Load factors +6.0, -4.0 recommended; +9.0, -6.0 ultimate.

PERFORMANCE* - Max level speed 70 mph, 113 kph. Never exceed speed 88 mph, 142 kph. Max cruising speed 60 mph, 97 kph. Economic cruising speed 45 mph, 72 kph. Stalling speed 24 mph, 39 kph. Max climb rate at sea level 600 ft/min, 3.1 m/s. Take-off distance 200 ft, 61 m. Landing distance 200 ft, 61 m. Service ceiling 14,000 ft, 4270 m. Range at average cruising speed 130 mile, 209 km. Other data NC.

*Under the following test conditions - Airfield altitude 5 ft, 1.5 m. Ground temperature 70°F, 21°C. Ground pressure NC. Ground windspeed 0 mph, 0 kph. Test payload 210 lb, 95 kg.

ULTRA EFFICIENT PRODUCTS

Ultra Efficient Products Inc, 1158 Lewis Avenue, Sarasota, Florida 33577; tel (813) 955-0710 or 365-1263.

ULTRA EFFICIENT PRODUCTS *INVADER MKIII-B*

(Three-axis)

Single-seat single-engined mid-wing monoplane with unconventional three-axis control (conventional three-axis control optional). Wing has unswept leading and trailing edges, and constant chord; V-tail. Pitch/yaw control by ruddervator; roll control by 40%-span ailerons; control inputs through stick for pitch/yaw/roll (optional: stick for pitch/roll and pedals for yaw). Cantilever wing; 18% wing profile; 100% double-surface. Undercarriage has three wheels in tricycle formation; no suspension on nosewheel and bungee suspension on main wheels. Push-right go-right nosewheel steering independent from yaw control (optional: connected to yaw control). No brakes. Wood/foam/aluminium-alloy tube/steel-tube airframe, partially enclosed (totally enclosed optional). Engine mounted above wing, driving pusher propeller.

Production status: current, over 250 sets of plans sold.

GENERAL - Conceived by Nick Leighty, the original *Invader* appeared at the '82 Sun 'n Fun and has been steadily developed ever since. By early 1983 the machine was being offered in two versions, the *Invader MkII* and the *Invader MkIII,* the principal difference being the undercarriage: tail-dragger or tricycle respectively. Yamaha 14 hp or Zenoah 20 hp engines were used initially, but Rotax power was adopted in 1983, the aircraft becoming *Invader MkIII-B* in the process. En route, the tail-dragger option disappeared.

All versions are structurally similar. The fuselage is made up of 4130 welded steel, with an aluminium-alloy tail boom. Wings use a geodesic structure with hot-wire cut white styrofoam ribs tied to the spar with spruce capstrips and covered with transparent Mylar, a similar principle being

used for the rudderators. In fact Nick likens building the aircraft to aeromodelling on a grand scale.

While this construction may be structurally efficient and is certainly aesthetic, the company admits that the ribs have only a four-year life if kept covered when out of use, and as little as a year if left in strong sunlight. Substituting Dacron for the Mylar - an option offered by the factory - presumably helps, but of course makes inspection harder.

Not just the aircraft's structure is unusual, for the *Invader MkIII-B* is one of the few ultralights with single-stick control, sideways movement of the stick operating both a ruddervator and its related aileron via a mixer. Conventional three-axis control is an option, as the pedals are fitted anyway for ground steering.

Customers can buy in various ways. Plans cost US$60 (US$75 overseas) and require up to 600 h, or the builder can save time with a raw materials kit for US$3495, including engine, instruments and preformed ribs. For US$5500 a quick-build kit can be had, requiring 100 h and containing prefabricated sub-assemblies, ready-to-run power pack, and all hardware, materials and adhesives. Finally, for those who only want to spend the 15 min rigging time, the company sells finished aircraft for US$6700.

EXTERNAL DIMENSIONS & AREAS - Length overall 18.0 ft, 5.49 m. Height overall 4.0 ft, 1.22 m. Wing span 31.5 ft, 9.60 m. Constant chord 4.6 ft, 1.39 m. Dihedral 10°. Sweepback 0°. Tailplane span 8.0 ft, 2.44 m. Ruddervator height NC. Total wing area 144 ft², 13.4 m². Total aileron area 18.0 ft², 1.67 m². Ruddervator area 20.0 ft², 18.6 m². Aspect ratio 6.9/1. Wheel track 4.0 ft, 1.22 m. Wheelbase 4.0 ft, 1.22 m. Nosewheel diameter overall 10 inch, 25 cm. Main wheels diameter overall 10 inch, 25 cm.

POWER PLANT - Rotax 277 engine. Max power 28 hp at 6200 rpm. Propeller diameter and pitch 56x24 inch, 1.42x0.61 m. Gear reduction, ratio 2.5/1. Max static thrust 170 lb, 77 kg. Power per unit area 0.19 hp/ft², 2.1 hp/m². Fuel capacity 5.0 US gal, 4.2 Imp gal, 18.9 litre.

WEIGHTS & LOADINGS - Empty weight 245 lb, 111 kg. Max take-off weight 475 lb, 215 kg. Payload 230 lb, 104 kg. Max wing loading 3.30 lb/ft², 16.0 kg/m². Max power loading 17.0 lb/hp, 7.7 kg/hp. Load factors +3.5, -3.5 recommended; +4.5, -4.5 ultimate.

PERFORMANCE* - Max level speed 60 mph, 97 kph. Never exceed speed 75 mph, 121 kph. Max cruising speed 50 mph, 80 kph. Economic cruising speed 45 mph, 72 kph. Stalling speed 26 mph, 42 kph. Max climb rate at sea level

700 ft/min, 3.6 m/s. Min sink rate 250 ft/min, 1.3 m/s at NC speed. Best glide ratio with power off 14/1 at 40 mph, 64 kph. Take-off distance** 150 ft, 46 m. Landing distance** 150 ft, 46 m. Service ceiling 10,000 ft, 3050 m. Range at average cruising speed >200 mile, >322 km. Noise level NC.

*Under the following test conditions - Test payload 170 lb, 77 kg. Other data NC.

**On grass.

ULTRALIGHT FLIGHT

Ultralight Flight Inc, PO Box 790, Mount Airy, North Carolina 27030; tel (919) 786-9000. Proprietor: Harold Brown.

West German agent: Rainbow Air Services, In der Rauschen 6, 6460 Gelnhausen 3.

ULTRALIGHT FLIGHT
PHANTOM
(Three-axis)

Single-seat single-engined high-wing monoplane with conventional three-axis control. Wing has unswept leading edge, swept forward trailing edge, and tapering chord; cruciform tail. Pitch control by elevator on tail; yaw control by fin-mounted rudder; roll control by full-span ailerons; control inputs through stick for pitch/roll and pedals for yaw. Wing braced from above by kingpost and cables, from below by cables; wing profile NACA 4412 modified; 100% double-surface. Undercarriage has three wheels in tricycle formation; no suspension on nosewheel and bungee suspension on main wheels. Push-right go-right nosewheel steering connected to yaw control. No brakes. Aluminium-alloy tube airframe, with pod. Engine mounted above wing, driving tractor propeller.

Production status: current, 575 produced.

GENERAL - If you judge an aircraft by the number of imitations it has spawned - and that's as good a definition as any - then the *Phantom* is a classic. One of the first heavy-duty high-performance ultralights on the market, the *Phantom* has an excellent safety record, due in part to its sturdy, almost overbuilt construction. This ruggedness puts the machine very close to the ultralight weight limit, but makes it one of the few ultralights genuinely capable of aerobatics; the example thrown around at various American airshows by Jack Britton may be beefed-up and highly modified, but even the production version has been static tested to +9.9g and -6.6g and is capable of going from 45° bank in one direction to 45° the other way in 1.5 s. Douglas Barth, flight testing the machine in the January '83 *Glider Rider,* described it as 'a delightfully uncommon aircraft designed for the common man'.

Conceived under the direction of John Dempsey, the aircraft carried off the outstanding design award at the '82 Oshkosh, a feat which the *Mirage,* Ultralight Flight's earlier design, had managed at the previous year's Sun 'n Fun. For some time both machines were offered, but the *Mirage* is now the preserve of Mirage Aircraft, leaving Ultralight Flight's current management - which only took over in mid '84 - with just the *Phantom* and its two-seat derivative in its stable.

Power comes from the Kawasaki TA440A, though a few examples were produced in Britain by the now defunct Skyriders company using Robin engines.

Price is US$5495 for a 35 h kit, and rigging time is 30 min.

EXTERNAL DIMENSIONS & AREAS - Length overall 16.5 ft, 5.02 m. Height overall 8.2 ft, 2.49 m. Wing span 28.5 ft, 8.68 m. Chord at root 5.2 ft, 1.60 m. Chord at tip 4.8 ft, 1.47 m. Dihedral 1.5°. Sweepback 0°. Tailplane span 8.0 ft, 2.44 m. Fin height 5.0 ft, 1.52 m. Total wing area 141 ft², 13.1 m². Total aileron area 19.8 ft², 1.84 m². Fin area 6.9 ft², 2.12 m². Rudder area 8.8 ft², 0.81 m². Tailplane area 12.7 ft², 1.18 m². Total elevator area 10.1 ft², 0.94 m². Aspect ratio 5.8/1. Wheel track 3.4 ft, 1.05 m. Wheelbase 5.0 ft, 1.52 m. Nosewheel diameter overall 12 inch, 30 cm. Main wheels diameter overall 12 inch, 30 cm.

POWER PLANT - Kawasaki TA440A engine. Max power 37 hp at 6000 rpm. Propeller diameter and pitch 58x22

inch, 1.47x0.56 m. V-belt reduction, ratio 1.9/1. Max static thrust 190 lb, 86 kg. Power per unit area 0.19 hp/ft², 2.8 hp/m². Fuel capacity 4.5 US gal, 3.8 Imp gal, 17.0 litre.

WEIGHTS & LOADINGS - Empty weight 254 lb, 115 kg. Max take-off weight 510 lb, 231 kg. Payload 256 lb, 116 kg. Max wing loading 3.62 lb/ft², 17.6 kg/m². Max power loading 13.8 lb/hp, 6.2 kg/hp. Load factors +6.6, -4.4 recommended; +9.9, -6.6 ultimate.

PERFORMANCE* - Max level speed 63 mph, 101 kph. Never exceed speed 100 mph, 161 kph. Max cruising speed 57 mph, 92 kph. Economic cruising speed 51 mph, 82 kph. Stalling speed 27 mph, 43 kph. Max climb rate at sea level 750 ft/min, 3.8 m/s. Min sink rate 500 ft/min at 39 mph, 2.5 m/s at 63 kph. Best glide ratio with power off 7/1 at 39 mph, 63 kph. Take-off distance 100 ft, 30 m. Landing distance 150 ft, 46 m. Service ceiling 14,500 ft, 4420 m. Range at average cruising speed 125 mile, 201 km. Noise level NC.

*Under the following test conditions - Test payload 170 lb, 77 kg. Other data NC.

ULTRALIGHT FLIGHT
PHANTOM II

(Three-axis)

Summary as Phantom *except: Side-by-side two-seater. Main wheel brakes. Partially enclosed.*

Production status: prototype.

GENERAL - In view of the ample reserves of strength in the *Phantom,* it's a natural for development into a two-seater, and that is just what Harold Brown is doing. The new machine will, we understand, be very similar to the solo version except for a larger engine (Rotax 503), brakes, more weather protection, greater span, and more dihedral. The fuel tank is also slightly bigger.
Price: US$8995.

EXTERNAL DIMENSIONS & AREAS - See *Phantom* except: Length overall NC. Height overall NC. Wing span 33.5 ft, 10.21 m. Dihedral 3°. Total wing area 168 ft², 15.6 m². Total aileron area NC. Aspect ratio 6.7/1. Wheel track NC. Wheelbase NC.

POWER PLANT - Rotax 503 engine. Max power 52 hp at NC rpm. Propeller diameter and pitch 68x34 inch, 1.73x0.86 m. Gear reduction, ratio 2.7/1. Max static thrust 350 lb, 159 kg. Power per unit area 0.31 hp/ft², 3.33 hp/m². Fuel capacity 5.0 US gal, 4.2 Imp gal, 18.9 litre.

WEIGHTS & LOADINGS - Empty weight 350 lb, 159 kg. Max take-off weight 800 lb, 363 kg. Payload 450 lb, 204 kg. Max wing loading 4.76 lb/ft², 23.3 kg/m². Max power loading 15.4 lb/hp, 7.0 kg/hp. Load factors +3.8, -2.5 recommended; +5.7, -3.8 ultimate.

PERFORMANCE* - Max level speed 63 mph, 101 kph. Never exceed speed 100 mph, 161 kph. Max cruising speed 59 mph, 95 kph. Economic cruising speed 52 mph, 84 kph. Stalling speed 33 mph, 53 kph. Max climb rate at sea level 775 ft/min, 3.9 m/s. Take-off distance 150 ft, 46 m. Landing distance 200 ft, 61 m. Range at average cruising speed 80 mile, 129 km. Other data NC.

*Under unspecified test conditions.

ULTRALIGHT TECHNOLOGY

Ultralight Technology Inc, 1775 S First St, Route 16, San Jose, California 95112.

ULTRALIGHT TECHNOLOGY
CAVALIER

(Three-axis)

Single-seat single-engined high-wing monoplane with conventional three-axis control. Cruciform tail. Pitch control by elevator; yaw control by fin-mounted rudder; roll control NC; control inputs through stick for pitch/roll and pedals for yaw. Wing braced from below by struts; 100% double-surface. Undercarriage has three wheels in tricycle formation. Composite-construction airframe, partially enclosed. Engine mounted at wing height, driving tractor propeller. Other details NC.

Production status: prototype.

GENERAL - Seen at the Los Angeles Expo in late '84, the *Cavalier* attracted attention because of its beautiful sleek lines and excellent finish. It is aimed at the experimental-category market rather than the ultralight sector, though it may be microlight-legal in some countries.
This composite-construction machine has its power pack on a boom out front; the tail boom is quite separate, emerging from the bottom of the partially enclosed cockpit, which could easily be made totally enclosed by the addition of windows.
As you can gather from the absence of data paragraphs and the gaps in our summary above, information to date (July '85) is very sparse. At the time of the show the company was aiming to get the machine onto the market by spring '85 at around US$10,000, but as we go to press no further news has emerged.

ULTRALITE PRODUCTS

UP Inc, 28011 Front St, PO Box 659, Temecula, California 92390; tel (714) 676-5652.

ULTRALITE PRODUCTS
ARROW P-3

GENERAL - Normally we would hesitate to include an aircraft about which so little is known as the *Arrow P-3,* but in this case we have no doubts. Ultralite Products, or UP as it usually known, is known to every hang-glider in the US, if not the world, as a major force in that sport. If UP is interested in the ultralight market, the fact is worth recording.
At the time of going to press, that was about all we could record, except to observe that their machine is certainly not Rogallo based. It uses a twin-boom fuselage with Tedlar covering on the tail surfaces and Dacron on the wings, and will not be put into production until the FAA's ultralight legislation is finalised. Beyond that, we'll have to wait...

Hal Adkins

Assembling the Cloud Dancer, *with its roll-up wings.*

ULTRA SAIL

Ultra Sail Inc, 58 Davis Street, Locust Valley, New York 11560; tel (516) 676-5210. President: Erwin Rodger. Vice-president: Roger Delura.

ULTRA SAIL *CLOUD DANCER*
(Three-axis)

Single-seat single-engined low-wing monoplane with conventional three-axis control. Wing has unswept leading and trailing edges, and constant chord; V-tail. Pitch/yaw control by ruddervator; roll control by 27%-span spoilers; control inputs through stick for pitch/roll and pedals for yaw. Cantilever wing; wing profile NC; 85% double-surface. Undercarriage has three wheels in taildragger formation; spring suspension on tailwheel and glass-fibre suspension on main wheels. Push-right go-right tailwheel steering connected to yaw control. No brakes. Aluminium-alloy tube airframe, partially enclosed. Engine mounted above wing, driving pusher propeller.

Production status: prototype.

GENERAL - One of the very few ultralights designed for soaring, rather than merely with soaring capability, the *Cloud Dancer* made its public debut at the aircraft recreational vehicle (ARV) competition held at Oshkosh in 1983.

With a glide ratio of 15/1 and an efficient power unit - the Rotax 277 with integral gearbox is used - long leisurely cross-countries are a real possibility in this machine, especially if there are a few thermals around and the engine can be switched off some of the time. To keep the drag down, designer Erwin Rodger used a cantilevered wing and an almost enclosed fuselage, full enclosure being an option. These features, combined with an unusually high (for an ultralight) aspect ratio of 11/1 allow the *Cloud Dancer* to glide well without resorting to a very low wing loading.

The wings use an I-beam spar and an aluminium-alloy D-cell leading edge, a patented design which unplugs from the fuselage and folds up. Derigging or rigging time is a genuine 10 min, and Erwin has got the figure down to 7.5 in demonstrations! Unidirectional glass-fibre is used for the main gear legs, both the undercarriage and fuselage having been tested to an impact of 11g.

Glider pilots will feel at home in the cockpit. The stick has an optional trim control on top and a squeeze control on the front which gives simultaneous movement of the spoilers without loss of roll control. The spoilers are said to work right down to the stall and give a 45° to 45° roll rate of 2.5 s, while the ruddervators work differentially, making co-ordinated flight possible with just spoilers and rudder.

Sold as a 20 h kit for US$6800 or ready to fly for US$7300, the *Cloud Dancer* can be had with electric start (US$250 extra), ballistic parachute (US$850), in-flight trim (US$50), car-top system (US$200), extra wide tyres (US$30) and wing and fuselage covers (US$100), as well as a variety of instruments.

EXTERNAL DIMENSIONS & AREAS - Length overall 17.0 ft, 5.18 m. Height overall 4.5 ft, 1.37 m. Wing span 38.5 ft, 11.7 m. Constant chord 3.4 ft, 1.04 m. Total dihedral 12°. Sweepback 0°. Tailplane span 6.6 ft, 2.01 m. Ruddervator height 2.8 ft, 0.85 m. Total wing area 134 ft², 12.4 m². Total aileron area 2.5 ft², 0.23 m². Effective fin area 11.2 ft², 1.04 m². Effective rudder area 5.6 ft², 0.52 m². Effective tailplane area 13.1ft², 1.22 m². Effective elevator area 6.6 ft², 0.61 m². Aspect ratio 11.1/1. Wheel track 5.0 ft, 1.52 m. Wheelbase 13.0 ft, 3.96 m. Tailwheel diameter overall 4 inch, 10 cm. Main wheels diameter overall 11 inch, 27cm.

POWER PLANT - Rotax 277 engine. Max power 27 hp at 6200 rpm. Propeller diameter and pitch 48x26 inch, 1.22x0.66 m. Gear reduction, ratio 2.0/1. Max static thrust 155 lb, 70 kg. Power per unit area 0.20 hp/ft², 2.2 hp/m². Fuel capacity 5.0 US gal, 4.2 Imp gal, 18.9 litre.

WEIGHTS & LOADINGS - Empty weight 248 lb, 112 kg. Max take-off weight 500 lb, 227 kg. Payload 252 lb, 114 kg. Max wing loading 3.73 lb/ft², 18.3 kg/m². Max power loading 18.5 lb/hp, 8.4 kg/hp. Load factors +3.5, -3.5 recommended; +5.5, -5.5 ultimate.

PERFORMANCE* - Max level speed 62 mph, 100 kph.

Never exceed speed 70 mph, 113 kph. Max cruising speed 55 mph, 88 kph. Economic cruising speed 40 mph, 64 kph. Stalling speed 28 mph, 45 kph. Max climb rate at sea level 600 ft/min, 3.1 m/s. Min sink rate 250 ft/min at 34 mph, 1.3 m/s at 55 kph. Best glide ratio with power off 15/1 at 42 mph, 68 kph. Take-off distance 100 ft, 30 m. Landing distance 150 ft, 46 m. Service ceiling 18,000 ft, 5490 m. Range at average cruising speed 200 mile, 322 km. Noise level NC.

Under the following test conditions - Airfield altitude 100 ft, 30 m. Ground temperature 70°F, 21°C. Ground pressure 1013 mB. Ground windspeed 10 mph, 16 kph. Test payload 200 lb, 91 kg.

US AIRCRAFT

US Aircraft, PO Box 325, Whiting, New Jersey 08759; tel (609) 726-1369. President: Robert Abel.

US AIRCRAFT *KUB*

(Three-axis)

Single-seat single-engined high-wing monoplane with conventional three-axis control. Wing has unswept leading and trailing edges, and constant chord; flaps fitted; cruciform tail. Pitch control by elevator on tail; yaw control by fully flying rudder; roll control by approx 60%-span ailerons; control inputs through stick for pitch/roll and pedals for yaw. Wing braced from below by struts; wing profile 'One on 12x8'; 100% double-surface. Undercarriage has three wheels in tricycle formation; axle-flex suspension on all wheels. Push-right go-right nosewheel steering connected to yaw control. Nosewheel brake. Aluminium-alloy tube airframe, totally enclosed. Engine mounted below wing, driving tractor propeller.

Production status: prototype.

GENERAL - With *Cub* lookalikes being so popular, it was only a matter of time before someone created a lightplane-like ultralight and actually revived the name, albeit with a different spelling. That someone is Robert Abel, who as you can read under the Eastern Ultralights heading has now left that company in the hands of brother Raymond so that he can get on with developing the *Kub*.
In fact there is a relationship with Eastern Ultralights' *Snoop* series, particularly the double-surfaced *Snoop+*, for although the two aircraft look utterly different, the *Kub* is still a tube and Dacron design underneath and uses a wing and tail of similar configuration. At the risk of being accused of over-simplification, the recipe is: take a *Snoop+*, ditch the kingpost in favour of struts, move the engine up front to drive a tractor prop, add a sturdy undercarriage and nosewheel brake, and cover the whole airframe in Dacron. The result looks rather like the covered versions of the defunct Gemini International *Hummingbird 103*, except that there is a cruciform tail instead of a V-shape.
At the time of writing the aircraft is in prototype form, with production scheduled for later in 1985 at a price of US$6790 for a 45 h kit which will be complete except for instruments. A British Skymaster parachute is standard equipment, not least because the 'parachute allowance' is needed to make this machine ultralight-legal.
Later will come a two-seater called the *Kub II,* which will use a 48 hp Rotax 503 and be certified as a homebuilt. Of very similar configuration, it will use a strengthened version of the *Kub's* wing but with a 10 inch (25 cm) increase in span, plus of course a wider cockpit. Data below refers to the prototype single-seater.

EXTERNAL DIMENSIONS & AREAS - Length overall 17.0 ft, 5.18 m. Height overall 7.0 ft, 2.13 m. Wing span 30.0 ft, 9.14 m. Constant chord* 4.0 ft, 1.22 m. Sweepback 0°. Tailplane span 7.5 ft, 2.29 m. Total wing area** 135 ft^2, 12.5 m^2. Tailplane area 16.0 ft^2, 1.49 m^2. Aspect ratio 7.5/1. Wheel track 5.2 ft, 1.58 m. Wheelbase 5.2 ft, 1.58 m. Other data NC.

POWER PLANT - Rotax 277 engine. Max power 28 hp at NC rpm. Propeller diameter and pitch 60x28 inch, 1.52x0.71 m. Gear reduction, ratio 2.6/1. Max static thrust NC. Power per unit area 0.21 hp/ft^2, 2.2 hp/m^2. Fuel capacity 5.0 US gal, 4.2 Imp gal, 18.9 litre.

WEIGHTS & LOADINGS - Empty weight 276 lb, 125 kg. Max take-off weight 576 lb, 261 kg. Payload 300 lb, 136 kg. Max wing loading 4.27 lb/ft^2, 20.9 kg/m^2. Max power loading 20.6 lb/hp, 9.3 kg/hp. Load factors NC.

PERFORMANCE*** - Never exceed speed 70 mph, 113 kph. Cruising speed 55 mph, 88 kph. Stalling speed with power off 26 mph, 42 kph. Stalling speed with power on and full flaps 24 mph, 39 kph. Max climb rate at sea level 800 ft/min, 4.1 m/s. Take-off distance 175 ft, 53 m. Landing distance 175 ft, 53 m. Other data NC.

Excluding ailerons and flaps.

**Including ailerons and flaps.*

***Under the following test conditions* - Ground windspeed 0 mph, 0 kph. Pilot weight 165 lb, 75 kg. Other data NC.

VOLMER AIRCRAFT

Volmer Aircraft, Box 5222, Glendale, California 91201; tel (818) 247-8718. Proprietor: Volmer Jensen.

VOLMER AIRCRAFT *VJ-24 Sunfun*

(Three-axis)

Single-seat single-engined high-wing monoplane with conventional three-axis control. Wing has unswept leading and trailing edges, and constant chord; cruciform tail. Pitch control by elevator on tail; yaw control by fin-mounted rudder; roll control by 36%-span ailerons; control inputs through stick for pitch/roll and pedals for yaw. Wing braced from struts; wing profile in-house; 90% double-surface. Undercarriage has three wheels in tail-dragger formation; no suspension on tailwheel and axle-flex suspension on main wheels. Push-right go-right tailwheel steering connected to yaw control. No brakes. Aluminium-alloy tube airframe, partially enclosed. Engine mounted at wing height, driving tractor propeller.

Production status: current, number completed NC.

GENERAL - Volmer Jensen, now 74 years young, is one of the true pioneers of the ultralight movement, designing the predecessor of the *VJ-24 Sunfun*, the *VJ-23 Swingwing*, in 1971 in conjunction with Irvin Culver. This first machine was a plans-built hang-glider of traditional construction, using steel tube, mahogany and spruce with Dacron covering, but soon a motorised version was produced, the *VJ-23E Swingwing,* using a 12 hp McCulloch Mc-101 mounted as a pusher in a pod above the wing.

To this aircraft goes the honour of the first ever microlight crossing of the English Channel, by Englishman Dave Cook on 9 May 1978, but despite this achievement the aircraft

suffered from a major fault in pilots' eyes - it took too long to build. Therefore the tube-and-Dacron *VJ-24 Sunfun* was introduced in 1974, its strut bracing making it easily distinguishable from its cantilevered predecessor. This too started life as a hang-glider, being produced in that form for three years before being motorised to become *VJ-24E Sunfun* foot-launched ultralight. McCulloch power was again used, but this time under the wing behind the pilot.

A further three years went by before the next major change - the *VJ-24W Sunfun.* This model differed from the *VJ-24E*

Compare this picture of an earlier, open VJ-24 *with the current version featured in the colour section.*

in two important ways - first, it had a fixed seat, so that the wheels acted as a conventional undercarriage rather than being used just to wheel the machine into its launch position, and second it had a tractor prop.

The aircraft offered today is essentially a refined version of the *VJ-24W,* the 'W' having somehow got lost along the way. But the essence of the machine remains the same: a true slow-flight aircraft, with delightfully responsive controls and a wing efficient enough to fly with fewer horsepower than any other in the industry. Latest models incorporate a nacelle around the pilot, 'Cessna type' landing gear, a steerable tailwheel, a sailplane-type rudder and a propeller brake, the latter to enable the pilot to stop the prop while the engine is idling and go quietly soaring.

Sold at one stage through the Airway Aircraft company, the plans are now once again marketed by Volmer Jensen himself, and cost US$200. Build cost is around US$2000 with Yamaha engine.

EXTERNAL DIMENSIONS & AREAS - Length overall 18.5 ft, 5.64 m. Height overall 5.5 ft, 1.68 m. Wing span 36.0 ft, 10.97 m. Constant chord 4.5 ft, 1.37 m. Dihedral 1°. Sweepback 0°. Tailplane span 10.0 ft, 3.05 m. Fin height 5.0 ft, 1.52 m. Total wing area 160 ft², 14.9 m². Aspect ratio 8.1/1. Wheel track 4.0 ft, 1.22 m. Tailwheel diameter overall 3 inch, 8 cm. Main wheels diameter overall 16 inch, 41 cm. Other data NC.

POWER PLANT - Yamaha KT-100S engine. Max power 15 hp at 10,000 rpm. Propeller diameter and pitch 54x24 inch, 1.37x0.61 m. Notched V-belt reduction, ratio 3.6/1. Max static thrust > 100 lb, > 45 kg. Power per unit area 0.09 hp/ft², 1.0 hp/m². Fuel capacity 1.5 US gal, 1.3 Imp gal, 5.7 litre.

WEIGHTS & LOADINGS - Empty weight 210 lb, 95 kg. Max take-off weight 410 lb, 186 kg. Payload 200 lb, 91 kg. Max wing loading 2.56 lb/ft², 12.5 kg/m². Max power loading 27.3 lb/hp, 12.4 kg/hp. Load factors +2.6, -NC recommended; +3.9, -NC ultimate.

PERFORMANCE* - Max level speed 40 mph, 64 kph. Never exceed speed 50 mph, 80 kph. Max cruising speed 30 mph, 48 kph. Economic cruising speed 30 mph, 48 kph. Stalling speed 20 mph, 32 kph. Max climb rate at sea level 350 ft/min, 1.8 m/s. Best glide ratio with power off 10/1 at 25 mph, 40 kph. Take-off distance 100 ft, 30 m. Landing distance 50 ft, 15 m. Range at average cruising speed 50 mile, 80 km. Other data NC.

*Under unspecified test conditions.

WICKS

Wicks Aircraft Supply, 410 Pine Street, Highland, Illinois 62249; tel (618) 654-7447.

WICKS
BARNSTORMER
(Three-axis)

Single-seat single-engined biplane with conventional three-axis control. Wings have unswept leading and trailing edges, and constant chord; conventional tail. Pitch control by elevator on tail; yaw control by fin-mounted rudder; roll control by full-span ailerons; con-

Glider Rider

▲

trol inputs through stick for pitch/roll and pedals for yaw. Wings braced by struts; wing profile NACA 23015; 100% double-surface. Undercarriage has three wheels in tricycle formation; bungee suspension on all wheels. Push-right go-right nosewheel steering connected to yaw control. Brakes on main wheels. Aluminium-alloy tube airframe, completely open. Engine mounted between wings, driving tractor propeller.

Production status: current, number completed NC.

GENERAL - This Mike Fisher design was first shown at Oshkosh in 1982, but is not marketed by his company Fisher Flying Products, which concentrates on the *FP* series of aircraft. Instead the *Barnstormer* is sold on his behalf by Wicks Aircraft Supply in the form of a basic kit without power pack. The *Barnstormer* makes a good homebuild project, as it has a relatively simple structure using 6061T6 tubing and 2024T3 sheet for the airframe, the wings being covered with 2.7 oz Stits Polyfiber. *Barnstormers* can be found with two different wing spans - either the standard 20.0 ft (6.09 m) span or a shortened span of 17.5 ft (5.33 m).

Being a homebuilt, individual examples will vary widely, but our data below is typical of a Kawasaki-engined *Barnstormer* developing 40 hp and using the standard wing span, the form in which many kit-built *Barnstormers* have been produced. Price of the kit is US$1426. No rigging time is quoted.

EXTERNAL DIMENSIONS & AREAS - Wing span 20.0 ft, 6.09 m (both wings). Constant chord 4.0 ft, 1.21 m (both wings). Sweepback 0°. Total wing area 154 ft², 14.3 m². Aspect ratio 5.4/1 (bottom wing); 5.0/1 (top wing). Nosewheel diameter overall 16 inch, 41 cm. Main wheels diameter overall 16 inch, 41 cm. Other data NC.

POWER PLANT - Kawasaki TA440 engine. Max power 40 hp at 6000 rpm. Propeller diameter and pitch 58xNC inch, 1.47xNC m. Reduction type NC. Max static thrust NC. Power per unit area 0.26 hp/ft², 2.8 hp/m². Fuel capacity 5.0 US gal, 4.2 Imp gal, 18.9 litre.

WEIGHTS & LOADINGS - Empty weight 220 lb, 100 kg. Max take-off weight 450 lb, 204 kg. Payload 230 lb, 104 kg.

Max wing loading 2.92 lb/ft², 14.3 kg/m². Max power loading 11.3 lb/hp, 5.1 kg/hp. Load factors NC.

PERFORMANCE* - Max level speed 60 mph, 97 kph. Cruising speed 40 mph, 64 kph. Other data NC.

*Under unspecified test conditions.

WICKS *BOOMERANG*

(Three-axis)

Single-seat single-engined high-wing monoplane with conventional three-axis control. Wing has unswept leading and trailing edges, and constant chord; cruciform tail. Pitch control by elevator on tail; yaw control by fin-mounted rudder; roll control by half-span ailerons; control inputs through stick for pitch/roll and pedals for yaw. Wing braced from below by struts; 100% double-surface. Undercarriage has three wheels in tail-dragger formation. Aluminium-alloy tube airframe, completely open. Engine mounted below wing, driving tractor propeller. Other details NC.

Production status: current, number completed NC.

GENERAL - Like the *Barnstormer*, the *Boomerang* is a Mike Fisher design intended for homebuilders and marketed on his behalf by Wicks Aircraft Supply. Though quite different in appearance, the appeal is similar - a simple design using readily available materials (the airframe materials and wing covering are as for the *Barnstormer*), which can be easily constructed by the homebuilder of average competence. Another parallel with its biplane stablemate is the option of a different-span wing; builders of *Boomerangs* can choose either the 28.0 ft (8.53 m) span in which form we detail it below, or can have a greater span of 32.0 ft (9.75 m) and correspondingly larger area, an option which allows the aircraft to be used in two-seat form.

Power packs vary too, but a 30 hp Kawasaki with 2.5 US gal (2.1 Imp gal, 9.5 litre) tank is typical and is thus used in our data below; 440 Kawasakis and double-size tanks have also been fitted. Price of the kit without power pack is US$1270 and rigging time is said to be only 10 min.

EXTERNAL DIMENSIONS & AREAS - Wing span 28.0 ft, 8.53 m. Constant chord 5.6 ft, 1.70 m. Sweepback 0°. Total wing area 156 ft², 14.5 m². Aspect ratio 5.0/1. Main

▼

Glider Rider

wheels diameter overall 20 inch, 51 cm. Other data NC.

POWER PLANT - Kawasaki 340 engine. Max power 30 hp at NC rpm. Propeller diameter and pitch 54x22 inch, 1.37x0.56 m. Reduction type NC, ratio 2.0/1. Max static thrust NC. Power per unit area 0.19 hp/ft², 2.1 hp/m². Fuel capacity 2.5 US gal, 2.1 Imp gal, 9.5 litre.

WEIGHTS & LOADINGS - Empty weight 191 lb, 86 kg. Max take-off weight 400 lb, 181 kg. Payload 209 lb, 95 kg. Max wing loading 2.56 lb/ft², 12.5 kg/m². Max power loading 13.3 lb/hp, 6.0 kg/hp. Load factors NC.

PERFORMANCE* - Cruising speed 40 mph, 64 kph. Stalling speed 17 mph, 27 kph. Other data NC.

*Under unspecified test conditions.

WICKS *WOODHOPPER*

(Two-axis)

Single-seat single-engined high-wing monoplane with two-axis control. Wing has unswept leading and trailing edges, and constant chord; cruciform tail. Pitch control by elevator on tail; yaw control by fin-mounted rudder; no separate roll control; control inputs through stick for pitch/yaw. Wing braced from above by kingpost and cables, from below by cables; wing profile NC; NC% double-surface. Undercarriage has tail-dragger formation; no suspension on any wheels. Push-right go-right tail steering connected to yaw control. No brakes. Wood and aluminium-alloy tube airframe, completely open. Engine mounted at wing height, driving tractor propeller.

Production status: current, number completed NC.

GENERAL - Originally designed by the late John Chotia of *Weedhopper* fame, the *Woodhopper* has since the demise of the Weedhopper company been sold by Wicks Aircraft Supply, in the form of a basic kit without power pack. In fact basic is a good word to describe the whole aircraft, for flying machines do not come much simpler than this. With wood and tube construction and an engine hung out front a la *Weedhopper*, this is a machine for calm evenings and light pilots, even though the specification claims a respectable payload.

One constructor who has flown the aircraft successfully is Robert B Miller of Nashville, Tennessee, who described the project in the May 1984 issue of *Ultralight*. Robert redesigned the entire control system and also made a number of detail mods to the machine, and it is clear from the article that the *Woodhopper*, even more than most homebuilts, is very much what the constructor makes it. In such circumstances, performance data can only be typical rather than accurate, but we quote below figures which the manufacturer expects constructors to achieve with a direct-drive engine of around 20 hp. Robert, incidentally, flies his with a 215 cc Cuyuna.

Price of the *Woodhopper* is US$1082 and construction time is given as 250-300 h, which for once doesn't sound too much of an underestimate.

EXTERNAL DIMENSIONS & AREAS - Wing span 32.0 ft, 9.75 m. Constant chord 4.9 ft, 1.50 m. Sweepback 0°. Total wing area 157 ft², 14.6 m². Aspect ratio 6.5/1. Other data NC.

POWER PLANT - Max power *20* hp. No reduction. Power per unit area *0.13* hp/ft², *1.4* hp/m². Other data NC.

WEIGHTS & LOADINGS - Empty weight 145 lb, 66 kg. Max take-off weight 375 lb, 170 kg. Payload 230 lb, 104 kg. Max wing loading 2.39 lb/ft^2, 11.6 kg/m^2. Max power loading *18.8* lb/hp, *8.5* kg/hp. Load factors NC.

PERFORMANCE* - Never exceed speed 45 mph, 72 kph. Cruising speed 35 mph, 56 kph. Stalling speed 20 mph, 32 kph. Other data NC.

*Under unspecified test conditions.

CATTO *GOLDWING ST*

See Catto.

FIRST STRIKE *BOBCAT*

See First Strike.

LIGHT MINIATURE AIRCRAFT *LM-1*

See Light Miniature Aircraft.

MITCHELL AEROSPACE *B-10 MITCHELL WING*

See Mitchell Aerospace.

SPORT FLIGHT ENGINEERING *SKY PUP*

See Sport Flight Engineering.

WOLFE

Wolfe Aviation Co, PO Box 59, Elyria, Ohio 44036; tel (216) 324-7621.

WOLFE *AIRWOLFE/Suitable Rogallo* (Weight-shift)

Single-seat single-engined flex-wing aircraft with weight-shift control. Rogallo wing. Pilot suspended below wing in trike unit, using bar to control pitch and roll/yaw by altering relative positions of trike unit and wing. Wing construction dependent on Rogallo chosen. Undercarriage has three wheels in tricycle formation; suspension NC on nosewheel and glass-fibre suspension on main wheels. Push-right go-left nosewheel steering independent from aerodynamic controls. No brakes. Aluminium-alloy tube trike unit, with pod. Engine mounted below wing, driving pusher propeller.

Production status: current, 10 completed.

GENERAL - Developed from the Cuyuna 215-engined *WAT* featured in our last edition and like the *WAT* sold only as an accessory to hang-gliders rather than as a complete

Yamaha- and Rotax-powered Wolfe trikes.

aircraft, the *Airwolfe's* specification is very much dependent on the pilot's fancy. Not only is there a choice of two engines, but the pilot can also opt for larger rear wheels, while of course the performance will depend considerably on the wing chosen.

Popular Rogallos are from Delta Wing, Flight Designs, and Wills Wings, but the trike unit has also seen service with at least one European glider.

However, two things stand out when comparing the *Airwolfe* with modern European trikes. First, its power unit - even the larger option - is unfashionably small by Old World standards, and second, there is no front strut. Even lightweight trikes in Europe use a wire tieing the nose of the trike unit to the hang point, while on anything heavier a strut is the norm. Wolfe Aviation says the strut is omitted to cut rigging time and give an uninterrupted view, but we have our doubts about the arrangement. On the plus side though, the company deserves full marks for providing a back-up hang-strap, an item which should be de rigeur but which is actually omitted on some otherwise unimpeachable designs.

Complete with foam and fabric pod, the *Airwolfe* trike unit costs US$1800 with Yamaha engine or US$2095 with a Rotax 277, the version described below. The 20 inch (51 cm) main wheels cost an extra US$30.

EXTERNAL DIMENSIONS & AREAS - Length overall*

6.5 ft, 1.98 m. Height overall* 7.0 ft, 2.13 m. Wheel track 5.0 ft, 1.52 m. Wheelbase 5.0 ft, 1.52 m. Nosewheel diameter overall 11 inch, 28 cm. Main wheels diameter overall 11 inch, 28 cm. Other data NC.

POWER PLANT - Rotax 277 engine. Max power 27 hp at 6000 rpm. Propeller diameter and pitch 50x27 inch, 1.27x0.69 m. Notched V-belt reduction, ratio 2.0/1. Max static thrust 175 lb, 79 kg. Power per unit area NC. Fuel capacity 2.0 US gal, 1.7 Imp gal, 7.6 litre.

WEIGHTS & LOADINGS - Empty weight* 128 lb, 58 kg. Other data NC.

PERFORMANCE - NC.

Trike unit only.

West Germany

Researched by
Willi Tacke of
Drachenflieger magazine

All pictures: Sigrid Kurz

We've stood the test...
by Norman Burr

In our first edition we included an introduction to West German ultralighting by Joachim Fassbender, President of the Deutsche Ultraleichtverband (German ultralight association). With the sport in West Germany being carefully regulated and pretty stable by comparison with other countries, we have decided to content ourselves with the following resume of that report, to leave room for some remarkable pictures of the one area of ultralighting where Joachim's country undoubtedly led the world - airworthiness testing procedures.

'Helmut Wilden's *Vowi 10* was undoubtedly the first German ultralight, but like many good ideas was ahead of its time, and remained a curiousity rather than a trendsetter. Produced in the early '70s, this three-axis machine weighed 290 lb (130 kg) empty, but nothing else deserving the descripion UL, as ultralights are known here, appeared for some years. When it did, it was a very different animal - the powered hang-glider.

Towards the end of the '70s, a number of pilots tried motorising their hang gliders, but they encountered just the same problems as their counterparts in other countries - feeble, unreliable engines, and thrust line problems. A decent engine was a priority, and D Konig and R Nolle delivered the goods in 1979, when they designed a motor specially for ultralight use and mated it to a *Fledge* wing. Now pilots could see all sorts of possibilities opening up, and around 20 began an experimental training programme run jointly by the hang gliding federation and the Department of Transport, a programme which culminated in West Germany's ultralight regulations in 1982 and the founding of the DULV the same year. The regulations include a requirement for pilot licensing, and are particularly strict as far as noise is concerned - 60 dB at 82 ft (25 m) from the line of flight of an aircraft flying at 500 ft (150 m). This figure was due to come down to 55 dB in 1985.'

For more information on ultralights in West Germany, contact: DULV, Obereschbach 9, 506 Bergisch-Gladbach 1. Drachenflieger magazine is at Ortlerstrasse 8, 8000 Munchen 70; tel (089) 769 92-0; tx 5-2 27 20.

Originally developed by Michael Schonherr and Ali Scmidt for testing hang gliders, the West German Gutesiegel test rig was adapted for use with triking Rogallos long before the British Hang Gliding Association finally succeeded in providing a similar service on the other side of the English Channel. As a result of this world lead, the West German standard has become an accepted benchmark in dozens of countries. Two cars are used - one for pitch and one for g-measuring. Our main pictures show the general arrangement of the rig, the others being a close-up of the wing mounting arrangements and two sequential shots illustrating what happens as a wing reaches breaking point. The rig can only be used for weight-shift and hybrid control machines: testing of two- and three-axis aircraft is the responsibility of the West German Aero Club.

In flight with the AN22; insets show the Point Aviation version at the Friedrichshafen show in '83, and the power pack with folding propeller.

ALBATROS

Albatros Ultra Flight GmbH Joachim Krenz, Eysseneckstrasse 19, 6000 Frankfurt am Main 1; tel 069/72 0451 work, 069/55 2556 home; tx 4189465. Proprietor: Joachim Krenz.

ALBATROS *AN22*
(Three-axis)

Single-seat single-engined high-wing monoplane with conventional three-axis control. Wing has unswept leading edge, swept forward trailing edge, and tapering chord; conventional tail. Pitch control by elevator on tail; yaw control by fin-mounted rudder; roll control by 70%-span ailerons; control inputs through stick for pitch/roll and pedals for yaw. Wing braced from below by struts; wing profile NACA 4415; 100% double-surface. Undercarriage has three wheels in tricycle formation with additional tailskid; no suspension on nosewheel and glass-fibre suspension on main wheels. Push-right go-right nosewheel steering connected to yaw control; also differential braking. Brakes on main wheels. Steel-tube airframe, completely open. Engine mounted below wing, driving pusher propeller.

Production status: prototype.

GENERAL - Originally designed by the much missed Swiss designer Albert Neukom, the *AN22* was listed in our first edition under Point Aviation, which at that time had the license to built it. The prototype made its first flights in March 1983, and Albert went on to build the first two examples to obtain certification in West Germany. Point Aviation showed the machine at the Aero 83 exhibition in Friedrichshafen and announced ambitious production plans for the model.

However, the *AN22* has since been taken over the Joachim Krenz's Albatros company and Joachim, much more cautiously, describes it as a prototype and has not released any price. Comparison of the data for the Point Aviation and Albatros versions reveals many airframe changes, notably a wing of smaller span and greater area than the original's 33.5 ft and 126 ft² (10.20 m and 11.8 m²). The intention seems to be to move away from Albert's gliding background into a more mainstream ultralight market, but happily the changes have not extended to the most distinctive feature of the aircraft, which remains one of the very few in the world to have its propeller mounted concentrically with the tail boom. Its most obvious competitor in this respect is the American *JB 1000,* made by Leaders International, but since this is a tail-dragger it does not really appeal to the same market.

On the *AN22,* the prop blades fold backwards parallel to the spar, to aid transportation, and are driven via a triple V-belt by the three-cylinder Konig so beloved of German and Swiss enthusiasts because of its quietness. Originally, Point Aviation envisaged two alternative power packs, a

220 cc Solo and a 260 cc Hirth, but these have been dropped. Aided by the novel folding prop, rigging time is claimed to be as little as 15 min, much better than average for a three-axis machine.

As you can read in our Swiss section, Albert Neukom did work on a two-seat version of this aircraft, but we have heard no news of it since his death. Our data below refers to the single-seater in standard form.

EXTERNAL DIMENSIONS & AREAS - Length overall 19.7 ft, 6.00 m. Height overall 6.9 ft, 2.10 m. Wing span 29.5 ft, 9.00 m. Chord at root 4.9 ft, 1.48 m. Chord at tip 4.5 ft, 1.38 m. Dihedral 3°. Sweepback 0°. Tailplane span 8.9 ft, 2.70 m. Fin height 4.8 ft, 1.45 m. Total wing area 145 ft², 13.5 m². Total aileron area 13.6 ft², 1.26 m². Fin area 8.9 ft², 0.83 m². Rudder area 6.7 ft², 0.62 m². Tailplane area 13.0 ft², 1.21 m². Total elevator area 13.1 ft², 1.22 m². Aspect ratio 6.3/1. Wheel track 4.9 ft, 1.50 m. Nosewheel diameter overall 12 inch, 30 cm. Main wheels diameter overall 12 inch, 30 cm. Other data NC.

POWER PLANT - Konig SC430 engine. Max power 24 hp at 4200 rpm. Propeller diameter and pitch 55xNC inch, 1.40xNC m. V-belt reduction, ratio 1.9/1. Max static thrust 165 lb, 75 kg. Power per unit area 0.17 hp/ft², 1.8 hp/m². Fuel capacity 5.3 US gal, 4.4 Imp gal, 20.0 litre.

WEIGHTS & LOADINGS - Empty weight 287 lb, 130 kg. Max take-off weight 527 lb, 239 kg. Payload 240 lb, 109 kg. Max wing loading 3.63 lb/ft², 17.7 kg/m². Max power loading 22.0 lb/hp, 10.0 kg/hp. Load factors +4.0, -2.0 recommended; +6.0, -3.0 ultimate.

PERFORMANCE* - Max level speed 56 mph, 90 kph. Never exceed speed 68 mph, 110 kph. Max cruising speed 44 mph, 70 kph. Economic cruising speed 40 mph, 65 kph. Stalling speed 28 mph, 45 kph. Max climb rate at sea level 390 ft/min, 2.0 m/s. Min sink rate 280 ft/min at 40 mph, 1.4 m/s at 65 kph. Best glide ratio with power off NC. Take-off distance 260 ft, 80 m. Landing distance 150 ft, 45 m. Service ceiling NC. Range at average cruising speed 137 mile, 220 km. Noise level 57 dB(A) at 490 ft, 150 m.

*Under the following test conditions - Airfield altitude 1148 ft, 350 m. Ground temperature 68°F, 20°C. Ground pressure 1015 mB. Ground windspeed 0 mph, 0 kph. Test payload 207 lb, 94 kg.

ALBATROS *MILAN*
(Three-axis)

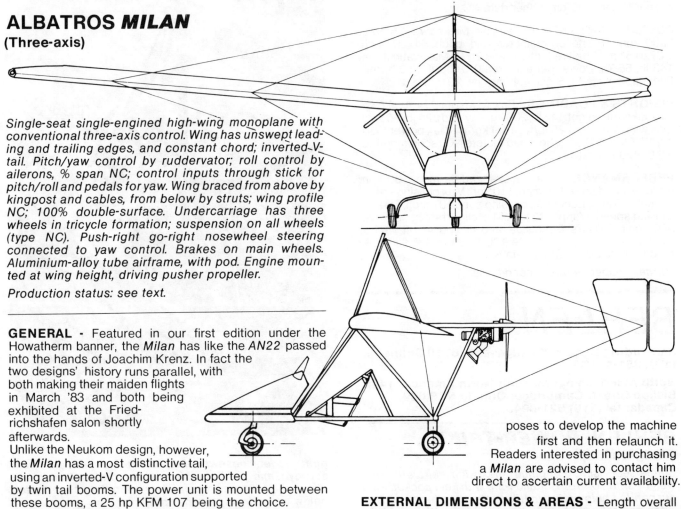

Single-seat single-engined high-wing monoplane with conventional three-axis control. Wing has unswept leading and trailing edges, and constant chord; inverted-V tail. Pitch/yaw control by ruddervator; roll control by ailerons, % span NC; control inputs through stick for pitch/roll and pedals for yaw. Wing braced from above by kingpost and cables, from below by struts; wing profile NC; 100% double-surface. Undercarriage has three wheels in tricycle formation; suspension on all wheels (type NC). Push-right go-right nosewheel steering connected to yaw control. Brakes on main wheels. Aluminium-alloy tube airframe, with pod. Engine mounted at wing height, driving pusher propeller.

Production status: see text.

GENERAL - Featured in our first edition under the Howatherm banner, the *Milan* has like the *AN22* passed into the hands of Joachim Krenz. In fact the two designs' history runs parallel, with both making their maiden flights in March '83 and both being exhibited at the Friedrichshafen salon shortly afterwards.

Unlike the Neukom design, however, the *Milan* has a most distinctive tail, using an inverted-V configuration supported by twin tail booms. The power unit is mounted between these booms, a 25 hp KFM 107 being the choice. Unfortunately, we have no details of the machine's present availability. When we wrote our first edition, Howatherm had two prototypes built and was laying down a production run of ten with a projected price of DM17,400. However, it is not clear whether Joachim Krenz has immediate plans to start production on his own premises, or whether he proposes to develop the machine first and then relaunch it. Readers interested in purchasing a *Milan* are advised to contact him direct to ascertain current availability.

EXTERNAL DIMENSIONS & AREAS - Length overall 18.0 ft, 5.50 m. Height overall 8.5 ft, 2.60 m. Wing span 34.4 ft, 10.50 m. Constant chord 3.9 ft, 1.20 m. Dihedral 4°. Sweepback 0°. Tailplane span 8.2 ft, 2.50 m. Fin height 4.8 ft, 1.45 m. Total wing area 136 ft², 12.6 m². Total aileron area 25.8 ft², 2.40 m². Tailplane area 32.3 ft², 3.00 m². Aspect ratio 8.8/1. Wheel track 4.9 ft, 1.50 m. Nosewheel

Rigging sequence for a typical Behlen trike unit: this particular example has the out of production Lloyd engine.

diameter overall 10 inch, 26 cm. Main wheels diameter overall 12 inch, 30 cm. Other data NC.

POWER PLANT - KFM 107 engine. Max power 25 hp at 6300 rpm. Propeller diameter and pitch 54x20 inch, 1.37x0.51 m. V-belt reduction, ratio 2.1/1. Max static thrust 143 lb, 65 kg. Power per unit area 0.18 hp/ft^2, 2.0 hp/m^2. Fuel capacity 5.3 US gal, 4.4 Imp gal, 20.0 litre.

WEIGHTS & LOADINGS - Empty weight *214* lb, *97* kg. Max take-off weight 442 lb, 200 kg. Payload *228* lb, *103* kg. Max wing loading 3.25 lb/ft^2, 15.9 kg/m^2. Max power loading 17.7 lb/hp, 8.0 kg/hp. Load factors NC recommended; +6.0, -3.0 ultimate.

PERFORMANCE* - Max level speed 62 mph, 100 kph. Never exceed speed 68 mph, 110 kph. Max cruising speed 56 mph, 90 kph. Economic cruising speed 37 mph, 60 kph. Stalling speed 27 mph, 43 kph. Max climb rate at sea level 390 ft/min, 2.0 m/s. Best glide ratio with power off 13/1 at NC speed. Take-off distance 100 ft, 30 m. Landing distance 100 ft, 30 m. Other data NC.

*Under unspecified test conditions.

BEHLEN

Karl-Ludwig Behlen, Weedgasse 6, 6719 Gollheim; tel 06351-41100.

North American agent: Hirth North America, 1425 Bishop Street, Cambridge, Ontario N1R 6J9, Canada; tel (519) 621-8940.

BEHLEN *POWER-TRIKE*
(Weight-shift)

Single-seat single-engined flex-wing aircraft with weight-shift control. Rogallo wing with keel pocket. Pilot suspended below wing in trike unit, using bar to control pitch and roll/yaw by altering relative positions of trike unit and wing. Wing braced from above by kingpost and cables, from below by cables; rigid cross-tube construction with 50% double-surface not enclosing cross-tube; preformed ribs. Undercarriage has three wheels in tricycle formation; no suspension on any wheels. Push-

right go-left nosewheel steering independent from aerodynamic controls. Nosewheel brake. Aluminium-alloy tube trike unit, completely open. Engine mounted below wing, driving pusher propeller.

Production status: current, see text for number completed.

GENERAL - With many years of hang-glider construction under his belt and a history of trike building going back to

1979, Karl-Ludwig Behlen was well placed to become West Germany's first officially approved ultralight manufacturer, and that's just what he achieved. Unlike many trike makers, Karl-Ludwig's machines are built largely in-house, and for a while even incorporated the company's own engine, the Lloyd LS400.

This twin-cylinder motor-industry sourced unit was modified by the Behlen company to aviation specification, in which form it produced 23 hp at 5500 rpm and weighed 61 lb (28 kg). It proved very popular in West Germany and the factory was kept busy producing not only engines for its own use but also units to re-engine existing machines, so that by spring 1983 more than 200 had passed through the company's hands. However, the engine is now a very old design, and Karl-Ludwig has abandoned it in favour of Hirth power, an arrangement which also gives him an outlet in North America through the engine company's agency there.

His trike units, unlike more modern designs, retain the robust duopole construction and feature a novel two-piece front strut, which allows them to fold without seat or strut being removed. As with many trike makers, a variety of seating arrangements, engine options and wing fitments have been supplied over the years; total production must now run into the hundreds, as by April '83, the last time the company gave us a figure, the tally had already reached 200-plus. We detail below the *Power-Trike* in the form in which it is sold on the North American market, with Hirth 2701 engine, single-seat and rigid cross-tube wing. The price there is US$3800, a similar machine in Europe costing DM12,000. For an additional DM480 an instrument panel with ASI, altimeter, and compass can be fitted.

EXTERNAL DIMENSIONS & AREAS - Wing span 30.6 ft, 9.32 m. Total wing area 154 ft², 14.3 m². Aspect ratio 6.1/1. Other data NC.

POWER PLANT - Hirth 2702 engine. Max power 36 hp at

A pair of Mistrals, both with optional pods. For another illustration see front cover.

NC rpm. Power per unit area 0.23 hp/ft², 2.5 hp/m². Fuel capacity 5.0 US gal, 4.2 Imp gal, 18.9 litre. Other data NC.

WEIGHTS & LOADINGS - Empty weight 233 lb, 106 kg. Max take-off weight 444 lb, 201 kg. Payload 211 lb, 96 kg. Max wing loading 2.88 lb/ft², 14.1 kg/m². Max power loading 12.3 lb/hp, 5.6 kg/hp. Load factors NC.

PERFORMANCE - Never exceed speed 78 mph, 126 kph. Other data NC.

BINDER

Binder Aviatik GmbH, Flugplatz Donaueschingen-Villingen, 7710 Donaueschingen; tel 0771-3078/9; tx 792 889 AVIAT D. Works manager: Heinz Westphal.

BINDER *MISTRAL*

(Three-axis)

Single-seat single-engined high-wing monoplane with conventional three-axis control. Wing has unswept leading and trailing edges, and constant chord; cruciform tail. Pitch control by elevator on tail; yaw control by fin-mounted rudder; roll control by full-span ailerons; control inputs through stick for pitch/roll and pedals for yaw. Wing braced from above by kingpost and cables, from below by cables; wing profile Mu 14%; 100% double-surface. Undercarriage has three wheels in tricycle formation with additional tailskid; no suspension on nosewheel and rubber suspension on main wheels. Push-right go-right nosewheel steering connected to yaw control. Nosewheel brake. Aluminium-alloy tube airframe, with optional pod. Engine mounted below wing, driving pusher propeller.

Production status: current, 13 completed by February '85.

GENERAL - As with Sonaca in Belgium and Zenith in France, the increasing maturity of ultralight aviation is attracting established general aviation companies into the sport, and Binder Aviatik is a classic example of this trend.

Established in 1960, this firm is the West German Piper agent and has been supplying West German enthusiasts with light and sport planes for a generation. In the early '80s, however, Binder became concerned at the falling sales of lightplanes. Saturation of the market, increased tax on aviation fuel, and higher costs all round were each taking their toll of the sales figures, and the company needed a new product to sell. A top quality ultralight seemed the answer.

Reasoning that 'today's ultralight customer can be tomorrow's Piper customer', the company set out to find a partner in the ultralight project, eventually settling on Ikarusflug Bodensee after rejecting various French firms, largely on the grounds of quality.

Ikarusflug Bodensee, which incidentally is not the same company as the Ikarus we list in this section, already had considerable experience at the ultralight and hang gliding end of the aviation spectrum and developed for Binder a neat, light, well mannered single seater with conventional tube and Dacron construction and full-span ailerons. With only 28 hp available, it is not particularly fast, but has been designed to give good handling, and thanks to the full-span ailerons can roll from 45° to 45° in a very respectable 2.5 s. Designed initially to the original West German ultralight limit of 220 lb (100 kg) empty, the engineers took advantage of the subsequent increase to 253 lb (115 kg) to strengthen the structure. Within this still tight limit, the designers have managed to provide an airframe which is quite strong for its weight, though it doesn't pretend to have the aerobatic qualities of the *Phantom* for example, while still leaving room for a four-cylinder Konig radial, mainwheel suspension, nosewheel brake and basic instrumentation - ASI, altimeter and compass. Another feature is a nosewheel which collapses on very heavy landing.

They called the new machine *BA 83* internally, after the Binder company initials and the year the project started, and later christened it *Mistral*. Design and construction of the first prototype took only four months and the first *Mistral* took to the air in October '83, gaining its airworthiness certificate the following June, the first three-axis machine to be put on the *Gutesiegel* test rig.

The machine is now manufactured in conjunction with Ikarusflug Bodensee and sold through the Binder organisation at a basic price of DM20,042. Options include a parking brake for DM175, a pod for DM625, and a parachute for DM2290, with a four-stroke option being considered for the future. The company does not see the home market as being able to absorb more than a few dozen *Mistrals,* and Binder's eyes are now fixed firmly on exports to countries where there is no indigenous ultralight industry.

EXTERNAL DIMENSIONS & AREAS - Length overall 19.3 ft, 5.88 m. Height overall 8.5 ft, 2.60 m. Wing span 30.8 ft, 9.40 m. Constant chord 4.9 ft, 1.48 m. Dihedral 2°. Sweepback 0°. Tailplane span 8.2 ft, 2.50 m. Total wing area 150 ft², 13.9 m². Aspect ratio 6.4/1. Wheel track 4.4 ft, 1.35 m. Nosewheel diameter overall 10 inch, 26 cm. Main wheels diameter overall 12 inch, 30 cm. Other data NC.

POWER PLANT - Konig SD570 engine. Max power 28 hp at 4000 rpm. Propeller diameter and pitch 55x37 inch, 1.40x0.95 m. Toothed-belt reduction, ratio 2.0/1. Max static thrust 154 lb, 70 kg. Power per unit area 0.19 hp/ft², 2.0 hp/m². Fuel capacity 5.3 US gal, 4.4 Imp gal, 20.0 litre.

WEIGHTS & LOADINGS - Empty weight 251 lb, 114 kg. Max take-off weight 509 lb, 231 kg. Payload 258 lb, 117 kg. Max wing loading 3.39 lb/ft², 16.6 kg/m². Max power loading 18.2 lb/hp, 8.3 kg/hp. Load factors +4.0, -2.0 recommended; +6.0, -3.0 ultimate.

PERFORMANCE* - Never exceed speed 68 mph, 110 kph. Economic cruising speed 44 mph, 70 kph. Stalling speed 28 mph, 45 kph. Max climb rate at sea level 300 ft/min, 1.5 m/s. Min sink rate 310 ft/min, 1.6 m/s at NC speed. Best glide ratio with power off 9/1 at 34 mph, 55 kph. Take-off distance 230 ft, 70 m. Landing distance 165 ft, 50 m. Range at average cruising speed 118 mile, 190 km. Noise level 59 dB at 490 ft, 150 m. Other data NC.

*Under the following test conditions - Airfield altitude 2231 ft, 680 m. Ground temperature 59°F, 15°C. Ground pressure 1013 mB. Ground windspeed 0 mph, 0 kph. Test payload 234 lb, 106 kg.

HOFFMANN

Wolf Hoffmann Flugzeugbau KG, Sportflugplatz, D-8870 Gunzberg; tel 08221/1417. Proprietor: Dipl-Ing Wolf D Hoffmann.

HOFFMANN *H 39 DIANA*
(Three-axis)

Single-seat single-engined high-wing monoplane with conventional three-axis control. Wing shape - see text; cruciform tail. Pitch control by elevator on tail; yaw control by fin-mounted rudder; roll control by half-span ailerons; control inputs through stick for pitch/roll and pedals for yaw. Wing braced from below by struts; wing profile Worthmann FX63-137; 100% double-surface. Undercarriage has three wheels in tricycle formation; suspension NC on nosewheel and glass-fibre suspension on main wheels. Push-right go-right nosewheel steering connected to yaw control. Nosewheel brake. Glass-fibre/carbon-fibre fuselage, partially enclosed. Engine mounted below wing, driving pusher propeller.

Production status: prototype.

GENERAL - Wolf Hoffmann is a gliding enthusiast and aeronautical engineer, and has to his credit the conventional motor glider *H 36 Dimona* of 1980, a side-by-side two-seater which has been on sale since summer '81. Naturally, when his thoughts turned to ultralights, the result was a very gliding-oriented machine, the *H 39 Diana*, which uses the same Worthmann FX63-137 profile and the same manufacturing techniques as his motor glider.
The soaring heritage is clearly visible in the rigging system, which uses the time-honoured glider arrangement of detachable wings, these being held by two bolts and

supported from underneath by two airfoil-section struts each side. The horizontal empennage is similarly bolted on, allowing the aircraft to be trailered easily. Wing design shows glider thinking too, with a constant chord inboard section incorporating air brakes, and a tapered outboard section incorporating ailerons.

Power comes from the four-cylinder Konig radial, limited to 26 hp at 3500 rpm instead of the normal 28 at 4000 rpm because it is direct driven.

The prototype was shown at the '83 Friedrichshafen exhibition, and though it didn't fly it created a great deal of interest, Wolf expecting to go into production that summer at a price of DM12,500. However, we understand that as recently as February '85 the aircraft was still in prototype form, and at the time of writing it is not clear when production will finally get under way, or at what price.

EXTERNAL DIMENSIONS & AREAS - Length overall 18.4 ft, 5.60 m. Height overall 5.7 ft, 1.75 m. Wing span 32.8 ft, 10.00 m. Chord at root 4.4 ft, 1.33 m. Chord at tip 3.1 ft, 0.93 m. Dihedral 4°. Sweepback 0°. Tailplane span 9.8 ft, 3.00 m. Fin height 3.9 ft, 1.20 m. Total wing area 135 ft^2, 12.5 m^2. Total aileron area 12.1 ft^2, 1.12 m^2. Fin area 6.2 ft^2, 0.58 m^2. Rudder area 4.1 ft^2, 0.38 m^2. Tailplane area 18.1 ft^2, 1.68 m^2. Total elevator area 7.8 ft^2, 0.72 m^2. Aspect ratio 8.0/1. Wheel track 4.9 ft, 1.50 m. Wheelbase 7.0 ft, 2.13 m. Nosewheel diameter overall 10 inch, 26 cm. Main wheels diameter overall 13 inch, 32 cm.

POWER PLANT - Konig SD570 engine. Max power 26 hp at 3500 rpm. Propeller diameter and pitch 42xNC inch, 1.07xNC m. No reduction. Max static thrust 132lb, 60kg. Power per unit area 0.19 hp/ft^2, 2.1 hp/m^2. Fuel capacity 5.3 US gal, 4.4 Imp gal, 20.0 litre.

WEIGHTS & LOADINGS - Empty weight 210 lb, 95 kg. Max take-off weight 475 lb, 215 kg. Payload 265 lb, 120 kg. Max wing loading 3.52 lb/ft^2, 17.2 kg/m^2. Max power loading 18.3 lb/hp, 8.3 kg/hp. Load factors NC recommended; +6.0, -3.0 ultimate.

PERFORMANCE* - Max level speed *62* mph, *100* kph. Never exceed speed *84* mph, *135* kph. Max cruising speed *62* mph, *100* kph. Economic cruising speed *44* mph, *70* kph. Stalling speed *24* mph, *38* kph. Max climb rate at sea level *590* ft/min, *3.0* m/s. Min sink rate *240* ft/min at *28* mph, *1.2* m/s at *45* kph. Best glide ratio with power off *15/1* at *40* mph, *65* kph. Take-off distance *130* ft, *40* m. Landing distance *115* ft, *35* m. Service ceiling *14,400* ft, *4400* m. Range at average cruising speed *93* mile, *150* km. Noise level NC.

*Under the following test conditions - Airfield altitude 0 ft, 0 m. Ground temperature 59°F, 15°C. Ground pressure NC. Ground windspeed 0 mph, 0 kph. Test payload 264 lb, 120 kg.

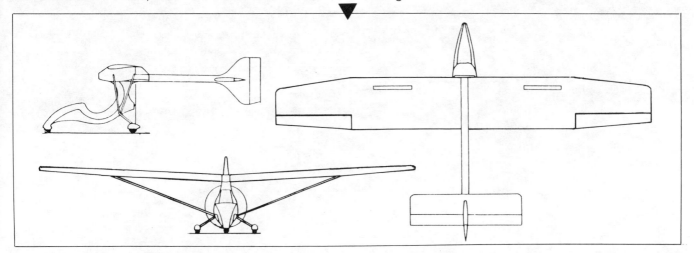

HOHENFLUG

HFL, Hohenflug Leichtflugzeugbau, In der March 3,
D-2120 Luneburg; tel 04131/36488.

HOHENFLUG *HFL*

(Three-axis)

Single-seat single-engined high-wing monoplane or biplane with conventional three-axis control. Wing(s) have unswept leading and trailing edges, and constant chord; two-fin tail. Pitch control by elevator on tail; yaw control by fin-mounted rudders; roll control by half-span ailerons (monoplane configuration), full-span ailerons on lower wing (biplane configuration); control inputs through stick for pitch/roll and pedals for yaw. Cantilever wing(s); wing profile Worthmann FX63-137; 100% double-surface. Undercarriage has three wheels in tricycle formation; suspension NC. Steerable nosewheel. Brakes NC. Airframe construction see text, completely open. Engine mounted below wing (monoplane configuration), between wings (biplane configuration), driving pusher propeller.

Production status: prototype.

GENERAL - Of all the ultralights in this book, the *HFL* is the only one which can be genuinely used as either a monoplane or biplane, the idea being to remove the outer half of the monoplane wing, complete with aileron, and install it beneath the inner half. Since this results in a biplane with lower wing of greater span than upper, an aerodynamic absurdity, an extension piece is then added to the upper wing.

The closest any other company has come to even attempting this 'two aircraft in one' philosophy is the American firm Atlantis, whose *Baby Chicken Hawk 277* can be converted into a biplane by adding an extra wing, the top one in this case being left alone. This undoubtedly changes the aircraft's handling and performance, but is hardly likely to produce the complete change of character offered to the *HFL* owner, who can opt for a high-aspect ratio soaring machine one day, or a responsive biplane the next. Moreover the Atlantis aircraft's simple tube and Dacron structure cannot compare with the sophistication of the composite-construction *HFL*.

Hard information on this fascinating machine is still unfortunately very sparse, but it is clear that the company has made real progress since the *HFL* was described in our first edition. The drawings we printed then are reproduced next to our 1985 photos, and show that in the intervening two years the designer has ditched the tubular empennage and conventional tail in favour of a two-fin arrangement supported by two large-diameter booms. Up front the tubular structure has been retained and extended to provide a mounting for a steerable nosewheel, the original tailskid being abandoned.

Little information is forthcoming about materials, except that the wings are made from carbon-fibre and unidirectional glass-fibre, and the only data which has been released relates to the original design; we reproduce it here in the absence of anything more up to date. Performance figures have been based on a calculated power

Structurally complete but obviously in need of finishing, the HFL in these 1985 photos is very different from the 1983 design in the drawings. Photos show the aircraft rigged as a biplane and half-rigged as a monoplane.

range of 20-28 hp, the engine type having yet to be decided. Data refers to the aircraft in monoplane configuration; where different, figures for the biplane are shown in parentheses.

No price or production dates are known.

EXTERNAL DIMENSIONS & AREAS - Length overall 16.4 ft, 5.00 m. Height overall 5.9 ft, 1.80 m. Wing span -(NC) ft, -(NC) m (bottom); 38.7(22.6) ft, 11.80(6.90) m (top). Constant chord -(3.6) ft, -(1.10) m (bottom wing); 3.6 ft, 1.10 m (top wing). Sweepback 0°. Total wing area 140(151) ft², 13.0(14.0) m². Aspect ratio -(NC)/1 (bottom wing); 10.7 (6.3)/1 (top wing). Wheel track 3.9 ft, 1.20 m. Other data NC.

POWER PLANT - Engine type NC. Max power *28* hp at NC rpm. Propeller diameter and pitch 45xNC inch, 1.13xNC m (3-blade). Reduction type and ratio NC. Max static thrust NC. Power per unit area *0.20(0.19)* hp/ft², *2.2(2.0)* hp/m². Fuel capacity 5.3 US gal, 4.4 Imp gal, 20.0 litre.

WEIGHTS & LOADINGS - Empty weight 199(203) lb, 90(92) kg. Max take-off weight 442 lb, 200 kg. Payload 243(239) lb, 110(108) kg. Max wing loading 3.15(2.92) lb/ft², 15.4(14.3) kg/m². Max power loading *15.8* lb/hp, *7.1* kg/hp. Load factors NC recommended; +4.9, -2.5 ultimate.

PERFORMANCE* - Never exceed speed *81* mph, *130* kph. Max cruising speed *50* mph, *80* kph. Stalling speed *27* mph, *43* kph. Max climb rate at sea level *400* ft/min, *2.0* m/s. Range at average cruising speed 124 mile, 200 km. Other data NC.

*Under unspecified test conditions.

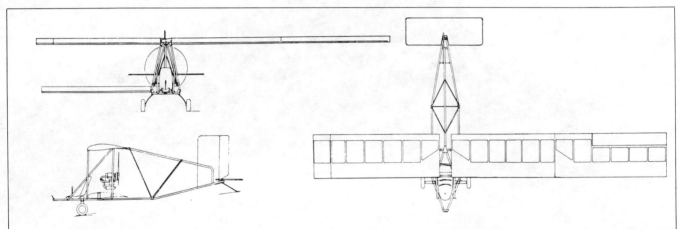

IKARUS

Comco GmbH, Ikarus-Deutschland, Tannenweg 20, 7031 Aidlingen 1; tel 07034 4081/4083.

Australian enquiries through:
ULA-Leichtflugzeuge, Pestalozzistrasse 42, 2090 Winsen-Luhe, West Germany. Contact: Dieter Horstmann.

Dutch agent: Mekura, Vleddermond 2, 9502 EH Stadskanaal. Also: Daan van Leeuwen Boomkamp, Oud Over 156, 3632 VH Loenen a.d. Vecht.

North American agent: Hirth North America, 1425 Bishop Street, Cambridge, Ontario N1R 6J9, Canada; tel (519) 621-8940.

IKARUS *FOX*

(Three-axis)

Single-seat single-engined high-wing monoplane with conventional three-axis control. Wing has unswept leading and trailing edges, and constant chord; cruciform tail. Pitch control by elevator on tail; yaw control by fin-mounted rudder; roll control by half-span ailerons; control inputs through stick for pitch/roll and pedals for yaw. Wing braced from above by kingpost and cables, from below by cables; wing profile NC; 100% double-surface. Undercarriage has three wheels in tricycle formation; no suspension on nosewheel and rubber suspension on main wheels. Push-right go-right nosewheel steering

connected to yaw control. Nosewheel brake. Aluminium-alloy tube airframe, with pod. Engine mounted at wing height, driving tractor propeller.

Production status: current, 80 completed by end of February '85.

GENERAL - Just as Albatros has acquired the rights to the Swiss *AN-22* design of Albert Neukom, so Ikarus is licensed to produce another Swiss machine - the *Fox*. There the parallel ends, however, for whereas the Albatros company is still at prototype stage, Ikarus' products are very much in production, and have been for two years.
The *Fox* story begins with the Swiss designer Hans Gigax, who in early 1981 made the maiden flight of his tube and Dacron *Microstar,* an aircraft which he later developed into the *Sherpa I.* The latter was a robust design intended from the outset to be easily capable of conversion to a two-seater, and made its first flight in May '82, while the two-seat version, the *Sherpa II,* flew for the first time on the way to the French homebuilders' meeting at Brienne-le-Chateau that July. Subsequently the rights were sold to Ikarus, a hang-glider manufacturer of many years' standing, and production of the single seater was well under way by the time our first edition went to press in May '83. A dimensionally identical dual version was just coming on stream, using a more powerful Hirth 276R instead of the *Sherpa I's* Hirth 263R, and kits for the solo machine were offered to convert it to dual specification.
Since then the single-and two-seat designs have diverged somewhat. The solo *Sherpa* has been dropped in favour of the structurally similar *Fox,* the most important improve-

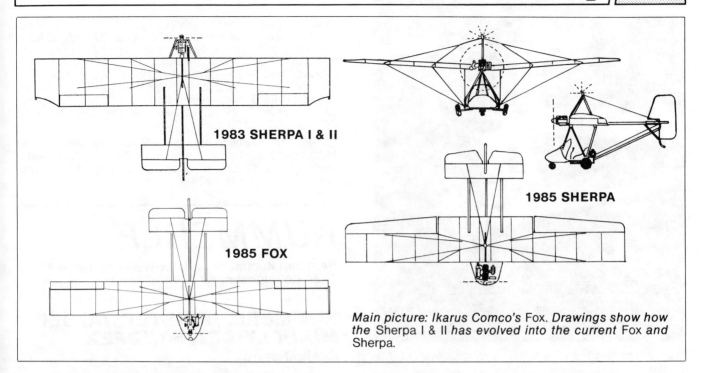

1983 SHERPA I & II

1985 SHERPA

1985 FOX

Main picture: Ikarus Comco's Fox. *Drawings show how the* Sherpa I & II *has evolved into the current* Fox *and* Sherpa.

ment being a redesigned wing of slightly smaller span. This is easily recognisable because the distinctive cutaway at the outboard end of the trailing edge has gone, allowing the ailerons to be increased in size and moved fully outboard to maximise their effect. A pod has been added as standard equipment.

A similar wing rethink on the two-seater has produced the current *Sherpa* from the original *Sherpa II,* though in this case the span remains the same. A further change on the dual machine is the substitution of a Rotax 462 for the Hirth 276R.

It is pleasant to report that the changes to the solo machine have actually resulted in a lower price - DM16,000 ready to fly against DM18,000 two years ago. A similar machine is sold in North America as the Tragelehen *Fox* through Hirth's agency there, retailing at US$4800 for an assembly kit. The dual machine is dearer now, DM20,500 against DM18,050 in '83, much of the increase probably being due to the superior power unit now fitted.

Data below refers to the *Fox;* figures for the *Sherpa* we list separately.

EXTERNAL DIMENSIONS & AREAS - Length overall 14.8 ft, 4.50 m. Height overall 7.7 ft, 2.35 m. Wing span 32.8 ft, 10.0 m. Constant chord 4.4 ft, 1.33 m. Dihedral 2.4°. Sweepback 0°. Tailplane span 9.8 ft, 3.00 m. Fin height NC. Total wing area 142 ft², 13.2 m². Total aileron area 13.5 ft², 1.25 m². Total fin and rudder area 10.0 ft², 0.93 m². Tailplane area 18.3 ft², 1.70 m². Total elevator area 9.7 ft², 0.90 m². Aspect ratio 7.6/1. Wheel track 4.3 ft, 1.25 m. Wheelbase NC. Nosewheel diameter overall 10 inch, 26 cm. Main wheels diameter overall 13 inch, 32 cm.

POWER PLANT - Hirth 263R engine. Max power 22 hp at 4000 rpm. Propeller diameter and pitch 63x39 inch, 1.60x1.00 m. Poly V-belt reduction, ratio 2.5/1. Max static thrust 154 lb, 70 kg. Power per unit area 0.15 hp/ft², 1.7 hp/m². Fuel capacity 3.2 US gal, 2.6 Imp gal, 12.0 litre.

WEIGHTS & LOADINGS - Empty weight 231 lb, 105 kg. Max take-off weight 507 lb, 230 kg. Payload 276 lb, 125 kg. Max wing loading 3.57 lb/ft², 17.4 kg/m². Max power loading 23.0 lb/hp, 10.5 kg/hp. Load factors +4.0, -2.0 recommended; +6.0, -4.0 ultimate.

PERFORMANCE* - Max level speed 53 mph, 85 kph. Never exceed speed 65 mph, 105 kph. Max cruising speed 50 mph, 80 kph. Economic cruising speed 44 mph, 70 kph. Stalling speed 26 mph, 42 kph. Max climb rate at sea level 390 ft/min, 2.0 m/s. Min sink rate 350 ft/min at 31 mph, 1.8 m/s at 50 kph. Best glide ratio with power off 8/1 at 34 mph, 55 kph. Take-off distance 115 ft, 35 m. Landing distance 115 ft, 35 m. Service ceiling 6560 ft, 2000 m. Range at average cruising speed 124 mile, 200 km. Noise level 55 dB(A) at 490 ft, 150 m.

*Under the following test conditions - Airfield altitude 1310 ft, 400 m. Ground temperature 59°F, 15°C. Ground pressure NC. Ground windspeed 0 mph, 0 kph. Test payload 198 lb, 90 kg.

IKARUS *SHERPA*
(Three-axis)

Summary as Fox *except: Side-by-side two-seater. Swept forward trailing edge, tapering chord. Rubber suspension on all wheels. Pod optional.*

Production status: current, 150 completed by end of February '85.

GENERAL - See *Fox* text.

EXTERNAL DIMENSIONS & AREAS - Length overall 16.4 ft, 5.00 m. Height overall 9.2 ft, 2.80 m. Wing span 34.4 ft, 10.50 m. Chord at root 4.9 ft, 1.50 m. Chord at tip 4.3 ft, 1.30 m. Dihedral 2.5°. Sweepback 0°. Tailplane span 10.5 ft, 3.20 m. Fin height NC. Total wing area 169 ft², 15.7 m². Total aileron area 20.0 ft², 1.86 m². Total fin and rudder area 14.5 ft², 1.35 m². Tailplane area 19.2 ft², 1.78 m². Total elevator area 15.3 ft², 1.42 m². Aspect ratio 7.0/1. Wheel track 5.9 ft, 1.80 m. Wheelbase NC. Nosewheel diameter

Rear suspension and cockpit arrangements of the Sherpa.

overall 10 inch, 26 cm. Main wheels diameter overall 16 inch, 40 cm.

POWER PLANT - Rotax 462 engine. Max power 40 hp at 4800 rpm. Propeller diameter and pitch 71x47 inch, 1.80x1.20 m. Poly V-belt reduction, ratio 2.8/1. Max static thrust 243 lb, 110 kg. Power per unit area 0.24 hp/ft², 2.5 hp/m². Fuel capacity 5.3 US gal, 4.4 Imp gal, 20.0 litre.

WEIGHTS & LOADINGS - Empty weight 309 lb, 140 kg. Max take-off weight 728 lb, 330 kg. Payload 419 lb, 190 kg. Max wing loading 4.31 lb/ft², 21.0 kg/m². Max power loading 18.2 lb/hp, 8.3 kg/hp. Load factors +4.0, -2.0 recommended; +6.0, -4.0 ultimate.

PERFORMANCE* - Max level speed 50 mph, 80 kph.

Never exceed speed 62 mph, 100 kph. Max cruising speed 44 mph, 70 kph. Economic cruising speed 37 mph, 60 kph. Stalling speed 28 mph, 45 kph. Max climb rate at sea level 390 ft/min, 2.0 m/s. Min sink rate 350 ft/min at 34 mph, 1.8 m/s at 55 kph. Best glide ratio with power off 8/1 at 34 mph, 55 kph. Take-off distance 165 ft, 50 m. Landing distance 165 ft, 50 m. Service ceiling 6560 ft, 2000 m. Range at average cruising speed 162 mile, 260 km. Noise level 58 dB(A) at 490 ft, 150 m.

*Under the following test conditions - Airfield altitude 1310 ft, 400 m. Ground temperature 72°F, 22°C. Ground pressure NC. Ground windspeed 6-12 mph, 10-20 kph. Test payload 419 lb, 190 kg.

KUMMERLE

Hermann Kummerle, Gustav-Werner-Strasse 2, 7124 Bonnigheim; tel 07143-23500.

KUMMERLE/FINSTERWALDER
MINI-FLY-SET/WINDFEX
(Weight-shift)

Single-seat single-engined flex-wing aircraft with weight-shift control. Rogallo wing with keel pocket. Pilot suspended below wing in harness, using bar to control pitch and roll/yaw by altering relative positions of pilot and wing. Wing braced from above by kingpost and cables, from below by cables; floating cross-tube construction with 60% double-surface enclosing cross-tube; preformed ribs. Undercarriage has two wheels plus tailball; no suspension on wheels or tailball. No ground steering. No brakes. Aluminium-alloy tube structure, completely open. Engine mounted below wing, driving pusher propeller.

Production status: current, number completed NC.

GENERAL - Aircraft don't come much simpler than Hermann Kummerle's *Mini-Fly-Set,* which we detail here mated to a Finsterwalder *Windfex* wing. Hermann's contribution is basically a power pack, which consists of a front-mounted engine driving a pusher prop through a long shaft, the latter being enclosed in a tube bolted to the A-frame at the front and to the wing's keel at the rear.

The only pure powered hang-glider in this book, as opposed to trikes, Hermann's machine is evocative of the earliest days of microlighting, when tiny engines were attached to hang gliders by pilots fed up with climbing hills before take-off. All sorts of engine positions were tried before the trike unit became almost universally accepted as the safest and most reliable method of powering a Rogallo, as it avoided the thrust-line changes inherent in wing-mounted engines, but the very existence of the *Mini-Fly-Set* proves that there are still some pilots who want something simpler and cheaper.

The aircraft can be foot- or wheel-launched and can be flown with a variety of wings, popular alternatives to the *Windfex* being the *Sierra II* and *Bullet C85.* Whichever of the three is chosen, the price of the complete aircraft is the same, at DM4300.

EXTERNAL DIMENSIONS & AREAS - Length overall* 11.8 ft, 3.60 m. Height overall 8.2 ft, 2.50 m. Wing span 32.2 ft, 9.80 m. Chord at root 8.2 ft, 2.50 m. Chord at tip 0 ft, 0 m. Nose angle 125°. Total wing area 179 ft², 16.7 m². Aspect

Main picture: Hermann Kummerle's Mini-Fly-Set *mated to an exposed-crosstube wing. Inset shows a close-up of the power pack.*

300 ft/min, 1.5 m/s. Min sink rate 240 ft/min at 22 mph, 1.2 m/s at 35 kph. Best glide ratio with power off 9/1 at 22 mph, 35 kph. Take-off distance 16 ft, 5 m. Landing distance 50 ft, 15 m. Service ceiling 6560 ft, 2000 m. Range at average cruising speed 75 mile, 120 km. Noise level 57 dB at 490 ft, 150 m.

*Power pack only.

**Under the following test conditions - Airfield altitude 820 ft, 250 m. Ground temperature 75°F, 24°C. Ground pressure 1010 mB. Ground windspeed 3 mph, 5 kph. Test payload 187 lb, 85 kg.

ratio 5.8/1. Wheel track 4.6 ft, 1.40 m. Tailball diameter overall 8 inch, 20 cm. Main wheels diameter overall 14 inch, 35 cm. Other data NC.

POWER PLANT - Sachs Dolmar 166 engine. Max power 8 hp at 7500 rpm. Propeller diameter and pitch 51x24 inch, 1.30x0.60 m. Micro V-belt reduction, ratio 3.2/1. Max static thrust 86 lb, 39 kg. Power per unit area 0.045 hp/ft^2, 0.48 hp/m^2. Fuel capacity 1.3 US gal, 1.1 Imp gal, 5.0 litre.

WEIGHTS & LOADINGS - Empty weight* 35 lb, 16 kg. Payload 198 lb, 90 kg. Load factors +6.0, -3.0 recommended; NC ultimate. Other data NC.

PERFORMANCE -** Max level speed 47 mph, 75 kph. Never exceed speed 53 mph, 85 kph. Max cruising speed 31 mph, 50 kph. Economic cruising speed 28 mph, 45 kph. Stalling speed 17 mph, 27 kph. Max climb rate at sea level

LTB-BOROWSKI

LTB-Borowski, Flugplatz, Winzel-Schramberg; tel 074221 53644.

LTB-BOROWSKI
AN-20 PICOLO
(Three-axis)

Single-seat single-engined high-wing monoplane with conventional three-axis control. Wing has swept back leading and trailing edges, and constant chord; T-tail.

Peter F Selinger

Pitch control by fully flying tail; yaw control by fin-mounted rudder; roll control by one-third span ailerons; control inputs through stick for pitch/roll and pedals for yaw. Cantilever wing; wing profile NC; 100% double-surface. Undercarriage has three wheels in tricycle formation; glass-fibre suspension on nosewheel and suspension NC on main wheels. Push-right go-right nosewheel steering. Nosewheel brake. Composite-construction fuselage, partially enclosed. Engine mounted above wing, driving pusher propeller.

Production status: prototype.

GENERAL - One glance at the picture accompanying this text is enough to explain the ancestry of this machine, for as its name suggests the *AN-20 Picolo* is a derivative of Albert Neukom's *AN-20B* which we feature in our Swiss section.

However, the West German company has not been content simply to copy Albert's creation, but instead has developed it into a cleaner, more elegant and much faster aircraft. The most noticeable change is the absence of the tubular structure which supported the wing and engine; this is rejected in favour of a redesigned fuselage incorporating mounting points for wing and power pack. The latter is moved up to get the prop into clean air, with a KFM 107 providing the push instead of the Konig used originally, while the wing is now fully cantilevered, the struts of the *AN-20B* having been removed.

These changes have added a full 66 lb (30 kg) to the weight, with the result that the *AN-20 Picolo* is just outside the FAI microlight definition, at least in the form described here. However, the aircraft is still in prototype form, so it is possible that production models will comply. No production schedule or price has been announced.

EXTERNAL DIMENSIONS & AREAS - NC.

POWER PLANT - KFM 107 engine. Max power 25 hp at NC rpm. Propeller diameter and pitch 59xNC inch, 1.50xNC m. V-belt reduction, ratio 3.0/1. Max static thrust NC. Power per unit area NC. Fuel capacity 5.3 US gal, 4.4 Imp gal, 20.0 litre.

WEIGHTS & LOADINGS - Empty weight 353 lb, 160 kg. Max take-off weight 573 lb, 260 kg. Payload 220 lb, 100 kg. Max wing loading NC. Max power loading 22.9 lb/hp, 10.4 kg/hp. Load factors +6.0, -3.0 recommended; NC ultimate.

PERFORMANCE* - Max level speed 106 mph, 170 kph. Never exceed speed 118 mph, 190 kph. Max cruising speed 87 mph, 140 kph. Economic cruising speed 68 mph, 110 kph. Stalling speed 34 mph, 54 kph. Max climb rate at sea level 390 ft/min, 2.0 m/s. Min sink rate 190 ft/min at 44 mph, 0.95 m/s at 70 kph. Best glide ratio with power off 22/1 at 56 mph, 90 kph. Take-off distance 260 ft, 80 m. Landing distance 165 ft, 50 m. Service ceiling NC. Range at average cruising speed NC. Noise level 60 dB at 490 ft, 150m.

*Under unspecified test conditions.

Main picture:
Mahe's Pfadfinder
in flight.

Insets detail
cockpit arrangement
and wing-warping
mechanism.

MAHE

Mahe, Flugplatz Schachtlder, 2370 Rendsburg;
tel 040/52 78737.

MAHE *PFADFINDER*

(Three-axis)

*Single-seat single-engined high-wing monoplane with
conventional three-axis control. Wing has unswept leading edge, swept forward trailing edge, and tapering
chord; conventional tail. Pitch control by fully flying tail;
yaw control by fully flying rudder; roll control by wing
warping; control inputs through stick for pitch/roll and
pedals for yaw. Wing braced from above by kingpost and
cables, from below by cables; wing profile NC; single-
surface. Undercarriage has three wheels in tail-dragger
formation; suspension NC on tailwheel and steel-spring
suspension on main wheels. No ground steering. Brakes*

*NC. Aluminium-alloy tube airframe, completely open.
Engine mounted below wing, driving tractor propeller.*

Production status: current, number completed NC.

GENERAL - Ron Wheeler's venerable *Scout* must have
spawned more derivatives than any other ultralight with the
exception of the famous *Quicksilver MX*. It is produced in
New Zealand by Canterbury Microlights, in Britain by
Flylite, and at one stage was also in production by the MAC
company in South Africa.

The *Pfadfinder* is West Germany's contribution to *Scout*
lore, and like the original *Scout* has evolved from the two-
axis control system featured in our last edition, a system
used on the earliest Australian machines back in 1976, to
conventional three-axis control with wing warping.

But the power unit sets this quasi-*Scout* apart from all the
others, as the *Pfadfinder* is the only one to use a three-
cylinder engine, a Konig SC430 with belt reduction and
pitch-adjustable prop. This gives the *Pfadfinder* a rather

better performance than we would have expected from such a simple single-surface machine.

To the best of our knowledge, the company's prices and accessories have not changed since our first edition went to press in May '83: DM13,560 ready to fly in West Germany, DM11,800 for export, and a range of options including floats for DM1400, instruments and a document and map case.

EXTERNAL DIMENSIONS & AREAS - Length overall 17.1 ft, 5.22 m. Height overall 6.9 ft, 2.09 m. Wing span 28.4 ft, 8.67 m. Chord at root 5.7 ft, 1.75 m. Chord at tip 1.3 ft, 0.41 m. Dihedral NC. Sweepback 0°. Elevator span 10.7 ft, 3.25 m. Fin height 4.9 ft, 1.50 m. Total wing area 125 ft^2, 11.6 m^2. Rudder area 8.3 ft^2, 0.77 m^2. Total elevator area 17.0 ft^2, 1.58 m^2. Aspect ratio 6.51. Wheel track 4.8 ft, 1.47 m. Wheelbase 12.5 ft, 3.78 m. Tailwheel diameter overall NC. Main wheels diameter overall 11 inch, 27 cm.

POWER PLANT - Konig SC430 engine. Max power 27 hp at 4400 rpm. Propeller diameter and pitch 51x* inch, 1.30x* m. Belt reduction, ratio 1.5/1. Max static thrust 155 lb, 70 kg. Power per unit area 0.22 hp/ft^2, 2.3 hp/m^2. Fuel capacity 2.6 US gal, 2.2 Imp gal, 10.0 litre.

WEIGHTS & LOADINGS - Empty weight 132 lb, 60 kg. Max take-off weight 375 lb, 170 kg. Payload 243 lb, 110 kg. Max wing loading 3.00 lb/ft^2, 14.7 kg/m^2. Max power loading 13.9 lb/hp, 6.3 kg/hp. Load factors NC recommended; +6.0, -NC ultimate.

PERFORMANCE -** Max level speed 56 mph, 90 kph. Never exceed speed 65 mph, 105 kph. Max cruising speed 56 mph, 90 kph. Economic cruising speed 47 mph, 75 kph. Stalling speed 28 mph, 45 kph. Max climb rate at sea level 500 ft/min, 2.5 m/s. Best glide ratio with power off 7/1 at

Warming up the Schwarze Trike; *this example is attached to a* Lightning Phase II *wing.*

NC speed. Take-off distance 130 ft, 40 m. Landing distance 80 ft, 25 m. Range at average cruising speed 112 mile, 180 km. Other data NC.

*Ground adjustable for pitch.

**Under unspecified test conditions.

NST

NST Maschinenbau (Norbert Schwarze), Theenhausener Strasse 28, 4806 Werther; tel 05203/7281.

French agent: Air Force Enterprise, 75014 Paris.

Norwegian agent: Johannsen Ragnar (address from manufacturer).

Swiss agent: Delta Plus, 1252 Meinier.

NST/PACIFIC WINGS
SCHWARZE TRIKE/VAMPIR II
(Weight-shift)

Single-seat single-engined flex-wing aircraft with weight-shift control. Rogallo wing with keel pocket. Pilot suspended below wing in trike unit, using bar to control pitch and roll/yaw by altering relative positions of trike unit and wing. Wing braced from above by kingpost and

cables, from below by cables; floating cross-tube construction with 80% double-surface enclosing cross-tube; preformed ribs. Undercarriage has four wheels; no suspension on nosewheels and glass-fibre suspension on main wheels. Push-right go-left nosewheel steering independent from aerodynamic controls. No brakes. Aluminium-alloy tube trike unit, completely open. Engine mounted below wing, driving pusher propeller.

Production status: current, number completed NC.

GENERAL - Unlike many trike unit manufacturers, Norbert Schwarze is not content to follow the monopole construction which has become almost an industry norm in the past couple of years, and has come up with a rather different machine.

Instead of the usual legs-straight stance, the pilot of the *Schwarze Trike* sits with knees bent and feet between two (yes, two) front wheels. This leaves room at the back of the trike unit for the motor to be hung well to the rear on three tubular supports, a long tailskid being provided to protect the prop if the pilot comes in with the nose too high. Whether this seating position is comfortable on cross-countries we do not know, but at least the pilot will find the *Schwarze Trike* a peaceful machine to fly. Not only is the engine very quiet, as are most West German ultralights, but what noise there is emanates from well astern.

The machine may be flown with a wide variety of wings, including Finsterwalder *Windfex IIM* (DM8685), Schonleber *Focus* (DM8900), La Mouette *Profil* (DM8950), Firebird *CX* and *Sierra,* Bicla *Spider,* Southdown International *Lightning Phase II* and the *Vampir II* by Pacific Wings (DM8772). We detail it here with the last of these, which incidentally is a European derivative of the defunct Pacific Kites *Vampyr* from New Zealand (see Ultra Flight Systems). All prices are for ready to fly machines, an option on all variants being a parachute for DM1650.

EXTERNAL DIMENSIONS & AREAS - Length overall 13.1 ft, 4.00 m. Wing span 30.8 ft, 9.40 m. Chord at root 13.1 ft, 4.00 m. Chord at tip 1.6 ft, 0.50 m. Dihedral 2°. Nose angle 135°. Depth of keel pocket 1.0 ft, 0.30 m. Total wing area 166 ft², 15.4 m². Aspect ratio 5.7/1. Wheel track 3.9 ft, 1.20 m. Nosewheel diameter overall 10 inch, 25 cm. Main wheels diameter overall 16 inch, 40 cm. Other data NC.

POWER PLANT - Solo 220 engine. Max power 18 hp at 6000 rpm. Propeller diameter and pitch 61x31 inch, 1.55x0.80 m. Poly V-belt reduction, ratio 3.0/1. Max static thrust 132 lb, 60 kg. Power per unit area 0.11 hp/ft², 1.2 hp/m². Fuel capacity 2.6 US gal, 2.2 Imp gal, 10.0 litre.

WEIGHTS & LOADINGS - Empty weight 154 lb, 70 kg. Max take-off weight 397 lb, 180 kg. Payload 243 lb, 110 kg. Max wing loading 2.39 lb/ft², 11.7 kg/m². Max power loading 22.1 lb/hp, 10.0 kg/hp. Load factors NC recommended; +6.0, -4.0 ultimate.

PERFORMANCE* - Max level speed 50 mph, 80 kph. Never exceed speed 50 mph, 80 kph. Max cruising speed 37 mph, 60 kph. Economic cruising speed 31 mph, 50 kph. Stalling speed 24 mph, 38 kph. Max climb rate at sea level 390 ft/min, 2.0 m/s. Min sink rate 350 ft/min at 28 mph, 1.8 m/s at 45 kph. Best glide ratio with power off 8/1 at 28 mph, 45 kph. Take-off distance 100 ft, 30 m. Landing distance 100 ft, 30 m. Service ceiling NC. Range at average cruising speed 124 mile, 200 km. Noise level 58 dB at 490 ft, 150 m.

*Under the following test conditions - Test payload 176 lb, 80 kg. Other data NC.

NST/PACIFIC WINGS
MINIMUM/VAMPIR II
(Weight-shift)

Single-seat single-engined flex-wing aircraft with weight-shift control. Rogallo wing with keel pocket. Pilot suspended below wing in trike unit, using bar to control pitch and roll/yaw by altering relative positions of trike unit and wing. Wing braced from above by kingpost and cables, from below by cables; floating cross-tube construction with 80% double-surface enclosing cross-tube; preformed ribs. Undercarriage has three wheels in tail-dragger formation; suspension NC on tailwheel and bungee suspension on main wheels. One main wheel steerable. Brakes NC. Tubular structure, completely open. Engine mounted below wing, driving pusher propeller.

Production status: current, 130 completed.

GENERAL - With the *Minimum* Norbert Schwarze has taken his interest in unconventional methods of powering Rogallos a stage further. Whereas his *Schwarze Trike* is still recognisable as a trike unit, the *Minimum* is closer to the powered hang gliders used at the dawn of ultralight aviation.

There is, however, one vital difference - the position of the power pack. Early attempts at powering hang gliders mounted the engine on the keel tube of the wing, resulting in a thrust line which changed as the pilot moved the bar fore and aft. This made them unstable in pitch, as a number of pioneers learned to their cost, and it was this instability which ensured that the trike was welcomed with open arms by flexwing pilots looking for a safe and reliable method of power flying. Norbert's *Minimum* is an attempt to have the best of both worlds - the 'pure' feel of prone flying with the stability of a trike. To achieve this he mounts the engine not on the keel but on a tubular structure attached at the top to the hang point and at the bottom to the pilot's harness, the structure being designed so that the engine is at the aircraft's centre of gravity in normal flight.

The resulting aircraft is not a trike in the normal sense of the word, and there is nothing like it in the whole of this book, though Rupert Sweet-Escott's *Nomad* (see Flight Research, British section) comes close, especially the prototype with its tail-dragger undercarriage.

Like the *Schwarze Trike,* the *Minimum* can be flown with a variety of wings, notably the *Spider* from Klaus Bichemeier's Bicla company, or the *Vampir II* from Pacific Wings, and costs DM8200 complete with either of these Rogallos. Our data below refers to the *Vampir II.*

EXTERNAL DIMENSIONS & AREAS - See *Schwarze Trike/Vampir II* except: Height overall 7.8 ft, 2.40 m. Wheel track depends on A-frame selected by pilot. Nosewheel diameter not applicable; tailwheel diameter overall 4 inch, 10 cm. Main wheels diameter overall 10 inch, 25 cm.

POWER PLANT - See *Schwarze Trike/Vampir II* except: Fuel capacity NC.

WEIGHTS & LOADINGS - Empty weight NC. Max take-off weight 375 lb, 170 kg. Payload NC. Max wing loading 2.26 lb/ft², 11.0 kg/m². Max power loading 20.8 lb/hp, 9.4 kg/hp. Load factors NC recommended; +6.0, -3.0 ultimate.

PERFORMANCE* - See *Schwarze Trike* except: Stalling speed 21 mph, 34 kph. Min sink rate 310 ft/min at 24 mph,

Willi Tacke

Willi Tacke

This Minimum *is flying with a* Spider *wing; inset shows power pack.*

1.6 m/s at 38 kph. Best glide ratio with power off 8.5/1 at 28 mph, 45 kph. Service ceiling >8200 ft, >2500 m. Range at average cruising speed 199 mile, 320 km. Noise level 60 dB at 490 ft, 150 m.

Under the following test conditions - Take-off weight 331 lb, 150 kg. Other data NC.

PLATZER

Dipl Ing M Platzer, Am Buschgraben 6, 3501 Ellenberg; tel 05665 2820.

PLATZER
MOTTE B2/B3 and MOTTE C

(Three-axis)

Single-seat single-engined high-wing monoplane with conventional three-axis control. Wing has swept back leading and trailing edges, and constant chord; cruciform tail. Pitch control by elevator on tail; yaw control by fully flying pendular rudder with separate fin; roll control by 60%-span ailerons; control inputs through stick for pitch/roll and pedals for yaw. Wing braced from above by kingpost and cables, from below by cables; wing profile Eigenkonstrukion (Motte B2/B3), Gottingen (Motte C); 100% double-surface. Undercarriage has three wheels in tail-dragger formation; no suspension on any wheels. Push-right go-right tailwheel steering connected to yaw control. No brakes. Aluminium-alloy tube airframe, completely open. Engine mounted at wing height, driving tractor propeller.

Production status: plans-built, 38 completed or under construction.

GENERAL - Designed for homebuilders, this uncomplicated tail-dragger machine presents the constructor with a choice of two models: the *Motte B2/B3*, with its tube and fabric wing, or the *Motte C,* which uses a traditional wooden wing.

Because the two wings have different profiles (see our summary above), the performance varies depending on the design chosen. It is difficult to quantify the difference because the picture is confused by the wide variety of power units which can be fitted, but it appears that the wood construction is a shade faster in cruise and around 10% more economical. On the other hand it needs rather more runway, and of course takes much longer to build. The same weight is quoted for both.

Herr Platzer tells us that the *Motte* will take any Hirth engine from 22 to 40 hp and accordingly has given us a range of performance figures for each wing type, based on tests done at the DULV (West German Ultralight Association) proving grounds at Kassel-Calden. Data below refers to the *Motte B2/B3;* where different, figures for the *Motte C* are shown in parentheses.

Plans for either version cost DM750, for which the buyer gets drawings, instructions and a log book.

EXTERNAL DIMENSIONS & AREAS - Length overall 15.6 ft, 4.74 m. Height overall 7.4 ft, 2.25 m. Wing span 26.9 ft, 8.20 m. Constant chord 4.7 ft, 1.43 m. Dihedral 4°. Sweepback 6°. Tailplane span 8.5 ft, 2.60 m. Fin height 3.3 ft, 1.00 m. Total wing area 126 ft², 11.7 m². Rudder area 9.7 ft², 0.90 m². Total tailplane and elevator area 27.8 ft², 2.58 m². Aspect ratio 5.7/1. Wheel track 4.6 ft, 1.40 m. Tailwheel diameter overall 5 inch, 12.5 cm. Main wheels diameter overall 16 inch, 40 cm. Other data NC.

POWER PLANT - Hirth engine. Max power 22-40 hp at rpm. Propeller diameter and pitch 55-71xNC inch, 1.40-1.80xNC m. Poly V-belt reduction, ratio 2.5/1. Max static thrust NC. Power per unit area 0.17-0.32 hp/ft², 1.9-3.4 hp/m². Fuel capacity 5.3 US gal, 4.4 Imp gal, 20.0 litre.

WEIGHTS & LOADINGS - Empty weight *198* lb, *90* kg. Max take-off weight 474 lb, 215 kg. Payload *276* lb, *125* kg. Max wing loading 3.76 lb/ft², 18.4 kg/m². Max power loading 21.5-11.9 lb/hp, 9.8-5.4kg/hp. Load factors +4.3, -2.5 recommended; +6.5, -3.75 ultimate.

PERFORMANCE* - Max level speed NC. Never exceed speed 78 mph, 126 kph. Max cruising speed 44-56 mph,

The tube and fabric winged version of the Motte, *the* B2/B3.

70-90 kph. Economic cruising speed 44-47(44-56) mph, 70-75(70-90) kph. Stalling speed 22 mph, 35 kph. Max climb rate at sea level 390-690 ft/min, 2.0-3.5 m/s. Min sink rate 370 ft/min at 37 mph, 1.9 m/s at 60 kph. Best glide ratio with power off NC/1 at 37(40) mph, 60(65) kph. Take-off distance 130-195(150-230) ft, 40-60(45-70) m. Landing distance 100-165(115-195) ft, 30-50(35-60) m. Service ceiling NC. Range at average cruising speed 124(137) mile, 200(220) km. Noise level** 56-57 dB at 330 ft, 100m.

*Under unspecified test conditions.

**With 24 hp engine.

SCHEIBE

Scheibe Flugzeugbau GmbH, August-Pfaltz-Strasse 23, Postfach 1829, 8060 Dachau bei Munchen; tel 08031/6813; tx 0526650.

SCHEIBE *ULI I*
(Three-axis)

Single-seat single-engined high-wing monoplane with conventional three-axis control. Wing has unswept leading and trailing edges, and constant chord; conventional tail. Pitch control by fully flying tail; yaw control by fully flying rudder; roll control by half-span ailerons; control inputs through stick for pitch/roll and pedals for yaw. Wing braced from above by kingpost and cables, from below by cables; wing profile NC; 100% double-surface. Undercarriage has three wheels in tail-dragger formation (tricycle formation optional); suspension NC on tailwheel and glass-fibre suspension on main wheels. Ground steering NC. No brakes. Steel-tube airframe, with optional pod. Engine mounted below wing, driving pusher propeller.

Production status: current, number completed NC.

GENERAL - Scheibe is one of the best known names in the gliding world, a well established firm founded by Egon

Main picture: Uli I *in flight. Inset: Ian Wheeler with the* Uli I *prototype.*

Scheibe in 1951. The company had some success with the *Mu-13E Bergfalke I* and then went on to produce a whole series of conventional gliders and motor gliders, such as the *SF-25C* and *C-S Falke, SF-25E Super Falke, SF-28A Tandem Falke, Bergfalke IV, SF-34 Delphin* and *SF-36.* Over 2300 machines had been produced by 1983, plus numerous kits for homebuilders.

So when this important firm announced in 1982 that it was entering the ultralight world, it was a significant event. Its first design, the *Uli I,* made its maiden flight at the end of '82 and was the subject of an article by Ian Wheeler in the mid-February '83 *Flightline.* That prototype had a tailskid rather than a tailwheel, and no pod, but by the Aero '83 show at Friedrichshafen shortly afterwards these matters had been remedied and a prospective price of around DM18,000 was announced. Two years later that price had risen to DM21,000 ready to fly.

The design is unusual in that it uses an airframe of welded-steel tubing, rather than the usual fabricated aluminium alloy, though the latter is retained for the wing spars. Ribs are foam, capped top and bottom with wood, and all flying surfaces are ceconite-covered. The distinctive latticework tail boom makes the *Uli I* easily recognisable.

EXTERNAL DIMENSIONS & AREAS - Length overall 18.0 ft, 5.50 m. Wing span 31.5 ft, 9.60 m. Constant chord 4.3 ft, 1.31 m. Sweepback 0°. Tailplane span 7.2 ft, 2.20 m. Total wing area 136 ft², 12.6 m². Aspect ratio 7.3/1. Wheel track 4.6 ft, 1.40 m. Other data NC.

POWER PLANT - Hirth 383 cc engine. Max power 22 hp at 4000 rpm. Propeller diameter and pitch 51xNC inch, 1.30xNC m. Belt reduction, ratio 1.8/1. Max static thrust NC. Power per unit area 0.16 hp/ft², 1.7 hp/m². Fuel capacity 5.3 US gal, 4.4 Imp gal, 20.0 litre.

WEIGHTS & LOADINGS - Empty weight 254 lb, 115 kg. Max take-off weight 485 lb, 220 kg. Payload 231 lb, 105 kg. Max wing loading 3.57 lb/ft², 17.5 kg/m². Max power loading 22.0 lb/hp, 10.0 kg/hp. Load factors NC recommended; +6.0, -3.0 ultimate.

PERFORMANCE* - Max level speed 53 mph, 85 kph. Never exceed speed 56 mph, 90 kph. Cruising speed 47 mph, 75 kph. Stalling speed 28 mph, 45 kph. Max climb rate at sea level 400 ft/min, 2.0 m/s. Min sink rate 310 ft/min at 35 mph, 1.6 m/s at 56 kph. Best glide ratio with power off 9/1 at NC speed. Take-off distance 150 ft, 46 m. Landing distance 100 ft, 30 m. Service ceiling NC. Range at average cruising speed 112 mile, 180 km. Noise level NC.

*Under unspecified test conditions.

SCHEIBE *ULTRA*
(Three-axis)
Summary similar to Uli I *except: Side-by-side two-seater.*

Production status: current, number completed NC.

GENERAL - In our first edition we featured a prototype tandem two-seater from Scheibe, called the *Uli II.* The company, however, has since decided that tandem seating is not the way to go with dual machines, and has abandoned the *Uli II* in favour of a new side-by-side aircraft, the *Ultra.*

Judging by the picture in our colour section, it appears that this new two-seater is similar in concept to the familiar *Uli I,* though it uses a more powerful Hirth engine and has a wing of greater span and area. Little other information is available.

Price: DM25,600 ready to fly.

EXTERNAL DIMENSIONS & AREAS - Wing span 36.7 ft, 11.20 m. Total wing area 161 ft², 15.0 m². Aspect ratio 8.4/1. Other data NC.

POWER PLANT - Hirth engine, model NC. Max power 35 hp at NC rpm. Power per unit area 0.22 hp/ft², 2.3 hp/m². Other data NC.

WEIGHTS & LOADINGS - Empty weight 331 lb, 150 kg. Max take-off weight 728 lb, 330 kg. Payload 397 lb, 180 kg. Max wing loading 4.52 lb/ft², 22.0 kg/m². Max power loading 20.8 lb/hp, 9.4 kg/hp. Load factors NC.

PERFORMANCE* - Max level speed 53 mph, 85 kph. Never exceed speed 56 mph, 90 kph. Cruising speed 47 mph, 75 kph. Stalling speed 28 mph, 45 kph. Other data NC.

*Under unspecified test conditions.

SCHMIDTLER BERND

Schmidtler Bernd, Wilhelmstrasse 14, 8 Munchen 40; tel 089 39 2817.

SCHMIDTLER *RANGER*
(Weight-shift)

Single-seat single-engined flex-wing aircraft with weight-shift control. Rogallo wing with keel pocket. Pilot suspended below wing in trike unit, using bar to control pitch and roll/yaw by altering relative positions of trike unit and wing. Wing braced from above by kingpost and cables, from below by cables; rigid cross-tube construction with single-surface; flexible ribs. Undercarriage has three wheels in tricycle formation; bungee suspension with telescopic legs on all wheels. Push-right go-left nosewheel steering independent from aerodynamic controls. No brakes. Aluminium-alloy tube trike unit, completely open. Engine mounted below wing, driving pusher propeller.

Production status: current, number completed NC.

GENERAL - Though it has been active for several years, the Schmidtler company escaped our first edition, so this is our first attempt at explaining the company's complicated range of trikes and wings.

The oldest design of trike unit in the company's stable is the *Ranger M,* a unique design which surrounds the pilot with a complete cage of tubing, making what must surely

Flashback to 27 May 1981, and the early days of the Ranger. Main picture shows the complete aircraft, inset shows the trike unit. Recent examples are very similar, apart from changes to the power pack.

be the most crash-resistant trike structure in this book. There is no base tube; instead two Pterodactyl-style horizontal tubes at armpit height join the duopoles at the rear to a double strut arrangement at the front. From these front joints two further tubes are angled down to brace the rear suspension assembly. Various other tubes further strengthen the structure.

In keeping with this old but interesting design, the company offers a similarly venerable wing, a completely single-surface Rogallo with flexible ribs and rigid cross-tube. Though not a high performance design, it remains popular with pilots who value light weight and portability, especially those who go free flying from mountainsides and don't fancy a long hike with a heavy, complex wing. Confusingly, this too is called *Ranger,* and when mated to the *Ranger M*

457

trike unit produces, predictably, the *Ranger* trike! For those preferring a more modern Rogallo, the company can supply Pacific Wings' *Vampir II*.

Customers wanting a *Ranger* pure and simple can choose from four engines - the air-cooled Konig SC430 (DM13,650) and Hirth 263 (DM12,450), or the liquid-cooled MKB 430A (DM14,250) and MKB 430B (DM14,450). Our data below refers to the *Ranger* with Konig SC430 engine; where different, figures for the other engines are shown in parentheses in that order. All these prices are for complete aircraft and include 14% tax. Electric start is available on the Hirth only, for an extra DM350.

Data for the *Ranger M/Vampir II* we list separately, only the MKB units being available in that case.

EXTERNAL DIMENSIONS & AREAS - Wing span 30.0 ft, 9.15 m. Total wing area 188 ft², 17.5 m². Aspect ratio 4.8/1. Wheel track *4.9* ft, *1.50* m. Wheelbase *5.9* ft, *1.80* m. Nosewheel diameter overall 16 inch, 40 cm. Main wheels diameter overall 16 inch, 40 cm. Other data NC.

POWER PLANT - Konig SC430 (Hirth 263) (MKB 430A) (MKB 430B) engine. Max power 24(22)(21)(20) hp at 4000(4200)(3700)(3300) rpm. Propeller diameter and pitch* 52xNC inch, 1.32xNC m. Toothed-belt (poly V-belt) (poly V-belt) (poly V-belt) reduction, ratio 1.7(1.8)(1.65)(1.65)/1. Max static thrust NC. Power per unit area 0.13(0.12)(0.11)(0.106) hp/ft², 1.4(1.3)(1.2)(1.1) hp/m². Fuel capacity 5.3 US gal, 4.4 Imp gal, 20.0 litre.

WEIGHTS & LOADINGS - Empty weight 154(165)(154) (154) lb, 70(75)(70)(70) kg. Max take-off weight 408 lb, 185 kg. Payload 254(243)(254)(254) lb, 115(110)(115)(115) kg. Max wing loading 2.17 lb/ft², 10.6 kg/m². Max power loading 17.0(18.5)(19.4)(20.4) lb/hp, 7.7(8.4)(8.8)(9.3) kg/hp. Load factors +4.0, -2.0 recommended; +6.0, -3.0 ultimate.

PERFORMANCE -** Max level speed 44 mph, 70 kph. Never exceed speed 48(44)(44)(44) mph, 78(70)(70)(70) kph. Max cruising speed 36 mph, 58 kph. Economic cruising speed 36 mph, 58 kph. Stalling speed 28 mph, 45 kph. Max climb rate at sea level 350(300)(300)(260) ft/min, 1.8(1.5)(1.5)(1.3) m/s. Range at average cruising speed 93(112)(112)(112) mile, 150(180)(180)(180) km. Noise level 60(60)(60)(55) dB at 490 ft, 150 m. Other data NC.

All props multi-blade: some three-blade, some four.

**Under the following test conditions - Airfield altitude 0 ft, 0 m. Ground temperature 59°F, 15°C. Ground pressure 1013 mB. Ground windspeed 0 mph, 0 kph. Test payload 254(243)(254)(254) lb, 115(110)(115)(115) kg.*

SCHMIDTLER/PACIFIC WINGS
RANGER M/VAMPIR II
(Weight-shift)

Summary as Ranger except: Floating cross-tube construction with approximately 80% double-surface enclosing cross-tube; preformed ribs.

Production status: current, number completed NC.

GENERAL - As explained under *Ranger*, this aircraft uses the same trike unit as that machine, but mates it to a more modern wing, the *Vampir II*. Only the remarkably quiet MKB engines are available with this combination, liquid-cooled units derived from Yamaha outboards by the West German Rotax distributor and named after the initials of the three engineers who developed them.

The *Ranger M/Vampir II* costs DM15,500 when fitted with the MKB 430B, complete and including 14% tax. No price is available for the 430A version but it is likely to be around DM200 cheaper. Data below refers to the latter variant; where different, figures for the 430B are shown in parentheses.

Like the *Ranger*, the *Ranger M/Vampir II* has full *Gutesiegel* approval. Astute readers may notice that the wing data quoted differs from that of the NST *Schwarze Trike/Vampir II*; this is because the wing is available in several different sizes.

EXTERNAL DIMENSIONS & AREAS - Wing span 32.2 ft, 9.80 m. Nose angle 128°. Total wing area 153 ft², 14.2 m². Aspect ratio 6.8/1. Wheel track *4.9* ft, *1.50* m. Wheelbase *5.9* ft, *1.80* m. Nosewheel diameter overall 16 inch, 40 cm. Main wheels diameter overall 16 inch, 40 cm. Other data NC.

POWER PLANT - See appropriate MKB-engined version of *Ranger* except: Power per unit area 0.14(0.13) hp/ft², 1.5(1.4) hp/m².

WEIGHTS & LOADINGS - Empty weight 174 lb, 79 kg. Max take-off weight 408 lb, 185 kg. Payload 234 lb, 106 kg. Max wing loading 2.67 lb/ft², 13.0 kg/m². Max power loading 19.4(20.4) lb/hp, 8.8(9.3) kg/hp. Load factors +4.0, -2.0 recommended; +6.0, -3.0 ultimate.

PERFORMANCE -** Max level speed** 50 mph, 80 kph. Never exceed speed** 50 mph, 80 kph. Max cruising speed 40 mph, 65 kph. Economic cruising speed 40 mph, 65 kph. Stalling speed 28 mph, 45 kph. Max climb rate at sea level NC(260) ft/min, NC(1.3) m/s. Range at average cruising speed 118(93) mile, 190(150) km. Noise level 60(55) dB at 490 ft, 150 m. Other data NC.

Under the following test conditions - Airfield altitude 0 ft, 0 m. Ground temperature 59°F, 15°C. Ground pressure 1013 mB. Ground windspeed 0 mph, 0 kph. Test payload 234 lb, 106 kg.

**Maximum permitted under West German law.*

SCHMIDTLER/BADER
ENDURO/FALKE V
(Weight-shift)

Single-seat single-engined flex-wing aircraft with weight-shift control. Rogallo wing with keel pocket. Pilot suspended below wing in trike unit, using bar to control pitch and roll/yaw by altering relative positions of trike unit and wing; hang point adjustable in flight. Wing braced from above by kingpost and cables, from below by cables; floating cross-tube construction with approximately 60% double-surface enclosing cross-tube; preformed ribs. Undercarriage has three wheels in tricycle formation; no suspension on nosewheel and gas strut suspension on main wheels. Push-right go-left nosewheel steering independent from aerodynamic controls. Optional nosewheel brake. Aluminium-alloy tube trike unit, completely open. Engine mounted below wing, driving pusher propeller.

Production status: current, number completed NC.

GENERAL - The *Enduro* is Schmidtler's trike unit for those who want something more conventionally constructed, being heavier and with a greater payload than the *Ranger M*. Herr Schmidtler, however, has been unable to resist adding some original touches to the design, and two items

Details of the Enduro's construction: gas strut rear suspension and cable run for the adjustable hang-point.

in particular set this trike unit apart from rival models. The most intriguing of these is the adjustable hang point, operated from a control behind the pilot. This is connected to a cable routed along the trike base tube, around a pulley above the nosewheel and then up to the wing, and allows the pilot to adjust the angle of attack to give hands-off flying at whatever cruise speed he or she chooses. The other notable feature is gas-strut suspension on the main wheels.

Like the *Ranger M,* the *Enduro* is available with a wide variety of wings and engines. The examples we list have been selected by the factory and start with the *Falke V* wing from Hansi Bader, which as you can see from the data below is available with a choice of two engines. The data refers to the Konig SD570-engined version; where different, figures for the Hirth 263 option are shown in parentheses. These two aircraft cost DM13,100 and DM12,100 respectively.

We list separately the *Enduro* with three alternative wings, all available only with the Hirth 263 engine: *Profil 17* by La Mouette (DM12,880), *Focus 18* by Ernst Schonleber (DM13,000), and *Euro III* from Christian Steinbach (DM11,950). All these aircraft have *Gutesiegel* certification and all are priced ready to fly and with 14% tax paid.

Finally we list two experimental machines which have yet to obtain certification, the *Enduro MKB 462* high-performance trike unit, and the *Enduro Doppelsitzer/Focus 20* two-seater.

EXTERNAL DIMENSIONS & AREAS - Wing span 33.5 ft, 10.2 m. Total wing area 180 ft², 16.7 m². Aspect ratio 6.2/1. Wheel track 5.0 ft, 1.52 m. Wheelbase 6.5 ft, 1.98 m. Nosewheel diameter overall 16 inch, 40 cm. Main wheels diameter overall 16 inch, 40 cm. Other data NC.

POWER PLANT - Konig SD570 (Hirth 263) engine. Max power 28(22) hp at 4000(4200) rpm. Propeller diameter and pitch* 61xNC inch, 1.54xNC m. Poly V-belt reduction, ratio 2.0(2.5)/1. Max static thrust NC. Power per unit area 0.16(0.12) hp/ft², 1.7(1.3) hp/m². Fuel capacity 5.3 US gal, 4.4 Imp gal, 20.0 litre.

WEIGHTS & LOADINGS - Empty weight 209(225) lb, 95(102) kg. Max take-off weight 467 lb, 212 kg. Payload 258(243) lb, 117(110) kg. Max wing loading 2.59 lb/ft², 12.7 kg/m². Max power loading 16.7(21.2) lb/hp, 7.6(9.6) kg/hp. Load factors +4.0, -2.0 recommended; +6.0, -3.0 ultimate.

PERFORMANCE - Max level speed*** 50 mph, 80 kph. Never exceed speed*** 50 mph, 80 kph. Max cruising speed 37 mph, 60 kph. Economic cruising speed 37 mph, 60 kph. Stalling speed 28 mph, 45 kph. Max climb rate at sea level 550(390) ft/min, 2.8(2.0) m/s. Range at average cruising speed 75(150) mile, 120(240) km. Noise level 60(58) dB at 490 ft, 150 m. Other data NC.

All props multi-blade: some three-blade, some four.

**Under the following test conditions - Airfield altitude 0 ft, 0 m. Ground temperature 59°F, 15°C. Ground pressure 1013 mB. Ground windspeed 0 mph, 0 kph. Test payload 258(243) lb, 117(110) kg.*

***Maximum permitted under West German law.*

SCHMIDTLER/LA MOUETTE ENDURO/PROFIL 17
(Weight-shift)

Summary as Enduro/Falke V *except: 60% double-surface.*

Production status: current, number completed NC.

GENERAL - See *Enduro/Falke V.*

EXTERNAL DIMENSIONS & AREAS - See *Enduro/Falke V* except: Length overall 16.4 ft, 5.00 m. Wing span 34.4 ft, 10.50 m. Chord at root 8.0 ft, 2.45 m. Chord at tip 3.1 ft, 0.95 m. Dihedral 1°. Nose angle 120°. Total wing area 175 ft², 16.3 m². Aspect ratio 6.8/1.

POWER PLANT - See Hirth 263-engined version of *Enduro/Falke V* except: Power per unit area 0.13 hp/ft², 1.3 hp/m².

WEIGHTS & LOADINGS - Empty weight 234 lb, 106 kg. Max take-off weight 443 lb, 201 kg. Payload 209 lb, 95 kg. Max wing loading 2.53 lb/ft², 12.3 kg/m². Max power loading 20.1 lb/hp, 9.1 kg/hp. Load factors +4.0, -2.0 recommended; +6.0, -3.0 ultimate.

PERFORMANCE* - See Hirth 263-engined version of *Enduro/Falke V* except: Max cruising speed 40 mph, 65 kph. Economic cruising speed 40 mph, 65 kph. Range at average cruising speed NC.

*Under the following test conditions - See Hirth 263-engined version of *Enduro/Falke V* except: Test payload 209 lb, 95 kg.

SCHMIDTLER/SCHONLEBER *ENDURO/FOCUS 18*
(Weight-shift)

Summary as Enduro/Falke V *except: Approximately 80% double-surface.*

Production status: current, number completed NC.

GENERAL - See *Enduro/Falke V.*

EXTERNAL DIMENSIONS & AREAS - See *Enduro/ Falke V* except: Wing span 35.8 ft, 10.90 m. Total wing area 194 ft², 18.0 m². Aspect ratio 6.6/1.

POWER PLANT - See Hirth 263-engined version of *Enduro/Falke V* except: Power per unit area 0.11 hp/ft², 1.2 hp/m².

WEIGHTS & LOADINGS - Empty weight 225 lb, 102 kg. Max take-off weight 500 lb, 227 kg. Payload 276 lb, 125 kg. Max wing loading 2.58 lb/ft², 12.6 kg/m². Max power loading 22.7 lb/hp, 10.3 kg/hp. Load factors +4.0, -2.0 recommended; +6.0, -3.0 ultimate.

PERFORMANCE* - See Hirth 263-engined version of *Enduro/Falke V.*

*Under the following test conditions - See Hirth 263-engined version of *Enduro/Falke V* except: Test payload 276 lb, 125 kg.

SCHMIDTLER/STEINBACH DELTA *ENDURO/EURO III*
(Weight-shift)

Summary as Enduro/Falke V *except: Approximately 50% double-surface.*

Production status: current, number completed NC.

GENERAL - See *Enduro/Falke V.*

EXTERNAL DIMENSIONS & AREAS - See *Enduro/ Falke V* except: Length overall 11.2 ft, 3.40 m. Wing span 31.5 ft, 9.60 m. Chord at root 9.8 ft, 3.00 m. Chord at tip 1.1 ft, 0.50 m. Nose angle 132°. Depth of keel pocket 0.7 ft, 0.20 m. Total wing area 183 ft², 17.0 m². Aspect ratio 5.4/1.

POWER PLANT - See Hirth 263-engined version of *Enduro/Falke V.*

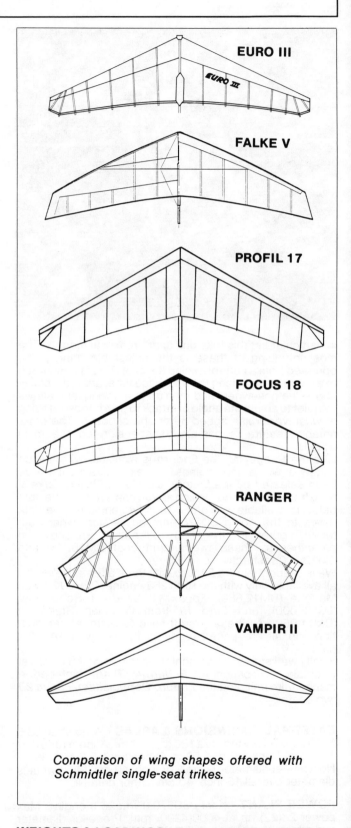

Comparison of wing shapes offered with Schmidtler single-seat trikes.

WEIGHTS & LOADINGS - Empty weight 245 lb, 111 kg. Max take-off weight 454 lb, 206 kg. Payload 209 lb, 95 kg. Max wing loading 2.48 lb/ft², 12.1 kg/m². Max power loading 20.6 lb/hp, 9.4 kg/hp. Load factors +4.0, -2.0 recommended; +6.0, -3.0 ultimate.

PERFORMANCE* - See Hirth 263-engined version of *Enduro/Falke V* except: Max cruising speed 34 mph, 55 kph. Economic cruising speed 34 mph, 55 kph. Range at average cruising speed *106* mile, *170* km.

*Under the following test conditions - See Hirth 263-engined version of *Enduro/Falke V* except: Test payload 209 lb, 95 kg.

SCHMIDTLER/SCHONLEBER *ENDURO DOPPELSITZER/ FOCUS 20*

(Weight-shift)

Summary as Enduro/Falke V *except: Side-by-side two-seater. Approximately 80% double-surface.*

Production status: one-off.

GENERAL - The *Enduro Doppelsitzer* is Schmidtler's first two-seater and is at the time of writing still incomplete. Structurally similar to the solo *Enduro*, with the same wheelbase, track, and wheel sizes, it will be mated to a *Focus 20* wing and will feature side-by-side seating. It has been designed to the same g-limits as the solo machines. Power unit has yet to be decided, and there is no word about whether a production run is planned.

EXTERNAL DIMENSIONS & AREAS - Wheel track 5.0 ft, 1.52 m. Wheelbase 6.5 ft, 1.98 m. Nosewheel diameter overall 16 inch, 40 cm. Main wheels diameter overall 16 inch, 40 cm. Other data NC.

POWER PLANT - Propeller diameter and pitch 61xNC inch, 1.54xNC m (4-blade). Fuel capacity 5.3 US gal, 4.4 Imp gal, 20.0 litre. Other data NC.

WEIGHTS & LOADINGS - Load factors +4.0, -2.0 recommended; +6.0, -3.0 ultimate. Other data NC.

PERFORMANCE - NC.

SCHMIDTLER *ENDURO MKB 462/Suitable Rogallo*

(Weight-shift)

Summary similar to Enduro/Falke V.

Production status: one-off.

GENERAL - This high-performance version of the *Enduro* was under development as we went to press and little data was available - even the wing type had not been decided. Power unit is the MKB 462. For background information on the trike unit, see *Enduro/Falke V.*

EXTERNAL DIMENSIONS & AREAS - Wheel track 5.0 ft, 1.52 m. Nosewheel diameter overall 16 inch, 40 cm. Main wheels diameter overall 16 inch, 40 cm. Other data NC.

POWER PLANT - MKB 462 engine. Max power 52 hp at NC rpm. Propeller diameter and pitch 61xNC inch, 1.54xNC m (4-blade). Poly V-belt reduction, ratio 2.0/1. Max static thrust NC. Power per unit area NC. Fuel capacity 5.3 US gal, 4.4 Imp gal, 20.0 litre.

WEIGHTS & LOADINGS - NC.

PERFORMANCE - NC.

THALHOFER

Thalhofer GmbH, Allmandstrasse 12, 7440 Nurtingen 7; tel 07022-54090.

THALHOFER *BRONCO*

(Three-axis)

Single-seat single-engined high-wing monoplane with conventional three-axis control. Wing has unswept leading and trailing edges, and constant chord; conventional tail. Pitch control by elevator on tail; yaw control by fin-mounted rudder; roll control by full-span ailerons; control inputs through stick for pitch/roll and pedals for yaw. Wing braced from below by struts; wing profile modified FX63-137; 100% double-surface. Undercarriage has three wheels in tricycle formation with additional tail-wheel; no suspension on nosewheel and rubber suspension on main wheels. Push-right go-right nosewheel steering connected to yaw control. Nosewheel brake. Aluminium-alloy tube airframe, completely open (partial enclosure optional). Engine mounted below wing, driving pusher propeller.

Production status: current, number completed NC.

GENERAL - This hang glider manufacturer built its first ultralight as long ago as 1976, but it was not until '83 that the first two *Bronco* prototypes took to the air. Considerable refinements have been incorporated since we described the aircraft in our first edition; in the interim the machine has acquired an attractive optional partial enclosure, complemented by wheel spats and an additional fairing between the enclosure and the wing, reaching back to the engine mounts.

The engine itself is pretty much unchanged, though a shade more powerful than before, but the wing is noticeably different. Though the same chord is retained, both wing span and area are increased, from 28.5 to 33.1 ft and from 114 to 129 ft^2 respectively (8.70-10.10 m, 10.6-12.0 m^2). Glide angle is now a very respectable 12/1. Completing the list of changes are the enlargement of the ailerons to full-span and the incorporation of a nosewheel brake. Ready to fly and including ASI, altimeter and compass, the *Bronco* costs DM21,500.

In our previous edition we mentioned also a side-by-side two-seater derivative which was planned for summer '83. The latest two-seater from Thalhofer, however, is of tandem layout (exactly the opposite route to the developments at Scheibe) but is still in prototype form at the time of going to press, so we have no further details. Data below refers to the solo machine in standard form.

EXTERNAL DIMENSIONS & AREAS - Length overall 18.7 ft, 5.70 m. Height overall 7.2 ft, 2.20 m. Wing span 33.1 ft, 10.10 m. Constant chord 3.9 ft, 1.20 m. Dihedral 2°. Sweepback 0°. Tailplane span 6.2 ft, 1.90 m. Fin height 3.6 ft, 1.10 m. Total wing area 129 ft^2, 12.0 m^2. Total aileron area 23.7 ft^2, 2.20 m^2. Total fin and rudder area 10.7 ft^2, 1.00 m^2. Total tailplane and elevator area 22.6 ft^2, 2.10 m^2. Aspect ratio 8.5/1. Wheel track 5.2 ft, 1.60 m. Wheelbase NC. Nosewheel diameter overall 12 inch, 30 cm. Main wheels diameter overall 20 inch, 50 cm.

POWER PLANT - Konig SC430 engine. Max power 27 hp at 4000 rpm. Propeller diameter and pitch 52xNC inch, 1.32xNC m (3-blade). Toothed-belt reduction, ratio 1.8/1.

461

Main picture shows Bronco *with enclosure but without wheel spats; inset shows machine in standard form.*

Max static thrust 170 lb, 77 kg. Power per unit area 0.21 hp/ft², 2.3 hp/m². Fuel capacity 5.3 US gal, 4.4 Imp gal, 20.0 litre.

WEIGHTS & LOADINGS - Empty weight 254 lb, 115 kg. Max take-off weight 540 lb, 245 kg. Payload 287 lb, 130 kg. Max wing loading 4.19 lb/ft², 20.4 kg/m². Max power loading 20.0 lb/hp, 9.1 kg/hp. Load factors +6.0, -3.0 recommended; NC ultimate.

PERFORMANCE* - Max level speed 68 mph, 110 kph. Never exceed speed 68 mph, 110 kph. Max cruising speed 56 mph, 90 kph. Economic cruising speed 47 mph, 75 kph. Stalling speed 27 mph, 43 kph. Max climb rate at sea level 390 ft/min, 2.0 m/s. Min sink rate 240 ft/min at 31 mph, 1.2 m/s at 50 kph. Best glide ratio with power off 12/1 at 40 mph, 65 kph. Take-off distance 230 ft, 70 m. Landing distance 165 ft, 50 m. Service ceiling NC. Range at average cruising speed 186 mile, 300 km. Noise level 59 dB at 490 ft, 150 m.

*Under the following test conditions - Airfield altitude 2300 ft, 700 m. Ground temperature 59°F, 15°C. Ground pressure 1010 mB. Ground windspeed 0 mph, 0 kph. Test payload 243 lb, 110 kg.

ULTRA-FLUG

Ultra-Flug Jagle GmbH, Weissenburger Strasse 43, 8078 Eichstatt; tel 08421-1004; tx D55 939. Chief personnel: Wolfgang, Karl and Walter Jagle; Wolfgang Hellweg.

ULTRA-FLUG
ULTRA-VECTOR H and ULTRA-VECTOR F
(Three-axis)

Summary similar to Sky King Vector 627SR *(see Canadian section) except: Ultra-Vector F has tractor propeller.*

Production status: current, approximately 1500 completed (total of all Vector *production - see text).*

GENERAL - Two good ways to judge the quality of a design are its ability to outlive the companies which produce it, and its ability to inspire overseas imitators/licensees. On both counts Klaus Hill's *Vector* emerges as one of ultralighting's great classics. Not only has the original has passed through four hands in North America - Skysports, Vector Aircraft Corp, Aerodyne and finally the present Canadian producer Sky King - it has also resulted in three overseas versions, by APCO in Israel, Avulnor in France and Ultra-Flug in West Germany.
Of these, the German example is the most interesting, not

Willi Tacke

West Germany's interpretation of the classic Vector can be had with pusher prop (main picture) or tractor prop (inset).

just because it offers a choice of two engines, but because the buyer also has a choice of tractor or pusher prop. The time-honoured *Vector* arrangement of front engine and pusher prop can be had with a Konig SC430, but those who don't fancy having a long driveshaft whirring just above their head can opt instead for a 22 hp Hirth with tractor prop, the two versions being known as *Ultra-Vector H* and *F* respectively. Our data below refers to the pusher version. Prices vary according to specification, but are around DM15,000. The use of the word 'Ultra' in the model title is probably more than just ego on the part of the company, as it helps to distinguish its product from the Israeli-made *Vector,* which is also sold in West Germany.

Power plant apart, the Ultra-Flug machines are very similar to the other variations on the *Vector* theme. Interestingly though, we have yet to find two sets of *Vector* dimensions from anywhere which agree! Short of hiring a hangar and airfreighting machines from all over the world at prodigious expense, there is no way we can compare the aircraft side by side and ascertain the actual differences in length, wing span etc. All we can do is print Ultra-Flug's data in good faith, just as we have with the other manufacturers, and express the hope that some *Vector* freak will pursue this fascinating but distinctly esoteric investigation on our behalf . . .

EXTERNAL DIMENSIONS & AREAS - Length overall 18.0 ft, 5.49 m. Height overall 8.0 ft, 2.43 m. Wing span 35.2 ft, 10.72 m. Dihedral 8°. Sweepback 0°. Total wing area 154 ft², 14.3 m². Aspect ratio 8.0/1. Wheel track 4.1 ft, 1.25 m. Other data NC.

POWER PLANT - Konig SC430 engine. Max power 26 hp at 4200 rpm. Propeller diameter and pitch 51xNC inch, 1.30xNC m. Toothed-belt reduction, ratio 1.5/1. Max static thrust 132 lb, 60 kg. Power per unit area 0.17 hp/ft², 1.8 hp/m². Fuel capacity 5.3 US gal, 4.4 Imp gal, 20.0 litre.

WEIGHTS & LOADINGS - Empty weight 115 lb, 254 kg. Max take-off weight 474 lb, 215 kg. Payload 220 lb, 100 kg. Max wing loading 3.08 lb/ft², 15.0 kg/m². Max power loading 18.2 lb/hp, 8.3 kg/hp. Load factors +6.0, -NC recommended; NC ultimate.

PERFORMANCE* - Max level speed 50 mph, 80 kph. Never exceed speed 56 mph, 90 kph. Max cruising speed 45 mph, 72 kph. Economic cruising speed 31 mph, 50 kph. Stalling speed 26 mph, 42 kph. Max climb rate at sea level 390 ft/min, 2.0 m/s. Min sink rate 300 ft/min at 31 mph, 1.5 m/s at 50 kph. Best glide ratio with power off 7/1 at 34 mph, 55 kph. Take-off distance 18 ft, 60 m. Landing distance 18 ft, 60 m. Service ceiling NC. Range at average cruising speed 124 mile, 200 km. Noise level 59 dB at 490 ft, 150 m.

*Under the following test conditions - Airfield altitude 0 ft, 0 m. Ground temperature 59°F, 15°C. Ground pressure 1013 mB. Ground windspeed 0 mph, 0 kph. Test payload 207 lb, 94 kg.

Willi Tacke

ULTRALEICHTE FLUGGERATEBAU

Ultraleichte Fluggeratebau GmbH, Twist 9, Am UL-Flugplatz, 4455 Wietmarschen; tel 05936 400.

ULTRALEICHTE FLUGGERATEBAU *WILDENTE*

(Three-axis)

Single-seat single-engined high-wing monoplane with conventional three-axis control. Wing has unswept leading and trailing edges, and constant chord; cruciform tail. Pitch control by elevator on tail; yaw control by fin-mounted rudder; roll control by half-span ailerons; control inputs through stick for pitch/roll and pedals for yaw. Wing braced from below by struts; wing profile Ga 549; 100% double-surface. Undercarriage has three wheels in tricycle formation; steel-spring suspension on nose-wheel and glass-fibre suspension on main wheels. Push-right go-right nosewheel steering connected to yaw control. Brakes on main wheels. Aluminium-alloy tube airframe, with pod. Engine mounted below wing, driving pusher propeller.

Production status: current, number completed NC.

GENERAL - The Aero '83 show at Friedrichshafen was a significant event for the ultralight fraternity, with many new designs making their first appearance, and not least among them was the *Wildente*. At that time, however, it had not flown, first airtime being logged on 16 April that year.

Since then the machine has gone into series production. It is notable for its welded tubular airframe, which is claimed to allow rigging and derigging in only 10 min, as well as offering excellent rigidity. On the minus side, it is likely to make repairs expensive, and mitigates against home-builders.

Perhaps because of this, the only price we have is for a ready to fly machine, which in February '85 cost DM22,600 including tax.

We have no word on the two-seater which the company said would appear during summer '83.

EXTERNAL DIMENSIONS & AREAS - Length overall 19.4 ft, 5.90 m. Wing span 34.4 ft, 10.50 m. Constant chord 4.9 ft, 1.50 m. Sweepback 0°X. Total wing area 166 ft², 15.4 m². Aspect ratio 7.2/1. Wheel track 5.1 ft, 1.55 m. Other data NC.

POWER PLANT - Hirth engine. Max power 28 hp at NC rpm. Power per unit area 0.17 hp/ft², 1.8 hp/m². Fuel capacity 5.3 US gal, 4.4 Imp gal, 20.0 litre. Other data NC.

WEIGHTS & LOADINGS - Empty weight 254 lb, 115 kg. Max take-off weight 485 lb, 220 kg. Payload 231 lb, 105 kg. Max wing loading 2.92 lb/ft², 14.3 kg/m². Max power loading 17.3 lb/hp, 7.9 kg/hp. Load factors NC recommended; +6.0, -3.0 ultimate.

PERFORMANCE* - Max level speed 62 mph, 100 kph. Cruising speed 40 mph, 65 kph. Stalling speed 26 mph, 42 kph. Min sink rate 310 ft/min, 1.6 m/s at NC speed. Best glide ratio with power off 9.5/1 at NC speed. Range at average cruising speed 162 mile, 260 km. Other data NC.

*Under unspecified test conditions.

VULCAN

Vulcan UL-Aviation, Kiefernweg 13, 8011 Poring; tel 08106-29148.

VULCAN *TRAVELER III*
(Two-axis)

Single-seat single-engined high-wing monoplane with two-axis control. Wing has swept back leading and trailing edges, and tapering chord; no tail, canard wing. Pitch control by fully flying canard; yaw control by tip rudders; no separate roll control; control inputs through stick for pitch/yaw. Wing braced from above by kingpost and cables, from below by cables; wing profile NC; double-

surface. Undercarriage has three wheels in tricycle formation; suspension NC on nosewheel and glass-fibre suspension on main wheels. Push-right go-left nosewheel steering independent from yaw control. Nosewheel brake. Aluminium-alloy tube airframe, completely open. Engine mounted below wing, driving pusher propeller.

Production status: current, 20 completed by March '83 (latest figure available).

GENERAL - Pterodactyl enthusiasts will immediately recognise the heritage of this machine, for it is yet another derivative of the famous *Fledgling* wing, designed by the late Klaus Hill and since flown with and without power in almost every conceivable configuration.

Of all these configurations, the canard is probably the most popular, and the West German company has produced a canard with a difference - two separate surfaces, one attached to each of the main horizontal tubes. The rest of the tubework is also Vulcan's own design, but the result is still faithful to the 'Dactyl spirit. Another Vulcan touch is the addition of trapezoidal vertical surfaces to the wing tips to act as winglets and reduce tip vortices.

Originally sold with either a *Fledge II* or *Fledge III* wing, the *Traveler* title being suffixed accordingly, the company is now concentrating on the latter version, which retails at DM17,250 ready to fly. Another change is the power unit, which was originally a Lloyd LS400, though many others were fitted over the years, including Cuyuna 430s as in the States. Now that the Lloyd is out of production, the standard engine is a Hirth 263.

EXTERNAL DIMENSIONS & AREAS - Height overall 6.4 ft, 1.95 m. Wing span 32.5 ft, 9.90 m. Nose angle 144°. Main wing area 157 ft², 14.6 m². Aspect ratio (of main wing) 6.7/1. Other data NC.

POWER PLANT - Hirth 263 engine. Max power 22 hp at NC rpm. Power per unit area 0.14 hp/ft², 1.5 hp/m². Fuel

West Germany's answer to the Pterodactyl - the Traveler. *Small pictures show the unique double canard and the winglets/tip rudder arrangement.*

capacity 5.3 US gal, 4.4 Imp gal, 20.0 litre. Other data NC.

WEIGHTS & LOADINGS - Empty weight 254 lb, 115 kg. Max take-off weight 485 lb, 220 kg. Payload 231 lb, 105 kg. Max wing loading 3.09 lb/ft², 15.1 kg/m². Max power loading 22.0 lb/hp, 10.0 kg/hp. Load factors NC.

PERFORMANCE* - Max level speed 50 mph, 80 kph. Cruising speed 37 mph, 60 kph. Stalling speed 22 mph, 35 kph. Best glide ratio with power off 10/1 at NC speed. Range at average cruising speed 114 mile, 183 km. Other data NC.

*Under unspecified test conditions.

WARNKE

UL-Technik Othmar Warnke, Junkersdamm 6, 2903 Danikhorst; tel 04403-1295.

WARNKE/SOUTHDOWN INTERNATIONAL
WARNKE TRIKE/LIGHTNING PHASE II
(Weight-shift)

Single-seat single-engined flex-wing aircraft with weight-shift control. Rogallo wing with fin. Pilot suspended below wing in trike unit, using bar to control pitch and roll/yaw by altering relative positions of trike unit and wing. Wing braced from above by kingpost and cables, from below by cables; floating cross-tube construction with 60% double-surface enclosing cross-tube; preformed ribs. Undercarriage has three wheels in tricycle formation; no suspension on any wheels. Push-right go-left nosewheel steering independent from aerodynamic controls. Optional nosewheel brake.

The Warnke Trike folded, rigged, and flying.

Aluminium-alloy tube trike unit, completely open. Engine mounted below wing, driving pusher propeller.

Production status: current, 62 completed by February '85.

GENERAL - As well as being the West German agent for the British firm Southdown International, whose famous *Puma Sprint* he sells as a trainer, Othmar Warnke also makes his own single-seat trike units.

Not surprisingly, when he comes to choose a wing for them, it is a Southdown product which he puts at the top of the list, the *Lightning Phase II,* which like all Southdown wings has a distinctive fin on its top surface. However, Othmar does offer alternatives, such as the Bicla *Spider* and *Arrow M,* and the *Steinbach* Euro III.

Undoubtedly the most novel feature of Othmar's machines is the centrifugal clutch, which ensures that the pilot can ride the thermals peacefully and efficiently, with the engine at idle but the prop stationary. The company can if required supply trikes without this device, in which case the reduction ratio is changed to 1.8/1 and the prop to 51x41 inch (1.30x1.05 m), the same Hirth 263 engine being used in either case. Our data below refers to a trike unit with clutch mated to a *Lightning Phase II* wing, a combination which costs DM11,450 ready to fly. With Bicla *Spider* the price is reduced to DM10,890 and with Steinbach *Euro III* it drops to DM10,427.

Options include electric start, nosewheel brake, floats, skis, and the British-made Skymaster parachute system.

EXTERNAL DIMENSIONS & AREAS - Length overall 12.5 ft, 3.80 m. Height overall 11.5 ft, 3.50 m. Wing span 32.5 ft, 9.90 m. Fin height 2.0 ft, 0.60 m. Total wing area 174 ft^2, 16.2 m^2. Aspect ratio 6.1/1. Wheel track 5.2 ft, 1.60 m. Nosewheel diameter overall 16 inch, 40 cm. Main wheels diameter overall 16 inch, 40 cm. Other data NC.

POWER PLANT - Hirth 263 A13 engine. Max power 22 hp at 4200 rpm. Propeller diameter and pitch 63x47 inch, 1.60x1.20 m. Poly V-belt reduction, ratio 2.5/1. Max static thrust 165 lb, 75 kg. Power per unit area 0.13 hp/ft^2, 1.4 hp/m^2. Fuel capacity 5.3 US gal, 4.4 Imp gal, 20.0 litre.

WEIGHTS & LOADINGS - Empty weight 227 lb, 103 kg. Max take-off weight 441 lb, 200 kg. Payload 214 lb, 97 kg. Max wing loading 2.53 lb/ft^2, 12.3 kg/m^2. Max power loading 20.0 lb/hp, 9.1 kg/hp. Standard Gutesiegel load factors.

PERFORMANCE* - Max level speed 50 mph, 80 kph. Never exceed speed 59 mph, 95 kph. Max cruising speed 37 mph, 60 kph. Stalling speed 26 mph, 42 kph. Min sink rate 300 ft/min at 29 mph, 1.5 m/s at 46 kph. Best glide ratio with power off 6/1 at NC speed. Take-off distance 80 ft, 25 m. Landing distance 100 ft, 30 m. Noise level 57.6 dB at 490 ft, 150 m. Other data NC.

*Under unspecified test conditions.

Yugoslavia

Researched by Bogoljub Jeremic, Secretary General of L'Union Aeronautique de Yougoslavie

Taking the Adriatic air
by Norman Burr

Although our information on Yugoslavian aircraft is rather sparse, this section is a great improvement on the Yugoslavian coverage of our first edition, which amounted to nil! For this change we have Bogoljub Jeremic to thank, secretary general of UAY, the Yugoslavian aero club, who distributed forms to homebuilders on our behalf.

We say homebuilders because the country has as yet no ultralights in series production, but this short section shows that the sport there is nevertheless very much alive. We feature here four homebuilts, three flexwings and one fixedwing, all using the Trabant engine so beloved of the Hungarian enthusiasts over the border.

There are, however, two obvious differences from the Hungarian approach: first, imported wings are quite common, whereas to the north they are all locally produced, and second there is some three-axis activity, albeit a minority.

For more information on ultralights in Yugoslavia, contact: L'Union Aeronautique de Yougoslavie (UAY), Uzun Mirkova 4/I, Boite Postale 872, Beograd; tel 626077 or 626235; telegrams Vazduhosavez - Beograd.

KONAVEC

Ivan Konavec, Milanova 10, 65222 Kobarid.

KONAVEC/LA MOUETTE
TRIKE NORMAL/AZUR 17
(Weight-shift)

Single-seat single-engined flex-wing aircraft with weight-shift control. Rogallo wing with keel pocket. Pilot suspended below wing in trike unit, using bar to control pitch and roll/yaw by altering relative positions of trike unit and wing. Wing braced from above by kingpost and cables, from below by cables; floating cross-tube construction with 50% double-surface enclosing cross-tube; preformed ribs. Undercarriage has three wheels in tricycle formation; no suspension on any wheels. Push-right go-left nosewheel steering independent from aerodynamic controls. Nosewheel brake. Aluminium-alloy tube trike unit, completely open. Engine mounted below wing, driving pusher propeller.

Production status: prototype.

GENERAL - Though it is out of production, the well proven *Azur 17* wing by the French company La Mouette is still flown in large numbers, and one at least has found its way to Yugoslavia and onto the top of Ivan Konavec's *Trike Normal*.

Ivan unfortunately hasn't sent us a picture of his machine, but we understand that it is a conventional monopole of aluminium-alloy tubing. Power comes from the East German Trabant car engine, almost the standard triking power plant in communist countries, and in this application it develops 26 hp.·ʻ

Ivan describes his machine as a prototype rather than a one-off, which makes us wonder whether there is some thought of series production. We'll find out in our third edition . . .

EXTERNAL DIMENSIONS & AREAS - Length overall 11.5 ft, 3.50 m. Height overall 9.8 ft, 3.00 m. Wing span 34.8 ft, 10.60 m. Chord at root 8.5 ft, 2.60 m. Chord at tip 2.0 ft, 0.60 m. Dihedral 4°. Nose angle 119°. Depth of keel pocket 1.0 ft, 0.30 m. Total wing area 178 ft², 16.5 m². Keel pocket area 2.2 ft², 0.20 m². Aspect ratio 6.8/1. Wheel track 4.9 ft, 1.50 m. Wheelbase 4.9 ft, 1.50 m. Nosewheel diameter overall 14 inch, 35 cm. Main wheels diameter overall 16 inch, 40 cm.

POWER PLANT - Trabant 600 engine. Max power 26 hp at NC rpm. Propeller diameter and pitch 49xNC inch, 1.24xNC m. No reduction. Max static thrust 154 lb, 70 kg. Power per unit area 0.15 hp/ft², 1.6 hp/m². Fuel capacity NC.

WEIGHTS & LOADINGS - Empty weight 220 lb, 100 kg. Max take-off weight 419 lb, 190 kg. Payload 198 lb, 90 kg. Max wing loading 2.35 lb/ft², 11.5 kg/m². Max power loading 16.1 lb/hp, 7.3 kg/hp. Load factors +3.0, -2.0 recommended; +5.0, -3.0 ultimate.

PERFORMANCE* - Never exceed speed 44 mph, 70 kph. Economic cruising speed 31 mph, 50 kph. Stalling speed 22 mph, 35 kph. Max climb rate at sea level 350 ft/min, 1.8 m/s. Min sink rate NC ft/min at 30 mph, NC m/s at 48 kph. Best glide ratio with power off 8/1 at NC speed. Take-off distance 150 ft, 45 m. Landing distance 150 ft, 45 m. Service ceiling 6560 ft, 2000 m. Range at average cruising speed 93 mile, 150 km. Other data NC.

*Under the following test conditions - Airfield altitude 490 ft, 150 m. Ground temperature 77°F, 25°C. Ground pressure 1014 mB. Ground windspeed 6 mph, 10 kph. Test payload NC.

PETKOVNIK

Janko Petkovnik, Speglova 22, 63320 T Velenje.

PETKOVNIK/FIREBIRD
Homebuilt/SIERRA
(Weight-shift)

Single-seat single-engined flex-wing aircraft with weight-shift control. Rogallo wing with keel pocket. Pilot suspended below wing in trike unit, using bar to control pitch and roll/yaw by altering relative positions of trike unit and wing. Wing braced from above by kingpost and cables, from below by cables; floating cross-tube construction with NC% double-surface enclosing cross-tube; preformed ribs. Undercarriage has three wheels in tricycle formation; no suspension on any wheels. Push-right go-left nosewheel steering independent from aerodynamic controls. Nosewheel brake. Aluminium-alloy tube trike unit, completely open. Engine mounted below wing, driving pusher propeller.

Production status: prototype.

GENERAL - Like Ivan Konavec's machine, Janko Petkovnik's trike sports an imported wing, in this case the *Sierra 175* from the West German company Firebird. The trike unit's specification seems to follow that of Ivan's very closely, with monopole construction, Trabant 600 engine, nosewheel brake, and no attempt at any pilot enclosure - hardly a surprising omission in view of the country's excellent weather.

Janko has also omitted to name his creation. There's no word of any production plans, though like Ivan he describes the aircraft as a prototype rather than a one-off.

EXTERNAL DIMENSIONS & AREAS - Length overall 12.5 ft, 3.80 m. Height overall 9.8 ft, 3.00 m. Wing span 35.8 ft, 10.90 m. Chord at root 9.8 ft, 3.00 m. Chord at tip 3.9 ft, 1.20 m. Nose angle 136°. Total wing area 180 ft², 16.7 m². Aspect ratio 7.1/1. Wheel track 4.9 ft, 1.50 m. Wheelbase 4.9 ft, 1.50 m. Nosewheel diameter overall 14 inch, 35 cm. Main wheels diameter overall 14 inch, 35 cm. Other data NC.

POWER PLANT - Trabant 600 engine. Max power 26 hp at 4200 rpm. Propeller diameter and pitch 47xNC inch, 1.20xNC m. No reduction. Max static thrust 154 lb, 70 kg. Power per unit area 0.14 hp/ft², 1.6 hp/m². Fuel capacity NC.

WEIGHTS & LOADINGS - Empty weight 220 lb, 100 kg. Max take-off weight 441 lb, 200 kg. Payload 220 lb, 100 kg. Max wing loading 2.45 lb/ft², 12.0 kg/m². Max power loading 17.0 lb/hp, 7.7 kg/hp. Load factors +3.0, -1.0 recommended; +6.0, -4.0 ultimate.

PERFORMANCE* - Never exceed speed 50 mph, 80 kph. Economic cruising speed 31 mph, 50 kph. Stalling speed 22 mph, 35 kph. Max climb rate at sea level 390 ft/min, 2.0 m/s. Min sink rate NC ft/min at 31 mph, NC m/s at 50 kph. Best glide ratio with power off 9/1 at NC speed. Take-off distance 150 ft, 45 m. Landing distance 130 ft, 40 m. Service ceiling 8200 ft, 2500 m. Range at average cruising speed 93 mile, 150 km. Other data NC.

*Under unspecified test conditions.

REMS

Lojze Rems, Zagorica 2, 61235 Radomlje.

REMS
Homebuilt/TAIFUN
(Weight-shift)

Single-seat single-engined flex-wing aircraft with weight-shift control. Rogallo wing with keel pocket. Pilot suspended below wing in trike unit, using bar to control pitch and roll/yaw by altering relative positions of trike unit and wing. Wing braced from above by kingpost and cables, from below by cables; floating cross-tube construction with NC% double-surface enclosing cross-tube; preformed ribs. Undercarriage has three wheels in tricycle formation; no suspension on any wheels. Push-right go-left nosewheel steering independent from aerodynamic controls. Nosewheel brake. Aluminium-alloy tube trike unit, completely open. Engine mounted below wing, driving pusher propeller.

Production status: prototype.

GENERAL - We are tempted to say that this is a 'standard' Yugoslavian homebuilt trike, in that it follows an almost identical formula to the two previous entries in this section, with direct-drive Trabant 600, monopole construction and an imported wing.

However, it is not quite that simple. Although the wing area and span are very close to the *Typhoon S4 Medium* from the British firm Pegasus, the other dimensions are significantly different, and we are left wondering whether we are in fact describing a *Typhoon* or simply a wing whose name and principal dimensions are similar. Unfortunately, deadlines do not permit us to investigate the matter further, so all we can do is print the wing name and data exactly as supplied, and hope that this conundrum can be sorted out for future editions.

EXTERNAL DIMENSIONS & AREAS - Length overall 11.5 ft, 3.50 m. Height overall 11.5 ft, 3.5 m. Wing span 32.8 ft, 10.00 m. Chord at root 8.2 ft, 2.50 m. Chord at tip 3.3 ft, 1.00 m. Nose angle 129°. Total wing area 167 ft², 15.5 m². Aspect ratio 6.5/1. Wheel track 4.6 ft, 1.40 m. Wheelbase 4.9 ft, 1.50 m. Nosewheel diameter overall 14 inch, 35 cm. Main wheels diameter overall 14 inch, 35 cm. Other data NC.

POWER PLANT - Trabant 600 engine. Max power 26 hp at 4200 rpm. Propeller diameter and pitch 49xNC inch, 1.24xNC m. No reduction. Max static thrust 154 lb, 70 kg. Power per unit area 0.16 hp/ft², 1.7 hp/m². Fuel capacity NC.

WEIGHTS & LOADINGS - Empty weight 220 lb, 100 kg. Max take-off weight 441 lb, 200 kg. Payload 220 lb, 100 kg. Max wing loading 2.64 lb/ft², 12.9 kg/m². Max power loading 17.0 lb/hp, 7.7 kg/hp. Load factors +3.0, -1.0 recommended; +5.0, -3.0 ultimate.

PERFORMANCE* - Never exceed speed 50 mph, 80 kph. Economic cruising speed 37 mph, 60 kph. Stalling speed 22 mph, 35 kph. Max climb rate at sea level 390 ft/min, 2.0 m/s. Min sink rate NC ft/min at 31 mph, NC m/s at 50 kph. Best glide ratio with power off 9/1 at NC speed. Take-off

distance 130 ft, 40 m. Landing distance 130 ft, 40 m. Service ceiling 8200 ft, 2500 m. Range at average cruising speed 93 mile, 150 km. Other data NC.

Under unspecified test conditions.

SLOBODAN & MILAN

Durin Slobodan & Durin Milan, Zabagska 43, 23000 Zrenjanin; tel 02325 680.

SLOBODAN & MILAN
KOMARAC III
(Three-axis)

Single-seat single-engined parasol-wing monoplane with conventional three-axis control. Wing has swept back leading and trailing edges, and constant chord; conventional tail. Pitch control by elevator on tail; yaw control by fin-mounted rudder; roll control by half-span ailerons; control inputs through stick for pitch/roll and pedals for yaw. Wing braced from below by struts; wing profile Durin; 100% double-surface. Undercarriage has two wheels plus tailskid; rubber suspension on tailskid and main wheels. No ground steering. No brakes. Aluminium-alloy angle airframe, partially enclosed. Engine mounted below wing, driving tractor propeller.

Production status: one-off.

GENERAL - Great minds think alike, even if they don't know each other, a fact which perennially plagues historians as they try to decide who to credit with a particular invention or discovery.

And so it is with ultralights. Replace the present parasol arrangement with a low wing, and the *Komarac* could easily be mistaken for Mike Fisher's *FP-303,* proof that if you set out to create a straightforward tail-dragger ultralight which uses easily available materials and yet is easy to build, the result will be no respecter of ideological divides. It seems highly unlikely that Mike knew of the Yugoslavian design when he created the *FP-303,* and it is absolutely certain that the Fisher product did not influence the Durin partnership, since the *Komarac* predates the *FP-303* by several years.

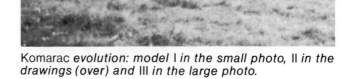

Komarac evolution: model I in the small photo, II in the drawings (over) and III in the large photo.

There have in fact been three *Komaracs* (the name means mosquito, incidentally), starting with the *Komarac I* which made its first flight as long ago as September 1975. As our unfortunately rather poor quality picture shows, this early effort bore little relationship to its successors, which ditched the tubular empennage in favour of a box-section fuselage. A little under four years later, in May '79, the *Komarac II* took to the air, and it is this machine which we illustrate in our colour section.

The following year came the latest variant and the one which we detail here, the *Komarac III,* very similar in appearance to its predecessor and retaining the same distinctive L-section aluminium-alloy structure. This incidentally is in contrast to the Mike Fisher design, which is an all-wood geodetic construction, and there's no doubt which is the more efficient structure, since the Yugoslavian machine weighs over half as much again as its American lookalike and is actually over the microlight limit in its present form. Nevertheless the figures below show that the *Komarac* has a thoroughly respectable performance for a 26 hp aircraft, especially when the age of the design is taken into account.

EXTERNAL DIMENSIONS & AREAS - Length overall 20.5 ft, 6.25 m. Height overall 5.9 ft, 1.80 m. Wing span 33.5 ft, 10.2 m. Constant chord 5.1 ft, 1.55 m. Dihedral 0°. Sweepback 1°. Tailplane span 10.7 ft, 3.25 m. Fin height 4.8 ft, 1.45 m. Total wing area 161 ft^2, 15.0 m^2. Aspect ratio 6.9/1. Wheel track 2.6 ft, 0.80 m. Main wheels diameter overall 16 inch, 40 cm. Other data NC.

Yugoslavia

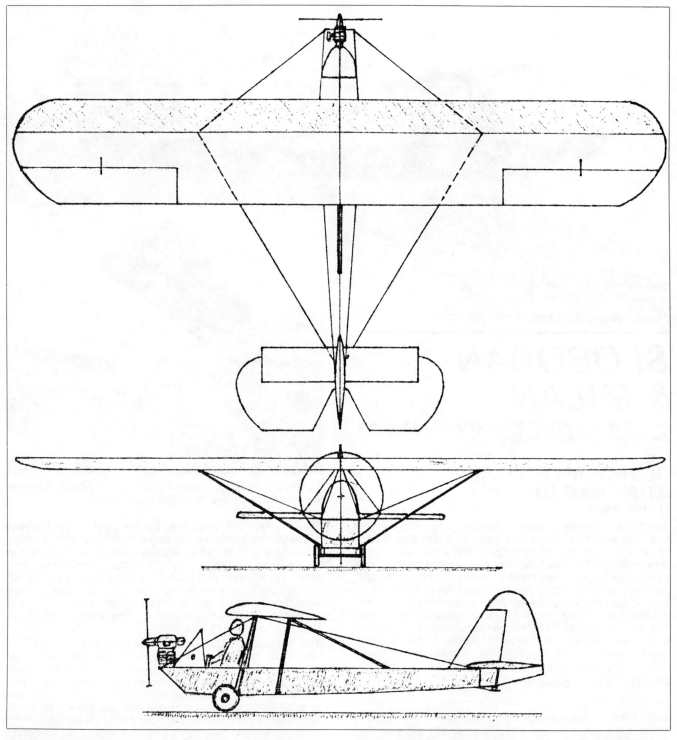

POWER PLANT - Trabant 601 engine. Max power 26 hp at 3600 rpm. Propeller diameter and pitch 51xNC inch, 1.30xNC m. No reduction. Max static thrust 154 lb, 70 kg. Power per unit area 0.16 hp/ft², 1.7 hp/m². Fuel capacity 5.8 US gal, 4.8 Imp gal, 22.0 litre.

WEIGHTS & LOADINGS - Empty weight 397 lb, 180 kg. Max take-off weight 661 lb, 300 kg. Payload 265 lb, 120 kg. Max wing loading 4.11 lb/ft², 20.0 kg/m². Max power loading 25.4 lb/hp, 11.5 kg/hp. Load factors +3.5, -3.0 recommended; +4.5, -3.5 ultimate.

PERFORMANCE* - Max level speed 68 mph, 110 kph.

Never exceed speed 81 mph, 130 kph. Max cruising speed 62 mph, 100 kph. Economic cruising speed 50 mph, 80 kph. Stalling speed 31 mph, 50 kph. Max climb rate at sea level 300 ft/min, 1.5 m/s. Min sink rate NC. Best glide ratio with power off 10/1 at 47 mph, 75 kph. Take-off distance 260 ft, 80 m. Landing distance 330 ft, 100 m. Service ceiling 6560 ft, 2000 m. Range at average cruising speed 124 mile, 200 km. Noise level NC.

*Under the following test conditions - Airfield altitude 262 ft, 80 m. Ground temperature 86°F, 30°C. Ground pressure 1000 mB. Ground windspeed 0 mph, 0 kph. Test payload 265 lb, 120 kg.

Other Countries

Researched by Norman Burr, Willi Tacke,
and Martin Velek

APCO (Israel)

APCO Aviation, PO Box 2124, Holon 58121; tel 053-34322; tx 35770/1 COIN IL EXT AXD. Factory address: 11 Hacadar Street, Industrial Zone, Netanya 42377.

APCO *VECTOR 627SR*

See Sky King Vector 627SR *(Canadian section).*

CONTINENTAL AEROLIGHTS (Netherlands)

Continental Aerolights, Atletenstraat 117, 7535 AT, Enschede; tel 53 311501.

CONTINENTAL AEROLIGHTS *EAGLE XL*
(Three-axis)

Summary as Ultrasport Eagle XL *(see Italian section).*
Production status: current, number completed NC.

GENERAL - Continental Aerolights is the Netherlands only commercial ultralight producer, and builds a version of ▼

the famous American canard machine, the *Eagle XL*. As we explain under Ultrasport in our Italian section, production of the *Eagle XL* has now ceased in its native USA (though the TFM lookalike is still available there), and world markets are being satisfied primarily from Italy.

However, Continental Aerolights builds its own version for sale to countries where strict noise limits outlaw the standard Rotax 377, substituting the 32 hp Hirth 2702-R03 instead. To the best of our knowledge, the aircraft are otherwise identical.

Princpal markets for the Dutch variant are West Germany, where it costs DM16,750 including tax and has full *Gutesiegel* approval, and of course the Netherlands.

EXTERNAL DIMENSIONS & AREAS - See Ultrasport *Eagle XL* (Italian section).

POWER PLANT - Hirth 2702-R03 engine. Max power 32 hp at 4200 rpm. Power per unit area 0.18 hp/ft^2, 2.0 hp/m^2. Fuel capacity 5.3 US gal, 4.4 Imp gal, 20.0 litre. Other data NC.

WEIGHTS & LOADINGS - Empty weight 247 lb, 112 kg. Max take-off weight 496 lb, 225 kg. Payload 249 lb, 113 kg. Max wing loading 2.83 lb/ft^2, 13.8 kg/m^2. Max power loading 15.5 lb/hp, 7.0 kg/hp. Load factors NC.

PERFORMANCE* - Max level speed 50 mph, 80 kph. Cruising speed 40 mph, 65 kph. Stalling speed 26 mph, 42 kph. Range at average cruising speed 100 mile, 161 km. Other data NC.

*Under unspecified test conditions.

CVUT (Czechoslovakia)

Aero Engineering Department, Technical University of Prague (CVUT), Prague.

CVUT
SP-1
(Three-axis)

Single-seat single-engined high-wing monoplane with conventional three-axis control. Wing has unswept leading and trailing edges, and constant chord; conventional tail. Pitch control by elevator on tail; yaw control by fin-mounted rudder; roll control by 30%-span ailerons; control inputs through stick for pitch/roll and pedals for yaw. Wing braced from below by struts; wing profile NC; 100% double-surface. Undercarriage has three wheels in tricycle formation; no suspension on nosewheel and bungee suspension on main wheels. Push-right go-left nosewheel steering independent from yaw control. No

Though dwarfed by its neighbours, the SP-1 stands proudly outside the hangar shortly after completion. For another picture, see colour section.

Letectvi Kosmonautika

brakes. *Aluminium-alloy tube/wood airframe, completely open. Engine mounted at wing height, driving pusher propeller.*

Production status: one-off.

GENERAL - Of the two Czech ultralights in this book, the *SP-1* is easily the most modern and could easily be mistaken for a homebuilder-style machine from a Western producer.

An amateur project under the sponsorship and technical guidance of the aero engineering department of the Prague Technical University, it is designed to *FAR 23* standards and uses a combination of alloy tubing and timber to produce a tidy looking aircraft which comes in just below the FAI microlight weight limit. In fact the structure does not look that heavy, so we suspect that the power unit is rather weightier than average. Martin Velek of *Kosmonautika* magazine tells us it is a two-stroke Walter A engine of 1976 vintage, incorporating gear reduction despite developing its 22 hp at only 2400 rpm.

Our data was prepared in early 1985, when the machine was still under test, so no performance figures are available.

EXTERNAL DIMENSIONS & AREAS - Length overall 18.6 ft, 5.68 m. Height overall 4.7 ft, 1.42 m. Wing span 34.8 ft, 10.60 m. Constant chord 4.0 ft, 1.22 m. Dihedral 1°. Sweepback 0°. Total wing area 139 ft^2, 12.9 m^2. Aspect ratio 8.7/1. Other data NC.

POWER PLANT - Walter A engine. Max power 22 hp at 2400 rpm. Propeller diameter and pitch 49xNC inch, 1.25xNC m. Gear reduction, ratio NC. Max static thrust 168 lb, 76 kg. Power per unit area 0.16 hp/ft^2, 1.7 hp/m^2. Fuel capacity 7.1 US gal, 5.9 Imp gal, 27.0 litre.

WEIGHTS & LOADINGS - Empty weight 322 lb, 146 kg. Max take-off weight 564 lb, 256 kg. Payload 243 lb, 110 kg. Max wing loading 4.06 lb/ft^2, 19.8 kg/m^2. Max power loading 25.6 lb/hp, 11.6 kg/hp. Load factors +6.0, -4.0 recommended; NC ultimate.

PERFORMANCE - NC.

HOKURIKU (Japan)

Hokuriku Gyros, Kawaguchi machi 1979-330, Kitauonuma Gun, Niigata Pre 949-75.

HOKURIKU
PROTOTYPE

(Three-axis)

Summary similar to Freedom Fliers Pterodactyl Ascender II+2 (see US section) except: Tandem seating.

Production status: see text.

GENERAL - Hokuriku is primarily a gyroplane company, but in mid '83 announced that it had completed what it called a 'reconstruction model' of a *Pterodactyl Ascender*. However, the aircraft is clearly not just a straight copy of

the American machine, because the seating arrangement is different. US two-seat 'Dactyls have side-by-side seating, and it seems certain that the tandem design is Hokuriku's own, since the only other aircraft of this genre which use it are George Killey's machines from South Africa. These are only produced in very small numbers, so it's unlikely that any have found their way to Japan.

Fitted with skis to cope with the deep snow found regularly in wintertime in that part of Japan, the aircraft is reported to have proved a useful training tool. Two up, the cruise is around 50 mph (80 kph), a figure which can be achieved on only 70% throttle if the pilot is flying solo. Unfortunately, we have no technical information on the machine, nor any word on whether it has gone into production, so we are omitting our data paragraphs in this case.

ICA (Romania)

Intreprinderea de Constructii Aeronautice, 2200 Brasov, Casuta postala Nr 198; tel 924 16719/ 16722; tx 61266. Director: Barbu Dumitru.

ICA *42/41*

(Weight-shift)

Single-seat single-engined flex-wing aircraft with weight-shift control. Rogallo wing with keel pocket. Pilot suspended below wing in trike unit, using bar to control pitch and roll/yaw by altering relative positions of trike unit and wing. Wing braced from above by kingpost and cables, from below by cables; bowsprit construction with 25% double-surface; preformed ribs. Undercarriage has three wheels in tricycle formation; rubber suspension on nosewheel and glass-fibre suspension on main wheels. Push-right go-left nosewheel steering independent from aerodynamic controls. Nosewheel brake. Aluminium-alloy tube trike unit, with optional pod. Engine mounted below wing, driving pusher propeller.

Production status: prototype.

GENERAL - One of the nicest things about editing *Berger-Burr's* is receiving friendly letters from people we've never met, and ICA is one such example.

We confess that we don't know a lot about ICA as a company, but judging by the diligence with which director Barbu Dumitru answered our request for information, and by the photograph of his product, this Romanian firm intends to be around the sport for a long time.

At present in prototype form, the ICA trike consists of the company's model *41* wing mated to its model *42* trike unit. The wing is unusual in that it is a bowsprit design (ie without cross-tube), a configuration familiar to the Flexiform *Striker's* many fans but not popular with other manufacturers, and the trike unit too shows many original touches. A duopole construction, it nevertheless manages to provide all three wheels with proper suspension, and also features an unusual nose structure, with the front strut clasped between two downward-angled tubes which meet the main structure under the base of the seat.

Not content with producing both trike unit and wing, Barbu also developed his own engine for the machine, a high-revving 15 hp unit with integral planetary reduction. Like the rest of the trike, the power unit looks very neatly engineered, at least as far as can be judged from our

photograph, and we feel sure would arouse much curiosity among British sub-70 kg enthusiasts if it turned up in the UK. At only 132 lb (60 kg) complete, the *42/41* is a real featherweight among trikes.

No details of price or availability have been revealed, but we have a hunch we have not heard the last of this interesting flexwing.

EXTERNAL DIMENSIONS & AREAS - Length overall 14.8 ft, 4.50 m. Height overall 11.5 ft, 3.50 m. Wing span 32.2 ft, 9.80 m. Chord at root 8.5 ft, 2.60 m. Chord at tip 3.0 ft, 0.90 m. Dihedral 4°. Nose angle 130°. Depth of keel pocket 1.0 ft, 0.30 m. Total wing area 178 ft², 16.5 m². Keel pocket area 3.2 ft², 0.30 m². Aspect ratio 5.8/1. Wheel track 4.9 ft, 1.50 m. Wheelbase 5.9 ft, 1.80 m. Nosewheel diameter overall 13 inch, 33 cm. Main wheels diameter overall 13 inch, 33 cm.

POWER PLANT - ICA-Brasov RB155-D engine. Max power 15 hp at 8300 rpm. Propeller diameter and pitch 53x31 inch, 1.34x0.80 m. Planetary gear reduction, ratio 5.2/1. Max static thrust 106 lb, 48 kg. Power per unit area 0.08 hp/ft², 0.9 hp/m². Fuel capacity 3.2 US gal, 2.6 Imp gal, 12.0 litre.

WEIGHTS & LOADINGS - Empty weight 132 lb, 60 kg. Max take-off weight 375 lb, 170 kg. Payload 243 lb, 110 kg. Max wing loading 2.11 lb/ft², 10.3 kg/m². Max power loading 25.0 lb/hp, 11.3 kg/hp. Load factors +4.0, -2.0 recommended; +6.0, -3.0 ultimate.

PERFORMANCE* - Max level speed 39 mph, 62 kph. Never exceed speed 47 mph, 75 kph. Max cruising speed 34 mph, 55 kph. Economic cruising speed 37 mph, 50 kph. Stalling speed 22 mph, 35 kph. Max climb rate at sea level 350 ft/min, 1.8 m/s. Min sink rate 300 ft/min at 25 mph, 1.5 m/s at 40 kph. Best glide ratio with power off 7/1 at 28 mph, 45 kph. Take-off distance 130 ft, 40 m. Landing distance 100 ft, 30 m. Service ceiling 4920 ft, 1500 m. Range at average cruising speed 124 mile, 200 km. Noise level 60 dB at 490 ft, 150 m.

*Under the following test conditions - Airfield altitude 1740 ft, 530 m. Ground temperature 59°F, 15°C. Ground pressure 955 mB. Ground windspeed 1 mph, 2 kph. Test payload 198 lb, 90 kg.

MIFENG (China)

Address NC.

MIFENG
MIFENG 2
(Three-axis)

Single-seat single-engined high-wing monoplane with conventional three-axis control. Wing shape NC; cruciform tail. Pitch control by elevator on tail; yaw control by fin-mounted rudder; roll control NC; control inputs through stick for pitch/roll and pedals for yaw. Wing braced from above by kingpost and cables, from below by cables; wing profile NC; 100% double-surface. Undercarriage has three wheels in tricycle formation; suspension NC. Ground steering NC. Nosewheel brake. Tubular airframe, with pod. Engine mounted below wing, driving pusher propeller.

Production status: see text.

GENERAL - The very sparse details which we give of China's first commercial ultralight design are drawn entirely from the *New Zealand Wings* magazine of December-January '84, which carried a picture caption of the *Mifeng 2* taken at a trade fair in Guangzhou.

The picture, which for copyright reasons we are unfortunately unable to reproduce, showed a modern, tidy tube and dacron design with pod, high wing and pusher prop, the empennage consisting of a single large-diameter tube. According to the caption, the machine was intended for export and had already attracted orders for 100 from Britain and a commitment to sell 1000 in the US over the next three years.

As we write, we are now halfway through that period and the *Mifeng 2* (the name means honeybee) has yet to appear on either market. Janic Geelen at *New Zealand Wings* tells us he can add nothing to the tantalising snippets he published originally, so we are left wondering what has happened to the project. We cannot print our usual data paragraphs because we have absolutely no technical information on the machine - not even the engine type, though a Catic would seem a safe bet since it is the only Chinese-made ultralight unit.

However, it is clear that the world's most populous country has at least realised the potential of ultralights, and that surely is an event worth recording . . .

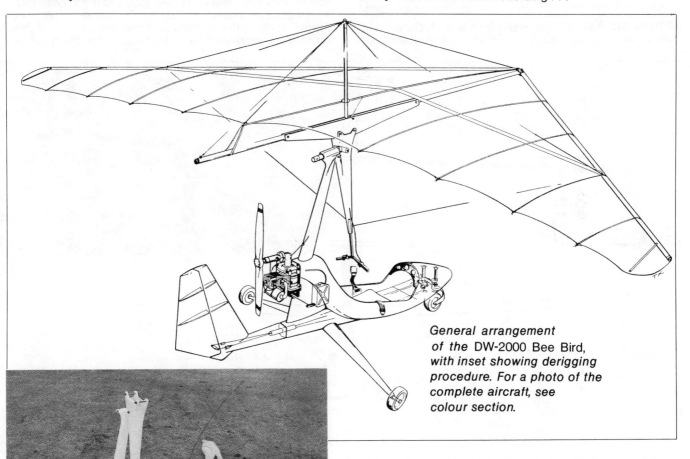

General arrangement of the DW-2000 Bee Bird, with inset showing derigging procedure. For a photo of the complete aircraft, see colour section.

MOTO HUNG (Japan)

Mitsukawa Corporation, address NC; tel 045-314 5578.

MOTO HUNG
DW-2000 BEE BIRD
(Hybrid)

Single-seat single-engined flex-wing aircraft with hybrid control. Rogallo wing with keel pocket; tail carries rudder and horizontal stabiliser. Pilot suspended below wing in trike unit, using inverted T-bar to control pitch and roll by altering relative positions of trike unit and wing; yaw control input by pedals. Wing braced from above by kingpost and cables, from below by cables; floating cross-tube construction with NC% double-surface enclosing cross-tube; preformed ribs. Undercarriage has three wheels in tricycle formation; suspension NC. Push-right go-left nosewheel steering connected to yaw control. Brakes NC. Composite-construction trike unit, partially enclosed. Engine mounted below wing, driving pusher propeller.

Production status: current, number completed NC.

GENERAL - Talk to progressive trike manufacturers and the conversation will invariably turn to semi-enclosed trike

units with composite construction; there seems no doubt about the way the industry will go in the next few years. When this happens, however, it will not be quite the revolution which the manufacturers would have us believe, because what they will in effect have created is a *DW-2000 Bee Bird* minus its yaw controls and with a conventional triking trapeze - and the *Bee Bird* is, amazingly, an 11 year-old design!

Admittedly it wasn't called that back in 1974, when Paris architect Jean-Marc Geiser designed it, nor did it have a modern CFX wing, but the trike unit was visually identical. The Motodelta *G-10,* as the original was called, was years ahead of its time, and was developed into the improved *G-11* model, some being built by the Centrair company (see French section) during the '70s. However, a series of production and marketing difficulties meant that the machine

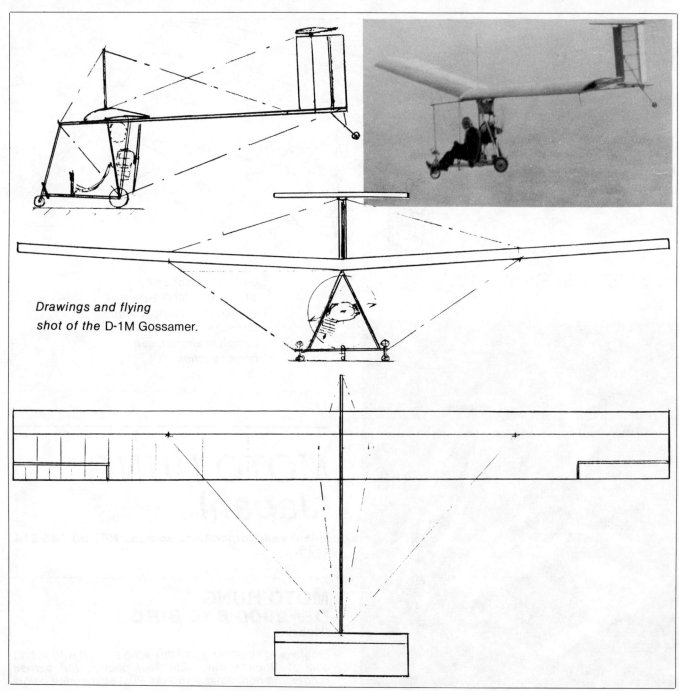

Drawings and flying
shot of the D-1M Gossamer.

Letectvi Kosmonautika

never reached its full potential, and while the Motodelta was faltering in the marketplace, the conventional trikes were improving by leaps and bounds and cutting its market away from underneath. By the time we wrote our first edition, the design was apparently dead, and though we did manage to squeeze a picture in to illustrate a Soviet aircraft of similar concept, the *G-11* was not listed in its own right.

Since then, we are happy to report that the machine is under new management in Japan, with a modern wing and a Zenoah engine (French models mainly used JPX PUL425s) but otherwise little changed. Sold in Japan at an undisclosed price, the aircraft has not as yet re-entered the European market, but the wheel could yet turn full circle for this historic hybrid.

EXTERNAL DIMENSIONS & AREAS - Wing span 35.8 ft, 10.90 m. Nose angle 121°. Total wing area 183 ft², 17.0 m². Aspect ratio 7.0/1. Other data NC.

POWER PLANT - Zenoah G25B engine. Max power 23 hp at NC rpm. Propeller diameter and pitch NC (3-blade). Gear reduction, ratio NC. Max static thrust 155 lb, 70 kg. Power per unit area 0.13 hp/ft², 1.4 hp/m². Fuel capacity NC.

WEIGHTS & LOADINGS - NC.

PERFORMANCE* - Max level speed 56 mph, 90 kph. Stalling speed 19 mph, 30 kph. Other data NC.

*Under unspecified test conditions.

OLSANSKY (Czechoslovakia)

Address NC.

OLSANSKY
D-1M GOSSAMER
(Three-axis)

Single-seat single-engined high-wing monoplane with conventional three-axis control. Wing has unswept leading and trailing edges, and constant chord; T-tail. Pitch control by fully flying tail; yaw control by fully flying rudder; roll control by 30%-span ailerons; control inputs through stick for pitch/roll and pedals for yaw. Wing braced from above by kingpost and cables, from below by cables; wing profile Worthmann FX72-MS150A; 100% double-surface. Undercarriage has three wheels in tricycle formation with additional tailwheel; no suspension on any wheels. No ground steering. No brakes. Wood airframe, completely open. Engine mounted below wing, driving pusher propeller.

Production status: one-off.

GENERAL - Although we don't know the date it first flew, this machine certainly represents one of Czechoslovakia's first attempts at ultralight aviation, and was designed purely as a one-off amateur project. We include it largely out of historical interest, for it is now several years old and has been retired to the country's aviation and space museum, for storage and eventual static display.

Apparently one reason for its retirement was its use of a Jawa motorcycle engine, which Martin Velek of *Kosmonautika* magazine tells us was too heavy.

EXTERNAL DIMENSIONS & AREAS - Length overall 16.4 ft, 5.00 m. Height overall 9.2 ft, 2.80 m. Wing span 36.7 ft, 11.20 m. Constant chord 3.6 ft, 1.10 m. Dihedral 3°. Sweepback 0°. Tailplane span 7.5 ft, 2.30 m. Rudder height 3.9 ft, 1.20 m. Total wing area 133 ft², 12.4 m². Total aileron area 9.3 ft², 0.86 m². Rudder area NC. Total elevator area 17.3 ft², 1.61 m². Aspect ratio 10.0/1. Wheel track 4.9 ft, 1.50 m. Wheelbase 4.6 ft, 1.40 m. Nosewheel diameter overall 10 inch, 25 cm. Main wheels diameter overall 12 inch, 30 cm.

POWER PLANT - Jawa 350 engine. Max power 23 hp at 5000 rpm. Propeller diameter and pitch 43x22 inch, 1.10x0.55 m. Double-roller chain reduction, ratio 1.6/1. Max static thrust 121 lb, 55 kg. Power per unit area 0.17 hp/ft², 1.9 hp/m². Fuel capacity 1.3 US gal, 1.1 Imp gal, 5.0 litre.

WEIGHTS & LOADINGS - Empty weight 220 lb, 100 kg. Max take-off weight 419 lb, 190 kg. Payload 198 lb, 90 kg. Max wing loading 3.15 lb/ft², 15.3 kg/m². Max power loading 18.2 lb/hp, 8.3 kg/hp. Load factors +4.0, -2.0 recommended; +4.0, -2.0 ultimate.

PERFORMANCE* - Max level speed *44* mph, *70* kph. Never exceed speed 56 mph, 90 kph. Max cruising speed 37 mph, 60 kph. Economic cruising speed 34 mph, 55 kph. Stalling speed 28 mph, 45 kph. Max climb rate at sea level 200 ft/min, 1.0 m/s. Min sink rate 350 ft/min at 31 mph, 1.8 m/s at 50 kph. Best glide ratio with power off *7.5/1* at 31 mph, 50 kph. Take-off distance *115* ft, *35* m. Landing distance *130* ft, *40* m. Service ceiling NC. Range at average cruising speed 25 mile, 40 km. Noise level NC.

*Under unspecified test conditions.

STEINBACH DELTA (Austria)

Steinbach Delta, 6382 Kirchdorf/T.577; tel 053 52 3383. Proprietor: Christian Steinbach.

STEINBACH DELTA
EURO TRIKE/EURO III
(Weight-shift)

Single-seat single-engined flex-wing aircraft with weight-shift control. Rogallo wing with keel pocket. Pilot suspended below wing in trike unit, using bar to control pitch and roll/yaw by altering relative positions of trike unit and wing. Wing braced from above by kingpost and cables, from below by cables; rigid cross-tube construction with 30% double-surface not enclosing cross-tube; preformed ribs. Undercarriage has three wheels in tricycle formation; no suspension on nosewheel and glass-fibre suspension on main wheels. Push-right go-left nosewheel steering independent from aerodynamic controls. Nosewheel brake. Aluminium-alloy tube trike

unit, completely open. Engine mounted below wing, driving pusher propeller.

Production status: current, 15 completed.

GENERAL - Steinbach is principally a wing maker, selling the bulk of its output to the neighboring West German market, but like Flexiform in Britain it does make complete trikes in fairly small numbers.

It is hard to define a typical Steinbach trike, not just because they are not mass produced but also because the specification can be varied considerably according to customers' wishes. The model we list here is a single-seater mated to the company's own *Euro III* wing, but some machines use the Steinbach *Spot II,* while still others are made with two-seats.

Price of the solo machine with *Euro III* is OS72,265, substitution of the *Spot II* adding OS3000 to this figure. No prices are available for the two-seaters.

EXTERNAL DIMENSIONS & AREAS - Length overall

Apart from its distinctive curved tubular engine mounts, Steinbach's Euro Trike is a straightforward modern monopole. This example is flying with a Euro III wing.

11.2 ft, 3.40 m. Height overall 8.5 ft, 2.60 m. Wing span 31.5 ft, 9.60 m. Chord at root 9.8 ft, 3.00 m. Chord at tip 1.1 ft, 0.50 m. Nose angle 132°. Depth of keel pocket 0.7 ft, 0.20 m. Total wing area 183 ft², 17.0 m². Aspect ratio 5.4/1.

POWER PLANT - Rotax 377 engine. Max power 34 hp at NC rpm. Power per unit area 0.19 hp/ft², 2.0 hp/m². Fuel capacity 5.3 US gal, 4.4 Imp gal, 20.0 litre. Other data NC.

WEIGHTS & LOADINGS - Empty weight 187 lb, 85 kg. Max take-off weight 485 lb, 220 kg. Payload 298 lb, 135 kg. Max wing loading 2.65 lb/ft², 12.9 kg/m². Max power loading 14.3 lb/hp, 6.5 kg/hp. Load factors NC recommended; +6.0, -3.0 ultimate.

PERFORMANCE - NC.

A new engine under test in West Germany, mounted on a Uli I from Scheibe, the company through which the engine is being marketed.

Engines

INTRODUCTION - Since our first edition was published the industry has tended to standardise on a few well proven units - notably Rotax, Robin, JPX, KFM and Cuyuna - and many of the older engines have been dropped. Nevertheless there is still a great variety of motors available, and we include in this section every engine currently used in any quantity in the ultralight industry, plus others which are not used in great numbers but which have obvious potential. Not included are many of the older engines which have fallen out of favour with ultralight builders (though in some cases they are still being used in a small way), and for details of these we refer readers to our first edition. On the other hand, in deference to their great popularity in the US, we have left in the Kawasakis, even though at the time of going to press they were out of production.

Most of the engines in this section are air-cooled two-strokes, but there are a few liquid-cooled designs, and a few four-strokes. Many of the four-strokes are Volkswagen-based, either using the 'half VW' concept or a full four cylinders. The VW unit has been a favourite among lightplane homebuilders for many years, and dozens of aviation conversions for it have been offered over the years. However, as most of the full four-cylinder versions are too heavy for ultralight use, we could not really justify including them, so we have contented ourselves with detailing one series of conversions, by the French firm JPX. We chose these because unlike most VW conversions they have found an ultralight application, on the AEIM range of trikes.

SPECIFICATIONS COMPARABILITY - The great problem with any attempt to provide engine data is that different manufacturers supply their engines in different forms, some offering just a bare bones unit, some a complete power pack right down the prop, and most something inbetween. Often an engine which sounds exceptionally light and compact can turn out to be anything but, when laden with reduction unit, exhaust, starter etc. To counter this problem, in this edition we detail at the beginning of each

◁ engine its 'standard specification', before going on to describe the engine *in that form*. The information is thus consistent *within each engine*.

This does not of course mean that readers can compare like with like (except in occasional cases where the standard specifications are identical), but at least users can see where engines differ and make allowances accordingly. Readers should note that our 'standard specification' is not necessarily the most basic form of the engine available; often it includes items which are theoretically optional but in practice essential for ultralight use.

PERFORMANCE COMPARABILITY - Power output, fuel consumption, induction system and exhaust system are all closely inter-related on two-strokes. Figures given are makers' test-bed figures and, in the case of engines sold without a full complement of induction and exhaust components, are best treated only as a guide. Because of the effect which installation arrangements can have on output, figures quoted in our aircraft descriptions will not necessarily agree with those quoted in this section. Remember too that some manufacturers claim their engines to be capable of reliably delivering maximum power continuously, whereas others do not.

Different methods of measuring power output give different results. Net figures, notably those measured on the DIN standard, can be up to 15% lower than SAE outputs. Where known, the method of measurement is stated.

Fuel consumption is dependent on revs and where a manufacturer has supplied a consumption figure at a particular engine speed, this has been used. Where a graph of consumption versus engine speed was supplied, we have selected the figure pertaining to cruise speed, which we have taken as 75% of the engine speed at which maximum power is developed.

On fan-cooled engines, both power output and fuel consumption can be improved by removing the fan and ducting, and for this reason some manufacturers of fan-cooled models will supply their products less these components. However, before using an engine in this form, readers are advised to discuss the proposed installation with the manufacturer, since deletion of the fan may adversely affect reliability, especially on pusher installations where there is no propwash to cool the engine.

COMPRESSION RATIOS AND FUELS - Compression ratio is one of the major factors affecting power output; basically, the greater the ratio, the greater the output. However, very high compressions demand high-octane fuel and can shorten engine life. It is impossible to be authoritative about suitable fuels for each engine because fuel quality and additives vary greatly from country to country, but as a general rule, regular grade automotive fuel (with appropriate oil mix, if a two-stroke) should suffice for engines with a compression ratio of 8.5/1 or less.

CARBURETTORS - Two basic types of carburettor are used for ultralights - the diaphragm type and the float type. Diaphragm carbuettors are light, simple and often incorporate an integral pump, but on the other hand need careful adjustment to take account of weather conditions. Float-type carburettors are relatively idiot-proof because the settings are fixed at the factory and cannot usually be adjusted, apart from the idling characteristics. This pre-setting can be a disadvantage at high altitudes, where a different jet may be needed to cope with rarified air.

IGNITION SYSTEMS - For ultralights the most popular method of electricity generation is the flywheel magneto, which can be linked to a variety of spark-generating devices. Simplest of these is the conventional contact breaker (often called 'points') which produces a hot powerful spark at minimal revs and thus permits easy starting even with a recoil starter. However, points need regular maintenance and should be replaced approximately every 200 h, so to overcome these disadvantages a variety of electronic and semi-electronic systems have evolved. Some of these do not work efficiently below 300-400 rpm, and are therefore best used in conjunction with an electric start. This in turn necessitates a battery, with accompanying weight and cost disadvantages.

ROTATION - Rotation is quoted as viewed from the output end.

DIMENSIONS - These are listed in order of length, width and height. In the case of in-line engines, they are measured with the cylinders vertically above the crankshaft.

For more information on engines, consult Ultralight Propulsion, *by Glenn Brinks, published by Ultralight Publications.*

AED

Advanced Engine Design. Mailing address: PO Box 589, Flint, Michigan 48501. Factory: G. 3283 S Dort Hway, Burton, Michigan 48529.

AED 340

Two-stroke flat twin. Standard specification includes: engine mountings, carburettor with integral pump, electric start without recoil, reduction system.

Mechanical - Capacity 334 cc. Bore and stroke 64x52 mm. Max power 30

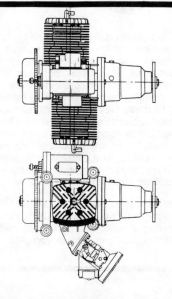

hp at 6300 rpm. Compression ratio 11/1. Crankshaft runs clockwise (2.1/1 reduction), anti-clockwise (3.1/1 reduction). Weight 64 lb, 29kg.

Fuel system - One OVC carburettor, one Mikuni pump. Fuel 2.5% two-stroke mix. Consumption at 75% power 2.4 US gal/h, 2.0 Imp gal/h, 9.1 litre/h.

Electrical system - Flywheel magneto. CDI ignition.

Cooling system - Free air.

Reduction system - Planetary gear, ratio 2.1 or 3.1/1.

Dimensions (lxwxh) - 18.5x19.7x 16.5 inch, 469x500x420 mm.

AED 680

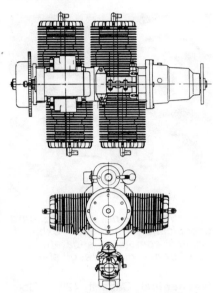

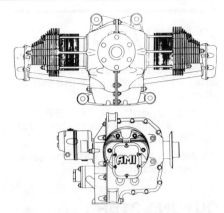

Two-stroke flat four. Standard specification as AED 340.

Mechanical - Capacity 668 cc. Bore and stroke 64x52 mm. Max power 70 hp at 6500 rpm. Compression ratio 11/1. Crankshaft runs clockwise (2.1/1 reduction), anti-clockwise (3.1/1 reduction). Weight 93 lb, 42kg.

Fuel system - Two OVC carburettors, each with Mikuni pump. Fuel 2.5% two-stroke mix. Consumption at 75% power 4.8 US gal/h, 4.0 Imp gal/h, 18.2 litre/h.

Electrical system - Flywheel magneto. CDI ignition.

Cooling system - Free air.

Reduction system - Planetary gear, ratio 2.1 or 3.1/1.

Dimensions (lxwxh) - 25.2x19.7x 16.5 inch, 640x500x420 mm.

AERO-MOTION

AeroMotion Inc, 1224 W South Park Avenue, Oshkosh, Wisconsin 54901, USA; tel (414) 233-0773.

AEROMOTION TWIN

Four-stroke flat twin. Standard specification includes: recoil start. Other details NC..

Mechanical - Capacity 1650 cc. Bore and stroke 102x102 mm. Max

power 52 hp at 3200 rpm. Weight 100 lb, 45 kg.

Fuel system - Fuel automotive gasoline.

Electrical system - Duplicated Slick flywheel magneto. Duplicated ignition. Duplicated spark plugs.

Cooling system - Free air.

Reduction system - Not necessary.

Dimensions (lxwxh) - 18.3x11.6x 31.0 inch, 464x294x787 mm.

ARROW

Arrow, Via Campi 23, 29100 Piacenza, Italy; tel 0523 23841.

French agent: Cosmos (see French section).

ARROW GT 500

Two-stroke flat twin. Standard specification includes: carburettor with integral pump, recoil start, reduction system.

Mechanical - Capacity 500 cc. Max power 60 hp. Weight 53 lb, 24 kg.

Fuel system - One carburettor. Consumption 1.3-2.1 US gal/h, 1.1-1.8 Imp gal/h, 5.0-8.0 litre/h.

Electrical system - Max generator output 12 V, 130 W LT. Electronic ignition.

Cooling system - Free air.

Reduction system - Planetary gear, gives max prop speed of 2600 rpm.

Options - Electric start.

CATIC

Catic, China - address NC. Enquiries to North American agent: Seaborne Trading Co, 21 Columbus Ave, San Francisco, California 94111; tel (415) 362-2900. Contact: Edwin Cheng.

CATIC HS-16

Two-stroke flat four. Standard specification includes: carburettor with integral pump, guy rope start.

Mechanical - Capacity 280 cc. Bore and stroke 40x42 mm. Max power 16 hp at 6000 rpm. Compression ratio 7.0/1. Crankshaft runs anti-clockwise on 3 needle and ball bearings. Weight 26 lb, 12 kg.

Fuel system - Two carburettors. Fuel 7% two-stroke mix. Consumption 2.4 US gal/h, 2.0 Imp gal/h, 8.9 litre/h.

Electrical system - Flywheel magneto.

Cooling system - Free air.

Dimensions (lxwxh) - 18.1x12.6x 10.8 inch, 460x320x275 mm.

CATIC HS-26

Two-stroke flat four. Standard specification includes: carburettor with integral pump, guy rope start.

Mechanical - Capacity 512 cc. Bore and stroke 56x52 mm. Max power 26 hp at 5500 rpm. Compression ratio 7.0/1. Crankshaft runs anti-clockwise on 3 needle and ball bearings. Weight 42 lb, 19 kg.

Fuel system - Two carburettors. Fuel 7% two-stroke mix. Consumption 3.8 US gal/h, 3.2 Imp gal/h, 14.5 litre/h.

Electrical system - Flywheel magneto.

Cooling system - Free air.

Dimensions (lxwxh) - 19.7x17.3x 13.8 inch, 500x440x350 mm.

COMER

Comer Bagnolo in piano, Reggio Emilia, Italy; tel (0522) 61642-617373; tx 531844 COMER I.

COMER DELTA 137

Two-stroke single. Standard specification includes: carburettor with integral pump, recoil start, reduction system, propeller.

Mechanical - Capacity 137 cc. Bore and stroke 66x40 mm. Max power 14 hp at 8500 rpm.

Fuel system - One diaphragm carburettor. Fuel two-stroke mix.

Electrical system - Electronic ignition.

Cooling system - Air with integral fan and ducting.

Reduction system - Integral chain with centrifugal clutch, ratio 2.8/1.

Dimensions - Power unit NC. Propeller 43x28 inch, 1.10x0.70 m.

CUYUNA

Cuyuna Engine Co, Ist St SW, Box 116, Crosby, Minnesota, USA.

French agent: SCFF, BP127, 06334 Grasse cedex; tel (93) 700264; tx 461531 F.

UK agent: Aerolite Aviation (see Eipper, US section).

CUYUNA 215R

Two-stroke single. Standard specification includes: exhaust-system complete, separate carburettor and pump, recoil start.

Mechanical - Capacity 214 cc. Bore and stroke 67x60 mm. Max power 20 hp at 6000 rpm. Compression ratio 12.5/1. Crankshaft runs anti-clockwise on 2 ball bearings. Weight 39 lb, 18 kg.

Fuel system - One Mikuni float carburettor. Fuel 4% two-stroke mix. Consumption at 5000 rpm 2.0 US gal/h, 1.7 Imp gal/h, 7.6 litre/h.

Electrical system - NGK flywheel magneto. Max output 12 V 150 W LT. Non-mechanically switched CDI ignition. Bosch W260 T-2, NGK BR8ES, or Champion N3 spark plug.

Cooling system - Air with integral fan and ducting.

Reduction system - Normally used, buyer to find.

Dimensions (lxwxh) - 12.7x12.8x 14.4 inch, 324x325x366 mm.

Options - 215D specification, includes extra crankshaft bearing, compulsory for direct-drive use; 215RR specification, with crankshaft end machined for reduction drive; 215F specification, with reverse-flow fan, compulsory for tractor use; electric start.

CUYUNA 430R

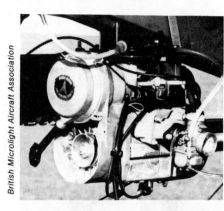

Two-stroke in-line twin. Standard specification includes: exhaust-system complete, separate carburettor and pump, recoil start.

Mechanical - Capacity 428 cc. Bore and stroke 67x60 mm. Max power 35 hp at 6000 rpm. Compression ratio 12.5/1. Crankshaft runs anti-clockwise on 4 ball bearings. Weight 62 lb, 28 kg.

Fuel system - Two Mikuni float carburettors. Fuel 4% two-stroke mix. Consumption at 4500 rpm 3.4 US gal/h, 2.9 Imp gal/h, 13.0 litre/h.

Electrical system - NGK flywheel magneto. Max output 12 V 150 W LT. Non-mechanically switched CDI ignition. Bosch W260 T-2, NGK BR8ES, or Champion N3 spark plugs.

Cooling system - Air with integral fan and ducting, axial flow.

Reduction system - Normally used, buyer to find.

Dimensions (lxwxh) - 14.7x11.4x 10.9 inch, 374x289x278 mm.

Options - 430D specification, includes extra crankshaft bearing, compulsory for direct-drive use; 430RR specification, with crankshaft end machined for reduction drive; 430F specification, with reverse-flow fan, compulsory for tractor use; high-performance package, develops 43 hp at 6500 rpm; electric start.

CUYUNA ULII-02

Two-stroke in-line twin. Standard specification as Cuyuna 430R.

Mechanical - See Cuyuna 430R except: Max power 37 hp at 6250 rpm. Crankshaft strengthened at output end. Weight 57 lb, 26 kg.

Fuel system - See Cuyuna 430R.

Electrical system - See Cuyuna 430R.

Cooling system - Air with integral fan and ducting, transverse flow.

Reduction system - Normally used, buyer to find.

Dimensions (lxwxh) - See Cuyuna 430R.

Options - Electric start.

DAWN STAR

Engines: Dawn Star Technologies Corp, 148 Northeast 28th St, Miami, Florida 33137, USA; tel (305) 573-0897.

Reduction drives: Nova Power Products, PO Box 36, Crosby, MN 56441, USA; tel (218) 546-6829.

DAWN STAR SP-440

Single-rotor Wankel. Standard specification includes: exhaust stub, carburettor but no pump, electric and recoil starters. NB: Flexible engine mounts not needed.

Mechanical - Capacity 440 cc. Generating radius 93 mm, eccentricity 13.5 mm, rotor width 66 mm. Max power 30.5 hp SAE at 5500 rpm. Crankshaft runs anti-clockwise on 4

bearings (3 plain for crankshaft, 1 ball for thrust). Weight 66 lb, 30 kg.

Fuel system - One Facet or Marvel-Schebler carburettor. Fuel automotive gasoline. Consumption 2.7 US gal/h, 2.3 Imp gal/h, 10.3 litre/h.

Electrical system - Bosch flywheel magneto. Max output 12 V 100 W LT. Magnetically switched CDI ignition. Champion N19V spark plug.

Cooling system - Air with integral fan and ducting. Oil cooler.

Reduction system - Normally used, factory-approved option.

Dimensions (lxwxh including output shaft) - 18.2x18.2x14.5 inch, 463x463x368 mm.

Options - Nova GearMate DS gear reduction (various ratios available from 2.0 to 3.1/1), deletion of recoil start.

DAWN STAR SP-440 HIGH OUTPUT

Single-rotor Wankel. Standard specification as Dawn Star SP-440.

Mechanical - See Dawn Star SP-440 except: Max power 37 hp SAE at 5500 rpm. Compression ratio 7.8/1.

All other information - See Dawn Star SP-440.

EMDAIR

Emdair Ltd, The Old Rectory, Guestling, nr Hastings, E Sussex TN35 4HT, UK; tel 0424 813457. Director: M R L Daniel.

US agent: H Allman, Flite-Lite Inc, PO Box, Miami, Florida 33159-3187; tel (305) 472-5863.

EMDAIR WESLAKE W44/60-77-02

Four-stroke flat twin. Standard specification includes: separate carburettors and pumps, electric start without recoil.

Mechanical - Capacity 1261 cc. Bore and stroke 95x89 mm. Max power 60 hp at 3400 rpm. Compression ratio 9.5/1. Crankshaft runs anti-clockwise. Weight 85 lb, 39 kg.

Fuel system - Two carburettors. Fuel automotive gasoline. Consumption at 2360 rpm 3.1 US gal/h, 2.6 Imp gal/h, 11.8 litre/h.

Electrical system - Alternator. Electronic ignition. Duplicated spark plugs.

Cooling system - Free air.

Reduction system - Not necessary.

Dimensions (lxwxh) - 15.5x27.9x 17.0 inch, 395x707x432 mm.

ENGINE DYNAMICS

Engine Dynamics Inc, 858 South State St, Salt Lake City, Utah 84111-9990, USA.

ENGINE DYNAMICS API O-500L

Four-stroke flat twin. Standard specification includes: carburettor, electric start without recoil.

Mechanical - Capacity 523 cc. Bore and stroke 81x51 mm. Max power 33 hp at 5500 rpm. Weight 44 lb, 20kg.

Fuel system - One diaphragm carburettor. Fuel automotive gasoline.

Engines

Electrical system - Flywheel magneto. Electronic ignition.

Cooling system - Free air.

Reduction system - Not necessary.

Dimensions (lxwxh) - 17.0x15.0x 15.0 inch, 432x381x381 mm.

Options - 12 V DC or 28 V DC integral alternator with rectifier. Shielded ignition system. Deletion of electric start.

FIELDHOUSE

Fieldhouse Engines Ltd, 2-4 Latimer St, Anstey, Leicester, UK; tel 0533 362613; tx 341023.

FIELDHOUSE 260A

Two-stroke single. Standard specification includes: exhaust-system complete, engine mountings, separate carburettor and pump, electric and recoil starters, reduction system.

Mechanical - Capacity 260 cc. Bore and stroke 72x64 mm. Max power 25 hp at 6000 rpm. Compression ratio 9/1. Crankshaft runs anti-clockwise on 3 ball bearings. Weight (excluding reduction and fan cooling) 44 lb, 20 kg.

Fuel system - One Amal float carburettor. Fuel 4% two-stroke mix.

Electrical system - Lucas alternator. Duplicated non-mechanically switched CDI ignition. Duplicated KLG spark plug.

Cooling system - Free air, or air with integral fan and ducting.

Reduction system - Gear, various ratios available.

Dimensions (lxwxh, excluding reduction and fan cooling) - 11.4x 13.0x15.0 inch, 290x330x380 mm.

FIELDHOUSE 525A

Two-stroke in-line twin. Standard specification as Fieldhouse HS260A except: separate carburettors and pumps.

Mechanical - Capacity 525 cc. Bore and stroke 72x64 mm. Max power 45 hp at 6000 rpm. Compression ratio 9/1. Crankshaft runs anti-clockwise on 5 ball bearings. Weight (excluding reduction and fan cooling) 73 lb, 33 kg.

Fuel system - Two Amal float carburettors. Fuel 4% two-stroke mix.

Electrical system - Lucas alternator. Duplicated non-mechanically switched CDI ignition. Duplicated KLG spark plugs.

Cooling system - Free air, or air with integral fan and ducting.

Reduction system - Gear, various ratios available.

Dimensions (lxwxh, excluding reduction and fan cooling) - 18.5x 13.8x15.7 inch, 470x350x400 mm.

FUJI

See Robin.

GLOBAL

Global Machine Tool Corp, 140 Ashwood Road, Hendersonville, N Carolina 28739, USA; tel (704) 692-2744.

Canadian agent: Canadian Sport Aviation Center, Rural Route 7, Hwy 10, Markdale, Ontario N0C 1H0; tel (519) 986-3113.

GLOBAL 7892

Four-stroke flat twin. Standard specification includes: exhaust-system complete, engine mountings, carburettor but no pump, neither electric nor recoil starters.

Mechanical - Capacity 1039 cc. Bore and stroke 92x78 mm. Max power 32 hp at 3250 rpm. Compression ratio 10/1. Crankshaft runs clockwise on plain bearings. Weight 76 lb, 35 kg.

Fuel system - One Bendix/Zenith float carburettor. Fuel automotive gasoline. Consumption 1.7 US gal/h, 1.4 Imp gal/h, 6.4 litre/h.

Electrical system - Flywheel magneto. Conventional contact-breaker. Bosch spark plugs.

Cooling system - Free air.

Reduction system - Not necessary.

Dimensions (lxwxh) - 14.7x30.0x 14.0 inch, 373x762x356 mm.

Options - Cockpit-adjustable carburettor, carburettor heat. Under development: electric start, dual ignition.

HEWLAND

Hewland Engineering Ltd, Boyn Valley Industrial Estate, Boyn Valley Road, Maidenhead, Berkshire SL6 4EQ, UK; tel 0628 32033; tx 847607. Directors: Mike Hewland, W C Greggains.

HEWLAND TWIN

Two-stroke in-line twin. Standard specification includes: separate

carburettors and pumps (interlinked), radiator and hoses, electric start without recoil, reduction system.

Mechanical - Capacity 507 cc. Bore and stroke 71x64 mm. Max power 52 hp at 6750 rpm. Compression ratio 11.0/1. Weight 76 lb, 34 kg.

Fuel system - Two Amal carburettors, model MkII. Fuel two-stroke mix. Consumption at 5800 rpm 2.9 US gal/h, 2.4 Imp gal/h, 10.8 litre/h.

Electrical system - Alternator. Duplicated electronic ignition. Duplicated spark plugs.

Cooling system - Liquid.

Reduction system - Helical gear, ratio 2.5/1.

Options - Alternative reduction ratios: 2.1/1, 2.7/1.

HEWLAND TRIPLE

Two-stroke in-line triple. Standard specification as Hewland Twin.

Mechanical - Capacity 760 cc. Bore and stroke 71x64 mm. Max power 77 hp at 6750 rpm. Compression ratio 11.0/1. Weight 110 lb, 50 kg.

Fuel system - Fuel two-stroke mix. Consumption at 40 hp output 3.6 US gal/h, 3.0 Imp gal/h, 13.6 litre/h.

Electrical system - Alternator. Duplicated electronic ignition. Duplicated spark plugs.

Cooling system - Liquid.

Reduction system - Helical gear, ratio 2.7/1.

HIRTH

Gobler Hirthmotoren, 7141 Benningen, Postfach, West Germany; tel 07144 6074.

French agent: Loravia, Aerodrome, 57110 Yutz; tel (8) 256 6371.

North American agent: Hirth North America, 1425 Bishop Street, Cambridge, Ontario N1R 6J9, Canada; tel (519) 621-8940.

HIRTH 263

Two-stroke in-line twin. Standard specification includes: exhaust stubs, carburettor, electric start without recoil.

Mechanical - Capacity 383 cc. Bore and stroke 66x56 mm. Max power 22 hp at 3900 rpm. Compression ratio 9.5/1. Crankshaft runs anti-clockwise. Weight 53 lb, 24 kg.

Fuel system - Bing carburettor. Fuel two-stroke mix.

Electrical system - Bosch dynamo magneto. Max output 12 V 123 W LT.

Cooling system - Free air.

Reduction system - Normally used, buyer to find.

Options - Muffler (adds 5.5 lb, 2.5 kg), recoil start.

HIRTH 276R

Two-stroke in-line twin. Standard specification includes: exhaust-system complete, carburettor but no pump, recoil start.

Mechanical - Capacity 438 cc. Bore and stroke 66x64 mm. Max power 40 hp at 7000 rpm. Compression ratio 11.0/1. Crankshaft runs anti-clockwise. Weight 71 lb, 33 kg.

Fuel system - One carburettor. Fuel two-stroke mix. Consumption 4.2 US gal/h, 3.5 Imp gal/h, 16.0 litre/h.

Electrical system - Bosch dynamo magneto. Conventional contact-breaker.

Cooling system - Air with integral fan and ducting.

Reduction system - Normally used, factory option.

Options - Electric start (adds approx 6 lb, 2.7 kg), 276RR specification with 1.8/1 mechanical reduction.

Note: Latest versions have redesigned crankshaft.

HIRTH HL2701

Two-stroke in-line twin. Standard specification includes: exhaust-system complete, carburettor and pump, electric start without recoil.

Mechanical - Capacity 493 cc. Bore and stroke 70x64 mm. Max power 43 hp at 6750 rpm. Compression ratio 11.0/1. Crankshaft runs clockwise on 5 needle-roller and ball bearings. Weight 66 lb, 30 kg.

Fuel system - One Mikuni or Walbro float or diaphragm carburettor. Fuel 4% two-stroke mix. Consumption 2.9 US gal/h, 2.4 Imp gal/h, 11.0 litre/h.

Electrical system - Bosch dynamo magneto. Max output 12 V 123 W LT. Conventional contact-breaker. Champion or Beru spark plugs.

Cooling system - Air with integral fan and ducting.

Reduction system - Normally used, factory option.

Dimensions (lxwxh) - 15.4x6.7x 13.0 inch, 390x170x330 mm.

Options - HL2701 RR170 specification, with 1.8/1 gear reduction and 47 inch (1.20 m) diameter propeller, adds 9 lb (4 kg) to weight, 3.1 inch (80 mm) to length, 3.9 inch (100 mm) to height. HL2701 RC240 specification, with 2.4/1 toothed-belt reduction and 55 inch (1.40 m) diameter propeller, adds 9 lb (4 kg) to weight, 2.4 inch (60 mm) to length, 4.3 inch (110 mm) to height. Deletion of fan and ducting.

HUNTING

See Fieldhouse.

ICARUS

See Skylark.

JCV

Butterfly Company (see Belgian section).

JCV

Two-stroke flat twin. Standard specification includes: recoil start. Other details NC.

Mechanical - Capacity 274 cc. Max power 22 hp at 6800 rpm.

Fuel system - Two carburettors. Fuel two-stroke mix.

Cooling system - Free air.

Reduction system - Can be used, factory option.

Options - Reduction system, ratio 1.8/1.

JONATHAN

Nanni (see Italian section).

JONATHAN ELITE

Two-stroke single. Standard specification includes: carburettor, recoil start, reduction system.

Mechanical - Capacity 171 cc. Bore and stroke 66x50 mm. Max power 22 hp at 7800 rpm. Weight 40 lb, 18kg.

Fuel system - One Dellorto carburettor, model OVC 34.30. Fuel 3% two-stroke mix.

Electrical system - Flywheel magneto. CDI ignition.

Cooling system - Free air.

Reduction system - Toothed-belt, ratio 3.3/1.

Options - Duplicated spark plug. Electric start.

JONATHAN EXPORT

Two-stroke single. Standard specification as Jonathan Elite.

Reduction system - Toothed-belt, ratio 2.5/1.

All other information - See Jonathan Elite (engines very similar, principal difference is cylinder orientation; compare Elite photo above with Export photo in Italian section under Nanni/Pegasus *Fox Mono*).

JPX

JPX, BP 13, ZI Nord, 72320 Vibraye, France; tel (43) 93 6174.

British agent: Flight Research (see British section).

JPX PUL212

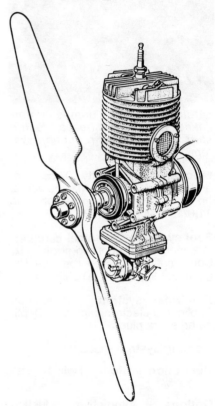

Two-stroke single. Standard specification includes: engine mountings, carburettor, neither electric nor recoil starter.

Mechanical - Capacity 212 cc. Bore and stroke 66x62 mm. Max power 15 hp at 6000 rpm. Compression ratio 8.3/1. Crankshaft runs anti-clockwise on needle-roller bearings. Weight 17 lb, 8 kg.

Fuel system - One Tillotson carburettor, model 22 mm. Fuel 2.5% two-stroke mix.

Electrical system - Novi flywheel magneto. Conventional contact-breaker.

Cooling system - Free air.

Reduction system - Not necessary.

Dimensions (lxwxh) - 5.7x12.9x 14.4 inch, 145x320x365 mm.

JPX PUL425

Flight Research

Two-stroke flat twin. Standard specification includes: engine mountings, carburettor but no pump, recoil start.

Mechanical - Capacity 425 cc. Bore and stroke 66x62 mm. Max power 22 hp at 4600 rpm. Compression ratio 8.3/1. Crankshaft runs anti-clockwise on needle-roller bearings. Weight 32 lb, 14.5 kg.

Fuel system - One Dellorto carburettor, model 30 mm. Fuel 2.5% two-stroke mix. Consumption 1.2-2.1 US gal/h, 1.0-1.8 Imp gal/h, 4.5-8.0 litre/h depending on engine speed.

Electrical system - Novi flywheel magneto. Conventional contact-breaker. NGK B9ES spark plugs.

Cooling system - Free air.

Reduction system - Not necessary.

Dimensions (lxwxh) - 11.8x16.9x 15.7 inch, 300x430x400 mm.

Options - Diaphragm pump, propeller, muffler.

JPX PAL865

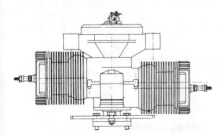

Two-stroke flat twin. Standard specification includes: engine mountings, separate carburettor and pump, electric start without recoil.

Mechanical - Capacity 865 cc. Bore and stroke 84x78 mm. Max power 33

hp at 3200 rpm. Compression ratio 9.0/1. Crankshaft runs clockwise. Weight 60 lb, 27 kg.

Fuel system - One Dellorto carburettor, model 34 mm. Fuel 2% two-stroke mix. Consumption 3.2-3.5 US gal/h, 2.7-2.9 Imp gal/h, 12.3-13.3 litre/h depending on engine speed.

Electrical system - Alternator. Max output 12 V 42 W LT. CDI ignition. Shielded platinum spark plugs.

Cooling system - Free air.

Reduction system - Not necessary.

Dimensions (lxwxh) - 15.8x24.0x 16.5 inch, 402x610x420 mm.

Options - Engine driven oil pump enabling use of automotive gasoline.

JPX 4T50 1600

Four-stroke flat four. Standard specification includes: engine mountings, separate carburettor and pump, neither electric nor recoil start.

Mechanical - Capacity 1583 cc. Bore and stroke 86x69 mm. Max power 50 hp at 3200 rpm. Compression ratio 7.8/1. Crankshaft runs clockwise. Weight 139 lb, 63 kg.

Fuel system - One Dellorto carburettor, model 34 mm. Fuel high-octane automotive gasoline. Consumption 3.6-4.2 US gal/h, 3.0-3.5 Imp gal/h, 13.6-15.9 litre/h.

Electrical system - Slick flywheel magneto, model 4266R.

Cooling system - Free air.

Reduction system - Not necessary.

Dimensions (lxwxh) - 25.6x 31.5xNC inch, 650x800xNC mm.

Options - 4T50A 1600 specification with electric starter and different engine mounts, adds 24 lb, 11 kg.

JPX 4T55AE 1875

Four-stroke flat four. Standard specification as 4T50 1600.

Mechanical - Capacity 1875 cc. Bore and stroke 93x69 mm. Max power 60 hp at 3200 rpm. Compression ratio 8.4/1. Crankshaft runs clockwise. Weight 139 lb, 63 kg.

Fuel system - See JPX 4T50 1600.

Electrical system - Slick flywheel magneto, model 4216R. Eyquem A755 spark plugs.

Cooling system - Free air.

Reduction system - Not necessary.

Dimensions (lxwxh) - See JPX 4T50 1600.

Options - 4T55A 1875 specification with electric starter and different engine mounts, adds 24 lb, 11 kg.

JPX 4T60A 2050

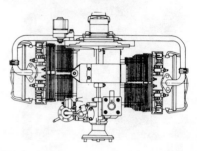

Four-stroke flat four. Standard specification includes: engine mountings, separate carburettor and pump, electric start without recoil.

Mechanical - Capacity 2050 cc. Bore and stroke 93x75 mm. Max power 65 hp at 3200 rpm. Compression ratio 8.2/1. Crankshaft runs clockwise. Weight 161 lb, 73 kg.

Fuel system - One Dellorto carburettor, model 34 mm. Fuel high-octane automotive gasoline or avgas.

Electrical system - See JPX 4T55AE 1875.

Cooling system - Free air.

Reduction system - Not necessary.

Dimensions (lxwxh) - 25.6x 31.7xNC inch, 650x805xNC mm.

Options - 4T60B 2050 specification with JPX electronic ignition.

KAWASAKI

Kawasaki, Japan. Engines out of production, but still available through US agent: Aerowood Aircraft Supply, 900 Wertz NW, Canton, Ohio 44708; tel (216) 455-3913.

KAWASAKI 340

Two-stroke in-line twin. Standard specification NC.

Mechanical - Capacity 339 cc. Max power 28 hp at 6500 rpm.

Fuel system - Fuel two-stroke mix.

Other data NC.

KAWASAKI TA440

Two-stroke in-line twin. Standard specification includes: carburettor with integral pump, electric start, reduction system.

Mechanical - Capacity 436 cc. Bore and stroke 68x60 mm. Max power 38.5 hp at 5000 rpm. Weight 78 lb, 35 kg.

Fuel system - One Mikuni carburettor, model 34 mm. Fuel two-stroke mix.

Electrical system - Flywheel magneto. CDI ignition.

Cooling system - Air with integral fan and ducting.

Reduction system - Quadruple notched V-belt, ratio 1.9/1.

KFM

KFM Division, IAME SpA, Via Lisbona 15, 24040 Zingonia, Italy.

Australian agent: Transavia Division, Transfield (NSW) Pty Ltd, 73 Station Road, Seven Hills, 2147 NSW; tel 624-4244; tx 70300 TRANSAC AA.

British agent: Ferrari Racing Services, 66-69 Link House, Fruit & Vegetable Market, New Covent Garden Market, London SW8; tel 01-720 8677.

Canadian agent: Ultraflight Sales (see Canadian section).

French agent: Sovame, 132 rue Rechossiere, 93300 Aubervilliers; tel 833 5626.

US agent: KFM Inc, Orange County Airport, RD 2, Box 8, Montgomery, New York 12549; tel (914) 457-3188. Alter-

natively: **Italmotion, PO Box 71, Monroe, New York 10950; tel (914) 783 7314; tx 178912 (attention Don Black).**

KFM 107ER

Foto Wells

Two-stroke flat twin. Standard specification includes: exhaust-system complete, engine mountings, air filter, separate carburettor and pump, electric start without recoil, reduction system.

Mechanical - Capacity 294 cc. Bore and stroke 60x52 mm. Max power 25 hp at 6300 rpm. Compression ratio 10.5/1. Crankshaft runs anti-clockwise on 2 ball and 1 needle-roller bearings. Weight 47 lb, 22 kg.

Fuel system - One diaphragm carburettor. Fuel 2.5% two-stroke mix. Consumption at 75% power 1.8 US gal/h, 1.5 Imp gal/h, 6.8 litre/h.

Electrical system - Motoplat flywheel magneto and alternator, dual coils. Max output 12 V 130 W LT. Electronic ignition.

Cooling system - Free air.

Reduction system - Triple V-belt, ratio 2.1/1.

Dimensions (lxwxh*) - 18.0x17.3x 15.8 inch, 457x440x401 mm.

Options - 107E specification, without reduction system (saves 7.3 lb, 3.3 kg); 107ERU specification, with crankshaft pulley but without rest of reduction system (for remote reduction installations, saves 6.4 lb, 2.9 kg); 107ERR specification, with reduction ratio 2.55/1.

*Height figure excludes air filter.

KFM 107 MAXI ER

Two-stroke flat twin. Standard specification as KFM 107ER.

Mechanical - Capacity 334 cc. Bore and stroke 64x52 mm. Max power 30 hp at 6300 rpm. Compression ratio 11.0/1. Crankshaft runs anti-clock-

wise on 2 ball and 1 needle-roller bearings. Weight 49.2 lb, 22.3 kg.

Fuel system - One Dellorto float carburettor, model OVC 36/33. Fuel 2.5% two-stroke mix. Consumption 2.2 US gal/h, 1.8 Imp gal/h, 8.3 litre/h.

Electrical system - See KFM 107ER except: Champion CJ6Y or CJ3 spark plugs.

Cooling system - See KFM 107ER.

Reduction system - See KFM 107ER.

Dimensions (lxwxh) - See KFM 107ER.

Options - As KFM 107ER, producing 107 Maxi E, 107 Maxi ERU, and 107 Maxi ERR specifications.

KFM 112

Foto Wells

Four-stroke flat four. Standard specification includes: exhaust-system complete, separate carburettor and pump, electric start without recoil.

Mechanical - Capacity 1286 cc. Bore and stroke 80x64 mm. Max power 50 hp at 3200 rpm. Compression ratio 9.2/1. Crankshaft runs anti-clockwise on 4 plain bearings. Weight 99 lb, 45 kg.

Fuel system - Two Dellorto float carburettors, model OVC 28/24. Fuel high-octane automotive gasoline or avgas. Consumption at 70% cruise 2.4 US gal/h, 2.0 Imp gal/h, 9.0 litre/h.

Electrical system - Flywheel magneto and alternator. Max output 12 V 100 W LT. Transistor-switched contact-breaker. Champion spark plugs.

Cooling system - Free air.

Reduction system - Not necessary.

Dimensions (lxwxh) - 23.4x23.4x 13.5 inch, 594x595x344 mm.

Options - Dual ignition. Detuned version with 45 hp at 2900 rpm.

Note: Still in prototype form at time of writing (August '85).

KIRK

Kirk Enginies Inc, PO Box 864, Waukegan, Illinois 60085, USA.

KIRK X-4, MODEL 25

Two-stroke radial four. Standard specification includes: exhaust-system complete, engine mountings, carburettor but no pump, neither electric nor recoil starters.

Mechanical - Capacity 413 cc. Bore and stroke 59x38 mm. Max power 25 hp at 5000 rpm. Compression ratio 7.0/1. Crankshaft runs anti-clockwise on 4 ball bearings. Weight 60 lb, 27 kg.

Fuel system - One Posa slide-valve carburettor, model 23 mm. Fuel leaded automotive gasoline. Consumption 2.1 US gal/h, 1.8 Imp gal/h, 7.9 litre/h.

Electrical system - Vertex flywheel magneto. Conventional contact-breaker. Champion J6J spark plugs.

Cooling system - Free air.

Reduction system - Not necessary.

Dimensions (lxwxh) - 31.0x16.3x 16.3 inch, 787x413x413 mm.

Options - Electric start. Alternator. Planetary gear reduction system, ratio 3.0/1.

Note: Engine still under development at time of writing (August '85).

KITE

Kite Industries of Arizona, 5820 N 72nd Drive, Glendale, Arizona 85303, USA.

KITE VW CONVERSION

Four-stroke flat twin. Standard specification depends on buyer - engine sold in plans form only, consists of standard VW flat four with two cylinders removed. Buyer supplies own power unit.

Mechanical - Capacity 917 cc. Max power 30 hp at 3000 rpm.

Fuel system - One carburettor. Fuel automotive gasoline.

Cooling system - Free air.

Reduction system - Not necessary.

Other data NC.

KONIG

Konig-Motorenbau KG, Friedrich-Olbricht-Damm 72, 1000 Berlin 13 (Charlottenburg-Nord), West Germany; tel 030 344 3071. Proprietor: Dieter Konig.

Australian agent: Geonic (see Australian section).

British agent: Chris Applebee Engineering, 471 Rayleigh Road, Thundersley, Essex; tel 0268 776642.

Canadian agent: Micro Aviation, 9A chemin des Erables, Limbour, Quebec J8V 1C1; tel (819) 827-1908.

KONIG SC430

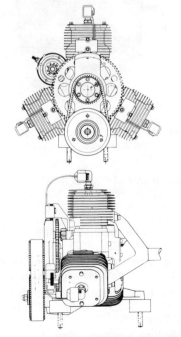

Two-stroke radial three. Standard specification includes: exhaust-system complete, engine mountings, separate carburettor and pump, electric start without recoil, reduction system.

Mechanical - Capacity 430 cc. Bore and stroke 66x42 mm. Max power 24 hp at 4200 rpm. Compression ratio 7.5/1. Crankshaft runs anti-clockwise on 3 ball bearings. Weight 42 lb, 19 kg.

Fuel system - One Gurtner float carburettor, model 22. Fuel 3% two-stroke mix. Consumption 2.4 US gal/h, 2.0 Imp gal/h, 9.0 litre/h.

Electrical system - Flywheel magneto. Triplicated non-mechanically switched CDI ignition. Champion L82Y spark plugs.

Cooling system - Free air.

Reduction system - Toothed-belt, ratio 1.75/1.

Dimensions (lxwxh) - 11.4x13.8x 14.2 inch, 290x350x360 mm.

Options - Deletion of reduction system (saves 6.6 lb, 3.0 kg). Propeller.

KONIG SD570

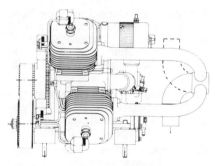

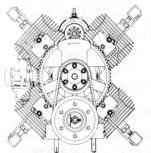

Two-stroke radial four. Standard specification as Konig SC430.

Mechanical - Capacity 570 cc. Bore and stroke 66x42 mm. Max power 28 hp at 4200 rpm. Compression ratio 7.5/1. Crankshaft runs anti-clockwise on 3 ball bearings. Weight 48.5 lb, 22.0 kg.

Fuel system - See Konig SC430 except: Consumption 2.9 US gal/h, 2.4 Imp gal/h, 11.0 litre/h.

Electrical system - See Konig

Engines

SC430 except: Quadruplicated non-mechanically switched CDI ignition.

Cooling system - See Konig SC430.

Reduction system - See Konig SC430.

Dimensions (lxwxh) - 13.4x12.6x 12.6 inch, 340x320x320 mm.

Options - Deletion of reduction system (saves 7.7 lb, 3.5 kg). Propeller.

KONIG SF930

Two-stroke radial four. Standard specification as Konig SC430.

Mechanical - Capacity 930 cc. Bore and stroke 70x60 mm. Max power 48 hp at 4200 rpm. Compression ratio 7.5/1. Crankshaft runs anti-clockwise on 4 ball bearings. Weight 79 lb, 36 kg.

Fuel system - One Bing float carburettor, model 25. Fuel 3% two-stroke mix. Consumption 4.8 US gal/h, 4.0 Imp gal/h, 18.0 litre/h.

Electrical system - Flywheel magneto. Non-mechanically switched CDI ignition. Champion L82R spark plugs.

Cooling system - Free air.

Reduction system - Toothed-belt, ratio 2.0/1.

Dimensions (lxwxh) - 17.3x16.1x 16.1 inch, 440x410x410 mm.

Options - Propeller.

LIL' BRUTE

Lil' Brute Ultralight Engines, 1660 Sheldon St, Unit D, Sun Valley, California 91352; tel (213) 768-0750 x7. Proprietor: Frank Spore.

LIL' BRUTE 720

Two-stroke flat four. Standard specification includes: electric start without recoil.

Mechanical - Capacity 720 cc. Max power 50 hp at 5500 rpm. Weight 42 lb, 19 kg.

Fuel system - One Mikuni carburettor. Fuel two-stroke mix.

Electrical system - Flywheel magneto. CDI ignition.

Cooling system - Free air.

Reduction system - Not necessary.

LIMBACH

Limbach Flugmotoren, Kotthausener Strasse 5, 5330 Konigswinter 21, Sassenberg, West Germany; tel 02244 2322; tx 889574 PLM D. Proprietor: Peter Limbach Snr.

US agent: Limbach Aircraft Corporation, PO Box 1201, Tulsa, Oklahoma 74101; tel (918) 832-9017; tx 821849 SSS INC UD.

LIMBACH L275E

Two-stroke flat twin. Standard specification includes: carburettors, neither electric nor recoil starters.

Mechanical - Capacity 274 cc. Bore and stroke 66x40 mm. Max power 25 hp at 7300 rpm. Compression ratio 10.0/1. Crankshaft runs clockwise on needle-roller bearings. Weight 16.5 lb, 7.5 kg.

Fuel system - Two diaphragm carburettors. Fuel 4% two-stroke mix.

Electrical system - Bosch transistorised 12 V. Bosch WK175 T6 spark plugs.

Cooling system - Free air.

Reduction system - Not necessary.

Options - Recoil start.

LOTUS

Lotus Cars Ltd, Norwich, Norfolk NR14 8EZ, UK; tel 0953 606531 or 608000.

LOTUS MAGNUM 2.25

Four-stroke flat twin. Standard specification includes: carburettor, recoil start, integral reduction system, propeller flanges.

Mechanical - Capacity 480 cc. Bore and stroke 72x59 mm. Max power 25 hp at 2500 rpm. Crankshaft runs anti-clockwise on 1 roller and 1 ball bearing. Weight 31 lb, 14 kg.

Fuel system - One carburettor. Fuel automotive gasoline. Consumption 1.8 US gal/h, 1.5 Imp gal/h, 6.8 litre/h.

Electrical system - Flywheel magneto. CDI ignition.

Cooling system - Free air.

Reduction system - Integral (cam drive), ratio 2.0/1.

Dimensions (lxwxh) - 17.0x20.8x 11.1 inch, 433x528x282 mm.

Options - Vibration damper. Electric starter. Alternator, 12 V 144 W. Extended propeller shaft.

LOTUS MAGNUM 4.50

Four-stroke flat four. Standard specification as Lotus Magnum 2.25.

Mechanical - Capacity 960 cc. Bore and stroke 72x59 mm. Max power 50

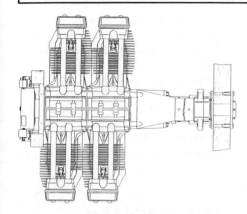

hp at 2500 rpm. Crankshaft runs anti-clockwise. Weight 56 lb, 25 kg.

Fuel system - One carburettor. Fuel automotive gasoline. Consumption 3.6 US gal/h, 3.0 Imp gal/h, 13.6 litre/h.

Electrical system - See Lotus Magnum 2.25.

Cooling system - See Lotus Magnum 2.25.

Reduction system - See Lotus Magnum 2.25.

Dimensions (lxwxh) - 21.9x20.8x 11.1 inch, 557x528x282 mm.

Options - See Lotus Magnum 2.25.

McCULLOCH

Address NC. Sales and service through McCulloch dealers worldwide.

McCULLOCH Mc101

Two-stroke single. Standard specification includes: carburettor with integral pump, neither electric nor recoil starters.

Mechanical - Capacity 123 cc. Bore and stroke 58x45 mm. Max power 12.5 hp at 9000 rpm. Crankshaft runs on 2 bearings. Weight 12.3 lb, 5.6 kg.

Fuel system - One McCulloch carburettor, model BDC. Fuel two-stroke mix.

Electrical system - Flywheel magneto.

Cooling system - Free air.

Reduction system - Normally used, buyer to find.

Options - Recoil start.

MKB

MKB, Muhlstrasse 33, 7151 Burgstall, West Germany; tel 07191 84155.

MKB 430A, 430B and 462

For details see various Schmidtler listings (West German section).

PONG DRAGON

All enquiries to First Class Aircraft (see US section).

PONG DRAGON 35-1.4

Four-stroke twin-row radial six. Standard specification includes: exhaust manifold, carburettors, neither electric nor recoil starters.

Mechanical - Capacity 1391 cc. Bore and stroke 81x45 mm. Max power 35 hp at 2450 rpm. Compression ratio 9.5/1. Crankshaft runs anti-clockwise. Weight 46 lb, 21 kg.

Fuel system - Six diaphragm carburettors. Fuel automotive gasoline.

Electrical system - Two Pong flywheel magnetos. Duplicated spark plugs.

Cooling system - Free air.

Reduction system - Not necessary.

Dimensions (lxwxh) - 13.4x15.4x 16.5 inch, 340x390x420 mm.

REBEL

Rebel Experimental Engines Inc, PO Box 805, Russellville, Arizona 72801, USA; tel (501) 968-5444.

REBEL TWIN 2-205

Two-stroke flat twin. Standard specification includes: engine mountings, air filter, carburettor but no pump, neither electric nor recoil starters, propeller flange.

Mechanical - Capacity 410 cc. Bore and stroke 67x57 mm. Max power 25 hp at 3500 rpm. Compression ratio 8.5/1. Crankshaft runs clockwise on 3 roller bearings. Weight 29.8 lb, 13.5 kg.

Fuel system - One Mikuni float carburettor. Fuel 2.5% two-stroke mix. Consumption 1.5 US gal/h, 1.3 Imp gal/h, 5.7 litre/h.

Electrical system - Flywheel magneto. Non-mechanically switched CDI ignition.

Cooling system - Free air.

Reduction system - Not necessary.

Dimensions (lxwxh) - 12.3x17.0x 11.0 inch, 311x432x279 mm.

Options - Recoil start/exhaust/propeller package (adds 5.5 lb, 2.5 kg). Electric start. Alternator.

REBEL TWIN 2-45

Four-stroke flat twin. Standard specification as Rebel Twin 2-205.

Mechanical - Capacity 1476 cc. Bore and stroke 110x78 mm. Max power 50 hp at 3800 rpm. Compression ratio 8.5/1. Crankshaft runs clockwise on 4 plain bearings.

Electrical system - Alternator. Duplicated non-mechanically switched

CDI ignition. Duplicated spark plugs.

Cooling system - Free air.

Reduction system - Not necessary.

Options - Propeller, exhaust, electric start.

ROBIN

Fuji Heavy Industries, Shinjukuku, Tokyo, Japan.

British agent: Aero-Tech (see British section).

French agent: Mecaworms, 9 rue Maryse Hilsz, 92300 Levallois-Perret; tel 739 3240; tx 620984.

ROBIN EC25PS

Two-stroke single. Standard specification includes: separate carburettor and pump, recoil start.

Mechanical - Capacity 244 cc. Bore and stroke 72x60 mm. Max power 19 hp SAE at 6000 rpm. Crankshaft runs anti-clockwise on 2 ball bearings. Weight 41 lb, 18.5 kg.

Fuel system - One Mikuni float carburettor. Fuel 3% two-stroke mix. Consumption 1.6 US gal/h, 1.3 Imp gal/h, 6.0 litre/h.

Electrical system - Flywheel magneto. Max output 12 V 75 W LT. Conventional contact-breaker. NGK BR8ES spark plug.

Cooling system - Air with integral fan and ducting.

Reduction system - Normally used, option through British and French agents.

Dimensions (lxwxh) - 13.0x13.5x 15.1 inch, 331x344x383 mm.

Options - Air filter. Engine mountings. Exhaust system. Twin V-belt reduction drive, ratio 1.8/1. Propeller. Electric start (adds 11 lb, 5 kg).

ROBIN EC34PM

Two-stroke in-line twin. Standard specification includes: separate carburettor and pump, recoil start.

Mechanical - Capacity 333 cc. Bore and stroke 62x56 mm. Max power 32 hp SAE at 6500 rpm. Crankshaft runs anti-clockwise on 3 ball bearings. Weight 63 lb, 29 kg.

Fuel system - Two Mikuni float carburettors. Fuel 3% two-stroke mix. Consumption 2.1 US gal/h, 1.8 Imp gal/h, 8.0 litre/h.

Electrical system - Flywheel magneto. Max output 12 V 75 W LT. Non-mechanically triggered CDI ignition. NGK BR9ES spark plugs.

Cooling system - See Robin EC25PS.

Reduction system - Normally used, option through British and French agents.

Dimensions (lxwxh*) - 16.7x12.9x 13.7 inch, 425x327x349 mm.

Options - Air filter. Engine mountings. Exhaust system. Toothed-belt reduction drive, ratio 2.2/1. Propeller. Electric start (adds 11 lb, 5 kg).

*Height figure is without spark plugs.

ROBIN EC34PL

Two-stroke in-line twin. Standard specification as EC34PM.

Mechanical - See Robin EC34PL except: Max power 55 hp SAE at 8500 rpm. Weight 68 lb, 31 kg.

Fuel system - See Robin EC34PM except: Consumption NC.

Electrical system - Flywheel magneto. Max output 12 V 90 W LT. Non-mechanically triggered CDI ignition.

Cooling system - Liquid.

Reduction system - Normally used, option through British and French agents.

Dimensions (lxwxh) - 17.2x13.4x 13.9 inch, 437x341x353 mm.

Options - Air filter. Engine mountings. Exhaust system. Reduction drive. Propeller.

Engine available to special order only.

ROBIN EC44PM

Two-stroke in-line twin. Standard specification includes separate carburettors and pump, electric and recoil starters.

Mechanical - Capacity 432 cc. Bore and stroke 68x60 mm. Max power 50 hp SAE at 6500 rpm. Crankshaft runs anti-clockwise on 3 ball bearings. Weight 86 lb, 39 kg.

Fuel system - See Robin EC34PM except: Consumption 2.6 US gal/h, 2.2 Imp gal/h, 10.0 litre/h.

Electrical system - See Robin EC34PM.

Cooling system - See Robin EC25PS.

Reduction system - Normally used, option through British and French agents.

Dimensions (lxwxh*) - 18.1x14.8x 15.0 inch, 461x377x380 mm.

Options - Air filter. Engine mountings. Exhaust system. Toothed-belt reduction drive, ratio 2.2/1. Propeller. Deletion of electric start (saves 11 lb, 5 kg).

*Height figure is without spark plugs.

ROBIN EC44PM 2*

Two-stroke in-line twin. Standard specification includes: separate carburettors and pump, recoil start.

Mechanical - Capacity 432 cc. Bore and stroke 68x60 mm. Max power 53 hp at 6750 rpm. Crankshaft runs anti-clockwise. Weight 66 lb, 30 kg.

Fuel system - See Robin EC34PM except: Consumption 2.6 US gal/h, 2.2 Imp gal/h, 10.0 litre/h.

Electrical system - See Robin EC34PM.

Cooling system - See Robin EC25PS.

Reduction system - Normally used, option through British and French agents.

Dimensions (lxwxh**) - 17.4x 13.3x13.9 inch, 443x338x354 mm.

Options - See Robin EC34PM.

*Sometimes called Robin EC44 2PM or EC44 2P1.

**Height figure is without spark plugs.

ROBIN EC51PL

Two-stroke in-line three. Standard specification includes: separate carburettors and pump, recoil start.

Mechanical - Capacity 500 cc. Bore and stroke 62x56 mm. Max power 75 hp at 8000 rpm. Crankshaft runs anti-clockwise. Weight 99 lb, 45 kg.

Fuel system - Three Mikuni float carburettors. Fuel two-stroke mix.

Electrical system - Flywheel magneto. Max output 12 V 120 W LT. Non-mechanically triggered CDI ignition.

Cooling system - Liquid.

Reduction system - Normally used, option through British and French agents.

Dimensions (lxwxh) - 21.7x14.0x 13.3 inch, 551x355x337 mm.

Options - See Robin EC34PL.

Engine available to special order only.

ROTAX

Bombardier-Rotax GmbH Motorenfabrik, Postfach 5, 4623 Gunskirchen, Austria; tel 07246 2710; tx 25546 BRGK A.

British agent: Cyclone Hovercraft Ltd, 8 Walton Road, Caldecotte, Milton Keynes MK7 8AE; tel 0908 647333. Director: Nigel Beale.

North American agent: Ron Shettler, Site 4, Comp 19, RR8, Vernon, British Columbia V1T 8L6; tel (604) 542-4151.

ROTAX 185

Two-stroke single. Standard specification includes: carburettor, recoil start.

Mechanical - Capacity 185 cc. Bore and stroke 62x61 mm. Max power 9.5 hp at 5800 rpm. Weight 25 lb, 11 kg.

Fuel system - One Tillotson diaphragm carburettor. Fuel two-stroke mix.

Electrical system - Bosch flywheel magneto.

Cooling system - Air with integral fan and ducting.

Reduction system - Can be used, buyer to find.

Dimensions (lxwxh) - 15.0x8.0x9.0 inch, 381x203x229 mm.

ROTAX 277

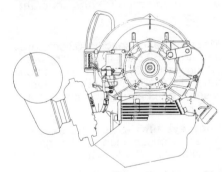

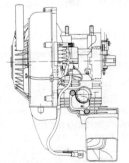

Two-stroke single. Standard specification includes: exhaust-system complete, air intake silencer/filter, separate carburettor and pump, recoil start.

Mechanical - Capacity 269 cc. Bore and stroke 72x66 mm. Max power* 26 hp at 6500 rpm. Compression ratio 11.8/1. Crankshaft runs clockwise on ball bearings. Weight 53 lb, 24 kg.

Fuel system - One Bing float carburettor, model 36 mm. Fuel 2% two-stroke mix. Consumption 2.0 US gal/h, 1.7 Imp gal/h, 7.5 litre/h.

Electrical system - Bosch flywheel magneto, model SCP1. Max output 12 V 75/23 W LT. Conventional contact-breaker. NGK B8ES spark plug.

Cooling system - Air with integral fan and ducting.

Reduction system - Normally used, factory option.

Dimensions (lxwxh) - 12.0x23.3x 16.8 inch, 305x593x426 mm.

Options - Electric start. Rectifier/regulator. Spark plug suppression. Lightweight engine. Deletion of fan and ducting (tractor installations only). Low-noise equipment including modified engine parts and special exhaust system with after-muffler, reduces power to 19 hp at 5500 rpm. Gear reduction system, ratios 2.0, 2.24, 2.58/1 available, 1.77 and 3.0/1 in preparation mid '85. Propeller flange.

*Measured without air-intake silencer.

ROTAX 377

Two-stroke in-line twin. Standard specification as Rotax 277.

Mechanical - Capacity 368 cc. Bore and stroke 62x61 mm. Max power* 35 hp at 6500 rpm. Compression ratio 11.6/1. Crankshaft runs clockwise on ball bearings. Weight 72 lb, 32.5 kg.

Fuel system - See Rotax 277 except: Consumption 2.1 US gal/h, 1.8 Imp gal/h, 8.0 litre/h.

Electrical system - Bosch flywheel magneto, model SCP2. Max output 12 V 140 W LT. Conventional contact-breaker. NGK B8ES spark plugs.

Cooling system - See Rotax 277.

Reduction system - Normally used, factory option.

Dimensions (lxwxh) - 16.0x20.6x 11.9 inch, 406x523x302 mm.

Options - Electric start. Rectifier/ regulator. Spark plug suppression. Lightweight engine. Deletion of fan and ducting (tractor installations only). Low-noise equipment including modified engine parts and special exhaust system with after-muffler, reduces power to 26 hp at 5500 rpm. Gear reduction system, ratios 2.0, 2.24, 2.58/1 available, 1.77 and 3.0/1 in preparation mid '85. Propeller flange. Aluminium cylinder cowl available at no extra cost. Two Bing float carburettors, model 32 mm (produce 39 hp at 7900 rpm, add 2.2 lb, 1.0 kg).

Measured without air-intake silencer.

ROTAX 447

Two-stroke in-line twin. Standard specification as Rotax 277.

Mechanical - Capacity 437 cc. Bore and stroke 67.5x61 mm. Max power* 40 hp at 6500 rpm. Compression ratio 9.6/1. Crankshaft runs clockwise on ball bearings. Weight 72 lb, 32.5 kg.

Fuel system - See Rotax 277 except: Consumption 2.1 US gal/h, 1.8 Imp gal/h, 8.0 litre/h.

Electrical system - See Rotax 377.

Cooling system - See Rotax 277.

Reduction system - Normally used, factory option.

Dimensions (lxwxh) - See Rotax 377.

Options - See Rotax 377 except: Low-noise equipment reduces power to 35 hp at 5500 rpm. Twin-carburettors not available.

Measured without air-intake silencer.

ROTAX 462

Two-stroke in-line twin. Standard specification includes: exhaust-system complete, air intake silencer/filter, separate carburettor and pump, recoil start, coolant pump.

Mechanical - Capacity 463 cc. Bore and stroke 69.5x61 mm. Max power* 52 hp at 6500 rpm. Compression ratio 11.5/1. Crankshaft runs clockwise on ball bearings. Weight 71 lb, 32.0 kg.

Fuel system - See Rotax 277 except: Consumption 2.4 US gal/h, 2.0 Imp gal/h, 9.0 litre/h.

Electrical system - See Rotax 377.

Cooling system - Liquid.

Reduction system - Normally used, factory option.

Options - Electric start. Rectifier/ regulator. Spark plug suppression. Lightweight engine. Low-noise equipment including modified engine parts and special exhaust system with after-muffler, reduces power to 38 hp at 5500 rpm. Gear reduction system, ratios 2.0, 2.24, 2.58/1 available, 1.77 and 3.0/1 in preparation mid '85. Propeller flange. Radiator.

Measured without air-intake silencer.

ROTAX 503

Two-stroke in-line twin. Standard specification as Rotax 277.

Mechanical - Capacity 497 cc. Bore and stroke 72x61 mm. Max power* 46 hp at 6500 rpm. Compression ratio 10.8/1. Crankshaft runs clockwise on ball bearings. Weight 79 lb, 35.8 kg.

Fuel system - See Rotax 277 except: Consumption 2.6 US gal/h, 2.2 Imp gal/h, 10.0 litre/h.

Electrical system - See Rotax 377.

Cooling system - See Rotax 277.

Reduction system - Normally used, factory option.

Dimensions (lxwxh) - 16.9x21.1x 13.9 inch, 429x535x353 mm.

Options - See Rotax 377 except: Low-noise equipment reduces power to 36 hp at 5500 rpm. Aluminium cylinder cowl not available. Twin-carburettors are 36 mm (produce 52 hp at 6500 rpm; add 2.2 lb, 1.0 kg; consume 3.2 US gal/h, 2.6 Imp gal/h, 12.0 litre/h).

Measured without air-intake silencer.

ROTAX 532

Two-stroke in-line twin. Standard specification as Rotax 462.

Mechanical - Capacity 521 cc. Bore and stroke 72x64 mm. Max power* 64 hp at 6500 rpm. Compression ratio 12.6/1. Crankshaft runs clockwise on ball bearings. Weight 71 lb, 32.0 kg.

Fuel system - Two Bing float carburettors, model 36 mm. Fuel 2% two-stroke mix. Consumption 3.4 US gal/h, 2.9 Imp gal/h, 13.0 litre/h.

Electrical system - See Rotax 377.

Cooling system - Liquid.

Reduction system - Normally used, factory option.

Options - See Rotax 462 except: Low-noise equipment not available.

Measured without air-intake silencer.

SCHEIBE

Address etc - see West German section.

SCHEIBE FOUR-STROKE

Four-stroke flat twin. Standard specification NC.

Mechanical - Capacity 500 cc. Max power 30 hp.

Reduction system - Not necessary.

No other details available at time of going to press - for photo, see introduction to this section.

SKYLARK

Addresses etc - see Skylark (Australian section).

SKYLARK MARK II

Two-stroke flat twin. Standard specification includes: carburettor but no pump, recoil start.

Mechanical - Capacity 320 cc. Bore and stroke 61x54 mm. Max power 24 hp at 5200 rpm. Compression ratio

8.0/1. Crankshaft runs on 3 ball bearings. Weight 31 lb, 14 kg.

Fuel system - One Tillotson diaphragm carburettor, model 34 mm. Fuel 5% two-stroke mix. Consumption 1.6 US gal/h, 1.3 Imp gal/h, 6.0 litre/h.

Electrical system - Flywheel magneto. Electronic ignition.

Cooling system - Free air.

Reduction system - Can be used, factory option.

Options - Mikuni carburettor, model 27 mm, with pump. Reduction drive. Exhaust system. Automatic decompression start.

SOLO

Solo Flightline Division, Dietrich CTA, Albstrasse 105, 7000 Stuttgart 70, West Germany; tel 0711 766313.

British agent: Various small-engine dealers.

French agent: Solo Moteurs, 194 rue des Ambassadeurs, 95610 Eragny sur Oise; tel (3) 037 2280.

US agent: Various small-engine dealers.

SOLO 335

Two-stroke single. Standard specification includes: exhaust-system complete, engine mountings, carburettor, recoil start, reduction system.

Mechanical - Capacity 210 cc. Bore and stroke 70x55 mm. Max power 19 hp at 6900 rpm. Crankshaft runs on ball bearings. Weight 38 lb, 17 kg.

Fuel system - One Bing float carburettor, model 22 mm. Fuel two-stroke mix. Consumption at 5200 rpm 1.0 US gal/h, 0.8 Imp gal/h, 3.9 litre/h.

Electrical system - Flywheel magneto. Conventional contact-breaker.

Cooling system - Air with integral fan and ducting.

Reduction system - Quadruple V-belt.

Dimensions (lxwxh) - 11.8x19.2x 22.6 inch, 300x487x573 mm.

SPITFIRE

See Advanced Engine Design.

VW

See introduction to this section.

WAM

Weslake Aero Marine Engines Ltd, Westland Works, Yeovil, Somerset BA20 2YD; tel 0935 75181; tx 46132.

WAM WAE 342

Two-stroke flat twin. Standard specification includes: carburettor, recoil start.

Mechanical - Capacity 342 cc. Bore and stroke 66x50 mm. Max power 30 hp at 7000 rpm. Compression ratio 9.2/1. Crankshaft runs anti-clockwise on 3 ball bearings. Weight 18.5 lb, 8.4 kg.

Fuel system - One Dellorto diaphragm carburettor with reed block. Fuel 4% two-stroke mix. Consumption *1.0* US gal/h, *0.8* Imp gal/h, *3.9* litre/h.

Electrical system - Flywheel magneto. CDI ignition.

Cooling system - Free air.

Reduction system - Can be used, factory option.

Dimensions (lxwxh*) - 14.8x 7.1x5.5 inch, 375x181x141 mm.

Options - Exhaust system, electric start, micro V-belt reduction drive.

Height figure measured above crankshaft centreline.

Note: Engine being redesigned at time of going to press (see Tirith, British section). Data above refers to original version; subsequent versions likely to be heavier.

WESLAKE

See Emdair.

YAMAHA

Yamaha, Japan. Sales and service through Yamaha karting dealers.

YAMAHA KT100S

Two-stroke single. Standard specification includes: carburettor with integral pump.

Mechanical - Capacity 98 cc. Bore and stroke 52x46 mm. Max power 15 hp at 10,000 rpm. Compression ratio 7.9-10.0/1. Weight 23 lb, 10.4 kg.

Fuel system - One carburettor. Fuel 4% two-stroke mix.

Electrical system - Flywheel magneto.

Cooling system - Free air.

Reduction system - Can be fitted, buyer to find.

ZENOAH

Komatsu Zenoah Co, 142-1 Sakuragaoka-2, Higashiyamato, Tokyo 189, Japan; tel 0425-61 2141; tx 2842 122.

French agent: Jardibois SA, JB Distribution, BP 7116, 18 rue Vaucanson, 44030 Nantes Cedex; tel (40) 461762.

US agent: Komatsu Zenoah Co, 24144 Sumac Drive, Golden, Colorado 80401; tel (303) 526-1250; tx 045 4520.

ZENOAH G25B-1

Two-stroke single. Standard specification includes: carburettor but no pump, recoil start.

Mechanical - Capacity 242 cc. Bore and stroke 72x59.5 mm. Max power 20 hp at 6500 rpm. Compression ratio 6.5/1. Crankshaft runs anti-clockwise on 3 ball bearings. Weight 39 lb, 17.5 kg.

Fuel system - One Keihin float carburettor, model G25. Fuel 4% two-stroke mix. Consumption 1.3 US gal/h, 1.1 Imp gal/h, 5.0 litre/h.

Electrical system - Flywheel magneto. Non-mechanically switched CDI ignition. N3C spark plug.

Cooling system - Free air.

Reduction system - Normally used, factory option.

Dimensions (lxwxh) - 12.3x11.6x 14.8 inch, 312x294x377 mm.

Options - Exhaust system. Fuel pump. Micro V-belt reduction drive. Propeller. G25B-2 specification, deletes recoil start (saves 3 lb, 1.5 kg).

ZENOAH G50C

Two-stroke flat twin. Standard specification includes: exhaust-system complete, carburettors but no pumps, recoil start.

Mechanical - Capacity 484 cc. Bore and stroke 72x59.5 mm. Max power 35 hp at 5300 rpm to 45 hp at 6500 rpm, depending on state of tune. Crankshaft runs anti-clockwise. Weight 67 lb, 31 kg.

Fuel system - Two Keihin float carburettors, model G50. Fuel 4% two-stroke mix. Consumption 2.1 US gal/h, 1.8 Imp gal/h, 8.0 litre/h.

Electrical system - See Zenoah G25B-1 except: separate ignition system for each cylinder.

Cooling system - Air with integral fan and ducting.

Reduction system - Normally used, factory option.

Dimensions (lxwxh) - 14.1x23.0x 14.8 inch, 357x583x377 mm.

Options - Fuel pump. Micro V-belt reduction drive, ratio 2.5/1. Propeller. G50D specification, free-air cooled (saves 9.5 lb, 5 kg)

Aircraft Index

Note: 1 This index covers aircraft only. Engines are arranged alphabetically in the Engines Section.

2 Numbers in bold indicate a listing. Numbers in light type indicate a mention.

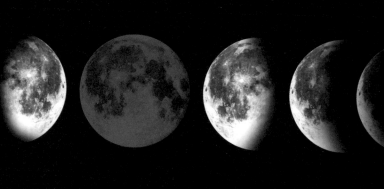

THE
APOLLO
MURDERS

CHRIS
HADFIELD

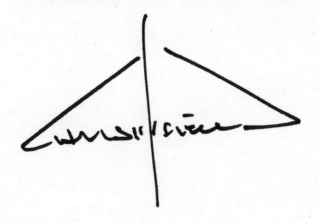

Quercus

THE
APOLLO
MURDERS

THE
APOLLO
MURDERS

CHRIS
HADFIELD

Quercus

First published in Great Britain in 2021 by

Quercus Editions Ltd
Carmelite House
50 Victoria Embankment
London EC4Y 0DZ

An Hachette UK company

A CIP catalogue record for this book is available
from the British Library

HB ISBN 978 1 52940 685 6
TPB ISBN 978 1 52940 682 5

10 9 8 7 6 5 4 3 2 1

Printed and bound in Great Britain by Clays Ltd, Elcograf S.p.A.

MIX
Paper from
responsible sources
FSC® C104740
FSC
www.fsc.org

Papers used by Quercus are from well-managed forests and other responsible sources.

To Helene
who hand-built the multicolored desk on which this book was written,
as well as our entire life together

Many of these people are real. Much of this actually happened.

PROLOGUE

Chesapeake Bay, 1968

I lost my left eye on a beautiful autumn morning with not a cloud in the sky.

I was flying an F-4 Phantom, a big, heavy jet fighter nicknamed the Double Ugly, with the nose section newly modified to hold reconnaissance cameras. The nose cone was now bulbous, which meant the air flowed differently around it, so I was taking it on a test flight over the Chesapeake Bay to recalibrate the speed sensing system.

I loved flying the Phantom. Pushing forward on the throttles created an instantaneous powerful thrust into my back, and pulling back steadily on the control stick arced the jet's nose up into the eternal blue. I felt like I was piloting some great winged dinosaur, laughing with effortless grace and freedom in three dimensions.

But today I was staying down close to the water to measure exactly how fast I was going. By comparing what my cockpit dials showed with the readouts from the technicians recording my pass from the shoreline, we could update the airplane's instruments to tell the truth of the new nose shape.

I pushed the small knob under my left thumb and said into my oxygen mask, "Setting up for the final pass, 550 knots."

The lead engineer's voice crackled right back through my helmet's earpieces. "Roger, Kaz, we're ready."

I twisted my head hard to spot the line-up markers, big orange reflective triangles on posts sticking up out of the water. I rolled the Phantom to the left, pulled to turn and align with the proper ground track, and pushed the throttles forward, just short of afterburner, to set speed at 550 knots. Nine miles a minute, or almost 1,000 feet with every tick of my watch's second hand.

The shoreline trees on my right were a blur as I eased the jet lower over the bay. I needed to cross in front of the measuring cameras at exactly 50 feet above the water. A very quick glance showed my speed at 540 and my altitude at 75, so I added a titch of power and eased the stick forward a hair before leveling off. As the first marker raced up and flicked past under my nose I pushed the button, and said, "Ready."

"Roger" came back.

As I was about to mark the crossing of the second tower, I saw the seagull.

Just a white-gray speck, but dead ahead. My first instinct was to push forward on the stick so I would miss it, but at 50 feet above the water, that would be a bad idea. My fist and arm muscles clenched, freezing the stick.

The seagull saw what was about to happen and, calling on millions of years of evolved avian instinct, dove to avoid danger, but it was too late. I was moving far faster than any bird.

We hit.

The technicians in the measuring tower were so tightly focused on their sighting equipment they didn't notice. They briefly wondered why I hadn't called "Ready" a second time and then "Mark" as I crossed the third tower, but they sat back from their instruments as the lead engineer calmly transmitted, "That's the last data point, Kaz. Nice flying. See you at the debrief."

In the cockpit, the explosion was stupendous. The gull hit just ahead and left of me, shattering the acrylic plastic canopy like a grenade. The 550-mile-an-hour wind, full of seagull guts and plexiglas shards, hit my chest and face full force, slamming me back against the ejection seat, then blowing me around in my harness like a ragdoll. I couldn't see a thing, blindly easing back on the stick to get up and away from the water.

My head was ringing from what felt like a hard punch in my left eye. I blinked fast to try to clear my vision, but I still couldn't see. As the jet climbed, I pulled the throttles back to midrange to slow down, and leaned forward against my straps to get my face out of the pummeling wind, reaching up with one hand to clear the guck out of my eyes. I wiped hard, left and right, clearing my right eye enough for me to glimpse the horizon. The Phantom was rolling slowly to the right, and still climbing. I moved the control stick to level off, wiped my eyes again, and glanced down at my glove. The light brown leather was soaked in fresh, red blood.

I bet that's not all from the seagull.

I yanked off the glove to feel around my face, fighting the buffeting wind. My right eye seemed normal, but my numb left cheek felt torn, and I couldn't see anything out of my left eye, which was now hurting like hell.

My thick green rubber oxygen mask was still in place over my nose and mouth, held there by the heavy jawline clips on my helmet. But my dark green visor was gone, lost somehow in the impact and the wind. I reached back and pivoted my helmet forward, wiggling and recentering it. I needed to talk to somebody, and fast.

"Mayday, Mayday, Mayday!" I yelled, mashing down the comm button with a thumb slippery with blood. "This is Phantom 665. I've had a birdstrike. Canopy's broken." I couldn't see well enough to change the radio frequency, and hoped the crew in the observation tower was still listening. The roar in the cockpit was so loud I couldn't hear any response.

Alternately wiping the blood that kept filling my right eye socket and jamming the heel of my hand hard into my left, I found I could see

enough to fly. I looked at the Chesapeake shoreline below me to get my
bearings. The mouth of the Potomac was a distinctive shape under
my left wing, and I used it to turn towards base, up the Maryland shore
to the familiar safety of the runways at Patuxent River Naval Air Station.

The bird had hit the left side of the Phantom, so I knew some of the
debris from the collision might have been sucked into that engine,
damaging it. I strained to see the instruments—at least I couldn't see
any yellow caution lights. *One engine's enough anyway*, I thought, and
started to set up for landing.

When I leaned hard to the left, the slipstream blew across my face,
keeping the blood from running into my good eye. I shouted again into
my mask: "Mayday, Mayday, Mayday, Phantom 665's lining up for an
emergency straight-in full stop, runway 31." Hoping someone was listening, and that other jets were getting out of my way.

As Pax River neared I pulled my hand away from my left eye and
yanked the throttles to idle, to slow enough to drop the landing gear.
The airspeed indicator was blurry too, but when I guessed the needle
was below 250 knots I grabbed the big red gear knob and slammed it
down. The Phantom made the normal clunking and shuddering vibrations as the wheels lowered and locked into place. I reached hard left
and slapped the flaps and slats down.

The wind in the cockpit was still my own personal tornado. I kept
leaning left, took one last swipe at my right eye to clear the blood, set
the throttles about two-thirds back, jammed my palm back into my
bleeding left eye socket, and lined up.

The F-4 has small bright lights by the windscreen that glow red when
you're at the right angle for landing, and it also sounds a reassuring
steady tone to say you're on-speed. I blessed the McDonnell Aircraft
engineers for their thoughtfulness as I clumsily set up on final. My depth
perception was all messed up, so I aimed about a third of the way down
the runway and judged the rate of descent as best I could. The ground
on either side of the runway came rushing up and slam! I was down,
yanking the throttle to idle and pulling up on the handle to release the

drag chute, squinting like hell to try to keep the Phantom somewhere near the middle of the runway.

I pulled the stick all the way back into my lap to help air-drag the 17-ton jet to a stop, pushing hard on the wheel brakes, trying to bring the far end of the runway into focus. It looked like it was coming up too fast, so I stood on the brakes, yanking against the leverage of the stick.

And suddenly it was over. The jet lurched to a stop, the engines were at idle, and I saw yellow fire trucks pulling onto the runway, racing towards me. Someone must have heard my radio calls. As the trucks pulled up I swapped hands on my injured eye, reached down to the throttles, raised the finger lifts and shut off both engines.

I leaned back against the ejection seat and closed my good eye. As the adrenaline left my body, excruciating pain took over, a searing fire centered in my left eye socket. The rest of me was numb, nauseous, soaking wet, totally limp.

The fire chief's ladder rattled against the side of the Phantom. And then I heard his voice next to me.

"Holy Christ," he said.

TO

THE

MOON

1

Houston, January 1973

Flat.

Flat, as far as the eye could see.

The plane had just descended below cloud and the hazy, humid South Texas air made the distances look shorter somehow. Kaz leaned forward to get a good look at his new posting. He'd been in the Boeing 727 seat for nearly four hours and his neck cracked as he craned it. Underneath him was a waterway snaking through an industrial maze of petroleum refineries and waterside cranes. His forehead touched the window as he tipped his head to track where it flowed into Galveston Bay, a glistening expanse of oily brown water that fed into the Gulf of Mexico, fuzzily visible on the horizon through the smog.

Not a garden spot.

As the plane descended towards the runway, he noticed each small correction the pilots made, silently evaluating their landing as the tires squawked onto the runway at Houston Intercontinental Airport. *Not bad*.

The Avis rental car was ready for him. He heaved his overfilled suitcase and satchel into the trunk, and carefully set his guitar on top. "I have too much gear," he muttered, but Houston was going to be home for a few months, so he'd packed what he figured he'd need.

Kaz glanced at his watch, now on Central time—midday Sunday traffic should be light—and climbed in. As he turned the key, he noticed the name of the model on the key fob. He smiled. They'd rented him a silver Plymouth Satellite.

The accident hadn't only cost Kaz an eye. Without binocular vision, he'd lost his medical as both a test pilot and an astronaut selectee who'd been assigned to fly on MOL, the military's planned Manned Orbiting Laboratory spy space station. His work and dreams had disappeared in a bloody flurry of feathers.

The Navy had sent him to postgraduate school to heal and to study space-borne electro-optics, and then used his analysis expertise inside National Security and Central Intelligence. He'd enjoyed the complexity of the work, applying his insight to help shape policy, but had watched with quiet envy as former military pilots flew on Apollo missions and walked on the Moon.

Yet Washington's ever-changing politics had now brought him here to Houston. President Richard Nixon was feeling the heat in an election year; some districts felt they'd already won the space race, and inflation and unemployment had both been rising. The Department of Defense was on Nixon's back, with uncertain direction as the Vietnam War was ending, and they were still incensed that he had canceled MOL. The National Reconnaissance Office had assured Nixon that their new Gambit-3 Key Hole satellites could take spy pictures better and more cheaply than astronauts on a space station.

But Nixon was a career politician, and easily found the advantageous middle ground: give the American public one more Moon flight, and let the Department of Defense and its vast budgetary resources pay the cost.

With DoD money behind it, Apollo 18 was redesignated as America's first all-military spaceflight, and its classified purpose was given to the

US Air Force to decide. Given his rare combination of test flying, MOL training and Washington intelligence work, the Navy sent Kaz to Texas to be the crew military liaison.

To keep an eye on things.

As he cruised south on I-45, Kaz was tempted to drive directly to NASA's Manned Spacecraft Center for a look, but instead he headed a bit farther west. Before leaving Washington, he'd made some phone calls and found a place to rent that sounded better than good, near a town called Pearland. He followed the signs towards Galveston, then turned off the big highway at the exit to FM 528.

The land was just as flat as it had seemed from the air, with mud-green cow pasture on both sides of the two-lane road, no gas stations, and no traffic. The sign for his turnoff was so small he almost missed it: Welcome to Polly Ranch Estates.

He followed the unpaved road, his tires crunching on crushed shells. There was a quick rumbling rhythm as the Plymouth crossed a cattle gate set in the road, aligned with a rusted barbed-wire fence strung left and right into the distance. Peering ahead, he saw two lone houses built on small rises in the ground, a pickup truck parked in front of the nearest one. He pulled into the other driveway, glanced in the rear-view mirror to make sure his glass eye was in straight, and opened the door. Stiff, he arched his back as he stood, stretching for a three-count. Too many years sitting on hard ejection seats.

The two houses were new, ranch-style bungalows, but with oddly high, wide garages. Kaz looked left and right—the road was arrow straight for several thousand feet. *Perfect.*

He headed for the house with the pickup, and as he took the stairs to the front door, it opened. A compact, muscular man in a faded green Ban-Lon golf shirt, blue jeans and pointed brown boots stepped out. Maybe mid-fifties, hair cut close in a graying crew cut, face seaming early with age. Had to be his new landlord, Frank Thompson, who'd said on the phone that he'd been an Avenger pilot in the Pacific theater and was now an airline captain with Continental.

"You Kaz Zemeckis?"

Kaz nodded.

"I'm Frank," he said, and held out his hand. "Welcome to Polly Ranch! You found us okay?"

Kaz shook the man's hand. "Yes, thanks. Your directions were good."

"Hold on a sec," Frank said and disappeared into his house. He came back out holding up a shiny bronze-colored key, then led the way down the steps and across the new grass between the houses. He unlocked Kaz's front door, stepped back, and held out the key to Kaz, letting him enter first.

A long, sloping ceiling joining the living room, dining area and kitchen. Saltillo tile floors, lots of windows front and back, dark paneling throughout, and a hallway leading off to the left, presumably to bedrooms. There was still a slight varnish smell in the air. It was fully furnished, perfect for his needs. Kaz liked it, and said so.

"Let's go have a look at the best room in the house," Frank said. He walked to the far end of the living room, opened an oversized wooden door and clicked on the lights.

They stepped into a full-sized hangar—50 feet wide, 60 deep, with a 14-foot ceiling. There were garage doors front and back, racks of fluorescent lights above, and a smooth-poured concrete floor. In the middle of it, spotless under the lights, was an orange-and-white, all-metal Cessna 170B, sitting lightly on its cantilever front gear and tailwheel.

"Frank, that's a beautiful plane. You sure you trust me to fly it?"

"With your background, no question. Want to take it up for a checkout now?"

The only answer to that question was yes.

After Frank pushed a button to open the garage doors, Kaz tucked his rental car into the side of the hangar, and they pushed the Cessna out and down onto the road.

They did a quick walkaround together. Kaz checked the oil, drained a bit of gas into a clear tube to check for water and carefully poured it out on a weed growing by the roadside. They climbed in and Frank talked him through the simple checklist, getting the engine started, watching pressures and temps, checking the controls. Kaz back-taxied to the far end of the road, where it led into a stand of trees. A touch of left brake and extra power and the plane snapped around smartly, lining up with the long, skinny runway.

Kaz checked the mags, and then raised his eyebrows expectantly at Frank, who nodded. Pushing the throttle smoothly all the way to the stop, Kaz checked the gauges, his feet dancing on the rudder pedals, keeping the plane exactly in the middle of the 20-foot-wide pavement. He rocked his head and upper body constantly left and right, so he could see the runway edges on both sides with his good eye. He held the control wheel full forward to raise the tail, then eased it gently back; the 170 lifted off effortlessly at 55 miles per hour. They were flying.

"Where to?" he asked, shouting slightly over the motor noise. Frank waved forward and to the right, and Kaz banked away from the two houses and headed east. He followed FM 528 back across I-45, and saw Galveston Bay for the second time that day, brown on the horizon.

"That's where you're going to be working!" Frank shouted, pointing ahead to the left. Kaz glanced through his side window, and for the first time, saw NASA's Manned Spacecraft Center—home of the Apollo program, astronaut training and Mission Control. It was far bigger than he'd expected—hundreds of acres of empty pasture stretching off to the west, and dozens of rectangular white and pale-blue buildings surrounded by parking lots, mostly empty since it was the weekend. In the middle was a long green park, crisscrossed with walking paths joining all the surrounding buildings and dotted with circular ponds.

"Looks like a college campus," he yelled at Frank.

"They designed it that way so they could give it back to Rice University when the Moon landings ended," Frank shouted back.

Not so fast, Kaz thought. If he did his job right and Apollo 18 went well, the Air Force might talk Nixon into flying Apollo 19 too.

———

Kaz pulled the throttle to idle, cut the mixture, and the Cessna's engine coughed and quit, the wooden propeller suddenly visible in front of them. The click of switches was unnaturally loud as Kaz shut off the electrics.

"Sweet plane, Frank," he said.

"You fly it better than I do. That's a skinny runway, and you made it look simple, first try. Glad she'll be getting some extra use—I'm away too much. Better for the engine."

Frank showed Kaz where the fuel tank sat against the side of the garage, and they dragged the long hose inside and topped off the wing tanks. There was a clipboard hanging on a hook just inside the door, and Kaz recorded date, flight time and fuel used. They both looked over at the silent plane, sharing an unspoken moment of appreciation for the joy of flight. Since becoming a pilot, Kaz felt he never really understood a place until he'd seen the lay of the land from the air, like a living map below him. It was as if the third dimension added a key piece, building an intuitive sense of proportion in his head.

Frank said, "I'll leave you to get settled," and headed back to his place. Kaz lowered the garage door behind him and unloaded the car.

He lugged his heavy suitcase down the L-shaped hallway and set it on the bed in the largest bedroom, pleased to see that it was king-sized. A glance to the left showed a big attached bathroom.

Feeling oddly like he had checked into a hotel, he unzipped the suitcase and started putting things away. He hung up his two suits, one gray, one black, plus a checked sport jacket, in the closet. Did the same with a half-dozen collared shirts, white and light blue, slacks, two ties. One pair of dress shoes, one pair of Adidas. Casual clothes and PT gear went into the lowboy dresser, along with socks and undershorts. Two novels and his traveling alarm clock on the bedside table. Shaving kit and eyeball care bag on the bathroom counter.

The last items in the suitcase were his faded orange US Navy flight suit and leather boots. He touched the black-and-white shoulder patch— the grinning skull and crossbones of the VF-84 Jolly Rogers, from his time flying F-4s off the USS *Independence* aircraft carrier. Just below it was sewn the much more formal crest of the USN Test Pilot School, where he had graduated top of his class. He rubbed a thumb across the gold of his naval aviator wings—a hard-earned, permanent measure of himself—then lifted the flight suit out, threaded the hanger into the arms, hung it in the closet and tucked his brown lace-up flight boots underneath.

The rattling bedside alarm woke him, his glass eye feeling gritty as he blinked at the sunrise. His first morning on the Texas Gulf Coast.

Kaz rolled out of bed and padded to the bathroom on the stone floor, cold under his bare feet. He relieved himself and then looked in the mirror, assessing what he saw. Six foot, 173 pounds (*need to buy a scale*), dark chest hair, pale skin. His parents were Lithuanian Jews who had fled the rising threat of Nazi Germany, emigrating to New York when Kaz was an infant. His face was like his dad's: broad forehead, big ears, a wide jaw leading to a slightly cleft chin. Thick dark eyebrows above pale-blue eyes, one real, one fake. The ocularist had done a nice job of matching the color. He turned his head to the right and leaned closer, pulling down slightly on the skin of his cheek. The scars were there, but mostly faded. After several surgeries (*five? six?*), the plastic surgeon had rebuilt the eye socket and cheekbone to a near-perfect match.

Good enough for government work.

He methodically went through his morning ritual, five minutes of stretching, sit-ups, back extensions and push-ups, straining his body until his muscles squawked. You get out of it what you put into it.

Feeling looser, he showered and shaved, and brushed his teeth. He rummaged in his eye bag, pulled out a small squeeze bottle and leaned back to put a few artificial tears into his fake eye. He blinked at himself rapidly, his good eye staring back with 20/12 vision.

That impressed them a long time ago during aircrew selection. *Eye like a hawk.*

2

Manned Spacecraft Center

"Houston, we have an electrical problem in the LM." Apollo Lunar Module Pilot Luke Hemming's voice was measured, calmly reporting the crisis he was observing.

"Roger, Luke, we're looking at it." The Capsule Communicator's voice, coming from Mission Control in Building 30 at the Manned Spacecraft Center, was equally calm, matching Luke's dispassionate urgency.

On the instrument panel in front of Luke, the Master Alarm light glowed bright red next to the window, where he couldn't miss it during their upcoming landing on the Moon. He pushed the red light in to extinguish it, resetting it for subsequent failures. Several multicolored lights were still illuminated on the Caution and Warning panel.

"What are you seeing, Luke?" Mission Commander Tom Hoffman leaned across to have a look, their shoulders touching in the confined cockpit.

"I think it's a bad voltage sensor," Luke said. "Volts show zero/off scale low, but amps look good." Tom peered around him at the gauges, and nodded.

The crew was hot mic, so the CAPCOM heard them. "Roger, Luke, we concur. Continue with Trans-Lunar Coast Activation."

Tom and Luke carried on bringing the lunar lander to life, taking advantage of what would be the relatively quiet three days after launch, during which they'd travel across the 240,000 miles of space between the Earth and the Moon.

Luke slid his pencil out of his shoulder pocket and made a quick note on the small notepad he'd clipped to the panel. He was tracking the failures as they accumulated; maintaining a running tally was the only way to keep it all straight in his head, especially as multiple systems failed. The Apollo 13 explosion had reinforced just how complicated the spaceship was, and how quickly things could go seriously wrong.

Tom checked his own handwritten list. "So, I see a sticky cabin dump valve, a misconfigured circuit breaker, failed biomed telemetry, and now a bad voltage sensor. I think we're still GO to continue with the full flight plan. Houston, you concur?"

"Roger, *Bulldog*, we'll watch that voltage and likely have some steps for you to take later, but you're still on track for lunar insertion and landing." Luke, a Marine Corps captain, had been the one to nickname the tough little spaceship "Bulldog" after the Marine Corps longtime mascot.

Tom and Luke finished the TLC checklist, deactivated the LM, and exited through the tunnel, closing the hatch behind them.

Michael Esdale, in his pilot seat in the Command Module, greeted them with a broad smile. He was the one who would be orbiting the Moon while Tom and Luke went down to the surface. "I'd about given up on you two," he said. "I made snacks, figuring you might be hungry after all that heavy switch throwing."

Tom squeezed past Michael into his seat on the left, while Luke settled in on Michael's right.

"How's *Pursuit* doing?" Tom asked.

"Ticking like a Timex," Michael answered. A US Navy test pilot, Michael had been the one to name the Command Module. As the world's first Black astronaut, he had decided to honor the WW2 Black fighter pilots, the Tuskegee Airmen, and their unit, the 99th Pursuit Squadron.

"These snacks are . . . simple," Luke said, popping a Ritz cracker with a square of cheese on top into his mouth.

"NASA's version of shit on a shingle," Michael said. "Maybe some Tang to wash it down?" Despite the TV ads, astronauts hadn't drunk Tang in space since Gemini in the mid-1960s. One of the early astronauts had vomited Tang during space motion sickness, and reported that it tasted even worse coming back up.

Tom pushed the transmit button. "What next, Houston?"

"Take a fifteen-minute bathroom break while we reset the sim. We'll pick up again in the Prep for Lunar Orbit Insertion."

"Sounds good," Tom replied. He pushed a small knob on his wrist-watch and the Apollo 18 crew clambered out of the Command Module simulator.

Kaz, who was watching them on the multiple consoles in the instructor station in the adjoining room, had allowed himself only a moment to think that it might have been him in that sim, prepping for Apollo 18. He'd flown with Luke and Michael, all test pilots together, out of Patuxent River; until the accident, he'd seen them nearly every day, and gone for a beer with them most nights. As he watched the experts create one malfunction after another for the crew to deal with—before the launch, it was crucial that Tom, Luke and Michael see all the possible things that could go wrong and learn how to deal with them—he felt a little rueful that he was about to throw them the biggest mission curve ball ever.

After the bathroom break he saw Michael and Luke head directly back to the sim, but Tom stopped for a quick check-in with the instructors. When he spotted Kaz, he came directly to him, a big smile on his face. "Well look who the cat dragged in! Kazimieras Zemeckis! You're even uglier than I remember."

Kaz shook his hand, smiling back. He didn't know Tom as well as the other two, but they'd been classmates in the same Test Pilot School group at Edwards Air Force Base in California's Mojave Desert. "Good to see you, Tom," he said. "You three are doing good work together."

"Yeah, we're getting there. These torturers here are making sure of that."

Kaz said, "I need to talk with you all after the sim." He paused. "Update from Washington."

Tom's forehead furrowed. He didn't like surprises, especially as the crew commander. He looked at his watch, and then nodded, curtly. "Okay. But time to head back in now. See you at the debrief."

As Kaz left the sim and walked out of Building 5, he had to stop for a moment to get his bearings. He looked at the parking lot ahead and the nine-story rectangular building on his right, and matched it with what he'd seen while flying over in the Cessna. He turned right across the open central quadrangle and headed towards the Mission Control Center.

From the outside, MCC looked like just another three-story block of stuccoed cement, with windows tinted dark against the Texas sun. He followed the path around to the entrance, where the architect had made a perfunctory effort to give the nation what they expected of their space program — angular concrete forms stuck onto the postmodern Brutalist cubes. *Government ugly.*

He reached into his sport jacket pocket to retrieve the new NASA ID badge he'd been issued that morning. A guard sitting in front of three heavy silver doors took it from him, checked the building access code and handed it back.

"Welcome to MCC," he said pleasantly, pushing a button. The clunk was loud as the nearest door unlocked. *Like a bank vault*, Kaz thought. *Let's see what valuables they're keeping inside.*

The immediate interior was as underwhelming as the exterior. Gray, fluorescent-lit corridors, functional linoleum and fading prints of the Earth and Moon in cheap black frames on the walls. Kaz followed the arrows on the small signs saying MCC. One of the two elevators had an Out of Order sign on it, so he looked around and took the stairs.

He showed his badge to another seated guard, who nodded and pointed with his thumb at the solid-looking door behind him. Kaz gave it a push, and then pushed harder at the unexpected weight. He closed it carefully behind him, trying not to make much noise. He was suddenly inside the hub of manned spaceflight, and the experts were at work.

He'd entered a room of pale-green consoles, each stacked progressively higher, like in a theater. The workstations all faced the three big screens on Kaz's left, glowing with yellow-orange hieroglyphics of numbers, acronyms and schematics. Behind each console Kaz could see a face, lit up by the displays, hazed by cigarette smoke. Each specialist was wearing a half headset, so they could hear both the radio conversation and the voices around them. Mission emblems of previous spaceflights, all the way back to Gemini 4, hung on the walls.

Kaz stood watching the Flight Control team as they communicated with the Apollo 18 crew, now back at work in Building 5. He spotted a familiar face, a fellow test pilot who raised a hand to wave Kaz over. He threaded his way up the tiered levels, trying not to disturb the concentration of the flight controllers.

Kaz ended up behind the CAPCOM console, where he shook hands with Chad Miller, the backup commander of Apollo 18.

"Welcome to Houston," Chad said softly. "You were over with the crew?"

Kaz nodded. "They're doing good."

The two men watched the room work for a minute. A cartoon-like graphic of *Pursuit* was projected on the big center screen up front. The ship was about to disappear behind the Moon, so Chad asked, "Need a coffee?" Kaz nodded, and the two quietly worked their way out of the room.

Chad Miller, like the rest of the Apollo 18 prime and backup crew-members, was a military test pilot. Clear blue eyes, sandy-brown hair, square shoulders filling his short-sleeved sky-blue polo shirt, tucked in smoothly at the narrow waist of his compact body. Gray slacks, brown belt, brown loafers. His strong hands and forearms flexed as he poured coffee into two white-enameled mugs. He wore his oversized Air Force–issued watch on his left wrist.

"Cream or sugar?"

"Black, thanks."

Chad handed him his cup and led him to a small briefing room, where he and Kaz leaned easily on the long table, catching up. They knew each other somewhat from test pilot days, but Chad had worked at Edwards and Kaz at Patuxent River, so they'd never flown together. Chad had a reputation in the small community as a superb pilot, the consummate stick-and-rudder man, with an unforgiving intolerance of incompetence in himself and others. It was a trait shared by many astronauts, and Kaz respected him for it—someone who could get shit done.

At a pause in conversation, Kaz posed the question that everyone asked the backup crew. "Think you'll fly?"

"Nah, Tom's just too damned healthy." Chad laughed. "And it looks like 18 will be the last Apollo. My last chance to walk on the Moon. I've wanted to do that ever since I was a kid."

Kaz nodded. "I know that feeling. But my days of flying any kind of high-performance machine are done—the Navy prefers a pilot with two eyes."

"Makes sense, I guess. Hopefully NASA will let you fly backseat T-38 while you're here."

Kaz agreed, then leaned to glance out the open door, making sure no one was listening in the hallway.

"You coming to the debrief after the sim?"

Chad nodded.

"There's something we've all got to talk about." Kaz paused. "The Russians have been busy."

3

East Berlin, 1957

The Russian Orthodox cathedral's vestry was cold. Father Hieromonk Ilarion shifted his weight and hitched up the shoulders of his robes to cover the back of his neck, grateful for the extra layer of long underwear he'd decided to put on that morning.

Sitting on a high stool, the weak winter light shining through the nearby stained-glass window, Father Ilarion carried on with his scrutiny of the US Army's partial listing of War Children—German orphans who had been adopted by American soldiers after World War II.

The process of obtaining this mimeographed copy of the list had frustrated even the patience of a hieromonk—over a year of navigating foreign military bureaucracy and its confidentiality concerns. Ilarion had written nine separate letters, each carefully translated for him by an English-speaking junior lector at the cathedral, and he had gone twice in person to meet with the ecumenical cleric at US Mission Berlin. A complicating factor was the Americans' unspoken embarrassment that their conquering soldiers had fathered thousands of illegitimate children in

Germany. As US-Soviet tensions in Berlin heightened, it had only gotten harder to maneuver.

Finally, the list had arrived in the post. But when he'd opened the US government envelope, his heart beating fast, he'd been disappointed to see that the personal details of the adoptive families had been blacked out. Now he sipped his tea and slowly ran his thumb down every page, taking his time, carefully considering each name, trying to pick up the trail that had gone so cold in the dozen years since 1945.

Every morning Ilarion gave thanks in his prayers for his new life as hieromonk; a simple, quiet and deeply contemplative existence that was a bulwark against his harsh childhood in war-torn Berlin and his firsthand experience of the atrocities that people could commit. Still, he felt deeply guilty about losing his brother. He had let down his dead parents by failing to take care of the little boy, and he wanted to find him, and if he needed help, to give it to him.

With his rudimentary English he was able at least to puzzle out the meaning of each column: name, sex, age, hair and eye color, date of birth if known, and date and place of adoption. Many of the children had been so young that all that was listed was a first name or no name at all. The saving grace was that before the war there hadn't been that large a Russian population living in Berlin—mostly émigrés who had fled the Communists, like his own parents. He silently thanked them for giving their sons traditional Russian names. It should be relatively easy to find a "Yuri" on a list with many boys named Hans or Wilhelm, though the names weren't grouped alphabetically, or by birth or adoption date; it was like the list had been pulled together from a random pile of adoption papers. It occurred to Father Ilarion that he had no way to tell if a page was lost or if an adoption had been missed. He sighed, and carried on.

When he found his thumb suddenly next to a row describing a boy named Yuri, it was so startling he gasped. His eyes flicked along the row, disbelieving. Might this be him?

The birthday was listed as unknown, and the boy's age estimated as seven. Date of adoption was 1947, but Ilarion couldn't tell if that meant when the boy was taken from Berlin or when the paperwork was completed. His brother had been born in 1935, so this one was too young. Still, he made a neat question mark in pencil beside the entry.

He found another Yuri, and made another mark. By the time he reached the bottom of the list, he had four possible leads, none of them perfect. Then he realized he had skipped the many children with no names listed. Slightly exasperated, he started again, this time looking at any male child orphaned in Berlin who was born around 1935. It was slower going, but after a half hour he reached the bottom again. He quickly flicked the pages, counting 23 possibles. He shook his head slightly. Not possibles. Children.

Father Ilarion took a short break to make more tea. As the kettle boiled he stretched his back, and twisted his hips to ease the pain in his shorter leg. It was how he had lost Yuri. He'd been badly injured working as a bricklayer on a building site, a trade he'd learned from his father. He hadn't been able to get word from the hospital to his little brother, and by the time he'd made it back to the basement where the brothers had been sheltering, Yuri was gone, along with the only picture they had of their mother and the locket she'd treasured. In the chaos of the war-torn city, he couldn't find him. But after years of searching through death records for any sign, he'd realized that Yuri could have been adopted, and started a whole new search. He held his hands close to the kettle, happy for the radiative warmth, then wrapped his warmed palms around his damaged thigh, which still hurt when he was cold or when the weather changed. When the kettle started whistling, he retrieved a hard biscuit from the tin on the shelf, poured the steaming water over his already used teabag, and returned to the desk.

Now to be a detective. His brother had been lost in the heart of Berlin. His date of birth of 1935 was definite, so he would have been nine, but Yuri had been small for his age, so maybe the authorities thought he was seven or eight. The other certainties: blue eyes and light-brown hair.

A thought struck him. American spellings of unfamiliar foreign names might vary, so he was going to have to recheck for Yuriy, or Juri, or anything similar. He pursed his lips at the extra work, then smiled as he thought of a quote from the endless comfort of his faith: *Until you have suffered much in your heart, you cannot learn humility.*

The monk went through the list again, prioritizing. He settled on two good matches, both Yuris with brown hair and blue eyes, seven maybes, and eleven long shots. He held the two pages with the closest matches up to his eyes, inspecting every bit of information carefully, and made a discovery. The Army functionary who had crossed out the family information had not been scrupulous. Some of the black lines were thin or wavered enough that parts of the letters were visible. Ilarion went to the window, flattened the printed sides of the two sheets against the glass and started copying everything he could discern.

He was able to make out a few more of the details about the adoptive parents, but he was going to need English-speaking help and an atlas to get any further. He went through the seven next-best prospects, and added their facts to his own list. The next step would be to ask the English-speaking junior lector to help him write to the Russian Orthodox Church in America, enclosing the list, and request that they contact the churches nearest to the boys' possible locations. There was at least a chance the local churches would know if anyone in the area had adopted a Russian-speaking German orphan. This was an opportunity to bring long-lost children into the fold, after all. To give each a link to their Russian heritage and faith. To make right the wrongs of war.

To find his brother.

4

Simferopol, Soviet Ukraine, 1973

It was not a beautiful machine.

A squatty silver bathtub, riding heavily on eight spoked wheels. Two scientific instruments mounted on the front like a cross between a ray gun and a Christmas ornament. Stereo video cameras gave it lobster eyes.

Even its name was more functional than poetic—Lunokhod. Moon Rover. Typical Ivan engineering, where practicality ruled design. Not much good for pretty, but pretty much good for strong.

Lunokhod had just landed on the Moon.

Thinking through the sequence of how to take the machine down the ramp and onto the Moon's surface, Gabdulkhai Latypov—Gabdul to his friends—rubbed the sweat off his palms onto his pants legs. He repositioned the procedures book on the console and cracked his thick knuckles. He double-checked that all status lights were green, then reached out and carefully grabbed the controller. Leaning forward, he rested both forearms on the console for stability, stared at the monitor and began.

He tipped the controller forward slightly, pushed the command button and let go. The controller sent an electrical pulse through the console to the giant satellite dish outside the building that pointed straight at the Moon. The signal traversed the 240,000 miles of empty space in 1.25 seconds and hit Lunokhod's small, pointy antenna. It sent the pulse to the rover's processor, which deciphered it and briefly powered all eight wheels.

Lunokhod jerked forward slightly, and stopped. A perfectly trained dog, far from home but still responding to its master.

The rover's twin cameras took an image of the barren landscape and sent it back across the quarter million miles to Gabdul's huge satellite dish in Simferopol, where it appeared on his fuzzy black-and-white TV monitor.

Ten seconds after he'd released the hand controller, Gabdul saw that Lunokhod had moved.

"Zhivoy!" he shouted, in triumph. It's alive! He could hear the stifled murmurs of relief and excitement from the ops crew standing behind him.

Gabdul carefully pushed the controller forward again, a longer command this time, following the practiced protocol to get the machine down onto the Moon. To get to work.

Gabdul had grown up near Simferopol, on the Crimean Peninsula. His family's Tatar heritage was obvious in his thick dark hair, his wide cheekbones and the glottal sounds of his multisyllabic name. As a teenager he'd stood outside in the Crimean dusk, watching in wonder as Sputnik had raced across the sky, visible proof of Soviet technical prowess and dominance. And when Gagarin orbited Earth four years later, Gabdul decided he was going to be a cosmonaut. Just like a million other Soviet young men.

As soon as he graduated high school, he joined the Soviet Air Forces, which would send him to technical college to study aviation engineering, and after that, he hoped, to flying school. But his origins

were a constant impediment. Gabdul had thought that Stalin's depor-
tation of 200,000 Crimean Tatars to Uzbekistan after the Great
Patriotic War was old history, but the bigotry in the military still ran
deep—ever deeper, he found, the closer he got to Moscow. Being an
ethnic minority from the edge of the Soviet Union made him second
class in a classless society.

Despite his graduating in first place, other students with last names
like Ivanov and Popov got all the opportunities. Repeatedly denied pilot
training, at 25 he found himself a lieutenant in the Soviet Air Forces,
working as a junior technical engineer at a space communications
ground station near Shchelkovo, on the distant outskirts of Moscow.

Then one day his captain spoke to him during a smoke break out in
the hall.

"Gabdulkhai Gimad'ovich," he'd begun formally, as the two of them
stood side by side, staring out the double-paned window at the blowing
snow whipping around the hulking silhouettes of the satellite dishes.
"There's a new program starting, and they need smart young electronics
engineers. Hush-hush for now, but apparently it will involve a lot of
extra training and travel. Are you interested?"

His captain already knew what Gabdul's answer would be.

Within weeks, he was called to the OKB-52 Machine Building Plant
in Moscow, for an interview and aptitude testing. He took his place in
the hallway with several other young engineers waiting for their names
to be called, hiding their nervousness behind impassive faces. The interview was straightforward: questions about his career, interests, family.
He made sure to mention his pride in his father's army service and his
own lifelong desire to serve the Soviet space program.

The practical testing was harder, and also puzzling. They had him
operate a forklift truck, driving it around a prescribed course on the
factory floor as they timed him. Then they hitched a trailer to it and
had him back that up, around a corner. Gabdul silently thanked his
father for having imparted that skill when he was teaching him to drive,
back home in Simferopol.

One of the evaluators took over as the driver, and they had Gabdul observe the forklift remotely through a TV monitor and issue instructions to the driver by radio. They repeated the test in dim lighting and then they only let Gabdul see the camera image every five seconds, covering and uncovering the screen with a clipboard. He wasn't sure what they were evaluating him on, but he tried to imagine himself as the driver and say the things that he would like to hear if he was operating the vehicle.

No one gave him any explanation, just stressed again as he was leaving that he was not to discuss the interview with anyone.

One uneasy week later, his captain came into the control room during his shift.

"Gabdulkhai Gimad'ovich!"

"Da?"

The other engineers looked up as Gabdul got to his feet.

"You are leaving us. The Soviet Air Forces, in their infinite wisdom, have decided that you have communicated with enough satellites. You will report to the Lavochkin NGO in Reutov in two days." He looked Gabdul in the eye. "They haven't told me what you will be doing, so it must be highly important. So important, in fact"—he fished around in his pants pocket and pulled out two dark-blue epaulettes with a thin light-blue stripe and three stars—"that you've been promoted to senior lieutenant!"

He stepped forward, unbuttoned Gabdul's faded epaulettes and replaced them with the stiff new ones. He stepped back, and returned Gabdul's stunned salute.

The captain broke into a broad smile. Looking around at the others, he said, "Rebyata! Sto gram!" This calls for vodka!

But at first Gabdul's new posting didn't feel important. When he got to the facility in Reutov, a senior official welcomed him and 18 other trainees by lecturing them on secrecy. Then he led them into a factory clean room, where they all donned caps and lab coats and were sent to stand next to technicians who were assembling a machine that would go to the Moon. The official waved his hand at the hulking silver thing, nearly as tall as he was, and spoke to them of its purpose, its complexity and their role as the handpicked team that would drive it.

Gabdul didn't know what to think. His dreams of flying in space were crashing down around him, lost forever, but maybe driving this beast on the Moon would be cool.

At the first smoke break, one of the trainees said out loud what several others were clearly thinking. "A toy car driver? That's not what I signed up for. I thought we were going to be cosmonauts!"

Gabdul sympathized, but also noticed he was the only Tatar in the group, and felt the significance of that.

Soon several quit in disappointment. Others failed out of the surprisingly complex, rigorous training. And Gabdul felt a growing sense of something like pride. Of all 240 million Soviet citizens, only he and this small, elite team would get to do this difficult job. The likelihood of a Soviet cosmonaut ever walking on the Moon was dwindling to near zero with the repeated failures of the heavy-lift N1 rocket. But Lunokhod was *real*, and soon to launch. Even better, the new lunar simulation field and Mission Control Center were being built in his hometown of Simferopol in the Crimea.

This was a unique challenge, and a chance to make his family proud: a Tatar, in his indigenous Crimean homeland, serving the Soviet Union's space program.

It might not be his feet that would stand on the Moon, but he, Gabdulkhai Latypov, son of Gimadutin, was about to kick up the lunar dust with wire-spoked wheels.

Gabdul had become a Moon explorer.

5

Washington, DC, 1973

Jim Schlesinger was fit to be tied, as usual.

He stood by the window of his seventh-floor office, staring angrily across the George Washington Parkway towards the Little Falls Dam on the Potomac River. As the brand-new director of the Central Intelligence Agency, he wanted change, and it was happening too slowly.

"Richardson!" he yelled, without turning from the window. He'd fired his incompetent predecessor's secretary the day he'd arrived, and now waited impatiently for her replacement. The door opened, and a tall, composed woman stepped in, notepad and pen in hand.

"Yes, sir?" After 18 years with the agency, Mona Richardson had worked her way up through many types of bosses, and was rapidly figuring out how to be effective with this one.

The DCI didn't look at her. "Look at this," he barked and pointed with his chin.

Mona joined him at the window.

"That's where they're supposed to be putting up the agency road sign," he said, staring down at the traffic. "Why is nothing happening?"

32

"I confirmed with Fairfax County Public Works yesterday, sir. They assured me that they had the sign printed as you requested, and that they would have it installed today. I'll follow up again."

He turned and looked at her, eyes dark under heavy brows, then shook his head. They needed a sign showing people where the nation's intelligence agency was located! "Bring me more coffee, please."

Mona nodded, quietly making her exit.

Schlesinger turned back to look outside. He reached into the pocket of his tweed jacket, found his pipe and clamped it hard between his teeth. He pulled his lighter from his other pocket and lit the pipe, puffing several times, exhaling slowly through his nose. Nixon was right, as usual. This praetorian guard of outdated, clubby, shoe-leather spies that he'd inherited was smug and self-serving. They needed weeding, and he was the man to do it.

He turned and grabbed a sheet of paper off his desk, reading down the list as he smoked.

He'd fired 837 people, mostly in the so-called Directorate of Plans— the CIA's clandestine arm. He'd terminated a dozen of its senior management personally, and had changed the name to Directorate of Operations. Cutting deadwood. Making sure these people didn't screw Nixon. And the country.

His time in the RAND Corporation and the White House budget office had shown him how technology was changing the world. The United States wasn't going to win the Cold War by using old methods. The two years he'd chaired the Atomic Energy Commission had only highlighted the power of that technology. *Mutually assured destruction?* He shook his head. MAD was right! America needed better. A CIA that pushed new tech to its limits in order to gather intelligence like no other nation could. Before it was too late.

He went back to the window, glancing up at the blue sky. *Our fighters and spy planes aren't keeping up either. We're just doing what we've always done. Someone needs to shake this place, hard. And let the hangers-on fall by the wayside.*

Mona knocked twice on the door and paused, as she'd been instructed. Hearing nothing, she entered with his fresh coffee, placing the tray silently on the desk. She snuck a glance at him, still staring out at the view. He was tall, with thick graying hair, a broad forehead and cleft chin. *A handsome man. If only he weren't such an arrogant ass.*

Schlesinger spoke without looking at her. "Get me Sam Phillips on the phone."

Twenty-three miles to the northeast, on the ninth floor of the National Security Agency, a truly ugly rectangular building on the Fort Meade Army base, General Sam Phillips studied an airplane model he kept on his office bookshelf—the P-38 Lightning. It was the fighter he'd flown over Germany in the war.

The design still amazed him. Big twin turbo-supercharged Allison V-12s cranking out 1,600 horsepower, turning in opposite directions to minimize torque. He'd loved how it had felt to push the throttles to the stops, letting those giant tractors pull him faster and faster. He'd had it up over 400 miles per hour once, out of bullets and outrunning an Me-109, racing for the safety of England.

He bent down and peered head-on at the model, and not for the first time. He shook his head slightly, marveling again at how the airplane almost disappeared from the front—what the wind saw. *No wonder she was so fast.* Beautiful, purposeful engineering. The Lockheed Skunk Works thought the same way he did. Results are what count.

He took one quick glance at the framed picture the Apollo 11 crew had signed for him of the US flag they'd planted on the Moon. Neil Armstrong had handwritten the dedication: "To General Sam Phillips, with thanks—without you, this flag would not be here." Then it was back to work.

"Phone call, General," his secretary called from the adjoining room. "CIA Director James Schlesinger, on Secure One." A beat. "Are you available?"

That's all I need. He sighed.

"Yes, put him through, please, Jan." The beige phone on his desk rang, an insistent blinking light indicating which line. He picked up the handset and pushed the button.

"Director Phillips speaking."

"Sam, we need to talk about a couple things."

"Good morning, Jim. How can I help you?"

"Help me? It's not me that needs help. It's this fiasco brewing in Russia."

Sam Phillips scanned quickly through his mind. Which fiasco? What mattered to the new CIA Director?

He guessed. "The upcoming Proton launch?"

Schlesinger exhaled loudly through his nose. "You know it. What are your SIGINT boys telling you?"

Phillips shook his head. His agency provided signals intelligence to the Department of Defense, not the CIA. He'd heard that Schlesinger wanted to gather all the country's intel organizations under the CIA's control—*his* control—including the military ones. This was a battle that eventually had to be fought. But for now, he'd offer cautious cooperation; the President had put Schlesinger there by choice. "Nothing significant since the last White House briefing with the Joint Chiefs of Staff." Mostly true.

He could feel Schlesinger's blood pressure rising over the phone.

"Your job isn't figuring out what's significant, Sam, it's gathering! Tell me the latest."

Phillips decided to flood the man with information that wasn't all that sensitive, hoping it would satisfy him.

"You know about the Soviets recently landing their rover at a location on the Moon they didn't reveal to the scientific community in advance. Well, they are also just finishing final assembly and checkout of their new space station, which they're publicly calling Salyut 2. As you know, Salyut 1 had to be deorbited when it ran out of fuel eighteen months ago. After the visiting Soyuz crew was killed due to malfunction during re-entry, they grounded their resupply fleet.

"We think Salyut 2 is actually a military spy station called Almaz. Our sources have been monitoring unusual hardware deliveries, and extra levels of security. Our best guess is that they're building an equivalent to what we intended to do with MOL—essentially a huge, manned camera. Something they can point here and there around the world and see details down to an unprecedented resolution level."

As he heard Schlesinger take a breath in order to speak, he carried on quickly.

"We won't know for certain when the launch will be until we see Almaz roll between certain buildings on its railcar at the Baikonur launch site. We have people and assets monitoring that, watching out especially for when they mate it to the Proton rocket itself. Our best guess is that launch will be in early April. So our mid-April target for Apollo 18 is looking good."

As he hoped, the info dump had been enough to pacify Schlesinger.

"Okay, Sam, the President and I want to know the moment you have visual confirmation."

Clearly he meant for General Phillips to note his familiarity with the president.

"If the Soviets get this Almaz into orbit in April, how are you going to keep what's going on at Area 51 a secret?" Schlesinger asked. "They'll see everything parked on the ramp, and more importantly, the HAVE BLUE testing."

Time for some shared responsibility, Phillips thought. "I agree, Jim. We'll need to change ops there. Use camouflage covers, dummy mock-ups, and no flying during Almaz overflights. It will interrupt our activities for about five minutes a few times per day."

Schlesinger didn't pick up the cue. There was no such thing as "we" or "our" in his mind. "You've got another option too, Sam."

Phillips heard the click of the pipe stem in Schlesinger's teeth.

"Stop them being able to look at the United States, or any of our interests, from orbit."

After he hung up, Phillips stood and thought for a full minute. Then he picked the phone back up to call Kaz Zemeckis.

6

Mission Control, Houston

Gene Kranz, buzz-cut, gruff and competent, looked around the conference room at the team gathered there. Young men, mostly, and a handful of women. He was the lead flight director assigned to Apollo 18. With launch only three months away, he'd summed up the day's work by telling them that he was pleased there had been no major screwups during the six-hour simulation, either by the all-rookie crew or the Mission Control team. Gene had been a flight director since the first Gemini mission, and after six Apollo Moon landings, he treated this one as almost routine, even though he knew that almost anything could go wrong.

"Any questions?" he asked.

Kaz raised his hand. "Flight, could I have a word with you and the crew after debrief is done?"

Gene made eye contact with each of his console engineers. No question marks on any of the faces. "Sure, I think that's now. Thanks. Everyone else, you're cleared to go." The room emptied like a class dismissed, leaving only Tom, Luke and Michael, the prime crew, and

Chad, the backup commander. They and Gene Kranz all looked at Kaz
expectantly as he walked to the blackboard at the front of the room and
picked up a piece of chalk.

"You all know that the Russians just landed a rover on the Moon,
right?" Kaz said. "Well, they're about to launch a thing called Almaz,
a space station designed exclusively for spying, like MOL was supposed to be." He turned and wrote "ALMAZ" in block letters.

"According to our best intel, Almaz's camera will be powerful enough
to easily see things down to the size of a small car." He let the national
security implications of that sink in for a few seconds. They were all
military men, including Gene, who'd flown fighters in Korea. They
knew of the secret testing going on out of sight at remote airfields like
Edwards in California and Area 51 in Nevada.

"Our sources say it looks like they'll be ready to launch Almaz in
early April, unmanned. Once they've made sure it's fully operational,
they'll send cosmonauts up on a Soyuz to crew it, and then they'll start
taking pictures." Kaz paused to let that sink in before drawing the line to
their own mission.

"The Joint Chiefs, with the approval of the president, want to use
Apollo 18 to take a close look at Almaz in Earth orbit before the Soviet
crew gets there. The Air Force just let NASA know on Friday, and I've
been sent down here to brief you ASAP."

Tom said, "Wait—are we still going to the Moon?" He sounded
rattled.

"Yes." Kaz turned to the chalkboard and drew a large circle. "Earth,"
he said, pointing. Then he drew a shape that looked like an off-kilter
hula hoop surrounding it. He pointed at the spot where the hoop's curve
was highest.

"The Soviets are launching Almaz from here, in Baikonur, fifty-two
degrees north of the equator." He traced the curve with his finger, showing where it descended behind the globe and reappeared in the south.
"Apollo 18 has to match that orbit, so after launch, you'll need to steer
up the Florida coast."

"Can't do it," Gene said immediately. "If we don't launch the Saturn V straight east out of Canaveral, we don't get the added speed of the Earth's spin, Kaz. Eighteen's too heavy. We're just making it as it is."

"Agreed." Kaz quickly sketched the Saturn V rocket, Apollo Command Module and Lunar Module, stacked for launch. "To lighten the load, we need to take everything off the mission that isn't absolutely needed."

He drew an X on the LM. "That means no experiments on this mission and minimal time for *Bulldog* on the lunar surface." Another X on *Bulldog*'s exterior. "We won't be carrying a rover." Kaz looked at each of them, then drew Xs on the Command Module and the rocket. "Bare minimum gear in *Pursuit*, and a stripped-down Saturn V too. We'll need to be creative, and Washington is looking to you for more ideas. Our best estimates show we can just make it."

Michael said, "Let me get this straight. We launch up the east coast, and instead of heading to the Moon, we stay in Earth orbit long enough to go find this"—he glanced at the blackboard—"Almaz." He looked back at Kaz. "We hang around taking pictures or whatever, and then we're GO for TLI?" Trans-Lunar Injection—firing the rocket motor that accelerated them to escape velocity out of Earth orbit, headed for the Moon.

"That's right," Kaz confirmed.

Luke Hemming spoke, his voice incredulous. "With no experiments to run and no rover, what are Tom and I doing on the Moon?"

"I was just about to get to that," Kaz said. "With the added time and fuel needed to intercept Almaz, they've stripped your time on the Moon to deal with only the highest military priorities. And those just changed."

"Christ!" Tom muttered, thinking of the new pressure his crew was going to be under for the next three months, made even more intense by the inevitable new layers of secrecy.

"The Soviets landed their rover in a crater called Le Monnier, on the edge of Mare Serenitatis." Kaz drew a second circle to represent the Moon, and two smaller circles to the upper right, labeling them "Serenitatis" and "Le Monnier." "It's about a hundred miles north of where

Apollo 17 landed—and it's not where the Soviets said they were going to land. The DoD wants you to go find out why the Russians are there."

He looked directly at Tom and Luke. "So, gentlemen, you are headed to Mare Serenitatis. The Sea of Serenity."

Luke rolled his eyes. "Idiots!" he muttered.

"Okay, it boils down to two main new objectives," Gene said. "One—do a rendezvous and close approach to this Almaz, and linger there long enough to accomplish the DoD's objectives." He thought a second. "Any idea what success looks like to them, how much maneuvering will be involved and how long we've got there?"

"On the order of an hour, maybe two," Kaz said. "You'll need to burn some fuel in order to position *Pursuit* to take detailed photos. Success is a close look-see. Nothing the Soviets would see as hostile."

"Then we land in the"—Gene glanced at the blackboard—"Le Monnier crater, where we do how many EVAs?" E-V-As, or Extra Vehicular Activities.

"Our first guess is that one moonwalk is all we'll have oxygen and fuel reserves for," Kaz replied.

Gene stared into space for several seconds, calculating. They hadn't saved Apollo 13 by guessing. "We'll see about that. But for now, we plan on one EVA. What exactly does the DoD want Tom and Luke to do on the Moon?"

Kaz counted on his fingers. "A detailed survey of the area. A close-up of the Soviet rover to check out its latest sensors and discern its purpose. Retrieval of rock and dust samples, to see what is so interesting to the Russians."

"Michael can get good area imagery passing overhead," Gene said. "We'll lower his orbit as close to the surface as we can."

Michael added, "I'll need another long lens for the Hasselblad." Gene nodded.

Kaz looked around at the group, now all deep in thought, revising, replanning, updating their options. *Like five high-speed problem-solving computers.*

Tom broke the silence. "A more fundamental ops question, Kaz. Who came up with this and who's actually in charge?"

Kaz paused. Spaceflight, like test flying, relied on the crew's sense of control. Al Shepard, America's first astronaut, had set the tone when he sat atop his Mercury rocket after hours of delay and said, "Why don't you fix your little problem and light this candle?" You couldn't tell a test pilot or an astronaut that their opinion mattered less than the people pulling the strings. Or a flight director, either, especially not one as experienced as Gene Krantz.

"We want to keep Apollo 18 as close to a normal mission as possible. Training, development, launch, flight ops and return will all be run by NASA, as usual. The difference will be at the management level. In addition to your Flight Ops Department here in Houston, representatives from the Air Force, the National Security Agency and the White House will work together. They'll have their people here starting later this week, and they'll be around throughout the flight."

Chad, who had remained quiet until now, laughed out loud. Kaz knew these men's years in the military had ingrained in them a mistrust of political meddling, especially with NSA spooks involved.

Luke shook his head, summarizing it in US Marine terms. "What a clusterfuck."

Tom looked around at his crew. "This is actually going to be pretty interesting, guys. We still have the mission components we've been training for, but with added pieces that make perfect sense for us as military astronauts. A chance to do some stuff that no other Apollo crew has done—rendezvous with a non-cooperative foreign target in Earth orbit, and run what is essentially a military reconnaissance op on the Moon."

Chad piped up. "It's going to require some really efficient flying. Previous missions' fuel reserve margins are going to have to be shaved all the way down the line." He looked pointedly at Michael, *Pursuit's* pilot, and Michael nodded soberly.

"So, Kaz, what exactly is your role in this?" Gene asked.

"They sent me down here as liaison—to translate what Washington wants for you, and to tell Washington what you can deliver. My aim is to free you guys up to concentrate on training while I run interference with management."

Luke was the one who laughed aloud this time. "Mismanagement."

Gene spoke again. "So you need to be in on everything for this to work, Kaz. We're going to be buried in the details, working the problem, building something that will hold together. I'm going to need you in Mission Control from here on out, attending all the sims."

Kaz nodded. "Of course, Gene. I figured as much, and that's what I told the folks in Washington would happen."

"Kaz, when you say 'Washington,' who do you mean?" Tom asked. "It's been—what, five years since your accident at Pax? Who exactly are you working for these days?"

"It's complicated. Legally, I still belong to the Navy. They paid for my graduate work at MIT after I recovered. But during my time there, the Air Force started asking me to advise directly on MOL and SIGINT issues. I ended up talking with the NSA multiple times, and have been called to brief the White House and the CIA, assessing Soviet space assets. I report directly to the Vice Chief of Naval Ops and do my best to keep my one eye focused on the big picture for him, but I spend a lot of time farmed out to other organizations."

Kaz made sure he had everyone's attention, then said, "One more thing. The official briefings with the NASA folks start here tomorrow. What I've told you now is for your ears only. Don't even tell your wives, please." The men all nodded. Of them, Gene, Tom and Michael were married.

Kaz turned to erase the blackboard, rubbing to remove all traces. So far, so good, but he knew just how complicated it was going to get. He expected Washington hadn't told them the half of it yet.

On the way out of the parking lot, Kaz realized there was nothing in the fridge back at Polly Ranch and started scouting around for restaurants.

He spotted a low red building that was so ramshackle it looked like something that had been dropped there from *The Wizard of Oz*. The parking lot was just an open area of grass, though the early-evening clientele had lined their vehicles up neatly with whoever had parked first. One of the cars was a Corvette Stingray, gold with black trim. Kaz had seen one like it in *LIFE* magazine; ever since the Mercury program, a Chevy dealer had been giving Corvettes to astronauts for one dollar each, considering it free advertising. *Must be an Apollo guy eating here.* He pulled in.

As he got out of the car, he spotted the small hand-painted sign: The Universal Joint, it read, with Best TX BBQ Since 1965 underneath.

Perfect.

The entrance was guarded by hip-height swinging doors in the shape of cowgirls, upholstered in red Naugahyde with heavy thumbtacks as sequins. He pushed the girls open and stepped into the low-lit, rough-hewn room. He walked carefully across the uneven flooring and took a seat on a red Naugahyde stool at the long wooden bar. "Eli's Coming" by Three Dog Night was playing loudly on the jukebox, just getting to the big choral crescendo. Kaz caught the eye of the ponytailed bartender, pointed at the Budweiser sign and held up a finger. She nodded, reached into a red cooler and pried off the cap as she brought it to him. She smiled briefly as she handed him a well-worn plasticized menu.

A door behind the bar opened directly to the outside, and Kaz realized the kitchen was just a charcoal barbecue on the back porch. He glanced at the menu and decided on the Universal TX BBQ Cheeseburger, with the works. *Eat what they do best.* He caught the waitress's eye, held the menu up and pointed, just as the jukebox changed to "A Horse with No Name." His order taken care of, Kaz took a long drink of the cold beer, happy for the quieter harmonies.

The wooden walls of the U-Joint were plastered with recent local history, a disordered collage of space mission pictures, astronaut crew photos, real estate advertising and Air Force recruiting signs from nearby Ellington Field. A helmeted mannequin in a Reno Air Races flight suit hung dustily from the ceiling. A group of after-work NASA engineers were playing pool at the lone table, lit by a low-hanging light promoting Coors beer. Small square-topped tables filled the place, four cheap chairs at each, almost all occupied. The Naugahyde cowgirls kept swinging. *The working spaceman's local*, Kaz thought.

"Coffee, please, Janie."

Kaz turned in the direction of the voice to find a short, black-haired man in black-framed glasses leaning on the bar on his blind side.

He noted that Ponytail's name was Janie. *Good to know*.

"This seat taken?" the man asked.

"All yours."

He nodded, and slid up onto the stool.

Janie set a steaming coffee in an enameled ivory mug in front of him. "Black, right, Doc?"

"You bet." He took an appreciative sip, then joined Kaz in surveying the room.

"Quite the place," Kaz offered.

The man looked at him closely for a moment. "You Kazimieras Zemeckis?"

Startled, Kaz nodded. "Have we met?"

The man's face creased in an apologetic smile. "Sorry, I'm JW McKinley, one of the NASA flight docs here. HQ medical sent us your Navy file over the weekend, and when I noticed the glass eye, I just figured."

Kaz said, "My Lithuanian maiden aunts and the IRS call me Kazimieras. Everyone else calls me Kaz."

"Glad to meet you, Kaz. I go by JW, or J-Dub if you're in a hurry."

As they toasted their new acquaintance, Kaz watched the way the doctor's shoulders rolled with thick muscle under his button-down shirt.

"You lift?"

"Just enough to keep from getting too fat. The men in my family are all built like fire hydrants." He paused as Rod Stewart started singing

"Maggie May," then said, "That birdstrike that took your eye must have been something else."

"It turned out poorly for the seagull."

The usual deflection didn't work with the doctor. Under JW's friendly questioning, Kaz found himself talking about the accident in a way he never had, confiding personal details about how the surgeries had felt and all the weirdnesses of getting a glass eye.

"You have a good bar-side manner, Doctor," he said at last. "Your turn—tell me about yourself."

JW smiled at him. "Not much to tell. I'm a Midwest kinda guy, the Air Force paid my way through medical school, I did some trauma work, and I've been a flight surgeon with NASA for the past four years."

"What school?"

"Stanford."

That was as good as it got.

"And the trauma work?"

"I spent eighteen months at the Cleveland Clinic, responding all over the state via helicopter."

Kaz gave a low whistle. "I'll bet you've seen some hairy stuff."

"Yeah, I sure have. Motor vehicle, burns, shootings. Even drownings on Lake Erie."

"What brought you to Houston?"

"I like space." JW smiled again. "Apollo's been an amazing four years."

Kaz turned his head at a sudden loud burst of laughter. He saw a short, tanned, balding man, a gap between his front teeth, holding court at a table by the wall.

JW followed his gaze. "That's Pete Conrad, Apollo 12 commander and moonwalker. He's Navy too. You know him?"

"I think I saw his Corvette outside. He left for NASA while I was still in flight school. I've never met him, but I always felt like I was following in his footsteps, only ten years after. Until the seagull, that is."

"He ejected from a T-38 last year," JW said. "Nighttime, weather here went bad, lost a generator, ran out of gas trying to get to Bergstrom.

His parachute set him down a hundred yards from the base ops building, and he didn't have a scratch."

"Better to be lucky than good. Or in Pete's case, both."

JW shot a discreet glance at Kaz's glass eye. "So how'd you end up in beautiful Houston-by-the-sea?"

"After the accident, the Navy thought maybe they would keep me flying in transports, but I said screw that and asked to go back to school." Kaz shrugged. "They sent me to MIT, then I did some time in Washington, and now I'm here to work with the 18 crew."

"What did you study at MIT?"

"I already had a master's in aerospace systems from the Navy PG school at Monterey. I really liked the science of sensors and electro-optics, so that's what I did at the Lincoln Lab in Boston."

"Wait—you have a doctorate from MIT?"

Kaz shrugged.

"And you said Washington too. Doing what?"

"The specifics are classified, but I ended up at the National Security Agency." Kaz drained his beer. "Turns out the NSA Director flew P-38s in the war and headed NASA's lunar landing program all through the 1960s. He's the one who took an interest in my work."

JW stared. "Holy cow! You're talking about Sam Phillips. He's a legend! You work directly for him?"

Kaz grinned and nodded. "But don't let that get around. Here I'm just another one-eyed ex-astronaut trying to help Apollo 18 get to the Moon."

His cheeseburger arrived, and he realized how hungry he was. But before he took a bite, he asked, "You eating?"

"Nah, I need to get home. Ferne's holding dinner for me. She'll have already fed our two little ones." JW drank the last of his coffee and slid down off the stool. "Nice to meet you, Dr. Zemeckis."

Kaz laughed and picked up his burger. "You too."

7

Lunar Receiving Laboratory, Houston

Kaz felt foolish. He'd asked for an 08:00 meeting with the NASA experts on what the Soviets might be looking for on the Moon, but now he couldn't find the building.

He glanced at his watch. *You've got six minutes.*

He drove up a divided straightaway inside the Manned Spacecraft Center for the second time, craning his neck to find the right building number. He finally spotted a large number 37 in shadow under an overhang. Then he realized he'd missed the parking lot, and had to circle the block to find the entrance. He quickly squeezed the Satellite into a spot between two aging VW Beetles—*scientists prefer Volkswagens?*—grabbed his bag and jogged to the entrance.

He saw people going into a conference room just off the main foyer and glanced at the government-issue wall clock, black hands on a round white face. NASA was big on keeping accurate time. With two minutes to spare, he followed them in and headed for the front of the room, setting his bag on the long veneer table around which the scientists had gathered. He took his notebook out of his back pocket, quickly reviewing the things he was hoping to find out, then raised a hand to get everyone's attention. The room quieted.

"Good morning, everyone. My name's Kaz Zemeckis." He omitted mentioning his military rank, knowing it sometimes rubbed scientists the wrong way. "I'm a former MOL astronaut, recently assigned as crew-government liaison for Apollo 18. I appreciate you all meeting with me."

He glanced around the room, making eye contact. *More facial hair than normal. And more women.* He spotted Chad Miller and nodded; part of the backup commander's job was to go to briefings Tom Hoffman didn't have time for.

"There are lots of details still to come, many of which are classified, but I wanted to start the Apollo 18 revised science discussion with you. I need to get smarter about moonrocks, and I hear this is the right place for that."

There were polite chuckles and nods around the table. The Lunar Receiving Laboratory had been purpose-built to quarantine returning astronauts in case they brought back an interplanetary plague from the Moon. When the first three Apollo crews all stayed healthy—it turned out that, as suspected, the Moon had no life, not even single-celled bacteria—the quarantine period was canceled. But Building 37 was also designed to house the moonrocks and dirt—*don't say dirt, they call it regolith*, Kaz corrected himself. Somewhere inside this building were racks full of bits of the Moon, 842 pounds in total, protected like the Crown Jewels. Actually, pound for pound, the moonrocks had cost more.

Kaz summarized the updated timeline of Apollo 18 for the group, and described the revised landing location, without specifying why it had changed. The lack of surprise on their faces told him that word had already gotten around. MSC was a small community, and the lunar scientists an even tighter subculture within it. They all knew that shifting political agendas were part of the deal.

"So," Kaz said, "what have we learned recently, from orbital photos, the Apollo returns here in this building or the Soviet robotic return samples, that would make you want to go have a close look at a place on the Moon where we've never set foot?"

The room contemplated the question. The Russians had successfully brought back small samples of lunar regolith on their unmanned Luna 16 and Luna 20 missions. Less than a pound in total, but they'd drilled over a foot deep to get it. Despite some published academic papers, no one knew for sure what the Soviets had found.

A tall woman with unruly long black hair raised her hand. "Astronaut Zemeckis, if I may?"

"Kaz, please."

She smiled slightly. "I'm Dr. Laura Woodsworth, one of the cosmochemists here in the lab."

Kaz nodded. She was slender and tanned, wearing a sleeveless floral print dress, with a small crucifix on a gold chain around her neck.

"We've learned more about the Moon in the past forty months than in the previous forty thousand years. Radiometric dating of the samples the missions brought back has shown us that the Moon is over four billion years old—quite close to the age of the Earth. Also, the Moon's regolith is not like Earth dust, which has been weathered by rain and wind. Instead, it's more like broken bits of glass, the result of billions of years of meteorite impact fragments."

Chad spoke up. "It's nasty stuff, Kaz, like loose sandpaper grit. Hard on machinery and spacesuits. The guys have dust stuck to their suits when they come back into the LM that makes them cough after they take their helmets off."

Kaz glanced down the table at him, wondering why Chad felt he needed to interject, but Laura nodded. "By looking at the chemistry of the rocks and dust, we're getting an idea that the interior of the Moon is more like Earth than we thought. A central heavy core, solidified magma surrounding that, and a crust on top. The crust is the gray color you see when you look up at the Moon."

Kaz felt a little like she was treating him as a know-nothing, but was also glad for the refresher. And this was a good way to build rapport with the scientists.

"One other thing before I get to your question," Laura said. "The Man in the Moon—the darker shapes you see—those are ancient lava flows. The light gray rock of the crust is anorthosite, and the darker areas are basalt. Also, the Moon is tidally locked. Do you know what that means?"

That Kaz didn't know. He shook his head.

"It means that the same side of the Moon always faces us. Only twenty-four humans—all Apollo astronauts—have seen the other side."

"Why always the same side?" Kaz asked.

"The Earth's gravity pulls hard enough on the Moon that it bulges a little towards us, like a stone tide going up and down. That internal friction, over time, slowed the Moon's spin, until eventually it got to perfect balance. Presto—we only see the one side."

Kaz held up his hands, slowly turning an imaginary Moon. "So what causes the lunar phases?"

"The Moon orbits around the Earth every 27.3 days. Depending on where the Moon is in its slow orbit, you might see it lit from the side—a crescent—or not at all."

"So, if the Moon spins just once every 27 days or so," Kaz said, "then an astronaut on the surface would be in sunlight for two weeks, and then darkness for two weeks?"

Laura beamed at him. "Yes!"

"How hot and cold does it get, then?"

"About two hundred and sixty degrees Fahrenheit at lunar noon, and minus two hundred and eighty at midnight."

Kaz whistled. "Good to know."

A man in a Hawaiian shirt and Elvis Presley sideburns, the look spoiled slightly by premature balding, spoke up. "Hi, Kaz, I'm Don Baldwin, the department head here. I've been thinking about your question about what we've learned recently. There's a couple things." He ran a hand over his head, front to back, flattening down his remaining hair.

"Some of the more recent asteroid impacts blasted pretty deep holes that haven't been covered by dust yet. They'd be a good place to study the underlying rock, to a depth we haven't been able to drill. We'll need to dig into our photo library at your revised coordinates to see if there are any new craters nearby."

Baldwin paused a moment to look hard at Kaz. His unspoken message was clear. His people hadn't chosen the location, but they'd make the best of it.

"There's another thing we're interested in. Laura, there"—Baldwin nodded at her—"spotted something surprising recently. Laura, why don't you tell him about it?"

She looked at Kaz. "A weird anomaly caught my eye as I was studying some high-res images of the surface, like a dark spot on the film. I had to double-check with a magnifying glass to be sure what I was seeing. But I found a hole in the Moon."

"What?"

"It looks to be a good size, maybe a hundred yards across." Laura flipped through her folder on the table. "I have a picture with me."

She passed an eight-by-ten black-and-white photo down the table to Kaz. He studied the glossy page with his good eye.

It looked like . . . a hole. Almost perfectly round, with the bottom partially lit by the angle of the sunshine. Like something had drilled a skylight.

Kaz looked up in puzzlement. "What made this?"

Laura deferred to her boss.

"We don't know for sure," Baldwin said. "If it was on Earth, our best guess would be a collapsed lava tube, where flowing magma bored a tunnel that later caved in. But how that could happen on the Moon is beyond us. We're forming theories."

Kaz peered closer. "How deep do you think it is?"

Laura answered this one. "We need more photos to be sure, but knowing the angle of the Sun at that time of the lunar day, our guess is, pretty deep—like a hundred yards."

Kaz looked at the hole with new respect.

"If you jumped in, with the Moon's low gravity, you'd slowly fall for eleven seconds. But you'd hit the bottom at forty miles per hour." She smiled. "I did the math."

Chad spoke again. "Yeah, I know I'm just the backup, but let's not try that. Hard on the suit."

Kaz handed the photo back to her. "So, you'd all like to see a cross-section of bedrock in a recent impact crater, and learn more about this hole. Are there more of them?"

"Probably," Baldwin said. "We're going back through all the photos. It took Laura's sharp eyes to spot this one, but now we know what we're looking for."

"Anything else?" Kaz asked.

A bespectacled younger man with shoulder-length hair and a wispy, drooping mustache spoke up. "What about KREEP?"

Kaz looked at him. "What's creep?"

"It's spelled K-R-E-E-P. K for potassium. REE for rare earth elements, and P for phosphorous." He shot Kaz a look, who nodded to show he knew what rare earth elements were. "They aren't actually all that rare, it's just that it's hard to find them in concentration anywhere. They're sort of evenly spread in the Earth's crust, due to their chemical nature. But on the Moon, we think they ended up solidifying into a rich layer just below the crust. Lots of the moonrocks in this building have KREEP basalts in them."

Kaz pondered. "Okay, but why is finding KREEP on the Moon important?"

"Theoretically, the same process that concentrated the KREEP should also sometimes enrich it with uranium and thorium. It may be feasible to mine radioactive elements on the Moon, which means we could power a Moon colony there."

Kaz was careful to keep his excitement to himself. Uranium on the Moon? Is that what the Soviet robot prospectors had found? Could this be the reason they had landed Lunokhod where they did? Finding out what the Soviets were looking for would be key in deciding exactly what the Apollo 18 crew was going to do on the Moon.

Kaz said, "Anything else I should know?"

Don Baldwin surveyed his team. "I think that's it, Lieutenant Commander." The dig was subtle, but the man was telling Kaz he'd done his homework and recognized the military component to all this.

Kaz didn't rise to the bait. "Well thanks, then, everyone. That was extremely informative. Chad and I will update the crew, and I'll be following up with you as we finalize mission planning."

Kaz caught up with Laura as they left the conference room.

"Think you'll find more holes?" he asked.

Laura turned to look at him, her gaze shifting from his right eye to his left and back again. "I expect so. If it happened once, then it can happen again. Pretty exciting to be in on discovering something totally new."

"I look forward to hearing what you find. I'm not in the MSC directory yet, so how about I give you my number?"

"Sure."

Kaz pulled out his notepad, copied his new number onto a blank page and carefully tore it out for her.

"At the rate we're looking," she said, "we should know within a couple days."

When she made no move to give him her number in return, Kaz took a chance.

"If you ever want to go flying, I have access to a little plane just west of here. Nice on a sunny day."

Laura looked at him, considering. "That sounds like fun," she said at last. "I'll give you a call on both."

He nodded. "Talk to you then."

Laura smiled at him, then turned and headed down the corridor. Kaz watched her as she strode purposefully away, her thick black hair swaying.

Kaz considered his actions; he wasn't usually so impulsive. He'd been engaged when the accident had happened, but the relationship hadn't survived his recovery, or rather the dark few months when he couldn't see a future path. He'd been careful about romantic entanglements ever since.

But there was something about Laura that he liked.

8

Lubyanka, Moscow

Espionage, like chess, is a game of patience and focus. Carefully move the pieces to ever-stronger positions, endure the setbacks, wait for the opportunities provided by the opponent and then—pounce.

Vitaly Kalugin, a long-term player at the spy game, sat down at his desk, preparing to start his day. Unlike the three men he shared the office with, Vitaly liked a neat desk. Next to his pen stand he kept a low wooden tray for incoming correspondence. He always made sure his outgoing tray was filled with the telexes and reports that he'd read and notated before he went home every night, to be sent on by the office runners to the next names on the lengthy distribution lists. The KGB was the single security agency for the entire Soviet Union, handling both domestic and foreign intelligence and counter-intelligence, while combating dissent and anti-Soviet activities. It made for a lot of reading every day.

He kept his beige phone on his left, where he could hold it and talk while writing with his right hand. An emptied ashtray was on the far right, his matches and cigarettes still in his jacket pocket. Vitaly unlocked his desk, set his lunch box into its deepest drawer, next to the half-empty bottle of Moskovskaya vodka. Irina always sent him to work with piro-zhki stuffed with meat and vegetables, a block of pale Russian cheese and pickled cucumbers or tomatoes. He got a hot lunch at the office stolovaya, but he liked to eat, and the extra food carried him through the long days.

The vodka was reserved for when there was something to celebrate, which there hadn't been for a while.

From the center drawer he retrieved a green baize-covered note-book and set it squarely in front of himself. In his filing cabinet against the wall there were dozens of identical notebooks, KGB-issue, each neatly hand-lettered on the spine with start and end dates. He flipped the current book open to a fresh page, tidily wrote the date in the top right corner, and then flipped back to his previous day's notes, quickly scanning to refresh his memory on the most current issues. He'd set water to boiling and got himself a cup of tea with two sugars, grabbed two pieces of dried cinnamon raisin toast from the communal tin, bal-anced them on the saucer and re-sat to begin working through his new stack of mail.

The KGB translation service was slow, but thorough. They provided a running supply of foreign periodicals and trade journals, and Vitaly was on the internal subscription for several. By the time they were delivered to his desk they were normally a few months out of date, but for his strategic purposes that was fine. They also made interesting read-ing, providing insight into not just what the enemy was doing, but how they explained it to themselves.

He pulled the next mimeographed, stapled bundle from his inbox and saw that it was *Stars and Stripes*, the long-running American mil-itary newspaper. His eyes darted around the paper quickly, hunting for patterns.

The front page was dominated by Vietnam War peace negotiations and US presidential election news. Nothing useful there. Vitaly licked his thumb and forefinger and turned the page, careful not to smudge the cheap ink. A photograph on page two caught his attention. It showed three men in different uniforms standing next to a model of a tall white rocket. The headline read

Military Astronauts — Moonbound!

The United States Air Force and the National Aeronautics and Space Administration today jointly named USAF Lieutenant Colonel Thomas H. Hoffman, USN Lieutenant Michael H. Esdale, and USMC Captain Lucas B. Hemming as the crew for Apollo 18, the last scheduled lunar landing mission.

Hoffman, commander, and Hemming, lunar module pilot, will explore the lunar surface, while Esdale, Command Module pilot, conducts extensive scientific experiments in lunar orbit. Esdale, who has a PhD degree in chemistry, will be the fourth holder of a doctorate to voyage to the Moon. He will also be the first Black astronaut.

Apollo 18 is scheduled for launch in April 1973. Final choice of the landing site has not yet been made. The 12-day mission will continue the emphasis on both lunar surface and lunar orbital science. Lunar surface stay time will be up to 68 hours, and three exploration periods of up to 7 hours each are possible. An Apollo Lunar Surface Experiments Package will be deployed. Mapping of the Moon and several scientific experiments will be continued from lunar orbit. Esdale will leave the spacecraft to retrieve film from cameras in the service module during the trip back to Earth.

Backup crewmen are USAF Major Chad Y. Miller, USN Lieutenant Robert L. Crippen and USMC Captain Robert F. Overmyer.

Vitaly traced the name as he reread it, his brain spinning. *My source is assigned to an Apollo spaceflight!* Kalugin had put the pieces in place more than a decade ago, but to see this news in print was somehow shocking. He took a sip of tea to hide his emotions from his three office mates, his brain racing.

Vitaly Sergeievich Kalugin's source! This was a wild dream he hadn't allowed himself to count on, even when the MOL program had been announced. The insight that they now could get into the actual hardware and operations of the US space program would be unprecedented. And this assignment also meant that his source would rise faster through the officer ranks in their military—several early astronauts were now generals. He'd also be front-of-line for future US spaceflights, including the reusable Space Shuttle their president had recently announced and the Skylab space station.

For the long game, this was a *superb* development. He leaned down to pull his desk drawer open and grabbed the bottle of vodka.

9

Ellington Field, Houston

Kaz and Chad stood next to each other at Ellington Field, the US Air Force base five miles north of the Manned Spacecraft Center. Ellington had been a military airfield since 1917 and was one of the reasons MSC was located in Houston.

Both of the men were wearing sunglasses and heavy black ear protectors against the blowing grit and noise. "What a crazy flying machine!" Kaz yelled. Chad nodded and gave him a thumbs-up. It was Chad's turn to fly the Lunar Landing Training Vehicle next.

It was a Rube Goldberg contraption that someone had once said looked like a flying bedstead. The nickname had stuck. The Bedstead had a jet engine that pointed straight up, and hydrogen peroxide thrusters mounted at all angles on an ungainly aluminum frame. The pilot's seat was open to the air, stuck incongruously on one end like a crane operator's shack. The vehicle had been designed and built in a hurry to train Apollo astronauts on how to land on the Moon, and it looked it. Hovering 200 feet in the air, held up by the raw power of

the downwards-thrusting turbojet, Tom Hoffman was practicing landings, the peroxide jets puffing bursts of smoke to the sides.

Like a nervous dragon, Kaz thought.

They watched as Tom followed the checklist profile, slowing forward speed as he descended, then settling the machine gently on its
four insect legs, jets puffing rapidly, exactly in the center of the painted
target X on the tarmac. This was as close to simulating the Moon's
one-sixth gravity as the NASA engineers and trainers could get.

Tom lifted off again, moving a few hundred yards away, setting up
for another practice run. An Air National Guard F-101 Voodoo interceptor jet noisily took off on the nearby main runway. Both men's eyes
turned to follow it. Pilots like airplanes.

Chad yelled an explanation at Kaz, who had never seen the training
vehicle in action. "Tom's setting the main engine to hold up five-sixths
of the weight now. Then he flies it using just the peroxide thrusters,
which gives it the same feel as the LM on the Moon. It's got close to the
same hand controllers as the LM, and the styrofoam walls block Tom's
view, like the real thing does."

Kaz leaned towards Chad. "How many crashes have they had? Three?"

"Yeah, but no one was hurt—she's got a good bang seat. You probably heard it's zero-zero."

Kaz nodded.

The ejection seat had been designed to save the pilot even if he
pulled the handle at zero altitude and zero airspeed. Most seats in jet
fighters needed forward speed and enough height to allow the parachute to properly inflate.

Tom landed again, bouncing slightly but right on target, and they
could see his hands going through the extra motions needed to shut it
down. The groundcrew, wearing heavy white protective gear, moved in
to safe the systems. They waved the fuel bowser truck in close and reeled
out its hose to refuel. A red USAF fire engine waited 100 feet away, just
in case.

Chad and Kaz took off their ear protectors, glad the noise had stopped. Chad popped his finger in his mouth and then held it up, testing the wind. "Still pretty light. Should be good for my flights too."

Tom walked towards them, his white helmet under his arm. He'd taken off his olive-green torso harness, which clipped solidly into the ejection seat; he was wearing the same all-white flight suit as Chad, made of thick Nomex in case the LLTV caught fire. He'd peeled back his white hood, extra fire protection for the back of his neck. Underneath, he was wearing all-cotton long underwear. It was hot, but a worthwhile precaution. Launch was under 10 weeks away, and even a minor injury could ground him.

They all shook hands.

"Not bad for an old guy, Tom," Chad teased, some edge in his voice. He was a year younger, and his Air Force career had followed Tom's throughout.

"I bounced that last landing a bit," Tom said.

"What's it fly like?" Kaz asked.

"Like you're balancing on top of a broomstick." Tom laughed. "Sort of like a helicopter, but no rotor to give all the cross-coupling and inertial effects. It's actually fairly stable. Until it isn't. In Lunar Sim Mode the jet engine pivots on gimbals, which helps fight wind gusts and keep the thrust vector pure vertical. It gets pretty twitchy. From what the other Apollo guys have said, the real LM is gonna be way smoother." He looked at Chad and smiled. "I'll tell you about it when I get back."

Chad reached into his leg pocket and took out his thin light-brown leather flying gloves. "Yeah, well, now it's the better pilot's turn." He winked at both men, picked up his helmet bag and walked confidently towards the contraption.

"Happy landings," Tom said to his back. For a moment, they both watched Chad, donning his green harness at the base of the yellow ladder.

Tom turned to Kaz. "So. What do you think?"

Kaz guessed what he meant. "I've known both your crewmembers for a long time. Michael comes across a little too informal sometimes, but he knows *Pursuit* inside out. He'll do fine. Luke is super-sharp and will serve you well in *Bulldog*, and outside walking with you on the Moon. Looks to me like everyone's coming along well."

Tom nodded, and held his gaze. He waited a beat. "But?"

They were watching Chad strap himself into the ejection seat.

"But . . . we're still not sure exactly when the Russians are going to launch Almaz, though it's still looking like early April. And we're not sure how high they're going to orbit it, but our best guess is that it'll be low for better camera resolution, and the stripped-down Saturn V can put you there, regardless. Also, we're not at all sure what their Lunokhod rover is doing in the Sea of Serenity. Our intel is lousy inside Moscow Mission Control, but we do know they've added even more layers of security. Which makes us think it's not just another lunar science mission."

Kaz glanced back at Chad, who was working through the steps of bringing the Bedstead back to life. "And we're not sure how long we can keep this quiet. So far the press hasn't caught on that there's anything different about this Apollo mission. But there are lots of people in the know—engineers, scientists, technicians. Heck, even the cleaning staff in the Vehicle Assembly Building must be able to see that you don't have a rover attached this time. Eventually your ugly face will be on the cover of *Newsweek* with a 'Secret Military Apollo Mission' caption. And then the Soviets will be hyper-alert."

Tom thought about it and said, "Add that to the training jerk-around that intercepting Almaz has caused, plus all the last-minute changes with the Moon landing site." He looked at Kaz, his face serious. "I'm not happy about it."

Kaz nodded, commiserating. "Are you getting heat from the Air Force too?" Kaz was well aware that the Pentagon had its own agenda, bolstered by an unassailable sense of self-importance. And, unlike with typical Apollo crews, they felt they could reach out directly to the former MOL astronauts.

"I'm getting phone calls every few days from Washington," Tom admitted. "But our crew secretary is the most polite stonewaller you've ever met. Al has drilled that into all his staff, and it works."

Al was Al Shepard, Chief of the Astronaut Office. One of the original Mercury 7 astronauts, the first American to fly in space, and a man who had walked on the Moon as commander of Apollo 14. He understood external pressures on flight crews like nobody else, and he ran things like the famous Navy Rear Admiral he was.

Kaz persisted. "What's Washington calling you about?"

"Oh, a mix of things. This is a real recruiting moment for the Air Force, especially with the mess in Vietnam. They want me to be the poster boy for their 'Tame the Wild Blue Yonder' advertising campaign." He smiled. "Al's helping me stiff-arm them, so they'll just have to take what they can get from NASA PR." He shook his head slightly. "They're also asking me what I'm going to do afterwards, maybe make me the commandant of the Air Force Academy, or the Test Pilot School at Edwards, though they'd have to promote me. But the truth is, I'd like to stay here if we can swing it. The kids are liking school, and Margaret likes Houston way better than the desert at Edwards. Maybe I'll leave the Air Force and hire on directly with NASA, work on Skylab and the Space Shuttle." He smiled. "Hell, if this flight goes okay, maybe even fly in space again, as a civilian next time."

Kaz nodded. He'd do the same thing in Tom's shoes.

Both men winced at a sudden roar from the Bedstead, and stuck their ear protectors on as Chad brought the jet engine back to life.

10

Manned Spacecraft Center

"Hi, Lieutenant Commander Zemeckis, it's Dr. Woodsworth."

Kaz had been deep in study of Lunar Lander systems, getting ready to support the crew during an upcoming sim, and had picked up his desk phone distractedly when it rang, still staring at the page.

Dr. Woodsworth? Hey, she actually called!

"Good morning, Dr. Woodsworth. Did you find any more holes in the Moon?"

"As a matter of fact, I did. Four so far! Everybody's pretty excited over here in the lab. I thought it might be worth showing you the pictures."

He glanced at his watch. "How about over lunch? Building 3 cafeteria, say, noon?"

Kaz grabbed a tray and walked along the steam line, choosing as he went. He had to admit that looking down at the NASA logo printed on his tray—the famous blue ball with a stylized spacecraft and orbit—gave him a ridiculous level of pleasure that he was actually here in Houston.

As he was paying the cashier, he scanned the tables. Laura, in her white silk blouse and pleated pale-blue skirt, was easy to spot among the male engineers.

"Good to see you, Laura," he said as he unloaded his lunch on the table she'd chosen by the window and set his tray on an empty chair. "Thanks for making time on short notice."

"A girl's gotta eat," she said.

She handed him the folder of pictures she'd brought, and picked up her sandwich.

He scanned them one by one. "The holes look so similar."

"Yes, that's a surprise to us as well. They all seem to be made the same way, but we haven't figured out how." She pointed to the one he was studying. "Notice that there's no ejecta around the hole, so they weren't made by impact."

Kaz spooned a mouthful of his soup, nodding. "Do you have a map that shows exactly where these are?"

"I thought you'd never ask." From the 3-ring binder next to her she unclipped a printed page, spun it around and set it beside the photos.

"The green triangles are the Apollo landing sites. The red ones are the Russian Luna landers. The yellows are where our unmanned Surveyor probes are." She touched a red fingernail to each. "And the black hand-drawn squares are the locations of the holes."

One of them was not too far from where Apollo 17 had landed. "Is that as close to the 17 site as it looks? Did the crew see anything?"

"It's many tens of miles from the farthest point the crew reached in the rover. Too bad we hadn't spotted these before they went."

She took a bite while she waited for Kaz to ask the obvious question.

"How close is it to where 18 is scheduled to land?"

"Close enough that Tom and Luke could maybe check it out if we give them enough time on the surface." She looked up at him. "Are we going to give them enough time?"

Kaz looked around pointedly at the lunchtime crowd. "That's up to the DoD to disclose, if and when they decide to. Sorry."

Laura stared at him for several seconds, and then shrugged. "We can wait." Then she smiled. "We're geologists."

Kaz decided it was time to change the subject. "What brought you to NASA?"

For a moment she hesitated, then met his eye. "I want to be an astronaut. And this place is astronaut mecca." She paused for a moment, clearly considering what more she would say. "I was still an undergrad when Kennedy made his Moon speech. I knew that girls weren't allowed to be fighter pilots, but I figured that other skills would be needed on the Moon too. While there are still no women in the astronaut corps, the fact that Dr. Schmitt flew on Apollo 17 shows I'm at least half-right."

Kaz knew that Schmitt, a geologist, had been selected in a new category of scientist-astronaut in 1965. He listened to the undercurrent of fierceness in her voice as she continued.

"Valentina Tereshkova flew in space solo for three days a decade ago. She showed that women can perform as well as men. The 1964 Civil Rights Act gives us legal protection against sex discrimination, so eventually NASA is going to be recruiting female astronauts. I intend to be one of them." She smiled then, and raised her eyebrows at him. "Well, you asked!"

Kaz knew what she was feeling. He'd been driven by the desire to fly in space ever since Gagarin and Al Shepard had opened the door in 1961. It was the main reason he'd gone to Test Pilot School, and only the accident had stopped his trajectory. But Laura was the first woman he'd met who felt as passionately as he did about the idea, or at least the first who'd told him about it.

He said, "It's been over a year since Nixon announced the new Space Shuttle. I understand it'll have a crew of seven, and I think I remember him saying 'men *and women* with work to do in space' in his speech.

Bound to take longer than they're predicting, but I bet that's your chance. And I'd vote for you."

"I'll take all the help I can get," she said, and laughed.

"Jack Schmitt had to learn to pilot NASA jets before they'd let him fly on Apollo," Kaz added. "And it looks like the Shuttle is going to be more of a pilot's machine than Apollo capsules ever were. Have you done much flying?"

Laura looked rueful. "Not yet. I got some scholarships, but I still had to pay my own way through nine years at UCLA. I've started flying lessons here, but they're expensive. And with all the Apollo missions back to back, there hasn't been much time."

"Don't forget I asked you to go flying. The house I'm renting comes with a little Cessna trainer in the garage, which my landlord is happy for me to fly. The street at the end of my driveway doubles as the run-way. I'd be glad to take you up."

Laura's gaze involuntarily flicked from his good eye to his glass one and back. She realized what she was doing, and looked down.

"Let's tackle this issue of me only having one eye," he said, not wanting to embarrass her, but also wanting it out of the way. "I've been flying with the Navy since college, fighters and test, and NASA's letting me into the back seat of the T-38s sometimes. You can trust me to fly a Cessna. We can go over all the basics you're getting in flight school."

Laura looked intently at him, then she nodded. "That's really kind of you. I'd love to."

Kaz checked his watch and glanced out the window. The weather was still good. No time like the present. "Sunset's a little after six these days. Got time for a flight right after work? Leave here, maybe, 4:30?"

"Today?" Laura said, but it didn't take her long to decide. "Where do you and the Cessna live?"

He had just turned the plane around in the hangar entrance when he spotted a white VW convertible Bug slowing to cross the cattle gate.

Wiping his hands on a rag, he watched as it shifted quickly up through all four gears on the straightaway, and then braked hard and turned smartly into his driveway. He waved at Laura to park to one side, pantomiming how the plane was going to roll out.

He smiled. *Scientists do love Volkswagens!*

As he watched her climb out of the car, Kaz saw that Laura had knocked off work early too, as she was now wearing bell-bottom jeans. He suddenly realized he was nervous, and that it had been a while since he'd felt that way.

"Found you!" she said. "I've never been out this way before."

"Glad you did." He glanced at his watch. "We have about an hour until sunset, so let's get flying. No lights on the runway here," he said, waving at the road, "so we need to land before it gets too dark."

"It's a taildragger," Laura said, as they walked around the plane, which was resting on its tailwheel with the nose sticking up into the air. "I've only ever flown planes with nose wheels."

"These have some advantages—the tailwheel acts like an anchor to keep you straight, especially landing on grass, and you don't carry the extra weight of a big, heavy wheel up front. Though you need to use your feet more on the rudder pedals."

They climbed in their respective side doors, and Kaz showed her where the release was to slide the seat forward. He was conscious of every movement of his hands as he helped her retrieve and attach the dangling shoulder strap, happy to be so close to her in the cockpit. He verbalized everything he was doing as he coasted down the driveway, started the engine, checked key instruments and lined up for takeoff.

He looked at her as she reached to touch the oil pressure and temperature instruments with her fingertip.

"Ready to go?"

She looked around the instrument panel methodically, finding and focusing on the airspeed, altitude and tachometer. "All set!"

Kaz nodded, then smoothly pushed the throttle all the way in and they began to roll. As the tires left the pavement, he glanced across at

her. Her face was alive with delight, eyes darting around the instruments and outside as the ground fell away.

The early-evening air was smooth, and he turned towards MSC,
leveled off and talked Laura through the basics of piloting the Cessna.
Then he let go, saying, "You have control."

She sat rigidly erect, focusing straight ahead. Kaz had her do some
gentle turns, and her posture relaxed slightly. He pointed out the
Spacecraft Center, and then Seabrook and Kemah as they crossed
the Galveston Bay shoreline.

"Want to do something fun and beautiful?"

She looked wide-eyed. "Sure."

"I have the aircraft." Kaz lowered the nose to pick up speed, and then
smoothly pulled hard up and to the right until they were looking down
the wing at the water, with airspeed slowed to bare flying speed. The
plane's nose gently followed the arc back down, and he reversed and did
the same thing in the other direction. The contrast between the noisy
rush of the dive and pull-up accentuated the ensuing grace and quiet as
they floated over the top. He did one more turn to the right, Laura
looking straight down out her side window at the dark waters of the bay.

She turned to him. "That's wonderful! Like a falling leaf!"

He nodded. "It's called a chandelle. Really reminds you that you're
flying."

He leveled off and let go of the controls. "All yours again. Let's reverse
and head back."

As she turned west, Kaz lowered the windscreen visors against the
sun on the horizon. The basic aerobatics had made him extra-aware of
his senses, as they always did, releasing a liberating feeling of three-
dimensional freedom. He leaned to point at MSC with his chin, his
shoulder touching hers in the small cockpit.

"Nobody down there got to experience that."

She followed his gaze, and didn't lean away. "We're lucky. Thanks for
asking me to go flying with you."

"Hey, you're the one flying!"

11

Simferopol, Soviet Ukraine

In the time of primordial hell, an ancient star, burning hotter and hotter as it ran out of fuel, suddenly exploded in a blinding, cataclysmic supernova. This enormous burst of energy was unleashed as a shockwave, rippling out into the galaxy now called the Milky Way. The unfathomably powerful waves pulsed through primal clouds of hydrogen and helium, scattering and pushing them together like flotsam on an interstellar ocean.

For the next 100 million years, these clouds were pulled into ever-bigger clumps by their tiny forces of gravity—an agonizingly slow ballet of gentle drifting and spinning and gathering into denser regions. The near-endless molecules of hydrogen and helium, colliding with higher and higher force, began to heat up and glow in what was becoming a central protostar. And somewhere around 4.6 billion years ago, the pressures and temperatures got to a critical level; atoms were crushed in on themselves, binding energies were released, and thermonuclear fusion suddenly began.

Let there be light.

What that brand-new Sun illuminated was a huge, swirling flat disk of the rubble of space—gas and dust and rocky remnants of previous

stellar explosions—all orbiting and collecting ever faster in the blackness. Far from the Sun, the low temperatures allowed volatile com-
pounds to stay frozen, as ice. They collided endlessly and joined into
ever-increasing lumps, gradually coalescing into the gas giant planets:
Jupiter, Saturn, Uranus and Neptune.

Closer to the Sun, though, the radiant heat turned the icy lumps
into comets with tails, vaporizing the frozen gases. Countless rocks
remained, crashing into each other, building larger and larger proto-
planets. Some asteroids were a dense mix of rocks and metal, while
others, from farther out, were lumpy balls of rubble held together by
frozen water. One by one, over millions of years, they looped and collided, settling into the winners of this stellar game of billiards—the
inner rocky planets Mercury, Venus, Mars and Earth.

But the massive gravitational pull of the two biggest planets, Jupiter
and Saturn, caused resonance and disruption. They yanked rocks from
the asteroid belt and the farthest regions of the outer Kuiper Belt, some
the size of the inner planets, and slung them in unstable orbits towards
the Sun. The resulting collisions were hugely powerful.

Earth was just a semi-molten ball of spinning rock, repeatedly bom-
barded by asteroids, ever growing in size. Over time the onslaught
lessened, as the debris diminished. But the biggest was saved for last.

On a normal day in the young planet's life, 4.5 billion years ago, it
was struck like never before. A planet the size of Mars, traveling at
9,000 miles per hour, slammed into the Earth.

The rock and ice of this attacker were violently plunged deep into
the Earth's mantle, forever merging the two planets into one. It spun the
Earth like a top, leaving it whipping around so fast that each day was just
five hours long. The flying debris of the impact splashed high into near
space, then fell back again as a rain of molten rock over the whole surface. But the inertia of the impactor was so high that great globs of itself,
and of the Earth, were thrown all the way into orbit. A ring of debris,
orbiting the planet, rapidly collected into one molten ball 2,000 miles
across, glowing in the night sky.

The Earth now had a Moon.

And inside that Moon, an untold wealth of minerals rose, sank and churned as it cooled.

"What's that?" Gabdul's navigator tapped Lunokhod's navigation camera screen with a fingertip. "There, to the left."

They both leaned close to the frozen image on the small black-and-white screen. Gabdul had commanded Lunokhod to stop.

He moved his head back and forth, trying to decipher the grainy image. "It looks like a rock and its shadow."

The navigator grunted. "I agree." He glanced at the rest of the science team, who nodded. "Give me a minute to replot you a course, and let's go have a look."

For moving around the surface they relied on three low-res TV cameras, but Lunokhod also had four high-resolution cams and one ultraviolet photometer, a photodetector, an X-ray spectrometer and radiation detectors. It even had a penetrometer to slam into the ground to measure for hardness.

It might be fun to bash this rock!

The navigator flicked through his well-worn orbital images of the area, including some brand-new photographs taken by Apollo 15 and 17, gleaned from an international planetary exploration conference in Moscow a few weeks earlier; an American scientist had unwittingly given the images and a Defense Mapping Agency lunar topographic chart to a senior Lunokhod engineer. The new detail was superb, and added to the navigator's confidence in telling Gabdul where to steer. He quickly laid out the route to get to a good science-gathering position near the rock, and then turned it into a sequence of operator commands.

Gabdul rehearsed the movements briefly, nodded to himself, positioned the hand controller to the side and pushed the command button. After six seconds he released, and they all stared at the monitor, waiting for the image to refresh.

The dark rock was now centered in the field of view. After the navigator nodded to him, Gabdul drove straight ahead, then checked the image again. He repeated the maneuver three times, until the rock was in perfect position at the bottom of the high-mounted navigation camera screen, then sent the command to switch to the lower panoramic cameras.

The team was used to the long pause between each command and the return image. It was part of their regular rhythm, a time to discuss what they were seeing, like dissecting the magic trick before the magician pulled the rabbit out of the hat. They hashed over why the rock was a different color than the surrounding regolith. Perhaps it had been dropped there somehow.

The assistant navigator laughed. "Maybe it's an alien turd!" The group chuckled, and then the new view appeared.

The two lower cameras, set apart like human eyes, gave a stereoscopic sense of depth. Looking closely, the navigator rejudged the distance and gave another command. Gabdul carefully moved the joystick, and Lunokhod rolled forward another meter and a half.

When the image updated, the navigator grunted, "Perfect!" He sat back, his job complete.

The science team swung into action. They recorded the imagery from the cameras onto videotape, and captured the data flowing down from the photometers on paper strip charts. So far no surprises: a rock, like many others.

Next, they sent commands to the RIFMA-M X-ray spectrometer, mounted low, like an insect's mandibles, under Lunokhod's front end. Its door pivoted open, uncovering small samples of radioactive tungsten and zirconium that unleashed an invisible cone of alpha and beta particles onto the Moon's surface. The focused spotlight excited mineral elements in the rock, causing each atom to release fluorescent X-rays. The return sensor sent these complex electronic signals across the void to the team in Simferopol, who saw them as distinct frequency lines on an oscilloscope. They ran a hard copy of the data so they could look closely at the rock's unique signature. They saw mostly magnesium, aluminum, silicon, some others—the proportions were a bit odd, but it was similar enough to other rocks.

Gabdul shrugged. "How about the magnetometer?" he asked, and got the thumbs-up.

At his command, a long, spindly pole that stuck out the top of Lunokhod slowly pivoted down until it was just a few inches above the rock, the small cross-shaped device on its end detecting the strength and direction of any local magnetic field. Again, none of the readings were out of the ordinary.

The lead scientist rubbed her hands together, readying for the next test. She truly loved this. It was the ultimate fieldwork, learning about a piece of the Moon that no human eyes had ever seen before today, the kind of pure exploration she'd been fantasizing about ever since she began her geology studies at Moscow University. So many papers were going to be written about what her team was discovering, and she would be co-author on them all. She'd get to attend international conferences, maybe even travel to America.

She kept her voice calm, as expected by the team. "Let's see what the Geiger counter can show us."

She watched as the heavy Geiger counter pivoted into position above the rock. *We couldn't have done this on Venus*, she thought. Only the Moon's one-sixth gravity allowed the weight of the sensor to be supported by such a delicate pole.

They maneuvered it incrementally closer, until she called, "That's enough! Let's power it up."

Her technician sent the command, all eyes fixed on the gauge as they waited the 10 seconds for a return signal.

Nothing. No radioactivity.

She frowned. "That's wrong. There's guaranteed to be background radiation at least. Send the command again."

This time the signal got through. The needle jumped to near full scale on the gauge. Her eyes widened. "Bozha moy!" she exclaimed. A rush of excitement coursed through her whole body. "It's radioactive!"

12

Ellington Field, Houston

"Is my hysterical palm tree ready?"

The ops desk clerk looked up at Tom Hoffman's grinning face. As a fighter pilot, Tom had long held helicopters in low-level contempt. To him, only the fact that he was going to walk on the Moon, and in order to do that he needed to practice landings in this backup training machine, made becoming a part-time helo pilot tolerable.

"Sure is, Tom." The ops clerk handed him the thick Bell 47G aircraft sign-out book: its daily certification of flight readiness. Tom scanned the completed maintenance actions, saw nothing new and scrawled his signature against the date. Then he retrieved his helmet and gloves from the counter, and stepped out onto the flight ramp at Ellington Field.

The sky was dotted with puffy cumulus clouds, winds were out of the south, and the March sun was surprisingly hot. The fishbowl—the enclosed full-bubble plexiglas canopy of the helo—was going to be scorching. Tom was glad he'd stopped for an extra drink at the water fountain.

The aircraft tech rolled a large red fire extinguisher close to the helicopter, a safety measure at every engine start. Tom dropped his helmet on the right seat, donned his gloves and did a quick walkaround. In the distance, he could see Luke taking his turn in the Bedstead, and he decided he'd fly over there and watch for a bit.

Tom climbed into the left seat, strapped into the four-point harness, put on his helmet and plugged in his comm cord. He pulled the checklist out of his leg pocket and quickly ran through the pre-start. He circled a raised finger at the groundcrew, started the engine and then checked all systems. Satisfied, he gave a salute, and watched the tech roll the fire extinguisher clear.

Tom took one last close look around the instrument panel—he still found flying helicopters unnatural and liked to be extra careful—then radioed Ellington Ground for taxi clearance. With that, he began the pilot's dance that makes helicopters fly.

In his left hand was the throttle. When he twisted it, like you would a motorcycle grip, the engine revved up. The Bell 47G only had 175 horsepower; with that little motor driving the two big spinning rotor blades overhead, it was all too easy to demand too much and over-torque the mechanical system.

The throttle was mounted on the end of a short pole, hinged at the far end. When he raised his hand, it changed the angle that the rotor blades above his head were biting into the air, making them lift harder. It was a simple, intuitive design—pull up, go up; push down, go down. Because it moved both rotor blades together, it was called the collective. Tom raised and lowered it once with the motor at idle, to make sure it was moving freely.

In his right hand, Tom held what looked and felt like the control stick in an airplane. Moving it around changed the angle of the rotor blades individually, to allow him to tip the helicopter forward and back, and to roll it left and right. Since the stick cycled each rotor blade through a full circle, it was called the cyclic. When he'd first seen the word, he'd pronounced it wrong, and had to learn to say it correctly. *Sigh-click*.

By pushing on the rudder pedals at his feet, he operated the small propeller mounted on the end of the long tail boom. It provided enough sideways force to counteract the spin of the main rotors, and let him fly in a straight line.

Tom took one last look around to make sure no one was near, and started raising the collective while twisting the throttle for more power. As the rotor blades lifted the helicopter's skids off the pavement, he pushed with his left foot to keep from turning. His right hand moved the cyclic constantly, to keep perfectly level. It had taken a lot of practice with a patient instructor to learn how to hover, but now, with concentration, Tom was good at it.

He moved the helicopter clear of the ramp and switched radio frequencies. "Ellington Tower, this is NASA 948. I'd like to head over to observe the LLTV, and then work east of the field for thirty minutes or so."

"Copy, 948, cleared as requested, no traffic in the pattern."

Tom clicked his mic button twice in acknowledgment, turned right and made a beeline straight at Luke, who was just lifting off in the LLTV, setting up for another practice lunar landing.

"Luke, Tom here in the fishbowl. Okay if I stay off to the side and watch?"

"Sure, Tom. I'm going to be doing normal patterns."

Tom maneuvered downwind so that his rotor wash wouldn't disrupt Luke's air. As Luke went through the landing profile, Tom mirrored the actions in his helo. On the real Moon landing, it would be him flying the LM, with Luke on his right, assisting.

Luke touched down smoothly.

Tom pushed his comm switch. "Not bad, for a Marine."

"Thanks, Boss."

"If you need any senior officer advice, just call. I'm headed east."

"Roger that. Happy motoring."

Tom chuckled. Just before he accelerated away towards Galveston Bay, he spotted Kaz standing where he had a good view of Luke's training session. Tom nodded to him, and got a thumbs-up in response.

Under him now were hundreds of acres of cow pasture just east of Ellington Field. A good place to fly and not bother anybody, apart from some Texas longhorns. He climbed to 1,000 feet, bouncing in turbulence as the heat of the day roiled up the air, conscious of the sweat trickling down his sides. In the real LM, the guidance computers would automatically bring him close to the Moon's surface. He'd take manual control 500 feet up, at 40 miles per hour, and 2,000 feet back from the landing site. They called it Low Gate, and he maneuvered the helo to set those conditions. Looking ahead, he chose a lone cow in an open area as his planned landing site.

The helicopter was shaking quite a bit now in the unsteady air, and Tom fought it to get the parameters set right. He pulled slightly on the collective to slow his descent, and eased back on the cyclic to set 40 miles per hour forward speed. His feet were playing the rudder pedals constantly to keep him pointed straight at the cow. He cross-checked speed and altitude, and spoke aloud the words he or Luke would say.

"Houston, *Bulldog*, 500 feet, down at"—he checked his vertical speed again—"15." He released slightly on the collective to descend and eased forward on the cyclic, eyes now fixed on the cow, 2,000 feet ahead.

There was a sudden, surprisingly violent jolt of turbulence, like he'd hit an air pocket, and Tom felt the helicopter rapidly fall. "Damn!" This was messing up his approach—there wouldn't be any downdrafts on the Moon. He pushed forward aggressively on the cyclic to hold forward speed.

It was the instinctive move of a high-time jet pilot, but entirely the wrong thing to do in a helicopter, a rookie mistake.

The linkage that connected Tom's right hand to the spinning rotor blade was complicated. The cyclic stick was attached to a series of hinges and pushrods, running down under his feet, up behind his back and out through the top of the fishbowl. It connected above the motor to a horn that protruded from the spinning main drive shaft, which was attached, via pitch control rods, up to the rotors. As Tom pushed on the cyclic, it pushed up on the horn, tipping the base mechanism to change the angle of the rotors.

But what Tom thought was turbulence had actually been a pitch rod holding nut, improperly tightened, working itself loose. The vibration and centrifugal forces had combined to undo the nut faster and faster, until it had come off completely, instantaneously disconnecting the pitch rod from that blade. With no more control, the rotor blade had gone flat, suddenly dropping the amount of lift it was providing to zero.

Tom's helicopter was now held aloft by just one of the spinning blades.

As Tom pushed forward hard on the cyclic and pulled on the collective, the remaining blade dug in hard, creating bone-shaking vibration, but also far too much force on the airframe. The torque brought the nose down faster than the big blades could follow as the long tail boom pivoted rapidly up. In an instant, the whirling blades struck the tail, their tips going 650 feet per second, slamming into the drive shaft of the tail rotor. It couldn't stand the impact and sheared off.

Tom felt the helicopter start to spin. The little Franklin engine kept churning out full horsepower as Tom maxed the throttle, torquing against the still-turning blades, spinning the fuselage up faster and faster. But the Bell 47G suddenly had no lift, and no directional control. It fell from 500 feet like a whirling one-ton stone. Tom's hands were still on the controls, demanding more lift, his feet on the pedals trying to counter the spin, as the broken remains of his helicopter slammed into the empty, hard pastureland. At impact, it was going 200 miles per hour, straight down.

He'd been flying for only 11 minutes, and the helicopter's two bulbous gas tanks were near full. The crash broke them free of their mounts, spraying the 80/87 aviation fuel over the hot motor in a mist. The mist instantly caught fire, and it spread to the ruptured tanks.

Tom was still strapped into his seat, his body already badly broken by the force of the impact, when the helicopter exploded into flame.

13

Ellington Field

Luke was the first to see the plume of heavy black smoke rising from the direction Tom had flown. But by the time he got on the radio to report it, the senior tower controller was already on the phone with the Ellington crash response team, and his deputy was calling Harris County Fire.

The rural crash site made access difficult. The base's responders drove to the eastern end of the airfield, unlocked a large gate and bumped cross-country towards the smoke. The Harris County fire trucks, sirens wailing, tacked towards the crash along graveled oil well access routes. Both teams had to cut barbed-wire cattle fences to get close. The Ellington crew arrived first, but it had taken them 14 minutes. By then the fuel had mostly burned off and the cattle had scattered to the field's edge, where they stood aligned, looking on, puzzled and alarmed.

Tom's helicopter had hit the ground upright, but the force of the impact had collapsed the landing skid on one side, so the aircraft was tipped on an angle. The rotors had broken at their central shaft, and now lay in a big inverted V across the wreckage. The tail boom was a twisted mess, like an electricity tower that had crumpled and fallen over.

Orange flame still licked around the charred central block of the
engine and transmission. The heat had torched the surrounding grass-
land, and the Ellington firefighters sprayed the site with water from
their truck, then crept closer. One of the Ellington crew jumped out to
use a portable extinguisher on the remaining flames, and then the fire
crew chief and his senior medic approached the cockpit.

Tom's body was still slumped in place, held by the Nomex shoulder
belts. His fire-retardant flight suit was only charred, and his blackened
helmet was still on his head. The crew chief moved closer. What he saw
inside the helmet made him quickly turn away.

The Harris County fire crew rolled up just as the Ellington medic
was checking Tom's body for vital signs. She looked up and shook her
head at both crews. With no one to rescue, the urgent pace slowed and
the two fire chiefs refocused their attention on maintaining the crash
site for the accident investigators and awaiting the county coroner.

After calling the fire crews, the tower controller had next called NASA
Ops, and the ops chief had scrambled a pickup truck with airframe
techs to head to the scene. Luke had quickly landed the LLTV and
come to stand, stunned, beside Kaz, each of them hoping for the best
and fearing the worst. Kaz flagged down the NASA pickup on the way
past, and he and Luke clambered into the back.

Luke looked ahead at the diminishing black plume, and then at Kaz.
Holding on as the truck bounced over the uneven ground, Kaz yelled
over the noise, "What did you see?"

"Only the smoke."

Kaz nodded. They were both test pilots. Fatal crashes were a frequent
part of the profession, which made understanding why one happened
all-important. It also gave them something to focus on, which helped
them deal with the personal tragedy and grief. "No use speculating until
we know more," Kaz said. "Hopefully Tom's there to tell us."

"Shit, Kaz, we're only a month from launch."

Kaz somberly held up crossed fingers.

The lack of action at the crash site told them the story before they'd even parked. The Ellington fire chief walked over to their truck, his face grave.

"The pilot was killed, I'm sorry to say. Because we're off the base and on county land, I need you to stay clear until the police get here." They heard a siren in the far distance. "That'll be them now."

Kaz, as senior rank present, turned to the NASA ops chief. "We need to get word right away to the Astronaut Office Chief, Center Director, Air Force Liaison Office, NASA HQ." He glanced at Luke and briefly held his gaze. "And Tom's family. Can I use your radio?"

They gathered in the Astronaut Office conference room, on the third floor of Building 4 at the Spacecraft Center. Every available astronaut was there, whether NASA or MOL, along with Gene Kranz and Dr. McKinley. Since Kaz had been at the crash site, Al Shepard asked him to speak first.

He took a deep breath. "As you've all heard, Tom Hoffman was killed this morning in a solo helo crash just east of Ellington. Luke and I were at the crash site twenty minutes after it happened, and could see no obvious cause.

"Luke is Tom's designated Casualty Assistance Calls Officer, so he's gone to the Hoffman house to stay with Margaret. I asked Doc McKinley to be here to speak to us, as he's just been out to the site and talked with the county coroner." Kaz nodded at JW.

"The coroner's report will take a day or two, but there's no doubt it was the impact that killed him. His back and neck were both broken, and it happened quick." JW looked around, making eye contact. "There was a subsequent fire, but Tom was already gone."

Several heads nodded. Death was new to no one in the room, and they all preferred to hear that it happened fast. They feared fire. When the Apollo 1 crew had burned to death in a plugs-out simulation six years previously, it had shaken everyone to the core.

Gene Kranz spoke up. "Gentlemen, this is a horrible day. We need to figure out why one of our training helicopters killed Tom, but we also have a launch scheduled for April 16. It's a miserable thing, and I hate it, but the brutal truth is that this is why we have backup crews."

He looked around the room for Al Shepard. "Management is extra-complex for Apollo 18, but we need a decision ASAP as to how the crews are going to be changed. As soon as that happens, we need to be ready to sprint."

Shepard nodded, and Kranz drove his point home. "We need to get the new crew assigned, and then this whole center needs to work day and night to turn them into the team that will leave Earth for the Moon in thirty-one days."

As the meeting broke up, Al Shepard gathered six of the astronauts in his office. After he closed the door, he said, "Guys, we have a lot to do, but let's have thirty seconds of silence to honor Tom Hoffman."

Some bowed their heads in prayer, and others stared into the distance. Kaz found himself painfully thinking about telling Tom that his face would be on a magazine cover. Not now, it wouldn't.

Shepard raised his head. "Thanks, fellas," he said, as they all turned to face him. He started to count points off on his fingers. "We've already kicked off the accident investigation, and we'll need an astronaut on that. I'm designating you, Bean"—Al Bean, a moonwalker on Apollo 12, nodded—"as you were in on Cernan's investigation." Astronaut Gene Cernan had survived a helicopter crash two years previously while flying too low at Cape Canaveral. Bean had helped dig out the cause of the accident while maintaining Cernan's astronaut career. Shepard had appreciated it.

He touched a second finger. "Luke's with Tom's family, but as of today I need him to focus on nothing but Apollo 18, so, Kaz, I'm asking you to take over as CACO."

Kaz said, "Will do."

A third finger. "Gene was right. We need a new crew roster for 18, and we need it now. We've done the same thing after other training crashes, and after the Apollo 1 fire, and when TK was grounded for 13."

Astronaut TK Mattingly had been inadvertently exposed to the measles three days before launch, and his place on Apollo 13 had been taken at the last minute by his backup, Jack Swigert.

"The MOL astronauts don't really work for me," Shepard said, "but I'm sure Washington and the Air Force are going to listen to what I recommend." He looked first at Chad Miller and then at Michael Esdale. "This close to launch, it's gonna be easier on everyone if we don't do a full crew swap. So my call is that Luke and Michael are still the crew, and the commander of Apollo 18 will now be Chad."

Chad's face remained impassive, but Kaz could see the rush of excitement in his eyes. All the new commander said to Shepard was "Thanks, Al."

"At my direction, the training team is already revamping the flow from here to launch," Shepard said, "to make sure Chad, Luke and Michael get exactly what they need. The helos will be grounded for a while, but otherwise we'll carry on with training and sims. The crew goes to the Cape on April 26, so that gives us"—all 13 eyes turned to look at the wall calendar—"ten days here at MSC." He looked at each man individually. "Any questions?"

They were military men. A death had occurred, they had acknowledged the loss, and now they had their new orders. They all shook their heads.

"All right then," Shepard said. "Let's get Apollo 18 ready to fly."

14

Timber Cove, Houston

"How do you want to handle this, Kaz?"

JW was in the passenger seat of the Satellite, thumbing through the folder of papers that Tom Hoffman had filed with the Astronaut Office in case of death.

Kaz took a deep breath and exhaled slowly. "I'll take the lead. We need to free up Luke to get back to work, make sure that Margaret is coping as well as can be expected—a big reason I asked you to come with me—and answer any questions she has about what happened and what's going on."

JW nodded, still scanning through the folder. "I've met Margaret a few times, and seen her boy and girl once when they came to the clinic." He looked across at Kaz, his face grim. "A lousy day."

Kaz turned off NASA Road 1 onto Kirby, and arced right on Old Kirby Road. The astronauts all tended to live in the three new waterfront neighborhoods that had been developed when the Spacecraft Center was built. The Hoffmans had chosen Timber Cove, and their snug cinderblock bungalow fronted on Taylor Lake. Kaz parked at the side of the road under some live oak trees, noting Luke's car in the driveway behind Margaret's station wagon.

They rang the doorbell, and Luke answered. The house was quiet and dimly lit. He led them into the living room, where the large bay window faced the brown bayou waters of the lake. The furnishings reflected the life the Air Force had given Tom: mismatched but comfortable sofa and chairs, a blond chestnut side table and folding screen from a tour in Okinawa, walls hung with smiling pictures of flying and family. A large mahogany stereo hi-fi and TV was against the paneled wall. Sitting on it was a wedding photo of Margaret in white and Tom in ROTC blues, the two of them young and laughing, ducking under an arch of raised swords.

Margaret was seated on the sofa, staring across the lake. Her eyes were red, but she wasn't crying now. She had her arms around her two children, who were tucked as close as they could get to her. The elder child, a girl, was crying quietly. The little boy was asleep. Margaret didn't seem to notice Kaz and JW come in.

Luke silently waved them into the kitchen.

He refilled the kettle. "I had Michael Esdale's wife, Dorothy, get the kids from school; she's standing by to come back as soon as Margaret's ready. I've been answering the phone and the door—all neighbors offering help. Word travels fast. Margaret's held together pretty well. I didn't tell her any specifics. Just that his helo had crashed, and he didn't make it." He got two mugs out of the paneled cupboard, and set a Nescafé freeze-dried coffee jar next to them. "Help yourself."

JW spooned out the crystals and when the kettle boiled, he poured, handing a mug to Kaz.

"Al doesn't want to shake up the whole crew," Kaz said after a small silence. "Chad's your new commander."

Luke nodded. "It makes sense. Minimizes the impact on the mission." He looked bleakly at the two men. "But he ain't no Tom Hoffman."

Kaz nodded. "They asked me to take over as CACO so you can get back to training." He paused. "You okay with that? Do you think Margaret will be?"

Luke shrugged. "When Tom asked me to be CACO, we never thought . . ." His voice broke. He turned away, and took two deep breaths. Then he said, "Right. If we're still going to the Moon, I'll need to get back to work. Let's go tell Margaret."

The March weather had turned to match the mood of the day, with low gray clouds moving in from the Gulf of Mexico. By dinnertime, it was raining steadily, with occasional downpours as waves of thicker clouds passed overhead. The fat raindrops made a continuous metallic din on the tin roof of the U-Joint, a background hum to the after-work wake that had gathered to honor Tom Hoffman.

The NASA Manned Spacecraft Center was a type of factory. It took in the strange raw materials of human dreams, ingenuity and tenacity, ran them through a labor-intensive assembly line of development, testing and training, and spat out astronauts and their support teams, ready for spaceflight. Regular as clockwork, best in the world.

When an accident happened, the assembly line slammed to a stop. It took internal inspections and tests to get the machinery running again, and while that was happening, the factory workers, with all their skills and creativity, were at loose ends.

The U-Joint's wet grass parking lot was filled with cars. Inside, there was a natural pecking order: Apollo space fliers sat at the tables, and junior engineers took the standing room out of respect for the astronauts' willingness to take risks.

The Apollo 18 crew, Chad, Luke and Michael, sat at their own table, the fourth chair empty. The three of them hadn't paid for any of their drinks; Janie just kept bringing them, all on the house.

Chad leaned towards the other two, elbows on the table, chin on his crossed hands. Despite the horrific circumstances, today was the start of his command, and he and these men were about to do something intensely dangerous and demanding together. He allowed himself a small smile and, attempting the first step towards a new relationship, said, "When did I first meet you two assholes, anyway?"

Michael let himself chuckle. "Pax River. Luke and I were still at Test Pilot School, and you and Tom were the Air Force hotshots who'd just been selected for the MOL program. You'd come to brief our class."

Luke looked up from the beer rings he'd been contemplating. "I think, to be accurate, we met at the Green Door." It was the Navy's equivalent of the U-Joint, a country bar in Southern Maryland, a favorite of the test pilots there. "Quite a legendary night, if I recall."

"Yeah, you're right. I remember now." Chad's tight smile faded. "Tom was there that night, with us—and he always will be."

The swinging doors banged open as Kaz and JW came in out of the rain, soaked, stomping their feet.

Chad waved a hand and pointed to the empty spot at the table. JW looked at Kaz questioningly, who by way of answer grabbed a chair off the stack by the jukebox and carried it over his head. Janie spotted them while bringing another round for the table, and stopped to add two whiskies, a beer and a coffee to her tray.

Luke spoke first after they got settled. "How are things with Margaret?"

"About what you'd expect. Dorothy's with her now." Kaz sipped his beer, looking around. "A good crowd."

Chad nodded. "Time to say something." He pushed his chair back and climbed up onto it, glass in hand. The room quickly hushed, all eyes turning to the lone figure on his chair. Someone turned down the sad song on the jukebox.

"Everyone charge their glasses, because today we lost one of our own." Chad turned his head slowly. "Look around. The walls of this place are covered with our history, and our heroes. Some made it to space, some even walked on the Moon. And many died trying. Spaceflight is hard, and it demands our best. Sometimes, even that isn't good enough. This morning we lost a friend, a test pilot, a husband and father, and a damned fine astronaut on his way to the Moon."

JW caught Chad's eye. He was still carrying Tom's folder, and he pulled a glossy eight-by-ten NASA portrait out of it and passed it up to Chad.

Chad held the photo above his head for all to see, saying, "Let's honor Tom Hoffman." He climbed down from his perch and headed for the wall reserved for the astronauts who had died. He found a space and carefully fixed the picture in place, stealing a couple of thumbtacks from the other photos. He raised his glass to Tom's portrait and said, quietly, "The Apollo 18 crew resolves that we will do our damnedest to make you proud."

He turned back to the crowd. "Ladies and gentlemen, we drink to a man gone too soon. So his loss will not be in vain, let's also drink to my crew's success on Apollo 18." He paused. "To Tom Hoffman!"

The room erupted in a toast that echoed from person to person.

Chad was too far away to notice the small tics of reaction on the faces of his two crew at his use of the word "my."

There was a moment of quiet, and to lighten the mood, Luke shouted, "Tom loved a good party, and now that he's on the wall, he won't miss this one. Drink up, everybody!"

The jukebox started back up, the pulsing keyboard of "Crocodile Rock" joining the rising voices of the crowd and the steady percussion of the rain on the roof.

Kaz spotted Laura through the smoke and crowd, grabbed his beer and made his way to her. She smiled when she saw him, and then caught herself. "I'm so sorry for the loss of your friend, Kaz."

"Thanks," he said. "It's a terrible thing. Can I get you a drink?"

She held up her nearly full mug by way of answer.

He touched her mug with his. "To Tom." They both drank.

"I never properly thanked you for taking me flying," she said. "I know it's normal for you, but it was a rare treat for me." She looked around sheepishly at the scientists in her group. "I've been boring everyone with the details, until today that is."

"You helped me remember my own joy in it."

"I'm glad," she said. She stared at her beer for a moment, then met his eye. "Do you think Tom's death will delay the mission?"

Kaz realized that most of the people in the room must be wondering the same thing. "No—we're going to get the crew trained with their new commander in time." He glanced towards the crew's table, where Chad was now sitting alone, staring at the wall where he'd just stuck up Tom's photo. Kaz realized that it was the first time he'd ever seen Chad lost in thought.

I don't blame him. It must really be sinking in.

He looked around for Luke and Michael, and found them at the center of a group of veteran astronauts, all drinking with purpose.

Laura frowned. "How do you do that?"

Kaz looked at her, puzzled. "Do what?"

"Recover so fast. Even in the Lunar Lab we've been zombies all day. It's why we came here tonight, in fact."

Kaz looked away. "It's hard for everyone," he said. He looked squarely back at Laura. "The speeches have been made, and you don't really want that beer. How about we leave?"

She glanced at her friends, then nodded. Kaz asked, "You have your Bug here?"

"Yes. Top's up, fortunately."

"Meet you at my place?"

Laura looked at him for a couple of seconds, then said, "Sure, why not?"

Both of them got drenched running from their cars into the house, and they sat on the couch with towels around their shoulders. Kaz opened a Chianti, rich and warm against the damp.

Laura took a sip, and sighed. Then asked, "So what's the answer to my question?"

Kaz had been thinking about it. "Truth is, we get used to the idea somehow." He looked out at the wet night, rain pouring down the window. "When my first good friend died on squadron, I couldn't accept it. He was a better pilot than I was, superb hands and feet, and more experienced. But on that one flight he came straight down out of low cloud at high speed and hit the water. There was nothing left."

He paused. "It made me mad. I wanted something to blame, *needed* something. So I dug hard into the details—recreating the accident, reviewing the plane maintenance records, looking at fleet reports for similar events. I developed a few probable theories. But eventually I realized that sometimes there's no answer. Flying high-performance machines is a dangerous profession, and occasionally it kills people."

He tipped his head to one side. "The grief is still there. I'll miss him forever—he should be here now, sharing in this life, a friend to laugh with into old age. It's unfair. Worse—it's random."

He took a mouthful of Chianti, swallowing slowly. "When the next friend died, the hole it caused inside me felt the same, but it seemed a little easier to bear. I'd learned the things I could do in response, and those I couldn't. When Tom crashed this morning, I felt that same, irre-trievable loss, and a wave of anger that maybe I'd missed taking some action that could have prevented it. I feel the need to find out what hap-pened so we don't repeat it, and the need to take care of his family."

He turned to look at her. "The wound is just as bad, but it's like I've developed a form of scar tissue so I can deal with it. I'll miss each of those guys for my whole life. But I'm still here. If it was me who had bought it, I'd expect them to stay focused; stay busy living too."

Laura raised her wineglass. "Here's to your friends, Kaz, the good men no longer here with you. Especially Tom." They touched glasses and drank them empty.

Then Kaz reflexively did another thing that helped him cope with loss: he pulled out his Gretsch archtop acoustic, a guitar he'd bought used in college and had dragged everywhere the Navy sent him.

They sat on the couch in the semi-darkness as he finger-picked his way through several of his favorites, singing softly, Laura joining in where she knew the words. He tried to avoid the sad ones, yet it felt like every song had certain lyrics that were magnified by Tom's death.

When he finished "Fire and Rain," James Taylor's soulful words echoing in the room, he looked at Laura in the half-light, leaned to pull her close and kissed her.

15

Washington, DC

When the 727's wheels thudded onto the concrete runway at Washington National, Kaz was already tired. It was noon in DC, but it had been a predawn departure from Polly Ranch, and the Eastern flight had been noisy and full, making it impossible for him to catch more sleep. Even his good eye felt gritty.

Now a Checker cab carried him across the 14th Street bridge into south DC, past the Jefferson Memorial and the Navy Yard, and then out into Maryland towards Baltimore. As the cab wound through the forest of the Patuxent Research Refuge, Kaz wondered, not for the first time, why Phillips had called for a face-to-face. The only change to the situation was Tom's death, three days previously. Adding a new commander to the mix made a big difference for the NASA trainers, but he didn't think it was something the NSA head should worry about. Unless there was something he didn't know.

He corrected himself: Sam Phillips was always dealing with things Kaz didn't know. The man faced a daily onslaught of intelligence from multiple sources and ever-changing advances in technology; the way the SIGINT was gathered could be just as important as the information itself. Then the head of the NSA had to sort the wheat from the chaff, feeding the key information, conclusions and recommendations up the chain to the military, who passed it via the Joint Chiefs to the President and other federal agencies.

Like the CIA.

Kaz squinted out the taxi window at the blur of trees. He'd heard about the CIA's new bull-in-a-china-shop boss, James Schlesinger. Could that be why he'd been summoned—in response to pressure from Nixon and his man at the CIA to take extra tactical advantage of Apollo 18's military agenda?

"C'mon in, Kaz!"

General Phillips, smiling warmly, stepped around his desk to greet him and they shook hands. Phillips's lean, pleasant face matched his tall, spare frame. The chest pocket of his short-sleeved white dress shirt had a notepad and a pen in it. His narrow brown tie, held with a clip, was tied in a neat Windsor knot. Pleated worsted pants were cinched high with a thin brown leather belt that matched his shiny brown shoes. A thoughtful military man in civilian clothing.

Jan appeared, unasked, carrying a tray with two coffees. Kaz thanked her and reached for his, grateful for caffeine. Phillips grabbed the other mug and led him to his small meeting table, where they sat. A green file folder, with TOP SECRET in red letters on its front, was already in the center of the table.

"How are you liking Texas?" Phillips asked.

"It's flat, hot and wet," Kaz said, smiling. "But I've been doing some flying, and it's been great to reconnect with Luke and Michael."

Phillips leaned to the left and called through the open door. "Jan, is Mo here yet?"

Kaz's mind raced ahead. "Mo" would be the overall military boss for Apollo 18—Admiral Maurice Weisner, the Vice Chief of Naval Operations.

"I'm just getting him a coffee now, General," Jan called back.

There was a knock on the frame of the door. "Permission to come aboard, Sam?"

Mo Weisner entered, smiling, cradling a coffee. Kaz stood to shake hands with the Admiral as Phillips waved him to the empty seat at the table. Weisner had been a junior officer in World War II whose ship had been sunk by Japanese torpedoes; he had lost 200 crewmates. After he'd retrained as a pilot, he'd torpedoed and sunk a Japanese destroyer escort, and gone on to command three squadrons. His gold naval wings, Distinguished Flying Crosses and other ribbons were neatly pinned above his name tag on his short-sleeved uniform shirt.

He sat and turned his heavy-lidded gaze on Kaz. "Good flight in?" The broad vowels of his Tennessee childhood made "in" a two-syllable word.

Kaz nodded. "Yes, sir, the Eastern breakfast flight." He held up his mug. "My fourth cup."

"I've read the prelim report of the crash," Weisner said, small talk over. He trained his intense brown eyes on Kaz. "They say no obvious cause. I heard you were there. Was it mechanical or did Tom make a mistake?"

"Weather was good, no other planes around, no sign of a birdstrike. My best guess is something failed in the machine. The accident board is sifting through the evidence."

Phillips and Weisner both nodded. As fixed-wing pilots, neither of them trusted helicopters.

"How's Miller doing?" Phillips asked.

"As you know, sir, he's been training alongside the crew in case something like this happened. He stepped right in and he knows his stuff," Kaz said.

"Sure, but are they gonna make it work?" Weisner asked. He'd led men in wartime. It was the key question.

"Tom was a special guy and he'd grown close to Luke and Michael. But Chad's up for it. Apollo 18 will be ready for launch."

Launch—the day the newly formed crew would leave Earth to do whatever these two senior officers decided.

Weisner glanced at Phillips, who said, "We've got some new intel about Almaz. We think they've significantly upgraded the optics." He lifted the pale-green folder and passed it to Kaz.

Inside was a collection of photographs, some with arrows and notes on them in silver and black ink. Kaz picked the first one up and tipped it into the strong light coming from the window. His dissertation at MIT had included an analysis of Soviet space assets, and his memory was clear on early designs for their space station.

"They've changed the mold line," he said, tracing his finger along the new shape of the spaceship's hull. One by one, he examined the remaining photos, looking closely at the print that showed the most magnification. "The optical window is different and the radiator arrangement has been shifted."

He looked up. "I agree with you, General. They've put a whole new capability in there." He thought a moment. "Do we have any ground-based intel on how good it might be?"

The senior men glanced at each other and, again, it was Phillips who spoke. "The CIA's been hearing some things that indicate the Soviets have used different parts suppliers and have also sent new scientific personnel to the assembly plant in Moscow."

Weisner continued. "Our best guess is they've made a significant improvement over the original design."

Kaz nodded, visualizing the components of the various systems. "The raw size of the optics in Almaz will outmatch their unmanned spy satellites, no question." He glanced back at the photographs. "That change in its outer shape means they could have put in reflective optics, using the whole interior diameter for focal length." He ran the numbers in his head. "Which means they could see things down to the sub-meter level. Maybe down to a little over a foot."

He looked up at Phillips and Weisner. "This version of Almaz could spot the two of you walking down the street and tell who's who."

"That's what my analysts have been telling me," Phillips said. "That kind of capability means we have to rethink our deployed assets all over the world, from what's on our ships' decks to our remote base activities to parking the President's car. Almaz is going to make us change and curtail what we're doing. We may have to start performing our critical ops at night, which will increase difficulty and decrease our chances of success."

Weisner said, "As you know, we've got some cutting-edge stuff going on in the high desert that's going to radically change warfare. But only if we can test and prove it in secrecy. You've been a test pilot, Kaz. You know what first flights are like in newly developed aircraft. There's no way we can do those in darkness."

Kaz set down the photos, no longer focusing on the technical details. He could feel where the conversation was heading.

"When does Almaz launch?" he asked.

Phillips said, "We've been watching their normal Proton preparations. Our best guess is in about two weeks. Somewhere in the first week of April."

"Then they'll need time to get Almaz checked out in orbit," Kaz said. "A camera that sophisticated will be too complex to load, point and operate remotely from the ground, so to get the capacity they want, they'll need to launch a crew on a Soyuz to rendezvous with the station and get the system working. The pictures will all be on wide-format film, which they'll need to deorbit in canisters or keep on board until the crew returns, maybe after a month or two."

He looked at the NSA chief. "Have you seen any indication of Soyuz crew launch prep?"

Phillips shook his head. "Not yet, no. We're still confident Apollo 18 is going to launch before the first Soyuz crew heads for Almaz."

"So as you've already figured out, that's our window," Weisner said, "when Almaz is parked in orbit, waiting for its crew." He looked hard at Kaz and added the key word. "Defenseless."

Kaz returned his stare. What these men were implying was clear, and stunning.

"So we won't just be taking close-ups of Almaz anymore."

Both senior officers shook their heads.

"You're ordering the crew of Apollo 18 to disable a Soviet spaceship?" They nodded.

A chill ran up his spine. Kaz said, "So for the first time in history the United States is going to take hostile military action in space."

16

MSC Headquarters, Houston

"We're going to do *what*?" Luke sounded both angry and incredulous.

Kaz had phoned ahead for an urgent meeting of the key players before he'd left Washington. The three crewmembers, along with Al Shepard and Gene Kranz, had gathered in Gene's office. The door was closed.

He'd brought the top-secret file back to Houston with him, and the men in the room were examining the new pictures of Almaz.

"This comes right from the Joint Chiefs, with the approval of the White House. Apollo 18 has been tasked to disable Almaz before its crew arrives."

Luke picked up one of the photos and stared at it. "How the hell are we gonna do that?"

"Good question. The NSA ops team had a few suggestions for vulnerable points we could get to with a cutting tool—antenna cables, radiator cooling lines, solar panel cables, docking targets, fuel lines. But this means we need to maneuver very close, and be ready for a space-walk when we get there."

Chad blew out sharply through his nose. "Does Washington understand what they're asking? This is going to be extremely dangerous."

"Yeah, I said the same thing, and the response is that they want 'all possible effort.'" Kaz mimed the quotation marks for emphasis. "The new CIA chief, Schlesinger, has made it highest priority, and he has the President's ear."

Gene Kranz was already thinking of the practicalities. "We've got some small bolt cutters in the spacewalk inventory, but we might need to get a bigger set on board. We can't cut anything that's got current running through it, but we could cut comms or cooling lines. Maybe fuel, depending."

They all considered that.

Michael asked the next obvious question. "Who's gonna go outside?"

Gene thought out loud. "The existing plan for you, Michael, to do the spacewalk on the way back from the Moon to retrieve *Pursuit's* external film canisters was already tight for weight margins. We'll likely have to trade that to get this done."

Michael shook his head. "But I'm going to have my hands full flying *Pursuit* close enough to Almaz to pull this off. I can't do the spacewalk at the same time." They all saw him realize what he'd just said: he was losing his spacewalk.

Gene nodded. "Agreed. That leaves Luke or Chad. I don't think we have the CO2 scrubbing reserves to send you both out, and Michael's going to need help maneuvering that close to another ship." He looked at both men, his mind ticking through the trade-offs.

Al Shepard spoke. "It needs to be Luke. Michael's the Command Module pilot, and Chad, as mission commander, needs to be inside honchoing all the moving parts."

Luke kept such a tight grip on his expression, Kaz couldn't tell what he was thinking. If it had been him, he would have been equal parts daunted and thrilled.

Chad stared at Al, his jaw clenched. "I don't like this. This is a third change of plan, and we've got less than four weeks until launch! We have no good way to simulate maneuvering so close to Almaz, and very little time to write and practice new procedures. This is a recipe to screw up before we even leave Earth orbit!"

Al nodded, his face serious. "You're right. And you may fail to disable that Soviet spy ship no matter what you do. But the reality is that this sort of op is why we *had* a MOL program, and you three were chosen specifically as a military crew to carry out military tasking. These orders are coming from the Joint Chiefs and the White House."

He looked at each man in turn. "This is now top priority. The least we're going to come away with is clear, close-up pictures of this thing. And with a little luck, Luke will hurt Almaz badly enough that we can protect America's secrets for a while yet."

Gene added, "We have procedures for fast rendezvous with non-cooperative targets from multiple Gemini flights, and we did maneuvering and orbital spacewalk tests during Apollo 9. The simulation hardware is still stored onsite, so we can put together enough reality to do some training. It won't be pretty, but I think we can be ready."

Kaz thought he better point out a fundamental concern. "These photos we're looking at here are top secret. We need the changes in training to be kept quiet, and a total media blackout during Almaz ops."

Gene said, "Right, I'll keep the team size to a minimum, and allow no TV coverage or visitors." He thought further. "There'll be people in Florida gathering to watch the launch, but I think it's best to black out the whole flight after that, not just the Almaz maneuver. NASA PR and the Air Force rep can deflect questions for us, citing national security if they have to."

Chad still looked like he'd eaten something sour. "We'll do it. But when we get there, I'm gonna have Michael keep *Pursuit* at a safe distance until we figure out what's actually possible. And if it turns out we can't do it, everybody will just have to be happy with more pretty pictures to add to Kaz's file."

He was the first to stand as the meeting broke up, and Luke and Michael followed him out the door.

17

Ellington Field, Houston

Apollo 18 was L minus 18 — 18 days from launch. Time to move operations from Texas to Florida, and the astronauts were flying themselves there.

Chad, strapped to his ejection seat in a blue and white NASA T-38 jet, leaned to the left to catch the eye of his groundcrew chief, and raised his right hand high above the cockpit, spinning his finger. Michael and Luke, in their own jets, saw the motion and did the same.

The groundcrew had parked air blowers, called "huffers," beside each of the three T-38s, and had connected the huffers' long hoses to the jets through doors in the planes' bellies. At the hand signal, they switched the huffers to max output, forcing air under high pressure into the T-38 engines, spinning the turbines like pinwheels. Once each engine got turning fast enough, the pilots brought their throttles to idle, letting jet fuel spray into the combustion chambers. Spark plugs flashed and the fuel/air mixture exploded into life, driving the turbines harder, sucking more air into the front intake of the motors. The groundcrew disconnected the huffers, and the engines wound up to working speed.

Kaz was in Chad's back seat, taking advantage of the ride to the Cape, and watched as the instrument panel came to life. Dr. McKinley, as the crew flight surgeon, was with Luke, and Michael's back seat carried an Air Force photographer—who already had his camera out, taking pictures of the start procedure.

Chad looked across at the other two pilots, and got a thumbs-up from each. He hit his mic: "Ellington Ground, this is NASA 18, flight of three, ready for taxi." Luke and Michael flicked their mic buttons briefly, and Kaz heard the two quick chirps in his helmet, confirming everyone was on frequency.

"Good morning, NASA 18 flight, altimeter is 30.12, set squawk 1818, cleared taxi for 35 Left. Have a great spaceflight."

"Copy 30.12, 35 Left, 1818 set. Will do, thanks."

All three pilots reached both hands up and motioned outwards with their thumbs, signaling the crew chiefs to pull the chocks clear of the main wheels. Once safely beyond the wingtip, the crewmen stood at attention and saluted. The pilots saluted back, pushed the throttles up and taxied clear.

Luke followed Chad, with Michael behind him, all offset slightly to avoid each other's jet engine blast. They left the ramp, turning right in close sequence, and headed along the taxiway to runway 35 Left.

Kaz stayed quiet, observing. Some pilots liked to chat, but Chad was all business. As they reached the wide pavement by the end of the runway, the other two jets pulled alongside. Kaz looked across at JW. Even under the helmet, oxygen mask and sunglasses, he could see the doctor's broad smile and knew what he was thinking: this crew was going to the Moon, and he was in the thick of it.

Chad leaned to check with Luke and Michael and saw them nod. Takeoff checks complete, everyone ready.

"Ellington Tower, NASA 18 flight of three, ready for takeoff 35 Left."

"Roger, NASA 18 flight, winds 350 at 11, cleared takeoff. Godspeed."

Chad clicked his mic button twice, closed his canopy and led the trio onto the runway, Luke lining up on his right wing, Michael on his left, both raising a thumb when in position.

Chad made a wind-up motion with his finger, and they moved their throttles ahead into a detent, giving full thrust just short of afterburner. He glanced left and right, then raised his chin and dropped it. At the signal, all three pilots released the toe brakes and jammed their throttles fully forward to the hard stop. Max thrust for takeoff.

The J85 engines responded instantly. Sparks flew, and like a giant blowtorch, the raw fuel ignited in the afterburners, yellow-gold flame visibly erupting out the exhaust at the rear. Now pushing with 6,000 pounds of thrust, the jets began to accelerate down the runway.

Chad pulled his throttles back a little bit to give the other two pilots some extra margin to hold position on his wings. As the airspeed indicator wound quickly up through 140 knots, he eased back on the stick, and the nose pivoted up. Kaz glanced out to see Michael and Luke doing the same. At 160 knots, the jets' thin, short wings were generating enough lift to raise the planes' main wheels off the runway. Chad paused a couple seconds, then raised the gear and flap handles. Staring intently to hold formation, the other pilots found the knobs blindly in their cockpits and did the same. All eyes watched the other airplanes' wheels fold up cleanly out of sight, the covering doors briskly snapping closed.

The transition was complete: the T-38s were no longer compromised beasts of the ground, but clean birds of the air, accelerating up into their natural environment.

The crews settled comfortably into position, tightly and naturally holding formation, a triangle of roaring metal climbing into the south Houston sky, pointed a little bit south of east. Headed to Cape Canaveral — and launch.

They leveled off at 37,000 feet, the sparkling blue waters of the Gulf of Mexico far below them, and Luke and Michael had drifted their jets out to loose formation. The T-38 had no autopilot, and the constant corrections needed to hold heading, altitude and airspeed were tiring. Soon Chad asked, "You want to fly, Kaz?"

"Glad to." Kaz lightly rested his hands on the stick and throttle, and glanced at the navigation chart on his knee for orientation.

"Great, thanks. You have control."

"I have it." Verbal confirmation was standard practice after several airplanes had gone out of control because each pilot thought the other was flying. Kaz shook the stick very slightly as a secondary confirmation, feeling the T-38 twitch in response.

Conversation in a two-seat jet is surreal and fragmented, yet strangely intimate, even with the background din of rushing air and noisy turbo-jet engines and having to keep a constant ear to the steady patter of Air Traffic Control. Both people face forward, so you can't see when the other is talking; the words just suddenly sound inside your helmet, almost as if they were your own thoughts.

Kaz had been thinking about the flying, and also about Laura, when Chad's voice snapped him out of his reverie. "Kazimieras Zemeckis— it's an unusual name. Where's your family from?"

"Lithuania. It's a Litvak name—Lithuanian Jewish. I was born in Vilnius just as the war started, and my family fled, managing to get one of the last passages to New York." A short pause, as they both listened to the muffled sounds of flight. Then Kaz added, "Good thing they did. By 1942, the Nazis had killed almost the whole community, seventy-five thousand Litvaks."

"So, you're a Jew?"

"Yes, but non-practicing." Why was Chad asking about this? He tried to lighten the mood. "My mother still hopes I'll find a nice Jewish girl to straighten me out."

Air Traffic Control called with a frequency change, transferring them from Houston to New Orleans as they worked their way eastward. The morning sun was bright in Kaz's eye, and he had his dark visor rotated down into place.

"Any other Jews in the program?"

Kaz was startled. Religion was not a normal topic of conversation among astronauts. Yes, the Apollo 8 crew had read from Genesis on Christmas Eve, during their return flight from the Moon, and Buzz Aldrin had taken Communion while on the surface. But this was a weird thing to ask in the cockpit.

"Uh, not that I know of."

Kaz knew that Chad had been raised in the Midwest, but where was this coming from?

"The Soviets have one," Chad said. "Boris Volynov. He got yanked from his first flight on Voskhod in '64, but eventually flew in '69."

Kaz shook his head. Why was that important? And why would Chad have noted it in the first place?

"Huh," he replied. "I didn't know that."

Chad continued. "Have you ever been blocked for an opportunity because you're Jewish?"

"Nah," Kaz said, now determined to lighten this up. "I just tried to come first at everything so no one could say no to me. And here I am today, riding with an Apollo commander on his way to launch!"

Chad grunted, and went silent.

Kaz made a note to check whether Chad had made similar off-color comments to Luke or Michael. The man was a great pilot, but maybe more of a redneck than Kaz had thought.

The long silty tendrils of the Mississippi Delta were passing off to their left, a web of sandbars like a chicken's claw reaching out into the Gulf of Mexico. Kaz turned slightly over the southern tip, heading 100 degrees, following the jet route. Michael's voice broke in. "Hey, Boss, the photog wants some formation shots with New Orleans in the background. Okay if you two close up, and we'll move around for good angles?"

"Sure," Chad said, and Luke brought his T-38 into tight formation. Kaz watched as Michael's jet moved around, getting pictures from several perspectives. They were halfway across the gulf when the photographer decided he had enough.

Chad took control back from Kaz as they entered an area of wispy cirrus cloud that was getting thicker, telling the other two pilots to move into closer formation.

As they crossed the Florida coast, Chad selected NASA Ops on the radio, turned down the squelch and called ahead. "This is NASA 18 flight, a hundred and twenty miles back. We should be there in fifteen minutes."

The responding voice was scratchy with static. "Good morning, 18 flight, we're ready for you, weather's good, plan on landing 31."

"Wilco, thanks." Chad switched back to Air Traffic Control, and asked to begin descent. Florida rolled quickly by underneath, the crew focusing on holding formation as they went in and out of cloud, the jets extra-sensitive at just barely under the speed of sound. As they crossed over Orlando, they switched back to Ops frequency.

"NASA, 18 flight, be there in five. We'd like a couple passes of the pad for photos, and then we'll come into the break for 31."

"Roger, 18 flight, no traffic, cleared as requested."

Chad pushed the jets lower as Merritt Island and the oversized buildings of the Kennedy Space Center came into view. Kaz peered ahead to the coastline, and spotted the massive white and black Saturn V rocket next to the orange framework gantry of its launch tower.

Michael moved his jet slightly away to give the photographer a good angle as they raced past the launch pad a couple hundred feet above the 500-foot tower. They made a wide dumbbell left turn over the Atlantic shore, coming down the coast for a second pass.

With all three jets now almost out of gas, Chad continued down the coast, turning to line up with runway 31. He waved Michael to the far side, moving the jets into echelon right, positioned like the last three fingers of his right hand. They flashed in close formation across the shore, down low and fast over the runway, and Chad broke hard up and left over the small crowd of NASA support crew and media waiting for them. Luke counted "thousand one" and yanked his jet left to follow, Michael doing the same in perfect sequence. They each slowed and dropped gear and flap as they headed downwind, and landed on the 10,000-foot runway, one behind the other.

Chad slowed to taxi speed so the others could catch up, and the three of them rolled in unison up to the waiting groundcrew. They turned in, parked neatly lined abreast and, at a nod from Chad, chopped throttles to Off together. The engines wound down quickly as they opened their canopies, and it was abruptly quiet. They started pulling off gloves and helmets, welcoming the salty Florida breeze on their faces.

They were here, and their rocketship was ready for them on the pad, pointed at the sky.

18

Baikonur, Kazakh Soviet Socialist Republic

The Syr Darya river winds for 1,400 miles, from its source high in the Kyrgyz Tian Shan, Mountains of Heaven, across the flat southern steppes of Kazakhstan, until it finally empties into the broad Aral Sea. The ice-fed headwaters gleam a surreal pale blue, carrying the reflective, finely ground silt of glaciers; the ancient Persians called it the True Pearl River. But by the time it twists down through the towns, reservoirs and endless agricultural irrigation schemes, its waters thicken to an opaque, oily brown. A nondescript-colored snake of a river bringing muddy water to soothe the thirst of the nomadic two-humped Bactrian camels.

The spring thaws and ice jams regularly cause it to overflow its banks, spreading its silt up across the surrounding gray land, turning the soil a fertile, rich brown. Kazakh farmers work its shores, growing crops and grazing their sheep, cattle and horses. Their word for the river's fertile soil was the name given to the town at a long, sweeping bend in the river. *Baikonur.* The rich, brown earth.

It wasn't just the river that had flowed from the east. The invasion and conquest of the region by Genghis Khan's Golden Horde was still

110

visible in the high cheekbones, black hair and epicanthic eyelids of the
Kazakh farmers. When the Tashkent railway opened in 1906, it brought
a wave of different invaders, from the northwest: the round-eyed, pale-
skinned ethnic Russians.

In 1955, the vast flatness of this southern land caught the eye of
the Soviet space program; Chief Designer Sergey Korolyov ordered the
construction of the Baikonur Cosmodrome. A new word, invented for
a whole new idea. Not just an aerodrome, but a *cosmodrome*: a gate-
way to the cosmos.

Sputnik roared off the Baikonur launch pad and into orbit just two
years later, its yellow rocket flame reflecting in the waters of the Syr
Daria. Four years after that, Vostok 1 carried Yuri Gagarin around the
world in 108 minutes.

But a dozen years had passed since that triumphant day—years
where the Soviet domination of the cosmos had waned, and decisive
leadership from the distant city of Moscow had faded. Even the first
spacewalk in orbit, by cosmonaut Alexei Leonov, was soon eclipsed by
the Americans who walked on the Moon.

Vladimir Chelomei, the current Chief Designer and the Director
of Spacecraft Factory OKB-52, stared for a moment down his long,
sharply pointed nose at his leather dress shoes and took a hard pull on
his cigarette, welcoming the acrid smoke deep into his lungs. "Desyat
lyet," he muttered to himself. Ten years. *And Korolyov's been dead for
seven of them.* Chelomei shook his head slowly. But now Korolyov's
mantle was his to take, once the Almaz military space station launched.

He and his team had first conceived of the rocket needed to lift
it in the early 1960s. It would be the Soviet answer to Apollo's Saturn V,
a way to win the space race and ensure that a Russian was the first man
on the Moon. Gagarin had been the first to space, after all, and a Soviet
man should have been the one to make the first footprints on the Moon.

But politicians aren't engineers. They'd bet on a different rocketship,
Vasily Mishin's ridiculous N1, with its 42 rocket motors. Of course it
had failed, during four agonizingly wasteful attempts in a row. It had

even destroyed its entire Baikonur launch pad! Chelomei had tried
everything within his power to change his nation's course, all the way to
appealing to Khrushchev himself. But Mishin's political connections
had prevailed.

Misplaced arrogance had cost Russia the Moon.

Not this time, Chelomei thought. They would win this second space
race, not just for science, but also for something much easier to understand: the national security of the Motherland itself.

Almaz. A powerful Soviet orbiting spy telescope, to be operated by
cosmonauts.

Chelomei was standing beside the rocket that would carry his spacecraft into orbit. It was 60 meters long, the enormous size seemingly
amplified by the fact that it was lying on its side on railcars. As he waited
for the Baikonur launch-pad train to start moving, he paced slowly past
the six huge exhaust nozzles and down the length of the behemoth.

The UR-500K monster rocket they'd dubbed the Proton was a proven
beast of a machine. *His* rocket. He stopped walking and looked to the
left and then the right, taking in the sight. The Proton was still hollow
and light, the huge fuel tanks kept empty until it was vertical on the
launch pad, ready to receive the full load of volatile hydrazine. Chelomei
knew every millimeter of it; he'd been key to the thousands of decisions
that had brought it into existence. He and his engineers had solved one
problem after another, even how to design it so it would fit on its railcars, able to squeeze through the railway tunnels between the factory in
Moscow and the launch pad in Baikonur.

He exhaled loudly through his nose and walked towards Proton's
pointed tip, to look at the real purpose of all this engineering: Almaz.
His baby, no matter the long gestation period, was in position at last,
attached with explosive bolts to the third stage of the rocket that would
push it to orbital speed. He glanced to his left. All of this complex
plumbing would be garbage then, the first and second stages tumbling
to crash onto the empty Kazakh/Altai steppes, the third stage falling into
the Pacific Ocean.

His eyes followed to the right, along the smooth shape of Almaz's protective shroud, sculpted down to the pointed metal tip that would be forced up through the air. The shroud wasn't just to help with the aerodynamics, though, but to disguise the shape of Almaz so it wouldn't give away its many secrets to curious launch guests and media cameras. Or the American satellites spying from above.

A klaxon sounded, interrupting his thoughts. He heard shouts of readiness from the workers along the rocket, and the deep rumble of the green and yellow diesel electric locomotive filled the hall. The giant sliding door just beyond the nozzles of the rocket began to move sideways on its tracks. He walked quickly towards the opening, ready to see the spectacle of his rocketship moving out into Baikonur's late March sunshine.

The phone rang on General Sam Phillips's desk. He leaned forward and saw one of the three secure lines flashing. He picked up the receiver and pushed the button.

"Phillips here."

"Sam, it's John McLucas. Got some good news." McLucas was head of the National Reconnaissance Office. "Looks like the Russkies have rolled their latest Proton out to the launch pad at Baikonur. We got lucky on timing with the KH-9 satellite we launched and caught them raising the rocket to vertical at the pad. We're pretty sure it's the launch you and Schlesinger were asking about."

Phillips glanced quickly at his desk calendar, counted days and nodded in satisfaction. The timing for Apollo 18 still made sense.

GO for launch.

They were a strange little group.

Three men, a woman and a boy dozed on the bench seats of two battered vehicles. Another man was awake, outside leaning on the rusting square front bumper of his olive-green ZIL-157 truck, staring at the sky. Occasionally he would glance at his aged watch and raise a pair of powerful binoculars, peering intently at the western horizon.

A good time to rest. The hard work would start soon.

His six-wheeled truck had a heavy winch mounted on the bumper, and strapped into the covered rear flatbed was an assortment of acetylene tanks, torches, cutting tools, hammers and wrenches.

The second vehicle was a four-wheel-drive UAZ-452 camper van, called a "bukhanka" for its homely resemblance to a loaf of bread. It had basic cooking facilities and fold-down cots, plus a heater for the cold nights. The early April days were only occasionally getting above freezing, and everyone was bulkily bundled in many layers of woolen clothing as they dozed, their heavy rubber boots lined with thick valenki felt.

The man on watch took a long, deep drag on his cigarette, welcoming the searing heat into his lungs. His name was Chot, and he was descended from the original inhabitants of these northern foothills of the Himalayas. The borders of four countries met just to the south of where the trucks were parked, and his features reflected the history of them all: Mongolia, China, Kazakhstan and the Soviet Union. His nationality was Soviet, but he was proudly Altaian.

He checked the time. "Oi!" he called, loudly. Chot's wife, son and brothers began to stir. Two p.m. in Baikonur. Time for a rocket launch.

The flight path of every Soviet rocketship on its way to space, ever since Sputnik, had passed directly over the Altai Oblast. As the rockets had gotten bigger, the Moscow designers had added multiple stages— sections that would boost the rocket in height and speed, and then, empty of fuel, separate and fall to Earth. Hulking cylinders of pressure tanks, engine bells, electronics and metal, tumbling violently to the ground on a regular basis. The Soviets knew roughly where the impacts would occur, and warned the villages directly under the predicted flight path to evacuate as needed. In reality, the Soviets played the odds, counting on the sparse population and political unimportance of the region to make any collateral damage of low concern. When there was a rocket failure, and the fuel-rich impact explosions led to loss of life, Moscow would pay recompense to the families and ensure there was no publicity. Cheap insurance to allow the space program to function.

Chot fixed his binoculars on the horizon. Having seen many launches, he knew exactly where to look. Sometimes the sun and cloud would align so that he could see the flame and smoke of the rocket itself, especially the larger ones. Today was the biggest: a Proton. He'd looked at the upper clouds and surface winds the night before, estimating from experience how they would affect the trajectory. The rocket's second stage would fall close to where he had positioned his family. If he had guessed wrong, some other group would find and claim the wreckage. He hoped he was right—the metal was worth a lot, and they needed the money.

There!

Through the binoculars he could see the actual smoke trail; squinting, he thought he could just make out the brightness of the flame. *Good.* No delays today. He checked his watch again, and went over the timing. The second stage would separate after about five minutes, and its fall to Earth would take another nine or so. In fourteen minutes, they'd know.

"Start the engines!" he called to his brothers, still staring hard through the binoculars to track the change in smoke that signified rocket staging. It was his job to spot the falling rocket body, and then there would be a race to get to the impact site. Whoever got there first had salvage rights. Just in case, each truck also carried a rifle.

He saw the smoke change, and knew his prize was now on its way. Letting the faint smoke of the third stage of the rocket drift out of sight to the east, he concentrated on where the falling section must be. Sometimes it would glint in the light as it tumbled down. He adjusted the binoculars slightly, hoping for a glimpse.

Was that a flash? He wasn't certain, but it was right where it was supposed to be. Chot could feel his heart racing. The rest of his family was staring upwards as well, everyone straining to see it first.

His young son had the sharpest eyes, and called out in his high voice, "I see it!" The boy pointed up and slightly south of where they were.

"Keep your eyes on it!" Chot ordered.

There was an odd roar of wind noise, a streak of something moving fast, and then an echoing thump of impact—a cloud of frozen dirt thrown up by the impact. "We're close!" he yelled, marking the direction. He jumped into the passenger seat of the ZIL, pointing out the direction for his brother.

I hope there's fire. They could use the smoke as a beacon.

And there it was! A small dark plume as the last of the hypergolic fuel burned itself out, released to the air by the impact. His brother saw it and pushed the truck to its limits, bouncing heavily over the rough ground, leaving the smaller van behind.

Chot scanned left and right, and saw no one else. A *great day!* His experience and cunning would provide for his family.

They came around a copse of evergreens to see the wreckage itself, largely intact on a long, sloping hillside, the smoke fading. No one else was here. The salvage was theirs!

His brother swung around and braked to a stop, carefully upwind to avoid the noxious fumes, and shut the truck off. In the distance they could see the bukhanka following their track. The hunt was over. Now they could get down to the business of stripping the carcass.

Chot looked to the sky. He didn't know where the rocket was going or what it was carrying, or even if there were people aboard, and in truth he didn't care. He was just happy that the Soviet Union had a space program.

It fed his family.

19

The Beach House, Cape Canaveral, Florida

"Pull!"

Kaz had already cocked the trap mechanism, rotating it back against the heavy spring. Hearing the yell, he yanked smoothly down on the nylon cord. An orange clay disk spun out of the track at the tip, arcing smoothly up and across in front of the beach house.

Blam!

The harsh, spitting sound of the 12-gauge shotgun echoed loudly off the clapboard and out across the beach, fading into the breaking surf of the Atlantic Ocean. The flying clay disk instantly disintegrated into shards. Hitting such a moving target took complete concentration, and was a fun distraction for three men about to undertake an unprecedented military mission in space.

"That's four dead pigeons out of five. Beat that!" Luke said, turning on the wooden deck to challenge Michael and Chad, lounging in their deck chairs. The grinding sound of the blender carried out onto the deck. JW was in the kitchen making margaritas.

Michael drained his beer and stood up, taking the gun and earmuffs from Luke. He yelled to Kaz. "You okay for five more?"

"All set!" Kaz, in the shade by the corner of the building, saluted him with his half-empty beer.

Michael put on the earmuffs, adjusting them around his sunglasses. He loaded two new shells into the shotgun barrels, braced his left foot, cocked and raised the gun to his shoulder and yelled, "Pull!"

The disc flew, and Michael tracked it with the long barrel, matching and leading its motion. He pulled the trigger, the recoil slamming the gun hard into his shoulder and cheek. The orange disk continued on its flight, falling and shattering amongst the saw palmetto.

"Uh-oh—bird away!" Luke called.

"I'm just getting sighted in." Michael repositioned and yelled "Pull!" again. He hit the next two, ending up with three out of five. "Looks like a silver medal for me," he said ruefully. "Your turn, Boss."

Chad moved his eyes lazily from one to the other. "You boys forget that I grew up on a farm. Varmint shooting was part of the job description." He set down the margarita JW had just handed him, and held a hand out for the gun. "Give me that."

As Chad loaded, JW walked down the porch stairs towards Kaz. He handed him a margarita, and toasted him with his iced tea.

Chad leaned over the railing. "You boys ready down there?"

"All set, Commander!" Kaz called.

Chad yelled, "Pull!" and pivoted, squeezing smoothly on the trigger, shattering the clay pigeon. Five tries, five hits.

He turned with a smirk. "And that, boys, is how it's done."

Luke and Michael raised their glasses in defeat as Chad put the shotgun back into its case and settled again into his chair. Kaz called up from below. "Sun's setting in an hour or so. Anyone up for a beach walk with me and JW?"

Chad waved his hand. "I'm easy here. You boys go right on ahead."

———

The narrow sandy path led 200 feet through the scrubby palmetto and sea oats before opening to the wide, pale sand of Neptune Beach on the Atlantic coast. The area had been home to a small seaside cottage community in the 1950s, but when the Air Force and NASA had started to expand space operations for Project Apollo, they'd acquired the land and torn down the small store, gas station and all but one of the scattered weatherboard houses. A far-thinking government official had spotted its solid foundations and new construction and decided to spare it from the bulldozers. NASA had christened the cottage the Astronaut Training and Rehabilitation Building to satisfy the fiduciary oversight of the Inspector General, but everyone knew it as the Beach House—a private place for crews to relax in the days leading up to launch. A rare island of no responsibility to counteract the mounting tension and extreme unspoken risk.

Kaz was glad Chad had decided not to come on the walk. He was still a little unsettled by the conversation they'd had on the trip from Houston, and was happy for some time with him out of earshot. As they all stopped to stare out to sea, he asked, as casually as he could, "So how's everybody getting along?"

Luke and Michael exchanged a glance, and Michael shrugged. "Things are different without Tom," he said, "but we're sorting it out."

Luke added, "Chad flies as well as he shoots."

Kaz said, "But he's not Tom, and he had to step in only three weeks before launch. It's got to be a lot to deal with."

Luke picked up a sand dollar and skipped it into the waves. "Well, he's got more of a temper on him than Tom did."

Michael nodded. "Yeah, he does. Plus, you can take the boy out of Wisconsin . . ."

"Anything Doc and I should know about?"

Michael glanced back at the beach house in the distance. "It's just that they've got their share of rednecks and tobacco chewers out there. Sometimes some of that attitude sneaks through."

"Chad keeps it in check for the most part," Luke said, leaning down for another sand dollar. He turned to Kaz. "It's not a popularity contest. Some of the early astronauts were right assholes to work with, but they knew how to get shit done. Michael and I have thick skins and a job to do."

Kaz turned to Michael. "Is there anything more than that? It would be good to know before you're all in space."

Michael shook his head. After a small silence, he said, "I'd prefer if he didn't call me 'boy' quite so much. But it's just how he was raised. We'll get through it."

Luke nodded. "We'll do fine." He looked out at the ocean. "But it sure would have been good to fly with Tom."

20

Ellington Field, Houston

As was often the case, the accident investigator was an unwelcome man.

When Tom Hoffman had crashed, NASA had immediately appointed an investigation board headed by the Chief of the Astronaut Office, Alan Shepard. The seven-member panel had moved quickly to cordon off and photograph the crash site, gathering and protecting all potential evidence. They were given unfettered access to Hoffman's Air Force and NASA medical records, as well as the coroner's report. They seized the maintenance history and daily sign-out log of the crashed helicopter, plus the Ellington Tower flight logs and audiotape of radio communications. The fuel truck had been impounded and sampled so they could check for possible contamination. The Houston Air Traffic Control Center provided radar tracking information of the helicopter's transponder, giving them exact speed and altitude. They consulted the Ellington Meteorological Office's record of the weather conditions, including temperature and wind, critical factors in rotary wing flight.

Once the body had been removed from the crash site, NASA maintenance techs had catalogued and retrieved all debris. The high vertical impact speed had kept the pieces of the helicopter in a surprisingly small area. The subsequent fire had reduced much of it to ash and rubble, including the light sheet-metal cabin and bubble canopy, but the seats, the tail rotor frame and the central heavy metal of the engine and transmission were relatively intact.

Piece by piece, the bits of wreckage were methodically photographed, tagged, loaded into a van and then laid out in a spotlessly cleaned and roped-off section of a secondary maintenance hangar. A silhouette of the helicopter was painted on the floor, and as each piece was identified, it was meticulously placed in its proper location.

Yet despite their methodical work, the NASA accident board had been unable to determine the root cause. The helo techs at Ellington Field had analyzed each charred piece but had found no obvious reason for the crash. A healthy pilot and a flightworthy aircraft had inexplicably fallen from the sky.

Al Shepard was frustrated with the inconclusive result. While the Apollo program was ending, Skylab and the Space Shuttle were starting. He needed any dirty laundry to be kept in-house in case a public hue and cry about cowboy astronaut antics or slipshod maintenance processes caused the already shrinking space budget to shrink further. He also owed an answer to Tom's family; he didn't want them to live with the ignominy of "probable pilot error" for the rest of their lives. But his team had found no smoking gun amidst the wreckage.

Shepard needed to get it resolved. As much as he disliked widening the circle, he called his ex-Navy contacts at the National Transportation Safety Board, and they sent their most seasoned investigator—a former Air Force Master Sergeant and senior instructor at the USAF Inspection and Safety Center, with a specialty in helicopters. A native Houstonian.

Miguel Fernandez stood between the two painted outlines, surveying the twisted, blackened metal. Extra lights had been erected on portable stands, and they starkly highlighted the angular debris, casting harsh shadows.

Looks like a dragonfly that fell into in a campfire, he thought.

Fernandez had flown in from Kirtland Air Force Base in Albuquerque the evening before, taking advantage of the travel to spend the night at his mom's place. His NASA guest pass had been waiting for him when he drove up to the Ellington hangar that morning. The reception at the ops desk had been cool, as it usually was in such circumstances. If Fernandez found something they'd missed, they were going to look bad. The duty officer had escorted him to the debris site, fetched him the coffee he'd requested, and left him on his own.

He sighed, and sipped the thick black liquid from the styrofoam cup. No one ever wanted to stick around and watch him work.

Fernandez had read the board's preliminary notes during the flight to Houston, thinking about the possible causes the investigators might have missed. He walked slowly amongst the wreckage, occasionally squatting, looking for signs that might prove any of his theories. After that first quick survey, he drained the last of the bitter coffee and retrieved his clipboard, pen and rubber gloves from his satchel. The many crashes he'd investigated had required him to develop a way to keep everything straight while missing nothing. He deliberately cleared his head of the morning's distractions and started focusing on the details.

After 45 minutes of stopping, bending, picking up parts in his gloved hand and peering at them through his high-powered reading glasses, he stepped out of the painted area at the tail boom. Fernandez was pretty sure he'd found the cause.

He tucked his clipboard back in his satchel, took his gloves off and carried his coffee cup back to the ops desk for a refill.

The duty officer looked hard at him, trying to determine if he'd discovered anything. "How's it going?" he finally asked.

"Nothing conclusive yet." Fernandez decided to reduce the hostility. "Your boys did a really nice job with the wreckage, very professional. Best I've seen anywhere." It wasn't true, but there was no harm in saying it.

A small smile appeared on the DO's face. "Thanks. I'll pass it on."

Miguel slowly walked back, sipping coffee as he mentally reviewed his inspection of each part. He set the cup on the floor and pulled the NASA board's summary notes from his bag. After he reread their recreation of the flight profile that had preceded the crash, he nodded. It all made sense.

He finished his coffee, then retrieved his Canon F-1 camera and 50 mm macro lens from his bag and also pulled out his magnifying glass and a clean pair of gloves. He slung the camera around his neck and walked to where the largest pieces sat—the engine, transmission and rotor hub. He stopped, took some establishing shots, donned his gloves and then bent down to look closely at the part he'd noticed earlier.

It was badly damaged. The force of the impact had broken the bolt and the mechanism, and the intensity of the fire, right there by the fuel tanks, had blackened and distorted the remnants. An easy thing to miss if a person hadn't seen something like it before and known to look.

He used the lens to get a magnified close-up, taking several frames from multiple angles. Then he picked up one of the pieces and took more photos. He brought the magnifying glass close, examining the shear plane of the broken bolt and the telltale marks on its remaining thread. He compared it to the remains of the matching bolt on the other side of the mechanism. He looked carefully around the nearby floor, verifying that the missing piece wasn't there somewhere.

He had a thought, and walked over to a rectangular painted area where the reconstruction team had laid out pieces of wreckage they weren't able to identify, and he sifted through each piece, just to be sure. It wasn't there, either.

The pitch-rod holding nut was missing.

Without it, the pilot wouldn't have been able to control the helicopter. As the nut loosened, the helo would have felt sloppier and vibrated more, but as soon as the nut popped off, the pilot would have lost pitch and roll control. Evidence of the rotors hitting the tail boom was obvious. The crash was inevitable.

But why had the nut come off? Critical components like this one were cinched to a specific torque and then lock-wired into place. The nut on the other side, though damaged, was still secure.

His examination with the magnifying glass had told him the answer, and the photos would verify it. The lock wire wasn't there. And the speed with which the nut had backed off revealed that it hadn't been torqued properly into place to begin with.

Fernandez looked around the tidy, professional NASA hangar, at the blue and white T-38s on stands and the technicians in white coveralls purposefully doing their maintenance work.

He saw two possible causes.

The first. Someone had skipped key steps in their procedures while installing the nut, and the confirming integrity check and sign-off had also missed it. Very unlikely. Both NASA and the Air Force used independent checks as part of standard procedure to keep just this sort of thing from happening.

The second cause. Someone had deliberately removed the lock wire and loosened the bolt. Someone with access to the helicopter after it had passed its daily inspection. Someone who was trusted inside the NASA organization.

That was much more probable—and the sabotage had led to death.

NASA had hoped he'd give them a simple answer so they could deal with it and get on with flying in space. But this was manslaughter at the very best, and homicide at the worst. Also, it crossed the jurisdictional boundaries of NASA, the Air Force and the NTSB, not to mention the local police. Once it came under the public scrutiny of a media fascinated by astronauts, it was going to get even uglier.

Fernandez had done his job and was sure of his conclusions. He mentally reviewed his reporting chain, deciding who to phone. He sure as hell wasn't going to tell anyone here. Time to hand this mess over to the powers that be.

The rest of it was above his pay grade.

21

Astronaut Crew Quarters, Kennedy Space Center

"Steak, eggs and toast? You sure about that, Boss?" Michael eyed Chad's full plate, willing himself not to picture what that food would look like if it came back up.

"I've never been motion sick in my life, and I'm not going to start today." Chad slid a sunny-side egg onto the steak, lifted both onto the buttered toast, cut a large bite and forked it all into his mouth. "Last decent meal we're gonna get for a while," he said, chewing.

Luke shrugged. "A wise old chief petty officer at sea once told me it's best to eat smooth food; makes it easier when you vomit." As Navy men, he and Michael had breakfasted on a banana each, water and coffee.

Al Shepard bemusedly watched Luke pour himself another cup. "Go easy on that, Marine. On my first flight I drank so much coffee I had to piss in my pressure suit, then lie on my back in the puddle, waiting for launch." He smiled at the memory. "A glorious first in space history."

Luke set the cup back down.

Kaz checked his watch. "About time to get dressed, fellas."

Luke and Michael pushed back from the table, then leaned into the kitchen to shake hands with the staff. Chad took one last forkful, and got up and followed them down the hall.

Al tapped Chad on the shoulder as he walked past. "Get your guys to take one last leak before they suit up."

A spaceship is, in essence, a bubble of Earth's air in the empty vacuum of space. The thin aluminum hull holds the internal pressure against the nothingness, so the crew can work comfortably wearing normal clothes, without oxygen masks. But during the riskier parts of flight, like launch and landing, when a sudden jar could pop a hull seal loose, astronauts need an extra layer of protection. Ever since Al Shepard's first flight, they'd worn a pressure suit, just in case—a form-fitting personal bubble of oxygen.

Hanging on racks in the suit-up room were three Apollo pressure suits, each custom-made for the crewmember, all of them in white to reflect the Sun's intense heat. To save weight and stowage space, Chad and Luke would wear the same suits to walk on the Moon.

Michael waddled out from the washroom, wearing a urine collection condom, heavy absorbent underwear, stick-on medical sensors and a full-body cooling suit woven with water recirculating tubes. Luke came out after him.

"Hey, Michael, your ass looks big," he said.

"Have you glanced in a mirror? You look like a snake that ate a toad!"

They padded to their suit techs, waiting patiently by tables loaded with spacesuit gear. A tall rack covered in dials and knobs stood nearby, ready to test pressurization and communication.

As the tallest of the three, Michael had the hardest time getting into his suit, a one-piece garment that opened from the back with a heavy zipper. He bent his head and narrowed his shoulders, squeezing in until his hands and feet found the arm and leg holes, finally stretching to full height as his head popped through the neck ring and his feet slid into the built-in booties.

He glanced at Chad and Luke, who were still squirming into their suits. "Every time I do that I feel like a baby climbing back into the womb."

Luke chuckled. "Freud would have a field day with you."

Michael pulled hard on a long, webbed tab between his legs, tugging the stiff zipper all the way around until it was sealed. His tech guided a black and white cloth cap over his head, and Michael pulled the chinstrap tight, getting the ear cups snug. He grabbed the flexible twin mic booms and bent them into place by the corners of his mouth; once he had his helmet on, there'd be no way to adjust them.

The tech raised his eyebrows. "Ready for air?"

Michael nodded, already overheating in the sealed rubber suit. The tech clipped a hose into a matching valve on Michael's chest and threw a switch on the control panel, and Michael could feel cool, dry air blowing through the suit, up and out around his neck.

"That's better," he said. He put his Omega Speedmaster watch on his wrist and pulled on thin white cotton gloves.

The tech held up a thick black rubber glove, and Michael pointed his fingers and thumb together to slide his hand inside. The tech expertly clicked the glove's pressure ring into place against the matching blue ring on the suit's left cuff, and then did the same with the glove and red ring on the right.

"Are they color-coded so we know our right from our left?" Michael asked. It was an old joke, but the tech laughed, cutting the guy some slack since he was about to go ride the world's biggest rocket.

Michael glanced at the wall clock. "Time to start breathing oxygen?"

The tech nodded and lifted Michael's helmet from the table. It looked like an inverted fishbowl with cloth stuck down one side. Michael took it from him and wiggled it over his head, the cloth section to the back, careful not to let the metal locking ring scrape the skin off his nose. He'd done that once in training, and now knew better.

The tech disconnected Michael's cooling airflow, locked the helmet latches in place and then hooked up recirculating oxygen and water lines. Michael was now relying on a machine to breathe, and would be until they landed back in the ocean at the end of the mission, over a week later.

The endless training and practice were over. Shit was getting real. He, Michael Henry Esdale, an unlikely little kid from South Chicago named for his two grandfathers, was about to get into a rocketship and blast off the face of the Earth. So many times he'd been told no in his life, a Black man trying to succeed in the white man's realm. It had been years of slogging to always be the best, to leave no doubt, and even then some people told him he was only here because of race politics. That he hadn't earned his opportunities, but had been handed them as some sort of favor. Michael shook his head to clear the thought. He'd earned his ticket, and it was him who was going to fly that thing.

The pure oxygen tasted dry and clean, and Michael felt his head clearing as his body absorbed the gas. Over the next few hours, the nitrogen in his blood would be gradually replaced by oxygen; that way, when he got to orbit and popped his helmet off in the low-pressure all-oxygen atmosphere, his blood nitrogen wouldn't suddenly bubble and give him the bends. As scuba divers knew, bubbles in the blood were bad, causing huge pain in the joints, and potentially death.

There were brown leather La-Z-Boy recliner chairs for each crewmember, and Michael settled into his while the tech cranked up the suit pressure, checking for leaks. As the suit stiffened, the neck ring of his helmet was pushed up to his mouth. It was uncomfortable, but workable; this is what it would be like during an emergency deorbit and splashdown. Michael moved his arms and flexed his fingers, picturing how he would reach switches against the hard resistance of the suit. The tech looked intently back and forth at the pressure gauges and a stopwatch, and eventually nodded in satisfaction. He twisted a large knob counterclockwise, and Michael gratefully felt the suit soften and his neck ring lower to its normal height. Suit check complete, he pulled out his launch emergencies checklist, flipping through it with his black-gloved hands.

Luke's voice carried to Michael through the communications lines. "Find anything new in there?"

Michael looked over, slightly sheepish. "Never too late to review."

In truth, Luke was happy to see it. Michael had the lion's share of the piloting to do after launch. They'd be heading immediately for Almaz, and Chad would be busy getting Luke and his suit and gear ready for the spacewalk. This was the first spaceflight for all of them and the pressure was intense to do things right.

Chad's voice cut in. "How are you boys doing?"

Luke leaned forward and twisted his suit so he could see Chad in his recliner. "No leaks, Boss." As the technician put the last of Luke's checklists and safety equipment into his suit's pockets, he added, "We must be getting close."

"Same here, Chad," Michael said, raising a thumb. "My suit fits like a glove."

"Especially the gloves," Luke joked.

The suit techs stepped back next to the consoles, their work complete. JW donned a headset and made one last assessment of medical status with each crewmember, while a NASA photographer walked around and took a few photos.

Al Shepard's voice came over the comms. "You gentlemen ready to go see your spaceship?"

Three hands immediately came up, thumbs raised.

"Right. Time to go get us a launch."

The ride to the pad was nine miles through palmetto scrub and a cluster of oversized rocket assembly buildings. As the van lumbered smoothly along the coral pavement, Chad spotted a bald eagle through his window. It swooped low along the road, spread its wings wide and landed in a large nest, high in a longleaf pine.

Like home, he thought. He'd loved watching birds on the farm, envying their effortless grace in flight. It was part of the reason he'd joined the Air Force; that and to prove himself, to make his parents proud. And now he was on his way to take his place among the greats. He looked down at his white pressure suit, a satisfied smile curling his lips. *I'm going to leave my footprints on the Moon.*

Al Shepard's voice broke in on his thoughts.

"Gentlemen, if I may." Al raised his hand to get everyone's attention. "It's time for the Astronaut's Prayer."

Chad had never heard of this, and from the expressions on his crewmembers' faces, they hadn't either.

His expression serious, Al looked each one of them intently in the eye, and then bowed his head. "Lord, please don't let these men fuck up." He raised his head, smirking, and they all joined him on the "Amen."

It was a joke, but it was also sincere.

The van slowed to a stop next to the Launch Control Center, a long, four-story white building. Al got up and shook hands with Chad and the other crew, wishing them luck, as did JW and Kaz, and then they all climbed out. They'd watch the launch through the fourth-floor windows of the LCC and then fly immediately back to Texas on a NASA Gulfstream jet to be in Mission Control in time for the rendezvous with Almaz. Chad was happy to see them go. It was his show now.

As the van pulled back out onto the road, the suit tech waved his hand to get their attention, and pointed forward. He knew what the view was about to be and wanted to be sure these men didn't miss it.

The van rounded the curve, and suddenly Chad could see the launch pad. Still three miles away, yet clearly visible high above the flood plain, the Saturn V rocket was like some ancient Egyptian monument to the gods, standing proudly next to Launch Pad 39A's gantry tower, gleaming white in the morning sunshine.

Their rocket. *His* rocket.

"Look at that!" Michael said in wonder, his voice muffled by the helmet.

The reality of it struck Chad like a face slap. No more simulations. It was time to show the world who he was.

The van rolled through the open gates at the base of the pad, and the driver downshifted to climb the long, sloping grade up to the rocket. The launch area was crisscrossed with train tracks and metal plates, and the van vibrated as it drove over them. The driver swung wide, stopped and then backed close to the tall gantry. He set the brake, climbed down, walked around and opened the wide rear door, facing the elevator that would take the crew up to the capsule atop the rocket.

Michael clambered out first, and the driver held out his hand.

"Boarding pass?" he demanded sternly. His face broke into a wide grin at the look on Michael's face, and he reached forward to shake his gloved hand. "Have a great flight, sir!"

He repeated the gag for Luke, who laughed obligingly. Chad stepped down, shook the man's hand and then leaned back so he could stare upwards along the full length of the Saturn V. The monstrous rocket was crackling and venting with the super-chilled oxygen being pumped into its tanks. An enormous, brooding dragon, about to belch fire and hurl itself up off the pad, into the blue of the Florida sky.

A white-suited tech was patiently holding the elevator door open. Chad tore his gaze away from the spectacle, trying to fix the image permanently into his memory, and led his crew into the elevator.

The Saturn V stood 363 feet, as tall as a 34-story building. The elevator was designed for freight, with just a framework of metal in place of walls, and the crew watched the rocket flash by as they climbed.

The thick first stage was 33 feet across—so big it couldn't fit on any road or railcar, and had been brought to KSC from the factory in New Orleans by barge, a thousand-mile trip that had taken 10 days. It was now filled with nearly 5 million pounds of oxygen and kerosene; once the engines lit, it would burn through the fuel at 15 tons a second.

The white skin of the rocket looked rough, as it was covered by a thin coating of ice. The chilled liquid oxygen inside it made the whole rocket cold, and when the humid Florida air condensed on the skin, it froze.

A *tall cold one*, Luke thought.

The ice would shatter and fall off as the engines lit.

The elevator clattered them up quickly past the black-and-white checkerboard pattern of the wide metal sleeve that protected the five second-stage motors and joined the two rocket segments together. The first stage was going to push with 160 million horsepower, and this hoop of metal had to be strong enough to handle the force and vibration.

As they passed the 20-story mark, the width of the rocket narrowed to the third stage, its hydrogen and oxygen tanks feeding a single engine that would push them out of Earth orbit to the Moon. Like the second stage, it had been built in California; both had traveled to the launch pad by ship through the Panama Canal.

Luke leaned forward and looked down. *Whoa!* He felt unexpected vertigo. The elevator was slowing as they reached the Command Module level, and he lifted his eyes towards the beach house to settle his gyros. He could see the thin strip of sand just beyond it, pale brown against the Atlantic waves.

The doors opened with a clang. Chad picked up his ventilator pack and strode off first. Michael followed, then Luke, walking along an outer railing and through a gantry door, then out to the final swing arm that led to their spaceship.

Michael leaned his helmet close to Luke's and yelled, "Like a gangplank!"

Chad had already started down the long, thin walkway of the swing arm. It was 320 feet above the launch pad, a latticework of orange-painted metal, with open sides and top. The metal grid of the floor was covered with rubber mats to block the dizzying view.

Luke yelled back, "You're next, Michael—now or never!"

At the far end of the walkway was a small, tent-like enclosure nestled against the sloping side of the spaceship. It was covered in white fabric, and, with NASA's typical artistic flair, it was called the White Room. It was just big enough for the suit techs to get one crewmember ready at a time. When Chad disappeared inside, Michael began walking.

He stayed solidly in the middle to avoid getting buffeted into the siderails by the wind. Like most pilots, he hated heights when he didn't have wings to support him. He kept his gaze focused on the White Room door at the end, and felt irrationally safer when it opened and he was able to step inside. Chad was already swinging himself into the capsule's darkened interior.

Luke took a few paces out onto the gantry and looked around while he waited his turn. His eyes followed the long crushed-gravel trail of the giant tracked crawler that had slowly carried the rocket-ship to the pad. At the far end were the Vehicle Assembly Building and the Launch Control Center; he peered at them, imagining the hundreds of engineers and technicians at their consoles, staring back at him through its windows.

He swung his gaze to the left, and could pick out the flag and crowds at the NASA Press Site. Squinting, he could just see the low, dark rect-angle of the digital countdown clock. Farther left, across the water of the Banana River, he could see glinting reflections from the thousands of cars that were parked there, the spectators jockeying for position on the beach. His parents were somewhere in that mass of people, and he raised a hand and waved to them, thinking of how they must be feeling and silently thanking them.

Movement caught his eye, and he realized the door had opened and a tech was waving at him. He hustled down the gantry.

The techs were fast and methodical as they checked Luke's suit. He handed them his ventilator and lifted his feet individually so they could slip off his protective yellow galoshes. Then he grabbed the handlebar above the hatch and swung his legs inside, fighting the bulky suit. Chad was already strapped into his seat on the left, and a tech was tightening Michael's restraint straps on the right. Since Luke would be doing the Almaz spacewalk soon after launch, he was in the center seat, nearest the hatch; it would simplify configuring his umbilical and getting himself efficiently outside. Lifting his weight, Luke slid on his back into place.

The tech leaned his face close and asked Luke to hold his breath so he could swap the hoses from the ventilator for the built-in ship lines. Luke could feel him making connections, and suddenly sound crackled in his headset. The tech leaned into Luke's sightline.

"One, two, three, how do you hear me, Luke?"

"Loud and clear, thanks."

The tech cinched down Luke's straps, double-checked that the checklists were still Velcroed and clipped in position, and gave his visor a wipe with a chamois cloth. Then he looked Luke in the eye.

"All good?"

"All set," Luke said.

As the tech retrieved the last of his equipment and gave the cabin a final once-over, Luke looked around. Lying on his back, he could turn his head left and right, its weight supported by his helmet. He listened to the low hiss of ship's oxygen flowing up and behind his head, feeling it blowing steadily down across his face to keep his visor from fogging. He glanced at Chad and then at Michael; both of them were all business, lit by the sunlight from the overhead windows as they focused on their instruments, double-checking against the checklists mounted in front of them.

Facing the crew was a complex array of over 600 switches, instruments and indicators that allowed them to control the spaceship, now as familiar to each of them as any airplane they'd ever flown. No one could reach all the switches, so they each had specific responsibilities. Squarely in front of Luke were the propulsion system, atmospheric control and the cluster of emergency lights that lit up in yellow and red to signal that something was wrong. There were still a few lights on, as the vehicle wasn't quite ready for launch, and Luke checked from memory that the pattern was correct.

He felt a tap on his helmet and leaned back to see the tech, his eyebrows raised in a polite question. Luke gave him a thumbs-up, and watched as he checked with Michael and then Chad. Then the tech waved, clambered carefully out and closed the hatch.

Luke looked at the digital mission timer squarely in front of him, counting down: two hours, ten minutes to launch.

Fifteen miles to the east, a ship called the *Kavkaz* waited patiently. She wasn't particularly big, and her hull was better suited to the landlocked Black Sea than the open waters of the Atlantic, but she was based on the classic Mayakovsky fishing trawler design and could handle the rougher seas well enough. Only 85 meters long, she had a more-than-ample 14-meter beam, and her 2,200-horsepower single-screw diesel could push her through the water at a useful but unimpressive 12.5 knots.

Kavkaz's true merit didn't rest on her hull and engine, though. It was in the gleaming white dome and multiple antenna towers mounted on her upper decks. She was a Primorye-class surveillance ship with high-speed satellite datalinks back to the Soviet Union, and she was patrolling the Florida coast just outside of the US 12-mile limit. And she had been tasked by HQ in Leningrad to observe this final Apollo launch.

The Captain was content. It was not a complex mission, and the mid-April Florida warmth was a very welcome break for his crew. They'd spent the previous two months in the North Sea, and when the orders had come to steam south, everyone had been glad. It was the twelfth Apollo launch, and they'd all been virtually identical. *Proshche parevoy repeh*, he thought. Simpler than a steamed turnip.

He'd told the chief communications officer to pipe the NASA countdown through the ship's loudspeakers, and every crewman who wasn't needed belowdecks was up on the rail, most with binoculars and cameras hanging around their necks.

The American voice echoed through the Soviet ship. "This is Apollo Saturn Launch Control. We've passed the thirty-six-minute mark in our countdown, and completed the range of safety command checks, all still going well. A short while ago Spacecraft Test Conductor Skip Chauvin asked Commander Chad Miller if the crew was comfortable up there, and Chad reported back that 'We're fine—it's a good morning.'"

The Captain, who spoke English passably, looked across the calm seas towards the Florida shore. *I agree, my fellow captain, it's a very good morning.*

The US Coast Guard cutter *Steadfast* was trailing the *Kavkaz* by a half mile, making sure they didn't stray too close. It was a cat-and-mouse game both of them had played many times before, and they were easy with it. The recently signed US-Soviet Incidents at Sea Agreement had made the rules clear for both sides: stay out of each other's way, follow the regulations and, most important of all, take no hostile-looking actions.

The Captain checked his watch: 15:00 in Moscow, 08:00 here in Florida. Just over a half hour until launch. He checked his binoculars and his camera as well. He didn't want to miss this.

The small black-and-white portable television was out of place in the Berlin cathedral. Alexander, now the senior lector for Father Ilarion, had brought it and set it up in the vestry at the monk's request. He extended the twin silver aerials, twisting and tilting them until he had a clear picture from the local station. He pushed the small buttons on top while the NASA announcer was talking, setting the volume. Alexander stepped back, and the picture faded. He grunted, readjusted the antennas and stepped back again. The picture held this time.

In truth, Alexander was excited for the chance to see the last Apollo launch, the last of America's planned manned Moon missions.

He heard the hieromonk coming down the hall and double-checked that the TV picture was still good. He'd positioned two chairs facing the screen.

"Pochti parah?" Father Ilarion asked. Is it almost time?

"Da. Minoot pietnadset." Yes—about 15 minutes.

The NASA announcer was speaking. "All still going well with the countdown at this time. The astronauts aboard the spacecraft have had a little chance to rest over the last few minutes. In the meantime, we have been performing final checks on the tracking beacons in the

Instrument Unit, which is used as the guidance system during the powered phase of flight."

"Shto skazal?" What's he saying?

The monk's grasp of English remained minimal. Alexander translated, summarizing as the NASA public affairs officer spoke. Ilarion leaned towards the small screen when they showed a close-up of the rocket on the pad. He frowned.

"What's that steam coming out of the ship?"

How should I know? Alexander thought with some exasperation. *Why do people think interpreters have knowledge beyond language?*

He guessed. "It's excess fuel as they fill the tanks to the brim."

Father Ilarion nodded. "What an amazing thing!"

They listened as Houston Mission Control started communications checks with the capsule. Alexander raised his hand, palm open, for silence.

"Apollo 18, this is Houston on VHF and S-band. How do you read? Over."

They both held their breath to listen for the voice crackling across the thousands of kilometers.

"Houston, Apollo 18. Have you loud and clear."

A wondering smile spread across Ilarion's face.

"This is Apollo Saturn Launch Control. We've passed the eleven-minute mark, all still GO at this time. The spacecraft is now on the full power of its fuel cells. The Commander has armed his rotational hand controller, and we have now gone to automatic on the Emergency Detection System. We're aiming for our planned liftoff at thirty-two minutes past the hour."

The voice echoed tinnily from the multiple small loudspeakers mounted on poles along the Banana River causeway. Cars were parked at all angles, thousands of them jammed together on the narrow strip between the road and the beach. With launch just 10 minutes away, the early-morning lineups at the food trucks and portable toilets had evaporated, and all faces were turning towards the launch pad, seven miles to the north. The morning sun was already hot, glaring down on the deck chairs, blankets and sunglasses of the excited crowd.

Laura sat on the back bumper of a Dodge van, holding a black coffee and rubbing the overnight grit from her eyes. She and three others from the Lunar Receiving Laboratory had made a last-minute decision to road-trip to the Cape for the launch, a monotonous, 15-hour five-state haul across I-10 and down I-75. Their NASA badges had gotten them early access to the causeway the night before, and they'd slept in the van backed right onto the beach, which meant she now had an unimpeded view straight across the water to the Saturn V.

Don Baldwin, his Hawaiian shirt adorned with rockets and clouds, sat next to her. "Got lucky on the weather."

She looked around at the blue sky and the light skiff of wind on the water, then stared across the water towards the rocket. "I'm glad we made the drive." She said it partly to convince herself; it had been an uncomfortable sleep. As the announcer called "Mark, T minus ten minutes and counting," she shook her head to clear it and sat up straighter.

The loudspeakers blared the familiar GO/NO-GO dialogue, STC querying each console in Launch Control for their readiness. Laura felt her gut clench as several of them reported problems, and then relax as they worked through them. She listened for Chad Miller to add his "GO," and then a different voice came on. "Apollo 18, this is the Launch Operations Manager. The launch team wishes you good luck and Godspeed."

She glanced at her watch, her heart starting to race. Four minutes to launch. Some of her experiments were inside that beast, and she'd helped to train the crew. She focused her camera lens on the rocketship, squeezed her finger on the shutter button and took the picture. Her thumb found the lever and advanced the film.

C'mon, baby, we scientists are ready! Time for all you engineers to do your stuff. Get that crazy monstrosity off the ground!

———

The Saturn V's F-1 engines were beasts with a power the world had never seen. Five of them waited at the bottom of the rocket, sleeping in suspended animation, their blood vessels dry, their hearts and bellies empty. Hungry and ready for the fuel and spark that would bring them to life.

Ten minutes before launch three valves had clicked open, allowing the first of the kerosene and chilled oxygen to gush down from the tanks, high above. This potential explosive power now waited to be mixed, just one valve away from exploding into the barely controlled hellfire that would push the massive weight up and away from the Earth.

Luke was aware that the pre-valves were open; he knew the entire sequence by heart. The giant dragon beneath them was awakening. He'd wondered how he would feel just before launch. *Not afraid*, he observed. *Good.* Either this thing was going to work or it wasn't. He felt . . . ready.

Movement on his right caught his eye. Michael's left knee was bobbing up and down, an unconscious release of pent-up emotion and energy. Luke was glad both of his knees were still.

He glanced at the clock. One minute to go. Sixty clicks of the second hand and the games would truly begin. He watched Chad reach and push the button to align the gyros, giving the rocket a final snapshot of orientation for accurate steering. It was the last crew step prior to launch.

Luke turned the page of his checklist and put his thumb next to the top of the table. Chad and Michael would be watching lights and instruments, but he'd be looking at height versus speed. The whole 11 minutes and 39 seconds was laid out in the table. When his thumb got to the bottom, they'd be 93 miles up, going 25,599 feet per second. 17,500 miles per hour. Five miles a second.

22

Launch Pad 39A, Kennedy Space Center

Starting the world's most powerful engine wasn't easy. It took about nine seconds to crank one up—the time an Olympic sprinter could run 100 yards. The time it takes to tie one shoe.

The most dangerous nine seconds of the whole flight.

The amount of fuel needed to push the Saturn V off the pad was staggering: 3,400 gallons every second. That required fuel pumps with their own jet engines, just to spin them fast enough. The rocketship had five of these jets pumping the kerosene and oxygen into the rocket chambers, where it would mix, explode and storm out the 12-foot-tall exhaust nozzles in a 5,800-degree, 160-million-horsepower inferno.

The crew's eyes were glued to the engine instruments as the clock counted down into single digits.

"T minus ten, nine, and we have ignition sequence start."

Four fireworks ignited inside each engine: two to spin up the fuel pump, and two to burn any flammable gases lurking in the exhaust nozzle.

"Six, five, four . . ."

Two big valves opened, and liquid oxygen poured from its high tank down through the spinning pump and into the rocket, gushing out the huge nozzle under its own weight like a frothy white waterfall. Two smaller valves clicked open, feeding oxygen and kerosene to fuel the jet engines, spinning the pumps up to high speed. The pressure in the main fuel lines suddenly jumped to 380 psi.

Conditions were set, with everything ready to ignite the rockets. Just needed some lighter fluid.

Two small discs burst under the high fuel pressure, and a slug of triethylboron/aluminum was pushed into the oxygen-rich rocket chambers. Like the ultimate spark plug, the fluids exploded on contact.

"Three, two . . ."

The middle engine lit first, followed quickly by the outer four; if all five had started at once, they would have torn the rocketship and launch pad apart. Two more big valves opened, and high-pressure kerosene poured into the growing maelstrom.

Luke felt the rippling vibration through his back and heard the deep, rumbling noise from 300 feet below. *Different than the simulator!* He glanced left to where Chad's eyes were focused. The five engine lights had gone out, confirming full thrust.

"One, zero, and liftoff, we have liftoff, at 7:32 a.m. Eastern Standard Time."

Hell, unleashed, creating 700 tons of thrust in each of the five engines—enough total power to lift more than 7 million pounds straight up. The ultimate deadlift.

The last of the ground umbilicals feeding the rocket disconnected and snapped back. The four heavy hold-down arms that had been clamping the base to the pad hissed in pneumatic relief and pivoted away.

The Saturn V was free.

Chad's eyes clicked around his instrument panel, confirming. The small, square Lift Off light was glowing, he could feel the vehicle moving, and the digital mission timer was counting upwards.

"The clock is running, Houston."

Apollo 18 had begun.

Father Ilarion's jaw had gone slack. What he was seeing on the small screen was far removed from his daily life, and yet the power and danger were palpable to him.

As the final 30 seconds before launch had ticked down, he'd grabbed Alexander's hand, squeezing hard. While the announcer's voice counted through the last 10 seconds, Ilarion's grip intensified until his entire arm was shaking, the flames from the engines filling the screen and the rocket lifting off the pad, agonizingly slowly.

"Slava Bogu!" Ilarion said in abject wonder. Praise God! His eyes remained locked on the flickering image, but he didn't understand what the NASA announcer was saying. "Is everything still all right, Alexander?"

"Yes, Father, the rocket is working perfectly. The astronauts are having the ride of their lives." He pried his hand out of the hieromonk's grip and shook his tingling fingers.

The two men watched without speaking, the blue TV light oddly illuminating the icons on the bare plaster walls as the image on the screen shrank to a wavering flame in the sky.

"Roll and pitch program, Houston."

The three crewmen were intensely hawking their instruments. The rocket had climbed clear of the launch tower and then turned to steer up the east coast; they could see the precision of it in the motion of the black-and-white ball of the artificial horizon. As Chad radioed the expected motions to Houston, Luke noticed the sunlight changing angle through the windows, confirming that the ship was guiding properly.

"Roger, 18. Thrust good on all five engines."

Hearing the voice of their CAPCOM was reassuring. It meant that a team of experts was comparing expected height and speed to what the ship was actually doing, and that they matched.

Luke traced his thumb along the table in his checklist, confirming what Houston was telling them. He tried to hold his hand steady against the deep, powerful throbs and fast, jittery shaking, but the vibrations made it hard to line up the numbers. The relentless roaring of the engines filled the cockpit with a symphonic cacophony punctuated by terse communications with the ground.

Luke leaned his head forward against the motors' thrust and caught Michael's eye. "How's that for a cat-shot?" he said, referring to the steam catapult that had once launched their jets from aircraft carriers.

Michael grinned. "Better!"

As the fuel rapidly burned and the vehicle got lighter, it accelerated faster and faster through the thinning air. Luke felt his head and arms getting pushed back as the g-force mounted. He leaned against the headrest, which was buzzing as the rocket shouldered itself through the atmosphere.

He checked his gauges. "Cabin pressure's dropping." Open valves were letting the air inside the cockpit vent as the pressure around the ship dropped with altitude. They'd let it fall all the way to 5 psi and then close the valves to hold it there, using pure oxygen for the rest of the flight. An elegant way to flush the spaceship of Florida air.

"Shake it, baby!" Michael's voice quavered slightly with the intensity of the vibration.

The air had been pushing back against their increasing speed, putting a heavier and heavier load on the structure of the ship. The engineering name for that pressure was Q, and they had just hit the speed and height where it was at maximum. Max Q. From now on, with the air getting rapidly thinner with height, the forces would drop. It was the heaviest load the rocket's structure was designed for, and Luke was glad to be safely through it. He gave Michael two thumbs up.

The CAPCOM's voice confirmed the good news: "18, you are GO for staging."

Soon the first stage of their rocket would run out of fuel and would shut down, separate and fall into the Atlantic. But for now the crew was still being crushed at nearly four times their weight, getting close to the design limit for the rocket itself. Rather than slam all five engines to a stop at once, the computer shut down the center motor to drop the forces while the remaining four burned the last of the fuel.

"Inboard cut-off," Chad reported. Luke instantly felt the load on his body lighten, like there was one less person lying on top of him. But the remaining four engines kept pushing as the ship got lighter, and the g-load rapidly climbed again.

"Christ!" he grunted. He'd pulled lots of g as a fighter pilot, but wasn't used to the relentless load of a rocket. It was getting hard to breathe against the steady weight.

"Hold on!" Chad yelled.

Wham! The crew was thrown forward against their straps as the four big engines stopped and the now-empty rocket body separated.

Slam! They were snapped back into their seats like they'd been rear-ended as the second stage lit, five new engines exploding into life.

"Holy shit!" Luke exclaimed. He'd been warned by previous crews of the violence of staging, but it was far more physical than he'd antici-pated. Like crashing into a wall.

"Looks like we got all five," Michael reported. The second-stage engines had lit properly, settling in to their six-minute push to near-orbital speed.

The NASA Public Affairs announcer spoke: "Apollo 18 now forty-six nautical miles in altitude, eighty nautical miles downrange. Coming up on tower jettison."

They no longer needed the nose-mounted rocket that had been poised to yank the capsule off the Saturn V in an emergency close to the ground. A small rocket in its tip fired for a second and pulled it clear, and it tumbled, unused, into the ocean.

The flash of the tower separating reminded Luke that they were now 50 miles above the surface—the imaginary line where the US Air Force had decided Earth's atmosphere legally ended. His thumb slid past the critical altitude in his checklist. "Congratulations, fellas, welcome to space! We're officially astronauts!"

"About frickin' time," Chad muttered.

The spectacle of the launch was magnificent from the Captain's ringside seat aboard the *Kavkaz*. As the American rocket rose off the pad, his men had broken into spontaneous cheers, and then again as they heard its rumble nearly a minute later. Their binoculars and cameras pivoted as one, tracking as it climbed almost perfectly vertically and then started to pitch over and head on its way.

A frown crossed the Captain's face as he studied the rocket through his own binoculars. He'd positioned the ship almost perfectly east of the launch pad so the rocket would pass directly overhead. Instead, it was accelerating unexpectedly to the right, moving north.

The sensors mounted on the antenna towers on his ship were grabbing multiple frequencies, including transmissions from the ascending rocket. His optical sensors were also tracking the bright light of its engines. He turned to his communications officer. "Do you have a solid directional lock on the rocket's transmissions?"

"Da."

"Get me their launch azimuth."

The comms officer set to work. He rapidly plotted the angle and estimated distance to the ascending Saturn V from the ship, building a series of points on his chart. He wished they also had a radar lock on the rocket, but they were restricted from pulsing energy at it. Still, with enough plot points, he should be able to figure out where Apollo 18 was headed. He expected the resulting line to be mostly easterly, like all previous Apollo launches. But as he added pencil marks, he stared at his chart: there was no denying the data. This line was tracking northeast.

As soon as he was certain he had it right, he aligned the straight edge of his chart protractor through the points, averaging the dispersion. He smoothly drew a pencil line on the chart, angling up from the Florida coast. He extended the line, and was intrigued to see it ran almost parallel to the coast of the Carolinas.

Flipping his protractor around, he took an accurate reading of the angle as it crossed the latitude and longitude grid lines. He sat back briefly and visualized the extended line all the way to the equator. He checked his numbers, and turned to report. The calculation had taken him less than 90 seconds.

"Tell me," the Captain said.

"Apollo 18 launched out of the Kennedy Space Center inclined at fifty-two degrees, meaning it was tipped fifty-two degrees from the equator." The comms officer had worked with the Soviet satellite fleet, and knew what that meant. "The same orbital inclination as our launches from Baikonur."

The Captain nodded. "Prepare an encrypted message for immediate LF transmission to HQ in Severomorsk," he said. He dictated the message, proofread the officer's transcription and signed off for urgent transmission, warning his communications officer, "Keep this information to yourself."

He turned back to stare at the sharp trail of smoke in the sky. *Where are you going, my fellow captain? Are you truly a moonship? Or do you have some other star to guide you?*

"18, Houston. You are GO for orbit—GO for orbit."

They were 1,100 miles from Kennedy, 110 miles above the Earth, still accelerating.

"Glad to hear those words, Houston," Chad replied. The second stage had done its work perfectly, and the third stage was now in the fine-tuning phase that would deliver them to the exact altitude and speed needed for their intercept of Almaz. They'd been rocketing for over 11 minutes, and this final stage was carefully pushing them with just a little over half a g.

"Almost there, boys," Michael said, his attention focused on the digital readouts and the timer as the speed climbed to over 25,000 feet per second.

And then it was over. The third stage shut itself down exactly on time, and the smooth, easy push of its single engine was instantly gone. For the first time in their lives, the three men were weightless.

Luke burst out laughing. "We're here!" He plucked his checklist off the Velcro and floated it in front of his helmet, gently spinning it. "Would you look at that!"

Michael leaned back and peered through his overhead windows. The blackness of space and the curve of the blue North Atlantic horizon filled his view. "Mother of God!" he said.

"Work to do, boys," Chad interjected, bursting their bubble. They each turned the page in their checklists and began the urgent steps that would convert their vehicle from a rocketship to a spaceship.

"Houston, we're with you on Launch page 2-10," Chad said.

A pause. No response.

"Houston, do you read?"

The returning call was scratchy and garbled.

Michael spoke. "I think I heard him repeat that we were GO for orbit there at the end."

Chad nodded. "Agreed. It's likely just bad comms through the North Atlantic relay ship." He glanced at his flight plan. "We'll have them back through the South Pacific ship in an hour or so."

Chad turned and looked at them both.

"Step one complete, boys. Now let's go find us a spy satellite."

23

Kennedy Space Center

The white and blue NASA helicopter was waiting in a roped-off area on the lawn beside Launch Control, its blades slowly turning. Kaz paused to look up at the last of the Saturn V's dispersing smoke, then grabbed the handrail and swung into the passenger bench seat in the back, next to Al Shepard. JW was already strapped in on the far side.

"What a launch!" Kaz shouted.

JW had a huge grin on his face, and Al nodded, unclipping the headphones from the bulkhead and cinching up his lap belt for the short ride to their jet, which would take them back to Mission Control in Houston.

The whine from the engines increased and the rotors spun up. The pilot was a Vietnam vet, and expertly plucked the helo off the ground, turning and pitching to accelerate to the south, towards Patrick Air Force Base.

Kaz looked down out the side window at the roads, already jammed all the way back to the causeway with departing cars and camper vans, thinking that Laura was somewhere down there in that mess. One day maybe he'd be on the ground watching her launch into space. The image made him smile.

The helicopter rapidly covered the 25 miles across the Banana River and along the sands of Cocoa Beach. Soon the Air Force housing and broad runways of Patrick filled the windscreen. The pilot brought the helicopter in fast, flared hard and set it down as light as a feather next to the NASA Gulfstream G-II that was waiting for them. He turned and nodded, nonchalant.

"Well flown," Al Shepard said. Kaz saw the pilot's neck flush red and knew that he'd dine out on that compliment from the first American in space for the rest of his life.

As they climbed out, Al raised a finger to Kaz. "Have them hold the jet. I need to make a phone call." He turned and walked briskly towards the hangar. Kaz and JW transferred the bags and climbed the airstairs onto the G-II.

The plane filled quickly as key Apollo mission personnel arrived at Patrick. By the time Al walked back across the tarmac, his was the last empty seat, next to Kaz. As he settled in, the plane's flight engineer raised the stairs and the pilots started taxiing.

Al didn't speak as the plane climbed away from Patrick, staring out the window as they headed west across the Gulf towards Houston. Finally he turned to Kaz, looking somber.

"Tell me again what you saw that day at Tom Hoffman's crash. From the moment you got to the field that morning."

Kaz didn't ask, but guessed this had something to do with the phone call Al had just made. He kept his tone factual, trying to recall the exact timeline of the morning and who he'd seen when. He described arriving at Ellington, walking through the hangar and then hitching a ride from the ops desk to watch the LLTV fly. He was starting into what he'd observed as Tom's helicopter flew past when Al interrupted him.

"Did you notice Tom's helo on the ground as you drove out to the LLTV site?"

Kaz thought back. "Not really. It was a decent day for weather; several jets had gone flying. The ramp was, maybe, half-full."

Al nodded. "Did you see anyone out on the ramp?" Then, before Kaz could answer, he asked, "Did you go out on the ramp?"

Kaz was startled. "Me? No, I didn't go out on the ramp, and there was nothing unusual that I remember." He closed both eyes, trying to picture it. "There was a T-38 starting, with the normal two groundcrew, one out front and one by the tail." He opened his eyes. "And a fuel truck."

Al looked at him. "Fueling what?"

Kaz shook his head slightly. "I'm not sure. It was driving out towards Tom's helo, but I'm not certain which aircraft it was headed for."

Al drilled further. "Who all did you see at ops and in the hangar?"

Kaz pictured his path, step by step. "Standard gate guard, a couple of the instructor pilots. Chad was there—he'd flown the LLTV before Luke. There was some sort of tour group with a NASA security guy. Normal faces at ops and maintenance."

He shrugged. "Sorry, Boss. I don't remember anything strange." He paused, then said, "Why you asking?"

Al looked around the plane. Everyone but them was dozing after the early-morning intensity of the launch. He leaned close and briefed Kaz on the facts of what the accident investigator had found.

Kaz made a low whistle. A backed-off bolt was someone's serious fuck-up. Or worse. He stared at Al, his eyes asking the next obvious question.

Al didn't answer, just said, "I don't think there's any point in telling the crew, do you?"

Kaz nodded. "And not the family, until we confirm the cause. Likely good if Gene Kranz knows, but otherwise this can wait till they get back."

He could see Al relax slightly. He pulled down the window shade, and tipped his chair back. "Agreed. I'll tell him. Now I'm going to shut my eyes until we get to Ellington. We've got a very busy few hours coming up." His voice was flat. "Looking forward to having Almaz behind them, and firing the engine to head towards the Moon."

Kaz's fake eye's socket was stinging with fatigue and the dry airplane air. He pushed the button to recline his own chair, and tried to find a comfortable position to doze, deliberately turning his mind away from all the troubling implications.

Navy pilots need to learn to nap anywhere, anytime. Soon both men were asleep.

The telex from the *Kavkaz* made the beige desktop machine in Severomorsk, home base of the Soviet Northern Fleet, chatter noisily as it printed the one-page message. The naval communications operator waited until the noise stopped, then leaned across to scan the security clearance and destination printed across the top. His eyes widened and he flicked his gaze away, deliberately not reading the contents.

He took extra care tearing it off the printer roll, and placed it neatly into a pinkish internal mail envelope marked ОСОБОЙ ВАЖНОСТИ—TOP SECRET. He hand-carried the envelope down the hall to the office of his superior, knocked briefly on the door, then set it into the man's inbox like it was hot to the touch. Keeping his gaze averted, he retreated quickly, glad to have done his part properly. Glad it wasn't his responsibility now.

His boss yawned, reading a message from a submarine commander who was taking his vessel back to dry dock. It was essentially a list of the major systems that needed work. He sighed, thinking, *Our fish are fast, but our parts don't last.* He scrawled his signature on the forwarding envelope, addressed it to the Severomorsk Quartermaster, put the multi-page message inside and flipped it into his outbox. He added an annotation to the tracking table in his green baize notebook, and reached across to his inbox for the new arrival.

Pink folder. TOP SECRET. *Atleechna!* Something worthwhile, hopefully!

He hadn't gone into Naval Communications and qualified for the highest security rating so he could push shopping lists around like a flunky clerk in a warehouse. He unwrapped the string holding the flap closed, and slid the page out.

He read it quickly once, and then again, more carefully. He thought for a minute, and then double-checked who the Captain of the *Kavkaz* had directed it to. He flicked his notebook open to the last page, to the list of naval departments and interfaces with other government organizations.

Nodding, he swiftly made a couple of neat notations on the routing envelope highlighting the urgency, and added a subsequent destination. As he started to slide the page back inside, he stopped and rechecked the message timestamp. Frowning, he glanced at his watch, and then reached for his desk phone. He ran his finger again down the list in his book, found a number and dialed it.

This one couldn't wait for internal mail. There was a potential real-time threat to the Motherland, and it was outside of the Navy's jurisdiction.

He listened to the ringing on the other end, rereading the message, preparing exactly what he was going to say.

It took three more phone calls and a total of 36 minutes for the *Kavkaz's* message to get cleared from Severomorsk through the bureaucratic layers all the way to Vladimir Chelomei, as the Almaz Program Director. The tinny telephone speaker on his desk rattled as the *Kavkaz* Captain's words were read to him verbatim, including the timestamp. Chelomei's thoughts clicked like tumblers as he unlocked what the information meant—what the Northern Fleet communications officer had grasped a small piece of.

Those American bastards are heading for my ship!

Gene Kranz leaned back in his chair and looked at his Instrumentation and Communications officer.

"INCO, why isn't 18 hearing us?"

Gene's voice was carried via headsets to everyone in Mission Control, but because of the military nature of the mission, it was blocked from going beyond the building.

"Not certain, FLIGHT. Likely a problem with the relay ship—we haven't had to station one this far north before. They got a good tracking lock, but voice is intermittent. Should be better when we pick up the South Pacific ship at seventy-two minutes."

Gene thought about it.

"FDO, how we looking?" Gene pronounced it "fido." FDO was the Flight Dynamics Officer, in charge of tracking the vehicle's position.

"Right on the money, FLIGHT. Perfect set-up for the rendezvous."

Gene nodded. "Let's work the updated tracking and start getting preliminary numbers for the first burn." The Apollo spaceship had launched into orbit perfectly aligned with Almaz, below and behind it, catching up. It was going to take two careful engine firings to raise the orbit enough so they could fly alongside. "Meanwhile, INCO, let's look hard at onboard comms so far, make sure we're not seeing anything wrong with 18's hardware."

"Copy, FLIGHT, in work."

Gene looked at the digital clocks on the front screen and addressed the whole room.

"When we pick them up over the South Pacific, Luke will be getting his suit ready to go outside, and we'll need to verify all systems are good to support that. We'll also be fifty minutes from the first burn, so we'll need updated tracking to get the right numbers on board.

"Let's be ready, people. This is an Apollo like no other."

The technician at Motorola was an expert with a soldering iron. She'd learned her skill in her dad's garage in Phoenix, the two of them building Heathkit radios and amplifiers together, him admiring her steadiness of hand and fierce concentration as she fed in the minimum amount of metal and flux for neat electrical connections.

When Motorola had hired her, she and her father had both taken great pride in the fact that she was now being trusted to assemble Apollo communications hardware. The complexity of circuitry required methodical assembly and exact handiwork, wiring and soldering each layer into place. The necessity for perfection demanded extra levels of inspection. After she'd bent over, staring intently through her protective glasses to accomplish a task, she'd move out of the way while a supervisor verified the quality of her work. Layer by layer, one soldered connection after another, they had built the main communications blocks for the Apollo Command and Service Modules.

She wore a cotton suit over her clothes, her hair tied up inside an elastic cap, to avoid stray strands or lint getting into the circuitry. Her mouth and nose were covered by a mask so that her humid breath didn't add any moisture. The room of technicians looked somehow robotic, all individuality blurred; anonymous pale-blue figures at electronics benches, intent on their work.

As she had leaned forward to accomplish one particular join, her mask bunched slightly under her nose. She ignored it, focusing on getting the tip of the soldering iron perfectly in place to heat the adjoining exposed wires. She wrinkled her nose at the tickling sensation caused by the mask and wiggled her pursed lips side to side. But it was no use, and she sneezed. She stifled it, as she had stifled other sneezes, focused on keeping her hands steady as she fed in the solder and flux.

She finished, pulled her hands away and tipped her head to one side, examining her work. She allowed herself a small smile under the mask. It looked perfect. She rolled her chair slightly away as the inspector leaned in to double-check. Satisfied as usual, he nodded, and made a checkmark in the long list on his clipboard. She adjusted the mask slightly away from her nostrils and continued working.

Unknowing.

Her stifled sneeze had jostled her arm and created an imperfection on the underside of the join. Like a pebble, a small ball of solder had cooled separately, trapped and hidden under a thin covering strand. A little sphere of metal, held securely in place against gravity.

Pursuit was the last Apollo Command Module to fly, and not all of its equipment was as rigorously tested as the first flights had been. The qualification process had already been proven, and money was tighter than ever. The original heavy vibration testing had been reduced to an approved laboratory shake test; the solder imperfection held through it, and the transponder passed its subsequent functional check flawlessly and was carefully installed in *Pursuit*'s avionics bay.

But the combination of actual launch vibration and acceleration shook it loose. The heavy forces at Max Q stressed the thin metal covering strand, and the sudden jolt of staging broke the ball free. The second-stage engines' acceleration pushed the small drop of solder into the adjoining circuit board and held it there. A tiny bit of metal, fallen out of harm's way, held in place by the forces of the launch.

When the third-stage motor shut off, the spacecraft was suddenly weightless, orbiting around the Earth. The little metal orb drifted gently up from its resting place, becoming a tiny conductive balloon in a playground of circuitry.

Small thrusters fired to point *Pursuit* in the right direction, giving a gentle acceleration to the ship. It moved sideways, floating the metal pebble into a new part of the transponder's circuitry. As Chad pushed the comm button to talk, the circuit was activated and shorted across two wires touching the solder ball, welding it into its new resting place. The electrical short dropped the current well below normal, and the signal didn't get through. Chad's voice dead-ended inside the box.

A stifled sneeze, 19 months earlier in Phoenix, Arizona, had caused the failure of the primary voice circuitry for *Pursuit*, Apollo 18's Command Module.

The crew was just talking to themselves.

Top Secret

CENTRAL INTELLIGENCE AGENCY—
UNITES STATES OF AMERICA

The President's Daily Brief—Addendum
16 April 1973—08:00 EST

FOR THE PRESIDENT ONLY

PRINCIPAL DEVELOPMENTS—Addendum

NASA reports a successful launch at 07:32 EST
this morning of Apollo 18, with an all-military
crew reporting to Vice Chief of Naval Operations,
Admiral Maurice Weisner, and the Joint Chiefs. Initial mission tasking is in support of the NSA and
CIA, to photo-document and, if possible, disable
the Soviet spy satellite Almaz ('Diamond'), which
launched from Baikonur USSR on 3 April. Almaz has
the most capable on-orbit optical spy capability
of any spacecraft, Soviet or American, estimated
to be able to resolve objects on the surface as
small as one foot. If operational, this would have
significant negative SIGINT impacts for the USA.

Almaz needs to be operated real-time by cosmonauts on board, required for film loading, unloading, processing and subsequent film de-orbit/ parachute return to the USSR. Almaz is as-yet unmanned and thus pre-operational, with no CIA/NSA indications of the upcoming cosmonaut launch date.

At approximately 10:35 today Apollo 18 astronaut Captain Lucas Hemming, USMC, will perform a solo spacewalk to photograph and disable Almaz by cutting external cables and/or cooling/fuel lines. Unlike all previous Apollo missions, there is a total public blackout of communications and crew activities during this 2-hour phase of flight, and potentially subsequent.

Once Almaz ops are complete, Apollo 18 will fire its engine to leave Earth orbit for the Moon at approximately 11:30 EST. Transit to the Moon will take 3 days. The flight profile will more closely resemble all previous Apollo missions from that point forward.

-Addendum End-

24

Pursuit, Earth Orbit

"Woo-hoo, sorry, guys. That one's a real stinker!"

The air pressure inside the cabin had dropped steadily, as planned, during launch, and was now holding at one-third of what it had been in Florida. The gases in everyone's guts had expanded, and all three of them were farting.

Michael winced. "Geez, Luke, keep that in your own spacesuit, would ya?"

"How's the alignment going, Michael?" Chad had jettisoned the exterior covers that protected the optical systems during launch, and Michael was sighting through the built-in cameras, carefully turning *Pursuit* to align with specific stars. When he was sure he had it exact, he entered the data into the navigation computer. They needed precise orientation for the upcoming maneuver to raise their orbit up to match Almaz.

"Looking good, Boss. The stars are right where they were in the sim."

"Well, that's a relief," Luke said. He was folding his launch seat out of the way to make room for his spacewalk. "That Saturn V sure gave us a hell of a ride!"

Michael chimed in. "I felt like a crash test dummy!"

Chad interrupted. "Boys, you got any snags we should tell Houston about?"

They both shook their heads at Chad, who was still strapped into the left seat. Making eye contact while weightless was new to them all; it was strange to have no common up or down as a reference.

Chad confirmed the S-band comm switch was in transmit/receive. He leaned to his right and watched as the radio signal strength jumped, showing communications lock with the *Rose Knot* relay ship, 106 miles below, off the Australia coast. He pushed the black transmit trigger on his rotational joystick.

"Houston, Apollo 18's back with you."

No response.

Chad rechecked his switches and leaned over to the communications sub-panel to verify that everything was set correctly. He called again, and frowned when Houston didn't respond. Michael floated over and tapped the keyboard display that showed digital uplink activity from the ship.

"Data's flowing fine, Boss."

The CAPCOM's voice broke in. "Apollo 18, it's Houston, how do you read?"

Both men exhaled in relief. "Try using your mic to answer," Chad told Michael, who pushed his trigger. "Loud and clear, Houston, how us?"

No response.

Michael pictured the communications system in his head, considering possible causes. "Data's good both ways, and we're hearing them fine. So we have a problem with voice downlink."

Chad agreed. "Houston, if you hear, we're swapping to VHF." He reached up and threw the switches to select the simpler, traditional aircraft radio system, and tried again.

"Houston, this is 18 on VHF, how do you hear?"

There was a light buzz of static in the headsets. Luke had stopped what he was doing to watch them work the problem. This had suddenly gone from annoying to serious. He said, "Can you send a null data command to let them know we're hearing them?"

"Good idea," Chad responded. He thought for a second, and then punched in five zeroes and pushed Enter. The computer rejected the command and the Operator Error light came on. He typed 11111, reselected S-band communications and waited for Houston to call again.

"Apollo 18, Houston, we see your null entry. How do you read?"

Chad pushed Enter. The Operator Error light came on again.

A smile spread on Michael's face. "You're setting up a code!"

Chad shrugged. "Let's see if they catch on." He ran his thumb down the flight plan. "We only have comms via this ship for another ninety seconds or so."

"Apollo 18, Houston. If you hear us, please retype all ones and Enter."

"Bingo!" Chad said, punching in the numbers.

The CAPCOM's voice sounded relieved. "18, we see that, thanks. All systems look good to us except downlink voice. It might be a weak transmit signal, so we'll try again on the big dish at White Sands in twenty-two minutes, and will have other ideas there. If you copy, press all zeroes and Enter."

Chad did as instructed.

"18, we see that. If you have any serious issues on board, type all ones. If nominal, type zeroes."

Chad sent five zeroes.

"Good to see, 18, thanks. Talk to you in twenty."

Chad turned to his crew.

"Looks like we're still on for now, but this is a primitive workaround. Luke, keep getting things set for the spacewalk. Michael, get out the comm system schematics. I do *not* want a simple comm problem to lose us the Moon."

Michael was by the window, his face lit by a faint glow. "I'm on it, but guys, stop for a minute and watch this. First sunrise in space."

Chad and Luke looked up through the windows to see the sunrise happening as they raced towards it at five miles a second, the faint purple glow of the night horizon quickly overtaken by the dawn.

Luke gasped as the Sun burst into view.

"That's the most beautiful thing I ever saw," Michael said reverently. "It's like someone just poured a rainbow onto the edge of the world."

"Nice," Chad said. "But it also means we've got ninety minutes. By the next sunrise, Almaz should be in our sights."

"Right," Luke said, and began gathering more gear for his spacewalk. "Where are you in EVA prep?"

"Doing good, Boss. I've got my long umbilical attached on the backpack, coiled for you to pay out as I go. Over-gloves and external visor are ready."

Luke rummaged in a narrow open locker, carefully retrieving a large, square Hasselblad camera with a stubby lens, mounted on a pistol grip. He clipped it into the frame built into the chest of his spacesuit, listening for the click, and then unclipped it and stowed it with his other gear. He reached back into the locker and pulled out yard-long orange bolt cutters. After the mission changed, he and an EVA tech had bought them at a Houston hardware store. They'd wired a small metal ring to one of the handles so Luke could make sure they didn't float away while he was outside. He tucked the tool under a bungee next to the camera.

Michael had unfolded the pull-out page with the communications system schematic from his thick reference checklist and was tracing wire lines on the diagram, looking for possible culprits. "Boss, check my thinking here. Our voice comm problem affected both of us, and only for downlink, so it's got to be a specific failure in a common location." He double-tapped a rectangle on the drawing. "My guess is inside the main USB transponder."

He flipped to a following page. "We can get at it in the avionics bay if we need to, but we'd need to tear things down some to get there."

Chad thought about it. "Let's wait and see what Houston says." He checked his watch. "Speaking of which."

Right on cue, a voice cut in on the cabin speaker. "Apollo 18, this is Houston via White Sands, how do you read?"

"Houston, I have you loud and clear." Chad paused. "How me?" The crew collectively held their breath.

"18, Houston, you're weak but readable. We're just confirming tracking now, will have the Almaz rendezvous burn pad up to you shortly."

"Copy, Houston." Weak but readable was good enough for now.

Gene Kranz wanted everyone in Mission Control to hear what he was about to say. "Everybody, listen up. This is FLIGHT. Give me a green when you're ready." He had a multicolored matrix on his console, with one small square for each officer in the room. When they each pushed the green button on their desks and Gene saw all lights turn to green on his, he knew he had everyone's undivided attention.

"INCO, talk to me. What's the workaround for 18's comm problem?" With the first maneuvering burn rapidly approaching, the room needed answers.

"FLIGHT, it's a weak signal on their return voice loop," INCO said. "Looks like a partial short somewhere, likely the connectors or inside the USB transponder box itself. For now, we'll have workable comms through the big antennas in Madrid and Canberra, as well as stateside. We'll have everything but return voice through all other sites. Once we get past the Almaz rendezvous and TLI burn, we have crew actions that should fix the problem."

Gene didn't like the word "should."

"INCO, what's your confidence in the crew repair actions?" Without there being a high probability they could fix the comm malfunction, he didn't want to fire the big engine that would take the ship out of the relative safety of Earth orbit and send them on an unstoppable three-day voyage across the void to the Moon. Counting three days there and three days back, it was basically a week of the crew's lives he'd be gambling with. He needed the communications to work.

"FLIGHT, worst case, we'll have what we just saw through White Sands—weak but readable. As we get farther from Earth it will get better, since we'll be in range of one or two of the big antennas on Earth all the time. No gaps. Also, deploying the high-gain antenna on *Pursuit* will help boost the signal."

Gene nodded. He had one more key question. "Will the Lunar Module have the same problem?"

"Nope, FLIGHT, the LM's independent."

Gene looked around the room. "We're about to talk to 18 again via Madrid, and then we have the first rendezvous burn." He paused. "Anyone have any concerns?"

Silence.

Not ideal, Gene thought. *But we've seen far worse. We found a way to get Apollo 13 safely back; we should be able to solve this little problem.*

"Good work, INCO," he said. "Everyone, let's uplink the rendezvous data ASAP. I'll be looking for a GO for the burn from each of you as soon as it's on board."

Gene raised his eyes to the front screen, watching the white projected image of the Apollo spacecraft crossing the North Atlantic west of Ireland. Just ahead of it was a red rectangle, tracing the same curved path across the globe.

What secrets do you hold, Almaz? We're about to go find out.

"Luke, you got everything stowed for the burn?"

Luke was hanging on to Chad's headrest, staring out the window at the orange dryness of the Sahara Desert. "Sure do, Boss. I'm ready to surf."

Michael leaned across to check the instruments in front of Chad. "Attitude looks good, Boss."

Chad nodded his agreement. The spacecraft had pivoted exactly in space to align with the instructions sent up from Mission Control. Next communications would be over Madagascar, but this engine firing to raise their orbit up to match Almaz was taking place in between ground sites. No one was watching except the crew.

"Michael, as soon as this burn's done, I'll get out of the left seat, and you can fly *Pursuit*."

"Roger that, I'm ready."

Their eyes were fixed on the digital counter.

"Ten seconds, Luke," Michael cautioned.

"All set, thanks." Luke had the Hasselblad in his free hand, and the electric film advance was whining and clunking as he snapped images out the window. "I can't believe this view of the Nile."

"Three, two, here we go," Chad said.

With a low rumble they could feel through the hull, the liquid hydrogen J-2 engine ignited 100 feet below their backs, instantly pushing with 200,000 pounds of thrust. Luke clattered against the aft bulkhead. "Whoa, Nellie!" he said, trying to keep the camera from banging the window.

"I told you to hold on!" Chad said.

A checklist detached itself from the Velcro with a ripping sound and sailed past Michael's head. Luke grabbed it out of the air and handed it back.

Michael said, "Temps and pressures look good, engine's gimballing fine." The single J-2 engine bell was pivoting precisely on its mount, ensuring the thrust was pushing *Pursuit* in the right direction. Through his seat, he could feel the small steering corrections and vibration. "Engine cut-off in fifteen seconds."

Chad raised his right hand and pointed to the pressure gauges. "Three, two, one." They confirmed that the timer and lights agreed.

"Good cut-off."

"Guys, as soon as you get a chance, take a look. You can see all the way from the Rift Valley to the Horn of Africa!"

Chad safed the switches, unbuckled his straps and carefully floated out of his seat. "Coming up for a look. Michael, the ship is yours."

"Aye aye, Captain! I have control." Michael floated into the left seat and loosely buckled himself in place. Their orbit was now shaped like an oval, with the high point raised to equal Almaz's altitude. They had one more engine firing over the Pacific so they'd match the Soviet ship's circular orbit exactly, and then they'd be in visual range for Michael to maneuver up close. He'd been practicing it in the sim relentlessly ever since Kaz had brought the orders from Washington, but today was the real thing. He noticed that his palms were damp and wiped them on the heavy cloth of his spacesuit, then gently held onto the hand controllers, picturing the motions he'd be making.

"Hey, Luke, what was that Astronaut's Prayer again?" he asked.

Luke laughed.

Michael exhaled to concentrate, and focused on what was coming.

Lord, please don't let me fuck this up.

Operating the ship had kept Chad fully occupied, and the seat straps had stopped him from fully sensing weightlessness; it had seemed more like an extra-realistic sim than actual spaceflight. But as he floated out of his seat to change positions with Michael, the reality of where he was physically struck him.

Whoa! His balance system was working hard, trying to sort out what was going on. He reached for the handrail next to the window, jerkily missing it once and then grabbing hard to steady himself. A wave of dizziness went through him, momentarily blurring his vision. He closed his eyes to let it pass.

Luke was floating next to him. "You good, Boss?"

"Never better," Chad said flatly, opening his eyes and focusing on the horizon. The medicos had warned him that he might feel motion sickness, but he'd spent a decade flying and testing fighters and had dismissed their concerns. Like all military pilots, he was proud of his iron stomach.

Luke tried to distract him by pointing out the window. "I wonder if there are people on that speck?" A tiny, circular volcanic island in the South Indian Ocean was passing underneath, its shadow pushed long across the ocean by the rapidly approaching sunset. Chad slowly pivoted his whole body to look, keeping his neck rigid to stop his head from moving.

He flicked his eyes down to see. "Real garden spot," he grunted. He closed his eyes again, slowly.

As they drove into orbital darkness, the light around them swiftly changed from bright white to orange to blood red, like a fading flare was illuminating their faces.

Chad gagged, his whole body convulsing as he tried to contain it. He fumbled in his leg pocket, yanking out a sick bag just in time to get it positioned over his face as the steak and eggs shot out of his mouth like a jet. Luke grimaced and pulled himself across the hatch to the other window. He poked Michael and silently pointed with his chin.

Did they really have to make the bag transparent?

They both winced and watched in morbid fascination as Chad gagged again, the vomit ricocheting off the far end of the bag and flying weightlessly back onto Chad's face. The cabin filled with the sour smell of vomit.

Luke pulled a cotton napkin out of his shoulder pocket and silently waved it to get Chad's attention.

Chad took it from him. He squeezed the sick bag closed with one hand and mopped his face from forehead to chin with the other.

Michael tried humor. "Well, at least we can't smell Luke's farts now."

Chad took one more swipe at his face and then stuffed the cloth into the sick bag, rolling and sealing the open end with the attached red twist tie. He pulled his own napkin out of his shoulder pocket and more carefully wiped his face and hands.

"I'll get you some water," Luke said. He squeezed past Chad to flick the pressurization switch, and pulled out the water dispenser, squirting it onto Chad's napkin.

"Thanks," Chad mumbled, wiping his face once more. He held up the half-full barf bag, a disgusted expression on his face. "What do we do with this for the next week?"

"I'll chuck it when I go outside," Luke said. "Maybe I can use it to disable Almaz."

"Very funny," Chad said as he Velcroed the sick bag next to the hatch, his newly empty stomach making him feel much better. He took a deep breath and checked his watch.

"We're going to have to start cabin depress soon for the EVA." He looked at Luke.

"Let's get you dressed for battle."

"Apollo 18, Houston, back with you through Madagascar. Looks like your burn was right on the money. We're genning up prelim numbers for your second burn now."

CAPCOM paused. "If you copy, type five balls."

Michael had the digital response ready and pushed Enter.

"We see that, and all systems look good. If you have any problems, type five ones."

Maybe this isn't so bad, Gene Kranz thought, sitting in his Flight Director chair. *Might be better for everyone if they can't tell us exactly what they're doing when we're close to Almaz.*

ALMAZ

25

Rendezvous, Earth Orbit

The Apollo crew had put their gloves and helmets back on, and the suits were stiffening as the pressure inside the capsule dropped in preparation for Luke's spacewalk. Luke was watching the vomit bag inflate with the air trapped inside it, and hoped it wouldn't leak or burst before they got to hard vacuum. He asked, "How you feeling, Boss?"

"I'm fine. Michael, how'd the burn look?"

"Right on the money. We should see Almaz ahead and above us soon."

As soon as Michael caught sight of the space station, he'd manually maneuver *Pursuit* up close and try to match speeds exactly so Luke could physically reach out and touch the Soviet ship.

Tricky flying, but Michael had talked at length with astronauts who'd done the same sort of thing during the Gemini program. Wally Schirra had got to within a foot of another Gemini ship, and easily held his position there.

Luke was in front of one window and Chad at another, both peering into the blackness. The horizon was a faint purple glow arcing around the Earth.

"We're still night for a few minutes," Chad said. "I don't see the ship yet. How soon until we get comms back with Houston?"

Michael held the Flight Plan in his overinflated left glove and clumsily ran his finger down the column. "We'll have them in ten minutes or so."

Chad thought about it. "The plan is to wait for Houston's GO to open the hatch, but if we see that we're getting there early, I'll make the call."

Luke floated away from the window to give Michael a clear view and grabbed onto *Pursuit*'s hatch opening handle. "I'm ready," he said.

The wooden door of Mission Control opened abruptly, and Al Shepard strode in. Kaz caught it swinging as he and JW followed, and quietly closed it behind them. Al had phoned from ops at Ellington, and the three of them were up to speed on *Pursuit*'s communications problem. They climbed the tiered steps past the floor-level console, heading to join the officers at their assigned positions: JW to SURGEON on the second level, Kaz beside him to assist the CAPCOM, and Al up two more levels to the center back at DFO, Director of Flight Ops. They each reached into cabinet drawers under the consoles and retrieved headsets, plugging in and becoming part of what was going on.

Gene Kranz waited until all three were settled and then took a moment to summarize mission status for everyone.

"As you can see on the screen, Apollo 18 is mid-Pacific and should have just completed the second burn, making them co-altitude with Almaz. They're also suited, with Luke Hemming ready for the EVA. Cabin depress should be just about complete to vacuum, waiting for our GO to open the hatch.

"As soon as we pick them back up off California, SURGEON, I want an immediate update on Luke's suit telemetry."

He looked to the front row at the Guidance Officer. "I'll need trajectory as soon as we can get it, to make sure the second burn went well and to run the calculations for the upcoming Trans-Lunar Injection burn.

We need to get those numbers on board prior to losing uplink—timing
is very tight. TLI is going to happen beyond comm range, and we need
to give the crew everything they need while we have them."

Gene glanced at the digital clock at the front of the room, then said,
"We'll pick them up in ten minutes, and TLI is set for thirty minutes
from now. Be ready, people. This is a critical half hour."

He glanced back at Al Shepard and raised his eyebrows to see if the
Chief Astronaut wanted to say anything. Al gave a curt nod of approval
and raised his right hand in a thumbs-up.

"Okay, back to work, everyone. Let's do this right."

"There it is!" Michael's voice was a mixture of awe and focus. "Right on
the money!"

As if a cloak had been suddenly pulled away, the rising Sun lit Almaz,
centered in *Pursuit's* windows. Chad had a stopwatch Velcroed on the
window frame. He aligned a small transparent ruler with the length of
Almaz, started the stopwatch and read the calculated distance to Michael.

"We're eleven hundred feet away. I'll have a closing rate for you
shortly."

"Roger," Michael responded, carefully firing the maneuvering jets
to hold Almaz centered in the window. "I think we're a little closer than
eleven hundred, and see a healthy closing rate."

Chad watched the second hand move on the stopwatch, thinking.
"Luke, we're only ten minutes or so from needing you in position. Let's
get the hatch open now."

"Roger that, Boss. In work." Luke double-checked that the rotary
switch was turned to Unlatch, and began pumping the handle. With
each stroke, the 15 rubber rollers that held the hatch tightly in place
rotated away from the structure.

Chad made another careful sighting with the ruler and checked it
against the stopwatch. "Looks like eight hundred feet, and closing
at"—he calculated—"five feet per second." He frowned. "I'll need a
couple more range marks before you can trust my speed calls."

"Understood," Michael said. He was happy that what he was seeing looked just like the visual simulator they'd set up for him in Houston. No surprises.

"All latches retracted, the hatch is loose. Opening it now." Luke had his left hand on Michael's seat, stabilizing as he pivoted the hatch out and open on its hinges. He glanced up, relieved to see the barf bag still secure on its Velcro. As he moved, his feet rotated quickly across the cabin and accidentally kicked Chad, tumbling him.

"Watch what you're doing!" Chad grabbed on to a bulkhead rail to stabilize himself, then repositioned in front of his window.

"Sorry, Boss." Luke cautiously moved his feet back between the two seats and began pulling himself up and through the hatch.

A voice in their headsets. "Apollo 18, this is Houston, how do you read?" Michael pushed the mic trigger. "Have you loud and clear, Houston, how me?"

Static. Gene Kranz looked at CAPCOM. "Did you get that?"

"Sorry, FLIGHT, no, unreadable." He looked at the forward screen. "They're still at max antenna range. It should get better as we get closer."

"Copy." Gene queried his other consoles, relieved to hear that the trajectory looked as expected, and the maneuvering fuel burn had been lower than budgeted.

JW said, "FLIGHT, this is SURGEON. Luke's heartbeat and respiration are high. I think he's started his spacewalk."

Gene looked at his Environmental Control officer for confirmation.

"FLIGHT, telemetry shows the hatch microswitches are open, and the cabin at vacuum. I agree, the EVA has begun."

Gene nodded, and glanced at the wall clock. "CAPCOM, tell them they have our GO for EVA."

As CAPCOM's voice passed the information through their headsets, Chad snorted. "No shit, Sherlock." After the kick from Luke had spun him, he was feeling queasy again. He focused on taking another distance measurement.

"Holy crap, this is beautiful!" Luke's lower torso and legs were still inside the capsule, but his head and shoulders were outside. "First things first." He cautiously twisted and reached down to dislodge the barf bag, and then carefully threw it in a straight line backwards to their direction of flight, so it would fall into a lower orbit. "Bomb's away!" He checked that his bolt cutters had floated out clear of the hatch on their tether, confirmed that his camera was secure and reached for the nearest handrail.

"Boss, you would not believe this view! I'm ready to move out if you're set to feed me umbilical as I go."

Chad said, "Michael, I show five hundred feet and three feet per second. You agree?"

"Yep, that matches what I see."

"Okay, Luke, I'm with you. Your umbilical's clear." Chad's voice sounded strained.

Luke smoothly pulled his feet clear and out, and pivoted his suited body like an obese rock climber, walking his hands along the rails that were mounted across *Pursuit* to the adjoining Service Module. A foot restraint was installed at the far end for him to click his boots into, so that he could have both hands free.

In case the CAPCOM could hear him, Michael reported, "Houston, 18, we're at four hundred feet and closing at two and a half. Luke just got outside and is getting into the foot restraint." No response.

He looked up again at Almaz, trying to judge how fast he was drifting towards it. He glanced across at Chad.

"You got a new data point for me, Boss?"

Chad didn't respond. Then both Luke and Michael heard him retching in their headsets.

Throwing up inside a sealed spacesuit was a misery. The flown astronauts who had told them about it had described the stink, the smeared visor, the stomach acid getting into their eyes, and trying not to inhale any of the floating chunks and bile.

Michael took another hard look at Almaz, assessing his approach speed. He gave two small decelerating pulses on the hand controller, and liked what he saw.

"Luke, how you doing?"

"Michael, it is fricking gorgeous out here! But I'm having trouble swinging around to get my feet in. Can you check that my umbilical isn't snagged?"

Michael looked at Chad again, who'd made no response to Luke's call. He released the controls and twisted in his seat, reaching as far as he could, feeling for the umbilical. It was pulled taut on the hatch mechanism, and he shook it like a garden hose to try to work it clear. He felt it give, and some extra length played out through his hand.

Luke said, "That did it, thanks! I'll get my feet in now."

Michael let go and his seat straps floated him back, centering him in position. He looked once more at Chad.

"Boss, how you doing?"

"I'm okay," Chad said thickly.

"Roger, if you can get me another data point, that'd be great." He hoped the task might help Chad work through his nausea.

"Apollo 18, Houston, comm check."

"Have you loud and clear, Houston, how us?" Michael said, then focused on the Soviet ship, correcting the sideways drift that had started while he was dealing with the umbilical.

His eyes caught unexpected movement. *What the hell is that?* A solar array turning? A comm antenna tracking them, maybe?

Luke's voice was in his ears. "Man! My left foot just won't . . . uhh . . . c'mon, twist in there!" His attention was focused down, trying to get into his foot restraint.

Michael peered hard at Almaz, trying to reconcile what he was seeing. "Houston, you hearing Luke? He's almost in position. Range and closure all good." *What is that?*

———

In Mission Control, the CAPCOM looked at Gene. "FLIGHT, I didn't get that, sorry." The voice comm from *Pursuit* was fading in and out.

Kaz pushed his mic button. "FLIGHT, I think I heard Luke say something, and pretty sure that Michael said good range and closure."

Gene nodded. "Let's just watch the data. They're busy enough without us calling for voice checks."

JW spoke, slight concern in his voice. "FLIGHT, SURGEON, Luke's heart rate and respiration are spiking."

"Roger, keep a close eye, let me know if it gets beyond limits."

Luke finally had his feet anchored. "There!" he said, the word a long exhale, heard by Michael and Chad, but lost in the bad connection with Mission Control. "That sure was harder than in the sim. Leaning back now."

He looked down and checked the camera on his chest. "Hasselblad's all set. Time to get some photos." To point the camera he needed to use his whole body, concentrating on alignment as he looked up at Almaz, about 200 feet away.

The bright white reflection off Almaz's exterior radiators momentarily blinded him. He squinted and turned to the side, away from the reflection, attempting to photograph one end of the Soviet spaceship.

The shape he saw was not what he expected.

"Hey, Michael, what's that end cone thing on Almaz? It's not like we briefed. It looks like some sort of add-on." He pushed the shutter trigger on the camera and started a slow pivot to the right to get the full, planned photo survey of the exterior. "Maybe it's some sort of return capsule?"

Chad was still keeping very still, fighting his nausea. Michael's hands were busy on their joysticks, slowing *Pursuit*'s closure rate, easing the two vessels closer together. He'd been glancing at all edges of Almaz to assess speed and angles at the same time as he was trying to figure out what he'd seen at the base of the solar array.

Just then, Luke spoke rapidly, his voice loud.

"Guys! There are two spacewalkers on Almaz! Houston, Almaz is manned! It has cosmonauts aboard, and two of them are outside!"

A beat as he considered that. "It's like they've been waiting for us!"

26

Almaz, Earth Orbit

Michael's voice was urgent. "Houston, 18, are you copying Luke's calls?"

Radio silence.

Christ! What do we do now?

"Boss, are you seeing this?"

Chad turned to face Michael, his visor smeared with vomit. The sudden motion triggered his nausea again, and he bent forward, pulsing weightlessly as he retched.

Michael shook his head in frustration and stared back through his window, slowing the approach, the vehicles drifting to within 50 feet of each other.

Luke's voice came through Michael's headset. "Okay, I've got a full photo survey done. The cosmonauts seem to be staying put. Maybe they're supposed to be observing us?"

Michael watched them; their visors were turned to his ship, both holding onto an Almaz handrail. "Maybe, Luke. I'll ease a little closer and set us up to fly slowly along the full length so you can get better-resolution photos. You got enough film left?"

"Yep, plenty." He paused, looking at the cosmonauts. "I don't think I should try to disable their ship. You guys agree?"

Michael looked across at Chad, still curled up on himself. Chad raised a thumb.

"Chad agrees, and so do I. Let's just get the close-ups, and then I'll maneuver us away."

Luke adjusted zoom and focus on the lens. "Maybe they'll wave on our way by."

"Almaz, Almaz, how do you hear me?" Chelomei's voice crackled in cosmonaut Andrei Mitkov's headset.

"We hear you clearly, Comrade Director. The American ship is ten meters away and slowly closing, with the hatch open and one space-walker outside. He has a large set of what look like bolt cutters with him. They are maneuvering now, repositioning forward, towards our re-entry capsule."

Chelomei's worst suspicions were confirmed. These men had been sent to attack his ship. "Mitkov! Be ready to physically stop the American from damaging Almaz. Take action as required."

"Understood. Both of us are moving forward towards the capsule now."

Chelomei whipped his head around at the flight director and shouted, "Where's that video feed?"

"We're just getting a solid relay lock now, Comrade Director. We'll have it on the front screen in a few seconds."

As if on command, a fuzzy black-and-white image appeared next to the Earth map at the front of the room. It showed a section of Almaz's curved hull against the blackness of space, with the broad arc of the Earth below.

"Where is the American ship? We need to turn to face it!" Chelomei had a plan, but he had to get Almaz properly aligned against the aggressors.

The flight director gestured impatiently at his comm tech, who spoke to the crew. "Almaz, we need updates on the relative position of the other ship, in orbital coordinates."

Mitkov paused from moving hand-over-hand along his vessel, and released one hand to pivot his whole spacesuit and look. The other cosmonaut paused behind him.

"They are aft and below us, five meters away now, co-aligned. Their command capsule is abeam our return capsule, holding distance steady, drifting forward slowly," he reported.

"Copy." The comm tech turned and looked questioningly at the flight director, who was holding his two hands up, picturing the orientation. He twisted one wrist, deciding on the needed rotation, then spoke urgently to the officer in charge of Almaz attitude control. "Start a max pitch rate pure down, and be ready to cancel the motion and track as soon as they come into the field of view."

The console officer rapidly typed on his keyboard and then paused briefly, his finger sliding across the screen to verify accuracy. With a small flourish, he raised his hand and stabbed the transmit button.

All eyes turned to the large screen, waiting for the video to reveal the attacking American vessel, squarely in Almaz's sights.

"Shit, they're moving, Michael!" Luke's voice was urgent.

Michael had been watching the Soviet spacewalkers as they slowly clambered along Almaz's hull, and he misunderstood. "Yeah, I see them. And it looks like their suits have backpacks, so no umbilicals."

"Not them, the whole ship! I just saw the thrusters fire. It's pivoting towards us!"

Michael moved his head left and right to take in the whole vessel. The blunt end was rotating downwards. He carefully tipped his joystick forward to match the rate, and then tapped his hand controller to start moving aft along Almaz.

"I see it, and am pitching to match. Should be good for you to start on the final photo pass anytime."

Luke took one more look at the two cosmonauts moving towards him, like white birds on an elephant's back, and then focused on his camera work. "Roger. Their pointy capsule is in my field of view now, starting pictures." He pressed the shutter trigger, carefully twisting his spacesuit to hold the image centered.

The CAPCOM's voice broke in. "Apollo 18, Houston, no response necessary, but your final TLI numbers are on board. New TIG is 3:25:00, need to get Luke inside prior-to. We should have you over Cape Town during the burn." A brief pause. "You have a GO for Trans-Lunar Injection."

Chad mutely raised his thumb again.

"Roger, Houston, 18 is GO for TLI," Michael said. He glanced at the clock and realized that was just 14 minutes away. He watched Almaz moving in the window and did a quick mental calculation.

"Luke, did you copy that call? You'll need to hustle inside as soon as this sweep is done so we can get the hatch closed prior to the burn."

"Copy, wilco, no sweat." A pause, and then Luke asked, "Michael, is Almaz pitching faster now?"

"Working on it," Michael responded, staring out the window. He'd added a couple pulses to his joystick to match rates with Almaz. *What were the Soviets up to?*

Luke's voice came again, and higher pitched. "Hey, the cosmonauts are getting pretty close to me. One of them's carrying a big monkey wrench, and the other has something like a drill!"

Chad straightened himself and rasped, "I'm gonna poke my head outside." He cautiously maneuvered under the hatch opening, trying not to trigger any more motion sickness, pivoting his whole body and moving his head and shoulders out into space.

"What the fuck?" Luke sounded incredulous. "Are these assholes coming for me?"

"What's going on?" Michael could only see the wide fuselage section of Almaz in his window.

Chad called, "The lead cosmonaut has pushed off of Almaz."

He watched in disbelief as the spacewalker floated across to *Pursuit* and grabbed a handrail near Luke. He moved closer, then swung his wrench towards Luke's visor.

"Luke, watch out, on your left!" Chad yelled.

Luke, his feet locked in their restraints, deflected the blow with his suited forearm and swung back with the bolt cutters. "You bastard!" he yelled.

The cosmonaut got his arm up in time to protect his visor, and the bolt cutters bounced off.

Now the second cosmonaut made the leap and began maneuvering towards Luke from the other side. He started twisting back and forth in the foot restraints, swinging the bolt cutters in an arc to keep them both at bay, his other hand held high to ward off blows.

Michael could hear Luke's grunting and harsh exhalations. "Boss, we need to get Luke inside now!"

"Agreed! Luke, pop your feet out of the restraints and I'll haul you clear!"

Michael pushed his transmit button. "Houston, if you're hearing this, the cosmonauts are on *Pursuit* and attacking Luke!"

Chelomei was yelling. "Increase the rotation rate! We have to get that ship in front of us!"

"Yes, Comrade Director." The pointing officer sent another command, firing Almaz's thrusters yet again. He checked the updated values. "We're at max design pitch rate for the solar panels now."

All eyes turned to the front screen. Rising up from the bottom of the video image was the conical white tip of the Apollo capsule.

Chelomei pointed to the screen. "Arm the R-23!"

The mechanisms officer, sitting one row ahead, responded. "Sending the command now."

As Almaz turned, the spacewalkers came into view—three fat figures in a clumsy slow-motion dance, intent on mutual destruction. The cosmonauts held tight to *Pursuit*'s handrails with one hand, swinging their makeshift weapons with their free arms, as the astronaut, one foot still braced, brandished his bolt cutters.

Bile rose in Chelomei's throat. His ship, *his* Almaz—so capable, so much of a threat that the Americans had decided to attack it in front of his eyes! He'd known this might happen. And he'd prepared for it.

He grabbed the headset off the desk and shouted into it. "Mitkov, both of you get back to Almaz. You need to be clear of the American ship, and fast!"

The grunting of the two cosmonauts in combat transmitted steadily, blocking the incoming call from Earth.

Chelomei tried again. "Mitkov, do you hear me? Return to Almaz!"

No response. The tech repeated the Director's words multiple times, urgently trying to get through.

Finally, Mitkov replied. "Moscow, I hear you! We're returning!"

Chelomei pivoted towards the flight director. "How much time do we have?"

"About thirty seconds, Comrade Director, forty-five maximum until we're out of antenna range."

They watched the screen, the Apollo ship remaining centered as the console operator reversed the thrusters on Almaz to hold steady. An astronaut was sticking out of the American hatch, guiding the umbilical of the spacewalker, who had got both feet free and was now floating up towards Almaz. One of the cosmonauts was traversing the gap between the vessels, the other still holding on to the American ship, ready to push off.

Chelomei spoke, his command loud enough for everyone to hear it without their headsets.

"At fifteen seconds, send the signal. All rounds! Fire the R-23!"

Vladimir Chelomei had not sent a defenseless ship into space.

The Kartech R-23 cannon was a unique design.

It had originally been built as the tail gun for the supersonic Tu-22 bomber, with a single short barrel to avoid the aircraft's turbulent airflow. As its bullets fired, the expanding gas from the explosion not only pushed the projectile out of the barrel, but also rotated a four-chamber revolver mechanism that loaded the next round. At full speed, the cannon spun at 2,600 rpm, a blistering 43 rotations every second.

It was the Soviet Union's fastest-firing single-barrel cannon, small, light and purpose-built. To keep its overall length short, the chambers loaded oddly, from the front, the pointy bullets encased in cylindrical galvanized metal sleeves, like deadly silver lipsticks.

For the cannon to fit onto Almaz, though, the engineers had to make it even smaller and lighter, choosing lower-caliber 14.5 mm bullets that allowed for a slimmer barrel and revolver. The entire space gun, loaded with 32 rounds, weighed just 70 pounds. Then, to further minimize mass and complexity, they'd removed the gun's aiming mount, simply bolting the R-23 to Almaz's hull. In order to line it up with the target, they had to turn the entire 20-ton space station.

The new design's rate of fire was 1,800 rpm; that meant all 32 bullets could be expended within one second. A brief hail of hardened steel through the emptiness of space, each spinning projectile traveling at over 2,000 feet per second.

All it needed was someone to pull the trigger.

With 15 seconds left in the comm pass, the Moscow technician pushed the button on his console to initiate the fire command. The signal traveled up via relay satellite and then down to the relay ship in the North Atlantic, which sent it directly back up to the receiving antenna on Almaz. The spaceship's decommutator routed the signal through Almaz's onboard wiring and amplified it into an electrical fire signal that the R-23 could recognize. It also sent a command to the ship's thrusters to ignite the maneuvering engines to counteract the impending recoil of the gun.

When the electrical signal reached its destination, the space cannon flashed into operational life.

The firing pin slammed into the percussion primer at the base of the loaded round, causing an instant explosion, which ignited the main nitrocellulose charge. The ensuing blast hurled the bullet down the rifled barrel and spun the revolver to accept the next round. Each successive round's explosion sped up the rotation until the cannon was turning at full speed.

As the chambers rotated, the used, empty cartridges flew out in a glittering trail of tiny satellites, slowly tumbling as their orbits decayed, to fall and burn up in the atmosphere.

But the sixteenth round jammed.

The problem was the strange bullet design. To securely hold the projectile in its unusual casing, a specially built machine at the OKB-16 factory squeezed the galvanized steel from both sides, crimping it solidly in place. Round 16 had an undetected bit of a broken high-tempered steel lock washer stuck to its underside, which the machine had crimped into its casing. The round looked normal, but the primer chamber was nearly penetrated.

As the rotating drive mechanism forced the defective round into the cannon's chamber, the casing crumpled, the primer chamber burst, and the heat and friction of the collapsing tube ignited it. The main charge sympathetically exploded, and the resulting sudden burst of expanding gas shattered the fast-spinning revolver.

Instantly, pieces flew in all directions—a deadly pinwheel shedding hardened steel parts. Some flew harmlessly off into space. But several were hurled into the pressure hull of Almaz, their ragged edges cutting through the thin aluminum as if it wasn't there. The air in the ship's main cabin started spewing out through the jagged holes.

One fragment followed an especially unlucky trajectory. Mounted just inside the hull was a bundle of tubes and cables carrying cooling glycol and electrical power, routed together for easy maintenance. A finger-sized piece of broken steel ripped through the bundle, cutting power to multiple Almaz systems and splitting fluid lines that immediately began spraying liquid into the rapidly dropping pressure inside the spacecraft.

Almaz was fatally wounded, a robot whale, mortally stabbed by its own explosive harpoon.

The 15 bullets that the cannon had successfully fired formed more of a spray pattern than the engineers had expected. Twelve of them had sailed past Apollo and the spacewalkers, destined to eventually fall to Earth and vaporize in the upper atmosphere.

One round nicked the edge of Apollo's open hatch door, scoring the metal and carrying away a small piece of the rubber seal that the North American Aviation technicians had carefully fitted and glued in place around its circumference.

Another collided with Luke's oxygen and power umbilical adapter, which attached to his suit just below his chest. Traveling at 850 meters per second, it tumbled through the delicate pressure regulator, wires and valves, tearing them open.

The third bullet struck senior cosmonaut Andrei Mitkov as he was floating back to Almaz. The bullet caught his helmet as neatly as if it had been fired by a sniper, hitting him squarely above his visor, creating a punctuation mark between the middle letters of CCCP.

The 175-gram projectile, designed to penetrate metal, passed through the successive layers of fiberglass, flesh, bone and brain as if they weren't there. The exit hole out the back of Mitkov's helmet was only slightly larger than the entry hole. A small spray of gray and red followed the bullet, quickly spreading and vaporizing in the vacuum of space.

Mitkov's body spun backwards with the force of the impact, tumbling like a rag doll until it struck Almaz. His lifeless arms flew forward on impact as if giving the ship a final embrace. His ivory-colored Yastreb suit deflated against his body as he slowly bounced clear, floating silently away towards the darkness.

The remaining cosmonaut, still clinging to *Pursuit*, watched in horror.

As the rapid darkness of the orbital sunset overtook it, Almaz slowly tumbled in space. The effect of firing the gun and trying to counteract it with the automated thrusters had been only a best guess by Chelomei's engineers. In reality, the forces had combined to add one last torquing moment to the ship as it died.

Inside the punctured hull, the pressure rapidly dropped to zero. Unlike the Apollo capsule, the main section of Almaz had never been intended to function in the vacuum of space. The spraying glycol from the severed coolant line had bubbled and evaporated as if it were boiling. The film canisters, with their hard-earned, precious first images carefully exposed and recorded on the wide celluloid filmstrips, had burst open. The temperature had dropped rapidly, and the ship's automated systems failed, one by one, as they vainly tried to keep critical systems warm on battery power.

A faint, thinning trail formed behind Almaz, where the venting atmosphere had spewed small fragments and liquid as the pressure had dropped. The hull's rotation had left a curved arc in the darkness. A keen observer might have been able to follow the track back to the slowly tumbling, lifeless body of the cosmonaut.

In Moscow, everyone was quiet at their consoles. Chelomei looked around, glowering. There'd been no time for confirmation that the cannon had fired, and the next communications ship was still 40 minutes away, over the South Pacific.

Questions tore at him. Had he made the right call? The Americans had been the aggressor! It had been *they* who had deliberately intercepted *his* ship, and they had put an astronaut outside carrying bolt cutters, irrefutable proof of destructive intent.

Chelomei clenched his jaw. All he'd done was react defensively, a course of action that had been cleared in advance. He'd been right to decide to arm Almaz. He'd known just what a valuable asset it was, and that it might come under attack. Events had now proven him correct.

He glanced at the timer on the front screen: 38 minutes until they could recontact Almaz and its crew. A little over half an hour to organize his thoughts, preparing for the inevitable avalanche of questions.

He began preparing his answers. The United States of America had attacked the Soviet Union in space. It was a purposeful, dangerous new escalation of the Cold War. Only *his* forethought had allowed them to be ready, and to respond. He nodded to himself. He was in the right and had acted as a soldier should.

Let them ask questions.

But first he had to talk to the crew to find out the result of his orders. Then everyone would be able to see how Almaz, how *he*, had helped change the course of Soviet history in space.

"What's going on?" Michael yelled. Almaz had spun faster than he could keep up and was now starting to roll. He'd pulsed his thrusters to keep clear, and was eyeing the countdown clock to the TLI burn that would take them towards the Moon.

"Bastards fired a gun at us!" Chad hissed, then choked as he suppressed another wave of nausea.

"They *what?*" Michael hurriedly rescanned his gauges. "I don't think they hit anything vital. All temps and pressures look normal." He rechecked the timer. "We have to get that hatch closed. Luke, are you in?"

"Almost," Chad grunted.

Michael focused on the small DSKY screen, double-checking the numbers as he maneuvered to the right orientation for the Trans-Lunar burn. Out of the corner of his eye, he saw Chad pull Luke into the center of the capsule and then reach past him to close the hatch.

"No time for cabin repress now, guys," Michael warned. "As soon as you get the hatch secured, hang on. We're almost at burn time. Chad, I need your eyes on the gauges with me."

Chad exhaled heavily as he worked to crank the hatch handle. "How soon do we get comms back?"

Michael awkwardly peeled his flight plan checklist off the Velcro, his glove still inflated against the vacuum in the cabin. "We'll pick up South Africa one minute into the burn. Unlikely they'll hear us, though."

Chad grunted an acknowledgment and eased himself across into the right-hand seat.

Michael's eyes flicked from instrument to instrument like a hawk watching potential prey. "Ignition in forty-five seconds. Attitude looks good, temps and pressures normal."

Chad was doing the same on the other side of the cockpit. "I see good attitude, 180, 312, 0," he said, sounding hoarse but much more in control. "I confirm a burn of 10,359.6 feet per second, duration 5:51." He paused. "Ullage settling."

"TIG in ten seconds." Michael glanced to his right. Luke was floating by the window, where he could see out. "Luke, hang tight," he called and locked his gaze back onto the gauges.

"Three, two, one, here we go!"

The single J-2 rocket engine burst back into life, to push them this time all the way up to escape velocity—fast enough to leave Earth orbit and coast to the Moon.

"Steer, baby, steer," Michael muttered. Pushed back into his seat, he could feel the guidance system adjusting the motor's exhaust direction, counteracting the fuel sloshing in the tanks.

"Tank pressures look good," Chad said. "No comms yet." Sunlight was flaring in the window as they approached sunset over the Central African coast.

Michael glanced back at Luke. "Good riddance to Almaz! Can you see it in the rear-view mirror?"

Luke, pressed by the acceleration into the rear wall of *Pursuit*, didn't answer.

"Luke, what went on out there? It sounded like a frickin' rodeo!"

Still no answer.

Both Chad and Michael twisted their suits to look at Luke. Michael reached to grab one of his feet and tried to pull him forward with one hand, against the push of the engines. "His suit feels soft!" he exclaimed in alarm.

Chad grabbed for his other foot, and they urgently pulled him forward. Michael spotted the bullet's damage. "His umbilical's wrecked!"

Luke's body turned, and Michael saw that his visor was clouded by condensation. He strained to see inside. "His eyes are closed."

"Shit!" Chad said, taking command at last. "The switches are on your side—start an emergency repress! I'll watch the burn."

Michael whipped to his left and moved the valves to let oxygen pour into the cabin. He watched the cabin pressure indicator, preparing to pop Luke's helmet off the moment it rose high enough.

The needle on the gauge stayed at zero. He tapped it rapidly, hoping the mechanism was stuck.

No response.

"Boss, I think we may have a cabin leak!"

The two men looked at each other across Luke's inert body, their thoughts racing.

"It's either the hatch didn't seat or a bullet hole," Chad said. "Hatch is quicker to check." He stared at Michael through the smears of vomit on his visor. "I'll keep watching the burn. You cycle and clear the hatch."

Michael unsnapped his harness and, fighting the force of the engine, closed the oxygen switches and reached behind him to the hatch handle, cranking fast to reopen it as quickly as he could. He watched as the mechanical rollers retracted, and pushed hard on the door as soon as they released. The darkness outside in contrast to the interior lights made it hard for him to see the rubber seal.

He rapidly traced the hatch edge and found the scored metal where the bullet had grazed it. He felt sick when he saw the torn rubber.

"Chad, looks like a small section of the door seal is missing! I'll grab the patch kit—I think it'll hold."

He had to move Luke out of the way to access the aft storage cupboard, cursing under his breath as he hunted for the right container. When he found it, he tore it open, pulling out the heavy plasticine-like block inside. Pivoting back up to the hatch, he rolled the sealant into place, making it extra thick where the rubber was missing and using his gloved thumb to smear it smooth along the metal. The patch kit container bounced free and floated through the hatch, out into the darkness. *Fuck!* He checked his work.

"Okay, Chad, I've got a good glob in there. Should do it. Closing the hatch now!"

Bracing with his other hand, he got a secure grip and pivoted the hatch towards himself, carefully keeping an eye on his makeshift repair to be sure it stayed in place.

As he had the hatch nearly closed, something blocked it. He pulled harder, then leaned back slightly to see the whole circumference, wondering what was in the way.

What Michael saw, he couldn't believe.

Pinched between the swinging hatch and the structure of *Pursuit* was a gloved hand.

Someone was trying to get in.

COSMONAUT

27

Pursuit, Trans-Lunar Burn

"How's it looking?" Gene Kranz's words were clipped with urgency.

Apollo 18 had just come into range of NASA's Deep Space Network satellite dish near Johannesburg, South Africa. The downlinked data was starting to appear on the Mission Control console screens, and Gene urgently wanted to know how the Trans-Lunar Injection engine firing was going.

"Burn's underway, FLIGHT." A pause as the Flight Dynamics console operator evaluated the rows of flashing numbers he was seeing. "Everything looks right on the money."

The Environmental Control officer spoke, mild surprise in his voice. "FLIGHT, EECOM here, they're still at vacuum."

Gene thought about it. Time had been tight, and the crew would have had no real need to deal with the distraction of repressurizing until after the burn.

"Copy, EECOM." He visualized what the crew was doing, double-checking. "Confirm the hatch shows closed?"

"Roger, FLIGHT."

So crew was inside, the ship was behaving itself, and they were on their way to the Moon. *Just need to get this damned comm snag fixed.*

"CAPCOM, let them know we're here, and that we see good numbers on the burn so far."

As CAPCOM keyed his mic to speak, the EECOM said, "FLIGHT, wait!"

Gene looked over the top of his console at the officer, who had turned so he could make direct eye contact. "The switches no longer show closed. The crew is opening the hatch during the TLI burn!"

Gene looked to his left. "SURGEON, you still getting Luke's data?"

JW shook his head. "FLIGHT, his signal seems intermittent. Not sure what to make of it."

Gene frowned. Biomedical sensors were notoriously unreliable, especially since the crew didn't like everyone knowing their heartbeat and often weren't too careful about attaching the electrodes. He looked at the front screen. There were still three minutes left in the burn, and that would take them almost to the end of the communications pass. Then they'd have a 23-minute gap until they could talk to them through Australia.

"CAPCOM, let's wait until there's forty-five seconds left in this comm pass to update the crew with what we're seeing."

Kaz, standing behind the CAPCOM, looked at Gene and nodded. Let the crew work the problem, but backstop them with the latest data from Mission Control before they went silent again.

"Listen up, all consoles," Gene said, pausing until conversation quieted. "Looks like we're headed to the Moon, but with bad comms and maybe a hatch problem. We still have Lunar Module extraction and S-IVB separation to get through before we'll have good two-way communication. We need to help the crew but stay out of their way until they get through this phase."

He paused and looked around at his team.

"I want a crisp update for them in twenty minutes. All systems abnormalities, and any changes to the flight plan." He turned to his left.

"And INCO, I want my comms back ASAP. We need to get this flight back to normal."

The glove was smooth and white, the rubberized fingers bulging with pressure as the cosmonaut held on against the accelerating spaceship.

"Chad! One of the cosmonauts is trying to get in!"

"What?" Chad pivoted his suit hard to see, pushing Luke's inert form out of his way. "Shit!"

He glanced back at the engine instruments. "We've got a minute left in the burn," he said, "and we've got to get air to Luke, fast. Bring the cosmonaut inside, and let's get the oxygen flowing ASAP!"

Michael pushed the hatch open and held out his gloved hand. The cosmonaut's other arm came arcing out of the darkness and grabbed it. Straining against the rocket's acceleration, he helped the cosmonaut inch into the cramped space. Michael yanked the Soviet suit's life-support backpack in last, trailing on its hoses, then squeezed up and around the cosmonaut's feet to check that his makeshift pressure seal repair was still in place. He pulled the hatch closed and lunged for the locking handle, rapidly cycling it, counting strokes.

As soon as it was locked, he pivoted and threw open the cabin repress switches to get some life-giving oxygen flowing. Sweating heavily, he reached down and pulled himself back into his seat.

Chad's voice cut in. "Three, two, one—burn's complete."

The sudden freedom of weightlessness was like coming inside out of a gale.

Michael kept his eyes glued to the cabin pressure gauge, which was rapidly climbing towards 5 psi. "Hatch seal's holding," he reported. As soon as it passed 3, he reached under the cosmonaut to get to Luke's helmet. Chad was already there, pulling at the neck latch. As the helmet came loose, Michael guided it up and off Luke's head.

Michael yanked off his right glove and jammed a finger up under Luke's jawline, feeling for a pulse.

Nothing.

He used his thumb to peel Luke's eyelid quickly back, but saw no response. He held his palm over Luke's nose and mouth. Nothing.

Unlatching and peeling off his own helmet, he grabbed Luke's jaw with his still-gloved left hand and pushed back on the top of his head with his right; sealing his lips over Luke's cold mouth, he blew hard into his lungs. He turned, hearing the rattle of the exhale, and then filled Luke's lungs again.

No response.

Bracing Luke with one hand, he slammed his other into Luke's chest, trying shock the heart back into action. The thickness of the spacesuit absorbed much of the blow. Their suited bodies bounced off the panels in weightlessness.

"Help me!" he yelled to Chad.

The two of them took turns slamming their gloved fists into Luke's chest, as Michael repeatedly blew more oxygen into his lungs.

But Luke's skin didn't pink up and his eyelids didn't flutter. Saliva floated from his slack mouth in a sticky, weightless web.

Lunar Module Pilot Luke Hemming, Captain in the United States Marine Corps, veteran of three hours of spaceflight and one spacewalk, was dead.

Bumping against them in the confined space, the cosmonaut was moving, hands twisting to open glove locks, then reaching for the neck handle that released the white helmet, CCCP printed in large red letters across its front.

Michael gathered the floating gloves, then helped to guide the helmet clear.

The cosmonaut, who was wearing a tight brown leather headset underneath, unclipped the chinstrap and peeled it off. Longish brown hair floated free in the weightlessness.

Michael frowned. The thick hair, matted after the spacewalk, was cut square across the front, in bangs. He saw no trace of a beard or sideburns. The guarded brown eyes now looking challengingly into his were unmistakably feminine.

The cosmonaut was a woman.

"Spasiba," she said evenly, nodding slightly. "Senk you."

Chad pivoted up from the other side of the cabin. He'd taken his helmet off, and the sharp smell of vomit came with him. "A woman! Good Christ!" He gestured at the jammed cabin, loose articles floating everywhere, the extra crewmember overfilling the already cramped confines. "What are we gonna do with *her*? Shit!"

Michael tried to take stock. "Luke is dead, the TLI burn's complete so we're going to the Moon regardless, our comms are still bad, and now we have a female Commie stowaway!"

Who was watching them both warily.

"We gotta get comms back ASAP." Chad grabbed his flight plan. "Next pass is Australia in"—he checked the digital timer—"four minutes. Maybe we'll get lucky and they'll hear us this time."

Michael said, "I need to pull the Lunar Module out of the S-IVB. And we've got to figure out what to do with—her." He looked at the cosmonaut and spoke deliberately, indicating himself. "My name is Michael." He pointed to her. "What is your name?"

She held his gaze. "My nem, Svetlana." She turned and looked at Chad, expectant.

"I'm Chad." He pointed at her, frowning. "You just wait there." He opened both hands, palms towards her to signify that her whole body needed to stay put. "Michael and I have work to do."

She stared back. Chad gave her a long look. *Must be a tough chick to hang on outside during all that.* He turned to Michael.

"You get into the LM extraction checklist. Before I do anything else, I need to clean up my suit."

Michael looked at the two of them, and at Luke's inert body. "What a shitshow."

The technician at Honeysuckle Creek had been waiting for this moment. It was 2:20 a.m. on Tuesday 17 April. The temperature outside had gone down to just above freezing, an early taste of Australia's approaching winter. She'd turned the antenna system heaters on and set up the automated tracking, and now she double-checked her watch.

Apollo 18 was to be the very last of the Moon missions. She hadn't been lucky enough to work any of the previous flights, and was excited to be part of this one. Though she just had to throw a few switches and wouldn't actually talk with the astronauts, she didn't care. She held her Kodak Pocket Instamatic camera at arm's length to try to get her face and the operator's console in the picture, smiled proudly and pushed the shutter. The flash lit up the empty room. Her mum was going to be so excited to see that photograph.

Setting the small camera on the desk, she rechecked the digital timer and pressed the mic button on her headset cord.

"Houston NETWORK, this is Honeysuckle Creek, all set for the Apollo 18 pass."

The voice crackled back through her earphones.

"Roger, Honeysuckle, acquisition should be at 02:25:30 your time. Appreciate the late-night help."

The Australian technician was thrilled to know she was talking directly to Mission Control in Houston. She listened to the status report.

"FLIGHT, Honeysuckle's ready, should have signal on time."

"Copy, NETWORK, thanks."

A shiver went down the Australian technician's back. *That was Gene Kranz, the man who saved Apollo 13!*

She watched the oscilloscope on her left, waiting for the spike that would show a return from the Apollo craft as it appeared over the horizon. Exactly on time, the display jumped. She made sure her voice was calm, matching the tone from Houston.

"NETWORK, Honeysuckle, I see it on the scope now. You should have comms and data shortly."

A pause.

"Yep, thanks, we're seeing it now."

The CAPCOM's voice came into the Honeysuckle technician's headset, halfway around the world.

"Apollo 18, Houston, we're with you through Australia. How do you read?"

All she heard was a burst of random noise.

"18, Houston, we heard some static, but you're still unreadable. Should be fixed when you get rid of the S-IVB, and the high-gain antenna deploys. We're evaluating trajectory now, but you're looking good for LM extraction. If you copy, type all zeroes."

There was a pause.

"Okay, 18, we see that, thanks."

A frown creased the Honeysuckle technician's forehead. She'd been half listening to the earlier Houston conversation about a comm problem, but hadn't realized the crew couldn't talk to Earth.

"Holy dooley!" she muttered.

"18, Houston, the LM extraction maneuver start time will be 3 plus 55 plus 27, separation time 10 minutes later."

Michael glanced at the timer, double-clicked his mic button and sent all zeroes, to acknowledge. "Maneuver starts in 90 seconds, Chad."

Chad nodded, carefully wiping out his suit with biocide.

The demands of the task helped Michael focus; he needed to physically separate *Pursuit*, flip it around and mate it with the lunar lander, still housed inside the S-IVB rocket, and then extract the lander. It was a delicate sequence he'd practiced thousands of times, but never like this. He pantomimed his upcoming hand movements on the controls, deliberately ignoring Luke's feet floating next to him and the cosmonaut—Svetlana—occasionally bumping into his shoulder.

"Apollo 18, we see the S-IVB maneuver is complete. You have a GO for T&D."

Transposition and docking. Time to put all that training to work. Michael reached forward and pushed the Launch Vehicle Separation button.

Bang! The sound of pyrotechnics rang through the ship as long lengths of explosive cord cut the metal structure joining them to the rocket. Michael felt Sveltlana turning in alarm. "It's okay," he said, giving her a reassuring thumbs-up. *Do Russians even know what that means?*

Chad was watching through his overhead window. Bits of metal and cover panels were drifting slowly clear. "Looks like a clean separation."

"Okay, here we go." Michael tipped back on his joystick and *Pursuit* responded, smoothly turning through a half circle to align for docking. The curve of the world rotated into view as he worked to center the Lunar Module in his window. The ship that Luke had named *Bulldog*. He pushed the thought out of his head.

"Moving in now." He pushed forward on the other joystick, and *Pursuit's* small thrusters fired in response, small pops of noise filling the cabin like someone was tapping on the hull with a hammer.

"18, Houston, as soon as you can we'd like you to deploy the high-gain. We expect that will resolve our comm problem."

Now that *Pursuit* was clear of the rocket, there was room to pivot out the large four-dish antenna.

"Roger, in work." Chad reached forward and threw the switches as Michael stared intently out his overhead window, maneuvering *Pursuit* closer to the docking target. Small pieces of debris and ice tumbled slowly across his view.

"Lots of small bits in the way, but *Bulldog* looks clean," Michael reported. The top of the Lunar Module protruded from the rocket body, harshly lit in the direct dawn sunlight.

No answer from Houston. Chad rechecked the antenna deploy indications.

"Switching the high-gain antenna to REACQ," he said, and flipped the switch down to force the antenna into reacquisition, making it search automatically for the radio signal from Earth.

"Almost there, Chad." Michael spoke intently, focused on hitting the target dead center. He stared unblinkingly out his window, making tiny adjustments with his hand controllers as *Bulldog* filled the field of view.

There was a metallic scraping sound, and they felt a small, sudden deceleration into their seat straps. Luke and Svetlana's suited forms bumped forward in the cockpit.

"Capture, Houston!" Michael reported with satisfaction.

Three small latches on the tip of *Pursuit*'s docking probe slid into place and clicked inside *Bulldog*'s docking mechanism, the indicators on the panel going from barber pole to gray. The two ships were mechanically attached.

Michael exhaled in quiet relief. He threw the switch to retract the docking probe, to pull in and solidly lock the ships together. They could hear the low grinding of gears. All that remained was to release *Bulldog* from the rocket body, and for Michael to back away and slide it out. Houston could then fire the thrusters on the rocket and move it safely clear.

"Apollo 18, we show a successful docking. Nicely done. Please give us a voice check." No hint in the CAPCOM's tone that this voice check was critical.

Chad glanced quickly at Michael, took a deep breath and pressed his comm trigger. "Houston, Apollo 18, how do you hear?"

The relief in the CAPCOM's voice was palpable in their headsets. "We have you loud and clear now, 18! How us?"

"Loud and clear also, Houston. Glad to be talking with you again." Chad paused, his voice going flat. "As soon as we can, I need to talk privately with the Director of Flight Ops."

He glanced at Luke's body, and at the cosmonaut.

"We've got some major issues to discuss."

28

Mission Control, Houston

Kaz pushed the button marked Speaker on the beige telephone on the desk in the Director of Flight Operations observation room. He heard the buzz of the dial tone, and then tapped in the Washington number. He glanced up through the window at the operators at their consoles, and then around at the other men in the room.

The faces were tense. Deke Slayton, a Mercury astronaut and the Flight Ops Director, was seated behind the desk, visibly pained and angry at the loss of another astronaut. Al Shepard was standing, staring at the large screen at the front of Mission Control. The Manned Spacecraft Center Director, Chris Kraft, stood next to him, a sheen of sweat on his broad forehead from the sprint he'd made from his office in the headquarters building.

They heard the phone ringing, and a female voice answered.

"National Security Agency, General Phillips's office."

"Hi, Jan, Kaz here in Houston, we need to talk to the General right now if possible."

"He's in a meeting. Just hold on a minute while I get him."

The voice of the CAPCOM talking with the Apollo crew came tinnily through a metal speaker on Deke's desk. They were working on opening the hatch between *Pursuit* and *Bulldog*, following the mission timeline as they awaited further instruction.

A sharp click from the speakerphone. "Kaz, Sam Phillips here. What's up?"

Kaz took a breath, quickly clarified who was in the room with him and then summarized the wild sequence of events that had just transpired in orbit.

Phillips had been the director of the Apollo program during several fatal astronaut plane crashes and the fire that had killed the Apollo 1 crew. He understood what Luke's death meant to these men.

"Deke, Al, Chris, I am so very sorry to hear this." They heard him exhale angrily through his nose. "Our intelligence let us down, badly. No one thought Almaz was manned, nor did we know it was armed. As NSA Director the failure is mine, and I am responsible for Captain Hemming's death. My deepest condolences."

Brief silence as Phillips thought further.

"We need to maintain the complete news blackout until we decide our path. I'll call the Joint Chiefs chairman now, and he's going to want an immediate briefing to the National Security Council and the President."

Al Shepard spoke. "Sam, we're working on what to do with Luke's body, and how the crew should deal with the cosmonaut. The only good news is that our spaceships are healthy, and we've got some time to regroup during the three days' coast to the Moon." He paused, glancing at Kraft and Slayton. "But we need a whole new plan for what to do when we get there."

"Yep, I hear you, Al. This will put way more fingers in the pie than anyone wanted. If you don't mind, I'm gonna need Kaz to keep us up to date and to be the one who passes sensitive direction up to the crew."

Al and Deke nodded. That made sense to them.

"Kaz, I'll need you back on the phone in a bit, to give an update at the Security Council meeting with the President."

"Understood, General. Meanwhile, I have a suggestion for what you might discuss with the Joint Chiefs."

This was why Phillips had recruited him. "Go ahead," he said.

"We badly need damage control with the Russians. For now, outside of Mission Control here, no one knows what's happened. Not even the Soviets, I'd guess, who must still be in the dark about what actually occurred, and specifically about the status of their two cosmonauts. We need to move fast to update them that one of their crew is alive, and to offer them a nuanced apology for the nightmare that happened at Almaz that offers them a potential benefit. Give them an option that they can take uphill to Brezhnev, along with the bad news."

He paused.

"We have a healthy orbiter and lander, three people alive on their way to the Moon, and the cosmonaut's and Luke's spacesuits—the crew confirmed that only the umbilical got damaged and his suit's okay. Michael Esdale can fly *Pursuit* around the Moon as planned, and Chad Miller is fully trained to fly *Bulldog* down to the surface."

Kaz made eye contact with the three men in the small room with him.

"The cosmonaut should fly in *Bulldog* with Chad, while Michael orbits in *Pursuit*. We can help the Soviets put the world's first woman on the Moon."

Time to get out of my suit, Svetlana decided.

The two astronauts had already doffed theirs, and had opened the forward hatch of their capsule. The thickset white one—*Tschad, he said he was called, and he acts like the commander*—had gone through into the connecting tunnel. The other, the Black one—*Mikhail*—was reading from a checklist and watching pressure gauges.

The third astronaut, suited with his helmet back on and strapped into the chair next to her, was dead, like Andrei was. She felt a surge of anger, but shook her head. "Pazhivyom, oovidim," she muttered. *I'm still alive, so let's see what's next.*

She unplugged the two hoses to her life-support backpack and wedged it and her helmet, gloves and comm cap behind the headrest of the Black astronaut's seat, against the underlying structure. He ignored her, focusing on activating the Lunar Module.

She was careful with her actions; on Chelomei's instructions, she and Andrei had brought weapons outside to defend the Almaz. She double-checked that hers was still safely concealed in her leg pocket. *Best keep that a secret for now.*

The Yastreb spacesuit was flexible, with an outer thermal coverall and a double inner rubber pressure liner. She slid down the long zipper, peeled back the Velcro flap and started unlacing, like undoing figure skates.

With the long laces floating free, she reached in near her belly and pulled out a rubber stub neck, held tightly closed with double-wrapped elastics. She released and unwound them, and then opened the neck, shaking it loose like the end of a large balloon. She worked her arms out of the sleeves, bent hard forward while prying the neck ring over her head, and emerged through the central opening. It reminded her of self-birth every time she did it. She pushed the upper half down around her hips and slid her legs out, turning and floating free.

She was now wearing only her byelyo—long white cotton underwear—and socks. She thought for a minute, then peeled the thermal coverall off the suit and put it on. *That feels better.* She rolled the inner pressure suit tightly so that the weapon was in the middle and tucked it beside her helmet.

Svetlana had been in space for two weeks, and had become adept in weightlessness. She pivoted smoothly, found a handhold on a support strut and floated silently next to Michael while she rolled up the cuffs on her oversized coveralls.

Michael glanced at her. "All okay?"

She nodded. "Da, okay."

———

Michael called down the tunnel to the Lunar Module. "How's it going, Chad?"

"All the latches look right, Michael. I think we're good to jettison the S-IVB."

Michael pushed the transmit button. "Houston, 18, we show good for separation."

"Roger, 18, concur, you are GO for Pyro Arm and extraction."

There was definite comfort in the familiar technical jargon and practiced actions. Michael set the switches to power the four explosive charges that would sever connection to the rocket body and push the *Bulldog* Lunar Module clear.

"Ready, Chad?"

"All set."

With Svetlana watching beside him, Michael leaned forward, flipped up the protective cover and raised the S-IVB SEP switch. There was a solid thumping sound, and they floated forward against the slight acceleration as springs and small thrusters pushed *Bulldog* free of its launch rocket. Michael stared up through his overhead window as the ships silently floated apart.

"There she goes, Houston, looks like a clean separation."

"Roger, Michael, good news. In a couple minutes we'll maneuver it clear of you."

Michael glanced at the cosmonaut and gave a quick nod, raising a thumb. She stared at him, unblinking.

I wonder if she's ever seen a Black man before.

With what sounded like forced nonchalance, the CAPCOM said, "Apollo 18, if now's a good time, the Flight Director would like to talk with you."

Chad poked his head out of the connecting tunnel to *Bulldog* and nodded at Michael to respond.

"Roger, Houston, we're listening." Michael realized that Svetlana didn't have a headset on. *Probably for the best. Who knows if she actually speaks English?*

Gene Kranz's familiar voice came into their headsets.

"Chad, Michael, I'm on a discreet comm loop, so we have some privacy. First of all, nice work on the TLI burn and S-IVB sep. Despite everything that's happened, you're on your way to the Moon.

"It's a terrible thing that we lost Luke, and my heart goes out to you both. No one here suspected there was a crew on Almaz, and we sure didn't know the ship was armed. Your reactions were a credit to the military services, and Luke will be forever honored by the Marine Corps as their first-ever combat fatality in space.

"Take any time you need to deal with it, but when you're ready, we have a few things."

Chad spoke. "Gene, we appreciate it." He looked at Michael, who shrugged. Death wasn't welcome, but it wasn't new to either man. "We're both okay with doing what needs to be done."

"Okay, thanks. As you can imagine, Washington is about to get involved, and we still have to decide what we're going to do when we get to the Moon—orbit and land, or just slingshot around and come straight back home. Those are going to be tough decisions, and Al, Deke and Kaz are working it on your behalf right now."

Chad and Michael nodded.

Gene continued. "For now, we need to decide what to do with Luke's body. The team is looking at options, but we recommend he stay sealed up in his suit for now." The message was clear: Luke's decomposing body would overwhelm the spaceship's air purifiers.

"We understand, Gene, thanks. His suit looks like it's airtight," Chad said. "I recommend we stay on the lunar orbit and landing trajectory for now, stick with the timeline. Keeps options open."

Michael glanced at him. *No way would Chad want to lose the moonwalk.*

"Agreed." Gene paused. "Is the cosmonaut listening? Does she speak English?"

"She's not on a headset, and it seems like she only knows a few words," Michael said.

Gene nodded. "For now I recommend you just treat her like a new crewmember, show her the critical safety and ops items, keep her out of trouble."

Svetlana noticed them both looking at her, and looked questioningly back.

"Makes sense, Gene," Chad said. "We'll let you know how it's going."

"Good. We're going to stay under total media blackout until told otherwise." The implied message: there was no need to limit what they said on the radio. "You two have any questions?"

Chad looked at Michael, who shook his head.

"Nope, thanks for the update."

CAPCOM spoke. "18, we're back with you, if you can pick up in 3-9 of the Flight Plan. We'd like the LM/CM Delta-P, and for you to get the cabin fan filter back on."

"Roger, Houston, in work." Michael flipped the page of the checklist and glanced at the cosmonaut. She calmly watched him, then turned to look at Chad. Michael saw her frown.

Looking over at Chad, Michael saw a faint smile on his commander's face. *What was that about?*

The phone rang on the flight director's console in Moscow. He picked it up and listened intently, making notes in his green daily logbook. He interrupted a couple of times to verify details, and then slowly set the phone down.

He turned to face Chelomei.

"Comrade Director, as you know, our ground stations have been listening for transmissions from the Apollo capsule."

Chelomei's stare burned into him. Ever since they'd sent the command to fire the gun on Almaz, they'd had no comms. It had been more than one full orbit, and neither of the relay ships had been able to get even basic telemetry data from the orbiting station. More ominously, there had been no word from the Almaz crew.

"Khvatit!" Chelomei spat. "Out with it!"

"It seems the Americans also had a comm problem, and recently got it fixed. Our interpreters are now hearing the Apollo crew clearly." He took a deep breath and then spoke in a rush. "The battle at Almaz killed one astronaut and one cosmonaut, and appears to have very badly damaged our ship. They referred to"—he checked his notes—"a 'trail of debris.'"

Chelomei's lips went thin.

"The Apollo Command Module was damaged but has been repaired, and they have fired their engine to leave Earth orbit for the Moon. They have extracted their lunar lander from the rocket body, as per normal. Somehow, after our crew's defense of Almaz, one cosmonaut was still clinging to the American ship as it turned for the Moon, and has since gotten inside."

He straightened in his chair. "Captain Andrei Mitkov is dead, Comrade, killed in battle. His body has floated free. Senior Lieutenant Svetlana Gromova is the one who is aboard the Apollo ship."

Chelomei wanted to scream. *Almaz a trail of debris. And Mitkov killed? The Americans did this!* He glared past the flight director, his thoughts reeling.

He took a lung-filling breath, held it and then forcefully exhaled, pushing it all out, clearing his mind. He pictured what was going to happen, assembling the logic. Since the Americans had not stayed in Earth orbit, they must still be intending to land on the Moon. And with only two astronauts, one would have to be in the lander, the other in the orbiting capsule.

So where would Gromova be?

What would I decide if I were the Americans? He nodded slightly. Having Gromova on the surface as an extra set of hands would be safer than a moonwalker being there solo. He thought through it again, weighing benefits, and reached the same conclusion. The Americans had to be thinking the same thing.

A Soviet on the Moon. From disaster, potential triumph!

But they were at the Americans' mercy. They couldn't even talk with Gromova unless NASA let them. Chelomei pictured the assets at his disposal, and what might be possible. He started a mental list of what was needed and who could provide it. He glanced at his watch and realized it was still evening. He grabbed the flight director console's phone and began making calls.

29

The White House

Bob Haldeman stood impatiently at the corner of the long, highly polished mahogany table in the West Wing of the White House. The hastily called National Security Council meeting was starting late. As President Nixon's fiercely loyal Chief of Staff, Haldeman was an unyielding taskmaster, and the delay made the veins in his forehead bulge below his tight crew cut.

Sam Phillips had arrived from his NSA office across town, and the Joint Chiefs Chairman and the Secretary of State were already at the table. Henry Kissinger, the head of the Council, had just taken his corner seat. CIA Chief James Schlesinger was still standing, pipe in hand, talking with Nixon. Haldeman placed a speakerphone in front of Nixon's chair to tie in to Houston and said, "Gentlemen, let's get seated, please."

Nixon looked at Haldeman, who nodded, and then walked around to sit midway up the side of the table, his chair bracketed by US and Presidential flags. He glanced at the phone on the table next to his cigar ashtray, and turned to Kissinger to begin.

"Mr. President, we have . . . a very tense situation . . . that has developed in space." Kissinger spoke like he was dictating a letter, in German-accented chunks. His gravelly voice was serious, his face impassive behind heavy-rimmed glasses.

"I will let Sam Phillips summarize what has occurred. But what we need to decide today is how to advise the Soviets, and how to turn this to our advantage."

Sam Phillips let that sink in before he spoke, and then he chronologically reviewed the events that had occurred that morning in space. As they listened, the faces of the men around the table darkened.

"The bastards!" muttered Schlesinger.

Sam continued. "I spoke with NORAD, and they're tracking multiple objects near the Almaz Space Station, confirming some sort of breakup. They estimate the lighter pieces will decay and burn up fairly quickly, and the main ship will re-enter Earth's atmosphere in about six weeks. A few dense pieces will likely make it to the surface, but the odds are they'll land in an ocean somewhere."

He made eye contact with Nixon. "Mr. President, if you concur, I'd like to get our rep in Mission Control on the line."

Nixon frowned. He hated ad hoc meetings and surprises. Haldeman and Kissinger prepared detailed daily written briefings for him, which he found much easier to deal with. But this was an unforeseen, serious event that required immediate action.

"Go ahead."

Haldeman walked around the table, reached carefully past the president and pushed the blinking button on the phone. Light static came through the speaker.

Sam Phillips said, "Kaz, I'm here with the President and National Security Council members. Can you hear us?"

"Yes, sir, loud and clear."

"I've summarized what you and I spoke about, but what we need is the latest info and recommendations from there at NASA." As he talked,

Phillips made eye contact with James Fletcher, the NASA Administrator, seated across from him.

Kaz was sitting in the Director of Flight Ops room, looking through the glass at Mission Control. *Christ, I'm talking to the President!* His heart raced, but he kept his voice calm, matching Sam's tone.

"Mr. President, this is Lieutenant Commander Kazimieras Zemeckis, MOL astronaut and military liaison to Apollo 18. As General Phillips has probably told you, both the Command Module and the Lunar Lander are healthy, and they're on their way to the Moon, arriving in orbit there in"—he glanced at the timer on the front screen—"sixty-nine hours. A little under three days.

"The crew is asking for direction on a few key issues, and NASA needs to decide a couple things soon, all at your direction, sir."

In preparing for the call, he'd tried to visualize the group he was talking to, and their concerns. "The main question is, do we land on the Moon or not? The military purpose of the landing is still strong—to determine what the Soviets have found there with their unmanned Lunokhod rover. It could have key tactical and scientific importance for America."

Nixon glanced at General Moorer, the Joint Chiefs Chairman, who nodded as Kaz continued.

"With the death of Captain Hemming, we lost the Lunar Module pilot, but Commander Miller can fly the LM to the surface and do a moonwalk solo, if needed. Lieutenant Esdale would operate the Command Module in orbit, as planned. The wild card is what to do with the cosmonaut. She apparently has no English, but the crew's been using sign language."

Kaz paused, thinking that was enough for the moment.

The men around the table were all looking in different directions, visualizing options. The CIA chief took his unlit pipe out of his mouth. "Lieutenant Commander Zemeckis, this is Jim Schlesinger. I want to hear *your* recommendation."

This is unreal, Kaz thought. *I'm just a frickin' pilot!* He took a breath.

"Sir, I think we should land and the cosmonaut should go to the surface too. We can store Captain Hemming's corpse in the cosmonaut's spacesuit like a body bag. The crew tells me she's about the same size as Luke, so she can wear his suit. She'd be more useful in the LM than orbiting with Lieutenant Esdale." He decided to be frank. "She's an unknown and a threat to the mission, whether we land or not, but this way we stick to the plan as closely as possible, and have the best chance to accomplish our key objectives."

Phillips turned to the President. "Sir, Kaz also pointed out to me that this would give us leverage to deal with the Russians. Trade their silence on what really happened at Almaz for a chance to have public American-Soviet cooperation."

Kissinger slowly nodded, then haltingly spoke. "We have been planning your summit with Brezhnev in June on preventing nuclear war. This would give us a good advantage."

Haldeman, the most political of Nixon's trusted men, looked the President in the eye and chose his words carefully. "With you having signed Title IX against sex discrimination, and the Supreme Court's Roe v. Wade decision, the women's libbers would *love* you for being the president that put a woman on the Moon." In front of this group, he didn't mention the recent worrisome developments in the Watergate investigation, but both he and Nixon recognized the looming need for increased popular support.

Kissinger's deep, reasoned voice cut in again. "I can call Dobrynin now to set up an urgent briefing with Brezhnev." Anatoly Dobrynin had been the Soviet ambassador in Washington for over a decade, and he and Kissinger met often.

Nixon looked around the room, waiting to see if anyone had anything else to add, probing his own thoughts. This was a lousy situation, but if they played it right, he might gain the kind of support he'd once felt when he congratulated Armstrong and Aldrin, live on national TV, as they stood on the Moon. They could spin the astronaut's death as something that had happened while rescuing a failing Russian spaceship; the man would be seen as a hero. They could use the fact that the Soviets had opened fire with Almaz, killing an astronaut who was merely taking pictures, as a key negotiating tool with the Politburo. And the world would know that the Russians couldn't walk on the Moon without America's help.

Win-win. He looked around to see all the men waiting for him to speak.

"Guys, let's not screw this up. We need to control the information carefully, and get Russian buy-in ASAP. I want NASA to minimize our risk by keeping the mission as short as possible to meet the military needs. But let's do it. Let's land Apollo 18, with a cosmonaut aboard, on the Moon."

That was nuts, Kaz thought, gathering his papers to walk back into Mission Control. Yawning and shaking his head to clear the exhaustion and adrenaline, he stopped to fill his coffee cup from the communal pot in the hallway, thinking about what steps this course of action required.

The crew needs an interpreter.

He climbed the steps to the Flight Director level, and walked over to Gene Kranz, catching the eye of Al Shepard behind the Flight Ops console. Kaz filled them both in on Nixon's approval. When he mentioned the interpreter, Gene said, smiling, "I'm a step ahead of you."

He raised his chin to point at the CAPCOM console, where a woman with long blond hair was standing, looking awkward. "That's Galena Northcutt. She works in the Mission Planning back room, has a math background and spoke Russian at home growing up. I've asked her to fill in until we can get someone here from the State Department."

The CAPCOM got Galena seated and showed her how to communicate with the crew. Kaz stepped around Gene's console and down one level to stand behind her. He retrieved his headset and plugged in to listen to Gene's updated briefing to the room.

"Gentlemen. And ladies." Gene glanced at Galena, the only woman there. "We've just received approval from the highest level to proceed as planned with Apollo 18. We still need to confirm with the Soviets, but the current intent is to have the cosmonaut on board"—he checked his papers for the name—"Svetlana Gromova, ride in place of Luke Hemming. I need TELMU to work suit-check and sizing, and Ops and Procedures to start revising checklists for the Commander to fly the LM without the usual help and to minimize total mission time."

TELMU was the console in charge of the spacewalking suit while on the lunar surface. The technicians nodded their heads at the Flight Director's instruction.

Gene continued. "We're fortunate to have a Russian speaker already on staff, to help CAPCOM and the crew communicate."

Galena looked around uncomfortably and waved.

"We'll gen up more translation help shortly, and the plan is undoubtedly going to shift as the Russians get involved."

He turned and looked at JW. "SURGEON, I need you to sort out a plan for Captain Hemming's body using the cosmonaut's spacesuit."

JW nodded. He'd already been looking up flesh decay rates and off-gassing concerns in a confined living area.

"That is all for now, people. Let's rethink our assumptions, given these new circumstances, and revise the plan to get the crew what they need and Apollo 18 safely to the surface of the Moon and back. CAPCOM, let's get the crew working the timeline, and offer up Miss Northcutt to help them talk to each other. Let's have Kaz talk to the crew directly on this, as he has the latest details."

The CAPCOM nodded.

"You ready?" Kaz asked Galena. Her eyes were wide, but she nodded. Kaz pushed the transmit button. "Apollo 18, Houston, how do you hear?"

Chad's voice came back through Kaz's headset. "Loud and clear, Houston."

"18, we'd like you to keep working the timeline, but meanwhile we have someone here to translate for you. My suggestion is to get the cosmonaut on a headset, and then we can act as relay for your conversation."

"Copy, Houston, in work."

Svetlana was floating next to Michael, watching with interest as he aligned the ship and methodically recorded the star angles into the computer. It intrigued her how similar it was to the system they had on Almaz. She felt the commander tug on her sleeve.

"Put this on," he said, holding out a headset on a long white cord. She held his gaze as she took it and slipped it into place over her ear, swinging the mic boom in front of her mouth. She frowned, wondering who she would be talking to.

"Houston, the cosmonaut has a headset on and should be able to hear you now." As he spoke, Chad showed her the volume thumbwheel on the cockpit side panel. She nodded and lowered it slightly.

Kaz looked at Galena. "Just repeat what I say in Russian, okay?" She nodded, moving her thumb on the unfamiliar transmit button.

"Svetlana, this is Mission Control Houston. How do you hear me?"

Galena repeated what he'd said in Russian. "Privyet Svetlana, zdyess tsenter upravlenia polyotami ve Houstonyeh. Kak nas slooshetyeh?"

Warily, Svetlana responded, and Galena translated for the room.

"She said, 'Houston, this is Senior Lieutenant Svetlana Gromova, I hear you.'"

Kaz nodded, and continued. "Tell her your name and that you're a NASA flight controller who speaks Russian. You're here to help interpret for her with the Apollo crew and with us in Mission Control. Also tell her we're contacting her team in Moscow to enable them to talk with her as soon as possible."

Galena blinked up at him. The CAPCOM slid a piece of paper and a pen in front of her, and she scribbled the key points and then broadcast it to Svetlana.

There was a pause, and then Svetlana spoke rapidly, Galena taking notes and translating.

"She'd like to know what happened to her crewmate, and to her ship. She also wants to know what's going to happen now."

Kaz looked at Gene, and at Al Shepard. Both men shrugged, as if to say "Tell her the truth." He pushed the transmit button.

"Apollo 18, for simplicity, let's just communicate like usual and allow time for Galena here to translate as we go, sentence by sentence." He paused while Galena interpreted.

"Senior Lieutenant Gromova, this is Lieutenant Commander Kaz Zemeckis. I am sorry to have to tell you that your crewmate has died, and that your spaceship was fatally damaged. We are glad you have survived and are safely aboard Apollo. The mission is continuing to the Moon, as planned, for now. We'll get you more details soon."

Galena translated. There was a pause, then he heard Svetlana quietly say, "Spasiba."

"Thank you," Galena translated.

Gene leaned back to Al's console, shaking his head. Both of them had flown jets in the Cold War and Korea, with Communists as their sworn enemy. Gene muttered, "I never thought I'd see the day."

38

Mission Control, Houston

JW took off his headset and walked up to talk directly with the Flight Director.

Gene gave him his full attention; SURGEON didn't come talk to him often. He beckoned to Kaz and Al Shepard to join them.

"I've been looking at postmortem decay rates," JW said. "Captain Hemming's body will currently be in autolysis, or self-digestion, as his membranes and cells break down. The gas from the bacteria and decay, especially in his gut, is going to get rapidly worse. His body could bloat to double its size, and the gas will vent through his anus and esophagus. The odors of putrefaction will be extremely unpleasant." JW was matter-of-fact, but Kaz felt himself trying not to think that this was Luke he was talking about.

JW continued. "The body will also be stiffening soon, with rigor mortis starting in the neck and torso. That will last about twenty-four hours. The limbs and joints will be too rigid to transfer into the other suit within an hour or two. Oh, and the bowels will have evacuated, so there will be urine and probably feces for the crew to deal with."

Gene raised a palm, signaling JW to stop. *Doctors.* "Sounds like the timeline is critical. What do you recommend?"

"We need to get Luke's body transferred into the cosmonaut's suit and sealed up ASAP. Then they need to store it someplace, hopefully cool, to slow bacterial activity. Maybe even vent it to vacuum, if possible, to kill the bugs."

"Maybe a burial at sea?" Al Shepard suggested. "It would be honorable that Luke's resting place was the surface of the Moon. Pretty sure *Bulldog* has enough weight margin for his body. And keeping him in *Pursuit* all the way back to Earth would add a bunch of risk—atmosphere contamination and re-entry weight and balance."

Gene nodded. He thanked the doctor, then stood squarely in front of his console and addressed the room. "Folks, we need to have the crew transfer Captain Hemming's body into the cosmonaut's pressure suit before they go to sleep for the night. It's already been a long day, I know, but once rigor mortis sets in, it will be too difficult. CAPCOM, please advise the crew, with translation."

Kaz stepped back down to his console and checked that Galena was ready. He spoke: "*Pursuit*, Houston, when you have a minute." Code for *This is important.*

Michael's ears perked up, and he caught Chad's eye. "Go ahead, Houston, *Pursuit*'s listening."

Kaz described the plan, and the reasons behind it. He had Galena translate the key details, especially the planned use of the cosmonaut's spacesuit.

Svetlana's head whipped around at that, looking at her stowed suit.

"*Pursuit* copies all, thanks." Michael said, his voice somber.

Svetlana floated abruptly in front of him, frowning. She waved a finger and shook her head, saying something forcefully in Russian. The only word Michael recognized was "nyet."

Galena listened to the rapid-fire, agitated voice, and translated for all in Mission Control to hear. "The cosmonaut says she can't allow her suit to be used by anyone but her. It's custom-sized, and she'll need it for re-entry and landing. She's demanding to talk to senior management in Moscow, or she won't authorize it."

The room was briefly silent as they digested this.

Gene Kranz shook his head. "Galena, tell her that we're working on getting a link with Moscow as fast as we can, but that she is a guest on an American vessel, and operational needs outweigh her concerns. Tell her we'll have a pressure suit to protect her for re-entry. And repeat what you say in English too, so the crew knows."

Galena read up Gene's words, and Chad replied immediately. "Houston, this puts us in an ugly situation here. She's mad, and blocking us from getting at her suit. I may have to force her out of the way while Michael grabs it."

Kaz raised his hand to get Gene's attention, and got a nod.

"Chad, Kaz here. It's going to take a while for you two to get Luke out of his suit. I recommend you start on that now, and hopefully we'll hear from Moscow while you're in process. Also, she'll likely get distracted at some point, and you can just grab it." He shrugged, as Gene raised a thumb.

"Copy, Houston, concur. We'll start now."

In Moscow Mission Control, known by its Russian acronym, "TsUP," the communication technician was listening to the American chatter coming back from the Apollo ship. "She's asking them to let her talk to us, Comrade Director. Something about not allowing them to use her Yastreb suit." The tech looked puzzled, trying to piece together the one-sided conversation, unable to hear the transmissions up from Houston.

Chelomei stared at him, thinking. *Her suit? Why would they want her suit? Was something wrong with theirs?*

He blew out sharply through his nose. *Damn, I need to talk to her!* He glanced at his watch. Nearly midnight. Another night sleeping on the cot in his office.

He stood, curtly telling the flight director, "I'll be back in the morning. Send someone to fetch me immediately if you hear any other developments." He turned on his heel without waiting for an answer and strode out of TsUP, his steps echoing loudly down the tiled hallway.

He needed to accelerate diplomacy at the highest level. As soon as Moscow woke back up, he'd call his contacts in the Kremlin.

Michael was undoing the umbilical hoses from Luke's suit. "Look here," he said, pointing. Chad leaned in, and saw the ragged metal where the bullet had split the oxygen feed line and regulator.

"That's what killed him." Chad scowled at the cosmonaut, who was glaring back at him as she hung on firmly to the crew headrest, covering her rolled-up spacesuit.

"Look at that Russian bear, showing her lack of gratitude," Chad said disgustedly. "All we did was save her life after they fired on us, and killed Luke here."

Michael had undone Luke's gloves and was pulling them off the lifeless fingers. The pale skin was already starting to blotch with death.

"Help me with the helmet," Michael said as he pinched and released the latch on the neck ring. The two of them guided it clear of Luke's head, the glass of the visor still fogged.

As the helmet came away, Luke's sightless eyes appeared, wide open and bloodshot. Chad looked away, muttering "Christ!"

Michael reached in and closed Luke's eyelids. "Sorry, buddy," he said. He turned the body over, peeled back the Velcro and snaps, and unzipped the suit's long pressure seal.

He reached an arm inside around Luke's body, bending him at the waist, and started prying the upper half of the suit off his shoulders. As he forced the neck ring over the back of Luke's head, the arms slid out of the sleeves and the upper torso popped free, loosely waving in weightlessness like a released jack-in-the-box, banging into structures, filling the confined space.

"Geez, Luke, you're scaring me!" Michael forced the joke to try to settle his own nerves. Svetlana had jammed herself into the far corner, as far clear as possible, now holding her spacesuit tightly rolled under her arm.

Chad grabbed Luke's boots and tugged, moving down the tunnel towards the LM. Michael disconnected the inner plumbing and electrical leads to Luke's body, and then helped work his legs clear.

The cockpit had become a jumble of floating bodies and gear. "I'll stow the suit in the LM," Chad decided, gathering the helmet and gloves and moving down the tunnel.

Michael began removing Luke's liquid-cooled long underwear, feeling like he should apologize to his friend. *This feels too personal.* He pulled down the long front zipper and peeled the stiff, tube-filled fabric away, relieved to see that Luke's low-fiber prelaunch diet had meant he hadn't shat himself. The underwear was damp with urine, but that would dry before the cosmonaut had to put it on. *Tolerable.*

"What are you doing?" Chad had reappeared and was looking past Michael at the cosmonaut. She had partially unrolled her suit and, smiling uncertainly, held it out.

Chad frowned. "Had a change of heart, did you?"

"Maybe she understands better now that we've got Luke out of his suit," Michael said.

"Yeah, maybe." Chad reached his hand out, beckoning, and she released her suit, floating it to him. He looked at her body and then at Luke's. "Let's hope this fits."

They unrolled the suit, flipping it around, inspecting the design differences. "Looks like the Russians enter from the front, through this balloon opening," Michael said. He raised his eyebrows at Svetlana, and she nodded. They fed Luke's legs inside, working them down into place, and then pulled the suit over his arms. Chad had to pry hard to get the helmet ring over Luke's head, as the body was stiffening, but with yanking and pushing, he made it work.

Svetlana held out her helmet. Chad took it and guided it over Luke's head, nestling it into its seal. There was an obvious over-center latch sticking out the side, and he lifted and clicked it into place, tugging and twisting on the helmet to check it was secure.

He looked up at her. "Gloves?" He flexed his fingers to demonstrate. She retrieved them from under the seat, and he slid them onto Luke's limp hands and locked the mechanism.

Michael had been trying to figure out how the air seal at the front of the suit worked. "I see that we need to pinch this internal body balloon closed, but what holds it?"

"Vapross?" Svetlana asked.

"Yeah, how do you Russians do this?"

She floated across and quickly gathered the loose rubber into successive folds with one hand, squeezing excess air from the suit with the other. Two rubber ties floated free, and with practiced motions she tightly wound them around the folds, tucking the bulbous end of each tie into a matching eyelet. She tucked the double-sealed balloon end inside the fabric of the suit, next to Luke's body.

Michael nodded, impressed. "Simple design." He pulled the outer fabric covering closed and began crisscrossing the laces tightly all the way up the torso.

Chad was looking at the umbilical connections, poking with his finger. "Let's hope these one-way valves keep Luke airtight."

Svetlana had chosen her moment. While the commander had been down the tunnel and Mikhail had his back turned, she'd grabbed the weapon from her bundled suit and tucked it flush against the backpack. She'd strapped it into place, muffled inside the thermal insulation cloth to avoid the clink of metal on metal. As she replaced the pack under the seat, she double-checked that the weapon was concealed.

Lucha sinitsa ve rookak chem zhuravel ve nyeba. She wasn't sure what was going to happen, but a bird in hand was definitely better than one in the sky.

She assumed they were lying to her about talking to someone in Moscow. If that happened, fine, but why would they allow it? Capitalist

Americans, with a cosmonaut as a captive prize on their ship? They were going to make a spectacle of her, exploit the opportunity and use her as a bargaining chip. Better to be ready.

Better to be armed.

Michael guided Luke's body up the tunnel to stow it in the LM, and in the sudden lull, Chad noticed he was hungry. And thirsty. The nausea had passed, and his body was telling him it was time to eat.

He leaned back and rummaged in the food locker, looking for packages that were marked for him with an identifying small red Velcro square. He found a brownie in a vacuum-sealed pouch, and the utensils container with scissors. As he was cutting the plastic open, he saw Svetlana watching him.

He realized it must have been a while since she'd eaten. "Hungry?" He held out the brownie.

She nodded. He handed her the package and found himself another. They chewed in silence.

He dug through the packets again and came out with a long, clear bag with grainy powder inside. He grabbed the water dispenser, a pistol-like contraption mounted on a hose, turned the red butterfly valve and carefully injected water into the bag through an opening in the bottom. He shook the bag to dissolve the powder and cautiously unrolled the drinking tube, biting its end closed between sips.

He filled a second one, read the label and floated it to her. "Pineapple grapefruit drink—you'll love it."

She'd been observing, and unrolled the tube and drank.

"Here, you can fend for yourself." Chad found one of Luke's food packages and held it out to her, pointing at the color-coded Velcro patch and then at her. "You—blue. Me—red." He jerked a thumb towards the LM. "Michael, white. Ironic, eh? You get it?"

She nodded as she took the package, rubbing the blue Velcro with her thumb. "Svetlana 'bloo.' Spasiba." She pronounced the English word like it had a new taste in her mouth.

"Yeah, whatever."

She used her fingers to squeeze the last of the juice up the drinking tube, and then rolled the empty package tightly together with the brownie packet. "Kuda?" she asked.

"In there." Chad pointed at a covered opening in the starboard wall. She jammed the empty plastic in and down, compacting the volume, and then held her hand out for his.

"Sure, toots. You clean up." He floated her his empties. She stuffed them away and then looked squarely at him.

"Tooalyet?" She pointed at her midsection and made a brushing-away motion with her fingers.

"Toilet? Right, you'll be needing that by now." He thought a moment. NASA had provided a condom-like adapter for the men to piss into, filling a urine bag. For shitting they had an open-mouthed plastic bag with a sticky seal that held it in place against their naked rear ends. Toilet paper and wet wipes were in attached bags.

Chad shrugged. She'd figure it out. He opened the storage locker and got her one of each.

She turned them over in her hands, nodding as she compared them to the similar Soviet equipment. *Muzhshini!* Men!

She floated to the far corner, turned away from Chad and started to peel off her coveralls.

"Oh, hey, hey!" he objected. "I don't need to watch you crap!" He turned and faced the port wall and went back to revising the landing checklist. "Try not to stink up the place."

Svetlana paused and looked around. One astronaut was in the LM and the other was now deliberately not watching her. The control panel of switches was in front of her. She made a mental note. *An excellent way to get privacy.*

She might need it.

31

Mission Control, Houston

EECOM had been looking at the effect of the sunlight on the side of the ship in the direct glare of the Sun, and temperatures were nearing peak allowable. The standard plan to deal with it was to slowly spin the ship once every 20 minutes, like a slow-motion barbecue spit. With all the problems, they had delayed starting the spin. "FLIGHT," he said, "before the crew goes to sleep, we need to set up rotisserie mode."

Gene asked, "INCO, what'll that do to my comms?"

"FLIGHT, the Hi-Gain antenna won't track as well while we spin, so it'll drift in and out." INCO peered over his console. "We can stop and start the spin when we need to talk, if FDO agrees."

The Flight Dynamics Officer checked a data table on his screen. "It'll use a bit more propellant, but our margins are good."

The astronauts' official sleep period wasn't for several hours yet, but they'd had to get up at 3:00 a.m. for the early-morning launch. The timeline called for a 90-minute nap, and Gene knew after the craziness of the flight so far, as their adrenaline ebbed, they'd need it. A thought occurred to him, and he waved Kaz up to his console. Al Shepard came around to listen.

"How should we handle sleep now?" Gene looked at Al. "Do you think one of them needs to stay awake to keep an eye on the Russian?"

"Absolutely," Al said. "I sure don't want a Commie floating around unsupervised inside our ship."

"I suggest a new sleep rotation cycle, Gene," Kaz offered. "Chad needs to be well rested for his moonwalk. That's our top priority. I expect the cosmonaut is on Moscow time, nine hours ahead, so she'll likely be ready for some shuteye about now too."

Gene nodded. "Let's keep Chad on the planned day/night schedule and move Michael to cover while Chad sleeps."

Kaz said, "I suggest *Bulldog* as the astronaut sleep area, so they get peace and quiet. The cosmonaut can just unplug her comms and sleep in *Pursuit* with whoever's awake."

Gene pushed his mic button. "EECOM, you're approved to set up Passive Thermal Control." He looked back at Kaz. "Let the crew know the new plan."

Kaz nodded and returned to the CAPCOM console, Al and Gene watching him. As a Navy pilot, Al was always ready to take a dig at the other armed services, and Gene was Air Force. He smiled and raised an eyebrow.

"Not bad for a one-eyed sailor."

"Sleep? How the hell do they expect me to go to sleep?"

Chad had listened to Kaz's instructions and was now looking at the new pencil marks he'd made in the Flight Plan. "I'm sure it sounds nice to them, sipping their coffees there in Houston, but it's nuts! How am I going to rest easy with Luke's corpse floating next to me and *her* running around?"

Svetlana glanced at him, frowning slightly at what might have caused his obvious anger. The interpreter hadn't translated the lengthy conversation the two Americans had just had with Houston.

By now Michael was used to Chad's temper. "No choice, Boss. It just makes sense. We've got to have you in tip-top form for hopping around on the Moon, especially when you'll be babysitting her. I'll have lots of time to catch up on my beauty sleep once I get the two of you undocked."

Svetlana looked from one to the other, and back again.

Chad said, "Yeah, okay." But the anger was still clear on his face. "You need any help getting us spinning?"

Michael held his nose to talk. "This is your captain speaking. I'll be putting the plane in rockabye mode for your sleeping pleasure. Please pull down the window shades and have a good rest, travelers. When you wake up, the stewardess"—he stuck out a thumb at Svetlana—"will be ready to serve you a delicious vacuum-packed meal. Sweet dreams, and we'll be there before you know it."

Chad smiled in spite of himself. "Clown."

Michael tapped the data screen. "Maybe take extra clothes with you. It's colder in *Bulldog*."

Chad nodded and rummaged in a locker for a jacket, then floated down the tunnel to the LM.

What was that all about? Svetlana wondered. She peered down the tunnel, and back at Mikhail. He glanced at her and brought his palms together beside his head, tipping it to one side. Then he pointed at the empty crew couch.

He wants me to sleep? She glanced at her watch and did a double take. It was one in the morning. She paused to assess how her body felt, and suddenly experienced a wave of fatigue. Michael had gone back to looking at the control panel, and she stole a look at the backpack, still securely wedged and barely visible under his seat.

Maybe a quick rest wouldn't be a bad idea. *Tiki chass.* Nap time.

She floated onto the right-hand couch and loosely strapped herself in. She took one last look his way, then closed her eyes. Within seconds her thoughts took her into sleep.

Michael glanced over at her inert form, and then leaned to look down the darkened tunnel. He reached over and shut off the cabin overhead lights, then punched in some hexadecimal code on his keyboard to set an alarm for 30 minutes, just in case he dozed off too.

We're on our way, and I'm flying the ship alone. But man, is this fucked up.

The inside of the lander was completely familiar to Chad after the hundreds of hours he and Luke had spent in the simulator. And yet, with weightlessness, it felt strange, like diving inside a ship underwater. With no gravity to define up and down, even this small space was disorienting. He looked around in the harsh sunlight, adjusting his mind to the weirdness. *Like a sideshow fun house.*

Michael had strapped Luke's body up against the ceiling with one of the sleep hammocks. He'd rotated the gold visor down on the helmet so Luke's face was covered. Better that way.

Chad fit the sunshades into place over the two large, triangular landing windows. The labels and tips of all the switches, coated with luminescent paint, glowed in the darkness. He opened a locker to retrieve the other hammock and sleeping bag, and wrapped them around himself, clipping a strap to a handrail to keep from drifting. He consciously uncoiled the muscles in his body, took a deep breath and smoothly exhaled it. He was glad the motion sickness had passed.

A thought struck him. NASA had encouraged them to bring a few small private items, and he'd had a copy made of his parents' wedding picture. He reached down inside the sleeping bag, unzipped his leg pocket and slid it carefully out.

The glowing panels illuminated the black-and-white photo softly. Chad angled it to see the faces. His father, a man he only vaguely remembered, looked at him confidently, hair freshly cut, dark suit ill-fitting, with the pants too short, obviously borrowed for the day. Money had been tight. Chad looked into his eyes. *Could you have imagined this, Father?*

As always, though, it was his mother he couldn't look away from. She'd worn her best dress, a dark print with a large bow at the neckline. She'd added a long white veil that reached all the way to her calves. He rubbed the photo with his thumb. Her highly polished black shoes gleamed over her dark stockings. She was clutching red roses, and not for the first time, Chad counted them. He could see six clearly and, with care, one more, partially covered. Seven roses, an odd number for good luck, bought by this man, for this woman, on a day filled with promise.

Chad brought the photo closer. Her expression captured him most of all.

His mother's face was round, her cheekbones high. Her wide-set eyes looked squarely at the camera. He could sense the joy of the day in the way she held her neck, so straight and proud. The veil wasn't hers, and she knew it, but the day was, and so was a future together with this man. Her broad, full-lipped mouth bore the gentlest of knowing smiles. A smile Chad could still see and feel in his memory.

He touched the likeness just below her eyes. *Were they brown, or blue like his?* He wished he could remember.

He felt against his chest for her locket, fumbling along the thin chain in the unfamiliarity of zero gravity, finding it floating up near his shoulder. He pulled it around and held it between his thumb and forefinger, turning it slowly. A simple silver pendant, engraved with a winter rose. He looked back at the newly married couple. *Did you buy this for her, Father?* It had been hers, worn against her warm skin. He touched it to his lips and tucked it back under his T-shirt.

He shook his head, sighed deeply and carefully guided the photo back down into his pocket, zipping it safely closed. He relaxed his arms and was slightly surprised to see them float up in front of him. He glanced at Luke's body, suspended above him.

Chad had always held his secrets close. It somehow thrilled him to know that no one ever suspected that he was anything but an over-achieving farm boy from Wisconsin, as all-American as you could get. Even the couple who had raised him seemed to have forgotten where he came from; they'd done their good deed and adopted a lost Russian boy from the rubble of Berlin, making amends for the wickedness of the

World War. They'd convinced themselves that he was too traumatized to remember much about the violence of his childhood before America, even though he was nine when they'd brought him home. Better to forget it, anyway, in an America that was so deeply anti-communist.

And Chad might have forgotten too, if his brother hadn't contacted him. Oleg, the brother he'd thought had died in the war, who'd left him so alone after their parents were killed. But in Chad's first year of college, Oleg had finally tracked him down. It had been a shock to hear his brother's voice again, even through an interpreter. Chad had found that his spoken Russian was rusty, but was amazed at how easily his comprehension of his mother tongue came back. His secretive nature made him careful not to let on how much he understood; Russia was the enemy, and he didn't really know his brother anymore, not really. It was smarter somehow to keep the interpreter between them. Smarter not to tell his adoptive parents, or anyone, about this connection to his past. And especially smart once his Air Force dreams started to come true and he was on track to fly in space.

And now the cosmonaut doesn't know I speak Russian. Even better, no one else does either. The power of that thought made him smile in the darkness. Pulling the cosmonaut into their ship had opened a Pandora's box of unexpected opportunity. Now that she was going to the Moon's surface with him, he just had to keep his eyes open and figure out what he could do with it.

For a tense hour or two after Luke had died, Chad had thought all his sacrifices were going to be for nothing—that the higher-ups would abort the Moon landing and order them home. His control had been dangerously thin, but now he realized that the cards were falling into place.

He had another thought, and his smile widened.

She's my wild card.

32

Lunar Surface

The rock had lain on the surface of the Moon since well before humanity had begun keeping time.

Throughout all recorded history, small meteoroids and asteroids had drifted through the solar system and smashed into the Moon, kicking up powdery dust that fell slowly in the low gravity, leaving an unblemished, dry beach surrounding this particular small, protruding, gray-brown rock.

Until recently.

In the weeks since the radioactivity had been detected—a possible nuclear power source on the Moon, a chance for the Soviets to regain the upper hand in the space race—the smooth plain had started to resemble a dirt bike rodeo.

Gabdul and his team in Simferopol had backed Lunokhod away and reapproached from all sides, photographing and analyzing this most interesting of rocks, the eight wire wheels churning the regolith. The two-week lunar night had slowed operations, as they'd closed up Lunokhod to keep it warm, but the recently risen Sun had kicked off a renewed frenzy of activity.

The rock was about the size of two fists, sticking up above the dirt. They'd started calling it "Ugol"—Russian for "ember"—glowing eternally. Careful to not disturb it, Gabdul had driven the cameras and scientific instruments as close as he safely could, peering from all angles. They had all wondered whether Ugol was just the tip of a larger boulder underneath; the Geiger counter had shown no significant radiation in the surrounding area, so maybe the lunar soil was a better insulator than they thought. But after much scientific and operational discussion, they'd decided on today's plan.

Gabdul was going to bump the rock.

Not a straightforward thing to do. No one had thought to put fenders on the rover, as the intent had been to *not* run into things. It would be a disaster to damage Lunokhod, or one of its key instruments. If Ugol was part of a deeper bedrock, banging into its unyielding surface could do permanent harm.

During the 13-day-long darkness of lunar night, the Simferopol crew had repeatedly gone out into their Moon simulation yard with the full-scale Lunokhod mock-up, working through options. Having unmoving cameras on Lunokhod made the challenge harder; getting close enough to hit the rock with the rover's heavy frame meant losing sight of it.

They'd decided to touch it firmly with one wheel. The titanium rims and stainless-steel mesh tires were tough, and if Ugol was simply resting on the surface, they should be able to dislodge it. But it was going to need delicate driving, and Lunokhod was heavy, even on the Moon.

After the lunar night had ended, they waited several more days because Gabdul insisted that the Sun be high in the sky to minimize long shadows, and so its glare wouldn't shine into the cameras.

On the simulation field, Gabdul had backed Lunokhod into position and practiced on the approach track countless times: he set the precise distance using camera views, knew to move the hand controller for exactly the right length of time and then give a full reversing input just before letting go. These maneuvers had proven to give the most impulse to the rock while minimizing the chances of damage.

It had taken patience, but today was finally the day.

Sitting at his console, Gabdul leaned forward, steadying his arm. He looked at his navigator, who nodded. The image on the screen showed they were exactly in position. Gabdul mouthed a quiet countdown. "Tree, dva, adeen, pusk!"

He smoothly moved his hand controller forward to its limit, held it firmly while counting in his head, swiftly brought it fully back into reverse and then released it. All eyes locked onto the small TV screen, waiting for the slow image refresh to show them what had happened.

The 10 seconds seemed interminable, as Gabdul muttered "Davai, davai!" under his breath—C'mon, c'mon!

The grainy screen flickered impassively to its new image. It showed nothing remarkable—just the soil beyond the stone and a bit of the horizon. But it was exactly what they'd simulated, with everything still level, nothing visibly wrong. Gabdul glanced at his systems technician, who had been worriedly scanning his updated data.

"Pa paryadkeh," he said at last. All seems in order.

Gabdul nodded, and smoothly pulled back on the controller, commanding Lunokhod to reverse enough for the cameras to reveal the result of their work. He counted rhythmically to three and released again. If all worked as in the simulation, it would show Ugol's new position; if it had moved, they should be able to detect it against the surrounding dirt.

The lead scientist had been standing back, but now she grabbed the back of Gabdul's chair and leaned in to look as the new image popped onto the monitor. She'd printed the previous screenshot, and held it up to compare the two side by side. Her eyes flicked back and forth, left and right, scanning for differences.

The new tire track was obvious. Where there had been undisturbed dust, now there was a darker waffle print, the soil kicked up from the sudden momentum reversal. Gabdul touched the edge of the stone on the paper and then the same point on the screen. "I think it moved!" he said, delighted.

The scientist leaned closer, inspecting where he'd pointed. Ugol's edge had been smooth against the dust, but now, in the bright sunlight, there was a darker stripe where they met.

"I think you're right, Gabdul. Ugol has shifted!"

She stepped back and straightened up, crossing her arms. So Ugol was *not* a solid part of a radioactive outcropping. This puzzling lump of a rock was not attached to a mother lode. She focused again on the screen, one hand on her chin, a fingertip tapping her high cheekbone. *How did you get to this place, little one? Did a heavy impact excavate you from deep in the Moon and chuck you up onto the surface? Are there more like you just below the surface?*

It was a planetary geologist's dream. *What are you, Ugol, where did you come from, and what can you teach us about the universe?*

33

Mission Control, Houston

It was shift change, and the number of people in Mission Control had doubled. Each console was overcrowded as the oncoming crew listened to the details of what had happened, making notes and asking questions, so they could seamlessly take over responsibility. An Apollo mission was like a nine-day multi-person relay race where no one could let the baton of technical information and decision-making drop.

Kaz was briefing the oncoming shift CAPCOM. The State Department Field Office had provided a Russian interpreter, who stood calmly beside them, absorbing all the new jargon.

Just before his shift went off headset, Gene Kranz spoke.

"People, that was a helluva day. You worked through many serious problems, some unprecedented in the history of manned spaceflight." He made eye contact with each console.

"We've got the tragedy to deal with, as well as the complexity of handling a new, non-English-speaking foreign crewmember. But the bottom line is we had a successful launch and have a resting crew, a healthy spaceship and a clear mission."

"The real work is just beginning. Get some sleep. See you back here in"—he checked his watch—"fifteen hours."

Kaz had given the U-Joint a long look as he drove home, but the idea of the noisy bar hadn't appealed to him, especially knowing that another astronaut from the Apollo 18 crew would soon be joining Tom on the honor wall. He'd stopped at the grocery for supplies instead. He wanted a stretch and an easy run, a quiet beer and a bite, and maybe some time with Laura. He turned up and into his Polly Ranch driveway, parked and glanced at his watch as he got out and closed the car door. She'd said she'd try to come over after the long drive back from Florida, maybe get in around eight.

Perfect.

He tossed his bag on the sofa and put the food in the fridge, wrinkling his nose at the house's stale air. *Smells like an absent bachelor's pad.* He opened the screened windows as he changed into PT gear, letting the early-evening breeze blow through.

The sun was nearing the horizon as he stepped out onto the driveway and started his 5BX stretching. The disrupted schedule at the Cape and the long periods of sitting had made him stiff. He'd learned it was best not to think about it; just put the body through the practiced 10 minutes of isometrics, work smoothly to the limits, ignore the creaks. Let his mind separate and wander.

But the day kept crowding into his mind. He pictured what the crew was doing in the capsule as he transitioned from stretching to sit-ups. He guessed they would not be sleeping easily. Chad with his quick temper not responding well to all the changes of plan, and Michael trying to be a calming influence, minding the ship and doing the right thing. Both men on edge with Luke's body hovering unavoidably and a female cosmonaut thrown into the mix.

A lot of tension on board.

He stood to do the back extensions, grimacing, then distracting himself by deliberately trying to reimagine the situation through the cosmonaut's eyes. *What had she just been through?* Her crewmate killed, Almaz wrecked and abandoned, the wild ride she must have had, holding on to the outside of a spaceship with its engine firing. *Like Slim Pickens in* Dr. Strangelove. *Craziness!*

He thought back to what he knew of women cosmonauts. He'd only heard of one, with a name that was oddly easy to remember because of its rhythm: Valentina Tereshkova. What was she—a skydiver and Air Force officer? She had made a short solo flight 10 years earlier, with the Soviets going heavy on the propaganda. But this woman—Svetlana— was likely very different. Working as part of a military spy crew, low-profile, long-duration; it would be a mistake to underestimate her.

He felt the grit of the pavement on his palms as he started into his push-ups, doing them in slow motion for maximum effect. The painful pull across his chest and in his shoulders was almost pleasant; unmistakable feedback that he was at his limit, working his muscles, feeling his own strength.

Tomorrow should be an easier day as the crew transited towards the Moon. Maybe fire the engines once to fine-tune their exact trajectory. A chance for the crew to settle in to the new reality and start focusing on replanning the upcoming landing.

A quiet day would be welcome.

He stood and easily jogged down the drive and turned onto the runway. He glanced at his watch. Forty-five minutes ought to be about right. He set a pace that he knew would get his pulse to 145 or so, and settled into the run.

He'd just cracked open a bottle of Lone Star, his hair still wet from the shower, when he heard the sound of a small engine climbing the driveway. He smiled, opened a second bottle and headed for the front door.

"I am so glad to be back," Laura said, smiling at him tiredly as she climbed out of her Beetle. She had on a new Walt Disney World T-shirt featuring Minnie Mouse posing self-consciously in a red dress, and was

carrying an overnight bag. When she reached him, she took the beer
and touched his bottle in a toast before taking a long, thirsty swallow.

With the sparkle returning to her eyes, she said, "If you also have
food, you're the perfect man."

"How about tuna on toast with pickles?" Kaz took her bag and held
the door, and she followed him into the kitchen.

"What did you think of the launch?" he asked as he made the sandwiches.

"We all said the countdown together," she told him with a grin, "and
when that Saturn V blasted off—the rolling noise of it!" She shook her
head, marveling. "It gave me an external heartbeat. And so bright—like
seeing another sun!"

Kaz carried the sandwiches over to the table and sat down with her,
delighting in her pure emotion. He'd been so wrapped up in the technical details, aware of all the dangers, and inside Launch Control,
protected from the sound, that he felt he'd somehow missed what she'd
seen. And a rare, shared experience. "I would have liked to have
watched it with you," he said.

She looked at him, a half smile on her lips. "Well, you had important
astronaut stuff to do. I was just a lunar geologist there for the fun of it."
She took a big bite of her sandwich, then washed it down with the last
of the beer. "You got another one of these?"

As he opened the fridge, she popped a pickle into her mouth, talking
around it. "How's the mission going?"

He brought her the beer. As the lead geologist for the flight, she
needed to know about Luke's death and also that a female cosmonaut
was going to be landing on the Moon, but still he took a moment before
he began to speak, wishing that he could sustain her feelings of wonder
just a little longer.

Her eyes went round at the news. "Luke is dead, killed in space? I
can't really take in how horrible that is. Are you okay?"

When Kaz shrugged and nodded, Laura said, "I guess we had this
conversation the night after Tom died."

Her brow furrowed as she thought through the implications. "This means a whole new plan for surface ops." Her frown deepened. "Sounds like less science is going to get done."

Kaz nodded again. "You're right. We need to come up with a new timeline tomorrow. One that Chad can support on his own, with maybe minimal help from the cosmonaut, Svetlana."

"Well, that's something, anyway," Laura said. "The first woman on the Moon."

There was a moment's silence as they sat and pictured it, then Laura's mouth cracked open suddenly in a wide yawn. She blinked. "The day's catching up with me." She stood and carried her plate and half-finished beer to the sink. She turned to meet Kaz's eyes.

"I'm going to have a quick shower. How about you meet me when I come out?"

34

The Kremlin, Moscow

It wasn't often that Vitaly Kalugin went inside the Kremlin. Rarer still that he was called there for an urgent meeting.

The Kremlin wasn't physically far from his KGB office; just a 15-minute walk from Lubyanka, past the ornate, onion-domed St. Basil's Cathedral on the corner of Red Square and through the primary business entrance at Spasskaya Bashnya, the Savior Tower. But on this fine April morning, he made it in 12. It was an important meeting. He glanced up at the large clock on the tower: 11:40. He wouldn't be late.

Kremlin means "fortress," and its 15-foot-thick, red brick walls implacably reinforced the name. Vitaly walked up to the guard at the base of the clock tower, showed his KGB badge and was allowed to enter. He followed the footpath through the deep gate and turned right.

It always surprised him how pastoral this fortress was inside its walls. Spring flowers were in bloom, and the long grove of trees, each neatly dedicated with a small sign to a Soviet hero, was coming into early leaf. The noisy gray grind of the vast city seemed suddenly distant, and the immensity of Mother Russia herself, still thawing from winter, almost unimaginable.

Vitaly checked the time yet again as he neared Building 14, the four-story yellow-and-white-painted Presidium. *I need to calm myself!* He deliberately slowed his pace before entering through the broad wooden doors and climbing the stone steps towards the meeting room.

The files were in his briefcase, clasped firmly in his left hand.

For an enormous, paper-driven bureaucracy, word had traveled fast. The night admin team at Lubyanka had taken the phone call asking what the KGB had on a cosmonaut, Senior Lieutenant Svetlana Yevgenyevna Gromova, and on two American military astronauts, Lieutenant Michael Esdale and Major Chad Miller. The immense filing system had churned on the names, flip cards leading to file folders in labyrinthine underground storage halls. Photostats had been made, the designated case officers identified, and papers distributed. When Vitaly had arrived at his desk that morning, early as usual, the Miller file had been on top of the pile in his inbox. A red bookmark was stapled to the front with "Srochna" typed on it. Urgent.

Vitaly had read the cover note, considered his moves over his first cup of tea and then started a cascade of revealing phone calls. All leading to now.

The hallway door was open. After a small pause, he entered the conference room.

The far wall was all windows, stretching from the low bank of radiators to the ceiling, to let in the natural light. The impact was marred somewhat by the drab view of an identical room across a small inner courtyard. Spider plants sat on the radiator sill, adding a touch of natural green. A long table paralleled the window. Apart from a young pomozhnitsa placing water glasses and teacups in front of each chair, he was alone.

He resisted the urge to recheck his watch. He chose an unassuming far corner seat, set down his briefcase and went to stand by the window. The server set up a tea trolley along the wall by the door and quietly left.

Vitaly looked out at the sunshine, reviewing the details in his mind, realizing this might be a watershed day in his career. He felt his heart start to race, and he scowled. *Uspokoisya! Quiet yourself!*

He heard a rumble of deep voices in the hall, and three people came in, led by a tall, wide man in a gray suit, his hair combed straight back off a broad forehead, thick, wire-rimmed glasses magnifying his tired eyes.

Vitaly was stunned. Andropov! The head of the KGB himself. The rumor was that he was soon to become a full Politburo member. What was he doing here? On the phone they'd said there'd be senior representation at the meeting, but he'd never thought it would be Yuri Vladimirovich himself. *Bozha moy! Am I ready for this?*

Keeping his face a calm mask, he dipped his head in respect. "Dobry dyen, zasluzheni Predsedatel." Good day, honored Chairman.

Andropov peered at him through his glasses. "Kalugin, da?"

Vitaly nodded. "Da. Counterintelligence agent, Special Service II, Vitaly Dmitriyevich."

Andropov nodded. "Sadeetyes." Sit.

Vitaly sat.

The KGB Chairman took the chair at the head of the table, gesturing with his chin at the two other men. He spoke very clearly, pronouncing the names in an educated accent. "Vladimir Alexandrovich Kryuchkov. Vladimir Nikolayevich Chelomei." He rightly assumed Vitaly would know who they were.

Vitaly met the eyes of each man, and again nodded in respect. Kryuchkov was head of the KGB First Chief Directorate, responsible for all operations abroad, including Vitaly's department. Chelomei was a senior director in the Soviet space program.

Kryuchkov, as Vitaly's boss, took the lead. His round face with its high-domed forehead was marked by a squashed nose, broken badly at some point long ago.

"Vitaly Dmitriyevich, please brief us on the situation." He used the patronymic to ease the gap in seniority, which helped to put Vitaly at ease.

He took a steadying breath. These were smart, accomplished, powerful men. *Where to start?*

He quickly summarized the events that had transpired in orbit over the past 20 hours. While he spoke he glanced at Chelomei for confirmation that he had his facts right; the man's furrowed brow and pursed mouth gave away nothing. But he didn't contradict him, either. *So far, so good.*

Moving to more familiar ground, he gave a quick intelligence summary of the woman cosmonaut and the American astronaut, Esdale. Their records were clean, nothing suspicious in the files. No leverage there.

The three senior men listened, their faces impassive. They knew he was keeping the key information for last.

"The third person in space, American Air Force Major Chad Miller, gives us the greatest opportunity." Vitaly's heart rate slowed as he explained in detail, recounting how he'd fostered agents in the heart of the Russian Orthodox Church around the world, looking for angles and access routes to the West. He shared the details of Miller's file, starting with the boy's adoption in Berlin. Andropov nodded slowly as he heard how Vitaly had used an agent, the church interpreter, to send money to the pilot, ostensibly from his long-lost brother, eager to help with the young man's expenses when the adoptive parents, farmers apparently, had run low. And how Miller had never refused such handouts. The KGB chief looked at Kryuchkov, who nodded back.

"That gives us a position of strength. Spasiba, Vitaly Dmitriyevich. This Miller would not want the Americans to find out where that money actually came from."

Vitaly inwardly thrilled at Andropov using his name.

Andropov turned to Chelomei. "Vladimir Nikolay'ich, I know little of space. I commiserate with you on the loss of our Almaz space station, and the tragic death of cosmonaut Mitkov. These are blatant acts of American aggression, and help set our course of action." His old eyes blinked behind the thick lenses. "Nyet huda byez dobra"—there is no bad without good. "What other levers do we have here?" he asked.

"Respected Chairman, despite the tragedy of today's events, I have good news from the Soviet space program." Vladimir Chelomei's deliberately formal phrasing lent import to what he was saying.

"With what I have learned from Agent Kalugin here, and an important discovery made just yesterday by the Lunokhod team that is exploring the Moon's surface, I think we may have a rare opportunity."

Having gained the room's attention, he laid out his plan.

Kryuchkov had lifelong experience in diplomacy and subterfuge. He quickly evaluated the idea, considering the weaknesses as he rubbed his broken nose with his forefinger.

"We need communications with the cosmonaut—*private* communication. Can we get it?"

"Da, Vladimir Alexandrovich," Chelomei said. The two men worked in different fields, but were roughly equivalent in power. Chelomei had reached the same conclusion earlier that day, and had issued orders. "I've thought of a way to reach her."

Andropov stood. "I will take this to the Politburo, and to the General Secretary." As KGB chief and his longtime protégé, Andropov was Brezhnev's most trusted ally. "The Americans will be contacting us shortly, no doubt."

He looked at each of the three men.

"Let's make sure we're ready."

"Father Ilarion, I have unusual news." Alexander, the diocese interpreter, spoke quietly, knowing it was the best way to get the hieromonk's attention in the morning, after prayers and liturgy.

Ilarion was finishing his light breakfast, tapping the last crumbs of his toast off the small plate into his teacup, careful to waste nothing. "Good news, Sascha?" He looked up at the younger man curiously. "What is it?"

"The accomplishments of your brother have come to the attention of the Church in Moscow. One of my fellow interpreters there was working with the American Embassy church members, and he called me to let you know. They think it does you and your family great honor, and have been speaking with officials at the Soviet space program."

Ilarion's eyes widened.

"It seems the Church wants you to come to Moscow, and has obtained permission for you to go to Mission Control, where you will be able to talk directly with your brother while he's on the Moon. It's a rare honor indeed and will be a wonderful surprise for him."

Father Ilarion looked stunned by the prospect of a trip to Moscow and a chance to talk to his brother in space. His stroked his beard as he considered it, his eyes blinking rapidly behind his thick lenses.

"They say there is an Interflug flight from Schönefeld Airport direct to Moscow Sheremetyevo every day," Alexander urged. "The space program will cover all costs and accommodation."

The monk's face clouded. "But surely my brother won't want surprises to interrupt what he's doing. He'll be too busy."

Alexander nodded. His KGB handler had anticipated this, and provided some suggestions.

"They say that they often have family members speak directly with cosmonauts, who can be lonely so far from home. Contact with family is good for morale, for their mental calmness." He added a specific suggested phrase. "Your brother would be the most distant member of the flock you've ever had the chance to give solace to."

Father Ilarion turned his head away, eyes unfocused, trying to imagine what his brother was seeing. He nodded slowly. "You're right, Sascha. Earth must be very small for him now."

He turned back to Alexander with his brows furrowed. "But his Russian is rusty, and I have no English. I'm also not a traveler. Would you be coming with me?"

Alexander felt a rush of victory, but managed to keep his face calm, his expression helpful. "Yes, Father, the officials at Mission Control recognized the difficulty and asked that an interpreter accompany you. I'd be honored to help."

35

Mission Control, Houston

In the end, the Moscow-Houston communication had been surprisingly simple to set up.

Kaz stood at the CAPCOM console with the State Department translator next to him. The doctors confirmed that despite the staggered sleep schedule, the crew had gotten a reasonable night's rest. At least the astronauts had; the cosmonaut wasn't wired for heartbeat.

They had a mid-course correction coming up soon—a quick engine firing to change the ship's direction very slightly, based on careful tracking of *Pursuit*'s path. It saved fuel to do it early—to steer exactly towards perfectly entering orbit around the Moon.

"*Pursuit*, Houston, I have the burn numbers when you're ready."

"Roger, Kaz, I'm ready to copy." Michael had the flight plan floating in front of him, his pencil poised to write in the blank table.

"Okay, Michael, it'll be posigrade 10.5 fps, burn duration 0:02, perilune will be 53.1 . . ." Kaz went through the values carefully, the Mission Control specialists listening attentively to make sure he made no errors. When he finished, Michael read them back, verbatim.

"That all sounds good, Michael." A pause. "Is Chad listening?"

Michael glanced across at Chad, in the opposite seat. Svetlana was floating at a window, alternately looking at the Earth and the Moon.

"He's not on headset, but can be. What's up?"

Kaz answered carefully. "After the burn, we're going to patch Moscow through by phone to talk with the cosmonaut. We'll have sentence-by-sentence translation, to make sure it's all kosher, but wanted to give you a heads-up to think about it."

Michael passed the message to Chad, who frowned and donned his headset.

"Kaz, Chad here. I need this conversation to be controlled. Who's going to cut it off if we don't like how it's going?"

Kaz looked back at Gene, behind the Flight Director console. He and Gene had discussed just this.

"We agree, Chad. INCO will have his finger on the switch to stop comms at any moment. We recommend you do the same."

Chad looked at the switches on his comm panel. "Yeah, I'm gonna pull the plug on her the second I don't like what I hear."

"Sounds about right," Kaz said. "Mid-course burn is in three minutes, and we'll have someone from their Mission Control tied in shortly after that."

Chad glanced at Svetlana, who had turned to face him. "Copy."

When the KGB interpreter standing next to him relayed what Chad had just said, Chelomei grunted.

Eavesdropping on transmissions from the Apollo craft was nothing new. Since the start of the Apollo Moon landings, Russia had been listening in. The Soviet Central Committee had ordered Moscow Scientific Research Institute No. 885 to build the huge, 32-meter-wide TNA-400 satellite dish that towered over the Simferopol complex. It had required some clever reverse engineering; the Soviet technicians had experimented with the signals from the early Apollo flights, carefully demodulating the carrier and subcarrier frequencies until they could pick out voice and data, and even watch the fuzzy television images sent from the distant craft. They couldn't hear the transmissions going up to Apollo, but during the eight hours each day when the Russian side of the Earth was facing the Moon, they received everything the spaceship sent back.

It wasn't a total secret. The CIA had learned about the new antenna when an SR-71 spy plane had taken high-altitude photographs of it. The top-secret report summarized: *A 105-foot dish antenna such as this one would permit communications and telemetry reception at lunar distances. The antenna is operational.*

But Director Chelomei had just added a capability that no one at NASA or the CIA knew about. For it to work, he needed to discern some specific details during today's hastily arranged telephone link. And if both Houston and the crew were ready to pull the plug at the sound of anything they didn't like, he'd have to be subtle. He impatiently waited as they did their course correction burn.

Kaz said, "Looks like a good burn, Apollo. You're on your way."

Michael agreed as he safed the engine systems. "Copy, Kaz, thanks. And we've got all three of us on headsets now, whenever you're ready. The Commander's standing by at Panel 6."

Chad's finger and thumb were gripping the S-band transmit/receive switch.

Kaz glanced at Gene Kranz, who nodded.

"Moscow, this is Houston Mission Control, comm check."

The interpreter repeated what Kaz had said, in Russian.

An unfamiliar male voice crackled into Kaz's headset. "Zdyess Moskva, kak shlooshetye nas?"

The interpreter translated. "Moscow here, how do you hear us?"

Kaz realized he'd been holding his breath, and exhaled. "We have you loud and clear, Moscow. Stand by to speak with Apollo 18." He looked across at INCO, nodding, and got a thumbs-up.

"Apollo 18, this is Houston. Mission Control Moscow is on comms with us. Go ahead, Moscow."

Gene Kranz shook his head slowly. *Bloody Commies talking to his spaceship.*

The interpreter translated the first burst of Russian: "Senior Lieutenant Gromova, this is TsUP, how do you hear?"

Svetlana responded. "TsUP, I hear you well."

Chelomei, sitting at the flight director console in Moscow, held the phone receiver firmly. "Svetlana Yevgenyevna, this is Director Chelomei. We are very glad to hear your voice. How is your health?"

She began to respond immediately, but Chad slammed the transmit switch to receive only, holding up a hand. "You need to wait for translation." They listened as the interpreter repeated what Chelomei had said.

Chad looked hard at her. "Okay?" he queried.

"Da, okay."

He selected the switch back to transmit/receive.

"Tovarisch Director, it's an honor to speak with you. My health is fine, thank you."

The pauses for translation made the conversation awkward.

"They have found you a place to sleep on board the small vessel?" An innocuous question.

"Da. There is room in the capsule for two, comfortable, with one of them sleeping in the lander."

Come on, woman, give me more details! Chelomei urged silently.

"They alternate, and considerately leave me my own lounge chair in the capsule." She added a personal note. "I'm adjusting to the Houston time zone."

Chelomei nodded his head. *Excellent.* She was getting it.

He expressed his deep condolences on the death of her commander, Mitkov, and congratulated her on her resourcefulness and strength in getting aboard the Apollo ship.

She paused, waiting for the translation, and then thanked him, adding a question. "They used my suit to entomb the dead astronaut, and its PM-9 life-support system is now stowed. Please confirm that I'll be wearing their spacesuit from now on."

Chelomei smiled broadly. *Clever girl.* The PM-9 wasn't the life-support backpack; it was the model number of the weapon that had been on board the Almaz. She'd found a way to let them know she was secretly armed. He kept his tone matter-of-fact.

"Da, they have told us the sizing will work for you in their suit. And if you haven't heard yet, they are planning for you to wear it in the lunar lander, and to have the honor of being the first Soviet citizen to step onto the Moon."

Svetlana had suspected that was the new plan, but this was her first confirmation. She looked at Chad, who nodded, and was surprised at the surge of excitement that suddenly rushed through her. *I'm going to walk on the Moon!*

Her voice quavered. "That is wonderful, Tovarisch Director! I will do my best to make everyone proud."

Chelomei played back in his mind what they'd just said; nothing sounded suspicious, and the woman had demonstrated that she was aware of hidden meanings. Time to get Miller's attention.

"We are certain you will, Sveta. Your brother in Berlin is especially proud of you."

Chad squinted at her as the interpreter translated. *She had a brother in Berlin?* That was a strange coincidence. But why had Moscow mentioned that?

Svetlana's face revealed nothing. "I'm delighted to hear that. Please pass my best to my whole family."

Enough for now, Chelomei thought. Time for platitudes, plus one last hint.

"We will be in daily contact, Svetlana Yevgenyevna, and look forward to speaking with you. Your ears can look forward to hearing the Russian language so far from home."

"Spasiba, Tovarisch Director. Until next time."

Chelomei nodded, satisfied. "Doh sledusheva." He placed the handset in the cradle, ticking through his mental checklist. All messages sent. Time to move on to the next step.

What the hell had they meant? Chad thought. The conversation had felt fishy, somehow. *Do they know about my brother? How could they?* He stared hard at Svetlana as he stowed her headset, but she met his gaze impassively.

He thought further. *If they do, then they probably know I speak Russian.* He continued to stare at her, considering all that had been said.

But she doesn't know.

He took a deep breath and exhaled through his nose.

Good.

"Hey, Chad, I just noticed something." Michael's voice was relaxed, subdued. He'd borne the brunt of the sleep shift so they could continuously monitor the cosmonaut, and he was tired.

"What's that?" Chad was reviewing LM procedures, penciling in what he was going to do differently to land on the Moon without Luke to help.

"It says here in the flight plan that we just hit exactly halfway. Old Mother Earth and the Moon are both"—he checked the book—"107,229 miles away." He floated to the window next to Svetlana and twisted to look at one, and then the other. He made hand motions to try to explain the concept to her, defining a length, cutting it in half, and then pointing at the Moon and Earth.

She watched his hands and then looked at his face, quizzically.

"I don't think she gets it," Michael said. "What do they teach them in cosmonaut school?"

Chad kept reading, ignoring him.

Michael imitated Chad's voice. "I don't know, Michael, my guess is Soviet doctrine, invasion routes, whitewashed history and bad fashion sense. You know, Commie stuff."

He answered himself. "Thank you, Chad, for that keen insight. I think the Command Module Pilot is getting a little punchy. My turn for some sleep."

Chad looked up, hearing the last part. "You sleeping in the LM?"

Michael looked at him, bemused. "Yeah, as planned, if you're okay holding down the fort here."

Chad glanced at Svetlana and turned back to his page. "Yeah, we're set."

Michael gave Houston a heads-up so the doctors could track his rest, and then floated down the tunnel, emerging into the small cabin of the LM. He wrapped himself in the bag and hammock and glanced up in the darkness at Luke.

"I miss you, buddy," he murmured. "I'm sorry you've joined the dead." *What a long strange trip it's been.*

The night shift in TsUP, a minimal skeleton crew of two technicians and an interpreter, were listening carefully and heard Michael's call to Houston. Director Chelomei had left strict instructions to record all communications from the Apollo craft. He wanted to know who was sleeping, and when.

The interpreter translated, and the shift lead carefully wrote the Cyrillic characters next to the time in the large green ledger they had started for cosmonaut Gromova's flight to the Moon and back:

00:30 *Moscow Standard Time*   *Esdale sleeping alone in the lunar module.*
                                Miller awake in command module.
                                No word from Gromova.

Not very interesting. But hopefully useful.

36

Timber Cove, Houston

The house was a truncated A-frame bungalow with an attached garage, set on the brackish shore of Taylor Lake, 10 minutes east of the Manned Spacecraft Center. When Kaz and Al Shepard arrived, there was already an ugly brown Dodge Polara in the driveway. The double whip antennas and driver's side searchlight gave it away as an unmarked police car. The Harris County Sheriff's car, in fact.

With everything that had happened in the 36 hours since launch, Kaz had pushed the findings of the crash investigator into the back of his mind. But now that Apollo 18 was safely on its way to the Moon, he'd faced the fact that out of everyone who might have sabotaged Tom's helicopter, three of the suspects—only two of them still alive—were on board the spaceship. Al Shepard had alerted the sheriff and asked him for discretion, agreeing to help him look for evidence to quickly clear the three as potential suspects.

As Kaz pulled in and parked, two men got out of the Polara. The driver was in uniform, 30ish, with a crew cut. The passenger was a strongly built man in his 50s in a rumpled suit and tie, heavy-rimmed glasses below a combed-back wave of hair, graying at the temples.

Al walked up to him and they shook hands. "Hi, Jack, thanks for coming."

Jack Heard had been the Houston police chief for 20 years, and had recently been elected sheriff of Harris County, which included Ellington Field airport, the rural scene of the helicopter crash and this house. Chad Miller's house.

"I'm happy to serve NASA and a hero of the nation, Al," Heard said, and turned to Kaz, his sharp cop's eyes flicking across his face, missing nothing through the thick lenses. "You must be Lieutenant Commander Zemeckis. Sorry to hear about the death of your friend."

Kaz was startled. Luke's death in orbit hadn't been made public. Then he realized the sheriff meant Tom Hoffman. He said, "Thanks," and they shook hands.

Heard said, "That's Deputy Buddy Beauchamp," nodding at the uniform, who tipped his head.

Kaz led them all towards the front door, taking in the cedar shake siding and the multicolored entryway glass.

"Major Miller own this house?" Heard asked.

Al replied. "No, apparently it belongs to some dentist who rented it to Chad fully furnished."

Kaz unlocked and opened the door, turned on the light, and they stepped into another world.

The living room floor was paved with ocher tile. The walls were covered to shoulder height in gold shag carpeting. The fluorescent light fixture Kaz turned on alternated between red, yellow and blue light. The far wall was all glass, facing onto a swimming pool with Taylor Lake beyond it. A basket chair hung on a long chain from the ceiling, and a bulbous, shellacked rock chimney rose from the gas fireplace. Gaudy masks hung on the walls above the shag carpet.

"Quite the place," Sherriff Heard said. "A dentist, you say?"

Kaz had never been in Chad's house and was trying to reconcile the hippie-Playboy décor with the abrupt, judgmental military man he knew. It was a rental, but still.

There was a pool table to their left, with a low, wood-framed couch. The sheriff said, "You two have a seat while Buddy and I have a quick look around. We shouldn't be long."

Al and Kaz sat.

"I'm glad the Astronaut Clinic has their own dentists," Al said, making Kaz smile. After a moment, he asked, "You didn't see Michael out at Ellington that day, right?"

Kaz shook his head. "No, just Luke, who was flying the LLTV, and Chad, who was leaving since he'd just flown it. Michael was scheduled for a medical check that morning, so I think that pretty much clears him."

Al nodded, staring at the gargoyle masks on the wall. Both men were considering the unspoken. Motive.

Heard and his deputy came back through, heading for the open wooden staircase that led upstairs. Heard jerked his chin towards the back of the main floor, beyond the kitchen. He smiled slightly. "You might want to have a peek in the master bedroom."

Al shrugged, and they peeled themselves up and out of the low sofa. They walked past the stone counters of the kitchen, down a short hallway and through the doorless bedroom entrance.

Both men stopped. Three walls were tiled floor to ceiling with gold-tinted mirrors. The fourth wall faced the lake. It was all glass, and curtainless. Life-sized statues of topless mermaids flanked a king-sized bed that was suspended off the floor on heavy gold-colored chains. A recessed wall unit was lined with the same mirrored tile, each shelf adorned with a variety of nude female figurines.

Kaz walked past the bed to the closet. Pulling open the sliding doors, he was somewhat relieved to see familiar single-man's items on the hangers and shelves, shoes tidily aligned along the floor. There was a flight suit, along with a couple of jackets, trousers and crisply pressed shirts. He slid the doors closed and came back to Al, shaking his head. "This place would give me the creeps," he said.

They heard a voice echoing off the stone-tiled floors. "Hey, guys, c'mon back here."

They found the two cops standing at the foot of the staircase, and as soon as they reached them, the sheriff ushered them back out to Kaz's car, leaving his deputy by the front door. Heard said, "We found some things in the bedroom that Major Miller was using as his home office. Beyond the deviant dentist furniture, I mean."

He glanced back at the house. "I've called for a couple more deputies to help do a thorough search. We'll use an unmarked and guys out of uniform, to keep the profile low for as long as we can." He eyed the neighboring houses. "We can be thankful for small mercies that there's a media blackout on the mission."

He looked at Kaz. "I still need to have a quick look at the other crewmen's homes, if you can let me into them."

Kaz nodded. "Of course." He glanced at Al. "Have you briefed the sheriff on what's been going on?"

"Yeah, Jack knows about Luke, in strictest confidence." Al glanced at Beauchamp, standing mutely by the front door. "But nobody else."

"I know what you're thinking, Kaz," Heard said. "This is going to escalate. But my job is pretty clear. A civil-registered helicopter flying from a Harris County airport crashed on county land, the pilot died, and indications are that there was sabotage. So I'm investigating a murder. The fact that one suspect is dead and two others are off the planet doesn't bother me." He briefly stuck out his lower lip, considering. "In fact, it's better. I know exactly where they are, and when they'll be back."

But Kaz was thinking beyond the investigation. He was going to have to tell Sam Phillips that the man who was about to walk on the Moon, to find out what the Soviets were up to there, was now a viable suspect in a murder.

37

Mission Control, Houston

"FLIGHT, EECOM."

Gene looked over his console. "Go ahead."

"FLIGHT, my back room has been working the numbers, and we've got a revised status."

This was interesting. EECOM handled oxygen consumption. With the leak in Luke's umbilical at Almaz and the need to repair the hatch seal, Gene had been waiting to see whether and how much it would impact the planned mission.

"I'm listening, EECOM."

"Now that the tank temps have stabilized and we've got an update on current consumption with the LM hatch open, it looks like we lost considerably more O2 than we thought. It's very tight for full duration."

Oxygen wasn't just the sole gas used in the spaceships for breathing, it also fed the fuel cells to generate electricity.

"How tight?"

"It depends how much we take from the LM tanks. Assuming we're still protecting for multiple spacewalks with two crewmembers, it takes us well into the red."

Gene had already been thinking that the military would have to be happy with just one moonwalk. A short one.

"If you model for just one, five-hour lunar surface walk, how do the numbers look?"

EECOM countered with a question. "Both crewmembers working outside the whole time?" It would increase oxygen consumption.

Gene pictured Chad's and Svetlana's likely tasks on the surface. Better to assume worst case. "Yes."

EECOM had a quick side conversation with the technicians in his back room. "FLIGHT, with that revised plan, and if we start using oxygen from the *Bulldog* tanks now for cabin air, we have green margins through splashdown."

"Good to hear, EECOM, thanks."

Kaz spoke up quickly. "FLIGHT, Michael's just gone to sleep in the LM, and the repress valve in there makes a loud bang. If EECOM can wait, I recommend we delay tapping *Bulldog*'s oxygen until he wakes up."

Gene nodded. "SURGEON, how much beauty sleep will he need?"

JW answered. "My best guess is about four hours, FLIGHT."

EECOM piped in immediately. "We can wait that long."

Gene decided. "Sounds good. CAPCOM, plan to wake Lieutenant Esdale at"—he glanced at the digital timer at the front of the room—"thirty-seven hours mission elapsed time."

"Houston, 18, with a problem."

Well, that's not what I want to hear. Kaz set down his coffee next to the console ashtray. He deliberately made his voice calm to respond. As CAPCOM, he knew that the way he said things affected the psychology of both the crew on orbit and the team in Mission Control; being aware of his tone was especially important considering the parallel murder investigation. "Problems are what we're here for—go ahead, Michael."

"Hey, Kaz. Chad and I have both noticed that Luke's spacesuit is bulging. Looks like maybe his body is decomposing and the gas pressure is building up in there. We're not sure where the pressure relief valve is in the cosmonaut's spacesuit, but we sure don't want it burping nasty gases into *Bulldog*."

"Copy, agreed, checking."

Chad caught Michael's eye. "How about we ask Princess here to show us where the suit vents its overpressure?"

Michael nodded. "How good's your sign language?"

Svetlana, dozing on the right side of the cockpit, felt someone shaking her. Opening her eyes, she saw the commander pointing at the other astronaut disappearing into the tunnel to the lunar lander. He waved his hand for her to follow.

Shto? She followed the feet into the tunnel.

Michael had floated up against *Bulldog*'s ceiling next to Luke's body, and Chad moved to his designated position on the left, where he'd fly it. Svetlana took the open position on the right and looked at them questioningly.

Mikhail was speaking, moving his hands around her Yastreb spacesuit. She could see that the suit had ballooned. The astronaut suddenly opened his fingers and made a sharp hissing sound, and then raised his shoulders with a questioning look on his face. He was pointing at the oxygen and comm connections on the suit's front. She found all the English words distracting. *What does he mean?*

The other astronaut frowned disapprovingly. He impatiently repeated the bursting motion with his hand, and made a harsh "Pssssss" sound that he tailed off.

Ah. She got it. Floating up next to the suit, she pointed to two fist-sized protruding round knobs over the left rib cage, and mimed a twisting motion with her hand. She then reached up to the helmet and touched a gray butterfly valve under the left ear. She mimicked pinching and turning it, and made the same hissing noise the astronauts had made.

Michael looked closely where she'd pointed. "I think the two chest valves are pressure regulators. They've got some Russian writing on them, and arrows to show direction of turn." He switched his inspection to the helmet. "This looks like a simple purge valve."

Chad had been silently sounding out the Cyrillic writing on the two chest valves. One said "Unscrew all the way for flight" and the other said "Screw in all the way." He spoke as if he was making an educated guess. "I bet one's for overpressure, and the other's for underpressure." There were no labels on the helmet valve. He pointed at it. "That one looks like just a manual open/close."

Michael nodded. "Makes sense."

Both men pondered the information.

"But what do we do if the stink inside starts coming out of one of these?" Michael shook his head. "Even after death we have to deal with Luke's farting."

Chad ignored the humor. He had an idea. "We've got the small tap line here in *Bulldog* we can put on the egress hatch pressure valve. We could wrap it tight with tape directly to this helmet valve, and crack them both open very slightly to suck the extra pressure out to vacuum."

Michael evaluated. "Yeah, that should work." He smiled. "It'll put us in the running for the duct tape hall of fame."

Chad donned the LM headset and pushed Transmit.

"Houston, we think we have a solution." He described what the cosmonaut had shown them, and his plan.

Kaz replied, "Roger, *Bulldog*, sounds like it might well work. Let us think about it."

Gene Kranz spoke. "EECOM, I want you to use the interpreter and get on the horn ASAP with whoever the suit specialists are in Moscow. Make sure we're understanding the valve function properly and get their input into the crew's manual vent idea."

Kaz waved the interpreter to the EECOM console. Gene spoke again.

"Meanwhile, CAPCOM, tell them to start building the setup on board. We can't wait too long."

They moved the suit cautiously, like a fragile balloon, down towards the floor of the lunar lander, strapping it into place. Chad screwed a metal tube onto the pressure valve on the square hatch while Michael peeled sections of tape off a large roll, carefully wrapping the tube to join the helmet purge valve.

Svetlana pictured the Yastreb suit schematics. *If they keep the flow rate low, it ought to work.* She looked around the cockpit. They'd been keeping her in the other part of the ship, and this was her first chance to see the lander in detail.

I'm going to land on the Moon in this!

The thought thrilled her. She'd graduated top of her class from the Moscow State Aviation Institute, and became an aerobatic instructor pilot as well as a test pilot at the Gromov School outside Moscow. Her father had been a decorated fighter pilot in the Great Patriotic War, and his influence had been key in her cosmonaut selection.

Papa will be so proud!

While the men were distracted, she looked closely at the lander's controls, picturing herself flying it. *That must be the rotational controller on the right, to turn the vehicle.* It looked like a joystick, similar to what she'd trained on in the Almaz return capsule. She looked on the left for the thrust controller, which would move the vehicle up and down and left and right. *That's it, no doubt.* It resembled a palm-sized drawer handle, mounted on a short, pivoting stick to move in all directions. She reached out to touch it.

"Hey, what are you doing! Get away from that!" Chad's face was a mask of rage. He pointed at her. "Don't touch nothin'!"

His meaning was clear, and she floated back to beyond arm's length. Both men watched her suspiciously.

No matter. I'd feel the same if these Americans were in my ship.

She continued her visual inspection. In front of both crew stations were familiar artificial horizons, the gray-and-black balls recessed into the instrument panel. They were surrounded by gauges. *Must be speed, height, systems pressures*, she reasoned. All flying machines were essentially the same; you just had to figure out how to get them started and how they wanted to kill you.

She realized that the triangular windows were mounted low, like in a helicopter, so they could look down while landing. She glanced around for seats, and couldn't even see fixtures on the floor where seats might be mounted. *We must fly this thing standing up!* A reasonable compromise for low lunar gravity, she acknowledged, but still it would be strange.

She looked at the commander. *Tschad*. He'd most likely be the one flying this lander with her. She doubted they'd trust a Black man to do it. *Mikhail. No, Michael*. She moved her lips, trying the English pronunciation.

Chad's voice came into the headsets in Mission Control. "Houston, *Bulldog*, we have the suit strapped down securely on the floor and the helmet purge sealed against the hatch line. Just let us know when we can open the valves."

Kaz glanced over at the EECOM console, where the tech and the interpreter were engrossed in a laborious technical conversation with TsUP.

"Roger, *Bulldog*. We're talking with the Moscow specialists now, and should have word shortly."

"Copy, Houston, but regardless what Moscow says, we're gonna take care of this. This suit is bulging, and we're the ones at risk here."

Kaz could hear him thinking, *You morons!*

"Roger, Chad. We'll get you that ASAP."

As soon as possible—the phrase echoed in Kaz's head. The whole idea of "possible" had changed in a hurry.

Five minutes later Kaz pushed the comm button. "18, Houston, Moscow has described the suit valving to us, and we're good here. You have a GO to vent Luke's suit to vacuum."

"Thanks, Kaz," Michael responded. "Here goes nothin'."

Michael cautiously turned the vent valve handle on the side of the white helmet, the large red CCCP letters at the edge of his vision. He heard a slight hissing sound as pressure equalized into the vent hose, and then quiet. He sniffed for leaks, wrinkling his nose, but smelled nothing.

He glanced at Chad. "All set, Boss?"

Svetlana was curiously observing the men messing with her old suit.

"Yep. But close it immediately if something isn't going right."

"Agreed."

Michael reached around the vent hose and began turning the knob on the Cabin Relief and Dump Valve test port. Houston had said it would take a full turn to start flow, and he carefully rotated it between his thumb and forefingers, like a safecracker. A hissing began, barely audible above the noise of *Bulldog*'s air recirculation fans. He stopped turning, and all three of them turned to watch Luke's suit.

At first, nothing. Then, gradually, like an air mattress deflating, the tension eased on the fabric, and the seams looked less distended. Michael was relieved to see the needle dropping in the pressure gauge on the suit's right wrist.

"Looks like it's working, Houston." He tapped the gauge to make sure it wasn't sticking. "As soon as the pressure gauge shows zero differential, I'll close the valves." He poked at the suit's cloth; it was no longer quite as stiff.

"Copy, Michael," he heard Kaz say. "Reminder to close the helmet valve first, then the hatch valve." That would suck any extra odors out of the vent hose and keep them from getting into the cabin.

Michael didn't want to take it too far or the suit's negative pressure relief valve would suck open and start pulling in cabin air. He increased the speed of his tapping on the pressure gauge, watching the needle slowly bounce towards zero.

"Looks like we're there." He closed the helmet valve, and then quickly reached and spun the hatch valve tightly closed.

Svetlana squeezed the suit lightly, near the elbow, where there was no internal bracing. "Prekrasna," she nodded. Excellent.

Chad spoke to Houston. "Kaz, that's complete, suit looks good now, but we're going to leave Luke connected to the hose, just in case we need to vent him again. It's Michael's turn to get some shut-eye. The cosmonaut and I are heading back into *Pursuit*."

"Copy, Chad, sounds good. Nice work, and sweet dreams, Michael."

In Moscow, Chelomei turned to his flight director.

"Listen to them for any word of Michael Esdale waking up."

The Moscow Electronics Research Institute engineers had initially told Chelomei that his request was impossible; there were too many unknowns, there wasn't time, and there was no way to test that it would work properly. But he had been unrelenting. "Just build the equipment!" he had yelled. He hated the inbuilt Soviet caution about running afoul of interdepartmental politics; it had allowed the Americans to beat them to the Moon.

The engineers in the end had hastily installed their thrown-together 13-cm S-band modulating uplink hardware alongside the huge TNA-400 antenna's listening gear. The modification would interweave TsUP's voice transmissions with the strong carrier frequency that it blasted skyward in a beam of electromagnetic energy, tightly focused towards the Moon by the towering dish antenna. It was like an invisible searchlight in the night, looking for the four small, circular receiving antennas sticking out of the aft section of *Pursuit*.

With luck, the processors inside the American ship would treat it as just another arriving signal to deal with. If the frequency and modulation matched closely enough to the American transmissions, it would pass through the filters, and the radio wave would be transformed into an electric signal that passed to a speaker—in this case the small one built into the commander's headset, over his left ear.

When the flight director reported that he was certain that the other astronaut was asleep, Chelomei pushed his mic button and spoke. Hoping it was only Commander Miller, but uncertain of who else might be listening, he chose his words carefully.

"Transmission test, transmission test, how do you hear me?" he said in a deliberately flat and bored tone, like an uninterested radio operator. He wasn't sure if the signal would be retransmitted by the spaceship back to Houston somehow, and didn't want to alert anyone.

Chad, who had been thumbing through the checklist for tomorrow's entry into lunar orbit, bolted upright, startled to hear the Russian language in his ear. It didn't repeat, and he snuck a glance at Svetlana, who was looking out the window at the growing Moon. Had he imagined it?

Chelomei repeated himself. "Transmission test, transmission test, how do you hear me?" He wondered whether Cosmonaut Gromova would also hear him, or only Miller. He checked the clock at the front of the room. Still 30 minutes of comms remaining until the Earth turned too far for his satellite dish to see the spacecraft.

Be patient, he counseled himself. *Miller needs time to decide what to do.*

Chad pictured the ship's comm system in his head, and rechecked the switch config. *What the fuck?* This wasn't just stray VHF radio delivering typical, unregulated noise from Earth; this was coming to him on their designated S-band frequency. To get through to his headset, it had to be a specifically modulated signal. The realization hit him. *Someone in Russia is calling us on purpose!*

But who? He kept his face calm, in case Svetlana looked at him.

Chelomei upped the stakes.

"Transmission test, transmission test. If you can hear me, respond with two microphone clicks."

Standing in TsUP, Chelomei listened intently. One click, by itself, could be anything; two would be deliberate. Three could make Houston wonder what was going on.

He waited.

Chad's Russian was rusty, but he was pretty sure he'd understood. Whoever was calling wanted two chirps on the mic.

A thought struck him, and he looked out the window at Earth. The Atlantic Ocean was facing him, but he could see from the western edge of Russia to the eastern edge of America. Someone in that part of the world had chosen this moment to contact him. He could just barely see where Moscow was in the darkness on the eastern side of the ball. *Had they known Michael was asleep and wouldn't be listening? Who would know that?*

He decided. Reaching for the transmit switch, he toggled it twice. Then listened.

In Houston, Kaz heard the clicks and perked up his ears since the noise of the mic always preceded a transmission from the ship. When no one spoke, he shrugged. *Just static.*

On the other side of the world, Chelomei heard the two clicks and was exultant. *I've made direct contact with the Apollo crew! They can hear me!* His eyes burned in triumph. Time to raise the stakes again.

"I hear your two clicks. And so does your brother. Don't reply. Listen for more in"—he glanced at the clock on the screen—"eighteen hours. After 16:30 Moscow time." He released the mic.

Chelomei reviewed what he'd said and nodded to himself. *That will give him food for thought.*

Chad was dumbfounded. *"And so does your brother"*?

That was the second time the Russians had mentioned him. It was obviously a threat of some kind, but what were they going to do? Chad pictured Oleg—Father Ilarion, he corrected himself—at his church in East Berlin, and looked out the window again, searching for Germany under the northern European clouds. *Why would they threaten me with my brother?*

What do they want?

The voice had said 16:30 Moscow time. Chad pictured the Earth turning, and realized the person communicating with him had to wait until the Earth spun enough to bring it back around. At least the next 18 hours would give gave him time to think.

He flicked through his flight plan and made a small mark at the designated time, noting that it was about when he was scheduled to wake from his next nap. Right, they wouldn't call while Michael was listening. That would be too hard to explain. He thought back. *They must have heard me telling Houston that Michael was going to sleep.*

He considered how to use this new information. He pictured his brother under threat, and took a long look at Svetlana, who was still engrossed with the view of the Moon. Eventually he nodded his head.

That must be it.

But what exactly do they know?

38

Into Lunar Orbit

"Good morning, *Pursuit*, this is Houston," Kaz said. "Sorry to wake some of you a little early, but it's Moon arrival day, and I have your LOI data anytime it's convenient."

LOI was Lunar Orbit Insertion, the firing of *Pursuit*'s main rocket engine to slow the ship down, allowing it to be captured by the Moon's gravity into a stable orbit.

They'd decided to have Svetlana sleep at the same time as Chad in *Bulldog*, so Michael had been solo, staring at the rapidly growing Moon and looking back at the tiny Earth, relishing having *Pursuit* to himself. The curve of the lunar surface's stark, ancient scars and deep shadows mesmerized him as they drew near, vastly more rugged and beautiful than the pictures he'd studied. It filled him with awe, knowing what they were about to do. "Morning, Kaz, the Moon is getting huge in my window. I've got my pencil poised, ready to copy."

"Roger. CM mass 62161, delta V 2911, ignition 75:49:50, burn duration 6 minutes, 2 seconds . . ."

As Michael scribbled the numbers in the table, he glanced at the clock. The burn was three hours away; just 180 minutes until they committed to staying at the Moon. Everything counting on the one engine to work perfectly.

He read the numbers carefully back to Kaz.

"That's a good copy, Michael. You'll make a fine stenographer someday."

"Roger that, Kaz. Good to have a fallback if this astronaut thing doesn't work out."

Floating in his hammock in *Bulldog*, Chad had his headset on, listening to the conversation. Svetlana was still asleep, floating below him, with Luke's body strapped to the floor.

He hadn't been able to sleep much, restless with wild dreams and uncertain thoughts. He looked at his watch, the Omega's hands glowing in the darkness, and added nine hours for Moscow time. *They're listening again now.*

It suddenly occurred to him that *he* was in control of this situation, no matter how it felt. Moscow could only transmit to them when he confirmed that Michael wasn't listening. No one would hear what they said except him. And *he* could choose when to respond with mic clicks. They wouldn't dare escalate and reveal their clandestine communications to Houston—they wanted this kept secret from the United States.

He looked down in the dimness at the sleeping cosmonaut, a blob of spit floating weightlessly from the corner of her mouth. Once she got on headset for them to head down to the surface, the game would change. He'd have to think about how to manage that. But for now, Moscow was his to manipulate.

He could hear Michael's voice calling through the tunnel. "Hey, sleepyheads, rise and shine. I've got breakfast ready, and we've got us a Moon to catch!"

As he took a bite of his cereal bar, Michael raised a topic he'd been brooding over. "What exactly are we going to do with Luke's body on the Moon?"

Chad was eating a sausage patty, and popped the last bite into his mouth. "Yeah, I have a few questions about that too."

Both he and Michael were wearing their headsets. Chad flicked the transmit switch on. "Houston, *Pursuit*."

"Go ahead, we're listening," Kaz replied.

"How are the fuel margins for carrying Luke's extra weight during landing, and where exactly do you want his body?"

"They've run the numbers here multiple times, and we're good on fuel, right through landing and abort scenarios. And the current plan is to have his body strapped down behind you, over the engine mount, for center of gravity."

Chad visualized how much space that would take up. He looked at the cosmonaut, who was sipping tea, watching them both. "When it's time to move him outside, is the woman staying inside *Bulldog*, or does Washington want her to get some surface time too?"

Kaz smiled slightly. Chad had his quirks and lived in a weird house, but he surely wasn't stupid. "Good question. We've been talking with the powers that be, and they think getting her feet onto the surface is important." It had been a heated discussion here at Mission Control, but the leverage it gave America to have enabled a Soviet to walk on the Moon was too important to pass up. Sam Phillips had said that Kissinger was insistent.

"She can help you move the body, and we're looking at regolith burial options. You'll see details of that in the new procedures. For now, though, we need you to resize Luke's suit to fit her. TELMU's standing by with expertise, and the interpreter's here. Let us know if you need help."

Chad looked at his watch again, picturing Moscow listening to what he'd said. *So far, so good.* "We have time before the LOI burn; we'll get at that as soon as she cleans up the breakfast dishes." He smiled. *This is fun.*

The inner long underwear with built-in cooling tubes fit reasonably well, Svetlana thought. The arms were a little long, but it was made of a stretchy material and clung to her everywhere else. Michael had turned his back as she changed, but the commander had blatantly watched her.

Tupitsa. He hasn't met Russian men.

The spacesuit was similar enough to the Soviet design that getting into it wasn't a problem. She thought the long pressure seal up her back was overly complicated and prone to leakage, but obviously it worked. The shoulders were a bit wide, and the two astronauts adjusted the sleeves, pulling internal tensioning strings and straps to shorten them to fit.

She'd worn many flight suits and spacesuits; they were always designed for men and fit poorly. She felt around inside: the boots were too big, the crotch was a little high, the hips a little narrow. It wasn't much worse than her Yastreb suit had been.

Michael got the interpreter to help, and walked her through the simple controls and purge on the front, the pressure gauge on her wrist and the backpack plumbing connections. She raised a hand in front of her face and wiggled the fingers, admiring the dexterity they had built into the design. *Better than our clumsy mittens.*

Michael asked her to flex her arms, moving his own to demonstrate. "Okay?"

She stretched both arms out straight, and then pulled them in to reach the controls on her chest. Her fingers slid back in the gloves, making it a bit clumsy, but she judged she could make them work. "Da, okay." Michael gave her a thumbs-up, and she returned the gesture with her gloved hand, a small smile on her face. *A trustworthy man.*

He undid the long zipper up her back, and she squirmed out of the suit, butt first, sliding her arms and legs out. As her head popped free, she caught Chad looking at her speculatively. She held his gaze for a moment, and then helped Michael bundle the suit. It reaffirmed her impression. *I need to watch out for that one.*

Both men suddenly looked slightly unfocused, and she realized they were listening to Houston. Michael handed her Luke's headset, and she slipped it back on, immediately hearing English chatter followed by the interpreter's Russian.

"Svetlana, please confirm you can hear clearly."

"Da, slushayu." *What's up now?*

She heard the CAPCOM's voice, and then the interpreter's.

"Chad, Michael, Svetlana, we're going to run through changes to tomorrow's timeline with serial translation, as all three of you will be involved. Let us know if you have any questions as we go. It's going to take a while, but I think we can get it in well before the LOI burn."

Chad's mind was racing on a parallel track, and he glanced out the window to confirm what his wristwatch had told him. Moscow was in sight, and would be listening to the crew's transmissions. He needed to clarify something.

"Hey, Kaz, just a thought, no need to translate, but in case the cosmonaut has a question, is Moscow on the phone as part of this briefing?"

Kaz waved a finger at the translator to not repeat in Russian. "No, we decided there's no need to let them listen in to our internal operations."

"Roger, makes sense, thanks." *I'm going to have to repeat the key info.* "We're ready to copy."

Kaz's voice. "Okay, great. I'm in the Lunar Surface Checklist, page 2-5. Chad, you'll be doing all the LMP actions here, with the interpreter ready for anything that only Svetlana can reach on her side of the cockpit." Kaz methodically read out the changes page by page, the interpreter repeating the gist in Russian, Chad and Michael penciling them in as he went.

"Kaz, confirm *Bulldog* undock time is 08:43?" Chad said. It was important for Moscow to know when they could call. Michael, in *Pursuit*, would be orbiting overhead every two hours; while he was behind the Moon, with his transmissions from Earth blocked, only *Bulldog* would hear Moscow.

"That's right, Chad, 08:43 central, Mission Elapsed Time of 97:12."

"Copy, thanks." They continued amending the checklist.

In TsUP, it was suppertime, but no one was eating. Chelomei was listening intently to the tone of the crew's responses and the translation by his interpreter, gathering information, trying to gauge the situation.

He nodded slowly as he heard Commander Miller clarify the time. *That is for us. Good boy.* He watched as the flight director wrote the undock time on the mission schedule sheet they had built. His trajectory team had already roughly calculated the orbiting ship's periods of communications blockage behind the Moon; they'd refine it once the decelerating burn was complete.

He thought ahead. There was key information he needed to get to the cosmonaut. And he needed to use the clergyman to apply pressure to the astronaut. But he had to be sure of the Americans' plan.

Glancing at the clock, he tried to will the voice in his ear to tell him what he needed to know. Not being able to hear what Houston was reading up to the crew was frustrating.

He heard Miller speak again, and then the translation came. "Copy, Kaz, I'll read back expected touchdown time and location."

This is it! He leaned over the console and grabbed a piece of paper and pen to ensure he copied down the key information as it was translated.

"*Bulldog* landing 11:17 Central, 99:45:40 MET, location 25.47 North, 30.56 East, next to a straight rille near the southeast rim of Le Monnier Crater."

Chelomei read the words and numbers he had written down, then pulled his notebook out of his breast pocket and quickly flipped the pages with his thumb, looking for what the technicians in Simfcropol had told him over the phone. He found his page of notes and held it next to the sheet on the console.

He cross-checked the numbers. The location was identical.

The Americans were going to land Apollo 18 right beside the Lunokhod rover.

Excellent.

Pursuit's rocket engine was twice as big as it needed to be. The design had been decided well before anyone at NASA knew for sure how much thrust they'd need, and by then it was too expensive to change. But extra margin was a good thing, because if the engine failed, the crew died. It was one throw of the dice. One solitary engine to slow the spaceship into orbit around the Moon and, a few days later, to get them going fast enough again to escape for Earth.

The engine's name was beyond mundane—the Service Propulsion System. But the SPS was about to fire, and the crew was on their own.

Svetlana was staring out the window at the surface of the Moon rolling past them, 50 miles below. The Sun was setting, and she held up her hand to block it as they raced into the darkness of the Moon's shadow. The low Sun angles exaggerated the shadows of the ridges and craters, making the strange sight even more bizarre.

"Bozhe moi!" she murmured, reverently. My God. *Can this be real?*

She glanced up into the blackness of the sky, seeing for herself that Earth was no longer visible; the Moon was in the way. That also meant all radio signals were blocked.

"Three minutes until ignition," Michael said. He was loosely strapped in his seat, checklist Velcroed to the panel, eyes intent on the instruments.

"Temps and pressures look good," Chad responded from the other seat. Without Houston to help monitor, it was up to the two of them to be ready to react to everything.

One of the problems the rocket engineers had to solve had been how to get the fuel out of the tank and into the motor in weightlessness; pumps don't work without gravity holding the liquid at the pump intake. They'd decided to pressurize the tanks with helium in order to squeeze the fuel through the lines to the motor—175 pounds per square inch, pushing the fuel against the valves, waiting for ignition time to snap open.

They also had to choose fuel that could be relied upon to burn: aerozine 50, a highly flammable, fishy-smelling clear liquid. The oxygen to burn it was waiting in the other tank, in a faintly orange-brown liquid called nitrogen tetroxide. When the two liquids touched each other they instantly exploded into flame. This hypergolic reaction meant they didn't need the added weight of spark plugs and electrics. As soon as the two mixed, *BOOM,* the engine would ignite.

Michael tugged on Svetlana's pantleg and mimed holding on to something. He didn't want her to be surprised by the acceleration and come tumbling onto them. She nodded and grabbed a handhold.

Chad was watching the clock. "Thirty seconds."

Michael typed in the command to enable ignition. Both astronauts' eyes were glued to the gauges, hands clutching emergency checklists, ready to respond instantly if the engine didn't behave.

The time on the digital clock hit zero. The valves clicked open, the aerozine and nitrogen tetroxide swirled together into the combustion chamber, burst into expanding flame and raced out the exhaust nozzle.

"Ignition!" The urgency of concentration was clear in Michael's voice.

Floating beside him, Svetlana silently mouthed "Pusk," the Russian equivalent. She was holding on tightly, but the acceleration was smaller than she expected, like drifting in a gentle, unseen current. She peered out the window and saw the glow of the flame reflected off the flat surfaces of the lunar lander. "Lem," she said quietly, the sound of the word foreign in her mouth.

"Chamber pressure's ninety, looks like it's running smooth." Chad's voice was clinical.

Michael was watching the digital displays. "Data looks good. Still in the tight limits."

Flame poured out the back of the oversized bell nozzle at the back of the ship, the two fluids burning a bright orange, an engine pushing backwards on a capsule with a lander mounted on its nose, slowing gradually to orbital speed around the Moon.

The computers sensed tiny changes in movement and made precise adjustments to the gimbals on the motor, pointing it in exactly the right direction, constantly recalculating speeds. Michael checked the clock.

"Four minutes to go."

He'd spent the past year learning everything about this ship, this *Pursuit*. It was his to fly, but it all hinged on this motor. *Burn, baby, burn.*

If the SPS failed, he'd have to use the engine on the lunar lander to somehow straighten things out and get them safely headed directly back

towards Earth. That's what they'd done on Apollo 13 after the oxygen
tank explosion, but they'd barely made it.

Pay attention!

"I show ninety seconds, Chad."

"Agreed." Chad had relaxed. In his experience, once an engine lit
it would normally keep going. They just had to be sure it shut down on
time, and then he could focus on what he was really here for. Getting to
the surface of the Moon. He glanced up and shook his head. *With her.*

"Five, four, three, two, one and . . . cut-off."

Michael's eyes flicked anxiously across the gauges, confirming that
the engine had shut down properly. He read the digital display carefully. "Looks like small residuals, no correction needed." In the simulator, as the engine thrust tailed off, it often left some small, undesirable
residual rates, and he'd had to manually null them. His fingers threw
the switches to safe the system, a grin spreading across his face.

"We're here!" He held up a hand, and Chad high-fived it.

"Well, that's just our superior cunning and skill, boy," Chad said.
"And now we can really get down to business."

Svetlana caught Michael's eye and held up a thumb, nodding slightly,
her eyebrows raised for confirmation.

He laughed with relief. "Da, we made it. We're in orbit around the
Moon!"

"Atleechna," she told him. Excellent.

Now she needed to hear from Moscow. She'd listened to the translated briefing from the Americans, but she wanted to hear it directly
from her bosses. She was certain they had separate plans for her, and it
was going to take all her wits to understand what they wanted without
letting on to the others what the interpreted words actually meant.

But they were *here*! Somehow she'd become the first Soviet to get to
the Moon, and tomorrow, she was going to step onto the lunar surface!

A rush of excitement went through her. She'd watched the near-
deification of Gagarin, the way he'd become one of the legendary figures
of Russian history. That was going to happen to her!

But not yet. As it had been her whole life, especially as a woman, first she had to perform. This time was perhaps the hardest of all: on a strange ship, in an unfamiliar suit, surrounded by a language she didn't understand.

What was it the first American who'd walked here below her had said? One small step?

She nodded to herself. *I can do this thing.* It was just one more step.

But first she needed to hear from Moscow.

39

Moscow

They were an odd-looking pair as they emerged into the Arrivals hall at Moscow's Sheremetyevo Airport. The bearded monk wore all black, a long, buttoned vest over his floor-length robes, simple black leather shoes visible as he walked, a black veil trailing from his tall kamilavka headdress. Laboring slightly beside him with a suitcase in each hand, the church interpreter was in a two-piece brown suit, square-toed shoes and a thigh-length tan trench coat cinched around his waist. It was always colder in Moscow than Berlin, and the April weather could still bite.

Father Ilarion had been quiet and thoughtful throughout the flight, observant of the newness of everything. Alexander had made sure to give him the window seat on the Interflug Tu-134. It had been noisy, seated just ahead of the engines, but Ilarion's face stayed glued to the round porthole window, watching East Germany give way to Poland, peering down at the Baltic Sea by Gdansk. His face filled with wonder as the view opened on the edge of the empty vastness of the Soviet Union.

When Moscow finally appeared, with the low gray shades of human history crowding on the switchback bends of the Moskva River, Alexander had leaned next to Father Ilarion to see the city, encircled by the early green of new leaves and grasses. The MKAD ring road surrounding Moscow in a near-perfect oval was a demarcation line separating natural from urban. The two men stared at the vast ranks of identical apartment blocks, the hulking cooling towers of the power plants and the concentric inner road patterns making a bullseye of Red Square and the Kremlin.

"Kremel, Sascha!" the monk had said, pointing for Alexander to see. The red of the high fortress walls stood out clearly against the dark pavement of Red Square and the glinting river. Neither man mentioned the enormous public swimming pool just to the west, built on the site where Stalin had torn down the Cathedral of Christ the Saviour—the pre-revolution home of the Orthodox Patriarchate.

No need to dwell on the past. This trip was about the future.

The driver was waiting for them in Arrivals, easily spotting the monk. He waved a hand, took the bags from Alexander and led them out to a squatty light-blue Moskvitch station wagon. He took care to set the bags down and solicitously open the rear door for the clergyman, politely lowering his head. He'd been told to make the monk feel important.

Traffic was light on the MKAD, and Father Ilarion's eyes darted in all directions, staring out the noisy little car's windows at the reality of Moscow, reading the overhead street signs as they flicked past. The driver took the Yaroslavl Highway to the right, towards the city center. In the distance, the Ostankino TV Tower dominated the skyline, its tapered silver bulges distinctive—the tallest tower in the world, a visual affirmation of Soviet pride and technical prowess.

As they neared Ostankino's base, a second tower appeared—a sweeping silver scimitar with a stylized rocket at its tip. Without being asked, the driver pulled the car into the adjoining parking lot and leaned forward to look up at the sight. "Pamyatnik pokorítelyam cosmosa," he said, simply. Monument to the conquerors of space.

"Would you like to have a look, Father?" Alexander asked.

"Da!" Ilarion craned his neck to look up through the side window. "My brother is now one of those conquerors," he said as he climbed out of the car's back seat.

The long, pyramid-like rectangular base of the monument was emblazoned with bold Soviet heroic figures in bas-relief, their muscular arms and stalwart male and female faces all pointing towards a cosmonaut in his spacesuit, climbing steps towards the heavens.

"Yuri Alekseyevich Gagarin. First man in space," Alexander said, pointing to the cosmonaut.

The monk stared at Gagarin's sculpted face, and then followed the majestic sweep of the titanium statue towards the sky. He blinked at the brightness.

"It's magnificent." He turned to look at the interpreter. "Sascha, I'm excited to talk to my brother. Do we know yet when it will happen?"

"Tomorrow, Father." Alexander explained that they needed to wait until the Moon was visible in the sky, so the signal would be able to get there and back from the Russian antennas. And tomorrow was also the day his brother would walk on the Moon. Tonight they would stay in quarters near TsUP Mission Control.

Tomorrow would be the biggest of days.

40

Office of the Chief Designer, Moscow

"Allo? Allo?"

Chelomei scowled, holding the receiver against his ear. *We can fly in space, but why can't we Soviets make phones that work?*

A series of static-filled clicks came through the line.

The information that Major Miller had transmitted down from Apollo had confirmed what he'd suspected. Somehow the Americans had precise information on the Lunokhod rover's location on the Moon, and had made it their landing target. The clear purpose of this US military lunar landing was glaringly revealed.

The question was why. They couldn't know about the lunar geology team's discoveries. They were too recent; the American ship's trajectory had to have been set several weeks in advance for crew training and launch timing. But they had intercepted Almaz with sabotage weapons in hand. Clearly this was the same thing: they wanted to see anything Lunokhod might have discovered, inspect the rover up close and then disable it. To stop Soviet progress on the Moon's surface.

The briefing he'd received on the most recent discovery significantly upped the stakes. It wasn't just lunar knowledge and Soviet technology they could now steal. A naturally occurring radioactive source on the Moon—if it was the right kind—meant many things, including power, and heat. It could enable the fundamental technology that would spur lunar settlement. And the knowledge had to remain the Soviet Union's alone.

He needed to protect what Lunokhod had found. Having a cosmonaut on the surface added tremendous leverage, and options. But he urgently needed details from the rover operations team in Simferopol, which is why he waited so impatiently on the phone.

Finally, a thin voice sounded in his earpiece. "Simferopol Luna Ops Command. Allo?"

"Director Chelomei here. Who is this?"

Gabdul sat bolt upright, stammering slightly. "S-S-Senior Lieutenant Gabdulkhai Latypov, Director. I'm the shift lead currently on console, primary Lunokhod operator, seconded from the Soviet Air Forces." *Stop babbling!* "And lead of the team that installed the Apollo uplink voice capability." Credentials were important. With his technical communications background, he'd been key in making the uplink voice work.

"Latypov, good." Chelomei had heard the name during the antenna modifications. "I have new information, and I need your team to be ready."

He quickly summarized the Apollo landing details, leaving out the fact that there would be a cosmonaut on the surface too. No need to overburden the rover drivers. "They'll be on the surface within twenty-four hours. How can Lunokhod best protect itself and what it has found?"

Gabdul was dumfounded that the director was asking his advice. His mind whirled as he considered options.

"Comrade Director, we have made fresh tracks all around Ugol—that's what we have named the rock. It will be obvious that we've been investigating it. Perhaps we could bury it with one of the probes? Or maybe push it into the nearby rille? Also, we need to protect Lunokhod itself."

An idea struck him and he quickly explained it.

Chelomei considered, and decided the plan was good for a couple of reasons. "Make ready to do it, Lieutenant Latypov. TsUP will be working closely with you tomorrow while the Americans are on the surface."

As Chelomei hung up, he glanced at his watch. The American, Esdale, should be going to sleep soon. He needed to brief Miller and Gromova, but he knew from the transmissions that they weren't keeping her on headset.

He closed his eyes and rubbed his forehead with his thumb and middle finger, his head aching with all the moving pieces and the lack of sleep. He stood and left his office, headed for TsUP.

I'll sleep when this is over.

"Transmission test, transmission test, how do you hear me?"

It was after midnight, and the Moscow Mission Control team was tired. Michael Esdale was finally napping, now that he had safely gotten his craft into lunar orbit. Despite the late hour, Chelomei had insisted on patience to ensure that Esdale was truly asleep, so he could send a message that would be heard by Miller alone. Out of extra caution, he'd decided to use the same innocuous call, and repeated it in deliberately bored Russian.

"Transmission test, transmission test, how do you hear me?" He listened for any response and glanced at the timer on the front screen. Just two minutes left before the ship would disappear behind the Moon. He decided it was worth the risk to assume Major Miller was hearing him and say what needed to be said.

"Listen to me carefully. We have your brother, Ilarion, here, and want him to remain safe. You will hear his voice tomorrow. Once you are on the Moon, we will brief you and Gromova with the exact details of what is needed." Chelomei had reasoned that she would have to be listening while they were in their spacesuits.

"If you understand, click your mic twice." The clock showed one minute before they lost signal.

Long seconds ticked by. Nothing.

Finally, *click, click.*

A slow, Cheshire cat smile spread on Chelomei's face. "We hear your response, and will talk to you tomorrow." He decided to dig in the knife slightly. "Sleep well."

In Houston, Kaz frowned. *That's the second time I've heard that.* He decided to check.

"18, Houston, did you call?"

Chad responded with palpable irritation. "No, we didn't call. We're trying to stay quiet, to let Michael sleep."

"Copy, apologies." Kaz kept his tone contrite, but he looked back at Gene Kranz and shrugged. They'd both heard the clicks.

"INCO, any idea where that sound came from?" Gene asked.

The communications operator was studying his displays. "Looks like from *Pursuit*, FLIGHT. Maybe they just bumped the switch." It was lame, but he couldn't see any other explanation.

"Copy, but let's keep an ear out for any recurrence," Gene said. "We don't need any more surprises in the comm system."

Kaz nodded along with INCO, but he was bothered. Clicking the mic twice was something pilots only did on purpose. But Chad had denied it. Was Michael awake and trying to get Kaz's attention? Why would he do that? Was it the cosmonaut? Or was there something going on with Chad?

In TsUP, the interpreter had translated Miller's irritated response to Houston.

Good boy, Chelomei thought. But he was going to have to be extra careful. He didn't want to make the Americans suspicious, at least not until after he had achieved his aim.

An idea popped into his head, and he smiled, tiredly. He had a better plan for next time.

41

Mission Control, Houston

"Everyone listen up, this is the Flight Director."

Conversations ceased in Mission Control, and faces turned to look at Gene Kranz, standing behind his console.

"Another excellent day, people. We're in lunar orbit with healthy spaceships, and have the landing and moonwalk tomorrow."

His eyes sought out each console operator as he spoke: "The crew needs to get some rest now, but so do you. After you all hand over to the night shift, I want you to head home and get a well-deserved sleep. I need you at the top of your game tomorrow. Sweet dreams, and see you in the morning."

Kaz leaned back to catch JW's eye. "U-Joint for a burger, Doc?"

JW smiled. "Outstanding plan."

Kaz had already called Laura, and spotted her Beetle as he drove into the bar's parking lot. Despite Gene Kranz's urging that they all have a quiet night, the lot was filling rapidly. As he walked through the swinging doors, he saw her waving, two fresh bottles of beer and a coffee on the table in front of her.

"Well, aren't you a sight for sore eye," Kaz joked as he sat.

She laughed and handed him his beer, raising hers in a toast, then shut one of her own eyes, appraising. "You look good too, in mono or stereo."

He rubbed his head and took a long, appreciative swig. "I look like a guy who was ready for this beer."

"I ordered us burgers." She spotted JW coming through the doors and waved him over. "One for the doc too."

"And they say cosmochemists aren't empathetic."

JW sat with a tired sigh. He nodded thanks for the coffee and took a sip, cradling the mug in his hands. "We three have a big day tomorrow," he said.

Laura nodded. "Enough of you boys flying spaceships and counting heartbeats, it's time to get down to what we're really here for. Extraterrestrial geology!"

Kaz pulled his chair closer and leaned in. The total blackout on news had been holding, and he didn't want to be overheard.

"Are the two of you ready for everything that could happen tomorrow?"

Laura frowned. "What don't I know, Kaz?"

"The thing is, we're not really sure." He began listing what was on his mind. "We're hoping to land within easy walking distance of the Soviet rover, to see what's been interesting them, but it might be a hike, depending where Chad touches down. And Chad is going to have to spend extra time ensuring the cosmonaut stays safe—she's had no training for a moonwalk. The Russians have asked for some senior politico to talk to her while she's on the surface, so that will tie up comms for a while. We've set schedule aside to place Luke's body on the surface, and have tried it out in the sim here, but we're not really sure how long it will take. And a lot of what we say is going to have to be repeated via the interpreter, which will also slow things down."

He looked at JW. "What did I miss?"

The doctor set his coffee down. "You're talking best case. We're gambling that Chad will find a way to work with Svetlana under stress. He's the only one who can fly the ship, or fix things when they break."

He looked at Kaz. "And we both know Chad's a . . . perfectionist."

And maybe something a lot worse, Kaz couldn't help but think, then cautioned himself to keep his mind open. Just because the sheriff had wanted to dig deeper didn't mean he had to jump to conclusions. He turned to Laura.

"I'm sorry, but all of this will steal potential science time. We're really gonna have to prioritize. What's your best guess about the terrain Chad'll be walking across?"

Laura stared back at him for a long, sober moment as she processed yet another change in the mission. She said, "It's in the corner of an old crater called Le Monnier that got inundated with lava at some point long ago. It doesn't have too many meteor craters in it, so the lava's fairly young, and flat. There's likely an even layer of dust on everything, with scattered rocks from more recent impacts. Should be okay for both landing and walking."

She took a drink of her beer. "Our orbital photos aren't great, but the most interesting thing we've seen nearby is a rille—a long, straight arroyo in the lava plain, just to the west."

JW asked, "How did it get there?"

"Likely as the lava cooled it contracted. Like mud when it dries out, it sometimes leaves straight cracks."

Kaz had been thinking. "Any further guesses on one of your holes in the Moon being close by?"

She nodded. "Yes, we've been looking at formation models. They're not common, but there's a fair chance that there might be some. If so, they've been too small to see from orbital cameras."

He nodded. Chad had been in on those briefings, so if he encountered such a hole it wouldn't be a surprise. Maybe worth warning the cosmonaut about, though.

"How steep are the sides likely to be?" JW was picturing potential injuries.

"The rille could be quite steep, since it's more of a crack than a valley, but it's likely been drifted in along the edges with millions of years of dust and rock. But if there's a hole, it's a pure vertical drop, like a well, or a Florida sinkhole. And we have no idea how stable the edges might be. Better to stay clear."

JW looked at Kaz. "With all the items they removed to save weight, how good will our camera views be?"

Kaz shrugged. "There's just the color TV camera, deployed on the side to watch them climb down the ladder. It'll be up to Chad to move that onto a tripod once they're both outside."

Laura, imagining how little of the science she hoped for might get done, was looking for options. "How long are you going to let them stay outside?"

JW answered. "That's determined by how fast they use up their oxygen, and exhale CO_2 for the suit to scrub. We have lots of data on Chad, but none on Svetlana, and she may have to work harder since it's not her own suit. Also, she might not get her biomed sensors attached correctly, so we could be guessing a bit."

Laura frowned. That wasn't an answer. "So, how long?"

They both looked at Kaz.

"Original plan with Chad and Luke was seven and a half hours, as you know. Now it's five hours." He saw her face fall, and said, "We might extend, depending on how they're doing, but I wouldn't count on it."

Another thought had been niggling at the back of Laura's mind. "Maybe you can't tell me, Kaz, but does Chad have military objectives that the geologists haven't been told about?"

Kaz looked around, then said, "That will depend on what we see when they land. It could end up being purely geology." *Not likely, though.*

She glanced at JW, who was carefully keeping his face impassive.

"I should play poker with you two. I'd clean you out." She smiled and shook her head as Janie arrived, balancing the three plates.

42

Bulldog, Lunar Orbit

Chad had been seething since the Russian call. His anger had made him restless all night, pouring through him in waves that invaded his dreams and kept cresting, right at the edge of his control.

He was the one who had qualified to command this spaceship. Who was this Soviet trying to tell *him* what to do? And to bring his brother into it? Floating in his hammock, he wanted to scream. He'd made his own life, taken his own actions to get to where he was supposed to be. He'd been the top test pilot in the US Air Force, and now at long last he was about to walk on the Moon. The small-thinking idiocy of that smug voice echoed in his head, the man trying to direct his actions like he was a puppet. "Sleep well," the arrogant bastard had said. How dare he!

When Chad finally had slept, he'd dreamt of Berlin. And it wasn't the first time for this dream—it was one he feared.

The colors in it were oddly faded, like he was inside an old newsreel. He was running, trying to keep up with his brother, as buildings burned and collapsed around them. He could hear the cries of a woman, but couldn't tell if she was behind or ahead of them. Were they running

towards her, or away? Where was his brother leading him? The faster
they ran, the less sure the footing became. He could hear his own
labored breathing over the female cries, and feel the blood pounding
in his temples.

Suddenly they were on a narrow track, running along the surviving
ramparts of the burning buildings. It became a balancing act to keep
up, to not put a foot wrong, yet still move so fast. The world around him
receded, and the narrow ridge of masonry that now supported them was
impossibly high in the sky, starkly lit in anti-aircraft lights, with smoky
haze far below.

He *had* to keep up! Every step treacherous, he pushed himself, calling to Oleg, "Medlenneya!" — Slow down! Please let me catch up. Please
don't leave me alone. He pushed his muscles to the limit, pounding
frantically along the thin, wobbling path until, finally, it collapsed underneath him and he tumbled. Helpless. Weightless. Lost.

And, as he always did at this point in the dream, he forced his eyes
open through sheer willpower. He couldn't allow himself to hit the
ground, and he didn't. Floating there, his heart still racing, he could
feel the sweat on his forehead. His awareness had saved him, again,
pulling him out of the terror.

But this time he wasn't alone. Someone was shaking him.

"Chad, Chad."

He felt the cold of the LM's air on his damp face.

"Chad, time to wake up, man," Michael was saying. "Houston's calling. Time to go make history."

The list of actions to ready the LM for undock and landing was long. As
Chad and Svetlana ate a hurried breakfast, Michael helped them get
suited. He made sure Svetlana got her heartbeat and breathing sensors
properly stuck to her skin, and pantomimed again the key controls on
the suit. She watched him carefully, then nodded, saying "Da," clearly
familiar with the type of equipment.

While the two finished suiting up, Michael set as many switches in

Bulldog as he could—Houston had decided that he would take Luke's role in activating the LM's system up to the point where he had to close the hatch for undock. He strapped Luke's body into place over the engine housing, relieved to see that no more gases had built up in the Soviet suit.

He was trying not to worry about Chad. When he'd woken him up, Chad had been thrashing in a nightmare. As he came to consciousness, his eyes had been wild, staring in raw, scowling fury at whatever he'd been dreaming. When he finally recognized Michael, Chad had thanked him and quickly gotten down to work. But what had upset Chad so much? Michael knew very little about what made the man tick, he realized, and that worried him too. He heard Chad and Svetlana coming down the tunnel, their bulky suits scraping the sides, and made himself small against the ceiling so they could get into position.

Michael started a small stopwatch, counting down to undock, and Velcroed it on the panel in front of them. It read 30 minutes—plenty of time for him to clear out and close the hatch. He helped them don their helmets and gloves, got a thumbs-up from each and backed his way out of the LM, carefully tending his loose items and comm cable. He attached the bulky probe-and-drogue metal apparatus that would allow *Bulldog* to redock onto the hatch when they returned from the Moon. He methodically wiped the rubber seal to make sure it was clean, closed the hatch and released the manual docking latches that had kept the vehicles securely joined.

As he turned to face into the capsule, he realized he was suddenly truly alone. The Command Module, *Pursuit*, named by him, was his to fly. A grin spread on his face as he imagined what the folks in Bronzeville, South Chicago, might be thinking, how proud his family would be. All he needed to do was to get *Bulldog* safely undocked, and he, Michael Henry Esdale, would be solo master and commander of his own ship, in orbit around the Moon.

He rechecked his flight plan and began setting *Pursuit*'s switches.

"Apollo 18, Houston," Kaz's voice intervened. "I have good news before you disappear behind the Moon. You are GO for undocking.

Also, we observed your rendezvous radar test—no issues. *Bulldog*, we have not seen you reset the digital autopilot."

"Thanks, Kaz, doing that now. I show myself"—Chad checked the timer—"fourteen minutes from undock. Talk to you when I come back around."

"Roger that, *Bulldog*."

Svetlana was standing next to Chad, the two of them held lightly in place on their feet by restraint cables clipped to rings on their hips. She'd wondered how they were going to stay in position without seats, and was impressed with the simplicity of the American solution. She found herself alternately watching Chad's hands moving switches and staring through the triangular window at the Moon racing by. They were just coming into sunset, and the lengthening shadows were mesmerizing. Especially given that soon she was going to be down there, walking on the surface.

Michael called, "Chad, when you're ready, I'll start extending the probe."

Undocking was controlled from *Pursuit*. Michael would be the one to extend the docking probe, release the latches and set *Bulldog* free. It would then be up to him to fire small thrusters and move safely clear.

"I'm all set here, Michael. You can let us go."

The phrasing caught Michael's ear, and he found himself suddenly humming "Let My People Go" as he threw the probe extend switch. His mother loved Paul Robeson's deep, mournful version of the song, but he preferred Louis Armstrong's upbeat take. As the gears of the mechanism were grinding, slowly pushing *Bulldog* away, Satchmo's words were playing in his head.

> *Go down, Moses, way down in Egypt land*
> *Tell old Pharaoh to let my people go.*

The mechanical sound stopped, and Michael peered hard through the window at *Bulldog*, relieved to see it moving slightly, independent of *Pursuit*. He pushed heavily on the extend switch to be sure, and pulled on the hand controller for three seconds to back away. He released both controls and watched with satisfaction as his ship separated cleanly from the LM. *Just like in the sim.*

"*Bulldog*, you are *free.*"

"Looks like a good sep, Michael," Chad said. "Starting my yaw and pitch now." He carefully moved his right joystick to pivot *Bulldog* around so Michael could inspect the exterior.

Michael stared through the dark windows, *Pursuit*'s interior light reflecting off the metal surfaces of *Bulldog*. "You look clean, Chad—all four legs extended, antennas pointing correctly."

"Good to hear. Checking the rendezvous radar now. Your transponder on?"

"Sure is. Ping away."

Chad reached down and selected Auto Track, and immediately saw the signal needle jump. He confirmed the tracking display bars were moving and the digital range was updating. They'd need that radar to find each other when *Bulldog* was returning from the lunar surface. "Good return, good tracking, showing range of point three miles." He looked out the window at *Pursuit* slowly moving away. "Matches what I see with my Mark One Eyeball."

"Agreed, Chad."

Michael looked ahead to the horizon, where the first light of sunrise was appearing. "We should have Houston back pretty soon. I'll be ready for landing landmark tracking."

Knowing exactly where to land was the most critical piece of information for the navigation computers. As *Pursuit* passed directly over the planned landing spot, one orbit before the landing, Michael would measure exact angles with a tracking telescope. The information would be added to data from the rendezvous radar and Earth antenna tracking, and fed back into the computer in *Bulldog*. That would give *Bulldog* the best possible information to begin descent.

Svetlana, looking ahead to the sunrise glowing on the Moon's far horizon, felt a bump on her arm. The astronaut had taken his gloves off and was removing his helmet. He gestured for her to do the same.

Now that undocking was done, it made sense. They could enjoy the unencumbered comfort for a while, then put them back on for landing. She watched how Chad stowed his gloves inside the helmet behind himself, bungeed to the floor, and did the same.

She stole a quick glance at his face, then stared for a moment longer when she realized he was completely focused on the instruments. He could have been any of the boys she had grown up with—the same round face, high cheekbones, deep-set eyes. *Where did your family come from, American?* She couldn't recall his family name.

Chad turned suddenly, holding her gaze. He looked pointedly at the NASA comm cap on her head and Luke's US flag on her shoulder. "Don't worry, toots," he said. "I won't forget who and what you are." She frowned, not understanding the words but not liking the tone.

Chad gave a short, derisive chuckle. "You just sit back and enjoy the ride. Watch how the best in the world do it."

He considered slipping a Russian word in to unsettle her further, but decided against it. *Cards are best kept close to the chest,* he reminded himself. And he might still need the extra leverage he gained by secretly knowing what the Russians were saying.

In Mission Control, Kaz was watching the timer count down to when *Pursuit* and *Bulldog* would pop out from behind the Moon. He glanced at the flight plan: they just had the tracking update and systems checks during this pass. When *Bulldog* went back behind the Moon, it would fire its engine to start descent. He read the expected time: touchdown at 11:17 a.m. Central. Lunchtime in Washington, 8:17 p.m. in Moscow. The Soviets would have to stay up late to talk to their cosmonaut on the surface.

It was time. "Apollo 18, Houston here, you should be seeing your home planet again now. How do you hear us?"

Michael answered first. "*Pursuit* has you loud and clear, Kaz. Happy to report we had a good undock."

"*Bulldog* has you five by five, Houston." Five out of five for strength of signal, and also for clarity of voice, Chad's standard military assessment of radio communications.

"We have you both the same. You'll be over the landing site in sixteen minutes if you want to have a good look, and *Bulldog*, we're ready to read you your DOI data." DOI was Descent Orbit Insertion—the engine burn that would lower *Bulldog* from 60 miles above the surface down to 6, setting up for the final descent.

Chad unclipped his checklist from the instrument panel and grabbed the pencil that floated with it, tethered by a string.

"*Bulldog's* ready to copy."

Kaz carefully read the long sequence of numbers specifying time of engine firing, vehicle orientation, plus abort information. The guidance engineers in Mission Control listened critically to Chad's response, and quickly responded when he finished. "FLIGHT, CONTROL, good readback."

Gene Kranz raised his thumb at Kaz.

"Good readback, *Bulldog*. We'd like to do a comm check with the cosmonaut, when you're ready."

Chad glanced at her. "She's listening."

Kaz nodded to the interpreter and began. "Senior Lieutenant Gromova, this is Houston, how do you read?"

Svetlana's head came up as she heard the Russian in her headset. Chad showed her the switch to throw on her control panel.

"Slishu vam yasna," she responded.

Kaz nodded at the translation. "Svetlana, we hear you clearly as well. We have the interpreter standing by at all times if you have questions. And once you're out on the surface, we'll be patching you through to Moscow for an official call of congratulations."

She listened to the interpreter. "Ponyala," she answered. "Understood." She'd been a pilot her entire adult life and didn't like chattiness on the radio. Or in normal conversation, for that matter.

Chad had been looking at her as she spoke. "What an ugly language," he said, shaking his head.

She squinted, uncertain what he disapproved of. "Shto?"

He snorted and turned away. Out his window he was starting to see the familiar landmarks leading up to the landing site they'd trained for. There was a grid painted on the layers of the tempered glass so he could visually cross-check with what the computer was telling him. He lined up his head with the references and watched the craters roll past at nearly a mile per second.

"Houston, *Bulldog*, I'm seeing the reference craters on the horizon. Looks a lot like the sim."

"*Pursuit's* seeing them as well, Kaz," Michael piped in. "Getting set here to update the computers."

"Houston copies both." Kaz looked across at JW. "Doc, you getting their heartbeats?"

JW decided it was good information for the whole room to know. "FLIGHT, SURGEON, we've got solid cardio and breathing telemetry from both crew in *Bulldog*."

"Let me know if you see anything unexpected," Gene replied.

Might be really important today, Kaz thought.

Michael had *Pursuit's* alignment telescope and sextant set up, ready to mark the data when he spotted the distinct features of the crater and the rille. He was hoping he might get lucky and see the Soviet rover as well. It would be critical info for Chad to use for manual landing.

As *Pursuit* flew closer, Michael took marks for the computer while looking unblinkingly through the eyepiece. When he passed overhead, he briefly saw glinting tracks in the area and a flash of silver dead center in the target zone. *Excellent!*

"Houston and *Bulldog*, *Pursuit* here. Landing landmark tracking complete, and happy to report that Lunokhod looks like it's right at the bullseye."

"Copy, Michael, good to hear. Hopefully won't be too long a walk for Chad."

"*Bulldog* here. I didn't spot anything through my window, but I'll set her down as close to Lunokhod as I can, next time we come around."

Svetlana was listening intently to the exchange. She could have sworn she'd heard them say "Lunokhod" twice, the familiar Russian sounds sticking out amongst the English. Could that be right? Was that their destination? Why were the Americans landing by the Soviet rover?

She scanned her memory for details of the Soviet Luna program, but she didn't remember much. Focused on her own mission, she'd paid only idle attention to robotic lunar geology research. In the translated planning meeting they'd had the night before, no one had said anything about Lunokhod. Could she have misheard?

She puzzled further. The astronaut in the suit she was now wearing had been carrying bolt cutters when he'd been outside at Almaz. That had shown hostile intent. Was this the second half of that same mission? To damage not only the Soviet orbital station, but also their vehicle on the Moon? She looked around inside the lander. Were those bolt cutters stowed in here? She couldn't see them, but with the stiffness of the suit, she couldn't turn her head properly to look everywhere.

She pictured what was going to happen after they landed. They'd said she would descend the ladder and stand on the surface while talking to someone in Moscow. But what would she do if Lunokhod was in sight and the astronaut started heading towards it?

Chad glanced at her and frowned. *Why are you looking so intent all of a sudden?* He saw her notice his scrutiny and immediately relax her face into its usual impassive mask.

He played back the past minute in his head. *Did you understand what we just said?* Maybe she spoke English after all, and was just playing dumb. He went through the instructions he'd received about the Soviet rover, then turned back to look through his window at the Moon's surface below, picturing exactly how it would go.

He was fine, he decided; she couldn't know his intentions. Even if she realized what was happening, she was weaker—there was no way she was going to stop him.

If there was a battle on the Moon, he would win.

—

It was a long, gradual descent begun in the shadowed silence of the far side of the Moon, the engine slowing *Bulldog* down, the gentle force of it pushing up through Chad's and Svetlana's feet.

Without Luke to assist, Houston had suggested that Chad relay his progress to Michael overhead so someone could double-check every needed action and help with emergencies.

Chad's voice was clipped and clinical. "H-dot's a little high. We're about 2 percent low on fuel."

Michael thought about it. "Yeah, I undocked you when we were a tad high, so that descent speed makes sense, and matches the burn rate."

"Concur."

"How does nav and guidance look?"

"PGNS and AGS compare." Chad pronounced the navigation acronyms "pings" and "ags."

"Copy. Looking good, Chad."

On *Bulldog*'s instrument panel, two small lights stopped glowing.

"I see the Altitude and Velocity lights are out now, showing a 3,400 delta-H. What do you think?"

Michael was following along in his checklist. "Sounds like the landing radar's got a good lock on height. I think you can accept the updated 3,400-foot difference it's giving you."

"Agreed. Accept. It's going in." Chad pushed the keyboard button.

This is happening! I'm going to land on the Moon!

Chad heard static in his headset, and then Kaz's voice from Mission Control, 250,000 miles away.

"*Bulldog*, Houston. You're GO at five, and your fuel quantity looks good here."

Five minutes since they'd started descent. Kaz checked the clock. Seven minutes to go.

In the front row of consoles, the engineers were having an urgent discussion with the experts in their back room over signs of a steadily building navigation error. The Flight Dynamics Officer spoke his concern. "FLIGHT, FDO. Tracking shows they're going to land 3,000 feet south of track."

Damn! Gene Kranz cursed. *We can't afford to be that far off!* "CAPCOM, give them a heads-up they'll need to steer that out manually."

Kaz agreed. "*Bulldog*, guidance is taking you half a mile left into the foothills."

Chad had been looking ahead at the planned landmarks and had noticed the trend as well. "Yeah, the mountains aren't quite where I expected. I'll redesignate."

In training he had repeatedly flown a robotic camera over a 15-by-15-foot model of the Moon, built by the US Geological Survey. It was a relief how familiar the actual view out the window looked. Carefully rotating his hand controller, he set the roll angle that would align the window marks with the correct reference craters. He watched to confirm the computer had accepted the update, and snapped his eyes back outside.

Show the world how to fly this thing!

Kaz was watching the downlinked data closely, picturing what Luke would have been telling Chad. "*Bulldog*, we see the update, and show 5,000 feet, engine at 41." A mile above the surface, engine at 41 percent power.

"Copy."

Kaz decided to just give key information to avoid being a distraction. "Two thousand feet, 42."

"Copy."

The Flight Director polled the room and heard no objections. All systems GO. Kaz relayed the vital bit of information.

"*Bulldog*, Houston, you're GO for landing."

"Copy, GO for landing." Chad could feel his heart pounding, even as he kept his fingers light on the controls.

At the SURGEON console, JW smiled. *That raised his heartbeat.*

"Five hundred feet, eighteen down." Just 500 feet up now, descending at 18 feet per second. Kaz spoke calmly, clearly.

"Copy."

"Two hundred fifty feet, eleven, 9 percent fuel remaining, all okay."

"Copy."

Svetlana was entranced by the practiced complexity of what was happening. She loved the wonderfully precise demands of the manual task. *I wish I were flying this!* She could see brown dust starting to blow in all directions below them, pushed away by the engine's down thrust. Through the hurtling bits, she caught sight of something silver ahead of them.

Chad's voice had a hint of triumph. "I have the rover in sight."

"Good to hear. A hundred feet, five."

The blowing dust was now streaming away below *Bulldog,* partially obscuring Lunokhod and the horizon. Chad snapped his focus inside the cockpit, eyes flicking across the instruments to keep control and hold the steady descent. He rapidly cross-checked outside, straining to see rocks through the dust storm, evaluating height and forward speed.

Kaz figured he had time for one last transmission. "Fifteen feet, one down, 6 percent fuel."

No response.

Fifteen long seconds ticked by.

Bam! The violence of the impact startled Svetlana. She'd been staring at the instruments, watching the artificial horizon and radar altitude, and was jolted by the sudden force up through her feet. She heard everything rattling in the ship, even through her helmet. She held her breath, waiting for alarms or for the vehicle to tip on a broken leg.

Nothing. Dead quiet. *Bulldog* sat solidly level. The astronaut was reaching and throwing switches. She leaned to look at his face through his visor. His mouth was curled in a smile, his eyes blazing.

"Houston, *Bulldog* is on the Moon."

THE

SEA OF

SERENITY

чз

Simferopol, Soviet Ukraine

The group was clustered around Gabdul's workstation, all trying to get a good view of his small black-and-white monitor. The vista had been largely unchanged for months: the flat plain of the lava flow in Le Monnier crater, the occasional rock, small craters, the gray of the lunar dust.

Spot, drive, look, repeat. It had become a routine—the geologists seeing something, the drivers maneuvering close, and then the sensors gleaning what information they could. Excellent, methodical science, but not a spectacle everyone would gather excitedly to watch.

Today was different.

With a little luck, they were going to see a spaceship land. Even the cook and waitress from their small canteen were shyly observing from the back.

The group peppered Gabdul with questions.

"Where will we first see it?"

He didn't know for sure, but said likely they would spot it against the blackness of the lunar sky while it was still flying.

"How did you know which direction to point?"

He said he had made an educated guess, based on the trajectory information they'd sent him from Mission Control in Moscow. When the crowd heard that Gabdul had been talking directly with Moscow, there was a small hush of awe.

"What if it lands behind Lunokhod?"

"Well, then I'll turn around," Gabdul answered wryly.

"Why does it take so long to refresh your TV screen?"

"Because it's not really TV," he explained. "It's just still images, and it takes a while to send all the little ones and zeroes across the four hundred thousand kilometers from the Moon to their big dish, outside."

"When will we see it?"

Good question. Gabdul rechecked the clock and turned up the volume from their Apollo audio receiver. Right on cue, a voice crackled through the speaker on his desk. "Copy, GO for landing."

One of the geologists who spoke some English had been designated as the group interpreter. The voice from the Moon had been scratchy, but she understood the last word. "Skazali prizemlyayutsya!" They said they're landing!

A murmur went through the gathering, and they refocused on the monitor. Gabdul's hand shot out, pointing. "There!" His finger indicated a small blob of light that had appeared on the screen. Everyone leaned forward.

Gabdul mentally counted the 10 seconds until the screen refreshed. When it did, the blob had moved higher in the image, becoming marginally bigger. Each successive refresh made it clearer, until he could start to pick out the shape of the craft. He was closest to the screen, and leaned in.

"Looks like a fat spider," he said. They heard the radio voice say something else, and waited for the translator, who was struggling with the poor audio quality and the unfamiliar jargon.

"I think he said he has seen something." She repeated the English sounds in her head, grasping for the words. Suddenly it clicked. "The rover, the rover, that's us! The astronauts see Lunokhod!"

Wow, Gabdul marveled. *We're looking at each other on the Moon.*

The next image was fuzzy, the lunar lander less distinct against the black. The following image was even worse.

"What's happening?" the interpreter asked.

Gabdul shook his head. He'd feared this. "It's dust, blown at us by their engine." He pushed a button to send a command he'd prepared, and the next image was black.

He turned and looked at the faces, all now frowning at him. "I've closed the covers over our cameras to protect them from the sharp bits of flying dust. Lunokhod is tough, but I don't want our lenses to get scratched." Heads nodded. That made sense. "As soon as we hear they've landed, we'll look again."

The English voice kept repeating one word, and the geologist interpreted. "He's just saying 'Copy,' over and over."

There was a long pause, finally broken by a terse statement in English. The geologist spoke excitedly. "Gabdul, open the lens covers! They've landed on the Moon!"

Gabdul made a small, fervent wish as he sent the command. *I hope we're pointed the right way!*

The signal traveled from his console outside to the enormous dish, sped across the void to the Moon in just over a second and worked its way through Lunokhod's logic circuitry. Two small motors began spinning, and the circular lens covers slowly pivoted down, out of the way. The camera's photo receptors gathered the light and sent the digitized raster scan, line by line, back to his console in Simferopol. Once it was assembled, the new image blinked onto his screen.

Everyone in the room made a noise. Some praised God and a couple said "Look at that!" But most just exhaled in wonder.

Gabdul hadn't guessed perfectly, but on the right-hand side of the screen, where there had been nothing but a flat, monotonous plain, there now stood a spaceship, glittering metallically in the sunlight.

He peered closely at the static image on the screen. It was going to take a while for the Americans to safe their ship, open the hatch and climb outside. So he made a suggestion. "Let's take a smoke break and go look at the Moon!" The group laughed, but many took his advice to head outside. It was 8:20 on a fine Crimean night, and the Moon was near full. A great way for them to reflect on what had just happened.

But as Gabdul lit a cigarette, stepped outside and looked up, he was mulling a new problem. There had been far more dust than he'd expected, and he needed to check Lunokhod's systems for damage. More importantly, though, some of the dust might have landed on top of his rover, where the solar arrays gathered the power that kept it alive and the radiator allowed the internal heat to escape. If there was too much dust, the vehicle could both overheat and run out of power. He stared at the Moon for a few seconds, thinking of ways to clear the dust.

But first, they had to deal with the Americans. The astronauts would soon be climbing down the ladder and walking towards his rover.

Let them come. He took a long drag, the harsh tobacco raw in his throat, the moonlight on his face. *I'm ready.*

44

Mission Control, Houston

The celebration in Mission Control had been enthusiastic but brief. Raised fists, a small roar of relief and hurrahs after the pent-up tension, followed by a few handshakes. Then back to work: make sure *Bulldog* was healthy and get the crew fully dressed and ready to go outside. The real point of the mission, just begun.

Kaz picked up the console phone to call Washington, as directed. He heard two rings, and then the clunking noise of a handset being picked up.

"National Security Agency, General Phillips's office."

"Hi, Jan, Kaz Zemeckis here. Is the General available?"

"He sure is, Lieutenant Commander Zemeckis. Just a second."

A click, followed by Phillips's calm, warm voice.

"Kaz! Good news, I hope?"

"Yes, sir, they're safely on the Moon as of 12:17 Eastern Time, just getting into preparation for their moonwalk now. Best guess is Chad will head down the ladder in about three hours."

"How close did they get to the Soviet rover?"

"We're not sure of the exact distance yet, but Chad landed within sight."

"Excellent! Like Pete did on Apollo 12." In November 1969, just after Phillips had left NASA, the second manned lunar landing had touched down 538 feet from an American probe called Surveyor 3, and the crew had retrieved pieces of it during their spacewalks.

"Yes, sir, a good piece of flying."

"Kaz, I booked the meeting with the Security Council for 15:30. Does that timing sound about right?"

Kaz looked at the flight plan. "Should be good, sir. We'll get an out-the-window description from Chad soon, and that will help set priorities. And we have the Soviet call to the cosmonaut booked for 16:30, to congratulate her once she's standing on the surface."

"Sounds good. How about once you reset the priorities you call me with an update?"

"Will do, sir."

"And Kaz—well done."

It had been a long, unsettled day for Father Ilarion.

He'd missed the chanting of the bell ringer that usually woke him, but his eyes had opened by habit at five a.m., in time for morning prayers. He'd read from his liturgical text in his room until seven. It was nearing the end of the 40-day Lenten fast leading up to Palm Sunday; as always by now, his hunger felt deeply purifying.

He had forgotten about the time zones, though, and was surprised when Alexander arrived at his door to say it was actually nine, time to leave for Ivanteevsky Deanery, the Orthodox church he'd arranged for them to visit before they had to go to Mission Control that night.

The seminarians had quietly welcomed Father Ilarion for prayers, followed by time for reflection and then conversation over a meager lunch. Afterwards, Alexander had made their excuses. They'd walked back to their quarters and, at his interpreter's urging, the monk had tried unsuccessfully to nap in preparation for what would be a late night. Eventually he had risen to observe Vespers and Matins in his room, feeling somehow inadequate conducting the ritual alone, and so far from home.

As suppertime approached, Alexander again knocked on his door. It was time to go.

As they arrived at TsUP, Ilarion leaned against his car window, peering up while they drove the length of the massive, four-story stone-and-glass building and pulled to a stop at the columned entrance.

"Are we here?" There was wonder in his voice. "It's huge, Sascha!"

"Yes, we are here, Father."

The sign over the double doors read Glory to the Soviet Conquest of Space. Underneath it, a man wearing no coat was smoking. He spotted the car, flicked his cigarette to the side and strode across to open the back door.

"Welcome to Mission Control, Father Ilarion. We've been eagerly awaiting you."

The monk's eyes went wide as he followed the man down a long, broad corridor, looking at the portraits on the walls of Director Korolyov, of cosmonauts Gagarin, Tereshkova and Leonov, and a parade of color views of the Earth from high above. *Our world from the heavens*, he marveled.

They rounded a corner, where their escort waved them into a small room with chairs and a sofa set around a low table with food, the dark paneling harshly lit by flickering fluorescent ceiling bulbs.

"Please be comfortable. Someone will be here shortly to bring you to TsUP." He turned and exited, closing the door behind him.

"What time is it, Sascha?" Ilarion asked. He'd lost track again.

"It is nearly 8:30, Father, well past time for supper. I suggest we eat a little and observe Compline before they come for us."

The table was laden with bread, cheese, sliced meat, tomatoes, parsley and cucumbers. Alex prepared two small plates, handing one to the monk, and poured them each a glass of water.

"Sascha," the monk asked, "is my brother already on the Moon?"

Alexander checked his watch. "He should be landing very soon, Father. Perhaps we will be able to watch it."

A boyish smile spread across Ilarion's face. "I would like that very much." He set his plate down and took just a small sip of water. "In truth, I am too excited to eat."

He closed his eyes and calmed himself by quietly chanting a prayer. It was Friday of Great Lent, and he included the memorized verses of the Penitential Office. At the end, he offered a special thanks for the privilege of the day, and a wish for the health and success of his brother.

As the monk opened his eyes, there was a knock on the door. It opened abruptly. The two of them stood as a strong-looking man in a suit entered, wearing an air of unmistakable authority and urgency. He flicked his eyes dismissively past Alexander to rest on the hieromonk.

"Father Ilarion, I am Director Chelomei, Vladimir Nikolayevich. Thank you for traveling all this way. It is an honor to have you in Mission Control."

The monk bowed his head, his high kamilavka and veil magnifying the motion.

"I am glad to tell you that your brother is safely on the Moon."

Ilarion's heart fell that he would not see it, but he gave no sign.

"Soon you will have a chance to speak with him directly. Would you come along with me now?"

The monk nodded and followed Chelomei, with Alexander trailing. They walked down another long corridor, this one ending at a set of wooden doors, where Chelomei stopped, turned and spoke formally. "Welcome to the Center for Control of Soviet Manned Spaceflight." He turned the knob, pushed the door open and gestured for the monk to enter first. The black-robed figure said "Spasiba" quietly and stepped into the heart of the Soviet space program.

It was much bigger than he had expected. *Like a cathedral.* There were rows of consoles to his left, each manned despite the late hour, and a sweeping semicircle of observers' chairs to his right, where a handful of people were seated. Terse, sporadic English came through a loudspeaker. Chelomei led them to the viewing chairs and asked the monk to sit.

"Please be comfortable, Father. Very soon you will speak with your brother." He flicked his finger for the interpreter to follow him, turned and walked quickly towards the center console. Ilarion sat, his gaze probing the strangeness of his surroundings.

The front of the room was dominated by a large, dark screen, showing a map of the Earth with several digital timers above it. An inset TV screen showed a grainy image of what he guessed to be the Moon's surface. The rows of consoles below it glowed green, silhouetting the operators. He noticed Director Chelomei and Alexander, now standing in the middle of the row, talking intently. Chelomei gestured with his hands, one fist forming a ball as the fingertip of the other circled it. The interpreter nodded his head and walked back to Ilarion.

"Father, it's time to talk with your brother. Unfortunately, the radio link is limited, so he won't be able to respond. But he will definitely be able to hear you. Director Chelomei thinks that after his long and dangerous voyage, your voice will be a great comfort to him, giving him strength before he steps outside to walk on the Moon."

The monk's brow furrowed in disappointment. "He won't be able to talk to me?"

Alex shook his head gently. "The Moon is so far away, Father, and he is in an American spaceship, which complicates communication. This is a rare privilege, just barely technically possible." Alexander turned and pointed at the TV screen. "You can just see his ship there — that shiny metal spider on the lunar surface."

Ilarion peered closely at the distant glowing image with eyes weakened from decades of reading in low light, barely making out a glint of reflection standing on the horizon. Suddenly he felt uncertain as to why he had come all this way.

"Are you ready, Father?" Alexander said, interrupting his bleak thoughts. "It will be such a wonderful surprise!"

The monk took a breath, setting his shoulders under the cassock, and nodded. "I am ready."

I did it! The triumph that coursed through Chad felt like fire. Under all the layers of his spacesuit, he could feel that he had an erection. He turned to Svetlana. "We're here!"

She abruptly turned her head and looked outside, uncomfortable with the intensity of his stare. *This is not a nice man. But a very skilled pilot.* She reached down surreptitiously and felt for the angular metal shape she'd transferred to the suit's leg pocket, just in case.

The dust had settled around the ship far more quickly than she'd expected. *Must be because there's no air.* She bounced a little on the balls of her feet inside the roominess of the suit. The strangeness of the low gravity was surprisingly unfamiliar, especially after her weeks in weightlessness. She felt clumsy in it.

Her gaze went to Lunokhod, silhouetted against the blackness of the horizon, harshly shadowed in the blazing sunlight. Chad was looking that way too, and pointed. "Lunokhod!" He pronounced it properly, the guttural sound of the "kho" very familiar in her ears. *Who taught you to say that?*

She turned to the window again and noticed glinting on the Moon's surface. She realized it was crisscrossing tire tracks surrounding the silver rover and trailing off into the distance. *They've been busy here.*

Kaz's voice broke into her thoughts. "*Bulldog*, you'll be glad to hear we've polled the room, and you're Stay for T-1."

Each Mission Control technician had verified that their systems had survived the landing and that they were safe to stay on the Moon for the first orbit of *Pursuit*, high above their heads.

Michael's voice came from *Pursuit*. "Good to hear. Stay there a while! I finally just got the place to myself, stretching my legs a bit."

Svetlana listened as Chad talked with Houston, obviously verifying pressures and throwing switches. He reached back and unlatched something behind her, pulling a water gun on its hose into view. He inserted it through the adapter on the side of his helmet, turned the red valve and took a long drink. Pulling it out, he offered it to her, and she mimicked what he had done, grateful for the liquid, suddenly aware of how thirsty breathing the dry oxygen in the suit had made her. She traced the hose back and restowed it.

"Cenk yu," she said. Chad ignored her, focused on working procedures with Houston. She looked back outside.

Why had they landed so near Lunokhod? In the briefing, the interpreter had said there was going to be just one moonwalk, so landing here must serve the main purpose of the mission. But the astronaut's death and her being on board had been a huge modification to their original plans. So was this new plan somehow related to her being there? She'd already reasoned that even though she was unfamiliar with the American equipment, they wouldn't have risked sending Chad to the surface alone; if he fell or had suit problems, they needed someone to assist him. But the only thing they'd told her that she was going to do was to climb down the ladder, stand on the Moon, talk to Moscow and go back inside *Bulldog*. Typical window dressing! What were they really doing here?

Once she was down the ladder, she realized, no one could stop her from moving around. She'd definitely walk the distance to Lunokhod and have a detailed look. The Soviet engineers would appreciate her description of what the months on the Moon had done to it. She also wanted to figure out the reason for all the tracks. She'd look for what the rover was looking for.

Michael's voice came through her headset. "Hey, *Bulldog* and Houston, *Pursuit's* about to go behind the Moon. I'll be back with you in forty-five minutes or so."

Kaz responded. "Copy, *Pursuit*, enjoy the solitude. See you at 101:19 mission time—that'll be 12:40, lunchtime here in Houston."

Michael clicked his mic twice in response.

Chelomei smiled at the sound. Almost time. As soon as the orbiting ship was blocked by the Moon, he'd be able to talk to the crew on the surface. He'd been thinking carefully about what to say and how best to use the monk. He looked up to see the interpreter and the black-robed figure making their way towards his console, and glanced at the TsUP clock. He decided to wait another five minutes, just to be sure. He raised an open hand for the pair to stay back, out of earshot.

In *Bulldog*, Chad heard Michael's call and thought about what that meant. He reached across and switched both him and Svetlana off hot mic. To respond, they'd need to push a transmit switch. He needed to be able to control what the cosmonaut said.

He checked the cabin pressure and began removing his gloves and helmet, gesturing for her to do the same. They'd need to eat, and then attach all the extra equipment to their suits before going outside. As he temp-stowed the gear, he went over the moonwalk plan in his head. *It's all on me.* This was why he'd loved flying single-seat fighters. Only his decisions mattered. His skills, his ideas, his actions. Every one of those nobodies in Houston—hell, in Moscow too—needed *him.* The power of it was exquisite. Only he had the whole picture, and everyone else had to ask him for what they wanted.

He looked at the cosmonaut as she lifted the helmet off her head. Especially her. *She's mine to control.*

They both heard the Russian voice simultaneously.

"Transmission test, transmission test, how do you hear me?" Chelomei paused briefly, and then said, "If you can hear me, call Houston for a comm check."

Svetlana's head whipped around to look at Chad.

He was looking directly at her, smiling oddly, as if he had anticipated her reaction. His eyes narrowed slightly, and he said one word to her. "Podozhdi!" The command for an underling to wait.

She was shocked. Had he just said a Russian word? She had to repeat it again in her head in order to believe it. He *had*, clearly, with no accent!

He held up his hand with a finger raised, staring at her intently—the clear signal to wait for him to do something.

Without breaking eye contact, he pushed the mic button on the control stick. "Houston, *Bulldog,* comm check."

Kaz answered by reflex. "Loud and clear, how us?"

Chad sneered, just a little, his eyes boring into hers. "Five by, thanks, just checking."

They waited. The voice spoke again in Russian.

"Thank you. Senior Lieutenant Gromova, if you can hear this transmission, cough twice."

Chad thought about it, then pointed at her and pushed the mic button.

Svetlana was confused, but coughed as requested, her mind reeling.

Chad released her mic and toggled his own. "Sorry, Houston, she's just coughing a bit in *Bulldog'*s dry air."

"Copy, Chad, let us know if it's a problem," Kaz responded. "SURGEON is standing by."

Chelomei was pleased—the astronaut was cooperating—but knew he had to keep it short. "Listen to me," he said. "You'll see we have parked Lunokhod in a very specific location. Just under the front of the rover, you'll find a good-sized stone. You will retrieve it without telling Houston, and stow it separately in your ship, so you know which one it is. Click your mic twice if you understand."

Chad pushed the mic button twice.

In Houston, Kaz heard the double click and a puzzled expression crossed his face. *Someone bumped the mic button again? What the hell?*

The Russian voice continued in Chad's and Svetlana's headsets. "We have your brother here, Major Miller. He is fine, but we hold him in our palm, like a dove."

Svetlana saw Chad's eyes narrow. *What the hell is going on?*

Chelomei waved for the cleric and interpreter to come closer. "Here is your brother," he said. He held the microphone up to the monk's mouth, pushed the button and nodded.

Ilarion was nervous, and Alexander quietly prompted him. "Speak to your brother, Father, he needs you."

Oddly, the monk felt like crying as he spoke. "Yuri? Yuri, they say you can hear me but cannot answer. That is okay." He felt the need to reassure his little brother as best he could.

Svetlana's eyes widened even further. *Yuri?* This new voice had called Chad by the name of Yuri. Was this American astronaut Russian?

"Yuri, I am so proud of you," the voice continued, full of emotion. "What you are doing is magnificent, and for all of mankind. You have taken great risks and traveled so far, and done our family honor, but also I will be so glad to see you safely back here on Earth."

Chelomei frowned slightly and made a spinning motion with one finger. Wrap it up.

The monk grew flustered. "Um, there was something I wanted to say to you, Yuri. Ah yes—you will need much strength to complete your voyage. Know that you have it from me, and more importantly, if our blessed mother were still alive, her pride would be pouring over you."

Alexander spoke softly. "Time to finish, Father."

"I bless you, and God is watching over you to make a safe return, my dear brother. Glory to the Father and to the Son and to the Holy Spirit, now and ever and forever. Amen."

Chelomei released the mic button and nodded at the interpreter, satisfied. That would do. He waved them back towards their seats, then pushed the mic button again. "You'll hear from us again officially via Houston while you're outside." He quickly reviewed whether he'd said all he wanted.

Enough. "Vsyo," he transmitted.

———

Chad was holding her gaze, his face unreadable.

She was incredulous. "Ti—ti gavorisch pa russki!" You—you speak Russian!

He gave no response, and his expression didn't change. He picked up his checklist, turned away and went back to working procedures.

Svetlana felt like she was falling. *What just happened?* She was sure the first voice she'd heard had been Director Chelomei's. How had he contacted them, and why couldn't they respond?

Was this astronaut a spy? If he was, then why were they threatening him with his brother?

Treat this like any emergency, she told herself. *I'm a test pilot, dammit! What do I know, and what should my actions be?*

She pictured how the comm system must work, imagining what her people must have built to intercept it. She glanced through the overhead window at the Earth to confirm that Russia was facing them—it was, just turning out of sight on the darkened side of the planet. She realized that they could listen to Moscow, but could not reply directly or the Americans would overhear them.

The small solution calmed her. She was gaining some control.

But how did Chad come to speak Russian? Had they taught him that in America? Not likely, given that he had a pious Russian brother who had called him Yuri.

He was still ignoring her, behaving as if nothing had happened, unclipping from his restraint cable and methodically retrieving items to get ready for the moonwalk. It was clear that he wasn't going to explain himself. That meant she had to find a path through this alone. Not giving away Chelomei's secrets, and scheming a way to do what he had just asked. Svetlana unclipped from her own restraint cable and looked around the unfamiliar landing ship, sizing up her options.

She was going to have to count on this astronaut. But she'd been right not to trust him.

—

Kaz took a sip of coffee. Years as a fighter test pilot had taught him to pay attention to the smallest, most insignificant breaks in any routine or expected course of action. Why had he heard a double click again? Michael was behind the Moon, so it wasn't him bumping the mic. It had to be coming from *Bulldog* on the surface. Could the cosmonaut be trying to get their attention? Did Soviets double-click? If it was Chad, why would he do that?

He squinted to moisten his eye; the air-conditioned air was so dry his eyelid was sticking. As he blinked to clear it, he looked up at the timer: two hours until hatch opening. The Security Council would meet shortly after that. He put down his cup and picked up the checklist. *Forget mic clicks for now. I need to be prepared.*

He glanced up as JW passed him, heading for the Flight Director console, and he stood to listen in. JW spoke quietly to the two of them. "A few minutes ago, for no reason I could see, both Chad's and Svetlana's heart rates spiked. Like something happened that surprised them both. Hers, especially—I saw a hundred and forty beats per minute. Yet per the timeline and after checking with other consoles, they were just standing there, doing a comm check with us, setting switches."

Gene took a deep pull on his cigarette, considering, and then stubbed it out in the full ashtray on his console. "Struggling to take their helmets off, maybe?"

JW shook his head. "We compared to previous flights, and it doesn't match. Plus, it was simultaneous. Like they both suddenly saw or heard something they weren't expecting." He paused. "We did hear the cosmonaut cough, but Chad called down about that."

Gene picked up his copy of the checklist, running his nicotine-stained finger down the timeline, finding nothing. He looked at Kaz. "Any ideas?"

"I wasn't going to mention it, but I also heard a double click from them around that time. I assumed one of them bumped the switch."

Gene paused, thinking. "How do their heart rates look now, Doc?"

"Hers is higher than it was, but acceptable. Chad's is back to normal."

"What do you recommend?"

"Nothing for now, FLIGHT. There's probably some simple answer. But it was out of the ordinary and I thought you should know."

JW looked at Kaz and raised his eyebrows. Kaz shrugged in agreement. Not serious enough to be alarming, and not enough info to respond in any way.

Gene decided. "Thanks, Doc. Keep watching them closely, especially the cosmonaut. Once they head outside, we need to be ready to order her back in if you don't like what you see. I don't want either of them anywhere near the cooling limits of the suit."

45

Bulldog

Having Luke's corpse in the way made their moonwalk suit-up awkward. As Chad retrieved the needed items, one by one, talking with Houston, it felt like he had to move the bulky, suited body every time. But at least, in one-sixth gravity, it was light.

Throughout, he was aware of Svetlana watching him, her face intense and wary, right beside him in the tiny space. He occasionally handed her an item and pantomimed what to do with it—which pocket it went into or how it mounted on her suit.

"Obyasni po russki!" she demanded. Explain in Russian!

He ignored her. She could figure it out, and no way was he admitting anything that gave her an advantage. *Control is everything.*

When he got to tool prep, he paused, considering. She'd seen Luke with the bolt cutters at Almaz, and she knew he'd landed *Bulldog* next to the Soviet rover on purpose. No doubt she'd already put two and two together, and might do something stupid. He decided to leave the cutters stowed until he figured out a way to get them outside without alerting her.

Chad meticulously checked their outsized backpacks. On the moonwalk all their life support would be contained in them, with no link to the mother ship. When he finished, he got her to assist him with donning his, and then he helped her with hers.

"Houston, we're putting the PLSSes on, and I'm about to start connecting the plumbing, if you can talk me through the procedures." He pronounced it "plisses"—the prosaically named Portable Life Support System.

"Will do, Chad. We're with you on page 2-6. Let's start with the O2 hoses." As Kaz read the checklist, Chad confirmed each connection and double-checked function.

The interpreter's voice came through in Russian. "Svetlana, how do you hear Houston?"

Chad pressed her mic button so she could reply. "I hear you well, how me?"

"Houston hears you well. Let us know if you have questions."

Hearing the Russian words finally broke Svetlana's composure. She grabbed Chad's shoulder and turned him so they were face to face. "This is stupid! Your brother said your name is Yuri! You speak Russian. Why are you pretending you don't?" Her Russian was rapid fire as she spit out the words.

Chad shrugged out from under her grip and squinted at her in apparent incomprehension. "What are you babbling about, toots?" He pointed to the US flag on her shoulder. "This is an American ship. A-mer-i-can." He pronounced each syllable. "Speak English!"

She exhaled in frustration. She was certain he'd said some Russian words to her and, more importantly, that he had understood Chelomei and the person Chelomei said was his brother. She took several deep breaths, calming herself, puzzling it out. Chad was ignoring it, but Chelomei must have something on him, and had chosen his moment carefully for leverage and so their interchange would stay a secret. Also, she realized, knowing that Chad spoke Russian might work to her advantage.

I'll play this game, she resolved. *For now.*

Chad was holding her helmet up, motioning that it was time to put it on. She guided it into place, the mechanism making a loud click as it locked into the suit's neck ring. Chad attached the visor assembly to it, and then donned his own. He handed gloves to her, and she put them on.

He moved switches on *Bulldog's* control panel and on the suits, and she felt cooling water flowing and heard the steady hiss of continuous communication, listening to the conversation between Chad and Houston in her helmet.

Chad grabbed her arm to check that her gloves were attached properly, and then reached for more switches. She felt air moving in the suit as it pressurized, and cleared her ears. *Feels just like our suits.*

Kaz's voice came into their headsets, verifying that the specialists in Houston who had been watching the suit data had verified no leaks. "Chad, both suits look tight at 3.8 psi delta."

Chad tugged on Svetlana's sleeve again and pointed to the pressure gauge on her wrist, nodding and holding up three fingers, then eight. "Roger, Kaz, both look steady here."

"*Bulldog,* you'll be glad to know you are GO for depress." Permission to vent the ship's oxygen out into the vacuum of space, in final preparation for the moonwalk.

"Copy, here it comes." Chad reached down between the two of them and rotated the hatch pressure handle to Open.

"*Bulldog,* we see pressure dropping. Rates look good."

Svetlana's suit was stiff, like a balloon. She wiggled her fingers, looking at them, marveling at the dexterity. *They have a better design.*

It took three minutes for the cabin pressure to go to zero. Chad tapped the gauge with his fingertip, watching the needle settle.

"Houston, I show nothing on the gauge. Opening the hatch now."

"Copy, *Bulldog.*"

He turned the handle, pulled hard to overcome the tiny bit of remaining air pressure and rotated the hatch inwards, pushing Svetlana out of the way to get it fully open. Sunlight streamed in around their booted feet.

He stood back up and turned the cooling system on for both suits—a water sprayer that instantly evaporated into the nothingness, like sweat, taking away heat.

"Sublimator waters are open, Houston."

JW had been watching Chad's heart rate with all the extra activity. "FLIGHT, Chad's heart is up around one-forty. Suggest he take a short break."

Gene Kranz nodded, and Kaz spoke. "Chad, just hold a second while we instruct Svetlana." Two birds. He nodded for the interpreter.

"Svetlana, Houston. Chad is about to exit and set up preliminary gear. We want you to stay where you are until instructed. If you get too cold or hot, let us know. Eventually, we'll have you come down the ladder. The entire moonwalk will be five hours max. Do you understand?"

"Ponyala."

Svetlana had squeezed back against the dead body, trying to make room as Chad turned and got down on his hands and knees to back out. His voice was labored with the effort.

"Houston, I'm climbing out now."

Kaz looked across at JW, who gave him a thumbs-up. "Copy, Chad, the doc's okay with your heart rate. Let us know as you deploy the MESA." The Modular Equipment Stowage Assembly would pivot down from the exterior of the lander when released, opening access to needed tools and uncovering the video camera that would transmit live Apollo 18 images from the Moon's surface.

Chad answered. "Okay, Kaz. Pulling the D-ring now." A short pause, with just his breathing audible. "There she goes."

Gene Kranz spoke. "INCO, let's get that TV image up ASAP."

"In work, FLIGHT."

All eyes turned to the front screen as the blank video image suddenly resolved into a familiar scene, the grainy white of the ladder angling down from the dark LM to the gray lunar surface. The bulk of Chad's white-suited legs were visible, his feet on the rungs.

In their back room, Laura and the geology team all leaned close to their monitors to see this first video image. As she figured out exactly where they had landed and what was on the surrounding terrain, Laura felt a wave of exhilaration course through her. *All right! We're here!*

A white object suddenly arced down through the scene, followed by another, falling slowly.

"Houston, I've chucked the equipment bags out. Climbing down to the surface now."

"Copy, Chad, we're all watching you through the MESA camera."

Chad paused a moment to take a deep breath, reveling. They *were* all watching. Watching *him*! He squeezed hard on the rung, through his glove. Feeling it, exulting in the reality of it. He turned his head inside the helmet, looking around to absorb the moment. *I'm about to step onto the fucking Moon!*

He bounced slightly in the weak gravity, his feet feeling for the last rung, and hopped down onto the circular foot of the LM's landing leg. Letting go with one hand, he turned, got his balance and stepped out onto the surface.

"Houston, this blue-eyed American boy is standing on the Moon."

His lips curled in triumph. All it had taken was a lifetime of hard work and the strategic loosening of one nut.

In DC, all eyes around the table were staring at the television in the corner.

Nixon rasped, "What's he doing now?"

Sam Phillips, the National Security Council meeting's space expert after his years leading Apollo at NASA, answered. "Major Miller has set up the TV camera, and he's now doing a visual survey around the lander. Shortly he'll start a traverse to the Soviet rover. He'll gather as many rocks as possible along the way to bring back for the geologists to analyze." Best to give the boss context.

"And the woman cosmonaut is waiting inside?"

"Yes, sir, until we're ready for the call from Russia, then she'll climb down the ladder to the surface." He checked his watch. "That's in about an hour from now. Miller will get the US flag set up in the meantime, and make sure the Soviet rover isn't in the shot, so we can rebroadcast it later."

Kissinger's bassoon voice rumbled. "You should talk to Miller first, Mr. President, and separately, to clearly show American preeminence."

Bob Haldeman piped in, "That's the way we have it set up, sir."

Nixon nodded. "What do we have to decide here today?"

Sam Phillips was the one to reply. "We don't like the Soviets gaining any advantage in discoveries on the Moon, and this new rover of theirs is far more capable than any that NASA has landed. It could work for months or even years, surviving the cold of lunar nights with its polonium-210 internal heater. Once Miller has had a close look at what it's doing and taken detailed pictures, we think he should disable it in a way that allows deniability. That needs to be done off camera and without the cosmonaut seeing. It needs to look like it was disabled by the blast of the *Bulldog*'s engine, for instance, rather than by deliberate action."

He was looking into the eyes of each of the men around the table. "The Soviets are only in contact with their rover when their big antenna in Simferopol is facing the Moon, and that ends in about an hour. Miller has bolt cutters on board, and we have some other ideas that might work as well. But with this Council's approval, Mr. President, by the time Apollo 18 blasts off the Moon tomorrow, Lunokhod will be dying, or dead."

Nixon didn't move, waiting for any dissenting voices. Silence.

He lifted his head to take a long look at Phillips, and then he nodded. "If you take no risks, you win no victories. Do it."

Inside *Bulldog*, Svetlana was bending as far as the suit would allow so she could watch what Chad was doing outside through the window.

The voice from Houston had instructed her to wait, but Moscow had given clear instructions about retrieving a specific rock from Lunokhod.

She stared at the rover on the horizon. How long would it take to walk that far? Could she trust the American to do what Moscow had asked?

No.

She'd studied how he'd climbed down the ladder. The hatch was wide open. But how would Houston react to her leaving the lander? If she could stay out of sight of the camera, how would they even know?

A thought occurred to her, and she studied the switches and circuit breakers in the cockpit. Her English was rudimentary, but a far-thinking high school teacher had forced her to learn the alphabet. She silently thanked her now as she sounded out the printed names, hunting for two specific letters and hoping their engineers had kept the labeling simple.

"Chyort!" she muttered. So many! Why hadn't she paid closer attention to the switches he'd moved before going outside? She paused to picture exactly where his hands had moved.

She found a row labeled Comm and sounded it out. English was so confusing; was the "C" hard or soft? She tried saying both, and suddenly realized that it was probably short for "communications," a technical English word she knew. Excitedly, she checked each of the breakers' names in the sub-row below it.

And there it was, the last one on the right side. Exactly like she'd hoped.

TV.

"Televizor" in Russian. He *had* reached for that one. She rapidly checked the rest of the panels to be sure it was the only circuit breaker labeled that way. She looked back at it closely. It was a standard design, meaning she'd just have to squeeze it between her thumb and two forefingers and pull. It would pop out, unpowering the TV camera. Houston wouldn't see her coming down the ladder.

But when to do it?

She looked back out the window, not seeing him. *Blyad!* Had he already headed for Lunokhod?

She twisted further and spotted movement on the far left. Chad was still near, unstowing something beside one of the lander's legs. It had two dinner-plate-sized, fat rubber tires on it, and he was unfolding long, parallel handles out and locking them into place.

Tachka, she decided. A wheelbarrow. For carrying things like tools. And rocks. That meant he was almost ready.

She touched the gun in her pocket. So was she.

At his console in Simferopol, Gabdul moved his hand controller carefully. Director Chelomei in Moscow was watching Lunokhod's video feed, and had demanded the best view he could give him; Gabdul was precisely turning the rover so its cameras were facing the Apollo lander, but without damaging the Ugol rock underneath.

There! That ought to do it. He stopped and looked at the slowly refreshing black-and-white still image to see if he'd gotten it right.

The metallic glint of the NASA ship was centered in the frame. "Otlichna," he muttered in satisfaction. Perfect.

He leaned close to the screen. He could just make out a white blob by the legs of the lander. As each new image processed, the blob was in a different place. *Spacewalker*, he concluded. He watched several successive frames. The blob was slowly getting clearer and larger. One of the images caught a reflective glint off the helmet's reflective coating. *And now he's headed our way.*

Chelomei's harsh voice came through the squawk box.

"I see the astronaut. Are you ready?"

"Da, Glavni Director. We are ready." Gabdul rubbed his palms on his legs to wipe off the sweat.

He quickly double-checked his command selections, watching the spacewalker get bigger with each image.

Not spacewalker, he corrected himself wryly. *Moonwalker.* "Lunokhod" in Russian. *Same as us.*

———

"Houston, Chad here, you'll want to see this." His voice was breathy with physical exertion.

Kaz looked intently at the front screen, watching the white of Chad's spacesuit against the moonscape as he bulkily walked towards Lunokhod, hauling the small handcart behind him.

"See what, Chad?"

The figure had stopped and was pointing off to the right.

"There's a really dark spot flush with the surface over there. Maybe a couple hundred feet away, hard to tell. Want me to go have a closer look?"

Kaz ran through possible explanations and mission priorities in his head.

"Chad, are there any rover tracks near what you're seeing?"

"Nope. Pristine Moon dirt. I mean, regolith."

Kaz nodded. If the Soviets hadn't investigated it, they likely hadn't seen it. He glanced at the Flight Director for a decision.

Gene said, "CAPCOM, Lunokhod survey is priority for now. Geology can wait a few more minutes—the rocks aren't going anywhere. Tell him we'll have him swing by it on the way back."

When Kaz passed the word, Chad shrugged. He'd been trying out different ways to walk, balancing the stiff bulk of the suit with the strange lightness of one-sixth gravity. Like the moonwalkers before him, he settled on a two-footed loping, hopping motion.

Kaz pushed a button on his comm panel to talk to the geology back room. "Laura, I'm sure you heard what Chad said."

Her excitement came through his headset. "Sure did! We think we see a smudge where he pointed, but need to get a closer look to know for sure. Can Michael zoom in and see anything when he passes overhead in *Pursuit*?"

"Good idea. He's just back on our side of the Moon again now. I'll ask him."

Kaz reset his comm switches. "*Pursuit*, Houston, welcome back Earthside. How was the view around back?"

The delight in Michael's voice was palpable. "Kaz, you can tell Pink Floyd I have *Dark Side of the Moon* playing full blast on cassette up here!"

Kaz smiled. "I'm just glad I don't have to hear you singing along. Meanwhile, you probably overheard Chad, but we'd like you to look closely at the landing site with the sextant telescope. Let us know if you see anything worth investigating."

"Already on it, wilco."

Michael floated down to the Nav panel, carefully grabbing the small joystick with his fingertips to point the telescope.

Kaz had an idea. "Svetlana, Houston, how are you doing?" The State Department interpreter translated.

"Normalna." Fine.

Kaz nodded for the interpreter to describe to her where to look. Svetlana leaned towards the window and peered hard off to the right of Lunokhod as directed, squinting against the harsh contrast of the light.

"There are dusty rolling hills and lots of small rocks," she said. "The Sun is not too high, so the shadows are fairly long." *Be methodical!* She followed the line of Chad's new footprints and deliberately searched to the right.

"I see one odd shadow, like a low spot. Maybe a small crater."

The interpreter translated for the room, and Kaz nodded thoughtfully. "Copy, thanks."

Svetlana looked back at Chad. *Time to do something.*

Chelomei had been listening intently. *What are the Americans seeing?* He looked at the timer: 40 minutes until the big dish in Simferopol could no longer see the Moon and they lost direct comms. On the screen, the astronaut was almost at Lunokhod. He heard him speak.

"Houston, I'm approaching the rover and starting to take pictures."

Chad turned his whole body to point the chest-mounted Hasselblad motor-drive camera, reaching underneath to squeeze the pistol grip trigger.

Kaz watched the distant figure shuffling slowly around the silver rover, small on the screen. "Copy, Chad. Those photos will be of great interest to our intel folks here."

"Kaz, it looks a lot like we expected: an eight-wheeled silver bathtub with a solar array lid open, a bunch of instruments dangling on arms out front." Chad completed his circuit and looked closely. "Three cameras on the front, and looks like a few wide-angle camera lenses on the side and back." He glanced up at the Earth. "They're probably looking at me right now."

Chelomei listened through his interpreter and nodded. Would this astronaut comply? Had the threat of harming his brother been enough? *Get the rock, and don't say anything!*

On the screen at the front of Mission Control, the TV video from *Bulldog* suddenly went blank.

From long experience, Gene Kranz gave it 30 seconds, allowing for a possible handover between ground antennas. When it persisted, he asked. "INCO, why'd we lose video?"

"FLIGHT, we're checking. Looks like it lost power."

Gene visualized the circuitry in his head. "Any other systems down?"

INCO was listening through his headset to the sudden blare of technical chatter in his back room, trying to filter out relevant information. "Don't think so. Electrical current drop matches just the camera power-down."

Gene rubbed his chin, frowning. During Apollo 12, Al Bean had inadvertently pointed the camera at the Sun while setting it up, and burned out the internal sensor. Doing the rest of the moonwalks blind had been a nightmare.

But doable.

"Okay, let me know what our troubleshooting options are. CAPCOM, let the EVA crew know. Everybody watch their data closely to make sure we don't have any cascading anomalies."

Kaz summarized the info to Chad and had the interpreter tell Svetlana, noting that it might affect her media event later.

After a short pause, JW spoke. "FLIGHT, SURGEON, I do have one other thing, probably unrelated. A few minutes ago, we lost the cosmonaut's biomed data. We've seen that happen before on other flights, and I wasn't too confident she'd get her sensors applied properly."

Gene frowned. "TELMU, is there any way we have a common cause between those two systems?"

Bulldog's electrical specialist shook his head. "No, FLIGHT, they're totally separate. Must be coincidence."

Gene Kranz scowled. He hated coincidences.

Michael's voice crackled from lunar orbit. "Houston, *Pursuit*, I just finished the overhead pass and am ready with observations."

Kaz thought they could use some good news. "Go ahead, *Pursuit*."

"It was easy to spot the long, straight line of the rille though the scope, and Lunokhod's tire tracks catch the light differently, so they helped as well. Pointing the sextant, I could just make out *Bulldog* on the surface." There was distinct pride in his voice. It had been finicky work. Some of the other Command Module pilots hadn't been able to do it.

"Nice work. You've got eyes like a hawk!"

"I looked where I think Chad meant and saw a few shadows. But one of them looked blacker and more distinct. Sort of crescent-shaped."

"Copy. Where is it relative to the LM?"

Michael pictured the long rille valley and the speck of *Bulldog*. "About halfway to the rille, and a bit north. Maybe have Chad aim thirty degrees or so left of *Bulldog* when he's walking back."

"Thanks, Michael, excellent intel, wilco."

Chad retrieved a long set of tongs from the handcart. With the video camera down, Houston was no longer watching him.

Too easy!

He walked around in front of Lunokhod, bent down in front of the lobster-like camera eyes and waved. He was confident that the tiny antenna on top couldn't be giving Moscow real-time video; they'd just be seeing fuzzy stills. He held his free hand up long enough for them to get an image.

Keep them guessing.

The rock they were interested in was supposed to be under the front end. He crouched as far as the suit would let him and reached in with the tongs. He probed a few times, pushing into the gritty resistance of the abrasive soil, feeling around until there was a hard stop. When he bent to try to see what he was running into, Lunokhod suddenly moved. Chad spasmed back clumsily in surprise, dropping the tongs, as all eight wheels spun and the rover lurched backwards for a yard or so. Then it stopped.

Shit!

"FLIGHT, SURGEON, we just saw a spike in Chad's heart rate. Without video, we recommend a check-in with him."

Gene nodded at Kaz.

"Hey, Chad, Kaz here, how's it going?"

Chad felt his heart pounding in his chest and guessed why they'd called. He deliberately calmed his voice. "All fine here on the Moon, thanks, Kaz. Just dropped the damned tool and tripped as I was retrieving rocks."

"Copy, no sweat. Since we've lost video, the Lunar Geology back room requests that you narrate as you go so they can track where each sample came from."

"Wilco, starting now."

He dropped into the patter they'd practiced in the sim, keeping it going as he looked back at the rover to see what its move had revealed. "The soil around Lunokhod is fine-grained, and much darker where the tracks have churned it up . . ."

An angular black rock was now sitting clear of Lunokhod's nose, jutting up out of the disturbed powdery regolith.

He pivoted his whole torso, the stiffness of the suit making it hard to see straight down, and finally spotted where the tongs had fallen. Other astronauts had warned him that picking things up off the surface was hard, and he didn't want to fall over. He bent his knees as far as he could, blindly reaching, and grabbed the metal shaft just as he started to topple over frontwards. He let the pressure of the suit bounce him back up and took a couple of steps to regain his balance.

"Whooee, Houston, just getting my balance here."

"Copy, Chad." Kaz looked at the timeline. "We're right on track. Once you've gathered enough samples so we can figure out what Lunokhod's been looking at, we'll have you start back towards *Bulldog*."

"Roger that. I'm going to start gathering local rocks with the tongs now." He squeezed the handle with both hands to open the tongs all the way, swung it into place over the rock and released, letting the springs clamp down. Lifting carefully, he turned and released it into the handcart.

It didn't look like much. He picked it up, turning it in the sunlight, startled by how light it felt. Sunlight glinted off internal crystals, and it had a dark, layered appearance, somewhere between deep red and black.

He looked around for similar rocks, but saw none.

How did you get here? And why are the Russkies so interested in you?

He pulled a plastic sample bag out of the larger duffel, carefully slid the rock in and rolled and twisted the wire top to seal it. He'd brought two collection bags, to make sure he kept this rock separate. Only he'd know which bag contained what.

He grabbed a collection rake from the cart and started gathering more samples, once more describing what he was seeing.

In Moscow, Chelomei had been watching the slow-motion sequence unfold, one still image at a time. He'd yelled at the technician in Simferopol to back Lunokhod up, and was gratified to see the result.

"Otlichna!" His plan had worked! The stone had been retrieved and was sitting there in the cart now on the first leg of its long journey back to Earth.

He glanced at the clock, seeing with surprise that it was already past midnight. He yawned hugely, suddenly aware of his exhaustion.

Kvatit. Enough. He gave the order to send the monk and his interpreter back to the hotel, since the American astronaut was behaving.

He just had time for a quick rest in his office before the joint press event with NASA. He nodded at the flight director, and turned to leave, thinking ahead to his next steps.

Gabdul's voice stopped him, sounding tinny through the squawk box on the Moscow flight director console.

"We see the second astronaut climbing down the ladder now."

What? Chelomei whipped around to face the image on the monitor. In the distance, beyond the nearby American and his handcart, there was a distinct blob of white against the angular shape of the lander.

He urgently queried the flight director. "Are we still hearing the astronaut?"

"Da, Comrade Director." He turned the volume up on the sound of the male voice steadily speaking.

The interpreter clarified. "He's talking about the geology of the samples he's gathering."

"Did the astronaut tell Lieutenant Gromova to come outside? Has she said anything recently?" It was frustrating not to be hearing what Houston had transmitted to the crew.

A headshake. "Nyet, Director."

What is she up to? He watched as the still images showed her leave the ladder and start walking. Towards Lunokhod.

46

Le Monnier Crater

Svetlana moved her head carefully, looking around the blocky structure of the LM up into the blackness of the sky, gauging the turn of the Earth. The western edge of Russia was still visible; she figured Moscow could see and hear them for another hour or so.

Good.

By squirming inside the suit, she'd dislodged the stick-on sensor from her ribs to hide her heart rate, and she was glad she had, given that she'd staggered when she'd let go of the ladder. She hadn't walked in weeks, and the oversized suit made her balance even worse. She'd grabbed the ladder again and held on until the dizziness passed.

Carefully, she let go and moved away from the LM, taking small steps. *Like a toddler learning to walk. I even have a diaper on!*

She cautiously followed the single line of tracks and twin wheel marks towards Lunokhod, feeling the blistering heat of the Sun through the fabric of her suit. *Take it easy, Sveta,* she counseled herself. She hoped the constant chatter between Chad and Houston would mask any extra breathing noises from her.

339

She kept her eyes on Chad in the distance. He was holding a long tool, alternately digging and working at the handcart, paying attention to Lunokhod and the soil around it. *Has he retrieved the rock?* She was able to move faster as she adapted, mimicking the gait she'd watched him use to move across the surface, willing him to keep his back turned.

She moved with purpose. Moscow had given orders. She was there to make sure he carried them out.

"FLIGHT, we're seeing odd data from Svetlana's EMU." The puzzlement in TELMU's voice was reflected on his face as he turned to look across the consoles at Gene Kranz. "Without her heart rate it's hard to tell, but it looks like she's moving around or something, breathing more, using more oxygen." His voice tailed off.

Gene's response was crisp. "Anything out of limits?"

The specific question got him back on secure ground. "No, FLIGHT, the suit is fine, all well within norms."

Gene pictured her in the LM, alone. She should be just standing there. What was she up to?

"CAPCOM, have the interpreter check in with the cosmonaut."

Kaz gave quick instructions, waiting for a gap in Chad's geology reporting, and the Russian language request went up.

"Svetlana, Houston. How are you doing?"

Svetlana abruptly stopped walking. Hearing Russian out here, unexpectedly, it felt like she'd been caught.

Why are they asking? Maybe they were seeing something in her suit data and she just needed to give them a reason for it.

"Normalna. I've been moving my arms and legs around to keep from falling asleep."

Kaz and the interpreter glanced at TELMU, who shrugged and nodded his head.

"Copy, thanks. The event with Moscow Mission Control will be in about an hour."

She made herself sound bored. "Gatova, spasiba." *I'm ready, thanks.*

She'd kept her eye on Chad during the exchange, but he'd been preoccupied with lifting a new sample and was still facing away. She started moving again and picked up the pace.

To Chelomei, it sounded like Houston was somehow okay with the cosmonaut being outside. *Can they not see her?* He watched the Lunokhod camera image as she began moving again.

He checked one of the timers at the front of the room; the orbiting capsule would be on the Earth side of the Moon for another 30 minutes. If he called now, that astronaut, the *Pursuit* pilot, would hear. He did the math. There'd be a half hour or so after *Pursuit* went behind the Moon when he could call. That was an ace up his sleeve, to be played if he needed it.

Patience, he told himself. But he hadn't gotten this far by being a patient man.

"There are many small crystalline rocks in this sample, an admixture of basaltic and anorthositic, up to maybe an inch across, maximum. Color and morphology appear to confirm they are largely made of the same material as the regolith." Chad continued his description as he tipped the collector on the rake into a bag.

"Copy, Chad," Kaz said in a monotone.

No wonder, Chad thought. *Geology is fucking boring.*

As he sealed the sample bag, he paused to look around at where he was. He turned his head deliberately, left and then right, like a male lion. Top of the food chain. He peered out onto the flat, gray-brown terrain and the perfect blackness of the lunar sky above. No one else had ever been here, in all of history, to see this. The power of that, the realization that it was only *him*, felt like a hit of narcotic. Victory running through his veins.

He twisted his neck inside the helmet, turning to look at the Earth. Of all those losers, only *he* had made it here.

Then he saw movement.

Another moonwalker, 50 feet away, coming towards him.

What the? How did she get outside? He ran the recent conversation with Houston back in his mind. They thought she was still in *Bulldog*!

He took a breath and opened his mouth to challenge her, but stopped. Secrets were good.

He raised both hands waist-high, palms up. *What are you doing?*

She continued towards him, raising one finger to her visor. The sign for silence.

He reached up and rotated the gold visor off his face, squinting hard against the glare. She watched, and did the same. Now they could read each other's facial expressions.

She gestured with her chin at Lunokhod and pantomimed scooping something solid up with her hand. She raised her eyebrows.

He stared at her, his face impassive. *No reason to make it easy for her.*

She held his gaze for a moment, and then looked away towards the rover, her lips tight with frustration. She reached past him to grab the tongs from the handcart, and walked towards Lunokhod, trying to read the disturbed soil and tracks. His footprints were all over, but the underlying wheel tracks showed where it had recently driven forward and backed up again.

Why?

As she was watching, the rover lurched into motion. It rolled straight towards her, slowly, and then stopped. She glanced at Chad, who stood watching her.

They're signaling me, she decided. As she watched, a slender arm pivoted down, touching the lunar surface in a darker, hollowed-out area, as if it were pointing. After 10 seconds the arm rotated back up, and the rover retreated again.

Svetlana nodded. She moved closer and probed at the disturbed soil with the tongs, grasping and releasing, finding only loose dust.

He had the stone.

She turned to him and pointed at the handcart with the tongs, jerking her chin for him to clarify, looking hard into his eyes.

He smiled broadly, shrugged and stared back at her as he spoke.

"Houston, I've got a pretty good sampling of everything in this area. How about I head back to *Bulldog* and start setting up the flag for the Rooskie press event?" He emphasized and pronounced the word carefully; in America, Rooskie was a derogative, but when said with a rolled "R" and the right weight, it was the word for "Russian" in her language.

A frown flashed across her face. She'd heard it, amongst the incomprehensible English. *Perfect.*

"Copy, Chad, sounds good. On the way back we'd like you to check out that darker spot you saw. Our best guess is about thirty degrees left of *Bulldog.*"

"Will do, just tying down the samples now."

Svetlana watched as he pulled the bungees across the bags and tools in the handcart, wondering what he had said. She'd clearly heard the Russian word, and he'd moved his head as he'd said it, to be sure she'd notice. What did he tell them? *Can't ask without giving myself away.*

He looked directly at her, reached up and rotated his gold visor back down over his face. He turned, grabbed the handle of the cart and started walking away.

She glanced at Lunokhod, motionless, still pointed at her. She walked around it, looking closely so she would be able to describe its status to Moscow when she got back. *Dusty, but all there.* Still holding the tongs, she turned and hustled clumsily after the astronaut.

Behind her, unobserved, Lunokhod's eight wheels began turning together. It picked up speed and followed them, like an oversized, lumbering pet chasing its master.

Or a wild animal tracking its prey.

"Houston, I'm keeping *Bulldog* at about one o'clock as I track back, but haven't seen anything yet." Chad was walking slowly; he didn't want any of the samples he'd gathered to bounce past the bungees and out of his cart. Especially the bag with the rock.

"That heading sounds about right, Chad." Kaz made a "V" with his hands, picturing what Chad was doing, remembering how long the traverse to Lunokhod had taken. "You should be coming up on it soon."

Laura was next to him at the console. He'd asked her to come sit in the front room to make it easier to discuss whatever geology Chad ran into, especially with the TV camera down.

"Okay, Houston, I'm seeing something now." Chad's voice tailed off.

Laura had both hands up on the console, her fists clenched in anticipation. As the seconds ticked by, her fingers slowly extended, palms up, and she turned to Kaz impatiently, eyes questioning.

He nodded and asked, "What are you seeing, Chad?"

"Uh, it's weird. Like a big sunken acne pockmark in the Moon. There's a downslope all around, and then what looks like a rocky round edge to it. Inside that I'm just seeing black. I think it's one of those holes the geologists were talking about."

A smile of triumph spread across Laura's face.

"Copy, Chad, that's the first one of those anybody's seen up close. Just hold position for a sec while we talk about it."

He stood up and gestured for Laura to do the same, turning to the flight director console.

Gene spoke: "What risks are we facing here, GEOLOGY?"

Laura fumbled for her mic switch, but then spoke confidently. "FLIGHT, from Chad's description, it sounds similar to the four holes we've got pictures of from lunar orbit. We hadn't spotted this specific one, but best guess is it's an old lava tube like we've studied in Hawaii, with a collapsed section where it's thin on top. It likely has sloping sides, not sure how steep."

Gene considered that. This could be one of the most important discoveries of the whole Apollo program. Access below the surface of the Moon, providing potential shelter from the temperature extremes and radiation on the exposed surface, might be a key to eventual lunar settlement. Also to understanding the geology of the Moon itself. But not enough to risk the crew. Especially with only one person outside. A trade-off, like everything in spaceflight. Purpose versus risk.

"What info would be most useful to you?"

Holy cow! Laura thought. Gene Kranz was asking her directly what to prioritize. She worked hard to keep her tone professional.

"Characteristics of the hole: size, surrounding debris differences, angles of repose, exposed bedrock. A look directly down inside would be the ultimate, to understand the interior lower wall structure — smooth or rough. If possible."

Gene put her on the spot. "How close would you walk to the edge?"

Laura swallowed, realizing that this was a pivotal moment in her life. All the years of study, the fieldwork, staring at photographs, writing endless grants and reports. All was in preparation for this.

"I recommend caution, FLIGHT. Nothing has disturbed that regolith in maybe a billion years. It's probably compacted and solid, but it could be ready for a landslide. Chad will be fine on the flat, but if it were me, I'd stay clear of where the slope gets at all steep."

Would I really? she wondered. Probably not. Geologists were explorers.

Gene nodded and looked at Kaz. "Let the crew know."

Close, but not too close, Chad summarized in his head. Typical. Everyone sitting in comfortable chairs, sipping coffee, congratulating themselves on their good judgment. Leaving the real risk to someone else.

To me.

He let go of the handcart and took a step forward, describing as he went, hyper-aware that everyone was hanging on his every word.

"Hard to judge distances, but the hole looks to be about fifty feet across and maybe fifteen feet below the surrounding plain. The slope steepens as it gets closer to the hole, interrupted by small ridgelines of bedrock sticking up. I'm going to walk along one of those outcroppings as they stay level closer to the edge."

"Okay, Chad, understood, but err on the side of caution. Where you are now is already giving us info we've never had before."

No shit. "I'm taking pictures as I go. The surface color is unchanged, and there's no perceptible difference in the soil surrounding the hole. Same mix of dust and stones."

He walked to his left, following a higher ridgeline that led towards the hole.

"Okay, I'm seeing deeper down into it now." He stretched in his suit, craning his neck. "I can see the far rim of the hole in the bedrock. The rim is thin—maybe a yard or so—and it's just black below."

Gene Kranz said, "Tell him that's far enough, CAPCOM."

Kaz transmitted, "Chad, hold there while we talk about it." He turned to Laura. "What do you think?"

"With the angle of the sunlight, he won't see the bottom unless he gets right to the edge." She left the implied decision to Kaz.

He held her gaze as he pushed the button. "Chad, once you're done taking photos, we'd like you to back away and head back to *Bulldog*. We'll have you come back to collect samples later if there's time."

Chad took a step closer, and then another, which brought him near enough to see the end of the harder rock that held up the narrow ridge he was on.

"Copy, Kaz."

He took another step, feeling a rush of exhilaration. This was the same as flying a jet close to the ground at high speed, away from where any prying eyes or radar could stop him. Feeling the danger of the trees and rocks whipping past, the risks all supremely controlled by him, and him alone. His skill. His decisions. He took another step.

Svetlana was watching, alarmed, and rapidly decided the risk of speaking was worth it. She'd known pilots like this, and they often crashed. She calculated that Houston would think she was watching out the windows of the lander.

"Ostorozhna!"

The female Russian voice cut through Chad's reverie. Still, he stayed where he was, defiantly, and decided to take one more step forward, to just a few yards from the edge. The ground was angling away from him now.

The translator clarified for the room. "She said, 'Be careful.'"

Kaz pictured her watching from the distance, seeing Chad doing something dangerous. He had no idea yet as to how Chad was going to achieve the new military aim of disabling Lunokhod discreetly with the cosmonaut there as a witness. Calmly, he instructed, "Chad, as you're walking back, please describe for the geologists what you saw."

Enough, Chad thought, his face breaking into a triumphant smile. *No one has ever done that!* He retraced his steps, turning when he had enough room. Ignoring Svetlana, he grabbed the cart's handle and started towards *Bulldog*. He said, "At my closest approach I could just see deep enough to catch sight of sunlight on the inner wall of the hole. It looked smooth and curved."

Svetlana followed him, shaking her head. When would he have stopped? *I'm on the Moon with a crazy man.* As she walked, she felt the reassuring weight of the pistol moving in her leg pocket.

Both of them were focused on the traverse back towards *Bulldog*, immersed in thought. Neither looked back to notice Lunokhod, starting and stopping with successive commands, moving in 10-second increments.

Following them.

In Simferopol, Gabdul glanced worriedly at the clock. Thirty minutes until they lost signal. It was helpful to have footprints to follow, as the team didn't have to analyze each image as it came down before sending another command to move. He just verified he was on track, adjusted direction, rolled forward for 10 seconds and then stopped. Repeat.

He wanted to get to whatever the astronauts had been looking at before the radio link dropped out. To give him time to think about it and maybe pass on a request to them while they were still on the Moon.

Part of the problem of building a tough, compact rover was that the topmost camera didn't stick up very high. The Moon was small enough

that the horizon dropped away rapidly, and he couldn't see very far
into the distance. It was like driving at night with the headlights on low
beams, and it made him uncomfortable when he had to hurry.

But Chelomei had ordered him to do it. And this was what he had
trained for. His quick responses had helped the astronaut find the
Ugol rock, and he'd even moved the magnetometer to show the other
astronaut where to dig around for any more fragments. Decisiveness
and finesse.

He jammed the stick forward again, counting *raz, dva, tree* in his
head, and on up to ten, and then released, waiting for the refreshed
image.

This one showed something odd, though. Only one set of footprints
now, and a low darkness beyond them. Better to move with more caution. He decided on five seconds forward, not ten. He eased ahead on
the stick, counted carefully and released.

He glanced up at the clock. Twenty minutes. Get a suite of images,
and some scientific samples. Then they'd have to wait until the Earth
brought them around again.

Until moonrise in Simferopol.

47

Le Monnier Crater

"Chad, we need you to check on the power to the TV camera, and then get the flag set up for the joint event with Washington and Moscow."

"Copy, Kaz." Chad glanced at Svetlana, who'd just arrived beside him at the lander. "You want me to bring the cosmonaut down the ladder first to make more room up there?"

Kaz looked at Gene. "We talked about it, Chad, and we'd prefer her to come down the ladder at the start of the joint event. So please leave her inside for now."

Chad shrugged. *People playing games.* "Copy."

He pointed at Svetlana and swung his finger around and up the ladder, towards the cockpit of *Bulldog*. She couldn't already be on the surface when he got the TV camera working again.

The interpreter's voice came into Svetlana's headset from Houston. "Lieutenant Gromova, the astronaut will be coming back up into the lander now to check on the TV system, and we'll have you come down to the surface to speak with Director Chelomei in about ten minutes."

Ah, that's why he's pointing.

"Ponyala," she said. She walked past Chad to climb the ladder, crawling on her hands and knees through the hatch.

Chad walked around the camera on its tripod, checking for loose connections. "Houston, all looks normal with the camera itself. I'm headed up the ladder now."

Svetlana stood and turned inside *Bulldog*, raising her gold visor and looking at the pulled TV circuit breaker. *Best to show ignorance*, she decided. She shuffled back and pressed into the dead body, making way as Chad crawled in and stood up.

He ran his fingers across the panels, quickly narrowing in on the black-and-white stripes of the protruding breaker. He turned deliberately, raised his visor and looked accusingly at her. She met his gaze steadily.

"Houston, I see the TV breaker is out. Did you see any overcurrents? My guess is the cosmonaut bumped it or snagged it somehow, being clumsy in here."

Kaz had already confirmed with the electrical back room. "No, Chad, no abnormal signatures, so we agree with you. You have permission for a reset."

"Copy, on my mark, three, two, one, mark." He pushed with his thumb and felt it click back into place.

Instant response. "Chad, we're seeing current flow and camera boot-up signal. Should have good video by the time you get back outside. We're about ten minutes from the Washington-Moscow event, if you can get the flag in place, please."

Five o'clock in Washington was 1:00 a.m. in Moscow. The lateness of the hour and the America-centric nature of the event had dissuaded any politicians from traveling from the Kremlin to TsUP. They'd delegated the task to Chelomei, and to the long-serving Soviet ambassador in Washington, Anatoly Dobrynin.

That suited Dobrynin fine. The press blackout meant that only a sanitized version of events would be made public, and even that wouldn't be released until after splashdown. He'd talked at length via secure phone with Andropov, the KGB head, and had clear direction from Brezhnev. They would create a triumphant way to present this in future. For now, they just needed a few key images and video recordings from the Moon.

And the always necessary calm of diplomacy.

Waiting for Dobrynin in the Oval Office was Henry Kissinger. The two had worked back-channel issues on behalf of their bosses for years together, and today was no different—protect national interests, maintain their deep, respectful friendship and make Nixon and Brezhnev look good.

"Anatoly Fyodorovich," Kissinger rumbled, his warmth genuine. "It is a pleasure to see you, especially on such an historic occasion."

Nixon got up from behind his broad, polished desk to greet the ambassador.

Dobrynin bowed his head with respect. "Mr. President, Mr. Kissinger, it is an honor to be invited here today." He'd been the ambassador since the Cuban Missile Crisis, and his Russian-accented English was flawless. He shook both men's hands, and Nixon waved him to sit in the gold chair at the corner of his desk. Kissinger took his accustomed place at the other corner.

The Oval Office had a formal, masculine feel. Nixon had hated the pale, limpid drapes that his predecessor, Johnson, had favored, and had replaced them with thick gold brocade curtains that matched his new deep-blue carpeting. Seated again in his black leather chair, he was flanked by US and Presidential flags, with a bust of Lincoln and a large photo of his family on the window table behind him. He preferred a clean desk. All that was in front of him was a neat briefing book, a pen-holder, his daily calendar and a black phone. One of its small lower buttons was blinking.

As the men chatted comfortably, Haldeman came through a side door, nodded at Dobrynin and walked around behind Nixon. He pushed the blinking button and adjusted the volume on the small speaker box. He'd wheeled a television in earlier, and he turned it on, getting the feed linked through from NASA. The image showed an astronaut standing on the Moon, flanked by the lunar lander on one side and the Stars and Stripes on the other. Haldeman leaned close and spoke in Nixon's ear, pointing to some writing in the briefing book. Nixon nodded, and Haldeman stepped back.

Kaz's voice came through the squawk box. "White House and Moscow Mission Control, this is Houston. Stand by for the event."

Kissinger and Dobrynin shifted in their chairs to be able to see the TV screen.

In Moscow, Chelomei checked his watch.

"Apollo 18, Houston, voice check."

Chad was facing the camera, his gold visor up so his face was visible, squinting in the bright sunlight. "18 has you loud and clear, Houston."

Kaz looked at the script the White House had sent. Nixon first.

"Mr. President, the comm is yours."

Nixon checked his briefing book. "Major Miller, this is President Nixon, your Commander in Chief. I can't tell you how proud I am, as an American, to be speaking with you, there on the Moon. Especially with the colors of the US flag so clear and bright next to you."

Chad's voice was scratchy through all the connections. "Mr. President, I am honored by the privilege of speaking with you, sir."

Nixon continued. "Chad, I know this mission you are commanding has been arduous, and has involved regrettable loss of life. Such is the cost of voyaging into the unknown. The nation and I offer you both our condolences and our gratitude as you work in the name of scientific discovery, and of peace."

Haldeman had written the words in consultation with Kissinger, knowing the Soviets would be listening.

"I am very pleased that we have found a way to use space exploration not just for technical human understanding, but also now for international cooperation. The world needs symbols of how we can work together, and you and NASA are leading the way. I have some Soviet representatives on the line who are eagerly looking forward to speaking with one of their own, there with you." He double-checked his script. "On their behalf I invite you now to welcome Senior Lieutenant Gromova, a female cosmonaut, to descend from the American lander onto the surface of the Moon."

In Moscow, Chelomei had been waiting for this moment. He spoke urgently via the squawk box to Gabdul, poised at his console in Simferopol, 1,200 kilometers to the south. "Now!"

Gabdul slammed his control stick forward and held it. Not the time for caution.

In Houston, the interpreter next to Kaz called for Svetlana to exit the lander. Her white form came into view on the screen as she smoothly backed down the rungs. She turned and strode over to stand on the opposite side of Chad from the flag. She glanced at him and raised her visor to match.

Nixon nodded at Dobrynin, who quietly said, "Mr. President, as this is so important a day for my country, with your permission I'm going to speak to the cosmonaut in Russian, and then in English."

Perfect, Haldeman thought, watching Nixon nod. *No doubt as to who is in charge.*

Behind the astronauts, a silver shape was slowly entering camera range. Kaz spotted it and spoke rapidly. "FLIGHT, their rover's approaching *Bulldog!*"

Gene Kranz's jaw was thrust forward, his eyes narrow. "I see it, CAPCOM." The Soviets were doing this on purpose. His mind clicked through possible dangers and potential reactions.

Dobrynin turned towards the screen and raised his voice for the speakerphone.

"Major Svetlana Yevgenyevna Gromova, this is Ambassador Dobrynin. I bring you the greatest of congratulations and honors from General Secretary Leonid Brezhnev, supreme leader of the Soviet Union. Your sacrifices, skills and accomplishments are already legendary, and will be a permanent source of pride for all of history. We salute you—the first Soviet citizen to walk on the Moon."

Major? I just got promoted two ranks. She responded formally.

"Thank you, Ambassador. I am deeply honored and forever grateful to be the fortunate first Soviet to be here, in this rare place, today."

In Simferopol, Gabdul had been counting aloud. As he hit "treedsit-shest," thirty-six, he released the hand controller. At full speed the rover should have traveled 20 meters. He looked to the screen for the updated still image, and said a quick prayer.

Dobrynin was still speaking. "Secretary Brezhnev asked me specifically to say he is greatly looking forward to welcoming you to the Kremlin on your safe return."

"Thank you, Ambassador," Svetlana said once more.

Dobrynin turned to Nixon. Neither man had been paying enough attention to the TV screen to notice the silver vehicle in the background. Haldeman had, though. He strode up closer to the television, frowning.

The Ambassador noticed Haldeman, but he was used to staying on topic while underlings dealt with distractions. "Mr. President, our nation celebrates with you in this shared cooperation, as we lead the world in space exploration. The support team in Moscow would also like to say a few words to Major Gromova."

Lunokhod was now squarely in the center of the TV image.

There were several clicking sounds as the phone lines were patched through, and then Chelomei's voice came clearly through the static. The Houston interpreter translated quickly as they spoke.

"Cosmonaut Major Gromova, this is Director Chelomei in TsUP. We salute your bravery, our first human explorer of the Moon, a true Soviet pathfinder and example to us all."

"Thank you, Tovarisch Director."

Haldeman turned to face the president. "Sir, they've driven their rover into the picture." Disgust at having been taken advantage of was thick in his voice. The three men around the desk leaned closer to the screen to see.

Chelomei delivered his coup de grace. "With your historic landing at this Soviet discovery site, with Lunokhod, which has already been exploring for three months, directly behind you, your name will forever join the ranks of Gagarin, Tereshkova and Leonov. Pozdravlyayem!"

Chad whipped around to look, startled to see Lunokhod now just 15 feet away, centered behind them. Svetlana had turned as well, and nodded at the tactic. *Smart move.*

She spoke in response. "It is with great pride that I follow such heroes of the Soviet Union, and in the tracks of Lunokhod. I thank you and every member of the support team, Director Chelomei. It is a great honor to be here on behalf of you all."

There was a pause. Kaz sensed the uncertainty as to who would speak next and stepped in. "Mr. President, back to you, sir."

Haldeman stepped forward quickly and whispered in Nixon's ear.

The President decided to ignore the rover. People were what mattered, not machinery. "The United States adds their congratulations, Major Gromova, on your historic human achievement. Major Miller, I'd personally like to thank you for skilfully piloting your ship to the surface and bringing another nation to the new world of the Moon."

Leave no doubt as to who did what.

"America wishes you and your crew a successful completion of tasks on the surface and a safe return home to Earth. We'll see you soon here at the White House."

"Thank you, Mr. President," Chad responded. "I look forward to it."

Kaz counted to five in case anyone had last things to say. Radio silence.

"Thank you, Mr. President, Ambassador Dobrynin and Director Chelomei. Apollo 18, Houston adds their congratulations, and that concludes the event."

In the Oval Office, Kissinger shook Dobrynin's hand, saying, "I'm certain you would have told us if you'd known they were going to drive the rover into view, Anatoly Fyodorovich." The men had many battles left yet to fight together. Not worth magnifying this one.

Dobrynin recognized the opening and spoke smoothly but loudly enough for Nixon to hear as well. "Yes, my apologies for the overzealous driving of our rover team. Even though they stayed at a safe distance, it seems they wanted some of the spotlight." He nodded to the president as he moved towards the door. "Secretary Brezhnev and I thank you again for the historic opportunity."

Nixon nodded back, but did not offer to shake the Ambassador's hand. He truly detested surprises.

In Moscow, despite the long day and the late hour, Chelomei wore an uncharacteristic smile, the seldom-used muscles squeezing his tired eyes nearly closed. It had worked!

His rocket, his rover, his ingenuity and tenacity had shown the Americans—the entire world—the true extent of Soviet capability. He had put a cosmonaut on the Moon. And a woman, something the Americans had never done! Forever there, recorded next to Soviet technology the Americans couldn't match, for all to see. A triumphant day for the Soviet Union!

He watched as the timer clicked over, signaling the relentless turn of the Earth's face away from the Moon and the end of the day's communications through his giant antenna in the Crimea. He nodded at the flight director, thanking him, and turned, walking out of TsUP.

As his steps echoed in the long hallway back to his office, he focused his weary thoughts forward. Lunokhod had discovered something valuable on the Moon, and he, Vladimir Chelomei, had found a way to get the Americans to unknowingly carry it back to Earth.

Still many problems to overcome. But he had more ideas up his sleeve.

With the press event over, Al Shepard walked up to Kaz's console in Mission Control and spoke quietly. "Got a minute?" He tipped his head towards the exit.

Kaz temporarily handed over to the evening shift CAPCOM, who had arrived early. He followed the Chief Astronaut to an empty briefing room. Al came straight to the point.

"How well do you know Chad?"

Kaz shrugged. He'd been expecting this. "We met during Test Pilot School nearly a decade ago, and then crossed paths again during MOL selection and training. But he's not really my kind of guy, and we didn't socialize much."

Al nodded slowly. The creases were deeply shadowed down both sides of his mouth. "He ever tell you anything about his childhood?"

Kaz looked away and down, recalling what he knew. "Not much. He's a Wisconsin redneck farm boy, went to the State U, I think, ROTC directly into the Air Force, pretty standard. First time I met his folks was at the launch, and they seemed just what you'd expect. No brothers or sisters. Chad never married, and I've never met a girlfriend. Bit of a loner." Kaz paused for a moment, then said, "Now that you ask, Al, I don't really know him that well at all."

"Yeah, me neither." Al looked into Kaz's good eye. "You know if he speaks any other languages?"

"I don't think so. Chad's an all-American type. Very Wisconsin, not too . . . nuanced, if you know what I mean."

Al nodded again. "One other question—any idea about his finances?"

Kaz shook his head. "He never seemed to buy anything flashy, and he paid for the round when it was his turn. I never heard him talk about money." As liaison, Kaz had gathered the necessary legal paperwork from all three crewmembers. "The will that he turned in before flight was just the standard fill-in-the-blanks military form, dead simple. He left everything to his folks."

Kaz decided to ask a question back. "Is there anything you know that will affect how I should be thinking for the rest of the flight?"

Al chewed his inner lip. "It's partly why I didn't ask Gene or the doc to join us. Crew concerns are *mine* to protect and solve, and the last thing I want to do is raise a red flag that distracts everyone from the mission. But the sheriff's investigation has brought a few things to light about Chad. Nothing conclusive yet, but we may well need to let some other folks in on the information soon. For now, I want you to watch what's happening with Apollo 18 extra closely."

Kaz nodded, suddenly thinking about the double clicks on the radio.

As Al turned to head back to Mission Control, Kaz asked him to wait. The recent discovery on the Moon had made him think of something else, and he quickly outlined his plan.

Al blinked several times, considering, and then nodded decisively. "Good idea, Kaz. Just need to call Vice Chief Mo Weisner, get his blessing from the Joint Chiefs. I'll do that, and you talk to FLIGHT and the EVA team."

48

Le Monnier Crater

As Chad climbed *Bulldog's* ladder, moving the two bags of geology samples up into the cabin, the conversation with the White House was playing over and over in his head. The president of the United States had called him by his first name and invited him to the White House! *A long way from the Wisconsin farm. Even farther from Berlin.* So what if the Soviets had driven their rover into the shot. Having it nearby just gave him more opportunity to disable it, and then they could blame any damage on the rocket blast at liftoff. *Idiots.* The Russians had played right into his hands.

He put the rock he'd retrieved from under Lunokhod by itself in a bag normally used for in-cabin tools, clipped into place under the computer entry panel. No one but him knew it was there. Then he moved the two duffels to the racks in the back, transferring the samples into hard-sided vacuum-sealed sample containers. He wedged the bolt cutters inside one of the empty duffels, happy that they just fit. He zipped the bag closed, checked that the cosmonaut was clear below and chucked it out onto the surface.

Now for Luke, and the new plan.

Houston had offered some suggestions for getting the body down to the surface, but Chad had decided to keep it simple. In the lighter Soviet suit, Luke only weighed 30 pounds on the Moon. Like picking up a medium-sized dog. No sweat.

But he didn't want Houston to watch.

He shifted the body forward along the floor until his feet were sticking out through the hatch, then reached up and pulled the TV circuit breaker. He bent and pushed Luke through, tucking the arms in and watching as the body slipped over the edge and fell, guided somewhat by the ladder. He quickly climbed down himself, finding Luke doubled over in a heap at the base. Svetlana watched as he straightened the body out and then climbed the ladder again, pushing the breaker back in.

Gene Kranz frowned as the TV image dropped out again. He waited for the team to diagnose the problem and tell him about it, and was about to push the button to ask, when the camera signal came back. As the image reappeared, he could see two suited figures standing beside a large bag on the ground. It took him a few seconds to recognize it as Luke's body, in the Soviet suit.

"FLIGHT, INCO, we had another TV camera dropout, but you can see it's back now. All indications normal, no action recommended."

"Copy, INCO, glad it didn't happen during the event with the President."

Kaz, seated at the console, quietly guessed what had actually happened. In Chad's place, he wouldn't have wanted a video record of the body tumbling down the ladder either.

Surprised, Svetlana had watched the astronaut push the body in her old spacesuit through the hatch, and had stayed clear as it had tumbled in slow motion down the ladder. Maybe Americans were less prissy than she'd thought.

Chad was now beckoning her towards the body. She glanced up at the Earth; the Soviet Union had rotated out of view.

She was on her own. *Might as well help.*

She joined him, and together they reached underneath the body, lifting, shuffling sideways and centering it crossways, face up, on the handcart.

Chad tapped on Svetlana's suit and pointed to Luke's feet, dangling almost to the ground. He motioned her to grab them, and walked around to the handle. He lifted it in one hand, glanced back and started walking. Past Lunokhod.

Towards the hole. Where the Americans now wanted their dead astronaut buried.

Standing by the door of Mission Control, the Navy officer's dark-blue dress uniform stood out, the heavy brass buttons glinting in the fluorescent light. His escort waited until the Flight Director waved them in, and then walked him up to Kaz at the CAPCOM console.

"Commander Zemeckis, this is Navy Chaplain Lieutenant Parham, serving with the Galveston Coast Guard." Duty complete, the escort nodded, turned and retreated.

The chaplain smiled apologetically, holding his white flattop hat under his arm. "Lieutenant junior grade, actually, sir," pointing at the thick and thin bars with the stylized cross on his sleeve.

Kaz smiled an acknowledgment. "That's okay, I'm only a lieutenant commander. And call me Kaz. Thanks for coming on short notice. Did they brief you on what we're doing?"

Parham nodded. "I'm honored to assist." JW had rolled an extra chair over from the SURGEON console for him, and Kaz waved for the chaplain to sit, plugging in a headset for him.

Kaz looked at the clock and the TV image of the two suited figures receding into the distance. "We'll get started in a couple minutes. We'd like you to keep it short, please, but by the book."

The chaplain nodded again, pulling folded papers from his breast pocket and smoothing them on the console. "Understood."

"Houston, we're almost at the rim, will get set up." Chad's voice sounded labored in their headsets. Wheeling the suited body had been more cumbersome than he'd expected, and they'd had to stop a few times to recenter it on the cart.

"Copy, Chad, let us know when you're ready." INCO zoomed the TV camera in as far as it would go; they could just see the two small, toy-like figures moving against the horizon.

Chad set the handle down, letting the cart's two front legs stabilize the weight, balanced just at the point where the slope steepened towards the pit. He reached into one of the cart's stowage bins and retrieved a thick white bundle with two heavy locking hooks. He attached one to a fabric tether ring on the Russian suit's hip, and the other to the attachment bracket on the front of his own suit. Reaching under the body, he pulled out the flag and unrolled it, laying it across Luke's chest. He leaned left and right, looking at the slope and visualizing his actions.

"Houston, Luke's in position, and we're ready."

Kaz gestured to the chaplain and they stood together, the rest of Mission Control following suit. The comm loops went quiet.

Kaz pressed his mic button and spoke, his voice reaching into all back rooms, and to Chad and Svetlana on the Moon. The orbiting *Pursuit* ship had just reappeared from around the far side, and Michael was quiet and listening as well.

"All hands bury the dead." The traditional call for ships to stop engines, and to lower flags to half-mast.

Chaplain Parham took his cue and read from Scripture. "I am the resurrection and the life, saith the Lord: he that believeth in me, though he were dead, yet shall he live: and whosoever liveth and believeth in me shall never die."

He paused and looked up at the TV image of the lonely figures on the Moon. He'd decided to change the traditional prayer's words slightly.

"We therefore commit Captain Luke Hemming's body to the depths of space, to be turned into corruption, looking for the resurrection of the body, when the Universe shall give up her dead, and the life of worlds to come, through our Lord Jesus Christ. Who at his coming shall change our vile body, that it may be like his glorious body, according to the mighty working, whereby he is able to subdue all things to himself."

His quiet "Amen" was echoed by voices throughout Mission Control, and 240,000 miles away by Chad and Michael. Svetlana silently mouthed her own amen, thinking of her crewmate, Andrei Mitkov, his body all alone, orbiting the world next to Almaz.

Kaz spoke as if on parade. "Atten—shun." He paused to give the moment its significance, then said, "Chad, you can commit Luke's body to the deep."

Chad lifted the flag off the body, handed it to Svetlana and with a quick two-handed motion tipped the cart abruptly to push Luke towards the pit, careful to keep his tethered line clear. The body arced several feet through the vacuum and fell to the surface halfway to the rim, rolling to a stop. Chad followed his previous footsteps out towards the promontory, unclipping the line from his suit, holding it clear in both hands. He turned to get good leverage and gave a sharp upwards tug. The body lifted and tumbled several more feet down the slope and stopped just short of the edge.

Chad eyed the footing and the angles, and walked back to the cart. He took two tethers out of a pocket, clipped them together lengthwise and attached one end to himself. He turned and quickly clipped the other end to the metal loop on Svetlana's suit. He beckoned for her to follow and started walking back towards the edge.

She held her ground, jerking him to a stop. She raised her visor and shook her head vehemently no.

Chad grabbed the tether in both hands and yanked, pulling her off balance, making her stumble towards him. He followed his tracks, tugging her onward to keep her from getting her feet set. She deliberately took a large hopping step and landed with one foot forward, the other behind her for stability, and stopped moving.

How crazy is he? She shook her head at him again. *Bad enough that he falls into the pit, but to drag me too?*

Chad looked at her, and again at Luke, lying in the dirt just beyond his reach. He lunged towards her, both hands up as if to strike, and as she took a reflexive step back, he dug in a foot and reversed direction, hard. Even though they were light in the lunar gravity, mass was still mass. The tether between them pulled taut, and she stumbled two more steps towards the hole before she caught herself.

It was far enough. He bent and picked up the line to the body, wrapping it around the thickness of his left glove so it wouldn't slip. He braced his feet, stabilized by the tight tether to Svetlana.

He saw her glancing at the hook releases and began counting backwards in Russian to unnerve her. "Tree, dva, udeen, nul!" He twisted and pulled with all his strength.

Luke's body jerked up off the surface and flew the remaining short distance towards the hole's edge, bouncing once and landing in a sitting position right at the rim. The arms continued the motion, flailing towards the yawning darkness. Slowly the body overbalanced, toppling towards the pit, accelerating as it leaned. Suddenly it was gone, leaving a fresh dark streak in the dirt where it had disturbed an eternity of meteorite dust.

But Chad had misjudged his balance. As he'd heaved, one foot had slipped out from under him. He fell on his side and bounced twice down the slope. The bulk of his suit kicked up a small cloud of dust, and the regolith shifted with him, pushed downhill for the first time in millennia. A small one-man landslide, momentarily jerked to a stop by the countering pull of the linked tethers to Svetlana.

Out of sight over the rim, Luke's body accelerated down slowly, freefalling in the one-sixth gravity. On Earth, after one second, it would have already dropped 16 feet, well out of sight, but on the Moon it had gone less than 3. Chad's tug, combined with his fall down the slope, had put an extra 6 feet of slack in the line.

Newton's laws of motion were universal. In 1.5 seconds, the slack was fully taken up by Luke's falling body. The line, still wrapped around Chad's hand, snapped straight and pulled tight.

Chad was just sorting out how he was going to climb back up the slope when the yank on the line pulled his left arm straight. He opened and spun his hand wildly, relieved to see the line unravel and whip clear, accelerate down the slope and with a flip of the end, disappear from sight.

But the damage was done. The unexpected jolt had pulsed through the tether and jerked Svetlana forward, and now she was scrabbling to get her feet back under her in the bulky, ill-fitting suit.

In Houston, Kaz was staring intently, trying to figure out what was happening to the small figures on the screen. Luke was no longer on the cart, but one of the suits was out of sight. He'd heard someone— Chad?—saying what sounded like a countdown, but in Russian. With the minister standing next to him, he needed to be respectful. *But what the fuck is going on?*

"Durok!" Svetlana grunted. Idiot! She twisted and planted her left foot into the sloping dirt, leaning away hard to counter the tether's pull. Chad was on his back, arms and legs splayed to try to stabilize. The shards of dust, rock and lunar sand under him caught and held in their new position at the pit's rim.

Motion stopped.

Just beyond the edge, the body accelerated as it fell, the cord snaking, into the shadowed darkness. In absolute silence, with no air friction to slow it, the fall took 11 seconds. Luke's body landed near the center of the pile of rubble that had fallen when the roof of the hole had caved in; at impact, his lifeless form was going 40 miles per hour, straight down. It bounced high once, turning, and then landed forever on its back, the Yastreb suit's tough plastic visor unbroken. Luke's sightless eyes stared upwards towards the small skylight in the blackness, shining with the eternity of the stars.

Chad pushed carefully with his left hand, rolling himself uphill onto his side. He dug his right shoulder in and bent his knees as far as the suit would allow. It gave a bit of slack in the tether, and Svetlana eased back to hold the tension.

Moving cautiously, Chad swung his left arm over and got onto his hands and knees. He tipped his head back hard inside the helmet and was just able to see the taut tether leading away towards the cosmonaut. Experimenting, he moved his left leg and right arm forward, and found the leverage to pry himself slightly up the hill. With the extra pulling from Svetlana, it worked. He shifted his weight and moved the other arm/leg, repeating the process, gaining a few more inches. A clumsy sniper crawl wearing a pressure suit.

Frowning, Kaz ran out of patience. "Chad, Houston, how's it going?"

Straining, Chad spoke. "Doing okay, Houston, just tripped and fell. Luke is on his way." As he alligatored his way up the slope, Svetlana moved back, keeping the line taut.

Kaz nodded at the chaplain to give the final benediction, and bowed his head.

"O God, by whose mercy the faithful departed find rest, send your holy Angel to watch over this distant grave," the chaplain said. "Through Christ our Lord. Amen."

Ceremony complete, Kaz shook hands with Parham and thanked him. The chaplain turned to shake hands with Gene Kranz and the doctor, and carefully walked down the steps and out the door.

Kaz squinted again at the front screen, seeing one figure standing and the other rocking to get up off their hands and knees.

"Apollo 18, the final step is the folding of the flag. Per protocol request from the Joint Chiefs, we'll be asking you to bring it back with you to be given to Luke's parents."

Chad shifted forward onto his hands, and then abruptly moved his weight back, bouncing to his feet, staggering a couple steps as he regained his balance. Svetlana unclipped the tether from her suit and threw it dismissively towards him, then turned her back.

The flag was lying where she'd dropped it. Chad coiled and stowed the tethers, picked up the flag and held it high as he folded it so the TV camera could see.

No need for them to know what just happened.

"Houston, we lowered Luke's body carefully over the edge and into the deep. I've folded his flag and am stowing it now."

"Copy, Chad, thanks. Geology would like you both to retrieve as many samples from around the hole as possible, to verify their theories on how it formed. Please take multiple images too." Kaz turned to the interpreter, who repeated the plan for Svetlana.

"Roger, Houston, in work." Chad looked down at the camera mounted on his chest, glad to see it was still in place, and brushed the dirt off. He handed the cosmonaut a soil collection bag and a scoop, and started his narration.

"The soil around the hole looks quite similar to the surrounding terrain, with no visible ejecta or ridges indicating impact." He took the rake and starting filling a bag, turning and clicking pictures as he moved. Collecting the rocks reminded him of being a kid on the farm, picking the stones the winter's frost had brought to the surface and moving them to the fencerows. *Less back-breaking on the Moon, though.*

As he worked, he realized that after this was done, there was only one task remaining on the surface.

He had to admit the sudden tumble towards the pit had startled him. But he'd anticipated it might happen, hooking the linked tether to the woman just in case. His own ingenuity had saved the day, as usual. Houston hadn't had any real plan to get Luke's body into the pit; they'd all counted on him to solve it. And, as usual, he had.

He glanced at *Bulldog* and the Soviet rover, and then at the cosmonaut, filling a bag with her scoop. He looked up to the Earth—Russia had rotated out of sight—and glanced at his wristwatch, strapped around the bulk of his pressurized sleeve. *Still lots of time.*

Time for him to do what they'd really come for.

49

Le Monnier Crater

The Soviet engineers had built Lunokhod to survive the Moon's temperature extremes. All the important and sensitive gear was protected like vital organs, safely nestled within the pressurized, insulated magnesium-alloy body. During the glaring sunlight of lunar day, a small fan blew cooling air up under a flat radiator at the top. With the protective lid and solar array pivoted open, the excess heat was shed to space. At nightfall, the lid swung closed over the radiator to keep the heat within, like a flower closing its petals. Inside, a small lump of radioactive polonium-210 provided warmth, the way a hot-water bottle warmed a bed. Awaiting the dawn.

Engineers at the RAND Corporation in Santa Monica had prepared a summary of Lunokhod systems that the DoD had analyzed for vulnerabilities. As Chad walked back towards *Bulldog*, trailing the handcart laden with bagged samples, he weighed the options they'd given him for disabling it. But really, it was up to him to figure it out. With a damned female cosmonaut watching over his shoulder.

While she'd been collecting the samples near the hole, he'd taken the bolt cutters out of the bag and strapped them down out of sight. Now, eyeing Lunokhod, another idea for disabling it occurred to him.

He turned around and waved at the cosmonaut. When he got her attention, he pointed up the ladder into *Bulldog*. He then motioned with both hands as if he was lifting the bag of rocks.

Svetlana considered. Helping to collect samples had made sense, because it gave her practical scientific experience to bring back to the cosmonaut program. She also figured that if she helped, the Soviet Union would have some leverage to demand a share of the lunar rocks and dirt.

Now he was asking her to help get them up the ladder. She shrugged. *Might as well.* She climbed, turned and faced him, reaching down as far as she could. As he hoisted the bulging bag up, she lunged for the straps, caught one and lifted.

Heavy, even here. She swung it back and forth, higher and higher, like a pendulum, and gave a good heave to get it up onto the platform. Climbing up the rungs, she pushed the sliding bag through the hatch and turned to look back at the astronaut. He pointed for her to enter, and then at himself, indicating he would follow.

In Houston, Kaz spoke. "*Bulldog*, we see you transferring the samples. We have about an hour max left on the surface, and show you doing well to finish on time." He had the interpreter translate. Svetlana saw that Chad was climbing the ladder behind her, so she turned and crawled through the hatch.

She pushed the bag all the way to the back and stood, lifting it with both hands onto the raised platform. She felt the astronaut bump into her from behind, and moved all the way up beside the bag. He pointed to a hard-sided, suitcase-like container in the narrow space.

He spoke evenly. "Houston, can you have the interpreter tell the cosmonaut to transfer the samples into the case while I do final button-up outside?" Svetlana listened to the Russian instructions, looked at the confined working quarters and nodded her acceptance. It would also give her a quick chance to look for the Lunokhod rock. She picked up the bag and wedged it into place as Chad turned to exit.

On the front screen in Mission Control, for the third time, the TV image went blank.

Chad backed out and down the ladder and walked to the handcart, glancing up at *Bulldog's* windows. He wheeled it a few feet around the corner, so he was out of sight in case she took time to watch him, and released the bungee holding the bolt cutters. He also grabbed the scoop tool. With one last glance up the ladder and at the unpowered TV camera, he loped quickly towards Lunokhod.

The recommendations from the military brass had been simple: don't cut any cable that might be carrying high voltage, but be sure to permanently kill the ability of the rover to function.

He decided to go with the simplest option first, the one he'd thought of while walking back to *Bulldog*. He bent and filled the scoop with the fine dust of the top surface layer and carefully poured it onto the flat of the rover's radiator. He was pleased to see how well it matched the color of the dust that had collected already, and added another scoopful, smoothing it evenly with his hand.

He took a pace back to survey his work. The thick layer of dust would stop the radiator from functioning properly, trapping the heat inside. With the Sun beating down and nowhere for the heat to go, the interior electronic components would cook. Hard to tell how fast, but a good first step. And when he turned the TV back on, nobody would be able to tell he'd done anything.

He stepped around the front of Lunokhod. There were thin, tele-scoping metal rods, like whiskers, slanting down from each of the four corners. *Too small for high-data transmission*, he reasoned, and left them alone. No sense dulling the bolt cutters on those.

He spotted several electronic devices, flush-mounted in multiple locations, and looked closely at each. He decided they were scientific sensors and discounted them as targets. *Looks like the intel was pretty accurate.*

Mounted high and clear on the front was a cone-shaped device, like a small silver Christmas tree. Beside it, pointing towards Earth, was a long, scalloped cylinder, resembling a kebab loaded with marsh-mallows. *Omni and high-gain communications antennas*, he recognized. He traced the wires leading to them, finding a location where he could slip the cutters under a protruding loop. He dropped the scoop and raised the bolt cutters, positioning his suited arms for leverage.

"Stop!" a voice loudly commanded. And then, "Smotri!" Look at me!

He turned. Standing between him and *Bulldog* was the cosmonaut. Glinting darkly in her hand was the distinctive angular black barrel of a snub-nosed pistol, pointed at him. The fatness of her gloved finger was wedged inside the guard, on the trigger.

"Nyet!" she said, pronouncing every letter.

His first thought was, *Where the hell did she get a pistol?*

His second was, *No way will she shoot me.* She didn't know how to fly *Bulldog*. To injure or kill him would be to sign her own death warrant. He raised his gold visor so she could see his face. Staring straight at her, he shook his head, a mocking smile spreading across his lips.

Kaz heard the urgent words from Svetlana and was puzzled when Chad didn't answer. The interpreter quickly translated what she'd said, but it didn't help him figure out what was going on. The lack of TV coverage didn't help. He gave it several seconds and then called.

"18, Houston, did you call?"

Svetlana took two paces forward, aimed carefully and pulled the trigger.

The Makarov Pistol was a proven Soviet design, standard military issue, and had been included in the Almaz return capsule's survival pack in case of off-target landings. It was modeled on the German Walther PP, but it was heavier, all steel, ruggedized with fewer moving parts for simplicity. As Svetlana pulled the trigger, the connecting rod released the spring-loaded hammer, driving the pointed firing pin hard into the center of the 9.27 mm cartridge loaded in the chamber. The impact ignited the mercury fulminate primer, sending a shower of sparks into the gunpowder, explosively burning it, the expanding gases pushing the round-nosed steel bullet up the short, rifled barrel. As it exited at the tip, the small, six-gram metal-jacketed projectile was traveling at just under 1,000 feet per second.

The explosion pushed the sliding bolt against a blowback spring, ejecting the empty casing and allowing the eight-round magazine inside the pistol's handle to push a fresh bullet up into the chamber. The heavy spring yanked the bolt forward, and the new round snicked home into place, ready for a second shot. Svetlana had trained on the firing range in Star City, and had squeezed her gloved fist tightly against the recoil. The gun kicked up, but by the time the new round was in the barrel, she was lowering it to aim again.

The small ejected empty steel casing arced high to Svetlana's right and behind her, glinting in the sunlight as it tumbled, finally raising a small cloud of dust as it hit the surface 120 feet away.

Chad saw the muzzle flash and instinctively jerked back. The bullet flashed past him, falling slowly in the light gravity with no air to slow it, eventually plowing a short furrow and creating a small new crater 1,300 feet behind him.

Svetlana had intended to miss. She wanted him to see that she was willing to shoot—to let him know that the pistol worked.

"Seriozna," she said, her voice flat. I'm serious.

JW spoke on the Mission Control internal loop. "FLIGHT, SURGEON, we just saw a big jump in Chad's heart rate."

Kaz nodded, and asked again, "18, did you call?"

Chad's thoughts were reeling. *Holy shit! That bullet barely missed!* He stayed still to reassure her, thinking fast, weighing the options. He couldn't tell Houston what was going on: there were too many secrets, and some of them the cosmonaut knew. He forced his voice to sound normal. "Hey, Houston, we're just working on something here. Disregard."

Kaz looked across at JW, who shrugged.

Svetlana waved twice with the pistol, gesturing for Chad to move away from Lunokhod, then aimed again at his head. She watched him step clear and decided it was time for her to take control.

Through the interpreter, she said, "Houston, this is Major Gromova. The lunar soil samples are stowed in their carrying case, and the astronaut and I are both back outside. How can I best help complete the moonwalk?" She beckoned with her free hand, pointing for Chad to hand her the bolt cutters.

Kaz turned to talk directly to Gene Kranz. "FLIGHT, I don't know if Chad disabled Lunokhod or not, and I'm still not sure how much English the cosmonaut understands."

Gene rubbed his hand over the back of his head, feeling the brush cut. "He should have had enough time while she was inside, and we need to keep deniability." He rubbed harder, then said, "He knows the priorities. Let's let him choose his moment."

Kaz nodded, and pushed his mic button. "Major Gromova, Houston, we copy, and will have tasks for you shortly." He held up a finger so the interpreter wouldn't translate what he said next. "Chad, just a reminder to complete mission priorities, and we're standing by with clean-up items when you're ready." *Innocuous enough.*

"Copy," Chad responded, watching the cosmonaut intently, trying to guess her mental state. She still had her gold visor down, which made the steady, aimed pistol seem more menacing. She gestured with her free hand again, more insistently.

Fine. There's still time.

He threw the cutters at her feet, warily, and walked past her. She bent awkwardly to pick them up, still aiming the pistol. As soon as she had them securely in hand, she reached down and slid the gun into her leg pocket.

Chad climbed the ladder to push the TV circuit breaker back in. "Houston, all priorities are complete, and I'm ready to start final cleanup."

She'll have to set those cutters down at some point. And she can't watch me the whole time.

Svolich! She shook her head, watching him climb the ladder. You bastard! Giving her a menial task while he went outside to damage Lunokhod—the arrogance!

She looked at the bolt cutters in her hand. Quickly she walked out of sight of the windows and dug in hard with her heel in an area of kicked-up soil to make a small trench. She dropped the cutters in and kicked loose dirt over top, stomping repeatedly across the area to camouflage it. She stepped back to look; just tracks in the dust, the same as those all around the lander. She glanced back at the ladder; Chad still hadn't descended.

She walked to the front of Lunokhod and bent to look closely at the area Chad had been studying. She traced the antenna wires carefully, seeing nothing disturbed or dangling. She stepped back and did one full circuit, checking the side power cables and wheels for damage, seeing none. He hadn't had that long; she'd hurried down the ladder when she'd spotted him by the rover, and had stopped him in the act.

She saw a scoop lying next to Lunokhod, and she grabbed it and walked back towards *Bulldog*, satisfied for now. But she'd have to remain vigilant. He'd try again, no doubt.

She weighed what she could do. Having watched him fly and land the LM, she was certain she couldn't operate it herself, even with verbal instruction from Houston. If he died, she died.

Was protecting Lunokhod worth her life? She was a soldier, and had sworn fealty to the Soviet Air Forces. Her childhood heroines, Lydia Litvyak and Yekaterina Budanova, both Great Patriotic War fighter aces, had died in battle. *How is this any different?* She looked around at the barren landscape and the low, rolling hills, the empty desolation. *But to die here?* They'd already retrieved the rock Moscow was interested in. Lunokhod had been exploring for three months already. *What would my death accomplish?*

He had come back outside and was stowing equipment. She scanned his spacesuit. Maybe she could damage his life-support backpack, which would force him to hurry inside the lander and connect to its umbilicals. Shooting the backpack might work, but it just as well might cut a vital line or rupture a pressure tank, or pass through and kill him instantly.

She looked up at the lander itself, seeking a vulnerability to exploit that would hasten their departure. *But what?* The legs and lower section had all been built just for landing and were here to stay; only the upper section would take off, and all its antennas and cables were far out of reach.

She thought back to the design of her own Yastreb spacesuit, which had an emergency oxygen tank to provide extra reserves in case the suit developed a leak. The American suit must have one too. Their engineers would have needed a solution to the same problem. But how to start a survivable leak in his suit? She looked at the scoop in her hand. Where could she find a sharp edge?

A Russian voice broke into her thoughts. "Major Gromova, Houston, we see you with the scoop and would like you to pass that to Major Miller to stow, please. And then we have some more actions, as requested, when you're ready."

"Ponyala, minutichkoo." Understood, just a minute.

He'd turned to face her, reaching a hand out for the scoop. She inspected the hoses on his chest as she passed it to him; they were a jumble of covered connectors. No way he'd let her get close enough to disconnect anything. She stepped back and told the interpreter to go ahead.

She was on the Moon with a man who had much to hide and who still had time to do damage.

Mission Control, Houston

Kaz rested his forehead in his left hand, his elbow propped on the console. He'd found that rubbing the outer edge of his left eye socket with the tip of his thumb helped ease the burning in his fake eye. He blinked several times to clear the grittiness; it had been a long day. They just needed to get the moonwalk cleaned up, the crew inside and the hatch closed. Then they could all take a break. Crew included.

He opened both eyes wide, like he was stretching them, and refocused, running his finger down the checklist items. There were only a few left.

"Chad, we just need you now to reposition the TV camera to a launch observation location, and then we should be good for the two of you to head inside."

"Copy, Kaz."

Chad turned, walked the length of the snaking white cable out to the TV camera and picked up its tripod. He backed up slowly until the cable was nearly taut, to give maximum clearance from the rocket blast. Looking down the lens at the LM and Lunokhod, he had a thought. He took several paces sideways, the cable dragging across the dust, ascribing an arc around *Bulldog*. He set the tripod down again and rechecked.

"Houston, that look okay to you?"

Kaz had been watching the camera bouncing wildly with the reposition. Now *Bulldog* was centered and Lunokhod was no longer in the frame, out of sight. No matter the suspicions swirling around Chad, the man was sharp.

"Looks good, 18, nice and square to watch your liftoff. Suggest one last look-around for any loose items, and then we think you're done on the surface."

"Wilco."

Chad started back. Svetlana was facing him by the base of the ladder. *Where did she hide the bolt cutters?* He'd looked everywhere during the close-out, even into the distance in case she'd thrown them. *Sneaky bitch!* It left him with only one option.

He turned abruptly, taking long, hopping strides towards Lunokhod. He'd looked at the angles; no way she could physically intercept him in time. And she wouldn't actually shoot him. It'd be sealing her own death warrant. Without him, she'd die badly, slowly suffocating as her oxygen ran out.

Svetlana didn't have much time to react. She took several fast steps towards Lunokhod to cut him off while he was still moving, and as he reached for Lunokhod, she braced herself with feet apart and carefully fired at the thickest part of the target. His intent was obvious, and she was a good shot; it was worth the risk.

The 9 mm bullet entered his life-support backpack from the left side. It went through the cloth covering and missed the aluminum frame entirely, penetrating the stainless-steel oxygen tank, rupturing it and instantly releasing the remaining 600 pounds per square inch into the vacuum of space with a brief burst of flame. The thin walls of the tank barely slowed the bullet, which tumbled on destructively through the plastic and wires of the power distribution bus, eventually slowing and stopping as it shattered into the multiple thick layers of the silver-zinc battery.

The force of the bullet and the explosively escaping oxygen pushed the backpack hard to the right, but Chad managed to correct the imbalance with his next stride, planting his right foot farther out, already slowing himself. He heard the warbling tone of a suit malfunction, and glanced down at the indicators on the top of the control unit on his chest; he saw he had low oxygen flow. *What the hell?*

First things first. He grabbed the rover's long, bulbous antenna in his right hand and the low, conical one in his left, and squeezed them together, like he was doing a chest press in the gym. He felt them both give way, the antennas and their mounting structures bending. He kept squeezing until they were pointed at each other, nearly touching. *Enough!*

In Houston, Kaz could only see *Bulldog*. Chad had headed out of frame to the right, and then he'd seen Svetlana move quickly in the same direction. Towards Lunokhod.

A voice broke urgently into the Mission Control loops. "FLIGHT, there are problems with Miller's suit. Looked like there was a sudden drop of tank pressure, and then we lost all signal. No data at all from it now."

Gene Kranz's jaw thrust forward. This was serious, especially with no visual on the crew. "CAPCOM, let's get a voice check ASAP."

Kaz pushed his mic button. "18, we're seeing a data dropout from Chad's suit. Comm check."

The tone had stopped sounding in Chad's headset, and he glanced at the pressure gauge on his right wrist; it showed only 3.4 psi, almost into the danger section. He turned towards the lander and saw Svetlana holding the pistol, and realized what had happened. *The slut shot me!* He mentally surveyed his body to see if he was injured. *No pain.*

"Easy, toots," he said, raising both hands, but he didn't hear his voice in his headset. He realized he couldn't hear his breathing either. His comms had died. He looked closely down at the control unit; his oxygen tank pressure was zero. *Shit!* He needed to open the emergency tanks on the top of his backpack before he breathed the last of the oxygen in his helmet. The steps were instinctive: he raised the lever on the control unit on the right side of his chest and slammed it into emergency position, and quickly reached across his body over his left rib cage and popped open the red purge valve. That let waste air escape, allowing the emergency oxygen to flow into his helmet, flushing the carbon dioxide buildup from his exhaled breath. He now had 30 minutes to get plugged into the lander's oxygen system. Less, if the suit itself was leaking. He started moving towards *Bulldog*.

Kaz pointed at the interpreter to repeat his comm check in Russian, and was relieved to hear Svetlana's voice in reply. "I hear you fine, Houston." She sounded angry.

"We hear you fine also. Chad, how do you copy?"

No response.

Kaz worked through the interpreter. "Major Gromova, we've lost comm with Major Miller. Can you apprise us of his status?"

Svetlana was at the front of Lunokhod, surveying the damage. *Dermo!* Shit! She hadn't protected the rover and she'd done unknown harm to the only person who could get them off this rock.

She glanced back at him. Maybe he was okay. "He's moving towards the lander, but I don't hear him saying anything."

Kaz assessed possibilities. Had Chad somehow damaged his suit while sabotaging Lunokhod? She must have seen what he was doing. Had she caused the suit problem? How best to handle it?

"Thank you, Major Gromova. We'd like you both to end the moonwalk now and return to the Lunar Lander for ingress. We need to get him plugged into the ship's systems to restore comms."

"Ponyala," she said, grunting as she grabbed the long antenna and heaved it back, trying to restore its original shape. The metal of its support mount twisted, and she pulled and looked up to align it with

Earth. She bent the smaller antenna as well, until it was near vertical. *Hopefully enough!*

She turned and saw that Miller was almost back at the lander. She glanced at the distant TV camera, pocketed the gun and loped after him.

There was an audible sigh of relief in Mission Control as Chad came into view. *Maybe just a data dropout,* Kaz thought. They watched as he went straight to the base of the ladder and began climbing, Svetlana following. The moving images were blurred, but they could see the white of Chad's suit disappearing as he crawled through the hatch. The cosmonaut was on the ladder, following.

Chad's anger roared in his ears. *You goddamned whore!* He got up off his hands and knees, turned inside *Bulldog,* reached down and closed and locked the hatch.

As soon as he could get oxygen flowing into *Bulldog,* the climbing cabin pressure would push against the wide, square surface of the hatch, holding it even more firmly in place. She could turn the handle on the outside, but no matter how hard she pushed against the pressure, soon she wouldn't be able to budge it.

Svetlana was trapped outside.

Her helmeted head was just clearing the top of the ladder when she saw the hatch swing closed. *Nyet!* She pulled hard on the railings with both hands and pivoted her body up onto the small porch, reaching to push the hatch back open, but it was already securely in place.

She leaned back to try to look up through the windows, but the space was too confined. *Would he actually leave me out here?*

She studied the bare metal face of the hatch. On the left there was a semicircle of gold foil and on the right a larger brown semicircle of bare fiberglass. There was writing across the center of the hatch, with what looked like instructions. *Instructions mean options. Think, girl!*

By the right half circle there were two orange lines painted like clock positions and words in block capitals. She puzzled out the English letters: Lock and Unlock. *Must be otkrit and zakrit,* open and close. There had to be an external control. She scrabbled at a rectangle inset into the fiberglass, and a Velcroed cover peeled off, revealing a metal handle. It was pivoted down, aligned with Lock. She grabbed it and twisted, but it didn't move.

She leaned hard forward and worked her fingers behind it until it was securely in her palm, and pivoted with her whole upper body, pulling with all her strength. It released, turning through the short arc, and with a push the hatch swung away from her. *I'm in!*

Chad was reaching up to turn the oxygen control rotary switch when he felt the opening hatch bump into his legs. He looked down in irritation. *Fuck!* He urgently needed to solve his suit problem.

He stepped clear so she could open the hatch all the way, and he grabbed and yanked on her backpack to get her through faster. Moving around her as she got to her feet, he bent and relatched the hatch closed, reached up to his right and pushed the Cabin Repress circuit breaker in. An unseen valve clicked open, and oxygen from *Bulldog's* tanks started flowing.

"FLIGHT, they've started cabin repress." The calm voice of the Systems Officer belied the release of tension in the room. The small interior size of *Bulldog* meant the crew would have breathable atmosphere in just over a minute, and could take off their helmets.

Chad watched as the cabin pressure climbed. When it hit 2.5 psi, he moved the lever on his suit to Off, and as it stabilized at 4.3, he started taking off his gloves.

Watching from the back of the cabin, Svetlana warily copied his actions. Had he really just tried to kill her? Or was closing the hatch his way of showing her who was boss? Her hands ached after the hours fighting the pressure in the ill-fitting gloves, and it was a relief to get them off and stow them in her left leg pocket.

He was hooking his suit up to the ship's hoses, his hands moving confidently as he bypassed the failed systems of his damaged backpack. Turning, he beckoned her closer, pointing at her hoses, reaching out.

They'd both raised their gold visors, and she watched his face as he worked. It was curiously expressionless, giving her no hint of what he was thinking.

He turned and threw some panel switches, and suddenly she could hear him breathing again.

"Houston, *Bulldog*, we're back inside, hooked up to the ship." He stared at her. "Not sure what happened with my suit comms, but we got everything done outside and are putting things away in here now. Both of us in good shape, ready for the rest period before we head up to dock with *Pursuit*."

Kaz nodded and then summarized, waiting as each sentence got translated. "The team here congratulates the two of you and thanks you for your teamwork during your historic moonwalk. The plan now is for a well-deserved eight hours sleep, with liftoff to redock tomorrow at 11:54 Houston time. Major Gromova, we have an interpreter here at all times, so call if you have any questions."

Svetlana looked at the watch on her suit, adding the nine hours for Moscow. "Ponyala, spaciba bolshoi." Copy, thanks very much.

She was planning ahead as she watched the astronaut taking off his helmet, ticking off the key items in her mind. Find the rock he'd taken from Lunokhod. Get launched, dock, fire the engine to head home and make it through re-entry. And somehow get herself and the rock back to Russia.

Transit time back to Earth would be three days—lots of opportunity to sort out a plan.

For now, though, she was locked inside this small place with a man she couldn't trust. A man she'd fired her gun at twice, and who'd latched the door with her outside.

First step was to survive this night, on the surface of the Moon.

51

Bulldog

"Help me," Chad said. He pointed at the buckles on the backpack straps. He'd wedged himself into the aft of the cabin, the weight of the backpack supported on the engine cover.

She looked at the attachments, reached in and popped them free. He stepped clear, flipped the backpack around and peeled back the thermal covering to survey the damage the bullet had caused.

A small neat hole had been punched on the left side where the round had entered the oxygen tank. On the opposing side, the metal had torn outwards with the escaping pressure, leaving an oval opening and sharp edges. Broken bits of plastic fell from the shattered circuit board and battery casing, tumbling slowly to the floor of the LM.

He raised his gaze to meet Svetlana's, shaking his head slightly.

"Bad girl."

He stuffed the backpack down beside the engine mount and turned to release the clips on hers, stowing it as well. He moved to the front of the cabin and connected black tubing to a connector on his suit. He had a condom-like cuff on his penis, and his urine had been collecting in a bag inside the suit all day. He turned a valve, and it was sucked out by partial vacuum into a LM storage tank.

He knew Svetlana was wearing a diaper under her suit. He looked at her as his urine transferred. "You can just keep pissing yourself," he said.

She replied rapidly in her native tongue. "I know you speak Russian. Why are you prattling on to me in English? It's stupid!"

He made an exaggerated face of not understanding. "Russia didn't get you to the Moon, toots. America did." He pointed to himself. "I did."

Svetlana exhaled loudly, watching as he turned to organize the stowage. He handed her a food packet and squirted water into his mouth from the dispensing gun. She realized she was hungry and stood chewing on the dried food as he unpacked the hammocks, bumping her out of the way, clipping them into place for the night.

The sample container where she'd stowed the bags of rocks and dust had been empty when she'd started; the Lunokhod rock hadn't been in it. There was a second hard-sided case on the aft shelf; it must be in there. She decided to just ask.

"Where did you stow the rock that Russia asked for?"

He ignored her.

"I know they have your brother in Moscow. And the Americans don't know about him, or the rock. Or that you speak Russian. Or that Moscow is talking to us secretly."

He kept his back to her.

"Stop!" she commanded in English, loudly. He turned and looked at her, his eyebrows exaggeratedly up. She continued in Russian. "You need me to keep your secrets. To get that rock to Russia, where it belongs." She suddenly realized the leverage she had, and the extra danger it put her in.

He nodded and replied, in English, "That puts you in a tough spot, doesn't it, sweet cheeks. You need me to get you home, and I'm the only one who actually has the whole picture."

A small smile curled the corners of his lips as he leaned his face towards hers and said one word, distinctly, in Russian. "Ostorozhna."

Be careful.

The unrelenting sunlight was shining directly on the metal hull of Lunokhod, parked next to *Bulldog* on the Moon's surface, and reflecting up off the ground around it on all sides. If there had been a thermometer touching the rover's exposed magnesium-alloy skin, it would have read 242 degrees Fahrenheit. The metal was conducting that heat through to the inside, where the energy from the lump of polonium and the quiescent electronics added to it. The small ventilation fan was earnestly doing its best, pulling the nitrogen air past all the warm surfaces and blowing it hopefully up to the radiator to cool.

Like a blanket, though, the layer of dirt that Chad had spread on the radiator's surface was holding the heat in. The bottom of the radiator was starting to get warm to the touch. Instead of cold air flowing back down from the top, with each passing minute the return air was getting hotter. A cycle feeding on itself, where even the small heat from the fan motor was making things worse.

Yet most of its systems were still asleep, patiently waiting for the big antenna on the far side of the Earth to rotate back into view. As soon as it did, small timers would go off, the high-gain antenna would move to point exactly to the planned angles, and Lunokhod would come fully to life, everything on, awaiting its next command.

As soon as that happened, the problem was going to get rapidly worse, turning the rover into a forced-air oven on the Moon, baking all its delicate circuits to death. Unless the team in Simferopol could recognize the problem and figure out a way to solve it.

A race with a thermometer.

Kaz was beat. He'd driven right past the U-Joint, headed for home and a much-needed night on his own.

He pulled the fridge door open and opted for what he saw; bacon, eggs, toast and beer. The sound and smell of the bacon starting to fry in the pan set his mouth watering; his first gulp of cold beer from the bottle cut through it perfectly. He broke two eggs in next to the bacon and pushed two slices of bread down in the toaster.

He looked out the window absently as he waited for the toast to pop, reviewing the day. It had been an unprecedented one, but the crew was safe and Luke's body had been buried with honor. He raised his beer before taking another swig and toasted him. *Here's to you, buddy.* He picked up the frying pan and swirled it slightly, freeing the still-runny eggs from sticking, then set it back down. He realized he felt deeply uneasy, the inner voice he'd learned to listen to as a pilot, the one that paid attention to subtleties and tried to make patterns out of the seeming randomness sending off various alarms.

What have I missed? He took another pull on the beer, deliberately letting his mind relax.

The recurring double clicks popped into his head. If that happened again, he was going to pounce on it and worry it until it was solved.

But the obvious major problem was Chad. Could he really have done such a wicked thing? How was it possible that he'd made it this far, with all the hoops he'd had to jump through, and still kept himself so secret? And why would he kill Tom? The only reason he could come up with was that Chad had been desperate to get on this mission. How did that even make sense? It wasn't as if the whole program was over. There'd still have been chances for an astronaut as technically gifted as Chad to get to space.

The toast popped as he tilted the bottle up and drained the last of the beer; he got the butter and another bottle out of the fridge. As he slid the bacon and eggs onto a plate, he realized how hungry he was, and ate rapidly until he was mopping up the last of the egg with the second piece of toast. He slid the plate and cutlery into open slots in the dishwasher and took the remaining half beer into the living room.

He picked up the Gretsch, letting his hands play whatever chords they chose as he looked out into the darkness. He recognized a couple of sad songs and exhaled, deeply, twice, feeling the exhaustion.

The last of the beer suddenly lost its appeal, and he set it down, put the guitar back into its stand and took himself to bed.

52

Simferopol, Soviet Ukraine

Sitting at his console in Simferopol, waiting for moonrise, Gabdul allowed himself to feel proud. It had been his idea to drive Lunokhod in a max-speed dash across the lunar dust to get close to the American lander. He'd pictured how the iconic photo would look: the first cosmonaut descending the ladder to the Moon, with Lunokhod posed heroically in the background. The established presence of Soviet technology as a perfect counterpoint to the American ship newly on the surface; a seasoned Russian explorer there to greet it. He just wished someone had thought to paint a large red hammer and sickle on the side of the rover.

Outside his operations building, the huge dish antenna was tipped up on its edge, pointed at the exact place on the southeastern horizon where the Moon was about to appear. As the three-quarter crescent wavered into view through the Earth's atmosphere, the first set of commands pulsed out through the amplifiers, bounced off the huge parabolic dish and raced to the Moon. Just 1.35 seconds later, the faint signal washed over Lunokhod's receiving antennas.

The long, bulbous high-gain receiving antenna missed it completely. Even with Svetlana's attempt to bend it back, the tightly focused receptor was no longer pointing in the right direction. But the smaller omni antenna turned out to be sturdier. It dutifully collected and passed on the commands from Earth, and Lunokhod came to life, the mechanical beast readying for its day's work.

Sitting at her console behind Gabdul, the antenna operator frowned. There was no systems signal coming back from the steerable high-gain antenna. It had been working perfectly the day before. She sent a test command for it to go through a search cycle, but nothing. Without the high-gain, they could only get limited, low-rate data back.

Beside her, the specialist engineer felt growing alarm as well. As the new data populated in the systems table on his screen, he saw that the temperatures were far higher than they should have been, with a couple already approaching limits. Both technicians spoke at the same time, summarizing what they were seeing.

Gabdul listened, his concern increasing. How could they have lost the high-gain and thermal control at the same time? Had his bouncing race across the surface broken something? The team rapidly pulled out schematic drawings, hunting for a common link. More importantly, looking for a solution. The internal temperatures were climbing alarmingly.

The systems engineer, looking closely at the data, recognized the pattern, but it made no sense. "It's as if the solar panel is closed over the radiator—we're getting near-zero cooling. But we're getting power from the array, which shows open, so that's not it." He looked at Gabdul. "Maybe the Americans already blasted off and covered us in dust?"

"They're not supposed to take off for a few more hours," Gabdul said, then asked the question that worried him. "Could our high-speed run or their moonwalking have kicked up enough dust to cause this?"

"Unlikely, but possible." The tech studied his data. "But if we don't do something soon, we're going to start losing systems."

Gabdul stared at his TV monitor. The small omni antenna had a very low data rate, and images were going to process very slowly. Whatever he did, it was going to have to be mostly blind. He made a decision and quickly briefed the team. He got reluctant nods from everyone; his proposed course of action was risky, but worth it, given the reality of what was happening.

Gabdul put his hand on the controller and began.

Chad kept his eyes closed after he woke up, listening for a minute to the reassuring mechanical sounds of the LM—the fans and pumps that were cycling the life-support systems, keeping him alive in this little bubble of air on the Moon. *Like I'm in a womb, listening to my mother's heartbeat.*

As he'd slept in the hammock, comfortably slung in the low gravity, he'd been dreaming of his mother, a familiar dream that he both longed for and hated. Oleg, his brother, pushing to do something, his mother in faded colors, her voice conveying more of an emotion than actual words. The three of them had been in a room somewhere in Berlin, Oleg demanding, their mother quietly urging caution. Even now, as he opened his eyes, he could feel the soothing effect of her loving voice. And the jagged unfairness of losing her.

And Oleg. What had happened to the tough, decisive older brother he remembered and dreamed of? The war and loss had somehow changed him, made him soft, turned him into this monk, Father Ilarion. Who was now being threatened by the Russians, and used as a lever against him.

He glanced at his watch. Time to get up.

He rolled onto his shoulder and reached to peel back the covering on his triangular window, letting harsh sunlight blast into the cabin. He leaned to look at the nearby horizon. *Strangest place I've ever woken up.* He glanced at the cosmonaut, crosswise below him, blinking in the bright light. *And with a woman, no less. Though not one I'd pick.*

Movement outside caught his eye. Lunokhod was rolling forward. As he watched, it abruptly stopped, as if they'd slammed on the brakes. It reversed, then immediately halted again. A small cloud of dust shook loose and fell.

He snorted. *Clever Russians.* Somehow they still had comms with their machine and were trying to shake the dirt off the radiator, like a cow shaking off flies. He watched it change direction jerkily a few more times, but very little dust was coming off now. *Driving all those motors will be heating it up even faster.* He was satisfied that he'd done his job and more. Hell, he'd gotten shot in the process.

So many secrets now. A fistful of cards held tight against his chest. And three days' ride home to decide how to play them.

He rolled out of the hammock, stretching against the suit as he stood. Yesterday's work had left bruises on his knees, shoulders and back, and his body protested the movement. But he didn't feel much different than he had as a teenager, the day after a wrestling tournament. Pain was just a reminder of victory.

"FLIGHT, Chad's awake." JW had been watching his console data for the change of heartbeat.

"Copy, SURGEON. CAPCOM, let's get them into the checklist ASAP, and headed towards launch."

Kaz nodded. "Good morning, *Bulldog*, we trust you had a good sleep, and when you're ready, we'd like an IMU Power-Up, on page 7-9 of the Surface book."

Chad acknowledged and threw the switches. *Time for me to do what I'm best at. Time to fly this thing.*

In Moscow, Chelomei had heard Miller's voice and waited impatiently for the orbiting vessel to disappear behind the Moon so the other astronaut—Esdale—wouldn't hear him. As soon as the TsUP flight director nodded, he pressed his mic button.

"Major Miller, listen to me carefully. I have a plan for your splashdown when you return to Earth." He quickly explained the key points of what he had set up with his contacts at the KGB and the Kremlin.

Chad had ceased moving, holding perfectly still, listening, rapidly weighing Chelomei's plan. Svetlana was watching him, listening as well.

Chelomei said, "I need you to be ready and make it happen. If you do not, we will reveal to your masters where all the money you thought your brother was sending you actually came from." He paused to let that new threat sink in, and then said, "If you understand, Major Miller, use the word 'Russia' in your next call to Houston."

All these years, you've been using my brother as a means to compromise me? Anger roared through him. *You asshole!* He pounded his clenched, gloved fists on the flat of the instrument panel.

I need to win this! He wrestled his thoughts back under control, his mind clicking into overdrive; yes, there was still a way to come out on top. In fact, this new demand gave him even more power over the course of events. He looked at the cosmonaut, warily staring back at him.

"Houston," Chad said, "it's been great here on the Moon, Russia and America working together like never before."

Kaz looked up, frowning. *Odd thing for Chad to say.* "Copy, Chad."

On the other side of the world, Chelomei smiled.

Svetlana stood on Chad's right in the cockpit, watching him go through the pages of checklist steps before launch, listening to the technical chatter with Houston. She pictured what the geometry would look like for them to blast off, rendezvous and dock. They'd offered translation, but she'd declined it as unnecessary. Better to just watch, listen and beware. She glanced at her watch—still over an hour to go.

She'd slept poorly, fully expecting that Chad would try to take the gun from her during the night. When she'd finally dozed off, she'd been clutching the pistol inside her leg pocket. But when he'd opened the window cover, waking her up, the hard metal was still there under her hand. It was an important win; once they docked, she'd have the other astronaut, Mikhail, always present as a witness, which would decrease the constant threat. Just three more days and nights to go.

Chad looked sharp and well rested, as if he'd had an untroubled sleep. Even with what Chelomei had said. *Psychopath,* she decided.

During a lull in the chatter with Houston, a Russian voice broke in. Chelomei again, from Moscow.

"Major Miller, we know you can hear this, no need to respond. We think your normal procedures have you opening the hatch once more to jettison unneeded items. When that happens, we need one of you to walk quickly to Lunokhod and brush the dust off the radiator. We just got word that it's overheating. This is critical."

Svetlana saw that Chad's hands stopped moving while Chelomei spoke, but his expression didn't change.

Dust on the radiator! She leaned to get a clear view of the rover. So that's why it had been moving around! But how had anything gotten on the upper surface? She thought back to her close inspection for damage. Had there been dust on top?

Chyort! She couldn't remember! *Did he put it there?*

She turned and looked at the pile of items on the floor behind them: a couple of duffle bags full of trash and their two backpacks. It made sense to throw them out so their engine didn't have to lift useless weight off the Moon. But neither of them could go outside now. Their hoses were plugged into the ship.

The astronaut hadn't reacted to Chelomei's demand and was back talking to Houston in English as if it had never happened. She looked again at Lunokhod in the distance, visualizing what it would be like at liftoff. She spoke quickly, before Chad shut off her mic.

"Houston, will our launch blast blow dust onto Lunokhod?"

Chad's arm shot out and flicked off the transmit switch, his face a mask of fury. "Don't you talk!" he yelled. She saw a spray of spit fog the lower part of his visor. But he'd been too slow.

The interpreter answered, translating what Kaz told him. "Major Gromova, the analysts here have looked at it, and they think the local blast from the upper stage motor will be mostly horizontal near Lunokhod, so should pose no dust threat."

Excellent, she thought, defiantly looking into Chad's eyes. Their launch would blow dust off the rover. *If Chelomei and his team read between the lines, they'll move it even closer!*

Chad was reaching to re-enable voice transmission when they heard Chelomei again.

"Thank you, Major Gromova, we understand. And if—"

The Russian voice cut off abruptly as Chad shut off all external communications. He spoke on intercom, his eyes blazing at Svetlana. "You try that again, I'll kill you!" His hand came up fast and punched her helmet, and her head banged into a handrail. She focused quickly to see if the plastic visor had broken, but saw only a new deep scratch on the outer surface.

"Ponyala?" he demanded.

She eyed him warily. "Da."

He turned back and threw the comm switches. "The cosmonaut's nodding, Houston, sorry for the interruption. I'm ready when you are for the depress and trash jettison."

She got out of his way as he opened the hatch and pushed the items out, watching through the windows to see if Moscow had understood her. With satisfaction, she saw that the rover was still moving in short bursts, each pulse getting it closer to the LM.

She smiled tightly.

There was no doubt that he was in charge. But she'd won another battle.

By design, *Bulldog* had just one chance to leave the Moon, a solitary rocket engine to lift the upper half clear of its heavy landing legs, get it going fast enough to catch up with *Pursuit* in orbit and dock.

Many things had to happen perfectly, in sequence. If any one of them failed, Chad and Svetlana would stay on the surface forever. Or perhaps worse, crash back into it. Either way, Michael would be flying his ship back to Earth alone.

It began with two bangs, as battery power ignited explosive charges. The larger of them shattered threaded nuts and drove a guillotine that severed all mechanical connections with the landing section. They were free. The smaller one then opened valves, letting high-pressure helium rush through small tubes connected to the propellant tanks. The helium squeezed the volatile liquids down into the engine, where they mixed and instantly exploded.

With a shower of sparks the engine fired, pushing *Bulldog* up and away from the surface of the Moon.

"I see pitch-over, Houston." Chad's voice was calm as 16 small steering thrusters pulsed, turning *Bulldog* from the pure vertical liftoff to aim towards *Pursuit.*

On Earth, Kaz was watching the data closely on his console monitor, listening to the technical confirmation on the comm loops. "You have good thrust, *Bulldog.*"

The sudden ignition of the motor had pushed Svetlana down into the floor with double her weight. *Like standing on Earth again.*

She leaned forward, looking down through her window to try to see what effect the rocket blast had had on Lunokhod, but couldn't tell. Within seconds the bottom half of the lander had disappeared from sight and they were accelerating towards rendezvous.

Chad was running his finger along a checklist table that showed altitude, attitude and climb speed, double-checking the steering computer. "*Bulldog*'s on track, Houston." The radio filled with static.

Kaz called *Pursuit.* "Michael, looks like our signal's getting messed up by their exhaust plume, as expected. Please relay that all numbers look good."

Michael had been staring at the Moon's surface, camera in hand, hoping to see the liftoff. "Will do, Kaz. I don't see them yet." He repeated Kaz's message to Chad.

Chad was watching his instruments. "Thanks, Michael, I have a solid radar lock on you. Guidance looks good. Engine shutdown time looks as planned at 7:18."

"I'm looking forward to the company! It's been quiet up here. Nice view, though."

"Copy that." Chad looked at the timeline. "We'll be docked in a couple of hours."

"I'll make some fresh coffee."

Ignoring the chatter, Svetlana was looking at the strange battered roughness of the Moon's surface falling away below them. As they accelerated towards the sunset, the shadows got longer, exaggerating the jagged peaks and smooth craters beneath her. *I'm like a fly over a skull*, she thought, trying to imprint the image into her memory. She twisted and looked up at Earth, the improbable blue orb suspended as if by magic in the blackness.

Her spaceflight was ending. She'd launched expecting to be on Almaz for months, yet now she'd be back in three days. A sudden pang of loss for her crewmate, Andrei, rushed through her. To command that spaceflight had been his life's dream.

She glanced at Chad, his eyes focused on the engine parameters and navigation instruments.

One thing at a time. First, they needed to get docked.

53

Moscow

Father Ilarion was troubled. His expectations for speaking with and honoring his brother, Yuri, had been so high, yet the day had been so strange. They'd gotten back to their quarters very late, and as he wearily rose for Matins, he had much to think on. And pray over.

Alexander was quieter than normal when he brought him breakfast. Ilarion asked if they would speak with Yuri again, and the interpreter said he didn't know, but that they needed to spend a few more days in Moscow, depending on how the space mission went.

"But why, Sascha?"

Alexander looked at the cleric. His kind face was creased with uncertainty, his discomfort with the disruption of his normal life evident in the deep cleft between his eyebrows. He decided the best course was to reassure.

"We have traveled so far to be here, Father. Director Chelomei thinks your presence could be very important for Yuri if he experiences any troubles during the remainder of the flight. He has requested that we stay for the sake of the mission."

Ilarion's face cleared. If he could help, he had purpose. Meanwhile, he could keep Yuri and his crewmates' success foremost in his prayers. He nodded slowly as he picked up the dry toast.

Bowing slightly, Alexander excused himself and stepped into the corridor, closing the door. There he stood up straight and took a deep breath. Chelomei had made it plain that he still needed the lever of threat against the cleric to get the American astronaut to do what was required.

He decided he needed to talk to his handler at Lubyanka to update him on the importance of *his* influence on what was happening on the Moon, and for the American's return. This was his chance to be recognized by the KGB for his work. His longtime loyalty and cleverness.

Alexander liked Father Ilarion. He hoped nothing bad would happen to him here. But this was his chance.

"Okay, Michael, I'm stopped, a hundred feet away. You're cleared to give *Pursuit* a spin."

"Copy, Chad, in work."

Michael had watched as *Bulldog* approached, a metallic insect rising from the surface of the Moon. He moved *Pursuit*'s hand controller to the side, gently rolling the ship like it was on a slow-motion barbecue spit. That would give Chad a chance to inspect the exterior for any micrometeorite damage before they fired the engine and headed across open space back towards Earth.

Svetlana watched *Pursuit* turn in front of them: the pointed, wide cone of the capsule at the front, the squatty silver cylinder of the main body, and the fat brown curve of the engine's exhaust nozzle at the rear. *Strannaya reeba*. What a strange fish.

"Looks clean as a whistle, Michael. Just hold her there, and I'll come in and dock."

"Good to hear." Michael nulled rates and re-engaged the autopilot to hold attitude. "You're cleared in."

Chad smiled as he began moving *Bulldog*'s controls. There was no one anywhere doing what he was doing now—docking his spaceship in orbit around the Moon. He pushed forward, closing the gap between the two vehicles.

Svetlana watched, appreciating the astronaut's ability, deeply disliking the man. She evaluated as he corrected the small misalignments, predicting his inputs, comparing them to what she would do.

On the outside of *Bulldog*, above her head, there was a cone-shaped indentation. Sticking out of *Pursuit* was an extended probe on a tripod; Chad was staring at a visual target to align the two. She heard Mikhail on the radio and recognized the words for numbers.

"Twenty-five feet, Chad."

"Copy."

"Twenty feet, rates look good."

"Agreed."

Pursuit grew in the LM's window like a flower blossoming as they neared.

"Ten feet, good alignment."

"Roger."

A pause as Chad made a last few inputs. Svetlana listened for the sound of metal on metal, hearing the scrape and thunk as they docked.

"Contact and capture!" Michael said. "Nice flying, Commander!"

"Thanks." It had been perfect. Chad safed the control system as he listened to the probe retraction mechanism pull the two ships together.

The specialists in Mission Control had all been watching closely, but Kaz had stayed radio silent, letting the crew do their work to get docked, one of the last major critical events.

"Congratulations, Apollo 18," he said. "Glad to see you reunited. If you look below you, you're just passing overhead your landing site at Le Monnier Crater. To let you know, we're planning to put a request in to the International Astronomical Union to name that local valley Hemming Rille, in honor of Luke." It had been Laura's idea, and Kaz had thought it fitting.

"Copy, Houston," Michael said. "He was a good man."

There was a moment's silence.

"Now let's get the hatch open and start heading for home."

Michael had cleaned house for their arrival. He'd gathered all the unneeded items and trash into one large transfer bag to leave in *Bulldog*, and had opened up *Pursuit's* lower lockers, ready to receive the all-important lunar rock and soil samples for return to Earth. The stowage was below the seats, to keep the added weight in a secure place for the high forces they'd face while re-entering Earth's atmosphere, and for stable floating in the ocean after splashdown.

In contrast, *Bulldog* was filthy, everything coated with the gritty lunar dust they'd brought in on their suits. Weightlessness was making it worse, as movement filled the cabin with the tiny, sharp, floating shards of countless meteorite impacts.

Previous crews had identified a need to clean the dust off items before transferring them out of the LM, and NASA engineers had rigged up a portable vacuum cleaner using a suit hose, fan and filter. Chad plugged it in, dragged it on its power cable through into *Bulldog* and held it out it to Svetlana.

"Here's where you turn it on, toots." He pointed to the silver switch on its side, and then at the walls and floor of *Bulldog*. "Now get cleaning."

He wants me to vacuum?

Instantly irritated, she crossed her arms. But she needed a reason to be in the LM, to watch every item being transferred. She realized that this would give her an excuse.

"Spasiba," she said, with a small nod, and reached out to take it. *Play his game.* She turned it on and the motor whirred tinnily to life.

Chad smirked. "Make sure you get into all the corners."

He turned and yelled down the tunnel. "Michael, you ready for transfer items?" A muffled voice called back affirmative, and he began collecting suit hardware, cameras and vacuum-sealed sample boxes to float through the hatch to *Pursuit*. Prior to transferring each one, he held it up for Svetlana to once-over with the vacuum.

"Look at us, a model of international cooperation," he said over the noise.

She ignored him, concentrating on the task. From the size of the hole in front of Lunokhod, the rock had not been big. She was certain the astronaut would have stowed it separately from the other samples. As she vacuumed, she considered possibilities. She now had the pistol tucked into the waistband of her underwear; maybe he'd done something similar with the rock? She looked at the white flight suit he'd put on; no obvious bulges. Their moonwalking suits were still bundled bulkily under bungees at the back of the LM; he'd have to pull them out for transfer, as they'd need to wear them again for re-entry.

In between cleaning transfer items, she vacuumed the cabin itself to keep the floating dust to a minimum. *Where else might he have put it?* The main stowage area was in the back; the front of the cockpit was spartan and functional. She looked along the edges of the instrument panel for any recesses, and her eyes settled on a small white bag clipped below the data entry panel. *Is that big enough? It's here somewhere, and he's going to try to bring it into the other ship without my knowing.* She just needed to be patient. And observant.

"Houston, *Pursuit*, I show us in LM jettison attitude: Roll 014, Pitch 038 and Yaw 344."

Kaz glanced to confirm the data on his console screen. "Looks good, Michael, you're GO for Pyro Arm. We show separation in thirty seconds."

Michael threw the switch and kept his hands floating near the controls. As soon as the pyrotechnic charges fired, the bit of air pressure they'd left in the tunnel would help to push *Bulldog* away, like a gust of wind on a sail. To be safe, he'd also fire *Pursuit*'s thrusters to get clear.

The digital timer hit zero, and there was a metallic bang as the docking mechanism and tunnel released.

"*Bulldog*'s away, Houston." Michael pulled back smoothly on the controller, hearing his maneuvering thrusters fire, watching through the window as the LM slowly receded. He released the knob, satisfied.

"Copy, *Pursuit*." Kaz left a small pause. "She was a good ship."

Chad was at his window, watching *Bulldog* against the blackness. "Sure was, Houston. You drive her gentle now."

The specialists in Mission Control were uplinking commands, ready to fire the small thrusters on *Bulldog* to steer it deliberately towards a controlled crash into the Moon. The force of the impact would echo through the solid rock and be picked up by seismic sensors installed during previous Apollo missions, mapping the shape of the inner mantle and core of the Moon.

Svetlana watched the two men as they stared out the windows, *They're so different*. She smiled wryly to herself. *Like black and white*.

She had vacuumed the spacesuits as Chad held them out for transfer, but had felt nothing in his suit's pockets. He'd sent her out of the LM before he finished collecting the last items, and had brought them all in one larger transfer bag, stowing it in a locker under the headrest of the left seat. *The rock has to be in there*.

She heard the voice from Houston again.

"*Pursuit*, when you're ready, I've got your coming-home PAD to read up to you."

Both men pulled themselves reluctantly from the window and peeled checklists off of Velcro, grabbing their floating tethered pencils.

Pursuit was Michael's ship, but Chad wanted to re-establish who was in command now that *Bulldog* was no longer attached. He was the one to respond. "Go ahead, Houston, *Pursuit* is ready to copy."

Kaz took a breath. "Okay, it's TEI-74, SPS G&N, weight 35768, plus 0.57, plus 0.88 . . ." As he carefully voiced the data, he pictured what each word meant, making sure it made sense to him. A mistake of even one digit or decimal place could be fatal. *Pursuit* was going to orbit back around behind the Moon, and, out of communication with Earth, the crew was going to point the ship in exactly the right direction for the big engine to fire. At precisely the right moment it would ignite and burn for 141 seconds; without the weight of the LM, that's all it would take to escape the Moon's gravity. By the time *Pursuit* reappeared, it would already be arcing high above the lunar surface, racing home.

He finished calling up the numbers. "Standing by for the readback, over."

Chad motioned with his chin at Michael to respond, and floated back to look out the window. *Bulldog* was rapidly becoming too small to see, soon to be just another memory, another vehicle that he had piloted well. Another event in his past.

He glanced up at the Earth. The past didn't matter. His future was three days away.

He felt a surge of confidence course through him. He just had to play his cards right. And he had a winning hand.

EARTHBOUND

54

Pursuit

Michael was looking forward out the windows at the Earth as *Pursuit* slowly turned in the sunlight. Svetlana was dozing, loosely strapped to her couch.

"Hey, Boss."

"What?" Chad looked up from the emergency entry procedures he was reading. The pages were pale red, highlighting their criticality.

"Did you ever think that since we fired *Pursuit*'s engine for the Trans-Earth Injection, we've really just been falling? Like a rock dropped from an enormous height, accelerating as Earth's gravity sucks us in, closer and closer?" There was awe in his voice.

Chad looked at him. "Nope."

Michael shrugged. "I just think it's cool."

Chad went back to his checklist. *Really? That's what he's thinking about?*

Kaz's voice crackled in his headset. "*Pursuit*, I've got your mid-course numbers when you're ready."

The huge antennas at Goldstone had been precisely tracking the spaceship, calculating exactly where it would enter the Earth's atmosphere; now the engineers in Houston wanted a small engine firing to adjust the trajectory a tiny bit.

Chad peeled Michael's headset off the console and held it out to him. "Houston's calling with mid-course data."

Michael grabbed a checklist and pushed the mic button. "Go ahead, Houston." Kaz read up the information, and Michael eased himself into the center seat to type in the data.

Kaz continued. "While I've got you, Michael, we'd like an updated stowage inventory so the guys here can finalize your center of mass for entry."

Michael stopped typing to respond. "Copy, Kaz, I'll get at it after the correction burn." Boring task, but an important one. Their capsule was going to hit the top of the Earth's atmosphere going just under 25,000 miles per hour, and had to fly itself through the thickening air, using friction to slow down. The only way to steer was to have the center of mass offset a foot or two so the capsule flew slightly crooked; that gave it a little bit of lift. By rolling the capsule left and right, the autopilot would be able to control where that lift was pointed and how fast they fell, which would determine how much g they pulled and where exactly they would splash down. If the computers failed, there was a backup system to manually roll the ship using just time and g-load. But it was all dependent on knowing where the crew had stowed the added weight of the moonrocks.

After the burn was complete, Michael dug around under the seats, opening lockers one by one. He was being methodical. The flight home was long. There was no sense rushing.

"Okay, Kaz, in locker A2 we've got"—he pulled the items out individually—"two sample return boxes and several bags." He hooked his toes under footloops to brace his body, and swung the first box left and right, estimating the mass by how much it resisted his motion and twisted his upper body. "My guess is the furthest forward-stowed box weighs fifty or sixty pounds." Not exact, but the best he could do.

The scientists were also interested in the characteristics of what the crew was bringing home. Per their request, Michael unclipped a thick silver tube from its bracket on a side panel, and twisted the upper section to turn it on. It resembled a foot-long flashlight, but in fact was a radiation-survey meter. He held the protruding rounded end close to the sample box and peered closely at the device's dial.

"Houston, the Geiger counter shows just background radiation levels." He checked each sample as he went, confirming what he'd been briefed to expect. The Moon's surface had been absorbing cosmic rays for billions of years, and they'd anticipated that it would have slightly elevated readings compared to Earth.

Svetlana saw that Michael's hands were full with multiple boxes and the sensor, and floated over.

"Pomotch?" she asked. Can I help? She snagged a bag that was floating free and held it for him to check for radioactivity.

Michael looked up in happy surprise. "Thanks!" Inventory was easier with two.

Feigning disinterest, Chad kept his head tilted towards his checklist while closely watching what they were doing out of the corner of his eye. He didn't want to highlight where he'd hidden the rock, and was confident that Michael's inventory would miss it. But he had a plan, just in case.

In Moscow, Chelomei was listening to the transmissions to Houston with rising concern. Their intelligence hadn't included the fact that the Americans had a portable radiation detector on board. He'd deliberately not told Miller and Gromova that the rock was radioactive when he'd ordered them to retrieve it, knowing they might overreact to having it inside their ship; now there was sudden, grave risk that the third crew-member, Esdale, would discover it and tell Houston.

His options were limited. If he transmitted a warning, Esdale would hear his voice — unacceptable. And even if he did, what could he say?

He pictured the sequence of possible events at splashdown, evaluating the different American actions if they knew it was on board. Slowly, his worry subsided. Their plan was robust enough.

Al Shepard walked down two levels from his management console in the rear of Mission Control and grabbed an empty seat between CAPCOM and SURGEON. He waved Kaz and JW closer.

"You two ready to go to Hawaii tomorrow?"

They nodded. "What time's the C-141 leave?" JW asked.

"Wheels up at six a.m. I'll be at Ellington by five thirty."

"Ouch," Kaz said.

Al nodded. "Yeah, I hear you. I'm planning to mostly sleep en route, plus we get four extra hours with the time difference. We'll land at Hickam around ten a.m. local, and then a Navy helo will take us out to the *New Orleans.*"

"Any surprise passengers coming from DC?" Kaz asked.

"Yeah. The Soviets are insisting they need a rep at splashdown to greet the cosmonaut, so they're sending an attaché from their consular staff." Al rolled his eyes. "I promised the Joint Chiefs we'll take good care of him, but Bob Carius, the skipper of the *New Orleans,* is gonna be just thrilled to have a spy on board."

JW frowned. "Any change to normal recovery ops as a result?"

"Nah, we'll do it by the book, Doc. As Crew Surgeon you'll be on the prime helo with the Navy divers and med techs as usual. Kaz and I will stay on the ship with the attaché, getting ready to grip and grin with the crew for the *Stars and Stripes* cameras. The *New Orleans* will bring us back into Pearl Harbor, and then we'll all fly back here Tuesday, including the attaché and the cosmonaut." He rubbed the side of his face, grimacing like he had a headache. "We still have to inform Luke's family, and then the media, and sort out military protocols to honor Luke, plus how to debrief lessons learned from the cosmonaut herself. But we still have a few days to set all that up."

JW smiled. "That's why they pay you the big bucks, Admiral."

"Yeah, right," Al said. "This'll be the last Moon mission, and the end of my time at NASA. A chance to go make some real money after thirty-two years with the government."

He tipped his head at Kaz and said, "Could you excuse us a minute, Doc?" JW nodded and wheeled his chair back over to his console.

Al moved closer to Kaz, speaking quietly below the hum of the room. "I wanted to update you on what Sheriff Heard's found. Stuff the Air Force should have caught a long time ago. You might know that Chad was adopted, a war orphan from Germany, raised by the ex-soldier who brought him out, on their family farm in Wisconsin. But at some point, sheriff's not sure when, it seems Chad was contacted by a surviving brother in East Berlin. Russian-born, it turns out, and a monk with the Orthodox Church there. He's been sending him money for years. And judging by Chad's bank accounts and the cash at his house, quite a bit more money recently."

He paused and looked at Kaz. "You ever play poker with Chad?"

Kaz shook his head. "No, I'm not a gambler."

"Yeah, me neither. But Chad's been playing some, locally, back room stuff. Quite a bit of money changes hands, apparently. Makes him vulnerable."

Kaz said nothing, thinking about what that meant.

"Bottom line, though, Heard has found no clear evidence tying Chad to the helo crash, or of him being involved in anything illegal. But several people are going to want to talk to him when he gets back. Including the Defense Intelligence Agency."

Kaz looked around the room, his eye pausing briefly on Gene Kranz. "Anyone here know this?"

"No. I need us to focus on getting Chad and the crew safely into the Pacific and then back here. The wheels of justice can wait until then."

55

Pacific Ocean

The radio signal began on the muddy banks of the springtime-swollen Amur River, just across from the eastern Soviet military-industrial city of Khabarovsk. The message had been coded for transmission at the Red Banner Pacific Fleet Intelligence Center just downriver, and now the pulsing electricity was traveling up 30 connected antenna towers, each nearly 800 feet tall. Like an entire orchestra of bass fiddles, the antennas throbbed deeply in unison, each vibrating, sending a low-frequency signal out into the surrounding air.

Very low.

The radio waves flowed out through the atmosphere, reflecting off the surrounding flatlands of the Amur River delta and 100 miles up to the electrically charged ionosphere, where their long wavelength bounced back down again. Trapped between the earth and sky, the Very Low Frequency signal followed the curve of the horizon across Sakhalin Island and the Sea of Okhotsk, and out over the Pacific Ocean.

Coded information, headed out to sea.

Most ships' antennas were far too short to pick up the signal and missed it as it passed by. But 50 feet below the water's surface, more than 6,000 kilometers away, a long trailing wire received it loud and clear. The electrical impulse passed through the deployed underwater antenna and into the ship, all the way forward to the communications chief's station. When he saw his yellow message light come on and the VLF needle jumping on the small screen, he turned to watch as the printer chugged to life, slowly tapping out the long, decoded message onto the thin roll of paper. He scanned the Cyrillic letters as they appeared.

New orders. He sighed. The Captain would not be pleased. They were already past due returning to their home port in Vladivostok, and a quick scan of the densely worded message looked like it would add at least another week at sea, maybe two.

But it was definitely not his job to scrutinize messages for Captain Serdyukov. He waited until the printer stopped, then carefully tore the paper off the machine just under End of Message and clipped it inside a folder marked Captain's Eyes Only. Locking the radio room hatch door, he turned up the narrow corridor towards the central post, in search of the captain of the nuclear-powered submarine K-252.

It was a Nalim-type sub, what the American Navy called Yankee class, 420 feet long, with a crew of 114 men, nuclear-powered, armed with 16 R-21 vertically launched ballistic missiles and 18 Type 53-65M wake-homing torpedoes. K-252 was a new ship; she'd been built two years previously just down the Amur River from Khabarovsk, and this was her second extended Pacific deployment. Captain Vasily Antonovich Serdyukov had commanded both.

As he was most hours of the day and night, Captain Serdyukov was seated in his brown leather swivel command chair, surrounded on all sides by the flat yellow panels of gauges and levers that gave him insight into and control over all systems of the sub. At the moment, they were moving quietly under the Pacific at 16 knots, 400 miles northeast of Hawaii, headed west. Towards home.

The comms chief stopped behind Serdyukov's right shoulder, checking if the Captain was busy, or perhaps dozing. The leather seat had a padded headrest for the relentless hours of work, and it was a mistake to waken Serdyukov if he was grabbing a nap during a quiet moment. He leaned forward to see if the Captain's eyes were closed.

They were. He looked closer at the face—the droopy eyelids, long nose and protruding chin of a tall man. Unusual in the submarine service, where the high hatches and low ceilings banged heads and knees mercilessly.

He decided the message's importance required him to clear his throat. The Captain's eyes instantly opened, flicking immediately across the gauges and digital readouts.

"Da, Pavel?" Captain Serdyukov's voice was deep.

The comms chief started in surprise. *How did he know it was me?* He stepped forward and handed over the message folder, nodded and returned immediately to his post, not wanting to be there when the Captain read the bad news.

Serdyukov opened the folder, scanned the message and then read it again, methodically. He leaned his head back to think. *This is a surprise.* The months of ballistic missile patrol up and down the American and Canadian coast had been successful, but also uneventful and monotonous. His ship had done well, but in essence, nothing had happened. Communications with the outside world had been rare, and the crew had turned inwards, busy with work and, in their highly regulated off-hours, making their own entertainment within the very limited confines of the ship. Except through the periscope, they hadn't seen another vessel, or any other people, since they'd left port. Food stores were getting low, and it was becoming increasingly harder to give the crew something to look forward to in the repetitive days. Arrival at home had been the next anticipated event.

He pictured what this message was going to mean for the ship. He would need to task his men to do things they had only practiced in drills and training exercises. Doing something very different, and with definite risk and potential consequences. Something clandestine and important. A smile curled his lips. The very essence of a submariner's purpose.

He reread the last lines of the message, which said further details would be sent shortly. But for now they had a specific destination, rough timing and expected actions. He began making a mental list of the skill sets of his men and the exercises they'd need to practice over the coming days. This was a chance for K-252 to distinguish herself as an outstanding ship of the Pacific Fleet, and for his crew to return to port with something to their credit besides bland reports of quiet patrols.

Captain Serdyukov was realistic; this had been his second command tour on the same boat. He knew there wouldn't be a third, and he was still only a captain of second rank. Successfully doing what the message described would go a long way to getting him promoted to full captain, able to wear the single thick bar and three stars on his shoulder that told everyone he was on his way to becoming an admiral. He nodded to himself. They needed to get this right.

He called the navigator over and gave him the updated coordinates. He watched as the information was typed into the inertial nav system, and felt the change of motion as the sub began to turn.

He'd have to brief his executive officer and the four department heads, and find some surface time for the specialist crewmen to practice operations. Their new orders were going to require patience, pinpoint accuracy and swift action.

He needed to get his men ready.

The sheltered harbors of the Hawaiian island of Oahu are a natural wonder. The inlets and bays reach deep inland, giving the islanders access to fresh water flowing down the steep slopes of the Koʻolau Range and protection from the ocean's storms. Food is abundant on the lush surrounding land, and under the bays' clear, still waters are pearl-producing oysters. Since before written history, Pacific sailors had found sanctuary in what the ancient Hawaiians called Wai Momi, the Waters of Pearl.

The harbor's entrance had been dredged and widened as ships got bigger, and the USS *New Orleans*, a flat-topped amphibious assault ship, required at least 30 feet of depth. As she exited Pearl Harbor and cleared Hammer Point, headed out to sea, she came left to exactly 154 degrees to stay in the center of the 1,000-foot-wide channel. Captain Bob Carius, standing by the forward windows of the conning tower, was relieved to see the depth sounder fall away rapidly, from 50 to 100, and then to over 1,000 feet as they cleared the island's shore. The brief stay at Pearl had been pleasant for the crew after a nine-month cruise, helping with Philippine flood relief and de-mining the coastal waters of North Vietnam as the last American combat troops were finally leaving. But he was looking forward to the tasking they'd received.

The *New Orleans* was sailing to recover the Apollo 18 crew.

Captain Carius wasn't sure what the post-Vietnam era was going to mean for the Pacific Fleet, but the *New Orleans* had acquitted herself well, and helping to bring the Apollo astronauts home was a definite feather in their cap. He'd even heard that Al Shepard, the first American in space and a Navy Rear Admiral, was going to be aboard to see the splashdown.

They passed the red and green harbor entrance buoys, and he relaxed, walking around the bridge, looking out at his ship. Most of the 700 crewmen had come up onto the large, flat deck as they'd left port, and he'd had the Apollo rescue helicopters proudly positioned on the bow to let everyone know where they were going. The maintainers had made sure that the Sikorsky SH-3A Sea Kings were freshly painted bright white, and the crews of Helicopter Sea Combat Squadron SIX had been practicing recovery procedures for several weeks.

They'd been waiting at Pearl for the exact location of the splashdown, and now NASA had given the Navy the coordinates: 300 miles north and a bit west of Oahu. An easy sail out, a little over a day to do final preparations on station, and they'd be ready.

Fun, really. Deploy the helos as soon as the capsule was under parachute, drop divers into the water next to it at splashdown, attach the flotation ring and help the crew into the rescue raft, hoist them aboard the *New Orleans* and welcome them back to Earth.

Unless something went wrong. He'd gotten a detailed briefing while in port, and he'd been running over his crew's readiness for multiple scenarios. There'd been storms in Apollo 11's planned landing area, and the rescue ship had to steam full-speed to meet the capsule hundreds of miles downrange. The Apollo 12 capsule had hit a wave hard at splashdown and an internal camera had broken loose; it hit an astronaut in the head, knocking him out. The ship's doctor had to give him six stitches. Apollo 15 had vented caustic hypergolic fuel that had melted parachute lines, collapsing one of its three canopies. And several capsules had landed upside down in the water, and the crew needed to quickly inflate emergency flotation balls to right them. From the briefing it was clear that Apollo 18 had had its share of serious trouble already, but he was confident that his ship and crew could deliver. They'd proven themselves on this cruise, in both war and peacetime, and they still had a couple of days for final polish. No matter what NASA threw at them, they'd be ready.

Carius leaned forward and looked up at the blue Hawaiian sky. This one should be a piece of cake.

Under the hot Sun on the surface of the Moon, Lunokhod was dying. Like a child with an uncontrollable fever, it was slowly shutting down internally, less and less capable to survive its own rising body heat.

Gabdul had worked frantically to try to save it just before the Apollo craft had lifted off. He'd alternated between driving and braking as violently as he could, trying to dislodge the layer of dust on the radiator, all while moving as close to the lander as possible, hoping its rocket blast might scour the flat surface clean. The team had talked quickly about the risk of debris damage, but it didn't matter. If they couldn't clear the dust, their mission was over.

They'd sent commands to close the camera covers just before liftoff, squinting their rover's eyes against the sandblast. But the light upper stage had left the surface so fast that it had blown only a little of the sand off; the rate of heating had slowed, but it hadn't stopped.

Gabdul had announced one last idea hurriedly, and had clicked the eyes back open while mashing the hand controller to full speed. His team had mapped a small, steep-sided crater a couple hundred meters away that they'd steered around on the way to the landing site. Now he was driving directly at it.

"I need the best timing countdown you can give me. Start at ten!" he urgently told his navigator. They needed to guess exactly right as they watched the new images slowly process, blurred with the bouncing motion, delayed by the enormous distance.

The navigator did his best, using every clue he could gather: forward speed readout, their nav map, the heading data and the latest looks at the lunar surface on the screen.

"Ten!" he said decisively. Then "Nine!"

He'd play the cadence right to the last, based on everything he saw. He said eight, seven and six quickly, and then five, four and three in an even rhythm. He could feel his heart racing, knowing this was all or nothing, based on too much guesswork.

"Dva . . . raz! Now, Gabdul, brake!"

Gabdul reversed hard, held it for two seconds and released his hand completely, listening to the small springs make a quick thocking sound as the hand controller returned itself to center. All eyes were glued to the screen.

His plan had been to bound over the edge at full speed and then lurch to a stop, driving the eight wheels backwards, encouraging the sand to slide off the top as Lunokhod came to rest on a steep angle.

The image resolved itself, drawing line by line from top to bottom on the monitor. All they could see was a screenful of lunar regolith, no horizon visible.

"We're in!" Gabdul turned to look at the rover's attitude sensor—a bit tipped left, but steeply nose-down. He read the number aloud, triumphant: "Thirty-five degrees!" That was basically the physical limit for a slope of loose regolith. They couldn't have done it any better. No one knew if they'd be able to drive out, but they'd done all they could.

Gabdul turned to the vehicle systems operator and asked the question on behalf of everyone. "Are we still getting hotter?"

The internal temperature readout was steady for many seconds. Longer than they'd seen during the race across the surface. Hopes rose. Then it clicked up by a tenth of a degree. And then another. And, as they all watched, by yet another.

It hadn't worked. The jolt hadn't shifted enough of the blanket of dust.

After three months of exploration, thousands of images and data points, and discovery of concentrated radioactivity on the Moon, the mission was over.

Lunokhod was in its grave.

Outside their building, the huge antenna that had brought the team the bad news pivoted, almost imperceptibly, its focused commands and patient listening circuits searching for a new signal. As soon as it found it, the self-tracking mechanism locked on and began following, steering precisely. The processors analyzed the timing and frequency shifts of the signals, and started doing the math. As it continued to track, the accuracy got better and better, until it had a solution threshold that could be trusted.

A second computer took that information and ran it through equations that included the mass and exact positions of the Moon and the spinning Earth, and used models of the friction that the atmosphere and shock waves would cause. It added the known characteristics of how previous missions had steered themselves, and how much g they had pulled as they descended.

In less than two minutes it had a result, and automatically transmitted it to the flight dynamics officer at his console in TsUP in Moscow. He looked at the screen with its table of flickering numbers, watching them update and become even more accurate with each passing second.

He leaned back and turned, waving to get the attention of the flight director. They now knew exactly where Apollo 18 was going to splash down.

56

Hickam Air Force Base, Hawaii

Kaz stretched and yawned as he stepped out of the dark interior of the C-141 transport plane, blinking at the bright Hawaiian sunshine, looking around the ramp and spotting the white Sea King helicopter waiting for them. He'd slept, but his lower back was aching; Air Force seats were built for troop transport, not comfort. As he stiffly walked down the airstairs, he could feel the heat reflecting up off the tarmac, his shirt starting to stick to him in the humid ocean air. Behind him, JW was noisily descending. A seaman met them at the bottom and took their hand luggage to transfer to the helo.

Al Shepard had gotten off first and was already taking the salute from the Sea King crew. Behind Al, waiting his turn, was the Soviet attaché, tall in a dark suit. In Houston, he'd introduced himself briefly as Roman Stepanov, his English good but thickly accented. He'd kept to himself during the flight, reading papers from his briefcase and dozing like the rest of them, even though each of the three Americans had moved to an empty seat in the Soviet's row during the flight to make conversation. Kaz had held out his hand across the seats. "Hi, I'm Kaz

Zemeckis, crew liaison. Been working in Mission Control throughout the flight." Stepanov, broad-shouldered and fit, had returned the handshake with a firm, dry grip and said, "Hello." The remaining hair on his prematurely bald head was neatly trimmed, his thick eyebrows were arched, and his small ears were a poor match for his large, hooked nose. His pale-gray eyes and thin mouth were expressionless. A thoughtful face.

"So did they brief you on what to expect during splashdown?"

"Yes." Stepanov held up a sheaf of papers on NASA letterhead.

A pause.

Kaz tried a different tack. "Been to Hawaii before?"

"No." Not unfriendly, just a clear vibe that he'd been doing something worthwhile and was politely waiting for Kaz to leave so he could get back to it. Like an interrupted professor.

"Okay, well, let me know if I can help."

The Russian had nodded and thanked him.

Not a chatterbox.

Kaz and the doctor climbed up into the helicopter and took their seats, opposite Al and the Russian, on the simple green webbing on metal frames that ran the length of the crew cabin. The crew chief gave them a short briefing on emergencies and handed them uninflated life jackets and earplugs as the five big rotor blades started turning above their heads.

The attaché listened attentively, then comfortably donned the safety equipment and did up the heavy shoulder and waist straps unaided.

Not Stepanov's first rodeo.

The Sea King lurched up off the pavement, pivoted in place, tipped forward and accelerated out to sea.

Chad looked out the window of *Pursuit*. The Moon behind him had shrunk to the size of a dime against the blackness. Ahead, what had been a thumbnail-sized marble, blue with white and green-brown highlights, was growing and resolving itself rapidly into the easily recognizable coastlines and country shapes of Earth; it felt like he was walking towards a lit globe on a darkened shelf.

He'd steered the ship to skim exactly against the side of that ball, where it would just brush the upper tendrils of the atmosphere. The ultimate high-stakes billiards shot: miss wide and they'd carom off into space with not enough oxygen to last until they could make it back. Hit with just a bit too much angle and the ship would dig in, disintegrating into flames under the violent deceleration.

He smiled at his reflection, repeating in the multilayered glass. He'd done everything perfectly. Been up for every challenge they'd thrown at him. And with the final test still coming, he was ready.

He glanced at Michael and Svetlana, thinking about the incomplete picture they each held in their heads, shaping their predictable choices and actions. He looked at Earth again, his smile growing wider. The Soviets thought they were directing what was going on—that they could control him! The Americans had arrogantly set the mission's parameters, yet needed someone who could actually do it.

I was chosen for this!

His life, from childhood until this exact moment, was like a movie script where he'd been the inevitable action hero.

Action hero. The words echoed in his head. He hadn't thought of himself that way before. But that's who he was. It was perfect. At every turn he'd taken the right action, moved forward, left the others behind— before they even knew what was happening.

And he was about to do it again. He had a plan that would achieve all the goals, and then some. He'd used this return trip, these two days when everyone else had just dozed and twiddled their thumbs, to dig into the details and come up with the right actions. His crew would be helpless to stop him.

He half closed his eyes and pictured it, his hands subtly performing the motions as if he were a conductor directing an orchestra. Reach here, move that, see this, say those words. A symphony of his own making, the ship responding, his actions setting the course of history.

A small thought popped into his reverie, unbidden. His smile faded and he frowned, picturing what it meant. He walked through the plan, seeing how it would unfold with this unwanted input, clicking through if/then statements, churning the wheel, checking the readout, then changing assumptions and rerunning it. Repeating until he had a way to make it work. As he saw the solution, his smile returned.

He checked his watch—enough time before tomorrow's main event.

One last look at himself in the window, the growing brightness of Earth highlighting his face, the endless darkness behind.

Action hero.

First nights on ships always kept Kaz awake. He wasn't sure why. Maybe it was the new sounds, the different motions of this particular hull in the water, the hardness of the thin Navy-issue mattress on the berth. From experience he knew it would be better the second night, and after a few days he'd sleep soundly. But for now, he was restless in the darkness of his small cabin aboard the USS *New Orleans*. He opened his eyes wide. *Weird*, he thought, not for the first time. An inner room on a ship with watertight closed hatches made for total darkness. He could feel that his eyelids were open, but his eye could see absolutely nothing.

A good place to think.

The sheriff hadn't found any proof that Chad had sabotaged Tom's helo, but the other information was troubling. Why had Chad never admitted to anyone that he was born into a Russian family, or that he'd retained enough of the language to stay in touch with this newly uncovered brother of his?

Kaz had learned that sometimes, to solve a problem, you had to take it back to basics and repicture it as if it were an exam question on a page. He tried phrasing it that way to himself.

A lander with two crew, American and Russian, is on the Moon. Above them, a spaceship with an American aboard is orbiting every 2 hours. Earth is a quarter million miles away, turning every 24 hours. Mission Control is in Houston, but has satellite dishes spaced around the globe to

talk continuously to the crew. Once in a while, Houston hears the crew
click their mic twice. Why?

Kaz blinked several times and turned his head against the hard
pillow. He could feel the stiff crispness of the pillowcase, no doubt
high-temp-washed and rough-pressed by a seaman somewhere in the
industrial bowels of the ship.

Nothing.

He tried another entry point. Why had the Soviets sent a KGB
officer? The way the guy was so quiet and calculating and the muscular bulk under the lousy suit were giveaways. Why wouldn't they send
a political, maybe the deputy ambassador, someone who they could
publicly identify in the PR pictures so they could wave the Soviet flag
in everyone's face? He recalled Stepanov's face—this guy wasn't here
for protocol. So what *was* he here for?

The cosmonaut was supposed to still be on Almaz, dutifully orbiting and photographing secret things around the planet, dropping film
to Earth in canisters. No one had planned on her being part of this
mission. So Stepanov was part of the reaction on their part, another
attempt to turn the situation to their advantage. But what did they have
control over, and what leverage could they use?

He stretched out on his back and scrunched the pillow under his
neck for support. The berth was just long enough that the top of his head
and his feet didn't touch the bulkheads. He closed his eyes and exhaled
to relax.

His eyes snapped open in the darkness. *Could that be it?*

He tried to remember the exact timing, reviewing when he'd been
on shift, mapping it out. He realized that it fit.

Christ!

The Soviets had been talking to the crew.

And the crew had responded.

57

Re-entry

Chad glanced at his small computer screen: 36,165 feet per second. He did the math. *Holy crap! I'm flying seven miles every second. Thirty-two times the speed of sound. Take THAT, Chuck Yeager!*

He leaned forward in his seat to look across at Michael, strapped in beside him, and the cosmonaut on the far right. "Get ready for the finest seven minutes of your life, kids."

The three of them had re-donned their spacesuits. NASA had learned that a Soviet crew of three had perished when re-entry vibrations and g-loads caused a cabin leak, and had added the safety measure for Apollo 18.

Pursuit was 75 miles high, just beginning to touch the outer atmosphere. Chad punched in the program code to check landing location, and compared it to the latitude and longitude Houston had given them. Identical. They were headed to an empty spot in the ocean, just a couple miles short of the USS *New Orleans*.

On the outside of the capsule, bad things were starting to happen. *Pursuit* was slamming into the rarefied air molecules with so much energy that it was ripping electrons free and tearing at its belly shield, burning off the outer layer. The mix of ionized gases clung to *Pursuit's* skin in a sheath of blowtorch flames; an electric plasma field, glowing yellow and orange and red, enveloped the ship in a hypersonic fireball.

"My God, look at that!" Michael was watching the flames lick and dance across the windows, the shadows flickering inside the capsule. "We're flying through a blast furnace!"

Svetlana let the chatter wash over her, probing how her body felt in anticipation of what was about to happen. She'd studied re-entry in detail at Star City, and had practiced repeatedly in the centrifuge trainer; to pass her cosmonaut flight qualification, she'd had to take over from the ship's computers and fly the simulated capsule by hand, all the way down to parachute opening. On an early training run she'd misjudged it, dug in too deeply and failed, pulling 14 g—beyond the limits of the simulator, barely survivable in real life. She knew how thin the margins were.

She looked at the horizon line in the overhead windows, judging their entry angle; it made sense to her. They were coming in belly first, slightly tipped up and rolled to the right, the computer ready to play the roll angle to control the g force. She nodded. *Just like I'd do it.*

Chad watched his entry monitoring panel, the large black arrow showing roll angle, the small digital readouts showing g and distance to go. He ran his thumb down the checklist and warned, "Here it comes!"

The sudden onslaught of force was vicious. In just 15 seconds the g slammed from zero to seven times their normal weight, pinning their heads hard back inside their helmets, forcing their arms down onto their chests, crushing them into their seats.

Svetlana could feel the skin of her face being pulled backwards, the strained tautness across her cheeks, her eyes watering to try to fight the brutality.

Michael gasped. "Hhhard to breathe!" he grunted. Pulling oxygen into his lungs felt like weight-lifting; he had to deliberately force his chest to expand, pushing his ribs forward.

Yet as soon as it was there it was gone, backing off to just 3 g as the capsule pulled out of its initial steep dive, settling into a shallower angle, racing and falling through the air. Chad knew the profile. "A couple minutes here, then we'll peak again."

They were on their own. The communications failure they'd had after launch had returned as soon as they'd jettisoned the lower Service Module, as expected. And even if the radios had been working, the glowing plasma field was blocking the antennas.

Pursuit was a fireball, plummeting earthward with the first step complete, now rolling precisely in readiness for the second g-spike.

Ever since the Apollo craft's launch day, the *Cosmonaut Yuri Gagarin* communications relay ship had been steaming northwards across the Pacific to be in position to observe splashdown. She was now just over the horizon from the USS *New Orleans*, her huge twin tracking antennas pointed along the expected entry trajectory. As the capsule emerged from the heavy g-load, still 170,000 feet up and racing towards the waiting ships, the *Gagarin*'s systems found it and locked on.

The antenna operator said, "We have it, Captain. Exactly on track."

The Captain nodded and pointed at his communications officer. "Let them know." The lieutenant typed rapidly, and the coded message left the ship, relaying up through distant satellites and back down on the other side of the world to TsUp in Moscow. There, the flight director waved for Chelomei's attention and pointed to his screen.

Chelomei read the text and nodded. *Pa paryadkeh.* So far, so good.

A hundred miles to the northeast of the *Gagarin*, Kaz was on the bridge of the *New Orleans*, standing beside Al Shepard and the attaché, Stepanov. He checked his watch and glanced at the timings in his notebook, providing a running commentary for Captain Carius. "They're six hundred miles out now, sir, with the second g-spike to go, expecting drogue chute opening in just under six minutes."

Carius nodded. "And how long until splashdown?"

"The drogue will pull out the three main parachutes, and then they'll be under those for another five minutes, so into the water in about ten minutes." With no radio communication, Kaz was just guessing, using predicted times. The *New Orleans* would receive the capsule's homing beacon as soon as the deploying parachutes triggered it. Then they'd know for sure.

Carius turned to his executive officer. "XO, what's 501's status?"

"She cleared the deck ten minutes ago with our team and the NASA doc on board, and is on station." The XO pointed forward and left of the bow, where the white of the Sea King helicopter was just visible above the blue horizon. Carius raised his binoculars and could make out the large 501 painted on her tail.

"The helo crew's reporting pretty choppy seas, Boss, five-foot swells."

Shepard gave a low whistle. "That's worse than it was for my crew, Bob. More like what they saw on Apollo 12." He grimaced. "Poor suckers're gonna puke."

Bob Carius smiled. "That's what you get when you fly Air Force astronauts, Admiral."

The Captain had one more question. "XO, we seeing anyone else in the area?"

The XO deliberately didn't look at Stepanov, who'd been listening, stone-faced. "We've got the Soviet comm relay ship, the *Gagarin*, just over a hundred miles out along the entry track. Normal enough, and to be expected with a cosmonaut on board this time." He didn't mention what the captain already knew: they'd deployed several sonobuoys but had heard no sounds of any submarine activity. No sub had ever shadowed a previous splashdown, but the *New Orleans* was an anti-sub ship, and the XO was just being thorough.

Carius smiled. "So apart from maybe needing some sick bags, I think the good ship *New Orleans* is ready to pipe aboard three new crewmembers."

———

Chad watched the g-meter carefully for the critical moment. He had to time this just right: early enough to have the desired effect, but too late for Michael to diagnose what was happening and take countering action. He could feel the capsule lofting slightly under him, the force letting up slightly prior to falling into thicker air and starting the second g-load.

Now!

He reached out with his left hand and flicked the switch to take spacecraft control away from the guidance computer. He was holding the hand controller in his right, and he rocked it hard sideways, towards his leg, commanding a turn. Small thrusters on the hull fired in response, and the capsule began to spin up to the left, like a slow-turning top.

Michael was alarmed. "What are you seeing?"

Chad put incredulity into his voice. "Did you miss it? Our beta was building rapidly! I've taken over for now, getting ready to go to Program 66 for ballistic."

Michael stared at the displays. *Our sideslip built up? Shit! How did I miss that?* He flipped the page in his checklist to the backup ballistic procedures. "Okay, I'm with you, Chad, on 2-6." He quickly thought about it. "With bad beta, though, I recommend against program ballistic, and that puts us in the starred block for manual EMS."

As Chad had expected, Michael was reacting just like they'd trained. "Copy, but let's try Program 66, to give the computer another chance. If no joy, I'll just take over manually again."

Michael weighed the odds. "Okay, agreed. I'm watching."

Chad released the hand controller and steadied his arm under the g-load as his finger poked at the small keyboard. Michael confirmed—"I see P66"—and Chad pushed the Proceed button. Their eyes locked onto the Entry Monitoring Systems panel.

Michael rapidly thought ahead. The ship was slowly rolling now, no longer generating continuous lift along its flight path; it had gone from flying under control like an airplane to just falling, arcing downwards like a thrown baseball.

"Hold on!" he shouted, and waved a hand near Svetlana to make sure she realized there was a serious problem. They were about to fall steeper into the thicker air and endure a lot more g than planned. As they fell faster, that air was going to slow their forward speed even more as well. There was nothing he could do.

Pursuit was going to land short.

At Kaena Point, on a high, windy ridge at the western tip of Oahu, an Air Force domed radar tracking antenna detected the subtle change in *Pursuit*'s motion. The data was automatically sent via undersea cable to Mission Control in Houston, appearing as numbers on the screen at the re-entry Guidance Officer's console.

"FLIGHT, GUIDO, the capsule's off trajectory." He watched for several seconds, listening to the rapid analysis in his headset from the experts in his back room. "We think it's gone to ballistic mode."

Damn! Gene Krantz thought. The weather briefer had talked about the rough sea state, and this meant the crew would be in the water longer than planned. "Copy, GUIDO, let me know when you have an updated splashdown location." He turned to his communications officer. "INCO, let's get the *New Orleans* that info ASAP."

Ninety seconds later the teletype machine began clacking in the communications cabin of the *New Orleans*. The Petty Officer tore off the page while reading it and hustled to hand it to the XO. He silently read it and handed it to the Captain, who frowned.

"This is from your boys in Houston," he said to the small group. "The capsule has gone into something called a backup ballistic mode, and is going to land short, apparently." He turned to the helmsman and handed him the paper. "Make for those new coordinates, full speed."

"How far short?" Kaz asked, evaluating causes for the unexpected change, already guessing the answer.

"About a hundred miles. We'll be there in four hours. The helo will take about an hour or so." He thought quickly. "XO, I don't think they'll have enough fuel now. Bring them aboard for a hot pit."

The Captain turned to Al Shepard. "Admiral, this just escalated. The new splashdown site is way too near that Soviet ship. I'm going to send two helos so we can have a few extra personnel on-site until the *New Orleans* can get there. Who from your team do you want to go?"

"The doc, of course, and Kaz. We'll need somebody on scene familiar with crew ops."

Stepanov spoke for the first time that morning. "I must go too."

The XO immediately shook his head and looked straight at the captain. "No way, Boss. We've already got all the skills we need, and Kaz is Navy-familiar. I don't need an embassy bureaucrat getting in the way." He glanced at Stepanov. "No offense."

Stepanov's expression said he took none. He spoke calmly. "Major Gromova doesn't speak English, and might be injured because of this new situation. There is no question. I must go also."

The Captain looked at his XO. "He's got a point, and our orders are clear that we provide full support to the cosmonaut. Put him on the same helo as Kaz, keep him out of trouble."

The XO started to speak, thought better of it and nodded. "Aye aye, sir." He nodded at the two men and headed rapidly towards the ladder leading down to the deck. "You come with me. We'll get you outfitted fast and on your way. We've got a lost space capsule to catch."

Kaz looked around inside the Sea King as it throbbed noisily, powering nose-low through the air at max speed towards the southwest. He was relieved that this wasn't a typical Apollo recovery crew, with safety divers and medicos. Filling the seats around Stepanov and himself were six large men, all wearing coveralls and heavy boots, each cradling an MP5 submachine gun on a shoulder strap, with a Colt M1911 pistol clipped on their webbed belt. The XO had decided that with the Soviet ship nearby there was potential for military action, and these men were the masters-at-arms of the *New Orleans*—the cross-trained sailors responsible for law enforcement at sea.

Sitting to Kaz's left was a black-haired man with a wide black mustache, the senior rate in the group. He'd shouted instructions as they'd hurried aboard the helo, and Kaz leaned close now to make himself heard through the earplugs, above the din.

"I'm Lieutenant Commander Kaz Zameckis, detailed with NASA. What briefing did your team get?"

"Petty Officer First Class Colombo, sir. We didn't get much of a briefing; the XO said the Apollo capsule has two astronauts and a cosmonaut aboard, be nearby for a show of force and take action only if needed." He looked at his men. "We had some pretty hairy times up the Vietnam coast and in the P.I., and have been training together this whole cruise. We're ready if something happens."

Kaz nodded. "Some of you may have to go into the water."

"Yep, we've got gear." He pointed at several large duffel bags inside the aft loading ramp. "I'll get the guys dressed when we're closer. No use overheating for now."

Kaz leaned farther, talking directly into the man's ear so he wouldn't be overheard. "If the XO didn't tell you, the guy with me is a Soviet attaché, likely military. Need to keep an eye on him."

Colombo nodded without looking and said, "My men can handle it."

Kaz sat back, satisfied. Stepanov was sitting motionless, staring straight ahead. Kaz thought back: the Russian had shown no surprise when they'd learned the capsule was landing short. Then again, he hadn't yet shown any emotion. *Did he somehow expect it?* Kaz had spent another full hour of the night in his bunk thinking through possibilities before finally falling asleep, and had briefed Al Shepard over breakfast. They'd agreed direct crew communication from Moscow might have been possible; this event only heightened the concern.

He turned back to the mustached Colombo.

"I'd like a gun as well."

Colombo turned and spoke into Kaz's ear. "We have extra in the bag. I'll get you one at a good moment."

58

Splashdown Zone

The g-load came on even more suddenly this time, like a skipping stone badly thrown into a pond; instead of skimming into the water at an angle, *Pursuit* was falling, nearly vertical, into the rapidly thickening air below. Michael called out the readings on the digital display, grunting more and more as the weight increased.

"There's five. Now six." He strained to take a quick breath. "Seven, eight . . . there's nine!" The flames on the other side of the glass deepened to an intense yellow, the cockpit glowing like it was on fire. On *Pursuit's* belly, the three-inch-thick protective plate of fiberglass and epoxy resin took the brunt of it, burning off and vaporizing in the 5,000-degree, friction-driven heat. Through the windows the three of them watched the roiling sheets of flame and continuous sparks of burnt resin whipping past.

And then they were through. The crushing force disappeared like someone had just lifted it off them, and the windows filled with the blue of the sky. The capsule was now simply a skydiver plummeting straight down at 250 miles an hour, 5 miles above the Pacific, waiting for her parachute to open.

Bang! The noise of small explosives came through their helmets as a metal cover blew off the top of *Pursuit* and two small drogue chutes mortared out behind it. The beyond-hurricane-force wind caught the fabric and snapped the unreefing chutes fully open, yanking the lines taut, pushing the crew hard down into their seats.

A brief new normal now, a momentary calm, as they fell in a 120-mile-per-hour vertical dive, waiting for the final event.

At 11,000 feet a small pressure sensor sent the command to cut the drogue lines and explosively fire three small parachutes; they caught the air and dragged out the big main chutes, which blossomed and filled the sky above their heads with red and white.

Michael raised two gloved fists, relief clear in his voice. "I see three good chutes!"

"Slava Bogu," Sveltana said quietly. Thank God.

On the top of *Pursuit*, a small VHF antenna pivoted clear and began transmitting the good news, a triumphant beacon signal for the rescue forces to home in. But the two helicopters were still beyond the horizon, 70 miles away, and missed it.

On the bridge of the *Gagarin*, the signal came clearly through the loudspeakers. The radio operator had been tracking the re-entry and quickly narrowed in on the exact location: "Bearing 037, Captain, range twelve kilometers." All heads turned to scan the bright sky, the Captain raising powerful binoculars to his eyes. "Vizhu," he said with satisfaction. I see it.

He turned back to the radio operator and nodded once. "Let them know."

The impact with the water was violent; *Pursuit*'s broad, flat underside made for a resounding belly flop, like squarely driving into a wall at 22 miles per hour.

"Christ!" Michael swore. "What a car crash!"

Pursuit plunged deeply, the salt water curling up around her in an enveloping wave. Then, like a cork, she bobbed immediately back up and tipped, yanked sideways by the parachutes caught in the wind.

The Apollo designers had recognized from the beginning that the capsule could function as a boat, but not very well. Ideally it would float upright, with the crew lying in their seats; they named that orientation Stable One. But in testing they'd also identified that the capsule could easily float inverted. They called that Stable Two.

Pursuit came to rest in the water upside down, swaying in the heavy waves. The crew hung in their straps as checklists fell to the top of the cockpit, banging against the metal of the tunnel hatch.

"Stable Two!" Michael called.

Chad threw the switches to cut the parachute lines. "Yeah, I see that. I'll get the float bags." He pushed in several circuit breakers and listened as two small compressors spun into life, pumping air into three inflatable bags attached to the top of *Pursuit*. They were designed to give the capsule added flotation and flip it upright.

What the engineers hadn't considered was the relentless effect of truly heavy seas. Waves kept breaking over the exposed flat bottom of *Pursuit*, flooding the compressor air inlets, overloading the built-in drains. The bags filled too slowly, getting pulled back and forth with each wave, the forces prying them against their mountings.

Perhaps if they'd filled fast enough the design would have worked and popped *Pursuit* up to Stable One. But the partially filled and still floppy bags were worked mercilessly back and forth by the powerful surges. Stressed to the limit, first the center bag tore, followed within seconds by the other two. The compressors kept running, futilely pumping air into the water next to the flapping remnants of the bags, the stream of bubbles rising around the sloped sides of the ship, popping on the surface between the waves.

Pursuit was going to stay upside down. And her rescue divers were still sitting in their Sea King helicopter, 65 miles away.

———

"Shit! This is taking too long." Chad's anger grew as he looked at the timer and then through the dark of the underwater windows, trying to spot the yellow of the filling bags. He double-checked his switches: no mistake.

"Yeah, the bags aren't working," Michael said. "And with the ballistic entry, help's gonna be a while getting here. I'm thinking we should get outside by ourselves." They were swaying left and right as the capsule rocked in the waves, their heads hanging down and their arms and legs dangling back and forth. After a week of weightlessness, he felt dizzy and disoriented, and had already had a twinge of nausea.

Fuck! Chad thought. *I flew this perfectly, and the stupid engineers can't design three balloons that work?* The motion was getting to him as well, and he shook his head to clear it. "Okay, I'm starting into unaided egress. I'll get the hatch and the raft, and you take care of her." He disconnected his suit hoses and comm line and twisted around to drag the survival raft kit out of its locker, dropping it down by the hatch. The motion made his head spin, and he blinked hard until things stabilized. He released his harness buckle and immediately flipped down towards the hatch, landing hard on his hands and knees. The air in the cockpit was getting warm and humid, and his visor was fogging, his body banging left and right with the wave motion. As he reached to open the hatch, he felt the first surge of nausea, and swallowed hard. Just as the hatch popped free and water rushed in around its edge seals, Chad vomited. Focused projectile vomiting, filling his visor in front of his face, splashing back into his nose and eyes, the gastric acid blinding him.

"Fuck!" he yelled, the "k" ending in a wet, retching cough and a second spasm. He grabbed blindly for his neck ring and released it, yanking the fouled helmet off his head, rubbing his eyes clear. He rotated the hatch out of the way, grabbed the survival kit, took a breath and rocked forward through the hatch, headfirst into the black water.

Behind him, Michael was vomiting as well. He'd peeled his helmet off when he'd felt it coming, and was using it as a bucket to throw up into while disconnecting himself and Svetlana. As soon as he saw Chad go out the hatch, he released his harness and reached up to release hers.

Svetlana still had her helmet on, and watched as Michael waved her urgently towards the water-filled hatch. *Weak Americans! Why are both these men sick?* She'd trained for emergency water egress in an inverted capsule in the Black Sea, and moved easily, grabbing the sides of the hatch with both hands, and thrusting herself through, feet-first. Behind her, Michael had one last look around, grabbed his survival kit, took a deep breath and pushed himself into the hatch.

All three of them were in the sea.

As Chad floated rapidly up, bareheaded, the tight rubber seal around his neck kept the water out of his spacesuit. Clutching the bulky survival kit tightly under his left arm, he pushed repeatedly with his right to fend off the sloping side of the capsule.

His lungs were screaming as he burst into the sunshine; instinctively he gulped for a huge breath just as a wave hit, slapping him in the face with a five-foot-high wall of water, smashing him into *Pursuit's* hard, curved edge. He raised his hands to protect his head, and the survival kit bounced out of his grasp, skittering across the belly of the capsule.

Shit! He coughed and retched up seawater, blinking his eyes against the saltiness, scrabbling for a handhold on the smooth, wet underside of the capsule. His gloved fingers blindly found a bolt hole and he pulled hard, sliding himself towards the floating kit. The next wave picked him up and slammed him again into *Pursuit*, the impact making him gasp. He swam clumsily through the surging water, kicking inside the stiffness of the suit, trying to focus and time it right. Just as a third wave hit, he reached hard with his right hand and felt his fingers close around the survival kit's handle. The crashing water tumbled them both clear of the capsule as he fumbled at the long zipper to open the bag and deploy the raft.

Svetlana's helmeted head bobbed up behind him, and she looked around, assessing, treading water hard to stay clear of the capsule. The trapped oxygen inside her suit would only be good for a few more breaths, and soon she'd have to take off her helmet. She spotted Chad 10 meters away and started swimming hard towards him, letting each wave push her as she stroked and kicked. She watched as he reached inside an oblong bag and pulled; a yellow raft started inflating, rapidly filling, unfolding itself into a long rectangle. Chad was pulling on its handles as it reached full-size, twisting and timing the waves to try to yank it under himself, and finally he flopped facedown into the center.

She kicked hard and found a strap trailing in the water. As soon as the next wave rolled past she grabbed the raft with both hands and pulled herself up and in, landing on top of Chad's legs. Both of them flailed to get on their backs in the center, to stabilize and not capsize in the heaving seas.

As Michael's bare head burst to the surface, he spun, spotted them and started side-stroking hard, his elbow crooked through the end strap of his kit bag. But the raft was floating on the surface, the wind blowing it along the foaming tops of the waves. Michael stole glances each time he crested the top of a wave, gauging his progress, and realized he was losing the race; the kit was dragging him down. "Hey!" he yelled as loudly as he could, trying to get their attention above the noise of the wind and water.

Svetlana was getting dizzy with the buildup of carbon dioxide in her suit. As she popped off her helmet, she heard Michael's voice. She raised her head over the bulbous side of the raft and spotted him splashing towards them, 10 meters away.

"Morskoy yakor?" she shouted at Chad. Is there a sea anchor? He looked at her uncomprehendingly, dazed with the nausea and his repeated hard impacts with *Pursuit*. *Useless!* She probed under him, searching for a bundle on a thick strap that had been in every raft she'd ever trained on. When she found it, she tore the package open and hurled it overboard, letting the jellyfish-shaped cloth anchor unfurl and start dragging. Immediately she felt a tug and then the entire raft pivoted, stabilizing and slowing against the wind and the waves.

She propped herself up on an elbow again to see Michael, and spotted him struggling, seemingly farther away. "Syudah!" she yelled twice, as loudly as she could. Over here! She waved her hand high, back and forth.

Christ, I'm not going to make it! Michael thought. Every time he'd caught a glimpse of the raft it was getting away from him. He decided to let go of his kit just as he heard the female voice scream, and changed his mind, keeping the strap inside his elbow. He strained again to look, and saw a hand waving. Kicking harder, he pulled as strongly as he could with his free arm, cupping his gloved hand to get the most out of every stroke. He stole another glance and the raft seemed slightly closer.

He heard her voice yelling again—"Da, Da!"—and kept pulling, timing his strokes with each wave, clumsily trying to bodysurf with the kit in between crests. He thought her calls were getting louder, and craned his head up, relieved to see the raft just 10 feet away. "Syudah!" she shouted again, with one of her arms over the side, reaching for him. He gave a final maximum-effort stroke and found her hand, their gloved fingers locking together. She reached over the edge with her other hand and grabbed the kit as he twisted to find a handrail. Kicking and heaving with the last of his strength, with Svetlana pulling on the back of his neck ring, he got his upper torso onto the inflated curve of the raft, and with one final kick, tumbled in against Chad and Svetlana.

A jumble of bodies crammed into a pitching three-man raft, being blown steadily away from their spacecraft towards the open, empty, wind-swept Pacific.

Michael spoke first, in heaving breaths, to Svetlana. "Thank you! How do you say it? Spasiba?"

"Nyeh za shto," she responded. It was nothing. She handed him the kit, anticipating what was inside.

Michael took a breath to gather himself. He unzipped the package, pulling out two heavy, army-green metal blocks. He held them up to her. "Radio!"

Svetlana nodded. "Znayoo." I know.

Michael twisted his wrist rings to release his gloves from the sleeves of the suit, and peeled the heavy wet fabric off his hands. He tucked them into his leg pockets, and with bare fingers slid the cylindrical battery into the radio, twisted the cap into place and clicked the thumbwheel to turn it on. Immediately there was an audible hiss of static, and he screwed on the whip antenna. He knew from training that they were now transmitting an emergency beacon signal, and that by pushing the button on the side, they could talk.

"Give me that," Chad said. "I'll call in the helos." He held out his hand.

Michael looked at him across the length of the raft, paused for a second and then shrugged. "You're the boss." He leaned forward, handing it over. Svetlana, watching the exchange, understood what had just happened. *Tipeechny.* Typical.

Chad held the radio up to his ear and pushed the button. "Rescue Forces, this is the Apollo 18 crew. We've exited the spacecraft and are secure in the raft." He looked back at *Pursuit* in the distance as the waves bobbed them up and down, and up at the Sun. "We've been blown about a hundred yards downwind, to the northeast, and are continuing to drift, with sea anchor deployed. Crew is fine, and so is the cosmonaut." He released the button and turned the thumbwheel up until he could clearly hear the static, waiting for a response.

There was none.

He was bringing the radio to his mouth to transmit again, when he saw the sea begin erupting between them and *Pursuit*. Michael and Svetlana had been watching his face as he talked; when they saw his change of expression, they whipped around to look.

It seemed like the waves were calming somehow, and then as if they were parting. The dark water went suddenly clear in the sunlight, weirdly distorting up and over some unseen shape, the waves turning white as they broke alongside it.

Emerging from the depths, the broad, jet-black hull of an enormous submarine crested out of the water. All three of them looked back along its length to the upthrust conning tower, its diving planes protruding out like stubby wings. There were no markings on the glistening black hull; it was like a monstrous metal whale, unexpectedly there beside them.

A head appeared over the edge of the conning tower, and a megaphone appeared. They heard a brief squeal and then a male voice hailed them in Russian, the sound distinct above the wind and the waves.

"Major Gromova, welcome back to Earth. We are launching a rescue boat. Stand by to be brought aboard."

"Holy shit!" Michael yelled. "Chad, I don't know what he just said, but we need Navy helo support ASAP!" As they watched, a hatch pivoted open on the submarine's forward deck, and men started climbing out onto the wet flat surface.

Chad nodded, his mind racing. He pushed the button again on the radio. "Rescue Forces, this is the Apollo 18 crew. A submarine has surfaced and they're taking the cosmonaut. Need assistance immediately."

Twenty-five miles away, the Sea King flight engineer hurried back from the cockpit, stopping in front of Kaz.

"Commander, we just got contact with the Apollo crew." He tilted his head towards the cockpit. "You're the senior officer, and the pilot needs you on the radio now, sir." He looked at Colombo. "You too, PO."

They followed him to the cockpit, where he handed Kaz headphones and showed him where the transmit button was. Colombo donned a second pair to listen.

"Apollo 18, Apollo 18, Kaz here, how do you read me?" Kaz spoke loudly above the helo's noise, holding one earphone tight against his head.

Chad's voice came back, crackling with static. "Kaz! We're in the raft, and there's a Commie submarine here! They're launching a boat to come take the cosmonaut."

Shit! Kaz turned and yelled to the pilot. "How long to get there?"

"We're twenty-four miles out—nine minutes."

Kaz pushed the mic button. "Copy, Chad, we'll be there in nine minutes. Two helos, one with . . ." He stopped himself, realizing that the Russian sub would be listening to their communications. He looked out the side window at the other chopper and turned to the flight engineer. "Is that helo on this freq?"

A nod.

"Helo 501, get Dr. McKinley on the radio." As he waited, Kaz talked urgently with the pilot and flight engineer, briefing possible options.

JW's voice was in the headsets. "Dr. McKinley's listening."

Kaz updated him on the situation and what he wanted them to do.

JW's voice was crisp. "Copy, Kaz, I'll let this crew know."

All eyes strained forward, trying to spot the splashdown site. The flight engineer tapped the pilot's shoulder, pointing slightly left. "There it is!"

Low in the water, barely visible on the horizon, the long black shape of the submarine glinted in the sunlight, its conning tower jutting squarely up. Just visible was the splash of yellow of the raft. Kaz talked hurriedly with Colombo, who went back to brief his men.

In the raft, Chad held the radio out to Michael. "You direct them in."

Michael took it, puzzled, as Chad grabbed the open survival kit and dragged it forward. Kaz's voice rattled loudly in Michael's hand. "We're seven minutes out. Sitrep."

Michael looked across at the sub. "They have a black Zodiac on deck, and it looks like two frogmen are getting in to head this way." He squinted, trying to see detail. "Looks like they're armed, Kaz!"

As Michael was speaking, Chad turned away from Svetlana, his suit blocking her view. He dug into the survival kit bag, found what he was looking for and slid it into his leg pocket. As he turned, she spoke to him in Russian.

"Where is it?"

He looked at her. "What?"

She spoke rapid-fire. "I know you understand me! Stop being an idiot. The stone! Where is Lunokhod's stone?"

Chad frowned, shaking his head. "Don't understand you, toots." He glanced at Michael. "Any idea what she wants?"

Michael shrugged. "Beats me." He looked across at the Soviet Zodiac, now in the water. "How do you want to handle this?"

They heard the outboard motor sputter to life and saw a white curl start under the Zodiac's bow. Chad yelled, "If that helo doesn't get here in time, then there's not much we can do. She belongs to them, and they came all this way to get her."

Svetlana looked back and forth at the two men, and then at the Zodiac. Time to act. She reached down, unzipped her leg pocket, pulled out the pistol and pointed it at Chad.

"We are out of time. Give me the stone. Now!"

Michael stared, incredulous, and pushed the transmit button on the radio as he yelled, "Chad, she's got a gun!"

"I see that." Chad's voice was calm as he looked directly at her, shaking his head slowly. "Whatever you want, girly, I don't have it." He pointed across the prow of the sub at *Pursuit*. "Did you forget something in the spaceship?" He pointed again. "Makeup, or something common?" He accented the last word.

Svetlana frowned. *Did he just say "kahmen"?* The Russian word for stone. She snorted in frustration and shouted at him again. "Stop playing games! Is the stone inside the capsule?"

Chad nodded yes. "That's right, toots, you keep babbling. Your cavalry's almost here to rescue you."

Michael felt paralyzed. *Where the fuck did she get a gun? And what does she want?* He kept his thumb on the mic button, holding it down.

The outboard motor whine of the submarine's inflatable Zodiac was loud now, pulsing as it neared, rising and falling with the waves. Svetlana kept the pistol trained on Chad as the boat pulled alongside. The large, wet-suited submariner in the bow looked at the scene in the raft and turned laughing to his only crewmate. In Russian he said, "Looks like she doesn't need our help." His smile was broad as they reached and grabbed for the handles on the raft. "Major Gromova, we're here to rescue you."

She unleashed a torrent of Russian at him. His smile disappeared. He looked back at the capsule in the distance, and then at the sky to the northeast. He reached down with his free hand and lifted a Kalashnikov submachine gun, cradling it, waving it urgently at Michael and Chad. He spoke in thickly accented English. "Get een!"

Michael looked to Chad, who raised his palms. The Soviet reached across and took the radio, handing it to the helmsman by the motor, then grabbed Michael's arm and tumbled him onto the Zodiac's plank floor.

Svetlana was still pointing her pistol, and she ordered Chad in Russian: "You next." Chad shrugged and climbed across, the sailor grabbing him by his suit's neck ring and pushing him into place next to Michael.

Svetlana pocketed her pistol, stood to haul in the sea anchor line with both hands and passed the end to the Russian. Timing it carefully with the surging waves, she stepped neatly between the boats. The helmsman revved the outboard, and with the raft now trailing, steered hard towards the bow of the submarine and the capsule beyond.

Thinking about what Svetlana had shouted at him, the lead sailor put his face close to Chad's, his large, black-suited body menacing. "Vere is it?"

Michael was watching. *Where is what? What's going on?*

Chad had a strange smile on his face. *Excellent! This one speaks English! That'll make it simple!* He glanced at Michael. "I think they want some of our moonrocks." He turned and looked into the sailor's face. "Never had any of their own, and now I guess they think they deserve some." He looked up at the Navy helicopters, just visible in the distance. "But it looks like we're gonna capture the flag, Ivan. What are you going to do about it?"

This is going to work, just like I figured! The Soviets could have their precious cosmonaftka back, but the US would get the real prize. And all because of him.

The slap was sudden and totally unexpected, making the impact feel worse; the sailor's full-handed blow rocked Chad's head violently to the side. The sailor spoke again, his accent thick. "I ask once more. Vere is the radioactivni kahmen—the radioactive stone?"

"Hey, you can't do that!" Michael protested. The sailor twisted and shoved him violently towards the bow, and the helmsman raised his Kalashnikov to hold him there. Chad was shaking his head slowly, his hand going to the spreading red mark on his cheek.

Svetlana looked sharply at the submariner. "Did you say the stone is radioactive?"

He nodded. "That's what Moscow told us."

She growled in frustration. *Idiots! Why didn't they tell me!*

She moved rapidly towards Chad and frisked his suit, probing forcefully for a distinctive rounded shape. She turned to the sailor. "Not there. It must still be in the capsule." She looked across at the helicopters, and down at the scuba tanks strapped to the floor next to her. *There's still time!* She spoke quickly, and the sailor began rapidly assembling and donning equipment.

She turned back to Chad. "If you don't answer right now, he's going to hit you again and then force you underwater to show him. Where did you hide the stone?"

Chad was still blinking to clear his head, and Michael answered for him. "He doesn't understand Russian, Svetlana! Leave him alone!"

She yelled at him. "Molchi!" Be silent! She turned back to Chad. "Last chance!"

He stared at her, dazed and defiant.

"Bah!" she said in frustration, and turned to the sailor. "He's yours. And hurry, before the Americans can get into the water!"

The two crewmen forced straps over Chad's arms, tightened the waist belt and mashed the rubber regulator against his lips. Chad kept his teeth closed, and the lead sailor shrugged. *He'll want to breathe eventually.* He pulled a long, sharp knife from his leg holster and reached in by Chad's neck, puncturing the airtight rubber seal, and then the two men lifted Chad up and threw him into the sea. The submariner had on his tank and flippers; he pulled on a mask, sat on the inflated edge and neatly pivoted over the side. Grabbing Chad by the neck ring, he dragged him underwater and started swimming hard, descending towards the inverted capsule.

JW's voice crackled into Kaz's ear. "Kaz, did you copy that?"

The voices had faded in and out during the long transmission from the Apollo 18 crew. "I heard something, Doc, but couldn't make it out."

"I think I heard Michael say something about a gun!"

Kaz nodded. "Yeah, it's no surprise that the Soviets are armed. We're ready here too."

"Copy." JW paused. "Be safe."

"Wilco."

Kaz took a final look out the forward windows of the Sea King. The pilot had slowed, approaching the situation cautiously. Behind him, Kaz heard the big side cargo door sliding open, and could feel the buffeting air from the rotors. He leaned forward to the pilot. "All set?"

The pilot nodded, focusing on positioning where they'd briefed. Kaz moved aft and yelled to Colombo, "The crew's all in the Soviet Zodiac now, and they're headed towards the capsule. Your men ready?" He glanced at the wet-suited figures, all standing, holding on to the overhead straps with one hand, their weapons with the other.

"Yep, all set." A large block was on the floor by the open door. The helo's flight engineer leaned out the side, talking on headset with the pilot, guiding him into position. As the Sea King slowed and then settled its belly into the water, he kicked the block out and tugged on its line. It released a large raft, which began rapidly inflating.

Kaz felt a tap on his shoulder and turned to see Stepanov standing next to him, shouting above the noise. "Commander Zemeckis, I need to be in that raft to assist my countrywoman."

Kaz shook his head. "No way."

Stepanov was intent. "Think. You will need translation."

Kaz quickly pictured what was likely to happen. *Shit, he's right, and the Captain had insisted.* He looked at the size of the Navy men. *Worth the risk.* He nodded reluctantly and held up an open hand. *Wait.*

Colombo was loading his team and their gear into the six-sided raft as it bounced up and down in the rough seas. He turned to Kaz, who indicated Stepanov and yelled "Translator!" and pointed out the door. Colombo shrugged and guided the Russian into waiting hands in the raft.

"You're next, sir!" he shouted. Kaz felt in his leg pocket for the Navy-issue Colt pistol the PO had given him, and stepped out into the raft, dropping to the floor for stability. Colombo followed immediately. The noise from the helicopter increased as its blades dug in and lifted it, dripping, out of the water. The downwash covered them with spray as the pilot maneuvered clear.

The first crewman into the raft had attached lines to *Pursuit*, and they pitched and heaved in the waves next to it.

Step one, Kaz thought. *Capsule upside down, but secured.* He turned to look downwind. The Zodiac had stopped 50 feet away, holding position using the little outboard, the yellow raft trailing, the sub in the distance. But something was wrong. He looked closely, frowning, counting: There weren't enough white and black suits! Where did the others go? *Shit!* What had he missed while they were boarding their raft?

He turned to Colombo. "I need to get inside the capsule. Now!"

With no mask on, Chad was blinded by the salt water. His lungs were starting to burn, demanding air, and he reached down and back, grabbing the scuba tank hose. He thrust the regulator into his mouth, exhaled sharply to clear the water out and then took a welcome deep breath, hearing the familiar ringing sound of compressed air feeding from the tank on his back.

He let himself be pulled along. *Might as well let this Russian tire himself out, doing all the work.* He patted down his suited leg, feeling for what he'd put into the pocket. *Good. Still there.*

With the cut rubber neck seal, water was flowing into his suit, bubbles working their way up past his face, making him heavy in the water. *Need to be careful. The bottom of this pool is a long way down.*

The sailor stopped pulling. Blinking his eyes, Chad could make out the shape of *Pursuit* silhouetted against the light from the surface. He felt strong hands pushing him, and suddenly his head was through the hatch and into the air still trapped inside the capsule. He spit out the regulator and raised himself up into the familiar cockpit.

Didn't think I'd be back here so soon.

He felt bumping from behind and squirmed himself to the side as the sailor emerged through the hatch, pulling off his mask. He reached down towards his fins, and when his hand came back up it was holding his long, curved diving knife. He held it close to Chad's face.

"Vere is the stone?"

Chad turned and pointed above the Russian. "In a bag up there, behind the R2 panel." When the sailor turned to look, Chad opened his pocket and slid his hand inside.

"Vere? You show me!"

"I will," Chad said. His hand arced up fast, clenching the machete he'd taken from the survival kit. With all his strength he twisted and slashed, aiming just below the Russian's chin into the exposed softness of his neck.

The submariner's instant, primal reaction was to lash back at the sudden pain and shock of being wounded. Taking Chad by surprise, he drove his diving knife hard forward, a spasm driven by a surge of adrenaline. The tip plunged through the layers of the white spacesuit, past the liquid cooling garment and deep into the flesh, muscle and gut of Chad's belly.

Blood spurted from both men's wounds and they fell back, stunned. Each did a fast internal assessment. *Is this it? Am I fatally hurt?* And then, *How will I know?* Chad's hands went slack and the machete fell, clattering onto the metal below.

In that brief frozen moment, bubbles appeared in the water at the hatch. A head came up through the surface, and when Svetlana raised her mask, she stared in disbelief. Blood was spurting from the severed artery in the sailor's neck, around the fist he had pushed into it, trying to staunch the flow. Chad was lying back on the instrument panel, his hands clutching at the handle of a knife buried in his stomach.

"You morons!" she screamed.

She pulled herself up next to the sailor and slapped his fumbling hand away, reaching in to see if she could apply direct pressure to stop the bleeding, but immediately saw there was no use. The cut was wide and deep; there were foaming pink bubbles and exposed meat and tendons where the knife had sliced through his trachea and jugular. Each gush of blood as his heart pumped was weaker. His eyes were wide, looking at her in disbelief. He tried to speak, but was unable, his air whistling out through the mortal wound.

She twisted in the small space to look at Chad, who was staring down with a concerned expression at the knife in his guts.

"How badly are you hurt?"

He looked up at her, saying nothing. The body of the sailor spasmed and slumped.

"Where is the stone?" she hissed.

Chad looked back down at the knife handle, puzzled, ignoring her.

After the two men had left the Zodiac she'd realized there was a better way to search for the stone. She spun now and reached up along the side of the instrument panel over her head, feeling for the tool Michael had used. Her fingers closed around the metal cylinder, and she pulled it down, twisting and turning it on. She looked at the dial of the Geiger counter, hearing it begin to click. She rapidly started moving from locker to locker, throwing open doors and reaching in, listening for a reaction.

She stopped as a better thought struck her. She turned and looked at Chad, who lay motionless, his eyes following her as she moved towards him. She touched the rounded end of the tube to the fabric of his suit, starting by his feet and moving up his legs, swinging it left and right.

As she passed his knees she heard extra clicks. Sweeping up his thighs the clicking increased, the noise becoming a continuous chatter. She kept going, up his torso, but the sound decreased, so she moved it back down until she got maximum signal.

The bastard had hidden the stone in his crotch. He looked at her, his skin ashen, and managed to smile. "Right by the family jewels."

How to get it out? The spacesuit's long zipper was in the back, clumsy to get at, and time was short.

She looked at the knife in his belly. It sickened her to think of pulling it out. *But how did he cut the sailor? There must be a second knife!* She glanced around below Chad and spotted the machete.

She pulled the cloth of Chad's suit taut and hurriedly began cutting. She hacked through the white outer cloth and the layers of metal-coated plastic. Her fingers dug in, making an opening as she sliced into the airtight rubberized nylon.

Chad tried to push her away. She grabbed the knife handle sticking out of his belly with her other hand, and twisted. He screamed, and she kept cutting.

The innermost layer was the toughest, with hundreds of plastic cooling tubes sewn into a tight mesh against his skin, but once she cut a small hole in the woven fabric it parted, and she was through. She saw fresh blood; she'd cut his upper leg. *No matter.*

She reached into the slit with both hands, opening it as wide as she could, and then slid one hand between his legs. She felt the cloth of a bag with a hardness inside it, and worked her fingers underneath, prying it out. Like extracting the head of a newborn, she squeezed it through the layers, and with a final yank, the bag came clear. She grabbed the Geiger counter and held it close to the blood-smeared surface; the clicking went crazy.

As she turned to stuff the bag into a leg pocket, Chad grabbed onto the neck ring of her spacesuit. "Dye minyeh!" His voice was strained, but his Russian was clear. "Give it to me!" In his free hand he held the machete she'd set down while extracting the bag.

She reached for the knife in his belly, but he slashed at her hand, cutting across her knuckles. "No, no, toots," he gasped. "I'm planning to live through this." He beckoned with his free hand and repeated his demand. "Dye minyeh!"

She twisted away from him in the confined space, reaching deeper into the leg pocket. Turning back, she raised the pistol and pointed it at him. "Nyet!"

A voice spoke loudly from below them. "Don't move!"

Kaz climbed into the cockpit, his pistol rock-steady, aiming at Svetlana's head.

59

Pursuit

"Well, isn't this a pretty little Mexican standoff," Chad grunted. "Or should I say Russian?" He smiled at his own joke, and grimaced.

Keeping his gun on Svetlana, Kaz flicked his gaze around the cockpit, taking in the bloodied wet-suited body and the knife in Chad's belly.

"You okay, Chad?"

"Never better, buddy." His voice was raspy.

"I know you speak Russian. Ask her what she wants."

"I do *what*, Kaz? How would I know how to speak Russian?"

Svetlana kept her gun trained on Chad, listening to the men.

"Chad, it's no longer a secret. We know you've been in contact with your brother in East Berlin for years, and that you've been communicating with the Soviets, even while you were on the Moon. Dammit, you speak Russian. Ask her!"

Chad's voice was slurring now. "I don't need to ask her anything, Kaz. She's already got what she wants. She just stuffed it into her pocket!"

Svetlana pivoted fast and fired point blank at Kaz; as he saw her move he squeezed his trigger. The two shots sounded in rapid succession, the noise deafening in the small space. Her bullet had spun Kaz, a sudden slam on his left side. She pushed forward past him, straightened her body and fell through the open hatch into the water.

He looked down, fearing the worst, seeing blood on his left upper arm. No pain yet. *Fuck!*

Colombo's head popped up through the hatch. "I just saw someone in a spacesuit swim out, and I heard shots! You okay, Commander?" He looked around the capsule, his eyes widening. "Holy shit!"

"Yeah, I just got dinged. But Chad needs a doctor ASAP, and I need to stop the cosmonaut. Go topside and call the other helo for medical help, now!"

"Aye aye, sir." Colombo disappeared.

Kaz looked at Chad, speaking rapidly. "We haven't got the proof yet, but we know you're guilty of Tom's helo sabotage, and that you've been taking money from the Soviets. Time to get your story straight, Chad. It's not going to be pretty."

He clumsily pulled his mask back on one-handed, shoved his regulator into his mouth and slid down through the hatch.

Guilty! Is that what Kaz said?

The word echoed in Chad's head, and he moaned. He wasn't guilty! He was a hero! He alone had found what the damned Russians wanted and had been bringing it back to the good guys. He looked at the bloody body on the other side of the cockpit. *Shit, I was stabbed defending it.*

He looked down at the handle of the knife protruding from his belly. A wave of pain surged through him, a burning agony like the center of his body was on fire. As it subsided he reached into the hole the cosmonaut had cut in his suit, then pulled his hand out, wiggling his wet fingers, looking at the dripping red of fresh blood. Realizing what it meant. Realizing what Kaz had said about sabotage and money, and what would happen to him now that they knew.

Get my story straight! He closed his eyes against another wave of pain, and everything went searingly, blindingly white in his head. It took longer to pass.

I'm an action hero! He visualized the words, like they were floating in front of him on the cover of a comic book. He nodded, a smile curling his lips. *I need to keep it that way.*

Time to take one more action.

He reached up and unlatched the locker near his head, pulling out the strap that was attached to one of the vacuum-sealed containers of moonrocks. He clipped the free end to the ring on his suit, then reached up again. The pain of pulling the heavy box out made him scream. He worked it past the edge, the agony a cascading roar in his head, until the box overbalanced, tumbling and banging violently past him, towards the hatch.

The tether yanked tight, hauling him after the box. The handle of the knife banged on metal as he was pulled through the hatch into the water; he shouted with the added pain, emptying his lungs. The weight dragged him clear of *Pursuit*, the white of his suit and red of his blood catching the fading light as he fell straight down into the blackness of the deep.

As consciousness faded, Chad reached up with his fingertips, feeling through the heavy cloth around his neck, finding the small, comforting lump of the silver pendant against his chest. His final thought before the world went black was of the gentle, loving smile of his mother.

In the raft beside the inverted capsule, the Soviet attaché had been watching and listening. He'd kicked his shoes off and worked his way around next to the jumble of diving equipment. As Colombo burst to the surface yelling urgently for a radio, Stepanov took advantage of the confusion. With all eyes turned away, he smoothly grabbed a tank, mask and fins, and rolled over the side. Easily donning the equipment underwater, he cleared his mask and looked around. Spotting what he was looking for, he pulled his switchblade from his pocket, flicked it open and swam hard in pursuit.

———

Kaz was kicking his fins as urgently as he could, pulling with his good arm, holding the pistol in his other hand, breathing heavily through the regulator. The salt water stung sharply in his wound. He'd glanced up to see the capsule and raft against the light, getting his bearings, and hoped he had the direction towards the Zodiac right. *She'll have done the same thing,* he reasoned. He strained his eyes forward, trying to spot her motion ahead of him.

How could my bullet have missed? She was right there! But she'd moved sideways as they shot, so it was possible. He hoped he'd at least winged her. Slowed her down.

He saw a flash of white ahead of him, and then another, and could see he was gaining on her. They'd chosen the same depth, about 15 feet down, just deep enough to not be easily seen from the surface. Both of them were swimming hard, but the bulk of her suit was slowing her. He listened to his labored breathing, the air squealing through the scuba valves as his lungs demanded continuous deep breaths, each stroke getting him nearer.

Kaz felt a sudden hard pull on his leg from behind, a strong hand grabbing and holding his calf. *What the fuck?* He spun in the water and recognized the gleaming bald head of Stepanov. One of his hands was gripping Kaz's leg, and the other was holding something that glinted in the watery light.

Kaz jackknifed hard, twisting and kicking violently, trying to free his leg from the attaché's grasp. Stepanov's arm arced towards Kaz's belly, a long, silver knife held firmly in his fist, the motion slowed by the resistance of the water. Kaz had to get inside the knife's trajectory; he grabbed Stepanov's shoulder strap and pulled violently, the pain searing in his arm. As their upper bodies slammed into each other, the knife curved in behind him and clanged hard into his tank.

Stepanov's grunt was audible through his mouthpiece. He released Kaz's thrashing leg and grabbed his webbed waist belt, stabilizing and then twisting his upper body. With the improved leverage, the knife

once more came slashing through the water. Kaz was bashing at
Stepanov's head with the pistol, knocking his mask off, but it had no
effect. The slicing blade was going to make contact. Out of options, Kaz
turned the pistol's hard metal nose against Stepanov's head and pulled
the trigger.

The explosion blew the water out the end of the barrel in an intense
high-speed blast wave that rocked the attaché's head sideways, away
from the muzzle. But the 45-caliber bullet behind the wave was still
going near normal exit speed, and it slammed into his skull at 750 feet
per second, tearing through bone and brain. Stepanov's body went
instantly limp, and the knife fell from his fingers, down into the abyss.

Kaz's heart was pounding. *Holy Christ!* He pushed Stepanov away
and turned to look for the cosmonaut, spotting the white of her suit.
She'd turned and was looking back at him. *Must have heard the gun-
shot*, he realized. Hoping he wasn't too late, he swam hard towards her.

He stopped far enough away to be mindful of the pistol in her hand,
and held his up as well. Bullets didn't travel far underwater, but surfacing would be a different game. A hard game to win.

He saw that Svetlana was now fumbling with her leg pocket. *Shit!* he
yelled, the word unrecognizable through his mouthpiece. He thrust
forward, kicking and pulling to swim below the cosmonaut, diving
deeper, looking up. As he watched, she let go of something white and
then started swimming hard for the surface.

The object was falling fast. He swam as hard as he could, willing
himself to intercept it, dropping the pistol and pulling the water with
both hands, ignoring the pain in his arm. His lungs couldn't draw
enough air out of the tank, and he was seeing red as the heavy object
fell past his depth. He gave one last pulsing heave with his arms and
legs, stretched out to his maximum reach, and grabbed for it, feeling
his fingers close on a cloth bag, heavy with weight.

Dazed with the effort and pain, Kaz just floated, suspended, inhal-
ing deeply. As he regained his breath, he carefully squeezed the bulky
bag into his coverall leg pocket with his good hand, listening to the

distinctive underwater whine of an outboard motor above. Looking straight up, he could see Svetlana splashing at the surface. And coming in fast from his right, the pointed black silhouette of the Zodiac.

He kicked hard, blowing excess air from his lungs as he ascended, watching as the boat coasted to a stop. Looking up, he saw the white-suited figure disappear out of the water and then oddly reappear, splayed and splashing, as if thrown back in. Just as he breached the surface, he heard the motor crank back up to full speed, and saw the boat turn abruptly and speed away.

Kaz swam through the waves towards the person in the water and was unsurprised to see that it was Michael, his suit over-buoyant, spread-eagling him faceup on the roiling surface. Kaz looked towards the sound of the Zodiac and spotted it pounding away through the crests towards the submarine.

"Michael, you okay?" His voice sounded odd to him, the words taken away by the wind.

"I'm fine, Kaz. So good to see you—that was nuts!"

Kaz's arm was screaming with pain in the motion of the waves. Holding on to the buoyancy of Michael's suit, he felt a surge of dizziness, dimming his vision. He heard the sound of a helicopter, and then some loud splashes next to him.

"Geez, Kaz, I leave you alone for ten minutes and look what happens!" JW was next to him in the water, supporting him, sliding a life jacket over his good arm. Two Navy divers were next to Michael. The Sea King dropped more divers and a raft; experienced hands grabbed Kaz under the arms and lifted him cleanly in, propping him against the inflated side, next to Michael. JW appeared beside him with scissors, neatly cutting off the sleeve of his coveralls at the shoulder and frowning at the bullet hole through his bicep.

He soaked the wound liberally with disinfectant, the added pain clearing Kaz's head, and quickly wrapped it in gauze and bandage and pulled it into a sling. He looked critically at his work. "That'll do for now."

Kaz fumbled for his leg pocket with his good hand, trying to pull out the white bag.

"Let me do that!" JW scolded. He worked it free and held it up, the weight swinging with the boat's motion.

"What's in there?" Michael asked.

"A good question," Kaz said. "Open it, Doc."

JW slid the zipper open, looked inside and glanced quizzically at Kaz. Frowning, he carefully reached in and pulled out a Soviet pistol by the tip of the barrel.

"Where did you find this?"

Kaz blinked twice, then scrambled to sit tall to see over the edge of the raft, turning to look at the submarine. The Zodiac was already stowed, and there were a few submariners working to close the forward hatch, the big boat beginning to move forward. A smaller, white-suited figure was standing facing him. She saluted suddenly, waved once and disappeared into the submarine.

Kaz watched for several long seconds after she'd gone, then raised his fingertips to the corner of his good eyebrow. He held them there for a moment, then lifted his hand and waved back.

60

Galveston Beach, Texas

"Hold my hand?"

It was evening, and the sun was just disappearing, the rich red light reflecting off the crests of the low, curling waves. Kaz had driven them out past the western edge of Galveston, beyond the lights, to where there was nothing but tall grass dunes, the flat of the coarse brown sand, and the endless Gulf of Mexico to the south. Small, stiff-legged birds hurried along the waterline, hunting for one last morsel before dark.

Laura slipped her hand into his, and they walked on the hard sand in silence, enjoying the quiet. Thankful for it.

Kaz looked up, and stopped. The Moon had waned to a delicate, thin arc, a sliver catching the sunlight. In the darkening sky he could barely make out the ghostly shadows of the flooded lava plains, and squinted to try to see the small circle of Mare Serenitatis. Luke's resting place.

Laura followed his gaze. "How did it go this morning?"

Kaz sighed. "I hate funerals," he said. "Arlington Cemetery is such a sad, beautiful place. But it was nice for the families. The Vice President came, and Sam Phillips. Michael gave a good speech at the graveside to honor his crewmates." Kaz looked bleakly at Laura. "Luke's parents just sat there in their seats, trying to understand what had happened to their boy. Admiral Weisner presented them with Luke's medals, including the Navy Cross." He paused. "Posthumous."

He could see tears welling in Laura's eyes. "Chad's folks were sitting beside them. Such nice people. So proud to be honoring their son, but forever sad that it had to be at Arlington." He started walking again. The military had decided to honor both men there, near where the other fallen astronauts had been buried. He and Al Shepard had reluctantly agreed.

"Much media there?" Laura asked.

Kaz shook his head. "No, none of the details of what happened have been released yet, and they asked to keep it just for family. They're calling the deaths 'classified under investigation' for now. As soon as Nixon and Brezhnev have a chance to meet, they'll make a formal announcement about Svetlana on the Moon, and find a way to spin it all so both sides look good." He shook his head. "So the two of *them* look good."

He glanced at Laura. "Have you had a look at the container of moon-rocks that made it back yet?"

She nodded, excitement creeping into her voice. "Sure have. We got the samples that were near Lunokhod, and mostly it's what we expected to see. But there were two small fragments that were a total surprise. A whole different type of morphology, like they were both broken off of one larger piece. And incredibly, when we checked closely, they're highly radioactive!" She shook her head. "As soon as we found that out, the military took charge, and everything's hush-hush until they decide what to do with the information."

Kaz kept walking, staring to the west, thinking. A small smile on his face.

Laura asked the question that everyone in the Lunar Receiving Lab had wanted to know. "Think this discovery will mean there'll be another Moon mission?"

Kaz nodded slowly. "Yes, I expect so. Maybe not another Apollo, but having a potential power source on the Moon will be too hard for the DoD to pass up. And with Lunokhod having originally found it, the Soviets will be hustling for a better look as well." He smiled at her. "Should be a bonanza for lunar geologists."

The last glow of the sunset was fading, and stars were starting to appear. Laura looked across at Kaz's sling as they turned to retrace their steps.

"How's the arm?"

"Healing fine. Clean in and out." He lifted his elbow, and grimaced slightly. "Still hurts a bit, but JW says I should have the sling off in a few days."

Laura shook her head. "Whenever they let you, you'll have to tell me everything that happened at splashdown."

"I will," he promised.

They were walking east now, and Laura suddenly raised her arm, pointing just above the horizon. "Look, Kaz! Mars!" The wavering light of the distant planet shone redly in the darkness. "From what the Mariner orbiters have been showing us, that'll be a *real* geologists' bonanza. And NASA's building a Mars lander they're calling Viking, to be there in a couple years!"

"But by then you'll be too busy training as a Space Shuttle astronaut," he reminded her.

"I sure hope so." She looked closely at him in the near-darkness, the distant lights of Galveston on his face. "What are *your* plans, mister?" She'd been thinking about it, but asked the question lightly.

"Funny you should ask. Sam Phillips talked to me this morning about a new project starting up out west, in Nevada. And he and NASA want me to stay here to support any future Moon flights and Skylab." He smiled, looking squarely at her. "Lots of good reasons to be here."

As they walked, the events of the morning rolled back into Kaz's head, like a newsreel. He quietly described it to her. "After the bugler played 'Taps,' the Blue Angels did the flypast. Six F-4 Phantoms, my old jet, tight in formation, low across the graveyard.

"Just as they passed overhead, one of the wingmen pulled hard up and away to honor Luke and Chad, leaving a hole in the formation for the missing man." He shook his head. "It breaks my heart every time."

He glanced back up at the Moon. The funeral had made him think of a small orphan boy, alone and afraid long ago. And an aging monk on the other side of the Berlin Wall, trying to make sense of it all.

He squeezed Laura's hand tightly and led them up off the beach, two joined figures in the darkness under the endless, star-filled sky.

AUTHOR'S NOTE

The Reality Behind The Apollo Murders

As I suggested at the outset of this novel, many of the characters, events and things in *The Apollo Murders* are real. Their inclusion made writing the book great fun, and a complex challenge. Here's a quick summary, to save you googling.

REAL CHARACTERS

Andropov, Yuri. Chairman of the KGB, went on to be General Secretary/ leader of the Soviet Union

Bean, Al. Apollo 12 and Skylab astronaut, painter

Carius, Bob. Captain of the USS *New Orleans*

Chauvin, C.A. "Skip." NASA Apollo Spacecraft Test Conductor at Kennedy Space Center

Chelomei, Vladimir. Chief Designer and Director of spacecraft factory OKB-52 for the Proton rocket and Almaz

Dobrynin, Anatoly. Soviet Ambassador to the US, 1962–86

Haldeman, Bob. White House Chief of Staff, 1969–73

Heard, Jack. Harris County Sheriff, 1973–1984

Kissinger, Henry. US National Security Advisor, 1969–75
Kraft, Chris. Manned Spacecraft Center Director, 1972-82
Kranz, Gene. Flight Director, NASA, 1962–94
Latypov, Gabdulkhai "Gabdul." Soviet Air Forces Senior Lieutenant,
    Lunokhod driver
Nixon, Richard. US President, 1969–74
Phillips, Sam. USAF General, Apollo Program Director, 1964–69,
    National Security Agency Director, 1972–73
Schlesinger, James. Central Intelligence Agency Director, 1973
Serdyukov, Vasily. Captain of the Soviet submarine K-252
Shepard, Al. USN Admiral, test pilot, first American astronaut
Slayton, Deke. NASA Director of Flight Crew Operations, astronaut
Weisner, Maurice "Mo." USN Admiral, Vice Chief of Naval
    Operations, 1972–73

ALMAZ SPACE STATION The Soviet spy space station in the story was
real, including the fact that it was armed with a Kartech R-23 machine gun.
It launched, unmanned, on 3 April 1973, but was fatally damaged after
two weeks by an explosion, and depressurized into a trail of debris before
a crew could be launched to dock with it. Its orbit decayed until it burned
up in the atmosphere on 28 May 1973. A subsequent Almaz station was
also armed with the R-23 gun, which was fired once in a successful test.

APOLLO 18 The US originally planned to launch Apollo 18 and 19,
and built most of the hardware, including the rockets, for both missions.
President Nixon canceled them both due to budgetary and other pressures after the near-disaster of Apollo 13.

AREA 51 A secret center for stealth technology development and testing captured Soviet fighter aircraft in Nevada.

FEMALE COSMONAUTS The first woman in space was Valentina
Tereshkova, who flew solo on Vostok 6 for nearly three days in 1963.

The next was Svetlana Savitskaya, a test pilot and 1970 world aerobatic champion. She flew in space twice in the early 1980s, including doing a spacewalk, and eventually retired from the Russian Air Force with the rank of major.

LUNOKHOD The Soviets landed several unmanned probes on the Moon. The Lunokhod rover in the story is real. It touched down in the Sea of Serenity on 15 January 1973, exploring and sending back extensive data. It accidentally brushed a crater wall on 9 May 1973, knocking moondust onto its radiator. It overheated and died two days later.

MANNED ORBITAL LABORATORY The US had a military spy space station program, and selected and trained test pilots for it, but it never flew, and was canceled in June 1969. Several of the MOL astronauts flew as part of the NASA astronaut corps. One of them would have been Major Robert H. Lawrence Jr., the first African-American astronaut, if he had not been killed in a USAF flying accident in 1967.

POLLY RANCH A real suburban Houston community based around a private runway, with houses and hangars combined. Several astronauts have lived there.

RADIOACTIVITY ON THE MOON The geology of the Moon as we understand it makes anything beyond low-level radioactive rock highly unlikely. Mars, though, with its immense Olympus Mons volcano and water processes, could well have concentrated radioactivity; we have found nearly 300 Martian meteorites on Earth, so some have very likely landed on the Moon.

RUSSIAN ORTHODOX CHURCH AND SPYING The KGB recruited translators inside the church in the 1970s in an attempt to entrap people of interest by maneuvering them into compromising situations.

SVETLANA'S PISTOL The Makarov Pistol was the Soviet Union's standard military and police sidearm for decades, and it was carried in the survival kit of their space capsules. In 1986 cosmonauts were issued a specially designed triple-barreled pistol called the TP-82 instead, with two 40-gauge shot and one 5.45 mm bullet. That's the weapon I trained with as a Soyuz pilot.

THE U-JOINT Fort Terry's Universal Joint was a favorite hangout during the Apollo era. During the Space Shuttle years, it became the Outpost. I spent many an evening there, and my picture joined the hundreds on the walls. It closed in 2009, and the building burned to the ground in 2010. I don't know where the swinging doors ended up.

TSUP MOSCOW MISSION CONTROL Soviet Mission Control, known by its acronym TsUP (ЦУП), is located in the Moscow suburb of Korolyov (Kaliningrad at the time of this book). It has been in operation since 1960, with an adjunct NASA office therein to support joint missions. I worked there multiple times.

YASTREB SPACEWALKING SUIT The suit that Svetlana and Andrei wore outside was real, developed at the time of the Almaz program. It was only used in space once, in 1969.

REFUGEE CHILD ADOPTIONS IN THE UNITED STATES Eleanor Roosevelt helped form USCOM, the United States Committee for the Care of European Children, which in conjunction with the Displaced Persons Act brought nearly 5,000 children orphaned in the Second World War to America.

ACKNOWLEDGMENTS

Writing this book took a daunting amount of research, often demanding expertise I'll never have. I want and need to thank each of these friends for their insights, help, ideas and corrections, and for earnestly trying to set me straight.

Shannon Abbott—schedule
Syd Burrows—the original one-eyed fighter pilot
Lindy Elkins-Tanton—planetary scientist
Paul Fjeld—artist and Apollo sage
David Forster—Polly Rancher
Tim Gregory—cosmochemist
Kata Hadfield—beloved daughter and trusted reader
Kristin Hadfield—beloved daughter and trusted reader
Walter Heneghan—helicopter pilot
Cheryl-Ann Horrocks—trusted reader
Alla Jiguirej—Star City oracle
Heather MacDonald—assistant
Mildred McElya—longtime Polly Rancher and
    Astronaut Office secretary
Leland Melvin—astronaut
Aaron Murphy—finance
Destin Sandlin—explainer of things
Rusty Schweickart—Apollo astronaut

Alex Shifrin—trusted reader
Judy Tanenbaum—trusted reader
Anatoly Zak—Russian Space Web

Most of all, enormous thanks and hugs to Jon Butler for the idea and the confidence, Rick Broadhead for his endless patience and attention to detail, and Anne Collins for her tenacity of clear purpose and enduring, unflagging support.